Content and Technology

 P9-DHT-803

CHAPTER 12

CONFLICT, NEGOTIATION, AND INTERGROUP BEHAVIOR

CHAPTER OUTLINE

A Definition of Conflict
Transitions in Conflict Thought
Functional vs. Dysfunctional Conflict
The Conflict Process
Negotiation
Intergroup Relations

> When two people in business always agree, one of them is unnecessary.
> —W. Wrigley, Jr.

Quit | Chapter Start | Contents | Video | Chapter End | Web Site | 1

"On Location"
Custom video cases shot
at **The Knitting Factory**
(30 minutes)

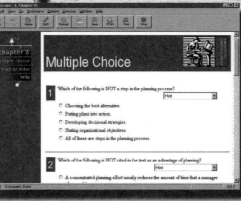

Student support site featuring

- News updates
- Interactive Study Guide
- Internet resources in OB

The student support site is accessible at
http://www.prenhall.com/robbinsorgbeh or
through a connection on the CD-ROM.

Eighth Edition

ORGANIZATIONAL BEHAVIOR

CONCEPTS ◆ CONTROVERSIES ◆ APPLICATIONS

STEPHEN P. ROBBINS
San Diego State University

PRENTICE HALL Upper Saddle River, New Jersey 07458

Acquisitions Editor: David Shafer
Assistant Editor: Lisamarie Brassini
Editorial Assistant: Christopher Stogdill
Editor-in-Chief: Natalie Anderson
Marketing Manager: Stephanie Johnson
Production Editor: Judith Leale
Managing Editor: Dee Josephson
Manufacturing Buyer: Kenneth J. Clinton
Manufacturing Supervisor: Arnold Vila
Manufacturing Manager: Vincent Scelta
Senior Designer: Ann France
Design Director: Patricia Wosczyk
Cover Design: Maureen Eide/Jill Little
Endpaper Design: Warren Fischbach
Cover Image: © Boris Lyubner/SIS

Copyright © 1998, 1996, 1993, 1991, 1989 by Prentice-Hall, Inc.
A Simon & Schuster Company
Upper Saddle River, New Jersey 07458

All rights reserved. No part of this book may be reproduced, in any form or by any means, without written permission from the Publisher.

Robbins, Stephen P.,
    Organizational behavior: concepts, controversies, applications /
  Stephen P. Robbins.   —8th ed.
     p. cm.
    Includes bibliographical references and index.
    ISBN 0-13-857459-6 (hard cover)
    1. Organizational behavior.   I. Title.
  HD58.7.R62   1997
  658.3—dc21   97-5407
                                               CIP

Prentice-Hall International (UK) Limited, London
Prentice-Hall of Australia Pty. Limited, Sydney
Prentice-Hall Canada, Inc., Toronto
Prentice-Hall Hispanoamericana, S.A., Mexico
Prentice-Hall of India Private Limited, New Delhi
Prentice-Hall of Japan, Inc., Tokyo
Simon & Schuster Asia Pte. Ltd., Singapore
Editora Prentice-Hall do Brasil, Ltda., Rio de Janeiro

Printed in the United States of America

10 9 8 7 6 5 4 3 2

Brief Contents

Contents

Preface

My publisher tells me that since its fifth edition this book has continually been the number-one-selling organizational behavior (OB) textbook in the United States and worldwide. Confirming the trend toward globalization of markets, this book actually sells more copies each year outside the U.S. than inside. For instance, the last edition (and its adaptations or translations) was the market leader in Australia, Hong Kong, Malaysia, the Philippines, India, Mexico, Brazil, Central America, and Scandinavia.

The previous comments, however, relate to the *past* editions. I expect you're more interested in what's in *this* edition. Therefore, let me highlight those features that adopters continue to tell me they like (and have been retained in this revision) as well as what's new.

Retained from the Previous Edition

◆ *Three-level model of analysis.* This book continues to organize OB around three levels of analysis. We begin with individual behavior and then move on to group behavior. Finally, we add the organization system to capture the full complexity of organizational behavior.

◆ *Writing style.* This text continues to present concepts in a clear and straight-forward manner. Considerable effort is made to carefully explain complex topics and to illustrate application through extensive use of examples.

◆ *Comprehensive literature coverage.* This book is regularly singled out for its comprehensive and up-to-date coverage of OB—from both academic journals as well as business periodicals. For instance, this book had a chapter on conflict in 1979 and a chapter on organizational culture in 1983. Additionally, it was one of the first OB books to include the topics of diversity, globalization, power and politics, negotiation, socialization, the demise of bureaucracy, the virtual organization, the bi-modal workforce, and the importance of building trust.

◆ *Pedagogy.* The eighth edition continues the tradition of providing the most complete assortment of pedagogy available in any OB book. This includes review and discussion questions, point-counterpoint debates, individual and group exercises, ethical dilemma exercises, case incidences and video cases, and an integrative part-ending case.

New to the Eighth Edition

Continuing the history of leadership in the market, users of previous editions will notice several significant changes.

◆ *First,* the material that previously was included in a separate chapter—"Responding to Global and Cultural Diversity"—has now been integrated throughout the text. As illustrated in Exhibit P-1, you'll find discussions of ethics, workforce diversity, and globalization covered in most chapters. This change is in keeping with my efforts at integrating issues rather than leaving them as isolated topics.

◆ *Second,* this edition represents the first attempt in organizational behavior texts to fully integrate technology. Each copy of OB 8/E includes a CD-ROM containing the text and video shot specifically for this text. In addition, there is an Internet connection to a text-specific web site

<http://www.prenhall.com/robbinsorgbeh>. There students can find an interactive study guide, links to additional organizational behavior sites, and up-to-date news articles linked to their texts.

As with the last edition, the text will be supported by **PHLIP**—Prentice Hall's Learning on the Internet Partnership—a faculty-support web site featuring Instructor's Manual, PowerPoint slides, current news articles, and links to related Internet sites.

◆ *Third,* based on the success of the ABC News videos (which have been retained and revised) we are introducing "On Location" videos. These are customized video cases shot specifically for this text, and intended to clearly demonstrate organizational behavior principles as they appear in real companies. **The Knitting Factory,** a small New York City based music label, is the featured company. Its global network and reliance on tech-

Exhibit P-1 Integrative Topics (with specific page references)

Chapter	Ethics	Diversity	Globalization
1	17–18, 32	13–14, 32–34	12–13
2		42–45	65–66
3	103, 117–19, 120, 126–27		116–17, 120
4	137	149–50	138, 140
5			167, 192–93
6	231–32	224	208, 210, 214, 217–18, 231
7		261–63, 264	261
8		299–300	294–96
9		330–32, 342–43	309–10, 315, 330, 332–34, 341–42
10	384–85	377–78	351–53, 382–83
11	422–23	395–96, 408–10, 430–31	395–96
12		445–47, 454	454–55
13	510–11		496
14	548–49		
15	575, 589–90	559, 561, 580–83, 590	558, 579–80, 586, 587
16	618	602	593–94, 600–01, 604
17			625–26, 637, 651–52, 671–72
Appendixes	A-2, A-23		

nology for rapid growth present interesting examples of individual, group, and organizational issues and concepts discussed in the text. These videos can be accessed on the enclosed CD-ROM and are also available on VHS for classroom use.

◆ *Fourth,* the entire research base from the seventh edition has been revised and updated for this edition.

◆ *Finally,* there are numerous changes and additions to many of the chapters. The most significant is the movement of stress management from the chapter on work design (old chapter 15) to the concluding chapter on organizational change (new chapter 17). The following list highlights what's new in this eighth edition:

Chapter 2: Foundations of Individual Behavior. New "Concepts to Skills" box on effective discipline skills.

Chapter 3: Perception and Individual Decision Making. Additional material on creativity in decision making, revised decision-making material emphasizing behavioral decision-making literature, and additional material on heuristics and decision-making styles.

Chapter 4: Values, Attitudes, and Job Satisfaction. Material on international cultural differences now included in this chapter and new material added on genetic influences on job satisfaction.

Chapter 6: Motivation: From Concepts to Applications. New material on employee recognition programs and on the challenges in motivating low-skilled service workers and people doing highly repetitive tasks.

Chapter 10: Leadership. New material on visionary leadership and team leadership, and on whether there is a moral dimension to leadership.

Chapter 14: Work Design. New section added on physical working conditions and work space design, and new material on team-based work design.

Chapter 15: Human Resource Management. New material on basic literacy training and on individualizing training; revised career development material, which reflects new emphasis on self-managed careers; and a new section on managing diversity.

Chapter 16: Organizational Culture. New "Concepts to Skills" box on reading an organization's culture.

Chapter 17: Organizational Change and Stress Management. New material on culture's effect on change efforts.

Glossary/Subject Index. The newly created "Glindex" integrates the subject index and the glossary. This now provides a one-stop location for finding and defining key terms and concepts.

Acknowledgments

A number of colleagues have been kind enough to review this revised edition and offer suggestions for improvement. I thank the following for their insights:

Joseph Martelli, The University of Findlay, Findlay, OH

Scott Lefaver, San Jose State University, San Jose, CA

Michael Whitty, Santa Clara University, Santa Clara, CA

Roya Ayman, Illinois Institute of Technology, Chicago, IL

Jane Whitney Gibson, Nova Southeastern University, Fort Lauderdale, FL

Matthew Lane, Portland State University, Portland, OR

Sheri Bischoff, Brigham Young University, Provo, UT

Regardless of how good the manuscript is that I turn in, it's only three or four floppy disks until my friends at Prentice Hall swing into action. Then PH's crack team of editors, production personnel, designers, marketing specialists, and sales representatives turn those couple of million digital characters into a bound textbook and see that it gets into faculty and students' hands. My thanks on this project go to David Shafer, Natalie Anderson, Jim Boyd, Sandy Steiner, Bill Oldsey, Stephanie Johnson, Judy Leale, Ann France, Christopher Stogdill, Lisamarie Brassini, Nancy Moudry, Teri Stratford, and all my friends at Prentice-Hall of Canada, Prentice Hall of Australia, Prentice Hall Hispanoamericana, Prentice Hall of Brazil, Prentice Hall of India, and Simon & Schuster Asia who have been so supportive of this book over its many editions.

A special thank you is extended to Rob Panco. Rob's openness and honesty continues to make this book's integrative case a unique feature among OB texts.

Finally, I want to acknowledge my wife, Laura Ospanik. Writing is a demanding activity. It is also something that I do by myself, hidden away in my office, almost every day of the year. Not many wives would understand such self-imposed isolation. As an artist, Laura does, and I want to use this space to publicly thank her for her tolerance and support.

Stephen P. Robbins

About the Author

STEPHEN P. ROBBINS received his Ph.D. from the University of Arizona. He previously worked for the Shell Oil Company and Reynolds Metals Company. Since completing his graduate studies, Dr. Robbins has taught at the University of Nebraska at Omaha, Concordia University in Montreal, the University of Baltimore, Southern Illinois University at Edwardsville, and San Diego State University. Dr. Robbins' research interests have focused on conflict, power, and politics in organizations, as well as the development of effective interpersonal skills. His articles on these and other topics have appeared in such journals as *Business Horizons,* the *California Management Review, Business and Economic Perspectives, International Management, Management Review, Canadian Personnel and Industrial Relations,* and *The Journal of Management Education.* In recent years, Dr. Robbins has been spending most of his professional time writing textbooks. His other Prentice Hall books include *Managing Today!, Management,* 5th edition (with Mary Coulter); *Fundamentals of Management,* 2nd edition (with David De Cenzo); *Essentials of Organizational Behavior,* 5th edition; *Training in InterPersonal Skills,* 2nd edition (with Phillip Hunsaker); *Organization Theory,* 3rd edition; and *Supervision Today!,* 2nd edition (with David De Cenzo). These books are used at more than 1,000 U.S. colleges and universities, as well as hundreds of schools in Canada, Australia, New Zealand, Singapore, Hong Kong, Malaysia, China, the Philippine Islands, Mexico, the Netherlands, and Scandinavia.

In Dr. Robbins' "other life," he participates in masters' track competitions. In 1995 he reaffirmed his title of "the world's fastest human—age 50 and over"—by winning the U.S. national indoor championships at 60 meters and 200 meters; winning the U.S. outdoor nationals at 100 meters and 200 meters; and capturing four gold medals (and setting three world records) at the XIth World Veteran Games. At the World Games, he won the 100-meter, 200-meter, and 400-meter dashes, and he anchored the victorious U.S. 4x1 relay team. Robbins was named the outstanding age-40-and-over male track and field athlete of 1995 by the Masters Track and Field Committee of USA Track & Field, the national governing body for athletics in the United States.

CHAPTER 1

Part One   Introduction

WHAT IS ORGANIZATIONAL BEHAVIOR?

CHAPTER OUTLINE
What Managers Do
Enter Organizational Behavior
Replacing Intuition with Systematic Study
Challenges and Opportunities for OB
Contributing Disciplines to the OB Field
There Are Few Absolutes in OB
Coming Attractions: Developing an OB Model

It's not what we don't know that gives us trouble, it's what we know that ain't so.
—W. Rogers

LEARNING OBJECTIVES

After studying this chapter, you should be able to

1 Define organizational behavior (OB)

2 Describe what managers do

3 Explain the value of the systematic study of OB

4 List the major challenges and opportunities for managers to use OB concepts

5 Identify the contributions made by major behavioral science disciplines to OB

6 Describe why managers require a knowledge of OB

7 Explain the need for a contingency approach to the study of OB

8 Identify the three levels of analysis in this book's OB model

David Kwok, a 1987 graduate of the University of California at Los Angeles. With a major in cognitive science, David works for a company called The Princeton Review that prepares students to take college and graduate school admission tests. At the age of 31, David directs fifty to sixty instructors at Princeton Review's Los Angeles office.

"My academic training in artificial intelligence didn't really prepare me for my biggest job challenge—understanding and motivating people," says David. "For instance, nothing at UCLA really emphasized how to get people psyched up. For me, people are the unknown part of the equation that determines how effective I am in my job. Other tasks, like scheduling or customer relations, give me very few headaches. What I've learned is that when things go wrong, it's almost always a people problem. I've worked hard to make our teaching staff feel like a small family and to learn techniques for getting them motivated. But it's been on-the-job training for me. I didn't learn any of this in school."

David Kwok has learned what most managers learn very quickly: A large part of the success in any management job is developing good interpersonal or people skills. Lawrence Weinbach, chief executive at the accounting firm of Arthur Andersen & Co., puts it this way: "Pure technical knowledge is only going to get you to a point. Beyond that, interpersonal skills become critical."[1]

Although practicing managers have long understood the importance of interpersonal skills to managerial effectiveness, business schools were slower to get the message. Until the late-1980s, business school curricula focused almost singularly on the technical aspects of management, emphasizing courses in economics, accounting, finance, and quantitative techniques. Course work in human behavior and people skills received minimal attention relative to the technical aspects of management. Over the past decade, however, business faculty have come to realize the importance that an understanding of human behavior plays in determining a manager's effectiveness, and required courses on people skills have been widely added to the curriculum. ◆

ecognition of the importance of developing managers' interpersonal skills is closely tied to the need for organizations to get and keep high-performing employees. For instance, the chief executive of Chrysler Corporation, Robert Eaton, sees his workforce as an asset that provides his company with a sustainable competitive advantage. "The only way we can beat the competition is with people," says Eaton. "That's the only thing anybody has. Your culture and how you motivate and empower and educate your people is what makes the difference."[2] The head of Starbucks, the rapidly growing Seattle-based coffee retailer, concurs: "Our only sustainable competitive advantage is the quality of our workforce."[3]

A study of 191 top executives at six Fortune 500 companies sought an answer to the question: Why do managers fail? The single biggest reason for failure, according to these executives, is poor interpersonal skills.[4] The Center for Creative Leadership in Greensboro, North Carolina, estimates that half of all managers and thirty percent of all senior managers have some type of difficulty with people.[5] Consistent with these findings are surveys that have sought to determine what skills college recruiters consider most important for the job effectiveness of MBA graduates.[6] These surveys consistently identify interpersonal skills as most important.

We have come to understand that technical skills are necessary, but insufficient, for succeeding in management. In today's increasingly competitive and demanding workplace, managers can't succeed on their technical skills alone. They also have to have good people skills. This book has been written to help both managers and potential managers develop those people skills.

What Managers Do

managers
Individuals who achieve goals through other people.

organization
A consciously coordinated social unit, composed of two or more people, that functions on a relatively continuous basis to achieve a common goal or set of goals.

Let's begin by briefly defining the terms *manager* and the place where managers work—the *organization*. Then let's look at the manager's job; specifically, what do managers do?

Managers get things done through other people. They make decisions, allocate resources, and direct the activities of others to attain goals. Managers do their work in an **organization**. This is a consciously coordinated social unit, composed of two or more people, that functions on a relatively continuous basis to achieve a common goal or set of goals. On the basis of this definition, manufacturing and service firms are organizations and so are schools, hospitals, churches, military units, retail stores, police departments, and local, state, and federal government agencies. The people who oversee the activities of others and who are responsible for attaining goals in these organizations are managers (although they're sometimes called *administrators*, especially in not-for-profit organizations).

◆ The people who oversee the activities of others and who are responsible for attaining goals in organizations are managers.

Management Functions

In the early part of this century, a French industrialist by the name of Henri Fayol wrote that all managers perform five management functions: They plan, organize, command, coordinate, and control.[7] Today, we have condensed those down to four: planning, organizing, leading, and controlling.

If you don't know where you're going, any road will get you there. Since organizations exist to achieve goals, someone has to define those goals and the means by which they can be achieved. Management is that someone. The **planning** function encompasses defining an organization's goals, establishing an overall strategy for achieving those goals, and developing a comprehensive hierarchy of plans to integrate and coordinate activities.

Managers are also responsible for designing an organization's structure. We call this function **organizing**. It includes the determination of what tasks are to be done, who is to do them, how the tasks are to be grouped, who reports to whom, and where decisions are to be made.

Every organization contains people, and it is management's job to direct and coordinate those people. This is the **leading** function. When managers motivate subordinates, direct the activities of others, select the most effective communication channels, or resolve conflicts among members, they are engaging in leading.

The final function managers perform is **controlling**. After the goals are set, the plans formulated, the structural arrangements delineated, and the people hired, trained, and motivated, there is still the possibility that something may go amiss. To ensure that things are going as they should, management must monitor the organization's performance. Actual performance must be compared with the previously set goals. If there are any significant deviations, it is management's job to get the organization back on track. This monitoring, comparing, and potential correcting is what is meant by the controlling function.

So, using the functional approach, the answer to the question, What do managers do? is that they plan, organize, lead, and control.

planning
Includes defining goals, establishing strategy, and developing plans to coordinate activities.

organizing
Determining what tasks are to be done, who is to do them, how the tasks are to be grouped, who reports to whom, and where decisions are to be made.

leading
Includes motivating subordinates, directing others, selecting the most effective communication channels, and resolving conflicts.

controlling
Monitoring activities to ensure they are being accomplished as planned and correcting any significant deviations.

Kim Woo-Choong (left), chairman and founder of South Korea's Daewoo Group, is personally involved in controlling product quality. His goal is to sell Daewoo cars, now mainly exported to Third World countries, in the United States. To achieve that goal, the company must improve the quality of its cars by reducing defects. Kim's frequent visits to the factory floor to personally inspect parts is a powerful signal to employees of the importance of monitoring product quality.

Management Roles

In the late 1960s, a graduate student at MIT, Henry Mintzberg, undertook a careful study of five executives to determine what these managers did on their jobs. On the basis of his observations of these managers, Mintzberg concluded that managers perform ten different, highly interrelated roles, or sets of behaviors attributable to their jobs.[8] As shown in Exhibit 1-1, these ten roles can be grouped as being primarily concerned with interpersonal relationships, the transfer of information, and decision making.

INTERPERSONAL ROLES All managers are required to perform duties that are ceremonial and symbolic in nature. When the president of a college hands out diplomas at commencement or a factory supervisor gives a group of high school students a tour of the plant, he or she is acting in a *figurehead* role. All managers also have a *leadership* role. This role includes hiring, training, motivating, and disciplining employees. The third role within the interpersonal grouping is the *liaison* role. Mintzberg described this activity as contacting outsiders who provide the manager with information. These may be individuals or groups inside or outside the organization. The sales manager who obtains information from the personnel manager in his or her own company has an internal liaison relationship. When that sales manager has contacts with other sales executives through a marketing trade association, he or she has an outside liaison relationship.

INFORMATION ROLES All managers, to some degree, collect information from organizations and institutions outside their own. Typically, they get information by reading magazines and talking with other people to learn of changes in the public's tastes, what competitors may be planning, and the like. Mintzberg called this the *monitor* role. Managers also act as a conduit to transmit information to organizational members. This is the *disseminator* role. Managers additionally perform a *spokesperson* role when they represent the organization to outsiders.

DECISIONAL ROLES Finally, Mintzberg identified four roles that revolve around the making of choices. In the *entrepreneur* role, managers initiate and oversee new projects that will improve their organization's performance. As *disturbance handlers*, managers take corrective action in response to unforeseen problems. As *resource allocators*, managers are responsible for allocating human, physical, and monetary resources. Last, managers perform a *negotiator* role, in which they discuss issues and bargain with other units to gain advantages for their own unit.

Management Skills

Still another way of considering what managers do is to look at the skills or competencies they need to successfully achieve their goals. Robert Katz has identified three essential management skills: technical, human, and conceptual.[9]

technical skills
The ability to apply specialized knowledge or expertise.

TECHNICAL SKILLS **Technical skills** encompass the ability to apply specialized knowledge or expertise. When you think of the skills held by professionals such as civil engineers or oral surgeons, you typically focus on their technical skills. Through extensive formal education, they have learned the

Exhibit 1-1 Mintzberg's Managerial Roles

Role	Description	Example
Interpersonal		
Figurehead	Symbolic head; required to perform a number of routine duties of a legal or social nature	Ceremonies, status requests, solicitations
Leader	Responsible for the motivation and direction of subordinates	Virtually all managerial activities involving subordinates
Liaison	Maintains a network of outside contacts who provide favors and information	Acknowledgment of mail, external board work
Informational		
Monitor	Receives wide variety of information; serves as nerve center of internal and external information of the organization	Handling all mail and contacts categorized as concerned primarily with receiving information
Disseminator	Transmits information received from outsiders or from other subordinates to members of the organization	Forwarding mail into organization for informational purposes; verbal contacts involving information flow to subordinates such as review sessions
Spokesperson	Transmits information to outsiders on organization's plans, policies, actions, and results; serves as expert on organization's industry	Board meetings; handling contacts involving transmission of information to outsiders
Decisional		
Entrepreneur	Searches organization and its environment for opportunities and initiates projects to bring about change	Strategy and review sessions involving initiation or design of improvement projects
Disturbance handler	Responsible for corrective action when organization faces important, unexpected disturbances	Strategy and review sessions involving disturbances and crises
Resource allocator	Making or approving significant organizational decisions	Scheduling; requests for authorization; budgeting; the programming of subordinates' work
Negotiator	Responsible for representing the organization at major negotiations	Contract negotation

Source: Adapted from *The Nature of Managerial Work* by H. Mintzberg. Copyright © 1973 by H. Mintzberg. Reprinted by permission of Addison-Wesley Educational Publishers Inc.

◆ Many people are technically proficient but interpersonally incompetent.

human skills
The ability to work with, understand, and motivate other people, both individually and in groups.

conceptual skills
The mental ability to analyze and diagnose complex situations.

special knowledge and practices of their field. Of course, professionals don't have a monopoly on technical skills, and not all technical skills have to be learned in schools or formal training programs. All jobs require some specialized expertise, and many people develop their technical skills on the job.

HUMAN SKILLS The ability to work with, understand, and motivate other people, both individually and in groups, describes **human skills**. Many people are technically proficient but interpersonally incompetent. They might be poor listeners, unable to understand the needs of others, or have difficulty managing conflicts. Since managers get things done through other people, they must have good human skills to communicate, motivate, and delegate.

CONCEPTUAL SKILLS Managers must have the mental ability to analyze and diagnose complex situations. These tasks require **conceptual skills**. Decision making, for instance, requires managers to spot problems, identify alternatives that can correct them, evaluate those alternatives, and select the best one. Managers can be technically and interpersonally competent yet still fail because of an inability to rationally process and interpret information.

Effective vs. Successful Managerial Activities

Fred Luthans and his associates looked at the issue of what managers do from a somewhat different perspective.[10] They asked the question, Do managers who move up most quickly in an organization do the same activities and with the same emphasis as managers who do the best job? You would tend to think that the managers who were the most effective in their jobs would also be the ones who were promoted fastest. But that's not what appears to happen.

Luthans and his associates studied more than 450 managers. What they found was that these managers all engaged in four managerial activities:

1. *Traditional management.* Decision making, planning, and controlling
2. *Communication.* Exchanging routine information and processing paperwork
3. *Human resource management.* Motivating, disciplining, managing conflict, staffing, and training
4. *Networking.* Socializing, politicking, and interacting with outsiders

The "average" manager in the study spent thirty-two percent of his or her time in traditional management activities, twenty-nine percent communicating, twenty percent in human resource management activities, and nineteen percent networking. However, the amount of time and effort that different managers spent on those four activities varied a great deal. Specifically, as shown in Exhibit 1-2, managers who were *successful* (defined in terms of the speed of promotion within their organization) had a very different emphasis than managers who were *effective* (defined in terms of the quantity and quality of their performance and the satisfaction and commitment of their subordinates). Among successful managers, networking made the largest relative contribution to success, and human resource management activities made the least relative contribution. Among effective managers, communication made the largest relative contribution and networking the least.

This study adds important insights to our knowledge of what managers

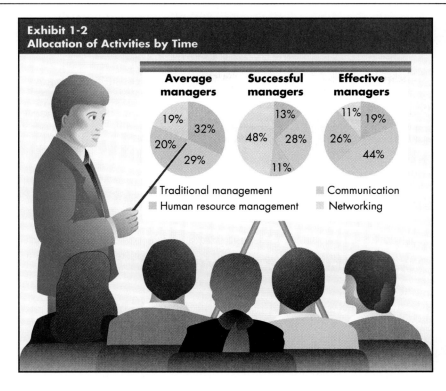

Exhibit 1-2
Allocation of Activities by Time

Average managers: Traditional management 32%, 19%, 20%, 29%
Successful managers: 13%, 28%, 48%, 11%
Effective managers: 11%, 19%, 26%, 44%

Traditional management
Human resource management
Communication
Networking

Source: Based on F. Luthans, R.M. Hodgetts, and S.A. Rosenkrantz, *Real Managers* (Cambridge, MA: Ballinger, 1988).

do. On average, managers spend approximately twenty to thirty percent of their time on each of the four activities: traditional management, communication, human resource management, and networking. However, successful managers don't give the same emphasis to each of those activities as do effective managers. In fact, their emphases are almost the opposite. This finding challenges the historical assumption that promotions are based on performance, vividly illustrating the importance that social and political skills play in getting ahead in organizations.

A Review of the Manager's Job

One common thread runs through the functions, roles, skills, and activities approaches to management: Each recognizes the paramount importance of managing people. As David Kwok found out when he became a manager at The Princeton Review, regardless of whether it's called "the leading function," "interpersonal roles," "human skills," or "human resource management, communication, and networking activities," it's clear that managers need to develop their people skills if they're going to be effective and successful.

Enter Organizational Behavior

We've made the case for the importance of people skills. But neither this book nor the discipline upon which it is based is called People Skills. The term that is widely used to describe the discipline is *Organizational Behavior*.

Organizational behavior (often abbreviated as OB) is *a field of study that investigates the impact that individuals, groups, and structure have on behavior within organizations for the purpose of applying such knowledge toward improving an organization's effectiveness.* That's a lot of words, so let's break it down.

organizational behavior (OB)
A field of study that investigates the impact that individuals, groups, and structure have on behavior within organizations, for the purpose of applying such knowledge toward improving an organization's effectiveness.

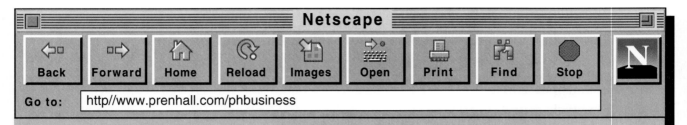

Netscape

| Back | Forward | Home | Reload | Images | Open | Print | Find | Stop |

Go to: http//www.prenhall.com/phbusiness

OB in the News

Building People Skills through an Executive Coach

Carolyn Piecherowski's problems began soon after she was promoted to comptroller of the Rosan Aerospace Fastener Division of Fairchild Corporation. Piecherowski, 45, had previously run an accounting department with eight subordinates but was used to issuing orders with little explanation. "I'd tell them, 'Do it the way I say. Don't worry about the whys.'" That style didn't work in her new job. After subordinates loudly complained, Piercherowski's boss took action. Did he reprimand her or consider replacing her? No! He hired an executive coach to help her improve her people skills.

The use of executive coaches to help managers improve their people skills is on the rise. Companies such as Texaco, AT&T, American Express, Coca-Cola, CitiBank, Sun Microsystems, and Northern Telecom are finding that these coaches can polish up the interpersonal skills of managers whose technical skills they don't want to lose. "Years ago, if you were good, you could get away with being abrasive," says one coach. "Nowadays people don't want to work with you." These coaches charge from $5,000 for a half-dozen 90-minute sessions to $100,000 for consultations that can last two years and involve fact-finding interviews with dozens of colleagues, customers, and even families.

Who are candidates for this type of coaching? Some are recently promoted managers, like Carolyn Piecherowski, with limited experience. The bulk of candidates, however, tend to be older white male bosses. They often adhere to command-and-control leadership styles that hinder their effectiveness, and they have difficulty overseeing workers under age 45 who are more diverse in terms of race, gender, and national origin.

Based on T. Gabriel, "Personal Trainers to Buff the Boss's People Skills," *New York Times*, April 28, 1996, pp. F1, F10.

Take It to the Net

We invite you to visit the Robbins page on the Prentice Hall Web site at:

http://www.prenhall.com/robbinsorgbeh

for this chapter's World Wide Web exercise.

Organizational behavior is a field of study. That statement means that it is a distinct area of expertise with a common body of knowledge. What does it study? It studies three determinants of behavior in organizations: individuals, groups, and structure. In addition, OB applies the knowledge gained about individuals, groups, and the effect of structure on behavior in order to make organizations work more effectively.

To sum up our definition, OB is concerned with the study of what people do in an organization and how that behavior affects the performance of the organization. And because OB is specifically concerned with employment-related situations, you should not be surprised to find that it emphasizes behavior as related to jobs, work, absenteeism, employment turnover, productivity, human performance, and management.

There is increasing agreement as to the components or topics that constitute the subject area of OB. Although there is still considerable debate as to the relative importance of each, there appears to be general agreement that OB includes the core topics of motivation, leader behavior and power, interpersonal communication, group structure and processes, learning, attitude development and perception, change processes, conflict, work design, and work stress.[11]

Replacing Intuition with Systematic Study

Each of us is a student of behavior. Since our earliest years, we have watched the actions of others and have attempted to interpret what we see. Whether or not you have explicitly thought about it before, you have been "reading" people almost all your life. You watch what others do and try to explain to yourself why they have engaged in their behavior. In addition, you have attempted to predict what they might do under different sets of conditions.

Generalizations about Behavior

You have already developed some generalizations that you find helpful in explaining and predicting what people do and will do. But how did you arrive at those generalizations? You did so by observing, sensing, asking, listening, and reading. That is, your understanding comes either directly from your own experience with things in the environment, or secondhand, through the experience of others.

How accurate are the generalizations that you hold? Some may represent extremely sophisticated appraisals of behavior and may prove highly effective in explaining and predicting the behavior of others. However, most of us also carry with us a number of beliefs that frequently fail to explain why people do what they do.[12] To illustrate, let's consider the following statements about work-related behavior:

◆ Most of us carry with us a number of beliefs that frequently fail to explain why people do what they do.

1. Happy workers are productive workers.
2. All individuals are most productive when their boss is friendly, trusting, and approachable.

3. The best leaders are those that exhibit consistent behavior, regardless of the situations they face.

4. Interviews are effective selection devices for separating job applicants who would be high-performing employees from those who would be low performers.

5. Everyone wants a challenging job.

6. You have to scare people a little to get them to do their jobs.

7. Because specific goals intimidate people, individuals work harder when asked just to do their best.

8. Everyone is motivated by money.

9. Most people are much more concerned with the size of their own salaries than with the size of other people's salaries.

10. The most effective work groups are devoid of conflict.

How many of these statements do you think are true? For the most part, they're all false, and we shall touch on each later in this text. But whether these statements are true or false is not really important at this time. What is important is that many of the views you hold concerning human behavior are based on intuition rather than fact. As a result, a systematic approach to the study of behavior can improve your explanatory and predictive abilities.

Consistency vs. Individual Differences

Casual or commonsense approaches to obtaining knowledge about human behavior are inadequate. In reading this text, you will discover that a systematic approach will uncover important facts and relationships and will provide a base from which more-accurate predictions of behavior can be made. Underlying this systematic approach is the belief that behavior is not random. It stems from and is directed toward some end that the individual believes, rightly or wrongly, is in his or her best interest.

Behavior generally is predictable if we know how the person perceived the situation and what is important to him or her. While people's behavior may not appear to be rational to an outsider, there is reason to believe it usually is intended to be rational and it is seen as rational by them. An observer often sees behavior as nonrational because the observer does not have access to the same information or does not perceive the environment in the same way.[13]

Certainly there are differences between individuals. Placed in similar situations, all people don't act exactly alike. However, there are certain fundamental consistencies underlying the behavior of all individuals that can be identified and then modified to reflect individual differences.

These fundamental consistencies are very important. Why? Because they allow predictability. When you get into your car, you make some definite and usually highly accurate predictions about how other people will behave. In North America, for instance, you would predict that other drivers will stop at stop signs and red lights, drive on the right side of the road, pass on your left, and not cross the solid double line on mountain roads. Notice that your predictions about the behav-

◆ There are certain fundamental consistencies underlying the behavior of all individuals that can be identified and then modified to reflect individual differences.

ior of people behind the wheels of their cars are almost always correct. Obviously, the rules of driving make predictions about driving behavior fairly easy.

What may be less obvious is that there are rules (written and unwritten) in almost every setting. Therefore, it can be argued that it's possible to predict behavior (undoubtedly, not always with 100 percent accuracy) in supermarkets, classrooms, doctors' offices, elevators, and in most structured situations. For instance, do you turn around and face the doors when you get into an elevator? Almost everyone does. But did you ever read that you're supposed to do this? Probably not! Just as I make predictions about automobile drivers (where there are definite rules of the road), I can make predictions about the behavior of people in elevators (where there are few written rules). In a class of sixty students, if you wanted to ask a question of the instructor, I predict that you would raise your hand. Why don't you clap, stand up, raise your leg, cough, or yell "Hey, over here!"? The reason is that you have learned that raising your hand is appropriate behavior in school. These examples support a major contention in this text: Behavior is generally predictable, and the *systematic study* of behavior is a means to making reasonably accurate predictions.

When we use the phrase **systematic study**, we mean looking at relationships, attempting to attribute causes and effects, and basing our conclusions on scientific evidence—that is, on data gathered under controlled conditions and measured and interpreted in a reasonably rigorous manner. (See Appendix B in the back of the book for a basic review of research methods used in studies of organizational behavior.)

Systematic study replaces **intuition**, or those "gut feelings" about "why I do what I do" and "what makes others tick." Of course, a systematic approach does not mean that those things you have come to believe in an unsystematic way are necessarily incorrect. Some of the conclusions we make in this text, based on reasonably substantive research findings, will only support what you always knew was true. But you'll also be exposed to research evidence that runs counter to what you may have thought was common sense. In fact, one of the challenges to teaching a subject like organizational behavior is to overcome the notion, held by many, that "it's all common sense."[14] You'll find that many of the so-called commonsense views you hold about human behavior are, on closer examination, wrong. Moreover, what one person considers common sense frequently runs counter to another's version of

systematic study
Looking at relationships, attempting to attribute causes and effects, and drawing conclusions based on scientific evidence.

intuition
A feeling not necessarily supported by research.

Psychologists at the Center for Creative Leadership systematically study the behavior of managers in a controlled environment. Through one-way glass, they observe, videotape, and evaluate managers' leadership skills. They also gather data by surveying the managers and their co-workers, bosses, and subordinates. The goal of this scientific study: to teach managers how to lead others in their organizations effectively.

common sense. Are leaders born or made? What is it that motivates people at work nowadays? You probably have answers to such questions, and individuals who have not reviewed the research are likely to differ on their answers. The point is that one of the objectives of this text is to encourage you to move away from your intuitive views of behavior toward a systematic analysis, in the belief that such analysis will improve your accuracy in explaining and predicting behavior.

Challenges and Opportunities for OB

Understanding organizational behavior has never been more important for managers. A quick look at a few of the dramatic changes now taking place in organizations supports this claim. For instance, the typical employee is getting older; more and more women and nonwhites are in the workplace; corporate downsizing and cost cutting are severing the bonds of loyalty that historically tied many employees to their employers; and global competition is requiring employees to become more flexible and to learn to cope with rapid change.

In short, there are a lot of challenges and opportunities today for managers to use OB concepts. In this section, we review some of the more critical issues confronting managers for which OB offers solutions—or at least some meaningful insights toward solutions.

The Creation of a Global Village

Twenty or thirty years ago, national borders acted to insulate most firms from foreign competitive pressures. At least three factors contributed to this insulation. First, politicians imposed heavy tariffs on imports, so it was difficult for firms to competitively sell goods outside their own country. Second, communist countries such as the Soviet Union, Poland, Hungary, and Yugoslavia were managed economies. Burdened by poor management systems and primitive manufacturing processes, firms in the Eastern bloc couldn't compete on price or quality against products manufactured by firms in capitalist countries. And third, the labor force in many countries—specifically places such as Japan, Korea, Taiwan, and Malaysia—lacked the skills to produce high-quality products that could compete against those manufactured by North American and European workers.

Organizations are no longer constrained by national borders. Trading blocks such as NAFTA and the European Union have significantly reduced tariffs and barriers to trade; capitalism is rapidly replacing government control in Eastern European companies; and North America and Europe no longer have a monopoly on high-skilled labor.

The world has truly become a global village. Burger King is owned by a British firm, and McDonald's sells hamburgers in Moscow. Exxon, a so-called American company, receives almost 75 percent of its revenues from sales outside the United States. Toyota makes cars in Kentucky; General Motors makes cars in Brazil; and Ford (which owns part of Mazda) transfers executives from Detroit to Japan to help Mazda manage its operations. The message? As multinational corporations develop operations worldwide, as companies develop joint ventures with foreign partners, and as workers increasingly chase job opportunities across national borders, managers have to become capable of working with people from different cultures.

Through foreign assignments, managers of the Coca-Cola Company learn how to work with people from different cultures. John Hunter, an Australian, became the company's top international executive after successfully building strong relationships with bottlers in many countries. Hunter is shown here mingling with customers in Mexico, a market that offers the global soft-drink marketer significant growth potential.

Globalization affects a manager's people skills in at least two ways. First, if you're a manager you're increasingly likely to find yourself in a foreign assignment. You'll be transferred to your employer's operating division or subsidiary in another country. Once there, you'll have to manage a workforce that is likely to be very different in needs, aspirations, and attitudes from the ones you were used to back home. Second, even in your own country, you're going to find yourself working with bosses, peers, and subordinates who were born and raised in different cultures. What motivates you may not motivate them. Your style of communication may be straightforward and open; they may find that style uncomfortable and threatening. If you're going to be able to work effectively with these people, you'll need to understand their culture and how it has shaped them and to learn to adapt your management style. As we discuss OB concepts throughout this book, we'll repeatedly focus on how cultural differences might require managers to modify their practices.

From "Everyone's the Same" to Workforce Diversity

One of the most important and broad-based challenges currently facing organizations is adapting to people who are different. The term we use for describing this challenge is *workforce diversity*. Whereas globalization focuses on differences between people from different countries, workforce diversity addresses differences among people within given countries.

Workforce diversity means that organizations are becoming more heterogeneous in terms of gender, race, and ethnicity. But the term

workforce diversity
The increasing heterogeneity of organizations with the inclusion of different groups.

encompasses anyone who varies from the so-called norm. In addition to the more obvious groups—women, African Americans, Hispanic Americans, Asian Americans—it also includes the physically disabled, gays and lesbians, and the elderly. Moreover, it's an issue in Canada, Australia, South Africa, Japan, and Europe as well as the United States. Managers in Canada and Australia, for instance, are having to adjust to large influxes of Asian workers. The "new" South Africa will increasingly be characterized by blacks' holding important technical and managerial jobs. Women, long confined to low-paying temporary jobs in Japan, are moving into managerial positions. And the creation of the European Union cooperative trade arrangement, which opened up borders throughout much of western Europe, has increased workforce diversity in organizations that operate in countries such as Germany, Portugal, Italy, and France.

We used to take a melting pot approach to differences in organizations, assuming people who were different would somehow automatically want to assimilate. But we now recognize that employees don't set aside their cultural values and lifestyle preferences when they come to work. The challenge for organizations, therefore, is to make themselves more accommodating to diverse groups of people by addressing their different lifestyles, family needs, and work styles. The melting pot assumption is being replaced by one that recognizes and values differences.[15]

Haven't organizations always included members of diverse groups? Yes, but they were a small percentage of the workforce and were, for the most part, ignored by large organizations. Moreover, it was assumed that these minorities would seek to blend in and assimilate. For instance, the bulk of the pre-1980s U.S. workforce were male Caucasians working full-time to support a nonemployed wife and school-aged children. Now such employees are the true minority! Currently, 45 percent of the U.S. labor force are women. Minorities and immigrants make up 22 percent.[16] As a case in point, Hewlett-Packard's workforce is 19 percent minorities and 40 percent women.[17] A Digital Equipment Corporation plant in Boston provides a partial preview of the future. The factory's 350 employees include men and women from 44 countries who speak 19 languages. When plant management issues written announcements, they are printed in English, Chinese, French, Spanish, Portuguese, Vietnamese, and Haitian Creole.

Workforce diversity has important implications for management practice. Managers will need to shift their philosophy from treating everyone alike to recognizing differences and responding to those differences in ways that will ensure employee retention and greater productivity while, at the same time, not discriminating. This shift includes, for instance, providing diversity training and revamping benefit programs to make them more "family-friendly." Diversity, if positively managed, can increase creativity and innovation in organizations as well as improve decision making by providing different perspectives on problems.[18] When diversity is not managed properly, there is potential for higher turnover, more-difficult communication, and more interpersonal conflicts.

Toward Improving Quality and Productivity

Tom Rossi manages in a tough business. He runs a light bulb plant in Mattoon, Illinois, for General Electric. His business has seen tough competition from manufacturers in the United States, Europe, Japan, and even China. To survive, he has had to cut fat, increase productivity, and improve quality. And he has succeeded. Over a recent five-year period, the Mattoon plant has averaged annual cost productivity improvements of approximately 8 percent. By focusing on continuous improvement, streamlining processes, and cutting costs, GE's Mattoon plant has remained viable and profitable.[19]

More and more managers are confronting the challenges that Tom Rossi is facing. They are having to improve their organization's productivity and the quality of the products and services they offer. Toward improving quality and productivity, they are implementing programs such as total quality management and reengineering—programs that require extensive employee involvement.

We discuss **total quality management (TQM)** throughout this book. As Exhibit 1-3 describes, TQM is a philosophy of management that is driven by the constant attainment of customer satisfaction through the continuous improvement of all organizational processes.[20] TQM has implications for OB because it requires employees to rethink what they do and become more involved in workplace decisions.

In times of rapid and dramatic change, it's sometimes necessary to approach improving quality and productivity from the perspective of "How would we do things around here if we were starting over from scratch?" That, in essence, is the approach of **reengineering**. It asks managers to reconsider how work would be done and their organization structured if they were starting over.[21] To illustrate the concept of reengineering, consider a manufacturer of roller skates. His product is essentially a shoe with wheels beneath it. The typical roller skate was a leather boot with shoelaces, attached to a steel platform that held four wooden wheels. If our manufacturer took a continuous improvement approach to change, he would look for small incremental improvements that he could introduce in his product. For instance, he might

total quality management (TQM)
A philosophy of management that is driven by the constant attainment of customer satisfaction through the continuous improvement of all organizational processes.

reengineering
Reconsiders how work would be done and the organization structured if they were being created from scratch.

Exhibit 1-3 What Is Total Quality Management?

1. *Intense focus on the customer.* The customer includes not only outsiders who buy the organization's products or services but also internal customers (such as shipping or accounts payable personnel) who interact with and serve others in the organization.

2. *Concern for continuous improvement.* TQM is a commitment to never being satisfied. "Very good" is not good enough. Quality can always be improved.

3. *Improvement in the quality of everything the organization does.* TQM uses a very broad definition of quality. It relates not only to the final product but also to how the organization handles deliveries, how rapidly it responds to complaints, how politely the phones are answered, and the like.

4. *Accurate measurement.* TQM uses statistical techniques to measure every critical performance variable in the organization's operations. These performance variables are then compared against standards or benchmarks to identify problems, the problems are traced to their roots, and the causes are eliminated.

5. *Empowerment of employees.* TQM involves the people on the line in the improvement process. Teams are widely used in TQM programs as empowerment vehicles for finding and solving problems.

consider adding hooks to the upper part of the boot for speed lacing; or changing the weight of leather used for improved comfort; or using different ballbearings to make the wheels spin more smoothly. Now most of us are familiar with in-line skates. They represent a reengineering approach to roller skates. The goal was to come up with a skating device that could improve skating speed, mobility, and control. Rollerblades fulfilled those goals in a completely different type of shoe. The upper was made of injected plastic, made popular in skiing. Laces were replaced by easy-close clamps. And the four wooden wheels, set in pairs of two, were replaced by four to six in-line plastic wheels. The reengineered result, which didn't look much like the traditional roller skate, proved universally superior. The rest, of course, is history. In-line skates have revolutionized the roller skate business.

Contemporary managers understand that, for any effort to improve quality and productivity to succeed, it must include their employees. These employees will not only be a major force in carrying out changes but increasingly will participate actively in planning them. OB offers important insights into helping managers work through those changes.

Improving People Skills

We opened this chapter by demonstrating how important people skills are to managerial effectiveness. We said, "This book has been written to help both managers and potential managers develop those people skills."

As you proceed through this text, we present relevant concepts and theories that can help you explain and predict the behavior of people at work. In addition, you'll also gain insights into specific people skills that you can use on the job. For instance, you'll learn how to be an effective listener, the proper way to give performance feedback, how to delegate authority, and how to create effective teams. Moreover, you'll have the opportunity to complete exercises that will give you insights into your own behavior, the behavior of others, and practice at improving your interpersonal skills.

From Management Control to Empowerment

If you pick up any popular business periodical nowadays, you'll read about the reshaping of the relationship between managers and the people they are supposedly responsible for managing. You'll find managers' being called coaches, advisers, sponsors, or facilitators.[22] In many organizations, employees have become associates or teammates.[23] And there's a blurring between the roles of managers and workers. Decision making is being pushed down to the operating level, where workers are being given the freedom to make choices about schedules, procedures, and solving work-related problems. In the 1980s, managers were encouraged to get their employees to participate in work-related decisions.[24] Now, managers are going considerably further by allowing employees full control of their work. Self-managed teams, in which workers operate largely without bosses, have become the rage of the 1990s.[25]

What's going on is that managers are empowering employees. They are putting employees in charge of what they do. And in so doing, managers are having to learn how to give up control and employees are having to learn how to take responsibility for their work and make appropriate decisions. In later chapters of this book we show how **empowerment** is changing leadership styles, power relationships, the way work is designed, and the way organizations are structured.

empowerment
Putting employees in charge of what they do.

From Stability to Flexibility

Managers have always been concerned with change. What's different nowadays is the length of time between changes. It used to be that managers needed to introduce major change programs once or twice a decade. Today, change is an ongoing activity for most managers. The concept of continuous improvement, for instance, implies constant change.

◆ Today, change is an ongoing activity for most managers.

In the past, managing could be characterized by long periods of stability, interrupted occasionally by short periods of change. Managing today would be more accurately described as long periods of ongoing change, interrupted occasionally by short periods of stability! The world that most managers and employees face today is one of permanent temporariness. The actual jobs that workers perform are in a permanent state of flux, so workers need to continually update their knowledge and skills to perform new job requirements.[26] For example, production employees at companies such as Caterpillar, Chrysler, and Reynolds Metals now need to know how to operate computerized production equipment. That was not part of their job description 15 years ago. Work groups are also increasingly in a state of flux. In the past, employees were assigned to a specific work group, and that assignment was relatively permanent. There was a considerable amount of security in working with the same people day in and day out. That predictability has been replaced by temporary work groups, teams that include members from different departments and whose members change all the time, and the increased use of employee rotation to fill constantly changing work assignments. Finally, organizations themselves are in a state of flux. They continually reorganize their various divisions, sell off poor-performing businesses, downsize operations, subcontract noncritical services and operations to other organizations, and replace permanent employees with temporaries.[27]

Today's managers and employees must learn to cope with temporariness. They have to learn to live with flexibility, spontaneity, and unpredictability. The study of OB can provide important insights into helping you better understand a work world of continual change, how to overcome resistance to change, and how best to create an organizational culture that thrives on change.

Improving Ethical Behavior

In an organizational world characterized by cutbacks, expectations of increasing worker productivity, and tough competition in the marketplace, it's not altogether surprising that many employees feel pressured to cut corners, break rules, and engage in other questionable practices.

Members of organizations are increasingly finding themselves facing **ethical dilemmas**, situations in which they are required to define right and wrong conduct.[28] For example, should they blow the whistle if they uncover illegal activities taking place in their company? Should they follow orders they don't personally agree with? Do they give an inflated performance evalu-

ethical dilemma
Situation in which an individual is required to define right and wrong conduct.

ation to an employee they like, knowing that such an evaluation could save that employee's job? Do they allow themselves to play politics in the organization if it will help their career advancement?

What constitutes good ethical behavior has never been clearly defined. And in recent years the line differentiating right from wrong has become even more blurred. Employees see people all around them engaging in unethical practices: Elected officials are indicted for padding their expense accounts or taking bribes; high-powered lawyers, who know the rules, are found to be avoiding payment of Social Security taxes for their household help; successful executives use insider information for personal financial gain; employees in other companies participate in massive cover-ups of defective military weapons. They hear these people, when caught, giving excuses like, "Everyone does it," or "You have to seize every advantage nowadays," or "I never thought I'd get caught."

Managers and their organizations are responding to this problem from several directions.[29] They're writing and distributing codes of ethics to guide employees through ethical dilemmas. They're offering seminars, workshops, and similar training programs to try to improve ethical behaviors. They're providing in-house advisers who can be contacted, in many cases anonymously, for assistance in dealing with ethical issues. And they're creating protection mechanisms for employees who reveal internal unethical practices.

◆ Today's manager needs to create an ethically healthy climate for his or her employees, where they can do their work productively and confront a minimal degree of ambiguity regarding what constitutes right and wrong behavior.

Today's manager needs to create an ethically healthy climate for his or her employees, where they can do their work productively and confront a minimal degree of ambiguity regarding what constitutes right and wrong behavior. We discuss ethics in several places in this book—for example, as it relates to decision making and politics in organizations. To help you define and establish your personal ethical standards, we include ethical dilemma exercises at the end of many chapters. By confronting ethical issues you might not have thought about before, and sharing your ideas with classmates, you can gain insights into your own ethical viewpoints, those of others, and the implications of various choices.

Contributing Disciplines to the OB Field

Organizational behavior is an applied behavioral science that is built upon contributions from a number of behavioral disciplines. The predominant areas are psychology, sociology, social psychology, anthropology, and political science.[30] As we shall learn, psychology's contributions have been mainly at the individual or micro level of analysis; the other four disciplines have contributed to our understanding of macro concepts such as group processes and organization. Exhibit 1-4 presents an overview of the major contributions to the study of organizational behavior.

Psychology

psychology
The science that seeks to measure, explain, and sometimes change the behavior of humans and other animals.

Psychology is the science that seeks to measure, explain, and sometimes change the behavior of humans and other animals. Psychologists concern themselves with studying and attempting to understand individual behavior.

Exhibit 1-4
Toward an OB Discipline

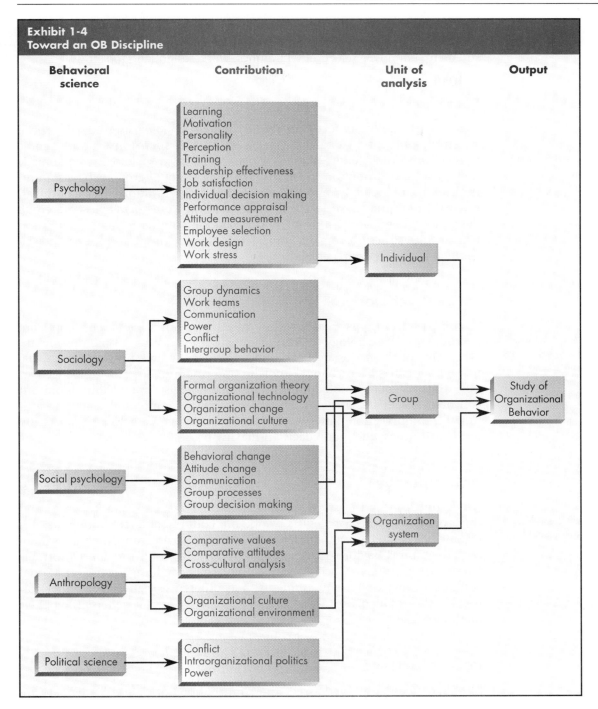

Those who have contributed and continue to add to the knowledge of OB are learning theorists, personality theorists, counseling psychologists, and, most important, industrial and organizational psychologists.

Early industrial and organizational psychologists concerned themselves with problems of fatigue, boredom, and other factors relevant to working conditions that could impede efficient work performance. More recently, their contributions have been expanded to include learning, perception, personality, training, leadership effectiveness, needs and motivational forces, job satisfaction, decision-making processes, performance appraisals, attitude measurement, employee selection techniques, work design, and job stress.

Sociology

sociology
The study of people in relation to their fellow human beings.

Whereas psychologists focus on the individual, sociologists study the social system in which individuals fill their roles; that is, **sociology** studies people in relation to their fellow human beings. Specifically, sociologists have made their greatest contribution to OB through their study of group behavior in organizations, particularly in formal and complex organizations. Some of the areas within OB that have received valuable input from sociologists are group dynamics, design of work teams, organizational culture, formal organization theory and structure, organizational technology, communications, power, conflict, and intergroup behavior.

Social Psychology

social psychology
An area within psychology that blends concepts from psychology and sociology and that focuses on the influence of people on one another.

Social psychology is an area within psychology, but it blends concepts from psychology and sociology. It focuses on the influence of people on one another. One of the major areas receiving considerable investigation from social psychologists has been change—how to implement it and how to reduce barriers to its acceptance. In addition, social psychologists are making significant contributions in the areas of measuring, understanding, and changing attitudes; communication patterns; the ways in which group activities can satisfy individual needs; and group decision-making processes.

Anthropology

anthropology
The study of societies to learn about human beings and their activities.

Anthropology is the study of societies to learn about human beings and their activities. Anthropologists' work on cultures and environments, for instance, has helped us understand differences in fundamental values, attitudes, and behavior between people in different countries and within different organizations. Much of our current understanding of organizational culture, organizational environments, and differences between national cultures is the result of the work of anthropologists or researchers using their methodologies.[31]

Political Science

political science
The study of the behavior of individuals and groups within a political environment.

Although frequently overlooked, the contributions of political scientists are significant to the understanding of behavior in organizations. **Political science** studies the behavior of individuals and groups within a political environment. Specific topics of concern include structuring of conflict, allocation of power, and how people manipulate power for individual self-interest.

Thirty years ago, little of what political scientists were studying was of interest to students of organizational behavior. But times have changed. We have become increasingly aware that organizations are political entities; if we are to be able to accurately explain and predict the behavior of people in organizations, we need to bring a political perspective to our analysis.

Exhibit 1-5
Drawing by Handelsman in *The New Yorker.* Copyright © 1986 by The New Yorker Magazine. Reprinted by permission.

"I'm a social scientist, Michael. That means I can't explain electricity or anything like that, but if you ever want to know about people I'm your man."

There Are Few Absolutes in OB

There are few, if any, simple and universal principles that explain organizational behavior. There are laws in the physical sciences—chemistry, astronomy, physics—that are consistent and apply in a wide range of situations. They allow scientists to generalize about the pull of gravity or to confidently send astronauts into space to repair satellites. But as one noted behavioral researcher aptly concluded, "God gave all the easy problems to the physicists." Human beings are complex. Because they are not alike, our ability to make simple, accurate, and sweeping generalizations is limited. Two people often act very differently in the same situation, and the same person's behavior changes in different situations. For instance, not everyone is motivated by money, and you behave differently at church on Sunday than you did at the beer party the night before.

◆ "God gave all the easy problems to the physicists."

That doesn't mean, of course, that we can't offer reasonably accurate explanations of human behavior or make valid predictions. It does mean, however, that OB concepts must reflect situational, or contingency, conditions. We can say that *x* leads to *y*, but only under conditions specified in *z* (the **contingency variables**). The science of OB was developed by using general concepts and then altering their application to the particular situation. So, for example, OB scholars would avoid stating that effective leaders should always seek the ideas of their subordinates before making a decision. Rather, we shall find that in some situations a participative style is clearly superior, but, in other situations, an autocratic decision style is more effective. In other words, the effectiveness of a particular leadership style is contingent upon the situation in which it is used.

As you proceed through this text, you'll encounter a wealth of research-based theories about how people behave in organizations. But don't expect to

contingency variables
Situational factors; variables that moderate the relationship between the independent and dependent variables and improve the correlation.

find a lot of straightforward cause-and-effect relationships. There aren't many! Organizational behavior theories mirror the subject matter with which they deal. People are complex and complicated, and so too must be the theories developed to explain their actions.

Consistent with the contingency philosophy, point-counterpoint debates are provided at the conclusion of each chapter. These debates are included to reinforce the fact that within the OB field there are many issues over which there is significant disagreement. Directly addressing some of the more controversial issues using the point-counterpoint format gives you the opportunity to explore different points of view, discover how diverse perspectives complement and oppose each other, and gain insight into some of the debates currently taking place within the OB field.[32]

So at the end of one chapter, you'll find the argument that leadership plays an important role in an organization's attaining its goals, followed by the argument that there is little evidence to support that claim. Similarly, at the end of other chapters, you'll read both sides of the debate on whether money is a motivator, clear communication is always desirable, and other controversial issues. These arguments are meant to demonstrate that OB, like many disciplines, has disagreements over specific findings, methods, and theories. Some of the point-counterpoint arguments are more provocative than others, but each makes some valid points that you should find thought-provoking. The key is to be able to decipher under what conditions each argument may be right or wrong.

> ◆ There are three levels of analysis in OB, and, as we move from the individual level to the group level to the organization systems level, we add systematically to our understanding of behavior in organizations.

Coming Attractions: Developing an OB Model

We conclude this chapter by presenting a general model that defines the field of OB, stakes out its parameters, and identifies its primary dependent and independent variables. The end result will be a "coming attraction" of the topics making up the remainder of this book.

An Overview

model
Abstraction of reality; simplified representation of some real-world phenomenon.

A **model** is an abstraction of reality, a simplified representation of some real-world phenomenon. A mannequin in a retail store is a model. So, too, is the accountant's formula: Assets = Liabilities + Owners' Equity. Exhibit 1-7 pre-

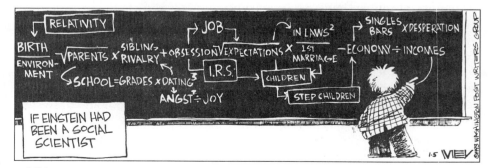

Exhibit 1-6
"Non-Sequitur" by Wiley in *The Washington Post*, January 5, 1993. Copyright © 1993, Washington Post Writers Group. Reprinted with permission.

sents the skeleton on which we will construct our OB model. It proposes that there are three levels of analysis in OB and that, as we move from the individual level to the organization systems level, we add systematically to our understanding of behavior in organizations. The three basic levels are analogous to building blocks; each level is constructed upon the previous level. Group concepts grow out of the foundation laid in the individual section; we overlay structural constraints on the individual and group in order to arrive at organizational behavior.

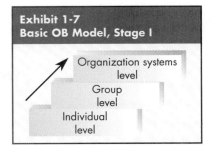

Exhibit 1-7
Basic OB Model, Stage I

Organization systems level
Group level
Individual level

The Dependent Variables

Dependent variables are the key factors that you want to explain or predict and that are affected by some other factor. What are the primary dependent variables in OB? Scholars tend to emphasize *productivity, absenteeism, turnover,* and *job satisfaction.* Because of their wide acceptance, we shall use those four as the critical dependent variables in an organization's human resources effectiveness. However, there is nothing magical about these dependent variables. They merely show that OB research has strongly reflected managerial interests over those of individuals or of society as a whole. Let's review those terms to ensure that we understand what they mean and why they have achieved the distinction of being OB's primary dependent variables.

dependent variable
A response that is affected by an independent variable.

PRODUCTIVITY   An organization is productive if it achieves its goals and does so by transferring inputs to outputs at the lowest cost. As such, **productivity** implies a concern for both **effectiveness** and **efficiency**.

A hospital, for example, is *effective* when it successfully meets the needs of its clientele. It is *efficient* when it can do so at a low cost. If a hospital manages to achieve higher output from its present staff by reducing the average number of days a patient is confined to a bed or by increasing the number of staff-patient contacts per day, we say that the hospital has gained productive

productivity
A performance measure including effectiveness and efficiency.

effectiveness
Achievement of goals.

efficiency
The ratio of effective output to the input required to achieve it.

In getting a shave from a flight attendant, British Airways' CEO Robert Ayling signals his plan to boost the airline's efficiency by shaving $1.5 billion in operating costs. Ayling plans to create a stripped-down profit machine focused on delivering top-grade service on global routes by asking 5,000 volunteers to leave the company, reducing costs in accounting and in baggage and cargo handling, and giving less profitable routes to smaller airlines to operate as franchises.

efficiency. A business firm is effective when it attains its sales or market share goals, but its productivity also depends on achieving those goals efficiently. Measures of such efficiency may include return on investment, profit per dollar of sales, and output per hour of labor.

We can also look at productivity from the perspective of the individual employee. Take the cases of Mike and Al, who are both long-distance truckers. If Mike is supposed to haul his fully loaded rig from New York to its destination in Los Angeles in 75 hours or less, he is effective if he makes the 3,000-mile trip within that time period. But measures of productivity must take into account the costs incurred in reaching the goal. That's where efficiency comes in. Let's assume that Mike made the New York to Los Angeles run in 68 hours and averaged 7 miles per gallon. Al, on the other hand, made the trip in 68 hours also but averaged 9 miles per gallon (rigs and loads are identical). Both Mike and Al were effective—they accomplished their goal—but Al was more efficient than Mike because his rig consumed less gas and, therefore, he achieved his goal at a lower cost.

In summary, one of OB's major concerns is productivity. We want to know what factors will influence the effectiveness and efficiency of individuals, of groups, and of the overall organization.

absenteeism
Failure to report to work.

ABSENTEEISM The annual cost of **absenteeism** has been estimated at over $40 billion for U.S. organizations and $12 billion for Canadian firms.[33] In Germany, absences cost industrial firms more than 60 billion Deutschmarks (U.S.$35.5 billion) each year.[34] At the job level, a one-day absence by a clerical worker can cost a U.S. employer up to $100 in reduced efficiency and increased supervisory workload.[35] These figures indicate the importance to an organization of keeping absenteeism low.

It is obviously difficult for an organization to operate smoothly and to attain its objectives if employees fail to report to their jobs. The work flow is disrupted, and often important decisions must be delayed. In organizations that rely heavily upon assembly-line production, absenteeism can be considerably more than a disruption; it can result in a drastic reduction in quality of output, and, in some cases, it can bring about a complete shutdown of the production facility. But levels of absenteeism beyond the normal range in any organization have a direct impact on that organization's effectiveness and efficiency.

Are *all* absences bad? Probably not! Although most absences have a negative impact on the organization, we can conceive of situations in which the organization may benefit by an employee's voluntarily choosing not to come to work. For instance, illness, fatigue, or excess stress can significantly decrease an employee's productivity. In jobs in which an employee needs to be alert—surgeons and airline pilots are obvious examples—it may well be better for the organization if the employee does not report to work rather than show up and perform poorly. The cost of an accident in such jobs could be prohibitive. Even in managerial jobs, where mistakes are less spectacular, performance may be improved when managers absent themselves from work rather than make a poor decision under stress. But these examples are clearly atypical. For the most part, we can assume that organizations benefit when employee absenteeism is low.

turnover
Voluntary and involuntary permanent withdrawal from the organization.

TURNOVER A high rate of **turnover** in an organization results in high recruiting, selection, and training costs. How high are those costs? A conservative estimate would be about $15,000 per employee.[36] A high rate of turnover can also disrupt the efficient running of an organization when knowledgeable and experienced personnel leave and replacements must be found and prepared to assume positions of responsibility.

All organizations, of course, have some turnover. In fact, if the "right" people are leaving the organization—the marginal and submarginal employees—turnover can be positive. It may create the opportunity to replace an underperforming individual with someone who has higher skills or motivation, open up increased opportunities for promotions, and add new and fresh ideas to the organization.[37] In today's changing world of work, reasonable levels of employee-initiated turnover facilitate organizational flexibility and employee independence, and they can lessen the need for management-initiated layoffs.

But turnover often involves the loss of people the organization doesn't want to lose. For instance, one study covering 900 employees who had resigned their jobs found that 92 percent earned performance ratings of "satisfactory" or better from their superiors.[38] So when turnover is excessive, or when it involves valuable performers, it can be a disruptive factor, hindering the organization's effectiveness.

JOB SATISFACTION   The final dependent variable we will look at is **job satisfaction**, which we define simply, at this point, as the difference between the amount of rewards workers receive and the amount they believe they should receive. (We expand considerably on that definition in chapter 4.) Unlike the previous three variables, job satisfaction represents an attitude rather than a behavior. Why, then, has it become a primary dependent variable? For two reasons: its demonstrated relationship to performance factors and the value preferences held by many OB researchers.

The belief that satisfied employees are more productive than dissatisfied employees has been a basic tenet among managers for years. Although much evidence questions that assumed causal relationship, it can be argued that advanced societies should be concerned not only with the quantity of life—that is, concerns such as higher productivity and material acquisitions—but also with its quality. Those researchers with strong humanistic values argue that satisfaction is a legitimate objective of an organization. Not only is

job satisfaction
A general attitude toward one's job; the difference between the amount of rewards workers receive and the amount they believe they should receive.

Companies are coming up with creative ways to increase job satisfaction. One way that Autodesk, a San Rafael, California-based software developer, keeps its employees satisfied is by allowing them to bring their dogs to work. The practice helps Autodesk maintain a loyal and motivated workforce that rates high on job satisfaction and productivity and low on turnover. Autodesk's dog lovers are shown here with their pets during lunchtime.

satisfaction negatively related to absenteeism and turnover, but, they argue, organizations have a responsibility to provide employees with jobs that are challenging and intrinsically rewarding. Therefore, although job satisfaction represents an attitude rather than a behavior, OB researchers typically consider it an important dependent variable.

The Independent Variables

independent variable
The presumed cause of some change in the dependent variable.

What are the major determinants of productivity, absenteeism, turnover, and job satisfaction? Our answer to that question brings us to the **independent variables**. Consistent with our belief that organizational behavior can best be understood when viewed essentially as a set of increasingly complex building blocks, the base, or first level, of our model lies in understanding individual behavior.

INDIVIDUAL-LEVEL VARIABLES It has been said that "managers, unlike parents, must work with used, not new, human beings—human beings whom others have gotten to first."[39] When individuals enter an organization, they are a bit like used cars. Each is different. Some are "low-mileage"—they have been treated carefully and have had only limited exposure to the realities of the elements. Others are "well-worn," having been driven over some rough roads. This metaphor indicates that people enter organizations with certain characteristics that will influence their behavior at work. The more obvious of these are personal or biographical characteristics such as age, gender, and marital status; personality characteristics; values and attitudes; and basic ability levels. These characteristics are essentially intact when an individual enters the workforce, and, for the most part, there is little management can do to alter them. Yet they have a very real impact on employee behavior. Therefore, each of these factors—biographical characteristics, personality, values and attitudes, and ability—will be discussed as independent variables in chapters 2 and 4.

There are four other individual-level variables that have been shown to affect employee behavior: perception, individual decision making, learning, and motivation. Those topics will be introduced and discussed in chapters 2, 3, 5, and 6.

GROUP-LEVEL VARIABLES The behavior of people in groups is more than the sum total of all the individuals acting in their own way. The complexity of our model is increased when we acknowledge that people's behavior when they are in groups is different from their behavior when they are alone. Therefore, the next step in the development of an understanding of OB is the study of group behavior.

Chapter 7 lays the foundation for an understanding of the dynamics of group behavior. That chapter discusses how individuals in groups are influenced by the patterns of behavior they are expected to exhibit, what the group considers to be acceptable standards of behavior, and the degree to which group members are attracted to each other. Chapter 8 translates our understanding of groups to the design of effective work teams. Chapters 9 through 12 demonstrate how communication patterns, leadership styles, power and politics, intergroup relations, and levels of conflict affect group behavior.

ORGANIZATION SYSTEMS LEVEL VARIABLES Organizational behavior reaches its highest level of sophistication when we add formal structure to our previous knowledge of individual and group behavior. Just as groups are more than the sum of their individual members, so are organizations more than the sum of their member groups. The design of the formal organization, work processes, and jobs; the organization's human resource policies and practices (that is, selection processes, training programs, performance appraisal methods); and the internal culture all have an impact on the dependent variables. These are discussed in detail in chapters 13 through 16.

Toward a Contingency OB Model

Our final model is shown in Exhibit 1-8 on page 28. It shows the four key dependent variables and a large number of independent variables, organized by level of analysis, that research indicates have varying effects on the former. As complicated as this model is, it still does not do justice to the complexity of the OB subject matter, but it should help explain why the chapters in this book are arranged as they are and help you to explain and predict the behavior of people at work.

For the most part, our model does not explicitly identify the vast number of contingency variables because of the tremendous complexity that would be involved in such a diagram. Rather, throughout this text we shall introduce important contingency variables that will improve the explanatory linkage between the independent and dependent variables in our OB model.

Note that we have included the concepts of change and stress in Exhibit 1-8, acknowledging the dynamics of behavior and the fact that work stress is an individual, group, and organizational issue. Specifically, in chapter 17 we will discuss the change process, ways to manage organizational change, key change issues for management in the 1990s, consequences of work stress, and techniques for managing stress.

Also note that Exhibit 1-8 includes linkages between the three levels of analysis. For instance, organization structure is linked to leadership. This link is meant to convey that authority and leadership are related; management exerts its influence on group behavior through leadership. Similarly, communication is the means by which individuals transmit information; thus, it is the link between individual and group behavior.

Summary and Implications for Managers

Managers need to develop their interpersonal, or people, skills if they are going to be effective in their jobs. Organizational behavior (OB) is a field of study that investigates the impact that individuals, groups, and structure have on behavior within an organization, and then it applies that knowledge to make organizations work more effectively. Specifically, OB focuses on how to improve productivity, reduce absenteeism and turnover, and increase employee job satisfaction.

We all hold generalizations about the behavior of people. Some of our generalizations may provide valid insights into human behavior, but many are erroneous. Organizational behavior uses systematic study to improve predictions of behavior that would be made from intuition alone. But, because

Exhibit 1-8
Basic OB Model, Stage II

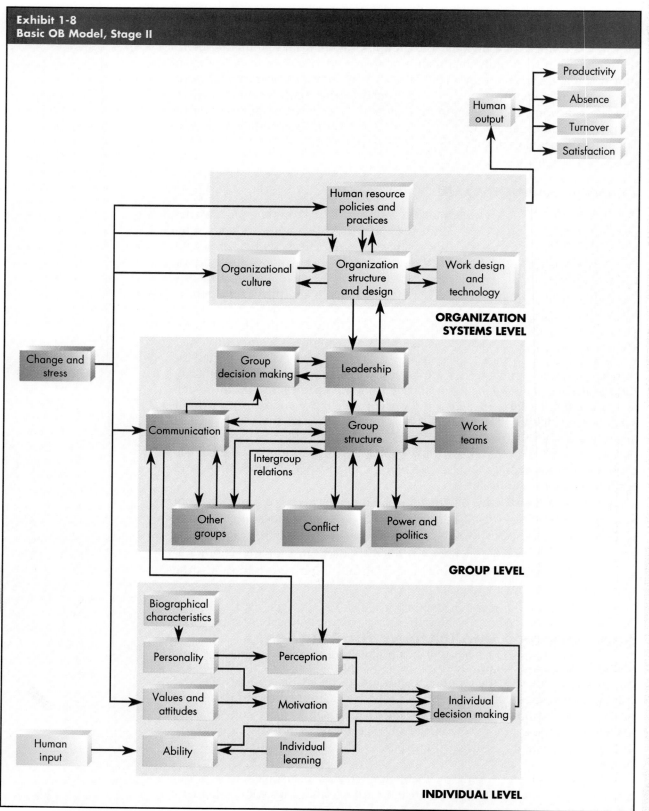

people are different, we need to look at OB in a contingency framework, using situational variables to moderate cause-effect relationships.

Organizational behavior offers both challenges and opportunities for managers. It recognizes differences and helps managers to see the value of workforce diversity and practices that may need to be changed when managing in different countries. It can help improve quality and employee productivity by showing managers how to empower their people as well as how to design and implement change programs. It offers specific insights to improve a manager's people skills. In times of rapid and ongoing change—what most managers face today—OB can help managers learn to cope in a world of temporariness and to manage a workforce that has undergone the trauma of downsizing. Finally, OB can offer managers guidance in creating an ethically healthy work climate.

For Review

1. "Behavior generally is predictable." Do you agree or disagree? Explain.

2. Define *organizational behavior*. Relate it to *management*.

3. What is an organization? Is the family unit an organization? Explain.

4. Identify and contrast the three general management roles.

5. What is TQM? How is it related to OB?

6. In what areas has psychology contributed to OB? Sociology? Social psychology? Anthropology? Political science? What other academic disciplines may have contributed to OB?

7. "Behavior is generally predictable, so there is no need to formally study OB." Why is that statement wrong?

8. What are the three levels of analysis in our OB model? Are they related? If so, how?

9. If job satisfaction is not a behavior, why is it considered an important dependent variable?

10. What are effectiveness and efficiency, and how are they related to organizational behavior?

For Discussion

1. Contrast the research comparing effective managers with successful managers. What are the implications from the research for practicing managers?

2. "The best way to view OB is through a contingency approach." Build an argument to support that statement.

3. Why do you think the subject of OB might be criticized as being "only common sense," when one would rarely hear such a criticism of a course in physics or statistics?

4. Millions of workers have lost their jobs due to downsizing. At the same time, many organizations are complaining that they can't find people to fill vacancies. How do you explain this apparent contradiction?

5. On a 1 to 10 scale measuring the sophistication of a scientific discipline in predicting phenomena, mathematical physics would probably be a 10. Where do you think OB would fall on the scale? Why?

The Case for a Structural Explanation of Organizational Behavior

If you want to really understand the behavior of people at work, you need to focus on social structure. Why? As one noted scholar put it, "The fundamental fact of social life is precisely that it is social—that human beings do not live in isolation but associate with other human beings."*

Far too much emphasis is placed on studying individual characteristics of people. We're not saying here that values, attitudes, personalities, and similar personal characteristics are irrelevant to understanding organizational behavior. Rather, our position is that you gain considerably more insight if you look at the structured relationships between individuals in organizations and how those relationships constrain certain actions and enable others to occur.

Organizations come with a host of formal and informal control mechanisms that, in effect, largely shape, direct, and constrain members' behavior. Let's look at a few examples.

Almost all organizations have formal documentation that limits and shapes behavior. This includes things such as policies, procedures, rules, job descriptions, and job instructions. This formal documentation sets standards of acceptable and unacceptable behavior. If you know an organization's major policies and have a copy of a specific employee's job description, you have a major leg up in being able to predict a good deal of that specific employee's on-the-job behavior.

Almost all organizations differentiate roles horizontally. By that I mean, they create unique jobs and departments. Toni is a sales representative for H. J. Heinz, calling on supermarkets. Frank also works for Heinz, but on an assembly line, where he monitors machines that fill pickle relish jars. The structure of these jobs alone allows me to predict that Toni will have a great deal more autonomy in deciding what she is going to do in her job and how she is going to do it than does Frank.

Organizations also differentiate roles vertically by creating levels of management. In so doing, they create boss-subordinate relationships that constrain subordinate behavior. In our nonwork lives we don't have "bosses" who can tell us what to do, evaluate us, and even fire us. But most of us do at work. And remember, bosses evaluate employee performance and typically control the allocation of rewards. So if I know what behaviors your boss prefers, I can gain insight into what behaviors you are most likely to exhibit.

When you join an organization, you are expected to adapt to its norms of acceptable behavior. The "rules" don't have to be written down to be powerful and controlling. An organization, for instance, may not have a formal dress code, but employees are expected to "dress appropriately"—which means adapting to the implied dress code norms. Merrill Lynch expects its brokers to dress appropriately: Men wear coats and ties and women wear similarly professional attire. Along the same lines, Microsoft's norms emphasize long work hours—60 to 70 hour workweeks are not unusual. These expectations are understood by employees, and employees modify their behavior accordingly.

The point is that you shouldn't forget the *organizational* part of organizational behavior. It doesn't sound very nice, but organizations are instruments of domination. They put people into job "boxes" that constrain what they can do and individuals with whom they can interact. To the degree that employees accept their boss's authority and the limits the organization places on their role, then that authority and those limits become constraints on the behavioral choices of organization members.

Some points in this argument are based on J. Pfeffer, "Organization Theory and Structural Perspectives on Management," *Journal of Management*, December 1991, pp. 789–803.

* P.M. Blau, *Inequality and Heterogeneity* (New York: Free Press, 1977), p. 1.

counterPoint

The Case for a Psychological Explanation of Organizational Behavior

The concept of an "organization" is an artificial notion. Organizations have physical properties, such as buildings, offices, and equipment, that tend to obscure the obvious fact that organizations are really nothing other than aggregates of individuals. As such, organizational actions are just the combined actions of individuals. In this section, we will argue that much of organizational behavior can be viewed as the collection of efforts by a set of quasi-independent actors.

Let me begin by acknowledging that organizations place constraints on employee behavior. But, despite those constraints, every job possesses a degree of discretion—areas in which rules, procedures, job descriptions, supervisory directives, and other formal constraints do not apply. Generally speaking, the higher one moves in the organization, the more discretion he or she has. Lower-level jobs tend to be more programmed than middle-management jobs; and middle managers have less discretion than do senior managers. But *every job* comes with some autonomy. And it is that autonomy that allows different people to do different things in the same job.

Casual observation leads all of us to the obvious conclusion that no two people in the same job behave in exactly the same way. Even in highly programmed jobs, such as assembly-line work in an automobile factory or processing claims in an insurance company, employee behavior varies. Why? Individual differences! College students certainly understand and act on this reality when they choose classes. If three instructors are all teaching Accounting 101 at the same time of day, most students will question their friends to find out the differences between the instructors. Even though they teach the same course as described in the college catalog, the instructors enjoy a considerable degree of freedom in how they meet their course objectives. Students know that, and they try to acquire accurate information that will allow them to select among the three. So despite the fact that the instructors are teaching the same course and the content of that course is explicitly defined in the organization's formal documentation (the college catalog), the students (and all the rest of us) know that the behavior of the three instructors will vary widely.

People go about doing their jobs in different ways. They differ in their interactions with their bosses and coworkers. They vary in terms of work habits—promptness in completing tasks, conscientiousness in doing quality work, cooperation with coworkers, ability to handle stressful situations, and the like. They vary by level of motivation and the degree of effort they are willing to exert on their job. They vary in terms of the creativity they display in doing their work. And they vary in terms of the importance they place on factors such as security, recognition, advancement, social support, challenging work assignments, and willingness to work overtime. What explains the variations? Individual psychological characteristics such as values, attitudes, perceptions, motives, and personalities.

The end result is that, in the quest to understand employee productivity, absenteeism, turnover, and satisfaction, you have to recognize the overwhelming influence that individual psychological factors play.

Some points in this argument are based on B. M. Staw, "Dressing Up Like an Organization: When Psychological Actions Can Explain Organizational Action," *Journal of Management*, December 1991, pp. 805–19.

Learning about Yourself Exercise

How Does Your Ethical Behavior Rate?

Below are 15 statements. Identify the frequency with which you do, have done, or would do these things in the future when employed full-time. Place the letter *R*, *O*, *S*, or *N* on the line before each statement.

R = REGULARLY; O = OCCASIONALLY; S = SELDOM; N = NEVER

_____ **1.** I come to work late and get paid for it.

_____ **2.** I leave work early and get paid for it.

_____ **3.** I take long breaks/lunches and get paid for it.

_____ **4.** I call in sick to get a day off when I'm not sick.

_____ **5.** I use the company phone to make personal long-distance calls.

_____ **6.** I do personal work on company time.

_____ **7.** I use the company copier for personal use.

_____ **8.** I mail personal things through the company mail.

_____ **9.** I take home company supplies or merchandise.

_____ **10.** I give company supplies or merchandise to friends, or I allow friends to take them without saying anything.

_____ **11.** I put in for reimbursement for meals that I did not actually eat, or trips that I did not take, or other fabricated expenses.

_____ **12.** I use the company car for personal business.

_____ **13.** I take my spouse/friend out to eat and charge it to the company expense account.

_____ **14.** I take my spouse/friend on business trips and charge the expense to the company.

_____ **15.** I accept gifts from customers/suppliers in exchange for giving them business.

Turn to page A-25 for scoring directions and key.

Source: R. N. Lussier, *Human Relations in Organizations: A Skill Building Approach*, 2nd ed. (Homewood, IL: Irwin, 1993), p. 297.

Working with Others Exercise

Workforce Diversity Exercise

Purpose To learn about the different needs of a diverse workforce.

Time required Approximately 40 minutes.

Participants and roles Divide the class into six groups of approximately equal size. Each group is assigned one of the following roles:

Nancy is 28 years old. She is a divorced mother of three children, aged 3, 5, and 7. She is the department head. She earns $37,000 a year on her job and receives another $3,600 a year in child support from her ex-husband.

Ethel is a 72-year-old widow. She works twenty-five hours a week to supplement her $8,000 annual pension. Including her hourly wage of $7.50, she earns $17,750 a year.

John is a 34-year-old black male born in Trinidad who is now a U.S. resident. He is married and the father of two small children. John attends college at night and is within a year of earning his bachelor's degree. His salary is $24,000 a year. His wife is an attorney and earns approximately $44,000 a year.

Lu is a 26-year-old physically impaired male Asian American. He is single and has a master's degree in education. Lu is paralyzed and confined to a wheelchair as a result of an auto accident. He earns $29,000 a year.

Maria is a single 22-year-old Hispanic. Born and raised in Mexico, she came to the United States only three months ago. Maria's English needs considerable improvement. She earns $18,000 a year.

Mike is a 16-year-old white male high school sophomore who works fifteen hours a week after school and during vacations. He earns $6.25 an hour, or approximately $4,875 a year.

The members of each group are to assume the character consistent with their assigned role.

Background   Our six participants work for a company that has recently installed a flexible benefits program. Instead of the traditional "one benefit package fits all," the company is allocating an additional 25 percent of each employee's annual pay to be used for discretionary benefits. Those benefits and their annual cost are listed below.

Supplementary health care for employee:

Plan A (No deductible and pays 90%) = $3,000
Plan B ($200 deductible and pays 80%) = $2,000
Plan C ($1,000 deductible and pays 70%) = $500

Supplementary health care for dependents (same deductibles and percentages as above):

Plan A = $2,000
Plan B = $1,500
Plan C = $500

Supplementary dental plan = $500

Life insurance:

> Plan A ($25,000 coverage) = $500
> Plan B ($50,000 coverage) = $1,000
> Plan C ($100,000 coverage) = $2,000
> Plan D ($250,000 coverage) = $3,000

Mental health plan = $500

Prepaid legal assistance = $300

Vacation = 2% of annual pay for each week, up to 6 weeks a year

Pension at retirement equal to approximately 50% of final annual earnings = $1,500

Four-day workweek during the three summer months (available only to full-time employees) = 4% of annual pay

Day-care services (after company contribution) = $2,000 for all of an employee's children, regardless of number

Company-provided transportation to and from work = $750

College tuition reimbursement = $1,000

Language class tuition reimbursement = $500

The Task
1. Each group has 15 minutes to develop a flexible benefits package that consumes 25 percent (and no more!) of their character's pay.
2. After completing step 1, each group appoints a spokesperson who describes to the entire class the benefits package they have arrived at for their character.
3. The entire class then discusses the results. How did the needs, concerns, and problems of each participant influence the group's decision? What do the results suggest for trying to motivate a diverse workforce?

Special thanks to Professor Penny Wright (San Diego State University) for her suggestions during the development of this exercise.

Thanks for 24 Years of Service. Now Here's the Door!

Russ McDonald graduated from the University of Michigan with his MBA in 1969. He had numerous job offers but chose General Motors for several reasons. The automobile industry offered terrific career opportunities, and GM was the world's number one car manufacturer. Salaries at GM were among the highest in corporate America, and a job at GM provided unparalleled security. A white-collar job with GM was the closest anybody could come to permanent employment, outside of working for the federal government.

Russ began his career at GM as a cost analyst at the company's Fisher Body division in Detroit. From there he proceeded through a long sequence of increased job responsibilities. By his 20th anniversary with the company he had risen to the position of assistant vice president of finance in the corporate treasury department. His salary was $124,000 a year, and, in a good year, he could expect a bonus of anywhere from $10,000 to $25,000. But those bonuses had become increasingly rare, because GM's profitability had declined throughout the 1980s. Increased foreign competition, aggressive action by

Ford and Chrysler, and GM's slow response to change had resulted in a serious erosion in the company's market position. When Russ joined the company, nearly one out of every two new cars sold in the United States was a GM product. By the late 1980s, that number was down to one in four. As a result, GM's management was taking drastic action to try to stop its decline in market share. It was closing inefficient plants, reorganizing divisions, introducing new production technologies, and making huge cuts in its staff. Tens of thousands of white-collar positions were eliminated. One of those was Russ McDonald's job. In the summer of 1993, less than a year short of his 25th anniversary with GM, he was given the opportunity to take early retirement. Russ saw the handwriting on the wall. If he didn't take early retirement, it would only be a matter of time—maybe a year or two at best—and he would be pushed out, and with a less attractive severance package. So he took the company's offer: nine months' pay plus lifetime health benefits for him and his family. Russ tried to put a positive spin on the situation. Maybe this was a blessing in disguise. He was only 49 years old. He had 24 years of experience with one of the world's foremost corporations. He would land on his feet with a company that was growing and offered opportunities that no longer existed at GM.

Russ's optimism had pretty well faded by New Year's Day of 1996. He had been out of work for nearly 30 months. He had responded to dozens of employment ads. He had sent out more than 200 résumés. He had talked with several executive recruiting firms, and he had spent more than $7,000 on employment counseling. All for naught. What he kept hearing was that his experience wasn't relevant to today's workplace; there were no opportunities in large companies; small companies wanted people who were flexible, and they considered corporate types like Russ as "mentally rigid." Even if there was a job for which Russ was qualified, he would have to take at least a 50 percent cut in pay, and employers were very uncomfortable offering someone such a relatively low salary; they figured Russ would be demotivated and likely to "jump ship" at the first opportunity.

Questions

1. How valid do you think the comments are that Russ is hearing?
2. If you were a small business executive in need of someone with extensive financial experience, would you consider Russ? Explain your position.
3. What suggestions might you make to Russ to help him find suitable employment?

David Vincent's New Career

Since 1990, 8,400 logging jobs have disappeared in Oregon. More efficient ways of tree cutting have pushed a lot of lumbermen out of the forest. One of those pushed out is 40-year-old David Vincent. Rather than seeking another logging job, David has decided to retrain for a completely new career. He's enrolled in a nursing program at his local community college.

"I get teased some," says David. "Nursing is a woman's occupation—or perceived that way. And my old lumberjack friends ask me if I question my masculinity." But David is a realist. He wants a future and he realizes there

VIDEO
CASE

ABCNEWS

isn't much of one for him in the logging business. "The reality of my situation is I have to survive. I have to adapt. The timber industry is on the skids; there's no work there for me anymore. And what I have to do is I'm going to have to adapt. I have to figure out a way of making a living and get on with my life." One place where there does seem to be opportunity is in health care. Since 1990, there are more than 6,000 new jobs in the Oregon health care industry. And David is determined to get one of them.

David isn't alone in his retraining efforts. Globalization, technology, and other forces are changing job structures and opportunities. Millions of Americans are doing what David is doing—retraining for new careers. Young Americans face the possibility of five, six, or seven different careers in their lifetime. For David Vincent, nursing will be his fourth.

For those workers who are afraid of change, unable to demonstrate flexibility, or unwilling to participate in retraining, their future may indeed be bleak.

Questions

1. What does this case say about the changing workforce?
2. What kind of personal attributes do you think would be related to success in the job of a logger? How about in the job of a nurse?
3. To what degree do you think your responses to question 2 are stereotypical?
4. How flexible do you think most people are in retraining for new careers? Discuss.

Source: Based on "Person in the News," *World News Tonight, ABC News;* aired March 18, 1994.

ROB PANCO: BACKGROUND AND REFLECTIONS*

Robert (Rob) Panco is thirty-seven years old. He is now a management consultant. Along the way to his current position, Rob's had some interesting work experiences, and he's been kind enough to share some of them with us. Specifically, he reflects on his career path as well as the challenges and problems related to OB that he encountered in his career.

You should find this progressive case (which appears at the end of each section of this book), valuable for at least two reasons. First, it will help you integrate many of the OB concepts introduced in this book. Unfortunately, textbooks have to be linear—moving sequentially through an artificially created set of independent chapters. The real world, however, is a juggling act of overlapping and highly interdependent activities. This case will make this interdependence clearer and help demonstrate how individual, group, and organization-system factors overlap. Second, this progressive case will show you the applicability of OB concepts to actual management practice. Most textbook examples or cases are short and designed to illustrate only one or two points. As an integrated and progressive story, the Rob Panco case will show you how one real-life manager has dealt with dozens of OB issues.

Exhibit I-1 provides a brief description of Rob Panco's background and career progression. But résumés leave a lot out. So let's begin by learning a bit about Rob's early life and career experiences.

If you had asked Rob during his senior year in high school what he planned on doing with his life, he'd have answered: "I'm going to be a professional musician." Toward that end, he had trained as a string bass player. When he went off to college—Duquesne University in Pittsburgh—it was with the intention to pursue his music interests. But things don't always work out as planned. During his first year, Rob came face to face with reality: There were lots of string bass players more talented than he was. If he pursued his passion, he could be a music teacher at best. Rob wanted more so he decided to change majors. He chose to work toward a degree in business, with specialization in marketing and management.

Why pursue a career in business? Rob wasn't sure. It might have been the influence of his father, who opened a State Farm insurance agency after spending 22 years in the U.S. Navy. Or it might have been the positive experiences he'd had working part-time in high school. From the age of 14 to 18, Rob worked evenings, weekends, and summers at a weekly newspaper. "I took the job initially to make money. I wanted to buy a $1400 string bass." He started by sweeping floors and washing presses. But, over time, he learned most of the jobs at the paper. For instance, he set type, pasted up ads, and perfected the skills of maintaining complex printing equipment. After graduating from high school, Rob continued working summers at the newspaper.

During his undergraduate college years, Rob gained experience selling shoes at Tom McAn, working in a Hallmark card store, and in similar jobs. It wasn't unusual for him to carry 18 units and work 30 hours a week during the

*Some facts, incidences, and quotes included in this progressive case have been slightly modified by the author to enhance student discussion and analysis.

Exhibit I-1 Résumé

ROBERT PANCO, JR.
446 Sheridan Avenue
New Brunswick, NJ 07114
(908) 792-1722

Education

M.B.A., Duquesne University (Pittsburgh, PA), 1984

B.S., Business Administration, Duquesne University.
   Major: Marketing/Management; Minor: Economics, 1982

Professional Experience

1/97–present	Independent Management Consultant
5/93–12/96	General Manager, M.E. Aslett Corp., New Jersey
10/92–4/93	Business Manager, M.E. Aslett Corp.
9/90–9/92	Project Manager/Consultant, AT&T Bell Laboratories, New Jersey
5/89–9/90	Senior Marketing Manager, AT&T Network Systems Regional Marketing, Maryland
10/88–4/89	Marketing Manager, AT&T Network Systems Regional Marketing
5/87–9/88	Market Planner, AT&T Network Systems Network Market Planning, New Jersey
6/86–4/87	Associate Market Planner, AT&T Network Systems Network Market Planning
6/83–6/86	Senior Consultant, Small Business Development Center; Duquesne University, Division of Continuing Education

Personal

Birthdate: January 20, 1960

Marital Status: Married, no children

school year. (He needed the money, but he also enjoyed working.) Rob also assumed leadership roles in campus activities. He was on the Student Activity Board (SAB) and singlehandedly fought to bring jazz concerts to campus. These concerts eventually became one of the SAB's few profit-making enterprises. But Rob's heavy schedule had a price. "My grades were never as high as they should have been," says Rob. "I was a B student when I should have been making A's."

After earning his undergraduate degree, and facing a weak job market, Rob entered graduate school to work on an MBA. Again, he combined studying with an outside job. In his first year, he spent 20 hours a week supervising students at the university's Student Union. In his second year, he spent 30 hours a week working in the university's Small Business Development Center. Both these jobs were valuable because they allowed Rob to apply what he was learning in his MBA program. Clearly, a pattern was emerging. This was a guy who wasn't happy unless he was keeping very busy.

Rob stayed at the Small Business Development Center for two years after earning his MBA. Then he left for a job at AT&T in New Jersey. In his first job there, he did market research on new products. After six months, he got his first promotion. A year later, he was chosen to head a temporary market-research project team made up of five peers. "This was a very challenging job," says Rob. "These people worked under my direction but reported to their departmental bosses. I had no real authority, yet I was responsible for the project. Ironically, it was a lot like my experience in running concerts in college. The people I oversaw were all volunteers. Managing peers and volunteers is very similar."

Rob's success in managing this project team led to his nomination and selection to AT&T's Leadership Continuity Program. This is a select group of individuals who show promise for significantly higher managerial responsibilities. As part of this program, Rob linked up with a senior executive who would become an informal mentor, participated in two continuing education programs a year, and gained favored status on future job assignments. In May 1989, Rob was transferred to Maryland as a senior marketing manager. Eighteen months later he returned to New Jersey as a project manager.

In October 1992, Rob joined M.E. Aslett Corporation as the company's business manager. Aslett is a small New Jersey-based packager of educational and professional reference books. It handles book projects from conception all the way up to, but excluding, the printing stage. Aslett's clients include Grolier Encyclopedia, World Book International, Prentice Hall, Harcourt Brace, and McGraw Hill. Seven months later, he took over as general manager where he oversaw the firm's operations—the production manager, network administrator, copy editors, proofreaders, desktop publishers, and color separators all reported directly to him.

When asked about his philosophy toward managing people, Rob says "You can't take honesty away. Don't mislead people. Be open and tell the truth." But he also mentions something that occasionally gets him into trouble: "I assume that other people love their work as much as I do. I like to learn, to keep moving forward. For instance, I set self-improvement goals for myself every quarter. I sometimes forget that other people aren't like me."

The comment that "other people aren't like me" prompted questions about workforce diversity at Aslett. "We had more women working there than men," Rob said, "and several of our people were single parents. In addition, we employed a couple of people from Great Britain, an African-American, and a Jamaican. For a company with only 20 people, I think we had a pretty diverse group."

When asked about his career goals, Rob's answer wasn't totally surprising. "I want to grow. I want to learn new things. I like working hard, but as long as I'm learning, I enjoy it. I want to do things that are fun." His current management consulting activities seem to fit well with his goal of continual learning.

Questions

1. How do you think Rob's early life experiences have influenced his career choices and his philosophy toward managing people?
2. Review Rob's last job at Aslett in terms of managerial functions, roles, and skills.
3. What challenges might Rob have faced with his diverse workforce at Aslett that he might not have had to deal with if he had a homogeneous workforce?
4. What do you think Rob meant when he said that "managing peers and volunteers is very similar"?

CHAPTER

FOUNDATIONS OF INDIVIDUAL BEHAVIOR

CHAPTER OUTLINE

Biographical Characteristics
Ability
Personality
Learning

"Be yourself" is the
worst advice you
can give some
people.
—T. Masson

LEARNING OBJECTIVES

After studying this chapter, you should be able to

1 Define the key biographical characteristics

2 Identify two types of ability

3 Explain the factors that determine an individual's personality

4 Describe the impact of job typology on the personality–job performance relationship

5 Summarize how learning theories provide insights into changing behavior

6 Distinguish between the four schedules of reinforcement

7 Clarify the role of punishment in learning

friends and colleagues describe the personality of Chrysler Corporation's president, Robert A. Lutz, they use terms such as *flamboyant, assertive,* and *daring.*[1] Lutz provides an excellent illustration of how an individual's personality shapes his or her behavior.

Robert Lutz was born in Zurich in 1932. He moved to New York City as a child, when his father, a banker, was transferred. He became a U.S. citizen at age 11. Because he moved around so much, he didn't finish high school until he was 22. But he wasn't letting grass grow under his feet. During his teenage years he learned to speak French, German, and Italian, as well as English.

Fascinated from an early age with motorcycles, cars, and planes—anything, in fact, that went fast— he joined the Marine Corps with the intention of becoming a fighter pilot. He flew jets for five years, then flew with the U.S. Marine Corps reserves while pursuing his higher education. By age 30, he had a BS and an MBA from the University of California at Berkeley.

In 1963, Lutz went to work for General Motors as a product planner. In his eight years with GM, he eventually moved up to become head of sales and marketing for GM's Opel unit in Germany. Then he spent three years in Munich as BMW's executive vice president of sales and marketing. From there, he went to Ford's European operations, where he quickly moved up the ranks to eventually head up Ford of Europe. At the age of 50, he returned to the United States as executive vice president of Ford's international operations. In 1986, at the age of 54, he was picked by Chrysler to become its President and Chief Operating Officer.

Lutz personifies Chrysler's image as Detroit's most aggressive auto maker. His flamboyant and strong personality probably cost him the chairmanship because of clashes with his previous boss. But his blunt opinions and bold approach to management make him a standout, and he is widely given credit for Chrysler's current success. He revamped Chrysler's engineering ranks into flexible, cross-functional teams and championed daring styling to match the sporty performance of models such as the Dodge Intrepid sedan and Ram pickup. His success in reorganizing the company's product development groups allows the company to develop cars faster and cheaper than its competition and has unleashed staffers' creativity, leading to better-looking, better-performing vehicles.

Neither age nor responsibilities have lessened Lutz's love for speed. In addition to owning a fleet of fast cars and motorcycles, he pilots his own helicopter and jet aircraft. His latest toy is a Czech-made L-39C Albatros jet fighter. On weekends, he and his wife can be found streaking across the Michigan sky at nearly 600 miles per hour. ◆

R obert Lutz's assertiveness and risk-seeking personality characteristics were in place long before he joined Chrysler Corp. But they play an important role in shaping his actions. Of course, Robert Lutz isn't unique. *All* our behavior is somewhat shaped by our personalities and experiences. In this chapter, we will look at four individual-level variables—biographical characteristics, ability, personality, and learning—and consider their effect on employee performance and satisfaction.

Biographical Characteristics

As discussed in the previous chapter, this text is essentially concerned with finding and analyzing the variables that have an impact on employee productivity, absence, turnover, and satisfaction. The list of those variables—as shown in Exhibit 1-8 on page 28—is long and contains some complicated concepts. Many of the concepts—motivation, say, or power and politics or organizational culture—are hard to assess. It might be valuable, then, to begin by looking at factors that are easily definable and readily available; data that can be obtained, for the most part, simply from information available in an employee's personnel file. What factors would these be? Obvious characteristics would be an employee's age, gender, marital status, and length of service with an organization. Fortunately, there is a sizable amount of research that has specifically analyzed many of these **biographical characteristics**.

biographical characteristics
Personal characteristics—such as age, gender, and marital status—that are objective and easily obtained from personnel records.

Age

The relationship between age and job performance is likely to be an issue of increasing importance during the next decade. Why? There are at least three reasons. First, there is a widespread belief that job performance declines with increasing age. Regardless of whether it's true or not, a lot of people believe it and act on it. Second is the reality that the workforce is aging. For instance, workers 55 and older are the fastest-growing sector of the labor force; between 1990 and 2005, their ranks are expected to jump 43.7 percent.[2] The third reason is recent U.S. legislation that, for all intents and purposes, outlaws mandatory retirement. Most U.S. workers today no longer have to retire at the age of 70.

What is the perception of older workers? Evidence indicates that employers hold mixed feelings.[3] They see a number of positive qualities that older workers bring to their jobs: specifically, experience, judgment, a strong work ethic, and commitment to quality. But older workers are also perceived as lacking flexibility and as being resistant to new technology. And in a time when organizations strongly seek individuals who are adaptable and open to change, the negatives associated with age clearly hinder the initial hiring of

McDonald's views older workers as willing to take on new responsibilities, patient, disciplined, and good role models for younger employees. Through its McMasters program, it recruits, trains, and develops people over 55. Studies indicate that, in general, older workers are more stable and (contrary to popular belief) no less productive than their younger co-workers.

older workers and increase the likelihood that they will be let go during downsizing. Now let's take a look at the evidence. What effect does age actually have on turnover, absenteeism, productivity, and satisfaction?

The older you get, the less likely you are to quit your job. That conclusion is based on studies of the age-turnover relationship.[4] Of course, it should not be too surprising. As workers get older, they have fewer alternative job opportunities. In addition, older workers are less likely to resign than are younger workers because their long tenure tends to provide them with higher wage rates, longer paid vacations, and more-attractive pension benefits.

It's tempting to assume that age is also inversely related to absenteeism. After all, if older workers are less likely to quit, won't they also demonstrate higher stability by coming to work more regularly? Not necessarily! Most studies do show an inverse relationship, but close examination finds that the age-absence relationship is partially a function of whether the absence is avoidable or unavoidable.[5] In general, older employees have lower rates of avoidable absence than do younger employees. However, they have higher rates of unavoidable absence, probably due to the poorer health associated with aging and the longer recovery period that older workers need when injured.

How does age affect productivity? There is a widespread belief that productivity declines with age. It is often assumed that an individual's skills—particularly speed, agility, strength, and coordination—decay over time and that prolonged job boredom and lack of intellectual stimulation all contribute to reduced productivity. The evidence, however, contradicts that belief and those assumptions. For instance, during a three-year period, a large hardware chain staffed one of its stores solely with employees over 50 and compared its results with those of five stores with younger employees. The store staffed by the over-50 employees was significantly more productive (measured in terms of sales generated against labor costs) than two of the other stores and held its own with the other three.[6] One comprehensive review of the research found that age and job performance were unrelated.[7] Moreover, that finding seems to be true for almost all types of jobs, professional and nonprofessional. The natural conclusion is that the demands of most jobs, even those with heavy manual labor requirements, are not extreme enough for any declines in physical skills due to age to have an impact on productivity; or, if there is some decay due to age, it is offset by gains due to experience.

Our final concern is the relationship between age and job satisfaction. On this issue, the evidence is mixed. Most studies indicate a positive association between age and satisfaction, at least up to age 60.[8] Other studies, however, have found a U-shaped relationship.[9] Several explanations could clear up these results, the most plausible being that these studies are intermixing professional and nonprofessional employees. When the two types are separated, satisfaction tends to continually increase among professionals as they age, whereas it falls among nonprofessionals during middle age and then rises again in the later years.

Gender

Few issues initiate more debates, misconceptions, and unsupported opinions than whether women perform as well on jobs as men do. In this section, we review the research on that issue.

◆ There are few, if any, important differences between men and women that will affect their job performance.

The evidence suggests that the best place to begin is with the recognition that there are few, if any, important differences between men and women that will affect *their job performance*. There are, for instance, no consistent male-female differences in problem-solving ability, analytical skills, competitive drive, motivation, sociability, or learning ability.[10] Psychological studies have found that women are more willing to conform to authority and that men are more aggressive and more likely than women to have expectations of success, but those differences are minor. Given the significant changes that have taken place in the last 25 years in terms of increasing female participation rates in the workforce and rethinking what constitutes male and female roles, you should operate on the assumption that there is no significant difference in job productivity between men and women. Similarly, there is no evidence indicating that an employee's gender affects job satisfaction.[11]

One issue that does seem to differ between genders, especially where the employee has preschool children, is preference for work schedules.[12] Working mothers are more likely to prefer part-time work, flexible work schedules, and telecommuting in order to accommodate their family responsibilities.

But what about absence and turnover rates? Are women less stable employees than men? First, on the question of turnover, the evidence is mixed.[13] Some studies have found that women have higher turnover rates; others have found no difference. There doesn't appear to be enough information from which to draw meaningful conclusions. The research on absence, however, is a different story. The evidence consistently indicates that women have higher rates of absenteeism than men do.[14] The most logical explanation for this finding is that the research was conducted in North America, and North American culture has historically placed home and family responsibilities on the woman. When a child is ill or someone needs to stay home to wait for the plumber, it has been the woman who has traditionally taken time off from work. However, this research is undoubtedly time-bound.[15] The historical role of the woman in caring for children and as secondary breadwinner has definitely changed since the 1970s, and a large proportion of men nowadays are as interested in day care and the problems associated with child care in general as are women.

Marital Status

There are not enough studies to draw any conclusions about the effect of marital status on productivity. But research consistently indicates that married employees have fewer absences, undergo less turnover, and are more satisfied with their jobs than are their unmarried coworkers.[16]

Marriage imposes increased responsibilities that may make a steady job more valuable and important. But the question of causation is not clear. It may very well be that conscientious and satisfied employees are more likely to be married. Another offshoot of this issue is that research has not pursued other statuses besides single or married. Does being divorced or widowed have an impact on an employee's performance and satisfaction? What about couples who live together without being married? These are questions in need of investigation.

Tenure

The last biographical characteristic we'll look at is tenure. With the exception of the issue of male-female differences, probably no issue is more subject to misconceptions and speculations than the impact of seniority on job performance.

Extensive reviews of the seniority-productivity relationship have been conducted.[17] If we define seniority as time on a particular job, we can say that the most recent evidence demonstrates a positive relationship between seniority and job productivity. So tenure, expressed as work experience, appears to be a good predictor of employee productivity.

The research relating tenure to absence is quite straightforward. Studies consistently demonstrate seniority to be negatively related to absenteeism.[18] In fact, in terms of both frequency of absence and total days lost at work, tenure is the single most important explanatory variable.[19]

Tenure is also a potent variable in explaining turnover. "Tenure has consistently been found to be negatively related to turnover and has been suggested as one of the single best predictors of turnover."[20] Moreover, consistent with research that suggests that past behavior is the best predictor of future behavior,[21] evidence indicates that tenure on an employee's previous job is a powerful predictor of that employee's future turnover.[22]

The evidence indicates that tenure and satisfaction are positively related.[23] In fact, when age and tenure are treated separately, tenure appears to be a more consistent and stable predictor of job satisfaction than is chronological age.

Ability

Contrary to what we were taught in grade school, we weren't all created equal. Most of us are to the left of the median on some normally distributed ability curve. Regardless of how motivated you are, it is unlikely that you can act as well as Meryl Streep, run as fast as Michael Johnson, write horror stories as

◆ Contrary to what we were taught in grade school, we weren't all created equal.

well as Stephen King, or sing as well as Whitney Houston. Of course, just because we aren't all equal in abilities does not imply that some individuals are inherently inferior to others. What we are acknowledging is that everyone has strengths and weaknesses in terms of ability that make him or her relatively superior or inferior to others in performing certain tasks or activities.[24] From management's standpoint, the issue is not whether people differ in terms of their abilities. They do! The issue is knowing how people differ in abilities and using that knowledge to increase the likelihood that an employee will perform his or her job well.

What does *ability* mean? As we will use the term, **ability** refers to an individual's capacity to perform the various tasks in a job. It is a current assessment of what one can do. An individual's overall abilities are essentially made up of two sets of factors: intellectual and physical abilities.

ability
An individual's capacity to perform the various tasks in a job.

Intellectual Abilities

intellectual ability
That required to do mental activities.

Intellectual abilities are those needed to perform mental activities. Intelligence quotient (IQ) tests, for example, are designed to ascertain one's general intellectual abilities. So, too, are popular college admission tests such as the SAT and ACT and graduate admission tests in business (GMAT), law (LSAT), and medicine (MCAT). The seven most frequently cited dimensions making up intellectual abilities are number aptitude, verbal comprehension, perceptual speed, inductive reasoning, deductive reasoning, spatial visualization, and memory.[25] Exhibit 2-1 describes those dimensions.

Exhibit 2-1 Dimensions of Intellectual Ability

Dimension	Description	Job Example
Number aptitude	Ability to do speedy and accurate arithmetic	Accountant: Computing the sales tax on a set of items
Verbal comprehension	Ability to understand what is read or heard and the relationship of words to each other	Plant manager: Following corporate policies
Perceptual speed	Ability to identify visual similarities and differences quickly and accurately	Fire investigator: Identifying clues to support a charge of arson
Inductive reasoning	Ability to identify a logical sequence in a problem and then solve the problem	Market researcher: Forecasting demand for a product in the next time period
Deductive reasoning	Ability to use logic and assess the implications of an argument	Supervisor: Choosing between two different suggestions offered by employees
Spatial visualization	Ability to imagine how an object would look if its position in space were changed	Interior decorator: Redecorating an office
Memory	Ability to retain and recall past experiences	Salesperson: Remembering the names of customers

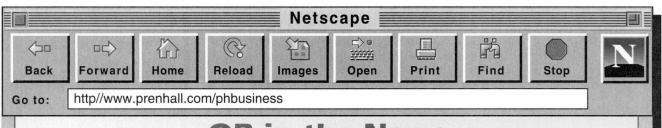

OB in the News

The *Bell Curve* Evidence

It was undoubtedly the most controversial social science book published during the first half of the 1990s. *The Bell Curve* (The Free Press, 1994) by Richard Herrnstein and Charles Murray presents evidence that IQ, not education or opportunity, is the key factor determining where a person ends up on the American social scale. What stirred up most reviewers, scientists, politicians, and journalists was the authors' claim that economic inequalities between racial groups are related to differences in average IQ levels between races. But we are interested only in that segment of their work that is related to the issue of IQ and job performance.

Herrnstein and Murray began by making six statements that they categorized as "beyond significant technical dispute": (1) There is such a thing as a general factor of cognitive ability on which human beings differ; (2) all standardized tests of academic aptitude or achievement measure this general factor to some degree, but IQ tests expressly designed for that purpose measure it most accurately; (3) IQ scores closely match whatever it is that people mean when they use the word *intelligent* or *smart* in ordinary language; (4) IQ scores are stable, although not perfectly so, over much of a person's life; (5) properly administered IQ tests are not demonstrably biased against social, economic, ethnic, or racial groups; and (6) a substantial portion of cognitive ability (no less than 40 percent and no more than 80 percent) is inherited through genes. Using these six points as a foundation, the authors then argued forcefully that IQ is a powerful predictor of job performance. Or to use their terms, "A smarter employee is, on average, a more proficient employee."

According to Herrnstein and Murray, all jobs require cognitive ability. This fact is relatively self-evident in professional occupations such as accounting or engineering. But it's also true for semi-skilled blue-collar jobs and holds, although weakly, even among people in unskilled manual jobs. For instance, they point out that there are better and worse busboys in restaurants. The really good ones use intelligence to solve job-related problems and to come up with solutions. But as jobs become more complex, IQ becomes more important in determining performance. This advantage holds over time. "The cost of hiring less intelligent workers may last as long as they stay on the job."

The views expressed by Herrnstein and Murray, by the way, aren't radical. At the peak of the controversy surrounding the publication of *The Bell Curve*, 52 of the most respected experts in intelligence research reaffirmed Herrnstein and Murray's conclusions in a *Wall Street Journal* editorial (December 13, 1994, p. A18).

Take It to the Net

We invite you to visit the Robbins page on the Prentice Hall Web site at:

http://www.prenhall.com/robbinsorgbeh

for this chapter's World Wide Web exercise.

Jobs differ in the demands they place on incumbents to use their intellectual abilities. Generally speaking, the more information-processing demands that exist in a job, the more general intelligence and verbal abilities will be necessary to perform the job successfully.[26] Of course, a high IQ is not a prerequisite for all jobs. In fact, for many jobs—in which employee behavior is highly routine and there are little or no opportunities to exercise discretion—a high IQ may be unrelated to performance. On the other hand, a careful review of the evidence demonstrates that tests that assess verbal, numerical, spatial, and perceptual abilities are valid predictors of job proficiency at all levels of jobs.[27] Therefore, tests that measure specific dimensions of intelligence have been found to be strong predictors of future job performance.

The major dilemma faced by employers who use mental ability tests for selection, promotion, training, and similar personnel decisions is that they may have a negative impact on racial and ethnic groups.[28] The evidence indicates that some minority groups score, on the average, as much as one standard deviation lower than whites on verbal, numerical, and spatial ability tests.

Physical Abilities

physical ability
That required to do tasks demanding stamina, dexterity, strength, and similar characteristics.

To the same degree that intellectual abilities play a larger role in complex jobs with demanding information-processing requirements, specific **physical abilities** gain importance for successfully doing less-skilled and more-standardized jobs. For example, jobs in which success demands stamina, manual dexterity, leg strength, or similar talents require management to identify an employee's physical capabilities.

Research on the requirements needed in hundreds of jobs has identified nine basic abilities involved in the performance of physical tasks.[29] These are described in Exhibit 2-2. Individuals differ in the extent to which they have each of these abilities. Not surprisingly, there is also little relationship between them: A high score on one is no assurance of a high score on others. High employee performance is likely to be achieved when management has ascertained the extent to which a job requires each of the nine abilities and then ensures that employees in that job have those abilities.

The Ability-Job Fit

Our concern is with explaining and predicting the behavior of people at work. In this section, we have demonstrated that jobs make differing demands on people and that people differ in the abilities they possess. Employee performance, therefore, is enhanced when there is a high ability-job fit.

◆ Employee performance is enhanced when there is a high ability-job fit.

The specific intellectual or physical abilities required for adequate job performance depend on the ability requirements of the job. So, for example, airline pilots need strong spatial-visualization abilities; beach lifeguards need both strong spatial-visualization abilities and body coordination; senior executives need verbal abilities; high-rise construction workers need balance; and journalists with weak reasoning abilities would likely have difficulty meeting minimum job-performance standards. Directing

Exhibit 2-2 Nine Basic Physical
Abilities

Strength Factors

1. Dynamic strength   Ability to exert muscular force repeatedly or continuously over time

2. Trunk strength   Ability to exert muscular strength using the trunk (particularly abdominal) muscles

3. Static strength   Ability to exert force against external objects

4. Explosive strength   Ability to expend a maximum of energy in one or a series of explosive acts

Flexibility Factors

5. Extent flexibility   Ability to move the trunk and back muscles as far as possible

6. Dynamic flexibility   Ability to make rapid, repeated flexing movements

Other Factors

7. Body coordination   Ability to coordinate the simultaneous actions of different parts of the body

8. Balance   Ability to maintain equilibrium despite forces pulling off balance

9. Stamina   Ability to continue maximum effort requiring prolonged effort over time

Source: Reprinted with permission of *HRMagazine* published by the Society for Human Resource Management, Alexandria, VA.

attention at only the employee's abilities or only the ability requirements of the job ignores the fact that employee performance depends on the interaction of the two.

What predictions can we make when the fit is poor? As alluded to previously, if employees lack the required abilities, they are likely to fail. If you are hired as a word processor and you cannot meet the job's basic keyboard typing requirements, your performance is going to be poor irrespective of your positive attitude or your high level of motivation. When the ability-job fit is out of sync because the employee has abilities that far exceed the requirements of the job, our predictions would be very different. Job performance is likely to be adequate, but there will be organizational inefficiencies and possible declines in employee satisfaction. Given that pay tends to reflect the highest skill level that employees possess, if an employee's abilities far exceed those necessary to do the job, management will be paying more than it needs to. Abilities significantly above those required can also reduce the employee's job satisfaction when the employee's desire to use his or her abilities is particularly strong and is frustrated by the limitations of the job.

Personality

Why are some people quiet and passive, while others are loud and aggressive? Are certain personality types better adapted for certain job types? What do we know from theories of personality that can help us explain and predict the

Body coordination, balance, stamina, and strength and flexibility factors are physical abilities required for job performance at Black Diamond Equipment in Salt Lake City. The rock-climbing equipment company ensures a high ability-job fit by hiring customers — sports enthusiasts who use its products and have a passion for climbing.

behavior of people like Robert Lutz at Chrysler, whom we described at the opening of this chapter? In this section, we will attempt to answer such questions.

What Is Personality?

When we talk of personality, we don't mean that a person has charm, a positive attitude toward life, a smiling face, or is a finalist for "Happiest and Friendliest" in this year's Miss America contest. When psychologists talk of personality, they mean a dynamic concept describing the growth and development of a person's whole psychological system. Rather than looking at parts of the person, personality looks at some aggregate whole that is greater than the sum of the parts.

The most frequently used definition of personality was produced by Gordon Allport more than sixty years ago. He said personality is "the dynamic organization within the individual of those psychophysical systems that determine his unique adjustments to his environment."[30] For our purposes, you should think of **personality** as the sum total of ways in which an individual reacts to and interacts with others. It is most often described in terms of measurable traits that a person exhibits.

personality
The sum total of ways in which an individual reacts and interacts with others.

Personality Determinants

An early argument in personality research was whether an individual's personality was the result of heredity or of environment. Was the personality predetermined at birth, or was it the result of the individual's interaction with his or her environment? Clearly, there is no simple black-and-white answer. Personality appears to be a result of both influences. In addition, today we recog-

From Concepts to Skills

Self-Awareness: Do You Know Yourself?

A famous cartoonist once attended a cocktail party with some friends. Someone asked him to draw a caricature of everyone present, which he proceeded to do with a few skilled strokes of his pencil. When the sketches were passed around for the guests to identify, everyone recognized the other persons, but hardly anyone recognized the caricature of himself.[31]

Many of us are like the people at that cocktail party. We really don't know our-

selves. But you can expand your self-awareness. And when you do, you will better understand your personal strengths and weaknesses and how you are perceived by others. You will also gain insights into why others respond to you as they do.

A major component in gaining self-understanding is finding out how you rate on key personality characteristics. Later in our discussion of personality, we will review six major personality attributes: locus of control, Machi-

avellianism, self-esteem, self-monitoring, risk taking, and the Type A personality. Included with the review will be a series of self-awareness questionnaires that have been designed to measure these personality characteristics. Individually, the questionnaires will give you insights into how you rate on each attribute. In aggregate, they will help you to better understand who you are.

nize a third factor—the situation. Thus, an adult's personality is now generally considered to be made up of both hereditary and environmental factors, moderated by situational conditions.

HEREDITY Heredity refers to those factors that were determined at conception. Physical stature, facial attractiveness, gender, temperament, muscle composition and reflexes, energy level, and biological rhythms are characteristics that are generally considered to be either completely or substantially influenced by who your parents were: that is, by their biological, physiological, and inherent psychological makeup. The heredity approach argues that the ultimate explanation of an individual's personality is the molecular structure of the genes, located in the chromosomes.

Three different streams of research lend some credibility to the argument that heredity plays an important part in determining an individual's personality. The first looks at the genetic underpinnings of human behavior and temperament among young children. The second addresses the study of twins who were separated at birth. The third examines the consistency in job satisfaction over time and across situations.

Recent studies of young children lend strong support to the power of heredity.[32] Evidence demonstrates that traits such as shyness, fear, and distress are most likely caused by inherited genetic characteristics. This finding suggests that some personality traits may be built into the same genetic code that affects factors such as height and hair color.

Researchers have studied more than 100 sets of identical twins who were separated at birth and raised separately.[33] If heredity played little or no part in determining personality, you would expect to find few similarities between the separated twins. But the researchers found a lot in common. For almost every behavioral trait, a significant part of the variation between the twins turned out to be associated with genetic factors. For instance, one set of twins who had been separated for 39 years and raised 45 miles apart were found to drive the same model and color car, chain-smoked the same brand of cigarette, owned dogs with the same name, and regularly vacationed within three blocks of each other in a beach community 1,500 miles away. Researchers have found that genetics accounts for about fifty percent of the personality differences and more than 30 percent of the variation in occupational and leisure interests.

Further support for the importance of heredity can be found in studies of individual job satisfaction. Research has uncovered an interesting phenomenon: Individual job satisfaction is remarkably stable over time. Even when employers or occupations change, job satisfaction remains relatively stable during one's lifetime.[34] This result is consistent with what you would expect if satisfaction is determined by something inherent in the person rather than by external environmental factors.

If personality characteristics were *completely* dictated by heredity, they would be fixed at birth and no amount of experience could alter them. If you were relaxed and easygoing as a child, for example, that would be the result of your genes, and it would not be possible for you to change those characteristics. But personality characteristics are not completely dictated by heredity.

ENVIRONMENT   Among the factors that exert pressures on our personality formation are the culture in which we are raised, our early conditioning, the norms among our family, friends, and social groups, and other influences that we experience. The environment we are exposed to plays a substantial role in shaping our personalities.

For example, culture establishes the norms, attitudes, and values that are passed along from one generation to the next and create consistencies over time. An ideology that is intensely fostered in one culture may have only moderate influence in another. For instance, North Americans have had the themes of industriousness, success, competition, independence, and the Protestant work ethic constantly instilled in them through books, the school system, family, and friends. North Americans, as a result, tend to be ambitious and aggressive relative to individuals raised in cultures that have emphasized getting along with others, cooperation, and the priority of family over work and career.

Careful consideration of the arguments favoring either heredity or environment as the primary determinant of personality forces the conclusion that both are important. Heredity sets the parameters or outer limits, but an individual's full potential will be determined by how well he or she adjusts to the demands and requirements of the environment.

SITUATION   A third factor, the situation, influences the effects of heredity and environment on personality. An individual's personality, although gener-

The cultural environment in which people are raised plays a major role in shaping personality. In India, children learn from an early age the values of hard work, frugality, and family closeness. This photo of the Harilela family illustrates the importance that Indians place on close family ties. Six Harilela brothers own real estate and hotels throughout Asia. Not only do the brothers work together, but their six families and that of a married sister also live together in a Hong Kong mansion.

ally stable and consistent, does change in different situations. The different demands of different situations call forth different aspects of one's personality. We should not, therefore, look at personality patterns in isolation.[35]

It seems only logical to suppose that situations will influence an individual's personality, but a neat classification scheme that would tell us the impact of various types of situations has so far eluded us. "Apparently we are not yet close to developing a system for clarifying situations so that they might be systematically studied."[36] However, we do know that certain situations are more relevant than others in influencing personality.

What is of interest taxonomically is that situations seem to differ substantially in the constraints they impose on behavior. Some situations—e.g., church, an employment interview—constrain many behaviors; other situations—e.g., a picnic in a public park—constrain relatively few.[37]

Furthermore, although certain generalizations can be made about personality, there are significant individual differences. As we shall see, the study of individual differences has come to receive greater emphasis in personality research, which originally sought out more general, universal patterns.

Personality Traits

The early work in the structure of personality revolved around attempts to identify and label enduring characteristics that describe an individual's behavior. Popular characteristics include shy, aggressive, submissive, lazy, ambitious, loyal, and timid. Those characteristics, when they are exhibited in a large number of situations, are called **personality traits**.[38] The more consistent the characteristic and the more frequently it occurs in diverse situations, the more important that trait is in describing the individual.

personality traits
Enduring characteristics that describe an individual's behavior.

Exhibit 2-3

Source: PEANUTS reprinted by permission of United Features Syndicate, Inc.

EARLY SEARCH FOR PRIMARY TRAITS Efforts to isolate traits have been hindered because there are so many of them. In one study, 17,953 individual traits were identified.[39] It is virtually impossible to predict behavior when such a large number of traits must be taken into account. As a result, attention has been directed toward reducing these thousands to a more manageable number.

One researcher isolated 171 traits but concluded that they were superficial and lacking in descriptive power.[40] What he sought was a reduced set of traits that would identify underlying patterns. The result was the identification of sixteen personality factors, which he called the *source*, or *primary*, *traits*. They are shown in Exhibit 2-4. These sixteen traits have been found to be generally steady and constant sources of behavior, allowing prediction of an individual's behavior in specific situations by weighing the characteristics for their situational relevance.

Myers-Briggs Type Indicator (MBTI)

A personality test that taps four characteristics and classifies people into one of 16 personality types.

THE MYERS-BRIGGS TYPE INDICATOR One of the most widely used personality frameworks is called the **Myers-Briggs Type Indicator (MBTI)**.[41] It is essentially a 100-question personality test that asks people how they usually feel or act in particular situations.

On the basis of the answers individuals give to the test, they are classified as extroverted or introverted (E or I), sensing or intuitive (S or N), thinking or feeling (T or F), and perceiving or judging (P or J). These classifications are then combined into sixteen personality types. (These types are different from the sixteen primary traits in Exhibit 2-4.) To illustrate, let's take several examples. INTJs are visionaries. They usually have original minds and great drive for their own ideas and purposes. They are characterized as skeptical, critical, independent, determined, and often stubborn. ESTJs are organizers. They are realistic, logical, analytical, decisive and have a natural head for business or mechanics. They like to organize and run activities. The ENTP type is a conceptualizer. He or she is innovative, individualistic, versatile, and attracted to entrepreneurial ideas. This person tends to be resourceful in solving challenging problems but may neglect routine assignments. A recent book that profiled thirteen contemporary businesspeople who created supersuccessful firms including Apple Computer, Federal Express, Honda Motors, Microsoft, Price Club, and Sony found that all thirteen are intuitive thinkers (NTs).[42] This result is particularly interesting because intuitive thinkers represent only about five percent of the population.

More than 2 million people a year take the MBTI in the United States alone. Organizations using the MBTI include Apple Computer, AT&T, Citi-

Exhibit 2-4 Sixteen Primary Traits

1.	Reserved	vs.	Outgoing
2.	Less intelligent	vs.	More intelligent
3.	Affected by feelings	vs.	Emotionally stable
4.	Submissive	vs.	Dominant
5.	Serious	vs.	Happy-go-lucky
6.	Expedient	vs.	Conscientious
7.	Timid	vs.	Venturesome
8.	Tough-minded	vs.	Sensitive
9.	Trusting	vs.	Suspicious
10.	Practical	vs.	Imaginative
11.	Forthright	vs.	Shrewd
12.	Self-assured	vs.	Apprehensive
13.	Conservative	vs.	Experimenting
14.	Group-dependent	vs.	Self-sufficient
15.	Uncontrolled	vs.	Controlled
16.	Relaxed	vs.	Tense

corp, Exxon, GE, 3M Co., plus many hospitals, educational institutions, and even the U.S. Armed Forces.

Ironically, there is no hard evidence that the MBTI is a valid measure of personality. But lack of evidence doesn't seem to deter its use in a wide range of organizations.

THE BIG FIVE MODEL The MBTI may lack for valid supporting evidence, but that can't be said for the five-factor model of personality—more typically called the "Big Five."[43] In recent years, an impressive body of research supports the notion that five basic personality dimensions underlie all others. The Big Five factors are:

◆ **Extraversion**. This dimension captures one's comfort level with relationships. Extraverts (high in extraversion) tend to be friendly and outgoing and to spend much of their time maintaining and enjoying a large number of relationships. Introverts tend to be reserved and to have fewer relationships, and they are more comfortable with solitude than most people are.

extraversion
A personality dimension describing someone who is sociable, talkative, and assertive.

◆ **Agreeableness**. This dimension refers to an individual's propensity to defer to others. High agreeable people value harmony more than they value having their say or their way. They are cooperative and trusting of others. People who score low on agreeableness focus more on their own needs than on the needs of others.

agreeableness
A personality dimension that describes someone who is good-natured, cooperative, and trusting.

◆ **Conscientiousness**. This dimension refers to the number of goals on which a person focuses. A high conscientious person pursues fewer goals, in a purposeful way, and tends to be responsible, persistent, dependable, and achievement-oriented. Those who score low on this dimension tend to be more easily distracted, pursuing many goals, and more hedonistic.

conscientiousness
A personality dimension that describes someone who is responsible, dependable, persistent, and achievement oriented.

◆ **Emotional stability**. This dimension taps a person's ability to withstand stress. People with positive emotional stability tend to be characterized as calm, enthusiastic, and secure. Those with high negative scores tend to be nervous, depressed, and insecure.

emotional stability
A personality dimension that characterizes someone as calm, enthusiastic, secure (positive) versus tense, nervous, depressed, and insecure (negative).

openness to experience
A personality dimension that characterizes someone in terms of imaginativeness, artistic sensitivity, and intellectualism.

◆ **Openness to experience**. The final dimension addresses one's range of interests. Extremely open people are fascinated by novelty and innovation. They tend to be imaginative, artistically sensitive, and intellectual. Those at the other end of the openness category appear more conventional and find comfort in the familiar.

In addition to providing a unifying personality framework, research on the Big Five also has found important relationships between these personality dimensions and job performance.[44] A broad spectrum of occupations were looked at: professionals (including engineers, architects, accountants, attorneys), police, managers, salespeople, and semiskilled and skilled employees. Job performance was defined in terms of performance ratings, training proficiency (performance during training programs), and personnel data such as salary level. The results showed that conscientiousness predicted job performance for all occupational groups. "The preponderance of evidence shows that individuals who are dependable, reliable, careful, thorough, able to plan, organized, hardworking, persistent, and achievement-oriented tend to have higher job performance in most if not all occupations."[45] For the other personality dimensions, predictability depended upon both the performance criterion and the occupational group. For instance, extraversion predicted performance in managerial and sales positions. This finding makes sense since those occupations involve high social interaction. Similarly, openness to experience was found to be important in predicting training proficiency, which, too, seems logical. What wasn't so clear was why positive emotional stability wasn't related to job performance. Intuitively, it would seem that people who are calm and secure would do better on almost all jobs than people who are anxious and insecure. The researchers suggested that the answer might be that only people who score fairly high on emotional stability retain their jobs. So the range among those people studied, all of whom were employed, would tend to be quite small.

Major Personality Attributes Influencing OB

In this section, we want to more carefully evaluate specific personality attributes that have been found to be powerful predictors of behavior in organizations. The first is related to where one perceives the locus of control in one's life. The others are Machiavellianism, self-esteem, self-monitoring, propensity for risk taking, and Type A personality. In this section, we shall briefly introduce these attributes and summarize what we know about their ability to explain and predict employee behavior.

internals
Individuals who believe that they control what happens to them.

externals
Individuals who believe that what happens to them is controlled by outside forces such as luck or chance.

locus of control
The degree to which people believe they are masters of their own fate.

LOCUS OF CONTROL Some people believe that they are masters of their own fate. Other people see themselves as pawns of fate, believing that what happens to them in their lives is due to luck or chance. The first type, those who believe that they control their destinies, have been labeled **internals**, whereas the latter, who see their lives as being controlled by outside forces, have been called **externals**.[46] A person's perception of the source of his or her fate is termed **locus of control**.

A large amount of research comparing internals with externals has consistently shown that individuals who rate high in externality are less satisfied with their jobs, have higher absenteeism rates, are more alienated from the work setting, and are less involved on their jobs than are internals.[47]

INCREASE YOUR SELF-AWARENESS: ASSESS YOUR LOCUS OF CONTROL

Instructions: Read the following statements and indicate whether you agree more with choice A or choice B.

A

1. Making a lot of money is largely a matter of getting the right breaks.
2. I have noticed that there is a direct connection between how hard I study and the grades I get.
3. The number of divorces indicates that more and more people are not trying to make their marriages work.
4. It is silly to think that one can really change another person's basic attitudes.
5. Getting promoted is really a matter of being a little luckier than the next person.
6. If one knows how to deal with people, they are really quite easily led.
7. The grades I make are the result of my own efforts; luck has little or nothing to do with it.
8. People like me can change the course of world affairs if we make ourselves heard.
9. A great deal that happens to me is probably a matter of chance.
10. Getting along with people is a skill that must be practiced.

B

1. Promotions are earned through hard work and persistence. _____
2. Many times, the reactions of teachers seem haphazard to me. _____
3. Marriage is largely a gamble.

   _____
4. When I am right I can convince others.

   _____
5. In our society, a person's future earning power is dependent upon his or her ability. _____
6. I have little influence over the way other people behave. _____
7. Sometimes I feel that I have little to do with the grades I get. _____
8. It is only wishful thinking to believe that one can readily influence what happens in our society. _____
9. I am the master of my fate.

   _____
10. It is almost impossible to figure out how to please some people. _____

Source: Adapted from J.B. Rotter, "External Control and Internal Control," *Psychology Today,* June 1971, p. 42. Copyright 1971 by the American Psychological Association. Adapted with permission.

Scoring Key: Give yourself 1 point for each of the following selections: 1B, 2A, 3A, 4B, 5B, 6A, 7A, 8A, 9B, and 10A. Scores can be interpreted as follows:

        8–10 = High internal locus of control
        6–7 = Moderate internal locus of control
         5 = Mixed
        3–4 = Moderate external locus of control
        1–2 = High external locus of control

Why are externals more dissatisfied? The answer is probably because they perceive themselves as having little control over those organizational outcomes that are important to them. Internals, facing the same situation, attribute organizational outcomes to their own actions. If the situation is unattractive, they believe that they have no one else to blame but themselves. Also, the dissatisfied internal is more likely to quit a dissatisfying job.

The impact of locus of control on absence is an interesting one. Internals believe that health is substantially under their own control through proper habits, so they take more responsibility for their health and have better health habits. Consequently, their incidences of sickness and, hence, of absenteeism, are lower.[48]

We shouldn't expect any clear relationship between locus of control and turnover, because there are opposing forces at work. "On the one hand, internals tend to take action and thus might be expected to quit jobs more readily. On the other hand, they tend to be more successful on the job and more satisfied, factors associated with less individual turnover."[49]

The overall evidence indicates that internals generally perform better on their jobs, but that conclusion should be moderated to reflect differences in jobs. Internals search more actively for information before making a decision, are more motivated to achieve, and make a greater attempt to control their environment. Externals, however, are more compliant and willing to follow directions. Therefore, internals do well on sophisticated tasks—which include most managerial and professional jobs—that require complex information processing and learning. In addition, internals are more suited to jobs that require initiative and independence of action. In contrast, externals should do well on jobs that are well structured and routine and in which success depends heavily on complying with the direction of others.

Machiavellianism
Degree to which an individual is pragmatic, maintains emotional distance, and believes that ends can justify means.

MACHIAVELLIANISM The personality characteristic of **Machiavellianism** (Mach) is named after Niccolo Machiavelli, who wrote in the sixteenth century on how to gain and use power. An individual high in Machiavellianism is pragmatic, maintains emotional distance, and believes that ends can justify means. "If it works, use it" is consistent with a high-Mach perspective.

A considerable amount of research has been directed toward relating high- and low-Mach personalities to certain behavioral outcomes.[50] High Machs manipulate more, win more, are persuaded less, and persuade others more than do low Machs.[51] Yet these high Mach outcomes are moderated by situational factors. It has been found that high Machs flourish (1) when they interact face to face with others rather than indirectly; (2) when the situation has a minimum number of rules and regulations, thus allowing latitude for improvisation; and (3) when emotional involvement with details irrelevant to winning distracts low Machs.[52]

Should we conclude that high Machs make good employees? That answer depends on the type of job and whether you consider ethical implications in evaluating performance. In jobs that require bargaining skills (such as labor negotiation) or that offer substantial rewards for winning (as in commissioned sales), high Machs will be productive. But if ends can't justify the means, if there are *absolute* standards of behavior, or if the three situational factors noted in the preceding paragraph are not in evidence, our ability to predict a high Mach's performance will be severely curtailed.

self-esteem
Individuals' degree of liking or disliking of themselves.

SELF-ESTEEM People differ in the degree to which they like or dislike themselves. This trait is called **self-esteem**.[53] The research on self-esteem (SE) offers some interesting insights into organizational behavior. For example, self-esteem is directly related to expectations for success. High SEs believe that they possess the ability they need in order to succeed at work.

Individuals with high self-esteem will take more risks in job selection and are more likely to choose unconventional jobs than people with low self-esteem.

INCREASE YOUR SELF-AWARENESS: HOW MACHIAVELLIAN ARE YOU?

Instructions: For each statement, circle the number that most closely resembles your attitude.

Statement	Disagree			Agree	
	A Lot	A Little	Neutral	A Little	A Lot
1. The best way to handle people is to tell them what they want to hear.	1	2	3	4	5
2. When you ask someone to do something for you, it is best to give the real reason for wanting it rather than giving reasons that might carry more weight.	1	2	3	4	5
3. Anyone who completely trusts anyone else is asking for trouble.	1	2	3	4	5
4. It is hard to get ahead without cutting corners here and there.	1	2	3	4	5
5. It is safest to assume that all people have a vicious streak, and it will come out when they are given a chance.	1	2	3	4	5
6. One should take action only when it is morally right.	1	2	3	4	5
7. Most people are basically good and kind.	1	2	3	4	5
8. There is no excuse for lying to someone else.	1	2	3	4	5
9. Most people more easily forget the death of their father than the loss of their property.	1	2	3	4	5
10. Generally speaking, people won't work hard unless they're forced to do so.	1	2	3	4	5

Source: R. Christie and F.L. Geis, *Studies in Machiavellianism.* © Academic Press 1970. Reprinted by permission.

Scoring Key: To obtain your Mach score, add the number you have checked on questions 1, 3, 4, 5, 9, and 10. For the other four questions, reverse the numbers you have checked: 5 becomes 1, 4 is 2, 2 is 4, and 1 is 5. Total your ten numbers to find your score. The higher your score, the more Machiavellian you are. Among a random sample of American adults, the national average was 25.

The most generalizable finding on self-esteem is that low SEs are more susceptible to external influence than are high SEs. Low SEs are dependent on the receipt of positive evaluations from others. As a result, they are more likely to seek approval from others and more prone to conform to the beliefs and behaviors of those they respect than are high SEs. In managerial positions, low SEs will tend to be concerned with pleasing others and, therefore, are less likely to take unpopular stands than are high SEs.

Not surprisingly, self-esteem has also been found to be related to job satisfaction. A number of studies confirm that high SEs are more satisfied with their jobs than are low SEs.

SELF-MONITORING A personality trait that has recently received increased attention is called **self-monitoring**.[54] It refers to an individual's ability to adjust his or her behavior to external, situational factors.

self-monitoring
A personality trait that measures an individual's ability to adjust his or her behavior to external, situational factors.

INCREASE YOUR SELF-AWARENESS: HOW'S YOUR SELF-ESTEEM?

Instructions: Answer each of the following questions *honestly*. Next to each question write a 1, 2, 3, 4, or 5 depending on which answer best describes you.

- 1 = Very often
- 2 = Fairly often
- 3 = Sometimes
- 4 = Once in a great while
- 5 = Practically never

_____ 1. How often do you have the feeling that there is nothing that you can do well?

_____ 2. When you talk in front of a class or group of people your own age, how often do you feel worried or afraid?

_____ 3. How often do you feel that you have handled yourself well at a social gathering?

_____ 4. How often do you have the feeling that you can do everything well?

_____ 5. How often are you comfortable when starting a conversation with people you don't know?

_____ 6. How often do you feel self-conscious?

_____ 7. How often do you feel that you are a successful person?

_____ 8. How often are you troubled with shyness?

_____ 9. How often do you feel inferior to most people you know?

_____ 10. How often do you feel that you are a worthless individual?

_____ 11. How often do you feel confident that your success in your future job or career is assured?

_____ 12. How often do you feel sure of yourself when among strangers?

_____ 13. How often do you feel confident that some day people will look up to you and respect you?

_____ 14. In general, how often do you feel confident about your abilities?

_____ 15. How often do you worry about how well you get along with other people?

_____ 16. How often do you feel that you dislike yourself?

_____ 17. How often do you feel so discouraged with yourself that you wonder whether anything is worthwhile?

_____ 18. How often do you worry about whether other people like to be with you?

_____ 19. When you talk in front of a class or a group of people of your own age, how often are you pleased with your performance?

_____ 20. How often do you feel sure of yourself when you speak in a class discussion?

Source: Developed by A.H. Eagly and adapted from J.R. Robinson and P.R. Shaver, *Measures of Social Psychological Attitudes* (Ann Arbor, MI: Institute of Social Research, 1973), pp. 79–80. With permission.

Scoring Key: Add up your score from the left column for the following ten items: 1, 2, 6, 8, 9, 10, 15, 16, 17, and 18. For the other ten items, reverse your scoring (i.e., a 5 becomes a 1; a 4 becomes a 2). The higher your score, the higher your self-esteem.

Individuals high in self-monitoring show considerable adaptability in adjusting their behavior to external situational factors. They are highly sensitive to external cues and can behave differently in different situations. High self-monitors are capable of presenting striking contradictions between their public persona and their private self. Low self-monitors can't disguise them-

INCREASE YOUR SELF-AWARENESS: ARE YOU A HIGH SELF-MONITOR?

Instructions: Indicate the degree to which you think the following statements are true or false by circling the appropriate number. For example, if a statement is always true, circle the 5 next to that statement.

5 = Certainly, always true
4 = Generally true
3 = Somewhat true, but with exceptions
2 = Somewhat false, but with exceptions
1 = Generally false
0 = Certainly, always false

1. In social situations, I have the ability to alter my behavior if I feel that something else is called for.	5 4 3 2 1 0
2. I am often able to read people's true emotions correctly through their eyes.	5 4 3 2 1 0
3. I have the ability to control the way I come across to people, depending on the impression I wish to give them.	5 4 3 2 1 0
4. In conversations, I am sensitive to even the slightest change in the facial expression of the person I'm conversing with.	5 4 3 2 1 0
5. My powers of intuition are quite good when it comes to understanding others' emotions and motives.	5 4 3 2 1 0
6. I can usually tell when others consider a joke in bad taste, even though they may laugh convincingly.	5 4 3 2 1 0
7. When I feel that the image I am portraying isn't working, I can readily change it to something that does.	5 4 3 2 1 0
8. I can usually tell when I've said something inappropriate by reading the listener's eyes.	5 4 3 2 1 0
9. I have trouble changing my behavior to suit different people and different situations.	5 4 3 2 1 0
10. I have found that I can adjust my behavior to meet the requirements of any situation I find myself in.	5 4 3 2 1 0
11. If someone is lying to me, I usually know it at once from that person's manner of expression.	5 4 3 2 1 0
12. Even when it might be to my advantage, I have difficulty putting up a good front.	5 4 3 2 1 0
13. Once I know what the situation calls for, it's easy for me to regulate my actions accordingly.	5 4 3 2 1 0

Source: R.D. Lennox and R.N. Wolfe, "Revision of the Self-Monitoring Scale," *Journal of Personality and Social Psychology,* June 1984, p. 1361. Copyright 1984 by the American Psychological Association. Reprinted by permission.

Scoring Key: To obtain your score, add up the numbers circled, except reverse scores for questions 9 and 12. On those, a circled 5 becomes a 0, 4 becomes 1, and so forth. High self-monitors are defined as those with scores of 53 or higher.

selves in that way. They tend to display their true dispositions and attitudes in every situation; hence, there is high behavioral consistency between who they are and what they do.

The research on self-monitoring is in its infancy, so predictions must be guarded. However, preliminary evidence suggests that high self-monitors tend to pay closer attention to the behavior of others and are more capable of conforming than are low self-monitors.[55] In addition, high self-monitoring managers tend to be more mobile in their careers and receive more promotions (both internal and cross-organizational).[56] We might also hypothesize that high self-monitors will be more successful in managerial positions in which individuals are required to play multiple, and even contradicting, roles. The high self-monitor is capable of putting on different "faces" for different audiences.

RISK TAKING People differ in their willingness to take chances. This propensity to assume or avoid risk has been shown to have an impact on how long it takes managers to make a decision and how much information they require before making their choice. For instance, seventy-nine managers worked on simulated personnel exercises that required them to make hiring decisions.[57] High risk-taking managers made more rapid decisions and used less information in making their choices than did the low risk-taking managers. Interestingly, the decision accuracy was the same for both groups.

While it is generally correct to conclude that managers in organizations are risk-aversive,[58] there are still individual differences on this dimension.[59] As

INCREASE YOUR SELF-AWARENESS: ARE YOU A RISK TAKER?

Instructions: For each of the following situations, you will be asked to indicate the minimum odds of success you would demand before recommending that one alternative be chosen over another. Try to place yourself in the position of the adviser to the central person in each of the situations.

1. Mr. B, a 45-year-old accountant, has recently been informed by his physician that he has developed a severe heart ailment. The disease would be sufficiently serious to force Mr. B to change many of his strongest life habits—reducing his work load, drastically changing his diet, giving up favorite leisure-time pursuits. The physician suggests that a delicate medical operation could be attempted that, if successful, would completely relieve the heart condition. But its success could not be assured, and, in fact, the operation might prove fatal.

Imagine that you are advising Mr. B. Listed below are several probabilities or odds that the operation will prove successful. Check the *lowest probability* that you would consider acceptable for the operation to be performed.

_____ Place a check here if you think that Mr. B should *not* have the operation no matter what the probabilities.

_____ The chances are 9 in 10 that the operation will be a success.

_____ The chances are 7 in 10 that the operation will be a success.

_____ The chances are 5 in 10 that the operation will be a success.

_____ The chances are 3 in 10 that the operation will be a success.

_____ The chances are 1 in 10 that the operation will be a success.

2. Mr. D is the captain of College X's football team. College X is playing its traditional rival, College Y, in the final game of the season. The game is in its final seconds, and Mr. D's team, College X, is behind in the score. College X has time to run one more play. Mr. D, the captain, must decide whether it would be best to settle for a tie score with a play that would be almost certain to work or, on the other hand, should he try a more complicated and risky play that would bring victory if it succeeded but defeat if it failed.

Imagine that you are advising Mr. D. Listed below are several probabilities or odds that the risky play will work. Check the *lowest probability* that you would consider acceptable for the risky play to be attempted.

(continued)

_____Place a check here if you think that Mr. D should *not* attempt the risky play no matter what the probabilities.

_____The chances are 9 in 10 that the risky play will work.

_____The chances are 7 in 10 that the risky play will work.

_____The chances are 5 in 10 that the risky play will work.

_____The chances are 3 in 10 that the risky play will work.

_____The chances are 1 in 10 that the risky play will work.

3. Ms. K is a successful businesswoman who has participated in a number of civic activities of considerable value to the community. Ms. K has been approached by the leaders of her political party as a possible congressional candidate in the next election. Ms. K's party is a minority party in the district, though the party has won occasional elections in the past. Ms. K would like to hold political office, but to do so would involve a serious financial sacrifice, since the party has insufficient campaign funds. She would also have to endure the attacks of her political opponents in a hot campaign.

Imagine that you are advising Ms. K. Listed below are several probabilities or odds of Ms. K's winning the election in her district. Check the *lowest probability* that you would consider acceptable to make it worthwhile for Ms. K to run for political office.

_____Place a check here if you think that Ms. K should *not* run for political office no matter what the probabilities.

_____The chances are 9 in 10 that Ms. K will win the election.

_____The chances are 7 in 10 that Ms. K will win the election.

_____The chances are 5 in 10 that Ms. K will win the election.

_____The chances are 3 in 10 that Ms. K will win the election.

_____The chances are 1 in 10 that Ms. K will win the election.

4. Ms. L, a 30-year-old research physicist, has been given a five-year appointment by a major university laboratory. As she contemplates the next five years, she realizes that she might work on a difficult, long-term problem that, if a solution could be found, would resolve basic scientific issues in the field and bring high scientific honors. If no solution were found, however, Ms. L would have little to show for her five years in the laboratory and it would be hard for her to get a good job afterward. On the other hand, she could, as most of her professional associates are doing, work on a series of short-term problems for which solutions would be easier to find but that are of lesser scientific importance.

Imagine that you are advising Ms. L. Listed below are several probabilities or odds that a solution will be found to the difficult, long-term problem that Ms. L has in mind. Check the *lowest probability* that you would consider acceptable to make it worthwhile for Ms. L to work on the more difficult long-term problem.

_____The chances are 1 in 10 that Ms. L will solve the long-term problem.

_____The chances are 3 in 10 that Ms. L will solve the long-term problem.

_____The chances are 5 in 10 that Ms. L will solve the long-term problem.

_____The chances are 7 in 10 that Ms. L will solve the long-term problem.

_____The chances are 9 in 10 that Ms. L will solve the long-term problem.

_____Place a check here if you think Ms. L should *not* choose the long-term, difficult problem, no matter what the probabilities.

Source: Adapted from N. Kogan and M.A. Wallach, *Risk Taking: A Study in Cognition and Personality* (New York: Holt, Rinehart & Winston, 1964), pp. 256–61.

Scoring Key: These situations were based on a longer questionnaire. Your results are an indication of your general orientation toward risk rather than a precise measure. To calculate your risk-taking score, add up the chances you were willing to take and divide by four. For any of the situations in which you would not take the risk regardless of the probabilities, give yourself a 10. The lower your number, the more risk-taking you are.

a result, it makes sense to recognize these differences and even to consider aligning risk-taking propensity with specific job demands. For instance, a high risk-taking propensity may lead to more effective performance for a stock trader in a brokerage firm because that type of job demands rapid decision making. On the other hand, a willingness to take risks might prove a major obstacle to an accountant who performs auditing activities. The latter job might be better filled by someone with a low risk-taking propensity.

TYPE A PERSONALITY Do you know any people who are excessively competitive and always seem to be experiencing a chronic sense of time urgency? If you do, it's a good bet that those people have a Type A personality. A person with a **Type A personality** is "*aggressively* involved in a *chronic, incessant* struggle to achieve more and more in less and less time, and, if required to do so, against the opposing efforts of other things or other persons."[60] In the North American culture, such characteristics tend to be highly prized and positively associated with ambition and the successful acquisition of material goods.

Type A personality
Aggressive involvement in a chronic, incessant struggle to achieve more and more in less and less time and, if necessary, against the opposing efforts of other things or other people.

TYPE A'S

1. are always moving, walking, and eating rapidly;
2. feel impatient with the rate at which most events take place;
3. strive to think or do two or more things at once;
4. cannot cope with leisure time;
5. are obsessed with numbers, measuring their success in terms of how many or how much of everything they acquire.

INCREASE YOUR SELF-AWARENESS: ARE YOU A TYPE A?

Instructions: Circle the number on the scale below that best characterizes your behavior for each trait.

1. Casual about appointments	1	2	3	4	5	6	7	8	Never late
2. Not competitive	1	2	3	4	5	6	7	8	Very competitive
3. Never feel rushed	1	2	3	4	5	6	7	8	Always feel rushed
4. Take things one at a time	1	2	3	4	5	6	7	8	Try to do many things at once
5. Slow doing things	1	2	3	4	5	6	7	8	Fast (eating, walking, etc.)
6. Express feelings	1	2	3	4	5	6	7	8	"Sit on" feelings
7. Many interests	1	2	3	4	5	6	7	8	Few interests outside work

Source: Adapted from R.W. Bortner, "Short Rating Scale as a Potential Measure of Pattern A Behavior," *Journal of Chronic Diseases,* June 1969, pp. 87–91. With permission.

Scoring Key: Total your score on the seven questions. Now multiple the total by 3. A total of 120 or more indicates that you are a hard-core Type A. Scores below 90 indicate that you are a hard-core Type B. The following gives you more specifics:

Points	Personality Type
120 or more	A+
106–119	A
100–105	A–
90–99	B+
Less than 90	B

In contrast to the Type A personality is the Type B, who is exactly opposite. Type B's are "rarely harried by the desire to obtain a wildly increasing number of things or participate in an endless growing series of events in an ever-decreasing amount of time."[61]

TYPE B'S

1. never suffer from a sense of time urgency with its accompanying impatience;
2. feel no need to display or discuss either their achievements or accomplishments unless such exposure is demanded by the situation;
3. play for fun and relaxation, rather than to exhibit their superiority at any cost;
4. can relax without guilt.

Type A's operate under moderate to high levels of stress. They subject themselves to more or less continuous time pressure, creating for themselves a life of deadlines. These characteristics result in some rather specific behavioral outcomes. For example, Type A's are fast workers, because they emphasize quantity over quality. In managerial positions, Type A's demonstrate their competitiveness by working long hours and, not infrequently, making poor decisions because they make them too fast. Type A's are also rarely creative. Because of their concern with quantity and speed, they rely on past experiences when faced with problems. They will not allocate the time that is necessary to develop unique solutions to new problems. They rarely vary in their responses to specific challenges in their milieu; hence, their behavior is easier to predict than that of Type B's.

Are Type A's or Type B's more successful in organizations? Despite the Type A's hard work, the Type B's are the ones who appear to make it to the top. Great salespersons are usually Type A's; senior executives are usually Type B's. Why? The answer lies in the tendency of Type A's to trade off quality of effort for quantity. Promotions in corporate and professional organizations "usually go to those who are wise rather than to those who are merely hasty, to those who are tactful rather than to those who are hostile, and to those who are creative rather than to those who are merely agile in competitive strife."[62]

Personality and National Culture

There are certainly no common personality types for a given country. You can, for instance, find high and low risk-takers in almost any culture. Yet a country's culture should influence the dominant personality characteristics of its population. Let's build this case by looking at two personality attributes—locus of control and the Type A personality.

There is evidence that cultures differ in terms of people's relationship to their environment.[63] In some cultures, such as those in North America, people believe that they can dominate their environment. People in other societies, such as Middle Eastern countries, believe that life is essentially preordained. Notice the close parallel to internal and external locus of control. We should expect a larger proportion of internals in the American and Canadian workforce than in the Saudi Arabian or Iranian workforce.

The prevalence of Type A personalities will be somewhat influenced by the culture in which a person grows up. There are Type A's in every country, but there will be more in capitalistic countries, where achievement and material success are highly valued. For instance, it is estimated that about 50 percent of the North American population is Type A.[64] This percentage shouldn't be too surprising. The United States and Canada both have a high emphasis on time management and efficiency. Both have cultures that stress accomplishments and acquisition of money and material goods. In cultures such as Sweden and France, where materialism is less revered, we would predict a smaller proportion of Type A personalities.

Matching Personalities and Jobs

personality–job fit theory
Identifies six personality types and proposes that the fit between personality type and occupational environment determines satisfaction and turnover.

In the discussion of personality attributes, our conclusions were often qualified to recognize that the requirements of the job moderated the relationship between possession of the personality characteristic and job performance. This concern with matching the job requirements with personality characteristics is best articulated in John Holland's **personality–job fit theory**.[65] The theory is based on the notion of fit between an individual's personality characteristics and his or her occupational environment. Holland presents six personality types and proposes that satisfaction and the propensity to leave a job depend on the degree to which individuals successfully match their personalities to an occupational environment.

Exhibit 2-5 Holland's Typology of Personality and Congruent Occupations

Type	Personality Characteristics	Congruent Occupations
Realistic: Prefers physical activities that require skill, strength, and coordination	Shy, genuine, persistent, stable, conforming, practical	Mechanic, drill press operator, assembly line worker, farmer
Investigative: Prefers activities that involve thinking, organizing, and understanding	Analytical, original, curious, independent	Biologist, economist, mathematician, news reporter
Social: Prefers activities that involve helping and developing others	Sociable, friendly, cooperative, understanding	Social worker, teacher, counselor, clinical psychologist
Conventional: Prefers rule-regulated, orderly, and unambiguous activities	Conforming, efficient, practical, unimaginative, inflexible	Accountant, corporate manager, bank teller, file clerk
Enterprising: Prefers verbal activities where there are opportunities to influence others and attain power	Self-confident, ambitious, energetic, domineering	Lawyer, real estate agent, public relations specialist, small business manager
Artistic: Prefers ambiguous and unsystematic activities that allow creative expression	Imaginative, disorderly, idealistic, emotional, impractical	Painter, musician, writer, interior decorator

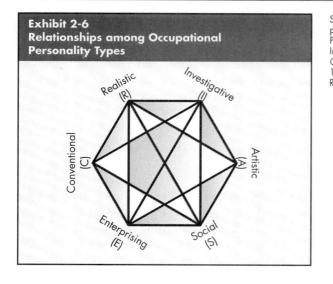

**Exhibit 2-6
Relationships among Occupational
Personality Types**

Source: Reprinted by special permission of the publisher, Psychological Assessment Resources, Inc., from *Making Vocational Choices,* Copyright 1973, 1985, 1992 by Psychological Assessment Resources, Inc. All rights reserved.

Each one of the six personality types has a congruent occupational environment. Exhibit 2-5 describes the six types and their personality characteristics and gives examples of congruent occupations.

Holland has developed a Vocational Preference Inventory questionnaire that contains 160 occupational titles. Respondents indicate which of these occupations they like or dislike, and their answers are used to form personality profiles. Using this procedure, research strongly supports the hexagonal diagram in Exhibit 2-6.[66] This figure shows that the closer two fields or orientations are in the hexagon, the more compatible they are. Adjacent categories are quite similar, whereas those diagonally opposite are highly dissimilar.

What does all this mean? The theory argues that satisfaction is highest and turnover lowest when personality and occupation are in agreement. Social individuals should be in social jobs, conventional people in conventional

Southwest Airlines uses the personality-job fit theory in hiring employees. It hires social personality types—fun-loving, friendly people who enjoy helping and entertaining customers—as flight attendants. Antics like a flight attendant popping out of a luggage bin delight customers and increase employee job satisfaction, which helps make Southwest the most consistently profitable U.S. airline.

jobs, and so forth. A realistic person in a realistic job is in a more congruent situation than is a realistic person in an investigative job. A realistic person in a social job is in the most incongruent situation possible. The key points of this model are that (1) there do appear to be intrinsic differences in personality among individuals, (2) there are different types of jobs, and (3) people in job environments congruent with their personality types should be more satisfied and less likely to voluntarily resign than should people in incongruent jobs.

LEARNING

The last topic we will introduce in this chapter is learning. It is included for the obvious reason that almost all complex behavior is learned. If we want to explain and predict behavior, we need to understand how people learn.

A Definition of Learning

learning
Any relatively permanent change in behavior that occurs as a result of experience.

What is **learning**? A psychologist's definition is considerably broader than the layperson's view that "it's what we did when we went to school." In actuality, each of us is continuously going "to school." Learning occurs all of the time. A generally accepted definition of learning is, therefore, *any relatively permanent change in behavior that occurs as a result of experience.* Ironically, we can say that changes in behavior indicate that learning has taken place and that learning is a change in behavior.

Obviously, the foregoing definition suggests that we shall never see someone "learning." We can see changes taking place but not the learning itself. The concept is theoretical and, hence, not directly observable:

> You have seen people in the process of learning, you have seen people who behave in a particular way as a result of learning and some of you (in fact, I guess the majority of you) have "learned" at some time in your life. In other words, we infer that learning has taken place if an individual behaves, reacts, responds as a result of experience in a manner different from the way he formerly behaved.[67]

Our definition has several components that deserve clarification. First, learning involves change. Change may be good or bad from an organizational point of view. People can learn unfavorable behaviors—to hold prejudices or to restrict their output, for example—as well as favorable behaviors. Second,

◆ Learning involves change.

the change must be relatively permanent. Temporary changes may be only reflexive and fail to represent any learning. Therefore, the requirement that learning must be relatively permanent rules out behavioral changes caused by fatigue or temporary adaptations. Third, our definition is concerned with behavior. Learning takes place when there is a change in actions. A change in an individual's thought processes or attitudes, if accompanied by no change in behavior, would not be learning. Finally, some form of experience is necessary for learning. Experience may be acquired directly through observation or practice, or it may be acquired indirectly, as through reading. The crucial test still remains: Does this experience result in a relatively permanent change in behavior? If the answer is Yes, we can say that learning has taken place.

Theories of Learning

How do we learn? Three theories have been offered to explain the process by which we acquire patterns of behavior. These are classical conditioning, operant conditioning, and social learning.

CLASSICAL CONDITIONING **Classical conditioning** grew out of experiments to teach dogs to salivate in response to the ringing of a bell, conducted at the turn of the century by a Russian physiologist, Ivan Pavlov.[68] A simple surgical procedure allowed Pavlov to measure accurately the amount of saliva secreted by a dog. When Pavlov presented the dog with a piece of meat, the dog exhibited a noticeable increase in salivation. When Pavlov withheld the presentation of meat and merely rang a bell, the dog did not salivate. Then Pavlov proceeded to link the meat and the ringing of the bell. After repeatedly hearing the bell before getting the food, the dog began to salivate as soon as the bell rang. After a while, the dog would salivate merely at the sound of the bell, even if no food was offered. In effect, the dog had learned to respond—that is, to salivate—to the bell. Let's review this experiment to introduce the key concepts in classical conditioning.

The meat was an *unconditioned stimulus*; it invariably caused the dog to react in a specific way. The reaction that took place whenever the unconditioned stimulus occurred was called the *unconditioned response* (or the noticeable increase in salivation, in this case). The bell was an artificial stimulus, or what we call the *conditioned stimulus*. Although it was originally neutral, after the bell was paired with the meat (an unconditioned stimulus), it eventually

classical conditioning
A type of conditioning in which an individual responds to some stimulus that would not ordinarily produce such a response.

THE FAR SIDE   By GARY LARSON

Unbeknownst to most students of psychology, Pavlov's first experiment was to ring a bell and cause his dog to attack Freud's cat.

Exhibit 2-7
Source: THE FAR SIDE copyright 1990 & 1991 FARWORKS, INC./Dist. by UNIVERSAL PRESS SYNDICATE. Reprinted with permission. All rights reserved.

produced a response when presented alone. The last key concept is the *conditioned response*. This describes the behavior of the dog; it salivated in reaction to the bell alone.

Using these concepts, we can summarize classical conditioning. Essentially, learning a conditioned response involves building up an association between a conditioned stimulus and an unconditioned stimulus. When the stimuli, one compelling and the other one neutral, are paired, the neutral one becomes a conditioned stimulus and, hence, takes on the properties of the unconditioned stimulus.

Classical conditioning can be used to explain why Christmas carols often bring back pleasant memories of childhood; the songs are associated with the festive Christmas spirit and evoke fond memories and feelings of euphoria. In an organizational setting, we can also see classical conditioning operating. For example, at one manufacturing plant, every time the top executives from the head office were scheduled to make a visit, the plant management would clean up the administrative offices and wash the windows. This went on for years. Eventually, employees would turn on their best behavior and look prim and proper whenever the windows were cleaned—even in those occasional instances when the cleaning was not paired with the visit from the top brass. People had learned to associate the cleaning of the windows with a visit from the head office.

Classical conditioning is passive. Something happens and we react in a specific way. It is elicited in response to a specific, identifiable event. As such, it can explain simple reflexive behaviors. But most behavior—particularly the complex behavior of individuals in organizations—is emitted rather than elicited. It is voluntary rather than reflexive. For example, employees choose to arrive at work on time, ask their boss for help with problems, or "goof off" when no one is watching. The learning of those behaviors is better understood by looking at operant conditioning.

operant conditioning
A type of conditioning in which desired voluntary behavior leads to a reward or prevents a punishment.

OPERANT CONDITIONING **Operant conditioning** argues that behavior is a function of its consequences. People learn to behave to get something they want or to avoid something they don't want. Operant behavior means voluntary or learned behavior in contrast to reflexive or unlearned behavior. The tendency to repeat such behavior is influenced by the reinforcement or lack of reinforcement brought about by the consequences of the behavior. Reinforcement, therefore, strengthens a behavior and increases the likelihood that it will be repeated.

What Pavlov did for classical conditioning, the Harvard psychologist B.F. Skinner did for operant conditioning.[69] Building on earlier work in the field, Skinner's research extensively expanded our knowledge of operant conditioning. Even his staunchest critics, who represent a sizable group, admit that his operant concepts work.

◆ Reinforcement strengthens a behavior and increases the likelihood that it will be repeated.

Behavior is assumed to be determined from without—that is, learned—rather than from within—reflexive or unlearned. Skinner argued that creating pleasing consequences to follow specific forms of behavior would increase the frequency of that behavior. People will most likely engage in desired behaviors if they are positively reinforced for doing so. Rewards are most effective if they immediately follow the desired response. In addition, behavior that is not rewarded, or is punished, is less likely to be repeated.

You see illustrations of operant conditioning everywhere. For example, any situation in which it is either explicitly stated or implicitly suggested that reinforcements are contingent on some action on your part involves the use of operant learning. Your instructor says that if you want a high grade in the course you must supply correct answers on the test. A commissioned salesperson wanting to earn a sizable income finds that doing so is contingent on generating high sales in her territory. Of course, the linkage can also work to teach the individual to engage in behaviors that work against the best interests of the organization. Assume that your boss tells you that if you will work overtime during the next three-week busy season, you will be compensated for it at the next performance appraisal. However, when performance appraisal time comes, you find that you are given no positive reinforcement for your overtime work. The next time your boss asks you to work overtime, what will you do? You'll probably decline! Your behavior can be explained by operant conditioning: If a behavior fails to be positively reinforced, the probability that the behavior will be repeated declines.

SOCIAL LEARNING   Individuals can also learn by observing what happens to other people and just by being told about something, as well as by direct experiences. So, for example, much of what we have learned comes from watching models—parents, teachers, peers, motion picture and television performers, bosses, and so forth. This view that we can learn through both observation and direct experience has been called **social-learning theory**.[70]

social-learning theory
People can learn through observation and direct experience.

Although social-learning theory is an extension of operant conditioning—that is, it assumes that behavior is a function of consequences—it also acknowledges the existence of observational learning and the importance of perception in learning. People respond to how they perceive and define consequences not to the objective consequences themselves.

The influence of models is central to the social-learning viewpoint. Four processes have been found to determine the influence that a model will have on an individual. As we will show later in this chapter, the inclusion of the following processes when management sets up employee training programs will significantly improve the likelihood that the programs will be successful:

1. *Attentional processes.* People learn from a model only when they recognize and pay attention to its critical features. We tend to be most influenced by models that are attractive, repeatedly available, important to us, or similar to us in our estimation.
2. *Retention processes.* A model's influence will depend on how well the individual remembers the model's action after the model is no longer readily available.
3. *Motor reproduction processes.* After a person has seen a new behavior by observing the model, the watching must be converted to doing. This process then demonstrates that the individual can perform the modeled activities.
4. *Reinforcement processes.* Individuals will be motivated to exhibit the modeled behavior if positive incentives or rewards are provided. Behaviors that are positively reinforced will be given more attention, learned better, and performed more often.

Shaping: A Managerial Tool

Because learning takes place on the job as well as prior to it, managers will be concerned with how they can teach employees to behave in ways that most

shaping behavior
Systematically reinforcing each successive step that moves an individual closer to the desired response.

benefit the organization. When we attempt to mold individuals by guiding their learning in graduated steps, we are **shaping behavior**.

Consider the situation in which an employee's behavior is significantly different from that sought by management. If management rewarded the individual only when he or she showed desirable responses, there might be very little reinforcement taking place. In such a case, shaping offers a logical approach toward achieving the desired behavior.

We *shape* behavior by systematically reinforcing each successive step that moves the individual closer to the desired response. If an employee who has chronically been a half-hour late for work comes in only twenty minutes late, we can reinforce that improvement. Reinforcement would increase as responses more closely approximated the desired behavior.

METHODS OF SHAPING BEHAVIOR There are four ways in which to shape behavior: through positive reinforcement, negative reinforcement, punishment, and extinction.

Following a response with something pleasant is called *positive reinforcement*. This would describe, for instance, the boss who praises an employee for a job well done. Following a response by the termination or withdrawal of something unpleasant is called *negative reinforcement*. If your college instructor asks a question and you don't know the answer, looking through your lecture notes is likely to preclude your being called on. This is a negative reinforcement because you have learned that looking busily through your notes prevents the instructor from calling on you. *Punishment* is causing an unpleasant condition in an attempt to eliminate an undesirable behavior. Giving an employee a two-day suspension from work without pay for showing up drunk is an example of punishment. Eliminating any reinforcement that is maintaining a behavior is called *extinction*. When the behavior is not reinforced, it tends to gradually be extinguished. College instructors who wish to discourage students from asking questions in class can eliminate this behavior in their students by ignoring those who raise their hands to ask questions. Hand-raising will become extinct when it is invariably met with an absence of reinforcement.

Both positive and negative reinforcement result in learning. They strengthen a response and increase the probability of repetition. In the preceding illustrations, praise strengthens and increases the behavior of doing a good job because praise is desired. The behavior of "looking busy" is similarly strengthened and increased by its terminating the undesirable consequence of being called on by the teacher. Both punishment and extinction, however, weaken behavior and tend to decrease its subsequent frequency.

Reinforcement, whether it is positive or negative, has an impressive record as a shaping tool. Our interest, therefore, is in reinforcement rather than in punishment or extinction. A review of research findings on the impact of reinforcement upon behavior in organizations concluded that

1. Some type of reinforcement is necessary to produce a change in behavior.
2. Some types of rewards are more effective for use in organizations than others.
3. The speed with which learning takes place and the permanence of its effects will be determined by the timing of reinforcement.[71]

Point 3 is extremely important and deserves considerable elaboration.

SCHEDULES OF REINFORCEMENT The two major types of reinforcement schedules are *continuous* and *intermittent*. A **continuous reinforcement** schedule reinforces the desired behavior each and every time it is demonstrated. Take, for example, the case of someone who has historically had trouble arriving at work on time. Every time he is not tardy his manager might compliment him on his desirable behavior. In an intermittent schedule, on the other hand, not every instance of the desirable behavior is reinforced, but reinforcement is given often enough to make the behavior worth repeating. This latter schedule can be compared to the workings of a slot machine, which people will continue to play even when they know that it is adjusted to give a considerable return to the gambling house. The intermittent payoffs occur just often enough to reinforce the behavior of slipping in coins and pulling the handle. Evidence indicates that the intermittent, or varied, form of reinforcement tends to promote more resistance to extinction than does the continuous form.[72]

An **intermittent reinforcement** can be of a ratio or interval type. *Ratio schedules* depend upon how many responses the subject makes. The individual is reinforced after giving a certain number of specific types of behavior. *Interval schedules* depend upon how much time has passed since the last reinforcement. With interval schedules, the individual is reinforced on the first appropriate behavior after a particular time has elapsed. A reinforcement can also be classified as fixed or variable. Intermittent techniques for administering rewards can, therefore, be placed into four categories, as shown in Exhibit 2-8.

When rewards are spaced at uniform time intervals, the reinforcement schedule is of the **fixed-interval** type. The critical variable is time, and it is held constant. This is the predominant schedule for almost all salaried workers in North America. When you get your paycheck on a weekly, semimonthly, monthly, or other predetermined time basis, you are rewarded on a fixed-interval reinforcement schedule.

If rewards are distributed in time so that reinforcements are unpredictable, the schedule is of the **variable-interval** type. When an instructor advises her class that pop quizzes will be given during the term (the exact number of which is unknown to the students) and the quizzes will account for twenty percent of the term grade, she is using a variable-interval schedule. Similarly, a series of randomly timed unannounced visits to a company office by the corporate audit staff is an example of a variable-interval schedule.

In a **fixed-ratio** schedule, after a fixed or constant number of responses are given, a reward is initiated. For example, a piece-rate incentive plan is a fixed-ratio schedule; the employee receives a reward based on the number of work pieces generated. If the piece rate for a zipper installer in a dressmaking factory is $5.00 a dozen, the reinforcement (money in this case) is fixed to the

continuous reinforcement
A desired behavior is reinforced each and every time it is demonstrated.

intermittent reinforcement
A desired behavior is reinforced often enough to make the behavior worth repeating but not every time it is demonstrated.

fixed-interval schedule
Rewards are spaced at uniform time intervals.

variable-interval schedule
Rewards are distributed in time so that reinforcements are unpredictable.

fixed-ratio schedule
Rewards are initiated after a fixed or constant number of responses.

Exhibit 2-8
Schedules of Reinforcement

	Interval	Ratio
Fixed	Fixed-interval	Fixed-ratio
Variable	Variable-interval	Variable-ratio

number of zippers sewn into garments. After every dozen is sewn in, the installer has earned another $5.00.

When the reward varies relative to the behavior of the individual, he or she is said to be reinforced on a **variable-ratio** schedule. Salespeople on commission are examples of individuals on such a reinforcement schedule. On some occasions, they may make a sale after only two calls on a potential customer. On other occasions, they might need to make twenty or more calls to secure a sale. The reward, then, is variable in relation to the number of successful calls the salesperson makes. Exhibit 2-9 depicts the four categories of intermittent schedules.

variable-ratio schedule
The reward varies relative to the behavior of the individual.

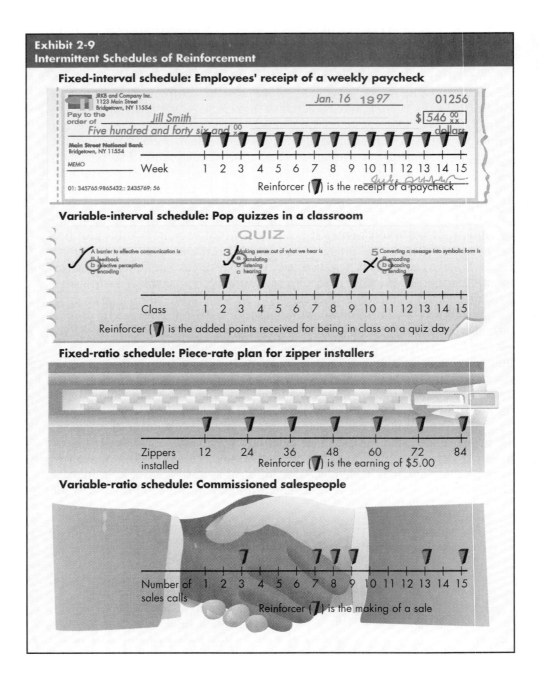

Exhibit 2-9
Intermittent Schedules of Reinforcement

Fixed-interval schedule: Employees' receipt of a weekly paycheck

Reinforcer (▼) is the receipt of a paycheck

Variable-interval schedule: Pop quizzes in a classroom

Reinforcer (▼) is the added points received for being in class on a quiz day

Fixed-ratio schedule: Piece-rate plan for zipper installers

Reinforcer (▼) is the earning of $5.00

Variable-ratio schedule: Commissioned salespeople

Reinforcer (▼) is the making of a sale

REINFORCEMENT SCHEDULES AND BEHAVIOR   Continuous reinforcement schedules can lead to early satiation, and under this schedule behavior tends to weaken rapidly when reinforcers are withheld. However, continuous reinforcers are appropriate for newly emitted, unstable, or low-frequency responses. In contrast, intermittent reinforcers preclude early satiation because they don't follow every response. They are appropriate for stable or high-frequency responses.

In general, variable schedules tend to lead to higher performance than fixed schedules. For example, as noted previously, most employees in organizations are paid on fixed-interval schedules. But such a schedule does not clearly link performance and rewards. The reward is given for time spent on the job rather than for a specific response (performance). In contrast, variable-interval schedules generate high rates of response and more stable and consistent behavior because of a high correlation between performance and reward and because of the uncertainty involved—the employee tends to be more alert since there is a surprise factor.

Some Specific Organizational Applications

We have alluded to a number of situations in which learning theory could be helpful to managers. In this section, we will briefly look at six specific applications: using lotteries to reduce absenteeism, substituting well pay for sick pay, disciplining problem employees, developing effective employee training programs, creating mentoring programs for new employees, and applying learning theory to self-management.

USING LOTTERIES TO REDUCE ABSENTEEISM   Management can use learning theory to design programs to reduce absenteeism. For example, New York Life Insurance Co. created a lottery that rewarded employees for attendance.[73] Each quarter, the names of all the headquarters employees who had no absences are placed in a drum. In a typical quarter, about 4,000 of the company's 7,500 employees have their names placed in the drum. The first ten names pulled earn a $200 bond, the next twenty earn a $100 bond, and seventy more receive a paid day off. At the end of the year, another lottery is held for those with twelve months of perfect attendance. Twelve prizes are awarded; two employees receive $1,000 bonds, and ten more earn five days off with pay.

This lottery follows a variable-ratio schedule. A good attendance record increases an employee's probability of winning, yet having perfect attendance is no assurance that an employee will be rewarded by winning one of the prizes. Consistent with the research on reinforcement schedules, this lottery resulted in lower absence rates. In its first ten months of operation, for instance, absenteeism was twenty-one percent lower than for the comparable period in the preceding year.

WELL PAY VS. SICK PAY   Most organizations provide their salaried employees with paid sick leave as part of the employee's fringe benefit program. But, ironically, organizations with paid sick leave programs experience almost twice the absenteeism of organizations without such programs.[74] The reality is that sick leave programs reinforce the wrong behavior—

◆ Sick leave programs reinforce the wrong behavior.

absence from work. When employees receive ten paid sick days a year, it is the unusual employee who isn't sure to use them all up, regardless of whether he or she is sick. Organizations should reward attendance not absence.

As a case in point, one Midwest organization implemented a well-pay program that paid a bonus to employees who had no absence for any given four-week period and then paid for sick leave only after the first eight hours of absence.[75] Evaluation of the well-pay program found that it produced increased savings to the organization, reduced absenteeism, increased productivity, and improved employee satisfaction.

Forbes magazine used the same approach to cut its health care costs.[76] It rewarded employees who stayed healthy and didn't file medical claims by paying them the difference between $500 and their medical claims, then doubling the amount. So if someone submitted no claims in a given year, he or she would receive $1,000 ($500 × 2). By rewarding employees for good health, *Forbes* cut its major medical and dental claims by over thirty percent.

EMPLOYEE DISCIPLINE Every manager will, at some time, have to deal with an employee who drinks on the job, is insubordinate, steals company property, arrives consistently late for work, or engages in similar problem behaviors. Managers will respond with disciplinary actions such as oral reprimands, written warnings, and temporary suspensions. But our knowledge about punishment's effect on behavior indicates that the use of discipline carries costs. It may provide only a short-term solution and result in serious side effects.

Disciplining employees for undesirable behaviors only tells them what *not* to do. It doesn't tell them what alternative behaviors are preferred. The result is that this form of punishment frequently leads to only short-term suppression of the undesirable behavior rather than its elimination. Continued use of punishment, rather than positive reinforcement, also tends to produce a fear of the manager. As the punishing agent, the manager becomes associated in the employee's mind with adverse consequences. Employees respond by "hiding" from their boss. Hence, the use of punishment can undermine manager-employee relations.

Discipline does have a place in organizations. In practice, it tends to be popular because of its ability to produce fast results in the short run. Moreover, managers are reinforced for using discipline because it produces an immediate change in the employee's behavior. The suggestions offered in the "From Concepts to Skills" box can help you to more effectively implement disciplinary action.

DEVELOPING TRAINING PROGRAMS Most organizations have some type of systematic training program. More specifically, U.S. corporations with 100 or more employees spent $52.2 billion in one recent year on formal training for 47.3 million workers.[77] Can these organizations draw from our discussion of learning in order to improve the effectiveness of their training programs? Certainly.

Social-learning theory offers such a guide. It tells us that training should offer a model to grab the trainee's attention; provide motivational properties; help the trainee to file away what he or she has learned for later use; provide opportunities to practice new behaviors; offer positive rewards for accomplishments; and, if the training has taken place off the job, allow the trainee some opportunity to transfer what he or she has learned to the job.

From Concepts to Skills

Effective Discipline Skills

The essence of effective disciplining can be summarized by the following eight behaviors.[78]

1. *Respond immediately.* The more quickly a disciplinary action follows an offense, the more likely it is that the employee will associate the discipline with the offense rather than with you as the dispenser of the discipline. It's best to begin the disciplinary process as soon as possible after you notice a violation.

2. *Provide a warning.* You have an obligation to give warning before initiating disciplinary action. This means that the employee must be aware of the organization's rules and accept its standards of behavior. Disciplinary action is more likely to be interpreted by employees as fair when they have received clear warning that a given violation will lead to discipline and when they know what that discipline will be.

3. *State the problem specifically.* Give the date, time, place, individuals involved, and any mitigating circumstances surrounding the violation. Be sure to define the violation in exact terms instead of just reciting company regulations or terms from a union contract. It's not the violation of the rules per se that you want to convey concern about. It's the effect that the rule violation has on the work unit's performance. Explain why the behavior can't be continued by showing how it specifically affects the employee's job performance, the unit's effectiveness, and the employee's colleagues.

4. *Allow the employee to explain his or her position.* Regardless of what facts you have uncovered, due process demands that you give the employee the opportunity to explain his or her position. From the employee's perspective, what happened? Why did it happen? What was his or her perception of the rules, regulations, and circumstances?

5. *Keep discussion impersonal.* Penalties should be connected with a given violation, not with the personality of the individual violator. That is, discipline should be directed at what the employee has done not at the employee.

6. *Be consistent.* Fair treatment of employees demands that disciplinary action be consistent. If you enforce rule violations in an inconsistent manner, the rules will lose their impact, morale will decline, and employees will likely question your competence. Consistency, however, need not result in treating everyone exactly alike; doing, that would ignore mitigating circumstances. But the responsibility is yours to clearly justify disciplinary actions that might appear inconsistent to employees.

7. *Take progressive action.* Choose a punishment that's appropriate to the crime. Penalties should get progressively stronger if, or when, an offense is repeated. Typically, progressive disciplinary action begins with a verbal warning and then proceeds through a written reprimand, suspension, a demotion or pay cut, and finally, in the most serious cases, dismissal.

8. *Obtain agreement on change.* Disciplining should include guidance and direction for correcting the problem. Let the employee state what he or she plans to do in the future to ensure that the violation won't be repeated.

CREATING MENTORING PROGRAMS It's the unusual senior manager who, early in his or her career, didn't have an older, more experienced mentor higher up in the organization. This mentor took the protégé under his or her wing and provided advice and guidance on how to survive and get ahead in the organization. Mentoring, of course, is not limited to the managerial ranks. Union apprenticeship programs, for example, do the same thing by preparing

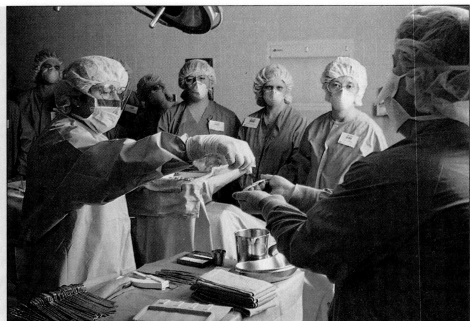

3M uses learning theory in designing off-the-job training programs. Employees at 3M's medical and surgical products plant visit the operating rooms of local hospitals to watch how doctors and nurses use the surgical tapes, prep solutions, and other products the employees make. From this interaction with customers, employees learn how important their jobs are in delivering high-quality products that completely satisfy customers.

individuals to move from unskilled apprentice status to that of skilled journeyman. A young electrician apprentice typically works under an experienced electrician for several years to develop the full range of skills necessary to effectively execute his or her job.

A successful mentoring program will be built on modeling concepts from social-learning theory. That is, a mentor's impact comes from more than merely what he or she explicitly tells a protégé. Mentors are role models. Protégés learn to convey the attitudes and behaviors that the organization wants by emulating the traits and actions of their mentors. They observe and then imitate. Top managers who are concerned with developing employees who will fit into the organization and with preparing young managerial talent for greater responsibilities should give careful attention to who takes on mentoring roles. The creating of formal mentoring programs—in which young individuals are officially assigned a mentor—allows senior executives to manage the process and increases the likelihood that protégés will be molded the way top management desires.

SELF-MANAGEMENT Organizational applications of learning concepts are not restricted to managing the behavior of others. These concepts can also be used to allow individuals to manage their own behavior and, in so doing, reduce the need for managerial control. This is called **self-management**.[79]

self-management
Learning techniques that allow individuals to manage their own behavior so that less external management control is necessary.

Self-management requires an individual to deliberately manipulate stimuli, internal processes, and responses to achieve personal behavioral outcomes. The basic processes involve observing one's own behavior, comparing the behavior with a standard, and rewarding oneself if the behavior meets the standard.

So how might self-management be applied? Here's an illustration. A group of state government blue-collar employees received eight hours of training in which they were taught self-management skills.[80] They were then shown how the skills could be used for improving job attendance. They were instructed on how to set specific goals for job attendance, both short-term and intermediate-term. They learned how to write a behavioral contract with themselves and identify self-chosen reinforcers. Finally, they learned the importance of self-monitoring their attendance behavior and administering incentives when they achieved their goals. The net result for these participants was a significant improvement in job attendance.

Summary and Implications for Managers

This chapter looked at four individual variables—biographical characteristics, ability, personality, and learning. Let's now try to summarize what we found and consider their importance for the manager who is trying to understand organizational behavior.

BIOGRAPHICAL CHARACTERISTICS Biographical characteristics are readily available to managers. For the most part, they include data that are contained in almost every employee's personnel file. The most important conclusions we can draw after our review of the evidence are that age seems to have no relationship to productivity; older workers and those with longer tenure are less likely to resign; and married employees have fewer absences, less turnover, and report higher job satisfaction than do unmarried employees. But what value can this information have for managers? The obvious answer is that it can help in making choices among job applicants.

ABILITY Ability directly influences an employee's level of performance and satisfaction through the ability-job fit. Given management's desire to get a compatible fit, what can be done?

First, an effective selection process will improve the fit. A job analysis will provide information about jobs currently being done and the abilities that individuals need to perform the jobs adequately. Applicants can then be tested, interviewed, and evaluated on the degree to which they possess the necessary abilities.

Second, promotion and transfer decisions affecting individuals already in the organization's employ should reflect the abilities of candidates. As with new employees, care should be taken to assess critical abilities that incumbents will need in the job and to match those requirements with the organization's human resources.

Third, the fit can be improved by fine-tuning the job to better match an incumbent's abilities. Often modifications can be made in the job that, while not having a significant impact on the job's basic activities, better adapts it to the specific talents of a given employee. Examples would be to change some of the equipment used or to reorganize tasks within a group of employees.

A final alternative is to provide training for employees. This is applicable to both new workers and present job incumbents. Training can keep the abilities of incumbents current or provide new skills as times and conditions change.

PERSONALITY A review of the personality literature offers general guidelines that can lead to effective job performance. As such, it can improve hiring, transfer, and promotion decisions. Because personality characteristics create the parameters for people's behavior, they give us a framework for predicting behavior. For example, individuals who are shy, introverted, and uncomfortable in social situations would probably be ill-suited as salespeople. Individuals who are submissive and conforming might not be effective as advertising "idea" people.

Can we predict which people will be high performers in sales, research, or assembly-line work on the basis of their personality characteristics alone? The answer is No. But a knowledge of an individual's personality can aid in reducing mismatches, which, in turn, can lead to reduced turnover and higher job satisfaction.

We can look at certain personality characteristics that tend to be related to job success, test for those traits, and use the data to make selection more effective. A person who accepts rules, conformity, and dependence and rates high on authoritarianism is likely to feel more comfortable in, say, a structured assembly-line job, as an admittance clerk in a hospital, or as an administrator in a large public agency than as a researcher or an employee whose job requires a high degree of creativity.

LEARNING Any observable change in behavior is prima facie evidence that learning has taken place. What we want to do, of course, is to ascertain if learning concepts provide us with any insights that would allow us to explain and predict behavior.

Positive reinforcement is a powerful tool for modifying behavior. By identifying and rewarding performance-enhancing behaviors, management increases the likelihood that they will be repeated.

Our knowledge about learning further suggests that reinforcement is a more effective tool than punishment. Although punishment eliminates undesired behavior more quickly than negative reinforcement does, punished behavior tends to be only temporarily suppressed rather than permanently changed. And punishment may produce unpleasant side effects such as lower morale and higher absenteeism or turnover. In addition, the recipients of punishment tend to become resentful of the punisher. Managers, therefore, are advised to use reinforcement rather than punishment.

Finally, managers should expect that employees will look to them as models. Managers who are constantly late to work, or take two hours for lunch, or help themselves to company office supplies for personal use should expect employees to read the message they are sending and model their behavior accordingly.

For Review

1. Which biographical characteristics best predict productivity? Absenteeism? Turnover? Satisfaction?

2. Describe the specific steps you would take to ensure that an individual has the appropriate abilities to satisfactorily do a given job.

3. What constrains the power of personality traits to precisely predict behavior?

4. What behavioral predictions might you make if you knew that an employee had (a) an external locus of control? (b) a low Mach score? (c) low self-esteem? (d) a Type A personality?

5. What is the Myers-Briggs Type Indicator?

6. What were the six personality types identified by Holland?

7. How might employees actually learn unethical behavior on their jobs?

8. Contrast classical conditioning, operant conditioning, and social learning.

9. Describe the four types of intermittent reinforcers.

10. If you had to take disciplinary action against an employee, how, specifically, would you do it?

For Discussion

1. "Heredity determines personality." (a) Build an argument to support this statement. (b) Build an argument against this statement.

2. "The type of job an employee does moderates the relationship between personality and job productivity." Do you agree or disagree with this statement? Discuss.

3. One day your boss comes in and he's nervous, edgy, and argumentative. The next day he is calm and relaxed. Does this behavior suggest that personality traits aren't consistent from day to day?

4. Learning theory can be used to explain behavior and to control behavior. Can you distinguish between the two objectives? Can you give any ethical or moral arguments why managers should not seek control over others' behavior? How valid do you think these arguments are?

5. What have you learned about "learning" that could help you to explain the behavior of students in a classroom if: (a) The instructor gives only one test—a final examination at the end of the course? (b) The instructor gives four exams during the term, all of which are announced on the first day of class? (c) The student's grade is based on the results of numerous exams, none of which are announced by the instructor ahead of time?

☞ Point ☜

The Value of Traits in Explaining Attitudes and Behavior

The essence of trait approaches in OB is that employees possess stable personality characteristics—such as dependency, anxiety, and sociability—that significantly influence their attitudes toward, and behavioral reactions to, organizational settings. People with particular traits tend to be relatively consistent in their attitudes and behavior over time and across situations.

Of course, trait theorists recognize that all traits are not equally powerful. *Cardinal traits* are defined as being so strong and generalized that they influence every act a person performs. For instance, a person who possesses dominance as a cardinal trait is domineering in virtually all of his or her actions. Evidence indicates that cardinal traits are relatively rare. More typical are *primary traits*. These are generally consistent influences on behavior, but they may not show up in all situations. So a person may be generally sociable but not display that primary trait in, say, large meetings. Finally, *secondary traits* are attributes that do not form a vital part of the personality but come into play only in particular situations. An otherwise assertive person may be submissive, for example, when confronted by his or her boss. For the most part, trait theories have focused on the power of primary traits to predict employee attitudes and behavior.

Trait theories do a fairly good job of meeting the average person's face-validity test. That is, they appear to be a reasonably accurate way to describe people. Think of friends, relatives, and acquaintances you have known for a number of years. Do they have traits that have remained essentially sta-

ble over time? Most of us would answer that question in the affirmative. If Cousin Anne was shy and nervous when we last saw her ten years ago, we would be surprised to find her outgoing and relaxed now.

In an organizational context, researchers have found that a person's job satisfaction in one given year was a significant predictor of his or her job satisfaction five years later, even when changes in occupational status, pay, occupation, and employer were controlled for.* This finding led the researchers to conclude that individuals possess a predisposition toward happiness, which significantly affects their job satisfaction in all types of jobs and organizations.

Here's a final point regarding the function of traits in organizations: Managers must have a strong belief in the power of traits to predict behavior. Otherwise, they would not bother testing and interviewing prospective employees. If managers believed that situations determined behavior, they would hire people almost at random and structure the situation properly. But the employee selection process in many organizations throughout the industrialized world places a great deal of emphasis on how applicants perform in interviews and on tests. Assume you are an interviewer and ask yourself: What am I looking for in job candidates? If you answered with terms such as *conscientious, hardworking, ambitious, confident, independent*, and *dependable*, you're a trait theorist!

Some of the points in this argument are from R.J. House, S.A. Shane, and D.M. Herold, "Rumors of the Death of Dispositional Research Are Vastly Exaggerated," *Academy of Management Review*, January 1996, pp. 203–24.

*B.M. Staw and J. Ross, "Stability in the Midst of Change: A Dispositional Approach to Job Attitudes," *Journal of Applied Psychology*, August 1985, pp. 469–80.

counterPoint

The Limited Power of Traits in Organizations

Few people would dispute the point that there are some stable individual attributes that affect experience in and reactions to the workplace. But trait theorists go beyond that generality and argue that individual behavior consistencies are widespread and account for much of the differences in behavior among people.

There are two important problems with using traits to explain a large proportion of behavior in organizations. First, a substantial amount of evidence shows that organizational settings are strong situations that have a large impact on employee attitudes and behavior. Second, a growing body of research indicates that individuals are highly adaptive and that personality traits change in response to organizational situations. Let's elaborate on each of those problems.

It has been well known for some time that the effects of traits are likely to be strongest in relatively weak situations and weakest in relatively strong situations. Organizational settings tend to be strong situations. Why? First, they have formal structures with rules, regulations, policies, and reward systems that define acceptable behavior and punish deviant behaviors. Second, they have informal norms that dictate appropriate behaviors. These formal and informal constraints lead employees to adopt attitudes and behaviors that are consistent with their organizational roles, thus minimizing the effects of personality traits.

By arguing that employees possess stable traits that lead to cross-situational consistency in their attitudes and behaviors, trait theorists are implying that individuals do not really adapt to different situations. But there is a growing body of evidence that an individual's traits are changed by the organizations that individual participates in. Thus, instead of remaining stable over time, an individual's personality is changed by all the organizations in which he or she has taken part. If the individual's personality changes as a result of exposure to organizational settings, in what sense can that individual be said to have traits that persistently and consistently affect his or her reactions to those very settings? Moreover, people demonstrate their situational flexibility when they change roles as they participate in different organizations. Employees often belong to many organizations. Bob is a corporate accountant during the day, presides over church meetings two nights a week, and coaches his daughter's soccer team on weekends. Most of us are like Bob; we belong to multiple organizations that often include very different kinds of members. We adapt to those different situations. Instead of being the prisoners of a rigid and stable personality framework as trait theorists propose, we regularly adjust our behavior and attitudes to reflect the requirements of various situations.

Based on A. Davis-Blake and J. Pfeffer, "Just a Mirage: The Search for Dispositional Effects in Organizational Research," *Academy of Management Review*, July 1989, pp. 385–400.

Learning about Yourself Exercise

What's Your Learning Style?

For each of the following, circle the number that is most true for you.

1. When I learn a subject, I like to learn the theory first and then work on concrete applications; or do you prefer to work on concrete applications first and then learn the theory behind what you have done?

1	2	3	4	5
Theory First				Applications First

2. When I learn a subject, I like to get the "big picture" first and then learn specific details; I like to see how what I am learning relates to what I have already learned; or do you prefer to learn the details first and then see how they are related to material you already know or have learned?

1	2	3	4	5
Big Picture First				Details First

3. I expect study group members to use group time to: (1) teach each other the "nitty-gritty" details and review problems; (2) ask each other questions to prepare for an exam; or (3) do everything that is necessary.

1	2	3

4. In drawing conclusions about a problem or case, I first seek facts and hard data before reaching a conclusion; or do you reach a conclusion and then seek facts that support your idea?

1	2	3	4	5
Data Then Conclusions				Conclusions Then Data

5. In drawing conclusions about a problem or case, I prefer to seek additional options and to postpone decision making as long as possible; or do you prefer to seek closure early and make a decision?

1	2	3	4	5
Seek Additional Options				Seek Early Closure

6. When I learn a subject I am satisfied to know the *what* of the subject; or do you also want to know the *why* of things?

1	2	3	4	5
What Only				What and Why

7. When confronted with a difficult task, I am willing to spend whatever time it takes to comprehend it; or do you set time limits, and if you haven't mastered the material you go on to another subject?

1	2	3	4	5
Whatever Time It Takes				Set Time Limits

8. In order for me to know a subject I must have "hands-on" experience.

1	2	3	4	5
Must Have Hands On				Hands On Unnecessary

9. When I learn a subject, I prefer that the instructor lays out material in a logical fashion; or do you prefer not to be told everything so that you have the opportunity to discover the ideas for yourself?

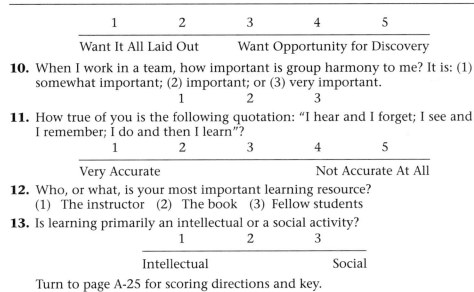

	1	2	3	4	5	
Want It All Laid Out					Want Opportunity for Discovery	

10. When I work in a team, how important is group harmony to me? It is: (1) somewhat important; (2) important; or (3) very important.

$$1 \qquad 2 \qquad 3$$

11. How true of you is the following quotation: "I hear and I forget; I see and I remember; I do and then I learn"?

	1	2	3	4	5	
Very Accurate					Not Accurate At All	

12. Who, or what, is your most important learning resource?
    (1) The instructor (2) The book (3) Fellow students

13. Is learning primarily an intellectual or a social activity?

$$1 \qquad 2 \qquad 3$$

	1	2	3	
Intellectual			Social	

Turn to page A-25 for scoring directions and key.

Source: This exercise is adapted from W.A. Kahn, "An Exercise of Authority," *Organizational Behavior Teaching Review*, vol. XIV, no. 2, 1989–90, pp. 28–42. Reprinted with permission.

Working with Others Exercise

Positive and Negative Reinforcement

This ten-step exercise takes approximately 20 minutes.

EXERCISE OVERVIEW (STEPS 1–4)

1. Two volunteers are selected to receive reinforcement from the class while performing a particular task. The volunteers leave the room.

2. The instructor identifies an object for the student volunteers to locate when they return to the room. (The object should be unobstructive but clearly visible to the class. Examples that have worked well include a small triangular piece of paper that was left behind when a notice was torn off a classroom bulletin board, a smudge on the chalkboard, and a chip in the plaster of a classroom wall.)

3. The instructor specifies the reinforcement contingencies that will be in effect when the volunteers return to the room. For negative reinforcement, students should hiss and boo when the first volunteer is moving away from the object. For positive reinforcement, they should cheer and applaud when the second volunteer is getting closer to the object.

4. The instructor should assign a student to keep a record of the time it takes each of the volunteers to locate the object.

VOLUNTEER 1 (STEPS 5 AND 6)

5. Volunteer 1 is brought back into the room and is told, "Your task is to locate and touch a particular object in the room and the class has agreed to help you. You can't use words or ask questions. Begin."

6. Volunteer 1 continues to look for the object until it is found, while the class assists by giving negative reinforcement.

VOLUNTEER 2 (STEPS 7 AND 8)

7. Volunteer 2 is brought back into the room and is told, "Your task is to locate and touch a particular object in the room and the

class has agreed to help you. You can't use words or ask questions. Begin."

8. Volunteer 2 continues to look for the object until it is found, while the class assists by giving positive reinforcement.

CLASS REVIEW (STEPS 9 AND 10)

9. The timekeeper will present the results on how long it took each volunteer to find the object.

10. The class will discuss:

   a. What was the difference in behavior of the two volunteers?

   b. What are the implications of this exercise to reinforcement schedules in organizations?

Source: Based on an exercise developed by Larry Michaelson of the University of Oklahoma. With permission.

Predicting Performance

CASE INCIDENT

Alix Maher is the new admissions director at a small, highly selective New England college. She has a bachelor's degree in education and a recent master's degree in educational administration. But she has no prior experience in college admissions.

Alix's predecessor, in conjunction with the college's admissions committee (made up of 5 faculty members), had given the following weights to student selection criteria: high school grades (40 percent); Scholastic Aptitude Test (SAT) scores (40 percent); extracurricular activities and achievements (10 percent); and the quality and creativity of a written theme submitted with the application (10 percent).

Alix has serious reservations about using SAT scores. In their defense, she recognizes that the quality of high schools varies greatly, so that the level of student performance that receives an A in American history at one school might earn only a C at a far more demanding school. Alix is also aware that the people who design the SATs, the Educational Testing Service, argue forcefully that these test scores are valid predictors of how well a person will do in college. Yet Alix has several concerns:

1. The pressure of the SAT exam is very great, and many students suffer from test anxiety. The results, therefore, may not be truly reflective of what a student knows.

2. There is evidence that coaching improves scores by between 40 and 150 points. Test scores, therefore, may adversely affect the chances of acceptance for students who cannot afford the $500 or $600 to take test-coaching courses.

3. Are SATs valid, or do they discriminate against minorities, the poor, and those who have had limited access to cultural growth experiences?

As Alix ponders whether she wants to recommend changing the college's selection criteria and weights, she is reminded of a recent conversation she had with a friend who is an industrial psychologist with a Fortune 100 company. He told her that his company regularly uses intelligence tests to help select from among job applicants. For instance, after the company's recruiters interview graduating seniors on college campuses and identify possible hirees, they give the applicants a standardized intelligence test. Those who fail to score at least in the 80th percentile are eliminated from the applicant pool.

Alix thinks that if intelligence tests are used by billion dollar corporations to screen job applicants, why shouldn't colleges use them? Moreover, since one of the objectives of a college should be to get its graduates placed in good jobs, maybe SAT scores should be given even higher weight than 40 percent in the selection decision. After all, if SATs tap intelligence and employers want intelligent job applicants, why not make college selection decisions predominantly on the basis of SAT scores? Or should her college replace the SAT with a pure intelligence test like the Wechsler Adult Intelligence Scale?

Questions

1. What do you think SATs measure: aptitude, innate ability, achievement potential, intelligence, ability to take tests, or something else?
2. If the best predictor of future behavior is past behavior, what should admissions directors use to identify the best-qualified applicants?
3. If you were Alix, what would you do? Why?

Emotional Intelligence

We've known for some time the value of academic intelligence to success in life. Yet it is not a perfect predictor. A lot of straight-A students and class valedictorians never live up to their potential. Daniel Goleman, a psychologist, believes that the missing element in the explanation is something called *emotional intelligence*.

"An IQ test is really a single measure of how verbally fluent you are," says Goleman. "It's how well you do math and logical reasoning." But a more powerful predictor of how well people will do in life is a measure of their emotional I.Q., which taps their emotional and social skills.

According to Goleman, there are four basic people skills everyone needs to master. First is the ability to handle anger. When you feel anger, do you know what to do with it? Second, can you soothe yourself when you're anxious? People with high emotional I.Q.s can control their emotions. Third, people need to be able to read other's feelings from nonverbal cues. It's valuable to be able to read the feelings of others so you can get along better with them. Finally, it's important to be able to delay gratification. "If you can't delay gratification," Goleman claims, "you are the kind of person who won't be able to pursue goals, who won't persist when things get tough, who won't be able to study and learn as well."

Researchers tested children on their ability to control their impulsiveness and then followed their progress over a 25 year period. The researchers found that on average those who wait do better in life. Says Goleman, "We followed kids who are impulsive through life and we see that they are the kids who are more likely to be in jail; they are the kids, if they are girls, who are more likely to get pregnant."

Goleman describes the characteristics possessed by engineers at Bell Labs who were rated as stars by their peers. The scientists considered stars to be better at relating to others. The difference depended on their emotional I.Q., not their academic I.Q.

Questions

1. Do you think there is anything an organization could do to improve an employee's emotional I.Q., once he or she is hired?
2. How could a knowledge of emotional I.Q. help managers to be more effective?

Source: Based on "Emotional I.Q.," *20/20, ABC News*; aired October 20, 1995.

VIDEO
CASE

ABCNEWS

PERCEPTION AND INDIVIDUAL DECISION MAKING

First umpire: "Some's balls and some's strikes and I calls 'em as they is."
Second umpire: "Some's balls and some's strikes and I calls 'em as I sees 'em."
Third umpire: "Some's balls and some's strikes but they ain't nothin' till I calls 'em."
— H. Cantril

LEARNING OBJECTIVES

After studying this chapter, you should be able to

1 Explain how two people can see the same thing and interpret it differently

2 List the three determinants of attribution

3 Describe how shortcuts can assist in or distort our judgment of others

4 Explain how perception affects the decision-making process

5 Outline the six steps in the rational decision-making model

6 Describe the actions of the boundedly rational decision maker

7 Identify the conditions in which individuals are most likely to use intuition in decision making

8 Describe four styles of decision making

9 Define heuristics and explain how they bias decisions

10 Explain the factors that influence ethical decision-making behavior

MARILYN Marks has been making a number of decisions in her effort to remake the company she heads, Dorsey Trailers Inc.[1]

Marks was trained as an accountant. But in 1987, at the age of 34, she and a small group of partners borrowed nearly $25 million to buy Dorsey Trailers in a leveraged buyout. At the time, there weren't a whole lot of people interested in purchasing Dorsey. Although it had earned $11 million in 1984, it had lost $2.4 million in 1986. And the future didn't look too promising for this manufacturer of specialized refrigerator, dump, and parcel truck trailers.

Marks saw something others didn't. She figured the company could be a money maker again if she could successfully cut costs. So, after taking over the company, that's where she began. For instance, Marks gave the 500 workers at the company's plant in Edgerton, Wisconsin, and their union, a choice: Give her wage and work rule concessions or she would shut the plant down. The union said no. "They thought we were just bluffing," says Marks. She wasn't. Within two years, all the plant's equipment had been shifted to a company operation in Alabama.

In the spring of 1990, disaster hit Marks and her company. Eighteen inches of rain had swelled Alabama's Pea River, the levee had cracked, and the company's Elba, Alabama, plant was completely washed out. And, unfortunately, Dorsey's flood insurance was inadequate to get the plant running again. Combined with financial losses of $4.4 million in 1988 and $9 million in 1989, Marks was forced to meet with lawyers to consider bankruptcy for Dorsey. At the last minute, she heard of a special relief program offered by the Small Business Administration for firms that employed a large percentage of a local area's work force. Dorsey's Elba operation met the requirements. The SBA quickly approved a $25 million loan for Dorsey, and the plant reopened four months after the flooding.

Marks seems to have had more than her fair share of disasters since taking over Dorsey. In addition to constant labor troubles, the flood, and financial losses, she has also faced major price increases in aluminum (a principal raw material in her business) and a decline in her traditional markets. But Marks continues to come up with aggressive strategies. She has overhauled the company's product line, eliminating several models and focusing on several specialty trailers. She has also started selling direct to big trucking firms, in addition to local distributors. This move has given her price flexibility for cutting deals and has won her several big customers, such as Tyson Foods and United Parcel Service.

In July 1994, Marks decided to take Dorsey Trailers public. She sold 41 percent of the company for $22 million. She and her partners pocketed $5 million, and the rest was used to reduce company debt. And the bottom line has been improving. In 1995, the company earned $5 million on sales of $230 million. Meanwhile, Marks continues her quest to cut costs and improve profitability at Dorsey. In November 1995, when union workers at a small Dorsey plant in Pennsylvania had been striking for almost six months, she bought a nonunion factory in Georgia. She then closed down the Pennsylvania plant and transferred all the work to the new Georgia site. ◆

M arilyn Marks's actions at Dorsey Trailers illustrate two often overlooked realities in decision making. First, what often looks like an isolated decision is almost always part of a much larger *stream of decisions*. Past history and precedents largely shape current and future choices. As a result, any specific decision is more accurately an accumulation of previous decisions—constrained and directed by choices that preceded it. Decisions that Marilyn Marks makes today at Dorsey Trailers reflect previous opportunities identified and crises encountered. Second, decisions reflect the decision styles of their makers. Marks's willingness to make bold and creative moves has largely shaped the company's current situation. Another executive, with similar competencies but a more conservative approach to decisions, might have taken Dorsey Trailers in a very different direction.

In this chapter, we'll describe how decisions in organizations are made. But first, we discuss perceptual processes and show how they are linked to individual decision making.

◆ The world as it is perceived is the world that is behaviorally important.

What Is Perception, and Why Is It Important?

perception
A process by which individuals organize and interpret their sensory impressions in order to give meaning to their environment.

Perception can be defined as a process by which individuals organize and interpret their sensory impressions in order to give meaning to their environment. However, what one perceives can be substantially different from objective reality. It need not be, but there is often disagreement. For example, it is possible that all employees in a firm may view it as a great place to work—favorable working conditions, interesting job assignments, good pay, an understanding and responsible management—but, as most of us know, it is very unusual to find such agreement.

Why is perception important in the study of OB? Simply because people's behavior is based on their perception of what reality is, not on reality itself. *The world as it is perceived is the world that is behaviorally important.*

Factors Influencing Perception

How do we explain that individuals may look at the same thing, yet perceive it differently? A number of factors operate to shape and sometimes distort perception. These factors can reside in the *perceiver*, in the object or *target* being perceived, or in the context of the *situation* in which the perception is made.

The Perceiver

When an individual looks at a target and attempts to interpret what he or she sees, that interpretation is heavily influenced by personal characteristics of the individual perceiver. Have you ever bought a new car and then suddenly noticed a large number of cars like yours on the road? It's unlikely that the number of such cars suddenly expanded. Rather, your own purchase has influenced your perception so that you are now more likely to notice them. This is an example of how factors related to the perceiver influence what he or she perceives. Among the more relevant personal characteristics affecting perception are attitudes, motives, interests, past experiences, and expectations.

Teri likes small classes because she enjoys asking a lot of questions of her teachers. Scott, on the other hand, prefers large lectures. He rarely asks questions and likes the anonymity that goes with being lost in a sea of bodies. On the first day of classes this term, Teri and Scott find themselves walking into the university auditorium for their introductory course in psychology. They both recognize that they will be among some 800 students in this class. But given the different attitudes held by Teri and Scott, it shouldn't surprise you to find that they interpret what they see differently. Teri sulks, while Scott's smile does little to hide his relief in being able to blend unnoticed into the large crowd. They both see the same thing, but they interpret it differently. A major reason is that they hold divergent *attitudes* concerning large classes.

Unsatisfied needs or *motives* stimulate individuals and may exert a strong influence on their perceptions. This fact was dramatically demonstrated in research on hunger.[2] Individuals in the study had not eaten for varying numbers of hours. Some had eaten an hour earlier; others had gone as long as 16 hours without food. These subjects were shown blurred pictures, and the results indicated that the extent of hunger influenced the interpretation of the blurred pictures. Those who had not eaten for 16 hours perceived the blurred images as pictures of food far more frequently than did those subjects who had eaten only a short time earlier.

This same phenomenon has application in an organizational context as well. It would not be surprising, for example, to find that a boss who is insecure perceives a subordinate's efforts to do an outstanding job as a threat to his or her own position. Personal insecurity can be transferred into the perception that others are out to "get my job," regardless of the intention of the subordinates. Likewise, people who are devious are prone to see others as also devious.

It should not surprise you that a plastic surgeon is more likely to notice an imperfect nose than a plumber is. The supervisor who has just been reprimanded by her boss for the high level of lateness among her staff is more likely to notice lateness by an employee tomorrow than she was last week. If you are preoccupied with a personal problem, you may find it hard to be attentive in class. These examples illustrate that the focus of our attention appears to be influenced by our *interests*. Because our individual interests differ considerably, what one person notices in a situation can differ from what others perceive.

Just as interests narrow one's focus, so do one's *past experiences*. You perceive those things to which you can relate. However, in many instances, your past experiences will act to nullify an object's interest.

Objects or events that have never been experienced before are more noticeable than those that have been experienced in the past. You are more likely to notice a machine that you have never seen before than a standard filing cabinet that is exactly like a hundred others you have previously seen. Similarly, you are more likely to notice the operations along an assembly line if this is the first time you have seen an assembly line. In the late 1960s and early 1970s, women and minorities in managerial positions were highly visible because, historically, those positions were the province of white males. Today, women and minorities are more widely represented in the managerial ranks, so we are less likely to take notice that a manager is female, African-American, Asian-American, or Latino.

Finally, *expectations* can distort your perceptions in that you will see what you expect to see. If you expect police officers to be authoritative, young people to be unambitious, personnel directors to "like people," or individuals holding public office to be unscrupulous, you may perceive them as such regardless of their actual traits.

The Target

Characteristics of the target that is being observed can affect what is perceived. Loud people are more likely to be noticed in a group than are quiet ones. So, too, are extremely attractive or unattractive individuals. Motion, sounds, size, and other attributes of a target shape the way we see it.

Diversity advocate Ernest Drew, CEO of Hoechst Celanese, set a goal to have at least 34 percent representation of women and minorities at all levels of his company by 2001. To influence managers' perceptions of women and minorities, Drew requires that his top 26 officers join two organizations in which they are a minority. Drew put the policy in place to help managers break out of their comfort zones and experience what it's like to be a minority so they learn "that all people are similar." Drew is a board member of black Hampton University and of SER-Jobs for Progress, a Hispanic association. He's shown here visiting with Hampton students.

Exhibit 3-1
Figure-Ground Illustrations

Because targets are not looked at in isolation, the relationship of a target to its background influences perception, as does our tendency to group close things and similar things together.

What we see is dependent on how we separate a figure from its general background. For instance, what you see as you read this sentence is black letters on a white page. You do not see funny-shaped patches of black and white because you recognize these shapes and organize the black shapes against the white background. Exhibit 3-1 dramatizes this effect. The object on the left may at first look like a yellow vase. However, if yellow is taken as the background, we see two purple profiles. At first observation, the group of objects on the right appears to be some purple modular figures against a yellow background. Closer inspection will reveal the word *FLY* once the background is defined as purple.

Objects that are close to each other will tend to be perceived together rather than separately. As a result of physical or time proximity, we often put together objects or events that are unrelated. Employees in a particular department are seen as a group. If two people in a four-member department suddenly resign, we tend to assume that their departures were related when, in fact, they may be totally unrelated. Timing may also imply dependence when, for example, a new sales manager is assigned to a territory and, soon after, sales in that territory skyrocket. The assignment of the new sales manager and the increase in sales may not be related—the increase may be due to the introduction of a new product line or to one of many other reasons—but there is a tendency to perceive the two occurrences as related.

Persons, objects, or events that are similar to each other also tend to be grouped together. The greater the similarity, the greater the probability that we will tend to perceive them as a common group. Women, blacks, or members of any other group that has clearly distinguishable characteristics in terms of features or color will tend to be perceived as alike in other, unrelated characteristics as well.

The Situation

The context in which we see objects or events is important. Elements in the surrounding environment influence our perceptions. I may not notice a 25-year-old female in an evening gown and heavy makeup at a nightclub on Saturday night. Yet that same woman so attired for my Monday morning management class would certainly catch my attention (and that of the rest of the class). Neither the perceiver nor the target changed between Saturday night

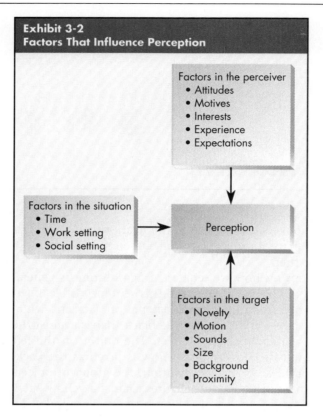

Exhibit 3-2
Factors That Influence Perception

Factors in the perceiver
- Attitudes
- Motives
- Interests
- Experience
- Expectations

Factors in the situation
- Time
- Work setting
- Social setting

Perception

Factors in the target
- Novelty
- Motion
- Sounds
- Size
- Background
- Proximity

and Monday morning, but the situation is different. Similarly, you are more likely to notice your subordinates goofing off if your boss from the head office happens to be in town. Again, the situation affects your perception. The time at which an object or event is seen can influence attention, as can location, light, heat, or any number of situational factors. Exhibit 3-2 summarizes the factors influencing perception.

Person Perception: Making Judgments about Others

Now we turn to the most relevant application of perception concepts to OB. This is the issue of *person perception*.

Attribution Theory

Our perceptions of people differ from our perceptions of inanimate objects such as desks, machines, or buildings because we make inferences about the actions of people that we don't make about inanimate objects. Nonliving objects are subject to the laws of nature, but they have no beliefs, motives, or intentions. People do. The result is that when we observe people, we attempt to develop explanations of why they behave in certain ways. Our perception and judgment of a person's actions, therefore, will be significantly influenced by the assumptions we make about that person's internal state.

Attribution theory has been proposed to develop explanations of the ways in which we judge people differently, depending on what meaning we attribute to a given behavior.[3] Basically, the theory suggests that when we observe an individual's behavior, we attempt to determine whether it was internally or externally caused. That determination, however, depends largely on three factors: (1) distinctiveness, (2) consensus, and (3) consistency. First, let's clarify the differences between internal and external causation and then we will elaborate on each of the three determining factors.

Internally caused behaviors are those that are believed to be under the personal control of the individual. *Externally* caused behavior is seen as resulting from outside causes; that is, the person is seen as having been forced into the behavior by the situation. If one of your employees is late for work, you might attribute his lateness to his partying into the wee hours of the morning and then oversleeping. This would be an internal attribution. But if you attribute his arriving late to a major automobile accident that tied up traffic on the road that this employee regularly uses, then you would be making an external attribution.

Distinctiveness refers to whether an individual displays different behaviors in different situations. Is the employee who arrives late today also the source of complaints by co-workers for being a "goof-off"? What we want to know is whether this behavior is unusual. If it is, the observer is likely to give the behavior an external attribution. If this action is not unusual, it will probably be judged as internal.

If everyone who is faced with a similar situation responds in the same way, we can say the behavior shows *consensus*. Our late employee's behavior would meet this criterion if all employees who took the same route to work were also late. From an attribution perspective, if consensus is high, you would be expected to give an external attribution to the employee's tardiness, whereas if other employees who took the same route made it to work on time, your conclusion as to causation would be internal.

Finally, an observer looks for *consistency* in a person's actions. Does the person respond the same way over time? Coming in ten minutes late for work is not perceived in the same way for the employee for whom it is an unusual case (she hasn't been late for several months) as it is for the employee for whom it is part of a routine pattern (she is regularly late two or three times a week). The more consistent the behavior, the more the observer is inclined to attribute it to internal causes.

Exhibit 3-3 on page 96 summarizes the key elements in attribution theory. It would tell us, for instance, that if your employee—Kim Randolph—generally performs at about the same level on other related tasks as she does on her current task (low distinctiveness), if other employees frequently perform differently—better or worse—than Kim does on that current task (low consensus), and if Kim's performance on this current task is consistent over time (high consistency), you or anyone else who is judging Kim's work is likely to hold her primarily responsible for her task performance (internal attribution).

One of the more interesting findings from attribution theory is that there are errors or biases that distort attributions. For instance, there is substantial evidence that when we make judgments about the behavior of other people, we have a tendency to underestimate the influence of external factors and

attribution theory
When individuals observe behavior, they attempt to determine whether it is internally or externally caused.

◆ There is a tendency for individuals to attribute their own successes to internal factors such as ability or effort while putting the blame for failure on external factors such as luck.

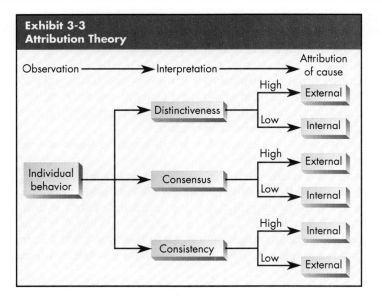

Exhibit 3-3
Attribution Theory

fundamental attribution error
The tendency to underestimate the influence of external factors and overestimate the influence of internal factors when making judgments about the behavior of others.

self-serving bias
The tendency for individuals to attribute their own successes to internal factors while putting the blame for failures on external factors.

overestimate the influence of internal or personal factors.[4] This is called the **fundamental attribution error** and can explain why a sales manager is prone to attribute the poor performance of her sales agents to laziness rather than to the innovative product line introduced by a competitor. There is also a tendency for individuals to attribute their own successes to internal factors such as ability or effort while putting the blame for failure on external factors such as luck. This is called the **self-serving bias** and suggests that feedback provided to employees in performance reviews will be predictably distorted by recipients depending on whether it is positive or negative.

Are these errors or biases that distort attributions universal across different cultures? We can't answer that question definitively, but there is some preliminary evidence that indicates cultural differences. For instance, a study of Korean managers found that, contrary to the self-serving bias, they tended to accept responsibility for group failure "because I was not a capable leader" instead of attributing it to group members.[5] Attribution theory was developed largely in the United States on the basis of experiments with Americans. But the Korean study suggests caution in making attribution theory predictions outside the United States, especially in countries with strong collectivist traditions.

Frequently Used Shortcuts in Judging Others

We use a number of shortcuts when we judge others. Perceiving and interpreting what others do is burdensome. As a result, individuals develop techniques for making the task more manageable. These techniques are frequently valuable—they allow us to make accurate perceptions rapidly and provide valid data for making predictions. However, they are not foolproof. They can and do get us into trouble. An understanding of these shortcuts can be helpful toward recognizing when they can result in significant distortions.

SELECTIVE PERCEPTION Any characteristic that makes a person, object, or event stand out will increase the probability that it will be perceived. Why? Because it is impossible for us to assimilate everything we see—only certain

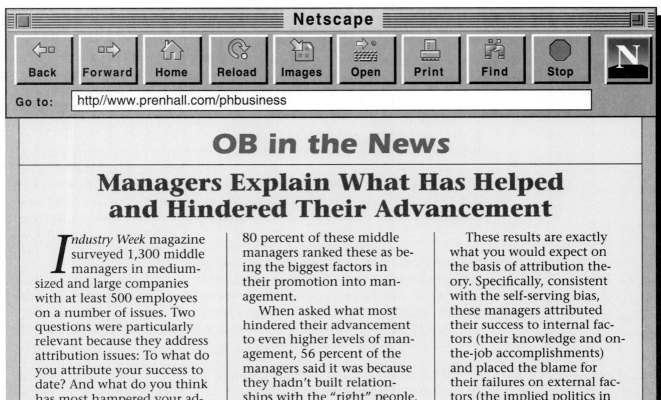

OB in the News

Managers Explain What Has Helped and Hindered Their Advancement

Industry Week magazine surveyed 1,300 middle managers in medium-sized and large companies with at least 500 employees on a number of issues. Two questions were particularly relevant because they address attribution issues: To what do you attribute your success to date? And what do you think has most hampered your advancement to even higher levels in your company?

Most managers attributed their advancement to their knowledge and on-the-job accomplishments. More than 80 percent of these middle managers ranked these as being the biggest factors in their promotion into management.

When asked what most hindered their advancement to even higher levels of management, 56 percent of the managers said it was because they hadn't built relationships with the "right" people. This group was followed by 23 percent who said that they were most hindered by insufficient education, intelligence, or knowledge of their business area.

These results are exactly what you would expect on the basis of attribution theory. Specifically, consistent with the self-serving bias, these managers attributed their success to internal factors (their knowledge and on-the-job accomplishments) and placed the blame for their failures on external factors (the implied politics in knowing the right people).

Based on D.R. Altany, "Torn between Halo and Horns," *Industry Week*, March 15, 1993, p. 19.

Take It to the Net

We invite you to visit the Robbins page on the Prentice Hall Web site at:

http://www.prenhall.com/robbinsorgbeh

for this chapter's World Wide Web exercise.

---

stimuli can be taken in. This tendency explains why, as we noted earlier, you are more likely to notice cars like your own or why some people may be reprimanded by their boss for doing something that, when done by another employee, goes unnoticed. Since we can't observe everything going on about us, we engage in **selective perception**. A classic example shows how vested interests can significantly influence which problems we see.

Dearborn and Simon performed a perceptual study in which 23 business executives read a comprehensive case describing the organization and activities of a steel company.[6] Six of the 23 executives were in the sales function, five in production, four in accounting, and eight in miscellaneous functions.

selective perception
People selectively interpret what they see on the basis of their interests, background, experience, and attitudes.

Each manager was asked to write down the most important problem he found in the case. Eighty-three percent of the sales executives rated sales important; only 29 percent of the others did so. This, along with other results of the study, led the researchers to conclude that the participants perceived aspects of a situation that were specifically related to the activities and goals of the unit to which they were attached. A group's perception of organizational activities is selectively altered to align with the vested interests they represent. In other words, when the stimuli are ambiguous, as in the steel company case, perception tends to be influenced more by an individual's base of interpretation (that is, attitudes, interests, and background) than by the stimulus itself.

But how does selectivity work as a shortcut in judging other people? Since we cannot assimilate all that we observe, we take in bits and pieces. But those bits and pieces are not chosen randomly; rather, they are selectively chosen according to our interests, background, experience, and attitudes. Selective perception allows us to "speed-read" others, but not without the risk of drawing an inaccurate picture. Because we see what we want to see, we can draw unwarranted conclusions from an ambiguous situation. If there is a rumor going around the office that your company's sales are down and that large layoffs may be coming, a routine visit by a senior executive from headquarters might be interpreted as the first step in management's identification of people to be fired, when in reality such an action may be the furthest thing from the mind of the senior executive.

halo effect
Drawing a general impression about an individual on the basis of a single characteristic.

HALO EFFECT   When we draw a general impression about an individual on the basis of a single characteristic, such as intelligence, sociability, or appearance, a **halo effect** is operating. This phenomenon frequently occurs when students appraise their classroom instructor. Students may give prominence to a single trait such as enthusiasm and allow their entire evaluation to be tainted by how they judge the instructor on that one trait. Thus, an instructor may be quiet, assured, knowledgeable, and highly qualified, but if his style lacks zeal, those students would probably give him a low rating.

The reality of the halo effect was confirmed in a classic study in which subjects were given a list of traits such as intelligent, skillful, practical, industrious, determined, and warm and were asked to evaluate the person to whom those traits applied.[7] When those traits were used, the person was judged to be wise, humorous, popular, and imaginative. When the same list was modified—cold was substituted for warm—a completely different set of perceptions was obtained. Clearly, the subjects were allowing a single trait to influence their overall impression of the person being judged.

The propensity for the halo effect to operate is not random. Research suggests that it is likely to be most extreme when the traits to be perceived are ambiguous in behavioral terms, when the traits have moral overtones, and when the perceiver is judging traits with which he or she has had limited experience.[8]

CONTRAST EFFECTS   There's an old adage among entertainers who perform in variety shows: Never follow an act that has kids or animals in it. Why? The common belief is that audiences love children and animals so much that you will look bad in comparison. In a similar vein, I remember when I was a college freshman and had to give a presentation in a speech class. I was scheduled to speak third that morning. After both of the first two speakers stammered, stumbled, and forgot their lines, I suddenly got a rush of confidence because I figured that even though my talk might not go too well, I'd probably get a pretty good grade. I was counting on the instructor's raising my evaluation after contrasting my speech with those that immediately preceded it.

These two examples demonstrate how **contrast effects** can distort perceptions. We don't evaluate a person in isolation. Our reaction to one person is often influenced by other persons we have recently encountered.

An illustration of how contrast effects operate is an interview situation in which one sees a pool of job applicants. Distortions in any given candidate's evaluation can occur as a result of his or her place in the interview schedule. The candidate is likely to receive a more favorable evaluation if preceded by mediocre applicants and a less favorable evaluation if preceded by strong applicants.

PROJECTION It is easy to judge others if we assume that they are similar to us. For instance, if you want challenge and responsibility in your job, you assume that others want the same. Or, you are honest and trustworthy, so you take it for granted that other people are equally honest and trustworthy. This tendency to attribute one's own characteristics to other people—which is called **projection**—can distort perceptions made about others.

People who engage in projection tend to perceive others according to what they themselves are like rather than according to what the person being observed is really like. When observing others who actually are like them, these observers are quite accurate—not because they are perceptive but because they always judge people as being similar to themselves. So when they finally do find someone who is like them, they are naturally correct. When managers engage in projection, they compromise their ability to respond to individual differences. They tend to see people as more homogeneous than they really are.

STEREOTYPING When we judge someone on the basis of our perception of the group to which he or she belongs, we are using the shortcut called **stereotyping**. F. Scott Fitzgerald engaged in stereotyping in his reported conversation with Ernest Hemingway when he said, "The very rich are different from you and me." Hemingway's reply, "Yes, they have more money," indicated that he refused to generalize characteristics about people on the basis of their wealth.

Generalization, of course, is not without advantages. It is a means of simplifying a complex world, and it permits us to maintain consistency. It is less difficult to deal with an unmanageable number of stimuli if we use stereotypes. As an example, assume you are a sales manager looking to fill a sales position in your territory. You want to hire someone who is ambitious and hardworking and who can deal well with adversity. You've had good success in the past by hiring individuals who participated in athletics during college. So you focus your search by looking for candidates who participated in collegiate athletics. In so doing, you have cut down considerably on your search time. Furthermore, to the extent that athletes *are* ambitious, hardworking, and able to deal with adversity, the use of this stereotype can improve your decision making. The problem, of course, is when we inaccurately stereotype.[9] All college athletes are *not necessarily* ambitious, hardworking, or good at

contrast effects
Evaluations of a person's characteristics that are affected by comparisons with other people recently encountered who rank higher or lower on the same characteristics.

projection
Attributing one's own characteristics to other people.

◆ People who engage in projection tend to perceive others according to what they themselves are like rather than according to what the person being observed is really like.

stereotyping
Judging someone on the basis of one's perception of the group to which that person belongs.

Exhibit 3-4
Drawing by William Steig; © 1987 The New Yorker Magazine. Reprinted by permission.

"I do not hate you. You're projecting."

dealing with adversity; just as all accountants are *not necessarily* quiet and introspective.

In organizations, we frequently hear comments that represent stereotypes based on gender, age, race, ethnicity, and even weight[10]: "Women won't relocate for a promotion"; "men aren't interested in child care"; "older workers can't learn new skills"; "Asian immigrants are hardworking and conscientious"; "overweight people lack discipline." From a perceptual standpoint, if people expect to see these stereotypes, that is what they will perceive, whether they are accurate or not.

Obviously, one of the problems of stereotypes is that they are widespread, despite the fact that they may not contain a shred of truth or that they may be irrelevant. Their being widespread may mean only that many people are making the same inaccurate perception on the basis of a false premise about a group.

Specific Applications in Organizations

People in organizations are always judging each other. Managers must appraise their subordinates' performances. We evaluate how much effort our co-workers are putting into their jobs. When a new person joins a work team, he or she is immediately "sized up" by the other team members. In many cases, these judgments have important consequences for the organization. Let's briefly look at a few of the more obvious applications.

EMPLOYMENT INTERVIEW A major input into who is hired and who is rejected in any organization is the employment interview. It's fair to say that

few people are hired without an interview. But the evidence indicates that interviewers make perceptual judgments that are often inaccurate. In addition,
agreement among interviewers is often poor; that is, different interviewers see
different things in the same candidate and thus arrive at different conclusions
about the applicant.

Interviewers generally draw early impressions that become very quickly
entrenched. If negative information is exposed early in the interview, it tends
to be more heavily weighted than if that same information comes out later.[11]
Studies indicate that most interviewers' decisions change very little after the
first four or five minutes of the interview. As a result, information elicited
early in the interview carries greater weight than does information elicited
later, and a "good applicant" is probably characterized more by the absence of
unfavorable characteristics than by the presence of favorable characteristics.

Importantly, who you think is a good candidate and who I think is one
may differ markedly. Because interviews usually have so little consistent structure and interviewers vary in terms of what they are looking for in a candidate, judgments of the same candidate can vary widely. If the employment interview is an important input into the hiring decision—and it usually
is—you should recognize that perceptual factors influence who is hired and
eventually the quality of an organization's labor force.

PERFORMANCE EXPECTATIONS There is an impressive amount of evidence
that demonstrates that people will attempt to validate their perceptions of reality, even when those perceptions are faulty.[12] This characteristic is particularly relevant when we consider performance expectations on the job.

The terms **self-fulfilling prophecy**, or *pygmalion effect*, have evolved
to characterize the fact that people's expectations determine their behavior. In
other words, if a manager expects big things from his people, they're not
likely to let him down. Similarly, if a manager expects people to perform minimally, they'll tend to behave so as to meet those low expectations. The result
then is that the expectations become reality.

self-fulfilling prophecy
When one person inaccurately perceives
a second person and the resulting
expectations cause the second person to
behave in ways consistent with the
original perception.

Mary Tjosvold (center), CEO of Mary
T. Inc., believes in the self-fulfilling
prophecy: Tjosvold expects big things
from her employees, and they meet
her high performance expectations.
Mary T. provides residential social
services for people with disabilities.
Tjosvold gives employee teams
decision-making responsibility in
servicing customers. She trusts her
employees to plan and implement
programs that meet Mary T.'s high
standards, and her employees
respond by accepting responsibility
and exercising self-direction.

An interesting illustration of the self-fulfilling prophecy is a study undertaken with 105 soldiers in the Israeli Defense Forces who were taking a fifteen-week combat command course.[13] The four course instructors were told that one-third of the specific incoming trainees had high potential, one-third had normal potential, and the potential of the rest was unknown. In reality, the trainees were randomly placed into those categories by the researchers. The results confirmed the existence of a self-fulfilling prophecy. Those trainees whom instructors were told had high potential scored significantly higher on objective achievement tests, exhibited more positive attitudes, and held their leaders in higher regard than did the other two groups. The instructors of the supposedly high-potential trainees got better results from them because the instructors expected it!

PERFORMANCE EVALUATION Although the impact of performance evaluations on behavior will be discussed fully in chapter 15, it should be pointed out here that an employee's performance appraisal is very much dependent on the perceptual process.[14] An employee's future is closely tied to his or her appraisal—promotions, pay raises, and continuation of employment are among the most obvious outcomes. The performance appraisal represents an assessment of an employee's work. Although the appraisal can be objective (for example, a salesperson is appraised on how many dollars of sales she generates in her territory), many jobs are evaluated in subjective terms. Subjective measures are easier to implement, they provide managers with greater discretion, and many jobs do not readily lend themselves to objective measures. Subjective measures are, by definition, judgmental. The evaluator forms a general impression of an employee's work. To the degree that managers use subjective measures in appraising employees, what the evaluator perceives to be good or bad employee characteristics or behaviors will significantly influence the outcome of the appraisal.

EMPLOYEE EFFORT An individual's future in an organization is usually not dependent on performance alone. In many organizations, the level of an employee's effort is given high importance. Just as teachers frequently consider how hard you try in a course as well as how you perform on examinations, so often do managers. An assessment of an individual's effort is a subjective judgment susceptible to perceptual distortions and bias. If it is true, as some claim, that "more workers are fired for poor attitudes and lack of discipline than for lack of ability,"[15] then appraisal of an employee's effort may be a primary influence on his or her future in the organization.

EMPLOYEE LOYALTY Another important judgment that managers make about employees is whether or not they are loyal to the organization. Despite the general decline in employee loyalty noted in chapter 1, few organizations appreciate it when employees, especially those in the managerial ranks, openly disparage the firm. Furthermore, in some organizations, if the word gets around that an employee is looking at other employment opportunities outside the firm, that employee may be labeled as disloyal and so may be cut off from all future advancement opportunities. The issue is not whether organizations are right in demanding loyalty. The issue is that many do, and that assessment of an employee's loyalty or commitment is highly judgmental.

What is perceived as loyalty by one decision maker may be seen as excessive conformity by another. An employee who questions a top-management decision may be seen as disloyal by some, yet caring and concerned by others. As a case in point, **whistle-blowers**—individuals who report unethical practices by their employer to outsiders—typically act out of loyalty to their organization but are perceived by management as troublemakers.[16]

whistle-blowers
Individuals who report unethical practices by their employer to outsiders.

The Link between Perception and Individual Decision Making

Individuals in organizations make **decisions**. That is, they make choices from among two or more alternatives. Top managers such as Marilyn Marks at Dorsey Trailers, for instance, determine their organization's goals, what products or services to offer, how best to finance operations, or where to locate a new manufacturing plant. Middle- and lower-level managers determine production schedules, select new employees, and decide how pay raises are to be allocated. Of course, making decisions is not the sole province of managers. Nonmanagerial employees also make decisions that affect their jobs and the organizations they work for. The more obvious of these decisions might include whether or not to come to work on any given day, how much effort to put forward once at work, and whether or not to comply with a request made by the boss. In addition, an increasing number of organizations in recent years have been empowering their nonmanagerial employees with job-related decision-making authority that historically was reserved for managers alone. Individual decision making, therefore, is an important part of organizational behavior. But how individuals in organizations make decisions and the quality of their final choices are largely influenced by their perceptions.

decisions
The choices made from among two or more alternatives.

Decision making occurs as a reaction to a **problem**. That is, there is a discrepancy between some *current* state of affairs and some *desired* state, requiring consideration of alternative courses of action. So if your car breaks down and you rely on it to get to school, you have a problem that requires a decision on your part. Unfortunately, most problems don't come neatly packaged with a label "problem" clearly displayed on them. One person's *problem* is another person's *satisfactory state of affairs*. One manager may view her division's 2 percent decline in quarterly sales to be a serious problem requiring immediate action on her part. In contrast, her counterpart in another division of the same company, who also had a 2 percent sales decrease, may consider that percentage quite satisfactory. So the awareness that a problem exists and that a decision needs to be made is a perceptual issue.

problem
A discrepancy between some current state of affairs and some desired state.

◆ How individuals in organizations make decisions and the quality of their final choices are largely influenced by their perceptions.

Moreover, every decision requires interpretation and evaluation of information. Data are typically received from multiple sources and they need to be screened, processed, and interpreted. Which data, for instance, are relevant to the decision and which are not? The perceptions of the decision maker will answer that question. Alternatives will be developed, and the strengths and weaknesses of each will need to be evaluated. Again, because alternatives don't come with "red flags" identifying them as such or with their strengths and weaknesses clearly marked, the individual decision maker's perceptual process will have a large bearing on the final outcome.

How Should Decisions Be Made?

Let's begin by describing how individuals should behave in order to maximize or optimize a certain outcome. We call this the *rational decision-making process*.

The Rational Decision-Making Process

rational
Refers to choices that are consistent and value maximizing.

rational decision-making
A decision-making model that describes how individuals should behave in order to maximize some outcome.

The optimizing decision maker is **rational**. That is, he or she makes consistent, value-maximizing choices within specified constraints.[17] These choices are made following a six-step **rational decision-making model**.[18] Moreover, specific assumptions underlie this model.

THE RATIONAL MODEL   The six steps in the rational decision-making model are listed in Exhibit 3-5.

The model begins by *defining the problem*. As noted previously, a problem exists when there is a discrepancy between an existing and a desired state of affairs.[19] If you calculate your monthly expenses and find you're spending $50 more than you allocated in your budget, you have defined a problem. Many poor decisions can be traced to the decision maker overlooking a problem or defining the wrong problem.

Once a decision maker has defined the problem, he or she needs to *identify the decision criteria* that will be important in solving the problem. In this step, the decision maker determines what is relevant in making the decision. This step brings the decision maker's interests, values, and similar personal preferences into the process. Identifying criteria is important because what one person thinks is relevant another person may not. Also keep in mind that any factors not identified in this step are considered irrelevant to the decision maker.

The criteria identified are rarely all equal in importance. So the third step requires the decision maker to *weight the previously identified criteria* in order to give them the correct priority in the decision.

The fourth step requires the decision maker to *generate possible alternatives* that could succeed in resolving the problem. No attempt is made in this step to appraise these alternatives, only to list them.

Once the alternatives have been generated, the decision maker must critically analyze and evaluate each one. This is done by *rating each alternative on each criterion*. The strengths and weaknesses of each alternative become evident as they are compared with the criteria and weights established in the second and third steps.

Exhibit 3-5 Steps in the Rational Decision-Making Model

1. Define the problem.
2. Identify the decision criteria.
3. Allocate weights to the criteria.
4. Develop the alternatives.
5. Evaluate the alternatives.
6. Select the best alternative.

The final step in this model requires *computing the optimal decision*. This is done by evaluating each alternative against the weighted criteria and selecting the alternative with the highest total score.

ASSUMPTIONS OF THE MODEL The rational decision-making model we just described contains a number of assumptions.[20] Let's briefly outline those assumptions.

1. *Problem clarity*. The problem is clear and unambiguous. The decision maker is assumed to have complete information regarding the decision situation.
2. *Known options*. It is assumed the decision maker can identify all the relevant criteria and can list all the viable alternatives. Furthermore, the decision maker is aware of all the possible consequences of each alternative.
3. *Clear preferences*. Rationality assumes that the criteria and alternatives can be ranked and weighted to reflect their importance.
4. *Constant preferences*. It's assumed that the specific decision criteria are constant and that the weights assigned to them are stable over time.
5. *No time or cost constraints*. The rational decision maker can obtain full information about criteria and alternatives because it's assumed that there are no time or cost constraints.
6. *Maximum payoff*. The rational decision maker will choose the alternative that yields the highest perceived value.

Improving Creativity in Decision Making

The rational decision maker needs **creativity**, that is, the ability to combine ideas in a unique way or to make unusual associations between ideas.[21] Why? Creativity allows the decision maker to more fully appraise and understand the problem, including seeing problems others can't see. However, creativity's most obvious value is in helping the decision maker identify all viable alternatives.

creativity
The ability to combine ideas in a unique way or to make unusual associations between ideas.

CREATIVE POTENTIAL Most people have creative potential that they can use when confronted with a decision-making problem. But to unleash that potential, they have to get out of the psychological ruts most of us get into and learn how to think about a problem in divergent ways.

We can start with the obvious. People differ in their inherent creativity. Einstein, Edison, Picasso, and Mozart were individuals of exceptional creativity. Not surprisingly, exceptional creativity is scarce. A study of lifetime creativity of 461 men and women found that fewer than 1 percent were exceptionally creative.[22] But 10 percent were highly creative and about 60 percent were somewhat creative. This suggests that most of us have creative potential, if we can learn to unleash it.

METHODS FOR STIMULATING INDIVIDUAL CREATIVITY Sometimes the most simple action can be very powerful. That seems to be true with stimulating creativity. Evidence indicates that the mere action of instructing someone to "be creative" and to avoid obvious approaches to a problem results in more unique ideas.[23] This *direct-instruction* method is based on evidence that people

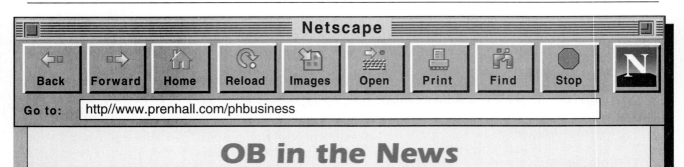

OB in the News

Creativity Killers

Teresa Amabile has spent 20 years researching and consulting on creativity in business organizations. Some of her clients include AT&T, Du Pont, Dow, Exxon, General Motors, and J. C. Penney. What she has found provides important insight to understanding how to stimulate or block individual creativity in organizations.

Although certain personality traits seem to regularly surface in exceptionally creative people, Dr. Amabile says "the social environment that people are working in can have an impact on their creativity and whether they will realize whatever potential they have for doing creative work."

She has identified five factors that act to block a manager's or employee's creativity:

1. *Expected evaluation*. Focusing on how your work is going to be evaluated.
2. *Surveillance*. Being watched while you are working.
3. *External motivators*. Emphasizing external, tangible rewards.
4. *Competition*. Facing a win-lose situation with other people.
5. *Constrained choice*. Being given limits on how you can do your work.

Given that the preceding factors tend to stifle creativity, Dr. Amabile offers the following suggestions for stimulating creativity in any individual:

1. Teach skill in the domain of endeavor through special training, education, or talent development.
2. Use creativity-relevant thinking skills, such as brainstorming or metaphor and analogy techniques, that allow an individual to come up with new ideas and new perspectives.
3. Foster motivation, indicating an inner drive or impulse to meet the challenge.

Based on T. Stevens, "Creativity Killers," *Industry Week*, January 23, 1995, p. 63.

Take It to the Net

We invite you to visit the Robbins page on the Prentice Hall Web site at:

http://www.prenhall.com/robbinsorgbeh

for this chapter's World Wide Web exercise.

tend to accept obvious solutions and this tendency prevents them from performing up to their capabilities. So the mere statement that unique and creative alternatives are sought acts to encourage such ideas. Or overtly telling yourself that you are going to seek out creative options should lead to an increase in unique alternatives.

Another technique is *attribute listing*.[24] In attribute listing, the decision maker isolates the major characteristics of traditional alternatives. Each major attribute of the alternative is then considered in turn and is changed in every conceivable way. No ideas are rejected, no matter how ridiculous they may seem. Once this extensive list is completed, the constraints of the problem are imposed in order to eliminate all but the viable alternatives.

Creativity can also be stimulated by practicing zig-zag or *lateral thinking*.[25] This is a replacement for the more traditional vertical thinking, where each step in the process follows the previous step in an unbroken sequence. Vertical thinking is often seen as rational thinking because it must be correct at every step and it deals only with what is relevant. With lateral thinking, individuals emphasize thinking sideways: not developing a pattern but restructuring a pattern. It's not sequential. For example, you could tackle a problem from the solution end rather than the starting end, and back into various beginning states. Lateral thinking doesn't have to be correct at each step. In fact, in some cases, it may be necessary to pass through a "wrong" area in order to reach a position from which a correct path may be visible. Finally, lateral thinking is not restricted to relevant information. It deliberately uses random or irrelevant information to bring about a new way of looking at the problem.

A final suggestion: *Synectics* uses analogies and inverted rationale to make the strange familiar and the familiar strange.[26] It operates on the assumption that most problems aren't new. The challenge is to view the problem in a new way. So you have to try to abandon the familiar or routine ways that you look at things. For instance, most of us think of hens laying eggs. But how many of us have considered that a hen is only an egg's way of making another egg? One of the most famous examples in which analogy resulted in a creative breakthrough was Alexander Graham Bell's observation that it might be possible to take concepts that operate in the ear and apply them to his "talking box." He noticed that the bones in the ear are operated by a delicate, thin membrane. He wondered why, then, a thicker and stronger piece of membrane shouldn't be able to move a piece of steel. Out of that analogy, the telephone was conceived.

How Are Decisions Actually Made in Organizations?

Are decision makers in organizations rational? Do they carefully assess problems, identify all relevant criteria, use their creativity to identify all viable alternatives, and painstakingly evaluate every alternative to find an optimizing choice? When decision makers are faced with a simple problem having few alternative courses of action, and when the cost of searching out and evaluating alternatives is low, the rational model provides a fairly accurate description of the decision process.[27] But such situations are the exception. Most decisions in the real world don't follow the rational model. For instance, people are usually content to find an acceptable or reasonable solution to their problem rather than an optimizing one. As such, decision makers generally make limited use of their creativity. Choices tend to be confined to the neighborhood of the problem symptom and to the neighborhood of the current alternative. As one expert in decision making recently concluded: "Most significant decisions are made by judgment, rather than by a defined prescriptive model."[28]

The following reviews a large body of evidence to provide you with a more accurate description of how most decisions in organizations are actually made.

Bounded Rationality

When you considered which college to attend, did you look at *every* viable alternative? Did you carefully identify all the criteria that were important in your decision? Did you evaluate each alternative against the criteria in order to find the optimum college? I expect the answers to these questions is probably "No." Well, don't feel bad. Few people made their college choice this way. Instead of optimizing, you probably satisficed.

When faced with a complex problem, most people respond by reducing the problem to a level at which it can be readily understood. This is because the limited information processing capability of human beings makes it impossible to assimilate and understand all the information necessary to optimize. So people *satisfice*; that is, they seek solutions that are satisfactory and sufficient.

Since the capacity of the human mind for formulating and solving complex problems is far too small to meet the requirements for full rationality, individuals operate within the confines of **bounded rationality**. They construct simplified models that extract the essential features from problems without capturing all their complexity.[29] Individuals can then behave rationally within the limits of the simple model.

How does bounded rationality work for the typical individual? Once a problem is identified, the search for criteria and alternatives begins. But the list of criteria is likely to be far from exhaustive. The decision maker will identify a limited list made up of the more conspicuous choices. These are the choices that are easy to find and that tend to be highly visible. In most cases, they will represent familiar criteria and previously tried-and-true solutions. Once this limited set of alternatives is identified, the decision maker will begin reviewing it. But the review will not be comprehensive—not all the alternatives will be carefully evaluated. Instead, the decision maker will begin with alternatives that differ only in a relatively small degree from the choice currently in effect. Following along familiar and well-worn paths, the decision maker proceeds to review alternatives only until he or she identifies an alternative that is "good enough"—one that meets an acceptable level of performance. The first alternative that meets the "good enough" criterion ends the search. So the final solution represents a satisficing choice rather than an optimum one.

One of the more interesting aspects of bounded rationality is that the order in which alternatives are considered is critical in determining which alternative is selected. Remember, in the fully rational decision-making model, all alternatives are eventually listed in a hierarchy of preferred order. Because all alternatives are considered, the initial order in which they are evaluated is irrelevant. Every potential solution would get a full and complete evaluation. But this isn't the case with bounded rationality. Assuming that a problem has more than one potential solution, the satisficing choice will be the first *acceptable* one the decision maker encounters. Since decision makers use simple and limited models, they typically begin by identifying alternatives that are obvious, ones with which they are familiar,

bounded rationality
Individuals make decisions by constructing simplified models that extract the essential features from problems without capturing all their complexity.

◆ The satisficing decision maker settles for the first solution that is "good enough."

and those not too far from the status quo. Those solutions that depart least from the status quo and meet the decision criteria are most likely to be selected. A unique and creative alternative may present an optimizing solution to the problem; however, it's unlikely to be chosen because an acceptable solution will be identified well before the decision maker is required to search very far beyond the status quo.

Intuition

Joe Garcia has just committed his corporation to spend in excess of $40 million to build a new plant in Atlanta to manufacture electronic components for satellite communication equipment. A vice president of operations for his firm, Joe had before him a comprehensive analysis of five possible plant locations developed by a site location consulting firm he had hired. This report ranked the Atlanta location third among the five alternatives. After carefully reading the report and its conclusions, Joe decided against the consultant's recommendation. When asked to explain his decision, Joe said, "I looked the report over very carefully. But in spite of its recommendation, I felt that the numbers didn't tell the whole story. Intuitively, I just sensed that Atlanta would prove to be the best bet over the long run."

Intuitive decision making, like that used by Joe Garcia, has recently come out of the closet and into some respectability. Experts no longer automatically assume that using intuition to make decisions is irrational or ineffective.[30] There is growing recognition that rational analysis has been overemphasized and that, in certain instances, relying on intuition can improve decision making.

What do we mean by intuitive decision making? There are a number of ways to conceptualize intuition.[31] For instance, some consider it a form of extrasensory power or sixth sense, and some believe it is a personality trait that a limited number of people are born with. For our purposes, we define **intuitive decision making** as an unconscious process created out of distilled experience. It doesn't necessarily operate independently of rational analysis; rather, the two complement each other.

intuitive decision making
An unconscious process created out of distilled experience.

Research on chess playing provides an excellent example of how intuition works.[32] Novice chess players and grandmasters were shown an actual, but unfamiliar, chess game with about 25 pieces on the board. After five or ten seconds, the pieces were removed and each was asked to reconstruct the pieces by position. On average, the grandmaster could put 23 or 24 pieces in their correct squares, while the novice was able to replace only six. Then the exercise was changed. This time the pieces were placed randomly on the board. Again, the novice got only about six correct, but so did the grandmaster! The second exercise demonstrated that the grandmaster didn't have any better memory than the novice. What he did have was the ability, based on the experience of having played thousands of chess games, to recognize patterns and clusters of pieces that occur on chessboards in the course of games. Studies further show that chess professionals can play 50 or more games simultaneously, where decisions often must be made in only seconds, and exhibit only a moderately lower level of skill than when playing one game under tournament conditions, where decisions take half an hour or longer. The expert's experience allows him or her to recognize a situation and draw upon previously learned information

◆ Intuition isn't independent of rational analysis. The two complement each other.

associated with that situation to quickly arrive at a decision choice. The result is that the intuitive decision maker can decide rapidly with what appears to be very limited information.

When are people most likely to use intuitive decision making? Eight conditions have been identified: (1) when a high level of uncertainty exists; (2) when there is little precedent to draw on; (3) when variables are less scientifically predictable; (4) when "facts" are limited; (5) when facts don't clearly point the way to go; (6) when analytical data are of little use; (7) when there are several plausible alternative solutions to choose from, with good arguments for each; and (8) when time is limited and there is pressure to come up with the right decision.[33]

Although intuitive decision making has gained in respectability since the early 1980s, don't expect people—especially in North America, Great Britain, and other cultures where rational analysis is the approved way of making decisions—to acknowledge they are using it. People with strong intuitive abilities don't usually tell their colleagues how they reached their conclusions. Since rational analysis is considered more socially desirable, intuitive ability is often disguised or hidden. As one top executive commented, "Sometimes one must dress up a gut decision in 'data clothes' to make it acceptable or palatable, but this fine-tuning is usually after the fact of the decision."[34]

Problem Identification

Problems don't come with flashing neon lights to identify themselves. And one person's *problem* is another person's *acceptable status quo*. So how do decision makers identify and select problems?

Problems that are visible tend to have a higher probability of being selected than ones that are important.[35] Why? We can offer at least two reasons. First, it's easier to recognize visible problems. They are more likely to catch a decision maker's attention. This explains why politicians are more likely to talk about the "crime problem" than the "illiteracy problem." Second, remember we're concerned with decision making in organizations. Decision makers want to appear competent and "on top of problems." This motivates them to focus attention on problems that are visible to others.

Don't ignore the decision maker's self-interest. If a decision maker faces a conflict between selecting a problem that is important to the organization and one that is important to the decision maker, self-interest tends to win out.[36] This also ties in with the issue of visibility. It's usually in a decision maker's best interest to attack high-profile problems. It conveys to others that things are under control. Moreover, when the decision maker's performance is later reviewed, the evaluator is more likely to give a high rating to someone who has been aggressively attacking visible problems than to someone whose actions have been less obvious.

Alternative Development

Since decision makers rarely seek an optimum solution, but rather a satisficing one, we should expect to find a minimal use of creativity in the search for alternatives. And that expectation is generally on target.

Efforts will be made to try to keep the search process simple. It will tend to be confined to the neighborhood of the current alternative. More complex search behavior, which includes the development of creative alternatives, will be resorted to only when a simple search fails to uncover a satisfactory alternative.

Rather than formulating new and unique problem definitions and alternatives, with frequent journeys into unfamiliar territory, the evidence indicates that decision making is incremental rather than comprehensive.[37] This means decision makers avoid the difficult task of considering all the important factors, weighing their relative merits and drawbacks, and calculating the value for each alternative. Instead, they make successive limited comparisons. This branch approach simplifies decision choices by comparing only those alternatives that differ in relatively small degrees from the choice currently in effect. This approach also makes it unnecessary for the decision maker to thoroughly examine an alternative and its consequences; one need investigate only those aspects in which the proposed alternative and its consequences differ from the status quo.

What emerges is a decision maker who takes small steps toward his or her objective. Acknowledging the noncomprehensive nature of choice selection, decision makers make successive comparisons because decisions are never made forever and written in stone, but rather decisions are made and remade endlessly in small comparisons between narrow choices.

Making Choices

In order to avoid information overload, decision makers rely on **heuristics** or judgmental shortcuts in decision making.[38] There are two common categories of heuristics—availability and representativeness. Each creates biases in judgment. Another bias that decision makers often have is the tendency to escalate commitment to a failing course of action.

heuristics
Judgmental shortcuts in decision making.

AVAILABILITY HEURISTIC Many more people suffer from fear of flying than fear of driving in a car. The reason is that many people think flying is more dangerous. It isn't, of course. With apologies ahead of time for this graphic example, if flying on a commercial airline was as dangerous as driving, the equivalent of two 747s filled to capacity would have to crash every week, killing all aboard, to match the risk of being killed in a car accident. But the media give a lot more attention to air accidents, so we tend to overstate the risk in flying and understate the risk in driving.

This illustrates an example of the **availability heuristic**, which is the tendency for people to base their judgments on information that is readily available to them. Events that evoke emotions, that are particularly vivid, or that have occurred more recently tend to be more available in our memory. As a result, we tend to be prone to overestimating unlikely events like an airplane crash. The availability heuristic can also explain why managers, when doing annual performance appraisals, tend to give more weight to recent behaviors of an employee than those behaviors of six or nine months ago.

availability heuristic
The tendency for people to base their judgments on information that is readily available to them.

REPRESENTATIVE HEURISTIC Literally millions of inner-city, African-American boys in the United States talk about the goal of playing basketball in the NBA. In reality, they have a better chance of becoming medical doctors than they do of playing in the NBA, but these kids are suffering from a **representative heuristic**. They tend to assess the likelihood of an occurrence by trying to match it with a preexisting category. They hear about a boy from

representative heuristic
Assessing the likelihood of an occurrence by drawing analogies and seeing identical situations where they don't exist.

their neighborhood ten years ago who went on to play professional basketball. Or they watch NBA games on television and think that those players are like them. We all are guilty of using this heuristic at times. Managers, for example, frequently predict the performance of a new product by relating it to a previous product's success. Or if three graduates from the same college were hired and turned out to be poor performers, managers may predict that a current job applicant from the same college will not be a good employee.

escalation of commitment
An increased commitment to a previous decision in spite of negative information.

ESCALATION OF COMMITMENT   Another bias that creeps into decisions in practice is a tendency to escalate commitment when a decision stream represents a series of decisions.[39] **Escalation of commitment** is an increased commitment to a previous decision in spite of negative information. For example, a friend of mine had been dating a woman for about four years. Although he admitted that things weren't going too well in the relationship, he informed me that he was going to marry the woman. A bit surprised by his decision, I asked him why. He responded: "I have a lot invested in the relationship!" Similarly, another friend was explaining why she was working on a doctorate in education, although she disliked teaching and didn't want to continue her career in education. She told me she really wanted to be a software programmer, but then she hit me with her escalation of commitment explanation: "I already have a master's in education and I'd have to go back and complete some deficiencies if I changed to work on a degree in software programming now."

It has been well documented that individuals escalate commitment to a failing course of action when they view themselves as responsible for the failure. That is, they "throw good money after bad" to demonstrate that their initial decision wasn't wrong and to avoid having to admit they made a mistake. Escalation of commitment is also congruent with evidence that people try to appear consistent in what they say and do. Increasing commitment to previous actions conveys consistency.

Escalation of commitment has obvious implications for managerial decisions. Many an organization has suffered large losses because a manager was

Quaker Oats CEO William Smithburg has a big problem. He decided to buy Snapple Beverage Corporation in 1994, paying a hefty $1.7 billion, a price financial analysts say was $1 billion too much. In 1995, Snapple lost $75 million. Smithburg's self-interest in boosting Snapple sales is enormous. He's attacking the problem by spending more money on Snapple advertising, introducing new products such as diet Snapple, and, as shown in this photo, personally promoting Snapple by handing out free samples.

determined to prove his or her original decision was right by continuing to commit resources to what was a lost cause from the beginning. Additionally, consistency is a characteristic often associated with effective leaders. So managers, in an effort to appear effective, may be motivated to be consistent when switching to another course of action may be preferable. In actuality, effective managers are those who are able to differentiate between situations in which persistence will pay off and situations in which it will not.

Individual Differences: Decision-Making Styles

Put Chad and Sean into the same decision situation and Chad almost always seems to take longer to come to a solution. Chad's final choices aren't necessarily always better than Sean's, he's just slower in processing information. Additionally, if there's an obvious risk dimension in the decision, Sean seems to consistently prefer a riskier option than does Chad. What this illustrates is that all of us bring our individual style to the decisions we make.

Research on decision styles has identified four different individual approaches to making decisions.[40] This model was designed to be used by managers and aspiring managers, but its general framework can be used with any individual decision maker.

The basic foundation of the model is the recognition that people differ along two dimensions. The first is their way of *thinking*. Some people are logical and rational. They process information serially. In contrast, some people are intuitive and creative. They perceive things as a whole. Note that these differences are above and beyond general human limitations such as we described regarding bounded rationality. The other dimension addresses a person's *tolerance for ambiguity*. Some people have a high need to structure information in ways that minimize ambiguity, while others are able to process many thoughts at the same time. When these two dimensions are diagrammed, they form four styles of decision making (see Exhibit 3-6 on page 114). These are: directive, analytic, conceptual, and behavioral.

People using the *directive* style have low tolerance for ambiguity and seek rationality. They are efficient and logical, but their efficiency concerns result in decisions made with minimal information and with few alternatives assessed. Directive types make decisions fast and they focus on the short run.

The *analytic* type has a much greater tolerance for ambiguity than do directive decision makers. This leads to the desire for more information and consideration of more alternatives than is true for directives. Analytic managers would be best characterized as careful decision makers with the ability to adapt to or cope with new situations.

Individuals with a *conceptual* style tend to be very broad in their outlook and consider many alternatives. Their focus is long range and they are very good at finding creative solutions to problems.

The final category—the *behavioral* style—characterizes decision makers who work well with others. They're concerned with the achievement of peers and subordinates and are receptive to suggestions from others, relying heavily on meetings for communicating. This type of manager tries to avoid conflict and seeks acceptance.

Although these four categories are distinct, most managers have characteristics that fall into more than one. It's probably best to think in terms of a manager's dominant style and his or her backup styles. Some managers rely

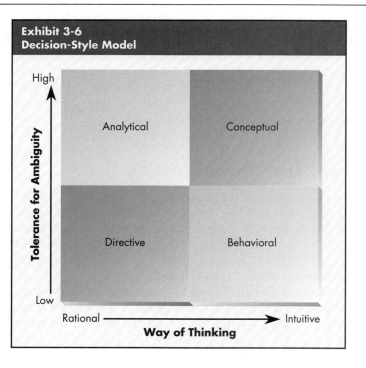

Exhibit 3-6
Decision-Style Model

Source: A.J. Rowe and J.D. Boulgarides, *Managerial Decision Making*, © 1992 Prentice Hall, Upper Saddle River, NJ, p. 29.

almost exclusively on their dominant style, however, more flexible managers can make shifts depending on the situation.

Business students, lower-level managers, and top executives tend to score highest in the analytic style. That's not surprising given the emphasis that formal education, particularly business education, gives to developing rational thinking. For instance, courses in accounting, statistics, and finance all stress rational analysis.

In addition to providing a framework for looking at individual differences, focusing on decision styles can be useful for helping you to understand how two equally intelligent people, with access to the same information, can differ in the ways they approach decisions and the final choices they make.

Organizational Constraints

The organization itself constrains decision makers. Managers, for instance, shape their decisions to reflect the organization's performance evaluation and reward system, to comply with the organization's formal regulations, and to meet organizationally imposed time constraints. Previous organizational decisions also act as precedents to constrain current decisions.

PERFORMANCE EVALUATION Managers are strongly influenced in their decision making by the criteria by which they are evaluated. If a division manager believes that the manufacturing plants under his responsibility are operating best when he hears nothing negative, we shouldn't be surprised to find his plant managers spending a good part of their time ensuring that negative information doesn't reach the division boss. Similarly, if a college dean believes that an instructor should never fail more than 10 percent of her students—to fail more reflects on the instructor's ability to teach—we should expect that new instructors, who want to receive favorable evaluations, will decide not to fail too many students.

REWARD SYSTEMS   The organization's reward system influences decision makers by suggesting to them what choices are preferable in terms of personal payoff. For example, if the organization rewards risk aversion, managers are more likely to make conservative decisions. From the 1930s through the mid-1980s, General Motors consistently gave out promotions and bonuses to those managers who kept a low profile, avoided controversy, and were good team players. The result was that GM managers became very adept at dodging tough issues and passing controversial decisions on to committees.

PROGRAMMED ROUTINES   David Gonzalez, a shift manager at a Taco Bell restaurant in San Antonio, Texas, describes constraints he faces on his job: "I've got rules and regulations covering almost every decision I make—from how to make a burrito to how often I need to clean the restrooms. My job doesn't come with much freedom of choice."

David's situation is not unique. All but the smallest of organizations create rules, policies, procedures, and other formalized regulations in order to standardize the behavior of their members. By programming decisions, organizations are able to get individuals to achieve high levels of performance without paying for the years of experience that would be necessary in the absence of regulations. David Gonzalez, for instance, earns about $21,000 a year, but he's only 20 years old and has no college exposure. To get the same quality of decisions from someone in David's job, without providing him or her with extensive operations manuals to follow, Taco Bell would need to hire managers with considerably more work experience and training—and probably have to pay them $35,000 or more per year.

SYSTEM-IMPOSED TIME CONSTRAINTS   Organizations impose deadlines on decisions. For instance, department budgets need to be completed by next Friday. Or the report on new-product development has to be ready for the executive committee to review by the first of the month. A host of decisions must be made quickly in order to stay ahead of the competition and keep customers satisfied. And almost all important decisions come with explicit deadlines. These conditions create time pressures on decision makers and often make it difficult, if not impossible, to gather all the information they might like to have before making a final choice. The rational model ignores the reality that, in organizations, decisions come with time constraints.

HISTORICAL PRECEDENTS   Rational decision making takes an unrealistic and insulated perspective. It views decisions as independent and discrete events. But that isn't the way it is in the real world! Decisions aren't made in a vacuum. They have a context. In fact, as noted at the beginning of this chapter, individual decisions are more accurately characterized as points in a stream of decisions.

Decisions made in the past are ghosts which continually haunt current choices. For instance, commitments made in the past constrain current options. To use a social situation as an example, the decision you might make after meeting "Mr. or Ms. Right" is more complicated if you're married than if you're single. Prior commitments—in this case, having chosen to get

Car makers impose time constraints on their design teams to deliver new models by specific deadlines. Members of the Honda Civic design team shown here are celebrating the successful completion of a project they started in 1992 to redesign the car for its 1996 product launch. The Japanese car, which is made at Honda's plant in the United States, represents a team effort that gathered cost-cutting ideas from designers and suppliers from both countries.

married—constrain your options. In a business context, Eastman Kodak is a good example of a firm which has had to live with its past mistakes.[41] Starting in the early 1970s, Kodak's management concluded that the days of silver halide photography were numbered. They predicted other technologies, such as electronic photography, would soon replace it. But instead of approaching the problem deliberately, Kodak management panicked. They took off in all directions, and today, virtually all of Kodak's problems can be traced to the decisions made and not made since then. Government budget decisions also offer an illustration of our point. It's common knowledge that the largest determining factor of the size of any given year's budget is last year's budget.[42] Choices made today, therefore, are largely a result of choices made over the years.

Cultural Differences

The rational model makes no acknowledgment of cultural differences. But Arabs, for instance, don't necessarily make decisions the same way that Canadians do. Therefore, we need to recognize that the cultural background of the decision maker can have significant influence on his or her selection of problems, depth of analysis, the importance placed on logic and rationality, or whether organizational decisions should be made autocratically by an individual manager or collectively in groups.[43]

Cultures, for example, differ in terms of time orientation, the importance of rationality, their belief in the ability of people to solve problems, and preference for collective decision making. Differences in time orientation help us understand why managers in Egypt will make decisions at a much slower and more deliberate pace than their American counterparts. While rationality is valued in North America, that's not true everywhere in the world. A North American manager might make an important decision intuitively, but he or she knows that it's important to appear to proceed in a rational fashion. This is because rationality is highly valued in the West. In countries such as Iran, where rationality is not admired, efforts to appear rational are not necessary.

Some cultures emphasize solving problems, while others focus on accepting situations as they are. The United States falls in the former category, while Thailand and Indonesia are examples of cultures that fall into the latter. Because problem-solving managers believe they can and should change situations to their benefit, American managers might identify a problem long before their Thai or Indonesian counterparts would choose to recognize it as such.

Decision making by Japanese managers is much more group oriented than in the United States. The Japanese value conformity and cooperation. So before Japanese CEOs make an important decision, they collect a large amount of information, which is then used in consensus-forming group decisions.

What about Ethics in Decision Making?

No contemporary discussion of decision making would be complete without inclusion of ethics because ethical considerations should be an important criterion in organizational decision making. In this final section, we present three different ways to ethically frame decisions and look at the factors that shape an individual's ethical decision-making behavior.

Three Ethical Decision Criteria

An individual can use three different criteria in making ethical choices.[44] The first is the *utilitarian* criterion, in which decisions are made solely on the basis of their outcomes or consequences. The goal of **utilitarianism** is to provide the greatest good for the greatest number. This view tends to dominate business decision making. It is consistent with goals like efficiency, productivity, and high profits. By maximizing profits, for instance, a business executive can argue he is securing the greatest good for the greatest number—as he hands out dismissal notices to 15 percent of his employees.

utilitarianism
Decisions are made so as to provide the greatest good for the greatest number.

◆ Utilitarianism dominates business decision making.

Another ethical criterion is to focus on *rights*. This calls on individuals to make decisions consistent with fundamental liberties and privileges as set forth in documents like the Bill of Rights. An emphasis on rights in decision making means respecting and protecting the basic rights of individuals, such as the right to privacy, to free speech, and to due process. For instance, use of this criterion would protect whistleblowers when they report unethical or illegal practices by their organization to the press or government agencies on the grounds of their right to free speech.

A third criterion is to focus on *justice*. This requires individuals to impose and enforce rules fairly and impartially so there is an equitable distribution of benefits and costs. Union members typically favor this view. It justifies paying people the same wage for a given job, regardless of performance differences, and using seniority as the primary determination in making layoff decisions.

Each of these three criteria has advantages and liabilities. A focus on utilitarianism promotes efficiency and productivity, but it can result in ignoring

Robert Holland, the former CEO of Ben & Jerry's Homemade Inc., made decisions based on the company's founding principle of balancing profits and social responsibility. When a Japanese firm offered to distribute Ben & Jerry's ice cream in Japan, Holland turned down the lucrative offer because the firm did not have a reputation for backing social causes. Holland said the only reason to take the opportunity was to make money, a decision that could be justified in utilitarian terms but would not have been compatible with the company's concern for social justice.

the rights of some individuals, particularly those with minority representation in the organization. The use of rights as a criterion protects individuals from injury and is consistent with freedom and privacy, but it can create an overly legalistic work environment that hinders productivity and efficiency. A focus on justice protects the interests of the underrepresented and less powerful, but it can encourage a sense of entitlement that reduces risk taking, innovation, and productivity.

Decision makers, particularly in for-profit organizations, tend to feel safe and comfortable when they use utilitarianism. A lot of questionable actions can be justified when framed as being in the best interests of "the organization" and stockholders. But many critics of business decision makers argue that this perspective needs to change.[45] Increased concern in society about individual rights and social justice suggests the need for managers to develop ethical standards based on nonutilitarian criteria. This presents a solid challenge to today's managers because making decisions using criteria such as individual rights and social justice involves far more ambiguities than using utilitarian criteria such as effects on efficiency and profits. This helps to explain why managers are increasingly criticized for their actions. Raising prices, selling products with questionable effects on consumer health, closing down plants, laying off large numbers of employees, moving production overseas to cut costs, and similar decisions can be justified in utilitarian terms. But that may no longer be the single criterion by which good decisions should be judged.

Factors Influencing Ethical Decision-Making Behavior

What accounts for unethical behavior in organizations? Is it immoral individuals or work environments that promote unethical activity? The answer is *both*! The evidence indicates that ethical or unethical actions are largely a function of both the individual's characteristics and the environment in which he or she works.[46]

Exhibit 3-7 presents a model for explaining ethical or unethical behavior. **Stages of moral development** assess a person's capacity to judge what is morally right.[47] The higher one's moral development, the less dependent he or she is on outside influences and, hence, the more he or she will be predisposed to behave ethically. For instance, most adults are at a mid-level of moral development—they're strongly influenced by peers and will follow an organization's rules and procedures. Those individuals who have progressed to the higher stages place increased value on the rights of others, regardless of the majority's opinion, and are likely to challenge organizational practices they believe are personally wrong.

We discussed *locus of control* in chapter 2. It's a personality characteristic that taps the extent to which people believe they are responsible for the events in their lives. Research indicates that people with an external locus of control (i.e., what happens to them in life is due to luck or chance) are less likely to take responsibility for the consequences of their behavior and are more likely to rely on external influences. Internals, on the other hand, are more likely to rely on their own internal standards of right or wrong to guide their behavior.

The *organizational environment* refers to an employee's perception of organizational expectations. Does the organization encourage and support ethical behavior by rewarding it or discourage unethical behavior by punishing it? Written codes of ethics, high moral behavior by senior management, realistic performance expectations, performance appraisals that evaluate means as well as ends, visible recognition and promotions for individuals who display high moral behavior, and visible punishment for those who act unethically are some examples of an organizational environment that is likely to foster high ethical decision making.

In summary, people who lack a strong moral sense are much less likely to make unethical decisions if they are constrained by an organizational environment that frowns on such behaviors. Conversely, very righteous individuals can be corrupted by an organizational environment that permits or encourages unethical practices.

stages of moral development
An assessment of a person's capacity to judge what is morally right.

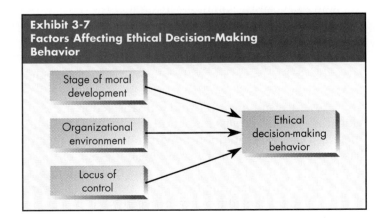

Exhibit 3-7
Factors Affecting Ethical Decision-Making Behavior

Stage of moral development

Organizational environment

Locus of control

Ethical decision-making behavior

What about National Culture?

What is seen as an ethical decision in China may not be seen as such in Canada. The reason is that there are no global ethical standards. Contrasts between Asia and the West provide an illustration.[48] Because bribery is commonplace in countries such as China, a Canadian working in China might face the dilemma: Should I pay a bribe to secure business if it is an accepted part of that country's culture?

While ethical standards may seem ambiguous in the West, criteria defining right and wrong are actually much clearer in the West than in Asia. Few issues are black-and-white there; most are gray. The need for global organizations to establish ethical principles for decision makers in countries such as India and China may be critical if high standards are to be upheld and if consistent practices are to be achieved.

Summary and Implications for Managers

Perception

Individuals behave in a given manner based not on the way their external environment actually is but, rather, on what they see or believe it to be. An organization may spend millions of dollars to create a pleasant work environment for its employees. However, in spite of these expenditures, if an employee believes that his or her job is lousy, that employee will behave accordingly. It is the employee's perception of a situation that becomes the basis for his or her behavior. The employee who perceives his or her supervisor as a hurdle reducer who helps him or her do a better job and the employee who sees the same supervisor as "big brother, closely monitoring every motion, to ensure that I keep working" will differ in their behavioral responses to their supervisor. The difference has nothing to do with the reality of the supervisor's actions; the difference in employee behavior is due to different perceptions.

The evidence suggests that what individuals *perceive* from their work situation will influence their productivity more than will the situation itself. Whether or not a job is actually interesting or challenging is irrelevant. Whether or not a manager successfully plans and organizes the work of his or her subordinates and actually helps them to structure their work more efficiently and effectively is far less important than how subordinates perceive the manager's efforts. Similarly, issues like fair pay for work performed, the validity of performance appraisals, and the adequacy of working conditions are not judged by employees in a way that assures common perceptions, nor can we be assured that individuals will interpret conditions about their jobs in a favorable light. Therefore, to be able to influence productivity, it is necessary to assess how workers perceive their jobs.

Absenteeism, turnover, and job satisfaction are also reactions to the individual's perceptions. Dissatisfaction with working conditions or the belief that there is a lack of promotion opportunities in the organization are judgments based on attempts to make some meaning out of one's job. The employee's conclusion that a job is good or bad is an interpretation. Managers must spend time understanding how each individual interprets reality and, where there is a significant difference between what is seen and what exists, try to eliminate the distortions. Failure to deal with the differences when individuals perceive the job in negative terms will result in increased absenteeism and turnover and lower job satisfaction.

Individual Decision Making

Individuals think and reason before they act. It is because of this that an understanding of how people make decisions can be helpful for explaining and predicting their behavior.

Under some decision situations, people follow the rational decision-making model. But for most people, and most nonroutine decisions, this is probably more the exception than the rule. Few important decisions are simple or unambiguous enough for the rational model's assumptions to apply. So we find individuals looking for solutions that satisfice rather than optimize, injecting biases and prejudices into the decision process, and relying on intuition.

Given the evidence we've described on how decisions are actually made in organizations, what can managers do to improve their decision making? We offer five suggestions.

First, analyze the situation. Adjust your decision-making style to the national culture you're operating in and to the criteria your organization evaluates and rewards. For instance, if you're in a country that doesn't value rationality, don't feel compelled to follow the rational decision-making model or even to try to make your decisions appear rational. Similarly, organizations differ in terms of the importance they place on risk, the use of groups, and the like. Adjust your decision style to ensure it's compatible with the organization's culture.

Second, be aware of biases. We all bring biases to the decisions we make. If you understand the biases influencing your judgment, you can begin to change the way you make decisions to reduce those biases.

Third, combine rational analysis with intuition. These are not conflicting approaches to decision making. By using both, you can actually improve your decision-making effectiveness. As you gain managerial experience, you should feel increasingly confident in imposing your intuitive processes on top of your rational analysis.

Fourth, don't assume that your specific decision style is appropriate for every job. Just as organizations differ, so too do jobs within organizations. And your effectiveness as a decision maker will increase if you match your decision style to the requirements of the job. For instance, if your decision-making style is directive, you'll be more effective working with people whose jobs require quick action. This style would match well with managing stockbrokers. An analytic style, on the other hand, would work well managing accountants, market researchers, or financial analysts.

Finally, use creativity-stimulation techniques. You can improve your overall decision-making effectiveness by searching for new and novel solutions to problems. This can be as elementary as telling yourself to think creatively and to specifically look for unique alternatives. Additionally, you can practice the attribute listing and lateral thinking techniques described in this chapter.

What can we conclude regarding ethics? For individuals already employed, managers can influence only the employee's work environment. So managers should overtly seek to convey high ethical standards to employees through the actions the managers take. By what managers say, do, reward, punish, and overlook, they set the ethical tone for their employees. When hiring new employees, managers have an opportunity to weed out ethically undesirable applicants. The selection process—for instance, interviews, tests, and background checks—should be viewed as an opportunity to learn about an individual's level of moral development and locus of control. This then can be used to identify individuals whose ethical standards might be in conflict with those of the organization or who are particularly vulnerable to negative external influences.

For Review

1. Define *perception*.
2. What is attribution theory? What are its implications for explaining organizational behavior?
3. What factors do you think might create the fundamental attribution error?
4. How does selectivity affect perception? Give an example of how selectivity can create perceptual distortion.
5. What is stereotyping? Give an example of how stereotyping can create perceptual distortion.
6. Give some positive results of using shortcuts when judging others.
7. What is the rational decision-making model? Under what conditions is it applicable?
8. Describe organizational factors that might constrain decision makers.
9. What role does intuition play in effective decision making?
10. Describe the three criteria individuals can use in making ethical decisions.

For Discussion

1. "That you and I agree on what we see suggests we have similar backgrounds and experiences." Do you agree or disagree? Discuss.
2. In what work-related situations do you think it is important to be able to determine whether others' behavior stems primarily from internal or external causes?
3. "For the most part, individual decision making in organizations is an irrational process." Do you agree or disagree? Discuss.
4. What factors do you think differentiate good decision makers from poor ones? Relate your answer to the six-step rational model.
5. Have you ever increased your commitment to a failed course of action? If so, analyze the follow-up decision to increase your commitment and explain why you behaved as you did.

When Hiring Employees: Emphasize the Positive

Hiring new employees requires managers to become salespeople. They have to emphasize the positive, even if it means failing to mention the negative aspects in the job. While there is a real risk of setting unrealistic expectations about the organization and about the specific job, that's a risk managers have to take. As in dealing with any salesperson, it is the job applicant's responsibility to follow the dictum *caveat emptor*—let the buyer beware!

Why should managers emphasize the positive when discussing a job with a prospective candidate? They have no choice! First, there is a dwindling supply of qualified applicants for many job vacancies; and second, this approach is necessary to meet the competition.

The massive restructuring and downsizing of organizations that began in the late 1980s has drawn attention to corporate layoffs. What has often been overlooked in this process is the growing shortage of qualified applicants for literally millions of jobs. Through the foreseeable future, managers will find it increasingly difficult to get qualified people who

can fill jobs such as legal secretary, nurse, accountant, salesperson, maintenance mechanic, computer-repair specialist, software programmer, social worker, physical therapist, environmental engineer, telecommunications specialist, and airline pilot. But managers will also find it harder to get qualified people to fill entry-level, minimum-wage jobs. There may be no shortage of physical bodies, but finding individuals who can read, write, perform basic mathematical calculations, and have the proper work habits to effectively perform these jobs isn't so easy. There is a growing gap between the skills workers have and the skills employers require. So managers need to *sell* jobs to the limited pool of applicants. And this means presenting the job and the organization in the most favorable light possible.

Another reason management is forced to emphasize the positive with job candidates is that this is what the competition is doing. Other employers also face a limited applicant pool. As a result, to get people to join their organizations, they are forced to put a positive "spin" on their descriptions of their organizations and the jobs they seek to fill. In this competitive environment, any employer who presents jobs realistically to applicants—that is, openly provides the negative aspects of a job along with the positive—risks losing most or all of the most desirable candidates.

When Hiring Employees: Balance the Positive with the Negative

Regardless of the changing labor market, managers who treat the recruiting and hiring of candidates as if the applicants must be sold on the job and exposed to only positive aspects set themselves up to have a work force that is dissatisfied and prone to high turnover.

Every applicant acquires, during the selection process, a set of expectations about the organization and about the specific job he or she hopes to be offered. When the information an applicant receives is excessively inflated, a number of things happen that have potentially negative effects on the organization. First, mismatched applicants who would probably become dissatisfied with the job and soon quit are less likely to select themselves out of the search process. Second, the absence of negative information builds unrealistic expectations. If hired, the new employee is likely to become quickly disappointed. And inaccurate perceptions lead to premature resignations. Third, new hires are prone to become disillusioned and less committed to the organization when they come face-to-face with the negatives in the job. Employees who feel they were tricked or misled during the hiring process are unlikely to be satisfied workers.

To increase job satisfaction among employees and reduce turnover, applicants should be given a realistic job preview, with both unfavorable and favorable information, before an offer is made. For example, in addition to positive comments, the candidate might be told that there are limited opportunities to talk with co-workers during work hours, or that erratic fluctuations in workloads create considerable stress on employees during rush periods.

Research indicates that applicants who have been given a realistic job preview hold lower and more realistic expectations about the job they'll be doing and are better prepared for coping with the job and its frustrating elements. The result is fewer unexpected resignations by new employees. In a tight labor market, retaining people is as critical as hiring them in the first place. Presenting only the positive aspects of a job to a recruit may initially entice him or her to join the organization, but it may be a marriage that both parties will quickly regret.

Information in this argument comes from J.A. Breaugh, "Realistic Job Previews: A Critical Appraisal and Future Research Directions," *Academy of Management Review*, October 1983, pp. 612–19; S.L. Premack and J.P. Wanous, "A Meta-Analysis of Realistic Job Preview Experiments," *Journal of Applied Psychology*, November 1985, pp. 706–20; B.M. Meglino, A.S. DeNisi, S.A. Youngblood, and K.J. Williams, "Effects of Realistic Job Previews: A Comparison Using an Enhancement and a Reduction Preview," *Journal of Applied Psychology*, May 1988, pp. 259–66; and R.J. Vandenberg and V. Scarpello, "The Matching Model: An Examination of the Processes Underlying Realistic Job Previews," *Journal of Applied Psychology*, February 1990, pp. 60–67.

Learning about Yourself Exercise

Decision-Making Style Questionnaire

PART I

Circle the response that comes closest to how you usually feel or act. There are no right or wrong responses to any of these items.

1. I am more careful about
   a. people's feelings   **b.** their rights

2. I usually get along better with
   a. imaginative people   **b.** realistic people

3. It is a higher compliment to be called
   a. a person of real feeling   **b.** a consistently reasonable person

4. In doing something with other people, it appeals more to me
   a. to do it in the accepted way   **b.** to invent a way of my own

5. I get more annoyed at
   a. fancy theories   **b.** people who do not like theories

6. It is higher praise to call someone
   a. a person of vision   **b.** a person of common sense

7. I more often let
   a. my heart rule my head   **b.** my head rule my heart

8. I think it is a worse fault
   a. to show too much warmth   **b.** to be unsympathetic

9. If I were a teacher, I would rather teach
   a. courses involving theory   **b.** factual courses

PART II

Which word in the following pairs appeals to you more? Circle *a* or *b*.

10. **a.** Compassion   **b.** Foresight
11. **a.** Justice   **b.** Mercy
12. **a.** Production   **b.** Design
13. **a.** Gentle   **b.** Firm
14. **a.** Uncritical   **b.** Critical
15. **a.** Literal   **b.** Figurative
16. **a.** Imaginative   **b.** Matter-of-fact

Turn to page A-26 for scoring directions and key.

Source: Based on a personality scale developed by D. Hellriegel, J. Slocum, and R.W. Woodman, *Organizational Behavior*, 3rd ed. (St. Paul, MN: West Publishing, 1983), pp. 127–41, and reproduced in J.M. Ivancevich and M.T. Matteson, *Organizational Behavior and Management*, 2nd ed. (Homewood, IL: BPI/Irwin, 1990), pp. 538–39.

Working with Others Exercise

Evaluating Your Interpersonal Perception

1. On a piece of paper, independently write down how you would describe *yourself* on the following dimensions:
   a. Friendliness
   b. Moodiness
   c. Sense of humor
   d. Career motivation
   e. Interpersonal skills
   f. Desire to be accepted by others
   g. Independence

2. Now form groups of three to five members. Evaluate each of the *other members* in your group (as best you can) on the same seven dimensions.

3. Going around the group so each member gets to participate, describe what each of you has written about Member A. After you have all provided your perceptions, Member A will share his or her own self-perceptions. Then do the same with Member B, and so forth, until all group members have received feedback and shared their own impressions.

4. The exercise concludes by each member analyzing the similarities and differences between their perceptions of themselves on the seven dimensions and how they're perceived by the other members of their group.

Ethical Dilemma Exercise

Five Ethical Decisions: What Would You Do?

Assume you're a middle manager in a company with about a thousand employees. How would you respond to each of the following situations?

1. You're negotiating a contract with a potentially very large customer whose representative has hinted that you could almost certainly be assured of getting his business if you gave him and his wife an all-expense-paid cruise to the Caribbean. You know the representative's employer wouldn't approve of such a "payoff," but you have the discretion to authorize such an expenditure. What would you do?

2. You have the opportunity to steal $100,000 from your company with absolute certainty that you would not be detected or caught. Would you do it?

3. Your company policy on reimbursement for meals while traveling on company business is that you will be repaid for your out-of-pocket costs, not to exceed $50 a day. You don't need receipts for these expenses—the company will take your word. When traveling, you tend to eat at fast-food places and rarely spend in excess of $15 a day. Most of your colleagues put in reimbursement requests in the range of $40

to $45 a day regardless of what their actual expenses are. How much would you request for your meal reimbursements?

4. You want to get feedback from people who are using one of your competitor's products. You believe you'll get much more honest responses from these people if you disguise the identity of your company. Your boss suggests you contact possible participants by using the fictitious name of the Consumer Marketing Research Corporation. What would you do?

5. You've discovered that one of your closest friends at work has stolen a large sum of money from the company. Would you: Do nothing? Go directly to an executive to report the incident before talking about it with the offender? Confront the individual before taking action? Make contact with the individual with the goal of persuading that person to return the money?

Several of these scenarios are based on D.R. Altany, "Torn between Halo and Horns," *Industry Week*, March 15, 1993, pp. 15–20.

Ben & Jerry's Reassesses Its Social Agenda

The senior management at Ben & Jerry's Homemade Inc. has a dilemma. Does the company have to forgo profits to follow its conscience?

Ben & Jerry's was born as a socially responsible company. It still is. Co-founder and chairman Ben Cohen, who with the other co-founder Jerry Greenfield owns 42 percent of the voting stock, continues to favor slower growth that won't harm relations with employees or the tiny Vermont communities where it operates. Cohen argues that his company shouldn't pursue a business opportunity unless there is some purpose beyond making money. The company's president and CEO, Robert Holland, Jr.,* generally agrees with this philosophy but is concerned that it may be hampering growth.

Health-conscious Americans are increasingly passing on superpremium ice cream. The result is lower sales and profits for Ben & Jerry's in the United States. Meanwhile, the Japanese are gobbling up premium ice cream like crazy. In 1995, Haagen-Dazs sold $300 million worth of product there. Yet when a top Japanese supplier offered Holland distribution of Ben & Jerry's in Japan, he said no. Why? The Japanese supplier did not have a reputation for backing social causes. "The only clear reason to take the opportunity," says Holland, "was to make money."

Holland and other top executives who have been brought in from mainstream companies such as American Express and The Limited believe Ben & Jerry's must expand its brand more aggressively. This creates a conflict with Cohen and many long-term employees who identify with the company's socially responsible stance.

Cohen's vision is of "values-led" capitalism, where returning something to customers, employees, and the community is as important as the bottom line. For instance, Ben & Jerry's donates 7.5 percent of its pretax profits to social causes. It also uses its purchasing clout to back its values: It buys milk and cream from Vermont family farms, even if it means paying significantly above market prices.

A recent example of Ben & Jerry's problem was its move into the market for upscale sorbets. The company came to market a year behind Haagen-Dazs, largely due to internal squabbles. Sorbets held no clear link to the company's social mission. Profits—and a good opportunity to extend the brand—

weren't enough. "Sorbets weren't high on Ben's agenda," says one director. The solution was to use organic fruit.

More recently, when the company planned to move into the French market, Cohen fought to stay out unless ads took a stand against the French government's policy of nuclear testing in the South Pacific. Holland argued against Cohen and, after much debate, prevailed.

Questions

1. What ethical decision criteria has Ben & Jerry's been using?
2. How does this criteria compare with most large companies?
3. Can Ben & Jerry's compete in a global economy by relying on its past values-led capitalistic perspective? Defend your position.
4. Analyze this case in terms of (a) decision-making styles, (b) stages of moral development, and (c) cultural differences.

Based on P.C. Judge, "Is It Rainforest Crunch Time?" *Business Week*, July 15, 1996, pp. 70–71.
*Holland actually left the company in the fall of 1996.

VIDEO CASE

ABCNEWS

Decision Making, Detective Style

They're the cold case squad. Two crusty, dogged, never-say-die homicide detectives in the Boston police department. Since they started work in 1991, they've closed the books on 29 homicides, many of which were all but given up on long ago. Much of their success is due to their skill in decision making.

Just what is a "cold case"? It's an old murder case that's never been solved. These are cases that no other police detective wants to touch because, in many cases, the trail leading to the murderer has "gone cold." Most of us would assume that the cold cases are just plain unsolvable and the murderer(s) have gotten away. But the two members of the cold case squad consider time to be their ally. There's a rule of thumb among homicide detectives that if a murder isn't solved within the first 48 to 72 hours, the odds of ever solving it drop dramatically. Even so, the cold case squad goes against conventional wisdom. "A certain number of these cases, they get better with age," says one detective, "because as relationships deteriorate, people are now willing to talk about a person that they wouldn't say a word about, years gone by."

And the cold case squad detectives listen to their hunches—to their instincts about a case. Although "working a hunch" is one of the basic skills of any good detective, the cold case squad often goes far beyond this. Their creativity at tracking suspected murderers and finding a trail to these individuals is nothing short of astonishing. For instance, they play with numerous variations of a suspect's name to see if that trail leads anywhere. They may substitute the suspect's middle name or use the suspect's mother's maiden name, or the suspect's nickname and try various combinations of these to see if anything comes of it. In one instance, the detectives had a case with no file, no fingerprints, no photographs. All they had was a little piece of paper that said "HAW Rebecca." Driving around one day, the thought hit them that HAW could stand for "Husband and Wife." Following up on this brainstorm, they eventually found enough evidence to convict the murderer.

One detective on the cold case squad spends his off hours playing chess on Harvard Square. He likens the game of chess to solving the murder investigations assigned to the cold case squad. According to him, being successful at chess means thinking about what your opponent is going to do and why he's doing it. You try to reflect on the last move and previous moves to see what he might do in the future. And it's the same technique the cold case squad uses as it investigates and attempts to solve these difficult-to-crack murder cases.

Questions

1. What creativity techniques might help the cold case squad in doing its job?
2. What could you learn from the cold case squad that is relevant to effective decision making?

Source: Based on "The Cold Case Squad," *ABC News Primetime*; aired on July 14, 1994.

4

VALUES, ATTITUDES, AND JOB SATISFACTION

CHAPTER OUTLINE
Values
Attitudes
Job Satisfaction

> When you prevent me from doing anything I want to do, that is persecution; but when I prevent you from doing anything you want to do, that is law, order and morals.
>
> —G. B. Shaw

LEARNING OBJECTIVES

After studying this chapter, you should be able to

1 Explain the source of an individual's value system

2 List the dominant values in today's workforce

3 Describe the three primary job-related attitudes

4 Summarize the relationship between attitudes and behavior

5 Identify the role consistency plays in attitudes

6 Clarify how individuals reconcile inconsistencies

7 Explain what determines job satisfaction

8 State the relationship between job satisfaction and behavior

9 Describe the current level of job satisfaction among Americans in the workplace

10 Identify four employee responses to dissatisfaction

NINA LUI (see photo) is an elementary school teacher at P.S. 234 in New York City. Lori Gaunt manages a bakery and café in Seattle. Two very different jobs, yet Nina and Lori share one thing in common: They both express very positive attitudes about their work.[1]

"I work in a terrific school," says Nina. "Collaboration is encouraged, and we're given the time to sit together and bounce ideas off one another—to be a think tank. There's a lot of debate and a sense of encouragement and support." Lori Gaunt's comments sound very similar, "I feel as if my opinions count a lot, and I've been instrumental in making changes. The owner isn't hands-off, but she loves what I do and tells me to run with it. It's neat to have that much freedom."

Are Nina's and Lori's attitudes toward work unusual nowadays? In a world where layoffs are a way of life and we read regularly about increased stress levels in the workplace, are Nina and Lori exceptions? Or do the majority of workers feel positive about their jobs? You might be surprised by the answers.

A recent Gallup poll surveyed Americans nationwide to find out their attitudes toward their jobs and their workplaces.[2] In spite of all the negative stories you may have read in the media, on a scale from 1 to 5, with 5 representing "extremely satisfied," 71 percent of the respondents rated their level of satisfaction with their place of employment at 4 or 5, while only 9 percent rated it at 1 or 2. Closer analysis of the findings indicated that a large part of these positive findings could be explained by the fact that jobs were generally meeting the primary needs of workers. They considered the following factors critical to their satisfaction and job performance: the opportunity to do what they do best; having their opinions count; and getting the opportunity to learn and grow. Sixty-two of the respondents indicated that in the previous seven days they had received recognition or praise for good work; and 84 percent said they had had the opportunity at work to learn and grow during the previous year.

These positive attitudes toward work are not an aberration. Studies consistently show that workers are satisfied with their jobs. This is applicable over time as well as across national boundaries. Regardless of which studies you choose to look at, when American workers are asked if they are satisfied with their jobs, the results tend to be very similar: Between 70 and 80 percent report they're satisfied with their jobs.[3] These numbers do tend to vary with age—with older workers reporting the highest satisfaction. But even young people—under age 25—report levels of satisfaction in excess of 70 percent.[4]

Although there was some concern in the late 1970s that satisfaction was declining across almost all occupational groups,[5] recent reinterpretations of these data and additional longitudinal studies indicate that job satisfaction levels have held steady for decades—through economic recessions as well as prosperous times.[6] Moreover, these results are generally applicable to other developed countries. For instance, comparable studies among workers in Canada, Great Britain, Switzerland, Germany, France, and Mexico indicate more positive than negative results.[7]

How does one explain these findings? One answer is that whatever it is people want from their jobs, they seem to be getting it. But two additional points should be added.

First, people don't select jobs randomly. They tend to gravitate toward jobs that are compatible with their interests, values, and abilities.[8] Because people are likely to seek jobs that provide a good person–job fit, reports of high satisfaction shouldn't be totally surprising. Second, based on our knowledge of cognitive dissonance theory, we might expect employees to resolve inconsistencies between dissatisfaction with their jobs and their staying with those jobs by not reporting the dissatisfaction. So these positive findings might be tainted by efforts to reduce dissonance. ◆

◆ Is capital punishment right or wrong? If a person likes power, is that good or bad? The answers to these questions are value laden.

In this chapter, we look more carefully at the concept of job satisfaction and what managers can do to increase it among their workers. First, however, we consider how values influence employee behavior.

Values

Is capital punishment right or wrong? How about racial quotas in hiring—are they right or wrong? If a person likes power, is that good or bad? The answers to these questions are value laden. Some might argue, for example, that capital punishment is right because it is an appropriate retribution for crimes like murder and treason. However, others might argue, just as strongly, that no government has the right to take anyone's life.

values
Basic convictions that a specific mode of conduct or end-state of existence is personally or socially preferable to an opposite or converse mode of conduct or end-state of existence.

Values represent basic convictions that "a specific mode of conduct or end-state of existence is personally or socially preferable to an opposite or converse mode of conduct or end-state of existence."[9] They contain a judgmental element in that they carry an individual's ideas as to what is right, good, or desirable. Values have both content and intensity attributes. The content attribute says that a mode of conduct or end-state of existence is *important*. The intensity attribute specifies *how important* it is. When we rank an individual's values in terms of their intensity, we obtain that person's **value system**. All of us have a hierarchy of values that forms our value system. This system is identified by the relative importance we assign to such values as freedom, pleasure, self-respect, honesty, obedience, and equality.

value system
A hierarchy based on a ranking of an individual's values in terms of their intensity.

Importance of Values

Values are important to the study of organizational behavior because they lay the foundation for the understanding of attitudes and motivation and because they influence our perceptions. Individuals enter an organization with preconceived notions of what "ought" and what "ought not" to be. Of course, these notions are not value free. On the contrary, they contain interpretations of right and wrong. Furthermore, they imply that certain behaviors or outcomes are preferred over others. As a result, values cloud objectivity and rationality.

Values generally influence attitudes and behavior.[10] Suppose that you enter an organization with the view that allocating pay on the basis of performance is right, whereas allocating pay on the basis of seniority is wrong or inferior. How are you going to react if you find that the organization you have just joined rewards seniority and not performance? You're likely to be disappointed—and this can lead to job dissatisfaction and the decision not to exert a high level of effort since "it's probably not going to lead to more money, anyway." Would your attitudes and behavior be different if your values aligned with the organization's pay policies? Most likely.

Sources of Our Value Systems

Where do our value systems come from? A significant portion is genetically determined. The rest is attributable to factors like national culture, parental dictates, teachers, friends, and similar environmental influences.

Studies of twins reared apart demonstrate that about 40 percent of the variation in work values is explained by genetics.[11] So the values of your biological parents play an important part in explaining what your values will be. Still the majority of the variation in values is due to environmental factors.

When we were children, why did many of our mothers tell us "you should always clean your dinner plate"? Why is it that, at least historically in North America, achievement has been considered good and being lazy has been considered bad? The answer is that, in every culture, certain values have developed over time and are continuously reinforced. Achievement, peace, cooperation, equity, and democracy are societal values that are considered desirable in North America. These values are not fixed, but when they change, they do so very slowly.

A significant portion of the values we hold is established in our early years—from parents, teachers, friends, and others. Many of your early ideas of what is right and wrong were probably formulated from the views expressed by your parents. Think back to your early views on such topics as education, sex, and politics. For the most part, they were the same as those expressed by your parents. As you grew up and were exposed to other value systems, you may have altered a number of your values. For example, in high school, if you desired to be a member of a social club whose values included the conviction that "every person should carry a gun," there is a good probability that you changed your value system to align with that of the members of the club, even if it meant rejecting your parents' value that "only gang members carry guns, and gang members are bad."

Interestingly, values are relatively stable and enduring.[12] This has been explained as a result of both their genetic component and the way in which they're learned.[13] Concerning this second point, we were told as children that certain behaviors or outcomes were always desirable or always undesirable. There were no gray areas. You were told, for example, that you should be honest and responsible. You were never taught to be just a little bit honest or a little bit responsible. It is this absolute or "black-or-white" learning of values, when combined with a significant portion of genetic imprinting, that more or less assures their stability and endurance.

The process of questioning our values, of course, may result in a change. We may decide that these underlying convictions are no longer acceptable. More often, our questioning merely acts to reinforce those values we hold.

Exhibit 4-1 Terminal and Instrumental Values in Rokeach Value Survey

Terminal Values	Instrumental Values
A comfortable life (a prosperous life)	Ambitious (hardworking, aspiring)
An exciting life (a stimulating, active life)	Broad-minded (open-minded)
A sense of accomplishment (lasting contribution)	Capable (competent, effective)
A world at peace (free of war and conflict)	Cheerful (lighthearted, joyful)
A world of beauty (beauty of nature and the arts)	Clean (neat, tidy)
Equality (brotherhood, equal opportunity for all)	Courageous (standing up for your beliefs)
Family security (taking care of loved ones)	Forgiving (willing to pardon others)
Freedom (independence, free choice)	Helpful (working for the welfare of others)
Happiness (contentedness)	Honest (sincere, truthful)
Inner harmony (freedom from inner conflict)	Imaginative (daring, creative)
Mature love (sexual and spiritual intimacy)	Independent (self-reliant, self-sufficient)
National security (protection from attack)	Intellectual (intelligent, reflective)
Pleasure (an enjoyable, leisurely life)	Logical (consistent, rational)
Salvation (saved, eternal life)	Loving (affectionate, tender)
Self-respect (self-esteem)	Obedient (dutiful, respectful)
Social recognition (respect, admiration)	Polite (courteous, well mannered)
True friendship (close companionship)	Responsible (dependable, reliable)
Wisdom (a mature understanding of life)	Self-controlled (restrained, self-disciplined)

Source: M. Rokeach, *The Nature of Human Values* (New York: The Free Press, 1973).

Exhibit 4-2 Mean Value Ranking of Executives, Union Members, and Activists (Top Five Only)	Executives		Union Members		Activists	
	Terminal	Instrumental	Terminal	Instrumental	Terminal	Instrumental
	1. Self-respect	1. Honest	1. Family security	1. Responsible	1. Equality	1. Honest
	2. Family security	2. Responsible	2. Freedom	2. Honest	2. A world of peace	2. Helpful
	3. Freedom	3. Capable	3. Happiness	3. Courageous	3. Family security	3. Courageous
	4. A sense of accomplishment	4. Ambitious	4. Self-respect	4. Independent	4. Self-respect	4. Responsible
	5. Happiness	5. Independent	5. Mature love	5. Capable	5. Freedom	5. Capable

Source: Based on W.C. Frederick and J. Weber, "The Values of Corporate Managers and Their Critics: An Empirical Description and Normative Implications," in W.C. Frederick and L.E. Preston (eds.), *Business Ethics: Research Issues and Empirical Studies* (Greenwich, CT: JAI Press, 1990), pp. 123–44.

Types of Values

Can we classify values? The answer is: Yes! In this section, we review two approaches to developing value typologies.

ROKEACH VALUE SURVEY   Milton Rokeach created the Rokeach Value Survey (RVS).[14] The RVS consists of two sets of values, with each set containing 18 individual value items. One set, called **terminal values**, refers to desirable end-states of existence. These are the goals that a person would like to achieve during his or her lifetime. The other set, called **instrumental values**, refers to preferable modes of behavior, or means of achieving the terminal values. Exhibit 4-1 gives common examples for each of these sets.

Several studies confirm that the RVS values vary among groups.[15] People in the same occupations or categories (e.g., corporate managers, union members, parents, students) tend to hold similar values. For instance, one study compared corporate executives, members of the steelworkers' union, and members of a community activist group. Although a good deal of overlap was found among the three groups,[16] there were also some very significant differences. (See Exhibit 4-2). The activists had value preferences that were quite different from those of the other two groups. They ranked "equality" as their most important terminal value; executives and union members ranked this value 14 and 13, respectively. Activists ranked "helpful" as their second-highest instrumental value. The other two groups both ranked it 14. These differences are important, since executives, union members, and activists all have a vested interest in what corporations do. "When corporations and critical stakeholder groups such as these [other] two come together in negotiations or contend with one another over economic and social policies, they are likely to begin with these built-in differences in personal value preferences. . . .   Reaching agreement on any specific issue or policy where these personal values are importantly implicated might prove to be quite difficult."[17]

terminal values
Desirable end-states of existence; the goals that a person would like to achieve during his or her lifetime.

instrumental values
Preferable modes of behavior or means of achieving one's terminal values.

CONTEMPORARY WORK COHORTS   Your author has integrated a number of recent analyses of work values into a four-stage model that attempts to capture the unique values of different cohorts or generations in the U.S. workforce.[18] (No assumption is made that this framework would universally apply across all cultures.)[19] Exhibit 4-3 proposes that employees can be segmented by the era in which they entered the workforce. Because most people start work between the ages of 18 and 23, the eras also correlate closely with the chronological age of employees.

Workers who grew up influenced by the Great Depression, World War II, U.S. leadership in world manufacturing, the Andrews Sisters, and the Berlin blockade entered the workforce from the mid-1940s through the late 1950s believing in the Protestant work ethic. Once hired, they tended to be loyal to their employer. In terms of the terminal values on the RVS, these employees are likely to place the greatest importance on a comfortable life and family security.

Employees who entered the workforce during the 1960s through the mid-1970s were influenced heavily by John F. Kennedy, the civil rights movement, the Beatles, the Vietnam war, and baby-boom competition. They brought with them a large measure of the "hippie ethic" and existential philosophy. They are more concerned with the quality of their lives than with the amount of money and possessions they can accumulate. Their desire for autonomy has directed their loyalty toward themselves rather than toward the organization that employs them. In terms of the RVS, freedom and equality rate high.

Individuals who entered the workforce from the mid-1970s through the late-1980s reflect the society's return to more traditional values, but with far greater emphasis on achievement and material success. As a generation, they were strongly influenced by Reagan conservatism, the defense buildup, dual-career households, and $150,000 starter homes. Born toward the end of the baby-boom period, these workers are pragmatists who believe that ends can justify means. They see the organizations that employ them merely as vehicles for their careers. Terminal values like a sense of accomplishment and social recognition rank high with them.

Exhibit 4-3 Dominant Values in Today's Workforce

Stage	Entered the Workforce	Approximate Current Age	Dominant Work Values
I. Protestant work ethic	Mid-1940s to late 1950s	55–75	Hard work, conservative; loyalty to the organization
II. Existential	1960s to mid-1970s	40–55	Quality of life, nonconforming, seeks autonomy; loyalty to self
III. Pragmatic	Mid-1970s to late 1980s	30–40	Success, achievement, ambition, hard work; loyalty to career
IV. Generation X	1990 to present	Under 30	Flexibility, job satisfaction, leisure time; loyalty to relationships

Our final category encompasses what has become known as generation X. Their lives have been shaped by globalization, economic stagnation, the fall of communism, MTV, AIDS, and computers. They value flexibility, life options, and the achievement of job satisfaction. Family and relationships are very important to this cohort. Money is important as an indicator of career performance, but they are willing to trade off salary increases, titles, security, and promotions for increased leisure time and expanded lifestyle options. In search of balance in their lives, these more recent entrants into the workforce are less willing to make personal sacrifices for the sake of their employer than previous generations were. On the RVS, they rate high on true friendship, happiness, and pleasure.

◆ The lives of generation X have been shaped by globalization, economic stagnation, the fall of communism, MTV, AIDS, and computers.

An understanding that individuals' values differ but tend to reflect the societal values of the period in which they grew up can be a valuable aid in explaining and predicting behavior. Employees in their thirties and sixties, for instance, are more likely to be conservative and accepting of authority than their existential co-workers in their forties. And workers under 30 are more likely than the other groups to balk at having to work weekends and more prone to leave a job in mid-career to pursue another that provides more leisure time.

Values, Loyalty, and Ethical Behavior

Did a decline in business ethics set in sometime in the late 1970s? The issue is debatable.[20] Nevertheless, a lot of people think so. If there has been a decline in ethical standards, perhaps we should look to our four-stage model of work cohort values (see Exhibit 4-3) for a possible explanation. After all, managers consistently report that the actions of their bosses is the most important factor influencing ethical behavior in their organizations.[21] Given this fact, the values of those in middle and upper management should have a significant bearing on the entire ethical climate within an organization.

Through the mid-1970s, the managerial ranks were dominated by Protestant-work-ethic types (Stage I) whose loyalties were to their employer. When faced with ethical dilemmas, their decisions were made in terms of what was best for their organization. Beginning in the mid-to-late 1970s, individuals with existential values began to rise into the upper levels of management. They were soon followed by pragmatic types. By the late 1980s, a large portion of middle- and top-management positions in business organizations were held by people from Stages II and III.

The loyalty of existentials and pragmatics is to self and careers, respectively. Their focus is inward and their primary concern is with "looking out for number one." Such self-centered values would be consistent with a decline in ethical standards. Could this help explain the alleged decline in business ethics beginning in the late 1970s?

The potential good news in this analysis is that recent entrants to the workforce, and tomorrow's managers, appear to be less self-centered. Since their loyalty is to relationships, they are more likely to consider the ethical implications of their actions on others around them. The result? We might look forward to an uplifting of ethical standards in business over the next decade or two merely as a result of changing values within the managerial ranks.

Values Across Cultures

In chapter 1, we described the new global village and said "managers have to become capable of working with people from different cultures." Because values differ across cultures, an understanding of these differences should be helpful in explaining and predicting behavior of employees from different countries. A comparison of American and Japanese cultures can help illustrate this point.[22]

American children are taught early the values of individuality and uniqueness. In contrast, Japanese children are indoctrinated to be "team players," to work within the group, and to conform. A significant part of an American student's education is to learn to think, analyze, and question. Their Japanese counterparts are rewarded for recounting facts. These different socialization practices reflect different cultures and, not surprisingly, result in different types of employees. The average U.S. worker is more competitive and self-focused than the Japanese worker. Predictions of employee behavior, based on U.S. workers, are likely to be off-target when they are applied to a population of employees—such as the Japanese—who prefer and perform better in standardized tasks, as part of a work team, with group-based decisions and rewards.

A FRAMEWORK FOR ASSESSING CULTURES One of the most widely referenced approaches for analyzing variations among cultures has been done by Geert Hofstede.[23] He surveyed more than 116,000 IBM employees in 40 countries about their work-related values. He found that managers and employees vary on five value dimensions of national culture. They are listed and defined as follows:

◆ **Power distance**. The degree to which people in a country accept that power in institutions and organizations is distributed unequally. Ranges from relatively equal (low power distance) to extremely unequal (high power distance).

◆ **Individualism** versus **collectivism**. Individualism is the degree to which people in a country prefer to act as individuals rather than as members of groups. Collectivism is the equivalent of low individualism.

◆ **Quantity of life** versus **quality of life**. Quantity of life is the degree to which values like assertiveness, the acquisition of money and material goods, and competition prevail. Quality of life is the degree to which people value relationships, and show sensitivity and concern for the welfare of others.[24]

◆ **Uncertainty avoidance**. The degree to which people in a country prefer structured over unstructured situations. In countries that score high on uncertainty avoidance, people have an increased level of anxiety, which manifests itself in greater nervousness, stress, and aggressiveness.

◆ **Long-term** versus **short-term orientation**. People in cultures with long-term orientations look to the future and value thrift and persistence. A short-term orientation values the past and present, and emphasizes respect for tradition and fulfilling social obligations.

Exhibit 4-4 on page 140 provides a summary of how a number of countries rate on these five dimensions. For instance, not surprisingly, most Asian

power distance
A national culture attribute describing the extent to which a society accepts that power in institutions and organizations is distributed unequally.

individualism
A national culture attribute describing a loosely knit social framework in which people emphasize only the care of themselves and their immediate family.

collectivism
A national culture attribute that describes a tight social framework in which people expect others in groups of which they are a part to look after them and protect them.

quantity of life
A national culture attribute describing the extent to which societal values are characterized by assertiveness and materialism.

quality of life
A national culture attribute that emphasizes relationships and concern for others.

uncertainty avoidance
A national culture attribute describing the extent to which a society feels threatened by uncertain and ambiguous situations and tries to avoid them.

long-term orientation
A national culture attribute that emphasizes the future, thrift, and persistence.

short-term orientation
A national culture attribute that emphasizes the past and present, respect for tradition, and fulfilling social obligation.

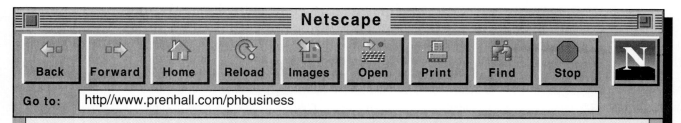

OB in the News

Ford Uses Generational "Value Groups" to Help Develop Cars

James C. Bulin, a mid-level design staffer at Ford Motor Co., has come up with an idea that is radically changing the way Ford designs its vehicles. He breaks potential buyers into generational value groups, then uses these data to tailor the design and marketing of a specific vehicle to a specific target audience.

Bulin has identified six distinct generations, each with shared traits and tastes that influence its car-buying habits. His six categories are:

Depression kids (born 1920–34). They always plan for a rainy day. They are also status seekers, preferring cars that are longer, lower, wider, and more colorful. They believe trucks belong on a farm or construction site.

Quiet generation (1935–45). Members of this generation prefer cars with individuality to generic look-alike vehicles. They have not embraced trucks, except for custom wheels.

Baby boomers (1946–64). They seek instant gratification and want others to think they make smart purchase decisions. They have embraced minivans and sport-utility vehicles.

Lost generation (1965–69). Members of this group feel disenfranchised because they grew up in the boomers' shadow. They're waiting for life to get better and are not affluent. They drive small sport-utility vehicles and off-beat niche vehicles.

Birth dearth (1970–77). These individual grew up in the rich 1980s and acquired a taste for excellence, which their jobs won't support. They drive sport-utility vehicles and practical sedans.

Baby boomlet (1978–present). Although they have a strong desire for the affluence of their parents' generation, they're unlikely to have as much money.

Their car choices are still forming.

Using these value groups, Bulin targeted the preferences of baby boomers. For instance, boomers equate strength with being trim and fit. So Ford made the F-150 look lean and muscular, narrowing the cab by 2 inches and lengthening it by 5 inches. They also added a rearward-swinging third door behind the front passenger door to ease entry and exit for boomers with growing children.

This approach has been remarkably effective. While the old model pickup got two-thirds of its sales from people over age 50, 80 percent of the new models are expected to be bought by boomers. Sales for the newly redesigned F-150s are up 18 percent over the older model.

Source: Based on K. Naughton, "How Ford's F-150 Lapped the Competition," *Business Week*, July 29, 1996, pp. 74–76.

Take It to the Net

We invite you to visit the Robbins page on the Prentice Hall Web site at:

http://www.prenhall.com/robbinsorgbeh

for this chapter's World Wide Web exercise.

Exhibit 4-4 Examples of Cultural Dimensions

Country	Power Distance	Individualism*	Quantity of Life**	Uncertainty Avoidance	Long-term Orientation***
China	High	Low	Moderate	Moderate	High
France	High	High	Moderate	High	Low
Germany	Low	High	High	Moderate	Moderate
Hong Kong	High	Low	High	Low	High
Indonesia	High	Low	Moderate	Low	Low
Japan	Moderate	Moderate	High	Moderate	Moderate
Netherlands	Low	High	Low	Moderate	Moderate
Russia	High	Moderate	Low	High	Low
United States	Low	High	High	Low	Low
West Africa	High	Low	Moderate	Moderate	Low

* A low score is synonymous with collectivism. ** A low score is synonymous with high quality of life. *** A low score is synonymous with a short-term orientation.
Source: Adapted from G. Hofstede, "Cultural Constraints in Management Theories," *Academy of Management Executive*, February 1993, p. 91.

countries are more collectivist than individualistic. On the other hand, the United States ranked highest among all countries surveyed on individualism.

IMPLICATIONS FOR OB Most of the concepts that currently make up the body of knowledge we call *organizational behavior* have been developed by Americans using American subjects within domestic contexts. A comprehensive study, for instance, of more than 11,000 articles published in 24 management and organizational behavior journals over a ten-year period revealed that approximately 80 percent of the studies were done in the United States and had been conducted by Americans.[25] Follow-up studies continue to confirm the lack of cross-cultural considerations in management and OB research.[26] What this means is that (1) not all OB theories and concepts are universally applicable to managing people around the world, especially in countries where work values are considerably different from those in the United States; and (2) you should take into consideration cultural values when trying to understand the behavior of people in different countries.

Attitudes

attitudes
Evaluative statements or judgments concerning objects, people, or events.

cognitive component of an attitude
The opinion or belief segment of an attitude.

affective component of an attitude
The emotional or feeling segment of an attitude.

Attitudes are evaluative statements—either favorable or unfavorable—concerning objects, people, or events. They reflect how one feels about something. When I say "I like my job," I am expressing my attitude about work.

Attitudes are not the same as values, but the two are interrelated. You can see this by looking at the three components of an attitude: cognition, affect, and behavior.[27]

The belief that "discrimination is wrong" is a value statement. Such an opinion is the **cognitive component** of an attitude. It sets the stage for the more critical part of an attitude—its **affective component**. Affect is the

From their earliest years, Japanese children are taught the value of working together. This socialization practice extends into the workplace, where employees work well as a team. The team of workers shown here at Japan's Yokogawa Electric, maker of industrial testing and measuring equipment, is able to make decisions about redesigning products in short periods of time while meeting the company's cost-cutting goals.

emotional or feeling segment of an attitude and is reflected in the statement "I don't like Jon because he discriminates against minorities." Finally, and we'll discuss this issue at considerable length later in this section, affect can lead to behavioral outcomes. The **behavioral component** of an attitude refers to an intention to behave in a certain way toward someone or something. So, to continue our example, I might choose to avoid Jon because of my feeling about him.

behavioral component of an attitude
An intention to behave in a certain way toward someone or something.

Viewing attitudes as made up of three components—cognition, affect, and behavior—is helpful toward understanding their complexity and the potential relationship between attitudes and behavior. But for clarity's sake, keep in mind that the term *attitude* essentially refers to the affect part of the three components.

Sources of Attitudes

Attitudes, like values, are acquired from parents, teachers, and peer group members. We are born with certain genetic predispositions.[28] Then, in our early years, we begin modeling our attitudes after those we admire, respect, or maybe even fear. We observe the way family and friends behave, and we shape our attitudes and behavior to align with theirs. People also imitate the attitudes of popular individuals and those they admire and respect. If the "right thing" is to favor eating at McDonald's, you're likely to hold that attitude.

In contrast to values, your attitudes are less stable. Advertising messages, for example, attempt to alter your attitudes toward a certain product or service: If the people at Ford can get you to hold a favorable feeling toward their cars, that attitude may lead to a desirable behavior (for them)—your purchase of a Ford product.

In organizations, attitudes are important because they affect job behavior. If workers believe, for example, that supervisors, auditors, bosses, and time-and-motion engineers are all in conspiracy to make employees work harder for the same or less money, then it makes sense to try to understand how these attitudes were formed, their relationship to actual job behavior, and how they might be changed.

Types of Attitudes

A person can have thousands of attitudes, but OB focuses our attention on a very limited number of job-related attitudes. These job-related attitudes tap positive or negative evaluations that employees hold about aspects of their work environment. Most of the research in OB has been concerned with three attitudes: job satisfaction, job involvement, and organizational commitment.[29]

◆ Most of the research in OB has been concerned with three attitudes: job satisfaction, job involvement, and organizational commitment.

JOB SATISFACTION The term *job satisfaction* refers to an individual's general attitude toward his or her job. A person with a high level of job satisfaction holds positive attitudes toward the job, while a person who is dissatisfied with his or her job holds negative attitudes about the job. When people speak of employee attitudes, more often than not they mean job satisfaction. In fact, the two are frequently used interchangeably. Because of the high importance OB researchers have given to job satisfaction, we'll review this attitude in considerable detail later in this chapter.

job involvement
The degree to which a person identifies with his or her job, actively participates in it, and considers his or her performance important to self-worth.

JOB INVOLVEMENT The term **job involvement** is a more recent addition to the OB literature.[30] While there isn't complete agreement over what the term means, a workable definition states that job involvement measures the degree to which a person identifies psychologically with his or her job and considers his or her perceived performance level important to self-worth.[31] Employees with a high level of job involvement strongly identify with and really care about the kind of work they do.

High levels of job involvement have been found to be related to fewer absences and lower resignation rates.[32] However, it seems to more consistently predict turnover than absenteeism, accounting for as much as 16 percent of the variance in the former.[33]

organizational commitment
The degree to which an employee identifies with a particular organization and its goals, and wishes to maintain membership in the organization.

ORGANIZATIONAL COMMITMENT The third job attitude we shall discuss is **organizational commitment**, which is defined as a state in which an employee identifies with a particular organization and its goals, and wishes to maintain membership in the organization.[34] So, high *job involvement* means identifying with one's specific job, while high *organizational commitment* means identifying with one's employing organization.

As with job involvement, the research evidence demonstrates negative relationships between organizational commitment and both absenteeism and turnover.[35] In fact, studies demonstrate that an individual's level of organizational commitment is a better indicator of turnover than the far more frequently used job satisfaction predictor, explaining as much as 34 percent of the variance.[36] Organizational commitment is probably a better predictor because it is a more global and enduring response to the organization as a whole than is job satisfaction.[37] An employee may be dissatisfied with his or her particular job and consider it a temporary condition, yet not be dissatisfied with the organization as a whole. But when dissatisfaction spreads to the organization itself, individuals are more likely to consider resigning.

Attitudes and Consistency

Did you ever notice how people change what they say so it doesn't contradict what they do? Perhaps a friend of yours has consistently argued that the quality of American cars isn't up to that of the imports and that he'd never own anything but a foreign import. But his dad gives him a late-model American-made car, and suddenly they're not so bad. Or, when going through sorority rush, a new freshman believes that sororities are good and that pledging a sorority is important. If she fails to make a sorority, however, she may say, "I recognized that sorority life isn't all it's cracked up to be, anyway!"

Research has generally concluded that people seek consistency among their attitudes and between their attitudes and their behavior. This means that individuals seek to reconcile divergent attitudes and align their attitudes and behavior so they appear rational and consistent. When there is an inconsistency, forces are initiated to return the individual to an equilibrium state where attitudes and behavior are again consistent. This can be done by altering either the attitudes or the behavior, or by developing a rationalization for the discrepancy.

For example, a recruiter for the ABC Company, whose job it is to visit college campuses, identify qualified job candidates, and sell them on the advantages of ABC as a place to work, would be in conflict if he personally

The enthusiasm of these Pep Boys employees demonstrates an attitude that fits with their company's philosophy of giving customers extraordinary "Banner Service." High organizational commitment means employees work hard to ensure that customers drive away happy with their car-repair and maintenance products and service. Committed employees are important to Pep Boys, as the company's reputation of offering excellent service facilitates the opening of new stores and service centers throughout the country.

believes the ABC Company has poor working conditions and few opportunities for new college graduates. This recruiter could, over time, find his attitudes toward the ABC Company becoming more positive. He may, in effect, brainwash himself by continually articulating the merits of working for ABC. Another alternative would be for the recruiter to become overtly negative about ABC and the opportunities within the firm for prospective candidates. The original enthusiasm that the recruiter may have shown would dwindle, probably to be replaced by open cynicism toward the company. Finally, the recruiter might acknowledge that ABC is an undesirable place to work, but think that, as a professional recruiter, his obligation is to present the positive side of working for the company. He might further rationalize that no workplace is perfect; therefore, his job is not to present both sides of the issue, but rather to present a rosy picture of the company.

Cognitive Dissonance Theory

Can we also assume from this consistency principle that an individual's behavior can always be predicted if we know his or her attitude on a subject? If Mr. Jones views the company's pay level as too low, will a substantial increase in his pay change his behavior, that is, make him work harder? The answer to this question is, unfortunately, more complex than merely a "Yes" or "No."

cognitive dissonance
Any incompatibility between two or more attitudes or between behavior and attitudes.

Leon Festinger, in the late 1950s, proposed the theory of **cognitive dissonance**.[38] This theory sought to explain the linkage between attitudes and behavior. Dissonance means an inconsistency. Cognitive dissonance refers to any incompatibility that an individual might perceive between two or more of his or her attitudes, or between his or her behavior and attitudes. Festinger argued that any form of inconsistency is uncomfortable and that individuals will attempt to reduce the dissonance and, hence, the discomfort. Therefore, individuals will seek a stable state where there is a minimum of dissonance.

Of course, no individual can completely avoid dissonance. You know that cheating on your income tax is wrong, but you "fudge" the numbers a bit every year, and hope you're not audited. Or you tell your children to brush after every meal, but *you* don't. So how do people cope? Festinger would propose that the desire to reduce dissonance would be determined by the *importance* of the elements creating the dissonance, the degree of *influence* the individual believes he or she has over the elements, and the *rewards* that may be involved in dissonance.

If the elements creating the dissonance are relatively unimportant, the pressure to correct this imbalance will be low. However, say that a corporate manager—Mrs. Smith—believes strongly that no company should pollute the air or water. Unfortunately, Mrs. Smith, because of the requirements of her job, is placed in the position of having to make decisions that would trade off her company's profitability against her attitudes on pollution. She knows that dumping the company's sewage into the local river (which we shall assume is legal) is in the best economic interest of her firm. What will she do? Clearly, Mrs. Smith is experiencing a high degree of cognitive dissonance. Because of the importance of the elements in this example, we cannot expect Mrs. Smith to ignore the inconsistency. There are several paths that she can follow to deal with her dilemma. She can change her behavior (stop polluting the river). Or she can reduce dissonance by concluding that the dissonant behavior is not so

Netscape

| ⇦🔲 Back | 🔲⇨ Forward | 🏠 Home | 🔄 Reload | 🖼 Images | ⇨ Open | 🖨 Print | 🔍 Find | ⬤ Stop |

Go to: http//www.prenhall.com/phbusiness

OB in the News

"How Do Tobacco Executives Live with Themselves?"

How do tobacco executives explain their responsibility for a product that kills more than 420,000 Americans a year? How do they reject the overwhelming evidence connecting smoking with lung and throat cancer, emphysema, and heart disease? By insisting that direct causation has not been proved? These executives are quick to point out to critics that their product is legal, that they don't encourage nonsmokers to take up smoking, and that what they are really promoting is freedom of choice.

The following is from an interview with Steven C. Parrish, 44, general counsel and senior vice president for external affairs, Philip Morris, U.S.A. He and his wife have a daughter, 11, and a son, 4. For the record, he does smoke cigarettes.

After graduating from the University of Missouri, Parrish joined a Kansas City law firm and represented Philip Morris. The company approached Parrish about working for it full time.

"Philip Morris is a great company in terms of its business success, its reputation, and all that sort of thing. The people really impressed me. And I really like representing the tobacco workers, who run the machinery and make the cigarettes. Really good people—the kind I thought I'd represent when I was growing up [in a small Missouri town]. . . . I didn't have any qualms about joining a tobacco company."

"A year or two ago, my daughter came home from school, and said, 'I have a homework assignment I need you to help me with. Tomorrow we're going to talk about drugs like marijuana, cocaine, and alcohol. We're also going to talk about cigarettes and whether or not they're addictive. I want to know what you think about cigarettes.' And I told her that a lot of people believe that cig-arette smoking is addictive but I don't believe it. And I told her the Surgeon General says some 40 million people have quit smoking on their own. But if she asked me about the health consequences, I would tell her that I certainly don't think it's safe to smoke. It's a risk factor for lung cancer. For heart disease. But it's a choice. We're confronted with choices all the time. Still, I'd have to tell her that it might be a bad idea. I don't know. But it might be."

"You might say that we ought to do everything we can do reasonably to make sure that nobody ever smokes another cigarette. But you wouldn't say that people who work for tobacco companies can't look themselves in the mirror because they're somehow lesser human beings than people who work for a drug company or a steel company."

Based on R. Rosenblatt, *The New York Times Magazine*, March 20, 1994, pp. 34–41.

Take It to the Net

We invite you to visit the Robbins page on the Prentice Hall Web site at:

http://www.prenhall.com/robbinsorgbeh

for this chapter's World Wide Web exercise.

important after all ("I've got to make a living, and in my role as a corporate decision maker, I often have to place the good of my company above that of the environment or society"). A third alternative would be for Mrs. Smith to change her attitude ("There is nothing wrong in polluting the river"). Still another choice would be to seek out more consonant elements to outweigh the dissonant ones ("The benefits to society from manufacturing our products more than offset the cost to society of the resulting water pollution").

The degree of influence that individuals believe they have over the elements will have an impact on how they will react to the dissonance. If they perceive the dissonance to be an uncontrollable result—something over which they have no choice—they are less likely to be receptive to attitude change. If, for example, the dissonance-producing behavior is required as a result of the boss's directive, the pressure to reduce dissonance would be less than if the behavior was performed voluntarily. While dissonance exists, it can be rationalized and justified.

Rewards also influence the degree to which individuals are motivated to reduce dissonance. High rewards accompanying high dissonance tend to reduce the tension inherent in the dissonance. The rewards act to reduce dissonance by increasing the consistency side of the individual's balance sheet.

These moderating factors suggest that just because individuals experience dissonance they will not necessarily move directly toward consistency, that is, toward reduction of this dissonance. If the issues underlying the dissonance are of minimal importance, if an individual perceives that the dissonance is externally imposed and is substantially uncontrollable by him or her, or if rewards are significant enough to offset the dissonance, the individual will not be under great tension to reduce the dissonance.

What are the organizational implications of the theory of cognitive dissonance? It can help to predict the propensity to engage in attitude and behavioral change. If individuals are required, for example, by the demands of their job to say or do things that contradict their personal attitude, they will tend to modify their attitude in order to make it compatible with the cognition of what they have said or done. Additionally, the greater the dissonance—after it has been moderated by importance, choice, and reward factors—the greater the pressures to reduce it.

Measuring the A–B Relationship

We have maintained throughout this chapter that attitudes affect behavior. The early research work on attitudes assumed that they were causally related to behavior; that is, the attitudes that people hold determine what they do. Common sense, too, suggests a relationship. Is it not logical that people watch television programs that they say they like or that employees try to avoid assignments they find distasteful?

However, in the late 1960s, this assumed relationship between attitudes and behavior (A–B) was challenged by a review of the research.[39] Based on an evaluation of a number of studies that investigated the A–B relationship, the reviewer concluded that attitudes were unrelated to behavior or, at best, only slightly related.[40] More recent research has demonstrated that the A–B relationship can be improved by taking moderating contingency variables into consideration.

MODERATING VARIABLES   One thing that improves our chances of finding significant A–B relationships is the use of both specific attitudes and specific behaviors.[41] It is one thing to talk about a person's attitude toward "preserving the environment" and another to speak of his or her attitude toward recycling. The more specific the attitude we are measuring, and the more specific we are in identifying a related behavior, the greater the probability that we can show a relationship between A and B. If you ask people today whether or not they are concerned about preserving the environment, most will probably say "Yes." That doesn't mean, however, that they separate out recyclable items from their garbage. The correlation between a question that asks about concern for protecting the environment and recycling may be only +.20 or so. But as you make the question more specific—by asking, for example, about the degree of personal obligation one feels to separate recyclable items—the A–B relationship is likely to reach +.50 or higher.

Another moderator is social constraints on behavior. Discrepancies between attitudes and behavior may occur because the social pressures on the individual to behave in a certain way may hold exceptional power.[42] Group pressures, for instance, may explain why an employee who holds strong antiunion attitudes attends prounion organizing meetings.

Still another moderating variable is experience with the attitude in question.[43] The A–B relationship is likely to be much stronger if the attitude being evaluated refers to something with which the individual has experience. For instance, most of us will respond to a questionnaire on almost any issue. But is my attitude toward starving fish in the Amazon any indication of whether or not I'd donate to a fund to save these fish? Probably not! Getting the views of college students, with no work experience, on job factors that are important in determining whether or not they would stay put in a job is an example of an attitude response that is unlikely to predict much in terms of actual turnover behavior.

SELF-PERCEPTION THEORY   Although most A–B studies yield positive results[44]—that attitudes do influence behavior—the relationship tends to be weak before adjustments are made for moderating variables. But requiring specificity, an absence of social constraints, and experience in order to get a meaningful correlation imposes severe limitations on making generalizations about the A–B relationship. This has prompted some researchers to take another direction—to look at whether or not behavior influences attitudes. This view, called **self-perception theory**, has generated some encouraging findings. Let's briefly review the theory.[45]

When asked about an attitude toward some object, individuals recall their behavior relevant to that object and then infer their attitude from their past behavior. So if an employee were asked about her feelings about being a training specialist at U.S. West, she would likely think, "I've had this same job at U.S. West as a trainer for ten years, so I must like it!" Self-perception theory, therefore, argues that attitudes are used, *after the fact*, to make sense out of an action that has already occurred rather than as devices that precede and guide action.

Self-perception theory has been well supported.[46] While the traditional attitude–behavior relationship is generally

self-perception theory
Attitudes are used after the fact to make sense out of an action that has already occurred.

◆   It seems that we are very good at finding reasons for what we do, but not so good at doing what we find reasons for.

positive, it is also weak. In contrast, the behavior–attitude relationship is quite strong. So what can we conclude? It seems that we're very good at finding reasons for what we do, but not so good at doing what we find reasons for.[47]

An Application: Attitude Surveys

attitude surveys
Eliciting responses from employees through questionnaires about how they feel about their jobs, work groups, supervisors, and/or the organization.

The preceding review should not discourage us from using attitudes to predict behavior. In an organizational context, most of the attitudes management would seek to inquire about would be ones with which employees have some experience. If the attitudes in question are specifically stated, management should obtain information that can be valuable in guiding their decisions relative to these employees. But how does management get information about employee attitudes? The most popular method is through the use of **attitude surveys**.[48]

Exhibit 4-5 illustrates what an attitude survey might look like. Typically, attitude surveys present the employee with a set of statements or questions. Ideally, the items are tailored to obtain the specific information that management desires. An attitude score is achieved by summing up responses to individual questionnaire items. These scores can then be averaged for job groups, departments, divisions, or the organization as a whole.

Results from attitude surveys can frequently surprise management. For instance, Michael Gilliland owns and operates a chain of 12 food markets.[49] He and his management team developed a ten-item job-satisfaction questionnaire, which they administer to all employees twice a year. Recently Gilliland was surprised to find the worst complaints coming from employees at the store with the best working conditions and the most benefits. Careful analysis of the results uncovered that, although the manager at this store was well liked, employees were frustrated because he was behind on their performance

Exhibit 4-5 Sample Attitude Survey

Please answer each of the following statements using the following rating scale:

5 = Strongly agree
4 = Agree
3 = Undecided
2 = Disagree
1 = Strongly disagree

Statement	Rating
1. This company is a pretty good place to work.	___
2. I can get ahead in this company if I make the effort.	___
3. This company's wage rates are competitive with those of other companies.	___
4. Employee promotion decisions are handled fairly.	___
5. I understand the various fringe benefits the company offers.	___
6. My job makes the best use of my abilities.	___
7. My workload is challenging but not burdensome.	___
8. I have trust and confidence in my boss.	___
9. I feel free to tell my boss what I think.	___
10. I know what my boss expects of me.	___

reviews and had failed to fire a particularly unproductive employee. As one of Gilliland's associates put it, "We'd assumed it would be the happiest store, but it wasn't."

A corporatewide attitude survey at BP Exploration revealed that employees were unhappy with the way their direct superiors managed them.[50] In response, management introduced a formal upward-appraisal system which allows the company's 12,000 employees to evaluate their boss's managerial performance. Now managers pay a lot more attention to the needs of their employees because their employees' opinions play an important part in determining the manager's future in the organization.

Using attitude surveys on a regular basis provides managers with valuable feedback on how employees perceive their working conditions. Consistent with our discussion of perceptions in the previous chapter, the policies and practices that management views as objective and fair may be seen as inequitable by employees in general or by certain groups of employees. That these distorted perceptions have led to negative attitudes about the job and organization should be important to management. This is because employee behaviors are based on perceptions, not reality. Remember, the employee who quits because she believes she is underpaid—when, in fact, management has objective data to support that her salary is highly competitive—is just as gone as if she had actually been underpaid. The use of regular attitude surveys can alert management to potential problems and employees' intentions early so that action can be taken to prevent repercussions.[51]

Attitudes and Workforce Diversity

Managers are increasingly concerned with changing employee attitudes to reflect shifting perspectives on racial, gender, and other diversity issues. A comment to a co-worker of the opposite sex, which 15 years ago might have been

Diversity training at Harvard Pilgrim Health Care emphasizes practical conflict management. The managed care organization uses real-life case studies of situations employees face daily. The training includes role-playing workshops to teach employees how to respond to differences among people with sensitivity and respect. Harvard Pilgrim serves a growing number of racial and ethnic minority customers and a large gay and lesbian population. Its diversity training helps employees in providing care to diverse customers who demand that health care workers are not judgmental.

From Concepts to Skills

Changing Attitudes

Can you change unfavorable employee attitudes? Sometimes! It depends on who you are, the strength of the employee's attitude, the magnitude of the change, and the technique you choose to try to change the attitude.[52]

Employees are most likely to respond to change efforts made by someone who is liked, credible, and convincing. If people like you, they're more apt to identify and adopt your message. Credibility implies trust, expertise, and objectivity. So you're more likely to change an employee's attitude if that employee sees you as believable, knowledgeable about what you're talking about, and unbiased in your presentation. Finally, successful attitude change is enhanced when you present your arguments clearly and persuasively.

It's easier to change an employee's attitude if he or she isn't strongly committed to it. Conversely, the stronger the belief about the attitude, the harder it is to change it. In addition, attitudes that have been expressed publicly are more difficult to change because it requires one to admit he or she has made a mistake.

It's easier to change attitudes when that change isn't very significant. To get an employee to accept a new attitude that varies greatly from his or her current position requires more effort. It may also threaten other deeply held attitudes and create increased dissonance.

All attitude-change techniques are not equally effective across situations. Oral persuasion techniques are most effective when you use a positive, tactful tone; present strong evidence to support your position; tailor your argument to the listener; use logic; and support your evidence by appealing to the employee's fears, frustrations, and other emotions. But people are more likely to embrace change when they can experience it. The use of training sessions where employees share and personalize experiences, and practice new behaviors, can be powerful stimulants for change. Consistent with self-perception theory, changes in behavior can lead to changes in attitudes.

taken as a compliment, can today become a career-limiting episode.[53] As such, organizations are investing in training to help reshape attitudes of employees.

A recent survey of U.S. organizations with 100 or more employees found that 47 percent of them sponsored some sort of diversity training.[54] Some examples: Police officers in Escondido, California receive 36 hours of diversity training each year. Pacific Gas & Electric Co. requires a minimum of four hours of training for its 12,000 employees. The Federal Aviation Administration sponsors a mandatory eight-hour diversity seminar for employees of its Western Pacific region.

What do these diversity programs look like and how do they address attitude change?[55] They almost all include a self-evaluation phase. People are pressed to examine themselves and to confront ethnic and cultural stereotypes they might hold. Then participants typically take part in group discussions or panels with representatives from diverse groups. So, for instance, a Hmong man might describe his family's life in Southeast Asia, and explain why they resettled in California; or a lesbian might describe how she discovered her sexual identity, and the reaction of her friends and family when she came out.

Additional activities designed to change attitudes include arranging for people to do volunteer work in community or social service centers in order to meet face-to-face with individuals and groups from diverse backgrounds and using exercises that let participants feel what it's like to be different. For example, when participants see the film *Eye of the Beholder*, where people are segregated and stereotyped according to their eye color, participants see what it's like to be judged by something they have no control over.

Job Satisfaction

We have already discussed job satisfaction briefly—earlier in this chapter as well as in chapter 1. In this section, we want to dissect the concept more carefully. How do we measure job satisfaction? What determines job satisfaction? What is its effect on employee productivity, absenteeism, and turnover rates? We answer each of these questions in this section.

Measuring Job Satisfaction

We've previously defined job satisfaction as an individual's general attitude toward his or her job. This definition is clearly a very broad one.[56] Yet this is inherent in the concept. Remember, a person's job is more than just the obvious activities of shuffling papers, waiting on customers, or driving a truck. Jobs require interaction with co-workers and bosses, following organizational rules and policies, meeting performance standards, living with working conditions that are often less than ideal, and the like.[57] This means that an employee's assessment of how satisfied or dissatisfied he or she is with his or her job is a complex summation of a number of discrete job elements. How, then, do we measure the concept?

The two most widely used approaches are a *single global rating* and a *summation score* made up of a number of job facets. The single global rating method is nothing more than asking individuals to respond to one question, such as "All things considered, how satisfied are you with your job?" Respondents then reply by circling a number between one and five that corresponds to answers from "highly satisfied" to "highly dissatisfied." The other approach—a summation of job facets—is more sophisticated. It identifies key elements in a job and asks for the employee's feelings about each. Typical factors that would be included are the nature of the work, supervision, present pay, promotion opportunities, and relations with co-workers.[58] These factors are rated on a standardized scale and then added up to create an overall job satisfaction score.

Is one of the foregoing approaches superior to the other? Intuitively, it would seem that summing up responses to a number of job factors would achieve a more accurate evaluation of job satisfaction. The research, however, doesn't support this intuition.[59] This is one of those rare instances in which simplicity wins out over complexity. Comparisons of one-question global ratings with the more lengthy summation-of-job-factors method indicate that the former is more valid. The best explanation for this outcome is that the concept of job satisfaction is inherently so broad that the single question actually becomes a more inclusive measure.

What Determines Job Satisfaction?

We now turn to the question: What work-related variables determine job satisfaction? An extensive review of the literature indicates that the more important factors conducive to job satisfaction are mentally challenging work, equitable rewards, supportive working conditions, and supportive colleagues.[60] To this list, we'd also add the importance of a good personality–job fit and an individual's genetic disposition (some people are just inherently upbeat and positive about all things, including their job).

MENTALLY CHALLENGING WORK Employees tend to prefer jobs that give them opportunities to use their skills and abilities and offer a variety of tasks, freedom, and feedback on how well they are doing. These characteristics make work mentally challenging. Jobs that have too little challenge create boredom, but too much challenge creates frustration and feelings of failure. Under conditions of moderate challenge, most employees will experience pleasure and satisfaction.[61]

EQUITABLE REWARDS Employees want pay systems and promotion policies that they perceive as being just, unambiguous, and in line with their expectations. When pay is seen as fair based on job demands, individual skill level, and community pay standards, satisfaction is likely to result. Of course, not everyone seeks money. Many people willingly accept less money to work in a preferred location or in a less demanding job or to have greater discretion in the work they do and the hours they work. But the key in linking pay to satisfaction is not the absolute amount one is paid; rather, it is the perception of fairness. Similarly, employees seek fair promotion policies and practices. Promotions provide opportunities for personal growth, more responsibilities, and increased social status. Individuals who perceive that promotion decisions are made in a fair and just manner, therefore, are likely to experience satisfaction from their jobs.[62]

SUPPORTIVE WORKING CONDITIONS Employees are concerned with their work environment for both personal comfort and facilitating doing a good job. Studies demonstrate that employees prefer physical surroundings that are not dangerous or uncomfortable. Temperature, light, noise, and other environmental factors should not be at either extreme—for example, having too much heat or too little light. Additionally, most employees prefer working relatively close to home, in clean and relatively modern facilities, and with adequate tools and equipment.

SUPPORTIVE COLLEAGUES People get more out of work than merely money or tangible achievements. For most employees, work also fills the need for social interaction. Not surprisingly, therefore, having friendly and supportive co-workers leads to increased job satisfaction. The behavior of one's boss also is a major determinant of satisfaction. Studies generally find that employee satisfaction is increased when the immediate supervisor is understanding and friendly, offers praise for good performance, listens to employees' opinions, and shows a personal interest in them.

◆ Having friendly and supportive co-workers leads to increased job satisfaction.

Supportive colleagues made Ronna Adams, a bookkeeper, feel like "Queen for a Day" when she celebrated her 20th anniversary with Walgreen's. Her co-workers honored her with a giant surprise party. Research indicates that supportive colleagues like Ronna's lead to increased job satisfaction. In an industry noted for high turnover, supportive colleagues contribute to keeping Walgreen's resignations low.

DON'T FORGET THE PERSONALITY–JOB FIT! In chapter 2, we presented Holland's personality–job fit theory. As you remember, one of Holland's conclusions was that high agreement between an employee's personality and occupation results in a more satisfied individual. His logic was essentially this: People with personality types congruent with their chosen vocations should find that they have the right talents and abilities to meet the demands of their jobs. Thus, they are more likely to be successful on those jobs and, because of this success, have a greater probability of achieving high satisfaction from their work. Studies to replicate Holland's conclusions have been almost universally supportive.[63] It's important, therefore, to add this to our list of factors that determine job satisfaction.

IT'S IN THE GENES As much as 30 percent of an individual's satisfaction can be explained by heredity.[64] Analysis of satisfaction data for a selected sample of individuals over a 50-year period found that individual results were consistently stable over time, even when these people changed the employer for whom they worked and their occupation. This and other research suggests that a significant portion of some people's satisfaction is genetically determined. That is, an individual's disposition toward life—positive or negative—is established by his or her genetic makeup, holds over time, and carries over into his or her disposition toward work. Given this evidence, it may well be that, at least for some employees, there isn't much managers can do to influence employee satisfaction. Manipulating job characteristics, working conditions, rewards, and the job fit may have little effect. This suggests managers should focus attention on employee selection: If you want satisfied workers, make sure you screen out the negative, maladjusted, troublemaking fault-finders who derive little satisfaction in anything about their jobs.[65]

The Effect of Job Satisfaction on Employee Performance

Managers' interest in job satisfaction tends to center on its effect on employee performance. Researchers have recognized this interest, so we find a large number of studies that have been designed to assess the impact of job satisfaction on employee productivity, absenteeism, and turnover. Let's look at the current state of our knowledge.

SATISFACTION AND PRODUCTIVITY A number of reviews were done in the 1950s and 1960s, covering dozens of studies that sought to establish the relationship between satisfaction and productivity.[66] These reviews could find no consistent relationship. In the 1990s, though the studies are far from unambiguous, we can make some sense out of the evidence.

The early views on the satisfaction–performance relationship can be essentially summarized in the statement "a happy worker is a productive worker." Much of the paternalism shown by managers in the 1930s, 1940s, and 1950s—forming company bowling teams and credit unions, having company picnics, providing counseling services for employees, training supervisors to be sensitive to the concerns of subordinates—was done to make workers happy. But belief in the happy worker thesis was based more on wishful thinking than hard evidence. A careful review of the research indicated that if there is a positive relationship between satisfaction and productivity, the correlations are consistently low—in the vicinity of +0.14.[67] This means that no more than 2 percent of the variance in output can be accounted for by employee satisfaction. However, introduction of moderating variables has improved the relationship.[68] For example, the relationship is stronger when the employee's behavior is not constrained or controlled by outside factors. An employee's productivity on machine-paced jobs, for instance, is going to be much more influenced by the speed of the machine than his or her level of satisfaction. Similarly, a stockbroker's productivity is largely constrained by the general movement of the stock market. When the market is moving up and volume is high, both satisfied and dissatisfied brokers are going to ring up lots of commissions. Conversely, when the market is in the doldrums, the level of broker satisfaction is not likely to mean much. Job level also seems to be an important moderating variable. The satisfaction–performance correlations are stronger for higher-level employees. Thus, we might expect the relationship to be more relevant for individuals in professional, supervisory, and managerial positions.

Another point of concern in the satisfaction–productivity issue is the direction of the causal arrow. Most of the studies on the relationship used research designs that could not prove cause and effect. Studies that have controlled for this possibility indicate that the more valid conclusion is that productivity leads to satisfaction rather than the other way around.[69] If you do a good job, you intrinsically feel good about it. Additionally, assuming that the organization rewards productivity, your higher productivity should increase verbal recognition, your pay level, and probabilities for promotion. These rewards, in turn, increase your level of satisfaction with the job.

The most recent research provides renewed support for the original satisfaction–performance relationship.[70] When satisfaction and productivity data are gathered for the organization as a whole, rather than at the individual level, we find that organizations with more satisfied employees tended to be more effective than organizations with less satisfied employees. If this conclusion can be reproduced in additional studies, it may well be that the reason we haven't gotten strong support for the *satisfaction causes productivity thesis* is that studies have focused on individuals rather than the organization and that individual-level measures of productivity don't take into consideration all the interactions and complexities in the work process.

SATISFACTION AND ABSENTEEISM We find a consistent negative relationship between satisfaction and absenteeism, but the correlation is moderate—usually less than +0.40.[71] While it certainly makes sense that dissatisfied employees are more likely to miss work, other factors have an impact on the relationship and reduce the correlation coefficient. For example, remember our discussion of sick pay versus well pay in chapter 2. Organizations that provide liberal sick leave benefits are encouraging all their employees—including those who are highly satisfied—to take days off. Assuming that you have a reasonable number of varied interests, you can find work satisfying and yet still take off work to enjoy a three-day weekend, tan yourself on a warm summer day, or watch the World Series on television if those days come free with no penalties. Also, as with productivity, outside factors can act to reduce the correlation.

An excellent illustration of how satisfaction directly leads to attendance, where there is a minimum impact from other factors, is a study done at Sears, Roebuck.[72] Satisfaction data were available on employees at Sears's two headquarters in Chicago and New York. Additionally, it is important to note that Sears's policy was not to permit employees to be absent from work for avoidable reasons without penalty. The occurrence of a freak April 2 snowstorm in Chicago created the opportunity to compare employee attendance at the Chicago office with attendance in New York, where the weather was quite nice. The interesting dimension in this study is that the snowstorm gave the Chicago employees a built-in excuse not to come to work. The storm crippled the city's transportation, and individuals knew they could miss work this day with no penalty. This natural experiment permitted the comparison of attendance records for satisfied and dissatisfied employees at two locations—one where you were expected to be at work (with normal pressures for attendance) and the other where you were free to choose with no penalty involved. If satisfaction leads to attendance, where there is an absence of outside factors, the more satisfied employees should have come to work in Chicago, while dissatisfied employees should have stayed home. The study found that on this particular April 2 absenteeism rates in New York were just as high for satisfied groups of workers as for dissatisfied groups. But in Chicago, the workers with high satisfaction scores had much higher attendance than did those with lower satisfaction levels. These findings are exactly what we would have expected if satisfaction is negatively correlated with absenteeism.

SATISFACTION AND TURNOVER Satisfaction is also negatively related to turnover, but the correlation is stronger than what we found for absenteeism.[73] Yet, again, other factors such as labor market conditions, expectations about alternative job opportunities, and length of tenure with the organization are important constraints on the actual decision to leave one's current job.[74]

Evidence indicates that an important moderator of the satisfaction–turnover relationship is the employee's level of performance.[75] Specifically, level of satisfaction is less important in predicting turnover for superior

Employee turnover is so high in the hair salon business that it's said stylists pass through salons like they are revolving doors. But Kay Hirai, owner of Studio 904 salons, found a way to keep her employees happy. Because in most salons stylists are paid in commissions and tips, they tend to guard their clients. Hirai has her stylists work as teams and pays them a salary plus benefits such as medical and dental coverage, paid vacations, and sick days. She posts daily, weekly, and monthly financial results and distributes 25 percent of her profits to employees as bonuses every two weeks. Hirai's stylists are happy because they are not competing with co-workers, and the salons benefit by an ever-growing client base.

performers. Why? The organization typically makes considerable efforts to keep these people. They get pay raises, praise, recognition, increased promotional opportunities, and so forth. Just the opposite tends to apply to poor performers. Few attempts are made by the organization to retain them. There may even be subtle pressures to encourage them to quit. We would expect, therefore, that job satisfaction is more important in influencing poor performers to stay than superior performers. Regardless of level of satisfaction, the latter are more likely to remain with the organization because the receipt of recognition, praise, and other rewards gives them more reasons for staying.

Consistent with our previous discussion, we shouldn't be surprised to find that a person's general disposition toward life also moderates the satisfaction–turnover relationship.[76] Specifically, some individuals generally gripe more than others and such individuals, when dissatisfied with their jobs, are less likely to quit than those who are more positively disposed toward life. So if two workers report the same level of job dissatisfaction, the one most likely to quit is the one with the highest predisposition to be happy or satisfied in general.

How Employees Can Express Dissatisfaction

One final point before we leave the issue of job satisfaction: Employee dissatisfaction can be expressed in a number of ways.[77] For example, rather than quit, employees can complain, be insubordinate, steal organizational property, or shirk a part of their work responsibilities. Exhibit 4-6 offers four responses that differ from one another along two dimensions: constructiveness/destructiveness and activity/passivity. They are defined as follows:[78]

exit
Dissatisfaction expressed through behavior directed toward leaving the organization.

◆ **Exit**: Behavior directed toward leaving the organization, including looking for a new position as well as resigning.

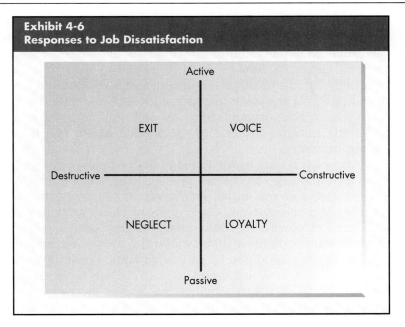

Exhibit 4-6
Responses to Job Dissatisfaction

Active

EXIT   VOICE

Destructive ——————————— Constructive

NEGLECT   LOYALTY

Passive

Source: C. Rusbult and D. Lowery, "When Bureaucrats Get the Blues," *Journal of Applied Social Psychology*, Vol. 15, No. 1(1985), p. 83. With permission.

◆ **Voice**: Actively and constructively attempting to improve conditions, including suggesting improvements, discussing problems with superiors, and some forms of union activity.

◆ **Loyalty**: Passively but optimistically waiting for conditions to improve, including speaking up for the organization in the face of external criticism and trusting the organization and its management to "do the right thing."

◆ **Neglect**: Passively allowing conditions to worsen, including chronic absenteeism or lateness, reduced effort, and increased error rate.

voice
Dissatisfaction expressed through active and constructive attempts to improve conditions.

loyalty
Dissatisfaction expressed by passively waiting for conditions to improve.

neglect
Dissatisfaction expressed through allowing conditions to worsen.

Exit and neglect behaviors encompass our performance variables—productivity, absenteeism, and turnover. But this model expands employee response to include voice and loyalty—constructive behaviors that allow individuals to tolerate unpleasant situations or to revive satisfactory working conditions. It helps us to understand situations, such as those sometimes found among unionized workers, where low job satisfaction is coupled with low turnover.[79] Union members often express dissatisfaction through the grievance procedure or through formal contract negotiations. These voice mechanisms allow the union members to continue in their jobs while convincing themselves that they are acting to improve the situation.

Summary and Implications for Managers

Why is it important to know an individual's values? Although they don't have a direct impact on behavior, values strongly influence a person's attitudes. So knowledge of an individual's value system can provide insight into his or her attitudes.

Given that people's values differ, managers can use the Rokeach Value Survey to assess potential employees and determine if their values align with the dominant values of the organization. An employee's performance and satisfaction are likely to be higher if his or her values fit well with the organization. For instance, the person who places high importance on imagination, independence, and freedom is likely to be poorly matched with an organization that seeks conformity from its employees. Managers are more likely to appreciate, evaluate positively, and allocate rewards to employees who "fit in," and employees are more likely to be satisfied if they perceive that they do fit. This argues for management to strive during the selection of new employees to find job candidates who not only have the ability, experience, and motivation to perform, but also a value system that is compatible with the organization's.

Managers should be interested in their employees' attitudes because attitudes give warnings of potential problems and because they influence behavior. Satisfied and committed employees, for instance, have lower rates of turnover and absenteeism. Given that managers want to keep resignations and absences down—especially among their more productive employees—they will want to do those things that will generate positive job attitudes.

Managers should also be aware that employees will try to reduce cognitive dissonance. More important, dissonance can be managed. If employees are required to engage in activities that appear inconsistent to them or that are at odds with their attitudes, the pressures to reduce the resulting dissonance are lessened when the employee perceives that the dissonance is externally imposed and is beyond his or her control or if the rewards are significant enough to offset the dissonance.

For Review

1. Contrast the Protestant work ethic, existential, pragmatic, and generation X typologies with the terminal values identified in the Rokeach Value Survey.
2. Contrast the cognitive and affective components of an attitude.
3. What is cognitive dissonance and how is it related to attitudes?
4. What is self-perception theory? How does it increase our ability to predict behavior?
5. What contingency factors can improve the statistical relationship between attitudes and behavior?
6. What role does genetics play in determining an individual's job satisfaction?
7. Are happy workers productive workers?
8. What is the relationship between job satisfaction and absenteeism? Turnover? Which is the stronger relationship?
9. How can managers get employees to more readily accept working with colleagues who are different from themselves?
10. Contrast exit, voice, loyalty, and neglect as employee responses to job dissatisfaction.

For Discussion

1. "Thirty-five years ago, young employees we hired were ambitious, conscientious, hardworking, and honest. Today's young workers don't have the same values." Do you agree or disagree with this manager's comments? Support your position.

2. Do you think there might be any positive and significant relationship between the possession of certain personal values and successful career progression in organizations like Merrill Lynch, the AFL-CIO, and the city of Cleveland's police department? Discuss.

3. "Managers should do everything they can to enhance the job satisfaction of their employees." Do you agree or disagree? Support your position.

4. Discuss the advantages and disadvantages of using regular attitude surveys to monitor employee job satisfaction.

5. When employees are asked whether they would again choose the same work or whether they would want their children to follow in their footsteps, typically less than half answer in the affirmative. What, if anything, do you think this implies about employee job satisfaction?

The Importance of High Job Satisfaction

The importance of job satisfaction is obvious. Managers should be concerned with the level of job satisfaction in their organizations for at least four reasons: (1) There is clear evidence that dissatisfied employees skip work more often and are more likely to resign; (2) dissatisfied workers are more likely to engage in destructive behaviors; (3) it has been demonstrated that satisfied employees have better health and live longer; and (4) satisfaction on the job carries over to the employee's life outside the job.

We reviewed the evidence between satisfaction and withdrawal behaviors in this chapter. That evidence was fairly clear. Satisfied employees have lower rates of both turnover and absenteeism. If we consider the two withdrawal behaviors separately, however, we can be more confident about the influence of satisfaction on turnover. Specifically, satisfaction is strongly and consistently negatively related to an employee's decision to leave the organization. Although satisfaction and absence are also negatively related, conclusions regarding the relationship should be more guarded.

Dissatisfaction is frequently associated with a high level of complaints and work grievances. Highly dissatisfied employees are more likely to resort to sabotage and passive aggression. For employees with limited alternative options, who would quit if they could, these forms of destructive actions act as extreme applications of neglect.

An often overlooked dimension of job satisfaction is its relationship to employee health. Several studies have shown that employees who are dissatisfied with their jobs are prone to health setbacks ranging from headaches to heart disease. Some research even indicates that job satisfaction is a bet-ter predictor of length of life than is physical condition or tobacco use. These studies suggest that dissatisfaction is not solely a psychological phenomenon. The stress that results from dissatisfaction apparently increases one's susceptibility to heart attacks and the like. For managers, this means that even if satisfaction didn't lead to less voluntary turnover and absence, the goal of a satisfied work force might be justifiable because it would reduce medical costs and the premature loss of valued employees by way of heart disease or strokes.

Our final point in support of job satisfaction's importance is the spin-off effect that job satisfaction has for society as a whole. When employees are happy with their jobs, it improves their lives off the job. In contrast, the dissatisfied employee carries that negative attitude home. In wealthy countries such as the United States, Canada, Great Britain, Australia, or Japan, doesn't management have a responsibility to provide jobs from which employees can receive high satisfaction? Some benefits of job satisfaction accrue to every citizen in society. Satisfied employees are more likely to be satisfied citizens. These people will hold a more positive attitude toward life in general and make for a society of more psychologically healthy people.

The evidence is impressive. Job satisfaction is important. For management, a satisfied work force translates into higher productivity due to fewer disruptions caused by absenteeism or good employees quitting, fewer incidences of destructive behavior, as well as lower medical and life insurance costs. Additionally, there are benefits for society in general. Satisfaction on the job carries over to the employee's off-the-job hours. So the goal of high job satisfaction for employees can be defended in terms of both dollars and cents and social responsibility.

Job Satisfaction Has Been Overemphasized

Few issues have been more blown out of proportion than the importance of job satisfaction at work.* Let's look closely at the evidence.

There is no consistent relationship indicating that satisfaction leads to productivity. And, after all, isn't productivity the name of the game? Organizations are not altruistic institutions. Management's obligation is to use efficiently the resources that it has available. It has no obligation to create a satisfied work force if the costs exceed the benefits. As one executive put it, "I don't care if my people are happy or not! Do they produce?"

It would be naive to assume that satisfaction alone would have a major impact on employee behavior. As a case in point, consider the issue of turnover. Certainly there are a number of other factors that have an equal or greater impact on whether an employee decides to remain with an organization or take a job somewhere else—length of time on the job, financial situation, and availability of other jobs, to name the most obvious. If I'm 55 years old, have been with my company 25 years, perceive few other opportunities in the job market, and have no other source of income besides my job, does my unhappiness have much impact on my decision to stay with the organization? No!

Did you ever notice who seems to be most concerned with improving employee job satisfaction? It's usually college professors and researchers! They've chosen careers that provide them with considerable freedom and opportunities for personal growth. They place a very high value on job satisfaction. The problem is that they impose their values on others. Because job satisfaction is important to them, they suppose that it's important to everyone. To a lot of people, a job is merely the means to get the money they need to do the things they desire during their nonworking hours. Assuming you work 40 hours a week and sleep eight hours a night, you still have 70 hours or more a week to achieve fulfillment and satisfaction in off-the-job activities. So the importance of job satisfaction may be oversold when you recognize that there are other sources—outside the job—where the dissatisfied employee can find satisfaction.

A final point against overemphasizing job satisfaction: Consider the issue in a contingency framework. Even if satisfaction were significantly related to performance, it's unlikely that the relationship would hold consistently across all segments of the work force. In fact, evidence demonstrates that people differ in terms of the importance that work plays in their lives. To some, the job is their central life interest. But for the majority of people, their primary interests are off the job. Non–job-oriented people tend not to be emotionally involved with their work. This relative indifference allows them to accept frustrating conditions at work more willingly. Importantly, the majority of the work force probably falls into this non–job-oriented category. So while job satisfaction might be important to lawyers, surgeons, and other professionals, it may be irrelevant to the average worker because he or she is generally apathetic about the job's frustrating elements.

*See, for instance, G. Bassett, "The Case Against Job Satisfaction," *Business Horizons*, May–June 1994, pp. 61–68.

Learning about Yourself Exercise

What Do You Value?

Following are 16 items. Rate how important each one is to you on a scale of 0 (not important) to 100 (very important). Write the number 0–100 on the line to the left of each item.

Not important	Somewhat important	Very important

0	10	20	30	40	50	60	70	80	90	100

_____ **1.** An enjoyable, satisfying job.

_____ **2.** A high-paying job.

_____ **3.** A good marriage.

_____ **4.** Meeting new people; social events.

_____ **5.** Involvement in community activities.

_____ **6.** My religion.

_____ **7.** Exercising, playing sports.

_____ **8.** Intellectual development.

_____ **9.** A career with challenging opportunities.

_____ **10.** Nice cars, clothes, home, and so on.

_____ **11.** Spending time with family.

_____ **12.** Having several close friends.

_____ **13.** Volunteer work for not-for-profit organizations, like the cancer society.

_____ **14.** Meditation, quiet time to think, pray, and so on.

_____ **15.** A healthy, balanced diet.

_____ **16.** Educational reading, television, self-improvement programs, and so on.

Turn to page A-26 for scoring directions and key.

Source: R.N. Lussier, *Human Relations in Organizations: A Skill Building Approach*, 2nd ed. (Homewood, IL: Richard D. Irwin, 1993). Used with permission.

Working with Others Exercise

Assessing Work Attitudes

Objective
To compare attitudes about the workforce.

Time
Approximately 30 minutes.

Procedure
Choose the best answers for the following five questions:

1. *Generally*, American workers

　　_____**a.** are highly motivated and hardworking

　　_____**b.** try to give a fair day's effort

　　_____**c.** will put forth effort if you make it worthwhile

　　_____**d.** try to get by with a low level of effort

　　_____**e.** are lazy and/or poorly motivated

2. The people *I have worked with*

　　_____**a.** are highly motivated and hardworking

　　_____**b.** try to give a fair day's effort

　　_____**c.** will put forth effort if you make it worthwhile

　　_____**d.** try to get by with a low level of effort

　　_____**e.** are lazy and/or poorly motivated

3. *Compared to foreign workers*, American workers are

　　_____**a.** more productive

　　_____**b.** equally productive

　　_____**c.** less productive

4. *Over the past 20 years*, American workers have (pick one)

　　_____**a.** improved in overall quality of job performance

　　_____**b.** remained about the same in quality of job performance

　　_____**c.** deteriorated in overall quality of job performance

5. If you have a low opinion of the U.S. workforce, give the one step (or action) that could be taken that would lead to the most improvement.

GROUP DISCUSSION

a. Break into groups of three to five members each. Compare your answers to the five questions.

b. For each question where one or more members disagree, discuss *why* each member chose his or her answer.

c. After this discussion, members are free to change their original answer. Did any in your group do so?

d. Your instructor will provide data from other student attitude responses to these questions, then lead the class in discussing the implications or accuracy of these attitudes.

Source: Based on D.R. Brown, "Dealing with Student Conceptions and Misconceptions About Worker Attitudes and Productivity," *Journal of Management Education*, May 1991, pp. 259–64.

Binney & Smith (Canada)

Binney & Smith (B&S) operates a plant in Lindsay, Ontario, to produce crayons. Their Crayola brand is familiar to almost all preschoolers and elementary school children in North America.

In 1992, the production goals for the Lindsay plant were doubled, to 4 million 16-stick boxes of assorted-color crayons. Little more than a year earlier, the plant produced about a quarter of that volume. Maybe somewhat surprisingly, employees have been very receptive to these much higher production goals. These employees, most of whom have been with the company for at least ten years, indicate that they're more excited about their jobs and more satisfied with their working lives than ever before.

Workers at B&S traditionally knew their own jobs well, and many of these jobs were repetitive and unchallenging. For instance, one job is to run the machine which glues labels to crayon sticks—172 labels per minute. The label-gluing machine operator was an expert at his job but knew little about the other jobs in the plant. To get the increased production, management redesigned the label-gluing machine operator's job and almost everybody else's.

Workers in the Lindsay plant now do their jobs in teams and are encouraged to learn the jobs of everyone else on their team. Team members regularly rotate jobs to increase their skills and reduce boredom. These teams have taken on the responsibility for solving their work problems. And employees in the plant now also have taken charge of tracking production, changing layouts as needed to solve quality problems, and conceiving and implementing cost-reduction ideas like recycling waste.

Employees receive no financial or material rewards for accepting these new changes. What they do get is increased recognition, the opportunity to learn new tasks, and greater control over their work. The results have been extremely encouraging for both employees and management. Employees have increased job satisfaction and self-esteem, and the plant more than doubled its profit in the first year of these new changes. Additionally, employees at Lindsay now have greater job security than they had before because the plant has eliminated the 15 to 25 percent cost disadvantage it previously labored under compared to the company's sister plants in the United States.

Questions

1. How does the B&S experience in its Lindsay plant compare with the evidence on the satisfaction–productivity relationship described in this chapter? Explain why it might confirm or contradict the research.

2. B&S's historical turnover rate has been very low. Why do you think that is? Shouldn't a plant with boring and repetitive jobs like gluing 172 labels a minute on crayon sticks have high absenteeism and turnover?

3. Explain why, in spite of tremendously high new production goals, B&S employees seem more satisfied with their jobs than ever.

Source: Based on J. Wells, "Winning Colours," *Report on Business Magazine*, July 1992; cited in S.P. Robbins, D.A. DeCenzo, and R. Stuart-Kotze, *Fundamentals of Management: Canadian Edition* (Scarborough, Ontario: Prentice Hall Canada, 1996), p. 246.

Age and Attitudes

U.S. federal laws consider anyone who is 40 years of age or older to be an older worker. This means that no organization has the right to discriminate against these individuals because of their age. Yet, as more and more organizations downsize and millions of middle-aged workers are pounding the pavement looking for work, examples of age discrimination are happening every day in every profession. Statistics, for example, show that it takes older job seekers 64 percent longer to find work than younger ones. Even though age discrimination is illegal, it appears to be such an ingrained part of our culture that we may not even recognize if and when we're doing it.

When you talk with people who hire, they'll tell you they don't discriminate. Then they list "certain realities" to face about older workers: They get sick more often, they don't stay with the company as long as younger workers do, and they can't work as hard. Of course, these realities are all false, but they nevertheless influence hiring decisions.

The actual performance of older workers is impressive. For instance, Days Inn deliberately recruited older workers to see how they performed. Days Inn found that the older workers stay with the company longer, take fewer sick days, and are just as productive as their younger counterparts.

Negative attitudes toward older workers have subtle influences on the way we perceive and behave toward them. For instance, in job interviews, differences can be seen in the treatment of younger and older applicants. In several staged interviews with pairs of applicants—one older and one younger—the younger women were accommodated more by the interviewer. The older women were subtly discouraged. In fact, in one-third of these 24 staged interviews, a startling difference in the way older and younger job applicants were treated could be seen. In another staged interview situation, one individual made up to look younger one time and older another found a job opening at a brokerage firm offered to his "younger" self even though this "person" had less job experience and didn't follow up on the interview with a letter or phone call. Although the interviewers didn't appear to purposefully discriminate (after all, it *is* illegal) against the older job applicants in the way they acted and in the questions they asked, differences in attitude could still be seen.

Questions

1. Describe the three components of an attitude and relate them to the views often held about older workers.

2. Is stereotyping part of the problem with attitudes about age? Explain.

3. What are the implications of this case for building a diverse workforce?

4. What can organizations do to lessen the negative attitudes that managers and employees might hold toward older workers?

Source: Based on "Age and Attitudes," *ABC News Primetime*; aired on June 9, 1994.

CHAPTER 5

BASIC MOTIVATION CONCEPTS

CHAPTER OUTLINE
What Is Motivation?
Early Theories of Motivation
Contemporary Theories of Motivation
Integrating Contemporary Theories of Motivation
Caveat Emptor: Motivation Theories Are Culture Bound

When someone says, "It's not the money, it's the principle," it's the money!
—Anonymous

LEARNING OBJECTIVES

After studying this chapter, you should be able to

1 Outline the motivation process

2 Describe Maslow's need hierarchy

3 Contrast Theory X and Theory Y

4 Differentiate motivators from hygiene factors

5 List the characteristics that high achievers prefer in a job

6 Summarize the types of goals that increase performance

7 State the impact of underrewarding employees

8 Clarify the key relationships in expectancy theory

9 Explain how the contemporary theories of motivation complement each other

programs have long been part of the corporate landscape in the United States and Europe. With the exception of Japan, that hasn't been true in Asia. But things are changing.[1] Companies in countries such as Singapore, Hong Kong, China, Taiwan, and India are introducing incentive-based motivation programs to boost morale and employee productivity. Hong Kong's DHL Ltd. provides an illustrative example.

DHL was looking for a way to increase the productivity of its sales staff. It began, in September 1995, by setting specific goal targets for each salesperson. Then, to motivate people to achieve their goals, DHL's management created a cash and travel incentive program. "Travel [such as all-expense paid holidays in Thailand] has all the ingredients to motivate and encourage," says Michael Thibouville, DHL's regional human resource director (see photo). Each salesperson was given a model air cargo container to fill up. Individuals who exceeded their monthly sales targets were given small blocks to fill their containers. These containers sit on the employees' desks as a visible reminder of how well they are doing.

DHL's sales staff has a choice of redeeming the blocks for cash or going for the travel prize. "The beauty of our incentive scheme is that it isn't competitive," says Thibouville. "We found that salespeople having problems with a particular deal would approach those who had filled up their [containers] for help. With the scheme, we're now able to share the best demonstrated sales practices while developing a consultant-style sales ability among staff."

Sales at DHL have exceeded targets since the incentive program's introduction. Within four months, 26 of its 36 sales staff beat their goals by 40 percent, two by 35 percent, and another two by 30 percent.

The management at DHL Ltd. is seeing some of the positive results that can accrue from a well-designed motivation system. Unfortunately, many managers still fail to understand the importance of motivation and creating a motivating work environment. In this chapter and the following chapter, we explain the basics of motivation and show you how to design effective motivation programs. ◆

What Is Motivation?

Maybe the place to begin is to say what motivation isn't. Many people incorrectly view motivation as a personal trait—that is, some have it and others don't. In practice, some managers label employees who seem to lack motivation as lazy. Such a label assumes that an individual is always lazy or is lacking in motivation. Our knowledge of motivation tells us that this just isn't true. What we know is that motivation is the result of the interaction of the individual and the situation. Certainly, individuals differ in their basic motivational drive. But the same employee who is quickly bored when pulling the lever on his drill press may pull the lever on a slot machine in Las Vegas for hours on end without the slightest hint of boredom. You may read a complete novel at one sitting, yet find it difficult to stay with a textbook for more than 20 minutes. It's not necessarily you—it's the situation. So as we analyze the concept of motivation, keep in mind that level of motivation varies both between individuals and within individuals at different times.

motivation
The willingness to exert high levels of effort toward organizational goals, conditioned by the effort's ability to satisfy some individual need.

We'll define **motivation** as the willingness to exert high levels of effort toward organizational goals, conditioned by the effort's ability to satisfy some individual need. While general motivation is concerned with effort toward *any* goal, we'll narrow the focus to *organizational* goals in order to reflect our singular interest in work-related behavior. The three key elements in our definition are effort, organizational goals, and needs.

The effort element is a measure of intensity. When someone is motivated, he or she tries hard. But high levels of effort are unlikely to lead to favorable job-performance outcomes unless the effort is channeled in a direction that benefits the organization.[2] Therefore, we must consider the quality of the effort as well as its intensity. Effort that is directed toward, and consistent with, the organization's goals is the kind of effort that we should be seeking. Finally, we will treat motivation as a need-satisfying process. This is depicted in Exhibit 5-1.

need
Some internal state that makes certain outcomes appear attractive.

A **need**, in our terminology, means some internal state that makes certain outcomes appear attractive. An unsatisfied need creates tension that stimulates drives within the individual. These drives generate a search behavior to find particular goals that, if attained, will satisfy the need and lead to the reduction of tension.

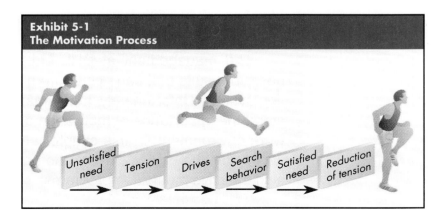

Exhibit 5-1
The Motivation Process

Unsatisfied need → Tension → Drives → Search behavior → Satisfied need → Reduction of tension

Therefore, we can say that motivated employees are in a state of tension. To relieve this tension, they exert effort. The greater the tension, the higher the effort level. If this effort successfully leads to the satisfaction of the need, tension is reduced. But since we are interested in work behavior, this tension-reduction effort must also be directed toward organizational goals. Therefore, inherent in our definition of motivation is the requirement that the individual's needs be compatible and consistent with the organization's goals. Where this does not occur, we can have individuals exerting high levels of effort that actually run counter to the interests of the organization. This, incidentally, is not so unusual. For example, some employees regularly spend a lot of time talking with friends at work in order to satisfy their social needs. There is a high level of effort, only it's being unproductively directed.

Early Theories of Motivation

The 1950s were a fruitful period in the development of motivation concepts. Three specific theories were formulated during this period, which although heavily attacked and now questionable in terms of validity, are probably still the best-known explanations for employee motivation. These are the hierarchy of needs theory, Theories X and Y, and the motivation-hygiene theory. As you'll see later in this chapter, we have since developed more valid explanations of motivation, but you should know these early theories for at least two reasons: (1) They represent a foundation from which contemporary theories have grown, and (2) practicing managers regularly use these theories and their terminology in explaining employee motivation.

◆ Probably the most well-known theory of motivation is Maslow's hierarchy of needs.

Hierarchy of Needs Theory

It's probably safe to say that the most well-known theory of motivation is Abraham Maslow's **hierarchy of needs**.[3] He hypothesized that within every human being there exists a hierarchy of five needs. These needs are:

1. *Physiological*: Includes hunger, thirst, shelter, sex, and other bodily needs
2. *Safety*: Includes security and protection from physical and emotional harm
3. *Social*: Includes affection, belongingness, acceptance, and friendship
4. *Esteem*: Includes internal esteem factors such as self-respect, autonomy, and achievement; and external esteem factors such as status, recognition, and attention
5. **Self-actualization**: The drive to become what one is capable of becoming; includes growth, achieving one's potential, and self-fulfillment

hierarchy of needs theory
There is a hierarchy of five needs—physiological, safety, social, esteem, and self-actualization—and as each need is substantially satisfied, the next need becomes dominant.

self-actualization
The drive to become what one is capable of becoming.

As each of these needs becomes substantially satisfied, the next need becomes dominant. In terms of Exhibit 5-2, the individual moves up the steps of the hierarchy. From the standpoint of motivation, the theory would say that although no need is ever fully gratified, a substantially satisfied need no

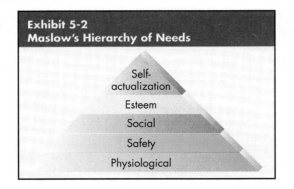

Exhibit 5-2
Maslow's Hierarchy of Needs

Self-actualization

Esteem

Social

Safety

Physiological

longer motivates. So if you want to motivate someone, according to Maslow, you need to understand what level of the hierarchy that person is currently on and focus on satisfying those needs at or above that level.

Maslow separated the five needs into higher and lower orders. Physiological and safety needs were described as **lower-order** and social, esteem, and self-actualization as **higher-order needs**. The differentiation between the two orders was made on the premise that higher-order needs are satisfied internally (within the person), whereas lower-order needs are predominantly satisfied externally (by such things as pay, union contracts, and tenure). In fact, the natural conclusion to be drawn from Maslow's classification is that in times of economic plenty, almost all permanently employed workers have their lower-order needs substantially met.

Maslow's need theory has received wide recognition, particularly among practicing managers. This can be attributed to the theory's intuitive logic and ease of understanding. Unfortunately, however, research does not generally validate the theory. Maslow provided no empirical substantiation, and several studies that sought to validate the theory found no support for it.[4]

Old theories, especially ones that are intuitively logical, apparently die hard. One researcher reviewed the evidence and concluded that "although of great societal popularity, need hierarchy as a theory continues to receive little empirical support."[5] Furthermore, the researcher stated that the "available research should certainly generate a reluctance to accept unconditionally the implication of Maslow's hierarchy."[6] Another review came to the same conclusion.[7] Little support was found for the prediction that need structures are organized along the dimensions proposed by Maslow, that unsatisfied needs motivate, or that a satisfied need activates movement to a new need level.

lower-order needs
Needs that are satisfied externally; physiological and safety needs.

higher-order needs
Needs that are satisfied internally; social, esteem, and self-actualization needs.

Theory X
The assumption that employees dislike work, are lazy, dislike responsibility, and must be coerced to perform.

Theory Y
The assumption that employees like work, are creative, seek responsibility, and can exercise self-direction.

Theory X and Theory Y

Douglas McGregor proposed two distinct views of human beings: one basically negative, labeled **Theory X**, and the other basically positive, labeled **Theory Y**.[8] After viewing the way in which managers dealt with employees, McGregor concluded that a manager's view of the nature of human beings is based on a certain grouping of assumptions and that he or she tends to mold his or her behavior toward subordinates according to these assumptions.

Under Theory X, the four assumptions held by managers are:

1. Employees inherently dislike work and, whenever possible, will attempt to avoid it.
2. Since employees dislike work, they must be coerced, controlled, or threatened with punishment to achieve goals.
3. Employees will avoid responsibilities and seek formal direction whenever possible.
4. Most workers place security above all other factors associated with work and will display little ambition.

In contrast to these negative views about the nature of human beings, McGregor listed the four positive assumptions that he called Theory Y:

1. Employees can view work as being as natural as rest or play.
2. People will exercise self-direction and self-control if they are committed to the objectives.
3. The average person can learn to accept, even seek, responsibility.
4. The ability to make innovative decisions is widely dispersed throughout the population and is not necessarily the sole province of those in management positions.

What are the motivational implications if you accept McGregor's analysis? The answer is best expressed in the framework presented by Maslow. Theory X assumes that lower-order needs dominate individuals. Theory Y assumes that higher-order needs dominate individuals. McGregor himself held to the belief that Theory Y assumptions were more valid than Theory X. Therefore, he proposed such ideas as participative decision making, responsible and challenging jobs, and good group relations as approaches that would maximize an employee's job motivation.

Unfortunately, there is no evidence to confirm that either set of assumptions is valid or that accepting Theory Y assumptions and altering one's actions accordingly will lead to more motivated workers. As will become evident later in this chapter, either Theory X or Theory Y assumptions may be appropriate in a particular situation.

Motivation-Hygiene Theory

The **motivation-hygiene theory** was proposed by psychologist Frederick Herzberg.[9] In the belief that an individual's relation to his or her work is a basic one and that his or her attitude toward this work can very well determine the individual's success or failure, Herzberg investigated the question, "What do people want from their jobs?" He asked people to describe, in detail, situations when they felt exceptionally *good* and *bad* about their jobs. These responses were tabulated and categorized. Factors affecting job attitudes as reported in 12 investigations conducted by Herzberg are illustrated in Exhibit 5-3 on page 172.

From the categorized responses, Herzberg concluded that the replies people gave when they felt good about their jobs were significantly different from the replies given when they felt bad. As seen in Exhibit 5-3, certain characteristics tend to be consistently related to job satisfaction (factors on the right side of the figure), and others to job dissatisfaction (the left side of the figure).

motivation-hygiene theory
Intrinsic factors are related to job satisfaction, while extrinsic factors are associated with dissatisfaction.

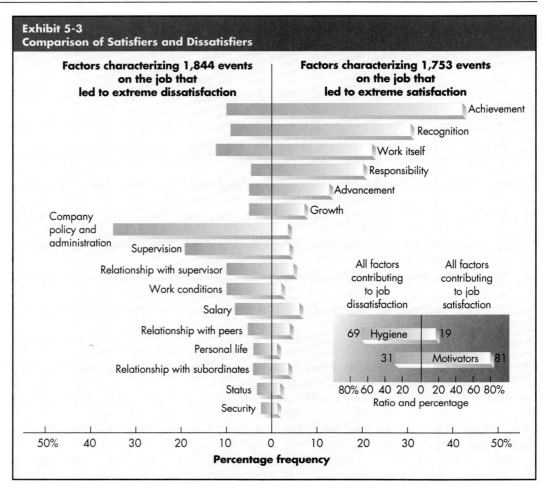

Exhibit 5-3
Comparison of Satisfiers and Dissatisfiers

Factors characterizing 1,844 events
on the job that
led to extreme dissatisfaction

Factors characterizing 1,753 events
on the job that
led to extreme satisfaction

Achievement
Recognition
Work itself
Responsibility
Advancement
Growth

Company policy and administration
Supervision
Relationship with supervisor
Work conditions
Salary
Relationship with peers
Personal life
Relationship with subordinates
Status
Security

All factors contributing to job dissatisfaction

All factors contributing to job satisfaction

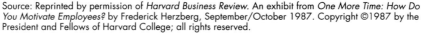

| 69 | Hygiene | 19 |
| 31 | Motivators | 81 |

80% 60 40 20 0 20 40 60 80%
Ratio and percentage

50% 40 30 20 10 0 10 20 30 40 50%
Percentage frequency

Source: Reprinted by permission of *Harvard Business Review.* An exhibit from *One More Time: How Do You Motivate Employees?* by Frederick Herzberg, September/October 1987. Copyright ©1987 by the President and Fellows of Harvard College; all rights reserved.

Intrinsic factors, such as achievement, recognition, the work itself, responsibility, advancement, and growth, seem to be related to job satisfaction. When those questioned felt good about their work, they tended to attribute these characteristics to themselves. On the other hand, when they were dissatisfied, they tended to cite extrinsic factors, such as company policy and administration, supervision, interpersonal relations, and working conditions.

The data suggest, says Herzberg, that the opposite of satisfaction is not dissatisfaction, as was traditionally believed. Removing dissatisfying characteristics from a job does not necessarily make the job satisfying. As illustrated in Exhibit 5-4, Herzberg proposes that his findings indicate the existence of a dual continuum: The opposite of "Satisfaction" is "No Satisfaction," and the opposite of "Dissatisfaction" is "No Dissatisfaction."

According to Herzberg, the factors leading to job satisfaction are separate and distinct from those that lead to job dissatisfaction. Therefore, managers who seek to eliminate factors that create job dissatisfaction can bring about peace, but not necessarily motivation. They will be placating their work force rather than motivating them. As a result, such characteristics as company policy and administration, supervision, interpersonal relations, working condi-

Exhibit 5-4
Contrasting Views of Satisfaction and Dissatisfaction

Traditional view

Satisfaction ——————————— Dissatisfaction

Herzberg's view

Motivators

Satisfaction ——————————— No satisfaction

Hygiene Factors

No dissatisfaction ——————————— Dissatisfaction

tions, and salary have been characterized by Herzberg as **hygiene factors.** When they are adequate, people will not be dissatisfied; however, neither will they be satisfied. If we want to motivate people on their jobs, Herzberg suggests emphasizing achievement, recognition, the work itself, responsibility, and growth. These are the characteristics that people find intrinsically rewarding.

The motivation-hygiene theory is not without its detractors. The criticisms of the theory include the following:

1. The procedure that Herzberg used is limited by its methodology. When things are going well, people tend to take credit themselves. Contrarily, they blame failure on the external environment.

2. The reliability of Herzberg's methodology is questioned. Since raters have to make interpretations, it is possible that they may contaminate the findings by interpreting one response in one manner while treating another similar response differently.

3. The theory, to the degree that it is valid, provides an explanation of job satisfaction. It is not really a theory of motivation.

4. No overall measure of satisfaction was utilized. In other words, a person may dislike part of his or her job, yet still think the job is acceptable.

5. The theory is inconsistent with previous research. The motivation-hygiene theory ignores situational variables.

6. Herzberg assumes that there is a relationship between satisfaction and productivity. But the research methodology he used looked only at satisfaction, not at productivity. To make such research relevant, one must assume a high relationship between satisfaction and productivity.[10]

Regardless of criticisms, Herzberg's theory has been widely read and few managers are unfamiliar with his recommendations. The popularity over the past 30 years of vertically expanding jobs to allow workers greater responsibility in planning and controlling their work can probably be largely attributed to Herzberg's findings and recommendations.

hygiene factors
Those factors—such as company policy and administration, supervision, and salary—that, when adequate in a job, placate workers. When these factors are adequate, people will not be dissatisfied.

Contemporary Theories of Motivation

The previous theories are well known but, unfortunately, have not held up well under close examination. However, all is not lost.[11] There are a number of contemporary theories that have one thing in common—each has a reasonable degree of valid supporting documentation. Of course, this doesn't mean that the theories we are about to introduce are unquestionably right. We call them "contemporary theories" not because they necessarily were developed recently, but because they represent the current state of the art in explaining employee motivation.

ERG Theory

ERG theory
There are three groups of core needs: existence, relatedness, and growth.

Clayton Alderfer of Yale University has reworked Maslow's need hierarchy to align it more closely with the empirical research. His revised need hierarchy is labeled **ERG theory**.[12]

Alderfer argues that there are three groups of core needs—existence, relatedness, and growth—hence, the label: ERG theory. The *existence* group is concerned with providing our basic material existence requirements. They include the items that Maslow considered to be physiological and safety needs. The second group of needs are those of *relatedness*— the desire we have for maintaining important interpersonal relationships. These social and status desires require interaction with others if they are to be satisfied, and they align with Maslow's social need and the external component of Maslow's esteem classification. Finally, Alderfer isolates *growth* needs—an intrinsic desire for personal development. These include the intrinsic component from Maslow's esteem category and the characteristics included under self-actualization.

Besides substituting three needs for five, how does Alderfer's ERG theory differ from Maslow's? In contrast to the hierarchy of needs theory, the ERG

Employees of Honeywell have many opportunities to satisfy their relatedness needs. They can build important interpersonal relationships by participating in a number of diversity advisory councils Honeywell has formed to accommodate its diverse global workforce that represents 47 cultures and 90 ethnic backgrounds. Employees can interact with others by serving on councils such as the Work and Family Council, Women's Council, Older Workers League, Black Employees Network, Hispanic Council, American Indian Council, and Council of Employees with Disabilities.

theory demonstrates that (1) more than one need may be operative at the same time, and (2) if the gratification of a higher-level need is stifled, the desire to satisfy a lower-level need increases.

Maslow's need hierarchy follows a rigid, steplike progression. ERG theory does not assume that there exists a rigid hierarchy where a lower need must be substantially gratified before one can move on. A person can, for instance, be working on growth even though existence or relatedness needs are unsatisfied; or all three need categories could be operating at the same time.

ERG theory also contains a frustration-regression dimension. Maslow, you'll remember, argued that an individual would stay at a certain need level until that need was satisfied. ERG theory counters by noting that when a higher-order need level is frustrated, the individual's desire to increase a lower-level need takes place. Inability to satisfy a need for social interaction, for instance, might increase the desire for more money or better working conditions. So frustration can lead to a regression to a lower need.

In summary, ERG theory argues, like Maslow, that satisfied lower-order needs lead to the desire to satisfy higher-order needs; but multiple needs can be operating as motivators at the same time, and frustration in attempting to satisfy a higher-level need can result in regression to a lower-level need.

ERG theory is more consistent with our knowledge of individual differences among people. Variables such as education, family background, and cultural environment can alter the importance or driving force that a group of needs holds for a particular individual. The evidence demonstrating that people in other cultures rank the need categories differently—for instance, natives of Spain and Japan place social needs before their physiological requirements[13]—would be consistent with ERG theory. Several studies have supported ERG theory,[14] but there is also evidence that it doesn't work in some organizations.[15] Overall, however, ERG theory represents a more valid version of the need hierarchy.

McClelland's Theory of Needs

You've got one beanbag and there are five targets set up in front of you. Each one is progressively farther away and, hence, more difficult to hit. Target A is a cinch. It sits almost within arm's reach of you. If you hit it, you get $2. Target B is a bit farther out, but about 80 percent of the people who try can hit it. It pays $4. Target C pays $8, and about half the people who try can hit it. Very few people can hit Target D, but the payoff is $16 if you do. Finally, Target E pays $32, but it's almost impossible to achieve. Which target would you try for? If you selected C, you're likely to be a high achiever. Why? Read on.

McClelland's theory of needs was developed by David McClelland and his associates.[16] The theory focuses on three needs: achievement, power, and affiliation. They are defined as follows:

◆ **Need for achievement**: The drive to excel, to achieve in relation to a set of standards, to strive to succeed

◆ **Need for power**: The need to make others behave in a way that they would not have behaved otherwise

◆ **Need for affiliation**: The desire for friendly and close interpersonal relationships

Some people have a compelling drive to succeed. They're striving for personal achievement rather than the rewards of success per se. They have a de-

McClelland's theory of needs
Achievement, power, and affiliation are three important needs that help explain motivation.

achievement need
The drive to excel, to achieve in relation to a set of standards, to strive to succeed.

power need
The desire to make others behave in a way that they would not otherwise have behaved in.

affiliation need
The desire for friendly and close interpersonal relationships.

sire to do something better or more efficiently than it has been done before. This drive is the achievement need (*nAch*). From research into the achievement need, McClelland found that high achievers differentiate themselves from others by their desire to do things better.[17] They seek situations where they can attain personal responsibility for finding solutions to problems, where they can receive rapid feedback on their performance so they can tell easily whether they are improving or not, and where they can set moderately challenging goals. High achievers are not gamblers; they dislike succeeding by chance. They prefer the challenge of working at a problem and accepting the personal responsibility for success or failure rather than leaving the outcome to chance or the actions of others. Importantly, they avoid what they perceive to be very easy or very difficult tasks. They want to overcome obstacles, but they want to feel that their success (or failure) is due to their own actions. This means they like tasks of intermediate difficulty.

High achievers perform best when they perceive their probability of success as being 0.5, that is, where they estimate that they have a 50-50 chance of success. They dislike gambling with high odds because they get no achievement satisfaction from happenstance success. Similarly, they dislike low odds (high probability of success) because then there is no challenge to their skills. They like to set goals that require stretching themselves a little. When there is an approximately equal chance of success or failure, there is the optimum opportunity to experience feelings of accomplishment and satisfaction from their efforts.

The need for power (*nPow*) is the desire to have impact, to be influential, and to control others. Individuals high in *nPow* enjoy being "in charge," strive for influence over others, prefer to be placed into competitive and status-oriented situations, and tend to be more concerned with prestige and gaining influence over others than with effective performance.

High achievers do well as managers at Enterprise Rent-a-Car. Enterprise hires competitive people who take personal responsibility for their actions, strive to succeed, and have a compelling drive to excel. Employees' pay is tied to the profits of their branch office. Employees are given the financial results of every branch office and every region, sparking lively intramural competition. High-achieving employees have helped make Enterprise the top car rental company in America.

The third need isolated by McClelland is affiliation (*nAff*). This need has received the least attention from researchers. Affiliation can be likened to Dale Carnegie's goals—the desire to be liked and accepted by others. Individuals with a high affiliation motive strive for friendship, prefer cooperative situations rather than competitive ones, and desire relationships involving a high degree of mutual understanding.

How do you find out if someone is, for instance, a high achiever? There are questionnaires that tap this motive,[18] but most research uses a projective test in which subjects respond to pictures.[19] Each picture is briefly shown to the subject and then he or she writes a story based on the picture. As an example, the picture may show a male sitting at a desk in a pensive position, looking at a photograph of a woman and two children that sits at the corner of the desk. The subject will then be asked to write a story describing what is going on, what preceded this situation, what will happen in the future, and the like. The stories become, in effect, projective tests that measure unconscious motives. Each story is scored and a subject's ratings on each of the three motives is obtained.

Relying on an extensive amount of research, some reasonably well-supported predictions can be made based on the relationship between achievement need and job performance. Although less research has been done on power and affiliation needs, there are consistent findings here, too.

First, as shown in Exhibit 5-5, individuals with a high need to achieve prefer job situations with personal responsibility, feedback, and an intermediate degree of risk. When these characteristics are prevalent, high achievers will be strongly motivated. The evidence consistently demonstrates, for instance, that high achievers are successful in entrepreneurial activities such as running their own businesses and managing a self-contained unit within a large organization.[20]

Second, a high need to achieve does not necessarily lead to being a good manager, especially in large organizations. People with a high achievement need are interested in how well they do personally and not in influencing others to do well. High-*nAch* salespeople do not necessarily make good sales managers, and the good general manager in a large organization does not typically have a high need to achieve.[21]

Third, the needs for affiliation and power tend to be closely related to managerial success. The best managers are high in their need for power and low in their need for affiliation.[22] In fact, a high power motive may be a requirement for managerial effectiveness.[23] Of course, what the cause is and what the effect is are arguable. It has been suggested that a high power need

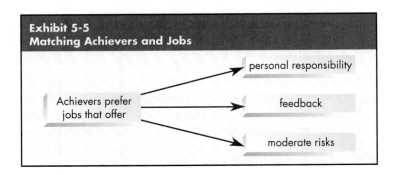

Exhibit 5-5
Matching Achievers and Jobs

Achievers prefer jobs that offer → personal responsibility
→ feedback
→ moderate risks

may occur simply as a function of one's level in a hierarchical organization.[24] The latter argument proposes that the higher the level an individual rises to in the organization, the greater is the incumbent's power motive. As a result, powerful positions would be the stimulus to a high power motive.

Finally, employees have been successfully trained to stimulate their achievement need. Trainers have been effective in teaching individuals to think in terms of accomplishments, winning, and success, and then helping them to learn how to *act* in a high achievement way by preferring situations where they have personal responsibility, feedback, and moderate risks. So if the job calls for a high achiever, management can select a person with a high *nAch* or develop its own candidate through achievement training.[25]

Cognitive Evaluation Theory

In the late 1960s, one researcher proposed that the introduction of extrinsic rewards, such as pay, for work effort that had been previously intrinsically rewarding due to the pleasure associated with the content of the work itself would tend to decrease the overall level of motivation.[26] This proposal—which has come to be called the **cognitive evaluation theory**—has been extensively researched, and a large number of studies have been supportive.[27] As we'll show, the major implications for this theory relate to the way in which people are paid in organizations.

cognitive evaluation theory
Allocating extrinsic rewards for behavior that had been previously intrinsically rewarded tends to decrease the overall level of motivation.

Historically, motivation theorists have generally assumed that intrinsic motivations such as achievement, responsibility, and competence are independent of extrinsic motivators like high pay, promotions, good supervisor relations, and pleasant working conditions. That is, the stimulation of one would not affect the other. But the cognitive evaluation theory suggests otherwise. It argues that when extrinsic rewards are used by organizations as payoffs for superior performance, the intrinsic rewards, which are derived from individuals doing what they like, are reduced. In other words, when extrinsic rewards are given to someone for performing an interesting task, it causes intrinsic interest in the task itself to decline.

Why would such an outcome occur? The popular explanation is that the individual experiences a loss of control over his or her own behavior so that the previous intrinsic motivation diminishes. Furthermore, the elimination of extrinsic rewards can produce a shift—from an external to an internal explanation—in an individual's perception of causation of why he or she works on a task. If you're reading a novel a week because your English literature instructor requires you to, you can attribute your reading behavior to an external source. However, after the course is over, if you find yourself continuing to read a novel a week, your natural inclination is to say, "I must enjoy reading novels because I'm still reading one a week!"

If the cognitive evaluation theory is valid, it should have major implications for managerial practices. It has been a truism among compensation specialists for years that if pay or other extrinsic rewards are to be effective motivators, they should be made contingent on an individual's performance. But, cognitive evaluation theorists would argue, this will only tend to decrease the internal satisfaction that the individual receives from doing the job. We have substituted an external stimulus for an internal stimulus. In fact, if cognitive evaluation theory is correct, it would make sense to make an individual's pay noncontingent on performance in order to avoid decreasing intrinsic motivation.

We noted earlier that the cognitive evaluation theory has been supported in a number of studies. Yet it has also met with attacks, specifically on the methodology used in these studies[28] and in the interpretation of the findings.[29] But where does this theory stand today? Can we say that when organizations use extrinsic motivators like pay and promotions to stimulate workers' performance they do so at the expense of reducing intrinsic interest and motivation in the work being done? The answer is not a simple "Yes" or "No."

Although further research is needed to clarify some of the current ambiguity, the evidence does lead us to conclude that the interdependence of extrinsic and intrinsic rewards is a real phenomenon.[30] However, its impact on employee motivation at work, in contrast to motivation in general, may be considerably less than originally thought. First, many of the studies testing the theory were done with students, not paid organizational employees. The researchers would observe what happens to a student's behavior when a reward that had been allocated is stopped. This is interesting, but it does not represent the typical work situation. In the real world, when extrinsic rewards are stopped, it usually means the individual is no longer part of the organization. Second, evidence indicates that very high intrinsic motivation levels are strongly resistant to the detrimental impacts of extrinsic rewards.[31] Even when a job is inherently interesting, there still exists a powerful norm for extrinsic payment.[32] At the other extreme, on dull tasks extrinsic rewards appear to increase intrinsic motivation.[33] Therefore, the theory may have limited applicability to work organizations because most low-level jobs are not inherently satisfying enough to foster high intrinsic interest and many managerial and professional positions offer intrinsic rewards. Cognitive evaluation theory may be relevant to that set of organizational jobs that falls in between—those that are neither extremely dull nor extremely interesting.

"What do you *mean* money isn't everything? This is a bank!"

Exhibit 5-6
Source: From *The Wall Street Journal*, February 8, 1995. With permission of Cartoon Features Syndicate.

Goal-Setting Theory

Gene Broadwater, coach of the Hamilton High School cross-country team, gave his squad these last words before they approached the line for the league championship race: "Each one of you is physically ready. Now, get out there and do your best. No one can ever ask more of you than that."

You've heard the phrase a number of times yourself: "Just do your best. That's all anyone can ask for." But what does "do your best" mean? Do we ever know if we've achieved that vague goal? Would the cross-country runners have recorded faster times if Coach Broadwater had given each a specific goal to shoot for? Might you have done better in your high school English class if your parents had said, "You should strive for 85 percent or higher on all your work in English" rather than telling you to "do your best"? The research on **goal-setting theory** addresses these issues, and the findings, as you will see, are impressive in terms of the effect that goal specificity, challenge, and feedback have on performance.

In the late 1960s, Edwin Locke proposed that intentions to work toward a goal are a major source of work motivation.[34] That is, goals tell an employee what needs to be done and how much effort will need to be expended.[35] The evidence strongly supports the value of goals. More to the point, we can say that specific goals increase performance; that difficult goals, when accepted, result in higher performance than do easy goals; and that feedback leads to higher performance than does nonfeedback.[36]

Specific hard goals produce a higher level of output than does the generalized goal of "do your best." The specificity of the goal itself acts as an internal stimulus. For instance, when a trucker commits to making 12 round-trip hauls between Toronto and Buffalo, New York each week, this intention gives him a specific objective to try to attain. We can say that, all things being equal, the trucker with a specific goal will outperform his or her counterpart operating with no goals or the generalized goal of "do your best."

goal-setting theory
The theory that specific and difficult goals lead to higher performance.

General Mills uses the goal-setting theory to motivate employees. When employees reach their goals, the company gives them a big reward. The team of Yoplait yogurt managers shown here each earned bonuses of up to $50,000 above their salaries for exceeding performance goals by 250 percent.

If factors like ability and acceptance of the goals are held constant, we can also state that the more difficult the goal, the higher the level of performance. However, it's logical to assume that easier goals are more likely to be accepted. But once an employee accepts a hard task, he or she will exert a high level of effort until it is achieved, lowered, or abandoned.

People will do better when they get feedback on how well they are progressing toward their goals because feedback helps to identify discrepancies between what they have done and what they want to do; that is, feedback acts to guide behavior. But all feedback is not equally potent. Self-generated feedback—where the employee is able to monitor his or her own progress—has been shown to be a more powerful motivator than externally generated feedback.[37]

If employees have the opportunity to participate in the setting of their own goals, will they try harder? The evidence is mixed regarding the superiority of participative over assigned goals.[38] In some cases, participatively set goals elicited superior performance, while in other cases, individuals performed best when assigned goals by their boss. But a major advantage of participation may be in increasing acceptance of the goal itself as a desirable one to work toward.[39] As we noted, resistance is greater when goals are difficult. If people participate in goal setting, they are more likely to accept even a difficult goal than if they are arbitrarily assigned it by their boss. The reason is that individuals are more committed to choices in which they have a part. Thus, although participative goals may have no superiority over assigned goals when acceptance is taken as a given, participation does increase the probability that more difficult goals will be agreed to and acted upon.

Are there any contingencies in goal-setting theory or can we take it as a universal truth that difficult and specific goals will always lead to higher performance? In addition to feedback, three other factors have been found to influence the goals–performance relationship. These are goal commitment, adequate self-efficacy, and national culture. Goal-setting theory presupposes that an individual is *committed* to the goal, that is, is determined not to lower or abandon the goal. This is most likely to occur when goals are made public, when the individual has an internal locus of control, and when the goals are self-set rather than assigned.[40] **Self-efficacy** refers to an individual's belief that he or she is capable of performing a task.[41] The higher your self-efficacy, the more confidence you have in your ability to succeed in a task. So, in difficult situations, we find that people with low self-efficacy are more likely to lessen their effort or give up altogether, while those with high self-efficacy will try harder to master the challenge.[42] In addition, individuals high in self-efficacy seem to respond to negative feedback with increased effort and motivation, whereas those low in self-efficacy are likely to lessen their effort when given negative feedback.[43] Finally, goal-setting theory is culture bound. It's well adapted to countries like the United States and Canada because its key components align reasonably well with North American cultures. It assumes that subordinates will be reasonably independent (not too high a score on power distance), that managers and subordinates will seek challenging goals (low in uncertainty avoidance), and that performance is considered important by both (high in quantity of life). So don't expect goal setting to necessarily lead to higher employee performance in countries such as Portugal or Chile, where the opposite conditions exist.

Our overall conclusion is that intentions—as articulated in terms of

self-efficacy
The individual's belief that he or she is capable of performing a task.

hard and specific goals—are a potent motivating force. Under the proper conditions, they can lead to higher performance. However, there is no evidence that such goals are associated with increased job satisfaction.[44]

Reinforcement Theory

reinforcement theory
Behavior is a function of its consequences.

A counterpoint to goal-setting theory is **reinforcement theory**. The former is a cognitive approach, proposing that an individual's purposes direct his or her action. In reinforcement theory, we have a behavioristic approach, which argues that reinforcement conditions behavior. The two are clearly at odds philosophically. Reinforcement theorists see behavior as being environmentally caused. You need not be concerned, they would argue, with internal cognitive events; what controls behavior are reinforcers—any consequence that, when immediately following a response, increases the probability that the behavior will be repeated.

Reinforcement theory ignores the inner state of the individual and concentrates solely on what happens to a person when he or she takes some action. Because it does not concern itself with what initiates behavior, it is not, strictly speaking, a theory of motivation. But it does provide a powerful means of analysis of what controls behavior, and it is for this reason that it is typically considered in discussions of motivation.[45]

We discussed the reinforcement process in detail in chapter 2. We showed how using reinforcers to condition behavior gives us considerable insight into how people learn. Yet we cannot ignore the fact that reinforcement has a wide following as a motivational device. In its pure form, however, reinforcement theory ignores feelings, attitudes, expectations, and other cognitive variables that are known to impact behavior. In fact, some researchers look at the same experiments that reinforcement theorists use to support their position and interpret the findings in a cognitive framework.[46]

Reinforcement is undoubtedly an important influence on behavior, but few scholars are prepared to argue that it is the only influence. The behaviors you engage in at work and the amount of effort you allocate to each task are affected by the consequences that follow from your behavior. If you are consistently reprimanded for outproducing your colleagues, you will likely reduce your productivity. But your lower productivity may also be explained in terms of goals, inequity, or expectancies.

Equity Theory

Jane Pearson graduated last year from the State University with a degree in accounting. After interviews with a number of organizations on campus, she accepted a position with one of the nation's largest public accounting firms and was assigned to their Boston office. Jane was very pleased with the offer she received: challenging work with a prestigious firm, an excellent opportunity to gain valuable experience, and the highest salary any accounting major at State was offered last year—$2,950 a month. But Jane was the top student in her class; she was ambitious and articulate and fully expected to receive a commensurate salary.

Twelve months have passed since Jane joined her employer. The work has proved to be as challenging and satisfying as she had hoped. Her employer is extremely pleased with her performance; in fact, she recently received a $200-a-month raise. However, Jane's motivational level has dropped dramatically in the past few weeks. Why? Her employer has just hired a fresh college graduate out of State University, who lacks the one-year experience Jane has gained, for $3,200 a month—$50 more than Jane now makes! It would be an understatement to describe Jane in any other terms than irate. Jane is even talking about looking for another job.

Jane's situation illustrates the role that equity plays in motivation. Employees make comparisons of their job inputs and outcomes relative to those of others. We perceive what we get from a job situation (outcomes) in relation to what we put into it (inputs), and then we compare our outcome–input ratio with the outcome–input ratio of relevant others. This is shown in Exhibit 5-7. If we perceive our ratio to be equal to that of the relevant others with whom we compare ourselves, a state of equity is said to exist. We perceive our situation as fair—that justice prevails. When we see the ratio as unequal, we experience equity tension. J. Stacy Adams has proposed that this negative tension state provides the motivation to do something to correct it.[47]

The referent that an employee selects adds to the complexity of **equity theory**. Evidence indicates that the referent chosen is an important variable in equity theory.[48] There are four referent comparisons that an employee can use:

equity theory
Individuals compare their job inputs and outcomes with those of others and then respond so as to eliminate any inequities.

1. *Self-inside*: An employee's experiences in a different position inside his or her current organization
2. *Self-outside*: An employee's experiences in a situation or position outside his or her current organization
3. *Other-inside*: Another individual or group of individuals inside the employee's organization
4. *Other-outside*: Another individual or group of individuals outside the employee's organization

Employees might compare themselves to friends, neighbors, co-workers, colleagues in other organizations, or past jobs they themselves have had. Which referent an employee chooses will be influenced by the information the employee holds about referents as well as by the attractiveness of the referent. This has led to focusing on four moderating variables—gender, length of tenure, level in the organization, and amount of education or professionalism.[49] Research shows that both men and women prefer same-sex comparisons. The research also demonstrates that women are typically paid less than men in comparable jobs and have lower pay expectations than men for the same work. So a female that uses another female as a referent tends to result in a lower comparative standard. This leads us to conclude that employees in jobs that are not sex segregated will make more cross-sex comparisons than

Exhibit 5-7 Equity Theory

Ratio Comparisons*	Perception
$O/I_A < O/I_B$	Inequity due to being underrewarded
$O/I_A = O/I_B$	Equity
$O/I_A > O/I_B$	Inequity due to being overrewarded

*Where O/I_A represents the employee; and O/I_B represents relevant others.

OB in the News

Compensation in the NBA

Imagine that you're making $3 million a year. A lot of money? Yes. But you're one of the best in your field and you spent ten years to get to this level of pay. Then you discover that one of your peers, whose statistics are far less impressive than yours, is making more money than you are. Worse yet, the company wants to pay some unproven hotshot five times what you're earning. Furious, you demand to renegotiate your contract. Welcome to the NBA in the 1990s!

With the escalation of salaries in the National Basketball Association, players have developed what former NBA coach Hubie Brown calls "petty jealousies." They can occur within a team or between teams. "When Shawn Kemp of Seattle gets a balloon payment of $20 million, guys like Cliff Robertson, Kevin Willis, and Charles Oakley feel that they are every bit as valuable to their teams as Kemp is to the Sonics," Brown says. "So they wonder: 'Where's my balloon payment?' "

The equity issue became prominent in the early 1990s when teams began giving astronomical contracts to first-round draft choices. In 1994, for instance, Milwaukee gave Glenn Robinson, the number-one pick overall, a $100 million deal. Dallas gave its top pick, guard Jason Kidd, $54 million in a nine-year contract—more money than established NBA guards John Stockton and Mark Price were making.

The equity issue was again placed in the spotlight in 1996, when dozens of NBA players became free agents. Shaquille O'Neal got a $120 million package from the Los Angeles Lakers. Michael Jordan re-signed for one year with the Chicago Bulls for $30 million, while Sonics All-Star guard Gary Payton accepted an $87.5 million deal to stay in Seattle. Bulls' free agent Dennis Rodman, who was making $2.5 million a year in 1996, quickly dismissed Chicago's initial offer of $6 million for the 1997 season. "I'll retire before I'd accept that offer," said Rodman. He finally signed for a little more than $9 million.

Based on J. Moore, "Managing Millionaires," *Seattle Post-Intelligencer*, November 3, 1994, p. C1; and S. Spencer, "Kemp Ready to Play Ball," *Seattle Post-Intelligencer*, October 23, 1996, p. D1.

Take It to the Net

We invite you to visit the Robbins page on the Prentice Hall Web site at:

http://www.prenhall.com/robbinsorgbeh

for this chapter's World Wide Web exercise.

those in jobs that are either male or female dominated. This also suggests that if women are tolerant of lower pay, it may be due to the comparative standard they use.

Employees with short tenure in their current organizations tend to have little information about others inside the organization, so they rely on their own personal experiences. On the other hand, employees with long tenure rely more heavily on co-workers for comparison. Upper-level employees, those in the professional ranks, and those with higher amounts of education tend to be more cosmopolitan and have better information about people in other organizations. Therefore, these types of employees will make more other-outside comparisons.

Based on equity theory, when employees perceive an inequity, they can be predicted to make one of six choices:[50]

1. Change their inputs (for example, don't exert as much effort)

2. Change their outcomes (for example, individuals paid on a piece-rate basis can increase their pay by producing a higher quantity of units of lower quality)

3. Distort perceptions of self (for example, "I used to think I worked at a moderate pace but now I realize that I work a lot harder than everyone else.")

4. Distort perceptions of others (for example, "Mike's job isn't as desirable as I previously thought it was.")

5. Choose a different referent (for example, "I may not make as much as my brother-in-law, but I'm doing a lot better than my Dad did when he was my age.")

6. Leave the field (for example, quit the job)

Equity theory recognizes that individuals are concerned not only with the absolute amount of rewards they receive for their efforts, but also with the relationship of this amount to what others receive. They make judgments as to the relationship between their inputs and outcomes and the inputs and outcomes of others. Based on one's inputs, such as effort, experience, education, and competence, one compares outcomes such as salary levels, raises, recognition, and other factors. When people perceive an imbalance in their outcome–input ratio relative to others, tension is created. This tension provides the basis for motivation, as people strive for what they perceive as equity and fairness.

> ◆ Equity theory recognizes that individuals are concerned not only with the absolute amount of rewards for their efforts but also with the relationship of this amount to what others receive.

Specifically, the theory establishes four propositions relating to inequitable pay:

1. *Given payment by time, overrewarded employees will produce more than will equitably paid employees.* Hourly and salaried employees will generate high quantity or quality of production in order to increase the input side of the ratio and bring about equity.

2. *Given payment by quantity of production, overrewarded employees will produce fewer, but higher-quality, units than will equitably paid employees.* Individuals paid on a piece-rate basis will increase their effort to achieve equity, which can result in greater quality or quantity. However, increases in quantity will only increase inequity, since every unit produced results in further overpayment. Therefore, effort is directed toward increasing quality rather than increasing quantity.

Defensive back Deion Sanders perceived an inequity due to being underrewarded. Sanders earned more than a million dollars a year with the San Francisco 49ers. But, unhappy with his pay relative to other defensive backs, Sanders joined the Dallas Cowboys for more than $5 million a year. Consistent with equity theory, Sanders sought a pay package that he perceived more fairly matched his performance on the field and his star status off the field.

3. *Given payment by time, underrewarded employees will produce less or poorer quality of output.* Effort will be decreased, which will bring about lower productivity or poorer-quality output than equitably paid subjects.

4. *Given payment by quantity of production, underrewarded employees will produce a large number of low-quality units in comparison with equitably paid employees.* Employees on piece-rate pay plans can bring about equity because trading off quality of output for quantity will result in an increase in rewards with little or no increase in contributions.

These propositions have generally been supported, with a few minor qualifications.[51] First, inequities created by overpayment do not seem to have a very significant impact on behavior in most work situations. Apparently, people have a great deal more tolerance of overpayment inequities than of underpayment inequities, or are better able to rationalize them. Second, not all people are equity sensitive. For example, there is a small part of the working population who actually prefer that their outcome–input ratio be less than the referent comparison. Predictions from equity theory are not likely to be very accurate with these "benevolent types."

It's also important to note that while most research on equity theory has focused on pay, employees seem to look for equity in the distribution of other organizational rewards. For instance, it's been shown that the use of high-status job titles as well as large and lavishly furnished offices may function as outcomes for some employees in their equity equation.[52]

Finally, recent research has been directed at expanding what is meant by equity or fairness.[53] Historically, equity theory focused on **distributive justice** or the perceived fairness of the *amount and allocation* of rewards among individuals. But equity should also consider **procedural justice**—the perceived fairness of the *process* used to determine the distribution of rewards. The evidence indicates that distributive justice has a greater influence on employee satisfaction than procedural justice, while procedural justice tends to

distributive justice
Perceived fairness of the amount and allocation of rewards among individuals.

procedural justice
The perceived fairness of the process used to determine the distribution of rewards.

affect an employee's organizational commitment, trust in his or her boss, and intention to quit.[54] So managers should consider openly sharing information on how allocation decisions are made, following consistent and unbiased procedures, and engaging in similar practices to increase the perception of procedural justice. By increasing the perception of procedural fairness, employees are likely to view their bosses and the organization as positive even if they're dissatisfied with pay, promotions, and other personal outcomes.

In conclusion, equity theory demonstrates that, for most employees, motivation is influenced significantly by relative rewards as well as by absolute rewards, but some key issues are still unclear.[55] For instance, how do employees handle conflicting equity signals, such as when unions point to other employee groups who are substantially *better off*, while management argues how much things have *improved*? How do employees define inputs and outcomes? How do they combine and weigh their inputs and outcomes to arrive at totals? When and how do the factors change over time? Yet, regardless of these problems, equity theory continues to offer us some important insights into employee motivation.

Expectancy Theory

Currently, one of the most widely accepted explanations of motivation is Victor Vroom's **expectancy theory**.[56] Although it has its critics,[57] most of the research evidence is supportive of the theory.[58]

Expectancy theory argues that the strength of a tendency to act in a certain way depends on the strength of an expectation that the act will be followed by a given outcome and on the attractiveness of that outcome to the individual. In more practical terms, expectancy theory says that an employee will be motivated to exert a high level of effort when he or she believes that effort will lead to a good performance appraisal; that a good appraisal will lead to organizational rewards like a bonus, a salary increase, or a promotion; and that the rewards will satisfy the employee's personal goals. The theory, therefore, focuses on three relationships (see Exhibit 5-8 on page 188).

expectancy theory
The strength of a tendency to act in a certain way depends on the strength of an expectation that the act will be followed by a given outcome and on the attractiveness of that outcome to the individual.

1. *Effort–performance relationship.* The probability perceived by the individual that exerting a given amount of effort will lead to performance.

2. *Performance–reward relationship.* The degree to which the individual believes that performing at a particular level will lead to the attainment of a desired outcome.

3. *Rewards–personal goals relationship.* The degree to which organizational rewards satisfy an individual's personal goals or needs and the attractiveness of those potential rewards for the individual.[59]

Expectancy theory helps explain why a lot of workers aren't motivated on their jobs and merely do the minimum necessary to get by. This is evident when we look at the theory's three relationships in a little more detail. We present them as questions employees need to answer in the affirmative if their motivation is to be maximized.

First, *if I give a maximum effort, will it be recognized in my performance appraisal?* For a lot of employees, the answer is "No." Why? Their skill level may be deficient, which means that no matter how hard they try, they're not likely to be a

◆ Expectancy theory helps explain why a lot of workers aren't motivated on their jobs and merely do the minimum necessary to get by.

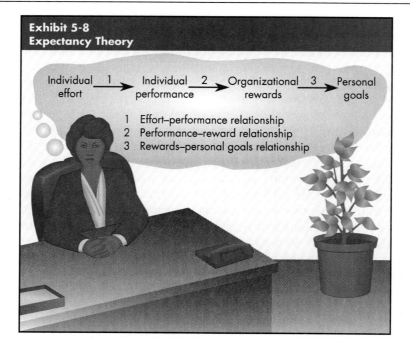

Exhibit 5-8
Expectancy Theory

Individual effort →1→ Individual performance →2→ Organizational rewards →3→ Personal goals

1 Effort–performance relationship
2 Performance–reward relationship
3 Rewards–personal goals relationship

high performer. The organization's performance appraisal system may be designed to assess nonperformance factors like loyalty, initiative, or courage, which means more effort won't necessarily result in a higher evaluation. Still another possibility is that the employee, rightly or wrongly, perceives that her boss doesn't like her. As a result, she expects to get a poor appraisal regardless of her level of effort. These examples suggest that one possible source of low employee motivation is the belief, by the employee, that no matter how hard she works, the likelihood of getting a good performance appraisal is low.

Second, *if I get a good performance appraisal, will it lead to organizational rewards?* Many employees see the performance–reward relationship in their job as weak. The reason, as we elaborate upon in the next chapter, is that organizations reward a lot of things besides just performance. For example, when pay is allocated to employees based on factors such as seniority, being cooperative, or for "kissing up" to the boss, employees are likely to see the performance–reward relationship as being weak and demotivating.

Finally, *if I'm rewarded, are the rewards ones that I find personally attractive?* The employee works hard in hope of getting a promotion but gets a pay raise instead. Or the employee wants a more interesting and challenging job but receives only a few words of praise. Or the employee puts in extra effort to be relocated to the company's Paris office but instead is transferred to Singapore. These examples illustrate the importance of the rewards being tailored to individual employee needs. Unfortunately, many managers are limited in the rewards they can distribute, which makes it difficult to individualize rewards. Moreover, some managers incorrectly assume that all employees want the same thing, thus overlooking the motivational effects of differentiating rewards. In either case, employee motivation is submaximized.

In summary, the key to expectancy theory is the understanding of an individual's goals and the linkage between effort and performance, between performance and rewards, and, finally, between the rewards and individual goal satisfaction. As a contingency model, expectancy theory recognizes that there is no universal principle for explaining everyone's motivations. Additionally, just because we understand what needs a person seeks to satisfy does not ensure that the individual perceives high performance as necessarily leading to the satisfaction of these needs.

Does expectancy theory work? Attempts to validate the theory have been complicated by methodological, criterion, and measurement problems. As a result, many published studies that purport to support or negate the theory must be viewed with caution. Importantly, most studies have failed to replicate the methodology as it was originally proposed. For example, the theory proposes to explain different levels of effort from the same person under different circumstances, but almost all replication studies have looked at different people. Correcting for this flaw has greatly improved support for the validity of expectancy theory.[60] Some critics suggest that the theory has only limited use, arguing that it tends to be more valid for predicting in situations where effort–performance and performance–reward linkages are clearly perceived by the individual.[61] Since few individuals perceive a high correlation between performance and rewards in their jobs, the theory tends to be idealistic. If organizations actually rewarded individuals for performance rather than according to such criteria as seniority, effort, skill level, and job difficulty, then the theory's validity might be considerably greater. However, rather than invalidating expectancy theory, this criticism can be used in support of the theory, for it explains why a significant segment of the workforce exerts low levels of effort in carrying out job responsibilities.

Don't Forget Ability and Opportunity

Robin and Chris both graduated from college a couple of years ago with their degrees in elementary education. They each took jobs as first-grade teachers, but in different school districts. Robin immediately confronted a number of obstacles on the job: a large class (42 students), a small and dingy classroom, and inadequate supplies. Chris's situation couldn't have been more different. He had only 15 students in his class, plus a teaching aide for 15 hours each week, a modern and well-lighted room, a well-stocked supply cabinet, six Macintosh computers for students to use, and a highly supportive principal. Not surprisingly, at the end of their first school year, Chris had been considerably more effective as a teacher than had Robin.

The preceding episode illustrates an obvious but often overlooked fact. Success on a job is facilitated or hindered by the existence or absence of support resources.

A popular, although arguably simplistic, way of thinking about employee performance is as a function of the interaction of ability and motivation; that is, performance = $f(A \times M)$. If either is inadequate, performance will be negatively affected. This helps to explain, for instance, the hardworking athlete or student with modest abilities who consistently outperforms his or her more gifted, but lazy, rival. So, as we noted in chapter 2, an individual's intelligence and skills (subsumed under the label *ability*) must be considered in addition to motivation if we are to be able to accurately explain and predict employee performance. But a piece of the puzzle is still missing. We need to add **opportunity to perform** to our equation—performance =

opportunity to perform
High levels of performance are partially a function of an absence of obstacles that constrain the employee.

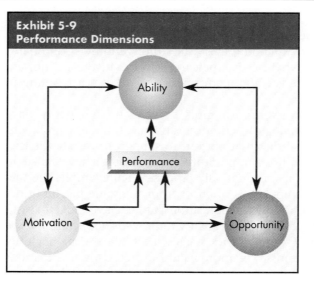

**Exhibit 5-9
Performance Dimensions**

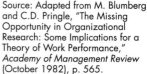

Source: Adapted from M. Blumberg and C.D. Pringle, "The Missing Opportunity in Organizational Research: Some Implications for a Theory of Work Performance," *Academy of Management Review* (October 1982), p. 565.

$f(A \times M \times O)$.[62] Even though an individual may be willing and able, there may be obstacles that constrain performance. This is shown in Exhibit 5-9.

When you attempt to assess why an employee may not be performing to the level that you believe he or she is capable of, take a look at the work environment to see if it's supportive. Does the employee have adequate tools, equipment, materials, and supplies? Does the employee have favorable working conditions, helpful co-workers, supportive work rules and procedures, sufficient information to make job-related decisions, adequate time to do a good job, and the like? If not, performance will suffer.

Integrating Contemporary Theories of Motivation

We've looked at a lot of motivation theories in this chapter. The fact that a number of these theories have been supported only complicates the matter. How simple it would have been if, after presenting several theories, only one was found valid. But these theories are not all in competition with one another! Because one is valid doesn't automatically make the others invalid. In fact, many of the theories presented in this chapter are complementary. The challenge is now to tie these theories together to help you understand their interrelationships.[63]

Exhibit 5-10 presents a model that integrates much of what we know about motivation. Its basic foundation is the expectancy model shown in Exhibit 5-8. Let's work through Exhibit 5-10.

We begin by explicitly recognizing that opportunities can aid or hinder individual effort. The individual effort box also has another arrow leading into it. This arrow flows out of the person's goals. Consistent with goal-setting theory, this goals–effort loop is meant to remind us that goals direct behavior.

Expectancy theory predicts that an employee will exert a high level of effort if he or she perceives that there is a strong relationship between effort and performance, performance and rewards, and rewards and satisfaction of per-

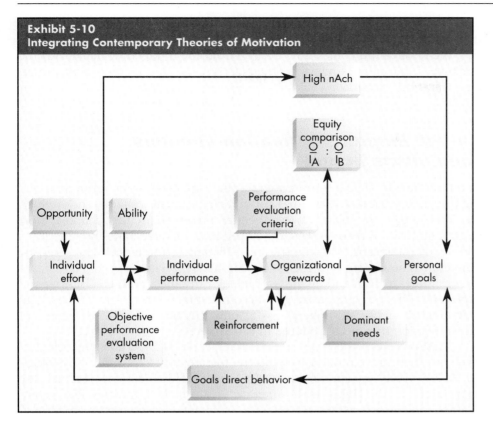

Exhibit 5-10
Integrating Contemporary Theories of Motivation

sonal goals. Each of these relationships, in turn, is influenced by certain factors. For effort to lead to good performance, the individual must have the requisite ability to perform, and the performance appraisal system that measures the individual's performance must be perceived as being fair and objective. The performance–reward relationship will be strong if the individual perceives that it is performance (rather than seniority, personal favorites, or other criteria) that is rewarded. If cognitive evaluation theory were fully valid in the actual workplace, we would predict here that basing rewards on performance should decrease the individual's intrinsic motivation. The final link in expectancy theory is the rewards–goals relationship. ERG theory would come into play at this point. Motivation would be high to the degree that the rewards an individual received for his or her high performance satisfied the dominant needs consistent with his or her individual goals.

A closer look at Exhibit 5-10 will also reveal that the model considers the achievement need and reinforcement and equity theories. The high achiever is not motivated by the organization's assessment of his or her performance or organizational rewards, hence, the jump from effort to personal goals for those with a high *nAch*. Remember, high achievers are internally driven as long as the jobs they are doing provide them with personal responsibility, feedback, and moderate risks. They are not concerned with the effort–performance, performance–rewards, or rewards–goal linkages.

Reinforcement theory enters our model by recognizing that the organization's rewards reinforce the individual's performance. If management has designed a reward system that is seen by employees as "paying off" for good performance, the rewards will reinforce and encourage continued good performance. Rewards also play the key part in equity theory. Individuals will compare the rewards (outcomes) they receive from the inputs they make with the outcome–input ratio of relevant others ($O/I_A : O/I_B$), and inequities may influence the effort expended.

Caveat Emptor: Motivation Theories Are Culture Bound

In our discussion of goal setting, we said that care needs to be taken in applying this theory because it assumes cultural characteristics that are not universal. This is true for many of the theories presented in this chapter. Most current motivation theories were developed in the United States by Americans and about Americans.[64] Maybe the most blatant pro-American characteristic inherent in these theories is the strong emphasis on what we defined in chapter 4 as individualism and quantity of life. For instance, both goal-setting and expectancy theories emphasize goal accomplishment as well as rational and individual thought. Let's take a look at how this bias has affected several of the motivation theories introduced in this chapter.

Maslow's need hierarchy argues that people start at the physiological level and then move progressively up the hierarchy in this order: physiological, safety, social, esteem, and self-actualization. This hierarchy, if it has any application at all, aligns with American culture. In countries like Japan, Greece, and Mexico, where uncertainty avoidance characteristics are strong, security needs would be on top of the need hierarchy. Countries that score high on quality-of-life characteristics—Denmark, Sweden, Norway, the Netherlands, and Finland—would have social needs on top.[65] We would pre-

While some cultural characteristics are not universal, it seems high achievers are in demand everywhere. Switzerland-based Nestlé, the world's largest branded food company, hires high achievers to sell its products in markets that span the globe. Cultural differences aside, Nestlé salespeople, such as the Red Hot Sales Force in Thailand shown here, are motivated by growth, achievement, responsibility, and recognition. These salespeople sell products to the American-style supermarkets and superstores sprouting up in developing nations. Nestlé is counting on the Red Hot group to increase profits and market share as competition in Thailand intensifies.

dict, for instance, that group work will motivate employees more when the country's culture scores high on the quality criterion.

Another motivation concept that clearly has an American bias is the achievement need. The view that a high achievement need acts as an internal motivator presupposes two cultural characteristics—a willingness to accept a moderate degree of risk (which excludes countries with strong uncertainty avoidance characteristics) and a concern with performance (which applies almost singularly to countries with strong quantity-of-life characteristics). This combination is found in Anglo-American countries like the United States, Canada, and Great Britain.[66] On the other hand, these characteristics are relatively absent in countries such as Chile and Portugal.

But don't assume there aren't *any* cross-cultural consistencies. For instance, the desire for interesting work seems important to almost all workers, regardless of their national culture. In a study of seven countries, employees in Belgium, Britain, Israel, and the United States ranked "interesting work" number one among 11 work goals. And this factor was ranked either second or third in Japan, the Netherlands, and Germany.[67] Similarly, in a study comparing job-preference outcomes among graduate students in the United States, Canada, Australia, and Singapore, growth, achievement, and responsibility were rated the top three and had identical rankings.[68] Both of these studies suggest some universality to the importance of intrinsic factors in motivation-hygiene theory.

Summary and Implications for Managers

The theories we've discussed in this chapter do not all address our four dependent variables. Some, for instance, are directed at explaining turnover, while others emphasize productivity. The theories also differ in their predictive strength. In this section, we (1) review the key motivation theories to determine their relevance in explaining our dependent variables, and (2) assess the predictive power of each.[69]

NEED THEORIES   We introduced four theories that focused on needs. These were Maslow's hierarchy, motivation-hygiene, ERG, and McClelland's needs theories. The strongest of these is probably the last, particularly regarding the relationship between achievement and productivity. If the other three have any value at all, that value relates to explaining and predicting job satisfaction.

GOAL-SETTING THEORY   There is little dispute that clear and difficult goals lead to higher levels of employee productivity. This evidence leads us to conclude that goal-setting theory provides one of the more powerful explanations of this dependent variable. The theory, however, does not address absenteeism, turnover, or satisfaction.

REINFORCEMENT THEORY   This theory has an impressive record for predicting factors like quality and quantity of work, persistence of effort, absenteeism, tardiness, and accident rates. It does not offer much insight into employee satisfaction or the decision to quit.

Exhibit 5-11 Power of Motivation Theories[a]

			THEORIES		
Variable	Need	Goal Setting	Reinforce-ment	Equity	Expectancy
Productivity	3[b]	5	3	3	4[c]
Absenteeism			4	4	4
Turnover				4	5
Satisfaction	2			2	

[a]Theories are rated on a scale of 1 to 5, 5 being highest.
[b]Applies to individuals with a high need to achieve.
[c]Limited value in jobs where employees have little discretionary choice.

Source: Based on F.J. Landy and W.S. Becker, "Motivation Theory Reconsidered," in L.L. Cummings and B.M. Staw (eds.), *Research in Organizational Behavior*, Vol. 9 (Greenwich, CT: JAI Press, 1987), p. 33.

EQUITY THEORY Equity theory deals with all four dependent variables. However, it is strongest when predicting absence and turnover behaviors and weak when predicting differences in employee productivity.

EXPECTANCY THEORY Our final theory focused on performance variables. It has proved to offer a relatively powerful explanation of employee productivity, absenteeism, and turnover. But expectancy theory assumes that employees have few constraints on their decision discretion. It makes many of the same assumptions that the rational model makes about individual decision making (see chapter 3). This acts to restrict its applicability.

For major decisions, like accepting or resigning from a job, expectancy theory works well because people don't rush into decisions of this nature. They're more prone to take the time to carefully consider the costs and benefits of all the alternatives. However, expectancy theory is not a very good explanation for more typical types of work behavior, especially for individuals in lower-level jobs, because such jobs come with considerable limitations imposed by work methods, supervisors, and company policies. We would conclude, therefore, that expectancy theory's power in explaining employee productivity increases where the jobs being performed are more complex and higher in the organization (where discretion is greater).

A GUIDE THROUGH THE MAZE Exhibit 5-11 summarizes what we know about the power of the more well-known motivation theories to explain and predict our four dependent variables. While based on a wealth of research, it also includes some subjective judgments. However, it does provide a reasonable guide through the motivation theory maze.

For Review

1. Does motivation come from within a person or is it a result of the situation? Explain.
2. What are the implications of Theories X and Y for motivation practices?
3. Compare and contrast Maslow's hierarchy of needs theory with (a) Alderfer's ERG theory and (b) Herzberg's motivation-hygiene theory.
4. Describe the three needs isolated by McClelland. How are they related to worker behavior?
5. Explain cognitive evaluation theory. How applicable is it to management practice?
6. What's the role of self-efficacy in goal setting?
7. Contrast distributive and procedural justice.
8. Identify the variables in expectancy theory.
9. Explain the formula: Performance $= f(A \times M \times O)$ and give an example.
10. What consistencies among motivation concepts, if any, apply cross-culturally?

For Discussion

1. "The cognitive evaluation theory is contradictory to reinforcement and expectancy theories." Do you agree or disagree? Explain.
2. "Goal setting is part of both reinforcement and expectancy theories." Do you agree or disagree? Explain.
3. Analyze the application of Maslow's and Herzberg's theories to an African or Caribbean nation where more than a quarter of the population is unemployed.
4. Can an individual be too motivated, so that his or her performance declines as a result of excessive effort? Discuss.
5. Identify three activities you really enjoy (for example, playing tennis, reading a novel, going shopping). Next, identify three activities you really dislike (for example, going to the dentist, cleaning the house, staying on a restricted-calorie diet). Using the expectancy model, analyze each of your answers to assess why some activities stimulate your effort while others don't.

Money Motivates!

The importance of money as a motivator has been consistently downgraded by most behavioral scientists. They prefer to point out the value of challenging jobs, goals, participation in decision making, feedback, cohesive work teams, and other nonmonetary factors as stimulants to employee motivation. We argue otherwise here—that money is *the* crucial incentive to work motivation. As a medium of exchange, it is the vehicle by which employees can purchase the numerous need-satisfying things they desire. Furthermore, money also performs the function of a scorecard, by which employees assess the value that the organization places on their services and by which employees can compare their value to others.*

Money's value as a medium of exchange is obvious. People may not work only for money, but take the money away and how many people would come to work? A recent study of nearly 2,500 employees found that while these people disagreed over what was their number-one motivator, they unanimously ranked money as their number two.** This study reaffirms that for the vast majority of the workforce, a regular paycheck is absolutely necessary in order to meet their basic physiological and safety needs.

As equity theory suggests, money has symbolic value in addition to its exchange value. We use pay as the primary outcome against which we compare our inputs to determine if we are being treated equitably. That an organization pays one executive $80,000 a year and another $95,000 means more than the latter's earning $15,000 a year more. It is a message, from the organization to both employees, of how much it values the contribution of each.

In addition to equity theory, both reinforcement and expectancy theories attest to the value of money as a motivator. In the former, if pay is contingent on performance, it will encourage workers to generate high levels of effort. Consistent with expectancy theory, money will motivate to the extent that it is seen as being able to satisfy an individual's personal goals and is perceived as being dependent upon performance criteria.

The best case for money as a motivator is a review of studies done by Ed Locke at the University of Maryland.*** Locke looked at four methods of motivating employee performance: money, goal setting, participation in decision making, and redesigning jobs to give workers more challenge and responsibility. He found that the average improvement from money was 30 percent; goal setting increased performance 16 percent; participation improved performance by less than 1 percent; and job redesign positively impacted performance by an average of 17 percent. Moreover, every study Locke reviewed that used money as a method of motivation resulted in some improvement in employee performance. Such evidence demonstrates that money may not be the *only* motivator, but it is difficult to argue that it *doesn't* motivate!

*K.O. Doyle, "Introduction: Money and the Behavioral Sciences," *American Behavioral Scientist*, July 1992, pp. 641–57.

**S. Caudron, "Motivation? Money's Only No. 2," *Industry Week*, November 15, 1993, p. 33.

***E.A. Locke, et al., "The Relative Effectiveness of Four Methods of Motivating Employee Performance," in *Changes in Working Life*, eds. K.D. Duncan, M.M. Gruneberg, and D. Wallis (London: John Wiley, Ltd., 1980), pp. 363–83.

Money Doesn't Motivate Most Employees Today!

Money can motivate *some* people under *some* conditions, so the issue isn't really whether or not money *can* motivate. The answer to that is: "It can!" The more relevant question is: Does money motivate most employees in the workforce today to higher performance? The answer to this question, we'll argue, is "No."

For money to motivate an individual's performance, certain conditions must be met. First, money must be important to the individual. Second, money must be perceived by the individual as being a direct reward for performance. Third, the marginal amount of money offered for the performance must be perceived by the individual as being significant. Finally, management must have the discretion to reward high performers with more money. Let's take a look at each of these conditions.

Money is not important to all employees. High achievers, for instance, are intrinsically motivated. Money should have little impact on these people. Similarly, money is relevant to those individuals with strong lower-order needs; but for most of the workforce, lower-order needs are substantially satisfied.

Money would motivate if employees perceived a strong linkage between performance and rewards in organizations. Unfortunately, pay increases are far more often determined by levels of skills and experience, community pay standards, the national cost-of-living index, and the organization's current and future financial prospects than by each employee's level of performance.

For money to motivate, the marginal difference in pay increases between a high performer and an average performer must be significant. In practice, it rarely is. For instance, a high-performing employee who currently is earning $35,000 a year is given a $200-a-month raise. After taxes, that amounts to about $35 a week. But this employee's $35,000-a-year co-worker, who is an average performer, is rarely passed over at raise time. Instead of getting an 8 percent raise, he is likely to get half of that. The net difference in their weekly paychecks is probably less than $20. How much motivation is there in knowing that if you work really hard you're going to end up with $20 a week more than someone who is doing just enough to get by? For a large number of people, not much! Research indicates that merit raises must be at least 7 percent of base pay for employees to perceive them as motivating. Unfortunately, recent surveys find nonmanagerial employees averaging merit increases of only 4.9 percent.*

Our last point relates to the degree of discretion that managers have in being able to reward high performers. Where unions exist, that discretion is almost zero. Pay is determined through collective bargaining and is allocated by job title and seniority, not level of performance. In nonunionized environments, the organization's compensation policies will constrain managerial discretion. Each job typically has a pay grade. Thus, a Systems Analyst III can earn between $3,825 and $4,540 a month. No matter how good a job that analyst does, her boss cannot pay her more than $4,540 a month. Similarly, no matter how poorly someone does in that job, he will earn at least $3,825 a month. In most organizations, managers have a very small area of discretion within which they can reward their higher-performing employees. So money might be theoretically capable of motivating employees to higher levels of performance, but most managers aren't given enough flexibility to do much about it.

For more on this argument, see B. Filipczak, "Can't Buy Me Love," *Training*, January 1996, pp. 29–34.

*See A. Mitra, N. Gupta, and G.D. Jenkins, Jr., "The Case of the Invisible Merit Raise: How People See Their Pay Raises," *Compensation & Benefits Review*, May–June 1995, pp. 71–76.

Learning about Yourself

What Motivates You?

Circle the number that most closely agrees with how you feel. Consider your answers in the context of your current job or past work experience.

	Strongly Disagree				Strongly Agree
1. I try very hard to improve on my past performance at work.	1	2	3	4	5
2. I enjoy competition and winning.	1	2	3	4	5
3. I often find myself talking to those around me about nonwork matters.	1	2	3	4	5
4. I enjoy a difficult challenge.	1	2	3	4	5
5. I enjoy being in charge.	1	2	3	4	5
6. I want to be liked by others.	1	2	3	4	5
7. I want to know how I am progressing as I complete tasks.	1	2	3	4	5
8. I confront people who do things I disagree with.	1	2	3	4	5
9. I tend to build close relationships with co-workers.	1	2	3	4	5
10. I enjoy setting and achieving realistic goals.	1	2	3	4	5
11. I enjoy influencing other people to get my way.	1	2	3	4	5
12. I enjoy belonging to groups and organizations.	1	2	3	4	5
13. I enjoy the satisfaction of completing a difficult task.	1	2	3	4	5
14. I often work to gain more control over the events around me.	1	2	3	4	5
15. I enjoy working with others more than working alone.	1	2	3	4	5

Turn to page A-27 for scoring directions and key.

Source: Based on R. Steers and D. Braunstein, "A Behaviorally Based Measure of Manifest Needs in Work Settings," *Journal of Vocational Behavior*, October 1976, p. 254; and R.N. Lussier, *Human Relations in Organizations: A Skill Building Approach* (Homewood, IL: Richard D. Irwin, 1990), p. 120.

Working with Others

What Do People Want from Their Jobs?

Each class member begins by completing the following questionnaire:

Rate the following 12 job factors according to how important each is to you. Place a number on a scale of 1 to 5 on the line before each factor.

Very important		Somewhat important		Not important
5	4	3	2	1

_____ **1.** An interesting job

_____ **2.** A good boss

_____ **3.** Recognition and appreciation for the work I do

_____ **4.** The opportunity for advancement

_____ **5.** A satisfying personal life

_____ **6.** A prestigious or status job

_____ **7.** Job responsibility

_____ **8.** Good working conditions

_____ **9.** Sensible company rules, regulations, procedures, and policies

_____**10.** The opportunity to grow through learning new things

_____**11.** A job I can do well and succeed at

_____**12.** Job security

This questionnaire taps the two dimensions in Herzberg's motivation-hygiene theory. To determine if hygiene or motivating factors are important to you, place the numbers 1–5 that represent your answers below.

Hygiene factors score	Motivational factors score
2. _____	1. _____
5. _____	3. _____
6. _____	4. _____
8. _____	7. _____
9. _____	10. _____
12. _____	11. _____
Total points _____	Total points _____

Add up each column. Did you select hygiene or motivating factors as being most important to you?

Now break into groups of five or six and compare your questionnaire results. (a) How similar are your scores? (b) How close did your group's results come to those found by Herzberg? (c) What motivational implications did your group arrive at based on your analysis?

This exercise is based on R.N. Lussier, *Human Relations in Organizations: A Skill Building Approach*, 2nd ed. Homewood, IL: Richard D. Irwin, 1993. With permission.

Lincoln Electric

A recent survey of large American companies found that nearly half had modified their compensation practices to link pay to performance. Many of these companies, in fact, had visited Cleveland-based Lincoln Electric Co. to look at its "model" pay-for-performance system.

Lincoln employs about 3,400 people and generates 90 percent of its sales from manufacturing arc-welding equipment and supplies. Founded in 1895, the company's legendary profit-sharing incentive system and resultant productivity record have received much attention from people who design motivation programs.

Factory workers at Lincoln receive piece-rate wages with no guaranteed minimum hourly pay. After working for the firm for two years, employees begin to participate in the year-end bonus plan. Determined by a formula that considers the company's gross profits, the employees' base piece rate, and merit rating, it has been one of the most lucrative bonus systems for factory workers in American manufacturing. The average size of the bonus over the past 55 years had been 95.5 percent of base wages!

The company has a guaranteed-employment policy, which it put in place in 1958. Since that time, it has not laid off a single worker. In return for job security, however, employees agree to several conditions. During slow times, they will accept reduced work periods. They also agree to accept work transfers, even to lower-paid jobs, if that is necessary to maintain a minimum of 30 hours of work per week.

You'd think the Lincoln Electric system would attract quality people, and it has. For instance, the company recently hired four Harvard MBAs to fill future management slots. But, consistent with company tradition, they started out, like everyone else, doing piecework on the assembly line.

Historically, Lincoln Electric's profit-sharing incentive system has provided positive benefits for the company as well as for its employees. In the early 1990s, one company executive estimated that Lincoln's overall productivity was about double that of its domestic competitors. To that point, the company had earned a profit every year since the depths of the 1930s Depression and had never missed a quarterly dividend. Lincoln also had one of the lowest employee turnover rates in U.S. industry.

But something interesting has recently happened at Lincoln Electric. The company is overhauling its pay system. Under pressure from institutional shareholders and independent board members, management has been looking for ways to improve earnings. The reason? Rapid growth and global competition resulted in the company losing money in 1992 and 1993, and employee bonuses have been dropping. In 1995, for instance, bonuses averaged 56 percent—the lowest in recent years. The result: Employees are disgruntled. Management decided it had to modify its pay system to make it more mainstream. One objective is to reduce the huge variations in worker pay—from roughly $32,000 to more than $100,000.

In early 1996, to revamp the pay scheme without stirring up resentment, management set up a committee to study the bonus program. It has told employees that a new formula is in the works. It wants employees to provide input by focusing more on their overall earnings, not just the percentage bonus they receive. For instance, senior management wants to start raising base pay and, simultaneously, to start reducing annual bonuses.

Questions

1. Use expectancy theory to explain the past success of Lincoln's pay system.
2. Using two or more motivation theories, explain problems with the historical system.
3. What problems, if any, do you think management should expect as a result of its announced changes in the pay system?

Based on S.J. Modic, "Fine-Tuning a Classic," *Industry Week*, March 6, 1989, pp. 15–18; C. Wiley, "Incentive Plan Pushes Production," *Personnel Journal*, August 1993, pp. 86–87; and Z. Schiller, "A Model Incentive Plan Gets Caught in a Vise," *Business Week*, January 22, 1996, pp. 89–92.

The Middle-Class Dream: Where Did It Go?

"We're working longer hours, it's taking two incomes versus one income. It's definitely taking more to achieve the American dream." "I work two jobs, not only during the week, but on the weekend." These comments capture a growing feeling among the American middle class. Middle-class Americans are losing their hope and optimism about the future, and they're having to work harder to maintain their middle-class status.

In 1986, 74 percent of working people expected their kids to be better off than they were. In 1991, that percentage was down to 66 percent. Now it's 54 percent. There's a definite loss of faith in the American dream. An increasing number of middle-class people—those who earn between $20,000 and $50,000 a year—don't expect their children to do better than they have. Today's workers increasingly believe they are not doing as well as their parents. Even people who are doing as well as their parents say they're working harder to keep that standard of living.

What has caused this drop in optimism? A number of factors: the need for two incomes to keep afloat; less free time to enjoy family; little or no savings or money for family vacations; high taxes; child-care expenses; fear that one family member will lose his or her job; the stress of trying to maintain middle-class status in times of stagnant wages; and making comparisons with families from the 1950s and 1960s, who seemed to live better, on only one income, and with less stress.

In the 30 years after World War II ended, the average American enjoyed a way of life unprecedented in history—a steady, rapidly growing real income and movement into the middle class. Skilled and unskilled workers alike came to expect job security and income growth. The last 20 years, however, have been a different story. For most Americans, since the mid-1970s there has really been wage stagnation and a failure of living standards to rise. For most families, it now takes two incomes to do what their parents did with one.

Take owning a home, for example. After World War II, low-cost housing was being built everywhere. Any young family with a few hundred dollars could have a piece of the American dream—a home of their own. Today a typical home costs nearly $100,000 and few young couples have the 20 percent needed for a traditional down payment. Among those who see a home in their near future, that home isn't much like their parents' or grandparents' homes. Instead of a small two-bedroom, one-bath starter home, today's family wants three or four bedrooms with multiple baths, a state-of-the-art kitchen, and a two-car garage. And few in the middle class can envision supporting such a home on one partner's income.

Is America on the verge of becoming a Third World nation? Will the middle class continue to shrink, while the rich get richer and the working poor become the new dominant class?

Questions

1. How might financial and personal strains discussed in the case influence employee motivation and behavior?

2. Contrast implications for motivating employees with middle-class incomes versus high-paid professionals.

3. What, if anything, can individual organizations do to alleviate the problems cited in this case?

Source: Based on "Middle Class—The Family Dream," *ABC Nightline*; aired on January 6, 1995.

6 MOTIVATION: FROM CONCEPTS TO APPLICATIONS

CHAPTER OUTLINE
Management by Objectives
Employee Recognition Programs
Employee Involvement Programs
Variable-Pay Programs
Skill-Based Pay Plans
Flexible Benefits
Special Issues in Motivation

Set me anything to do as a task, and it is inconceivable the desire I have to do something else.
—G. B. Shaw

LEARNING OBJECTIVES

After studying this chapter, you should be able to

1 Identify the four ingredients common to MBO programs

2 Explain why managers might want to use employee involvement programs

3 Contrast participative management with employee involvement

4 Define quality circles

5 Explain how ESOPs can increase employee motivation

6 Contrast gainsharing and profit sharing

7 Describe the link between skill-based pay plans and motivation theories

8 Explain how flexible benefits turn benefits into motivators

9 Contrast the challenges of motivating professional employees versus low-skilled employees

10 Contrast the challenges in motivating professional employees with temporary workers

SHAMEE Samad and Jamie Sokalsky have struck gold. But that's appropriate since they work for Barrick Gold Corporation of Toronto. The world's most profitable and third-largest gold mining operation, Barrick employees are enjoying the benefits from the company's generous stock-option program.[1]

Barrick introduced the idea of supplementing regular paychecks with stock in 1984. At the time, the company was strapped for cash so management decided to use stock options as a way to attract and motivate its employees. But in contrast to most stock-option plans, Barrick's plan covers all 5,000 employees, not just upper-level managers. So far, the program has seemed to be a winner for both employees and the company.

Ms. Samad, for example, has been an accounts payable clerk with the company for ten years—she joined Barrick as a 19-year-old, fresh out of high school. In her first year with the company, she earned stock options worth $11,000, on top of her $24,000 salary. In the decade she's been with Barrick, Samad has cashed in $51,000 from options she's been granted and still holds another $64,000 worth. Mr. Sokalsky, meanwhile, has only been with the company for two years. As corporate treasurer, however, he's already racked up $320,000 worth of options. Not bad considering that his annual salary is just over $100,000.

Do stock options motivate? Ms. Samad thinks they do. "If I have to come in early or stay late, I do it. No questions asked." And the company has come a long way from the days when it was strapped for money. A share of Barrick stock bought in 1983 at an initial price of $1.75 is now worth more than $42. The company has consistently outperformed other gold producers even during some very lean years in the gold business. A fall in gold prices to a three-year low in 1989, for example, hardly left a dent, as Barrick's earnings were up 21 percent and its share price rose 94 percent. The following year, earnings were up 73 percent and Barrick shares climbed another 38 percent, even as the Toronto Stock Exchange's Gold and Silver Index declined more than 20 percent. ◆

I n this chapter, we want to focus on how to apply motivation concepts. We want to link theories to practice. For it's one thing to be able to regurgitate motivation theories. It's often another to see how, as a manager, you could use them.

In the following pages, we review a number of motivation techniques and programs that have gained varying degrees of acceptance in practice. For example, we discuss variable-pay plans such as the stock-option program used by Barrick. And for each of the techniques and programs we review, we specifically address how they build on one or more of the motivation theories covered in the previous chapter.

Management by Objectives

Goal-setting theory has an impressive base of research support. But as a manager, how do you make goal setting operational? The best answer to that question is: Install a management by objectives (MBO) program.

What Is MBO?

management by objectives (MBO)
A program that encompasses specific goals, participatively set, for an explicit time period, with feedback on goal progress.

Management by objectives emphasizes participatively set goals that are tangible, verifiable, and measurable. It's not a new idea. In fact, it was originally proposed by Peter Drucker more than 40 years ago as a means of using goals to motivate people rather than to control them.[2] Today, no introduction to basic management concepts would be complete without a discussion of MBO.

MBO's appeal undoubtedly lies in its emphasis on converting overall organizational objectives into specific objectives for organizational units and individual members. MBO operationalizes the concept of objectives by devising a process by which objectives cascade down through the organization. As depicted in Exhibit 6-1, the organization's overall objectives are translated into specific objectives for each succeeding level (that is, divisional, departmental, individual) in the organization. But because lower-unit managers jointly participate in setting their own goals, MBO works from the "bottom up" as well as from the "top down." The result is a hierarchy of objectives that links objectives at one level to those at the next level. And for the individual employee, MBO provides specific personal performance objectives.

◆ No introduction to basic management concepts would be complete without a discussion of MBO.

There are four ingredients common to MBO programs. These are goal specificity, participative decision making, an explicit time period, and performance feedback.[3]

The objectives in MBO should be concise statements of expected accomplishments. It's not adequate, for example, to merely state a desire to cut costs, improve service, or increase quality. Such desires have to be converted into tangible objectives that can be measured and evaluated. To cut departmental costs *by 7 percent,* to improve service by ensuring that all telephone orders are processed *within 24 hours of receipt,* or to increase quality by keeping returns to *less than 1 percent of sales* are examples of specific objectives.

The objectives in MBO are not unilaterally set by the boss and then assigned to subordinates. MBO replaces imposed goals with participatively de-

Exhibit 6-1
Cascading of Objectives

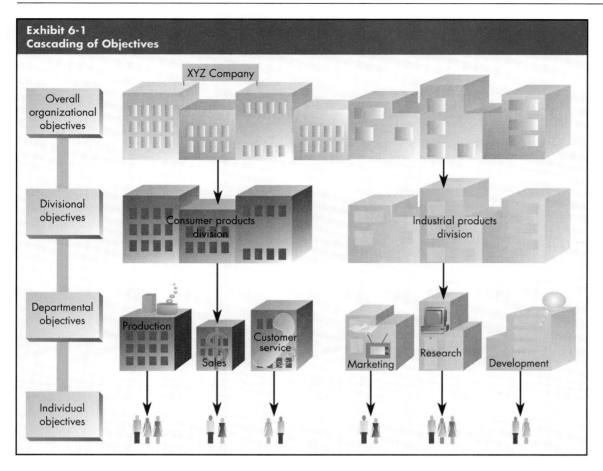

termined goals. The superior and subordinate jointly choose the goals and agree on how they will be measured.

Each objective has a specific time period in which it is to be completed. Typically the time period is three months, six months, or a year. So managers and subordinates have specific objectives and stipulated time periods in which to accomplish them.

The final ingredient in an MBO program is feedback on performance. MBO seeks to give continuous feedback on progress toward goals. Ideally, this is accomplished by giving ongoing feedback to individuals so they can monitor and correct their own actions. This is supplemented by periodic managerial evaluations, when progress is reviewed. This applies at the top of the organization as well as at the bottom. The vice president of sales, for instance, has objectives for overall sales and for each of his or her major products. He or she will monitor ongoing sales reports to determine progress toward the sales division's objectives. Similarly, district sales managers have objectives, as does each salesperson in the field. Feedback in terms of sales and performance data is provided to let these people know how they are doing. Formal appraisal meetings also take place at which superiors and subordinates can review progress toward goals and further feedback can be provided.

Linking MBO and Goal-Setting Theory

Goal-setting theory demonstrates that hard goals result in a higher level of individual performance than do easy goals, that specific hard goals result in higher levels of performance than do no goals at all or the generalized goal of "do your best," and that feedback on one's performance leads to higher performance. Compare these findings with MBO.

MBO directly advocates specific goals and feedback. MBO implies, rather than explicitly states, that goals must be perceived as feasible. Consistent with goal setting, MBO would be most effective when the goals are difficult enough to require the person to do some stretching.

The only area of possible disagreement between MBO and goal-setting theory relates to the issue of participation—MBO strongly advocates it, while goal-setting theory demonstrates that assigning goals to subordinates frequently works just as well. The major benefit to using participation, however, is that it appears to induce individuals to establish more difficult goals.

MBO in Practice

How widely used is MBO? Reviews of studies that have sought to answer this question suggest that it's a popular technique. You'll find MBO programs in many business, health care, educational, government, and nonprofit organizations.[4]

MBO's popularity should not be construed to mean that it always works. There are a number of documented cases where MBO has been implemented but failed to meet management's expectations.[5] A close look at these cases, however, indicates that the problems rarely lie with MBO's basic components. Rather, the culprits tend to be factors such as unrealistic expectations regarding results, lack of top-management commitment, and an inability or unwillingness by management to allocate rewards based on goal accomplishment. Nevertheless, MBO provides managers with the vehicle for implementing goal-setting theory.

Employee Recognition Programs

Laura Schendell only makes $5.50 an hour working at her fast-food job in Pensacola, Florida, and the job isn't very challenging or interesting. Yet Laura talks enthusiastically about her job, her boss, and the company that employs her. "What I like is the fact that Guy (her supervisor) appreciates the effort I make. He compliments me regularly in front of the other people on my shift, and I've been chosen "Employee of the Month" twice in the past six months. Did you see my picture on that plaque on the wall?"

Organizations are increasingly recognizing what Laura Schendell is acknowledging: Recognition can be a potent motivator.

What Are Employee Recognition Programs?

Employee recognition programs can take numerous forms. The best ones use multiple sources and recognize both individual and group accomplishments. Convex Computer Corporation, a supercomputer manufacturer based in Texas that employs 1,200 people, provides an excellent illustration of a comprehensive recognition program.[6]

These managers of insurance company USF&G are thrilled to be recognized for their work accomplishments. USF&G honors outstanding employees by giving them a prestigious company award for exhibiting leadership qualities. Winners of the "Seven C's of Leadership" awards are recognized for their excellence in communication, confidence, character, comprehension, conviction, courage, and competency.

On a quarterly basis, Convex's vice president of operations recognizes individuals who have been nominated by their managers as having gone "above and beyond the call of duty." Annually, individuals may nominate their peers for the Customer Service Award, which recognizes such categories as risk taking, innovation, cost reduction, and overall customer service. And at the department level, recognition takes the form of team or department T-shirts, coffee mugs, banners, or pictures. Supervisors have used movie tickets, Friday afternoon bowling get-togethers, time off, and cash awards to acknowledge such achievements as three months of defect-free assembly, five years of perfect attendance, and completing a project early.

Linking Recognition Programs and Reinforcement Theory

A few years ago, 1,500 employees were surveyed in a variety of work settings to find out what they considered to be the most powerful workplace motivator. Their response? Recognition, recognition, and more recognition![7]

Consistent with reinforcement theory, rewarding a behavior with recognition immediately following that behavior is likely to encourage its repetition. Recognition can take many forms. You can personally congratulate an employee in private for a good job. You can send a handwritten note or an e-mail message acknowledging something positive that the employee has done. For employees with a strong need for social acceptance, you can publicly recognize accomplishments. And to enhance group cohesiveness and motivation, you can celebrate team successes. You can use meetings to recognize the contributions and achievements of successful work teams.

Employee Recognition Programs in Practice

In today's highly competitive global economy, most organizations are under severe cost pressures. That makes recognition programs particularly attractive. In contrast to most other motivators, recognizing an employee's superior performance often costs little or no money. Maybe that's why a recent survey of 3,000 employers found that two-thirds use or plan to use special recognition awards.[8]

One of the most well-known and widely used recognition devices is the use of suggestion systems. Employees offer suggestions for improving processes or cutting costs and are recognized with small cash awards. The Japanese have been especially effective at making suggestion systems work. For instance, a typical high-performing Japanese plant in the auto components business generates 47 suggestions per employee a year and pays approximately the equivalent of U.S. $35 per suggestion. In contrast, a comparable Western factory generates about one suggestion per employee per year, but pays out $90 per suggestion.[9]

Employee Involvement Programs

The Donnelly Corporation, a major supplier of glass products to automobile manufacturers, uses committees of elected representatives to make all key decisions affecting Donnelly employees.[10] At a General Electric lighting plant in Ohio, work teams perform many tasks and assume many of the responsibilities once handled by their supervisors. In fact, when the plant was faced with a recent decline in the demand for the tubes it produces, the workers decided first to slow production and eventually to lay themselves off. Marketing people at USAA, a large insurance company, meet in a conference room for an hour every week to discuss ways in which they can improve the quality of their work and increase productivity. Management has implemented many of their suggestions. Childress Buick, an automobile dealer in Phoenix, allows its salespeople to negotiate and finalize deals with customers without any approval from management. The laws of Germany, France, Denmark, Sweden, and Austria require companies to have elected representatives from their employee groups as members of their boards of directors.[11]

The common theme through the preceding examples is that they all illustrate employee involvement programs. In this section, we clarify what we mean by employee involvement, describe some of the various forms that it takes, consider the motivational implications of these programs, and show some applications.

What Is Employee Involvement?

Employee involvement has become a convenient catchall term to cover a variety of techniques.[12] For instance, it encompasses such popular ideas as employee participation or participative management, workplace democracy, empowerment, and employee ownership. Our position is, although each of these ideas has some unique characteristics, they all have a common core—that of employee involvement.

What specifically do we mean by **employee involvement**? We define it as a participative process that uses the entire capacity of employees and is designed to encourage increased commitment to the organization's success.[13] The underlying logic is that by involving workers in those decisions that affect them and by increasing their autonomy and control over their work lives, employees will become more motivated, more committed to the organization, more productive, and more satisfied with their jobs.[14]

employee involvement
A participative process that uses the entire capacity of employees and is designed to encourage increased commitment to the organization's success.

Does that mean that participation and employee involvement are synonyms for each other? No. Participation is a more limited term. It's a subset within the larger framework of employee involvement. All of the employee involvement programs we describe include some form of employee participation but the term *participation*, per se, is too narrow and limiting.

Examples of Employee Involvement Programs

In this section we review four forms of employee involvement: participative management, representative participation, quality circles, and employee stock ownership plans.

PARTICIPATIVE MANAGEMENT The distinct characteristic common to all **participative management** programs is the use of joint decision making. That is, subordinates actually share a significant degree of decision-making power with their immediate superiors.

Participative management has, at times, been promoted as a panacea for poor morale and low productivity. One author has even argued that participative management is an ethical imperative.[15] But participative management is not appropriate for every organization or every work unit. For it to work, there must be adequate time to participate, the issues in which employees get involved must be relevant to their interests, employees must have the ability (intelligence, technical knowledge, communication skills) to participate, and the organization's culture must support employee involvement.[16]

Why would management want to share its decision-making power with subordinates? There are a number of good reasons. As jobs have become more complex, managers often don't know everything their employees do. Thus, participation allows those who know the most to contribute. The result can be better decisions. The interdependence in tasks that employees often do today also requires consultation with people in other departments and work units.

participative management
A process where subordinates share a significant degree of decision-making power with their immediate superiors.

Through its Employee Involvement program, Ford Motor Company empowers employees to make decisions that are best for customers and shareholders. Ford wants its employees to keep learning, and to be empowered to make decisions at the level closest to the action. Participation in decision making increases employees' commitment to Ford's goals of breakthroughs in product design and engineering, cost reduction, quality improvement, manufacturing efficiency, and overall productivity.

This increases the need for teams, committees, and group meetings to resolve issues that affect them jointly. Participation additionally increases commitment to decisions. People are less likely to undermine a decision at the time of its implementation if they shared in making that decision. Finally, participation provides intrinsic rewards for employees. It can make their jobs more interesting and meaningful.

Dozens of studies have been conducted on the participation–performance relationship. The findings, however, are mixed.[17] When the research is reviewed carefully, it appears that participation typically has only a modest influence on variables such as employee productivity, motivation, and job satisfaction. Of course, that doesn't mean that the use of participative management can't be beneficial under the right conditions. What it says, however, is that the use of participation is no sure means for improving employee performance.

representative participation
Workers participate in organizational decision making through a small group of representative employees.

REPRESENTATIVE PARTICIPATION Almost every country in Western Europe has some type of legislation requiring companies to practice **representative participation**. That is, rather than participate directly in decisions, workers are represented by a small group of employees who actually participate. Representative participation has been called "the most widely legislated form of employee involvement around the world."[18]

The goal of representative participation is to redistribute power within an organization, putting labor on a more equal footing with the interests of management and stockholders.

works councils
Groups of nominated or elected employees who must be consulted when management makes decisions involving personnel.

The two most common forms which representative participation takes are works councils and board representatives.[19] **Works councils** link employees with management. They are groups of nominated or elected employees who must be consulted when management makes decisions involving personnel. For example, in the Netherlands, if a Dutch company is taken over by another firm, the former's works council must be informed at an early stage, and if the council objects, it has 30 days to seek a court injunction to stop the takeover.[20] **Board representatives** are employees who sit on a company's board of directors and represent the interests of the firm's employees. In some countries, large companies may be legally required to make sure that employee representatives have the same number of board seats as stockholder representatives.

board representatives
A form of representative participation; employees sit on a company's board of directors and represent the interests of the firm's employees.

◆ Representative participation is the most widely legislated form of employee involvement around the world.

The overall influence of representative participation on working employees seems to be minimal.[21] For instance, the evidence suggests that works councils are dominated by management and have little impact on employees or the organization. And while this form of employee involvement might increase the motivation and satisfaction of those individuals who are doing the representing, there is little evidence that this trickles down to the operating employees whom they represent. Overall, "the greatest value of representative participation is symbolic. If one is interested in changing employee attitudes or in improving organizational performance, representative participation would be a poor choice."[22]

QUALITY CIRCLES "Probably the most widely discussed and undertaken formal style of employee involvement is the quality circle."[23] The quality circle concept is frequently mentioned as one of the techniques that Japanese firms utilize that has allowed them to make high-quality products at low costs. Originally begun in the United States and exported to Japan in the 1950s, the quality circle became quite popular in North America and Europe during the 1980s.[24]

What is a **quality circle**? It's a work group of eight to ten employees and supervisors who have a shared area of responsibility. They meet regularly—typically once a week, on company time and on company premises—to discuss their quality problems, investigate causes of the problems, recommend solutions, and take corrective actions. They take over the responsibility for solving quality problems, and they generate and evaluate their own feedback. But management typically retains control over the final decision regarding implementation of recommended solutions. Of course, it is not presumed that employees inherently have this ability to analyze and solve quality problems. Therefore, part of the quality circle concept includes teaching participating employees group communication skills, various quality strategies, and measurement and problem analysis techniques. Exhibit 6-2 describes a typical quality circle process.

Do quality circles improve employee productivity and satisfaction? A review of the evidence indicates that they are much more likely to positively affect productivity. They tend to show little or no effect on employee satisfaction; and while many studies report positive results from quality circles on productivity, these results are by no means guaranteed.[25] The failure of many quality circle programs to produce measurable benefits has also led to a large number of them to be discontinued.

quality circle
A work group of employees who meet regularly to discuss their quality problems, investigate causes, recommend solutions, and take corrective actions.

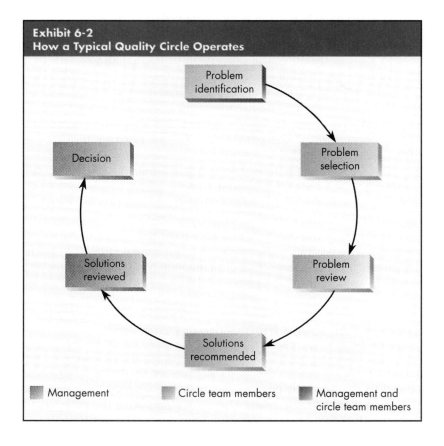

Exhibit 6-2
How a Typical Quality Circle Operates

Problem identification → Problem selection → Problem review → Solutions recommended → Solutions reviewed → Decision

☐ Management ☐ Circle team members ☐ Management and circle team members

One author has gone as far as to say that while quality circles were the management fad of the 1980s, they've "become a flop."[26] He offers two possible explanations for their disappointing results. First is the little bit of time that actually deals with employee involvement. "At most, these programs operate for one hour per week, with the remaining 39 hours unchanged. Why should changes in 2.5 percent of a person's job have a major impact?"[27] Second, the ease of implementing quality circles often worked against them. They were seen as a simple device that could be added on to the organization with few changes required outside the program itself. In many cases, the only significant involvement by management was funding the program. So quality circles became an easy way for management to get on the employee involvement bandwagon. And, unfortunately, the lack of planning and top-management commitment often contributed to quality circle failures.

employee stock ownership plans (ESOPs)

Company-established benefit plans in which employees acquire stock as part of their benefits.

EMPLOYEE STOCK OWNERSHIP PLANS The final employee involvement approach we'll discuss is **employee stock ownership plans (ESOPs)**.[28]

Employee ownership can mean any number of things from employees owning some stock in the company where they work to the individuals working in the company owning and personally operating the firm. Employee stock ownership plans are company-established benefit plans in which employees acquire stock as part of their benefits. Approximately 20 percent of Polaroid, for example, is owned by its employees. Forty percent of Canadian-based Spruce Falls, Inc. is owned by its employees. Employees own 71 percent of Avis Corporation. And Weirton Steel is 100 percent owned by its employees.[29]

In the typical ESOP, an employee stock ownership trust is created. Companies contribute either stock or cash to buy stock for the trust and allocate the stock to employees. While employees hold stock in their company, they usually cannot take physical possession of their shares or sell them as long as they're still employed at the company.

The research on ESOPs indicates that they increase employee satisfaction.[30] In addition, they frequently result in higher performance. For instance, one study compared 45 ESOPs against 238 conventional companies.[31] The ESOPs outperformed the conventional firms both in terms of employment and sales growth.

ESOPs have the potential to increase employee job satisfaction and work motivation. But for this potential to be realized, employees need to psychologically experience ownership.[32] That is, in addition to merely having a financial stake in the company, employees need to be kept regularly informed on the status of the business and also have the opportunity to exercise influence over the business. The evidence consistently indicates that it takes ownership *and* a participative style of management to achieve significant improvements in an organization's performance.[33]

Linking Employee Involvement Programs and Motivation Theories

Employee involvement draws on a number of the motivation theories discussed in the previous chapter. For instance, Theory Y is consistent with participative management, while Theory X aligns with the more traditional autocratic style of managing people. In terms of motivation-hygiene theory,

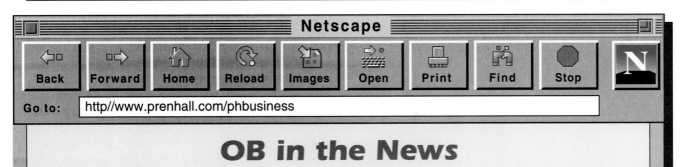

OB in the News

Employee Ownership Is Working at United Airlines

In July 1994, United Airlines' employees bought their company for $5 billion. In the first 18 months following the purchase, the evidence indicates that this ESOP is working. As the largest airline in the United States, United is outperforming most of its rivals—gaining market share from number-two American Airlines and number-three Delta Air Lines, and posting fatter operating margins and higher stock gains. For instance, United's stock has soared 120 percent since the buyout, compared to a 46 percent gain for the Standard & Poor's airline-industry average (which includes American, Delta, Southwest, and USAir).

At the employee level,

United has seen similarly positive results. Productivity of the company's 83,000 employees has risen and grievances are way down. Additionally, employees have enjoyed a marked increase in their net worth as the price of their stock has more than doubled.

A good part of the credit for this success belongs to Gerald Greenwald, a former Chrysler executive, who was hired by the employees for United's top-management spot. The company that Greenwald inherited had a long history of autocratic management. He immediately began changing that by increasing employee involvement in all aspects of the company. For instance, he created a half-dozen em-

ployee task teams to examine everything from reducing workers' sick time to improving cash management. Maybe his most visible action was his effort to pull employees into the decision on whether or not United should acquire USAir. Instead of the usual secrecy surrounding merger talks, Greenwald actively sought union leaders' input. They recounted the disasterous record of most airline mergers, mostly due to the difficulty of combining union seniority lists. Greenwald listened intently—and killed the bid.

Based on S. Chandler, "United We Own," *Business Week*, March 18, 1996, pp. 96–100.

Take It to the Net

We invite you to visit the Robbins page on the Prentice Hall Web site at:

http://www.prenhall.com/robbinsorgbeh

for this chapter's World Wide Web exercise.

employee involvement programs could provide employees with intrinsic motivation by increasing opportunities for growth, responsibility, and involvement in the work itself. Similarly, the opportunity to make and implement decisions, and then seeing them work out, can help satisfy an employee's needs for responsibility, achievement, recognition, growth, and enhanced self-esteem. So employee involvement is compatible with ERG theory and efforts to stimulate the achievement need.

Employee Involvement Programs in Practice

Germany, France, Holland, and the Scandinavian countries have firmly established the principle of industrial democracy in Europe, and other nations, including Japan and Israel, have traditionally practiced some form of representative participation for decades. Participative management and representative participation were much slower to gain ground in North American organizations. But nowdays, employee involvement programs that stress participation have become the norm. While some managers continue to resist sharing decision-making power, the pressure is on managers to give up their autocratic decision-making style in favor of a more participative, supportive, coaching-like role.

What about quality circles? How popular are they in practice? The names of companies that have used quality circles reads like a *Who's Who of Corporate America*: Hewlett-Packard, Digital Equipment, Westinghouse, General Electric, Texas Instruments, Inland Steel, Xerox, Eastman Kodak, Polaroid, Procter & Gamble, Control Data, General Motors, Ford, IBM, Motorola, American Airlines, and TRW.[34] But, as we noted, the success of quality circles has been far from overwhelming. They were popular in the 1980s, largely because they were easy to implement. In more recent years, many organizations have dropped their quality circles and replaced them with more comprehensive team-based structures (which we discuss in chapter 8).

What about ESOPs? They have become the most popular form of employee ownership. They've grown from just a handful in 1974 to around 10,000 now, covering approximately 10 million employees. Many well-known companies, including Anheuser-Busch, Procter & Gamble, and Polaroid, have implemented ESOPs.[35] But so too have many not so-well-known companies. Phelps County Bank in Rolla, Missouri, for instance, employs only 55 people. While the bank's ESOP has been in place for 13 years, the average employee's ownership balance exceeds $70,000. Connie Beddoe, a teller who annually earns less than $20,000, has managed to save almost three times that amount through her ESOP after seven years at the bank.[36]

Variable-Pay Programs

Allied-Signal has recently changed its compensation program for production workers at its Forstoria, Ohio, spark-plug plant.[37] The company cut the traditional 3 percent annual raise to 2 percent, but it created the opportunity for employees to earn more if they can increase productivity. Specifically, the plant's 1,200 employees will get their former 3 percent raise if they raise productivity 6 percent a year. If they push productivity up 9 percent, they get a 6 percent raise.

Dana Murray got a surprise in her recent paycheck. Her employer, Bookman's Used Books of Arizona, had established a bonus system linked to increases in the company's profits. As the firm's marketing manager, she knew business had been good but was not privy to financial details. She expected an extra thousand dollars or so as her part of Bookman's semiannual bonus payout. To her surprise, her bonus check was for more than $6,000—almost 20 percent of her base pay.

Traders at Bayerische Vereinsbank, Germany's fourth largest bank, earn 75,000 marks (about $55,000) a year in base pay. They also can earn as much as a 50,000-mark bonus if they meet their individual performance goals.[38]

Charles Sanford, CEO of Bankers Trust, took a 57 percent cut in his salary and bonus in 1994.[39] This is because his pay package is closely tied to his company's performance and Bankers Trust's return-on-equity was sliced in half in 1994.

The common thread in each of the previous examples is that they all illustrate variable-pay programs.

What Are Variable-Pay Programs?

Piece-rate plans, wage incentives, profit sharing, bonuses, and gainsharing are all forms of **variable-pay programs**. What differentiates these forms of compensation from more traditional programs is that instead of paying a person only for time on the job or seniority, a portion of an employee's pay is based on some individual and/or organizational measure of performance. Unlike more traditional base-pay programs, variable pay is not an annuity. There is no guarantee that just because you made $60,000 last year that you'll make the same amount this year. With variable pay, earnings fluctuate up and down with the measure of performance.[40]

> **variable-pay programs**
> A portion of an employee's pay is based on some individual and/or organizational measure of performance.

It is precisely the fluctuation in variable pay that has made these programs attractive to management. It turns part of an organization's fixed labor costs into a variable cost, thus reducing expenses when performance declines. Additionally, by tying pay to performance, earnings recognize contribution rather than being a form of entitlement. Low performers find, over time, that their pay stagnates, while high performers enjoy pay increases commensurate with their contribution.

Four of the more widely used variable-pay programs are piece-rate wages, bonuses, profit sharing, and gainsharing.

Piece-rate wages have been around for nearly a century. They have long been popular as a means for compensating production workers. In **piece-rate pay plans** workers are paid a fixed sum for each unit of production completed. When an employee gets no base salary and is paid only for what he or she produces, this is a pure piece-rate plan. People who work ball parks selling peanuts and soda pop frequently are paid this way. They might get to keep 25 cents for every bag of peanuts they sell. If they sell 200 bags during a game, they make $50. If they sell only 40 bags, their take is a mere $10. The harder they work and the more peanuts they sell, the more they earn. Many organizations use a modified piece-rate plan, where employees earn a base hourly wage plus a piece-rate differential. So a legal typist might be paid $6 an hour plus 20 cents per page. Such modified plans provide a floor under an employee's earnings, while still offering a productivity incentive.

> **piece-rate pay plans**
> Workers are paid a fixed sum for each unit of production completed.

Bonuses can be paid exclusively to executives or to all employees. For instance, annual bonuses in the millions of dollars are not uncommon in American corporations. Robert A. Watson, for example, received a $10 million incentive bonus in 1993 for his success in dismantling Westinghouse's financial operation.[41] Increasingly, bonus plans are taking on a larger net within organizations to include lower-ranking employees. One of the most ambitious bonus systems has recently been put in place by Levi Strauss.[42] If the company reaches cumulative cash flow of $7.6 billion for the next six years, each of the company's 37,500 employees in 60 countries, regardless of position, will get a full year's pay as a bonus. Levi Strauss estimates the potential cost of this bonus for the firm at about $750 million.

Profit-sharing plans are organizationwide programs that distribute compensation based on some established formula designed around a company's profitability. These can be direct cash outlays or, particularly in the case of top managers, allocated as stock options. When you read about executives like Michael Eisner, the CEO at Disney, earning over $200 million in one year, almost all of this comes from cashing in stock options previously granted based on company profit performance.

The variable-pay program that has gotten the most attention in recent years is undoubtedly **gainsharing**.[43] This is a formula-based group incentive plan. Improvements in group productivity—from one period to another—determine the total amount of money that is to be allocated. The division of productivity savings can be split between the company and employees in any number of ways, but 50-50 is pretty typical.

Isn't gainsharing the same thing as profit sharing? They're similar but not the same thing. By focusing on productivity gains rather than profits, gainsharing rewards specific behaviors that are less influenced by external factors. Employees in a gainsharing plan can receive incentive awards even when the organization isn't profitable.

Do variable-pay programs work? Do they increase motivation and productivity? The answer is a qualified "Yes." Gainsharing, for example, has been found to improve productivity in a majority of cases and often has a positive impact on employee attitudes. An American Management Association study of 83 companies that used gainsharing also found, on average, that grievances dropped 83 percent, absences fell 84 percent, and lost-time accidents decreased by 69 percent.[44] The downside of variable pay, from an employee's perspective, is its unpredictability. With a straight base salary, employees know what they'll be earning. Adding in merit and cost-of-living increases, they can make fairly accurate predictions about what they'll be making next

profit-sharing plans
Organizationwide programs that distribute compensation based on some established formula designed around a company's profitability.

gainsharing
An incentive plan where improvements in group productivity determine the total amount of money that is allocated.

At Geon Company, a producer of polyvinyl chloride resins, gainsharing keeps employees focused on continuous improvement so that the company can keep its competitive advantage as a low-cost producer. Each Geon location has a plant-specific gainsharing program that is tied to improvement in productivity, quality, and manufacturing. In recent years, the plan paid out an average of 11 percent of salaries in bonuses.

year and the year after. They can finance cars and homes based on reasonably solid assumptions. That's more difficult to do with variable pay. Your group's performance might slip this year or a recession might undermine your company's profits. Depending how your variable pay is determined, these can cut your income. Moreover, people begin to take repeated annual performance bonuses for granted. A 15 or 20 percent bonus, received three years in a row, begins to become expected in the fourth year. If it doesn't materialize, management will find itself with some disgruntled employees on its hands.

Linking Variable-Pay Programs and Expectancy Theory

Variable pay is probably most compatible with expectancy theory predictions. Specifically, individuals should perceive a strong relationship between their performance and the rewards they receive if motivation is to be maximized. If rewards are allocated completely on nonperformance factors—such as seniority or job title—then employees are likely to reduce their effort.

The evidence supports the importance of this linkage, especially for operative employees working under piece-rate systems. For example, one study of 400 manufacturing firms found that those companies with wage incentive plans achieved 43 to 64 percent greater productivity than those without such plans.[45]

Group and organizationwide incentives reinforce and encourage employees to sublimate personal goals for the best interests of their department or the organization. Group-based performance incentives are also a natural extension for those organizations that are trying to build a strong team ethic. By linking rewards to team performance, employees are encouraged to make extra efforts to help their team succeed.

Variable-Pay Programs in Practice

Variable pay is a concept that is rapidly replacing the annual cost-of-living raise. "There is a veritable explosion in variable-pay plans," says one consultant.[46] One reason, as cited earlier, is its motivational power—but don't ignore the cost implications. Bonuses, gainsharing, and other variable-based reward programs avoid the fixed expense of permanent salary boosts.

Pay for performance has been "in" for compensating managers for more than a decade. The new trend has been expanding this practice to nonmanagerial employees. Hughes Electronics, IBM, Wal-Mart, Pizza Hut, and John Deere are just a few examples of companies using variable-pay with rank-and-file employees.[47] In 1995, nearly 50 percent of all U.S. companies had some form of variable-pay plan for nonexecutives—nearly double the share of only four years earlier. An additional 26 percent said they were considering such plans.[48]

◆ Variable pay is rapidly replacing the annual cost-of-living raise.

Variable-pay plans that use bonuses are also becoming increasingly popular in Canada.[49] In 1992, typical senior executives in Canada could expect bonuses equal to 9.7 percent of their salaries. In 1996, that had almost doubled to 18.5 percent. And the growth in bonuses was even greater among hourly employees. The average bonus for an hourly worker during the same time period went from 1.1 percent of base pay to 5.8 percent. About 35 percent of Canadian companies now have companywide variable-pay incentive plans.

Gainsharing's popularity seems to be narrowly focused among large, unionized manufacturing companies.[50] It is currently being used in about 2,000 companies including such major firms as Bell & Howell, American Safety Razor, Champion Spark Plug, Cincinnati Milacron, Eaton, Firestone Tire, Hooker Chemical, and Mead Paper.[51]

Among firms that haven't introduced performance-based compensation programs, common concerns tend to surface.[52] Managers fret over what should constitute performance and how it should be measured. They have to overcome the historical attachment to cost-of-living adjustments and the belief that they have an obligation to keep all employees' pay in step with inflation. Other barriers include salary scales keyed to what the competition is paying, traditional compensation systems that rely heavily on specific pay grades and relatively narrow pay ranges, and performance appraisal practices that produce inflated evaluations and expectations of full rewards. Of course, from the employees' standpoint, the major concern is a potential drop in earnings. Pay for performance means employees have to share in the risks as well as the rewards of their employer's business.

Skill-Based Pay Plans

Organizations hire people for their skills, then typically put them in jobs and pay them based on their job title or rank. For example, the director of corporate sales earns $120,000 a year, the regional sales managers make $75,000, and the district sales managers get $60,000. But if organizations hire people because of their competencies, why don't they pay them for those same competencies? Some organizations do.

Workers at American Steel & Wire can boost their annual salaries by up to $12,480 by acquiring as many as ten skills. At AT&T's Universal Card service center in Jacksonville, Florida, the best-paid customer representatives have rotated through four to six troubleshooting assignments over two or three years, becoming adept at solving any billing, lost card, or other problem a credit card holder runs into. New employees at a Quaker Oats' pet food plant in Topeka, Kansas start at $8.75 an hour, but can reach a top rate of $14.50 when they master ten to twelve skills like operating lift trucks and factory computer controls. Salomon Brothers, a major brokerage firm, is using a skills-based pay system to turn narrowly trained and independent specialists into well-rounded product experts and to encourage them to be team players. Frito-Lay Corporation ties its compensation for managers to progress they make in developing their skills in leadership, group process facilitation, and communications.[53]

What Are Skill-Based Pay Plans?

skill-based pay
Pay levels are based on how many skills employees have or how many jobs they can do.

Skill-based pay is an alternative to job-based pay. Rather than having an individual's job title define his or her pay category, **skill-based pay** (or also sometimes called *competency-based pay*) sets pay levels on the basis of how many skills employees have or how many jobs they can do.[54] For instance, at Polaroid Corporation, the highest pay you can earn as a machine operator is

$14 an hour. However, because the company has a skill-based pay plan, if machine operators broaden their skills to include additional skills like material accounting, maintenance of equipment, and quality inspection, they can earn up to a 10 percent premium. If they can learn some of their supervisor's skills, they can earn even more.[55]

What's the appeal of skill-based pay plans? From management's perspective: flexibility. Filling staffing needs is easier when employee skills are interchangeable. This is particularly true today, as many organizations cut the size of their workforce. Downsizing requires more generalists and fewer specialists. While skill-based pay encourages employees to acquire a broader range of skills, there are also other benefits. It facilitates communication across the organization because people gain a better understanding of others' jobs. It lessens dysfunctional "protection of territory" behavior. Where skill-based pay exists, you're less likely to hear the phrase, "It's not my job!" Skill-based pay additionally helps meet the needs of ambitious employees who confront minimal advancement opportunities. These people can increase their earnings and knowledge without a promotion in job title. Finally, skill-based pay appears to lead to performance improvements. A broad-based survey of *Fortune* 1000 firms found that 60 percent of those with skill-based pay plans rated their plans as successful or very successful in increasing organizational performance, while only 6 percent considered them unsuccessful or very unsuccessful.[56]

What about the downside of skill-based pay? People can "top out"—learning all the skills the program calls for them to learn. This can frustrate employees after they've become challenged by an environment of learning, growth, and continual pay raises. Skills can become obsolete. When this happens, what should management do? Cut employee pay or continue to pay for skills that are no longer relevant? There is also the problem created by paying people for acquiring skills for which there may be no immediate need. This happened at IDS Financial Services.[57] The company found itself paying people more money even though there was little immediate use for their new skills. IDS eventually dropped its skill-based pay plan and replaced it with one that equally balances individual contribution and gains in work team productivity. Finally, skill-based plans don't address level of performance. They deal only with the issue of whether or not someone can perform the skill. For some skills, such as checking quality or leading a team, level of performance may be equivocal. While it's possible to assess how well employees perform each of the skills and combine that with a skill-based plan, that is not an inherent part of skill-based pay.

Linking Skill-Based Pay Plans to Motivation Theories

Skill-based pay plans are consistent with several motivation theories. Because they encourage employees to learn, expand their skills, and grow, they are consistent with ERG theory. Among employees whose lower-order needs are substantially satisfied, the opportunity to experience growth can be a motivator.

Paying people to expand their skill levels is also consistent with research on the achievement need. High achievers have a compelling drive to do things better or more efficiently. By learning new skills or improving the skills they already hold, high achievers will find their jobs more challenging.

There is also a link between reinforcement theory and skill-based pay. Skill-based pay encourages employees to develop their flexibility, to continue to learn, to cross-train, to be generalists rather than specialists, and to work cooperatively with others in the organization. To the degree that management wants employees to demonstrate such behaviors, skill-based pay should act as a reinforcer.

Skill-based pay may additionally have equity implications. When employees make their input–outcome comparisons, skills may provide a fairer input criterion for determining pay than factors such as seniority or education. To the degree that employees perceive skills as the critical variable in job performance, the use of skill-based pay may increase the perception of equity and help optimize employee motivation.

Skill-Based Pay in Practice

A number of studies have investigated the use and effectiveness of skill-based pay. The overall conclusion, based on these studies, is that skill-based pay is expanding and that it generally leads to higher employee performance and satisfaction.

For instance, between 1987 and 1993, the percentage of *Fortune* 1000 firms using some form of skill-based pay increased from 40 percent to 60 percent.[58]

A survey of 27 companies that pay employees for learning extra skills found 70 to 88 percent reported higher job satisfaction, product quality, or productivity. Some 70 to 75 percent cited lower operating costs or turnover.[59]

Additional research has discovered some other interesting trends. The increased use of skills as a basis for pay appears particularly strong among organizations facing aggressive foreign competition and those companies with shorter product life cycles and speed-to-market concerns.[60] Also, skill-based pay is moving from the shop floor to the white-collar workforce, and sometimes as far as the executive suite.[61]

◆ Skill-based pay is moving from the shop floor to the white-collar workforce.

Skilled-based pay appears to be an idea whose time has come. As one expert noted, "Slowly, but surely, we're becoming a skill-based society where your market value is tied to what you can do and what your skill set is. In this new world where skills and knowledge are what really counts, it doesn't make sense to treat people as jobholders. It makes sense to treat them as people with specific skills and to pay them for those skills."[62]

Flexible Benefits

Todd Evans and Allison Murphy both work for PepsiCo, but they have very different needs in terms of fringe benefits. Todd is married, has three young children, and a wife who is at home full time. Allison, too, is married, but her husband has a high-paying job with the federal government, and they have no children. Todd is concerned about having a good medical plan and enough life insurance to support his family if he weren't around. In contrast, Allison's husband already has her medical needs covered on his plan, and life insurance is a low priority for both her and her husband. Allison is more interested in extra vacation time and long-term financial benefits like a tax-deferred savings plan.

What Are Flexible Benefits?

Flexible benefits allow employees to pick and choose from among a menu of benefit options. The idea is to allow each employee to choose a benefit package that is individually tailored to his or her own needs and situation. It replaces the traditional "one-benefit-plan-fits-all" programs that have dominated organizations for more than 50 years.[63]

The average organization provides fringe benefits worth approximately 40 percent of an employee's salary. Traditional benefit programs were designed for the typical employee of the 1950s—a male with a wife and two children at home. Less than 10 percent of employees now fit this stereotype. While 25 percent of today's employees are single, a third are part of two-income families without any children. As such, these traditional programs don't tend to meet the needs of today's more diverse workforce. Flexible benefits, however, do meet these diverse needs. An organization sets up a flexible spending account for each employee, usually based on some percentage of his or her salary, and then a price tag is put on each benefit. Options might include inexpensive medical plans with high deductibles; expensive medical plans with low or no deductibles; hearing, dental, and eye coverage; vacation options; extended disability; a variety of savings and pension plans; life insurance; college tuition reimbursement plans; and extended vacation time. Employees then select benefit options until they have spent the dollar amount in their account.

flexible benefits
Employees tailor their benefit program to meet their personal needs by picking and choosing from a menu of benefit options.

Vacation options are part of Xerox Corporation's flexible benefits. The company has a sabbatical program that allows employees to take paid leaves of absence and work for charitable organizations. Xerox employee William Lankford, a customer service engineer, took a ten-month sabbatical to build homes for Habitat for Humanity in the woods of southern Maryland. Xerox believes the sabbatical program helps it retain and attract better employees.

Linking Flexible Benefits and Expectancy Theory

Giving all employees the same benefits assumes all employees have the same needs. Of course, we know this assumption is false. Thus, flexible benefits turn the benefits' expenditure into a motivator.

Consistent with expectancy theory's thesis that organizational rewards should be linked to each individual employee's goals, flexible benefits individualize rewards by allowing each employee to choose the compensation package that best satisfies his or her current needs. The fact that flexible benefits can turn the traditional homogeneous benefit program into a motivator was demonstrated at one company when 80 percent of the organization's employees changed their benefit packages when a flexible plan was put into effect.[64]

Flexible Benefits in Practice

In the early 1990s, about 38 percent of large companies had flexible benefits programs.[65] Flexible benefits also appear to be increasingly available in companies with fewer than 50 employees.[66]

Now, let's look at the benefits and drawbacks. For employees, flexibility is attractive because they can tailor their benefits and levels of coverage to their own needs. The major drawback, from the employee's standpoint, is that the costs of individual benefits often go up, so fewer total benefits can be purchased.[67] For example, low-risk employees keep the cost of medical plans low for everyone. As they are allowed to drop out, the high-risk population occupies a larger segment and the costs of medical benefits go up. From the organization's standpoint, the good news is that flexible benefits often produce savings. Many organizations use the introduction of flexible benefits to raise deductibles and premiums. Moreover, once in place, costly increases in things like health insurance premiums often have to be substantially absorbed by the employee. The bad news for the organization is that these plans are more cumbersome for management to oversee and administering the programs is often expensive.

Special Issues in Motivation

Various groups provide specific challenges in terms of motivation. In this section we look at some of the unique problems faced in trying to motivate professional employees, contingent workers, the diverse workforce, low-skilled service workers, and people doing highly repetitive tasks.

Motivating Professionals

In contrast to a generation ago, the typical employee today is more likely to be a highly trained professional with a college degree than a blue-collar factory worker. These professionals receive a great deal of intrinsic satisfaction from their work. They tend to be well paid. So what, if any, special concerns should you be aware of when trying to motivate a team of engineers at Intel, a software designer at Microsoft, or a group of CPAs at Price Waterhouse?

Professionals are typically different from nonprofessionals.[68] They have a strong and long-term commitment to their field of expertise. Their loyalty is

French computer services giant CAP Gemini Sogeti motivates its 17,000 software engineers and technicians by giving them the tools they need to tackle and solve challenging problems. The company's intranet, called Knowledge Galaxy, puts critical resources and expertise within every employee's reach, keeping the global workforce current on the latest technologies. CAP Gemini even installed an Internet cafe at its Paris headquarters, shown here, so employees can surf the Net during their breaks.

more often to their profession than to their employer. To keep current in their field, they need to regularly update their knowledge, and their commitment to their profession means they rarely define their workweek in terms of 8 to 5 and five days a week.

What motivates professionals? Money and promotions typically are low on their priority list. Why? They tend to be well paid and they enjoy what they do. In contrast, job challenge tends to be ranked high. They like to tackle problems and find solutions. Their chief reward in their job is the work itself. Professionals also value support. They want others to think what they're working on is important. Although this may be true for all employees, because professionals tend to be more focused on their work as their central life interest, nonprofessionals typically have other interests outside of work that can compensate for needs not met on the job.

The foregoing description implies a few guidelines to keep in mind if you're trying to motivate professionals. Provide them with ongoing challenging projects. Give them autonomy to follow their interests and allow them to structure their work in ways that they find productive. Reward them with educational opportunities—training, workshops, attending conferences—that allow them to keep current in their field. Also reward them with recognition, and ask questions and engage in other actions that demonstrate to them you're sincerely interested in what they're doing.

An increasing number of companies are creating alternative career paths for their professional/technical people, allowing employees to earn more money and status, without assuming managerial responsibilities. At Merck & Co., IBM, and AT&T, the best scientists, engineers, and researchers gain titles such as fellow and senior scientist. Their pay and prestige are comparable to those of managers but without the corresponding authority or responsibility.[69]

Motivating Contingent Workers

We noted in chapter 1 that one of the more comprehensive changes taking place in organizations is the addition of temporary or contingent employees. As downsizing has eliminated millions of "permanent" jobs, an increasing number of new openings are for part-time, contract, and other forms of temporary workers. For instance, in 1995, approximately 6 million Americans, or 4.9 percent of those with jobs, considered themselves as part of the contingent workforce.[70] These contingent employees don't have the security or stability that permanent employees have. As such, they don't identify with the organization or display the commitment that other employees do. Temporary workers also are typically provided with little or no health care, pensions, or similar benefits.[71]

There is no simple solution for motivating temporary employees. For that small set of temps who prefer the freedom of their temporary status—some students, working mothers, seniors—the lack of stability may not be an issue. Additionally, temporariness might be preferred by those highly compensated doctors, engineers, accountants, and financial planners who don't want the demands of a stable job. But these are the exceptions. For the most part, temporary employees are so involuntarily.

What will motivate involuntarily temporary employees? An obvious answer is the opportunity for permanent status. In those cases where permanent employees are selected from the pool of temporaries, temporaries will often work hard in hopes of becoming permanent. A less obvious answer is the opportunity for training. The ability of a temporary employee to find a new job is largely dependent on his or her skills. If the employee sees that the job he or she is doing for you can help develop salable skills, then motivation is increased. From an equity standpoint, you should also consider the repercussions of mixing permanent and temporary workers where pay differentials are significant. When temps work alongside permanent employees who earn more, and get benefits too, for doing the same job, the performance of temps is likely to suffer. Separating such employees or converting all employees to a variable-pay or skill-based pay plan might help lessen this problem.

Motivating the Diversified Workforce

Not everyone is motivated by money. Not everyone wants a challenging job. The needs of women, singles, immigrants, the physically disabled, senior citizens, and others from diverse groups are not the same as a white American male with three dependents. A couple of examples can make this point clearer. Employees who are attending college typically place a high value on flexible work schedules. Such individuals may be attracted to organizations that offer flexible work hours, job sharing, or temporary assignments. A father may prefer to work the midnight to 8 A.M. shift in order to spend time with his children during the day when his wife is at work.

If you're going to maximize your employees' motivation, you've got to understand and respond to this diversity. How? The key word to guide you should be flexibility. Be ready to design work schedules, compensation plans, benefits, physical work settings, and the like to reflect your employees' varied needs. This might include offering child and elder care, flexible work hours, and job sharing for employees with family responsibilities. It also might include offering flexible leave policies for immigrants who want occasionally to make extensive return trips to their homelands, or creating work teams for employees who come from countries with a strong collectivist orientation, or allowing employees who are going to school to vary their work schedules from semester to semester.

Motivating Low-Skilled Service Workers

One of the most challenging motivation problems in industries such as retailing and fast food is: How do you motivate individuals who are making very low wages and who have little opportunity to significantly increase their pay in either their current jobs or through promotions? These jobs are typically filled with people who have limited education and skills, and pay levels are little above minimum wage.

Traditional approaches for motivating these people have focused on providing more flexible work schedules and filling these jobs with teenagers and retirees whose financial needs are less. This has met with less than enthusiastic results. For instance, turnover rates of 200 percent or more are not uncommon for businesses like McDonald's. Taco Bell, PepsiCo's Mexican fast-food chain, has tried to make some of its service jobs more interesting and challenging but with limited results.[72] It has experimented with incentive pay and stock options for cashiers and cooks. These employees also have been given broader responsibility for inventory, scheduling, and hiring. But over a four-year period, this experiment has only reduced annual turnover from 223 percent to 160 percent.

What choices are left? Unless pay and benefits are significantly increased, high turnover probably has to be expected in these jobs. This can be somewhat offset by widening the recruiting net, making these jobs more appealing, and raising pay levels. You might also try some nontraditional approaches as well. To illustrate, Judy Wicks has found that celebrating employees' outside interests has dramatically cut turnover among waiters at her White Dog Café in Philadelphia.[73] For instance, to help create a close and family-like work climate, Wicks sets aside one night a year where employees exhibit their art, read their poetry, explain their volunteer work, and introduce their new babies.

Motivating People Doing Highly Repetitive Tasks

Our final category considers employees who do standardized and repetitive jobs. For instance, working on an assembly line or transcribing court reports are jobs that workers often find boring and even stressful.

Motivating individuals in these jobs can be made easier through careful selection. People vary in their tolerance for ambiguity. Many individuals prefer jobs that have a minimal amount of discretion and variety. Such individuals are obviously a better match to standardized jobs than individuals with strong needs for growth and autonomy. Standardized jobs should also be the first considered for automation.

Many standardized jobs, especially in the manufacturing sector, pay well. This makes it relatively easy to fill vacancies. While high pay can ease recruitment problems and reduce turnover, it doesn't necessarily lead to highly motivated workers. And realistically, there are jobs that don't readily lend themselves to being made more challenging and interesting or to being redesigned. Some tasks, for instance, are just far more efficiently done on assembly lines than in teams. This leaves limited options. You may not be able to do much more than try to make a bad situation tolerable by creating a pleasant work climate. This might include providing clean and attractive work surroundings, ample work breaks, the opportunity to socialize with colleagues during these breaks, and empathetic supervisors.

Summary and Implications for Managers

We've presented a number of motivation theories and applications in this and the previous chapter. While it's always dangerous to synthesize a large number of complex ideas into a few simple guidelines, the following suggestions summarize the essence of what we know about motivating employees in organizations.

RECOGNIZE INDIVIDUAL DIFFERENCES Employees have different needs. Don't treat them all alike. Moreover, spend the time necessary to understand what's important to each employee. This will allow you to individualize goals, level of involvement, and rewards to align with individual needs.

USE GOALS AND FEEDBACK Employees should have hard, specific goals, as well as feedback on how well they are faring in pursuit of those goals.

ALLOW EMPLOYEES TO PARTICIPATE IN DECISIONS THAT AFFECT THEM Employees can contribute to a number of decisions that affect them: setting work goals, choosing their own benefits packages, solving productivity and quality problems, and the like. This can increase employee productivity, commitment to work goals, motivation, and job satisfaction.

LINK REWARDS TO PERFORMANCE Rewards should be contingent on performance. Importantly, employees must perceive a clear linkage. Regardless of how closely rewards are actually correlated to performance criteria, if individuals perceive this relationship to be low, the results will be low performance, a decrease in job satisfaction, and an increase in turnover and absenteeism statistics.

CHECK THE SYSTEM FOR EQUITY Rewards should also be perceived by employees as equating with the inputs they bring to the job. At a simplistic level, this should mean that experience, skills, abilities, effort, and other obvious inputs should explain differences in performance and, hence, pay, job assignments, and other obvious rewards.

For Review

1. Relate goal-setting theory to the MBO process. How are they similar? Different?
2. What is an ESOP? How might it positively influence employee motivation?
3. Explain the roles of employees and management in quality circles.
4. What are the pluses of variable-pay programs from an employee's viewpoint? From management's viewpoint?
5. Contrast job-based and skill-based pay.
6. What is gainsharing? What explains its recent popularity?
7. What motivates professional employees?
8. What motivates contingent employees?
9. Is it possible to motivate low-skilled service workers? Discuss.
10. What can you do, as a manager, to increase the likelihood that your employees will exert a high level of effort?

For Discussion

1. Identify five different criteria by which organizations can compensate employees. Based on your knowledge and experience, do you think performance is the criterion most used in practice? Discuss.

2. "Recognition may be motivational for the moment but it doesn't have any staying power. It's an empty reinforcer. Why? Because they don't take recognition at the Safeway or Sears!" Do you agree or disagree? Discuss.

3. "Performance can't be measured, so any effort to link pay with performance is a fantasy. Differences in performance are often caused by the system, which means the organization ends up rewarding the circumstances. It's the same thing as rewarding the weather forecaster for a pleasant day." Do you agree or disagree with this statement? Support your position.

4. What drawbacks, if any, do you see in implementing flexible benefits? (Consider this question from the perspective of both the organization and the employee.)

5. Your text argues for recognizing individual differences. It also suggests paying attention to members of diversity groups. Is this contradictory? Discuss.

The Case for Pay Secrecy

"Oh, and one last point," said the director of human resources to the new employee. "We treat salary information as a private matter around here. What you make is your business and no one else's. We consider it grounds for termination if you tell anyone what you make."

This policy of pay secrecy is the norm in most organizations, though in the majority of cases, it's communicated informally. The message trickles down and new employees quickly learn from their boss and peers not to inquire about what other people make or to openly volunteer their own salary. However, in some companies, pay secrecy is a formal policy. For instance, at Electronic Data Systems Corporation new employees sign a form acknowledging several policies, one of which states that employees are allowed to disclose their salaries, but if such disclosure leads to disruption, they can be fired. It doesn't take a genius to predict that this policy effectively stifles discussion of pay at EDS.

For those raised in democratic societies, it may be tempting to surmise that there is something inherently wrong with pay secrecy. On the other hand, if it's wrong, why do the vast majority of successful corporations in democracies follow the practice? There are a number of logical reasons why organizations practice pay secrecy and why they are likely to continue to do so.

First, pay is privileged information to both the organization and the individual employee. Organizations hold many things privileged—manufacturing processes, product formulas, new-product research, marketing strategies—and U.S. courts have generally supported the argument that pay rightly belongs in this category. Salary information has been held to be confidential and the property of management. Employees who release such data can be discharged for willful misconduct. Moreover, most employees want their pay kept secret.

Many people's egos are tied to their paycheck. They are as comfortable discussing their specific pay as they are providing details of their sex life to strangers. Employees have a right to privacy, and this includes ensuring that their pay is kept secret.

Second, pay secrecy lessens the opportunity for comparisons among employees and the exposure of perceived inequities. No pay system will ever be perceived as fair by everyone. One person's "merit" is another person's "favoritism." Knowledge of what other employees are making only highlights perceived inequities and causes disruptions.

Third, pay differences are often perfectly justified, yet only for subtle, complicated, or difficult to explain reasons. For instance, people doing similar jobs were hired under different market conditions. Or two managers have similar titles, although one supervises ten people while the other supervises twenty. Or one person earns more today than a co-worker because of responsibilities held or contributions made to the organization in a different job several years earlier.

Fourth, pay secrecy saves embarrassing underpaid and underperforming employees. By definition, half of an organization's workforce is going to be below average. What kind of organization would be so cold and insensitive as to publicly expose those in the lower half of the performance distribution?

Finally, pay secrecy gives managers more freedom in administering pay because every pay differential doesn't have to be explained. A policy of openness encourages managers to minimize differences and allocate pay more evenly. Since employee performance in an organization tends to follow a normal distribution, only through pay secrecy can managers feel comfortable in giving large rewards to high performers and little or no rewards to low performers.

Based on J. Solomon, "Hush Money," The *Wall Street Journal*, April 18, 1990, pp. R22–R24; and K. Tracy, M. Renard, and G. Young, "Pay Secrecy: The Effects of Open and Secret Pay Policies on Satisfaction and Performance," in A. Head and W.P. Ferris (eds.), *Proceedings of the 28th Annual Meeting of the Eastern Academy of Management*, Hartford, CT, May 1991, pp. 248–51.

Let's Make Pay Information Open to All!

Open pay policies make good sense. They already exist for employees of most public institutions and for top executives in all publicly held corporations. A few private-sector companies have also seen the benefits that can accrue from making the pay of all employees public knowledge. For instance, the software maker NeXT Inc. (recently purchased by Apple Computer) has lists of all its employees' salaries hanging in company offices for anyone to consult.

Why do open pay policies make good sense? We can articulate at least five reasons.

First, such pay policies open communication and build trust. As an executive at NeXT stated, "Anything less than openness doesn't establish the same level of trust." If the organization can be open about such a sensitive issue as pay, it makes employees believe that management can be trusted about other concerns that are not so sensitive. In addition, if an organization's pay system is fair and equitable, employees report greater satisfaction with pay and with pay differentials where pay is open.

Second, an employee's right to privacy needs to be balanced against his or her right to know. Laws to protect an employee's right to know have become more popular in recent years, especially in the area of hazardous working conditions. The case can be made that the right to a free flow of information includes the right to know what others in one's organization earn.

Third, pay secrecy is often supported by organizations not to prevent embarrassment of employees but to prevent embarrassment of management. Pay openness threatens exposing system inequities caused by a poorly developed and administered pay system. An open pay system not only says to employees that management believes its pay policies are fair; but is itself a mechanism for increasing fairness. When true inequities creep into an open pay system, they are much more likely to be quickly identified and corrected than when they occur in pay-secrecy systems. Employees will provide the checks and balances on management.

Fourth, what management calls "freedom" in administering pay is really a euphemism for "control." Pay secrecy allows management to substitute favoritism for performance criteria in pay allocations. To the degree that we believe that organizations should reward good performance rather than good political skills, open pay policies take power and control away from managers. When pay levels and changes are public knowledge, organizational politics is less likely to surface.

Finally, and maybe most importantly, pay secrecy obscures the connection between pay and performance. Both equity and expectancy theories emphasize the desirability of linking rewards to performance. To maximize motivation, employees should know how the organization defines and measures performance, and the rewards attached to differing levels of performance. Unfortunately, when pay information is kept secret, employees make inaccurate perceptions. Even more unfortunately, those inaccuracies tend to work against increasing motivation. Specifically, research has found that people overestimate the pay of their peers and their subordinates and underestimate the pay of their superiors. So where pay is kept secret, actual differences tend to be discounted, which reduces the motivational benefits of linking pay to performance.

Based on E.E. Lawler III, "Secrecy About Management Compensation: Are There Hidden Costs?" *Organizational Behavior and Human Performance*, May 1967, pp. 182–89; J. Solomon, "Hush Money," *Wall Street Journal*, April 18, 1990, pp. R22–R24; and K. Tracy, M. Renard, and G. Young, "Pay Secrecy: The Effects of Open and Secret Pay Policies on Satisfaction and Performance," in A. Head and W.P. Ferris (eds.), *Proceedings of the 28th Annual Meeting of the Eastern Academy of Management*, Hartford, CT, May 1991, pp. 248–51.

Learning about Yourself Exercise

How Equity Sensitive Are You?

The following questions ask what you'd like your relationship to be with any organization for which you might work. For each question, divide ten points between the two answers (a and b) by giving the most points to the answer that is most like you and the fewest points to the answer that is least like you. You can, if you'd like, give the same number of points to both answers. And you can use zeros if you'd like. Just be sure to use all ten points on each question. Place your points in the blank next to each letter.

In any organization where I might work:

1. It would be more important for me to:
_____ **a.** Get from the organization
_____ **b.** Give to the organization

2. It would be more important for me to:
_____ **a.** Help others
_____ **b.** Watch out for my own good

3. I would be more concerned about:
_____ **a.** What I receive from the organization
_____ **b.** What I contribute to the organization

4. The hard work I would do should:
_____ **a.** Benefit the organization
_____ **b.** Benefit me

5. My personal philosophy in dealing with the organization would be:
_____ **a.** If you don't look out for yourself, nobody else will
_____ **b.** It's better to give than to receive

Turn to page A-27 for scoring direction and key.

Source: Courtesy of Prof. Edward W. Miles, Georgia State University, and Dean Richard C. Huseman, University of Central Florida. With permission.

Working with Others Exercise

Goal-Setting Task

Purpose This exercise will help you learn how to write tangible, verifiable, measurable, and relevant goals as might evolve from an MBO program.

Time Approximately 20 to 30 minutes.

Instructions 1. Break into groups of three to five.

2. Spend a few minutes discussing your class instructor's job. What does he or she do? What defines good performance? What behaviors will lead to good performance?

3. Each group is to develop a list of five goals that, although not established participatively with your instructor, you believe might be developed in an MBO program at your college. Try to select goals that seem most critical to the effective performance of your instructor's job.

4. Each group will select a leader who will share his or her group's goals with the entire class. For each group's goals, class discussion should focus on their: (a) specificity, (b) ease of measurement, (c) importance, and (d) motivational properties.

Ethical Dilemma Exercise

Are American CEOs Paid Too Much?

Critics have described the astronomical pay packages given to American CEOs as "rampant greed." They note that during the 1980s, CEO compensation jumped by 212 percent, while factory workers saw their pay increase by just 53 percent. During the same decade, the average earnings per share of the Standard & Poor's 500 companies grew by only 78 percent. In recent years, the average salary and bonus for a chief executive of a major U.S. corporation has been running at about 150 times the average factory worker's pay!

High levels of executive compensation seem to be widespread in the United States. In 1994, for instance, Stephen C. Hilbert of Conseco took home $39.6 million; Colgate-Palmolive's Reuben Mark was paid $13.4 million; and Coca-Cola's Roberto Goizueta earned $12.2 million. A recent survey examined the compensation of the two highest-paid executives at 361 large U.S. corporations. A record number, 501 of these 722 executives, earned more than $1 million.

How do you explain these astronomical pay packages? Some say this represents a classic economic response to a situation in which the demand is great for high-quality top-executive talent and the supply is low. Other arguments in favor of paying executives $1 million a year or more are: the need to compensate people for the tremendous responsibilities and stress that go with such jobs, the motivating potential that seven- and eight-figure annual incomes provide to senior executives and those who might aspire to be, and the influence of senior executives on the company's bottom line.

Executive pay is considerably higher in the United States than in most other countries. American CEOs typically make two or three times as much as their counterparts in Canada, Europe, and Asia. In 1994, for instance, European CEOs made about 47 percent of what their U.S. counterparts earned. Million-dollar incomes for executives still make headline news in Canada.

Critics of executive pay practices in the United States argue that CEOs choose board members whom they can count on to support ever-increasing pay for top management. If board members fail to "play along," they risk losing their positions, their fees, and the prestige and power inherent in board membership.

Is high compensation of U.S. executives a problem? If so, does the blame for the problem lie with CEOs or with the shareholders and boards that knowingly allow the practice? Are American CEOs greedy? Are these CEOs acting unethically? What do you think?

Source: J.M. Pennings, "Executive Reward Systems: A Cross-National Comparison," *Journal of Management Studies*, March 1993, pp. 261–80; E.S. Hardy, "America's Highest-Paid Bosses," *Forbes*, May 22, 1995, pp. 180–82; I. McGugan, "A Crapshoot Called Compensation," *Canadian Business*, July 1995, pp. 67–70; and J. Flynn, "Continental Divide Over Executive Pay," *Business Week*, July 3, 1995, pp. 40–41.

"What Am I Going to Do about Stella McCarthy?"

Jim Murray had worked as a cost accountant at Todd Brothers Chevrolet for nearly three years. When his boss retired in the spring of 1997, Ross Todd, the company's president, asked Jim to take over the accounting department. As the company controller, Jim supervises four people: Stella McCarthy, Judy Lawless, Tina Rothschild, and Mike Sohal.

Six months have passed since Jim took over his new job. As he expected, Judy, Tina, and Mike have been easy to work with. All have been in their jobs for at least four years. They know their jobs backward and forward, and they require very little of Jim's time.

Stella McCarthy, unfortunately, is a completely different story. Stella was hired about three months before Jim got his promotion. Her age and education aren't significantly different from his other three employees—she's in her early 30s with an undergraduate degree in accounting. But in recent weeks she has become his number-one headache.

Stella's job is to handle general accounting records. She also acts as the accounting's link to the service department. Stella provides advice and support to service on anything having to do with credit, cost control, the computer system, and the like.

The first sign of a problem began three weeks ago. Stella called in sick on both Monday and Tuesday. When she showed up for work on Wednesday morning, she looked like she hadn't slept in days. Jim called her into his office and, in an informal manner, began trying to find out what was going on. Stella was open. She admitted she hadn't been ill. She called in sick because she didn't have the emotional strength to come to work. She volunteered that her marriage was in trouble. Her husband had a serious drinking problem but wouldn't seek help. He had lost his third job in as many months on that last Friday. She was concerned about her children and her finances. Stella has a seven-year-old son from a previous marriage and twin daughters who are three years old. Jim tried to console Stella. He encouraged her to keep her spirits up and reminded her that the company's health plan provided six free counseling sessions. He suggested she consider using them.

Since that initial encounter, little seems to have changed with Stella. She's used up three more sick days. When she comes to the office, it's clear her mind is somewhere else. She is spending an inordinate amount of time on the telephone, and Jim suspects it's almost all related to personal matters. Twice in the past week, Jim has noticed Stella crying at her desk.

Yesterday was the third working day of the new month, and Stella should have completed the closing of last month's books. That is an important part of Stella's job. This morning, soon after Stella arrived, Jim asked her for the closing numbers. Stella got up and, with tears welling in her eyes, went to the ladies' room. Jim saw last month's books on Stella's desk. He opened them up. They were incomplete. Stella had missed her deadline, and Jim wasn't sure when he would have the final figures to give to Ross Todd.

Questions

1. Do any motivation techniques appear relevant to helping Jim deal with Stella? If so, what are they?
2. From an ethical perspective, how far do you think Jim should go in dealing with Stella's personal problems?
3. If you were Jim, what would you do?

What Motivates Elizabeth Dole?

Her husband failed in November 1996 to win the presidency. Ironically, she may end up in the White House yet—but in the Oval Office rather than as First Lady. The person we're talking about is Elizabeth Hanford Dole. She holds one of the most impressive résumés in Washington.

Elizabeth Hanford grew up in a prosperous and prominent family that schooled her in southern charm. She attended college at Duke, where she was president of her class. Then she took two degrees at Harvard, including law. In law school, she was one of only 23 women in a class of 539. After Harvard, she went to Washington. A registered Democrat, she went to work for Lyndon Johnson as a consumer advocate. When she married Bob Dole, she changed parties and became a Republican. Then she rose through the ranks of several Republican administrations. She became head of the Federal Trade Commission; assistant to the president for public liaison; secretary of transportation in the Reagan administration; then secretary of labor under George Bush. Most recently, she has been the president of the American Red Cross.

People constantly compare Elizabeth Dole to Hillary Rodham Clinton. The comparisons are striking. Both are highly intelligent and articulate. Both were class presidents in college. Both went to Ivy League law schools, and both have a history of independence in their political, professional, and personal life. But for some reasons, the same critics who have come down hard on Hillary Rodham Clinton have generally gone easy on Mrs. Dole. Why? The answer isn't clear. Elizabeth Dole is as ambitious or more so than Mrs. Clinton. But she's been more successful at camouflaging her career ambitions. Whereas Mrs. Clinton is often seen as too strong, too intelligent, too driven, Mrs. Dole seems less threatening. She comes across as the more traditional kind of wife. Yet she has never believed that she should sacrifice her career for that of her husband. Quite the contrary. Although Mrs. Clinton gave up her lucrative law practice when her husband became president, Mrs. Dole made it clear from the onset that, were her husband to be elected president, she planned to carry on full-time as head of the Red Cross. It was Elizabeth Dole, not Hillary Clinton, who chose to pass on being a mother.

Questions

1. What drives Elizabeth Dole?
2. Contrast her motivations to Hillary Rodham Clinton. How are they similar? Different?
3. How have societal expectations shaped Elizabeth Dole's behavior?
4. Why is it permissible for Bob Dole or Bill Clinton to show overt ambition, but such actions are frowned upon when exhibited by an equally qualified female?

Source: Based on "The Other Half," *ABC News Nightline*; aired on April 17, 1996.

ROB PANCO: MANAGING INDIVIDUALS

Before you can understand others, you need to understand yourself. With that in mind, Rob Panco was asked to describe his strengths and weaknesses. "On the positive side, I'm very opportunistic. I'm good at exploiting opportunities. I'm a positive person. I'm realistic. Broad-minded. I can deal with different opinions and change my mind when I need to. I'm also driven to succeed." When asked to identify what he thought his faults might be, Rob said, "I take too much responsibility for other people's performance and happiness. When I was a full-time manager, I wanted to provide my people with safety nets. Sometimes people perform best when they work without a net. Nurturing is good, but too much isn't. This tendency created problems when I delegated assignments. On one side, sometimes I didn't provide enough instructions with my delegation. This was particularly a problem with younger project leaders. On the other side, I was frequently paranoid when I delegated something. I'd be afraid that it would get screwed up. I worry a lot. I think this reflects the fact that I'm not always 100 percent sure of myself. I go through phases of insecurity. I feel overly responsible for people. Friends describe me as having confidence without arrogance. But when I was general manager at Aslett, I had a lot of responsibility, and I probably worried too much about people making mistakes and screwing things up."

The discussion with Rob then turned to his experiences at Aslett and the topics of selecting new employees, his decision-making style, his views on motivation, the importance he places on measuring employee attitudes, and ethical dilemmas he may have faced.

"In 1993 and 1994, business was very good. Sales were increasing and we needed to expand our staff. To find an ideal job candidate, I always started by looking at the specific job to be done. Essentially, I'd break jobs into one of two categories. For entry-level jobs, I looked for people who showed promise and were trainable. I could then mold them into the type of employee I wanted. For experienced workers and managers, I was more concerned with the fit between them and us. Their attitudes and ways of doing things were established, so I needed to be sure that they'd fit well with our organization. For example, I had been interviewing candidates to fill the position of production manager. I was looking for four things in this position. First, they had to have the ability to do the functional task. Second, they needed raw talent. By that I mean they had to show me evidence that they could successfully apply their ability. Third, I wanted some evidence of professional ambition. And fourth, I looked at their personal dynamics. Would they fit into our culture? Personality wise, the kind of people I wanted were those with enthusiasm, team players—I didn't want any heroes—and individuals committed to growth.

"Of course, like everyone, I've made some mistakes in hiring," Rob admitted. "For instance, I had to let one person go. He was late a lot. He lacked motivation. I had hired Dan right out of high school and I thought I could shape him into a real good employee. He was OK for about six months. Then the problems started. He wanted to leave at exactly 5 P.M. to be with his friends. He was resistant to new technologies. I encouraged him to take advantage of our training opportunities, but he wasn't interested. I talked with him about these problems on a monthly basis. I even talked with Hank, who Dan sort of modeled himself after. Hank told me that Dan lacked motivation and was hurting company morale. This confirmed to me that Dan didn't fit in. So I let him go. In another instance, I hired a woman as my financial assistant who did marvelously in the interview, had good references, and exactly the experience I was looking for. But Anne was just lethargic. She was slow, inaccurate, and her productivity was unsatisfactory. I had to fire her. Interestingly, I went back to Anne's original file and reviewed her application, references, and my interview notes. Nothing suggested that she wouldn't be a top performer. Sometimes you just can't predict how an employee is going to turn out!

"This discussion of hiring makes a good segue to the topic of decision making. I consider myself very rational. I'm a fact-based decision maker. Two things I think characterize my decision making. First, I'm flexible. I listen to others. I may not agree with you, but I'm open to letting you sell me on your position. I believe in others giving me input. But I don't believe in decisions by committee. Second, I follow what I call my '12-hour rule.' I never rush big decisions that have a lasting impact. When people would ask me right after a proposal what I was going to do, I'd say 'I don't know yet.' I like to sleep on decisions and then make a commitment."

Motivating employees is a key issue for most managers and Rob was no exception. "I may be wrong, but I think money is less of a factor in the '90s than it was in the 1980s. Now quality of work life is a prime motivator. At Aslett, no one earned less than $25,000 a year. So everyone had their basic financial needs met. Let me qualify my earlier comment. For people in the $25,000 to $35,000 range, money matters. It's less important for people who make over $35,000. And today, with so many dual-career couples, people just aren't going to jump through hoops in order to get an extra $1,000 or $2,000 salary increase. Also keep in mind that times have changed. The 10 percent annual cost-of-living raise is becoming extinct. At Aslett, we relied more on annual bonuses based on company and personal performance. In 1994, for instance, bonuses ranged from 1 to 10 percent of a person's salary. Additionally, I looked for creative ways to motivate people. As an example, I gave one person two days off with pay as a reward for an outstanding job. Most people appreciate recognition, so I used that. One employee got a write-up in a local paper for her success in fund-raising for charity. I put that article up on the wall in the lunch room. I also tried to modify work schedules to reflect individual differences. I worked with my single parents to give them leaves and schedules that helped them meet their personal needs. Oh yeah, and we gave all employees ten holidays a year. Only six of them were universally taken by everybody. The other four were floating days. Individuals could choose which holidays they wanted to take. Some took Martin Luther King Day as their holiday. One former military guy took Veteran's Day. Several of our Jewish employees took Rosh Hashanah and/or Yom Kippur."

Rob was asked whether the slowdown in business that Aslett faced in 1995 influenced motivation. Sales flattened and profits turned to losses. In December 1994, Aslett employed 16 full-time people. Two years later that number was down to nine. "It was surprising to me how people adapted to the decline in business," Rob said. "Most of the reductions in staff came through voluntary attrition. Those who couldn't handle the increased workloads, insecurity, and ambiguity resigned. One guy, for instance, left for a more traditional corporate job. In late 1995, when business picked up, a number of employees complained because we didn't hire any new people. I explained that the new equipment we'd installed allowed increases in productivity. But people didn't seem to understand that, while they were producing more, it was due to technology rather than them working harder.

"One of my more memorable problems was with Nick," Rob continued. "The product line that Nick worked on was going to be obsolete in a year or so. I made that clear to Nick and told him he needed to retrain. He resisted and resisted. But I didn't threaten him. I treated him like an adult. I just said, 'Nick. You may not have a job around here if your product line goes away. Whether or not you retrain to handle the new equipment is up to you.' That approach worked. He informally retrained himself by taking several of the new machines home with him on weekends and learning how to use them."

M.E. Aslett didn't use attitude surveys. Rob talked about three means by which he kept track of employee attitudes. "I tapped employee attitudes informally. There were two people who regularly came in to my office, talked with me, and gave me feedback on what people were thinking and saying. These people were very open with me. They spoke their mind. And they were pretty accurate at tapping into the mood." Rob got formal feedback on attitudes through project debriefings and performance reviews. Most projects at Aslett were done in teams. At the completion of a project, he debriefed the group. "I have to admit I didn't get that much out of those debriefings," says Rob, "but it was a good motivating tool. It gave people a feeling of contributing." Finally, Rob used the feedback from performance reviews and evaluations to monitor how employees felt about factors such as supervision, their job, and the organization itself.

When Rob was asked to identify ethical dilemmas he'd faced, he mentioned two. A publisher wanted him to publish a book that he felt was obviously outdated. Since he would be the editor of record, he didn't want to be associated with such a project. A second had to do with laying off a full-time employee and then rehiring someone to fill that slot but on a temporary basis. He wasn't sure whether such a decision, which made good business sense, was ethically appropriate.

Questions

1. To what degree do you think Rob should have felt responsible for his employee's performance and happiness?
2. What do you think of the four criteria Rob used in the selection of a production manager? What personality characteristics, if any, do you think might be related to success in that job?
3. How well did Rob handle his problems with Dan?
4. What pluses could Rob's "12-hour rule" provide? How about negatives?

5. What theories could help to explain Rob's motivation practices?

6. What do you think of the means by which Rob kept tabs on employee attitudes?

7. Is it unethical to fire a full-time employee and replace him or her with a temporary? What obligations, if any, does an employer have to a permanent employee?

CHAPTER 7

Part Three   The Group

FOUNDATIONS OF GROUP BEHAVIOR

> One of the truly remarkable things about work groups is that they can make 2 + 2 = 5. Of course, they also have the capability of making 2 + 2 = 3.
> — S.P.R.

LEARNING OBJECTIVES

After studying this chapter, you should be able to

1. Differentiate between formal and informal groups
2. Compare two models of group development
3. Explain how group interaction can be analyzed
4. Identify the key factors in explaining group behavior
5. Explain how role requirements change in different situations
6. Describe how norms exert influence on an individual's behavior
7. Define *social loafing* and its effect on group performance
8. Identify the benefits and disadvantages of cohesive groups
9. List the strengths and weaknesses of group decision making
10. Contrast the effectiveness of interacting, brainstorming, nominal, and electronic meeting groups

THE pulp and paper products industry in Canada has been under cost pressures for more than a decade. One particular player in this industry, MacMillan Bloedel Ltd. (MacBlo), has responded by closing mills, shutting down machines, and cutting its workforce down from 25,000 to 13,000. These efforts at downsizing have helped MacBlo, but the company still continues to post annual losses.[1]

If you think these cutbacks at MacBlo haven't set well with the company's unions, you'd be right. In fact, the company and its unions have a long history of antagonism. Three times during the 1980s, union locals hit the company with wildcat strikes. Each time the company sued the offending local and won cash awards and workplace concessions. The regional vice president of one union—the Communications, Energy, and Paperworkers Union of Canada—says, "There is not a great trust relationship here."

MacBlo's management led by CEO Robert Findlay (see photo), is trying to change its labor relations climate by getting workers more involved in company decision making. Its woodlands and mill managers now share detailed financial data and production plans in regular meetings with workers. Joint union–management committees have been created to solicit suggestions for improving productivity. Some division managers are even taking union representatives along on sales trips so they can see, firsthand, the industry's competitive conditions.

Management's efforts to improve relations with its union members haven't met with a great deal of success. Union leaders openly question management's motives. They claim that joint committees just dupe union members into making suggestions that increase productivity at the cost of jobs. They also use examples like the company's plan to discontinue bus service at one of the mills, which precipitated a one-day wildcat strike by 725 loggers, as evidence that the company just doesn't care about its employees. ◆

The labor–management problems at MacMillan Bloedel illustrate the importance of understanding groups in the workplace. The behavior of individuals in groups is something more than the sum total of each acting in his or her own way. In other words, when individuals are in groups, they act differently than they do when they're alone. So, for instance, the employee that would individually accept change and cooperate with management might become belligerent and try to hinder that change if he or she is a union member and the union seeks to maintain the status quo.

Union members are just one example of a work group. As we show in this chapter, organizations are made up of a number of formal and informal groups. And an understanding of these groups is critical to explaining organizational behavior.

Defining and Classifying Groups

group
Two or more individuals, interacting and interdependent, who have come together to achieve particular objectives.

A **group** is defined as two or more individuals, interacting and interdependent, who have come together to achieve particular objectives. Groups can be either formal or informal. By **formal groups**, we mean those defined by the organization's structure, with designated work assignments establishing tasks. In formal groups, the behaviors that one should engage in are stipulated by and directed toward organizational goals. The six members making up an airline flight crew are an example of a formal group. In contrast, **informal groups** are alliances that are neither formally structured nor organizationally determined. These groups are natural formations in the work environment that appear in response to the need for social contact. Three employees from different departments who regularly eat lunch together are an example of an informal group.

formal group
A designated work group defined by the organization's structure.

informal group
A group that is neither formally structured nor organizationally determined; appears in response to the need for social contact.

It's possible to subclassify groups as command, task, interest, or friendship groups.[2] Command and task groups are dictated by the formal organization, whereas interest and friendship groups are informal alliances.

command group
A manager and his or her immediate subordinates.

A **command group** is determined by the organization chart. It is composed of the subordinates who report directly to a given manager. An elementary school principal and her 12 teachers form a command group, as do the director of postal audits and his five inspectors.

task group
Those working together to complete a job task.

Task groups, also organizationally determined, represent those working together to complete a job task. However, a task group's boundaries are not limited to its immediate hierarchical superior. It can cross command relationships. For instance, if a college student is accused of a campus crime, it may require communication and coordination among the dean of academic affairs, the dean of students, the registrar, the director of security, and the student's advisor. Such a formation would constitute a task group. It should be noted that all command groups are also task groups, but because task groups can cut across the organization, the reverse need not be true.

People who may or may not be aligned into common command or task groups may affiliate to attain a specific objective with which each is concerned. This is an **interest group**. Employees who band together to have their vacation schedules altered, to support a peer who has been fired, or to seek improved working conditions represent the formation of a united body to further their common interest.

interest group
Those working together to attain a specific objective with which each is concerned.

Groups often develop because the individual members have one or more

Because speed and flexibility are important to the success of MagneTek in supplying electrical products to the growing worldwide market, the company has formed task groups to complete customer orders. The task groups shown here work as teams that adapt quickly to changes in the size, schedule, and complexity of customer orders.

common characteristics. We call these formations **friendship groups**. Social alliances, which frequently extend outside the work situation, can be based on similar age or ethnic heritage, support for Notre Dame football, or the holding of similar political views, to name just a few such characteristics.

friendship group
Those brought together because they share one or more common characteristics.

Informal groups provide a very important service by satisfying their members' social needs. Because of interactions that result from the close proximity of workstations or task interactions, we find workers playing golf together, riding to and from work together, lunching together, and spending their breaks around the water cooler together. We must recognize that these types of interactions among individuals, even though informal, deeply affect their behavior and performance.

There is no single reason why individuals join groups. Because most people belong to a number of groups, it's obvious that different groups provide different benefits to their members. Exhibit 7-1 on page 242 summarizes the most popular reasons people have for joining groups.

Stages of Group Development

For 30 years or more, we thought that most groups followed a specific sequence in their evolution and we thought that we knew what that sequence was. But we were wrong. Recent research indicates that there is no standardized pattern of group development. In this section, we review the better-known five-stage model of group development, and then the more recently discovered punctuated-equilibrium model.

The Five-Stage Model

From the mid-1960s, it was believed that groups passed through a standard sequence of five stages.[3] As shown in Exhibit 7-2 on page 242, these five stages have been labeled forming, storming, norming, performing, and adjourning.

Exhibit 7-1 Why Do People Join Groups?

Security

By joining a group, individuals can reduce the insecurity of "standing alone." People feel stronger, have fewer self-doubts, and are more resistant to threats when they are part of a group.

Status

Inclusion in a group that is viewed as important by others provides recognition and status for its members.

Self-Esteem

Groups can provide people with feelings of self-worth. That is, in addition to conveying status to those outside the group, membership can also give increased feelings of worth to the group members themselves.

Affiliation

Groups can fulfill social needs. People enjoy the regular interaction that comes with group membership. For many people, these on-the-job interactions are their primary source for fulfilling their needs for affiliation.

Power

What cannot be achieved individually often becomes possible through group action. There is power in numbers.

Goal Achievement

There are times when it takes more than one person to accomplish a particular task—there is a need to pool talents, knowledge, or power in order to complete a job. In such instances, management will rely on the use of a formal group.

forming
The first stage in group development, characterized by much uncertainty.

storming
The second stage in group development, characterized by intragroup conflict.

norming
The third stage in group development, characterized by close relationships and cohesiveness.

The first stage, **forming**, is characterized by a great deal of uncertainty about the group's purpose, structure, and leadership. Members are "testing the waters" to determine what types of behavior are acceptable. This stage is complete when members have begun to think of themselves as part of a group.

The **storming** stage is one of intragroup conflict. Members accept the existence of the group, but there is resistance to the constraints that the group imposes on individuality. Furthermore, there is conflict over who will control the group. When this stage is complete, there will be a relatively clear hierarchy of leadership within the group.

The third stage is one in which close relationships develop and the group demonstrates cohesiveness. There is now a strong sense of group identity and camaraderie. This **norming** stage is complete when the group struc-

Exhibit 7-2
Stages of Group Development

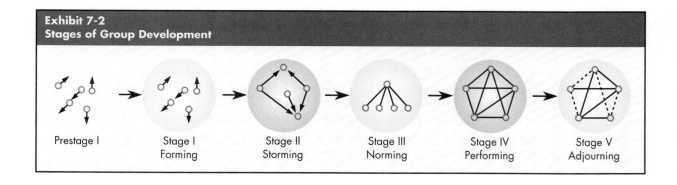

| Prestage I | Stage I Forming | Stage II Storming | Stage III Norming | Stage IV Performing | Stage V Adjourning |

ture solidifies and the group has assimilated a common set of expectations of what defines correct member behavior.

The fourth stage is **performing**. The structure at this point is fully functional and accepted. Group energy has moved from getting to know and understand each other to performing the task at hand.

For permanent work groups, performing is the last stage in their development. However, for temporary committees, teams, task forces, and similar groups that have a limited task to perform, there is an **adjourning** stage. In this stage, the group prepares for its disbandment. High task performance is no longer the group's top priority. Instead, attention is directed toward wrapping up activities. Responses of group members vary in this stage. Some are upbeat, basking in the group's accomplishments. Others may be depressed over the loss of camaraderie and friendships gained during the work group's life.

Many interpreters of the five-stage model have assumed that a group becomes more effective as it progresses through the first four stages. While this assumption may be generally true, what makes a group effective is more complex than this model acknowledges. Under some conditions, high levels of conflict are conducive to high group performance. So we might expect to find situations where groups in Stage II outperform those in Stages III or IV. Similarly, groups do not always proceed clearly from one stage to the next. Sometimes, in fact, several stages go on simultaneously, as when groups are storming and performing at the same time. Groups even occasionally regress to previous stages. Therefore, even the strongest proponents of this model do not assume that all groups follow its five-stage process precisely or that Stage IV is always the most preferable.

Another problem with the five-stage model, in terms of understanding work-related behavior, is that it ignores organizational context.[4] For instance, a study of a cockpit crew in an airliner found that, within ten minutes, three strangers assigned to fly together for the first time had become a high-performing group. What allowed for this speedy group development was the strong organizational context surrounding the tasks of the cockpit crew. This context provided the rules, task definitions, information, and resources needed for the group to perform. They didn't need to develop plans, assign roles, determine and allocate resources, resolve conflicts, and set norms the way the five-stage model predicts. Because much group behavior in organizations takes place within a strong organizational context, it would appear that the five-stage development model may have limited applicability in our quest to understand work groups.

performing
The fourth stage in group development, when the group is fully functional.

adjourning
The final stage in group development for temporary groups, characterized by concern with wrapping up activities rather than task performance.

The Punctuated-Equilibrium Model

Studies of more than a dozen field and laboratory task force groups confirmed that groups don't develop in a universal sequence of stages.[5] But the timing of when groups form and change the way they work is highly consistent. Specifically, it's been found that (1) the first meeting sets the group's direction; (2) the first phase of group activity is one of inertia; (3) a transition takes place at the end of the first phase, which occurs exactly when the group has used up half its allotted time; (4) the transition initiates major changes; (5) a second phase of inertia follows the transition; and (6) the group's last meeting is characterized by markedly accelerated activity. These findings are shown in Exhibit 7-3 on page 244.

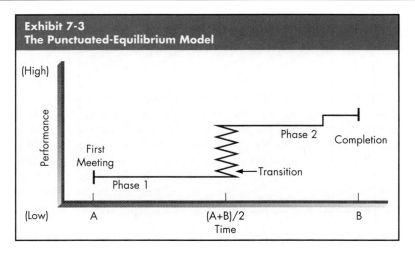

Exhibit 7-3
The Punctuated-Equilibrium Model

The first meeting sets the group's direction. A framework of behavioral patterns and assumptions through which the group will approach its project emerges in this first meeting. These lasting patterns can appear as early as the first few seconds of the group's life.

Once set, the group's direction becomes "written in stone" and is unlikely to be reexamined throughout the first half of the group's life. This is a period of inertia—that is, the group tends to stand still or become locked into a fixed course of action. Even if it gains new insights that challenge initial patterns and assumptions, the group is incapable of acting on these new insights in Phase 1.

One of the more interesting discoveries made in these studies was that each group experienced its transition at the same point in its calendar—precisely halfway between its first meeting and its official deadline—despite the fact that some groups spent as little as an hour on their project while others spent six months. It was as if the groups universally experienced a midlife crisis at this point. The midpoint appears to work like an alarm clock, heightening members' awareness that their time is limited and that they need to "get moving."

This transition ends Phase 1 and is characterized by a concentrated burst of changes, dropping of old patterns, and adoption of new perspectives. The transition sets a revised direction for Phase 2.

Phase 2 is a new equilibrium or period of inertia. In this phase, the group executes plans created during the transition period.

The group's last meeting is characterized by a final burst of activity to finish its work.

We can use this model to describe some of your experiences with student teams created for doing group term projects. At the first meeting, a basic timetable is established. Members size up one another. They agree they have nine weeks to do their project. The instructor's requirements are discussed and debated. From that point, the group meets regularly to carry out its activities. About four or five weeks into the project, however, problems are confronted. Criticism begins to be taken seriously. Discussion becomes more open. The group reassesses where it's been and aggressively moves to make necessary changes. If the right changes are made, the next four or five weeks find the group developing a first-rate project. The group's last meeting, which will probably occur just before the project is due, lasts longer than the others. In it, all final issues are discussed and details resolved.

In summary, the punctuated-equilibrium model characterizes groups as exhibiting long periods of inertia interspersed with brief revolutionary changes triggered primarily by their members' awareness of time and deadlines. Or, to use the terminology of the five-stage group development model, the group begins by combining the forming and norming stages, then goes through a period of low performing, followed by storming, then a period of high performing, and, finally, adjourning.

Sociometry: Analyzing Group Interaction

Shirley Goldman knew the formal work groups in the branch bank she managed. The tellers made up one group, the loan processors another, administrative support personnel still another, and the task force she had created for suggesting ways to improve customer service was a fourth. What Shirley didn't feel as confident about were the informal groups in her branch. Who were in these groups? Who were their informal leaders? How might these groups be affecting communication in the bank or creating potential conflicts? To get answers to these questions, Shirley decided to use a technique she learned in business school. It's called **sociometry** and it's an analytical tool for studying group interactions.[6]

Sociometry seeks to find out who people like or dislike and with whom they would or would not wish to work. How do you get that information? Through the use of interviews or questionnaires. For instance, employees might be asked: (1) With whom in your organization would you like to associate in the process of carrying out your job? or (2) Name several organization members with whom you would like to spend some of your free time.

This information can then be used to create a **sociogram**. This is a diagram that graphically maps the preferred social interactions obtained from the interviews or questionnaires. Before we actually work through an example, let's define some key terms that you need to know when discussing and analyzing a sociogram:[7]

- ◆ **Social networks**. Specific sets of linkages among a defined set of individuals.
- ◆ **Clusters**. Groups that exist within social networks.
- ◆ **Prescribed clusters**. Formal groups like departments, work teams, task forces, crews, or committees.
- ◆ **Emergent clusters**. Informal, unofficial groups.
- ◆ **Coalitions**. Clusters of individuals who temporarily come together to achieve a specific purpose.
- ◆ **Cliques**. Relatively permanent informal groupings that involve friendship.
- ◆ **Stars**. Individuals with the most linkages in a network.
- ◆ **Liaisons**. Individuals who connect two or more clusters but are not members of any cluster.
- ◆ **Bridges**. Individuals who serve as linking pins by belonging to two or more clusters.
- ◆ **Isolates**. Individuals who are not connected to a social network.

sociometry
An analytical technique for studying group interactions.

sociogram
A diagram that graphically maps the preferred social interactions obtained from interviews or questionnaires.

social networks
A specific set of linkages among a defined set of individuals.

clusters
Groups that exist within social networks.

prescribed clusters
Formal groups like departments, work teams, task forces, or committees.

emergent clusters
Informal, unofficial groups.

coalitions
A cluster of individuals who temporarily come together to achieve a specific purpose.

cliques
Relatively permanent informal groups that involve friendship.

stars
Individuals with the most linkages in a network.

liaisons
Individuals in a social network who connect two or more clusters but are not members of any cluster.

bridges
Individuals in a social network who serve as linking pins by belonging to two or more clusters.

isolates
Individuals who are not connected to a social network.

Shirley Goldman has just completed a sociometric survey of the 11 people who work in her Bank of America branch in Sacramento, California. She has had each employee fill out a questionnaire identifying with whom they would like to spend more time. Now Shirley has translated those preferences into the simplified sociogram shown in Exhibit 7-4. Each employee is shown as a circle. The arrow from B to A means B chose A. The two-headed arrow connecting A and D means both chose each other.

What information can Shirley deduce from this sociogram? A is the star. F is an isolate. D is a bridge. There don't appear to be any liaisons. In addition to the four prescribed clusters, two emergent clusters seem to exist. And without more information, Shirley can't tell if these emergent clusters are coalitions or cliques.

So what, if anything, can Shirley do with this information? It can help her predict communication patterns. For instance, D is likely to act as an information conduit between the tellers and the administrative support group. Similarly, Shirley shouldn't be surprised that F is out of the gossip loop and tends to rely almost exclusively on formal communication to know what's happening in the branch. If Shirley was going on vacation and needed to pick someone to temporarily run the branch, a good choice might be A because this person seems to be well liked. When conflicts occur between the tellers

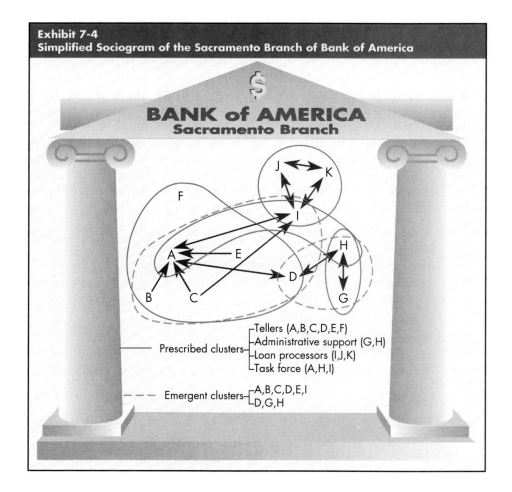

Exhibit 7-4
Simplified Sociogram of the Sacramento Branch of Bank of America

and the administrative support group, a bridge like D might be the best person to help resolve them.

Before we leave the topic of sociometry, some research relating to turnover, conflict, and diversity should be briefly mentioned. First, turnover is likely to be linked to emergent clusters.[8] Employees who perceive themselves as members of common clusters tend to act in concert—they're likely to stay or quit as a group. Second, strong interpersonal relationships between members tend to be associated with lower conflict levels.[9] So since members of emergent clusters tend to interact more with each other, there should be less conflict among these members. Finally, women and minorities tend to form coalitions and cliques, and are less likely than their white male counterparts to become liaisons or bridges.[10]

Toward Explaining Work Group Behavior

Why are some group efforts more successful than others? The answer to that question is complex, but it includes variables such as the ability of the group's members, the size of the group, the level of conflict, and the internal pressures on members to conform to the group's norms. Exhibit 7-5 presents the major components that determine group performance and satisfaction.[11] It can help you sort out the key variables and their interrelationships.

Work groups don't exist in isolation. They are part of a larger organization. A research team in Dow's plastic products division, for instance, must live within the rules and policies dictated from the division's headquarters and Dow's corporate offices. So every work group is influenced by external conditions imposed from outside it. The work group itself has a distinct set of resources determined by its membership. This includes such things as intelligence and motivation of members. It also has an internal structure that defines member roles and norms. These factors—group member resources and structure—determine interaction patterns and other processes within the group. Finally, the group process–performance/satisfaction relationship is moderated by the type of task that the group is working on. In the following pages, we'll elaborate on each of the basic boxes identified in Exhibit 7-5.

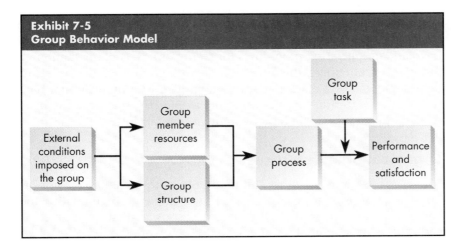

**Exhibit 7-5
Group Behavior Model**

External Conditions Imposed on the Group

To begin understanding the behavior of a work group, you need to view it as a subsystem embedded in a larger system.[12] That is, when we realize that groups are a subset of a larger organization system, we can extract part of the explanation of the group's behavior from an explanation of the organization to which it belongs.

Organization Strategy

An organization's overall strategy, typically put into place by top management, outlines the organization's goals and the means for attaining these goals. It might, for example, direct the organization toward reducing costs, improving quality, expanding market share, or shrinking the size of its overall operations. The strategy that an organization is pursuing, at any given time, will influence the power of various work groups, which, in turn, will determine the resources that the organization's top management is willing to allocate to it for performing its tasks. To illustrate, an organization that is retrenching through selling off or closing down major parts of its business is going to have work groups with a shrinking resource base, increased member anxiety, and the potential for heightened intragroup conflict.[13]

◆ Groups are a subset of a larger organization system.

Authority Structures

Organizations have authority structures that define who reports to whom, who makes decisions, and what decisions individuals or groups are empowered to make. This structure typically determines where a given work group is placed in the organization's hierarchy, the formal leader of the group, and formal relationships between groups. So while a work group might be led by someone who emerges informally from within the group, the formally designated leader—appointed by management—has authority that others in the group don't have.

Formal Regulations

Organizations create rules, procedures, policies, job descriptions, and other forms of regulations to standardize employee behavior. Because McDonald's has standard operating procedures for taking orders, cooking hamburgers, and filling soda containers, the discretion of work group members to set independent standards of behavior is severely limited. The more formal regulations that the organization imposes on all its employees, the more the behavior of work group members will be consistent and predictable.

Organizational Resources

Some organizations are large and profitable, with an abundance of resources. Their employees, for instance, will have modern, high-quality tools and equipment to do their jobs. Other organizations aren't as fortunate. When organizations have limited resources, so do their work groups. What a group actually accomplishes is, to a large degree, determined by what it is capable of accomplishing. The presence or absence of resources such as money, time, raw materials, and equipment—which are allocated to the group by the organization—have a large bearing on the group's behavior.

Human Resource Selection Process

Members of any work group are, first, members of the organization of which the group is a part. Members of a cost-reduction task force at Boeing first had to be hired as employees of the company. So the criteria that an organization uses in its selection process will determine the kinds of people that will be in its work groups.

Performance Evaluation and Reward System

Another organizationwide variable that affects all employees is the performance evaluation and reward system.[14] Does the organization provide employees with challenging, specific performance objectives? Does the organization reward the accomplishment of individual or group objectives? Since work groups are part of the larger organizational system, group members' behavior will be influenced by how the organization evaluates performance and what behaviors are rewarded.

Organizational Culture

Every organization has an unwritten culture that defines standards of acceptable and unacceptable behavior for employees. After a few months, most employees understand their organization's culture. They know things like how to dress for work, whether or not rules are rigidly enforced, what kinds of questionable behaviors are sure to get them into trouble and which are likely to be overlooked, the importance of honesty and integrity, and the like. While

Juggling with serving spades, tossing scoops of ice cream to one another behind the counter, break-dancing on the freezer top, and even wearing pajamas to work is acceptable behavior for crew members at Amy's Ice Creams shops in Austin and Houston, Texas. These antics are part of the dominant organizational culture created by owner Amy Miller. Miller differentiates her premium-ice-cream shops from competitors by selling entertainment as well as excellent products and service. The corporate culture of creating fun for customers is the source of the company's success.

many organizations have subcultures—often created around work groups—with an additional or modified set of standards, they still have a dominant culture that conveys to all employees those values the organization holds dearest. Members of work groups have to accept the standards implied in the organization's dominant culture if they are to remain in good standing.

Physical Work Setting

Finally, we propose that the physical work setting that is imposed on the group by external parties has an important bearing on work group behavior.[15] Architects, industrial engineers, and office designers make decisions regarding the size and physical layout of an employee's work space, the arrangement of equipment, illumination levels, and the need for acoustics to cut down on noise distractions. These create both barriers and opportunities for work group interaction. It's obviously a lot easier for employees to talk or "goof off" if their work stations are close together, there are no physical barriers between them, and their supervisor is in an enclosed office 50 yards away.

Group Member Resources

A group's potential level of performance is, to a large extent, dependent on the resources that its members individually bring to the group. In this section, we want to look at two resources that have received the greatest amount of attention: abilities and personality characteristics.

Abilities

Part of a group's performance can be predicted by assessing the task-relevant and intellectual abilities of its individual members. It's true that we occasionally read about the athletic team composed of mediocre players who, because of excellent coaching, determination, and precision teamwork, beats a far more talented group of players. But such cases make the news precisely because they represent an aberration. As the old saying goes, "The race doesn't always go to the swiftest nor the battle to the strongest, but that's the way to bet." A group's performance is not merely the summation of its individual members' abilities. However, these abilities set parameters for what members can do and how effectively they will perform in a group.

◆ Abilities set the parameters for what members can do and how effectively they will perform in a group.

What predictions can we make regarding ability and group performance? First, evidence indicates that individuals who hold crucial abilities for attaining the group's task tend to be more involved in group activity, generally contribute more, are more likely to emerge as the group leaders, and are more satisfied if their talents are effectively utilized by the group.[16] Second, intellectual ability and task-relevant ability have both been found to be related to overall group performance.[17] However, the correlation is not particularly high, suggesting that other factors, such as the size of the group, the type of tasks being performed, the actions of its leader, and level of conflict within the group, also influence performance.

The nine salespeople shown here with their coach (seated) are part of the Top Producer Group 2, a division of The Mutual Life Insurance Company of New York. They are the company's top agents, and they share personality characteristics that make their group the company's highest achievers. Groups members are energetic, competitive, goal-oriented, sociable, self-reliant, and independent. Taken together, these characteristics influence the group's performance.

Personality Characteristics

There has been a great deal of research on the relationship between personality traits and group attitudes and behavior. The general conclusion is that attributes that tend to have a positive connotation in our culture tend to be positively related to group productivity, morale, and cohesiveness. These include traits such as sociability, self-reliance, and independence. In contrast, negatively evaluated characteristics such as authoritarianism, dominance, and unconventionality tend to be negatively related to the dependent variables.[18] These personality traits affect group performance by strongly influencing how the individual will interact with other group members.

Is any one personality characteristic a good predictor of group behavior? The answer to that question is "No." The magnitude of the effect of any *single* characteristic is small, but taking personality characteristics *together*, the consequences for group behavior are of major significance.

Group Structure

Work groups are not unorganized mobs. They have a structure that shapes the behavior of members and makes it possible to explain and predict a large portion of individual behavior within the group as well as the performance of the group itself. What are some of these structural variables? They include formal leadership, roles, norms, group status, group size, composition of the group, and the degree of group cohesiveness.

Formal Leadership

Almost every work group has a formal leader. He or she is typically identified by titles such as unit or department manager, supervisor, foreman, project leader, task force head, or committee chair. This leader can play an important part in the group's success—so much so, in fact, that we have devoted an entire chapter to the topic of leadership. In chapter 10, we review the research on leadership and the effect that leaders have on individual and group performance variables.

Roles

Shakespeare said, "All the world's a stage, and all the men and women merely players." Using the same metaphor, all group members are actors, each playing a **role**. By this term, we mean a set of expected behavior patterns attributed to someone occupying a given position in a social unit. The understanding of role behavior would be dramatically simplified if each of us chose one role and "played it out" regularly and consistently. Unfortunately, we are required to play a number of diverse roles, both on and off our jobs. As we shall see, one of the tasks in understanding behavior is grasping the role that a person is currently playing.

For example, Bill Patterson is a plant manager with Electrical Industries, a large electrical equipment manufacturer in Phoenix. He has a number of roles that he fulfills on that job—for instance, Electrical Industries employee, member of middle management, electrical engineer, and the primary company spokesperson in the community. Off the job, Bill Patterson finds himself in still more roles: husband, father, Catholic, Rotarian, tennis player, member of the Thunderbird Country Club, and president of his homeowners' association. Many of these roles are compatible; some create conflicts. For instance, how does his religious involvement influence his managerial decisions regarding layoffs, expense account padding, and providing accurate information to government agencies? A recent offer of promotion requires Bill to relocate, yet his family very much wants to stay in Phoenix. Can the role demands of his job be reconciled with the demands of his husband and father roles?

The issue should be clear: Like Bill Patterson, we all are required to play a number of roles, and our behavior varies with the role we are playing. Bill's behavior when he attends church on Sunday morning is different from his behavior on the golf course later that same day. So different groups impose different role requirements on individuals.

role
A set of expected behavior patterns attributed to someone occupying a given position in a social unit.

ROLE INDENTITY There are certain attitudes and actual behaviors consistent with a role, and they create the **role identity**. People have the ability to shift roles rapidly when they recognize that the situation and its demands clearly require major changes. For instance, when union stewards were promoted to supervisory positions, it was found that their attitudes changed from prounion to promanagement within a few months of their promotion. When these promotions had to be rescinded later because of economic difficulties in the firm, it was found that the demoted supervisors had once again adopted their prounion attitudes.[19]

role identity
Certain attitudes and behaviors consistent with a role.

ROLE PERCEPTION One's view of how one is supposed to act in a given situation is a **role perception**. Based on an interpretation of how we believe we are supposed to behave, we engage in certain types of behavior.

Where do we get these perceptions? We get them from stimuli all around us—friends, books, movies, television. Many current law enforcement officers learned their roles from reading Joseph Wambaugh novels or watching Dirty Harry movies. Tomorrow's lawyers will certainly be influenced by the actions of attorneys in the O.J. Simpson double-murder trial. Of course, the primary

role perception
An individual's view of how he or she is supposed to act in a given situation.

reason that apprenticeship programs exist in many trades and professions is to allow beginners to watch an "expert," so that they can learn to act as they are supposed to.

ROLE EXPECTATIONS **Role expectations** are defined as how others believe you should act in a given situation. How you behave is determined to a large extent by the role defined in the context in which you are acting. The role of a U.S. senator is viewed as having propriety and dignity, whereas a football coach is seen as aggressive, dynamic, and inspiring to his players. In the same context, we might be surprised to learn that the neighborhood priest moonlights during the week as a bartender because our role expectations of priests and bartenders tend to be considerably different. When role expectations are concentrated into generalized categories, we have role stereotypes.

In the workplace, it can be helpful to look at the topic of role expectations through the perspective of the **psychological contract**. There is an unwritten agreement that exists between employees and their employer. This psychological contract sets out mutual expectations—what management expects from workers, and vice versa.[20] In effect, this contract defines the behavioral expectations that go with every role. Management is expected to treat employees justly, provide acceptable working conditions, clearly communicate what is a fair day's work, and give feedback on how well the employee is doing. Employees are expected to respond by demonstrating a good attitude, following directions, and showing loyalty to the organization.

What happens when role expectations as implied in the psychological contract are not met? If management is derelict in keeping up its part of the bargain, we can expect negative repercussions on employee performance and satisfaction. When employees fail to live up to expectations, the result is usually some form of disciplinary action up to and including firing.

The psychological contract should be recognized as a "powerful determiner of behavior in organizations."[21] It points out the importance of accurately communicating role expectations. In chapter 16, we discuss how organizations socialize employees in order to get them to play out their roles in the way management desires.

ROLE CONFLICT When an individual is confronted by divergent role expectations, the result is **role conflict**. It exists when an individual finds that compliance with one role requirement may make more difficult the compliance with another.[22] At the extreme, it would include situations in which two or more role expectations are mutually contradictory.

Our previous discussion of the many roles Bill Patterson had to deal with included several role conflicts—for instance, Bill's attempt to reconcile the expectations placed on him as a husband and father with those placed on him as an executive with Electrical Industries. The former, as you will remember, emphasizes stability and concern for the desire of his wife and children to remain in Phoenix. Electrical Industries, on the other hand, expects its employees to be responsive to the needs and requirements of the company. Although it might be in Bill's financial and career interests to accept a relocation, the conflict comes down to choosing between family and career role expectations.

All of us have faced and will continue to face role conflicts. The critical issue, from our standpoint, is how conflicts imposed by divergent expectations within the organization impact on behavior. Certainly, they increase internal tension and frustration. There are a number of behavioral responses

role expectations
How others believe a person should act in a given situation.

psychological contract
An unwritten agreement that sets out what management expects from the employee, and vice versa.

role conflict
A situation in which an individual is confronted by divergent role expectations.

one may engage in. For example, one can give a formalized bureaucratic response. The conflict is then resolved by relying on the rules, regulations, and procedures that govern organizational activities. For example, a worker faced with the conflicting requirements imposed by the corporate controller's office and his own plant manager decides in favor of his immediate boss—the plant manager. Other behavioral responses may include withdrawal, stalling, negotiation, or, as we found in our discussion of dissonance in chapter 4, redefining the facts or the situation to make them appear congruent.

AN EXPERIMENT: ZIMBARDO'S SIMULATED PRISON   One of the more illuminating role experiments was done by Stanford University psychologist Philip Zimbardo and his associates.[23] They created a "prison" in the basement of the Stanford psychology building; hired at $15 a day two dozen emotionally stable, physically healthy, law-abiding students who scored "normal average" on extensive personality tests; randomly assigned them the role of either "guard" or "prisoner"; and established some basic rules. The experimenters then stood back to see what would happen.

At the start of the planned two-week simulation, there were no measurable differences between those individuals assigned to be guards and those chosen to be prisoners. Additionally, the guards received no special training in how to be prison guards. They were told only to "maintain law and order" in the prison and not to take any nonsense from the prisoners: Physical violence was forbidden. To simulate further the realities of prison life, the prisoners were allowed visits from relatives and friends. Although the mock guards worked eight-hour shifts, the mock prisoners were kept in their cells around the clock and were allowed out only for meals, exercise, toilet privileges, headcount lineups, and work details.

It took the "prisoners" little time to accept the authority positions of the guards, or the mock guards to adjust to their new authority roles. After the

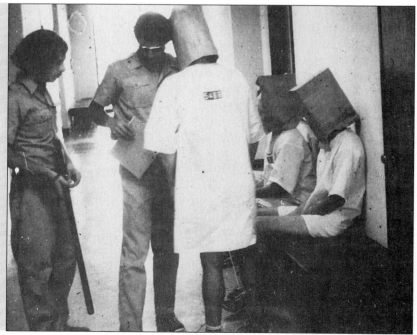

Students at Stanford University playing roles of "guard" and "prisoner" in a simulated prison experiment demonstrate how quickly individuals learn new roles different from their personalities and without any special training.

guards crushed a rebellion attempt on the second day, the prisoners became increasingly passive. Whatever the guards "dished out," the prisoners took. The prisoners actually began to believe and act as if they were, as the guards constantly reminded them, inferior and powerless. And every guard, at some time during the simulation, engaged in abusive, authoritative behavior. For example, one guard said, "I was surprised at myself . . . I made them call each other names and clean the toilets out with their bare hands. I practically considered the prisoners cattle, and I kept thinking: 'I have to watch out for them in case they try something.'" Another guard added, "I was tired of seeing the prisoners in their rags and smelling the strong odors of their bodies that filled the cells. I watched them tear at each other on orders given by us. They didn't see it as an experiment. It was real and they were fighting to keep their identity. But we were always there to show them who was boss."

The simulation actually proved too successful in demonstrating how quickly individuals learn new roles. The researchers had to stop the experiment after only six days because of the pathological reactions that the participants were demonstrating. And remember, these were individuals chosen precisely for their normalcy and emotional stability.

What should you conclude from this prison simulation? The participants in this prison simulation had, like the rest of us, learned stereotyped conceptions of guard and prisoner roles from the mass media and their own personal experiences in power and powerlessness relationships gained at home (parent–child), in school (teacher–student), and in other situations. This, then, allowed them easily and rapidly to assume roles that were very different from their inherent personalities. In this case, we saw that people with no prior personality pathology or training in their roles could execute extreme forms of behavior consistent with the roles they were playing.

Norms

Did you ever notice that golfers don't speak while their partners are putting on the green or that employees don't criticize their bosses in public? Why? The answer is: "Norms!"

All groups have established **norms**, that is, acceptable standards of behavior that are shared by the group's members. Norms tell members what they ought and ought not to do under certain circumstances. From an individual's standpoint, they tell what is expected of you in certain situations. When agreed to and accepted by the group, norms act as a means of influencing the behavior of group members with a minimum of external controls. Norms differ among groups, communities, and societies, but they all have them.[24]

norms
Acceptable standards of behavior within a group that are shared by the group's members.

Formalized norms are written up in organizational manuals setting out rules and procedures for employees to follow. By far, the majority of norms in organizations are informal. You don't need someone to tell you that throwing paper airplanes or engaging in prolonged gossip sessions at the water cooler are unacceptable behaviors when the "big boss from New York" is touring the office. Similarly, we all know that when we're in an employment interview discussing what we didn't like about our previous job, there are certain things we shouldn't talk about (difficulty in getting along with co-workers or our supervisor), while it's very appropriate to talk about other things (inadequate opportunities for advancement or unimportant and meaningless work). Evidence suggests that even high school students recognize that in such interviews certain answers are more socially desirable than others.[25]

COMMON CLASSES OF NORMS A work group's norms are like an individual's fingerprints—each is unique. Yet there are still some common classes of norms that appear in most work groups.[26]

Probably the most common class of norms is *performance norms*. Work groups typically provide their members with explicit cues on how hard they should work, how to get the job done, their level of output, appropriate levels of tardiness, and the like.[27] These norms are extremely powerful in affecting an individual employee's performance—they are capable of significantly modifying a performance prediction that was based solely on the employee's ability and level of personal motivation.

A second category encompasses *appearance norms*. This includes things like appropriate dress, loyalty to the work group or organization, when to look busy, and when it's acceptable to goof off. Some organizations have formal dress codes. However, even in their absence, norms frequently develop to dictate the kind of clothing that should be worn to work. Presenting the appearance of loyalty is important in many work groups and organizations. For instance, in many organizations, especially among professional employees and those in the executive ranks, it is considered inappropriate to be openly looking for another job.

Another category concerns *social arrangement norms*. These norms come from informal work groups and primarily regulate social interactions within the group. With whom group members eat lunch, friendships on and off the job, social games, and the like are influenced by these norms.

A final category relates to *allocation of resources norms*. These norms can originate in the group or in the organization and cover things like pay, assignment of difficult jobs, and allocation of new tools and equipment.

THE "HOW" AND "WHY" OF NORMS *How* do norms develop? *Why* are they enforced? A review of the research allows us to answer these questions.[28]

Norms typically develop gradually as group members learn what behaviors are necessary for the group to function effectively. Of course, critical events in the group might short-circuit the process and act quickly to solidify new norms. Most norms develop in one or more of the following four ways: (1) *Explicit statements made by a group member*—often the group's supervisor or a powerful member. The group leader might, for instance, specifically say that no personal phone calls are allowed during working hours or that coffee breaks are to be kept to ten minutes. (2) *Critical events in the group's history*. These set important precedents. A bystander is injured while standing too close to a machine and, from that point on, members of the work group regularly monitor each other to ensure that no one other than the operator gets within five feet of any machine. (3) *Primacy*. The first behavior pattern that emerges in a group frequently sets group expectations. Friendship groups of students often stake out seats near each other on the first day of class and become perturbed if an outsider takes "their" seats in a later class. (4) *Carry-over behaviors from past situations*. Group members bring expectations with them from other groups of which they have been members. This can explain why work groups typically prefer to add new members who are similar to current ones in background and experience. This is likely to increase the probability that the expectations they bring are consistent with those already held by the group.

But groups don't establish or enforce norms for every conceivable situation. The norms that the group will enforce tend to be those that are important to it. But what makes a norm important? (1) *If it facilitates the group's sur-*

vival. Groups don't like to fail, so they look to enforce those norms that increase their chances for success. This means that they'll try to protect themselves from interference from other groups or individuals. (2) *If it increases the predictability of group members' behaviors*. Norms that increase predictability enable group members to anticipate each other's actions and to prepare appropriate responses. (3) *If it reduces embarrassing interpersonal problems for group members*. Norms are important if they ensure the satisfaction of their members and prevent as much interpersonal discomfort as possible. (4) *If it allows members to express the central values of the group and clarify what is distinctive about the group's identity*. Norms that encourage expression of the group's values and distinctive identity help to solidify and maintain the group.

CONFORMITY   As a member of a group, you desire acceptance by the group. Because of your desire for acceptance, you are susceptible to conforming to the group's norms. There is considerable evidence that groups can place strong pressures on individual members to change their attitudes and behaviors to conform to the group's standard.[29]

Do individuals conform to the pressures of all the groups to which they belong? Obviously not, because people belong to many groups and their norms vary. In some cases, they may even have contradictory norms. So what do people do? They conform to the important groups to which they belong or hope to belong. The important groups have been referred to as **reference groups** and are characterized as ones where the person is aware of the others; the person defines himself or herself as a member, or would like to be a member; and the person feels that the group members are significant to him or her.[30] The implication, then, is that *all* groups do not impose equal conformity pressures on their members.

The impact that group pressures for **conformity** can have on an individual member's judgment and attitudes was demonstrated in the now-classic studies by Solomon Asch.[31] Asch made up groups of seven or eight people, who sat in a classroom and were asked to compare two cards held by the experimenter. One card had one line, the other had three lines of varying length. As shown in Exhibit 7-6, one of the lines on the three-line card was identical to the line on the one-line card. Also as shown in Exhibit 7-6, the difference in line length was quite obvious; under ordinary conditions,

reference groups
Important groups to which individuals belong or hope to belong and with whom's norms individuals are likely to conform.

conformity
Adjusting one's behavior to align with the norms of the group.

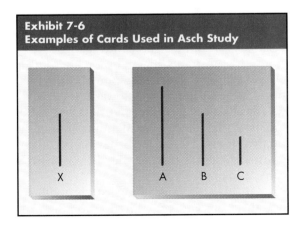

Exhibit 7-6
Examples of Cards Used in Asch Study

subjects made fewer than 1 percent errors. The object was to announce aloud which of the three lines matched the single line. But what happens if the members in the group begin to give incorrect answers? Will the pressures to conform result in an unsuspecting subject (USS) altering his or her answer to align with the others? That was what Asch wanted to know. So he arranged the group so that only the USS was unaware that the experiment was "fixed." The seating was prearranged: The USS was placed so as to be the last to announce his or her decision.

The experiment began with several sets of matching exercises. All the subjects gave the right answers. On the third set, however, the first subject gave an obviously wrong answer—for example, saying "C" in Exhibit 7-6. The next subject gave the same wrong answer, and so did the others until it got to the unknowing subject. He knew "B" was the same as "X," yet everyone has said "C." The decision confronting the USS was this: Do you publicly state a perception that differs from the preannounced position of the others in your group? Or do you give an answer that you strongly believe is incorrect in order to have your response agree with that of the other group members?

The results obtained by Asch demonstrated that over many experiments and many trials, subjects conformed in about 35 percent of the trials; that is, the subjects gave answers that they knew were wrong but that were consistent with the replies of other group members.

What can we conclude from this study? The results suggest that there are group norms that press us toward conformity. We desire to be one of the group and avoid being visibly different. We can generalize further to say that when an individual's opinion of objective data differs significantly from that of others in the group, he or she is likely to feel extensive pressure to align his or her opinions to conform with those of the others.

Status

While teaching a college course on adolescence, the instructor asked the class to list things that contributed to status when they were in high school. The list was long and included being an athlete or a cheerleader and being able to cut class without getting caught. Then the instructor asked the students to list things that didn't contribute to status. Again, it was easy for the students to create a long list: getting straight A's, having your mother drive you to school, and so forth. Finally, the students were asked to develop a third list—those things that didn't matter one way or the other. There was a long silence. At last one student in the back row volunteered, "In high school, nothing didn't matter."[32]

status
A socially defined position or rank given to groups or group members by others.

Status—that is, a socially defined position or rank given to groups or group members by others—permeates society far beyond the walls of high school. It would not be extravagant to rephrase the preceding quotation to read, "In the status hierarchy of life, nothing doesn't matter." We live in a class-structured society. Despite all attempts to make it more egalitarian, we have made little progress toward a classless society. Even the smallest group will develop roles, rights, and rituals to differentiate its members. Status is an important factor in understanding human behavior because it is a significant motivator and has major behavioral consequences when individuals perceive a disparity between what they believe their status to be and what others perceive it to be.

In his classic restaurant study, William F. Whyte demonstrated the importance of status.[33] Whyte proposed that people work together more smoothly if high-status personnel customarily originate action for lower-status personnel. He found a number of instances in which the initiating of action by lower-status people created a conflict between formal and informal status systems. In one instance he cited, waitresses were passing their customers' orders directly on to countermen—which meant that low-status servers were initiating action for high-status cooks. By the simple addition of an aluminum spindle to which the order could be hooked, a buffer was created between the lower-status waitresses and the higher-status countermen, allowing the latter to initiate action on orders when they felt ready.

Whyte also noted that in the kitchen, supply men secured food supplies from the chefs. This was, in effect, a case of low-skilled employees initiating action to be taken by high-skilled employees. Conflict was stimulated when supply men, either explicitly or implicitly, urged the chefs to "get a move on." However, Whyte observed that one supply man had little trouble with the chefs because he gave the order and asked that the chef call him when it was ready, thus reversing the initiating process. In his analysis, Whyte suggested several changes in procedures that aligned interactions more closely with the accepted status hierarchy and resulted in substantial improvements in worker relations and effectiveness.

STATUS AND NORMS Status has been shown to have some interesting effects on the power of norms and pressures to conform. For instance, high-status members of groups often are given more freedom to deviate from norms than are other group members.[34] High-status people also are better able to resist conformity pressures than their lower-status peers. An individual who is highly valued by a group but who doesn't much need or care about the social rewards the group provides is particularly able to pay minimal attention to conformity norms.[35]

The previous findings explain why many star athletes, famous actors, top-performing salespeople, and outstanding academics seem oblivious to appearance or social norms that constrain their peers. As high-status individuals, they're given a wider range of discretion. But this is true only as long as the high-status person's activities aren't severely detrimental to group goal achievement.[36]

STATUS EQUITY It is important for group members to believe that the status hierarchy is equitable. When inequity is perceived, it creates disequilibrium that results in various types of corrective behavior.[37]

The concept of equity presented in chapter 5 applies to status. People expect rewards to be proportionate to costs incurred. If Dana and Anne are the two finalists for the head nurse position in a hospital, and it is clear that Dana has more seniority and better preparation for assuming the promotion, Anne will view the selection of Dana to be equitable. However, if Anne is chosen because she is the daughter-in-law of the hospital director, Dana will believe an injustice has been committed.

The trappings that go with formal positions are also important elements in maintaining equity. When we believe there is an inequity between the perceived ranking of an individual and the status accouterments that person is given by the organization, we are experiencing status incongruence. Examples of this kind of incongruence are the more desirable office location being held by a lower-ranking individual and paid country club membership being provided by the company for division managers but not for vice presidents. Pay incongruence has long been a problem in the insurance industry, where top sales agents often earn two to five times more than senior corporate executives. The result is that it is very hard for insurance companies to entice successful agents into management positions. Our point is that employees expect the things an individual has and receives to be congruent with his or her status.

Groups generally agree within themselves on status criteria and, hence, there is usually high concurrence in group rankings of individuals. However, individuals can find themselves in a conflict situation when they move between groups whose status criteria are different or when they join groups whose members have heterogeneous backgrounds. For instance, business executives may use personal income or the growth rate of their companies as determinants of status. Government bureaucrats may use the size of their budgets. Professional employees may use the degree of autonomy that comes with their job assignment. Blue-collar workers may use years of seniority. In groups made up of heterogeneous individuals or when heterogeneous groups are forced to be interdependent, status differences may initiate conflict as the group attempts to reconcile and align the differing hierarchies. As we'll see in the next chapter, this can be a particular problem when management creates teams made up of employees from across varied functions within the organization.

Size

Does the size of a group affect the group's overall behavior? The answer to this question is a definite "Yes," but the effect depends on what dependent variables you look at.[38]

The evidence indicates, for instance, that smaller groups are faster at completing tasks than are larger ones. However, if the group is engaged in problem solving, large groups consistently get better marks than their smaller counterparts. Translating these results into specific numbers is a bit more hazardous, but we can offer some parameters. Large groups—with a dozen or more members—are good for gaining diverse input. So if the goal of the group is fact finding, larger groups should be more effective. On the other hand, smaller groups are better at doing something productive with that input. Groups of approximately seven members, therefore, tend to be more effective for taking action.

One of the most important findings related to the size of a group has been labeled **social loafing**. Social loafing is the tendency for individuals to expend less effort when working collectively than when working individually.[39] It directly challenges the logic that the productivity of the group as a whole should at least equal the sum of the productivity of each individual in that group.

A common stereotype about groups is that the sense of team spirit spurs individual effort and enhances the group's overall productivity. In the late 1920s, a German psychologist named Ringelmann compared the results of individual and group performance on a rope-pulling task.[40] He expected that the group's effort would be equal to the sum of the efforts of individuals within the group. That is, three people pulling together should exert three times as much pull on the rope as one person, and eight people should exert eight times as much pull. Ringelmann's results, however, did not confirm his expectations. Groups of three people exerted a force only two-and-a-half times the average individual performance. Groups of eight collectively achieved less than four times the solo rate.

social loafing
The tendency for individuals to expend less effort when working collectively than when working individually.

◆ Large groups are good for gaining diverse input but smaller groups are better at doing something productive with that input.

Replications of Ringelmann's research with similar tasks have generally supported his findings.[41] Increases in group size are inversely related to individual performance. More may be better in the sense that the total productivity of a group of four is greater than that of one or two people, but the individual productivity of each group member declines.

What causes this social loafing effect? It may be due to a belief that others in the group are not carrying their fair share. If you see others as lazy or inept, you can reestablish equity by reducing your effort. Another explanation is the dispersion of responsibility. Because the results of the group cannot be attributed to any single person, the relationship between an individual's input and the group's output is clouded. In such situations, individuals may be tempted to become "free riders" and coast on the group's efforts. In other words, there will be a reduction in efficiency where individuals think that their contribution cannot be measured.

The implications for OB of this effect on work groups are significant. Where managers utilize collective work situations to enhance morale and teamwork, they must also provide means by which individual efforts can be identified. If this is not done, management must weigh the potential losses in productivity from using groups against any possible gains in worker satisfaction.[42] However, this conclusion has a Western bias. It's consistent with individualistic cultures, like the United States and Canada, that are dominated by self-interest. It is not consistent with collective societies where individuals are motivated by in-group goals. For instance, in studies comparing employees from the United States with employees from the People's Republic of China and Israel (both collectivist societies), the Chinese and Israelis showed no propensity to engage in social loafing. In fact, the Chinese and Israelis actually performed better in a group than when working alone.[43]

The research on group size leads us to two additional conclusions: (1) Groups with an odd number of members tend to be preferable to those with an even number; and (2) groups made up of five or seven members do a pretty good job of exercising the best elements of both small and large groups.[44] Having an odd number of members eliminates the possibility of ties when votes are taken. And groups made up of five or seven members are large enough to form a majority and allow for diverse input, yet small enough to avoid the negative outcomes often associated with large groups, such as domination by a few members, development of subgroups, inhibited participation by some members, and excessive time taken to reach a decision.

Composition

Most group activities require a variety of skills and knowledge. Given this requirement, it would be reasonable to conclude that heterogeneous groups—those composed of dissimilar individuals—would be more likely to have diverse abilities and information and should be more effective. Research studies generally substantiate this conclusion.[45]

When a group is heterogeneous in terms of gender, personalities, opinions, abilities, skills, and perspectives, there is an increased probability that the group will possess the needed characteristics to complete its tasks effectively.[46] The group may be more conflict laden and less expedient as diverse positions are introduced and assimilated, but the evidence generally supports the conclusion that heterogeneous groups perform more effectively than do those that are homogeneous.

But what about diversity created by racial or national differences? The evidence indicates that these elements of diversity interfere with group processes, at least in the short term.[47] Cultural diversity seems to be an asset on tasks that call for a variety of viewpoints. But culturally heterogeneous groups have more difficulty in learning to work with each other and solving problems. The good news is that these difficulties seem to dissipate with time. While newly formed culturally diverse groups underperform newly formed culturally homogeneous groups, the differences disappear after about three months. The reason is that it takes diverse groups a while to learn how to work through disagreements and different approaches to solving problems.

An offshoot of the composition issue has recently received a great deal of attention by group researchers. This is the degree to which members of a group share a common demographic attribute, such as age, sex, race, educational level, or length of service in the organization, and the impact of this attribute on turnover. We call this variable **group demography**.

We discussed individual demographic factors in chapter 2. Here we consider the same type of factors, but in a group context. That is, it is not whether a person is male or female or has been employed with the organization a year rather than ten years that concerns us now, but rather the individual's attribute in relationship to the attributes of others with whom he or she works. Let's work through the logic of group demography, review the evidence, and then consider the implications.

Groups and organizations are composed of **cohorts**, which we define as individuals who hold a common attribute. For instance, everyone born in 1960 is of the same age. This means they also have shared common experiences. People born in 1970 have experienced the information revolution, but not the Korean conflict. People born in 1945 shared the Vietnam War, but not the Great Depression. Women in U.S. organizations today who were born before 1945 matured prior to the women's movement and have had substantially different experiences from women born after 1960. Group demography, therefore, suggests that such attributes as age or the date that someone joins a specific work group or organization should help us to predict turnover. Essentially, the logic goes like this: Turnover will be greater among those with dis-

group demography
The degree to which members of a group share a common demographic attribute, such as age, sex, race, educational level, or length of service in the organization, and the impact of this attribute on turnover.

cohorts
Individuals who, as part of a group, hold a common attribute.

Pepsi-Cola International's marketing team members in Great Britain share a common demographic attribute—they're all young. To execute its plan of increasing international soft drink sales, Pepsi is banking on youthful cohorts who have a passion for change, can embrace risk, act quickly, innovate constantly, and aren't afraid to break the rules of soft drink marketing.

similar experiences because communication is more difficult. Conflict and power struggles are more likely, and more severe when they occur. The increased conflict makes group membership less attractive, so employees are more likely to quit. Similarly, the losers in a power struggle are more apt to leave voluntarily or be forced out.

Several studies have sought to test this thesis, and the evidence is quite encouraging.[48] For example, in departments or separate work groups where a large portion of members entered at the same time, there is considerably more turnover among those outside this cohort. Also, where there are large gaps between cohorts, turnover is higher. People who enter a group or an organization together, or at approximately the same time, are more likely to associate with one another, have a similar perspective on the group or organization, and thus be more likely to stay. On the other hand, discontinuities or bulges in the group's date-of-entry distribution are likely to result in a higher turnover rate within that group.

The implication of this line of inquiry is that the composition of a group may be an important predictor of turnover. Differences per se may not predict turnover. But large differences within a single group will lead to turnover. If everyone is moderately dissimilar from everyone else in a group, the feelings of being an outsider are reduced. So, it's the degree of dispersion on an attribute, rather than the level, that matters most.

We can speculate that variance within a group in respect to attributes other than date of entry, such as social background, gender differences, and levels of education, might similarly create discontinuities or bulges in the distribution that will encourage some members to leave. To extend this idea further, the fact that a group member is a female may, in itself, mean little in predicting turnover. In fact, if the work group is made up of nine women and one man, we'd be more likely to predict that the lone male would leave. In the executive ranks of organizations, however, where females are in the minority, we would predict that this minority status would increase the likelihood that female managers would quit.

Cohesiveness

Groups differ in their **cohesiveness**, that is, the degree to which members are attracted to each other and are motivated to stay in the group.[49] For instance, some work groups are cohesive because the members have spent a great deal of time together, or the group's small size facilitates high interaction, or the group has experienced external threats that have brought members close together. Cohesiveness is important because it has been found to be related to the group's productivity.[50]

Studies consistently show that the relationship of cohesiveness and productivity depends on the performance-related norms established by the group. If performance-related norms are high (for example, high output, quality work, cooperation with individuals outside the group), a cohesive group will be more productive than will a less cohesive group. But if cohesiveness is high and performance norms are low, productivity will be low. If cohesiveness is low and performance norms are high, productivity increases but less than in the high cohesiveness–high norms situation. Where cohesiveness and performance-related norms are both low, productivity will tend to fall into the low-to-moderate range. These conclusions are summarized in Exhibit 7-7, on page 265.

cohesiveness
Degree to which group members are attracted to each other and are motivated to stay in the group.

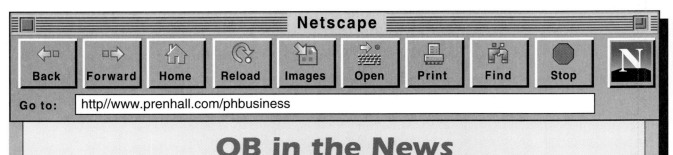

OB in the News

Workforce Diversity and Cliques

Leslie Meltzer Aronzon, a Los Angeles investment broker, remembers the incident well. It was right after she and four colleagues had been in an intense negotiating session with an important client. As they were walking along discussing their potential responses, the conversation came to an abrupt halt. Aronzon's associates had all veered off and disappeared into the men's room. When the men came out of the restroom, "they had decided what we should do." The incident again reminded Aronzon that she was a woman in a mostly male profession.

"A lot of guys in my office hang out together on weekends and share information. They even call each other with tips," Aronzon said. "They don't discriminate against me consciously, but they do discriminate."

Paul Muniz, a claims processor for a Los Angeles insurance firm, notices how people of similar backgrounds tend to congregate together at work. "My best friends at work tend to be other people from Mexico. You see Latinos clustering together, Vietnamese people together, black people together." Muniz says that he and his friends speak Spanish to one another because "we feel we can express ourselves better in Spanish. But I try to be careful not to overdo it, because sometimes people who don't speak Spanish think we're saying something important that they should be in on."

Workplace cliques are perfectly natural and usually understandable but inherently exclusive, and despite today's emphasis on diversity awareness, they are phenomena that corporate America cannot control.

It can be like high school all over again, except that at work, people break into cliques according to age, marital status, gender, race and position rather than looks, athletic ability, and popularity with the opposite sex.

Still, cliques can affect you as deeply at the workplace as they did in high school, determining not only your lunch crowd and your access to gossip, but such critical matters as your assignments, promotions, and salary. Unlike high school cliques, which thankfully disintegrate at graduation, office groupings don't meet such neat and convenient ends.

Based on S. Christian, "Out of the 'In' Crowd," *Los Angeles Times,* May 16, 1994, p. II-7.

Take It to the Net

We invite you to visit the Robbins page on the Prentice Hall Web site at:

http://www.prenhall.com/robbinsorgbeh

for this chapter's World Wide Web exercise.

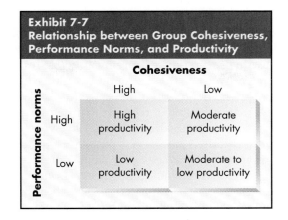

Exhibit 7-7
Relationship between Group Cohesiveness, Performance Norms, and Productivity

What can you do to encourage group cohesiveness? You might try one or more of the following suggestions: (1) Make the group smaller. (2) Encourage agreement with group goals. (3) Increase the time members spend together. (4) Increase the status of the group and the perceived difficulty of attaining membership in the group. (5) Stimulate competition with other groups. (6) Give rewards to the group rather than to members. (7) Physically isolate the group.[51]

Group Processes

The next component of our group behavior model considers the processes that go on within a work group—the communication patterns used by members for information exchanges, group decision processes, leader behavior, power dynamics, conflict interactions, and the like. Chapters 9 through 12 elaborate on many of these processes.

Why are processes important to understanding work group behavior? One way to answer this question is to return to the topic of social loafing. We found that $1 + 1 + 1$ doesn't necessarily add up to three. In group tasks where each member's contribution is not clearly visible, there is a tendency for individuals to decrease their effort. Social loafing, in other words, illustrates a process loss as a result of using groups. But group processes can also produce positive results. That is, groups can create outputs greater than the sum of their inputs. Exhibit 7-8 illustrates how group processes can impact on a group's actual effectiveness.[52]

Synergy is a term used in biology that refers to an action of two or more substances that results in an effect that is different from the individual summation of the substances. We can use the concept to better understand group processes.

synergy
An action of two or more substances that results in an effect that is different from the individual summation of the substances.

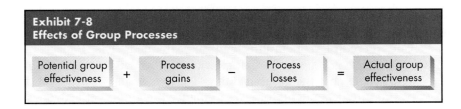

Exhibit 7-8
Effects of Group Processes

Potential group effectiveness + Process gains − Process losses = Actual group effectiveness

Social loafing, for instance, represents negative synergy. The whole is less than the sum of its parts. On the other hand, research teams are often used in research laboratories because they can draw on the diverse skills of various individuals to produce more meaningful research as a group than could be generated by all of the researchers working independently. That is, they produce positive synergy. Their process gains exceed their process losses.

Another line of research that helps us to better understand group processes is the social facilitation effect.[53] Have you ever noticed that performing a task in front of others can have a positive or negative effect on your performance? For instance, you privately practice a complex springboard dive at your home pool for weeks. Then you do the dive in front of a group of friends and you do it better than ever. Or you practice a speech in private and finally get it down perfect, but you "bomb" when you have to give the speech in public.

social facilitation effect
The tendency for performance to improve or decline in response to the presence of others.

The **social facilitation effect** refers to this tendency for performance to improve or decline in response to the presence of others. While this effect is not entirely a group phenomenon—people can work in the presence of others and not be members of a group—the group situation is more likely to provide the conditions for social facilitation to occur. The research on social facilitation tells us that the performance of simple, routine tasks tend to be speeded up and made more accurate by the presence of others. Where the work is more complex, requiring closer attention, the presence of others is likely to have a negative effect on performance.[54] So what are the implications of this research in terms of managing process gains and losses? The implications relate to learning and training. People seem to perform better on a task in the presence of others if that task is very well learned, but poorer if it is not well learned. So process gains will be maximized by training people for simple tasks in groups, while training people for complex tasks in individual private practice sessions.

◆ People perform better on a task in the presence of others if that task is very well learned.

Group Tasks

Imagine, for a moment, that there are two groups at a major oil company. The job of the first is to consider possible location sites for a new refinery. The decision is going to affect people in many areas of the company—production, engineering, marketing, distribution, purchasing, real estate development, and the like—so key people from each of these areas will need to provide input into the decision. The job of the second group is to coordinate the building of the refinery after the site has been selected, the design finalized, and the financial arrangements completed. Research on group effectiveness tells us that management would be well advised to use a larger group for the first task than for the second.[55] The reason is that large groups facilitate pooling of information. The addition of a diverse perspective to a problem-solving committee typically results in a process gain. But when a group's task is coordinating and implementing a decision, the process loss created by each additional member's presence is likely to be greater than the process gain he or she makes. So the size–performance relationship is moderated by the group's task requirements.

The preceding conclusions can be extended: The impact of group processes on the group's performance and member satisfaction is also moderated by the tasks that the group is doing. The evidence indicates that the complexity and interdependence of tasks influence the group's effectiveness.[56]

Tasks can be generalized as either simple or complex. Complex tasks are ones that tend to be novel or nonroutine. Simple ones are routine and standardized. We would hypothesize that the more complex the task, the more the group will benefit from discussion among members on alternative work methods. If the task is simple, group members don't need to discuss such alternatives. They can rely on standardized operating procedures for doing the job. Similarly, if there is a high degree of interdependence among the tasks that group members must perform, they'll need to interact more. Effective communication and minimal levels of conflict, therefore, should be more relevant to group performance when tasks are interdependent.

These conclusions are consistent with what we know about information-processing capacity and uncertainty.[57] Tasks that have higher uncertainty—those that are complex and interdependent—require more information processing. This, in turn, puts more importance on group processes. So just because a group is characterized by poor communication, weak leadership, high levels of conflict, and the like, it doesn't necessarily mean that it will be low performing. If the group's tasks are simple and require little interdependence among members, the group still may be effective.

Group Decision Making

The belief—characterized by juries—that two heads are better than one has long been accepted as a basic component of North American and many other countries' legal systems. This belief has expanded to the point that, today, many decisions in organizations are made by groups, teams, or committees. In this section, we want to review group decision making.

Groups vs. the Individual

Decision-making groups may be widely used in organizations, but does that imply that group decisions are preferable to those made by an individual alone? The answer to this question depends on a number of factors. Let's begin by looking at the strengths and weaknesses of groups.[58]

STRENGTHS OF GROUP DECISION MAKING Groups generate *more complete information and knowledge*. By aggregating the resources of several individuals, groups bring more input into the decision process. In addition to more input, groups can bring heterogeneity to the decision process. They offer *increased diversity of views*. This opens up the opportunity for more approaches and alternatives to be considered. The evidence indicates that a group will almost always outperform even the best individual. So groups generate *higher-quality decisions*. Finally, groups lead to *increased acceptance of a solution*. Many decisions fail after the final choice is made because people don't accept the solution. Group members who participated in making a decision are likely to enthusiastically support the decision and encourage others to accept it.

WEAKNESSES OF GROUP DECISION MAKING In spite of the pluses noted, group decisions have their drawbacks. They're *time consuming*. They typically take more time to reach a solution than would be the case if an individual were making the decision alone. There are *conformity pressures* in groups. The desire by group members to be accepted and considered an asset to the group can result in squashing any overt disagreement. Group discussion can be *dominated by one or a few members*. If this dominant coalition is composed of low- and medium-ability members, the group's overall effectiveness will suffer. Finally, group decisions suffer from *ambiguous responsibility*. In an individual decision, it's clear who is accountable for the final outcome. In a group decision, the responsibility of any single member is watered down.

EFFECTIVENESS AND EFFICIENCY Whether groups are more effective than individuals depends on the criteria you use for defining effectiveness. In terms of *accuracy*, group decisions will tend to be more accurate. The evidence indicates that, on the average, groups make better-quality decisions than individuals.[59] However, if decision effectiveness is defined in terms of *speed*, individuals are superior. If *creativity* is important, groups tend to be more effective than individuals. And if effectiveness means the degree of *acceptance* the final solution achieves, the nod again goes to the group.[60]

But effectiveness cannot be considered without also assessing efficiency. In terms of efficiency, groups almost always stack up as a poor second to the individual decision maker. With few exceptions, group decision making consumes more work hours than if an individual were to tackle the same problem alone. The exceptions tend to be those instances where, to achieve comparable quantities of diverse input, the single decision maker must spend a great deal of time reviewing files and talking to people. Because groups can include members from diverse areas, the time spent searching for information can be reduced. However, as we noted, these advantages in efficiency tend to be the exception. Groups are generally less efficient than individuals. In deciding whether to use groups, then, consideration should be given to assessing whether increases in effectiveness are more than enough to offset the losses in efficiency.

In summary, groups offer an excellent vehicle for performing many of the steps in the decision-making process. They are a source of both breadth and depth of input for information gathering. If the group is composed of individuals with diverse backgrounds, the alternatives generated should be more extensive and the analysis more critical. When the final solution is agreed upon, there are more people in a group decision to support and implement it. These pluses, however, can be more than offset by the time consumed by group decisions, the internal conflicts they create, and the pressures they generate toward conformity.

Groupthink and Groupshift

Two by-products of group decision making have received a considerable amount of attention by researchers in OB. As we'll show, these two phenomena have the potential to affect the group's ability to appraise alternatives objectively and arrive at quality decision solutions.

The first phenomenon, called **groupthink**, is related to norms. It describes situations in which group pressures for conformity deter the group from critically appraising unusual, minority, or unpopular views. Groupthink is a disease that attacks many groups and can dramatically hinder their performance. The second phenomenon we shall review is called **groupshift**. It indicates that in discussing a given set of alternatives and arriving at a solution, group members tend to exaggerate the initial positions that they hold. In some situations, caution dominates, and there is a conservative shift. More

groupthink
Phenomenon in which the norm for consensus overrides the realistic appraisal of alternative courses of action.

groupshift
A change in decision risk between the group's decision and the individual decision that members within the group would make; can be either toward conservatism or greater risk.

often, however, the evidence indicates that groups tend toward a risky shift. Let's look at each of these phenomena in more detail.

GROUPTHINK   A number of years ago I had a peculiar experience. During a faculty meeting, a motion was placed on the floor stipulating each faculty member's responsibilities in regard to counseling students. The motion received a second, and the floor was opened for questions. There were none. After about 15 seconds of silence, the chairperson asked if he could "call for the question" (fancy terminology for permission to take the vote). No objections were voiced. When the chair asked for those in favor, a vast majority of the 32 faculty members in attendance raised their hands. The motion was passed, and the chair proceeded to the next item on the agenda.

Nothing in the process seemed unusual, but the story is not over. About 20 minutes following the end of the meeting, a professor came roaring into my office with a petition. The petition said that the motion on counseling students had been rammed through and requested the chairperson to replace the motion on the next month's agenda for discussion and a vote. When I asked this professor why he had not spoken up less than an hour earlier, he gave me a frustrated look. He then proceeded to tell me that in talking with people after the meeting, he realized there actually had been considerable opposition to the motion. He didn't speak up, he said, because he thought he was the only one opposed. Conclusion: The faculty meeting we had attended had been attacked by the deadly groupthink "disease."

◆ When groupthink occurs, people keep silent about misgivings and silence is seen as agreement.

Have you ever felt like speaking up in a meeting, classroom, or informal group, but decided against it? One reason may have been shyness. On the other hand, you may have been a victim of groupthink, the phenomenon that occurs when group members become so enamored of seeking concurrence that the norm for consensus overrides the realistic appraisal of alternative courses of action and the full expression of deviant, minority, or unpopular views. It describes a deterioration in an individual's mental efficiency, reality testing, and moral judgment as a result of group pressures.[61]

We have all seen the symptoms of the groupthink phenomenon:

1. Group members rationalize any resistance to the assumptions they have made. No matter how strongly the evidence may contradict their basic assumptions, members behave so as to reinforce those assumptions continually.

2. Members apply direct pressures on those who momentarily express doubts about any of the group's shared views or who question the validity of arguments supporting the alternative favored by the majority.

3. Those members who have doubts or hold differing points of view seek to avoid deviating from what appears to be group consensus by keeping silent about misgivings and even minimizing to themselves the importance of their doubts.

4. There appears to be an illusion of unanimity. If someone doesn't speak, it's assumed that he or she is in full accord. In other words, abstention becomes viewed as a "Yes" vote.[62]

In studies of historic American foreign policy decisions, these symptoms were found to prevail when government policy-making groups failed—

unpreparedness at Pearl Harbor in 1941, the U.S. invasion of North Korea, the Bay of Pigs fiasco, and the escalation of the Vietnam War. Importantly, these four groupthink characteristics could not be found where group policy decisions were successful—the Cuban missile crisis and the formulation of the Marshall Plan.[63]

Groupthink appears to be closely aligned with the conclusions Asch drew in his experiments with a lone dissenter. Individuals who hold a position that is different from that of the dominant majority are under pressure to suppress, withhold, or modify their true feelings and beliefs. As members of a group, we find it more pleasant to be in agreement—to be a positive part of the group—than to be a disruptive force, even if disruption is necessary to improve the effectiveness of the group's decisions.

Are all groups equally vulnerable to groupthink? The evidence suggests not. Researchers have focused on three moderating variables—the group's cohesiveness, its leader's behavior, and its insulation from outsiders—but the findings have not been consistent.[64] At this point, the most valid conclusions we can make are: (1) Highly cohesive groups have more discussion and bring out more information, but it's unclear whether or not such groups discourage dissent; (2) groups with impartial leaders who encourage member input generate and discuss more alternative solutions; (3) leaders should avoid expressing a preferred solution early in the group's discussion because this tends to limit critical analysis and significantly increase the likelihood that the group will adopt this solution as the final choice; and (4) insulation of the group leads to fewer alternatives being generated and evaluated.

GROUPSHIFT In comparing group decisions with the individual decisions of members within the group, evidence suggests that there are differences.[65] In some cases, the group decisions are more conservative than the individual decisions. More often, the shift is toward greater risk.[66]

What appears to happen in groups is that the discussion leads to a significant shift in the positions of members toward a more extreme position in the direction in which they were already leaning before the discussion. So conservative types become more cautious and the more aggressive types take on more risk. The group discussion tends to exaggerate the initial position of the group.

The groupshift can be viewed as actually a special case of groupthink. The decision of the group reflects the dominant decision-making norm that develops during the group's discussion. Whether the shift in the group's decision is toward greater caution or more risk depends on the dominant prediscussion norm.

The greater occurrence of the shift toward risk has generated several explanations for the phenomenon.[67] It's been argued, for instance, that the discussion creates familiarization among the members. As they become more comfortable with each other, they also become more bold and daring. Another argument is that our society values risk, that we admire individuals who are willing to take risks, and that group discussion motivates members to show that they are at least as willing as their peers to take risks. The most plausible explanation of the shift toward risk, however, seems to be that the group diffuses responsibility. Group decisions free any single member from accountability for the group's final choice. Greater risk can be taken because even if the decision fails, no one member can be held wholly responsible.

So how should you use the findings on groupshift? You should recognize that group decisions exaggerate the initial position of the individual members,

Exhibit 7-9
Source: S. Adams, *Build a Better Life by Stealing Office Supplies* (Kansas City, MO, Andrews & McMeal, 1991), p. 31. DILBERT reprinted with permission of United Feature Syndicate, Inc.

that the shift has been shown more often to be toward greater risk, and that whether or not a group will shift toward greater risk or caution is a function of the members' prediscussion inclinations.

Group Decision-Making Techniques

The most common form of group decision-making takes place in **interacting groups**. In these groups, members meet face-to-face and rely on both verbal and nonverbal interaction to communicate with each other. But as our discussion of groupthink demonstrated, interacting groups often censor themselves and pressure individual members toward conformity of opinion. Brainstorming, the nominal group technique, and electronic meetings have been proposed as ways to reduce many of the problems inherent in the traditional interacting group.

Brainstorming is meant to overcome pressures for conformity in the interacting group that retard the development of creative alternatives.[68] It does this by utilizing an idea-generation process that specifically encourages any and all alternatives, while withholding any criticism of those alternatives.

interacting groups
Typical groups, where members interact with each other face-to-face.

brainstorming
An idea-generation process that specifically encourages any and all alternatives, while withholding any criticism of those alternatives.

In a typical brainstorming session, a half-dozen to a dozen people sit around a table. The group leader states the problem in a clear manner so that it is understood by all participants. Members then "free-wheel" as many alternatives as they can in a given length of time. No criticism is allowed, and all the alternatives are recorded for later discussion and analysis. That one idea stimulates others and that judgments of even the most bizarre suggestions are withheld until later encourage group members to "think the unusual." Brainstorming, however, is merely a process for generating ideas. The following two techniques go further by offering methods of actually arriving at a preferred solution.[69]

nominal group technique
A group decision-making method in which individual members meet face-to-face to pool their judgments in a systematic but independent fashion.

The **nominal group technique** restricts discussion or interpersonal communication during the decision-making process, hence, the term *nominal*. Group members are all physically present, as in a traditional committee meeting, but members operate independently. Specifically, a problem is presented and then the following steps take place:

1. Members meet as a group but, before any discussion takes place, each member independently writes down his or her ideas on the problem.
2. After this silent period, each member presents one idea to the group. Each member takes his or her turn, presenting a single idea until all ideas have been presented and recorded. No discussion takes place until all ideas have been recorded.
3. The group now discusses the ideas for clarity and evaluates them.
4. Each group member silently and independently rank-orders the ideas. The idea with the highest aggregate ranking determines the final decision.

The chief advantage of the nominal group technique is that it permits the group to meet formally but does not restrict independent thinking, as does the interacting group.

The most recent approach to group decision making blends the nominal group technique with sophisticated computer technology.[70] It's called the **electronic meeting**. Once the technology is in place, the concept is simple. Up to 50 people sit around a horseshoe-shaped table, empty except for a series of computer terminals. Issues are presented to participants and they type their responses onto their computer screen. Individual comments, as well as aggregate votes, are displayed on a projection screen in the room.

electronic meeting
A meeting where members interact on computers, allowing for anonymity of comments and aggregating of votes.

The major advantages of electronic meetings are anonymity, honesty, and speed. Participants can anonymously type any message they want and it flashes on the screen for all to see at the push of a participant's board key. It

◆ Electronic meetings offer anonymity, honesty, and speed.

also allows people to be brutally honest without penalty. And it's fast because chitchat is eliminated, discussions don't digress, and many participants can "talk" at once without stepping on one another's toes. The future of group meetings undoubtedly will include extensive use of this technology.

Each of these four group decision techniques has its own set of strengths and weaknesses. The choice of one technique over another will depend on what criteria you want to emphasize and the cost-benefit trade-off. For instance, as Exhibit 7-10 indicates, the interacting group is good for building group cohesiveness, brainstorming keeps social pressures to a minimum, the nominal group technique is an inexpensive means for generating a large number of ideas, and electronic meetings process ideas fast.

Exhibit 7-10 Evaluating Group Effectiveness

Effectiveness Criteria	Type of Group			
	Interacting	Brainstorming	Nominal	Electronic
Number of ideas	Low	Moderate	High	High
Quality of ideas	Low	Moderate	High	High
Social pressure	High	Low	Moderate	Low
Money costs	Low	Low	Low	High
Speed	Moderate	Moderate	Moderate	High
Task orientation	Low	High	High	High
Potential for interpersonal conflict	High	Low	Moderate	Low
Feelings of accomplishment	High to low	High	High	High
Commitment to solution	High	Not applicable	Moderate	Moderate
Develops group cohesiveness	High	High	Moderate	Low

Source: Based on J.K. Murnighan, "Group Decision Making: What Strategies Should You Use?", *Management Review*, February 1981, p. 61.

Summary and Implications for Managers

We've covered a lot of territory in this chapter. Since we essentially organized our discussion around the group behavior model in Exhibit 7-5, let's use this model to summarize our findings regarding performance and satisfaction.

Performance

Any predictions about a group's performance must begin by recognizing that work groups are part of a larger organization and that factors such as the organization's strategy, authority structure, selection procedures, and reward system can provide a favorable or unfavorable climate for the group to operate within. For example, if an organization is characterized by distrust between management and workers, it is more likely that work groups in that organization will develop norms to restrict effort and output than will work groups in an organization where trust is high. So managers shouldn't look at any group in isolation. Rather, they should begin by assessing the degree of support external conditions provide the group. It is obviously a lot easier for any work group to be productive when the overall organization of which it is a part is growing and it has both top management's support and abundant resources. Similarly, a group is more likely to be productive when its members have the requisite skills to do the group's tasks and the personality characteristics that facilitate working well together.

A number of structural factors show a relationship to performance. Among the more prominent are role perception, norms, status inequities, the size of the group, its demographic makeup, the group's task, and cohesiveness.

From Concepts to Skills

Conducting a Group Meeting

Group meetings have a reputation for inefficiency. For instance, noted economist, John Kenneth Galbraith, has said, "Meetings are indispensable when you don't want to do anything."

When you're responsible for conducting a meeting, what can you do to make it more efficient and effective? Follow these 12 steps:[71]

1. *Prepare a meeting agenda.* An agenda defines what you hope to accomplish at the meeting. It should state the meeting's purpose; who will be in attendance; what, if any, preparation is required of each participant; a detailed list of items to be covered; the specific time and location of the meeting; and a specific finishing time.

2. *Distribute the agenda in advance.* Participants should have the agenda enough ahead of time so they can adequately prepare for the meeting.

3. *Consult with participants before the meeting.* An unprepared participant can't contribute to his or her full potential. It is your responsibility to ensure that members are

prepared, so check with them ahead of time.

4. *Get participants to go over the agenda.* The first thing to do at the meeting is to have participants review the agenda, make any changes, then approve the final agenda.

5. *Establish specific time parameters.* Meetings should begin on time and have a specific time for completion. It is your responsibility to specify these time parameters and to hold to them.

6. *Maintain focused discussion.* It is your responsibility to give direction to the discussion; to keep it focused on the issues; and to minimize interruptions, disruptions, and irrelevant comments.

7. *Encourage and support participation of all members.* To maximize the effectiveness of problem-oriented meetings, each participant must be encouraged to contribute. Quiet or reserved personalities need to be drawn out so their ideas can be heard.

8. *Maintain a balanced style.* The effective group leader pushes when nec-

essary and is passive when need be.

9. *Encourage the clash of ideas.* You need to encourage different points of view, critical thinking, and constructive disagreement.

10. *Discourage the clash of personalities.* An effective meeting is characterized by the critical assessment of ideas, not attacks on people. When running a meeting, you must quickly intercede to stop personal attacks or other forms of verbal insult.

11. *Be an effective listener.* You need to listen with intensity, empathy, objectivity, and do whatever is necessary to get the full intended meaning from each participant's comments.

12. *Bring proper closure.* You should close a meeting by summarizing the group's accomplishments; clarifying what actions, if any, need to follow the meeting; and allocating follow-up assignments. If any decisions are made, you also need to determine who will be responsible for communicating and implementing them.

There is a positive relationship between role perception and an employee's performance evaluation.[72] The degree of congruence that exists between an employee and his or her boss in the perception of the employee's job influences the degree to which that employee will be judged as an effective performer by the boss. To the extent that the employee's role perception fulfills the boss's role expectations, the employee will receive a higher performance evaluation.

Norms control group member behavior by establishing standards of right and wrong. If managers know the norms of a given group, it can help to explain the behaviors of its members. Where norms support high output, managers can expect individual performance to be markedly higher than where group norms aim to restrict output. Similarly, acceptable standards of absenteeism will be dictated by the group norms.

Status inequities create frustration and can adversely influence productivity and the willingness to remain with an organization. Among those individuals who are equity sensitive, incongruence is likely to lead to reduced motivation and an increased search for ways to bring about fairness (i.e., taking another job).

The impact of size on a group's performance depends upon the type of task in which the group is engaged. Larger groups are more effective at fact-finding activities. Smaller groups are more effective at action-taking tasks. Our knowledge of social loafing suggests that if management uses larger groups, efforts should be made to provide measures of individual performance within the group.

We found the group's demographic composition to be a key determinant of individual turnover. Specifically, the evidence indicates that group members who share a common age or date of entry into the work group are less prone to resign.

We also found that cohesiveness can play an important function in influencing a group's level of productivity. Whether or not it does depends on the group's performance-related norms.

The primary contingency variable moderating the relationship between group processes and performance is the group's task. The more complex and interdependent the tasks, the more that inefficient processes will lead to reduced group performance.

Satisfaction

As with the role perception–performance relationship, high congruence between a boss and employee, as to the perception of the employee's job, shows a significant association with high employee satisfaction.[73] Similarly, role conflict is associated with job-induced tension and job dissatisfaction.[74]

Most people prefer to communicate with others at their own status level or a higher one rather than with those below them.[75] As a result, we should expect satisfaction to be greater among employees whose job minimizes interaction with individuals who are lower in status than themselves.

The group size–satisfaction relationship is what one would intuitively expect: Larger groups are associated with lower satisfaction.[76] As size increases, opportunities for participation and social interaction decrease, as does the ability of members to identify with the group's accomplishments. At the same time, having more members also prompts dissension, conflict, and the formation of subgroups which all act to make the group a less pleasant entity of which to be a part.

For Review

1. Compare and contrast command, task, interest, and friendship groups.
2. What might motivate you to join a group?
3. Define *sociometry* and explain its value to managers.
4. What is the relationship between a work group and the organization of which it is a part?
5. What are the implications of Zimbardo's prison experiment for OB?
6. Explain the implications from the Asch experiments.
7. What are the implications of Whyte's restaurant study for OB?
8. How are status and norms related?
9. How can a group's demography help you to predict turnover?
10. What is *groupthink*? What is its effect on decision-making quality?

For Discussion

1. How could you use the punctuated-equilibrium model to better understand group behavior?
2. Identify five roles you play. What behaviors do they require? Are any of these roles in conflict? If so, in what way? How do you resolve these conflicts?
3. "High cohesiveness in a group leads to higher group productivity." Do you agree or disagree? Explain.
4. What effect, if any, do you expect that workforce diversity has on a group's performance and satisfaction?
5. If group decisions consistently achieve better-quality outcomes than those achieved by individuals, how did the phrase "a camel is a horse designed by a committee" become so popular and ingrained in the culture?

Designing Jobs around Groups

It's time to take small groups seriously, that is, to use groups, rather than individuals, as the basic building blocks for an organization. I propose that we should design organizations from scratch around small groups rather than the way we have traditionally done it—around individuals.

Why would management want to do such a thing? At least seven reasons can be identified. First, small groups seem to be good for people. They can satisfy important membership needs. They can provide a moderately wide range of activities for individual members. They can provide support in times of stress and crisis. They are settings in which people can learn not only cognitively but empirically to be reasonably trusting and helpful to one another. Second, groups seem to be good problem-finding tools. They seem to be useful in promoting innovation and creativity. Third, in a wide variety of decision situations, groups make better decisions than individuals do. Fourth, they are great tools for implementation. Groups gain commitment from their members so that group decisions are likely to be willingly carried out. Fifth, they can control and discipline individual members in ways that are often extremely difficult through impersonal quasi-legal disciplinary systems. Sixth, as organizations grow large, small groups appear to be useful mechanisms for fending off many of the negative effects of large size. They help to prevent communication lines from growing too long, the hierarchy from growing too steep, and the individual from getting lost in the crowd. There is also a seventh, but altogether different, kind of argument for taking groups seriously. Groups are natural phenomena and facts of organizational life. They can be created, but their spontaneous development cannot be prevented.

Operationally, how would an organization that was truly designed around groups function? One answer to this question is merely to take the things that organizations do with individuals and apply them to groups. The idea would be to raise the level from the atom to the molecule and select groups rather than individuals, train groups rather than individuals, pay groups rather than individuals, promote groups rather than individuals, fire groups rather than individuals, and so on down the list of activities that organizations have traditionally carried on in order to use human beings in their organizations.

In the past, the human group has been primarily used for patching and mending organizations that were built around the individual. The time has come for management to discard the notion that individuals are the basic building blocks of organizations and to redesign organizations around groups. Importantly, a number of organizations seem to be moving in this direction. Hundreds of major companies, including Saturn Corp., Federal Express, and Microsoft, have essentially designed their current operations around small groups.

Based on H.J. Leavitt, "Suppose We Took Groups Seriously," in E.L. Cass and F.G. Zimmer (eds.), *Man and Work in Society* (New York: Van Nostrand Reinhold, 1975), pp. 67–77.

Jobs Should Be Designed around Individuals

The argument that organizations can and should be designed around groups might hold in a socialistic society but not in capitalistic countries like the United States, Canada, Australia, Germany, and the United Kingdom. The following response directly relates to the United States and American workers, although it is probably generalizable to other economically advanced capitalistic countries. In fact, given the political changes in Eastern Europe and the increasing acceptance of profit-motivated businesses, the case for the individually oriented organization may be applicable throughout the world.

America was built on the ethic of the individual. This ethic has been pounded into Americans from birth. The result is that it is deeply embedded in the psyche of every American. Americans strongly value individual achievement. They praise competition. Even in team sports, they want to identify individuals for recognition. Sure, they enjoy group interaction. They like being part of a team, especially a winning team. But it is one thing to be a member of a work group while maintaining a strong individual identity and another to sublimate one's identity to that of the group. The latter is inconsistent with the values of American life.

The American worker likes a clear link between his or her individual effort and a visible outcome. It is not happenstance that the United States, as a nation, has a considerably larger proportion of high achievers than exists in most of the world. America breeds achievers, and achievers seek personal responsibility. They would be frustrated in job situations where their contribution is commingled and homogenized with the contributions of others.

Americans want to be hired based on their individual talents. They want to be evaluated on their individual efforts. They also want to be rewarded with pay raises and promotions based on their individual performances. Americans believe in an authority and status hierarchy. They accept a system where there are bosses and subordinates. They are not likely to accept a group's decision on such issues as their job assignments and wage increases. It's harder to imagine that they would be comfortable in a system where the sole basis for their promotion or termination would be the performance of their group.

One of the best examples of how fully the individual ethic has permeated the American psyche is the general lack of enthusiasm that college students display toward group term papers. For years I've offered students the option to write term papers individually or as members of a small group. I tell the class that they can do the paper alone, in which case I would expect something around 20 to 25 pages in length. Or they can do the paper in groups, but that I'd expect the length to expand commensurately. The only qualifier I state is that we can't do both. The class has to decide whether they want to do individual or group papers and everyone has to abide by that decision. I can tell you that I have never had a class where the majority voluntarily chose the group-paper option! But I'm not surprised. Isn't this consistent with the stereotype of the individualistic American, motivated by his or her self-interest? Of someone who wants to rise or fall based on his or her own work performance? Yes! Is this a future full-time employee who would be satisfied, and reach his or her full productive capacity, in a group-centered organization? I don't think so!

Learning about Yourself Exercise

Are You Attracted to the Group?

Most of us have written a term paper. Some have been individual assignments. That is, the instructor expected each student to hand in a separate paper and your grade was determined solely by your own effort and contribution. But sometimes instructors assign group term papers, where students must work together on the project and share in the grade.

Think back to a recent experience in doing a group term paper. Now envision yourself at about the halfway point in the completion of that group assignment. Using your mind-set at this halfway point, answer the following 20 questions. This questionnaire measures your feelings about that work group.*

	AGREE DISAGREE
1. I want to remain a member of this group.	1 2 3 4 5 6 7 8 9
2. I like my group.	1 2 3 4 5 6 7 8 9
3. I look forward to coming to the group.	1 2 3 4 5 6 7 8 9
4. I don't care what happens in this group.	1 2 3 4 5 6 7 8 9
5. I feel involved in what is happening in my group.	1 2 3 4 5 6 7 8 9
6. If I could drop out of the group now, I would.	1 2 3 4 5 6 7 8 9
7. I dread coming to this group.	1 2 3 4 5 6 7 8 9
8. I wish it were possible for the group to end now.	1 2 3 4 5 6 7 8 9
9. I am dissatisfied with the group.	1 2 3 4 5 6 7 8 9
10. If it were possible to move to another group at this time, I would.	1 2 3 4 5 6 7 8 9
11. I feel included in the group.	1 2 3 4 5 6 7 8 9
12. In spite of individual differences, a feeling of unity exists in my group.	1 2 3 4 5 6 7 8 9
13. Compared to other groups, I feel my group is better than most.	1 2 3 4 5 6 7 8 9
14. I do not feel a part of the group's activities.	1 2 3 4 5 6 7 8 9
15. I feel it would make a difference to the group if I were not here.	1 2 3 4 5 6 7 8 9
16. If I were told my group would not meet today, I feel bad.	1 2 3 4 5 6 7 8 9
17. I feel distant from the group.	1 2 3 4 5 6 7 8 9
18. It makes a difference to me how this group turns out.	1 2 3 4 5 6 7 8 9
19. I feel my absence would not matter to the group.	1 2 3 4 5 6 7 8 9
20. I would not feel bad if I had to miss a meeting of this group.	1 2 3 4 5 6 7 8 9

Turn to page A-27 for scoring directions and key.

*Reproduced from N.J. Evans and P.A. Jarvis, "The Group Attitude Scale: A Measure of Attraction to Group," *Small Group Behavior*, May 1986, pp. 203–16. Reprinted by permission of Sage Publications, Inc.

Working with Others Exercise

Assessing Occupational Status

Rank the following 20 occupations from most prestigious (1) to least prestigious (20):

_____Accountant
_____Air traffic controller
_____Coach of a college football team

_____Coach of a college women's basketball team
_____Electrical engineer
_____Environmental scientist

_____Freelance financial consultant		_____Physician	
_____Lawyer		_____Plumber	
_____Manager of a British clothing manufacturer		_____Real estate salesperson	
_____Manager of a U.S. automobile plant		_____Sports agent	
_____Mayor of a large city		_____Teacher in a public elementary school	
_____Minister		_____U.S. Army colonel	
_____Pharmacist		_____Used car salesperson	

Now form into groups of three to five students each. Answer the following questions:

a. How closely did your top five choices (1–5) match?

b. How closely did your bottom five choices (16–20) match?

c. What occupations were generally easiest to rate? Which were most difficult? Why?

d. What does this exercise tell you about criteria for assessing status?

e. What does this exercise tell you about stereotypes?

The Law Offices of Dickinson, Stilwell, and Gardner (DSG)

James Dickinson and Richard Stilwell opened their El Paso, Texas law office in 1963. It has since grown to employ two dozen people. Dickinson is now deceased and Stilwell is semiretired. The firm's senior managing partner is now Charles Gardner. Gardner has been with the firm for more than 20 years.

Today, the law office of DSG has five partners and 12 full-time associates. Additionally, the firm employs an administrative manager (Linda Mendoza) and an assistant administrative manager, a receptionist, four secretaries, and two legal interns who work 20 hours a week doing research.

El Paso is a largely Hispanic community. For a variety of reasons, DSG has historically not done a very effective job of hiring and keeping Hispanic employees. Until very recently, none of the partners were Hispanic and only two of the associates were. Five months ago, the firm lured a prominent Hispanic lawyer, Francisco Jauregui, away from a competitor. Jauregui was brought in as a partner, at a base salary higher than any other DSG employee, with the exception of Charles Gardner.

The hiring of Jauregui has created a number of interpersonal issues at DSG. Many of the associates are unhappy. They feel the company hired Jauregui solely because he was one of the few big-name Hispanic lawyers in El Paso and could open doors for the firm into the Hispanic community. The associates were also concerned that the hiring of a new partner from the outside would lower the likelihood that they would make partner.

It was also clear that a clique was forming within the firm. It was made up of Jauregui, Ms. Mendoza, the two Hispanic associates, and one of the secretaries (all of whom are Hispanic by background). Morale has suffered in recent months. Privately, several employees have made complaints to Gardner such as "Linda gives favored treatment to Francisco and the Hispanic associates," "the Hispanic associates are suddenly working on the most visible and important cases within the firm," and "there's no future around here if you're not Hispanic."

Questions

1. Analyze this case using sociometric techniques.

2. What do you think you can learn from this case about diversity and group behavior?

3. What should Gardner do to deal with this dilemma?

Group Pressures Inside the FAA

Gregory May was a man with influence. He had a $1.5 million contract to perform diversity training for the Federal Aviation Administration. Approximately 4,000 people, including hundreds from the management ranks, had taken his course. He was perceived to be very close to senior FAA managers and was believed to share personal information with those managers about FAA employees. More importantly, doing well in May's training program was required to get ahead in the FAA. If you didn't get Mr. May's approval for completing the course in good standing, your career could be derailed, and if you objected to some of the things in Mr. May's course, you could get fired.

Given the importance of this course to FAA employees, you'd think the course itself would have been well thought out and professionally conducted. Well, you'd have thought wrong! Air traffic controllers, for instance, were subjected to bizarre sessions where they were forced to reveal their innermost sexual secrets. People would be expected to share details of painful experiences from their youth, often to the point where they were in tears. They had to undergo weird rituals. For instance, Mr. May would bark out orders such as "sit down," "stand up," "sit down" for hours on end. He wanted complete obedience from participants. In another exercise, he would tie individuals of the same sex together and make them go to the bathroom and shower together. When one complained that the exercise embarrassed him, May tossed it off and said, "Learn from it." In still another exercise, May made male air traffic controllers run a gauntlet of women who groped the men's private parts. All of this was in the name of teaching diversity.

Did people complain? A few did. Did they disobey? Not many. Said one former FAA employee, "I was a single parent with two small children, and they're 100 percent dependent on me, and my income. And there was no way I was going to give up a 12-year career working with the FAA." So they did what they were told for fear they would lose their jobs.

May is no longer performing diversity training for the FAA. A government investigation has been undertaken to find out what went on and to ensure it doesn't happen again. But, meanwhile, thousands of FAA employees spent several years being tormented by Mr. May under the guise of sensitizing workers to diversity issues.

Questions

1. Can you make any argument favoring this type of diversity training?

2. What are the ethical implications in this case?

3. What does this case say about group pressures to conform?

4. What, if anything, does this case say about group influence on training effectiveness?

5. What, if anything, could senior management have done to prevent employee abuse and protect employees' rights from people like May?

Source: Based on "A Cult and Its Influence within the FAA," *ABC Nightline;* aired February 21, 1995.

UNDERSTANDING WORK TEAMS

CHAPTER OUTLINE

Is it true that everyone's responsibility is, in reality, nobody's responsibility?
   —Anonymous

LEARNING OBJECTIVES

After studying this chapter, you should be able to

1 Explain the growing popularity of teams in organizations

2 Contrast teams with groups

3 Identify three types of teams

4 Demonstrate the linkage between group concepts and high-performing teams

5 Identify ways managers can build trust among team members

6 Explain how organizations can create team players

7 Describe the advantages and disadvantages of diversity to work teams

8 Explain how management can keep teams from becoming stagnant and rigid

COACHES of U.S. squads at the 1996 Olympics in Atlanta understood the importance of building effective teams.[1] Talented groups that failed to develop teamwork were typically eliminated early in the competition. As Steven Segaloff, coxswain of the eight-man boat for the men's rowing team, commented, "Rowing takes chemistry to the nth degree because if a single guy has an off day, we lose." After an early victory, Segaloff observed, "We calmed one another down, kept each other focused, and worked in near perfect harmony."

Many of the coaches began building their teams long before they arrived in Atlanta. For instance, the women's volleyball team (see photo) went to Hawaii a few months earlier for a team-bonding rope-climbing course. The women's gymnastic team held pizza parties and sock hops.

The challenge facing coaches was finding the right balance between allowing individuals to show their unique talents while, at the same time, minimizing grudges, big egos, personality conflicts, and misunderstandings. The strongest teams successfully balanced the "I" and the "we." "Players who lose their individuality inside the team become weaknesses because they don't have a sense of their unique role," says a sports psychologist. "That means they tend to hesitate and not assert themselves when their particular abilities are called for." Women's basketball coach Tar VanDerveer met one-on-one with each team member regularly before the games to talk about the player's aspirations. "It's better to have everything out in the open, so we know where everyone's coming from and there are no hidden agendas," she explains. Coaches of the women's field hockey team counseled each player so she understood what her particular role would be, and that role wasn't always athletic. A player might be invaluable as the team clown who brings levity to tense situations or the team confidant who can offer good advice.

Individual attitudes are also critical for team success. Women's soccer coach Tony DiCicco said he sent the obvious choice for one bottom position on the national team home in 1995 because, even though she wouldn't have played much, she still could have thrown teamwork off with her negative, confrontational manner. However, he put her on the '96 Olympic team—not because of better skills but because her attitude improved.

Coaches were also clear to differentiate between friendships and good team chemistry. They didn't want to build cliques of best buddies. Such cliques can undermine performance because people who like one another often go along with one another's lousy ideas in order to keep relations amicable. "Great chemistry is the ability to get through the good, the bad, and the ugly on an even keel," said women's field hockey coach Pam Hixon. "And the only way to do that is to air all conflict and resolve it as soon as possible." ◆

Coaches of athletic teams have long understood the importance of building teamwork. However, that hasn't necessarily been true for business firms. One reason, of course, is that business organizations have traditionally been organized around individuals. That's no longer true. Teams have increasingly become the primary means for organizing work in contemporary business firms.

Why Have Teams Become So Popular?

Twenty years ago, when companies like Volvo, Toyota, and General Foods introduced teams into their production processes, it made news because no one else was doing it. Today, it's just the opposite. (See Exhibit 8-1.) It's the organization that *doesn't* use teams that has become newsworthy. Pick up almost any business periodical today and you'll read how teams have become an essential part of the way business is being done in companies like General Electric, AT&T, Hewlett-Packard, Motorola, Apple Computer, Shiseido, Federal Express, Chrysler, Saab, 3M Co., John Deere, Texas Instruments, Australian Airlines, Johnson & Johnson, Dayton Hudson, Shenandoah Life Insurance Co., Florida

Exhibit 8-1 Teams in Practice

| | | Number of Employees | | | | |
	All sizes	100–499	500–999	1,000–2,499	2,500–9,900	10,000 or More
Percentage of U.S. organizations in which some employees are members of a working group identified as a team	78	77	84	82	83	83
In organizations that have teams, average percentage of employees who are members	61	65	48	40	49	52

Based on a cross section of 1,800 U.S. organizations with 100 or more employees.

Source: Reprinted with permission from the October 1995 issue of *TRAINING* Magazine. © 1995, Lakewood Publications, Minneapolis, MN. All rights reserved.

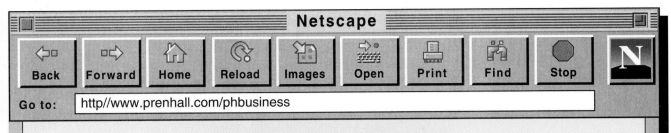

OB in the News

Teamwork in the Oil Fields

In 1992, Texaco Inc. appointed Stephen J. Hadden as assistant manager of its declining century-old Kern River (California) oil field. His task was to help breathe new life into its operations.

The turnaround began with an experiment that Hadden conducted in 1992 and early 1993. He assembled a group of 25 engineers, geologists, and technicians, putting them through a nine-month brainstorming session. The objective: to propose ways to improve operations. He was impressed with the number and quality of their suggestions. In 1994, when Hadden was promoted to the field's top-management spot, he decided his people were capable of operating under a team system. So he abolished the operation's old hierarchical lines of authority.

He told workers and managers alike that sharing ideas, not protecting turf, should become their number-one priority. He created 62 teams of nine members each, including foremen and production engineers, technicians, geologists, field workers, and even outside contractors. Many were assigned to two or more teams. Each group was responsible for a certain number of wells. The teams began meeting each morning to discuss problems and new ideas for solving them. On the job, employees were given new powers to act on their own and the freedom to communicate with other departments without management approval. Hadden also gave the teams unrestricted access to a new central computer that stored data on all aspects of operations.

"You challenge the way you've thought about everything before," says the assistant division manager. "The question that was asked repeatedly was, 'Have we exhausted every opportunity?'"

The team system has resulted in a minor miracle. Production, which had slipped to 80,000 barrels a day in the early 1990s, increased to 91,000 by 1995, and was on its way toward surpassing 100,000 by 1998. Kern River has increased its recovery rate to 66 percent of all oil from 50 percent, and expects to push it up to 80 percent. Officials say they're also tapping oil that had been missed in previous extraction efforts. In three years, production per worker has surged from 150 barrels a day to 250. And Texaco has raised its estimate of recoverable oil at Kern River by 66 million barrels, giving the field another decade of production.

"We're getting oil that we never knew was there," says the president of Texaco Exploration and Production. "It's become a growth opportunity. It's hard to believe."

Based on A. Salpukas, "New Ideas for U.S. Oil," *New York Times*, November 16, 1995, p. C1.

Take It to the Net

We invite you to visit the Robbins page on the Prentice Hall Web site at:

http://www.prenhall.com/robbinsorgbeh

for this chapter's World Wide Web exercise.

Power & Light, and Emerson Electric. Even the world-famous San Diego Zoo has restructured its native habitat zones around cross-departmental teams.

How do we explain the current popularity of teams? The evidence suggests that teams typically outperform individuals when the tasks being done require multiple skills, judgment, and experience.[2] As organizations have restructured themselves to compete more effectively and efficiently, they have turned to teams as a way to better utilize employee talents. Management has found that teams are more flexible and responsive to changing events than are traditional departments or other forms of permanent groupings. Teams have the capability to quickly assemble, deploy, refocus, and disband.

But don't overlook the motivational properties of teams. Consistent with our discussion in chapter 6 of the role of employee involvement as a motivator, teams facilitate employee participation in operating decisions. For instance, some assembly-line workers at John Deere are part of sales teams that call on customers.[3] These workers know the products better than any traditional salesperson; and by traveling and speaking with farmers, these hourly workers develop new skills and become more involved in their jobs. So another explanation for the popularity of teams is that they are an effective means for management to democratize their organizations and increase employee motivation.

Teams vs. Groups: What's the Difference?

Groups and teams are not the same thing. In this section, we want to define and clarify the difference between a work group and a work team.[4]

In the last chapter, we defined a *group* as two or more individuals, interacting and interdependent, who have come together to achieve particular objectives. A **work group** is a group that interacts primarily to share information and to make decisions to help each member perform within his or her area of responsibility.

Work groups have no need or opportunity to engage in collective work that requires joint effort. So their performance is merely the summation of each group member's individual contribution. There is no positive synergy that would create an overall level of performance that is greater than the sum of the inputs.

A **work team** generates positive synergy through coordinated effort. Their individual efforts results in a level of performance that is greater than the sum of those individual inputs. Exhibit 8-2 highlights the differences between work groups and work teams.

These definitions help clarify why so many organizations have recently restructured work processes around teams. Management is looking for that positive synergy that will allow their organizations to increase performance.

The extensive use of teams creates the *potential* for an organization to generate greater outputs with no increase in inputs. Notice, however, we said "potential." There is nothing inherently magical in the creation of teams that ensures the achievement of this positive synergy. Merely calling a *group* a *team* doesn't automatically increase its performance. As we show later in this chapter, successful or high-performing teams have certain common characteristics. If management hopes to gain increases in organizational performance through the use of teams, it will need to ensure that its teams possess these characteristics.

work group
A group that interacts primarily to share information and to make decisions to help each other perform within his or her area of responsibility.

work team
A group whose individual efforts result in a performance that is greater than the sum of those individual inputs.

◆ A work team generates positive synergy through coordinated effort.

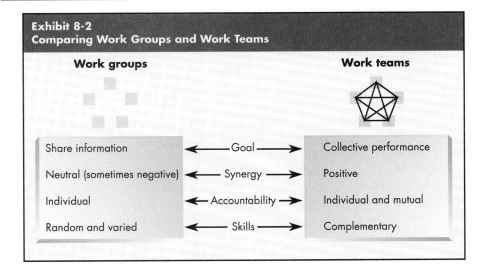

Exhibit 8-2
Comparing Work Groups and Work Teams

Work groups		Work teams
Share information	←—Goal—→	Collective performance
Neutral (sometimes negative)	←—Synergy—→	Positive
Individual	←—Accountability—→	Individual and mutual
Random and varied	←—Skills—→	Complementary

Types of Teams

Teams can be classified based on their objective. The three most common forms of teams you're likely to find in an organization are *problem-solving teams*, *self-managed teams*, and *cross-functional teams* (see Exhibit 8-3).

Problem-Solving Teams

If we look back 15 years or so, teams were just beginning to grow in popularity, and most of these teams took similar form. These were typically composed of 5 to 12 hourly employees from the same department who met for a few hours each week to discuss ways of improving quality, efficiency, and the work environment.[5] We call these **problem-solving teams**.

In problem-solving teams, members share ideas or offer suggestions on how work processes and methods can be improved. Rarely, however, are these teams given the authority to unilaterally implement any of their suggested actions.

One of the most widely practiced applications of problem-solving teams during the 1980s were quality circles.[6] As described in chapter 6, these are work teams of eight to ten employees and supervisors who have a shared area of responsibility and meet regularly to discuss their quality problems, investigate causes of the problems, recommend solutions, and take corrective actions.

problem-solving teams
Groups of 5 to 12 employees from the same department who meet for a few hours each week to discuss ways of improving quality, efficiency, and the work environment.

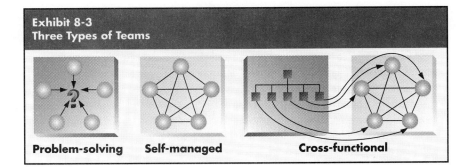

Exhibit 8-3
Three Types of Teams

Problem-solving **Self-managed** **Cross-functional**

Self-Managed Work Teams

Problem-solving teams were on the right track but they didn't go far enough in getting employees involved in work-related decisions and processes. This led to experimentations with truly autonomous teams that could not only solve problems but implement solutions and take full responsibility for outcomes.

self-managed work teams
Groups of 10 to 15 people who take on responsibilities of their former supervisors.

Self-managed work teams are groups of employees (typically 10 to 15 in number) who take on the responsibilities of their former supervisors.[7] Typically, this includes planning and scheduling of work, collective control over the pace of work, making operating decisions, and taking action on problems. Fully self-managed work teams even select their own members and have the members evaluate each other's performance. As a result, supervisory positions take on decreased importance and may even be eliminated. At GE's locomotive-engine plant in Grove City, Pennsylvania, there are about 100 self-managed teams and they make most of the plant's decisions. They arrange the maintenance, schedule the work, and routinely authorize equipment purchases. One team spent $2 million and the plant manager never flinched. At the L-S Electrogalvanizing Co., in Cleveland, the entire plant is run by self-managed teams. They do their own scheduling, rotate jobs on their own, establish production targets, set pay scales that are linked to skills, fire co-workers, and do the hiring. "I never meet a new employee until his first day on the job," says the plant's general manager.[8]

Xerox, General Motors, Coors Brewing, PepsiCo, Hewlett-Packard, Honeywell, M&M/Mars, and Aetna Life are just a few familiar names that have implemented self-managed work teams. Approximately one in five U.S. employers

When the San Diego Zoo reorganized exhibits into bioclimatic zones that integrate animals and plants in cageless areas resembling their native habitat, it also changed the way employees work. Instead of working the traditional way, where keepers tend the animals and gardeners tend the plants, the zoo formed self-managed teams that are responsible for operating and maintaining their exhibit. The Tiger River team shown here includes mammal and bird specialists, horticulturalists, and maintenance and construction workers. Self-managed teams are helping the zoo achieve two of its key goals: enriching the visitor experience and improving employees' quality of work life.

now uses this form of teams and experts predict that 40 to 50 percent of all U.S. workers could be managing themselves through such teams by decade's end.[9]

Business periodicals have been chock full of articles describing successful applications of self-managed teams. Texas Instruments' defense group gives self-directed teams credit for helping it win the Malcolm Baldrige National Quality Award and for allowing it to achieve the same level of sales with 25 percent fewer employees.[10] Aid Association for Lutherans, one of the largest insurance and financial service companies in the United States, claims that self-managed teams were primarily responsible for helping to increase employee satisfaction and allowing the company to increase business volume by 50 percent over a four-year period while cutting workforce staff by 15 percent.[11] The Edy's Grand Ice Cream plant in Fort Wayne, Indiana, introduced self-managed teams in 1990, and attributes to them the plant's 39 percent reduction in costs and 57 percent increase in productivity.[12]

In spite of these impressive stories, a word of caution needs to be offered here. Some organizations have been disappointed with the results from self-managed teams. For instance, employees at Douglas Aircraft Co. (part of McDonnell Douglas), which has been undergoing large layoffs, have revolted against self-managed teams. They've come to view cooperating with the team concept as an exercise in assisting one's own executioner.[13] The overall research on the effectiveness of self-managed work teams has not been uniformly positive.[14] For example, individuals on these teams do tend to report higher levels of job satisfaction. However, counter to conventional wisdom, employees on self-managed work teams seem to have higher absenteeism and turnover rates than do employees working in traditional work structures. The specific reasons for these findings are unclear, which implies a need for additional research.

Cross-Functional Teams

The Boeing Company used the latest application of the team concept to develop its 777-jet. This application is called **cross-functional teams**. These are teams made up of employees from about the same hierarchical level, but from different work areas, who come together to accomplish a task.[15]

Many organizations have used horizontal, boundary-spanning groups for years. For example, IBM created a large task force in the 1960s—made up of employees from across departments in the company—to develop the highly successful System 360. And a **task force** is really nothing other than a temporary cross-functional team. Similarly, **committees** composed of members from across departmental lines are another example of cross-functional teams.

But the popularity of cross-discipline work teams exploded in the late 1980s. All the major automobile manufacturers—including Toyota, Honda, Nissan, BMW, GM, Ford, and Chrysler—have turned to these forms of teams in order to coordinate complex projects. For example, the Neon, Chrysler's ground-breaking subcompact, was developed completely by a cross-functional team. The new model was delivered in a speedy 42 months and for a fraction of what any other manufacturer's small car has cost.[16]

Motorola's Iridium Project illustrates why so many companies have turned to cross-functional teams.[17] This project is developing a huge network that will contain 66 satellites. "We realized at the beginning that there was no way we could manage a project of this size and complexity in the traditional

cross-functional teams
Employees from about the same hierarchical level, but from different work areas, who come together to accomplish a task.

task force
A temporary cross-functional team.

committees
Groups made up of members from across departmental lines.

way and still get it done on time," says the project's general manager. For the first year and a half of the project, a cross-functional team of 20 Motorola people met every morning. This has since been expanded to include diverse expertise from people in dozens of other companies as well, such as McDonnell Douglas, Raytheon, Russia's Khrunichev Enterprise, Lockheed Martin, Scientific-Atlanta, and General Electric.

In summary, cross-functional teams are an effective means for allowing people from diverse areas within an organization (or even between organizations) to exchange information, develop new ideas and solve problems, and coordinate complex projects. Of course, cross-functional teams are no picnic to manage.[18] Their early stages of development are often very time consuming as members learn to work with diversity and complexity. It takes time to build trust and teamwork, especially among people from different backgrounds, with different experiences and perspectives. Later in this chapter, we'll discuss ways managers can help facilitate and build trust among team members.

Linking Teams and Group Concepts: Toward Creating High-Performance Teams

In the previous chapter, we introduced a number of basic group concepts. Let's now build on that introduction and look at how our knowledge of group processes can help us create more effective or high-performance teams.[19]

Size of Work Teams

The best work teams tend to be small. When they have more than about 10 to 12 members, it becomes difficult to get much done. Group members have trouble interacting constructively and agreeing on much. Large numbers of people usually can't develop the cohesiveness, commitment, and mutual accountability necessary to achieve high performance. So in designing effective teams, managers should keep them to under a dozen people. If a natural working unit is larger and you want a team effort, consider breaking the group into subteams.

◆ **The best work teams tend to be small.**

Abilities of Members

To perform effectively, a team requires three different types of skills. First, it needs people with *technical expertise*. Second, it needs people with the *problem-solving and decision-making skills* to be able to identify problems, generate alternatives, evaluate those alternatives, and make competent choices. Finally, teams need people with good listening, feedback, conflict resolution, and other *interpersonal skills*.[20]

No team can achieve its performance potential without developing all three types of skills. The right mix is crucial. Too much of one at the expense of others will result in lower team performance. But teams don't need to have all the complementary skills in place at their beginning. It's not uncommon for one or more members to take responsibility to learn the skills in which the group is deficient, thereby allowing the team to reach its full potential.

Allocating Roles and Promoting Diversity

Teams have different needs, and people should be selected for a team on the basis of their personalities and preferences. High-performing teams properly match people to various roles. For example, the basketball coaches who continually win over the long term have learned how to size up prospective players, identify their strengths and weaknesses, and then assign them to positions that best fit with their skills and allow them to contribute most to the overall team's performance. Coaches recognize that winning teams need a variety of skills—for example, ball handlers, power scorers, three-point shooters, defensive specialists, and shot blockers.

We can identify nine potential team roles (see Exhibit 8-4). Successful work teams have people to fill all these roles and have selected people to play in these roles based on their skills and preferences.[21] (On many teams, individuals will play multiple roles.) Managers need to understand the individual strengths that each person can bring to a team, select members with their strengths in mind, and allocate work assignments that fit with members' preferred styles. By matching individual preferences with team role demands, managers increase the likelihood that the team members will work well together.

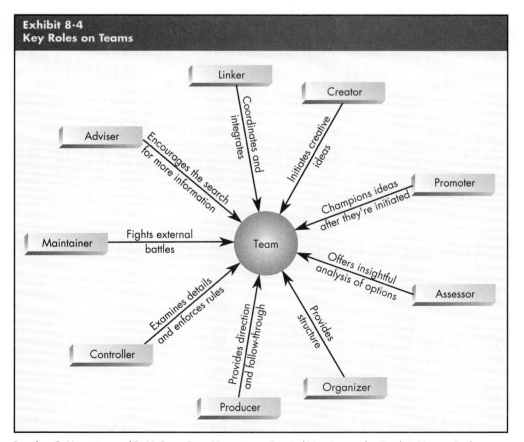

Exhibit 8-4
Key Roles on Teams

Based on C. Margerison and D. McCann, *Team Management: Practical New Approaches* (London: Mercury Books, 1990).

Having a Commitment to a Common Purpose

Does the team have a meaningful purpose to which all members aspire? This purpose is a vision. It's broader than specific goals. Effective teams have a common and meaningful purpose that provides direction, momentum, and commitment for members.

The development team at Apple Computer that designed the Macintosh, for example, was almost religiously committed to creating a user-friendly machine that would revolutionize the way people used computers. Production teams at Saturn Corp. are driven and united by the common purpose of building an American automobile that can successfully compete in terms of quality and price with the best of Japanese cars.

Members of successful teams put a tremendous amount of time and effort into discussing, shaping, and agreeing upon a purpose that belongs to them both collectively and individually. This common purpose, when accepted by the team, becomes the equivalent of what celestial navigation is to a ship captain—it provides direction and guidance under any and all conditions.

Establishing Specific Goals

Successful teams translate their common purpose into specific, measurable, and realistic performance goals. Just as we demonstrated in chapter 5 how goals lead individuals to higher performance, goals also energize teams. These specific goals facilitate clear communication. They also help teams maintain their focus on getting results. Thermos Corp., for example, created a cross-functional team in the fall of 1990 with the specific task of designing and building an innovative barbecue grill.[22] They agreed that they would create a new grill that looked like a handsome piece of furniture, didn't require pollutants like charcoal lighter, and cooked food that tasted good. The team also agreed on a rock-solid deadline. They wanted to have their grill ready for the big National Hardware Show in August 1992. So they had a little less than two years to plan, design, and build their new product. And that's exactly what they did. They created the Thermos Thermal Electric Grill, which has since won four design awards and become one of the most successful new product launches in the company's history.

Leadership and Structure

Goals define the team's end targets. But high-performance teams also need leadership and structure to provide focus and direction. Defining and agreeing upon a common approach, for example, ensures that the team is unified on the means for achieving its goals.

Team members must agree on who is to do what and ensure that all members contribute equally in sharing the workload. Additionally, the team needs to determine how schedules will be set, what skills need to be developed, how the group will resolve conflicts, and how the group will make and modify decisions. Agreeing on the specifics of work and how they fit together to integrate individual skills requires team leadership and structure. This, incidentally, can be provided directly by management or by the team members themselves as they fulfill promoter, organizer, producer, maintainer, and linker roles (refer back to Exhibit 8-4).

Performance goals energized this team of Mattel toy designers. It had just five months to design and develop a new car for the Hot Wheels line so it could be shown at the New York Toy Fair. While most toy cars take 18 months to perfect, this team of artists, designers, and computer experts developed the new Top Speed model in time to unveil it to the 20,000 buyers who attended the toy show.

Social Loafing and Accountability

We learned in the previous chapter that individuals can hide inside a group. They can engage in social loafing and coast on the group's effort because their individual contributions can't be identified. High-performing teams undermine this tendency by holding themselves accountable at both the individual and team level.

Successful teams make members individually and jointly accountable for the team's purpose, goals, and approach. They are clear on what they are individually responsible for and what they are jointly responsible for.

Appropriate Performance Evaluation and Reward Systems

How do you get team members to be both individually and jointly accountable? The traditional, individually oriented evaluation and reward system must be modified to reflect team performance.[23]

Individual performance evaluations, fixed hourly wages, individual incentives, and the like are not consistent with the development of high-performance teams. So in addition to evaluating and rewarding employees for their individual contributions, management should consider group-based appraisals, profit sharing, gainsharing, small-group incentives, and other system modifications that will reinforce team effort and commitment.

Developing High Mutual Trust

High-performance teams are characterized by high mutual **trust** among members. That is, members believe in the integrity, character, and ability of each other. But as you know from personal relationships, trust is fragile. It takes a long time to build, can be easily destroyed, and is hard to regain.[24] Also, since trust begets trust and distrust begets distrust, maintaining trust requires careful attention by management.

trust
A characteristic of high-performance teams where members believe in the integrity, character, and ability of each other.

Exhibit 8-5
Dimensions of Trust

Integrity

Openness   Competence
        Trust

Loyalty   Consistency

integrity
Honesty and truthfulness.

competence
Technical and interpersonal knowledge and skill.

consistency
Reliability, predictability, and good judgment in handling situations.

loyalty
Willingness to protect and save face for a person.

openness
Willingness to share ideas and information freely.

Recent research has identified five dimensions that underly the concept of trust (see Exhibit 8-5):[25]

◆ **Integrity**: Honesty and truthfulness
◆ **Competence**: Technical and interpersonal knowledge and skills
◆ **Consistency**: Reliability, predictability, and good judgment in handling situations
◆ **Loyalty**: Willingness to protect and save face for a person
◆ **Openness**: Willingness to share ideas and information freely

In terms of trust among team members, it's been found that the importance of these five dimensions is relatively constant: integrity > competence > loyalty > consistency > openness.[26] Moreover, integrity and competence are the most critical characteristics that an individual looks for in determining another's trustworthiness. Integrity seems to be rated highest because "without a perception of the other's 'moral character' and 'basic honesty,' other dimensions of trust were meaningless."[27] The high ranking of competence is probably due to the need for peer interaction by team members in order to successfully complete their job responsibilities.

Turning Individuals into Team Players

To this point, we've made a strong case for the value and growing popularity of teams. But many people are not inherently team players. They're loners or people who want to be recognized for their individual achievements. There are also a great many organizations that have historically nurtured individual accomplishments. They have created competitive work environments where only the strong survive. If these organizations adopt teams, what do they do about the selfish, "I-got-to-look-out-for-me" employees that they've created? Finally, as we discussed in chapter 4, countries differ in terms of how they rate on individualism and collectivism. Teams fit well with countries that score high on collectivism. But what if an organization wants to introduce teams into a work population that is made up largely of individuals born and raised in a highly individualistic society? As one writer so aptly put it, in describing

From Concepts to Skills

Building Trust

Managers and team leaders have a significant impact on a team's trust climate. As a result, managers and team leaders need to build trust between themselves and team members. The following summarizes ways you can build trust.[28]

Demonstrate that you're working for others' interests as well as your own. All of us are concerned with our own self-interest, but if others see you using them, your job, or the organization for your personal goals to the exclusion of your team, department, and organization's interests, your credibility will be undermined.

Be a team player. Support your work team both through words and actions. Defend the team and team members when they're attacked by outsiders. This will demonstrate your loyalty to your work group.

Practice openness. Mistrust comes as much from what people don't know as from what they do know. Openness leads to confidence and trust. So keep people informed, explain your decisions, be candid about problems, and fully disclose relevant information.

Be fair. Before making decisions or taking actions, consider how others will perceive them in terms of objectivity and fairness. Give credit where it's due, be objective and impartial in performance evaluations, and pay attention to equity perceptions in reward distributions.

Speak your feelings. Managers and leaders who convey only hard facts come across as cold and distant. By sharing your feelings, others will see you as real and human. They will know who you are and will increase their respect for you.

Show consistency in the basic values that guide your decision making. Mistrust comes from not knowing what to expect. Take the time to think about your values and beliefs. Then let them consistently guide your decisions. When you know your central purpose, your actions will follow accordingly, and you'll project a consistency that earns trust.

Maintain confidences. You trust those you can confide in and rely on. So if people tell you something in confidence, they need to feel assured that you won't discuss it with others or betray that confidence. If people perceive you as someone who "leaks" personal confidences or someone who can't be depended upon, you won't be perceived as trustworthy.

Demonstrate competence. Develop the admiration and respect of others by demonstrating technical and professional ability and good business sense. Pay particular attention to developing and displaying your communication, team-building, and other interpersonal skills.

the role of teams in the United States: "Americans don't grow up learning how to function in teams. In school we never receive a team report card or learn the names of the team of sailors who traveled with Columbus to America."[29] This limitation would obviously be just as true of Canadians, British, Australians, and others from highly individualistic societies.

The Challenge

The previous points are meant to dramatize that one substantial barrier to using work teams is individual resistance. An employee's success is no longer defined in terms of individual performance. To perform well as team members, individuals must be able to communicate openly and honestly, to confront differences and resolve conflicts, and to sublimate personal goals for the good of the team. For many employees, this is a difficult—sometimes impossible—task. The challenge of creating team players will be greatest where (1) the national culture is highly individualistic and (2) the teams are being introduced into an established organization that has historically valued individual achievement. This describes, for instance, what faced managers at AT&T, Ford, Motorola, and other large U.S.-based companies. These firms prospered by hiring and rewarding corporate stars, and they bred a competitive climate that encouraged individual achievement and recognition. Employees in these types of firms can be jolted by this sudden shift to the importance of team play.[30] A veteran employee of a large company, who had done well working alone, described the experience of joining a team: "I'm learning my lesson. I just had my first negative performance appraisal in 20 years."[31]

On the other hand, the challenge for management is less demanding when teams are introduced where employees have strong collectivist values—such as in Japan or Mexico—or in new organizations that use teams as their initial form for structuring work. Saturn Corp., for instance, is an American organization owned by General Motors. The company was designed around teams from its inception. Everyone at Saturn was hired with the knowledge that they would be working in teams. The ability to be a good team player was a basic hiring qualification that all new employees had to meet.

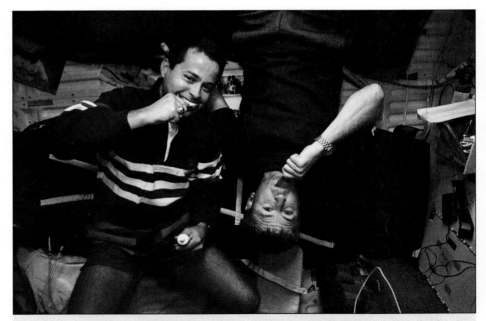

NASA knows that turning individuals into team players takes time and training. Astronauts are high-achieving individuals who undergo an extremely competitive selection process to become astronauts. But when they become part of a shuttle crew, they must work harmoniously with other crew members to achieve their mission's goal. NASA shapes astronauts into team players by training them to work together—including brushing their teeth together—every day for a year or two before their shuttle mission. By stressing that the mission's success depends on teamwork, NASA teaches astronauts how to compromise and make decisions that benefit the entire team.

Shaping Team Players

The following summarizes the primary options managers have for trying to turn individuals into team players.

SELECTION Some people already possess the interpersonal skills to be effective team players. When hiring team members, in addition to the technical skills required to fill the job, care should be taken to ensure that candidates can fulfill their team roles as well as technical requirements.

Many job candidates don't have team skills. This is especially true for those socialized around individual contributions. When faced with such candidates, managers basically have three options. The candidates can undergo training to "make them into team players." If this isn't possible or doesn't work, the other two options are to transfer the individual to another unit within the organization, without teams (if this possibility exists); or don't hire the candidate. In established organizations that decide to redesign jobs around teams, it should be expected that some employees will resist being team players and may be untrainable. Unfortunately, such people typically become casualties of the team approach.

TRAINING On a more optimistic note, a large proportion of people raised on the importance of individual accomplishment can be trained to become team players. Training specialists conduct exercises that allow employees to experience the satisfaction that teamwork can provide. They typically offer workshops to help employees improve their problem-solving, communication, negotiation, conflict-management, and coaching skills. Employees also learn the five-stage group development model described in chapter 7. At Bell Atlantic, for example, trainers focus on how a team goes through various stages before it finally gels. And employees are reminded of the importance of patience—because teams take longer to make decisions than if employees were acting alone.[32]

Emerson Electric's Speciality Motor Division in Missouri, for instance, has achieved remarkable success in getting its 650-member workforce not only to accept, but to welcome, team training.[33] Outside consultants were

Playfair, Inc. of Berkeley, California, is a training firm that specializes in developing exercises that help employees enjoy the satisfaction that teamwork can provide. In this photo, Playfair's founder Matt Weinstein (right) and staff members have fun doing an exercise they developed. It involves using craft materials to design a sculpture that represents a company's vision.

brought in to give workers practical skills for working in teams. After less than a year, employees have enthusiastically accepted the value of teamwork.

REWARDS The reward system needs to be reworked to encourage cooperative efforts rather than competitive ones. For instance, Hallmark Cards, Inc. added an annual bonus based on achievement of team goals to its basic individual-incentive system. Trigon Blue Cross Blue Shield changed its system to reward an even split between individual goals and teamlike behaviors.[34]

Promotions, pay raises, and other forms of recognition should be given to individuals for how effective they are as a collaborative team member. This doesn't mean individual contribution is ignored; rather, it is balanced with selfless contributions to the team. Examples of behaviors that should be rewarded include training new colleagues, sharing information with teammates, helping to resolve team conflicts, and mastering new skills that the team needs but in which it is deficient.

Lastly, don't forget the intrinsic rewards that employees can receive from teamwork. Teams provide camaraderie. It's exciting and satisfying to be an integral part of a successful team. The opportunity to engage in personal development and to help teammates grow can be a very satisfying and rewarding experience for employees.

Contemporary Issues in Managing Teams

In this section, we address three issues related to managing teams: (1) How do teams facilitate the adoption of total quality management? (2) What are the implications of workforce diversity on team performance? and (3) How does management reenergize stagnant teams?

Teams and Total Quality Management

One of the central characteristics of total quality management (TQM) is the use of teams. But why are teams an essential part of TQM?

The essence of TQM is process improvement, and employee involvement is the linchpin of process improvement. In other words, TQM requires management to give employees the encouragement to share ideas and act on what they suggest. As one author put it, "None of the various TQM processes and techniques will catch on and be applied except in work teams. All such techniques and processes require high levels of communication and contact, response and adaptation, and coordination and sequencing. They require, in short, the environment that can be supplied only by superior work teams."[35]

Teams provide the natural vehicle for employees to share ideas and to implement improvements. As stated by Gil Mosard, a TQM specialist at McDonnell Douglas: "When your measurement system tells you your process is out of control, you need teamwork for structured problem solving. Not everyone needs to know how to do all kinds of fancy control charts for performance tracking, but everybody does need to know where their process stands so they can judge if it is improving."[36] Examples from Ford Motor Co. and Amana Refrigeration, Inc. illustrate how teams are being used in TQM programs.[37]

Wainwright Industries is a team-oriented company, and its teams played a critical role in the company winning a Malcolm Baldrige National Quality Award. Wainwright's teams are small, about six members plus a team leader, so members can easily share ideas and implement improvements. The company's owners believe that teams help create an environment in which employees take more ownership in each other and in the company.

Ford began its TQM efforts in the early 1980s with teams as the primary organizing mechanism. "Because this business is so complex, you can't make an impact on it without a team approach," noted one Ford manager. In designing its quality problem-solving teams, Ford's management identified five goals. The teams should (1) be small enough to be efficient and effective; (2) be properly trained in the skills their members will need; (3) be allocated enough time to work on the problems they plan to address; (4) be given the authority to resolve the problems and implement corrective action; and (5) each have a designated "champion" whose job it is to help the team get around roadblocks that arise.

At Amana, cross-functional task forces made up of people from different levels within the company are used to deal with quality problems that cut across departmental lines. The various task forces each have a unique area of problem-solving responsibility. For instance, one handles in-plant products, another deals with items that arise outside the production facility, and still another focuses its attention specifically on supplier problems. Amana claims the use of these teams has improved vertical and horizontal communication within the company and substantially reduced both the number of units that don't meet company specifications and the number of service problems in the field.

Teams and Workforce Diversity

Managing diversity on teams is a balancing act (see Exhibit 8-6). Diversity typically provides fresh perspectives on issues but it makes it more difficult to unify the team and reach agreements.

The strongest case for diversity on work teams is when these teams are engaged in problem-solving and decision-making tasks.[38] Heterogeneous teams bring multiple perspectives to the discussion, thus increasing the likelihood that the team will identify creative or unique solutions. Additionally, the lack of a common perspective usually means diverse teams spend more time discussing issues, which decreases the chances that a weak alternative

Exhibit 8-6 Advantages and Disadvantages of Diversity

Advantages	Disadvantages
Multiple perspectives	Ambiguity
Greater openness to new ideas	Complexity
Multiple interpretations	Confusion
Increased creativity	Miscommunication
Increased flexibility	Difficulty in reaching a single agreement
Increased problem-solving skills	Difficulty in agreeing on specific actions

Source: From *International Dimensions of Organizational Behavior*, 2nd ed., by Nancy J. Adler. Copyright © 1991. By permission of South-Western College publishing, a division of International Thomsen Publishing, Inc., Cincinnati, OH 45227.

will be chosen. However, keep in mind that the positive contribution that diversity makes to decision-making teams undoubtedly declines over time. As we pointed out in the previous chapter, diverse groups have more difficulty working together and solving problems, *but this dissipates with time*. Expect the value-added component of diverse teams to increase as members become more familiar with each other and the team becomes more cohesive.

Studies tell us that members of cohesive teams have greater satisfaction, lower absenteeism, and lower attrition from the group.[39] Yet cohesiveness is likely to be lower on diverse teams.[40] So here is a potential negative of diversity: It is detrimental to group cohesiveness. But again, referring to the last chapter, we found that the relationship between cohesiveness and group productivity was moderated by performance-related norms. We suggest that if the norms of the team are supportive of diversity, then a team can maximize the value of heterogeneity while, at the same time, achieving the benefits of high cohesiveness.[41] This makes a strong case for team members to participate in diversity training.

Reinvigorating Mature Teams

Just because a team is performing well at a given point in time is no assurance that it will continue to do so.[42] Effective teams can become stagnant. Initial enthusiasm can give way to apathy. Time can diminish the positive value from diverse perspectives as cohesiveness increases.

In terms of the five-stage development model introduced in the previous chapter, teams don't automatically stay at the "performing stage." Familiarity breeds apathy. Success can lead to complacency. And maturity brings less openness to novel ideas and innovation.

Mature teams are particularly prone to suffer from groupthink. Members begin to believe they can read everyone's mind so they assume they know what everyone is thinking. As a result, team members become reluctant to express their thoughts and less likely to challenge each other.

Another source of problems for mature teams is that their early successes are often due to having taken on easy tasks. It's normal for new teams to begin by taking on those issues and problems that they can handle most easily. But as time passes, the easy problems become solved and the team has to begin to confront more difficult issues. At this point, the team has typically developed entrenched processes and routines, and members are reluctant to change the "perfect" system they've already worked out. The results can often be disasterous. Internal team processes no longer work smoothly. Communication bogs down. Conflicts increase because problems are less likely to have obvious solutions. And team performance can drop dramatically.

What can be done to reinvigorate mature teams? We can offer four suggestions: (1) *Prepare members to deal with the problems of maturity*. Remind team members that they're not unique—all successful teams have to confront maturity issues. They shouldn't feel let down or lose their confidence in the team concept when the initial euphoria subsides and conflicts surface. (2) *Offer refresher training*. When teams get into ruts, it may help to provide them with refresher training in communication, conflict resolution, team processes, and similar skills. This can help members regain confidence and trust in one another. (3) *Offer advanced training*. The skills that worked with easy problems may be insufficient for more difficult ones. So mature teams can often benefit from advanced training to help members develop stronger problem-solving, interpersonal, and technical skills. (4) *Encourage teams to treat their development as a constant learning experience*. Like TQM, teams should approach their own development as part of a search for continuous improvement. Teams should look for ways to improve, to confront member fears and frustrations, and to use conflict as a learning opportunity.

◆ Teams should approach their own development as part of a search for continuous improvement.

Summary and Implications for Managers

Few trends have influenced employee jobs as much as the massive movement to introduce teams into the workplace. The shift from working alone to working on teams requires employees to cooperate with others, share information, confront differences, and sublimate personal interests for the greater good of the team.

High-performing teams have been found to have common characteristics. They tend to be small. They contain people with three different types of skills: technical, problem solving and decision making, and interpersonal. They properly match people to various roles. These teams have a commitment to a common purpose, establish specific goals, and have the leadership and structure to provide focus and direction. They also hold themselves accountable at both the individual and team levels by having well-designed evaluation and reward systems. Finally, high-performing teams are characterized by high mutual trust among members.

Because individualistic organizations and societies attract and reward individual accomplishment, it is more difficult to create team players in these environments. To make the conversion, management should try to select individuals with the interpersonal skills to be effective team players, provide training to develop teamwork skills, and reward individuals for cooperative efforts.

Once teams are mature and performing effectively, management's job isn't over. This is because mature teams can become stagnant and complacent. Managers need to support mature teams with advice, guidance, and training if these teams are to continue to improve.

For Review

1. How can teams increase employee motivation?
2. Contrast *self-managed* and *cross-functional* teams.
3. List and describe nine team roles.
4. How do high-performing teams minimize social loafing?
5. How do high-performing teams minimize groupthink?
6. What are the five dimensions that underly the concept of trust?
7. Under what conditions will the challenge of creating team players be greatest?
8. What role do teams play in TQM?
9. Contrast the pros and cons of having diverse teams.
10. How can management invigorate stagnant teams?

For Discussion

1. Don't teams create conflict? Isn't conflict bad? Why, then, would management support the concept of teams?
2. Are there factors in the Japanese society that make teams more acceptable in the workplace than in the United States or Canada? Explain.
3. What problems might surface in teams at each stage in the five-stage group development model?
4. How do you think member expectation might affect team performance?
5. Would you prefer to work alone or as part of a team? Why? How do you think your answer compares with others in your class?

Point

The Value of Teams

The value of teams is now well known. Let's summarize the primary benefits that experts agree can result from the introduction of work teams.

Increased employee motivation. Work teams enhance employee involvement. They typically make jobs more interesting. They help employees meet their social needs. They also create social pressures on slackers to exert higher levels of effort in order to remain in the team's good graces. Consistent with the research on social facilitation, individuals are likely to perform better when they're in the presence of other people.

Higher levels of productivity. Teams have the potential to create positive synergy. In recent years, the introduction of teams in most organizations has been associated with cuts in staff. What management has done is to use the positive synergy to get the same or greater output from fewer people. This translates into higher levels of productivity.

Increased employee satisfaction. Employees have a need for affiliation. Working in teams can help meet this need by increasing worker interactions and creating camaraderie among team members. Moreover, people who are part of a satisfying team climate cope better with stress and enjoy their jobs more.

Common commitment to goals. Teams encourage individuals to sublimate their individual goals for those of the group. The process of developing a common purpose, committing to that purpose, and agreeing upon specific goals—combined with the social pressures exerted by the team—result in a high unity of commitment to team goals.

Improved communication. Self-managed teams create interpersonal dependencies that require members to interact considerably more than when they work on jobs alone. Similarly, cross-functional teams create interfunctional dependencies and increase organizationwide communication.

Expanded job skills. The implementation of teams almost always comes with expanded job training. Through this training, employees build their technical, decision-making, and interpersonal skills.

Organizational flexibility. Teams focus on processes rather than functions. They encourage cross-training, so members can do each other's jobs, and expansion of skills. It's not unusual for compensation on teams to be based on the number of skills a member has acquired. This expansion of skills increases organizational flexibility. Work can be reorganized and workers allocated, as needed, to meet changing conditions.

Does the introduction of teams *always* achieve these benefits? No! For instance, a study by Ernst & Young found that forming teams to investigate and improve products and processes led to measurable improvement only in organizations that were performing poorly in their markets in terms of profit, productivity, and quality.* In medium-performing companies, the study found, bottom-line results were unaffected by team activities. In high-performing companies, the introduction of new team-based work systems actually lowered performance.

There are obviously contingency factors that influence the acceptance and success of teams. Some examples might be: tasks that benefit from combining multiple skills; when the market will pay a premium for improved quality or innovation; with employees who value continual learning and enjoy complex tasks; and where management–employee relations already have a strong basis of mutual trust. Nevertheless, we can't ignore the reality that the team movement currently has tremendous momentum and reflects management's belief that teams can be successful in a wide range of settings.

*Cited in R. Zemke, "Rethinking the Rush to Team Up," *Training*, November 1993, p. 56.

The Tyranny of a Team Ideology

Beliefs about the benefits of teams have achieved an unquestioned place in the study of organizations. But teams are no panacea. Let's take a critical look at four of the assumptions that seem to underly this team ideology.

Mature teams are task oriented and have successfully minimized the negative influences of other group forces. Task-oriented teams still experience antitask behavior, and indeed have much in common with other types of groups. For instance, they often suffer from infighting over assignments and decision outcomes, low participation rates, and member apathy.

Individual, group, and organizational goals can all be integrated into common team goals. Contrary to what team advocates assume, people are not so simply motivated by the sociability and self-actualization supposedly offered by work teams. These teams suffer from competitiveness, conflict, and hostility. And rarely do team members support and help one another as difficult ideas and issues are worked through. Additionally, contrary to the notion that teams increase job satisfaction, the evidence suggests that individuals experience substantial and continuing stress as team members. Rarely is the team experience satisfying. Moreover, certain types of workers and certain types of work are better suited to solitary work situations, and individuals with particular work styles will never perform well on a team. For the hard-driving, competitive person who thrives on individual achievement, the cult of the team player is likely to produce only frustration and stress.

Participative or shared leadership is always effective. The team ideology oversimplifies the requirement for leadership. It downplays the importance of leadership by suggesting that high-performing teams can dispense with, or ignore, leadership concerns. It assumes that the team's commitment to a common goal unites all team action and thus reduces the need for leadership. Group process theorists are unanimous that all groups will experience phases of identifying with, rejecting, and working through relations with authority. This process cannot be eliminated simply by eliminating leaders from groups. The abdication of leadership can, in effect, paralyze teams.

The team environment drives out the subversive forces of politics, power, and conflict that divert groups from efficiently doing their work. Recipes for effective teams rate them on the quality of decision making, communication, cohesion, clarity and acceptance of goals, acceptance of minority views, and other criteria. Such recipes betray the fact that teams are made up of people with self-interests who are prepared to make deals, reward favorites, punish enemies, and engage in similar behaviors to further those self-interests. The result is that teams are political entities, where members play power games and engage in conflicts. Neither training nor organizational actions will alter the intrinsically political nature of teams.

The argument here has been that the team ideology, under the banner of benefits for all, ignores that teams are frequently used to camouflage coercion under the pretense of maintaining cohesion; conceal conflict under the guise of consensus; convert conformity into a semblance of creativity; delay action in the supposed interests of consultation; legitimize lack of leadership; and disguise expedient arguments and personal agendas. Teams do not necessarily provide fulfillment of individual needs, nor do they necessarily contribute to individual satisfaction and performance or organizational effectiveness. On the contrary, it's likely that the infatuation with teams and making every employee part of a team results in organizations not getting the best performance from many of their members.

Based on A. Sinclair, "The Tyranny of a Team Ideology," *Organization Studies*, Vol. 13, No. 4 (1992), pp. 611–26.

Learning about Yourself Exercise

Do Others See Me as Trustworthy?

To get some insight into how others may view your trustworthiness, complete this questionnaire. First, however, identify the person that will be evaluating you (i.e., a work colleague, friend, supervisor, team leader).

Use the following scale to score each question:

Strongly Disagree   1   2   3   4   5   6   7   8   9   10   Strongly Agree

Score

1. I can be expected to play fair.   _____

2. You can confide in me and know I will keep what's told to me in confidence.   _____

3. I can be counted on to tell the truth.   _____

4. I would never intentionally misrepresent my point of view to others.   _____

5. If I promise to do a favor, I can be counted on to carry out that promise.   _____

6. If I have an appointment with someone, I can be counted on to show up promptly.   _____

7. If I'm lent money, I can be counted on to pay it back as soon as possible.   _____

Turn to page A-28 for scoring directions and key.

Source: Based on C. Johnson-George and W.C. Swap, "Measurement of Specific Interpersonal Trust: Construction and Validation of a Scale to Assess Trust in a Specific Other," *Journal of Personality and Social Psychology*, December 1982, pp. 1306–17.

Working with Others Exercise

Building Effective Work Teams

Objective
This exercise is designed to allow class members to (a) experience working together as a team on a specific task and (b) analyze this experience.

Time
Teams will have 90 minutes to engage in steps 2 and 3 that follow. Another 45–60 minutes will be used in class to critique and evaluate the exercise.

Procedure
1. Class members are assigned to teams of about six people.
2. Each team is required to:
   a. Determine a team name   **b.** Compose a team song
3. Each team is to try to find the following items on its scavenger hunt:
   a. A picture of a team
   b. A newspaper article about a group or team
   c. A piece of apparel with the college name or logo

    d. A set of chopsticks
    e. A ball of cotton
    f. A piece of stationery from a college department
    g. A bottle of Liquid Paper
    h. A floppy disk
    i. A cup from McDonald's
    j. A dog leash
    k. A utility bill
    l. A calendar from last year
    m. A book by Ernest Hemingway
    n. An ad brochure for a Ford product
    o. A test tube
    p. A pack of gum
    q. An ear of corn
    r. A Garth Brooks tape or CD

4. After 90 minutes, all teams are to be back in the classroom. (A penalty, determined by the instructor, will be imposed on late teams.) The team with the most items on the list will be declared the winner. The class and instructor will determine whether or not the items meet the requirements of the exercise.

5. Debriefing of the exercise will begin by having each team engage in self-evaluation. Specifically, it should answer the following:
    a. What was the team's strategy?
    b. What roles did individual members perform?
    c. How effective was the team?
    d. What could the team have done to be more effective?

6. Full class discussion will focus on issues such as:
    a. What differentiated the more effective teams from the less effective teams?
    b. What did you learn from this experience that is relevant to the design of effective teams?

Source: Adapted from M.R. Manning and P.J. Schmidt, "Building Effective Work Teams: A Quick Exercise Based on a Scavenger Hunt," *Journal of Management Education*, August 1995, pp. 392–98. With permission.

XEL Communications

XEL Communications is a small fish in a big pond. The company employs 180 people and manufactures custom circuit boards. It competes against the likes of Northern Telecom and AT&T.

Bill Sanko and his partners bought the company from GTE Corp. GTE is its major customer, but Bill wants to cut down its dependence on GTE. He needs to sell more to the Baby Bells and to big industrial customers that operate their own phone systems.

Bill's problem is that to compete successfully for new business he has to dramatically improve XEL's agility. He wants lightning turnaround of orders, quicker than any big company could manage. He wants speedy response to customer needs. All done with close attention to cost. Unfortunately, XEL is not designed for speed or flexibility. Its costs are also too high to give the firm a competitive advantage.

For example, on the shop floor, it takes XEL eight weeks to get a product through the production cycle—from start-up to finished product. This ties up a lot of money in inventory and frustrates customers who want quick delivery. Sanko believes that high-performing teams could cut this down to four days or less. The company's structure is also burdensome. Line workers report to supervisors, who report to unit or departmental managers, who report on up the ladder to Sanko and a crew of top executives. This high vertical structure delays decision making and increases expenses. "If a hardware engineer needs some software help, he goes to his manager," Sanko says. "The manager says, 'Go write it up.' Then the hardware manager takes the software manager to lunch and they talk about it."

Sanko has decided to reorganize his company around self-managed teams. He thinks a well-designed team structure can help him better satisfy his customers by cutting cycle time from eight weeks to four days, significantly improve quality, cut assembly costs by 25 percent, and reduce inventory costs by 50 percent. Ambitious goals? You bet! But Sanko thinks it's possible. Moreover, achieving these goals might be necessary if his company is to survive.

Questions

1. Describe, in detail, the steps you think Sanko should take in planning and implementing self-managed teams.
2. What problems should Sanko be on the lookout for?

Source: Based on J. Case, "What the Experts Forgot to Mention," *INC.*, September 1993, pp. 66–78.

Assembly Line Teams at Square D

Square D is a manufacturer of electrical equipment. Its Lexington, Kentucky, plant introduced teams in 1988 in order to improve quality, speed orders, and increase productivity.

Every day begins with a team meeting at the Lexington plant. The 800 employees are divided into 20- to 30-person self-managed teams. Each team is like its own little factory within the factory. Team members control their own work and make decisions without checking with management. The teams are fully responsible for their products from start to finish.

The decision by management to introduce teams in 1988 wasn't made in a vacuum. Management recognized that employees would need training in order to effectively convert from a system where people did narrow, specialized tasks on an assembly line and never saw the finished product. That training has included exercises to help employees learn how to work as part of a team, solve problems, handle new technology, and service customers better. The plant continues to spend 4 percent of its payroll on training.

The results at Lexington are impressive. Employees no longer have to wait for maintenance personnel when equipment breaks down. They can fix their own machines. Employees exhibit newfound pride in their work and greater commitment to doing a good job. Management is pleased with the 75 percent reduction in the rejection rate and the ability to process orders in an average of three days versus six weeks under the old system.

Questions

1. Not all efforts to introduce teams are successful. Is there anything in the case of Square D that suggests why this program is doing so well?
2. What is there about team processes that can explain how self-managed teams could dramatically cut rejection rates and processing time from what had existed previously with high specialization?

Source: Based on "Assembly Line Teams Are Better Trained and More Efficient," *ABC World News Tonight*; aired February 24, 1993.

CHAPTER 9

COMMUNICATION

I didn't say that I
didn't say it. I said
that I didn't say that
I said it. I want to
make that very clear.
—G. Romney

LEARNING OBJECTIVES

After studying this chapter, you should be able to

1 Define *communication*

2 Identify factors affecting the use of the grapevine

3 List common barriers to effective communication

4 Describe an effective communication program in an organization
   undergoing dramatic changes

5 Outline the behaviors related to effective active listening

6 Contrast the meaning of talk for men versus women

7 Describe potential problems in cross-cultural communication

8 Discuss how technology is changing organizational communication

CAN the misunderstanding of a few words literally mean the difference between life and death? They can in the airline business. A number of aviation disasters have been largely attributed to problems in communication.[1] Consider the following:

History's worst aviation disaster occurred in 1977 at foggy Tenerife in the Canary Islands. The captain of a KLM flight thought the air traffic controller had cleared him to take off. But the controller intended only to give departure instructions. Although the language spoken between the Dutch KLM captain and the Spanish controller was English, confusion was created by heavy accents and improper terminology. The KLM Boeing 747 hit a Pan Am 747 at full throttle on the runway, killing 583 people.

In 1980, another Spanish controller at Tenerife gave a holding pattern clearance to a Dan Air flight from Manchester, England. But the controller said "turn to the left" when he should have said "turns to the left"—making circles instead of a single turn. The jet banked into a mountain, killing 146.

In 1990, Colombian Avianca pilots, after several holding patterns caused by bad weather, told controllers as they neared New York Kennedy Airport that their Boeing 707 was "running low on fuel." Controllers hear those words all the time, so they took no special action. While the pilots knew there was a serious problem, they failed to use a key phrase—"fuel emergency"—which would have obligated controllers to direct the Avianca flight ahead of all others and clear it to land as soon as possible. The people at Kennedy never understood the true nature of the pilots' problem. The jet ran out of fuel and crashed 16 miles from Kennedy. Seventy-three people died.

In 1993, Chinese pilots flying a U.S.-built MD-80 tried to land in fog at Urumqi, in northwest China. They were baffled by an audio alarm from the jet's ground proximity warning system. A cockpit recorder picked up one pilot's last words: "What does 'pull up' mean?" The plane hit power lines and crashed, killing 12.

On December 20, 1995, American Airlines Flight 965 was approaching the Cali, Colombia airport. The pilot expected to hear either the words "cleared as filed" (meaning follow the flight plan filed before leaving Miami) or "cleared direct" (meaning fly straight from where you are to Cali, a slightly different route from the flight plan). But the pilot heard neither. The con-troller intended to clear him "as filed" but said "cleared to Cali." The pilot interpreted that as a direct clearance. When he checked back, the controller said "affirmative." Both were obviously confused. The plane crashed, killing 160 people. ◆

The preceding examples tragically illustrate how miscommunication can have deadly consequences. In this chapter, we'll show (obviously not in as dramatic a fashion) that good communication is essential to any group's or organization's effectiveness.

Research indicates that poor communication is probably the most frequently cited source of interpersonal conflict.[2] Because individuals spend nearly 70 percent of their waking hours communicating—writing, reading, speaking, listening—it seems reasonable to conclude that one of the most inhibiting forces to successful group performance is a lack of effective communication. (See Exhibit 9-1.)

No group can exist without communication: the transference of meaning among its members. It is only through transmitting meaning from one person to another that information and ideas can be conveyed. Communication, however, is more than merely imparting meaning. It must also be understood. In a group where one member speaks only German and the others do not know German, the individual speaking German will not be fully understood. Therefore, **communication** must include both the *transference and the understanding of meaning.*

communication
The transference and understanding of meaning.

◆ An idea, no matter how great, is useless until it is transmitted and understood by others.

An idea, no matter how great, is useless until it is transmitted and understood by others. Perfect communication, if there were such a thing, would exist when a thought or an idea was transmitted so that the mental picture perceived by the receiver was exactly the same as that envisioned by the sender. Although elementary in theory, perfect communication is never achieved in practice, for reasons we shall expand upon later.

Before making too many generalizations concerning communication and problems in communicating effectively, we need to review briefly the functions that communication performs and describe the communication process.

Functions of Communication

Communication serves four major functions within a group or organization: control, motivation, emotional expression, and information.[3]

Communication acts to *control* member behavior in several ways. Organizations have authority hierarchies and formal guidelines that employees are required to follow. When employees, for instance, are required to first communicate any job-related grievance to their immediate boss, to follow their job description, or to comply with company policies, communication is performing a control function. But informal communication also controls behavior. When work groups tease or harass a member who produces too much (and makes the rest of the group look bad), they are informally communicating with, and controlling, the member's behavior.

Exhibit 9-1

Source: *Business Week*, May 16, 1994, p. 8. Reprinted by special permission. Copyright ©1994 by McGraw-Hill, Inc.

Communication fosters *motivation* by clarifying to employees what is to be done, how well they are doing, and what can be done to improve performance if it's subpar. We saw this operating in our review of goal-setting and reinforcement theories in chapter 5. The formation of specific goals, feedback on progress toward the goals, and reinforcement of desired behavior all stimulate motivation and require communication.

For many employees, their work group is a primary source for social interaction. The communication that takes place within the group is a fundamental mechanism by which members show their frustrations and feelings of satisfaction. Communication, therefore, provides a release for the *emotional expression* of feelings and for fulfillment of social needs.

The final function that communication performs relates to its role in facilitating decision making. It provides the *information* that individuals and groups need to make decisions by transmitting the data to identify and evaluate alternative choices.

No one of these four functions should be seen as being more important than the others. For groups to perform effectively, they need to maintain some form of control over members, stimulate members to perform, provide a means for emotional expression, and make decision choices. You can assume that almost every communication interaction that takes place in a group or organization performs one or more of these four functions.

The Communication Process

Communication can be thought of as a process or flow. Communication problems occur when there are deviations or blockages in that flow. In this section, we describe the process in terms of a communication model, consider how distortions can disrupt the process, and introduce the concept of communication apprehension as another potential disruption.

A Communication Model

Before communication can take place, a purpose, expressed as a message to be conveyed, is needed. It passes between a source (the sender) and a receiver. The message is encoded (converted to symbolic form) and is passed by way of some medium (channel) to the receiver, who retranslates (decodes) the

Communication at Home Depot is designed to give employees information, build their morale, and provide a release for the emotional expression of their feelings. Company founders Bernard Marcus and Arthur Blank spend about 40 percent of their time in stores talking with employees, who are encouraged to express their opinions without fear of being fired or demoted. During a closed circuit television program called "Breakfast with Bernie and Art," Marcus (shown here) and Blank speak to the employees from one of their stores, updating them on corporate news, sharing sales and profits results, and answering their questions.

communication process
The steps between a source and a receiver that result in the transference and understanding of meaning.

encoding
Converting a communication message to symbolic form.

message initiated by the sender. The result is a transference of meaning from one person to another.[4]

Exhibit 9-2 depicts the **communication process**. This model is made up of seven parts: (1) the communication source, (2) encoding, (3) the message, (4) the channel, (5) decoding, (6) the receiver, and (7) feedback.

The source initiates a message by **encoding** a thought. Four conditions have been described that affect the encoded message: skill, attitudes, knowledge, and the social-cultural system.

My success in communicating to you is dependent upon my writing skills; if the authors of textbooks are without the requisite writing skills, their messages will not reach students in the form desired. One's total communicative success includes speaking, reading, listening, and reasoning skills as well. As we discussed in chapter 4, our attitudes influence our behavior. We hold predisposed ideas on numerous topics, and our communications are affected by these attitudes. Furthermore, we are restricted in our communicative activ-

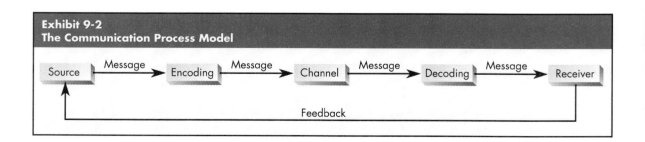

Exhibit 9-2
The Communication Process Model

Source → Message → Encoding → Message → Channel → Message → Decoding → Message → Receiver

Feedback

ity by the extent of our knowledge of the particular topic. We cannot communicate what we don't know, and should our knowledge be too extensive, it's possible that our receiver will not understand our message. Clearly, the amount of knowledge the source holds about his or her subject will affect the message he or she seeks to transfer. And, finally, just as attitudes influence our behavior, so does our position in the social-cultural system in which we exist. Your beliefs and values, all part of your culture, act to influence you as a communicative source.

The **message** is the actual physical product from the source encoding. "When we speak, the speech is the message. When we write, the writing is the message. When we paint, the picture is the message. When we gesture, the movements of our arms, the expressions on our face are the message."[5] Our message is affected by the code or group of symbols we use to transfer meaning, the content of the message itself, and the decisions that we make in selecting and arranging both codes and content.

message
What is communicated.

The **channel** is the medium through which the message travels. It is selected by the source, who must determine which channel is formal and which one is informal. Formal channels are established by the organization and transmit messages that pertain to the job-related activities of members. They traditionally follow the authority network within the organization. Other forms of messages, such as personal or social, follow the informal channels in the organization.

channel
The medium through which a communication message travels.

The receiver is the object to whom the message is directed. But before the message can be received, the symbols in it must be translated into a form that can be understood by the receiver. This is the **decoding** of the message. Just as the encoder was limited by his or her skills, attitudes, knowledge, and social-cultural system, the receiver is equally restricted. Just as the source must be skillful in writing or speaking, the receiver must be skillful in reading or listening, and both must be able to reason. One's knowledge, attitudes, and cultural background influence one's ability to receive, just as they do the ability to send.

decoding
Retranslating a sender's communication message.

The final link in the communication process is a **feedback loop**. "If a communication source decodes the message that he encodes, if the message is put back into his system, we have feedback."[6] Feedback is the check on how successful we have been in transferring our messages as originally intended. It determines whether or not understanding has been achieved.

feedback loop
The final link in the communication process; puts the message back into the system as a check against misunderstandings.

Sources of Distortion

Unfortunately, most of the seven components in the process model have the potential to create distortion and, therefore, impinge upon the goal of communicating perfectly. These sources of distortion explain why the message that is decoded by the receiver is rarely the exact message that the sender intended.

If the encoding is done carelessly, the message decoded by the sender will have been distorted. The message itself can also cause distortion. The poor choice of symbols and confusion in the content of the message are frequent problem areas. Of course, the channel can distort a communication if a poor one is selected or if the noise level is high. The receiver represents the final potential source for distortion. His or her prejudices, knowledge, perceptual skills, attention span, and care in decoding are all factors that can result in interpreting the message somewhat differently than envisioned by the sender. (See Exhibit 9-3.)

Communication Apprehension

communication apprehension
Undue tension and anxiety about oral communication, written communication, or both.

Another major roadblock to effective communication is that some people—an estimated 5 to 20 percent of the population[7]—suffer from debilitating **communication apprehension** or anxiety. Although lots of people dread speaking in front of a group, communication apprehension is a more serious problem because it affects a whole category of communication techniques. People who suffer from it experience undue tension and anxiety in oral communication, written communication, or both.[8] For example, oral apprehensives may find it extremely difficult to talk with others face-to-face or become extremely anxious when they have to use the telephone. As a result, they may rely on memos or letters to convey messages when a phone call would not only be faster but more appropriate.

Studies demonstrate that oral-communication apprehensives avoid situations that require them to engage in oral communication.[9] We should expect to find some self-selection in jobs so that such individuals don't take positions, such as teacher, where oral communication is a dominant requirement.[10] But almost all jobs require some oral communication. And of greater concern is the evidence that high-oral-communication apprehensives distort the communication demands of their jobs in order to minimize the need for communication.[11] So we need to be aware that there is a set of people in organizations who severely limit their oral communication and rationalize this practice by telling themselves that more communication isn't necessary for them to do their job effectively.

Exhibit 9-3   Empty Words That Create Distortions

Many young people today use a vocabulary of "filler words" that contribute to imprecise language. The following words and phrases distort communication because they're confusing and ambiguous to many listeners:

Like you know
See
So
OK
Like oh my God
I mean
Basically
And all that
And everything like that
And whatever
'n' stuff

The following dialog captures the problem:

"Like you know, I was so out of it. I was all, like, Duhhh! I mean, like oh my God. OK, so I said basically what's happening? OK, so I told him I'd be there and everything like that, you know? And he's all like not absolutely certain 'n stuff. It was totally an experience."

Communication Fundamentals

A working knowledge of communication requires a basic understanding of some fundamental concepts. In this section, we review those concepts. Specifically, we look at the flow patterns of communication, compare formal and informal communication networks, describe the importance of nonverbal communication, consider how individuals select communication channels, and summarize the major barriers to effective communication.

Direction of Communication

Communication can flow vertically or laterally. The vertical dimension can be further divided into downward and upward directions.[12]

DOWNWARD Communication that flows from one level of a group or organization to a lower level is a downward communication.

When we think of managers communicating with subordinates, the downward pattern is the one we usually think of. It is used by group leaders and managers to assign goals, provide job instructions, inform underlings of policies and procedures, point out problems that need attention, and offer feedback about performance. But downward communication doesn't have to be oral or face-to-face contact. When management sends letters to employees' homes to advise them of the organization's new sick leave policy, it is using downward communication.

UPWARD Upward communication flows to a higher level in the group or organization. It is used to provide feedback to higher-ups, inform them of progress toward goals, and relay current problems. Upward communication keeps managers aware of how employees feel about their jobs, co-workers, and the organization in general. Managers also rely on upward communication for ideas on how things can be improved.

Lee Kun Hee, chairman of the South Korean conglomerate Samsung, uses downward communication to deliver what he calls "shock therapy" to his 180,000 employees. To correct customer complaints about defective products, unappealing designs, and poor after-sales service, Lee prepared 300 hours of videotapes and 750 hours of audiotapes that tell employees what they must do to improve the quality of Samsung products. Lee, shown here on video, told employees to "Change everything but your wives and children."

Some organizational examples of upward communication are performance reports prepared by lower management for review by middle and top management, suggestion boxes, employee attitude surveys, grievance procedures, superior–subordinate discussions, and informal "gripe" sessions where employees have the opportunity to identify and discuss problems with their boss or representatives of higher management.

For example, Federal Express prides itself on its computerized upward communication program.[13] All 68,000 employees annually complete climate surveys and reviews of management. This program was cited as a key human resources strength by the Malcom Baldrige National Quality Award examiners when Federal Express won the honor.

LATERAL When communication takes place among members of the same work group, among members of work groups at the same level, among managers at the same level, or among any horizontally equivalent personnel, we describe it as lateral communications.

Why would there be a need for horizontal communications if a group or organization's vertical communications are effective? The answer is that horizontal communications are often necessary to save time and facilitate coordination. In some cases, these lateral relationships are formally sanctioned. Often, they are informally created to short-circuit the vertical hierarchy and expedite action. So lateral communications can, from management's viewpoint, be good or bad. Since strict adherence to the formal vertical structure for all communications can impede the efficient and accurate transfer of information, lateral communications can be beneficial. In such cases, they occur with the knowledge and support of superiors. But they can create dysfunctional conflicts when the formal vertical channels are breached, when members go above or around their superiors to get things done, or when bosses find out that actions have been taken or decisions made without their knowledge.

Formal vs. Informal Networks

communication networks
Channels by which information flows.

formal networks
Task-related communications that follow the authority chain.

informal network
The communication grapevine.

Communication networks define the channels by which information flows. These channels are one of two varieties—either formal or informal. **Formal networks** are typically vertical, follow the authority chain, and are limited to task-related communications. In contrast, the **informal network**—usually better known as the grapevine—is free to move in any direction, skip authority levels, and is as likely to satisfy group members' social needs as it is to facilitate task accomplishments.

FORMAL SMALL-GROUP NETWORKS Exhibit 9-4 on page 318 illustrates three common small-group networks. These are the chain, wheel, and all channel. The chain rigidly follows the formal chain of command. The wheel relies on the leader to act as the central conduit for all the group's communication. The all-channel network permits all group members to actively communicate with each other.

As Exhibit 9-5 demonstrates, the effectiveness of each network depends on the dependent variable you are concerned about. For instance, the structure of the wheel facilitates the emergence of a leader, the all-channel network is best if you are concerned with having high member satisfaction, and the

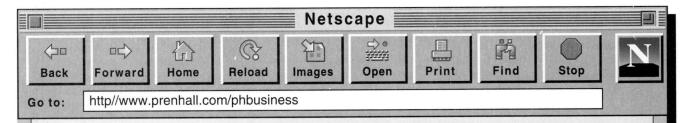

OB in the News

Empowering Employees by Opening Up Communication

In 1980, a long strike had nearly forced the closing of Missouri-based Springfield ReManufacturing Co. (SRC), a subsidiary of then International Harvester. To cut its losses, Harvester sold SRC, which reassembles diesel engines, to a group of investors. The new management needed to radically change the company if it was going to survive. That radical change came in the form of what has become known as *open-book management*. The goal was to get every employee to think like an owner. To achieve this end, management trained employees to understand the company's financials, shared those numbers routinely with the workforce, and provided bonuses and incentive pay based on profit improvement. For instance, each week SRC shuts down its machines for 30 minutes while its 800 employees break into small groups and study the latest financial statements. Every employee at SRC can now interpret profit and loss statements as well as most accountants.

The results of open-book management have been nothing short of sensational at SRC. In 1981, the company lost $61,000 on sales of $16 million. In 1994, the company earned $6 million on sales of $100 million.

Open-book management is drawing attention from other companies that are trying to empower their employees. "It's the next logical step after you've given self-directed teams the power to make decisions owners once had," says Donald Robb, a division manager at R.R. Donnelley & Sons Co. "It integrates all of the other things we've been doing and gives some focus to it."

Dozens of companies, from Allstate Insurance to sportswear maker Patagonia, have implemented open-book management. Allstate's Business Insurance Group, for instance, used open-book management to boost return on equity from 2.9 percent to 16.5 percent in just three years. The unit's 3,500 employees were trained to understand the importance of key financial measures and then were provided with the information on a regular basis. "It got employees involved and committed, and it gave them some ownership," says the unit's president. "They understood they had an impact on the bottom line."

Based on J. Fierman, "Winning Ideas from Maverick Managers," *Fortune*, February 6, 1995, pp. 66–80; and J.A. Byrne, "Management Meccas," *Business Week*, September 18, 1995, pp. 126–28.

Take It to the Net

We invite you to visit the Robbins page on the Prentice Hall Web site at:

http://www.prenhall.com/robbinsorgbeh

for this chapter's World Wide Web exercise.

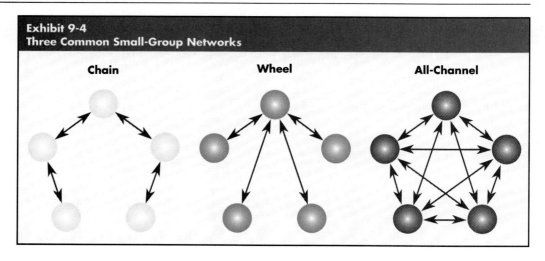

Exhibit 9-4
Three Common Small-Group Networks

Chain   Wheel   All-Channel

chain is best if accuracy is most important. Exhibit 9-5 leads us to the conclusion that no single network will be best for all occasions.

THE INFORMAL NETWORK The previous discussion of networks emphasized formal communication patterns, but the formal system is not the only communication system in a group or between groups. Now let's turn our attention to the informal system, where information flows along the well-known grapevine and rumors can flourish.

The grapevine has three main characteristics.[14] First, it is not controlled by management. Second, it is perceived by most employees as being more believable and reliable than formal communiques issued by top management. Third, it is largely used to serve the self-interests of those people within it.

One of the most famous studies of the grapevine investigated the communication pattern among 67 managerial personnel in a small manufacturing firm.[15] The basic approach used was to learn from each communication recipient how he or she first received a given piece of information and then trace it back to its source. It was found that, while the grapevine was an important source of information, only 10 percent of the executives acted as liaison individuals, that is, passed the information on to more than one other person. For example, when one executive decided to resign to enter the insurance business, 81 percent of the executives knew about it, but only 11 percent transmitted this information on to others.

Exhibit 9-5 Small-Group Networks and Effectiveness Criteria

	Networks		
Criteria	Chain	Wheel	All–Channel
Speed	Moderate	Fast	Fast
Accuracy	High	High	Moderate
Emergence of a leader	Moderate	High	None
Member satisfaction	Moderate	Low	High

Two other conclusions from this study are also worth noting. Information on events of general interest tended to flow between the major functional groups (that is, production, sales) rather than within them. Also, no evidence surfaced to suggest that members of any one group consistently acted as liaisons; rather, different types of information passed through different liaison persons.

An attempt to replicate this study among employees in a small state government office also found that only a small percentage (10 percent) acted as liaison individuals.[16] This is interesting, since the replication contained a wider spectrum of employees—including rank-and-file as well as managerial personnel. However, the flow of information in the government office took place within, rather than between, functional groups. It was proposed that this discrepancy might be due to comparing an executive-only sample against one that also included rank-and-file workers. Managers, for example, might feel greater pressure to stay informed and thus cultivate others outside their immediate functional group. Also, in contrast to the findings of the original study, the replication found that a consistent group of individuals acted as liaisons by transmitting information in the government office.

Is the information that flows along the grapevine accurate? The evidence indicates that about 75 percent of what is carried is accurate.[17] But what conditions foster an active grapevine? What gets the rumor mill rolling?

It is frequently assumed that rumors start because they make titillating gossip. Such is rarely the case. Rumors have at least four purposes: to structure and reduce anxiety; to make sense of limited or fragmented information; to serve as a vehicle to organize group members, and possibly outsiders, into coalitions; and to signal a sender's status ("I'm an insider and, with respect to this rumor, you're an outsider") or power ("I have the power to make you into an insider").[18] Research indicates that rumors emerge as a response to situations that are important to us, where there is ambiguity, and under conditions that arouse anxiety.[19] Work situations frequently contain these three elements, which explains why rumors flourish in organizations. The secrecy and competition that typically prevail in large organizations—around such issues as the appointment of new bosses, the relocation of offices, and the realignment of work assignments—create conditions that encourage and sustain rumors on the grapevine. A rumor will persist either until the wants and expectations creating the uncertainty underlying the rumor are fulfilled or until the anxiety is reduced.

◆ **The evidence indicates that 75 percent of what is carried on the grapevine is accurate.**

What can we conclude from this discussion? Certainly the grapevine is an important part of any group or organization's communication network and well worth understanding.[20] It identifies for managers those confusing issues that employees consider important and anxiety provoking. It acts, therefore, as both a filter and a feedback mechanism, picking up the issues that employees consider relevant. Perhaps more important, again from a managerial point of view, it seems possible to analyze grapevine information and to predict its flow, given that only a small set of individuals (around 10 percent) actively passes on information to more than one other person. By assessing which liaison individuals will consider a given piece of information to be relevant, we can improve our ability to explain and predict the pattern of the grapevine.

Can management entirely eliminate rumors? No! What management

Exhibit 9-6 Suggestions for Reducing the Negative Consequences of Rumors

1. Announce timetables for making important decisions.
2. Explain decisions and behaviors that may appear inconsistent or secretive.
3. Emphasize the downside, as well as the upside, of current decisions and future plans.
4. Openly discuss worst-case possibilities—it is almost never as anxiety provoking as the unspoken fantasy.

Source: Adapted from L. Hirschhorn, "Managing Rumors," in L. Hirschhorn (ed.), *Cutting Back* (San Francisco: Jossey-Bass, 1983), pp. 54–56. With permission.

should do, however, is minimize the negative consequences of rumors by limiting their range and impact. Exhibit 9-6 offers a few suggestions for minimizing those negative consequences.

Nonverbal Communications

Anyone who has ever paid a visit to a singles bar or a nightclub is aware that communication need not be verbal in order to convey a message. A glance, a stare, a smile, a frown, a provocative body movement—they all convey meaning. This example illustrates that no discussion of communication would be complete without a discussion of **nonverbal communications**. This includes body movements, the intonations or emphasis we give to words, facial expressions, and the physical distance between the sender and receiver.

nonverbal communications
Messages conveyed through body movements, the intonations or emphasis we give to words, facial expressions, and the physical distance between the sender and receiver.

kinesics
The study of body motions.

The academic study of body motions has been labeled **kinesics**. It refers to gestures, facial configurations, and other movements of the body. It is a relatively new field, and it has been subject to far more conjecture and popularizing than the research findings support. Hence, while we acknowledge that body movement is an important segment of the study of communication and behavior, conclusions must be necessarily guarded. Recognizing this qualification, let us briefly consider the ways in which body motions convey meaning.

It has been argued that every body movement has a meaning and that no movement is accidental.[21] For example, through body language,

> We say, "Help me, I'm lonely. Take me, I'm available. Leave me alone, I'm depressed." And rarely do we send our messages consciously. We act out our state of being with nonverbal body language. We lift one eyebrow for disbelief. We rub our noses for puzzlement. We clasp our arms to isolate ourselves or to protect ourselves. We shrug our shoulders for indifference, wink one eye for intimacy, tap our fingers for impatience, slap our forehead for forgetfulness.[22]

While we may disagree with the specific meaning of these movements, body language adds to and often complicates verbal communication. A body position or movement does not by itself have a precise or universal meaning, but when it is linked with spoken language, it gives fuller meaning to a sender's message.

If you read the verbatim minutes of a meeting, you could not grasp the impact of what was said in the same way you could if you had been there or saw the meeting on video. Why? There is no record of nonverbal communication. The *intonations* or emphasis given to words or phrases is missing.

The *facial expression* of the instructor will also convey meaning. A snarling face says something different from a smile. Facial expressions, along with intonations, can show arrogance, aggressiveness, fear, shyness, and other characteristics that would never be communicated if you read a transcript of what had been said.

The way individuals space themselves in terms of *physical distance* also has meaning. What is considered proper spacing is largely dependent on cultural norms. For example, what is businesslike distance in some European countries would be viewed as intimate in many parts of North America. If someone stands closer to you than is considered appropriate, it may indicate aggressiveness or sexual interest. If farther away than usual, it may mean disinterest or displeasure with what is being said.

It is important for the receiver to be alert to these nonverbal aspects of communication. You should look for nonverbal cues as well as listen to the literal meaning of a sender's words. You should particularly be aware of contradictions between the messages. The boss may say that she is free to talk to you about that raise you have been seeking, but you may see nonverbal signals that suggest that this is not the time to discuss the subject. Regardless of what is being said, an individual who frequently glances at her wristwatch is giving the message that she would prefer to terminate the conversation. We misinform others when we express one emotion verbally, such as trust, but nonverbally communicate a contradictory message that reads, "I don't have confidence in you." These contradictions often suggest that "actions speak louder (and more accurately) than words."

◆ Actions often speak louder (and more accurately) than words.

Choice of Communication Channel

Bucknell University, a 3,600-student campus in central Pennsylvania, regularly uses e-mail to convey career-center, athletics-department, and general-interest announcements to students. But the administration was widely criticized recently for insensitivity by using this communication channel to transmit the news that a fellow student had apparently committed suicide. "We enjoy a close-knit, friendly atmosphere at Bucknell, and it hurts everyone when a tragedy occurs," said the school paper's editor in an editorial. "In these situations, only a sympathetic method of conveying information can soften the blow of bad news."[23] The school's administration had erred by selecting the wrong channel for its message.

Why do people choose one channel of communication over another—for instance, a phone call instead of a face-to-face talk? One answer might be: Anxiety! As you will remember, some people are apprehensive about certain kinds of communication. What about the 80 to 95 percent of the population who don't suffer from this problem? Is there any general insight we might be able to provide regarding choice of communication channel? The answer is a qualified "Yes." A model of media richness has been developed to explain channel selection among managers.[24]

Recent research has found that channels differ in their capacity to convey information. Some are rich in that they have the ability to (1) handle multiple cues simultaneously, (2) facilitate rapid feedback, and (3) be very personal. Others are lean in that they score low on these three factors. As Exhibit 9-7 illustrates, face-to-face talk scores highest in terms of **channel richness** because it provides for the maximum amount of information to be

channel richness
The amount of information that can be transmitted during a communication episode.

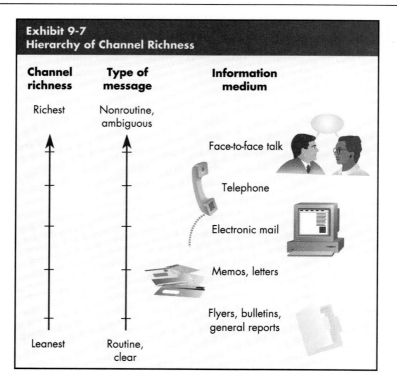

Exhibit 9-7
Hierarchy of Channel Richness

Channel richness	Type of message	Information medium
Richest	Nonroutine, ambiguous	Face-to-face talk
		Telephone
		Electronic mail
		Memos, letters
Leanest	Routine, clear	Flyers, bulletins, general reports

transmitted during a communication episode. That is, it offers multiple information cues (words, postures, facial expressions, gestures, intonations), immediate feedback (both verbal and nonverbal), and the personal touch of "being there." Impersonal written media such as bulletins and general reports rate lowest in richness.

The choice of one channel over another depends on whether the message is routine or nonroutine. The former types of messages tend to be straightforward and have a minimum of ambiguity. The latter are likely to be complicated and have the potential for misunderstanding. Managers can communicate routine messages efficiently through channels that are lower in richness. However, they can communicate nonroutine messages effectively only by selecting rich channels. Referring back to our opening example at Bucknell University, it appears that the administration's problem was using a channel relatively low in richness (e-mail) to convey a message that, because of its nonroutine nature and complexity, should have been conveyed using a rich communication medium.

Evidence indicates that high-performing managers tend to be more media sensitive than low-performing managers.[25] That is, they're better able to match appropriate media richness with the ambiguity involved in the communication.

The media richness model is consistent with organizational trends and practices during the past decade. It is not just coincidence that more and more senior managers have been using meetings to facilitate communication and regularly leaving the isolated sanctuary of their executive offices to manage by walking around. These executives are relying on richer channels of communication to transmit the more ambiguous messages they need to convey. The past decade has been characterized by organizations closing facilities, imposing large layoffs, restructuring, merging, consolidating, and introducing new products and services at an accelerated pace—all nonroutine messages high in ambiguity and requiring the use of channels that can convey a large amount of information. It is not surprising, therefore, to see the most effective managers expanding their use of rich channels.

Barriers to Effective Communication

We conclude our discussion of communication fundamentals by reviewing some of the more prominent barriers to effective communication of which you should be aware.

FILTERING **Filtering** refers to a sender manipulating information so that it will be seen more favorably by the receiver. For example, when a manager tells his boss what he feels his boss wants to hear, he is filtering information. Does this happen much in organizations? Sure! As information is passed up to senior executives, it has to be condensed and synthesized by underlings so those on top don't become overloaded with information. The personal interests and perceptions of what is important by those doing the synthesizing are going to result in filtering. As a former group vice president of General Motors described it, the filtering of communications through levels at GM made it impossible for senior managers to get objective information because "lower-level specialists provided information in such a way that they would get the answer they wanted. I know. I used to be down below and do it."[26]

The major determinant of filtering is the number of levels in an organization's structure. The more vertical levels in the organization's hierarchy, the more opportunities there are for filtering.

SELECTIVE PERCEPTION We have mentioned selective perception before in this book. It appears again because the receivers in the communication process selectively see and hear based on their needs, motivations, experience, background, and other personal characteristics. Receivers also project their interests and expectations into communications as they decode them. The employment interviewer who expects a female job applicant to put her family ahead of her career is likely to see that in female applicants, regardless of whether the applicants feel that way or not. As we said in chapter 3, we don't see reality; rather, we interpret what we see and call it reality.

DEFENSIVENESS When people feel that they're being threatened, they tend to react in ways that reduce their ability to achieve mutual understanding. That is, they become defensive—engaging in behaviors such as verbally attacking others, making sarcastic remarks, being overly judgmental, and questioning others' motives. So when individuals interpret another's message as threatening, they often respond in ways that retard effective communication.

filtering
A sender's manipulation of information so that it will be seen more favorably by the receiver.

◆ The meaning of words are not in the words; they are in us.

LANGUAGE Words mean different things to different people. "The meanings of words are not in the words; they are in us."[27] Age, education, and cultural background are three of the more obvious variables that influence the language a person uses and the definitions he or she gives to words. Rap-artist

From Concepts to Skills

Effective Listening

Too many people take listening skills for granted.[28] They confuse hearing with listening. What's the difference? Hearing is merely picking up sound vibrations. Listening is making sense out of what we hear. That is, listening requires paying attention, interpreting, and remembering sound stimuli.

The average person normally speaks at the rate of 125 to 200 words per minute. However, the average listener can comprehend up to 400 words per minute. This leaves a lot of time for idle mind-wandering while listening. For most people, it also means they've acquired a number of bad listening habits to fill in the "idle time."

The following eight behaviors are associated with effective listening skills. If you want to improve your listening skills, look to these behaviors as guides:

1. *Make eye contact.* How do you feel when somebody doesn't look at you when you're speaking? If you're like most people, you're likely to interpret this as aloofness or disinterest. We may listen with our ears, but others tend to judge whether we're really listening by looking at our eyes.

2. *Exhibit affirmative head nods and appropriate facial expressions.* The effective listener shows interest in what is being said. How? Through nonverbal signals. Affirmative head nods and appropriate facial expressions, when added to good eye contact, convey to the speaker that you're listening.

3. *Avoid distracting actions or gestures.* The other side of showing interest is avoiding actions that suggest your mind is somewhere else. When listening, don't look at your watch, shuffle papers, play with your pencil, or engage in similar distractions. They make the speaker feel you're bored or uninterested. Maybe more importantly, they indicate that you aren't fully attentive and may be missing part of the message that the speaker wants to convey.

4. *Ask questions.* The critical listener analyzes what he or she hears and asks questions. This behavior provides clarification, ensures understanding, and assures the speaker that you're listening.

5. *Paraphrase.* Paraphrasing means restating what the speaker has said in your own words. The effective listener uses phrases like: "What I hear you saying is. . . or "Do you mean . . . ?" Why rephrase what's already been said? Two reasons! First, it's an excellent control device to check on whether you're listening carefully. You can't paraphrase accurately if your mind is wandering or if you're thinking about what you're going to say next. Second, it's a control for accuracy. By rephrasing what the speaker has said in your own words and feeding it back to the speaker, you verify the accuracy of your understanding.

6. *Avoid interrupting the speaker.* Let the speaker complete his or her thought before you try to respond. Don't try to second-guess where the speaker's thoughts are going. When the speaker is finished, you'll know it!

7. *Don't overtalk.* Most of us would rather speak our own ideas than listen to what someone else says. Too many of us listen only because it's the price we have to pay to get people to let us talk. While talking may be more fun and silence may be uncomfortable, you can't talk and listen at the same time. The good listener recognizes this fact and doesn't overtalk.

8. *Make smooth transitions between the roles of speaker and listener.* When you're a student sitting in a lecture hall, you find it relatively easy to get into an

(continued)

effective listening frame of mind. Why? Because communication is essentially one-way: The teacher talks and you listen. But the teacher–student dyad is atypical. In most work situations, you're continually shifting back and forth between the roles of speaker and listener. The effective listener, therefore, makes transitions smoothly from speaker to listener and back to speaker. From a listening perspective, this means concentrating on what a speaker has to say and practicing not thinking about what you're going to say as soon as you get your chance.

Snoop Doggy Dogg and political-analyst/author William F. Buckley, Jr., both speak English. But the language each uses is vastly different from the other. In fact, the typical "person on the street" might have difficulty understanding either of these individuals' vocabulary.

In an organization, employees usually come from diverse backgrounds and, therefore, have different patterns of speech. Additionally, the grouping of employees into departments creates specialists who develop their own jargon or technical language. In large organizations, members are also frequently widely dispersed geographically—even operating in different countries—and individuals in each locale will use terms and phrases that are unique to their area. And the existence of vertical levels can also cause language problems. The language of senior executives, for instance, can be mystifying to operative employees not familiar with management jargon.

The point is that while you and I speak a common language—English—our usage of that language is far from uniform. If we knew how each of us modified the language, communication difficulties would be minimized. The problem is that members in an organization usually don't know how others with whom they interact have modified the language. Senders tend to assume that the words and terms they use mean the same to the receiver as they do to them. This, of course, is often incorrect, thus creating communication difficulties.

In Practice: Effective Employee Communications in Leading Companies Undergoing Dramatic Changes

As we've noted throughout this book, organizations around the world are restructuring in order to reduce costs and improve competitiveness. Almost all *Fortune* 100 companies, for instance, have scaled back the size of their labor force in the last half-dozen years through attrition and layoffs.

A recent study looked at employee communications programs in ten leading companies that had successfully undertaken major restructuring programs.[29] The companies were chosen because they had developed reputations for having excellent internal communication programs. The authors were interested in seeing if there were some common factors that determined the effectiveness of these firms' employee communications. The authors specifically chose companies that had undergone restructuring and reorganizations because they believed that the true test of a firm's communication effectiveness was how well it worked in times of major organizational change.

The authors found eight factors that were related to the effectiveness of employee communications in these ten firms. Since the companies studied came from a variety of industries and organizational settings, the authors propose that these eight characteristics should apply to many types of organizations.

Let's take a look at these eight factors because they provide some research-based guidance to managers in helping decide how best to communicate with employees.

The CEO Must Be Committed to the Importance of Communication

The most significant factor to a successful employee-communications program is the chief executive's leadership. He or she must be philosophically and behaviorally committed to the notion that communicating with employees is essential to the achievement of the organization's goals. If the organization's senior executive is committed to communication through his or her words and actions, it "trickles down" to the rest of the organization.

In addition to espousing a philosophical commitment to employee communications, the CEO must be a skilled and visible communications role model and be willing to personally deliver key messages. The CEOs in this study spent a significant amount of their time talking with employees, responding to questions, listening to their concerns, and conveying their vision of the company. Importantly, they tended to do this "in person." They didn't delegate this task to other managers. By personally championing the cause of good communication, they lessen employee fears about changes that are being implemented and set the precedent for other managers to follow.

Managers Match Actions and Words

Closely related to CEO support and involvement is managerial action. As we've noted previously, actions speak louder than words. When the implicit messages that managers send contradict the official messages as conveyed in formal communications, the managers lose credibility with employees. Employees will listen to what management has to say regarding changes being made and where the company is going, but these words must be backed up by matching actions.

Ed Clark, president and CEO of Canada Trust, shows his commitment to communication by personally visiting CT's 400 branch locations. His philosophy is that you can't sit in an office and tell people what to do. He frequently holds pizza and ginger ale sessions with employees. Clark's approachable style and ability to explain complex issues without talking down to listeners has earned him the loyalty of employees.

Commitment to Two-Way Communication

Ineffective programs are dominated by downward communication. Successful programs balance downward and upward communication.

How does a firm promote upward communication and stimulate employee dialogue? The company that displayed the highest commitment to two-way communication used interactive television broadcasts that allowed employees to call in questions and get responses from top management. Company publications had question-and-answer columns and employees were encouraged to submit questions. The company developed a grievance procedure that processed complaints quickly. Managers were trained in feedback techniques and then were rewarded for using them.

General Electric and Hallmark are two companies that have perfected two-way communication. GE, for instance, launched a companywide town meeting effort in the late 1980s. Managers give credit to these meetings for "uncovering all kinds of crazy stuff we were doing."[30] And Hallmark regularly selects 50 to 100 nonmanagement employees at random for a 90-minute face-to-face discussion with the company's CEO.[31]

Emphasis on Face-to-Face Communication

In times of uncertainty and change—which characterize major restructuring efforts—employees have lots of fears and concerns. Is their job in jeopardy? Will they have to learn new skills? Is their work group going to be disbanded? Consistent with our previous discussion of channel richness, these messages are nonroutine and ambiguous. The maximum amount of information can be transmitted through face-to-face conversation. Because the firms in this study were all undergoing significant changes, their senior executives got out and personally carried their messages to operating employees. Candid, open, face-to-face communication with employees presents executives as living, breathing people who understand the needs and concerns of the workers.

Shared Responsibility for Employee Communications

Top management provides the "big picture"—where the company is going. Supervisors link the big picture to their work group and to individual employees. Every manager has some responsibility in ensuring that employees are well informed; with the implications for changes becoming more specific as they flow down the organization hierarchy.

People prefer to hear about the changes that might affect them from their boss, not from their peers or from the grapevine. This requires top management to keep middle and lower managers fully apprised of planned changes. And it means that middle and lower-level managers must quickly share information with their work group in order to minimize ambiguity.

Dealing with Bad News

Organizations with effective employee communications aren't afraid to confront bad news. In fact, they typically have a high bad-news to good-news ratio. This doesn't mean that these firms have more problems; rather that they don't penalize the "bearer of bad news."

Increasingly, many corporations are using their company publications to keep employees current on setbacks as well as upbeat news. Allied-Signal's *Horizons* magazine, for instance, carried a recent article by the company's president on the loss of a major bid from Northrop.[32]

All organizations will, at times, have product failures, delivery delays, customer complaints, or similar problems. The issue is how comfortable people feel in communicating those problems. When bad news is candidly reported, a climate is created in which people aren't afraid to be truthful and good news gains increased credibility.

The Message Is Shaped for Its Intended Audience

Different people in the organization have different information needs. What is important to supervisors may not be so to middle managers. Similarly, what is interesting information to someone in product planning may be irrelevant to someone in accounting.

What information do individuals and groups want to know? When do they need to know it? In what form (at home, newsletter, e-mail, team meeting) is the best way for them to receive it? Employees vary in the type of information they need and the most effective way for them to receive it. Managers need to recognize this and design their communication program accordingly.

Treat Communication as an Ongoing Process

These leading companies viewed employee communications as a critical management process. This is illustrated by five common activities in which these firms engaged.

MANAGERS CONVEY THE RATIONALE UNDERLYING DECISIONS As change occurs more frequently, and their future becomes less certain, employees increasingly want to know the rationale underlying the decisions and changes that are being made. *Why* is this occurring? *How* will this affect me?

As the historical social contract that traded employee loyalty for job security has eroded, employees have new expectations from management. In times of permanent employment, comprehensive explanations of management decisions weren't as critical for employees because no matter what the changes, their jobs were relatively secure. But under the new covenant, with workers assuming a much greater responsibility for their own careers, employees feel a need for more information so they can make intelligent career decisions. Employees are looking for something from management to make up the difference between what they used to have guaranteed and what they have now. One of those things is information.

TIMELINESS IS VITAL It's important for managers to communicate what they know, when they know it. Employees don't want to be treated as children, parceled out bits of information piece by piece or kept from information for fear that it might be misconstrued. Give people the facts as soon as they become available. This lessens the power of the grapevine and increases management's credibility. The cost of not communicating in a timely manner is disaffection, anger, and loss of trust.

The management of Arco Chemical Company's European operations staged this photo to illustrate the importance of quickly sharing information with employees. Rapid communication is key to customer excellence throughout Arco Chemical, where teams from multiple departments share feedback from customer surveys and visits to customer locations.

New technologies make speedy communications possible. Federal Express, as a case in point, has built a $10 million internal television network so it can communicate quickly with employees. When FedEx purchased Flying Tigers in 1989, the company's chief executive was on the air with the announcement just minutes after the announcement hit the financial wires.[33]

COMMUNICATE CONTINUOUSLY Communication should be continuous, particularly during periods of change or crisis. When employees need information and it's not forthcoming, they'll fall back on informal channels to fill the void, even if those channels provide only unsubstantiated rumors. In those organizations where management strives to keep the information continuously flowing, employees are also more forgiving of the occasional error or omission.

LINK THE "BIG PICTURE" WITH THE "LITTLE PICTURE" Truly effective communication does not occur until employees understand how the "big picture" affects them and their jobs. Changes in the economy, among competitors in the industry, or in the organization as a whole must be translated into implications for each location, department, and employee. This responsibility falls most directly on employees' direct supervisors.

DON'T DICTATE THE WAY PEOPLE SHOULD FEEL ABOUT THE NEWS Employees don't want to be told how they should interpret and feel about change. Trust and openness are not enhanced by claims like "These new changes are really exciting!" or "You're going to like the way that the department is being restructured!" More often than not, these attempts to sway opinion only provoke antagonistic responses.

It's more effective to communicate, "who, what, when, where, why, and how" and then let employees draw their own conclusions.

Current Issues in Communication

We close this chapter by addressing four current issues: Why do men and women often have difficulty communicating with each other? What are the implications of the "politically correct" movement on communications in organizations? How can individuals improve their cross-cultural communications? And how is electronics changing the way people communicate with each other in organizations?

Communication Barriers between Women and Men

Research by Deborah Tannen provides us with some important insights into the differences between men and women in terms of their conversational styles.[34] In particular, she has been able to explain why gender often creates oral communication barriers.

The essence of Tannen's research is that men use talk to emphasize status, while women use it to create connection. Tannen states that communication is a continual balancing act, juggling the conflicting needs for intimacy and independence. Intimacy emphasizes closeness and commonalities. Independence emphasizes separateness and differences. But here's the kick: Women speak and hear a language of connection and intimacy; men speak and hear a language of status and independence. So, for many men, conversations are primarily a means to preserve independence and maintain status in a hierarchical social order. For many women, conversations are negotiations for closeness in which people try to seek and give confirmation and support. A few examples will illustrate Tannen's thesis:

◆ **Men use talk to emphasize status, while women use it to create connection.**

Men frequently complain that women talk on and on about their problems. Women criticize men for not listening. What's happening is that when men hear a problem, they frequently assert their desire for independence and control by offering solutions. Many women, on the other hand, view telling a problem as a means to promote closeness. The women present the problem to gain support and connection, not to get the male's advice. Mutual understanding is symmetrical. But giving advice is asymmetrical—it sets the advice giver up as more knowledgeable, more reasonable, and more in control. This contributes to distancing men and women in their efforts to communicate.

Men are often more direct than women in conversation. A man might say, "I think you're wrong on that point." A woman might say, "Have you looked at the marketing department's research report on that point?" (the implication being that the report will show the error). Men frequently see female indirectness as "covert" or "sneaky," but women are not as concerned as men with the status and one-upmanship that directness often creates.

Finally, men often criticize women for seeming to apologize all the time. Men tend to see the phrase "I'm sorry" as a weakness because they interpret the phrase to mean the woman is accepting blame, when he knows she's not to blame. The woman also knows she is not to blame. The problem is that women typically use "I'm sorry" to express regret: "I know you must feel bad about this; I do, too."

"Politically Correct" Communication

What words do you use to describe a colleague who is wheelchair bound? What terms do you use in addressing a female customer? How do you communicate with a brand-new client who is not like you? The right answers can mean the difference between losing a client, an employee, a lawsuit, a harassment claim, or a job.[35]

Most of us are acutely aware of how our vocabulary has been modified to reflect political correctness. For instance, most of us have cleansed the words *handicapped*, *blind*, and *elderly* from our vocabulary—and replaced them with terms like *physically challenged*, *visually impaired*, and *senior*. The *Los Angeles Times*, for instance, allows its journalists to use the term *old age* but cautions that the onset of old age varies from "person to person," so a group of 75-year-olds aren't necessarily all old.[36]

We must be sensitive to others' feelings. Certain words can and do stereotype, intimidate, and insult individuals. In an increasingly diverse workforce, we must be sensitive to how words might offend others. But there's a downside to political correctness. It's shrinking our vocabulary and making it more difficult for people to communicate. To illustrate, you probably know what these four terms mean: *death*, *quotas*, *dwarfs*, and *women*. But each of these words also has been found to offend one or more groups. They've been replaced with terms like *negative-patient-care outcome*, *educational equity*, *vertically challenged*, and *people of gender*. The problem is that this latter group of terms is much less likely to convey a uniform message than the words they replaced. You know what death means; I know what death means; but can you be sure that "negative-patient-care outcome" will be consistently defined as

THE FAR SIDE   By GARY LARSON

Larson 6-9   © 1994 FarWorks, Inc./Dist. by Universal Press Syndicate

"Well, actually, Doreen, I rather resent being called a 'swamp thing.' ...I prefer the term 'wetlands-challenged mutant.'"

Exhibit 9-8

Source: THE FAR SIDE copyright © 1994 Farworks, Inc. Dist. by Universal Press Syndicate. Reprinted with permission. All rights reserved.

synonymous with death? No! For instance, the phrase could also mean a longer stay than expected in the hospital or notification that your insurance company won't pay your hospital bill.

Some critics, for humor's sake, enjoy carrying political correctness to the extreme. Even those of us with thinning scalps, who aren't too thrilled at being labeled "bald," have to smirk when we're referred to as "follically challenged." But our concern here is with how politically correct language is contributing a new barrier to effective communication.

Words are the primary means by which people communicate. When we eliminate words from usage because they're politically incorrect, we reduce our options for conveying messages in the clearest and most accurate form. For the most part, the larger the vocabulary used by a sender and a receiver, the greater the opportunity to accurately transmit messages. By removing certain words from our vocabulary, we make it harder to communicate accurately. When we further replace these words with new terms whose meanings are less well understood, we have reduced the likelihood that our messages will be received as we had intended them.

We must be sensitive to how our choice of words might offend others. But we also have to be careful not to sanitize our language to the point where it clearly restricts clarity of communication. There is no simple solution to this dilemma. However, you should be aware of the trade-offs and the need to find a proper balance.

Cross-Cultural Communication

Effective communication is difficult under the best of conditions. Cross-cultural factors clearly create the potential for increased communication problems. This is illustrated in Exhibit 9-9. A gesture that is well understood and acceptable in one culture can be meaningless or lewd in another.[37]

One author has identified four specific problems related to language difficulties in cross-cultural communications.[38]

First, there are *barriers caused by semantics*. As we've noted previously, words mean different things to different people. This is particularly true for people from different national cultures. Some words, for instance, don't translate between cultures. Understanding the word *sisu* will help you in communicating with people from Finland, but this word is untranslatable into English. It means something akin to "guts" or "dogged persistence." Similarly, the new capitalists in Russia may have difficulty communicating with their British or Canadian counterparts because English terms such as *efficiency*, *free market*, and *regulation* are not directly translatable into Russian.

Second, there are *barriers caused by word connotations*. Words imply different things in different languages. Negotiations between Americans and Japanese executives, for instance, are made more difficult because the Japanese word *hai* translates as "yes," but its connotation may be "yes, I'm listening," rather than "yes, I agree."

Third are *barriers caused by tone differences*. In some cultures, language is formal, in others it's informal. In some cultures, the tone changes depending on the context: people speaking differently at home, in social situations, and at work. Using a personal, informal style in a situation where a more formal style is expected can be embarrassing and off-putting.

Fourth, there are *barriers caused by differences among perceptions*. People who speak different languages actually view the world in different ways.

Exhibit 9-9
Hand Gestures Mean Different Things in Different Countries

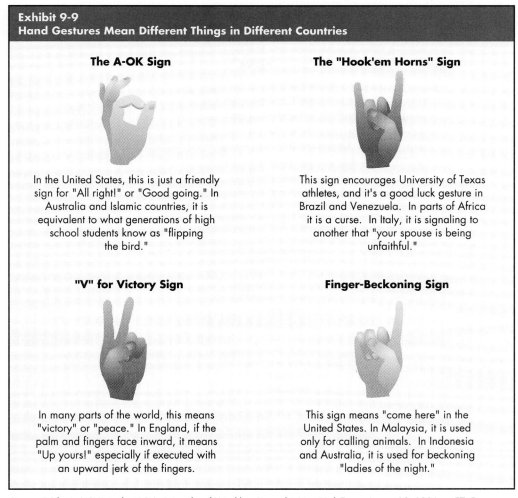

The A-OK Sign

In the United States, this is just a friendly sign for "All right!" or "Good going." In Australia and Islamic countries, it is equivalent to what generations of high school students know as "flipping the bird."

The "Hook'em Horns" Sign

This sign encourages University of Texas athletes, and it's a good luck gesture in Brazil and Venezuela. In parts of Africa it is a curse. In Italy, it is signaling to another that "your spouse is being unfaithful."

"V" for Victory Sign

In many parts of the world, this means "victory" or "peace." In England, if the palm and fingers face inward, it means "Up yours!" especially if executed with an upward jerk of the fingers.

Finger-Beckoning Sign

This sign means "come here" in the United States. In Malaysia, it is used only for calling animals. In Indonesia and Australia, it is used for beckoning "ladies of the night."

Source: "What's A-O.K. in the U.S.A. Is Lewd and Worthless Beyond," *New York Times*, August 18, 1996, p. E7. From Roger E. Axtell, GESTURES: The Do's and Taboos of Body Language Around the World. Copyright © 1991. This material is used by permission of John Wiley & Sons, Inc.

Eskimos perceive snow differently because they have many words for it. Thais perceive "no" differently than Americans because the former have no such word in their vocabulary.

When communicating with people from a different culture, what can you do to reduce misperceptions, misinterpretations, and misevaluations? Following these four rules can be helpful:[39]

1. *Assume differences until similarity is proven.* Most of us assume that others are more similar to us than they actually are. But people from different countries often are very different from us. So you are far less likely to make an error if you assume others are different from you rather than assuming similarity until difference is proven.

2. *Emphasize description rather than interpretation or evaluation.* Interpreting or evaluating what someone has said or done, in contrast to description, is based more on the observer's culture and background than on the observed situation. As a result, delay judgment until you've had sufficient time to observe and interpret the situation from the differing perspectives of all the cultures involved.

3. *Practice empathy*. Before sending a message, put yourself in the recipient's shoes. What are his or her values, experiences, and frames of reference? What do you know about his or her education, upbringing, and background that can give you added insight? Try to see the other person as he or she really is.

4. *Treat your interpretations as a working hypothesis*. Once you've developed an explanation for a new situation or think you empathize with someone from a foreign culture, treat your interpretation as a hypothesis that needs further testing rather than as a certainty. Carefully assess the feedback provided by recipients to see if it confirms your hypothesis. For important decisions or communiqués, you can also check with other foreign and home-country colleagues to make sure that your interpretations are on target.

Electronic Communications

Until the last 15 or to 20 years, there were very few technological breakthroughs that significantly affected organizational communications. Early in this century, the telephone dramatically reduced personal, face-to-face communication. The popularization of the photocopy machine in the late 1960s was the death bell for carbon paper and made the copying of documents faster and easier. But beginning in the early 1980s, we've been subjected to an onslaught of new electronic technologies that are largely reshaping the way we communicate in organizations.[40] These include pagers, facsimile machines, video conferencing, electronic meetings, e-mail, cellular phones, voice messaging, and palm-sized personal communicators.

Electronic communications no longer make it necessary for you to be at your work station or desk to be "available." Pagers, cellular phones, and personal communicators allow you to be reached when you're in a meeting, during your lunch break, while visiting in a customer's office across town, or during a golf game on Saturday morning. The line between an employee's work and nonwork life is no longer distinct. In the electronic age, all employees can theoretically be "on call" 24 hours a day.

Organizational boundaries become less relevant as a result of electronic communications. Why? Because networked computers—that is, computers that are interlinked to communicate with each other—allow employees to jump vertical levels within the organization, work full time at home or someplace other than an organizationally operated facility, and carry ongoing communications with people in other organizations. The market researcher who wants to discuss an issue with the vice president of marketing (who is three levels up in the hierarchy), can by-pass the people in between and send an e-mail message directly. And in so doing, the traditional status hierarchy, largely determined by level and access, becomes essentially negated. Or that same market researcher may choose to live in the Cayman Islands and work at home via telecommuting rather than do his or her job in the company's Chicago office. And when an employee's computer is linked to suppliers' and customers' computers, the boundaries separating organizations become further blurred. Hundreds of suppliers, for instance, are linked into Wal-Mart's computers. This allows people at companies like Levi Strauss to be able to monitor Wal-Mart's inventory of

◆ Organizational boundaries become less relevant as a result of electronic communications.

Investment bank Morgan Stanley distributes data and information to employees at its 37 offices around the world on the company's intranet, an internal corporate web. For example, the global network allows traders in Japan to receive up-to-the-minute information on securities transactions from colleagues in New York. Morgan Stanley has also connected its "hoot and holler" worldwide voice messaging system to its intranet, allowing salespeople to receive messages from their workstation speakers on the trading floor.

Levi jeans and to replace merchandise as needed, clouding the distinction between Levi and Wal-Mart employees.

Although the telephone allowed people to transmit verbal messages instantly, it's only been very recently that this same speed became available for the written word. In the mid-1960s, organizations were almost completely dependent on interoffice memos for internal, on-site messages, and on wire services and the post office for external messages. Then came overnight express delivery and fax machines. Today, with almost all organizations having introduced e-mail and an increasing number providing their employees with access to the Internet, written communications can be transmitted with all the speed of the telephone.

Electronic communications have revolutionized both the ability to access other people and to reach them almost instantaneously. Unfortunately, this access and speed have come with some costs. Electronic mail, for instance, doesn't provide the nonverbal communication component that the face-to-face meeting does. Nor does e-mail convey the emotions and nuances that come through from verbal intonations in telephone conversations. Similarly, it's been noted that meetings have historically served two distinct purposes—fulfilling a need for group affiliation and serving as a forum for completing task work.[41] Video conferences and electronic meetings do a good job at supporting tasks but don't address affiliation needs. For people with a high need for social contact, a heavy reliance on electronic communications is likely to lead to lower job satisfaction.

Summary and Implications for Managers

A careful review of this chapter finds a common theme regarding the relationship between communication and employee satisfaction: the less the uncertainty, the greater the satisfaction. Distortions, ambiguities, and incongruities all increase uncertainty and, hence, they have a negative impact on satisfaction.[42]

The less distortion that occurs in communication, the more that goals, feedback, and other management messages to employees will be received as they were intended.[43] This, in turn, should reduce ambiguities and clarify the group's task. Extensive use of vertical, lateral, and informal channels will increase communication flow, reduce uncertainty, and improve group performance and satisfaction. We should also expect incongruities between verbal and nonverbal communiqués to increase uncertainty and to reduce satisfaction.

Findings in the chapter further suggest that the goal of perfect communication is unattainable. Yet, there is evidence that demonstrates a positive relationship between effective communication (which includes factors such as perceived trust, perceived accuracy, desire for interaction, top-management receptiveness, and upward information requirements) and worker productivity.[44] Choosing the correct channel, being an effective listener, and utilizing feedback may, therefore, make for more effective communication. But the human factor generates distortions that can never be fully eliminated. The communication process represents an exchange of messages, but the outcome is meanings that may or may not approximate those that the sender intended. Whatever the sender's expectations, the decoded message in the mind of the receiver represents his or her reality. And it is this "reality" that will determine performance, along with the individual's level of motivation and his or her degree of satisfaction. The issue of motivation is critical, so we should briefly review how communication is central in determining an individual's degree of motivation.

You will remember from expectancy theory that the degree of effort an individual exerts depends on his or her perception of the effort–performance, performance–reward, and reward–goal satisfaction linkages. If individuals are not given the data necessary to make the perceived probability of these linkages high, motivation will suffer. If rewards are not made clear, if the criteria for determining and measuring performance are ambiguous, or if individuals are not relatively certain that their effort will lead to satisfactory performance, then effort will be reduced. So communication plays a significant role in determining the level of employee motivation.

A final implication from the communication literature relates to predicting turnover. The use of realistic job previews acts as a communication device for clarifying role expectations (see the "Counterpoint" in chapter 3). Employees who have been exposed to a realistic job preview have more accurate information about that job. Comparisons of turnover rates between organizations that use the realistic job preview versus either no preview or only presentation of positive job information show that those not using the realistic preview have, on average, almost 29 percent higher turnover.[45] This makes a strong case for managers to convey honest and accurate information about a job to applicants during the recruiting and selection process.

For Review

1. Describe the functions that communication provides within a group or organization. Give an example of each.

2. Contrast encoding and decoding.

3. Describe the communication process and identify its key components. Give an example of how this process operates with both oral and written messages.

4. Identify three common small-group networks and give the advantages of each.

5. What is *kinesics*? Why is it important?

6. What characterizes a communication that is rich in capacity to convey information?

7. What conditions stimulate the emergence of rumors?

8. Describe how political correctness can hinder effective communication.

9. List four specific problems related to language difficulties in cross-cultural communication.

10. What are the managerial implications from the research contrasting male and female communication styles?

For Discussion

1. "Ineffective communication is the fault of the sender." Do you agree or disagree? Discuss.

2. What can you do to improve the likelihood that your communiqués will be received and understood as you intend?

3. How might managers use the grapevine for their benefit?

4. Using the concept of channel richness, give examples of messages best conveyed by e-mail, by face-to-face communication, and on the company bulletin board.

5. Why do you think so many people are poor listeners?

The Case for Mutual Understanding: The Johari Window

The Johari Window (named after its creators, Joseph Luft and Harry Ingram) is a popular model, used by training specialists, for evaluating communication styles. The essence of the model is the belief that mutual understanding improves perceptual accuracy and communication.

The model classifies an individual's tendencies to facilitate or hinder interpersonal communication along two dimensions: exposure and feedback. Exposure is defined as the extent to which an individual openly and candidly divulges feelings, experiences, and information when trying to communicate. Feedback is the extent to which an individual successfully elicits exposure from others. As shown in Exhibit 9-A, these dimensions translate into four "windows"—open, blind, hidden, and unknown. The *open* window is information known to you as well as others. The *blind* window encompasses certain things about you that are apparent to others but not to yourself. This is the result of no one ever telling you or because you're defensively blocking them out. The *hidden* window is information known by you and unknown by others. It encompasses those feelings that we're aware of but don't share with others for fear they'll think less of us or possibly use the information against us. The *unknown* window includes feelings, experience, and information that neither you nor others are aware of.

Although there is no substantive body of research to support the following conclusion, the Johari Window model argues for more open communication on the assumption that people understand each other better when the amount of information in the open area increases. If you accept this conclusion, how would you increase the open area? According to Luft and Ingram, you do this through disclosure and feedback. By increasing self-disclosure, you reveal your inner feelings and experiences. In addition, the evidence suggests that self-disclosure encourages others to be similarly forthcoming and open. So disclosure breeds more disclosure. When others provide feedback on their insights into your behavior, you reduce your blind window.

Although advocates of the Johari Window encourage a climate of openness, where individuals self-disclose freely with each other, they recognize that there are conditions where guarded communication may be appropriate. These include transitory relationships, where one party has violated trust in the past, in competitive situations, or where the culture of the organization doesn't support openness. Although critics might argue that one or more of those conditions just about covers almost all communication situations in organizations, proponents of the Johari Window are more optimistic. They see openness, authenticity, and honesty to be valued qualities in interpersonal relationships. Although they don't say so directly, they imply that it's in the self-interest of the individual to expand the size of the open window by increasing self-disclosure and by being willing to listen to feedback from others even if it's unflattering.

Based on J. Luft, *Group Processes*, 3rd ed. (Palo Alto, CA: Mayfield Publishing, 1984), pp. 11–20; and J. Hall, "Communication Revisited," *California Management Review*, Fall 1973, pp. 56–67.

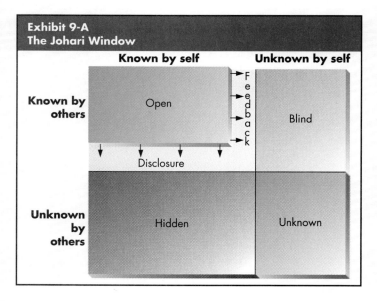

Exhibit 9-A
The Johari Window

	Known by self	Unknown by self
Known by others	Open	Blind
Unknown by others	Hidden	Unknown

Feedback

Disclosure

The Case for Ambiguous Communication

The argument for mutual understanding and openness, while honorable, is incredibly naive. It assumes that communicators actually want to achieve mutual understanding and that openness is the preferred means toward that end. Unfortunately, that argument overlooks a very basic fact: It's often in the sender's and/or receiver's best interest to keep communication ambiguous.

"Lack of communication" has become the explanation for every problem in an organization. If the newly "empowered" workforce is unmotivated, it's a communication problem. If the quality-improvement program fails to garner the promised benefits, it's a communication problem. If employees ignore or abuse customers despite training that instructs them otherwise, it's a communication problem.

We're continually hearing that problems would go away if we could "just communicate better." Some of the basic assumptions underlying this view need to be looked at carefully.

One assumption is that better communication will necessarily reduce strife and conflict. But each individual's definition of better communication, like his or her definition of virtuous conduct, becomes that of having the other party accept his or her views, which would reduce conflict at that party's expense. A better understanding of the situation might serve only to underline the differences rather than to resolve them. Indeed, many of the techniques thought of as poor communication were apparently developed with the aim of bypassing or avoiding confrontation.

Another assumption that grows from this view is that when a conflict has existed for a long time and shows every sign of continuing, lack of communication must be one of the basic problems. Usually, if the situation is examined more carefully,

plenty of communication will be found; the problem is, again, one of equating communication with agreement.

Still a third assumption is that it is always in the interest of at least one of the parties to an interaction, and often of both, to attain maximum clarity as measured by some more or less objective standard. Aside from the difficulty of setting up this standard—whose standard? and doesn't this give him or her control of the situation?—there are some sequences, and perhaps many of them, in which it is in the interests of both parties to leave the situation as fuzzy and undefined as possible. This is notably true in culturally or personally sensitive and taboo areas involving prejudices, preconceptions, and so on, but it can also be true when the area is merely a new one that could be seriously distorted by using old definitions and old solutions.

Too often we forget that keeping communications fuzzy cuts down on questions, permits faster decision making, minimizes objections, reduces opposition, makes it easier to deny one's earlier statements, preserves freedom to change one's mind, helps to preserve mystique and hide insecurities, allows one to say several things at the same time, permits one to say "No" diplomatically, and helps to avoid confrontation and anxiety.

If you want to see the fine art of ambiguous communication up close, all you have to do is watch a television interview with a politician who is running for office. The interviewer attempts to get specific information, while the politician tries to retain multiple possible interpretations. Such ambiguous communications allow the politician to approach his or her ideal image of being "all things to all people."

Based on C.O. Kursh, "The Benefits of Poor Communication," *The Psychoanalytic Review,* Summer–Fall 1971, pp. 189–208; E.M. Eisenberg and M.G. Witten, "Reconsidering Openness in Organizational Communication," *Academy of Management Review,* July 1987, pp. 418–26; and B. Filipczak, "Obfuscation Resounding," *Training,* July 1995, pp. 29–36.

Learning about Yourself Exercise

Listening Self-Inventory

Go through this 15-item questionnaire twice. The first time, mark the yes or no box next to each question. Mark as truthfully as you can in light of your behavior in recent meetings or gatherings you attended. The second time, mark a plus (+) next to your answer if you are satisfied with that answer, or a minus (−) next to the answer if you wish you could have answered that question differently.

	Yes	No	+ or −
1. I frequently attempt to listen to several conversations at the same time.	___	___	___
2. I like people to give me only the facts and then let me make my own interpretations.	___	___	___
3. I sometimes pretend to pay attention to people.	___	___	___
4. I consider myself a good judge of nonverbal communications.	___	___	___
5. I usually know what another person is going to say before he or she says it.	___	___	___
6. I usually end conversations that don't interest me by diverting my attention from the speaker.	___	___	___
7. I frequently nod, frown, or whatever to let the speaker know how I feel about what he or she is saying.	___	___	___
8. I usually respond immediately when someone has finished talking.	___	___	___
9. I evaluate what is being said while it is being said.	___	___	___
10. I usually formulate a response while the other person is still talking.	___	___	___
11. The speaker's delivery style frequently keeps me from listening to content.	___	___	___
12. I usually ask people to clarify what they have said rather than guess at the meaning.	___	___	___
13. I make a concerted effort to understand other people's point of view.	___	___	___
14. I frequently hear what I expect to hear rather than what is said.	___	___	___
15. Most people feel that I have understood their point of view when we disagree.	___	___	___

Turn to page A-28 for scoring directions and key.

Source: E.C. Glenn and E.A. Pood, "Listening Self-Inventory," *Supervisory Management*, January 1989, pp. 12–15. With permission.

Working with Others Exercise

An Absence of Nonverbal Communication

This exercise will help you to see the value of nonverbal communication to interpersonal relations.

1. The class is to split up into pairs (Party A and Party B).

2. Party A is to select a topic from the following list:
   a. Managing in the Middle East is significantly different from managing in North America.
   b. Employee turnover in an organization can be functional.
   c. Some conflict in an organization is good.
   d. Whistleblowers do more harm than good for an organization.
   e. Bureaucracies are frustrating to work in.
   f. An employer has a responsibility to provide every employee with an interesting and challenging job.
   g. Everyone should register to vote.
   h. Organizations should require all employees to undergo regular tests for AIDS.
   i. Organizations should require all employees to undergo regular drug tests.
   j. Individuals who have majored in business or economics make better employees than those who have majored in history or English.
   k. The place where you get your college degree is more important in determining career success than what you learn while you're there.
   l. Effective managers often have to lie as part of their job.
   m. It's unethical for a manager to purposely distort communications to get a favorable outcome.

3. Party B is to choose his or her position on this topic (for example, arguing *against* the view that "some conflict in an organization is good). Party A now must automatically take the opposite position.

4. The two parties have ten minutes in which to debate their topic. The catch is that individuals can only communicate verbally. They may *not* use gestures, facial movements, body movements, or any other nonverbal communication. It may help for each party to sit on his or her hands to remind them of their restrictions and to maintain an expressionless look.

5. After the debate is over, the class should discuss the following:
   a. How effective was communication during these debates?
   b. What barriers to communication existed?
   c. What purposes does nonverbal communication serve?
   d. Relate the lessons learned in this exercise to problems that might occur when communicating on the telephone or through e-mail.

Have We Got a Communication Problem Here?

"I don't want to hear your excuses. Just get those planes in the air," Jim Tuchman was screaming at his gate manager. As head of American Airlines' operations at the Mexico City airport, Tuchman has been consistently frustrated by

C A S E
INCIDENT

the attitude displayed by his native employees. Transferred from Dallas to Mexico City only three months ago, Tuchman was having difficulty adjusting to the Mexican style of work. "Am I critical of these people? You bet I am! They don't listen when I talk. They think things are just fine and fight every change I suggest. And they have no appreciation for the importance of keeping on schedule."

If Tuchman is critical of his Mexico City staff, it's mutual. They universally dislike him. Here's a few anonymous comments made about their boss: "He's totally insensitive to our needs." "He thinks if he yells and screams, that things will improve. We don't see it that way." "I've been working here for four years. Before he came here, this was a good place to work. Not anymore. I'm constantly in fear of being chewed out. I feel stress all the time, even at home. My husband has started commenting on it a lot."

Tuchman was brought in specifically to tighten up the Mexico City operation. High on his list of goals is improving American's on-time record in Mexico City, increasing productivity, and improving customer service. When Tuchman was asked if he thought he had any problems with his staff, he replied, "Yep. We just can't seem to communicate."

Questions

1. Does Jim Tuchman have a communication problem? Explain.
2. What suggestions, if any, would you make to Jim to help him improve his managerial effectiveness?

ABCNEWS

Does Women's Communication Style Hinder Them in Business?

Deborah Tannen says there's a distinct difference between the genders in the way they communicate. She calls them male and female rituals and she says they can get in the way of achieving work-related goals.

One of Tannen's findings relates to directness. Tannen says women often tend to avoid directness and cast themselves in an inferior light. This is seen in the following conversation between two *Money* Magazine writers, Lesley Alderman and Gary Belsky.

Gary: Well, do you have anything that you're considering?
Lesley: Here are things we . . . we were . . . that we've been thinking about. I'm just throwing things up.
Gary: Go on.
Lesley: So that's good. Then this one's really out, but . . . you're going to think I'm completely insane . . . but you know, there's like this whole like spiritual kind of drive thing. I can see you . . . like you're saying, "Oh, no." I don't even know if that's the angle, exactly. I'm not sure if that's the angle. All I'm saying is . . . I'm sort of throwing that out something . . .
Gary: OK.
Lesley: Maybe there's something in that. It's a little way out, perhaps.

Another gender-related ritual is apologizing. Women tend to apologize when they haven't done anything wrong. Why? They use it as a ritual way to get into the interaction. Men, on the other hand, seem to apologize only when they absolutely need to.

Tannen says women use a communication style that allows others to save face. They avoid directness and prefer subtlety. This can create real problems in organizations. Female managers may appear to be lacking confidence. They may also appear to be tentative when giving orders. According to Tannen, these conversational rituals can be the basis for underestimating a woman's capabilities. She can be seen as incompetent, whereas she thinks she's being considerate. She can be seen as lacking in confidence, whereas she feels she's simply being a good person by not flaunting her authority.

Women may be in a "can't win" situation. If they try to be considerate through indirectness, they may receive lower performance evaluations. Their bosses may assume they are not aggressive or confident enough to handle their jobs. But if they talk too much like men, they suffer because their bosses and subordinates may see them as too aggressive.

Questions

1. Do you think gender stereotypes of communication styles can be generalized to the entire workforce?
2. Do you think these gender styles are influenced by national culture? Explain.
3. Do you think adults can unlearn specific gender-related communication styles? Defend your position.
4. What suggestions would you make so women can communicate more effectively at work?
5. What suggestions would you make for men?

Source: Based on "He Says She Says," *20/20, ABC News*; aired on October 21, 1994.

10

LEADERSHIP

CHAPTER OUTLINE

LEARNING OBJECTIVES

After studying this chapter, you should be able to

1 Describe the nature of leadership

2 Summarize the conclusions of trait theories

3 Identify the limitations of behavioral theories

4 Describe Fiedler's contingency model

5 Summarize the path-goal theory

6 State the situational leadership theory

7 Explain leader-member exchange theory

8 Describe the leader-participation model

9 Explain why no one leadership style is ideal in all situations

10 Differentiate between transactional and transformational leaders

Lead, follow, or get out of the way!
—Anonymous

one person make a difference in an organization's performance? The Seattle Public School District thinks so. It recently hired John Stanford, a retired U.S. Army major general holding none of the usual educational credentials, with a mandate to lead a makeover of its failing urban school system.[1]

Beginning as a pilot, Stanford rose through the ranks of the U.S. Army. Then he served as the county executive for Fulton County, Georgia, where he cut bureaucratic inefficiencies, lowered taxes, and attracted new businesses. When interviewed by the Seattle school board, he told them, "Give me a mission and I will get it done." The board passed over more conventional candidates and chose the 58-year-old Stanford. He hasn't disappointed them.

He took over a school district with test scores that were stuck at the national average for five years. This was in spite of per-pupil spending that had risen almost 12 percent over this period and increases of 22 percent in average teacher pay. Between a swollen bureaucracy and an aggressive teachers' union, little of the extra money had seen its way into Seattle's classrooms. Over a 30-year period, Seattle's public school enrollment had dropped from 100,000 students to fewer than 50,000. In addition, a full third of Seattle's parents were sending their kids to private schools, compared to only 13 percent nationally.

In his first year on the job, Stanford has made a difference. His initial focus has been to convey a single mission for schools: to educate children, not provide cushy jobs for bureaucrats. Aware of the symbolic nature of leadership, he began his new job by visiting all 97 schools in the system—meeting with children, teachers, and parents to convey his mission. He encouraged parents to read for 30 minutes a day to their children, and he successfully reached out to the business community to donate books and money. He's also learned to use his job as a role model. He tells kids, "I make $175,000 a year, and so can you if you read, read, read."

Additionally, Stanford made a number of major organizational changes in his first year on the job. Pre-Stanford principals had been evaluated on the number of expulsions their school had. This led most of them to be lenient with troublemakers. Stanford changed the rules. He also shuffled a third of the principals to new assignments and threatened firing those whose school's educational performance didn't shape up.

There is still a lot more on Stanford's agenda. He plans to end crosstown busing for racial balance. He claims busing hasn't worked—the proportion of white students in the public schools has fallen to 40 percent as whites moved to the suburbs or sent their kids to private schools. He wants to reduce centralization and introduce competition. He wants principals to compete for teachers, and pick their own staff.

They'd bear responsibility for their schools' security and maintenance, even for the food in the cafeteria. "Principals as CEOs" is his slogan. Stanford also plans to allocate budgets to principals on the basis of students. Each student will be worth about $4,600. No students, no money. More students, more money.

Stanford realizes he faces serious opposition to some of his ideas, especially from teachers and their union. But ever the optimist, Stanford says he's not worried. "People will respond to leadership." ◆

As John Stanford is demonstrating in Seattle, leaders can make a difference. In this chapter, we want to look at the various studies on leadership to determine what makes an effective leader and what differentiates leaders from nonleaders. But first let's clarify what we mean by the term *leadership*.

What Is Leadership?

Few terms in OB inspire less agreement on definition than *leadership*. As one expert put it, "there are almost as many definitions of leadership as there are persons who have attempted to define the concept."[2]

Although almost everyone seems to agree that leadership involves an influence process, differences tend to center around whether leadership must be noncoercive (as opposed to using authority, rewards, and punishments to exert influence over followers) and whether it is distinct from management.[3] The latter issue has been a particularly heated topic of debate in recent years, with most experts arguing that leadership and management are different.

For instance, Abraham Zaleznik of the Harvard Business School argues that leaders and managers are very different kinds of people.[4] They differ in motivation, personal history, and how they think and act. Zaleznik says that managers tend to adopt impersonal, if not passive, attitudes toward goals, whereas leaders take a personal and active attitude toward goals. Managers tend to view work as an enabling process involving some combination of people and ideas interacting to establish strategies and make decisions. Leaders work from high-risk positions—indeed, they are often temperamentally disposed to seek out risk and danger, especially when opportunity and reward appear high. Managers prefer to work with people; they avoid solitary activity because it makes them anxious. They relate to people according to the role they play in a sequence of events or in a decision-making process. Leaders, who are concerned with ideas, relate to people in more intuitive and empathic ways.

John Kotter, a colleague of Zaleznik at Harvard, also argues that leadership is different from management, but for other reasons.[5] Management, he proposes, is about coping with complexity. Good management brings about order and consistency by drawing up formal plans, designing rigid organization structures, and monitoring results against the plans. Leadership, in contrast, is about coping with change. Leaders establish direction by developing a vision of the future; then they align people by communicating this vision and inspiring them to overcome hurdles. Kotter sees both strong leadership and strong management as necessary for optimum organizational effectiveness. But he believes that most organizations are underled and overmanaged. He claims we need to focus more on developing leadership in organizations because the people in charge today are too concerned with keeping things on time and on budget and with doing what was done yesterday, only doing it 5 percent better.

So where do we stand? We will use a broad definition of leadership—one that can encompass all the current approaches to the subject. Thus, we define **leadership** as the ability to influence a group toward the achievement of goals. The source of this influence may be formal, such as that provided by the possession of managerial rank in an organization. Since management positions come with some degree of formally designated authority, a person may assume a leadership role simply because of the position he or she holds in the organization. But not all leaders are managers; nor, for that matter, are all managers leaders. Just because an organization provides its managers with certain formal rights is no assurance that they will be able to lead effectively. We find that nonsanctioned leadership—that is, the ability to influence that arises outside the formal structure of the organization—is often as important or more important than formal influence. In other words, leaders can emerge from within a group as well as by formal appointment to lead a group.

leadership
The ability to influence a group toward the achievement of goals.

◆ Not all leaders are managers nor are all managers leaders.

Transition in Leadership Theories

The leadership literature is voluminous, and much of it is confusing and contradictory. In order to make our way through this "forest," we'll consider a number of approaches to explaining what makes an effective leader. We begin with the search to find universal personality traits that leaders had to some greater degree than nonleaders. A second approach tried to explain leadership in terms of the behavior that a person engaged in. Both approaches have been described as "false starts," based on their erroneous and oversimplified conception of leadership.[6] A third looked to contingency models to explain the inadequacies of previous leadership theories in reconciling and bringing together the diversity of research findings. In this chapter, we present the contributions and limitations of the trait, behavioral, and contingency approaches to leadership, introduce some of the more recent advances in leadership, review a number of contemporary issues related to applying leadership concepts, and conclude by considering the value of the leadership literature for practicing managers.

Trait Theories

When Margaret Thatcher was prime minister of Great Britain, she was regularly singled out for her leadership. She was described in terms such as confident, iron-willed, determined, and decisive. These terms are traits and,

trait theories of leadership
Theories that sought personality, social, physical, or intellectual traits that differentiated leaders from nonleaders.

whether Thatcher's advocates and critics recognized it at the time, when they described her in such terms they became trait-theorist supporters.

The media has long been a believer in **trait theories of leadership**. They identify people like Margaret Thatcher, Ronald Reagan, Nelson Mandela, Ted Turner, and Colin Powell as leaders, then describe them in terms such as *charismatic, enthusiastic*, and *courageous*. Well the media isn't alone. The search for personality, social, physical, or intellectual attributes that would describe leaders and differentiate them from nonleaders goes back to the 1930s and research done by psychologists.

Research efforts at isolating leadership traits resulted in a number of dead ends. For instance, a review of 20 different studies identified nearly 80 leadership traits, but only five of these traits were common to four or more of the investigations.[7] If the search was intended to identify a set of traits that would always differentiate leaders from followers and effective from ineffective leaders, the search failed. Perhaps it was a bit optimistic to believe that there could be consistent and unique traits that would apply universally to all effective leaders, no matter whether they were in charge of the Seattle public schools, the Mormon Tabernacle Choir, General Electric, Ted's Malibu Surf Shop, the Brazilian national soccer team, or Oxford University.

If, however, the search was intended to identify traits that were consistently associated with leadership, the results can be interpreted in a more impressive light. For example, six traits on which leaders tend to differ from nonleaders are ambition and energy, the desire to lead, honesty and integrity, self-confidence, intelligence, and job-relevant knowledge.[8] Additionally, recent research provides strong evidence that people who are high self-

Randy Jones ranks high in the traits associated with leadership. His ambition, energy, desire to lead, self-confidence, intelligence, and knowledge of publishing increases the likelihood of his success as the leader in establishing *Worth* as a new financial management magazine. Jones is also a high self-monitor, taking the lead in promoting his new product, whether it's participating in event marketing (shown here), dining with influential political and media people, or working with his sales reps in making presentations to win advertisers.

monitors—that is, are highly flexible in adjusting their behavior in different situations—are much more likely to emerge as leaders in groups than low self-monitors.[9] Overall, the cumulative findings from more than half a century of research lead us to conclude that some traits increase the likelihood of success as a leader, but none of the traits *guarantee* success.[10]

Why hasn't the trait approach proven more successful in explaining leadership? We can suggest at least four reasons. It overlooks the needs of followers, it generally fails to clarify the relative importance of various traits, it doesn't separate cause from effect (for example, are leaders self-confident or does success as a leader build self-confidence?), and it ignores situational factors. These limitations have led researchers to look in other directions. Although there has been some resurgent interest in traits during the past decade,[11] a major movement away from traits began as early as the 1940s. Leadership research from the late 1940s through the mid-1960s emphasized the preferred behavioral styles that leaders demonstrated.

Behavioral Theories

The inability to strike "gold" in the trait "mines" led researchers to look at the behaviors that specific leaders exhibited. They wondered if there was something unique in the way that effective leaders behave. For example, Robert Crandall, chairman of American Airlines, and Paul B. Kazarian, the former chairman of Sunbeam-Oster, both have been very successful in leading their companies through difficult times.[12] And they both rely on a common leadership style—tough-talking, intense, autocratic. Does this suggest that autocratic behavior is a preferred style for *all* leaders? In this section, we look at four different **behavioral theories of leadership** in order to answer that question. First, however, let's consider the practical implications of the behavioral approach.

behavioral theories of leadership Theories proposing that specific behaviors differentiate leaders from nonleaders.

If the behavioral approach to leadership were successful, it would have implications quite different from those of the trait approach. If trait research had been successful, it would have provided a basis for *selecting* the "right" persons to assume formal positions in groups and organizations requiring leadership. In contrast, if behavioral studies were to turn up critical behavioral determinants of leadership, we could *train* people to be leaders. The difference between trait and behavioral theories, in terms of application, lies in their underlying assumptions. If trait theories were valid, then leadership is basically inborn: You either have it or you don't. On the other hand, if there were specific behaviors that identified leaders, then we could teach leadership—we could design programs that implanted these behavioral patterns in individuals who desired to be effective leaders. This was surely a more exciting avenue, for it meant that the supply of leaders could be expanded. If training worked, we could have an infinite supply of effective leaders.

Ohio State Studies

The most comprehensive and replicated of the behavioral theories resulted from research that began at Ohio State University in the late 1940s.[13] These researchers sought to identify independent dimensions of leader behavior. Beginning with over a thousand dimensions, they eventually narrowed the list

Aaron Feuerstein, owner of Malden Mills, rates high on consideration behavior. After a fire destroyed one of the company's mills, Feuerstein tried to minimize the human suffering of his employees by continuing to pay out some $15 million in wages and benefits when they no longer had a place to work. He also promised to rebuild the factory so employees could return to their jobs. For his humanitarian efforts, Feuerstein was honored by President Clinton and showered with gratitude by employees. In this photo, a thankful employee gives Feuerstein a hug and kiss in appreciation of her employer's generosity.

into two categories that substantially accounted for most of the leadership behavior described by subordinates. They called these two dimensions *initiating structure* and *consideration*.

initiating structure
The extent to which a leader is likely to define and structure his or her role and those of subordinates in the search for goal attainment.

Initiating structure refers to the extent to which a leader is likely to define and structure his or her role and those of subordinates in the search for goal attainment. It includes behavior that attempts to organize work, work relationships, and goals. The leader characterized as high in initiating structure could be described as someone who "assigns group members to particular tasks," "expects workers to maintain definite standards of performance," and "emphasizes the meeting of deadlines." Robert Crandall and Paul Kazarian exhibit high initiating structure behavior.

consideration
The extent to which a leader is likely to have job relationships characterized by mutual trust, respect for subordinates' ideas, and regard for their feelings.

Consideration is described as the extent to which a person is likely to have job relationships that are characterized by mutual trust, respect for subordinates' ideas, and regard for their feelings. He or she shows concern for followers' comfort, well-being, status, and satisfaction. A leader high in consideration could be described as one who helps subordinates with personal problems, is friendly and approachable, and treats all subordinates as equals. The current chairman of Southwest Airlines, Herb Kelleher, rates high on consideration behavior. His leadership style is very people oriented, emphasizing friendliness and empowerment.

Extensive research, based on these definitions, found that leaders high in initiating structure and consideration (a "high-high" leader) tended to achieve high subordinate performance and satisfaction more frequently than those who rated low on either consideration, initiating structure, or both. However, the "high-high" style did not always result in positive consequences. For example, leader behavior characterized as high on initiating structure led to greater rates of grievances, absenteeism, and turnover and lower levels of job satisfaction for workers performing routine tasks. Other studies found that high consideration was negatively related to performance ratings of the leader by his or her superior. In conclusion, the Ohio State studies suggested that the "high-high" style generally resulted in positive outcomes, but enough exceptions were found to indicate that situational factors needed to be integrated into the theory.

University of Michigan Studies

Leadership studies undertaken at the University of Michigan's Survey Research Center, at about the same time as those being done at Ohio State, had similar research objectives: to locate behavioral characteristics of leaders that appeared to be related to measures of performance effectiveness.

The Michigan group also came up with two dimensions of leadership behavior that they labeled **employee oriented** and **production oriented**.[14] Leaders who were employee oriented were described as emphasizing interpersonal relations; they took a personal interest in the needs of their subordinates and accepted individual differences among members. The production-oriented leaders, in contrast, tended to emphasize the technical or task aspects of the job—their main concern was in accomplishing their group's tasks, and the group members were a means to that end.

employee-oriented leader
One who emphasizes interpersonal relations.

production-oriented leader
One who emphasizes technical or task aspects of the job.

The conclusions arrived at by the Michigan researchers strongly favored the leaders who were employee oriented in their behavior. Employee-oriented leaders were associated with higher group productivity and higher job satisfaction. Production-oriented leaders tended to be associated with low group productivity and lower job satisfaction.

The Managerial Grid

A graphic portrayal of a two-dimensional view of leadership style was developed by Blake and Mouton.[15] They proposed a **Managerial Grid** based on the styles of "concern for people" and "concern for production," which essentially represent the Ohio State dimensions of consideration and initiating structure or the Michigan dimensions of employee oriented and production oriented.

Managerial Grid
A nine-by-nine matrix outlining 81 different leadership styles.

The grid, depicted in Exhibit 10-1 on page 352, has nine possible positions along each axis, creating 81 different positions in which the leader's style may fall. The grid does not show results produced but, rather, the dominating factors in a leader's thinking in regard to getting results.

Based on the findings of Blake and Mouton, managers were found to perform best under a 9,9 style, as contrasted, for example, with a 9,1 (authority type) or 1,9 (country club type) style.[16] Unfortunately, the grid offers a better framework for conceptualizing leadership style than for presenting any tangible new information in clarifying the leadership quandary, since there is little substantive evidence to support the conclusion that a 9,9 style is most effective in all situations.[17]

Scandinavian Studies

The three behavioral approaches we've just reviewed were essentially developed between the late 1940s and early 1960s. These approaches evolved during a time when the world was a far more stable and predictable place. In the belief that these studies fail to capture the more dynamic realities of today, researchers in Finland and Sweden have been reassessing whether there are only two dimensions that capture the essence of leadership behavior.[18] Their basic premise is that in a changing world, effective leaders would exhibit **development-oriented** behavior. These are leaders who value experimentation, seek new ideas, and generate and implement change.

development-oriented leader
One who values experimentation, seeking new ideas, and generating and implementing change.

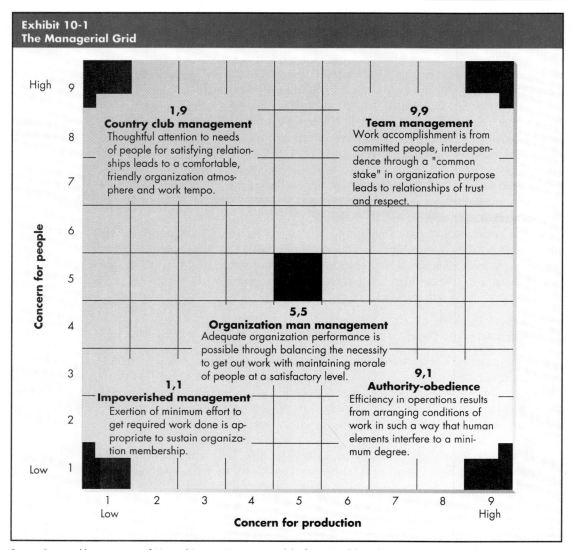

Exhibit 10-1
The Managerial Grid

Source: Reprinted by permission of *Harvard Business Review:* An exhibit from "Breakthrough in Organization Development" by R.R. Blake, J.S. Mouton, L.B. Barnes, and L.E. Greiner (November-December 1964). Copyright © 1964 by the President and Fellows of Harvard College; all rights reserved.

For instance, these Scandinavian researchers reviewed the original Ohio State data. They found that the Ohio State people included development items such as "pushes new ways of doing things," "originates new approaches to problems," and "encourages members to start new activities." But these items, at the time, didn't explain much toward effective leadership. It could be, the Scandinavian researchers proposed, that this was because developing new ideas and implementing change were not critical *in those days.* In today's dynamic environment, this may no longer be true. So the Scandinavian researchers have been conducting new studies looking to see if there is a third dimension—development orientation—that is related to leader effectiveness.

The early evidence is positive. Using samples of leaders in Finland and Sweden, the researchers have found strong support for development-oriented leader behavior as a separate and independent dimension. That is, the previous behavioral approaches that focused in on only two behaviors may not appropriately capture leadership in the 1990s. Moreover, while initial conclusions need to be guarded without more confirming evidence, it also appears that leaders who demonstrate development-oriented behavior have more satisfied subordinates and are seen as more competent by those subordinates.

Summary of Behavioral Theories

We've described the most important attempts to explain leadership in terms of the behavior exhibited by the leader. In general, they've had modest success in identifying consistent relationships between patterns of leadership behavior and group performance. What seems to be missing is consideration of the *situational* factors that influence success or failure. For example, Robert Crandall and Herb Kelleher have both been effective leaders of airlines, yet their styles are almost diametrically opposed. How can that be? The answer is that American and Southwest are very different companies, operating in different markets with very different labor forces. The behavioral theories fail to take this into account. Jesse Jackson is certainly an effective leader of black causes in the *1990s*, but would his style have been equally effective in the *1890s*? Probably not! Situations change and leadership styles need to change with them. Unfortunately, the behavioral approaches don't recognize changes in situations.

Contingency Theories

Bob Knight, the men's head basketball coach at Indiana University, consistently uses an intense, task-oriented leadership style that intimidates players, officials, the media, and university administrators. But his style works with

Bob Knight, the highly successful basketball coach at Indiana University, generally confirms Fiedler's belief that a person's leadership style is fixed. Knight's intense, task-oriented style seems unvarying. He regularly argues with referees and once threw a chair across the floor to protest a call. In one season he benched all his starters in a key conference game because they weren't practicing intensely enough. He even kicked his own son off the team for a rules infraction.

the Indiana teams he recruits. Knight has one of the most impressive win-loss records of any active major college basketball coach. But would this same style work if Bob Knight were counsel-general of the United Nations or project manager for a group of Ph.D.-software designers at Microsoft? Probably not! Observations such as this have directed researchers to look at more adaptive approaches to leadership.

It became increasingly clear to those who were studying the leadership phenomenon that predicting leadership success was more complex than isolating a few traits or preferable behaviors. The failure to obtain consistent results led to a focus on situational influences. The relationship between leadership style and effectiveness suggested that under condition *a*, style *x* would be appropriate, while style *y* would be more suitable for condition *b*, and style *z* for condition *c*. But what were the conditions *a*, *b*, *c*, and so forth? It was one thing to say that leadership effectiveness was dependent on the situation and another to be able to isolate those situational conditions.

There has been no shortage of studies attempting to isolate critical situational factors that affect leadership effectiveness. For instance, popular moderating variables used in the development of contingency theories include the degree of structure in the task being performed, the quality of leader–member relations, the leader's position power, subordinates' role clarity, group norms, information availability, subordinate acceptance of leader's decisions, and subordinate maturity.[19]

Several approaches to isolating key situational variables have proven more successful than others and, as a result, have gained wider recognition. We shall consider five of these: the Fiedler model, Hersey and Blanchard's situational theory, leader-member exchange theory, and the path-goal and leader-participation models.

Fiedler Model

Fiedler contingency model
The theory that effective groups depend upon a proper match between a leader's style of interacting with subordinates and the degree to which the situation gives control and influence to the leader.

least preferred co-worker (LPC) questionnaire
An instrument that purports to measure whether a person is task or relationship oriented.

The first comprehensive contingency model for leadership was developed by Fred Fiedler.[20] The **Fiedler contingency model** proposes that effective group performance depends upon the proper match between the leader's style of interacting with his or her subordinates and the degree to which the situation gives control and influence to the leader. Fiedler developed an instrument, which he called the **least preferred co-worker (LPC) questionnaire**, that purports to measure whether a person is task or relationship oriented. Furthermore, he isolated three situational criteria—leader-member relations, task structure, and position power—that he believes can be manipulated so as to create the proper match with the behavioral orientation of the leader. In a sense, the Fiedler model is an outgrowth of trait theory, since the LPC questionnaire is a simple psychological test. However, Fiedler goes significantly beyond trait and behavioral approaches by attempting to isolate situations, relating his personality measure to his situational classification, and then predicting leadership effectiveness as a function of the two.

This description of the Fiedler model is somewhat abstract. Let's now look at the model more closely.

IDENTIFYING LEADERSHIP STYLE Fiedler believes a key factor in leadership success is the individual's basic leadership style. So he begins by trying to find out what that basic style is. Fiedler created the LPC questionnaire for this purpose. It contains 16 contrasting adjectives (such as pleasant–unpleasant, efficient–inefficient, open–guarded, supportive–hostile). The questionnaire then asks respondents to think of all the co-workers they have ever had and to describe the one person they *least enjoyed* working with by rating him or her on a scale of 1 to 8 for each of the 16 sets of contrasting adjectives. Fiedler believes that based on the respondents' answers to this LPC questionnaire, he can determine their basic leadership style. If the least preferred co-worker is described in relatively positive terms (a high LPC score), then the respondent is primarily interested in good personal relations with this co-worker. That is, if you essentially describe the person you are least able to work with in favorable terms, Fiedler would label you *relationship oriented*. In contrast, if the least preferred co-worker is seen in relatively unfavorable terms (a low LPC score), the respondent is primarily interested in productivity and thus would be labeled *task oriented*. About 16 percent of respondents score in the middle range.[21] Such individuals cannot be classified as either relationship oriented or task oriented and thus fall outside the theory's predictions. The rest of our discussion, therefore, relates to the 84 percent who score in either the high or low range of the LPC.

Fiedler assumes that an individual's leadership style is fixed. As we'll show in a moment, this is important because it means that if a situation requires a task-oriented leader and the person in that leadership position is relationship oriented, either the situation has to be modified or the leader removed and replaced if optimum effectiveness is to be achieved. Fiedler argues that leadership style is innate to a person—you *can't* change your style to fit changing situations!

◆ Fiedler assumes that an individual's leadership style is fixed.

DEFINING THE SITUATION After an individual's basic leadership style has been assessed through the LPC, it is necessary to match the leader with the situation. Fiedler has identified three contingency dimensions that, he argues, define the key situational factors that determine leadership effectiveness. These are **leader–member relations**, **task structure**, and **position power**. They are defined as follows:

1. *Leader–member relations*: The degree of confidence, trust, and respect subordinates have in their leader
2. *Task structure*: The degree to which the job assignments are procedurized (that is, structured or unstructured)
3. *Position power*: The degree of influence a leader has over power variables such as hiring, firing, discipline, promotions, and salary increases

The next step in the Fiedler model is to evaluate the situation in terms of these three contingency variables. Leader–member relations are either good or poor, task structure is either high or low, and position power is either strong or weak.

Fiedler states the better the leader–member relations, the more highly structured the job, and the stronger the position power, the more control or influence the leader has. For example, a very favorable situation (where the leader would have a great deal of control) might involve a payroll manager who is well respected and whose subordinates have confidence in her (good leader–member relations), where the activities to be done—such as wage computation, check writing, report filing—are specific and clear (high task structure), and the job provides considerable freedom for her to reward and

leader–member relations
The degree of confidence, trust, and respect subordinates have in their leader.

task structure
The degree to which job assignments are procedurized.

position power
Influence derived from one's formal structural position in the organization; includes power to hire, fire, discipline, promote, and give salary increases.

punish her subordinates (strong position power). On the other hand, an unfavorable situation might be the disliked chairperson of a voluntary United Way fund-raising team. In this job, the leader has very little control. Altogether, by mixing the three contingency variables, there are potentially eight different situations or categories in which leaders could find themselves.

MATCHING LEADERS AND SITUATIONS With knowledge of an individual's LPC and an assessment of the three contingency variables, the Fiedler model proposes matching them up to achieve maximum leadership effectiveness.[22] Based on Fiedler's study of over 1,200 groups, in which he compared relationship- versus task-oriented leadership styles in each of the eight situational categories, he concluded that task-oriented leaders tend to perform better in situations that were *very favorable* to them and in situations that were *very unfavorable* (see Exhibit 10-2). So Fiedler would predict that when faced with a category I, II, III, VII, or VIII situation, task-oriented leaders perform better. Relationship-oriented leaders, however, perform better in moderately favorable situations—categories IV through VI.

Given Fiedler's findings, how would you apply them? You would seek to match leaders and situations. Individuals' LPC scores would determine the type of situation for which they were best suited. That "situation" would be defined by evaluating the three contingency factors of leader–member relations, task structure, and position power. But remember that Fiedler views an individual's leadership style as being fixed. Therefore, there are really only two ways in which to improve leader effectiveness.

First, you can change the leader to fit the situation—as in a baseball game, a manager can reach into the bullpen and put in a right-handed pitcher or a left-handed pitcher, depending on the situational characteristics of the hitter. So, for example, if a group situation rates as highly unfavorable but is currently led by a relationship-oriented manager, the group's performance could be improved by replacing that manager with one who is task oriented. The second alternative would be to change the situation to fit the leader. That

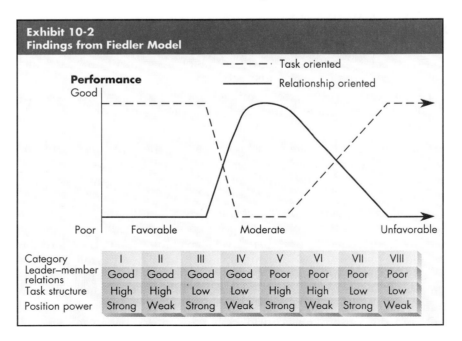

Exhibit 10-2
Findings from Fiedler Model

Category	I	II	III	IV	V	VI	VII	VIII
Leader–member relations	Good	Good	Good	Good	Poor	Poor	Poor	Poor
Task structure	High	High	Low	Low	High	High	Low	Low
Position power	Strong	Weak	Strong	Weak	Strong	Weak	Strong	Weak

could be done by restructuring tasks or increasing or decreasing the power that the leader has to control factors such as salary increases, promotions, and disciplinary actions. To illustrate, assume a task-oriented leader is in a category IV situation. If this leader could increase his or her position power, then the leader would be operating in category III and the leader–situation match would be compatible for high group performance.

EVALUATION As a whole, reviews of the major studies that tested the overall validity of the Fiedler model lead to a generally positive conclusion. That is, there is considerable evidence to support at least substantial parts of the model.[23] But additional variables are probably needed if an improved model is to fill in some of the remaining gaps. Moreover, there are problems with the LPC and the practical use of the model that need to be addressed. For instance, the logic underlying the LPC is not well understood and studies have shown that respondents' LPC scores are not stable.[24] Also, the contingency variables are complex and difficult for practitioners to assess. It's often difficult in practice to determine how good the leader–member relations are, how structured the task is, and how much position power the leader has.[25]

COGNITIVE RESOURCE THEORY: AN UPDATE ON FIEDLER'S CONTINGENCY MODEL More recently, Fiedler and an associate, Joe Garcia, reconceptualized the former's original theory[26] to deal with "some serious oversights that need to be addressed."[27] Specifically, they are concerned with trying to explain the process by which a leader obtains effective group performance. They call this reconceptualization **cognitive resource theory**.

They begin by making two assumptions. First, intelligent and competent leaders formulate more effective plans, decisions, and action strategies than less intelligent and competent leaders. Second, leaders communicate their plans, decisions, and strategies through directive behavior. Fiedler and Garcia then show how stress and cognitive resources such as experience, tenure, and intelligence act as important influences on leadership effectiveness.

The essence of the new theory can be boiled down to three predictions: (1) Directive behavior results in good performance only if linked with high intelligence in a supportive, nonstressful leadership environment; (2) in highly stressful situations, there is a positive relationship between job experience and performance; and (3) the intellectual abilities of leaders correlate with group performance in situations that the leader perceives as nonstressful.

Fiedler and Garcia admit that their data supporting cognitive resource theory are far from overwhelming. And the limited number of studies to test the theory have, to date, generated mixed results.[28] Clearly, more research is needed. Yet, given the impact of Fiedler's original contingency model of leadership on organizational behavior, the new theory's link to this earlier model, and the new theory's introduction of the leader's cognitive abilities as an important influence on leadership effectiveness, cognitive resource theory should not be dismissed out of hand.

cognitive resource theory
A theory of leadership that states that a leader obtains effective group performance by first making effective plans, decisions, and strategies, and then communicating them through directive behavior.

Hersey and Blanchard's Situational Theory

Paul Hersey and Ken Blanchard have developed a leadership model that has gained a strong following among management development specialists.[29] This model—called **situational leadership theory**—has been used as a major training device at such *Fortune* 500 companies as BankAmerica, Caterpillar,

situational leadership theory
A contingency theory that focuses on followers' readiness.

IBM, Mobil Oil, and Xerox; it has also been widely accepted in all the military services.[30] Although the theory has undergone limited evaluation to test its validity, we include it here because of its wide acceptance and its strong intuitive appeal.

Situational leadership is a contingency theory that focuses on the followers. Successful leadership is achieved by selecting the right leadership style, which Hersey and Blanchard argue is contingent on the level of the followers' readiness. Before we proceed, we should clarify two points: Why focus on the followers? What is meant by the term *readiness*?

> ◆ Situational leadership is a contingency theory that focuses on the followers.

The emphasis on the followers in leadership effectiveness reflects the reality that it is the followers who accept or reject the leader. Regardless of what the leader does, effectiveness depends on the actions of his or her followers. This is an important dimension that has been overlooked or underemphasized in most leadership theories. The term *readiness*, as defined by Hersey and Blanchard, refers to the extent to which people have the ability and willingness to accomplish a specific task.

Situational leadership uses the same two leadership dimensions that Fiedler identified: task and relationship behaviors. However, Hersey and Blanchard go a step further by considering each as either high or low and then combining them into four specific leader behaviors: telling, selling, participating, and delegating. They are described as follows:

Telling (high task–low relationship). The leader defines roles and tells people what, how, when, and where to do various tasks. It emphasizes directive behavior.

Selling (high task–high relationship). The leader provides both directive behavior and supportive behavior.

Participating (low task–high relationship). The leader and follower share in decision making, with the main role of the leader being facilitating and communicating.

Delegating (low task–low relationship). The leader provides little direction or support.

The final component in Hersey and Blanchard's theory is defining four stages of follower readiness:

R1. People are both unable and either unwilling or too insecure to take responsibility to do something. They are neither competent nor confident.

R2. People are unable but willing to do the necessary job tasks. They are motivated but currently lack the appropriate skills.

R3. People are able but unwilling or too apprehensive to do what the leader wants.

R4. People are both able and willing to do what is asked of them.

Exhibit 10-3 integrates the various components into the situational leadership model. As followers reach high levels of readiness, the leader responds by not only continuing to decrease control over activities, but also by continuing to decrease relationship behavior as well. At stage R1, followers need clear and specific directions. At stage R2, both high-task and high-relationship behavior is needed. The high-task behavior compensates for the followers' lack of ability, and the high-relationship behavior tries to get the followers

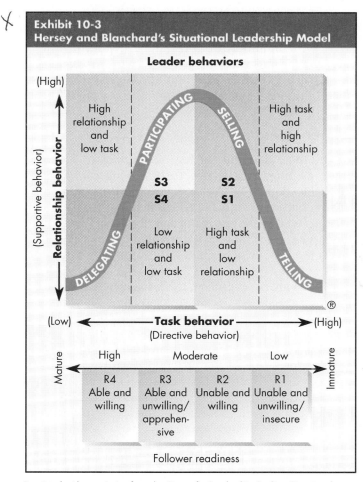

Exhibit 10-3
Hersey and Blanchard's Situational Leadership Model

Reprinted with permission from the Center for Leadership Studies. Situational Leadership® is a registered trademark of the Center for Leadership Studies, Escondido, California. All rights reserved.

psychologically to "buy into" the leader's desires. R3 represents motivational problems that are best solved by a supportive, nondirective, participative style. Finally, at stage R4, the leader doesn't have to do much because followers are both willing and able to take responsibility.

The astute reader might have noticed the high similarity between Hersey and Blanchard's four leadership styles and the four extreme "corners" in the Managerial Grid. The telling style equates to the 9,1 leader; selling equals 9,9; participating is equivalent to 1,9; and delegating is the same as the 1,1 leader. Is situational leadership, then, merely the Managerial Grid with one major difference—the replacement of the 9,9 ("one style for all occasions") contention with the recommendation that the "right" style should align with the readiness of the followers? Hersey and Blanchard say "No!"[31] They contend that the grid emphasizes *concern* for production and people, which are attitudinal dimensions. Situational leadership, in contrast, emphasizes task and relationship *behavior*. In spite of Hersey and Blanchard's claim, this is a pretty minute differentiation. Understanding of the situational leadership theory is probably enhanced by considering it as a fairly direct adaptation of the grid framework to reflect four stages of follower readiness.

Finally, we come to the critical question: Is there scientific evidence to support situational leadership theory? As noted earlier, the theory has received little attention from researchers,[32] but on the basis of the research to date, conclusions must be guarded. Some researchers provide partial support for the theory,[33] while others find no support for its assumptions.[34] As a result, any enthusiastic endorsement should be cautioned against.

Leader–Member Exchange Theory

For the most part, the leadership theories we've covered to this point have largely assumed that leaders treat all their subordinates in the same manner. But think about your experiences in groups. Did you notice that leaders often act very differently toward different subordinates? Did the leader tend to have favorites who made up his or her "in-group"? If you answered "Yes" to both these questions, you're acknowledging what George Graen and his associates have observed, which creates the foundation for their leader–member exchange theory.[35]

leader–member exchange (LMX) theory
Leaders create in-groups and out-groups, and subordinates with in-group status will have higher performance ratings, less turnover, and greater satisfaction with their superior.

The **leader–member exchange (LMX) theory** argues that because of time pressures, leaders establish a special relationship with a small group of their subordinates. These individuals make up the in-group—they are trusted, get a disproportionate amount of the leader's attention, and are more likely to receive special privileges. Other subordinates fall into the out-group. They get less of the leader's time, fewer of the preferred rewards that the leader controls, and have superior–subordinate relations based on formal authority interactions.

The theory proposes that early in the history of the interaction between a leader and a given subordinate, the leader implicitly categorizes the subordinate as an "in" or an "out" and that relationship is relatively stable over time.[36] Just precisely how the leader chooses who falls into each category is unclear, but there is evidence that leaders tend to choose in-group members because they have personal characteristics (for example, age, gender, attitudes) that are similar to the leader, a higher level of competence than out-group members, and/or an extroverted personality.[37] (See Exhibit 10-4.) LMX theory

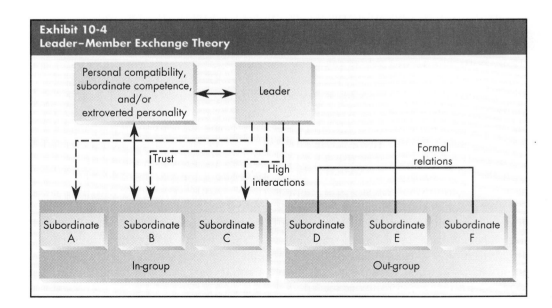

Exhibit 10-4
Leader–Member Exchange Theory

predicts that subordinates with in-group status will have higher performance ratings, less turnover, and greater satisfaction with their superiors.

Research to test LMX theory has been generally supportive.[38] More specifically, the theory and research surrounding it provide substantive evidence that leaders do differentiate among subordinates, that these disparities are far from random, and that in-group and out-group status is related to employee performance and satisfaction.[39]

Path-Goal Theory

Currently, one of the most respected approaches to leadership is the path-goal theory. Developed by Robert House, path-goal theory is a contingency model of leadership that extracts key elements from the Ohio State leadership research on initiating structure and consideration and the expectancy theory of motivation.[40]

The essence of the theory is that it's the leader's job to assist followers in attaining their goals and to provide the necessary direction and/or support to ensure that their goals are compatible with the overall objectives of the group or organization. The term *path-goal* is derived from the belief that effective leaders clarify the path to help their followers get from where they are to the achievement of their work goals and make the journey along the path easier by reducing roadblocks and pitfalls.

According to **path-goal theory**, a leader's behavior is *acceptable* to subordinates to the degree that it is viewed by them as an immediate source of satisfaction or as a means of future satisfaction. A leader's behavior is *motivational* to the degree that it (1) makes subordinate need satisfaction contingent on effective performance and (2) provides the coaching, guidance, support, and rewards that are necessary for effective performance. To test these statements, House identified four leadership behaviors. The *directive leader* lets subordinates know what is expected of them, schedules work to be done, and gives specific guidance as to how to accomplish tasks. This closely parallels the Ohio State dimension of initiating structure. The *supportive leader* is friendly and shows concern for the needs of subordinates. This is essentially synonymous with the Ohio State dimension of consideration. The *participative leader* consults with subordinates and uses their suggestions before making a decision. The *achievement-oriented leader* sets challenging goals and expects subordinates to perform at their highest level. In contrast to Fiedler's view of a leader's behavior, House assumes that leaders are flexible. Path-goal theory implies that the same leader can display any or all of these behaviors depending on the situation.

As Exhibit 10-5 on page 362 illustrates, path-goal theory proposes two classes of situational or contingency variables that moderate the leadership behavior–outcome relationship—those in the environment that are outside the control of the subordinate (task structure, the formal authority system, and the work group) and those that are part of the personal characteristics of the subordinate (locus of control, experience, and perceived ability). Environmental factors determine the type of leader behavior required as a complement if subordinate outcomes are to be maximized, while personal characteristics of the subordinate determine how the environment and leader behavior are interpreted. So the theory proposes that leader behavior will be ineffective when it is redundant with sources of environmental structure or incongruent with subordinate characteristics.

path-goal theory
The theory that a leader's behavior is acceptable to subordinates insofar as they view it as a source of either immediate or future satisfaction.

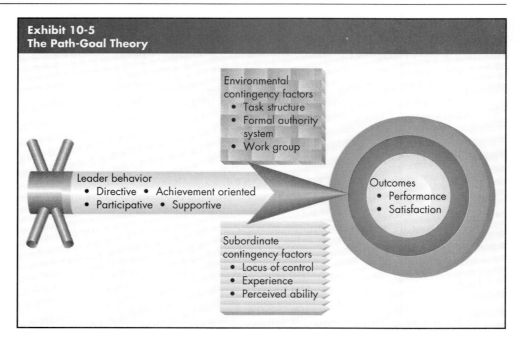

Exhibit 10-5
The Path-Goal Theory

The following are some examples of hypotheses that have evolved out of path-goal theory:

◆ Directive leadership leads to greater satisfaction when tasks are ambiguous or stressful than when they are highly structured and well laid out.

◆ Supportive leadership results in high employee performance and satisfaction when subordinates are performing structured tasks.

◆ Directive leadership is likely to be perceived as redundant among subordinates with high perceived ability or with considerable experience.

◆ The more clear and bureaucratic the formal authority relationships, the more leaders should exhibit supportive behavior and deemphasize directive behavior.

◆ Directive leadership will lead to higher employee satisfaction when there is substantive conflict within a work group.

◆ Subordinates with an internal locus of control (those who believe they control their own destiny) will be more satisfied with a participative style.

◆ Subordinates with an external locus of control will be more satisfied with a directive style.

◆ Achievement-oriented leadership will increase subordinates' expectancies that effort will lead to high performance when tasks are ambiguously structured.

Research to validate hypotheses such as these is generally encouraging.[41] The evidence supports the logic underlying the theory. That is, employee performance and satisfaction are likely to be positively influenced when the leader compensates for things lacking in either the employee or the work setting. However, the leader who spends time explaining tasks when those tasks are already clear or when the employee has the ability and experience to handle them without interference is likely to be ineffective because the employee will see such directive behavior as redundant or even insulting.

What does the future hold for path-goal theory? Its framework has been tested and appears to have moderate to high empirical support. We can, however, expect to see more research focused on refining and extending the theory by incorporating additional moderating variables.[42]

Leader-Participation Model

Back in 1973, Victor Vroom and Phillip Yetton developed a **leader-participation model** that related leadership behavior and participation to decision making.[43] Recognizing that task structures have varying demands for routine and nonroutine activities, these researchers argued that leader behavior must adjust to reflect the task structure. Vroom and Yetton's model was normative—it provided a sequential set of rules that should be followed for determining the form and amount of participation desirable in decision making, as dictated by different types of situations. The model was a complex decision tree incorporating seven contingencies (whose relevance could be identified by making "Yes" or "No" choices) and five alternative leadership styles.

More recent work by Vroom and Arthur Jago has resulted in a revision of this model.[44] The new model retains the same five alternative leadership styles but expands the contingency variables to twelve, ten of which are answered along a five-point scale. Exhibit 10-6 on page 364 lists the twelve variables.

The model assumes that any of five behaviors may be feasible in a given situation—Autocratic I (AI), Autocratic II (AII), Consultative I (CI), Consultative II (CII), and Group II (GII):

> **leader-participation model**
> A leadership theory that provides a set of rules to determine the form and amount of participative decision making in different situations.

- ◆ AI. You solve the problem or make a decision yourself using whatever facts you have at hand.

- ◆ AII. You obtain the necessary information from subordinates and then decide on the solution to the problem yourself. You may or may not tell them about the nature of the situation you face. You seek only relevant facts from them, not their advice or counsel.

- ◆ CI. You share the problem with relevant subordinates one-on-one, getting their ideas and suggestions. However, the final decision is yours alone.

- ◆ CII. You share the problem with your subordinates as a group, collectively obtaining their ideas and suggestions. Then you make the decision that may or may not reflect your subordinates' influence.

- ◆ GII. You share the problem with your subordinates as a group. Your goal is to help the group concur on a decision. Your ideas are not given any greater weight than those of others.

Vroom and Jago have developed a computer program that cuts through the complexity of the new model. But managers can still use decision trees to select their leader style if there are no shades of gray (that is, when the status of a variable is clear-cut so that a "Yes" or "No" response will be accurate), there are no critically severe time constraints, and subordinates are not geographically dispersed. Exhibit 10-7 on page 365 illustrates one of these decision trees.

Research testing of the original leader-participation model was very encouraging.[45] Because the revised model is new, its validity still needs to be assessed. But the new model is a direct extension of the 1973 version and it's also consistent with our current knowledge of the benefits and costs of

Exhibit 10-6 Contingency Variables in the Revised Leader-Participation Model

QR: Quality Requirement
How important is the technical quality of this decision?

1	2	3	4	5
No Importance	Low Importance	Average Importance	High Importance	Critical Importance

CR: Commitment Requirement
How important is subordinate commitment to the decision?

1	2	3	4	5
No Importance	Low Importance	Average Importance	High Importance	Critical Importance

LI: Leader Information
Do you have sufficient information to make a high-quality decision?

1	2	3	4	5
No	Probably No	Maybe	Probably Yes	Yes

ST: Problem Structure
Is the problem well structured?

1	2	3	4	5
No	Probably No	Maybe	Probably Yes	Yes

CP: Commitment Probability
If you were to make the decision by yourself, is it reasonably certain that your subordinates would be committed to the decision?

1	2	3	4	5
No	Probably No	Maybe	Probably Yes	Yes

GC: Goal Congruence
Do subordinates share the organizational goals to be attained in solving this problem?

1	2	3	4	5
No	Probably No	Maybe	Probably Yes	Yes

CO: Subordinate Conflict
Is conflict among subordinates over preferred solutions likely?

1	2	3	4	5
No	Probably No	Maybe	Probably Yes	Yes

SI: Subordinate Information
Do subordinates have sufficient information to make a high-quality decision?

1	2	3	4	5
No	Probably No	Maybe	Probably Yes	Yes

TC: Time Constraint
Does a critically severe time constraint limit your ability to involve subordinates?

1	5
No	Yes

GD: Geographical Dispersion
Are the costs involved in bringing together geographically dispersed subordinates prohibitive?

1	5
No	Yes

MT: Motivation—Time
How important is it to you to minimize the time it takes to make the decision?

1	2	3	4	5
No Importance	Low Importance	Average Importance	High Importance	Critical Importance

MD: Motivation—Development
How important is it to you to maximize the opportunities for subordinate development?

1	2	3	4	5
No Importance	Low Importance	Average Importance	High Importance	Critical Importance

Source: V.H. Vroom and A.G. Jago, (eds.), *THE NEW LEADERSHIP: Managing Participation in Organizations,* ©1988. Reprinted with permission of Prentice Hall, Inc., Upper Saddle River, NJ.

Exhibit 10-7
The Revised Leadership-Participation Model
(Time-Driven Decision Tree Group Problems)

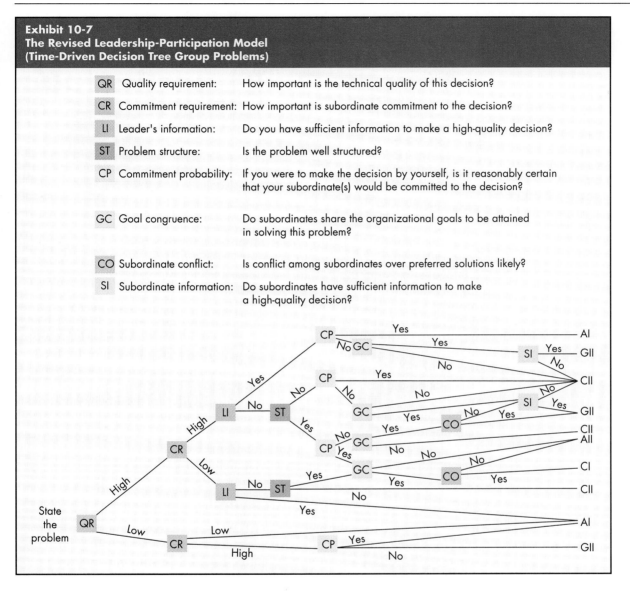

QR	Quality requirement:	How important is the technical quality of this decision?
CR	Commitment requirement:	How important is subordinate commitment to the decision?
LI	Leader's information:	Do you have sufficient information to make a high-quality decision?
ST	Problem structure:	Is the problem well structured?
CP	Commitment probability:	If you were to make the decision by yourself, is it reasonably certain that your subordinate(s) would be committed to the decision?
GC	Goal congruence:	Do subordinates share the organizational goals to be attained in solving this problem?
CO	Subordinate conflict:	Is conflict among subordinates over preferred solutions likely?
SI	Subordinate information:	Do subordinates have sufficient information to make a high-quality decision?

participation. So, at this time, we have every reason to believe that the revised model provides an excellent guide to help managers choose the most appropriate leadership style in different situations.

Two last points before we move on. First, the revised leader-participation model is very sophisticated and complex, which makes it impossible to describe in detail in a basic OB textbook. But the variables identified in Exhibit 10-6 provide you with some solid insights about which contingency variables you need to consider when choosing your leadership style.

Second, the leader-participation model confirms that leadership research should be directed at the situation rather than the person. It probably makes more sense to talk about autocratic and participative *situations* than about autocratic and participative *leaders*. As did House in his path-goal theory, Vroom, Yetton, and Jago argue against the notion that leader behavior is inflexible. The leader-participation model assumes that the leader can adjust his or her style to different situations.

Exhibit 10-8

Source: B. Parker and J. Hart, *Let There Be Reign* (Greenwich, CT: Fawcett Books, 1972). By permission of Johnny Hart and Creators Syndicate, Inc.

The cartoon in Exhibit 10-8 proposes adjusting the individual to the coat, rather than vice versa. In terms of leadership, we can think of "coat" as analogous to "situation." If an individual's leadership style range is very narrow, as Fiedler proposes, we are required to place that individual into the appropriate-size situation if he or she is to lead successfully. But there is another possibility: If House and Vroom-Yetton-Jago are right, the individual leader has to assess the situation that is available and adjust his or her style accordingly. Whether we should adjust the situation to fit the person or fix the person to fit the situation is an important issue. The answer is probably that it depends on the leader—specifically, on whether that person rates high or low on self-monitoring.[46] As we know, individuals differ in their behavioral flexibility. Some people show considerable ability to adjust their behavior to external, situational factors; they are adaptable. Others, however, exhibit high levels of consistency regardless of the situation. High self-monitors are generally able to adjust their leadership style to suit changing situations.

Sometimes Leadership Is Irrelevant!

In keeping with the contingency spirit, we want to conclude this section by offering this notion: the belief that some leadership style *will always* be effective *regardless* of the situation may not be true. Leadership may not always be important. Data from numerous studies collectively demonstrate that, in many situations, whatever behaviors leaders exhibit are irrelevant. Certain individual, job, and organizational variables can act as *substitutes* for leadership or *neutralize* the leader's effect to influence his or her subordinates.[47]

Neutralizers make it impossible for leader behavior to make any difference to subordinate outcomes. They negate the leader's influence. Substitutes, on the other hand, make a leader's influence not only impossible but also unnecessary. They act as a replacement for the leader's influence. For instance, characteristics of subordinates such as their experience, training, "professional" orientation, or indifference toward organizational rewards can substitute for, or neutralize the effect of, leadership. Experience and training, for instance, can replace the need for a leader's support or ability to create structure and reduce task ambiguity. Jobs that are inherently unambiguous and routine or that are intrinsically satisfying may place fewer demands on the leadership variable. Organizational characteristics like explicit formalized goals, rigid rules and procedures, and cohesive work groups can replace formal leadership (see Exhibit 10-9).

Exhibit 10-9 Substitutes and Neutralizers for Leadership		
Defining Characteristics	**Relationship-Oriented Leadership**	**Task-Oriented Leadership**
Individual		
Experience/training	No effect on	Substitutes for
Professionalism	Substitutes for	Substitutes for
Indifference to rewards	Neutralizes	Neutralizes
Job		
Highly structured task	No effect on	Substitutes for
Provides its own feedback	No effect on	Substitutes for
Intrinsically satisfying	Substitutes for	No effect on
Organization		
Explicit formalized goals	No effect on	Substitutes for
Rigid rules and procedures	No effect on	Substitutes for
Cohesive work groups	Substitutes for	Substitutes for

Source: Based on S. Kerr and J.M. Jermier, "Substitutes for Leadership: Their Meaning and Measurement," *Organizational Behavior and Human Performance*, December 1978, p. 378.

This recent recognition that leaders don't always have an impact on subordinate outcomes should not be that surprising. After all, we have introduced a number of variables—attitudes, personality, ability, and group norms, to name but a few—that have been documented as having an effect on employee performance and satisfaction. Yet supporters of the leadership concept have tended to place an undue burden on this variable for explaining and predicting behavior. It is too simplistic to consider subordinates as guided to goal accomplishments solely by the behavior of their leader. It is important, therefore, to recognize explicitly that leadership is merely another independent variable in our overall OB model. In some situations, it may contribute a lot to explaining employee productivity, absence, turnover, and satisfaction, but in other situations, it may contribute little toward that end.

Looking for Common Ground: What Does It All Mean?

The topic of leadership certainly doesn't lack for theories. But from an overview perspective, what does it all mean? Let's try to identify commonalities among the leadership theories and attempt to determine what, if any, practical value the theories hold for application to organizations.

Careful examination discloses that the concepts of "task" and "people"—often expressed in more elaborate terms that hold substantially the same meaning—permeate most of the theories.[48] The task dimension is called just that by Fiedler, but it goes by the name of "initiating structure" for the Ohio State group, "directive leadership" by path-goal supporters, "production orientation" by the Michigan researchers, and "concern for production" by Blake and Mouton. The people dimension gets similar treatment, going under such aliases as "consideration," "employee-oriented," "supportive," or "relationship-oriented" leadership. With the obvious exception posed by the

Scandinavian studies, leadership behavior tends to be reduced to two dimensions—task and people—but researchers continue to differ as to whether the orientations are two ends of a single continuum (you could be high on one or the other but not both) or two independent dimensions (you could be high or low on both).

Although one well-known scholar argues that virtually every theory has also "wrestled with the question of how much a leader should share power with subordinates in decision making,"[49] there is far less support for this contention. The situational leadership theory and the leader-participation model address this issue, but the task–people dichotomy appears to be far more encompassing.

Leadership theorists don't agree on the issue of whether a leader's style is fixed or flexible. For example, Fiedler takes the former position, while Vroom, Yetton, and Jago argue for the latter. As previously noted, our position is that both are probably right—it depends on the leader's personality. High self-monitors are more likely to adjust their leadership style to changing situations than are low self-monitors.[50] So the need to adjust the situation to the leader in order to improve the leader–situation match seems to be necessary only with low self-monitoring individuals.

How should we interpret the findings presented so far in this chapter? Some traits have proved, over time, to be modest predictors of leadership effectiveness. But knowing that a manager possesses intelligence, ambition, self-confidence, or the like would by no means assure us that his or her subordinates would be productive and satisfied employees. The ability of these traits to predict leadership success is just not that strong.

The early task–people approaches (such as the Ohio State, Michigan, and Managerial Grid theories) also offer us little substance. The strongest statement one can make based on these theories is that leaders who rate high in people orientation should end up with satisfied employees. The research is too mixed to make predictions regarding employee productivity or the effect of a task orientation on productivity and satisfaction.

The most important contribution of the Fiedler model may well be that it initiated a more rigorous search to identify contingency variables in leadership. While this model is no longer at the cutting edge of leadership theories, several of the situational variables that Fiedler originally identified continue to surface in more recent contingency theories.

Hersey and Blanchard's situational leadership theory is straightforward, intuitively appealing, and important for its explicit recognition that the subordinate's ability and motivation are critical to the leader's success. Yet, in spite of its wide acceptance by practitioners, the mixed empirical support renders the theory, at least at this time, more speculative than substantive.

Leader–member exchange theory looks at leadership from a different angle. It focuses on in-groups and out-groups. Given the impressive evidence that in-group employees have higher performance and satisfaction than out-group members, the theory provides valuable insight for predicting leader effect as long as we know whether an employee is an "in" or an "out."

Studies testing the original Vroom-Yetton version of the leader-participation model were supportive. Given that the revised Vroom-Jago version is a sophisticated extension of the original model, we should expect it to be even better. But the complexity of the model is a major limitation to its usage. With five styles and twelve contingency variables, it is difficult to use as a day-to-day guide for practicing managers. Still, leadership and decision making are

Rhonda Fryman is a team leader at Toyota Motor Manufacturing's plant in Georgetown, Kentucky. She exemplifies Toyota's philosophy of striving to create a warm, caring atmosphere with a high degree of respect for employees, which leads to their high levels of motivation and productivity. Consistent with the contingency models, Fryman is an effective leader because she assists her team in meeting their daily production goals and provides direction and support in achieving Toyota's quality goals.

complex issues requiring a complex process. To hope for some easy but valid model may be wishful thinking. The important conclusion here seems to be that where we find leaders who follow the model, we should expect also to find productive and satisfied employees.[51]

Finally, the path-goal model provides a framework for explaining and predicting leadership effectiveness that has developed a solid, empirical foundation. It recognizes that a leader's success depends on adjusting his or her style to the environment the leader is placed in, as well as to the individual characteristics of followers. In a limited way, path-goal theory validates contingency variables in other leadership theories. For example, its emphasis on task structure is consistent with the Fiedler contingency model and Vroom and Jago's leader-participation model (remember their question: Is the problem well structured?). Path-goal theory's recognition of individual characteristics is also consistent with Hersey and Blanchard's focus on the experience and ability of followers.

The Most Recent Approaches to Leadership

We conclude our review of leadership theories by presenting four more recent approaches to the subject. These are an attribution theory of leadership, charismatic leadership, transactional versus transformational leadership, and visionary leadership. If there is one theme to the approaches in this section, it is that they all deemphasize theoretical complexity and look at leadership more the way the average "person on the street" views the subject.

Attribution Theory of Leadership

In chapter 3, we discussed attribution theory in relation to perception. Attribution theory has also been used to help explain the perception of leadership.

Attribution theory, as you remember, deals with people trying to make sense out of cause-effect relationships. When something happens, they want to attribute it to something. In the context of leadership, attribution theory says that leadership is merely an attribution that people make about other individuals.[52] Using the attribution framework, researchers have found that people characterize leaders as having such traits as intelligence, outgoing personality, strong verbal skills, aggressiveness, understanding, and industriousness.[53] Similarly, the high-high leader (high on both initiating structure and consideration) has been found to be consistent with attributions of what makes a good leader.[54] That is, regardless of the situation, a high-high leadership style tends to be perceived as best. At the organizational level, the attribution framework accounts for the conditions under which people use leadership to explain organizational outcomes. Those conditions are extremes in organizational performance. When an organization has either extremely negative or extremely positive performance, people are prone to make leadership attributions to explain the performance.[55] This helps to account for the vulnerability of CEOs when their organizations suffer a major financial setback, regardless of whether or not they had much to do with it. It also accounts for why these CEOs tend to be given credit for extremely positive financial results—again, regardless of how much or how little they contributed.

◆ **Effective leaders are generally considered consistent or unwavering in their decisions.**

One of the more interesting themes in the **attribution theory of leadership** literature is the perception that effective leaders are generally considered consistent or unwavering in their decisions.[56] That is, one of the explanations for why Ronald Reagan (during his first term as president) was perceived as a leader was that he was fully committed, steadfast, and consistent in the decisions he made and the goals he set. It can also help explain some of the criticism targeted at President Bill Clinton. He is seen by many as "wishy-washy" on the issues and as continually changing his mind.

attribution theory of leadership
Proposes that leadership is merely an attribution that people make about other individuals.

Charismatic Leadership Theory

charismatic leadership
Followers make attributions of heroic or extraordinary leadership abilities when they observe certain behaviors.

Charismatic leadership theory is an extension of attribution theory. It says that followers make attributions of heroic or extraordinary leadership abilities when they observe certain behaviors.[57] Studies on charismatic leadership have, for the most part, been directed at identifying those behaviors that differentiate charismatic leaders from their noncharismatic counterparts. Some examples of individuals frequently cited as being charismatic leaders include John F. Kennedy, Martin Luther King, Jr., Walt Disney, Mary Kay Ash (founder of Mary Kay Cosmetics), Ross Perot, Steve Jobs (co-founder of Apple Computer), Ted Turner, Lee Iacocca (former chairman of Chrysler), Jan Carlzon (chairman of SAS Airlines), and General Norman Schwarzkopf.

Several authors have attempted to identify personal characteristics of the charismatic leader. Robert House (of path-goal fame) identified three: extremely high confidence, dominance, and strong convictions in his or her beliefs.[58] Warren Bennis, after studying 90 of the most effective and successful leaders in the United States, found that they had four common competencies: They had a compelling vision or sense of purpose; they could communicate that vision in clear terms that their followers could readily identify with; they demonstrated consistency and focus in the pursuit of their vision; and they knew their own strengths and capitalized on them.[59] The most comprehensive analysis, however, has been completed by Conger and Kanungo at McGill University.[60] Among their conclusions, they propose that charismatic leaders

Exhibit 10-10 Key Characteristics of Charismatic Leaders

1. *Self-confidence.* They have complete confidence in their judgment and ability.
2. *A vision.* This is an idealized goal that proposes a future better than the status quo. The greater the disparity between this idealized goal and the status quo, the more likely that followers will attribute extraordinary vision to the leader.
3. *Ability to articulate the vision.* They are able to clarify and state the vision in terms that are understandable to others. This articulation demonstrates an understanding of the followers' needs and, hence, acts as a motivating force.
4. *Strong convictions about the vision.* Charismatic leaders are perceived as being strongly committed, and willing to take on high personal risk, incur high costs, and engage in self-sacrifice to achieve their vision.
5. *Behavior that is out of the ordinary.* Those with charisma engage in behavior that is perceived as being novel, unconventional, and counter to norms. When successful, these behaviors evoke surprise and admiration in followers.
6. *Perceived as being a change agent.* Charismatic leaders are perceived as agents of radical change rather than as caretakers of the status quo.
7. *Environment sensitivity.* These leaders are able to make realistic assessments of the environmental constraints and resources needed to bring about change.

Source: Based on J.A. Conger and R.N. Kanungo, "Behavioral Dimensions of Charismatic Leadership," in J.A. Conger and R.N. Kanungo, *Charismatic Leadership* (San Francisco: Jossey-Bass, 1988), p. 91.

have an idealized goal that they want to achieve, a strong personal commitment to their goal, are perceived as unconventional, are assertive and self-confident, and are perceived as agents of radical change rather than managers of the status quo. Exhibit 10-10 summarizes the key characteristics that appear to differentiate charismatic leaders from noncharismatic ones.

Attention has recently been focused on trying to determine how charismatic leaders actually influence followers. The process begins by the leader articulating an appealing vision. This vision provides a sense of continuity for followers by linking the present with a better future for the organization. The leader then communicates high performance expectations and expresses confidence that followers can attain them. This enhances follower self-esteem and self-confidence. Next, the leader conveys, through words and actions, a new set of values and, by his or her behavior, sets an example for followers to imitate. Finally, the charismatic leader makes self-sacrifices and engages in unconventional behavior to demonstrate courage and convictions about the vision.[61]

What can we say about the charismatic leader's effect on his or her followers? There is an increasing body of research that shows impressive correlations between charismatic leadership and high performance and satisfaction among followers.[62] People working for charismatic leaders are motivated to exert extra work effort and, because they like their leader, express greater satisfaction.

If charisma is desirable, can people learn to be charismatic leaders? Or are charismatic leaders born with their qualities? While a small minority still think charisma cannot be learned, most experts believe that individuals can be trained to exhibit charismatic behaviors and can thus enjoy the benefits that accrue to being labeled "a charismatic leader."[63] For instance, one set of authors proposes that a person can learn to become charismatic by following a three-step process.[64] First, an individual needs to develop the aura of charisma by maintaining an optimistic view; using passion as a catalyst for generating enthusiasm; and communicating with the whole body, not just with words. Second, an individual draws others in by creating a bond that inspires others to follow. And third, the individual brings out the potential in followers by tapping into their emotions. This approach seems to work as evidenced by researchers who've succeeded in actually scripting undergraduate business students to "play" charismatic.[65] The students were taught to articulate an overarching goal, communicate high performance expectations, exhibit confidence in the ability of subordinates to meet these expectations, and empathize with the needs of their subordinates; they learned to project a powerful, confident, and dynamic presence; and they practiced using a captivating and engaging voice tone. To further capture the dynamics and energy of charisma, the leaders were trained to evoke charismatic nonverbal characteristics: They alternated between pacing and sitting on the edges of their desks, leaned toward the subordinate, maintained direct eye contact, and had relaxed postures and animated facial expressions. These researchers found that these students could learn how to project charisma. Moreover, subordinates of these leaders had higher task performance, task adjustment, and adjustment to the leader and to the group than did subordinates who worked under groups led by noncharismatic leaders.

One last word on this topic: Charismatic leadership may not always be needed to achieve high levels of employee performance. It may be most appropriate when the follower's task has an ideological component.[66] This may explain why, when charismatic leaders surface, it is more likely to be in politics, religion, wartime, or when a business firm is introducing a radically new product or facing a life-threatening crisis. Such conditions tend to involve ideological concerns. Franklin D. Roosevelt offered a vision to get Americans out of the Great Depression. Steve Jobs achieved unwavering loyalty and commitment from the technical staff he oversaw at Apple Computer during the late 1970s and early 1980s by articulating a vision of personal computers that would dramatically change the way people lived. General "Stormin Norman" Schwarzkopf's blunt, passionate style, absolute confidence in his troops, and a vision of total victory over Iraq made him a hero in the free world following Operation Desert Storm in 1991. Charismatic leaders, in fact, may become a liability to an organization once the crisis and need for dramatic change subside.[67] Why? Because then the charismatic leader's overwhelming self-confidence often becomes a liability. He or she is unable to listen to others, becomes uncomfortable when challenged by aggressive subordinates, and begins to hold an unjustifiable belief in his or her "rightness" on issues. Philippe Kahn's charismatic style, for instance, was an asset during the years of rapid growth of software-database company Borland International. But Borland's CEO became a liability as the company matured. His dictatorial style, arrogance, and reckless decision making have put the company's future in jeopardy.[68]

Transactional vs. Transformational Leadership

The final stream of research we'll touch on is the recent interest in differentiating transformational leaders from transactional leaders.[69] As you'll see, because transformational leaders are also charismatic, there is some overlap between this topic and our previous discussion of charismatic leadership.

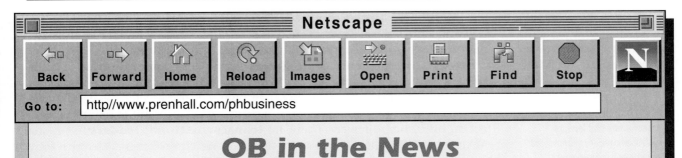

Netscape

| Back | Forward | Home | Reload | Images | Open | Print | Find | Stop | N |

Go to: http//www.prenhall.com/phbusiness

OB in the News

Herb Kelleher: The Charismatic Leader at Southwest Airlines

Southwest Airlines has grown from 198 employees in 1971 to 13,000 employees and more than $2 billion in revenues. It has been profitable for 23 consecutive years and has the lowest cost per passenger mile of any major airline. A large part of Southwest's success belongs to its chairman, CEO, president, and founder, Herb Kelleher (he asks everyone to call him Herb).

Don't confuse Herb Kelleher with any of those serious executives running American, Delta, and other major airlines. No, he's one of a kind! He's the company hellraiser, jokester, and cheerleader—all rolled into one. Give him the opportunity and he'll party with employees into the wee hours of the morning, dress up as Elvis or the Easter Bunny, or lead employees in company cheers. His unorthodox style, plus his unconditional commitment to his employees, has created a "family feeling" among Southwest's workforce that translates into employees who are willing to pitch in wherever needed, to walk—or fly—the extra mile. Pilots sometimes man the boarding gate if things are running slow; ticket agents voluntarily haul luggage if it will help get planes into the air faster. And Herb strives to maintain the same family atmosphere the company had when he knew every employee by their first name. Headquarters walls are filled with company and employee photos and memorabilia. "If you're sick, if you lose a relative, if you get married, if you have a baby, you hear from us," says Herb. Southwest also holds Christmas parties on different dates in its four major locations so employees in each city can talk with corporate executives.

Herb's "I-care" style consistently wins points with employees. According to an executive at Northwest Airlines, "Herb has somehow managed to get union people to identify personally with his company." The following incident captures Kelleher's unique style of labor relations. A Wall Street analyst tells of the time he was having lunch in the company cafeteria. Kelleher, seated at a table across the room with several female employees, suddenly leapt to his feet, kissed one of the women with gusto, and began leading the entire crowd in a series of cheers. When the analyst asked what was going on, one of the executives at his table explained that Kelleher had at that moment negotiated a new contract with Southwest's flight attendants.

Based on K. Labich, "Is Herb Kelleher America's Best CEO?" *Fortune*, May 2, 1994, pp. 44–52; and M.A. Verespej, "Flying His Own Course," *Industry Week*, November 20, 1995, pp. 22–24.

Take It to the Net

We invite you to visit the Robbins page on the Prentice Hall Web site at:

http://www.prenhall.com/robbinsorgbeh

for this chapter's World Wide Web exercise.

transactional leaders
Leaders who guide or motivate their followers in the direction of established goals by clarifying role and task requirements.

transformational leaders
Leaders who provide individualized consideration and intellectual stimulation, and who possess charisma.

Most of the leadership theories presented in this chapter—for instance, the Ohio State studies, Fiedler's model, path-goal theory, and the leader-participation model—have concerned **transactional leaders**. These kinds of leaders guide or motivate their followers in the direction of established goals by clarifying role and task requirements. There is also another type of leader who inspires followers to transcend their own self-interests for the good of the organization, and who is capable of having a profound and extraordinary effect on his or her followers. These are **transformational leaders** like Leslie Wexner of The Limited retail chain and Jack Welch at General Electric. They pay attention to the concerns and developmental needs of individual followers; they change followers' awareness of issues by helping them to look at old problems in new ways; and they are able to excite, arouse, and inspire followers to put out extra effort to achieve group goals. Exhibit 10-11 briefly identifies and defines the four characteristics that differentiate these two types of leaders.

Transactional and transformational leadership should not, however, be viewed as opposing approaches to getting things done.[70] Transformational leadership is built *on top of* transactional leadership—it produces levels of subordinate effort and performance that go beyond what would occur with a transactional approach alone. Moreover, transformational leadership is more than charisma. "The purely charismatic [leader] may want followers to adopt the charismatic's world view and go no further; the transformational leader will attempt to instill in followers the ability to question not only established views but eventually those established by the leader."[71]

The evidence supporting the superiority of transformational leadership over the transactional variety is overwhelmingly impressive. For instance, a number of studies with U.S., Canadian, and German military officers found, at every level, that transformational leaders were evaluated as more effective

Exhibit 10-11 Characteristics of Transactional and Transformational Leaders

Transactional Leader

Contingent Reward: Contracts exchange of rewards for effort, promises rewards for good performance, recognizes accomplishments.

Management by Exception (active): Watches and searches for deviations from rules and standards, takes corrective action.

Management by Exception (passive): Intervenes only if standards are not met.

Laissez-Faire: Abdicates responsibilities, avoids making decisions.

Transformational Leader

Charisma: Provides vision and sense of mission, instills pride, gains respect and trust.

Inspiration: Communicates high expectations, uses symbols to focus efforts, expresses important purposes in simple ways.

Intellectual Stimulation: Promotes intelligence, rationality, and careful problem solving.

Individualized Consideration: Gives personal attention, treats each employee individually, coaches, advises.

Source: B.M. Bass, "From Transactional to Transformational Leadership: Learning to Share the Vision," *Organizational Dynamics*, Winter 1990, p. 22. Reprinted, by permission of publisher. American Management Association, New York. All rights reserved.

than their transactional counterparts.[72] And managers at Federal Express who were rated by their followers as exhibiting more transformational leadership were evaluated by their immediate supervisors as higher performers and more promotable.[73] In summary, the overall evidence indicates that transformational leadership is more strongly correlated than transactional leadership with lower turnover rates, higher productivity, and higher employee satisfaction.[74]

Visionary Leadership

The term *vision* recurred throughout our discussion of charismatic leadership, but visionary leadership goes beyond charisma. In this section, we review recent revelations about the importance of visionary leadership.

Visionary leadership is the ability to create and articulate a realistic, credible, attractive vision of the future for an organization or organizational unit that grows out of and improves upon the present.[75] This vision, if properly selected and implemented, is so energizing that it "in effect jump-starts the future by calling forth the skills, talents, and resources to make it happen."[76]

A review of various definitions finds that a vision differs from other forms of direction setting in several ways: "A vision has clear and compelling imagery that offers an innovative way to improve, which recognizes and draws on traditions, and connects to actions that people can take to realize change. Vision taps people's emotions and energy. Properly articulated, a vision creates the enthusiasm that people have for sporting events and other leisure time activities, bringing the energy and commitment to the workplace."[77]

The case in favor of visionary leadership has been made by many writers. For instance: "the 21st-century organization virtually demands visionary leadership. It cannot function without it, for an organization driven by accelerating technological change, staffed by a diverse, multicultural mix of highly intelligent knowledge workers, facing global complexity, a vast kaleidoscope of individual customer needs, and the incessant demands of multiple constituencies would simply self-destruct without a common sense of direction."[78] Another argues that vision is "the glue that binds individuals into a group with a common goal . . . when shared by employees, [it] can keep an entire company moving forward in face of difficulties, enabling and inspiring leaders and employees alike."[79]

A survey of 1,500 senior leaders, 870 of them CEOs from 20 different countries, additionally attests to the growing importance of visionary leadership.[80] The leaders were asked to describe the key traits or talents desirable for a CEO in the year 2000. The dominant characteristic most frequently mentioned was that the CEO must convey a "strong sense of vision." Ninety-eight percent rated this trait as "most important." Another study contrasted 18 visionary companies with 18 comparable nonvisionary firms over a 65-year period.[81] The visionary companies were found to have outperformed the comparison group by six times on standard financial criteria and their stocks outperformed the general market by 15 times.

The key properties of a vision seem to be inspirational possibilities that are value centered, realizable, with superior imagery and articulation.[82] Visions should be able to create possibilities that are inspirational, unique, and offer a new order that can produce organizational distinction. A vision is likely to fail if it doesn't offer a view of the future that is clearly and

visionary leadership
The ability to create and articulate a realistic, credible, attractive vision of the future for an organization or organizational unit that grows out of and improves upon the present.

demonstrably better for the organization and its members. Desirable visions fit the times and circumstances and reflect the uniqueness of the organization. People in the organization must also believe that the vision is attainable. The vision should be perceived as challenging yet doable. Visions that have clear articulation and powerful imagery are more easily grasped and accepted.

What do visions look like? They're typically easier to talk about than to actually create, but here are a few examples: "To be the single source software provider to the financial services industry." "To be the leading African American owned promotional and public relations firm in the USA." "To become the most customer responsive producer of automobile interior trim in North America."[83] Here are some additional organization-specific examples.[84] Walt Disney single-handedly reinvented the idea of an amusement park when he described his vision of Disneyland in the early 1950s. Rupert Murdoch was one of the first people to see the future of the communication industry by combining entertainment and media. Through his News Corporation, Murdoch has successfully integrated a broadcast network, television stations, movie studio, publishing, and global satellite distribution. Mary Kay Ash's vision of women as entrepreneurs selling products that improved their self-image gave impetus to her cosmetics company. Scandinavian Airlines CEO, Jan Carlzon, used the notion of "50,000 daily moments of truth" to depict the emphasis to be placed on customer service. Carlzon wanted every employee to ensure that each "moment of truth"—those instances where customers come into contact with employees—would be a positive experience for SAS customers. H. Wayne Huizenga, who began picking up garbage with a beat-up old truck, envisioned potential in waste disposal and built Waste Management (now WMX). Then Huizenga bought into a small Dallas video-store chain, saw the future was in big stores, and turned the small chain into Blockbuster Video (now part of Viacom). Steve Jobs created a vision for Apple Computer, which energized employees around the idea of not just building computers but dramatically changing the world. Charles Schwab is currently attempting to redefine financial services by combining discount prices with comprehensive offerings.

What skills do visionary leaders exhibit? Once the vision is identified, these leaders appear to have three qualities that are related to effectiveness in their visionary roles.[85]

First is the ability to explain the vision to others. The leader needs to make the vision clear in terms of required actions and aims through clear oral and written communication. The best vision is likely to be ineffective if the leader isn't a strong communicator. Ronald Reagan—the so-called "great communicator"—used his years of acting experience to help him articulate a simple vision for his presidency: a return to a happier and more prosperous times through less government, lower taxes, and a strong military.

The second skill needed is to be able to express the vision not just verbally but through the leader's behavior. This requires behaving in ways that continually convey and reinforce the vision. Herb Kelleher at Southwest Airlines lives and breathes his commitment to customer service. He's famous within the company for jumping in, when needed, to help check in passengers, load baggage, fill in for flight attendants or do anything else to make the customer's experience more pleasant.

The third skill is being able to extend the vision to different leadership contexts. This is the ability to sequence activities so the vision can be applied

Herb Kelleher, chief executive of Southwest Airlines, has the three qualities that make a visionary leader effective. First, as a strong communicator, he articulates his vision of giving customers excellent service by expecting employees to help whenever and wherever they're needed. Second, as shown here, he reinforces his vision by pitching in to help. And third, he's able to extend his vision to all employees, whether they are a pilot, flight attendant, luggage handler, or ticket agent.

in a variety of situations. For instance, the vision has to be as meaningful to the people in accounting as to those in marketing, and to employees in Prague as well as in Pittsburgh.

Contemporary Issues in Leadership

Do men and women rely on different leadership styles? If so, is one style inherently superior to the other? What unique demands do teams place on leaders? How is the current popularity of *empowerment* affecting the way managers lead? Since leaders aren't leaders unless they have followers, what can managers do to make employees more effective followers? How does national culture affect the choice of leadership style? Is there a biological basis for leadership? Is there a moral dimension to leadership?

In this section, we briefly address these seven contemporary issues in leadership.

Gender: Do Males and Females Lead Differently?

An extensive review of the literature suggests two conclusions regarding gender and leadership.[86] First, the similarities between men and women tend to outweigh the differences. Second, what differences there are seem to be that women fall back on a more democratic leadership style, while men feel more comfortable with a directive style.

The similarities among men and women leaders shouldn't be completely surprising. Almost all the studies looking at this issue have used managerial positions as being synonymous with leadership. As such, gender differences apparent in the general population don't tend to be as evident because of career self-selection and organization selection. Just like people who choose careers in law enforcement or civil engineering have a lot in common, individuals who choose managerial careers also tend to have commonalities. People with traits associated with leadership—such as intelligence, confidence, and sociability—are more likely to be perceived as leaders and encouraged to pursue careers where they can exert leadership. This is true regardless of gender. Similarly, organizations tend to recruit and promote people into leadership positions who project leadership attributes. The result is that, regardless of gender, those who achieve formal leadership positions in organizations tend to be more alike than different.

Despite the previous conclusion, studies indicate some differences in the inherent leadership styles between women and men. Women tend to adopt a more democratic leadership style. They encourage participation, share power and information, and attempt to enhance followers' self-worth. They prefer to lead through inclusion and rely on their charisma, expertise, contacts, and interpersonal skills to influence others. Men, on the other hand, are more likely to use a directive command-and-control style. They rely on the formal authority of their position for their influence base. However, consistent with our first conclusion, these findings need to be qualified. The tendency for female leaders to be more democratic than males declines when women are in male-dominated jobs. Apparently, group norms and masculine stereotypes of leaders override personal preferences so that women abandon their feminine styles in such jobs and act more autocratically.

Given that men have historically held the great majority of leadership positions in organizations, it's tempting to assume that the existence of the noted differences between men and women would automatically work to favor men. It doesn't. In today's organizations, flexibility, teamwork, trust, and information sharing are replacing rigid structures, competitive individualism, control, and secrecy. The best managers listen, motivate, and provide support to their people. And many women seem to do those things better than men. As a specific example, the expanded use of cross-functional teams in organizations means that effective managers must become skillful negotiators. The leadership styles women typically use can make them better at negotiating, as they are less likely to focus on wins, losses, and competition, as do men. They tend to treat negotiations in the context of a continuing relationship—trying hard to make the other party a winner in its own and other's eyes.

Providing Team Leadership

Leadership is increasingly taking place within a team context. As teams grow in popularity, the role of the leader in guiding team members takes on heightened importance.[87] And the role of team leader is different from the traditional leadership role performed by first-line supervisors. J.D. Bryant, a supervisor at Texas Instruments' Forest Lane plant in Dallas, found that out.[88] One day he was happily overseeing a staff of 15 circuit-board assemblers. The next day he was informed the company was moving to teams and that he was to become a "facilitator." "I'm supposed to teach the teams everything I know and then let them make their own decisions," he said. Confused about his new role, he admitted "there was no clear plan on what I was supposed to do." In this section, we consider the challenge of being a team leader, review the new roles that team leaders take on, and offer some tips on how to increase the likelihood that you can perform effectively in this position.

Many leaders are not equipped to handle the change to teams. As one prominent consultant noted, "even the most capable managers have trouble making the transition because all the command-and-control type things they were encouraged to do before are no longer appropriate. There's no reason to have any skill or sense of this."[89] This same consultant estimated that "probably 15 percent of managers are natural team leaders; another 15 percent could never lead a team because it runs counter to their personality. [They're unable to sublimate their dominating style for the good of the team.] Then there's that huge group in the middle: Team leadership doesn't come naturally to them, but they can learn it."[90]

The challenge for most managers, then, is to learn how to become an effective team leader. They have to learn skills such as the patience to share information, to trust others, to give up authority, and understanding when to intervene. Effective leaders have mastered the difficult balancing act of knowing when to leave their teams alone and when to intercede. New team leaders may try to retain too much control at a time when team members need more autonomy, or they may abandon their teams at times when the teams need support and help.[91]

A recent study of 20 organizations that had reorganized themselves around teams found certain common responsibilities that all leaders had to assume. These included coaching, facilitating, handling disciplinary problems, reviewing team/individual performance, training, and communication.[92] Many of these responsibilities apply to managers in general. A more meaningful way to describe the team leader's job is to focus on two priorities: managing the team's external boundary and facilitating the team process.[93] We've broken these priorities down into four specific roles.

First, team leaders are *liaisons with external constituencies*. These include upper management, other internal teams, customers, and suppliers. The leader represents the team to other constituencies, secures needed resources, clarifies others' expectations of the team, gathers information from the outside, and shares this information with team members.

Second, team leaders are *troubleshooters*. When the team has problems and asks for assistance, team leaders sit in on meetings and help try to resolve the problems. This rarely relates to technical or operation issues because the team members typically know more about the tasks being done than does the team leader. Where the leader is most likely to contribute is by asking penetrating questions, helping the team talk through problems, and by getting needed resources from external constituencies. For instance, when a team in an aerospace firm found itself short-handed, its team leader took responsibility for getting more staff. He presented the team's case to upper management and got the approval through the company's human resources department.

Third, team leaders are *conflict managers*. When disagreements surface, they help process the conflict. What's the source of the conflict? Who is involved? What are the issues? What resolution options are available? What are the advantages and disadvantages of each? By getting team members to address questions such as these, the leader minimizes the disruptive aspects of intrateam conflicts.

Finally, team leaders are *coaches*. They clarify expectations and roles, teach, offer support, cheerlead, and whatever else is necessary to help team members improve their work performance.

Leading Through Empowerment

An important trend has developed over the past decade that has immense implications for leadership. That trend is for managers to embrace **empowerment**. More specifically, managers are being advised that effective leaders

empowerment
Putting employees in charge of what they do.

From Concepts to Skills

Coaching

Effective managers are increasingly being described as *coaches* rather than *bosses*. They are expected to provide instruction, guidance, advice, and encouragement to help employees improve their job performance. If a manager wants to transform himself or herself into a coach, what needs to be done? More specifically, what actions characterize effective coaching?

There are three general skills that managers should exhibit if they are to help their employees generate breakthroughs in performance.[94] The following reviews these general skills and the specific behaviors associated with each.

1. *Ability to analyze ways to improve an employee's performance and capabilities.* A coach looks for opportunities for an employee to expand his or her capabilities and improve performance.
   a. Observe your employee's behavior on a day-to-day basis.
   b. Ask questions of the employee: Why do you do a task this way? Can it be improved? What other approaches might be used?
   c. Show genuine interest in the person as an individual, not merely as an employee. Respect his or her individuality. More important than any technical expertise you can provide about improving job performance is the insight you have into the employee's uniqueness.
   d. Listen to the employee. You can't understand the world from an employee's perspective unless you listen.

2. *Ability to create a supportive climate.* It's the coach's responsibility to reduce barriers to development and facilitate a climate that encourages performance improvement.
   a. Create a climate that contributes to a free and open exchange of ideas.
   b. Offer help and assistance. Give guidance and advice when asked.
   c. Encourage your employees. Be positive and upbeat. Don't use threats.
   d. Focus on mistakes as learning opportunities. Change implies risk and employees must not feel that mistakes will be punished. When failure occurs, ask: "What did we learn that can help us in the future?"
   e. Reduce obstacles. What factors do you control that, if eliminated, would help the employee to improve his or her job performance?
   f. Express to the employee the value of his or her contribution to the unit's goals.
   g. Take personal responsibility for the outcome, but don't rob employees of their full responsibility. Validate the employees' efforts when they succeed, and point to what was missing when they fail. Never blame the employees for poor results.

3. *Ability to influence employees to change their behavior.* The ultimate test of coaching effectiveness is whether or not an employee's performance improves. However, this is not a static concept. We are concerned with ongoing growth and development.
   a. Encourage continual improvement. Recognize and reward small improvements and, consistent with TQM, treat coaching as helping employees to continually work toward improvement. There are no absolute upper limits to an employee's job performance.
   b. Use a collaborative style. Employees will be more responsive to accepting change if they participate in identifying and choosing among improvement ideas.
   c. Break difficult tasks down into simpler ones. By breaking down more complex jobs into a series of tasks of increasing difficulty, dis-

couraged employees are more likely to experience success. Achieving success on simpler tasks encourages them to take on more difficult ones.	**d.** Model the qualities that you expect from your employees. If you want openness, dedication, commitment, and responsibility from your employees, you must	demonstrate these qualities yourself. Your employees will look to you as a role model, so make sure your deeds match your words.

share power and responsibility with their employees.[95] The empowering leader's role is to show trust, provide vision, remove performance-blocking barriers, offer encouragement, motivate, and coach employees. The list of companies that have jumped on the "empowerment bandwagon" includes such world-famous corporations as General Electric, Intel, Ford, Saturn, Scandinavian Airline Systems, Harley-Davidson, Goodyear, and Conrail. Many have introduced empowerment as part of their corporatewide efforts in implementing total quality management.[96]

Does this wholesale embracing of shared leadership strike you as a bit strange, given the attention that has been focused on contingency approaches to leadership? If it doesn't, it should. Why? Because empowerment proponents are essentially advocating a noncontingent approach to leadership. Directive, task-oriented, autocratic leadership is out, and empowerment is in.

The problem with the current empowerment movement is that it ignores the extent to which leadership can be shared and the conditions facilitating the success of shared leadership. Because of factors such as downsizing, higher employee skills, commitment of organizations to continuous training, implementation of total quality management programs, and introduction of self-managed teams, there seems to be no doubt that an increasing number of situations call for a more empowering approach to leadership. But not *all* situations! Blanket acceptance of empowerment, or *any* universal approach to leadership, is inconsistent with the best and most current evidence we have on the subject.[97]

◆ The problem with the current empowerment movement is that it ignores the extent to which leadership can be shared and the conditions facilitating success of shared leadership.

What about Followership?

When someone was once asked what it took to be a great leader, he responded: Great followers! While the response may have seemed sarcastic, it has some truth. We have long known that many managers can't lead a horse to water. But, then again, many subordinates can't follow a parade.

Only recently have we begun to recognize that in addition to having leaders who can lead, successful organizations need followers who can follow.[98] In fact, it's probably fair to say that all organizations have far more followers than leaders, so ineffective followers may be more of a handicap to an organization than ineffective leaders.

Exhibit 10-12

Source: THE FAR SIDE copyright 1990 & 1991 Farworks, Inc./Dist. by Universal Press Syndicate. Reprinted with permission. All rights reserved.

"Well, what d'ya know! . . . *I'm* a follower, too!"

What qualities do effective followers have? One writer focuses on four.[99]

1. *They manage themselves well.* They are able to think for themselves. They can work independently and without close supervision.

2. *They are committed to a purpose outside themselves.* Effective followers are committed to something—a cause, a product, a work team, an organization, an idea—in addition to the care of their own lives. Most people like working with colleagues who are emotionally, as well as physically, committed to their work.

3. *They build their competence and focus their efforts for maximum impact.* Effective followers master skills that will be useful to their organizations, and they hold higher performance standards than their job or work group requires.

4. *They are courageous, honest, and credible.* Effective followers establish themselves as independent, critical thinkers whose knowledge and judgment can be trusted. They hold high ethical standards, give credit where credit is due, and aren't afraid to own up to their mistakes.

National Culture as an Added Contingency Variable

One general conclusion that surfaces from our discussion of leadership is that effective leaders don't use any single style. They adjust their style to the situation. While not mentioned explicitly in any of the theories we presented, certainly national culture is an important situational factor determining which leadership style will be most effective.[100] We propose that you consider it as another contingency variable. It can help explain, for instance, why executives at the highly successful Asia Department Store in central China blatantly brag about practicing "heartless" management, require new employees to undergo two to four weeks of military training with units of the People's Liberation Army in order to increase their obedience, and conduct the store's inhouse training sessions in a public place where employees can openly suffer embarrassment from their mistakes.[101]

National culture affects leadership style by way of the subordinate. Leaders cannot choose their styles at will. They are constrained by the cultural conditions that their subordinates have come to expect. For example, a manipulative or autocratic style is compatible with high power distance, and we find high power distance scores in Arab, Far Eastern, and Latin countries. Power distance rankings should also be good indicators of employee willingness to accept participative leadership. Participation is likely to be most effective in such low power distance cultures as exist in Norway, Finland, Denmark, and Sweden. Not incidentally, this may explain (a) why a number of leadership theories (the more obvious being ones like the University of Michigan behavioral studies and the leader-participation model) implicitly favor the use of a participative or people-oriented style; (b) the emergence of development-oriented leader behavior found by Scandinavian researchers; and (c) the recent enthusiasm in North America with empowerment. Remember that most leadership theories were developed by North Americans, using North American subjects; and the United States, Canada, and Scandinavian countries all rate below average on power distance.

Is There a Biological Basis for Leadership?

Is it possible that leader behavior lies in the body's hormones and in the brain's neurotransmitters? While this may take the study of leadership out of the behavioral laboratory and into the chemistry lab, there is increasing evidence indicating that leadership has biological roots.[102]

A growing body of research suggests that the best leaders are not necessarily the smartest, strongest, or most aggressive of a group but rather those who are most proficient at handling social interactions. That finding isn't particularly surprising. However, the researchers have found that effective leaders possess a unique biochemical mixture of hormones and brain chemistry that helps them build social alliances and cope with stress.

◆ There is increasing evidence indicating that leadership has biological roots.

Two chemicals—serotonin and testosterone—have received most of the attention. Increased levels of the former appear to improve sociability and control aggression. Higher levels of the latter increase competitive drive.

Studies with monkeys find that (1) dominant monkeys—the leaders (whether male or female)—have a higher level of serotonin than do their subordinates; and (2) when that leader is removed from the group, the new leader that takes charge shows a marked increase in levels of serotonin. Researchers believe that high levels of serotonin promote leadership by controlling aggressive and antisocial impulses, as well as reducing overreaction to petty or irrelevant stresses. The direction of causation, however, isn't clear: High levels of serotonin may stimulate leadership and/or leadership may result in a rise in serotonin.

Testosterone also seems to play a role in leadership. Studies with baboons find that leaders experience a sudden rise in testosterone levels when legitimate threats appear. In subordinates, the level of testosterone goes down during a crisis.

But enough about monkeys. How about humans? A study in a college fraternity found males in the highest leadership positions had the highest level of serotonin. Researchers have also found that testosterone levels rise in top tennis players before competitive matches. The high levels seem to make the tennis players more assertive and motivated to win. It's been found that testosterone also rises *after* status-enhancing achievements such as winning a promotion or earning a degree, and women in professional jobs have higher levels of the hormone.

The step from laboratory to workplace isn't as far as you might think. For instance, the highly popular antidepressant Prozac (its sales now exceed $2 billion a year and its manufacturer estimates that more than 21 million people worldwide have used it) is one of a new class of drugs called serotonin reuptake inhibitors. It zeros in on one neurotransmitter, serotonin, lifting mood and lessening anxiety by keeping pools of the chemical available in the brain for nerve cells to use and reuse. Prozac raises serotonin and improves the sociability of its users. Additionally, patches—similar to those worn by people trying to quit smoking—are now available to help them increase testosterone levels. Although we certainly aren't suggesting that individuals turn to pills or patches as a means to increase their leadership opportunities, the possibilities are nevertheless thought provoking.

Is There a Moral Dimension to Leadership?

The topic of leadership and ethics has surprisingly received little attention. Only very recently have ethicists and leadership researchers begun to consider the ethical implications in leadership.[103] Why now? One reason may be the growing general interest in ethics throughout the field of management. Another reason may be the discovery by probing biographers that many of our past leaders—such as Martin Luther King, Jr., John F. Kennedy, and Franklin D. Roosevelt—suffered from ethical shortcomings. Regardless, no contemporary discussion of leadership is complete without addressing its ethical dimension.

Ethics touches on leadership at a number of junctures. Transformational leaders, for instance, have been described by one authority as fostering moral virtue when they try to change the attitudes and behaviors of followers.[104] Charisma, too, has an ethical component. Unethical leaders are more likely to use their charisma to enhance *power over* followers, directed toward self-serving ends. Ethical leaders are considered to use their charisma in a socially constructive way to *serve* others.[105] There is also the issue of abuse of power by leaders, for example, when they give themselves large salaries and bonuses while, at the same time, they seek to cut costs by laying off long-time employees. And, of course, the topic of trust explicitly deals with honesty and integrity in leadership.

Leadership effectiveness needs to address the *means* that a leader uses in trying to achieve goals as well as the content of those goals. GE's Jack Welch, for instance, is consistently described as a highly effective leader because he has succeeded in achieving outstanding returns for shareholders. But Welch is also widely regarded as one of the world's toughest managers. He is regularly listed high on *Fortune*'s annual list of the most hated and reviled executives.

Similarly, Bill Gates's success in leading Microsoft to domination of the world's software business has been achieved by means of an extremely demanding work culture. Microsoft's culture demands long work hours by employees and is intolerant of individuals who want to balance work and their personal life. Additionally, ethical leadership must address the content of a leader's goals. Are the changes that the leader seeks for the organization morally acceptable? Is a business leader effective if he or she builds an organization's success by selling products that damage the health of its users? This question might be asked of tobacco executives. Or is a military leader successful by winning a war that should not have been fought in the first place?

Leadership is not value free. Before we judge any leader to be effective, we should consider both the means used by the leader to achieve his or her goals and the moral content of those goals.

Summary and Implications for Managers

Leadership plays a central part in understanding group behavior, for it's the leader who usually provides the direction toward goal attainment. Therefore, a more accurate predictive capability should be valuable in improving group performance.

In this chapter, we described a transition in approaches to the study of leadership—from the simple trait orientation to increasingly complex and sophisticated transactional models, such as path-goal and leader-participation models. With the increase in complexity has also come an increase in our ability to explain and predict behavior.

A major breakthrough in our understanding of leadership came when we recognized the need to include situational factors. Recent efforts have moved beyond mere recognition toward specific attempts to isolate these situational variables. We can expect further progress to be made with leadership models, but in the last decade, we have taken several large steps—large enough that we now can make moderately effective predictions as to who can best lead a group and explain under what conditions a given approach (such as task oriented or people oriented) is likely to lead to high employee performance and satisfaction.

In addition, the study of leadership has expanded to include more heroic and visionary approaches to leadership. As we learn more about the personal characteristics that followers attribute to charismatic and transformational leaders, and about the conditions that facilitate their emergence, we should be better able to predict when followers will exhibit extraordinary commitment and loyalty to their leaders and to those leaders' goals.

Finally, we addressed a number of contemporary issues in leadership. We learned, for instance, that male and female leadership styles tend to be more alike than different, but that women's propensity to rely on shared leadership is more in line with organizational needs in the 1990s than the directive style often preferred by men. Effective team leaders were found to perform four roles: They act as liaisons with external constituencies, they are troubleshooters, they manage conflict, and they coach team members. Empowered leadership was shown to be increasingly popular, but managers should not assume that empowering employees is the ideal leadership style for all occasions. Also, consistent with the contingency approach, managers should be sure to consider national culture as an important variable in choosing a leadership style. On a more controversial note, recent evidence on the link between biology and leadership suggests that the subject of leadership is not the sole province of psychologists and sociologists. In the future, improved understanding of the leadership phenomena may increasingly come from chemists or pharmacologists. Finally, we propose that leadership is not value free. So we should look at the moral content of a leader's goals and the means he or she uses to achieve those goals.

For Review

1. Trace the development of leadership research.
2. Describe the strengths and weaknesses in the trait approach to leadership.
3. What is the Managerial Grid? Contrast its approach to leadership with the approaches of the Ohio State and Michigan groups.
4. What was the contribution of the Scandinavian studies to the behavioral theories?
5. How do Hersey and Blanchard define *readiness*? Is this contingency variable included in any other contingency theory of leadership?
6. When might leaders be irrelevant?
7. Why do you think effective female and male managers often exhibit similar traits and behaviors?
8. What characteristics define an effective follower?
9. Explain the biological basis for leadership effectiveness.
10. What is moral leadership?

For Discussion

1. Develop an example where you operationalize the Fiedler model.
2. Contrast the situational leadership theory with the Managerial Grid.
3. Develop an example where you operationalize path-goal theory.
4. Reconcile Hersey and Blanchard's situational leadership theory, path-goal theory, and substitutes for leadership.
5. What kind of activities could a full-time college student pursue that might lead to the perception that he or she is a charismatic leader? In pursuing those activities, what might the student do to enhance this perception of being charismatic?

Leaders Make a Real Difference!

There can be little question that the success of an organization, or any group within an organization, depends largely on the quality of its leadership. Whether in business, government, education, medicine, or religion, the quality of an organization's leadership determines the quality of the organization itself. Successful leaders anticipate change, vigorously exploit opportunities, motivate their followers to higher levels of productivity, correct poor performance, and lead the organization toward its objectives.

The importance relegated to the leadership function is well known. Rarely does a week go by that we don't hear or read about some leadership concern: "President Fails to Provide the Leadership America Needs!" "The Republican Party Searches for New Leadership!" "Eisner Leads Disney Turnaround!" A review of the leadership literature led two academics to conclude that the research shows "a consistent effect for leadership explaining 20 to 45 percent of the variance on relevant organizational outcomes."*

Why is leadership so important to an organization's success? The answer lies in the need for coordination and control. Organizations exist to achieve objectives that are either impossible or extremely inefficient to achieve if done by individuals acting alone. The organization itself is a coordination and control mechanism. Rules, policies, job descriptions, and authority hierarchies are illustrations of devices created to facilitate coordination and control. But leadership, too, contributes toward integrating various job activities, coordinating communication between organizational subunits, monitoring activities, and controlling deviations from standard. No amount of rules and regulations can replace the experienced leader who can make rapid and decisive decisions.

The importance of leadership is not lost on those who staff organizations. Corporations, government agencies, school systems, and institutions of all shapes and sizes cumulatively spend billions of dollars every year to recruit, select, evaluate, and train individuals for leadership positions. The best evidence, however, of the importance organizations place on leadership roles is exhibited in salary schedules. Leaders are routinely paid ten, twenty, or more times the salary of those in nonleadership positions. The head of General Motors earns more than $1.5 million annually. The highest skilled auto worker, in contrast, earns under $50,000 a year. The president of this auto worker's union makes better than $100,000 a year. Police officers typically make around $30,000 to $45,000 a year. Their boss probably earns 25 percent more, and his or her boss another 25 percent. The pattern is well established. The more responsibility a leader has, as evidenced by his or her level in the organization, the more he or she earns. Would organizations voluntarily pay their leaders so much more than their nonleaders if they didn't strongly believe that leaders make a real difference?

*D.V. Day and R.G. Lord, "Executive Leadership and Organizational Performance: Suggestions for a New Theory and Methodology," *Journal of Management*, Fall 1988, pp. 453–64.

Leaders Don't Make a Difference!

Given the resources that have been spent on studying, selecting, and training leaders, you'd expect there would be overwhelming evidence supporting the positive effect of leadership on organizational performance. But that's not the case!

Currently, the two most popular approaches to leadership are contingency models and the study of charisma. For the most part, both operate under the naive assumption that through selection and/or training, leaders can learn to exhibit certain behaviors that, when properly matched to the situation, will result in improved employee and organizational performance. There are a number of flaws in this assumption.

First, leaders exist in a social system that constrains their behavior. They have to live with role expectations that define behaviors that are acceptable and unacceptable. Pressures to conform to the expectations of peers, subordinates, and superiors all limit the range of behaviors that a leader can exhibit.

Second, organizational rules, procedures, policies, and historical precedents all act to limit a leader's unilateral control over decisions and resources. Hiring decisions, for instance, must be made according to procedures. And budget allocations are typically heavily influenced by previous budget precedents.

Third, there are factors outside the organization that leaders can't control but which have a large bearing on organizational performance. For example, consider the executive in a home construction firm. Costs are largely determined by the operations of the commodities and labor markets, and demand is largely dependent on interest rates, availability of mortgage money, and economic conditions that are affected by governmental policies over which the executive has little control. Or consider the case of school superintendents. They have little control over birth rates and community economic development, both of which profoundly affect school system budgets. While a leader may react to problems as they arise or attempt to forecast and anticipate external changes, he or she has little influence over the environment. On the contrary, the environment typically puts significant limits and constraints on the leader.

Finally, the trend in recent years is toward leaders playing a smaller and smaller role in organizational activities. Important decisions are increasingly made by committees, not individuals. Additionally, the widespread popularity of employee involvement programs, the empowerment movement, and self-managed work teams has contributed to reducing any specific leader's influence.

There is a basic myth associated with leadership. We believe in attribution—when something happens, we believe something has *caused* it. Leaders play that role in organizations, and the fact that leaders earn higher pay than nonleaders is a symbolic gesture that organizations have created to further add to the impression that leaders make a difference. So while leaders may not really matter, the *belief* in leadership does. Although leaders take the credit for successes and the blame for failures, a more realistic conclusion would probably be that, except in times of rapid growth, change, or crisis, leaders don't make much of a difference in an organization's actual performance. But people want to believe that leadership is the cause of performance changes, particularly at the extremes.

Ideas in this argument came from J. Pfeffer, "The Ambiguity of Leadership," *Academy of Management Review*, January 1977, pp. 104–11; A.B. Thomas, "Does Leadership Make a Difference to Organizational Performance?" *Administrative Science Quarterly*, September 1988, pp. 388–400; C.C. Manz and H.P. Sims, Jr., "SuperLeadership: Beyond the Myth of Heroic Leadership," *Organizational Dynamics*, Spring 1991, pp. 18–35; and G. Gemmill and J. Oakley, "Leadership: An Alienating Social Myth?" *Human Relations*, February 1992, pp. 113–29.

Learning about Yourself Exercise

What's Your Basic Leadership Style?

We all have a basic leadership style to which we are already predisposed. This exercise will help you gain insight into your inherent or preferred leadership style.

The following describes eight hypothetical situations in which you have to make a decision affecting you and members of your work group. For each, indicate which one of four actions you are most likely to take by writing the letter corresponding to that action in the space provided.

A. Let the members of the group decide themselves what to do.

B. Ask the members of the group what to do, but make the final decision yourself.

C. Make the decision yourself, but explain your reasons.

D. Make the decision yourself, telling the group exactly what to do.

_____ **1.** In the face of financial pressures, you are forced to make budget cuts for your unit. Where do you cut?

_____ **2.** To meet an impending deadline, someone in your work group will have to work late one evening to finish the draft of an important report. Who will it be?

_____ **3.** As coach of a company softball team, you are required to trim your squad to 25 players from 30 currently on the roster. Who goes?

_____ **4.** Employees in your department have to schedule their summer vacations so as to keep the office appropriately staffed. Who decides first?

_____ **5.** As chair of the social committee, you are responsible for determining the theme for the annual company party. How do you do so?

_____ **6.** You have an opportunity to buy or rent an important piece of equipment for your company. After gathering all the facts, how do you make the choice?

_____ **7.** The office is being redecorated. How do you decide on the color scheme?

_____ **8.** Along with your associates, you are taking a visiting dignitary to dinner. How do you decide which restaurant to go to?

Turn to page A-28 for scoring directions and key.

Source: Adapted from J. Greenberg, *Managing Behavior in Organizations* (Upper Saddle River, NJ: Prentice Hall, 1996), pp. 228–29. With permission.

Working with Others Exercise

Practicing to Be Charismatic

People who are charismatic engage in the following behaviors:

1. *Project a powerful, confident, and dynamic presence.* This has both verbal and nonverbal components. They use a captivating and engaging voice tone. They convey confidence. They also talk directly to people, maintaining direct eye contact, and holding their body posture in a way that says they're sure of themselves. They speak clearly, avoid stammering, and avoid sprinkling their sentences with noncontent phrases such as "ahhh" and "you know."

2. *Articulate an overarching goal.* They have a vision for the future, unconventional ways of achieving the vision, and the ability to communicate the vision to others.

   The vision is a clear statement of where they want to go and how they're going to get there. They are able to persuade others how the achievement of this vision is in the others' self-interest.

   They look for fresh and radically different approaches to problems. The road to achieving their vision is novel but also appropriate to the context.

   They not only have a vision but they're able to get others to buy into it. The real power of Martin Luther King, Jr. was not that he had a dream, but that he could articulate it in terms that made it accessible to millions.

3. *Communicate high performance expectations and confidence in others' ability to meet these expectations.* They demonstrate their confidence in people by stating ambitious goals for them individually and as a group. They convey absolute belief that they will achieve their expectations.

4. *Are sensitive to the needs of followers.* Charismatic leaders get to know their followers individually. They understand their individual needs and are able to develop intensely personal relationships with each. They do this through encouraging followers to express their points of view, being approachable, genuinely listening to and caring about their followers' concerns, and by asking questions so they can learn what is really important to them.

Now that you know what charismatic leaders do, you get the opportunity to practice projecting charisma.

a. The class should break into pairs.

b. Student A's task is to "lead" Student B through a new-student orientation to your college. The orientation should last about 10 to 15 minutes. Assume Student B is new to your college and is unfamiliar with the campus. Remember, Student A should attempt to project himself or herself as charismatic.

c. Roles now reverse and Student B's task is to "lead" Student A in a 10- to 15-minute program on how to study more effectively for college exams. Take a few minutes to think about what has worked well for you and assume that Student B is a new student interested in improving his or her study habits. Again remember that Student B should attempt to project himself or herself as charismatic.

d. When both role plays are complete, each pair should assess how well they did in projecting charisma and how they might improve.

Source: This exercise is based on J.M. Howell and P.J. Frost, "A Laboratory Study of Charismatic Leadership," *Organizational Behavior and Human Decision Processes*, April 1989, pp. 243–69.

The Case against Vision

Robert J. Eaton had big shoes to fill. He took the post of chairman at Chrysler Corp. that had previously been held by "Mr. Charisma," Lee Iacocca. Iacocca had taken over the top spot at Chrysler in 1980, when the company was on the verge of bankruptcy. In only a few short years, Iacocca had turned Chrysler into a money-making machine.

Iacocca's style was bold and visionary. He developed several grand strategies for Chrysler. To get the company immediately profitable, he created a basic compact model—the K car—and used its platform to create a host of new cars including the incredibly successful minivan. To fill the need for subcompacts, he began importing cars from Japan and putting Chrysler Corp. nameplates on them.

But that was then and this is now. Robert Eaton has joined an impressive group of chief executives who no longer buy the notion that leaders need to provide grand visions or long-term strategies for their companies. In its place, they are emphasizing the short-term bottom line.

"Internally, we don't use the word *vision*," says Eaton. "I believe in quantifiable short-term results—things we can all relate to—as opposed to some esoteric thing no one can quantify."

That view is also being articulated by CEOs at Apple Computer, IBM, Aetna Life & Casualty, and General Motors. When asked for his recipe for an IBM comeback, the recently appointed chairman, Louis V. Gerstner, said, "The last thing IBM needs right now is a vision."

It appears that, at least among some leaders, grand visions are out of fashion. They're concentrating on the nuts and bolts of running their businesses.

Questions

1. Isn't this short-term focus likely to hurt companies in the longer term?

2. What's the purpose of a grand vision? What takes its place if a company's leader doesn't provide it?

3. Don't organizations need radical new ideas to win in the marketplace?

4. Eaton says his goal for Chrysler is "getting a little bit better every single day." Is that a viable goal for a real "leader"?

Source: Based on D. Lavin, "Robert Eaton Thinks 'Vision' Is Overrated and He's Not Alone," *The Wall Street Journal*, October 4, 1993, p. A1.

VIDEO
CASE

ABCNEWS

Leadership and Bill Gates

It is literally impossible for a month to go by and *not* have Bill Gates leering at you from the cover of one or more business periodicals. As co-founder and chairman of Microsoft, he seems to be everybody's pick as one of America's foremost corporate leaders. First a little background on Gates, then some comments from a recent interview.

Gates grew up in Seattle, Washington. His father was a prominent attorney and his mother a supporter of community cultural and educational activities. He attended a prestigious private school, went off to Harvard for college, but quit to start a business. He and his friend from high school, Paul Allen, began a business writing software for the first personal computers. While executives at the big computer companies like IBM, Digital, and Control Data saw no future in PCs, Gates and Allen disagreed. They envisioned a world where everyone would own one or more personal computers. And as part of Gates's vision, he saw his company, Microsoft, providing the basic operating software and programming software for these new machines.

Of course, history has proven Gates right. PCs became the computer of choice by both business and individuals. Meanwhile, almost all those PCs have Microsoft software inside them. And Microsoft has become a company valued at more than General Motors. As Microsoft's largest stockholder, Gates is worth in excess of $20 billion.

In 1995, Gates published his first book, *The Road Ahead*. It was an immediate best seller. Not a biography, the book essentially described Gates's interpretation of what has happened, so far, in the communication revolution and his vision of what the future holds. Several chapters describe how he and Allen saw the potential for PCs well before the large computer companies. Gates tells how he believed he had no choice but to drop out of Harvard—while he loved college, he figured time was of the essence. If he and Allen didn't move quickly to begin writing software for PCs, the opportunity would be filled by someone else. Ironically, that concern with moving quickly to grab opportunities continues today. Microsoft, the company, reflects the ambition, aggressiveness, and paranoia of its co-founder and chairman. Never satisfied to rest on its accomplishments, Microsoft behaves like a company fighting for survival. And as it does, it makes life miserable for its competitors.

One of the more interesting topics in Gates's book is his description of what he thinks most of us will be carrying around with us in a few years—a wallet-sized PC. This "appliance" will do almost anything for you. It will allow you to check on your bank balance, get a stock quote, access your e-mail, talk with friends or business associates, send messages to people, make flight reservations, check highway traffic patterns, or search the Internet for shopping bargains. It will even provide you with digital currency. You won't have to carry money with you since your wallet PC will be your money source. And the appliance will allow you to transfer funds from your bank account to the wallet PC when the latter gets low on money.

Critics of Gates fear the power he is amassing at Microsoft. Some even think he wants to rule the world. He laughs off that claim, but one can't ignore the power that comes from controlling the operating systems of 80 to 90 percent of all computers and having the wealth to buy just about anything or anybody. When asked why so many people are worried about him and Microsoft, he says he thinks it's because of the focus on the information revolution and the change it is bringing about. "It is bringing change, and change does cause problems. People are afraid of change. You know, the status quo, even though you can complain about it, you like a lot of things that are going on. And so Microsoft, almost iconically, represents this pace of change, and doing new things, and people imagine that we actually know exactly how it's going to unfold, which certainly isn't the case."

Questions

1. Bill Gates is at the top of nearly everyone's list of corporate leaders. Why?

2. What characteristics make Gates a transformational leader?

3. Do you think if Bill Gates had finished Harvard, earned an MBA, and joined IBM, he would have risen rapidly up the IBM ranks? Do you think he would have been seen as a leader at IBM? Explain.

Source: Based on "The World According to Gates," *ABC News Nightline*; aired November 23, 1995.

POWER AND POLITICS

You can get much farther with a kind word and a gun than you can with a kind word alone.
—A. Capone

LEARNING OBJECTIVES

After studying this chapter, you should be able to

1 Contrast *leadership* and *power*

2 Define the four bases of power

3 Clarify what creates dependency in power relationships

4 List seven power tactics and their contingencies

5 Explain how sexual harassment is about the abuse of power

6 Describe the importance of a political perspective

7 List those individual and organizational factors that stimulate political behavior

8 Identify seven techniques for managing the impression one makes on others

9 Explain how defensive behaviors can protect an individual's self-interest

10 List the three questions that can help determine if a political action is ethical

A sexually harassing climate can make work intolerable, and when employees want to keep their jobs, it puts those being harassed in a situation of powerlessness. As studies of sexual harassment continually recognize, sexual harassment isn't about sex. It's about the abuse of power. The recent situation at the Mitsubishi Motors plant in Normal, Illinois tragically illustrates this point.[1]

Opened in 1987, female employees at the Mitsubishi plant had been complaining about sexual misbehavior on the factory floor since 1992, but those complaints were essentially ignored by management. In December 1994, 29 female employees had enough. They wanted to keep their jobs—which with overtime and shift-premium pay could run as high as $60,000 a year—but they also wanted the relentless sex discrimination, sexual harassment, and sexual abuse by colleagues and supervisors to stop. They took their charges to the Equal Employment Opportunity Commission (EEOC). An investigation confirmed the women's charges. There was clear evidence of "pervasive sexual harassment that management was well aware of" but did little to control. Some examples included: obscene, crude sketches of genital organs and sex acts, and names of female workers scratched into unpainted car bodies moving along the assembly line. Women were called sluts and whores and subjected to groping, forced sex play, and male flashing. Explicit sexual graffiti were scrawled on rest-area and bathroom walls. One male line supervisor stated, "I don't want any bitches on my line. Women don't belong in the plant."

In May 1996, the EEOC filed suit against Mitsubishi. If the courts rule in favor of the EEOC, Mitsubishi could be held liable for compensatory and punitive damages in excess of $150 million. Additionally, the company has been hit by a class-action suit on behalf of the 29 women.

Following the EEOC suit, you'd think that corporate management would have moved quickly to correct the plant's sexist environment and to appease female employees. It didn't. Quite the opposite. It chose to fight. It urged employees to speak up in defense of the company—and their

395

jobs—by setting up a free phone bank with numbers of local news outlets and the names, biographies, and phone numbers of elected representatives. It even organized a demonstration to support the company outside the EEOC offices in Chicago (see photo) and coerced employees by giving them the "choice": They could sign up for a free round trip to the Chicago protest rally on one of the 50 Mitsubishi-chartered buses, get a free box lunch, and win the approval of their bosses. Or they

could report to the idled plant, clearly identifying themselves as disloyal.

Although executives at company headquarters in Tokyo claim to have begun actions to improve conditions at the Normal plant, a recent incident indicates the hostile and abusive work environment continues. Opening her locker to start her 5:30 A.M. shift, Terry Paz, one of the 29 complainants, found a handwritten note reading, "Die, bitch, you'll be sorry." She left the plant fearing for her life. ◆

P ower has been described as the last dirty word. It is easier for most of us to talk about money than it is to talk about power. People who have it deny it, people who want it try not to appear to be seeking it, and those who are good at getting it are secretive about how they got it.[2] OB researchers have learned a lot in recent years about how people gain and use power in organizations. In this chapter, we present you with their findings.

A major theme throughout this chapter is that power is a natural process in any group or organization. As such, you need to know how it's acquired and exercised if you're going to fully understand organizational behavior. Although you may have heard the phrase that "power corrupts, and absolute power corrupts absolutely," power is not always bad. As one author has noted, most medicines can kill if taken in the wrong amount and thousands die each year in automobile accidents, but we don't abandon chemicals or cars because of the dangers associated with them. Rather, we consider danger an incentive to get training and information that'll help us to use these forces productively.[3] The same applies to *power*. It's a reality of organizational life and it's not going to go away. Moreover, by learning how power works in organizations, you'll be better able to use your knowledge to help you be a more effective manager.

◆ Power has been described as the last dirty word.

A Definition of Power

power
A capacity that A has to influence the behavior of B so that B acts in accordance with A's wishes.

Power refers to a capacity that A has to influence the behavior of B, so that B acts in accordance with A's wishes.[4] This definition implies a *potential* that need not be actualized to be effective and a *dependency* relationship.

Power may exist but not be used. It is, therefore, a capacity or potential. One can have power but not impose it.

dependency
B's relationship to A when A possesses something that B requires.

Probably the most important aspect of power is that it is a function of **dependency**. The greater B's dependence on A, the greater is A's power in the relationship. Dependence, in turn, is based on alternatives that B perceives and the importance that B places on the alternative(s) that A controls. A person can have power over you only if he or she controls something you desire. If you want a college degree and have to pass a certain course to get it, and your current instructor is the only faculty member in the college who teaches that course, he or she has power over you. Your alternatives are highly limited

396

and you place a high degree of importance on obtaining a passing grade. Similarly, if you're attending college on funds totally provided by your parents, you probably recognize the power that they hold over you. You're dependent on them for financial support. But once you're out of school, have a job, and are making a solid income, your parents' power is reduced significantly. Who among us, though, has not known or heard of the rich relative who is able to control a large number of family members merely through the implicit or explicit threat of "writing them out of the will"?

Contrasting Leadership and Power

A careful comparison of our description of power with our description of leadership in the previous chapter reveals that the two concepts are closely intertwined. Leaders use power as a means of attaining group goals. Leaders achieve goals, and power is a means of facilitating their achievement.

What differences are there between the two terms? One difference relates to goal compatibility. Power does not require goal compatibility, merely dependence. Leadership, on the other hand, requires some congruence between the goals of the leader and those being led. A second difference relates to the direction of influence. Leadership focuses on the downward influence on one's subordinates. It minimizes the importance of lateral and upward influence patterns. Power does not. Still another difference deals with research emphasis. Leadership research, for the most part, emphasizes style. It seeks answers to such questions as: How supportive should a leader be? How much decision making should be shared with subordinates? In contrast, the research on power has tended to encompass a broader area and focus on tactics for gaining compliance. It has gone beyond the individual as exerciser because power can be used by groups as well as by individuals to control other individuals or groups.

◆ **Leaders achieve goals, and power is a means of facilitating their achievement.**

Bases of Power

Where does power come from? What is it that gives an individual or a group influence over others? The answer to these questions is a five-category classification scheme identified by French and Raven.[5] They proposed that there were five bases or sources of power: coercive, reward, legitimate, expert, and referent (see Exhibit 11-1 on page 398).

Coercive Power

The **coercive power** base is defined by French and Raven as being dependent on fear. One reacts to this power out of fear of the negative results that might occur if one failed to comply. It rests on the application, or the threat of application, of physical sanctions such as the infliction of pain, the generation of frustration through restriction of movement, or the controlling by force of basic physiological or safety needs.

coercive power
Power that is based on fear.

Of all the bases of power available to man, the power to hurt others is possibly most often used, most often condemned, and most difficult to control . . . the state relies on its military and legal resources to

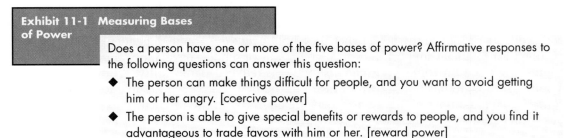

Source: G. Yukl and C.M. Falbe, "Importance of Different Power Sources in Downward and Lateral Relations," *Journal of Applied Psychology*, June 1991, p. 417. With permission.

intimidate nations, or even its own citizens. Businesses rely upon the control of economic resources. Schools and universities rely upon their rights to deny students formal education, while the church threatens individuals with loss of grace. At the personal level, individuals exercise coercive power through a reliance upon physical strength, verbal facility, or the ability to grant or withhold emotional support from others. These bases provide the individual with the means to physically harm, bully, humiliate, or deny love to others.[6]

At the organizational level, A has coercive power over B if A can dismiss, suspend, or demote B, assuming that B values his or her job. Similarly, if A can assign B work activities that B finds unpleasant or treat B in a manner that B finds embarrassing, A possesses coercive power over B.

Reward Power

reward power
Compliance achieved based on the ability to distribute rewards that others view as valuable.

The opposite of coercive power is **reward power**. People comply with the wishes or directives of another because doing so produces positive benefits; therefore, one who can distribute rewards that others view as valuable will have power over those others. These rewards can be anything that another person values. In an organizational context, we think of money, favorable performance appraisals, promotions, interesting work assignments, friendly colleagues, important information, and preferred work shifts or sales territories.

Coercive power and reward power are actually counterparts of each other. If you can remove something of positive value from another or inflict something of negative value upon him or her, you have coercive power over that person. If you can give someone something of positive value or remove something of negative value, you have reward power over that person. Again, as with coercive power, you don't need to be a manager to be able to exert influence through rewards. Rewards such as friendliness, acceptance, and praise are available to everyone in an organization. To the degree that an individual seeks such rewards, your ability to give or withhold them gives you power over that individual.

Legitimate Power

In formal groups and organizations, probably the most frequent access to one or more of the power bases is one's structural position. This is called **legitimate power**. It represents the power a person receives as a result of his or her position in the formal hierarchy of an organization.

Positions of authority include coercive and reward powers. Legitimate power, however, is broader than the power to coerce and reward. Specifically, it includes acceptance by members of an organization of the authority of a position. When school principals, bank presidents, or army captains speak (assuming that their directives are viewed to be within the authority of their positions), teachers, tellers, and first lieutenants listen and usually comply.

legitimate power
The power a person receives as a result of his or her position in the formal hierarchy of an organization.

Expert Power

Expert power is influence wielded as a result of expertise, special skill, or knowledge. Expertise has become one of the most powerful sources of influence as the world has become more technologically oriented. As jobs become more specialized, we become increasingly dependent on experts to achieve goals. So, while it is generally acknowledged that physicians have expertise and hence expert power—most of us follow the advice that our doctor gives us—you should also recognize that computer specialists, tax accountants, solar engineers, industrial psychologists, and other specialists are able to wield power as a result of their expertise.

expert power
Influence based on special skills or knowledge.

"*I was just going to say 'Well, I don't make the rules.' But, of course, I do make the rules.*"

Exhibit 11-2
Source: Drawing by Leo Cullum in *The New Yorker*. Copyright © 1986 The New Yorker Magazine. Reprinted by permission.

Microsoft Chairman William Gates has legitimate power as co-founder and chairman of Microsoft. His expert power is based on his software development expertise. Gates also has referent power, because his employees look up to him and admire his incredible accomplishments.

referent power
Influence based on possession by an individual of desirable resources or personal traits.

Referent Power

The last category of influence that French and Raven identified was **referent power**. Its base is identification with a person who has desirable resources or personal traits. If I admire and identify with you, you can exercise power over me because I want to please you.

Referent power develops out of admiration of another and a desire to be like that person. In a sense, then, it is a lot like charisma. If you admire someone to the point of modeling your behavior and attitudes after him or her, this person possesses referent power over you. Referent power explains why celebrities are paid millions of dollars to endorse products in commercials. Marketing research shows that people like Bill Cosby, Elizabeth Taylor, and Michael Jordan have the power to influence your choice of photo processors, perfume, and athletic shoes. With a little practice, you and I could probably deliver as smooth a sales pitch as these celebrities, but the buying public doesn't identify with you and me. In organizations, if you are articulate, domineering, physically imposing, or charismatic, you hold personal characteristics that may be used to get others to do what you want.

Dependency: The Key to Power

Earlier in this chapter it was said that probably the most important aspect of power is that it is a function of dependence. In this section, we show how an understanding of dependency is central to furthering your understanding of power itself.

The General Dependency Postulate

Let's begin with a general postulate: *The greater B's dependency on A, the greater the power A has over B*. When you possess anything that others require but that you alone control, you make them dependent upon you and, therefore, you gain power over them.[7] Dependency, then, is inversely proportional to the alternative sources of supply. If something is plentiful, possession of it will not increase your power. If everyone is intelligent, intelligence gives no special advantage. Similarly, among the superrich, money is no longer power. But, as the old saying goes, "In the land of the blind, the one-eyed man is king!" If you can create a monopoly by controlling information, prestige, or anything that others crave, they become dependent on you. Conversely, the more that you can expand your options, the less power you place in the hands of others. This explains, for example, why most organizations develop multiple suppliers rather than give their business to only one. It also explains why so many of us aspire to financial independence. Financial independence reduces the power that others can have over us.

Steven Appleton provides an example of the role that dependency plays in a work group or organization.[8] Appleton became CEO of Boise-based chip maker Micron Technology in 1994 at age 34. After a number of run-ins with the company's overbearing board of directors, composed of six Idaho agribusiness tycoons, Appleton was abruptly fired in January 1996. But the board quickly realized that they needed Appleton back when their handpicked successor quit after just a couple of days. To make matters worse, more than 20 executives confronted the board and threatened to resign if Appleton wasn't reinstated. Meanwhile, Appleton wasn't sitting around fretting over his loss. He had taken off for Los Angeles, had begun growing a goatee, and started planning a biplane trip to Australia. The board pleaded with Appleton to come back. He did, but on his terms. His eight-day "retirement" came to an end when the board agreed to his demands—including an end to intrusions by the board, resignation of his primary board protagonist, and sweetened severance packages to protect managers who had voiced their frustrations.

What Creates Dependency?

Dependency is increased when the resource you control is important, scarce, and nonsubstitutable.[9]

IMPORTANCE If nobody wants what you've got, it's not going to create dependency. To create dependency, therefore, the thing(s) you control must be perceived as being important. It's been found, for instance, that organizations actively seek to avoid uncertainty.[10] We should, therefore, expect that those individuals or groups who can absorb an organization's uncertainty will be perceived as controlling an important resource. For instance, a study of industrial organizations found that the marketing departments in these firms were consistently rated as the most powerful.[11] It was concluded by the researcher that the most critical uncertainty facing these firms was selling their products. This might suggest that during a labor strike, the organization's negotiating representatives have increased power, or that engineers, as a group, would be more powerful at Intel than at Procter & Gamble. These inferences appear to be generally valid. Labor negotiators do become more powerful within the personnel area and the organization as a whole during periods of labor strife. An organization such as Intel, which is heavily technologically oriented, is highly dependent on its engineers to maintain its products' technical advantages and quality. And, at Intel, engineers are clearly a powerful group. At Procter & Gamble, marketing is the name of the game, and marketers are the most

◆ Dependency is increased when the resource you control is important, scarce, and nonsubstitutable.

powerful occupational group. These examples support not only the view that the ability to reduce uncertainty increases a group's importance and, hence, its power but also that what's important is situational. It varies between organizations and undoubtedly also varies over time within any given organization.

SCARCITY As noted previously, if something is plentiful, possession of it will not increase your power. A resource needs to be perceived as scarce to create dependency.

This can help to explain how low-ranking members in an organization who have important knowledge not available to high-ranking members gain power over the high-ranking members. Possession of a scarce resource—in this case, important knowledge—makes the high-ranking member dependent on the low-ranking member. This also helps to make sense out of behaviors of low-ranking members that otherwise might seem illogical, such as destroying the procedure manuals that describe how a job is done, refusing to train people in their jobs or even to show others exactly what they do, creating specialized language and terminology that inhibit others from understanding their jobs, or operating in secrecy so an activity will appear more complex and difficult than it really is.

The scarcity–dependency relationship can further be seen in the power of occupational categories. Individuals in occupations in which the supply of personnel is low relative to demand can negotiate compensation and benefit packages which are far more attractive than can those in occupations where there is an abundance of candidates. College administrators have no problem today finding English instructors. The market for corporate finance teachers, in contrast, is extremely tight, with the demand high and the supply limited. The result is that the bargaining power of finance faculty allows them to negotiate higher salaries, lighter teaching loads, and other benefits.

NONSUBSTITUTABILITY The more that a resource has no viable substitutes, the more power that control over that resource provides. Higher education again provides an excellent example. In universities where there are strong pressures for the faculty to publish, we can say that a department head's power over a faculty member is inversely related to that member's publication record. The more recognition the faculty member receives through publication, the more mobile he or she is. That is, since other universities want faculty who are highly published and visible, there is an increased demand for his or her services. Although the concept of tenure can act to alter this relationship by restricting the department head's alternatives, those faculty members with little or no publications have the least mobility and are subject to the greatest influence from their superiors.

Identifying Where the Power Is

Mike Cisco got a summer job, between his junior and senior years in college, working in the lab at Phoenix Lutheran Hospital. As a chemistry major, Mike had never taken any courses in management or organizational behavior, but he had seen pictures of organization charts before. So on that first day at work, when the assistant in the human resources department gave Mike his orientation and showed him where the lab fit on the hospital's organization chart, he felt pretty good. The lab ranked pretty high up on the chart.

OB in the News

The Power of Subordinates

Watch out from below! Bosses aren't the only people in organizations with power. Subordinates have power too. They can effectively undermine your effectiveness and credibility with subtle actions like criticizing you to customers, peers, or bosses, or by excluding you from important decisions.

A New York advertising executive was hired to manage a major consumer-products account. He was chosen over Ms. Drew, an internal candidate, who had developed the account's brand strategy. Naively, the new executive assumed that Ms. Drew, who was now one of his employees, would support him during his first big meeting with the client. He assumed incorrectly. At the meeting, he rec-

ommended against creating an extension of the brand. To his shock, Ms. Drew literally slumped in her chair, undermining him openly. Her efforts to undermine him didn't end there. She continued to defy the executive and hurt his ability to perform by using her strong ties to the other agency people that he needed. One creative director, for instance, failed to attend a critical meeting with one of the executive's big customers—and the agency lost the account. Unable to gain credibility with his colleagues or clients, the executive was soon shuttled to another assignment. He quit a year later. And Ms. Drew? She got a promotion!

This incident illustrates that when a manager takes a new job or assignment, he or

she needs to identify subversive subordinates early and take steps to win them over. Individuals who are particularly likely to become subversives include subordinates that had unsuccessfully sought the manager's job and close allies to the person that the new manager is replacing. Also keep in mind that it may be easier for managers to win over subversives than to fire them. These Benedict Arnolds often have formed powerful friendships with senior executives who will protect them in a "shoot-out." Moreover, these ties with senior executives can be used to convey negative information about the way their manager is performing.

Based on J.E. Rigdon, "Look Out Below for Deadly Hits on Your Career," *The Wall Street Journal*, May 25, 1994, p. B1.

Take It to the Net

We invite you to visit the Robbins page on the Prentice Hall Web site at:

http://www.prenhall.com/robbinsorgbeh

for this chapter's World Wide Web exercise.

After about a week or so at the hospital, Mike noticed that the lab's manager didn't seem to have near the clout that the managers of marketing and finance had. And what puzzled Mike was that all three managers ranked at the same level on the hospital's organization chart.

Mike's first theory was that the marketing and finance managers were more aggressive individuals, but that clearly wasn't the case. It was obvious to almost everyone at the hospital that Mike's manager was smarter, more articulate, and more forceful than the other two managers. So Mike was at a loss to figure out why the marketing and finance managers seemed to be considered more important than his manager.

Mike got his answer over lunch during the second week. Traci Chou, a summer intern in the admissions office who was also working on her masters in business administration, clarified it for him. "The organization chart is deceptive. It doesn't tell you where the power is around here," Traci stated. "Ten years ago, the lab was equal to or maybe more important than finance or marketing, but not anymore. As competition has increased in the health care industry, hospitals have had to learn how to cut costs, do more with less, and develop new sources of revenue. This has resulted in expanding the power of departments like finance and marketing around here."

How do you determine where the power is in an organization at any given point in time? We can answer this question from both the departmental and individual manager levels.

At the department level, answers to the following questions will give you a good idea of how powerful that department is: What proportion of the organization's top-level managers came up through the department? Is the department represented on important interdepartmental teams and committees? How does the salary of the senior manager in the department compare with others at his or her level? Is the department located in the headquarters building? What's the average size of offices for people working in the department compared to offices in other departments? Has the department grown in number of employees relative to other departments? How does the promotion rate for people in the department compare to other units? Has the department's budget allocation been increasing relative to other departments?[12]

At the level of the individual manager, there are certain symbols you should be on the lookout for that suggest that a manager has power.[13] These include the ability to intercede favorably on behalf of someone in trouble in the organization, to get approval for expenditures beyond the budget, to get items on the agenda at major meetings, and to get fast access to top decision makers in the organization.

Software engineers at Oracle Corporation are important and powerful. Their technical expertise and inventiveness are critical to Oracle's future success, and the company provides them with every resource to facilitate their work. Oracle, the world's second-largest software company, plans to become a major player on the information superhighway and is counting on its engineers to develop the software that will make the communications and computer systems work together. The team of engineers shown here built the successful Video Server, a program that provides different digitized films to different locations at different times.

Power Tactics

This section is a logical extension of our previous discussions. We've reviewed where power comes from. Now, we move to the topic of **power tactics** to learn how employees translate their power bases into specific actions. Recent research indicates that there are standardized ways by which powerholders attempt to get what they want.[14]

power tactics
Ways in which individuals translate power bases into specific actions.

When 165 managers were asked to write essays describing an incident in which they influenced their bosses, co-workers, or subordinates, a total of 370 power tactics grouped into 14 categories were identified. These answers were condensed, rewritten into a 58-item questionnaire, and given to over 750 employees. These respondents were not only asked how they went about influencing others at work but also for the possible reasons for influencing the target person. The results, which are summarized here, give us considerable insight into power tactics—how managerial employees influence others and the conditions under which one tactic is chosen over another.[15]

The findings identified seven tactical dimensions or strategies:

◆ *Reason*: Use of facts and data to make a logical or rational presentation of ideas

◆ *Friendliness*: Use of flattery, creation of goodwill, acting humble, and being friendly prior to making a request

◆ *Coalition*: Getting the support of other people in the organization to back up the request

◆ *Bargaining*: Use of negotiation through the exchange of benefits or favors

◆ *Assertiveness*: Use of a direct and forceful approach such as demanding compliance with requests, repeating reminders, ordering individuals to do what is asked, and pointing out that rules require compliance

◆ *Higher authority*: Gaining the support of higher levels in the organization to back up requests

◆ *Sanctions*: Use of organizationally derived rewards and punishments such as preventing or promising a salary increase, threatening to give an unsatisfactory performance evaluation, or withholding a promotion

The researchers found that employees do not rely on the seven tactics equally. However, as shown in Exhibit 11-3, the most popular strategy was the use of reason, regardless of whether the influence was directed upward or downward. Additionally, the researchers uncovered four contingency variables that affect the selection of a power tactic: the manager's relative power, the manager's objectives for wanting to influence, the manager's expectation of the target person's willingness to comply, and the organization's culture.

A manager's relative power impacts the selection of tactics in two ways. First, managers who control resources that are valued by others, or who are perceived to be in positions of dominance, use a greater variety of tactics than do those with less power. Second, managers with power use assertiveness with greater frequency than do those with less power. Initially, we can expect that most managers will attempt to use simple requests and reason. Assertiveness is a backup strategy, used when the target of influence refuses or appears reluctant to comply with the request. Resistance leads to managers using more directive strategies. Typically, they shift from using simple requests to insisting that their demands be met. But the manager with relatively little power is more likely to stop trying to influence others when he or she encounters

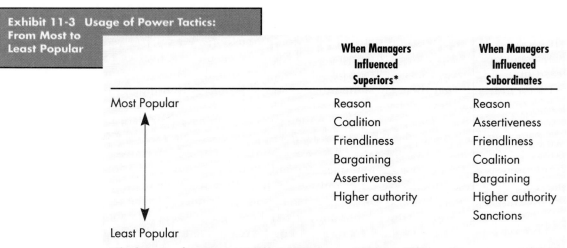

Exhibit 11-3 Usage of Power Tactics: From Most to Least Popular

	When Managers Influenced Superiors*	When Managers Influenced Subordinates
Most Popular	Reason	Reason
	Coalition	Assertiveness
	Friendliness	Friendliness
	Bargaining	Coalition
	Assertiveness	Bargaining
	Higher authority	Higher authority
Least Popular		Sanctions

*The dimension of sanctions is omitted in the scale that measures upward influence

Source: Reprinted, by permission of the publisher, from "Patterns of Managerial Influence: Shotgun Managers, Tacticians, and Bystanders," by D. Kipnis et al. *Organizational Dynamics*, Winter 1984, p. 62. © 1984 Periodicals Division, American Management Association, New York. All rights reserved.

resistance because he or she perceives the costs associated with assertiveness as unacceptable.

Managers vary their power tactics in relation to their objectives. When managers seek benefits from a superior, they tend to rely on kind words and the promotion of pleasant relationships; that is, they use friendliness. In comparison, managers attempting to persuade their superiors to accept new ideas usually rely on reason. This matching of tactics to objectives also holds true for downward influence. For example, managers use reason to sell ideas to subordinates and friendliness to obtain favors.

The manager's expectations of success guide his or her choice of tactics. When past experience indicates a high probability of success, managers use simple requests to gain compliance. Where success is less predictable, managers are more tempted to use assertiveness and sanctions to achieve their objectives.

Finally, we know that cultures within organizations differ markedly—for example, some are warm, relaxed, and supportive; others are formal and conservative. The organizational culture in which a manager works, therefore, will have a significant bearing on defining which tactics are considered appropriate. Some cultures encourage the use of friendliness, some encourage reason, and still others rely on sanctions and assertiveness. So the organization itself will influence which subset of power tactics is viewed as acceptable for use by managers.

Power in Groups: Coalitions

Those "out of power" and seeking to be "in" will first try to increase their power individually. Why share the spoils if one doesn't have to? But if this proves ineffective, the alternative is to form a coalition. There is strength in numbers.

The natural way to gain influence is to become a powerholder. Therefore, those who want power will attempt to build a personal power base. But, in

Ellen Wessel (right) is founder and president of Moving Comfort, a manufacturer of women's athletic wear. She has created a corporate culture that encourages the use of kind words and friendliness. The environment at Moving Comfort is warm and relaxed because Wessel is supportive in empowering employees to make decisions. She views employees as goodwill ambassadors for her company and attributes the company's rapid growth to giving employees the freedom to make things happen.

many instances, this may be difficult, risky, costly, or impossible. In such cases, efforts will be made to form a coalition of two or more "outs" who, by joining together, can combine their resources to increase rewards for themselves.[16]

Historically, blue-collar workers in organizations who were unsuccessful in bargaining on their own behalf with management resorted to labor unions to bargain for them. In recent years, white-collar employees and professionals have increasingly turned to unions after finding it difficult to exert power individually to attain higher wages and greater job security.

What predictions can we make about coalition formation?[17] First, coalitions in organizations often seek to maximize their size. In political science theory, coalitions move the other way—they try to minimize their size. They tend to be just large enough to exert the power necessary to achieve their objectives. But legislatures are different from organizations. Specifically, decision making in organizations does not end just with selection from among a set of alternatives. The decision must also be implemented. In organizations, the implementation of and commitment to the decision is at least as important as the decision itself. It's necessary, therefore, for coalitions in organizations to seek a broad constituency to support the coalition's objectives. This means expanding the coalition to encompass as many interests as possible. This coalition expansion to facilitate consensus building, of course, is more likely to occur in organizational cultures where cooperation, commitment, and shared decision making are highly valued. In autocratic and hierarchically controlled organizations, this search for maximizing the coalition's size is less likely to be sought.

Another prediction about coalitions relates to the degree of interdependence within the organization. More coalitions will likely be created where there is a great deal of task and resource interdependence. In contrast, there

Individuals had little success in attempting to influence local, state, and federal legislation to protect the rights of those suffering from AIDS. However, coalitions like ACTUP have successfully increased public awareness and lobbied for greater rights protection.

will be less interdependence among subunits and less coalition formation activity where subunits are largely self-contained or resources are abundant.

Finally, coalition formation will be influenced by the actual tasks that workers do. The more routine the task of a group, the greater the likelihood that coalitions will form. The more that the work that people do is routine, the greater their substitutability for each other and, thus, the greater their dependence. To offset this dependence, they can be expected to resort to a coalition. We see, therefore, that unions appeal more to low-skill and nonprofessional workers than to skilled and professional types. Of course, where the supply of skilled and professional employees is high relative to their demand or where organizations have standardized traditionally nonroutine jobs, we would expect these incumbents to find unionization attractive.

Sexual Harassment: Unequal Power in the Workplace

The issue of sexual harassment got increasing attention by corporations and the media in the 1980s because of the growing ranks of female employees, especially in nontraditional work environments. But it was the congressional hearings in the fall of 1991 in which law professor Anita Hill graphically accused Supreme Court nominee Clarence Thomas of sexual harassment that challenged organizations to reassess their harassment policies and practices.[18]

sexual harassment
Unwelcome advances, requests for sexual favors, and other verbal or physical conduct of a sexual nature.

Legally, **sexual harassment** is defined as unwelcome advances, requests for sexual favors, and other verbal or physical conduct of a sexual nature. A 1993 Supreme Court decision helped to clarify this definition by adding that the key test for determining if sexual harassment has occurred is whether comments or behavior in a work environment "would reasonably be perceived, and is perceived, as hostile or abusive."[19] But there continues to be disagreement as to what *specifically* constitutes sexual harassment. Organizations have generally made considerable progress in the last few years toward limiting overt forms of sexual harassment of female employees (an obvious exception being the Mitsubishi plant described at the opening of this chapter!). This includes unwanted physical touching, recurring requests for dates when it is made clear the woman isn't interested, and coercive threats that a woman will lose her job if she refuses a sexual proposition. The problems today are likely to surface around more subtle forms of sexual harassment—unwanted looks or comments, off-color jokes, sexual artifacts like nude calendars in the workplace, or misinterpretations of where the line between "being friendly" ends and "harassment" begins.

Most studies confirm that the concept of power is central to understanding sexual harassment.[20] This seems to be true whether the harassment comes from a supervisor, a co-worker, or even a subordinate.

The supervisor–employee dyad best characterizes an unequal power relationship, where position power gives the supervisor the capacity to reward and coerce. Supervisors give subordinates their assignments, evaluate their performance, make recommendations for salary adjustments and promotions, and even decide whether or not an employee retains his or her job. These decisions give a supervisor power. Since subordinates want favorable performance reviews, salary increases, and the like, it's clear supervisors control resources that most subordinates consider important and scarce. It's also worth noting that individuals who occupy high-status roles (like management positions) sometimes believe that sexually harassing female subordinates is merely an extension of their right to make demands on lower-status individuals. Because of power inequities, sexual harassment by one's boss typically creates the greatest difficulty for those who are being harassed. If there are no witnesses, it is her word against his. Are there others this boss has harassed and, if so, will they come forward? Because of the supervisor's control over resources, many of those who are harassed are afraid of speaking out for fear of retaliation by the supervisor.

◆ Organizations have made considerable progress in the last few years toward limiting overt forms of sexual harassment of female employees.

Although co-workers don't have position power, they can have influence and use it to sexually harass peers. In fact, although co-workers appear to engage in somewhat less severe forms of harassment than do supervisors, co-workers are the most frequent perpetrators of sexual harassment in organizations. How do co-workers exercise power? Most often it's by providing or withholding information, cooperation, and support. For example, the effective performance of most jobs requires interaction and support from co-workers. This is especially true nowadays as work is assigned to teams. By threatening to withhold or delay providing information that's necessary for the successful achievement of your work goals, co-workers can exert power over you.

Although it doesn't get nearly the attention that harassment by a supervisor does, women in positions of power can be subjected to sexual harassment from males who occupy less powerful positions within the organization. This is usually achieved by the subordinate devaluing the woman through highlighting traditional gender stereotypes (such as helplessness, passivity, lack of career commitment) that reflect negatively on the woman in power. A subordinate may engage in such practices to attempt to gain some power over the higher-ranking female or to minimize power differentials.

The topic of sexual harassment is about power. It's about an individual controlling or threatening another individual. It's wrong. Moreover, it's illegal. But you can understand how sexual harassment surfaces in organizations if you analyze it in power terms.

Politics: Power in Action

When people get together in groups, power will be exerted. People want to carve out a niche from which to exert influence, to earn awards, and to advance their careers.[21] When employees in organizations convert their power into action, we describe them as being engaged in politics. Those with good political skills have the ability to use their bases of power effectively.[22]

Definition

There has been no shortage of definitions for organizational politics. Essentially, however, they have focused on the use of power to affect decision making in the organization or on behaviors by members that are self-serving and organizationally nonsanctioned.[23] For our purposes, we shall define **political behavior** in organizations as *those activities that are not required as part of one's formal role in the organization, but that influence, or attempt to influence, the distribution of advantages and disadvantages within the organization.*[24]

This definition encompasses key elements from what most people mean when they talk about organizational politics. Political behavior is *outside* one's specified job requirements. The behavior requires some attempt to use one's *power* bases. Additionally, our definition encompasses efforts to influence the goals, criteria, or processes used for *decision making* when we state that politics is concerned with "the distribution of advantages and disadvantages within the organization." Our definition is broad enough to include such varied political behaviors as withholding key information from decision makers, whistleblowing, spreading rumors, leaking confidential information about organizational activities to the media, exchanging favors with others in the organization for mutual benefit, and lobbying on behalf of or against a particular individual or decision alternative. Exhibit 11-4 provides a quick measure to help you assess how political your workplace is.

A final comment relates to what has been referred to as the "legitimate–illegitimate" dimension in political behavior.[25] **Legitimate political behavior** refers to normal everyday politics—complaining to your supervisor, bypassing the chain of command, forming coalitions, obstructing organizational policies or decisions through inaction or excessive adherence to rules, and developing contacts outside the organization through one's professional activities. On the other hand, there are also **illegitimate political behaviors** that violate the implied rules of the game. Those who pursue such extreme activities are often described as individuals who "play hardball." Illegitimate activities include sabotage, whistleblowing, and symbolic protests such as wearing unorthodox dress or protest buttons, and groups of employees simultaneously calling in sick.

The vast majority of all organizational political actions are of the legitimate variety. The reasons are pragmatic: The extreme illegitimate forms of political behavior pose a very real risk of loss of organizational membership or extreme sanctions against those who use them and then fall short in having enough power to ensure that they work.

political behavior
Those activities that are not required as part of one's formal role in the organization, but that influence, or attempt to influence, the distribution of advantages and disadvantages within the organization.

legitimate political behavior
Normal everyday politics.

illegitimate political behavior
Extreme political behavior that violates the implied rules of the game.

Exhibit 11-4 A Quick Measure of How Political Your Workplace Is

How political is your workplace? Answer the 12 questions using the following scale:

SD = Strongly disagree
D = Disagree
U = Uncertain
A = Agree
SA = Strongly agree

1. Managers often use the selection system to hire only people who can help them in their future. _____

2. The rules and policies concerning promotion and pay are fair; it is how supervisors carry out the policies that is unfair and self-serving. _____

3. The performance ratings people receive from their supervisors reflect more of the supervisors' "own agenda" than the actual performance of the employee. _____

4. Although a lot of what my supervisor does around here appears to be directed at helping employees, it is actually intended to protect my supervisor. _____

5. There are cliques or "in-groups" which hinder effectiveness around here. _____

6. My co-workers help themselves, not others. _____

7. I have seen people deliberately distort information requested by others for purposes of personal gain, either by withholding it or by selectively reporting it. _____

8. If co-workers offer to lend some assistance, it is because they expect to get something out of it. _____

9. Favoritism rather than merit determines who gets ahead around here. _____

10. You can usually get what you want around here if you know the right person to ask. _____

11. Overall, the rules and policies concerning promotion and pay are specific and well defined. _____

12. Pay and promotion policies are generally clearly communicated in this organization. _____

This questionnaire taps the three salient dimensions that have been found to be related to perceptions of politics: supervisor behavior; co-worker behavior; and organizational policies and practices. To calculate your score, for items 1–10, give yourself 1 point for Strongly disagree; 2 points for Disagree; and so forth (through 5 points for Strongly agree). For items 11 and 12, reverse the score (i.e., 1 point for Strongly agree, etc.) Sum up the total: the higher the total score, the greater degree of perceived organizational politics.

Source: G.R. Ferris, D.D. Frink, D.P.S. Bhawuk, J. Zhou, and D.C. Gilmore, "Reactions of Diverse Groups to Politics in the Workplace," *Journal of Management*, vol. 22, no. 1, 1996, pp. 32–33.

The Reality of Politics

Politics is a fact of life in organizations. People who ignore this fact of life do so at their own peril. But why, you may wonder, must politics exist? Isn't it possible for an organization to be politics free? It's *possible*, but most unlikely.

Organizations are made up of individuals and groups with different values, goals, and interests.[26] This sets up the potential for conflict over resources. Departmental budgets, space allocations, project responsibilities, and salary adjustments are just a few examples of the resources about whose allocation organizational members will disagree.

Resources in organizations are also limited, which often turns potential conflict into real conflict. If resources were abundant, then all the various constituencies within the organization could satisfy their goals. But because they are limited, not everyone's interests can be provided for. Furthermore, whether true or not, gains by one individual or group are often *perceived* as being at the expense of others within the organization. These forces create a competition among members for the organization's limited resources.

◆ Politics is a fact of life in organizations.

Maybe the most important factor leading to politics within organizations is the realization that most of the "facts" that are used to allocate the limited resources are open to interpretation. What, for instance, is *good* performance? What's an *adequate* improvement? What constitutes an *unsatisfactory* job? One person's view that an act is a "selfless effort to benefit the organization" is seen by another as a "blatant attempt to further one's interest."[27] The manager of any major league baseball team knows a .400 hitter is a high performer and a .125 hitter is a poor performer. You don't need to be a baseball genius to know you should play your .400 hitter and send the .125 hitter back to the minors. But what if you have to choose between players who hit .280 and .290? Then other factors—less objective ones—come into play: fielding expertise, attitude, potential, ability to perform in the clutch, loyalty to the team, and so on. More managerial decisions resemble choosing between a .280 and a .290 hitter than deciding between a .125 hitter and a .400 hitter. It is in this large and ambiguous middle ground of organizational life—where the facts *don't* speak for themselves—that politics flourish (see Exhibit 11-5).

Finally, because most decisions have to be made in a climate of ambiguity—where facts are rarely fully objective, and thus are open to interpretation—people within organizations will use whatever influence they can to taint the facts to support their goals and interests. That, of course, creates the activities we call *politicking*.

Therefore, to answer the earlier question of whether or not it is possible for an organization to be politics free, we can say: "Yes," if all members of that organization hold the same goals and interests, if organizational resources are not scarce, and if performance outcomes are completely clear and objective. But that doesn't describe the organizational world that most of us live in!

Factors Contributing to Political Behavior

Not all groups or organizations are equally political. In some organizations, for instance, politicking is overt and rampant, while in others, politics plays a small role in influencing outcomes. Why is there this variation? Recent research and observation have identified a number of factors that appear to encourage political behavior. Some are individual characteristics, derived from

Exhibit 11-5 Politics Is in the Eye of the Beholder

A behavior that one person labels as "organizational politics" is very likely to be characterized as an instance of "effective management" by another. The fact is not that effective management is necessarily political, although in some cases it might be. Rather, a person's reference point determines what he or she classifies as organizational politics. Take a look at the following labels used to describe the same phenomenon. These suggest that politics, like beauty, is in the eye of the beholder.

"Political" label	"Effective management" label
1. Blaming others	1. Fixing responsibility
2. "Kissing up"	2. Developing working relationships
3. Apple polishing	3. Demonstrating loyalty
4. Passing the buck	4. Delegating authority
5. Covering your rear	5. Documenting decisions
6. Creating conflict	6. Encouraging change and innovation
7. Forming coalitions	7. Facilitating teamwork
8. Whistleblowing	8. Improving efficiency
9. Scheming	9. Planning ahead
10. Overachieving	10. Competent and capable
11. Ambitious	11. Career minded
12. Opportunistic	12. Astute
13. Cunning	13. Practical minded
14. Arrogant	14. Confident
15. Perfectionist	15. Attentive to detail

This exhibit is based on T.C. Krell, M.E. Mendenhall, and J. Sendry, "Doing Research in the Conceptual Morass of Organizational Politics," paper presented at the Western Academy of Management Conference, Hollywood, CA, April 1987.

the unique qualities of the people the organization employs; others are a result of the organization's culture or internal environment. Exhibit 11-6 on page 414 illustrates how both individual and organizational factors can increase political behavior and provide favorable outcomes (increased rewards and averted punishments) for both individuals and groups in the organization.

INDIVIDUAL FACTORS At the individual level, researchers have identified certain personality traits, needs, and other factors that are likely to be related to political behavior. In terms of traits, we find that employees who are high self-monitors, possess an internal locus of control, and have a high need for power are more likely to engage in political behavior.[28]

The high self-monitor is more sensitive to social cues, exhibits higher levels of social conformity, and is more likely to be skilled in political behavior than the low self-monitor. Individuals with an internal locus of control, because they believe they can control their environment, are more prone to take a proactive stance and attempt to manipulate situations in their favor. Not surprisingly, the Machiavellian personality—which is characterized by the will to manipulate and the desire for power—is comfortable using politics as a means to further his or her self-interest.

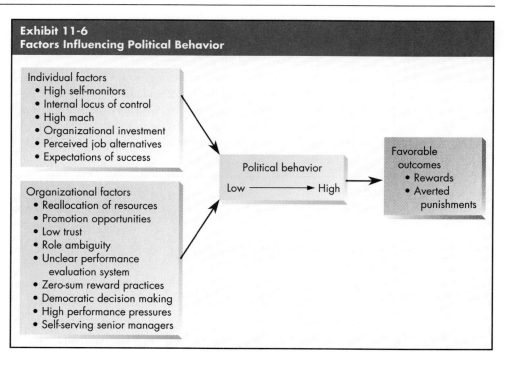

Exhibit 11-6
Factors Influencing Political Behavior

Individual factors
- High self-monitors
- Internal locus of control
- High mach
- Organizational investment
- Perceived job alternatives
- Expectations of success

Organizational factors
- Reallocation of resources
- Promotion opportunities
- Low trust
- Role ambiguity
- Unclear performance evaluation system
- Zero-sum reward practices
- Democratic decision making
- High performance pressures
- Self-serving senior managers

Political behavior
Low ——————→ High

Favorable outcomes
- Rewards
- Averted punishments

Additionally, an individual's investment in the organization, perceived alternatives, and expectations of success will influence the degree to which he or she will pursue illegitimate means of political action.[29] The more that a person has invested in the organization in terms of expectations of increased future benefits, the more a person has to lose if forced out and the less likely he or she is to use illegitimate means. The more alternative job opportunities an individual has—due to a favorable job market or the possession of scarce skills or knowledge, a prominent reputation, or influential contacts outside the organization—the more likely he or she is to risk illegitimate political actions. Finally, if an individual has a low expectation of success in using illegitimate means, it is unlikely that he or she will attempt to do so. High expectations of success in the use of illegitimate means are most likely to be the province of both experienced and powerful individuals with polished political skills and inexperienced and naive employees who misjudge their chances.

ORGANIZATIONAL FACTORS Political activity is probably more a function of the organization's characteristics than of individual difference variables. Why? Because many organizations have a large number of employees with the individual characteristics we listed, yet the extent of political behavior varies widely.

Although we acknowledge the role that individual differences can play in fostering politicking, the evidence more strongly supports that certain situations and cultures promote politics. More specifically, when an organization's resources are declining, when the existing pattern of resources is changing, and when there is opportunity for promotions, politics is more likely to surface.[30] In addition, cultures characterized by low trust, role ambiguity, unclear performance evaluation systems, zero-sum reward allocation practices, democratic decision making, high pressures for performance, and self-serving senior managers will create breeding grounds for politicking.[31]

When organizations downsize to improve efficiency, reductions in resources have to be made. Threatened with the loss of resources, people may engage in political actions to safeguard what they have. But any changes, especially those that imply significant reallocation of resources within the organization, are likely to stimulate conflict and increase politicking.

Promotion decisions have consistently been found to be one of the most political in organizations. The opportunity for promotions or advancement encourages people to compete for a limited resource and to try to positively influence the decision outcome.

The less trust there is within the organization, the higher the level of political behavior and the more likely that the political behavior will be of the illegitimate kind. So high trust should suppress the level of political behavior in general and inhibit illegitimate actions in particular.

Role ambiguity means that the prescribed behaviors of the employee are not clear. There are fewer limits, therefore, to the scope and functions of the employee's political actions. Since political activities are defined as those not required as part of one's formal role, the greater the role ambiguity, the more one can engage in political activity with little chance of it being visible.

The practice of performance evaluation is far from a perfected science. The more that organizations use subjective criteria in the appraisal, emphasize a single outcome measure, or allow significant time to pass between the time of an action and its appraisal, the greater the likelihood that an employee can get away with politicking. Subjective performance criteria create ambiguity. The use of a single outcome measure encourages individuals to do whatever is necessary to "look good" on that measure, but often at the expense of performing well on other important parts of the job that are not being appraised. The amount of time that elapses between an action and its appraisal is also a relevant factor. The longer the time period, the more unlikely that the employee will be held accountable for his or her political behaviors.

The more that an organization's culture emphasizes the zero-sum or win-lose approach to reward allocations, the more employees will be motivated to engage in politicking. The zero-sum approach treats the reward "pie" as fixed so that any gain one person or group achieves has to come at the expense of another person or group. If I win, you must lose! If $10,000 in annual raises is to be distributed among five employees, then any employee who gets more than $2,000 takes money away from one or more of the others. Such a practice encourages making others look bad and increasing the visibility of what you do.

In the last 25 years, there has been a general move in North America and among most developed nations toward making organizations less autocratic. Managers in these organizations are being asked to behave more democratically. They're told that they should allow subordinates to advise them on decisions and that they should rely to a greater extent on group input into the decision process. Such moves toward democracy, however, are not necessarily embraced by all individual managers. Many managers sought their positions in order to have legitimate power so as to be able to make unilateral decisions. They fought hard and often paid high personal costs to achieve their influential positions. Sharing their power with others runs directly against their desires. The result is that managers, especially those who began their careers in the 1950s and 1960s, may use the required committees, conferences, and group meetings in a superficial way, as arenas for maneuvering and manipulating.

General Electric wants its managers to share their power with employees. GE is breaking down autocratic barriers between labor and management that "cramp people, inhibit creativity, waste time, restrict visions, smother dreams, and above all, slow things down." GE expects managers to behave more democratically by fostering teamwork and rewarding employees who suggest ideas for improvement. This photo illustrates GE's move toward democracy, as a manager at the company's plant in Louisville, Kentucky, and an employee work together to improve the plant's profitability.

The more pressure that employees feel to perform well, the more likely they are to engage in politicking. When people are held strictly accountable for outcomes, this puts great pressure on them to "look good." If a person perceives that his or her entire career is riding on next quarter's sales figures or next month's plant productivity report, there is motivation to do whatever is necessary to make sure the numbers come out favorably.

Finally, when employees see the people on top engaging in political behavior, especially when they do so successfully and are rewarded for it, a climate is created that supports politicking. Politicking by top management, in a sense, gives permission to those lower in the organization to play politics by implying that such behavior is acceptable.

Impression Management

We know that people have an ongoing interest in how others perceive and evaluate them. For example, North Americans spend billions of dollars on diets, health club memberships, cosmetics, and plastic surgery—all intended to make them more attractive to others.[32] Being perceived positively by others should have benefits for people in organizations. It might, for instance, help them initially to get the jobs they want in an organization and, once hired, to get favorable evaluations, superior salary increases, and more rapid promotions. In a political context, it might help sway the distribution of advantages in their favor.

impression management
The process by which individuals attempt to control the impression others form of them.

The process by which individuals attempt to control the impression others form of them is called **impression management**.[34] It's a subject that only quite recently has gained the attention of OB researchers.[35]

Is everyone concerned with impression management (IM)? No! Who, then, might we predict to engage in IM? No surprise here! It's our old friend, the high self-monitor.[36] Low self-monitors tend to present images of them-

From Concepts to Skills

Politicking

Forget, for a moment, the ethics of politicking and any negative impressions you may have of people who engage in organizational politics. If you wanted to be more politically adept in your organization, what could you do? The following eight suggestions are likely to improve your political effectiveness.[33]

1. *Frame arguments in terms of organizational goals.* Effective politicking requires camouflaging your self-interest. No matter that your objective is self-serving; all the arguments you marshal in support of it must be framed in terms of the benefits that will accrue to the organization. People whose actions appear to blatantly further their own interests at the expense of the organization's are almost universally denounced, are likely to lose influence, and often suffer the ultimate penalty of being expelled from the organization.

2. *Develop the right image.* If you know your organization's culture, you understand what the organization wants and values from its employees—in terms of dress, associates to cultivate and those to avoid; whether to appear risk taking or risk aversive, the preferred leadership style, the importance placed on getting along

well with others, and so forth. Then you are equipped to project the appropriate image. Because the assessment of your performance is not a fully objective process, style as well as substance must be attended to.

3. *Gain control of organizational resources.* The control of organizational resources that are scarce and important is a source of power. Knowledge and expertise are particularly effective resources to control. They make you more valuable to the organization and, therefore, more likely to gain security, advancement, and a receptive audience for your ideas.

4. *Make yourself appear indispensable.* Because we're dealing with appearances rather than objective facts, you can enhance your power by appearing to be indispensable. That is, you don't have to really be indispensable as long as key people in the organization believe that you are. If the organization's prime decision makers believe there is no ready substitute for what you are giving the organization, they are likely to go to great lengths to ensure that your desires are satisfied.

5. *Be visible.* Because performance evaluation has a

substantial subjective component, it's important that your boss and those in power in the organization be made aware of your contribution. If you are fortunate enough to have a job that brings your accomplishments to the attention of others, it may not be necessary to take direct measures to increase your visibility. But your job may require you to handle activities that are low in visibility, or your specific contribution may be indistinguishable because you're part of a team endeavor. In such cases—*without appearing to be tooting your own horn or creating the image of a braggart*—you'll want to call attention to yourself by highlighting your successes in routine reports, having satisfied customers relay their appreciation to senior executives in your organization, being seen at social functions, being active in your professional associations, developing powerful allies who speak positively about your accomplishments, and similar tactics. Of course, the skilled politician actively and successfully lobbies to get those projects that will increase his or her visibility.

6. *Develop powerful allies.* It helps to have powerful people in your camp.

(continued)

Cultivate contacts with potentially influential people above you, at your own level, and in the lower ranks. They can provide you with important information that may not be available through normal channels. Additionally, there will be times when decisions will be made in favor of those with the greatest support. Having powerful allies can provide you with a coalition of support if and when you need it.

7. *Avoid "tainted" members.* In almost every organization, there are fringe members whose status is questionable. Their performance and/or loyalty is suspect. Keep your distance from such individuals. Given the reality that effectiveness has a large subjective component, your own effectiveness might be called into question if you're perceived as being too closely associated with tainted members.

8. *Support your boss.* Your immediate future is in the hands of your current boss. Since he or she evaluates your performance, you will typically want to do whatever is necessary to have your boss on your side. You should make every effort to help your boss succeed, make her look good, support her if she is under siege, and spend the time to find out what criteria she will be using to assess your effectiveness. Don't undermine your boss. And don't speak negatively of her to others.

selves that are consistent with their personalities, regardless of the beneficial or detrimental effects for them. In contrast, high self-monitors are good at reading situations and molding their appearances and behavior to fit each situation.

Given that you want to control the impression others form of you, what techniques could you use? Exhibit 11-7 summarizes some of the more popular IM techniques and provides an example of each.

Keep in mind that IM does not imply that the impressions people convey are necessarily false (although, of course, they sometimes are).[37] Excuses and acclaiming, for instance, may be offered with sincerity. Referring to the examples used in Exhibit 11-7, you can *actually* believe that ads contribute little to sales in your region or that you are the key to the tripling of your division's sales. But misrepresentation can have a high cost. If the image claimed is false, you may be discredited.[38] If you "cry wolf" once too often, no one is likely to believe you when the wolf really comes. So the impression manager must be cautious not to be perceived as insincere or manipulative.[39]

Are there *situations* where individuals are more likely to misrepresent themselves or more likely to get away with it? Yes—situations that are characterized by high uncertainty or ambiguity.[40] These situations provide relatively little information for challenging a fraudulent claim and reduce the risks associated with misrepresentation.

Only a limited number of studies have been undertaken to test the effectiveness of IM techniques, and these have been essentially limited to determining whether or not IM behavior is related to job interview success. This makes a particularly relevant area of study since applicants are clearly attempting to present positive images of themselves and there are relatively objective outcome measures (written assessments and typically a hire–don't hire recommendation).

The evidence is that IM behavior works.[41] In one study, for instance, interviewers felt that those applicants for a position as a customer service representative who used IM techniques performed better in the interview, and they seemed somewhat more inclined to hire these people.[42] Moreover, when the

Exhibit 11-7 Impression Management (IM) Techniques

Conformity

Agreeing with someone else's opinion in order to gain his or her approval.

Example: A manager tells his boss, "You're absolutely right on your reorganization plan for the western regional office. I couldn't agree with you more."

Excuses

Explanations of a predicament-creating event aimed at minimizing the apparent severity of the predicament.

Example: Sales manager to boss, "We failed to get the ad in the paper on time, but no one responds to those ads anyway."

Apologies

Admitting responsibility for an undesirable event and simultaneously seeking to get a pardon for the action.

Example: Employee to boss, "I'm sorry I made a mistake on the report. Please forgive me."

Acclaiming

Explanation of favorable events to maximize the desirable implications for oneself.

Example: A salesperson informs a peer, "The sales in our division have nearly tripled since I was hired."

Flattery

Complimenting others about their virtues in an effort to make oneself appear perceptive and likable.

Example: New sales trainee to peer, "You handled that client's complaint so tactfully! I could never have handled that as well as you did."

Favors

Doing something nice for someone to gain that person's approval.

Example: Salesperson to prospective client, "I've got two tickets to the theater tonight that I can't use. Take them. Consider it a thank-you for taking the time to talk with me."

Association

Enhancing or protecting one's image by managing information about people and things with which one is associated.

Example: A job applicant says to an interviewer, "What a coincidence. Your boss and I were roommates in college."

Source: Based on B.R. Schlenker, *Impression Management* (Monterey, CA: Brooks/Cole, 1980); W.L. Gardner and M.J. Martinko, "Impression Management in Organizations," *Journal of Management*, June 1988, p. 332; and R.B. Cialdini, "Indirect Tactics of Image Management: Beyond Basking," in R.A. Giacalone and P. Rosenfeld (eds.), *Impression Management in the Organization* (Hillsdale, NJ: Lawrence Erlbaum Associates, 1989), pp. 45–71.

researchers considered applicants' credentials, they concluded that it was the IM techniques alone that influenced the interviewers. That is, it didn't seem to matter if applicants were well or poorly qualified. If they used IM techniques, they did better in the interview.

Another employment interview study looked at whether certain IM techniques work better than others.[43] The researchers compared applicants who used IM techniques that focused the conversation on themselves (called a *controlling style*) to applicants who used techniques that focused on the interviewer (referred to as a *submissive style*). The researchers hypothesized that applicants who used the controlling style would be more effective because of the

◆ Job applicants who used impression management techniques did better in interviews.

implicit expectations inherent in employment interviews. We tend to expect job applicants to use self-enhancement, self-promotion, and other active controlling techniques in an interview because they reflect self-confidence and initiative. The researchers predicted that these active controlling techniques would work better for applicants than submissive tactics like conforming their opinions to those of the interviewer and offering favors to the interviewer. The results confirmed the researchers' predictions. Those applicants who used the controlling style were rated higher by interviewers on factors such as motivation, enthusiasm, and even technical skills—and they received more job offers. A more recent study confirmed the value of a controlling style over a submissive one.[44] Specifically, recent college graduates that used more self-promotion tactics got higher evaluations by interviewers and more follow-up job site visits, even after adjusting for grade point average, gender, and job type.

Defensive Behaviors

defensive behaviors
Reactive and protective behaviors to avoid action, blame, or change.

Organizational politics includes protection of self-interest as well as promotion. Individuals often engage in reactive and protective "defensive" behaviors to avoid action, blame, or change.[45] This section discusses common varieties of **defensive behaviors**, classified by their objective.

AVOIDING ACTION   Sometimes the best political strategy is to avoid action. That is, the best action is no action! However, role expectations typically dictate that one at least give the impression of doing something. Here are six popular ways to avoid action:

1. *Overconforming.* You strictly interpret your responsibility by saying things like, "The rules clearly state . . . " or "This is the way we've always done it." Rigid adherence to rules, policies, and precedents avoids the need to consider the nuances of a particular case.
2. *Passing the buck.* You transfer responsibility for the execution of a task or decision to someone else.
3. *Playing dumb.* This is a form of strategic helplessness. You avoid an unwanted task by falsely pleading ignorance or inability.
4. *Depersonalization.* You treat other people as objects or numbers, distancing yourself from problems and avoiding having to consider the idiosyncrasies of particular people or the impact of events on them. Hospital physicians often refer to patients by their room number or disease in order to avoid becoming too personally involved with them.
5. *Stretching and smoothing.* Stretching refers to prolonging a task so that you appear to be occupied—for example, you turn a two-week task into a four-month job. Smoothing refers to covering up fluctuations in effort or output. Both these practices are designed to make you appear continually busy and productive.
6. *Stalling.* This "foot-dragging" tactic requires you to appear more or less supportive publicly while doing little or nothing privately.

AVOIDING BLAME   What can you do to avoid blame for actual or anticipated negative outcomes? You can try one of the following six tactics:

1. *Buffing*. This is a nice way to refer to "covering your rear." It describes the practice of rigorously documenting activity to project an image of competence and thoroughness. "I can't provide that information unless I get a formal written requisition from you," is an example.

2. *Playing safe*. This encompasses tactics designed to evade situations that may reflect unfavorably on you. It includes taking on only projects with a high probability of success, having risky decisions approved by superiors, qualifying expressions of judgment, and taking neutral positions in conflicts.

3. *Justifying*. This tactic includes developing explanations that lessen your responsibility for a negative outcome and/or apologizing to demonstrate remorse.

4. *Scapegoating*. This is the classic effort to place the blame for a negative outcome on external factors that are not entirely blameworthy. "I would have had the paper in on time but my computer went down—and I lost everything—the day before the deadline."

5. *Misrepresenting*. This tactic involves the manipulation of information by distortion, embellishment, deception, selective presentation, or obfuscation.

6. *Escalation of commitment*. One way to vindicate an initially poor decision and a failing course of action is to escalate support for the decision. By further increasing the commitment of resources to a previous course of action, you indicate that the previous decision was not wrong. When you "throw good money after bad," you demonstrate confidence in past actions and consistency over time.

AVOIDING CHANGE Finally, there are two forms of defensiveness frequently used by people who feel personally threatened by change:

1. *Resisting change*. This is a catch-all name for a variety of behaviors, including some forms of overconforming, stalling, playing safe, and misrepresenting.

2. *Protecting turf*. This is defending your territory from encroachment by others. As one purchasing executive commented, "Tell the people in production that it's our job to talk with vendors, not theirs."

EFFECTS OF DEFENSIVE BEHAVIOR In the short run, extensive use of defensiveness may well promote an individual's self-interest. But in the long run, it more often than not becomes a liability. This is because defensive behavior frequently becomes chronic or even pathological over time. People who constantly rely on defensiveness find that, eventually, it is the only way they know how to behave. At that point, they lose the trust and support of their peers, bosses, subordinates, and clients. In moderation, however, defensive behavior can be an effective device for surviving and flourishing in an organization because it is often deliberately or unwittingly encouraged by management.

In terms of the organization, defensive behavior tends to reduce effectiveness. In the short run, defensiveness delays decisions, increases interpersonal and intergroup tensions, reduces risk taking, makes attributions and evaluations unreliable, and restricts change efforts. In the long term, defensiveness leads to organizational rigidity and stagnation, detachment from the organization's environment, an organizational culture that is highly politicized, and low employee morale.

The Ethics of Behaving Politically

We conclude our discussion of politics by providing some ethical guidelines for political behavior. While there are no clear-cut ways to differentiate ethical from unethical politicking, there are some questions you should consider.

Exhibit 11-8 illustrates a decision tree to guide ethical actions.[46] The first question you need to answer addresses self-interest versus organizational goals. Ethical actions are consistent with the organization's goals. Spreading untrue rumors about the safety of a new product introduced by your company, in order to make that product's design team look bad, is unethical. However, there may be nothing unethical if a department head exchanges favors with her division's purchasing manager in order to get a critical contract processed quickly.

The second question concerns the rights of other parties. If the department head described in the previous paragraph went down to the mail room during her lunch hour and read through the mail directed to the purchasing manager—with the intent of "getting something on him" so he'll expedite your contract—she would be acting unethically. She would have violated the purchasing manager's right to privacy.

The final question that needs to be addressed relates to whether or not the political activity conforms to standards of equity and justice. The department head that inflates the performance evaluation of a favored employee and deflates the evaluation of a disfavored employee—then uses these evaluations to justify giving the former a big raise and nothing to the latter—has treated the disfavored employee unfairly.

Unfortunately, the answers to the questions in Exhibit 11-8 are often argued in ways to make unethical practices seem ethical. Powerful people, for example, can become very good at explaining self-serving behaviors in terms of the organization's best interests. Similarly, they can persuasively argue that unfair actions are really fair and just. Our point is that immoral people can justify almost any behavior. Those who are powerful, articulate, and persuasive are most vulnerable because they are likely to be able to get away with unethical practices successfully. When faced with an ethical dilemma regarding organizational politics, try to answer the questions in Exhibit 11-8 truth-

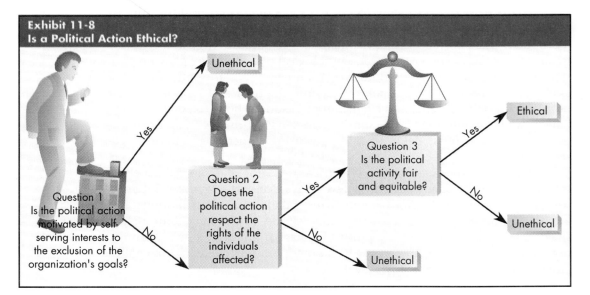

Exhibit 11-8
Is a Political Action Ethical?

Question 1
Is the political action motivated by self-serving interests to the exclusion of the organization's goals?

Yes → Unethical
No →

Question 2
Does the political action respect the rights of the individuals affected?

Yes →
No → Unethical

Question 3
Is the political activity fair and equitable?

Yes → Ethical
No → Unethical

fully. If you have a strong power base, recognize the ability of power to corrupt. Remember, it's a lot easier for the powerless to act ethically, if for no other reason than they typically have very little political discretion to exploit.

Summary and Implications for Managers

If you want to get things done in a group or organization, it helps to have power. As a manager who wants to maximize your power, you will want to increase others' dependence on you. You can, for instance, increase your power in relation to your boss by developing knowledge or a skill that he needs and for which he perceives no ready substitute. But power is a two-way street. You will not be alone in attempting to build your power bases. Others, particularly subordinates, will be seeking to make you dependent on them. The result is a continual battle. While you seek to maximize others' dependence on you, you will be seeking to minimize your dependence on others. And, of course, others you work with will be trying to do the same.

Few employees relish being powerless in their job and organization. It's been argued, for instance, that when people in organizations are difficult, argumentative, and temperamental it may be because they are in positions of powerlessness, where the performance expectations placed on them exceed their resources and capabilities.[47]

There is evidence that people respond differently to the various power bases.[48] Expert and referent power are derived from an individual's personal qualities. In contrast, coercion, reward, and legitimate power are essentially organizationally derived. Since people are more likely to enthusiastically accept and commit to an individual whom they admire or whose knowledge they respect (rather than someone who relies on his or her position to reward or coerce them), the effective use of expert and referent power should lead to higher employee performance, commitment, and satisfaction. Evidence indicates, for instance, that employees working under managers who use coercive power are unlikely to be committed to the organization and more likely to resist the managers' influence attempts.[49] In contrast, expert power has been found to be the most strongly and consistently related to effective employee performance.[50] For example, in a study of five organizations, knowledge was the most effective base for getting others to perform as desired.[51] Competence appears to offer wide appeal, and its use as a power base results in high performance by group members. The message here for managers seems to be: Develop and use your expert power base!

The power of your boss may also play a role in determining your job satisfaction. "One of the reasons many of us like to work for and with people who are powerful is that they are generally more pleasant—not because it is their native disposition, but because the reputation and reality of being powerful permits them more discretion and more ability to delegate to others."[52]

The effective manager accepts the political nature of organizations. By assessing behavior in a political framework, you can better predict the actions of others and use this information to formulate political strategies that will gain advantages for you and your work unit.

We can only speculate at this time on whether or not organizational politics is positively related to *actual* performance. However, there seems to be ample evidence that good political skills are positively related to high performance evaluations and, hence, to salary increases and promotions. We can comment more confidently on the relationship between politics and employee satisfaction. The more political that employees perceive an organization to be, the lower their satisfaction.[53] However, this conclusion needs to be moderated to reflect the employees' level in the organization.[54] Lower-ranking employees, who lack the power base and the means of influence needed to benefit from the political game, perceive organizational politics as a source of frustration and indicate lower satisfaction. But higher-ranking employees, who are in a better position to handle political behavior and benefit from it, don't tend to exhibit this negative attitude.

A final thought on organizational politics: Regardless of level in the organization, some people are just significantly more "politically astute" than are others. Although there is little evidence to support or negate the following conclusion, it seems reasonable that the politically naive or inept are likely to exhibit lower job satisfaction than their politically astute counterparts. The politically naive and inept tend to feel continually powerless to influence those decisions that most affect them. They look at actions around them and are perplexed at why they are regularly "shafted" by colleagues, bosses, and "the system."

For Review

1. What is power? How do you get it?
2. Contrast power tactics with power bases. What are some of the key contingency variables that determine which tactic a powerholder is likely to use?
3. Which of the five power bases lie with the individual? Which are derived from the organization?
4. State the general dependency postulate. What does it mean?
5. What creates dependency? Give an applied example.
6. What is a coalition? When is it likely to develop?
7. How are power and politics related?
8. Define political behavior. Why is politics a fact of life in organizations?
9. What factors contribute to political activity?
10. Define sexual harassment. Who is most likely to harass a female employee: her boss, co-worker, or subordinate?

For Discussion

1. Based on the information presented in this chapter, what would you do as a recent college graduate entering a new job to maximize your power and accelerate your career progress?
2. "More powerful managers are good for an organization. It is the powerless, not the powerful, who are the ineffective managers." Do you agree or disagree with this statement? Discuss.
3. You're a sales representative for an international software company. After four excellent years, sales in your territory are off 30 percent this year. Describe three defensive responses you might use to reduce the potential negative consequences of this decline in sales.
4. "Sexual harassment should not be tolerated at the workplace." "Workplace romances are a natural occurrence in organizations." Are both of these statements true? Can they be reconciled?
5. Which impression management techniques have you used? What ethical implications are there in using impression management?

Point

It's a Political Jungle Out There!

Nick is a talented television camera operator. He has worked on a number of popular television shows, including *Designing Women, Murphy Brown*, and *NYPD Blue*, over a ten-year period. But he's had trouble keeping those jobs. While most other camera operators and production employees are rehired from one season to the next, Nick seems to never be called back for a second year. It isn't that Nick isn't competent. Quite the contrary. His technical knowledge and formal education are typically more impressive than the directors he works for. Nick's problem is that he frequently disagrees with the camera angles that directors want him to set up and he has no qualms about expressing his displeasure to those directors. He also feels some need to offer unsolicited suggestions to directors and producers on how camera placements and shots can be improved.

Roy is also a camera operator. Like Nick, Roy sees directors and producers regularly making decisions that he doesn't agree with. But Roy holds his tongue and does what he's told. He recently finished his sixth straight year as the lead camera operator on one of television's most successful situation comedies.

Roy gets it. Nick doesn't. Nick has failed to recognize the reality that organizations are political systems. And while Roy is secure in his job, Nick's career continues to suffer because of his political naiveté.

It would be nice if all organizations or formal groups within organizations could be described as supportive, harmonious, objective, trusting, collaborative, or cooperative. A nonpolitical perspective can lead one to believe that employees will always behave in ways consistent with the interests of the organization, and that competence and high performance will always be rewarded. In contrast, a political view can explain much of what may seem to be irrational behavior in organizations. It can help to explain, for instance, why employees withhold information, restrict output, attempt to "build empires," publicize their successes, hide their failures, distort performance figures to make themselves look better, and engage in similar activities that appear to be at odds with the organization's desire for effectiveness and efficiency.

For those who want tangible evidence that "it's a political jungle out there" in the real world, let's look at two studies. The first analyzed what it takes to get promoted fast in organizations. The second addressed the performance appraisal process.

As previously described in Chapter 1, Luthans and his associates* studied more than 450 managers. They found that these managers engaged in four managerial activities: traditional management (decision making, planning, and controlling), communication (exchanging routine information and processing paperwork), human resource management (motivating, disciplining, managing conflict, staffing, and training), and networking (socializing, politicking, and interacting with outsiders). Those managers who got promoted fastest spent 48 percent of their time networking. The average managers spent most of their efforts on traditional management and communication activities and only 19 percent of their time networking. We suggest that this provides strong evidence of the importance that social and political skills play in getting ahead in organizations.

Longenecker and his associates** held in-depth interviews with 60 upper-level executives to find out what went into performance ratings. What they found was that executives frankly admitted to deliberately manipulating formal appraisals for political purposes. Accuracy was not a primary concern of these executives. Rather, they manipulated the appraisal results in an intentional and systematic manner to get the outcomes they wanted.

---

*F. Luthans, R.M. Hodgetts, and S.A. Rosenkrantz, *Real Managers* (Cambridge, MA: Ballinger, 1988).

**C.O. Longenecker, D.A. Gioia, and H.P. Sims, Jr., "Behind the Mask: The Politics of Employee Appraisal," *Academy of Management Executive*, August 1987, pp. 183–94.

Corporate Politics: What You See Is What You Get!

Organizational behavior currently appears to be undergoing a period of fascination with workplace politics. Proponents argue that politics is inevitable in organizations—that power struggles, alliance formations, strategic maneuverings, and cutthroat actions are as endemic to organizational life as work schedules and meetings. But is organizational politics inevitable? Maybe not. The existence of politics may be a perceptual interpretation.*

A recent study suggests that politics are more myth and interpretation than reality.** In this study of 180 experienced managers, 92 men and 88 women completed questionnaires. They analyzed a series of decisions and indicated the degree to which they thought the decisions were influenced by politics. They also completed a measure that assessed political inevitability. This included items such as "Politics is a normal part of any decision-making process" and "Politics can have as many helpful outcomes for the organizations as harmful ones." Additionally, the questionnaire asked respondents their beliefs about power and control in the world at large. Finally, respondents provided data on their income, job responsibilities, and years of managerial experience.

The study found that beliefs about politics affected how respondents perceived organizational events. Those managers who held strong beliefs in the inevitability of politics tended to see their own organization and the decision situations in the questionnaire in highly political terms. Moreover, there was evidence suggesting that these beliefs encompass not only beliefs about politics but also about power and control in the world at large. Managers who viewed the world as posing difficult and complex problems and ruled by luck also tended to perceive events as highly politicized. That is, they perceived organizations as part of a disorderly and unpredictable world where politics is inevitable.

Interestingly, not *all* managers saw organizations as political jungles. It was typically the inexperienced managers, with lower incomes and more limited responsibilities, who held this view. The researchers concluded that because junior managers often lack clear understandings of how organizations really work, they tend to interpret events as irrational. It's through their attempts to make sense of their situations that these junior managers may come to make political attributions.

This study attempted to determine whether the corporate political jungle is myth, reality, or a matter of interpretation. The popular press often presents the political jungle as the dominant corporate reality where gamesmanship and manipulation are key to survival. However, the findings of this study suggest that a manager's political reality is somewhat mythical in nature, partially constructed through his or her beliefs about politics' inevitability and about power and control in the world. More specifically, it's the inexperienced managers—those who are likely to hold the fewest and least accurate interpretations of organizational events—who perceive the extent of organizational politics to be greatest.

So if there is a corporate political jungle, it appears to be mostly in the eyes of the young and inexperienced. Because they tend to have less understanding of organizational processes and less power to influence outcomes, they are more likely to see organizations through a political lens. More experienced and higher-ranking managers, on the other hand, are more likely to see the corporate political jungle as a myth.

---

*See, for instance, C.P. Parker, R.L. Dipboye, and S.L. Jackson, "Perceptions of Organizational Politics: An Investigation of Antecedents and Consequences," *Journal of Management*, vol. 21, no. 5, 1995, pp. 891–912; and G.R. Ferris, D.D. Frink, M.C. Galang, J. Zhou, K.M. Kacmar, and J.L. Howard, "Perceptions of Organizational Politics: Prediction, Stress-Related Implications, and Outcomes," *Human Relations*, February 1996, pp. 233–66.

**Cited in C. Kirchmeyer, "The Corporate Political Jungle: Myth, Reality, or a Matter of Interpretation," in C. Harris and C.C. Lundberg (eds.), *Proceedings of the 29th Annual Eastern Academy of Management* (Baltimore, 1992), pp. 161–64.

Learning about Yourself Exercise

How Political Are You?

To determine your political tendencies, please answer the following questions. Check the answer that best represents your behavior or belief, even if that particular behavior or belief is not present all the time.

	True	False
1. You should make others feel important through an open appreciation of their ideas and work.	_____	_____
2. Because people tend to judge you when they first meet you, always try to make a good first impression.	_____	_____
3. Try to let others do most of the talking, be sympathetic to their problems, and resist telling people that they are totally wrong.	_____	_____
4. Praise the good traits of the people you meet and always give people an opportunity to save face if they are wrong or make a mistake.	_____	_____
5. Spreading false rumors, planting misleading information, and backstabbing are necessary, if somewhat unpleasant, methods to deal with your enemies.	_____	_____
6. Sometimes it is necessary to make promises that you know you will not or cannot keep.	_____	_____
7. It is important to get along with everybody, even with those who are generally recognized as windbags, abrasive, or constant complainers.	_____	_____
8. It is vital to do favors for others so that you can call in these IOUs at times when they will do you the most good.	_____	_____
9. Be willing to compromise, particularly on issues that are minor to you, but major to others.	_____	_____
10. On controversial issues, it is important to delay or avoid your involvement if possible.	_____	_____

Turn to page A-28 for scoring directions and key.

Source: J.F. Byrnes, "The Political Behavior Inventory." With permission.

Working with Others Exercise

Understanding Power Dynamics

1. Creation of groups

Students are to turn in a dollar bill (or similar value of currency) to the instructor and are divided into three groups based on criteria given by the instructor, assigned to their workplaces, and instructed to read the following rules and tasks. The money is divided into thirds, giving two-thirds of it to the top group, one-third to the middle group, and none to the bottom group.

2. Conduct exercise

Groups go to their assigned work places and have 30 minutes to complete their tasks.

Rules

a. Members of the top group are free to enter the space of either of the other groups and to communicate whatever they wish, whenever they wish. Members of the middle group may enter the space of the lower group when they wish but must request permission to enter the top group's space (which the top group can refuse). Members of the lower group may not disturb the top group in any way unless specifically invited by the top. The lower group does have the right to knock on the door of the middle group and request permission to communicate with them (which can also be refused).

b. The members of the top group have the authority to make any change in the rules that they wish, at any time, with or without notice.

Tasks

a. Top Group: To be responsible for the overall effectiveness and learning from the exercise, and to decide how to use its money.

b. Middle Group: To assist the Top Group in providing for the overall welfare of the organization, and to decide how to use its money.

c. Bottom Group: To identify its resources and to decide how best to provide for learning and the overall effectiveness of the organization.

3. Debriefing

Each of the three groups chooses two representatives to go to the front of the class and discuss the following questions:

a. Summarize what occurred within and among the three groups.

b. What are some of the differences between being in the Top Group versus being in the Bottom Group?

c. What can we learn about power from this experience?

d. How accurate do you think this exercise is to the reality of resource allocation decisions in large organizations?

Source: This exercise is adapted from L. Bolman and T.E. Deal, *Exchange*, vol. 3, no. 4, 1979, pp. 38–42. Reprinted by permission of Sage Publications, Inc.

Damned If You Do; Damned If You Don't

Fran Gilson has spent 15 years with the Thompson Grocery Company.* Starting out as a part-time cashier while attending college, Fran has risen up through the ranks of this 50-store grocery store chain. Today, at the age of 34, she is a regional manager, overseeing seven stores and earning nearly $80,000 a year. Fran also thinks she's ready to take on more responsibility. About five weeks ago, she was contacted by an executive-search recruiter inquiring about her interest in the position of vice president and regional manager for a national drugstore chain. She would be responsible for more than 100 stores in five states. She agreed to meet with the recruiter. This led to two meetings with top executives at the drugstore chain. The recruiter called Fran two days ago to tell her she was one of the two finalists for the job.

The only person at Thompson who knows Fran is looking at this other job is her good friend and colleague, Ken Hamilton. Ken is director of finance for the grocery chain. "It's a dream job," Fran told Ken. "It's a lot more responsibility and it's a good company to work for. The regional office is just 20 miles from here so I wouldn't have to move, and the pay is first rate. With the performance bonus, I could make nearly $200,000 a year. But best of all, the job provides terrific visibility. I'd be their only female vice president. The job would allow me to be a more visible role model for young women and give me a bigger voice in opening up doors for women and ethnic minorities in retailing management."

Since Fran considered Ken a close friend and wanted to keep the fact that she was looking at another job secret, she asked Ken last week if she could use his name as a reference. Said Ken, "Of course. I'll give you a great recommendation. We'd hate to lose you here, but you've got a lot of talent. They'd be lucky to get someone with your experience and energy." Fran passed Ken's name on to the executive recruiter as her only reference at Thompson. She made it very clear to the recruiter that Ken was the only person at Thompson who knew she was considering another job. Thompson's top management is old-fashioned and places a high value on loyalty. If anyone heard she was talking to another company, it might seriously jeopardize her chances for promotion. But she trusted Ken completely. It's against this backdrop that this morning's incident became more than just a question of sexual harrassment. It became a full-blown ethical and political dilemma for Fran.

Jennifer Chung has been a financial analyst in Ken's department for five months. Fran met Jennifer through Ken. The three have chatted together on a number of occasions in the coffee room. Fran's impression of Jennifer is quite positive. In many ways, Jennifer strikes Fran as a lot like she was ten years ago. This morning, Fran came to work around 6:30 A.M. as she usually does. It allows her to get a lot accomplished before "the troops" roll in at 8 A.M. At about 6:45, Jennifer came into Fran's office. It was immediately evident that something was wrong. Jennifer was very nervous and uncomfortable, which was most unlike her. She asked Fran if they could talk. Fran sat her down and listened to her story.

What Fran heard was hard to believe, but she had no reason to think Jennifer was lying. Jennifer said that Ken began making off-color comments to her when they were alone within a month after Jennifer joined Thompson. From there it got progressively worse. Ken would leer at her. He put his arm over her shoulder when they were reviewing reports. He patted her rear. Every time one of these occurrences happened, Jennifer would ask him to stop and not do it again, but it fell on deaf ears. Yesterday, Ken reminded Jennifer that her six-month probationary review was coming up. "He told me that if I didn't sleep with him that I couldn't expect a very favorable evaluation." She told Fran that all she could do was go to the ladies' room and cry.

Jennifer said that she had come to Fran because she didn't know what to do or whom to turn to. "I came to you, Fran, because you're a friend of Ken's and the highest ranking woman here. Will you help me?" Fran had never heard anything like this about Ken before. About all she knew regarding his personal life was that he was in his late 30s, single, and involved in a long-term relationship.

Questions

1. Analyze Fran's situation in a purely legalistic sense. You might want to talk to friends or relatives who are in management or the legal profession for advice in this analysis.

2. Analyze Fran's dilemma in political terms.

3. Analyze Fran's situation in an ethical sense. What is the *ethically* right thing for her to do? Is that also the *politically* right thing to do?

4. If you were Fran, what would *you* do?

*The identity of this organization and the people described are disguised for obvious reasons.

Power, Sexual Harassment, and the CIA

By the time "Janet" finished her training with the U.S. Central Intelligence Agency in Virginia, she looked like the perfect spy. Outgoing and affable, she slipped easily into foreign cultures—a legacy from having grown up overseas. In college, in Tokyo, Janet became fluent in Japanese. Now, skilled in picking locks and servicing film drops, the 26-year-old spy eagerly awaited her first assignment abroad. But the old boys of the CIA were not eager to have Janet among their ranks. Women spies have never been fully accepted in the hard-drinking, macho world of the agency's clandestine service, known as the Directorate of Operations, or DO. Janet quit the agency in 1988 out of frustration.

Today, the women of the CIA refuse to quit. Angered by a male-dominated climate and inequality in promotions and assignments, the CIA's female spies are demanding changes. Such reform is one of the many challenges facing newly appointed CIA director John Deutch.

To many, the issue goes beyond money and fairness. The agency's old-boy mentality wastes some of its most talented people, many CIA women say, while it hampers the basic mission of the CIA. "They really protect their own," says Lynne Larkin, a seven-year veteran who recently resigned over a job discrimination issue. The old-boy network, Larkin says, contributes to an atmosphere in which people feel they can break the rules without repercussion. "They have this idea that they're not really held accountable," says Larkin. "Abuse not only continues but tends to get worse."

For Janet, the discrimination was blatant. Her first assignment in Tokyo became the joke of the CIA station. She was assigned as a "port caller," an officer who recruits sailors, usually off of Third World ships, to photograph Chinese ports and North Korean vessels when they sail into "denied areas"— places U.S. spies cannot gain access to. Usually, the port caller job is reserved for swaggering jocks, not a 5-foot-6-inch, 125-pound female officer. For Janet, the station chief slapped on a special restriction: She was forbidden to go into bars or to drink while recruiting sailors. The job was a recipe for failure. "He clearly felt that if I was given a hard enough time, maybe they wouldn't send in another woman for a while," she says. Janet wouldn't be outsmarted, however. With some ingenuity, she devised a scheme to phone a ship's radio operator when a new vessel docked. Then, pretending to work for a publishing company, she invited the sailors ashore. Face to face, Janet persuaded them to take photos for pay. Within a year, Janet became the station's top recruiter. But her bosses didn't appreciate her efforts. After failing to win another overseas posting, Janet claimed that the station chief had altered her performance report, in violation of CIA policy. Today, some 300 women have threatened a class-action suit against the CIA, citing similar discriminatory practices.

Sexual harassment has been an even bigger problem at the CIA. Nearly 50 percent of all white women have reported being sexually harassed. Like a throwback to the 1950s, a fixation with nude photographs and crude sexual jokes is common among some male case officers. Women complain of a hostile work environment rife with insensitive or derogatory comments, jokes, signs, and posters.

Women who try to fight the old boys through official channels often encounter a fierce backlash. There is a strong perception within the DO that those who complained received no help or, worse, jeopardized their careers. "Jennifer," who had an otherwise stellar career in the DO, found her promotion path blocked after she officially complained that a male boss, at a staff meeting, had referred to "minorities, women and other two-headed animals." "If you complain, you are seen as betraying the system," she says.

Questions

1. Describe the hostile environment for women in the CIA.
2. How does this case demonstrate that sexual harassment is closely intertwined with power?
3. If you were John Deutch, what actions would you take to deal with the problems of discrimination and sexual harassment at the CIA?

Source: Based on "Women of the CIA Come Forward," *ABC News Nightline*; aired June 7, 1995.

12

CONFLICT, NEGOTIATION, AND INTERGROUP BEHAVIOR

> When two people in business always agree, one of them is unnecessary.
> —W. Wrigley, Jr.

LEARNING OBJECTIVES

After studying this chapter, you should be able to

1 Define *conflict*

2 Differentiate between the traditional, human relations, and interactionist views of conflict

3 Outline the conflict process

4 Describe the five conflict-handling intentions

5 Contrast distributive and integrative bargaining

6 Describe the five steps in the negotiation process

7 Explain the factors that affect intergroup relations

8 Identify methods for managing intergroup relations

SHEA & Gould was one of New York's best-known law firms.[1] It was founded in the mid-1960s by the man for whom Shea Stadium (home of the New York Mets) was named— William A. Shea, a confidant of governors, mayors, and corporate chieftains until his death in 1991—and Milton H. Gould. Among the firm's prestigious clients were the Mets, the New York Yankees, Apple Computer, Marine Midland Bank, and Toys "Я" Us. In early 1994, Shea & Gould had 80 partners, 200 lawyers, and offices in New York, Los Angeles, Washington, and Miami.

Mr. Shea and Mr. Gould had complementary talents. Shea was known more for his leadership skills than legal prowess, while Gould was a remarkably talented lawyer. Together they made a formidable team. Their firm grew and prospered in the 1970s and 1980s. At its peak, Shea & Gould had 350 lawyers and played a leading role in New York politics, banking, real estate, and sports.

A number of large and medium-sized law firms have closed their doors in the past decade as competition has increased and major clients have been lost. It isn't totally surprising then to learn that Shea & Gould's partners voted to dissolve their firm in January 1994. What is striking about this dissolution is that it had nothing to do with the firm's finances. Revenue in 1993 was $85 million, up from $83 million the year before. The firm, in fact, was still highly profitable for its partners. What brought the demise of Shea & Gould was that these partners couldn't get along with each other!

The problems at Shea & Gould began in the mid-1980s, when the founding partners began to cede control to younger lawyers. Some partners, accustomed to years of strong leadership by Shea and Gould, challenged the new power structure. Cliques and factions formed around legal disciplines, as well as around age groups and clients. Lawyers specializing in securities litigation lobbied for their interests, while lawyers who worked on legal matters for Big Six accounting firms fought for theirs. Younger partners clustered together against older partners, and no one group or alliance was strong enough to gain control over the whole firm. As the conflict escalated in December 1993, five partners resigned. A number of others were rumored to be actively looking at opportunities at other firms.

In January 1994, the partners gave up the fight and voted to dissolve the firm. A well-known consultant to the legal profession concluded that "this was a firm that had basic and principled differences among the partners that were basically irreconcilable." That same consultant also addressed the partners at their last meeting: "You don't have an economic problem," he said. "You have a personality problem. You hate each other!" ◆

◆ All conflicts aren't bad. Conflict has a positive side as well as a negative side.

Conflict can be a serious problem in *any* organization. It might not bring about the demise of a firm—as happened at Shea & Gould—but it certainly can hurt an organization's performance as well as lead to the loss of many good employees. However, as we show in this chapter, all conflicts aren't bad. Conflict has a positive side as well as a negative side. We explain the differences in this chapter and provide a guide to help you understand how conflicts develop. We also present two other topics in this chapter, both closely related to conflict—negotiation and intergroup relations. But let's begin by clarifying what we mean by conflict.

A Definition of Conflict

There has been no shortage of definitions of conflict.[2] Despite the divergent meanings the term has acquired, several common themes underlie most definitions. Conflict must be *perceived* by the parties to it; whether or not conflict exists is a perception issue. If no one is aware of a conflict, then it is generally agreed that no conflict exists. Additional commonalities in the definitions are opposition or incompatibility and some form of interaction.[3] These factors set the conditions that determine the beginning point of the conflict process.

conflict
A process that begins when one party perceives that another party has negatively affected, or is about to negatively affect, something that the first party cares about.

We can define **conflict**, then, as a process that begins when one party perceives that another party has negatively affected, or is about to negatively affect, something that the first party cares about.[4]

This definition is purposely broad. It describes that point in any ongoing activity when an interaction "crosses over" to become an interparty conflict. It encompasses the wide range of conflicts that people experience in organizations—incompatibility of goals, differences over interpretations of facts, disagreements based on behavioral expectations, and the like. Finally, our definition is flexible enough to cover the full range of conflict levels—from overt and violent acts to subtle forms of disagreement.

Transitions in Conflict Thought

It is entirely appropriate to say that there has been "conflict" over the role of conflict in groups and organizations. One school of thought has argued that conflict must be avoided—that it indicates a malfunctioning within the group. We call this the *traditional* view. Another school of thought, the *human relations* view, argues that conflict is a natural and inevitable outcome in any group and that it need not be evil, but rather has the potential to be a positive force in determining group performance. The third, and most recent, perspective proposes not only that conflict *can* be a positive force in a group but explicitly argues that some conflict is *absolutely necessary* for a group to perform effectively. We label this third school the *interactionist* approach. Let's take a closer look at each of these views.

The Traditional View

The early approach to conflict assumed that all conflict was bad. Conflict was viewed negatively, and it was used synonymously with such terms as *violence*, *destruction*, and *irrationality* to reinforce its negative connotation. Conflict, by definition, was harmful and was to be avoided.

The **traditional** view was consistent with the attitudes that prevailed about group behavior in the 1930s and 1940s. Conflict was seen as a dysfunctional outcome resulting from poor communication, a lack of openness and trust between people, and the failure of managers to be responsive to the needs and aspirations of their employees.

traditional view of conflict
The belief that all conflict is harmful and must be avoided.

The view that all conflict is bad certainly offers a simple approach to looking at the behavior of people who create conflict. Since all conflict is to be avoided, we need merely direct our attention to the causes of conflict and correct these malfunctionings in order to improve group and organizational performance. Although research studies now provide strong evidence to dispute that this approach to conflict reduction results in high group performance, many of us still evaluate conflict situations utilizing this outmoded standard. So, too, do many boards of directors.

The board of Sunbeam-Oster followed the traditional approach when they fired the company's chairman, Paul Kazarian, in 1993.[5] Three years earlier, Kazarian took over the company when it was in bankruptcy. He sold off losing businesses, restructured the remaining appliance operation, and turned a $40 million loss in 1990 into a $47 million profit in 1991. A few days before he was fired, the company reported a 40 percent jump in quarterly profits. But Kazarian's "crime" was that he rubbed a lot of people in the company the wrong way. He aggressively confronted managers, employees, and suppliers. People complained that his style was abrasive. Kazarian, however, defended his actions as necessary: "You don't change a company in bankruptcy without making a few waves. I wasn't there to be a polite manager. I was there to create value for stockholders."

The Human Relations View

The **human relations** position argued that conflict was a natural occurrence in all groups and organizations. Since conflict was inevitable, the human relations school advocated acceptance of conflict. Proponents rationalized its existence: It cannot be eliminated, and there are even times when conflict may benefit a group's performance. The human relations view dominated conflict theory from the late 1940s through the mid-1970s.

human relations view of conflict
The belief that conflict is a natural and inevitable outcome in any group.

The Interactionist View

While the human relations approach accepted conflict, the **interactionist** approach encourages conflict on the grounds that a harmonious, peaceful, tranquil, and cooperative group is prone to becoming static, apathetic, and

interactionist view of conflict
The belief that conflict is not only a positive force in a group but that it is absolutely necessary for a group to perform effectively.

These employees of ME International, a manufacturer of metal grinding balls, illustrate the interactionist view of conflict. The president of ME challenged his workers to develop a statement of corporate values. He hired consultant Rob Lebow (standing, center) to maintain an ongoing minimum level of conflict during the process by encouraging employees to express personal beliefs and opinions and openly question and disagree with others' ideas. Such conflict kept employees self-critical and creative, improving their performance in determining a set of shared values and in choosing the words that best reflect those values.

nonresponsive to needs for change and innovation. The major contribution of the interactionist approach, therefore, is encouraging group leaders to maintain an ongoing minimum level of conflict—enough to keep the group viable, self-critical, and creative.

Given the interactionist view—and it is the one that we shall take in this chapter—it becomes evident that to say conflict is all good or bad is inappropriate and naive. Whether a conflict is good or bad depends on the type of conflict. Specifically, it's necessary to differentiate between functional and dysfunctional conflicts.

Functional vs. Dysfunctional Conflict

The interactionist view does not propose that *all* conflicts are good. Rather, some conflicts support the goals of the group and improve its performance; these are **functional**, constructive forms of conflict. Additionally, there are conflicts that hinder group performance; these are **dysfunctional** or destructive forms of conflict. The conflict among partners at the law firm of Shea & Gould was clearly in the dysfunctional category.

Of course, it is one thing to argue that conflict can be valuable for the group, and another to be able to tell if a conflict is functional or dysfunctional.[6] The demarcation between functional and dysfunctional is neither clear nor precise. No one level of conflict can be adopted as acceptable or unacceptable under all conditions. The type and level of conflict that creates healthy and positive involvement toward one group's goals today may, in another group or in the same group at another time, be regarded as highly dysfunctional.

functional conflict
Conflict that supports the goals of the group and improves its performance.

dysfunctional conflict
Conflict that hinders group performance.

The criterion that differentiates functional from dysfunctional conflict is group performance. Since groups exist to attain a goal or goals, it is the impact that the conflict has on the group, rather than on any individual member, that determines functionality. Of course, the impact of conflict on the individual and its impact on the group are rarely mutually exclusive, so the ways that individuals perceive a conflict may have an important influence on its effect on the group. However, this need not be the case, and when it is not, our focus will be on the group. So whether an individual group member perceives a given conflict as being personally disturbing or positive is irrelevant. For example, a group member may perceive an action as dysfunctional, in that the outcome is personally dissatisfying to him or her. However, for our analysis, that action would be functional if it furthers the objectives of the group. So while many people at Sunbeam-Oster thought the conflicts created by Paul Kazarian were dysfunctional, Kazarian was convinced they were functional because they improved Sunbeam's performance.

The Conflict Process

The **conflict process** can be seen as comprising five stages: potential opposition or incompatibility, cognition and personalization, intentions, behavior, and outcomes. The process is diagrammed in Exhibit 12-1.

conflict process
Five stages: potential opposition or incompatibility; cognition and personalization; intentions; behavior; and outcomes.

Stage I: Potential Opposition or Incompatibility

The first step in the conflict process is the presence of conditions that create opportunities for conflict to arise. They *need not* lead directly to conflict, but one of these conditions is necessary if conflict is to arise. For simplicity's sake, these conditions (which also may be looked at as causes or sources of conflict) have been condensed into three general categories: communication, structure, and personal variables.[7]

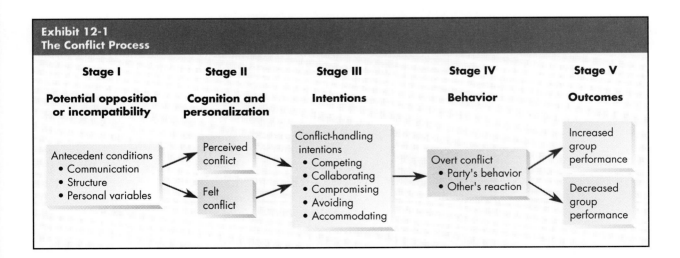

Exhibit 12-1
The Conflict Process

COMMUNICATION   Susan had worked in purchasing at Bristol-Myers Squibb for three years. She enjoyed her work in large part because her boss, Tim McGuire, was a great guy to work for. Then Tim got promoted six months ago and Chuck Benson took his place. Susan says her job is a lot more frustrating now. "Tim and I were on the same wavelength. It's not that way with Chuck. He tells me something and I do it. Then he tells me I did it wrong. I think he means one thing but says something else. It's been like this since the day he arrived. I don't think a day goes by when he isn't yelling at me for something. You know, there are some people you just find it easy to communicate with. Well, Chuck isn't one of those!"

Susan's comments illustrate that communication can be a source of conflict. It represents those opposing forces that arise from semantic difficulties, misunderstandings, and "noise" in the communication channels. Much of this discussion can be related back to our comments on communication in chapter 9.

One of the major myths that most of us carry around with us is that poor communication is the reason for conflicts—"if we could just communicate with each other, we could eliminate our differences." Such a conclusion is not unreasonable, given the amount of time each of us spends communicating. But, of course, poor communication is certainly not the source of all conflicts, though there is considerable evidence to suggest that problems in the communication process act to retard collaboration and stimulate misunderstanding.

> ◆ One of the major myths that most of us carry around with us is that poor communication is the major reason for conflicts.

A review of the research suggests that semantic difficulties, insufficient exchange of information, and noise in the communication channel are all barriers to communication and potential antecedent conditions to conflict. Specifically, evidence demonstrates that semantic difficulties arise as a result of differences in training, selective perception, and inadequate information about others. Research has further demonstrated a surprising finding: The potential for conflict increases when either too little or too much communication takes place. Apparently, an increase in communication is functional up to a point, whereupon it is possible to overcommunicate, with a resultant increase in the potential for conflict. Too much information as well as too little can lay the foundation for conflict. Furthermore, the channel chosen for communicating can have an influence on stimulating opposition. The filtering process that occurs as information is passed between members and the divergence of communications from formal or previously established channels offer potential opportunities for conflict to arise.

STRUCTURE   Charlotte and Teri both work at the Portland Furniture Mart—a large discount furniture retailer. Charlotte is a salesperson on the floor; Teri is the company credit manager. The two women have known each other for years and have much in common—they live within two blocks of each other, and their oldest daughters attend the same middle school and are best friends. In reality, if Charlotte and Teri had different jobs they might be best friends themselves, but these two women are consistently fighting battles with each other. Charlotte's job is to sell furniture and she does a heck of a job. But most of her sales are made on credit. Because Teri's job is to make sure the company minimizes credit losses, she regularly has to turn down the credit application of a customer to whom Charlotte has just closed a sale. It's nothing personal between Charlotte and Teri—the requirements of their jobs just bring them into conflict.

The conflicts between Charlotte and Teri are structural in nature. The term *structure* is used, in this context, to include variables such as size, degree of specialization in the tasks assigned to group members, jurisdictional clarity, member–goal compatibility, leadership styles, reward systems, and the degree of dependence between groups.

Research indicates that size and specialization act as forces to stimulate conflict. The larger the group and the more specialized its activities, the greater the likelihood of conflict. Tenure and conflict have been found to be inversely related. The potential for conflict tends to be greatest where group members are younger and where turnover is high.

The greater the ambiguity in precisely defining where responsibility for actions lies, the greater the potential for conflict to emerge. Such jurisdictional ambiguities increase intergroup fighting for control of resources and territory.

Groups within organizations have diverse goals. For instance, purchasing is concerned with the timely acquisition of inputs at low prices, marketing's goals concentrate on disposing of outputs and increasing revenues, quality control's attention is focused on improving quality and ensuring that the organization's products meet standards, and production units seek efficiency of operations by maintaining a steady production flow. This diversity of goals among groups is a major source of conflict. When groups within an organization seek diverse ends, some of which—like sales and credit at Portland Furniture Mart—are inherently at odds, there are increased opportunities for conflict.

There is some indication that a close style of leadership—tight and continuous observation with general control of others' behaviors—increases conflict potential, but the evidence is not particularly strong. Too much reliance on participation may also stimulate conflict. Research tends to confirm that participation and conflict are highly correlated, apparently because participation encourages the promotion of differences. Reward systems, too, are found to create conflict when one member's gain is at another's expense. Finally, if a group is dependent on another group (in contrast to the two being mutually independent) or if interdependence allows one group to gain at another's expense, opposing forces are stimulated.

PERSONAL VARIABLES Did you ever meet someone to whom you took an immediate disliking? Most of the opinions they expressed, you disagreed with. Even insignificant characteristics—the sound of their voice, the smirk when they smiled, their personality—annoyed you. We've all met people like that. When you have to work with such individuals, there is often the potential for conflict.

Our last category of potential sources of conflict is personal variables. As indicated, they include the individual value systems that each person has and the personality characteristics that account for individual idiosyncrasies and differences.

The evidence indicates that certain personality types—for example, individuals who are highly authoritarian and dogmatic, and who demonstrate low esteem—lead to potential conflict. Most important, and probably the most overlooked variable in the study of social conflict, is differing value systems.

Value differences, for example, are the best explanation of such diverse issues as prejudice, disagreements over one's contribution to the group and the rewards one deserves, and assessments of whether this particular book is any good. That John dislikes African-Americans and Dana believes John's position indicates his ignorance, that an employee thinks he is worth $45,000 a year but his boss believes him to be worth $40,000, and that Ann thinks this book is interesting to read while Jennifer views it as trash are all value judgments. And differences in value systems are important sources for creating the potential for conflict.

Stage II: Cognition and Personalization

If the conditions cited in Stage I negatively affect something that one party cares about, then the potential for opposition or incompatibility becomes actualized in the second stage. The antecedent conditions can only lead to conflict when one or more of the parties are affected by, and aware of, the conflict.

As we noted in our definition of conflict, perception is required. Therefore, one or more of the parties must be aware of the existence of the antecedent conditions. However, because a conflict is **perceived** does not mean that it is personalized. In other words, "A may be aware that B and A are in serious disagreement . . . but it may not make A tense or anxious, and it may

perceived conflict
Awareness by one or more parties of the existence of conditions that create opportunities for conflict to arise.

Positive emotions played a key role in shaping perceptions when a new member joined the world-famous Tokyo String Quartet. The chemistry among the original members, all Japanese musicians, was incredibly strong, as they had practiced and performed together for decades. When one of the original violinists left the group, a Canadian took his place and, with an outsider's perspective, began questioning everything the ensemble did, from musical selections to tour destinations. Rather than perceiving the new violinist's ideas in a negative way, the other members framed the conflict as a potential win-win situation. They took a positive approach, viewing the situation as an opportunity to see themselves more objectively and as a challenge to make the group more creative and innovative.

have no effect whatsoever on A's affection toward B."[8] It is at the **felt** level, when individuals become emotionally involved, that parties experience anxiety, tension, frustration, or hostility.

Keep in mind two points. First, Stage II is important because it's where conflict issues tend to be defined. This is the place in the process where the parties decide what the conflict is about.[9] And, in turn, this "sense making" is critical because the way a conflict is defined goes a long way toward establishing the sort of outcomes that might settle it. For instance, if I define our salary disagreement as a zero-sum situation—that is, if you get the increase in pay you want, there will be just that amount less for me—I am going to be far less willing to compromise than if I frame the conflict as a potential win-win situation (i.e., the dollars in the salary pool might be increased so that both of us could get the added pay we want). So the definition of a conflict is important, for it typically delineates the set of possible settlements. Our second point is that emotions play a major role in shaping perceptions.[10] For example, negative emotions have been found to produce oversimplification of issues, reductions in trust, and negative interpretations of the other party's behavior.[11] In contrast, positive feelings have been found to increase the tendency to see potential relationships among the elements of a problem, to take a broader view of the situation, and to develop more innovative solutions.[12]

Stage III: Intentions

Intentions intervene between people's perceptions and emotions and their overt behavior. These intentions are decisions to act in a given way.[13]

Why are intentions separated out as a distinct stage? You have to infer the other's intent in order to know how to respond to that other's behavior. A lot of conflicts are escalated merely by one party attributing the wrong intentions to the other party. Additionally, there is typically a great deal of slippage between intentions and behavior, so that behavior does not always accurately reflect a person's intentions.

Exhibit 12-2 represents one author's effort to identify the primary conflict-handling intentions. Using two dimensions—*cooperativeness* (the degree to which one party attempts to satisfy the other party's concerns) and *assertiveness* (the degree to which one party attempts to satisfy his or her own concerns)—five conflict-handling intentions can be identified: *competing* (assertive and uncooperative), *collaborating* (assertive and cooperative), *avoiding* (unassertive and uncooperative), *accommodating* (unassertive and cooperative), and *compromising* (midrange on both assertiveness and cooperativeness).[14]

COMPETING When one person seeks to satisfy his or her own interests, regardless of the impact on the other parties to the conflict, he or she is **competing**. Examples include intending to achieve your goal at the sacrifice of the other's goal, attempting to convince another that your conclusion is correct and his or hers is mistaken, and trying to make someone else accept blame for a problem.

COLLABORATING When the parties to conflict each desire to fully satisfy the concerns of all parties, we have cooperation and the search for a mutually beneficial outcome. In **collaborating**, the intention of the parties is to solve the problem by clarifying differences rather than by accommodating various points of view. Examples include attempting to find a win-win solution that

felt conflict
Emotional involvement in a conflict creating anxiety, tenseness, frustration, or hostility.

intentions
Decisions to act in a given way in a conflict episode.

competing
A desire to satisfy one's interests, regardless of the impact on the other party to the conflict.

collaborating
A situation where the parties to a conflict each desire to satisfy fully the concerns of all parties.

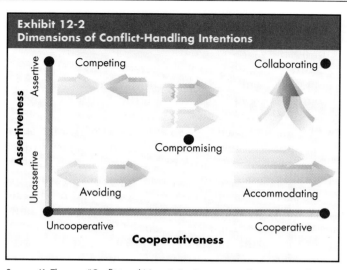

Exhibit 12-2
Dimensions of Conflict-Handling Intentions

Source: K. Thomas, "Conflict and Negotiation Processes in Organizations," in M.D. Dunnette and L.M. Hough (eds.), *Handbook of Industrial and Organizational Psychology,* 2nd ed., vol. 3 (Palo Alto, CA: Consulting Psychologists Press, 1992), p. 668. With permission.

allows both parties' goals to be completely achieved and seeking a conclusion that incorporates the valid insights of both parties.

AVOIDING   A person may recognize that a conflict exists and want to withdraw from it or suppress it. Examples of **avoiding** include trying to just ignore a conflict and avoiding others with whom you disagree.

avoiding
The desire to withdraw from or suppress a conflict.

ACCOMMODATING   When one party seeks to appease an opponent, that party may be willing to place the opponent's interests above his or her own. In other words, in order for the relationship to be maintained, one party is willing to be self-sacrificing. We refer to this intention as **accommodating**. Examples are a willingness to sacrifice your goal so the other party's goal can be attained, supporting someone else's opinion despite your reservations about it, and forgiving someone for an infraction and allowing subsequent ones.

accommodating
The willingness of one party in a conflict to place the opponent's interests above his or her own.

COMPROMISING   When each party to the conflict seeks to give up something, sharing occurs, resulting in a compromised outcome. In **compromising**, there is no clear winner or loser. Rather, there is a willingness to ration the object of the conflict and accept a solution that provides incomplete satisfaction of both parties' concerns. The distinguishing characteristic of compromising, therefore, is that each party intends to give up something. Examples might be willingness to accept a raise of $1 an hour rather than $2, to acknowledge partial agreement with a specific viewpoint, and to take partial blame for an infraction.

compromising
A situation in which each party to a conflict is willing to give up something.

Intentions provide general guidelines for parties in a conflict situation. They define each party's purpose. Yet, people's intentions are not fixed. During the course of a conflict, they might change because of reconceptualization or because of an emotional reaction to the behavior of the other party. However, research indicates that people have an underlying disposition to handle conflicts in certain ways.[15] Specifically, individuals have preferences among the five conflict-handling intentions just described; these preferences tend to be relied upon quite consistently, and a person's intentions can be predicted rather well from a combination of intellectual and personality characteristics. So it may be more appropriate to view the five conflict-handling intentions as relatively fixed rather than as a set of options from which individuals choose to fit an appropriate situation. That is, when confronting a conflict situation, some people want to win it all at any cost, some want to find an optimum solution, some want to run away, others want to be obliging, and still others want to "split the difference."

Stage IV: Behavior

When most people think of conflict situations, they tend to focus on Stage IV. Why? Because this is where conflicts become visible. The behavior stage includes the statements, actions, and reactions made by the conflicting parties.

These conflict behaviors are usually overt attempts to implement each party's intentions. But these behaviors have a stimulus quality that is separate from intentions. As a result of miscalculations or unskilled enactments, overt behaviors sometimes deviate from original intentions.[16]

It helps to think of Stage IV as a dynamic process of interaction. For example, you make a demand on me; I respond by arguing; you threaten me; I threaten you back; and so on. Exhibit 12-3 provides a way of visualizing conflict behavior. All conflicts exist somewhere along this continuum. At the lower part of the continuum, we have conflicts characterized by subtle, indirect, and highly controlled forms of tension. An illustration might be a student questioning in class a point the instructor has just made. Conflict inten-

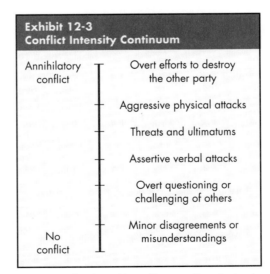

Exhibit 12-3
Conflict Intensity Continuum

Annihilatory conflict — Overt efforts to destroy the other party

— Aggressive physical attacks

— Threats and ultimatums

— Assertive verbal attacks

— Overt questioning or challenging of others

No conflict — Minor disagreements or misunderstandings

Source: Based on S.P. Robbins, *Managing Organizational Conflict: A Nontraditional Approach* (Upper Saddle River, NJ: Prentice Hall, 1974), pp. 93–97; and F. Glasl, "The Process of Conflict Escalation and the Roles of Third Parties," in G.B.J. Bomers and R. Peterson (eds.), *Conflict Management and Industrial Relations* (Boston: Kluwer-Nijhoff, 1982), pp. 119–40.

Exhibit 12-4 Conflict Management Techniques

Conflict Resolution Techniques

Problem solving	Face-to-face meeting of the conflicting parties for the purpose of identifying the problem and resolving it through open discussion.
Superordinate goals	Creating a shared goal that cannot be attained without the cooperation of each of the conflicting parties.
Expansion of resources	When a conflict is caused by the scarcity of a resource—say, money, promotion opportunities, office space—expansion of the resource can create a win-win solution.
Avoidance	Withdrawal from, or suppression of, the conflict.
Smoothing	Playing down differences while emphasizing common interests between the conflicting parties.
Compromise	Each party to the conflict gives up something of value.
Authoritative command	Management uses its formal authority to resolve the conflict and then communicates its desires to the parties involved.
Altering the human variable	Using behavioral change techniques such as human relations training to alter attitudes and behaviors that cause conflict.
Altering the structural variables	Changing the formal organization structure and the interaction patterns of conflicting parties through job redesign, transfers, creation of coordinating positions, and the like.

Conflict Stimulation Techniques

Communication	Using ambiguous or threatening messages to increase conflict levels.
Bringing in outsiders	Adding employees to a group whose backgrounds, values, attitudes, or managerial styles differ from those of present members.
Restructuring the organization	Realigning work groups, altering rules and regulations, increasing interdependence, and making similar structural changes to disrupt the status quo.
Appointing a devil's advocate	Designating a critic to purposely argue against the majority positions held by the group.

Source: Based on S.P. Robbins, *Managing Organizational Conflict: A Nontraditional Approach* (Upper Saddle River, NJ: Prentice Hall, 1974), pp. 59–89.

sities escalate as they move upward along the continuum until they become highly destructive. Strikes, riots, and wars clearly fall in this upper range. For the most part, you should assume that conflicts that reach the upper ranges of the continuum are almost always dysfunctional. Functional conflicts are typically confined to the lower range of the continuum.

If a conflict is dysfunctional, what can the parties do to deescalate it? Or, conversely, what options exist if conflict is too low and needs to be increased? This brings us to **conflict management** techniques. Exhibit 12-4 lists the major resolution and stimulation techniques that allow managers to control conflict levels. Notice that several of the resolution techniques were earlier described as conflict-handling intentions. This, of course, shouldn't be surprising. Under ideal conditions, a person's intentions should translate into comparable behaviors.

conflict management
The use of resolution and stimulation techniques to achieve the desired level of conflict.

Stage V: Outcomes

The action-reaction interplay between the conflicting parties results in consequences. As our model (see Exhibit 12-1) demonstrates, these outcomes may be functional in that the conflict results in an improvement in the group's performance, or dysfunctional in that it hinders group performance.

FUNCTIONAL OUTCOMES How might conflict act as a force to increase group performance? It is hard to visualize a situation where open or violent aggression could be functional. But there are a number of instances where it is possible to envision how low or moderate levels of conflict could improve the effectiveness of a group. Because people often find it difficult to think of instances where conflict can be constructive, let's consider some examples and then review the research evidence.

Conflict is constructive when it improves the quality of decisions, stimulates creativity and innovation, encourages interest and curiosity among group members, provides the medium through which problems can be aired and tensions released, and fosters an environment of self-evaluation and change. The evidence suggests that conflict can improve the quality of decision making by allowing all points, particularly the ones that are unusual or held by a minority, to be weighed in important decisions.[17] Conflict is an antidote for groupthink. It doesn't allow the group passively to "rubber-stamp" decisions that may be based on weak assumptions, inadequate consideration of relevant alternatives, or other debilities. Conflict challenges the status quo and therefore furthers the creation of new ideas, promotes reassessment of group goals and activities, and increases the probability that the group will respond to change.

For examples of companies that have suffered because they had too little functional conflict, you don't have to look further than Sears, Roebuck and General Motors.[18] Much of the problems that beset both of these companies throughout the 1970s and 1980s can be traced to a lack of functional conflict. They hired and promoted individuals who were "yes men," loyal to the organization to the point of never questioning company actions. Managers were, for the most part, conservative white Anglo-Saxon males raised in the midwestern United States who resisted change—they preferred looking back to past successes rather than forward to new challenges. Moreover, both firms kept their senior executives sheltered in their respective Chicago and Detroit headquarters' offices, protected from hearing anything they didn't want to hear, and a "world away" from the changes that were dramatically altering the retailing and automobile industries.

Research studies in diverse settings confirm the functionality of conflict. Consider the following findings.

Raymond Floyd (right), site manager at Exxon Chemical Company's plant in Baytown, Texas, believes that cultural diversity creates a more energized and productive workforce. Floyd builds high-performance work teams by training employees to recognize and understand the inherent differences in cultures that influence what individuals believe and how they behave. The training helps employees value differences and appreciate the special contributions of diverse cultural perspectives in improving business processes. The plant, honored as one of America's best, benefits by receiving some 24,000 improvement ideas from employees each year.

The comparison of six major decisions made during the administration of four different U.S. presidents found that conflict reduced the chance that groupthink would overpower policy decisions. The comparisons demonstrated that conformity among presidential advisors was related to poor decisions, while an atmosphere of constructive conflict and critical thinking surrounded the well-developed decisions.[19]

There is evidence indicating that conflict can also be positively related to productivity. For instance, it was demonstrated that, among established groups, performance tended to improve more when there was conflict among members than when there was fairly close agreement. The investigators observed that when groups analyzed decisions that had been made by the individual members of that group, the average improvement among the high-conflict groups was 73 percent greater than was that of those groups characterized by low-conflict conditions.[20] Others have found similar results: Groups composed of members with different interests tend to produce higher-quality solutions to a variety of problems than do homogeneous groups.[21]

The preceding leads us to predict that the increasing cultural diversity of the workforce should provide benefits to organizations. And that's what the evidence indicates. Research demonstrates that heterogeneity among group and organization members can increase creativity, improve the quality of decisions, and facilitate change by enhancing member flexibility.[22] For example, researchers compared decision-making groups composed of all-Anglo individuals with groups that also contained members from Asian, Hispanic, and black ethnic groups. The ethnically diverse groups produced more effective and more feasible ideas and the unique ideas they generated tended to be of higher quality than the unique ideas produced by the all-Anglo group.

Similarly, studies of professionals—systems analysts and research and development scientists—support the constructive value of conflict. An investigation of 22 teams of systems analysts found that the more incompatible groups were likely to be more productive.[23] Research and development scientists have been found to be most productive where there is a certain amount of intellectual conflict.[24]

Conflict can even be constructive on sports teams and in unions. Studies of sports teams indicate that moderate levels of group conflict contribute to team effectiveness and provide an additional stimulus for high achievement.[25] An examination of local unions found that conflict between members of the local was positively related to the union's power and to member loyalty and participation in union affairs.[26] These findings might suggest that conflict within a group indicates strength rather than, as in the traditional view, weakness.

DYSFUNCTIONAL OUTCOMES The destructive consequences of conflict upon a group or organization's performance are generally well known. A reasonable summary might state: Uncontrolled opposition breeds discontent, which acts to dissolve common ties, and eventually leads to the destruction of the group. And, of course, there is a substantial body of literature to document how conflict—the dysfunctional varieties—can reduce group effectiveness.[27] Among the more undesirable consequences are a retarding of communication, reductions in group cohesiveness, and subordination of group goals to the primacy of infighting between members. At the extreme, conflict can bring group functioning to a halt and potentially threaten the group's survival.

This discussion has again returned us to the issue of what is functional and what is dysfunctional. Research on conflict has yet to clearly identify those situations where conflict is more likely to be constructive than destructive. However, there is growing evidence that the type of group activity is a significant factor determining functionality.[28] The more nonroutine the tasks of the group, the greater the probability that internal conflict will be constructive. Groups that are required to tackle problems demanding new and novel approaches—as in research, advertising, and other professional activities—will benefit more from conflict than will groups performing highly routine activities—for instance, those of work teams on an automobile assembly line.

CREATING FUNCTIONAL CONFLICT We briefly mentioned conflict stimulation as part of Stage IV of the conflict process. Since the topic of conflict stimulation is relatively new and somewhat controversial, you might be wondering: If managers accept the interactionist view toward conflict, what can they do to encourage functional conflict in their organizations.[29]

There seems to be general agreement that creating functional conflict is a tough job, particularly in large American corporations. As one consultant put it, "A high proportion of people who get to the top are conflict avoiders. They don't like hearing negatives, they don't like saying or thinking negative things. They frequently make it up the ladder in part because they don't irritate people on the way up." Another suggests that at least seven out of ten people in American business hush up when their opinions are at odds with those of their superiors, allowing bosses to make mistakes even when they know better.

Such anticonflict cultures may have been tolerable in the past but not in today's fiercely competitive global economy. Those organizations that don't encourage and support dissent may not survive into the twenty-first century.

OB in the News

Spectrum Associates Purposely Builds Conflict into Its Structure

Spectrum Associates is a small but rapidly growing software company. In 1988, the company's first year of operations, revenues were only $404,000. Five years later revenues were $25 million.

Spectrum's founders attribute a large part of the company's success to the way it's structured. The firm is designed to create conflict. All product teams and support groups compete against each other for internal resources and outside markets.

"We've kept the company growing by making sure nobody gets comfortable," says one of the founders. The company simulates internally what all companies face externally. By setting internal groups against each other, the company simulates "the pricing pressure, the delivery pressure, and the growth pressure that we encounter in the marketplace." The result is a workforce in a perpetual state of readiness. "It keeps us healthy. A little insecurity can be very healthy."

The company only hires self-starters. New employees are told that "the company is not your parent. It's just a facility where you can come and lower your risks significantly because you have benefits, you have a base salary. But you're on your own." Recruits are encouraged to "grow your own business" within Spectrum. If it succeeds, you share in the wealth. If it fails, try again.

Spectrum's competitive culture is a shock for some. One employee, for example, said she wasn't prepared to have her own colleagues blocking her shots. "It took me a while to realize that meant convincing the salespeople to flip work to me instead of to someone else in the organization—that it meant bidding more aggressively to get a job."

But "it's not a free-for-all" says one co-founder. "Yeah, people compete, but they do it in groups. One individual is not out there trying to do in another person." The two owners referee squabbles as they arise, but they refuse to formalize boundaries or set rules. "Behind it all there's a very healthy thing going on, which is a struggle to do what's right for the customer," argues one of the founders. "When I talk to customers, I can say, 'Look, what do you want? The best quality, the best price, and the best delivery. It so happens that we're organized in such a way that we can guarantee all that.'"

Spectrum has created a bunch of different businesses competing for the organization's limited resources. In contrast to the typical firm whose competition is with outside companies, Spectrum's people have to compete against products created by its own internal groups.

Based on A. Murphy, "The Enemy Within," *INC.*, March 1994, pp. 58–69.

Take It to the Net

We invite you to visit the Robbins page on the Prentice Hall Web site at:

http://www.prenhall.com/robbinsorgbeh

for this chapter's World Wide Web exercise.

Let's look at some of the approaches organizations are taking to encourage their people to challenge the system and develop fresh ideas.

Hewlett-Packard rewards dissenters by recognizing go-against-the-grain types, or people who stay with the ideas they believe in even when those ideas are rejected by management. Herman Miller Inc., an office-furniture manufacturer, has a formal system in which employees evaluate and criticize their bosses. IBM also has a formal system that encourages dissension. Employees can question their boss with impunity. If the disagreement can't be resolved, the system provides a third party for counsel.

Royal Dutch Shell Group, General Electric, and Anheuser-Busch build devil's advocates into the decision process. For instance, when the policy committee at Anheuser-Busch considers a major move, such as getting into or out of a business or making a major capital expenditure, it often assigns teams to make the case for each side of the question. This process frequently results in decisions and alternatives that previously hadn't been considered.

The governor of Maryland stimulates conflict and invigorates his organization by requiring state cabinet officials to swap jobs for one month every year, then write reports and suggestions based on their experiences.

One common ingredient in organizations that successfully create functional conflict is that they reward dissent and punish conflict avoiders. The president of Innovis Interactive Technologies, for instance, fired a top executive who refused to dissent. His explanation: "He was the ultimate yes-man. In this organization, I can't afford to pay someone to hear my own opinion." But the real challenge for managers is when they hear news that they don't want to hear. The news may make their blood boil or their hopes collapse, but they can't show it. They have to learn to take the bad news without flinching. No tirades, no tight-lipped sarcasm, no eyes rolling upward, no gritting of teeth. Rather, managers should ask calm, even-tempered questions: "Can you tell me more about what happened?" "What do you think we ought to do?" A sincere "Thank you for bringing this to my attention" will probably reduce the likelihood that managers will be cut off from similar communications in the future.

> ◆ One common ingredient in organizations that successfully create functional conflict is that they reward dissent and punish conflict avoiders.

Negotiation

Negotiation permeates the interactions of almost everyone in groups and organizations. There's the obvious: Labor bargains with management. There's the not so obvious: Managers negotiate with subordinates, peers, and bosses; salespeople negotiate with customers; purchasing agents negotiate with suppliers. And there's the subtle: A worker agrees to answer a colleague's phone for a few minutes in exchange for some past or future benefit. In today's team-based organizations, where members are increasingly finding themselves having to work with colleagues over whom they have no direct authority and with whom they may not even share a common boss, negotiation skills become critical.

We'll define **negotiation** as a process in which two or more parties exchange goods or services and attempt to agree upon the exchange rate for them.[30] Note that we use the terms *negotiation* and *bargaining* interchangeably.

negotiation
A process in which two or more parties exchange goods or services and attempt to agree upon the exchange rate for them.

In this section, we'll contrast two bargaining strategies, provide a model of the negotiation process, ascertain the role of personality traits on bargaining, review cultural differences in negotiation, and take a brief look at third-party negotiations.

Bargaining Strategies

There are two general approaches to negotiation—*distributive bargaining* and *integrative bargaining*.[31] These are compared in Exhibit 12-5.

DISTRIBUTIVE BARGAINING You see a used car advertised for sale in the newspaper. It appears to be just what you've been looking for. You go out to see the car. It's great and you want it. The owner tells you the asking price. You don't want to pay that much. The two of you then negotiate over the price. The negotiating strategy you're engaging in is called **distributive bargaining**. Its most identifying feature is that it operates under zero-sum conditions. That is, any gain I make is at your expense, and vice versa. Referring back to the used car example, every dollar you can get the seller to cut from the car's price is a dollar you save. Conversely, every dollar more the seller can get from you comes at your expense. So the essence of distributive bargaining is negotiating over who gets what share of a fixed pie.

Probably the most widely cited example of distributive bargaining is in labor–management negotiations over wages. Typically, labor's representatives come to the bargaining table determined to get as much money as possible out of management. Since every cent more that labor negotiates increases management's costs, each party bargains aggressively and treats the other as an opponent who must be defeated.

The essence of distributive bargaining is depicted in Exhibit 12-6. Parties A and B represent two negotiators. Each has a *target point* that defines what he or she would like to achieve. Each also has a *resistance point*, which marks the lowest outcome that is acceptable—the point below which they would break off negotiations rather than accept a less favorable settlement. The area between these two points makes up each's aspiration range. As long as there is some overlap between A and B's aspiration ranges, there exists a settlement range where each one's aspirations can be met.

distributive bargaining
Negotiation that seeks to divide up a fixed amount of resources; a win-lose situation.

Exhibit 12-5 Distributive vs. Integrative Bargaining

Bargaining Characteristic	Distributive Bargaining	Integrative Bargaining
Available resources	Fixed amount of resources to be divided	Variable amount of resources to be divided
Primary motivations	I win, you lose	I win, you win
Primary interests	Opposed to each other	Convergent or congruent with each other
Focus of relationships	Short term	Long term

Source: Based on R.J. Lewicki and J.A. Litterer, *Negotiation* (Homewood, IL: Irwin, 1985), p. 280.

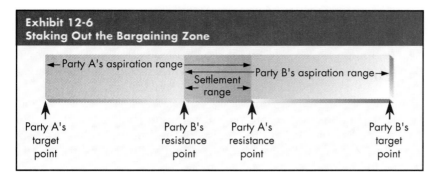

Exhibit 12-6
Staking Out the Bargaining Zone

When engaged in distributive bargaining, one's tactics focus on trying to get one's opponent to agree to one's specific target point or to get as close to it as possible. Examples of such tactics are persuading your opponent of the impossibility of getting to his or her target point and the advisability of accepting a settlement near yours; arguing that your target is fair, while your opponent's isn't; and attempting to get your opponent to feel emotionally generous toward you and thus accept an outcome close to your target point.

INTEGRATIVE BARGAINING A sales representative for a women's sportswear manufacturer has just closed a $15,000 order from a small clothing retailer. The sales rep calls in the order to her firm's credit department. She is told that the firm can't approve credit to this customer because of a past slow-pay record. The next day, the sales rep and the firm's credit manager meet to discuss the problem. The sales rep doesn't want to lose the business. Neither does the credit manager, but he also doesn't want to get stuck with an uncollectable debt. The two openly review their options. After considerable discussion, they agree on a solution that meets both their needs: The credit manager will approve the sale, but the clothing store's owner will provide a bank guarantee that will ensure payment if the bill isn't paid within sixty days.

This sales–credit negotiation is an example of **integrative bargaining**. In contrast to distributive bargaining, integrative problem solving operates under the assumption that there exists one or more settlements that can create a win-win solution.

integrative bargaining
Negotiation that seeks one or more settlements that can create a win-win solution.

In terms of intraorganizational behavior, all things being equal, integrative bargaining is preferable to distributive bargaining. Why? Because the former builds long-term relationships and facilitates working together in the future. It bonds negotiators and allows each to leave the bargaining table feeling that he or she has achieved a victory. Distributive bargaining, on the other hand, leaves one party a loser. It tends to build animosities and deepen divisions when people have to work together on an ongoing basis.

Why, then, don't we see more integrative bargaining in organizations? The answer lies in the conditions necessary for this type of negotiation to succeed. These include parties who are open with information and candid about their concerns, a sensitivity by both parties to the other's needs, the ability to trust one another, and a willingness by both parties to maintain flexibility.[32] Since these conditions often don't exist in organizations, it isn't surprising that negotiations often take on a win-at-any-cost dynamic.

The Negotiation Process

Exhibit 12-7 provides a simplified model of the negotiation process. It views negotiation as made up of five steps: (1) preparation and planning; (2) definition of ground rules; (3) clarification and justification; (4) bargaining and problem solving; and (5) closure and implementation.[33]

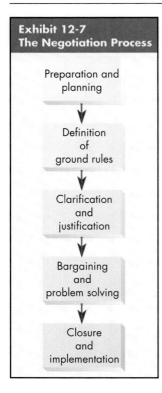

**Exhibit 12-7
The Negotiation Process**

Preparation and planning

↓

Definition of ground rules

↓

Clarification and justification

↓

Bargaining and problem solving

↓

Closure and implementation

BATNA
The best alternative to a negotiated agreement; the lowest acceptable value to an individual for a negotiated agreement.

PREPARATION AND PLANNING Before you start negotiating, you need to do your homework. What's the nature of the conflict? What's the history leading up to this negotiation? Who's involved and what are their perceptions of the conflict?

What do you want from the negotiation? What are *your* goals? If you're a purchasing manager at Dell Computer, for instance, and your goal is to get a significant cost reduction from your supplier of keyboards, make sure that this goal stays paramount in your discussions and doesn't get overshadowed by other issues. It often helps to put your goals in writing and develop a range of outcomes—from "most hopeful" to "minimally acceptable"—to keep your attention focused.

You also want to prepare an assessment of what you think the other party to your negotiation's goals are. What are they likely to ask for? How entrenched are they likely to be in their position? What intangible or hidden interests may be important to them? What might they be willing to settle on? When you can anticipate your opponent's position, you are better equipped to counter his or her arguments with the facts and figures that support your position.

Use the information you've gathered to develop a strategy. Like a chess match, expert chess players have a strategy. They know ahead of time how they will respond to any given situation. As part of your strategy, you should determine yours and the other side's *Best Alternative To a Negotiated Agreement* (**BATNA**).[34] Your BATNA determines the lowest value acceptable to you for a negotiated agreement. Any offer you receive that is higher than your BATNA is better than an impasse. Conversely, you shouldn't expect success in your negotiation effort unless you're able to make the other side an offer they find more attractive than their BATNA. If you go into your negotiation having a good idea of what the other party's BATNA is, even if you're not able to meet theirs, you might be able to get them to change it.

DEFINITION OF GROUND RULES Once you've done your planning and developed a strategy, you're ready to begin defining the ground rules and procedures with the other party over the negotiation itself. Who will do the negotiating? Where will it take place? What time constraints, if any, will apply? To what issues will negotiation be limited? Will there be a specific procedure to follow if an impasse is reached? During this phase, the parties will also exchange their initial proposals or demands.

CLARIFICATION AND JUSTIFICATION When initial positions have been exchanged, both you and the other party will explain, amplify, clarify, bolster, and justify your original demands. This needn't be confrontational. Rather, it is an opportunity for educating and informing each other on the issues, why they are important, and how each arrived at their initial demands. This is the point where you might want to provide the other party with any documentation that helps support your position.

From Concepts to Skills

Negotiating

Once you've taken the time to assess your own goals, considered the other party's goals and interests, and developed a strategy, you're ready to begin actual negotiations. The following suggestions should improve your negotiating skills.[35]

Begin with a positive overture. Studies on negotiation show that concessions tend to be reciprocated and lead to agreements. As a result, begin bargaining with a positive overture—perhaps a small concession—and then reciprocate your opponent's concessions.

Address problems, not personalities. Concentrate on the negotiation issues, not on the personal characteristics of your opponent. When nego-

tiations get tough, avoid the tendency to attack your opponent. It's your opponent's ideas or position that you disagree with, not him or her personally. Separate the people from the problem, and don't personalize differences.

Pay little attention to initial offers. Treat an initial offer as merely a point of departure. Everyone has to have an initial position. These initial offers tend to be extreme and idealistic. Treat them as such.

Emphasize win-win solutions. Inexperienced negotiators often assume that their gain must come at the expense of the other party. As noted with integrative bargaining, that needn't be the case. There are often win-win solutions. But assuming a zero-sum game means missed

opportunities for trade-offs that could benefit both sides. So if conditions are supportive, look for an integrative solution. Frame options in terms of your opponent's interests and look for solutions that can allow your opponent, as well as yourself, to declare a victory.

Create an open and trusting climate. Skilled negotiators are better listeners, ask more questions, focus their arguments more directly, are less defensive, and have learned to avoid words and phrases that can irritate an opponent (i.e., "generous offer," "fair price," "reasonable arrangement"). In other words, they are better at creating the open and trusting climate necessary for reaching an integrative settlement.

BARGAINING AND PROBLEM SOLVING The essence of the negotiation process is the actual give-and-take in trying to hash out an agreement. Concessions will undoubtedly need to be made by both parties. The "From Concepts to Skills" box on negotiating directly addresses some of the actions you should take to improve the likelihood that you can achieve a good agreement.

CLOSURE AND IMPLEMENTATION The final step in the negotiation process is formalizing the agreement that has been worked out and developing any procedures that are necessary for implementation and monitoring. For major negotiations—which would include everything from labor–management negotiations, to bargaining over lease terms, to buying a piece of real estate, to negotiating a job offer for a senior-management position—this will require hammering out the specifics in a formal contract. For most cases, however, closure of the negotiation process is nothing more formal than a handshake.

Issues in Negotiation

We conclude our discussion of negotiation by reviewing four contemporary issues in negotiation: the role of personality traits, gender differences in negotiating, the effect of cultural differences on negotiating styles, and the use of third parties to help resolve differences.

THE ROLE OF PERSONALITY TRAITS IN NEGOTIATION Can you predict an opponent's negotiating tactics if you know something about his or her personality? It's tempting to answer "Yes" to this question. For instance, you might assume that high risk takers would be more aggressive bargainers who make fewer concessions. Surprisingly, the evidence doesn't support this intuition.[36]

Overall assessments of the personality–negotiation relationship finds that personality traits have no significant direct effect on either the bargaining process or negotiation outcomes. This conclusion is important. It suggests that you should concentrate on the issues and the situational factors in each bargaining episode and not on your opponent's personality.

GENDER DIFFERENCES IN NEGOTIATIONS Do men and women negotiate differently? The answer appears to be "No."[37]

A popular stereotype held by many is that women are more cooperative, pleasant, and relationship oriented in negotiations than are men. The evidence doesn't support this belief. Comparisons between experienced male and female managers find women are neither worse nor better negotiators, neither more cooperative nor open to the other, and neither more nor less persuasive nor threatening than are men.

The belief that women are "nicer" than men in negotiations is probably due to confusing gender and the lack of power typically held by women in most large organizations. The research indicates that low-power managers, regardless of gender, attempt to placate their opponents and to use softly persuasive tactics rather than direct confrontation and threats. Where women and men have similar power bases, there shouldn't be any significant differences in their negotiation styles.

While gender may not be relevant in terms of negotiation outcomes, women's attitudes toward negotiation and toward themselves as negotiators appear to be quite different from men's. Managerial women demonstrate less confidence in anticipation of negotiating and are less satisfied with their performance after the process is complete, despite the fact that their performance and the outcomes they achieve are similar to men.

This latter conclusion suggests that women may unduly penalize themselves by failing to engage in negotiations when such action would be in their best interests.

CULTURAL DIFFERENCES IN NEGOTIATIONS Although there appears to be no significant direct relationship between an individual's personality and negotiation style, cultural background does seem to be relevant. Negotiating styles clearly vary across national cultures.[38]

The French like conflict. They frequently gain recognition and develop their reputations by thinking and acting against others. As a result, the French tend to take a long time in negotiating agreements and they aren't overly concerned about whether their opponents like or dislike them.[39] The Chinese also draw out negotiations but that's because they believe negotiations never end. Just when you think you've pinned down every detail and reached a final solution with a Chinese executive, that executive might smile and start the process all over again. Like the Japanese, the Chinese negotiate to develop a relationship and a commitment to work together rather than to tie up every loose end.[40] Americans are known around the world for their impatience and their desire to be liked. Astute negotiators from other countries often turn these characteristics to their advantage by dragging out negotiations and making friendship conditional on the final settlement.

The cultural context of the negotiation significantly influences the amount and type of preparation for bargaining, the relative emphasis on task versus interpersonal relationships, the tactics used, and even where the negotiation should be conducted. To further illustrate some of these differences, let's look at two studies comparing the influence of culture on business negotiations.

The first study compared North Americans, Arabs, and Russians.[41] Among the factors that were looked at were their negotiating style, how they responded to an opponent's arguments, their approach to making concessions, and how they handled negotiating deadlines. North Americans tried to persuade by relying on facts and appealing to logic. They countered opponents' arguments with objective facts. They made small concessions early in the negotiation to establish a relationship, and usually reciprocated opponent's concessions. North Americans treated deadlines as very important. The Arabs tried to persuade by appealing to emotion. They countered opponent's arguments with subjective feelings. They made concessions throughout the bargaining process and almost always reciprocated opponents' concessions. Arabs approached deadlines very casually. The Russians based their arguments on asserted ideals. They made few, if any, concessions. Any concession offered by an opponent was viewed as a weakness and almost never reciprocated. Finally, the Russians tended to ignore deadlines.

The second study looked at verbal and nonverbal negotiation tactics exhibited by North Americans, Japanese, and Brazilians during half-hour bargaining sessions.[42] Some of the differences were particularly interesting. For instance, the Brazilians on average said "No" 83 times, compared to five times for the Japanese and nine times for the North Americans. The Japanese displayed more than five periods of silence lasting longer than ten seconds during the 30-minute sessions. North Americans averaged 3.5 such periods; the Brazilians had none. The Japanese and North Americans interrupted their opponent about the same number of times, but the Brazilians interrupted 2.5 to 3 times more often than the North Americans and the Japanese. Finally, while the Japanese and the North Americans had no physical contact with their opponents during negotiations except for handshaking, the Brazilians touched each other almost five times every half-hour.

THIRD-PARTY NEGOTIATIONS   To this point, we've discussed bargaining in terms of direct negotiations. Occasionally, however, individuals or group representatives reach a stalemate and are unable to resolve their differences through direct negotiations. In such cases, they may turn to a third party to help them find a solution. There are four basic third-party roles: mediator, arbitrator, conciliator, and consultant.[43]

A **mediator** is a neutral third party who facilitates a negotiated solution by using reasoning and persuasion, suggesting alternatives, and the like. Mediators are widely used in labor–management negotiations and in civil court disputes.

mediator
A neutral third party who facilitates a negotiated solution by using reasoning, persuasion, and suggestions for alternatives.

The overall effectiveness of mediated negotiations is fairly impressive. The settlement rate is approximately 60 percent, with negotiator satisfaction at about 75 percent. But the situation is the key to whether or not mediation will succeed; the conflicting parties must be motivated to bargain and resolve their conflict. Additionally, conflict intensity can't be too high; mediation is most effective under moderate levels of conflict. Finally, perceptions of the mediator are important; to be effective, the mediator must be perceived as neutral and noncoercive.

arbitrator
A third party to a negotiation who has the authority to dictate an agreement.

An **arbitrator** is a third party with the authority to dictate an agreement. Arbitration can be voluntary (requested) or compulsory (forced on the parties by law or contract).

The authority of the arbitrator varies according to the rules set by the negotiators. For instance, the arbitrator might be limited to choosing one of the negotiator's last offers or to suggesting an agreement point that is nonbinding, or free to choose and make any judgment he or she wishes.

The big plus of arbitration over mediation is that it always results in a settlement. Whether or not there is a negative side depends on how "heavy-handed" the arbitrator appears. If one party is left feeling overwhelmingly defeated, that party is certain to be dissatisfied and unlikely to graciously accept the arbitrator's decision. Therefore, the conflict may resurface at a later time.

conciliator
A trusted third party who provides an informal communication link between the negotiator and the opponent.

A **conciliator** is a trusted third party who provides an informal communication link between the negotiator and the opponent. This role was made famous by Robert Duval in the first *Godfather* film. As Don Corleone's adopted son and a lawyer by training, Duval acted as an intermediary between the Corleone family and the other Mafioso families.

Conciliation is used extensively in international, labor, family, and community disputes. Comparing its effectiveness to mediation has proven difficult because the two overlap a great deal. In practice, conciliators typically act as more than mere communication conduits. They also engage in fact finding, interpreting messages, and persuading disputants to develop agreements.

consultant as negotiator
An impartial third party, skilled in conflict management, who attempts to facilitate creative problem solving through communication and analysis.

A **consultant** is a skilled and impartial third party who attempts to facilitate problem solving through communication and analysis, aided by his or her knowledge of conflict management. In contrast to the previous roles, the consultant's role is not to settle the issues but, rather, to improve relations between the conflicting parties so that they can reach a settlement themselves. Instead of putting forward specific solutions, the consultant tries to help the parties learn to understand and work with each other. Therefore, this approach has a longer-term focus: to build new and positive perceptions and attitudes between the conflicting parties.

Intergroup Relations

For the most part, the concepts we've discussed from Chapter 7 on have dealt with intragroup activities. For instance, the previous material in this chapter emphasized interpersonal and intragroup conflict as well as interpersonal negotiations. But we need to understand relationships between groups as well as within groups.[44] In this section, we'll focus on intergroup relationships. These are the coordinated bridges that link two distinct organizational groups.[45] As we'll show, the efficiency and quality of these relationships can have a significant bearing on one or both of the groups' performances and their members' satisfaction.

Factors Affecting Intergroup Relations

Successful intergroup performance is a function of a number of factors. The umbrella concept that overrides these factors is *coordination*. Each of the following can affect efforts at coordination.

    INTERDEPENDENCE   The first overriding question we need to ask is: Do the groups really need coordination? The answer to this question lies in determining the degree of interdependence that exists between the groups. That is, do the groups depend on each other and, if so, how much? The three most frequently identified types of interdependence are pooled, sequential, and reciprocal.[46] Each requires an increasing degree of group interaction (see Exhibit 12-8).

    When two groups function with relative independence but their combined output contributes to the organization's overall goals, **pooled interdependence** exists. At a firm such as Apple Computer, for instance, this would describe the relationship between the product development department and the shipping department. Both are necessary if Apple is to develop new products and get those products into consumers' hands, but each is essentially separate and distinct from the other. All other things being equal, coordination requirements between groups linked by pooled interdependence are less than with sequential or reciprocal interdependence.

    The purchasing and parts assembly departments at Apple are **sequentially interdependent**. One group—parts assembly—depends on another—purchasing—for its inputs, but the dependency is only one way. Purchasing is not directly dependent on parts assembly for its inputs. In sequential interdependence, if the group that provides the input doesn't perform its job properly, the group that is dependent on the first will be significantly affected. In our Apple example, if purchasing fails to order an important component that goes into the assembly process, then the parts assembly department may have to slow down or temporarily close its assembly operations.

pooled interdependence
Where two groups function with relative independence but their combined output contributes to the organization's overall goals.

sequential interdependence
One group depends on another for its input but the dependency is only one way.

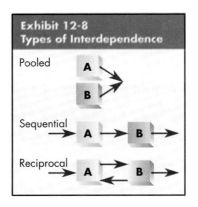

Coordination among groups is essential to satisfying customer needs at Chadick & Kimball. The Washington, D.C., design firm specializes in developing corporate identity programs. The projects require reciprocal interdependence of designers and the firm's marketing staff. Marketers interact with customers to determine their needs and exchange this information with the designers who create the programs.

reciprocal interdependence
Where groups exchange inputs and outputs.

The most complex form of interdependence is **reciprocal**. In these instances, groups exchange inputs and outputs. For example, sales and product development groups at Apple are reciprocally interdependent. Salespeople, in contact with customers, acquire information about their future needs. Sales then relays this back to product development so they can create new computer products. The long-term implications are that if product development doesn't come up with new products that potential customers find desirable, sales personnel are not going to get orders. So there is high interdependence—product development needs sales for information on customer needs so it can create successful new products, and sales depends on the product development group to create products that it can successfully sell. This high degree of dependency translates into greater interaction and increased coordination demands.

TASK UNCERTAINTY The next coordination question is: What type of tasks are the groups involved in? For simplicity's sake, we can think of a group's tasks as ranging from highly routine to highly nonroutine.[47] (See Exhibit 12-9.)

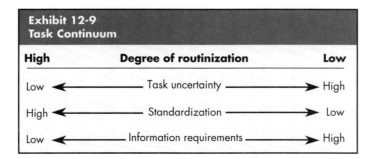

Exhibit 12-9
Task Continuum

High	Degree of routinization	Low
Low ⟵———	Task uncertainty	———⟶ High
High ⟵———	Standardization	———⟶ Low
Low ⟵———	Information requirements	———⟶ High

Highly routine tasks have little variation. Problems that group members face tend to contain few exceptions and are easy to analyze. Such group activities lend themselves to standardized operating procedures. For example, manufacturing tasks in a tire factory are made up of highly routine tasks. At the other extreme are nonroutine tasks. These are activities that are unstructured, with many exceptions and problems that are hard to analyze. Many of the tasks undertaken by marketing research and product development groups are of this variety. Of course, a lot of group tasks fall somewhere in the middle or combine both routine and nonroutine tasks.

The key to **task uncertainty** is that nonroutine tasks require considerably more processing of information. Tasks with low uncertainty tend to be standardized. Further, groups that do standardized tasks do not have to interact much with other groups. In contrast, groups that undertake tasks that are high in uncertainty face problems that require custom responses. This, in turn, leads to a need for more and better information. We would expect the people in the marketing research department at Goodyear Tire & Rubber to interact much more with other departments and constituencies—marketing, sales, product design, tire dealers, advertising agencies, and the like—than would people in Goodyear's manufacturing group.

task uncertainty
The greater the uncertainty in a task, the more customized the response. Conversely, low uncertainty encompasses routine tasks with standardized activities.

      TIME AND GOAL ORIENTATION   How different are the groups in terms of their members' background and thinking? This is the third question relevant to the degree of coordination necessary between groups. Research demonstrates that a work group's perceptions of what is important may differ on the basis of the time frame that governs their work and their goal orientation.[48] This can make it difficult for groups with different perceptions to work together.

Exhibit 12-10

Source: CATHY copyright Cathy Guisewite. Reprinted with permission of Universal Press Syndicate. All rights reserved.

Why might work groups have different time and goal orientations? Top management historically divided work up by putting common tasks into common functional groups and assigning these groups specific goals. Then people were hired with the appropriate background and skills to complete the tasks and help the group achieve its goals. This differentiation of tasks and hiring of specialists made it easier to coordinate intragroup activities, but it made it increasingly difficult to coordinate interaction between groups.

To illustrate how orientations differ between work groups, manufacturing personnel have a short-term time focus. They worry about today's production schedule and this week's productivity. In contrast, people in research and development focus on the long run. They're concerned about developing new products that may not be produced for several years. Similarly, work groups often have different goal orientations. As we noted earlier in the chapter, sales typically wants to sell anything and everything. Goals center on sales volume and increasing revenue and market share. Although customers' ability to pay for the sales made by the sales group is not its concern, the people in the credit department want to ensure that sales are made only to creditworthy customers. These differences in goals often make it difficult for sales and credit to communicate. It also makes it harder to coordinate their interactions.

Methods for Managing Intergroup Relations

What coordination methods are available for managing intergroup relations? There are a number of options; the seven most frequently used are identified in Exhibit 12-11. These seven are listed on a continuum, in order of increasing cost.[49] They also are cumulative in the sense that succeeding methods higher on the continuum add to, rather than are substituted for, lower methods. In most organizations, the simpler methods listed at the lower end of the continuum are used in conjunction with the more complex methods listed at the

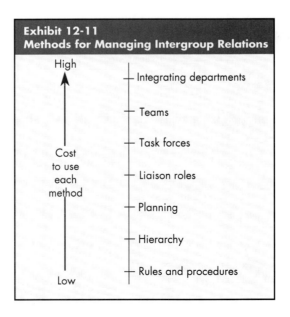

Exhibit 12-11
Methods for Managing Intergroup Relations

High

Cost to use each method

Low

- Integrating departments
- Teams
- Task forces
- Liaison roles
- Planning
- Hierarchy
- Rules and procedures

upper end. For instance, if a manager is using teams to coordinate intergroup relations, that manager is also likely to be using rules and procedures.

RULES AND PROCEDURES The most simple and least costly method for managing intergroup relations is to establish, in advance, a set of formalized rules and procedures that will specify how group members are to interact with each other. In large organizations, for example, standard operating procedures are like to specify that when additional permanent staff are needed in any department, a "request for new staff" form is to be filled with the human resources department. Upon receipt of this form, human resources begins a standardized process to fill the request. Notice that such rules and procedures minimize the need for interaction and information flow between the departments or work groups. The major drawback to this method is that it works well only when intergroup activities can be anticipated ahead of time and when they recur often enough to justify establishing rules and procedures for handling them. Under conditions of high uncertainty and change, rules and procedures alone may not be adequate to guarantee effective coordination of intergroup relations.

> ◆ The most simple and least costly method for managing intergroup relations is to establish rules and procedures.

HIERARCHY If rules and procedures are inadequate, the use of the organization's hierarchy becomes the primary method for managing intergroup relations. What this means is that coordination is achieved by referring problems to a common superior higher in the organization. In a college, if the chairpersons for the English and speech communication departments can't agree on where the new courses in debate will be taught, they can take the issue to the college dean for a resolution. The major limitation to this method is that it increases demands on the common superior's time. If all differences were resolved by this means, the organization's chief executive would be overwhelmed with resolving intergroup problems, leaving little time for other matters.

PLANNING The next step up the continuum is the use of planning to facilitate coordination. If each work group has specific goals for which it is responsible, then each knows what it is supposed to do. Intergroup tasks that create problems are resolved in terms of the goals and contributions of each group. In a state motor vehicle office, each of the various work groups—testing and examinations, driving permits, vehicle registration, cashiering, and the like—has a set of goals that defines its area of responsibility and acts to reduce intergroup conflicts. Planning tends to break down as a coordination device where work groups don't have clearly defined goals or where the volume of contacts between groups is high.

LIAISON ROLES Liaison roles are specialized roles designed to facilitate communication between two interdependent work units. In one organization, where accountants and engineers had a long history of conflict, management hired an engineer with an MBA degree and several years of experience in public accounting. This person could speak the language of both groups and understood their problems. After this new liaison role was established, conflicts

Pharmaceutical giant Merck & Co. created a human resources task force after it acquired Medco Containment Services, a pharmacy benefits management firm. Task force members, including Katherine Harrison of Merck (left) and Cynthia Gilhooly of Medco, worked on many issues related to the firms' cultural, managerial, and business integration. Members of the temporary team shared information about compensation and benefits, employee relations, employee development, management approaches, and work environments.

that had previously made it difficult for the accounting and engineering departments to coordinate their activities were significantly reduced. The major drawback to this coordination device is that there are limits to any liaison person's ability to handle information flow between interacting groups, especially where the groups are large and interactions are frequent.

TASK FORCES　A task force is a temporary group made up of representatives from a number of departments. It exists only long enough to solve the problem it was created to handle. After a solution is reached, task force participants return to their normal duties.

Task forces are an excellent device for coordinating activities when the number of interacting groups is more than two or three. For example, when Audi began receiving numerous complaints about its cars accelerating when the transmission was put in reverse, even though drivers swore that their feet were firmly on the brakes, the company created a task force to assess the problem and develop a solution. Representatives from design, production, legal, and engineering departments were brought together. After a solution was determined, the task force was disbanded.

TEAMS　As tasks become more complex, additional problems arise during the act of execution. Previous coordination devices are no longer adequate. If the delays in decisions become long, lines of communication become extended, and top managers are forced to spend more time on day-to-day operations, the next response is to use permanent teams. They are typically formed around frequently occurring problems—with team members maintaining a responsibility to both their primary functional department and to the team. When the team has accomplished its task, each member returns full time to his or her functional assignment.

Boeing uses a cross-functional team to coordinate investigations of air crashes. When a Boeing aircraft is involved in an accident, the company immediately dispatches a team made up of members from various departments—including design, production, legal, and public relations. Whenever an accident occurs, designated members of the team immediately drop their current departmental tasks, go directly to the accident site, and join the other team members to begin their investigation.

INTEGRATING DEPARTMENTS When intergroup relations become too complex to be coordinated through plans, task forces, teams, and the like, organizations may create integrating departments. These are permanent departments with members formally assigned to the task of integration between two or more groups. While they're permanent and expensive to maintain, they tend to be used when an organization has a number of groups with conflicting goals, nonroutine problems, and intergroup decisions that have a significant impact on the organization's total operations. They are also excellent devices to manage intergroup conflicts for organizations facing long-term retrenchments. When organizations are forced to shrink in size—as has recently occurred in a wide range of industries—conflicts over how cuts are to be distributed and how the smaller resource pie is to be allocated become major and ongoing dilemmas. The use of integrating departments in such cases can be an effective means for managing these intergroup relations.

Summary

It may help to put this discussion in perspective by considering methods for managing intergroup relations in terms of effectiveness.

Researchers state that the effectiveness of intergroup relations can be evaluated in terms of efficiency and quality.[50] Efficiency considers the costs to the organization of transforming an intergroup conflict into actions agreed to by the groups. Quality refers to the degree to which the outcome results in a well-defined and enduring exchange agreement. Using these definitions, the seven methods introduced in this section were presented, in order, from most efficient to least efficient. That is, ignoring outcomes for a moment, rules and procedures are less costly to implement than hierarchy, hierarchy is less costly than planning, and so forth. But, of course, keeping costs down is only one consideration. The other element of effectiveness is quality, or how well the coordination device works in facilitating interaction and reducing dysfunctional conflicts. As we've shown, the least costly alternative may not be adequate. So managers have a number of options at their disposal for managing intergroup relations. But since they tend to be cumulative, with costs rising as you move up the continuum in Exhibit 12-11, the most effective coordination device will be the one lowest on the continuum that facilitates an enduring integrative exchange.

Summary and Implications for Managers

Many people automatically assume that conflict is related to lower group and organizational performance. This chapter has demonstrated that this assumption is frequently incorrect. Conflict can be either constructive or destructive to the functioning of a group or unit. As shown in Exhibit 12-12, levels of

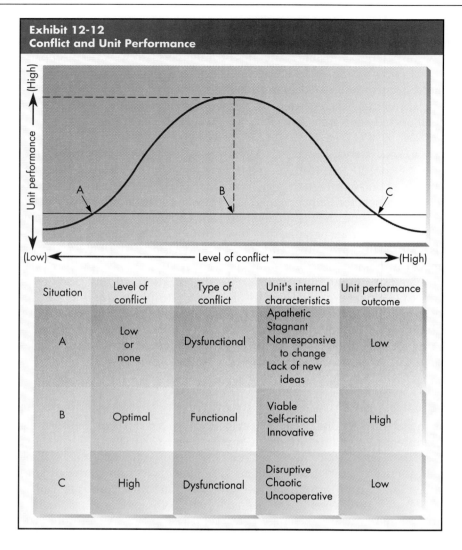

Exhibit 12-12
Conflict and Unit Performance

Situation	Level of conflict	Type of conflict	Unit's internal characteristics	Unit performance outcome
A	Low or none	Dysfunctional	Apathetic Stagnant Nonresponsive to change Lack of new ideas	Low
B	Optimal	Functional	Viable Self-critical Innovative	High
C	High	Dysfunctional	Disruptive Chaotic Uncooperative	Low

conflict can be either too high or too low. Either extreme hinders performance. An optimal level is where there is enough conflict to prevent stagnation, stimulate creativity, allow tensions to be released, and initiate the seeds for change, yet not so much as to be disruptive or deter coordination of activities.

Inadequate or excessive levels of conflict can hinder the effectiveness of a group or an organization, resulting in reduced satisfaction of group members, increased absence and turnover rates, and, eventually, lower productivity. On the other hand, when conflict is at an optimal level, complacency and apathy should be minimized, motivation should be enhanced through the creation of a challenging and questioning environment with a vitality that makes work interesting, and there should be the amount of turnover needed to rid the organization of misfits and poor performers.

What advice can we give managers faced with excessive conflict and the need to reduce it? Don't assume there's one conflict-handling intention that will always be best! You should select an intention appropriate for the situation. The following provides some guidelines:[51]

Use *competition* when quick, decisive action is vital (in emergencies); on important issues, where unpopular actions need implementing (in cost cutting, enforcing unpopular rules, discipline); on issues vital to the organization's welfare when you know you're right; and against people who take advantage of noncompetitive behavior.

Use *collaboration* to find an integrative solution when both sets of concerns are too important to be compromised; when your objective is to learn; to merge insights from people with different perspectives; to gain commitment by incorporating concerns into a consensus; and to work through feelings that have interfered with a relationship.

Use *avoidance* when an issue is trivial, or more important issues are pressing; when you perceive no chance of satisfying your concerns; when potential disruption outweighs the benefits of resolution; to let people cool down and regain perspective; when gathering information supersedes immediate decision; when others can resolve the conflict more effectively; and when issues seem tangential or symptomatic of other issues.

Use *accommodation* when you find you're wrong and to allow a better position to be heard, to learn, and to show your reasonableness; when issues are more important to others than yourself and to satisfy others and maintain cooperation; to build social credits for later issues; to minimize loss when you are outmatched and losing; when harmony and stability are especially important; and to allow subordinates to develop by learning from mistakes.

Use *compromise* when goals are important but not worth the effort of potential disruption of more assertive approaches; when opponents with equal power are committed to mutually exclusive goals; to achieve temporary settlements to complex issues; to arrive at expedient solutions under time pressure; and as a backup when collaboration or competition is unsuccessful.

Negotiation was shown to be an ongoing activity in groups and organizations. Distributive bargaining can resolve disputes but it often negatively affects one or more negotiators' satisfaction because it is focused on the short term and because it is confrontational. Integrative bargaining, in contrast, tends to provide outcomes that satisfy all parties and that build lasting relationships.

Intergroup conflicts can also affect an organization's performance. Emphasis at this level, however, has tended to focus on dysfunctional conflicts and methods for managing them. Where organizational performance depends on effective group relations and where there is high interdependence between groups, management needs to ensure that the proper integrative device is put in place. However, consistent with the interactionist perspective on conflict, there is no reason to believe that all intergroup conflicts are dysfunctional. Some minimal levels of conflict can facilitate critical thinking among group members, make a group more responsive to the need for change, and provide similar benefits that can enhance group and organizational performance.

For Review

1. What are the disadvantages to conflict? What are its advantages?
2. What is the difference between functional and dysfunctional conflict? What determines functionality?
3. Under what conditions might conflict be beneficial to a group?
4. What are the components in the conflict process model? From your own experiences, give an example of how a conflict proceeded through the five stages.
5. How could a manager stimulate conflict in his or her department?
6. What defines the settlement range in distributive bargaining?
7. Why isn't integrative bargaining more widely practiced in organizations?
8. How do men and women differ, if at all, in their approaches to negotiation?
9. What can you do to improve your negotiating effectiveness?
10. How do you assess the effectiveness of intergroup relations?

For Discussion

1. Do you think competition and conflict are different? Explain.
2. "Participation is an excellent method for identifying differences and resolving conflicts." Do you agree or disagree? Discuss.
3. Assume a Canadian had to negotiate a contract with someone from Spain. What problems might he or she face? What suggestions would you make to help facilitate a settlement?
4. From your own experience, describe a situation you were involved in where the conflict was dysfunctional. Describe another example, from your experience, where the conflict was functional. Now analyze how other parties in both conflicts might have interpreted the situation in terms of whether the conflicts were functional or dysfunctional.
5. Discuss the mechanisms for resolving intergroup conflicts between students and faculty on your campus. Are they effective? How could they be improved?

⬌ Point ⬌

Conflict Is Good for an Organization

We've made considerable progress in the last 25 years toward overcoming the negative stereotype given to conflict. Most behavioral scientists and an increasing number of practicing managers now accept that the goal of effective management is not to eliminate conflict. Rather, it's to create the right intensity of conflict so as to reap its functional benefits.

Since conflict can be good for an organization, it is only logical to acknowledge that there may be times when managers will purposely want to increase its intensity. Let's briefly review how stimulating conflict can provide benefits to the organization.

◆ *Conflict is a means by which to bring about radical change.* It's an effective device by which management can drastically change the existing power structure, current interaction patterns, and entrenched attitudes.

◆ *Conflict facilitates group cohesiveness.* While conflict increases hostility between groups, external threats tend to cause a group to pull together as a unit. Intergroup conflicts raise the extent to which members identify with their own group and increase feelings of solidarity, while, at the same time, internal differences and irritations dissolve.

◆ *Conflict improves group and organizational effectiveness.* The stimulation of conflict initiates the search for new means and goals and clears the way for innovation. The successful solution of a conflict leads to greater effec-

tiveness, to more trust and openness, to greater attraction of members for each other, and to depersonalization of future conflicts. In fact, it has been found that as the number of minor disagreements increases, the number of major clashes decreases.

◆ *Conflict brings about a slightly higher, more constructive level of tension.* This enhances the chances of solving the conflicts in a way satisfactory to all parties concerned. When the level of tension is very low, the parties are not sufficiently motivated to do something about a conflict.

These points are clearly not comprehensive. As noted in the chapter, conflict provides a number of benefits to an organization. However, groups or organizations devoid of conflict are likely to suffer from apathy, stagnation, groupthink, and other debilitating diseases. In fact, more organizations probably fail because they have *too little* conflict, not because they have too much. Take a look at a list of large organizations that have failed or suffered serious financial setbacks over the past decade or two. You see names like E.F. Hutton, General Motors, Western Union, Gimbel's, Kmart, Morrison Knudsen, Eastern Airlines, Greyhound, and Digital Computer. The common thread through these companies is that they stagnated. Their managements became complacent and unable or unwilling to facilitate change. These organizations could have benefited by having had more conflict—the functional kind.

The points presented here were influenced by E. Van de Vliert, "Escalative Intervention in Small-Group Conflicts," *Journal of Applied Behavioral Science*, Winter 1985, pp. 19–36.

All Conflicts Are Dysfunctional!

It may be true that conflict is an inherent part of any group or organization. It may not be possible to eliminate it completely. However, just because conflicts exist is no reason to deify them. All conflicts are dysfunctional, and it is one of management's major responsibilities to keep conflict intensity as low as humanly possible. A few points will support this case.

◆ *The negative consequences from conflict can be devastating.* The list of negatives associated with conflict is awesome. The most obvious are increased turnover, decreased employee satisfaction, inefficiencies between work units, sabotage, labor grievances and strikes, and physical aggression.

◆ *Effective managers build teamwork.* A good manager builds a coordinated team. Conflict works against such an objective. A successful work group is like a successful sports team; each member knows his or her role and supports his or her teammates. When a team works well, the whole becomes greater than the sum of the parts. Management creates teamwork by minimizing internal conflicts and facilitating internal coordination.

◆ *Competition is good for an organization, but not conflict.* Competition and conflict should not be confused with each other. Conflict is behavior directed against another party, whereas competition is behavior aimed at obtaining a goal without interference from another party. Competition is healthy; it's the source of organizational vitality. Conflict, on the other hand, is destructive.

◆ *Managers who accept and stimulate conflict don't survive in organizations.* The whole argument on the value of conflict may be moot as long as the majority of senior executives in organizations view conflict traditionally. In the traditional view, any conflict will be seen as bad. Since the evaluation of a manager's performance is made by higher-level executives, those managers who do not succeed in eliminating conflicts are likely to be appraised negatively. This, in turn, will reduce opportunities for advancement. Any manager who aspires to move up in such an environment will be wise to follow the traditional view and eliminate any outward signs of conflict. Failure to follow this advice might result in the premature departure of the manager.

Learning about Yourself Exercise

What Is Your Primary Conflict-Handling Intention?

Indicate how often you rely on each of the following tactics by circling the number that you feel is most appropriate.

		Rarely				Always
1.	I argue my case with my co-workers to show the merits of my position.	1	2	3	4	5
2.	I negotiate with my co-workers so that a compromise can be reached.	1	2	3	4	5
3.	I try to satisfy the expectations of my co-workers.	1	2	3	4	5
4.	I try to investigate an issue with my co-workers to find a solution acceptable to us.	1	2	3	4	5
5.	I am firm in pursuing my side of the issue.	1	2	3	4	5
6.	I attempt to avoid being put on the spot and try to keep my conflict with my co-workers to myself.	1	2	3	4	5
7.	I hold on to my solution to a problem.	1	2	3	4	5
8.	I use give-and-take so that a compromise can be made.	1	2	3	4	5
9.	I exchange accurate information with my co-workers to solve a problem together.	1	2	3	4	5
10.	I avoid open discussion of my differences with my co-workers.	1	2	3	4	5
11.	I accommodate the wishes of my co-workers.	1	2	3	4	5
12.	I try to bring all our concerns out in the open so that the issues can be resolved in the best possible way.	1	2	3	4	5
13.	I propose a middle ground for breaking deadlocks.	1	2	3	4	5
14.	I go along with the suggestions of my co-workers.	1	2	3	4	5
15.	I try to keep my disagreements with my co-workers to myself in order to avoid hard feelings.	1	2	3	4	5

Turn to page A-28 for scoring directions and key.

Source: This is an abbreviated version of a 35-item instrument described in M.A. Rahim, "A Measure of Styles of Handling Interpersonal Conflict," *Academy of Management Journal*, June 1983, pp. 368–76.

Working with Others Exercise

A Negotiation Role Play

This role play is designed to help you develop your negotiating skills. The class is to break into pairs. One person will play the role of Terry, the department supervisor. The other person will play Dale, Terry's boss.

The Situation: Terry and Dale work for Nike in Portland, Oregon. Terry supervises a research laboratory. Dale is the manager of research and development. Terry and Dale are former college runners who have worked for Nike for more than six years. Dale has been Terry's boss for two years.

One of Terry's employees has greatly impressed Terry. This employee is Lisa Roland. Lisa was hired 11 months ago. She is 24 years old and holds a master's degree in mechanical engineering. Her entry-level salary was $37,500 a year. She was told by Terry that, in accordance with corporation policy, she would receive an initial performance evaluation at six months and a comprehensive review after one year. Based on her performance record, Lisa was told she could expect a salary adjustment at the time of the one-year evaluation.

Terry's evaluation of Lisa after six months was very positive. Terry commented on the long hours Lisa was putting in, her cooperative spirit, the fact that others in the lab enjoyed working with her, and that she was making an immediate positive impact on the project she had been assigned. Now that Lisa's first anniversary is coming up, Terry has again reviewed Lisa's performance. Terry thinks Lisa may be the best new person the R&D group has ever hired. After only a year, Terry has ranked Lisa as the number-three performer in a department of 11.

Salaries in the department vary greatly. Terry, for instance, has a basic salary of $67,000, plus eligibility for a bonus that might add another $5,000 to $8,000 a year. The salary range of the 11 department members is $30,400 to $56,350. The lowest salary is a recent hire with a bachelor's degree in physics. The two people that Terry has rated above Lisa earn base salaries of $52,700 and $56,350. They're both 27 years old and have been at Nike for three and four years, respectively. The median salary in Terry's department is $46,660.

Terry's Role: You want to give Lisa a big raise. While she's young, she has proven to be an excellent addition to the department. You don't want to lose her. More importantly, she knows in general what other people in the department are earning and she thinks she's underpaid. The company typically gives one-year raises of 5 percent, although 10 percent is not unusual and 20 to 30 percent increases have been approved on occasion. You'd like to get Terry as large an increase as Dale will approve.

Dale's Role: All your supervisors typically try to squeeze you for as much money as they can for their people. You understand this because you did the same thing when you were a supervisor, but your boss wants to keep a lid on costs. He wants you to keep raises for recent hires generally in the 5 to 8 percent range. In fact, he's sent a memo to all managers and supervisors saying this. However, your boss is also very concerned with equity and paying people what they're worth. You feel assured that he will support any salary recommendation you make, as long as it can be justified. Your goal, consistent with cost reduction, is to keep salary increases as low as possible.

The Negotiation: Terry has a meeting scheduled with Dale to discuss Lisa's performance review and salary adjustment. Take a couple of minutes to think through the facts in this exercise and to prepare a strategy. Then you have up to 15 minutes to conduct your negotiation. When your negotiation is complete, the class will compare the various strategies used and pair outcomes.

Not Your Dream Team

Mallory Murray hadn't had much experience working as part of a team. A recent graduate of the University of Alabama, her business program had focused primarily on individual projects and accomplishments. What little exposure she had had to teams were in her organizational behavior, marketing research, and strategy formulation courses. When she interviewed with ThinkLink, an educational software firm out of Gainesville, Florida, she didn't give much concern to the fact that ThinkLink made extensive use of cross-functional teams. During on-site interviews, she told interviewers and managers alike that she had limited experience on teams. But she did tell them she worked well with people and thought that she could be an effective team player. Unfortunately, Mallory Murray was mistaken.

Mallory joined ThinkLink as an assistant marketing manager for the company's high school core programs. These are essentially software programs designed to help students learn algebra and geometry. Mallory's boss is Lin Chen (marketing manager). Other members of the team she is currently working with include Todd Schlotsky (senior programmer), Laura Willow (advertising), Sean Traynor (vice president for strategic marketing), Joyce Rothman (co-founder of ThinkLink, who now only works part-time in the company; formerly a high-school math teacher; the formal leader of this project), and Harlow Gray (educational consultant).

After her first week on the job, Mallory was seriously thinking about quitting. "I never imagined how difficult it would be working with people who are so opinionated and competitive. Every decision seems to be a power contest. Sean, Joyce, and Harlow are particularly troublesome. Sean thinks his rank entitles him to the last word. Joyce thinks her opinions should carry more weight because she was instrumental in creating the company. And Harlow views everyone as less knowledgeable than he is. Because he consults with a number of software firms and school districts, Harlow's a 'know-it-all.' To make things worse, Lin is passive and quiet. He rarely speaks up in meetings and appears to want to avoid any conflicts."

"What makes my job particularly difficult," Mallory went on, "is that I don't have any specific job responsibilities. It seems that someone else is always interfering with what I'm doing or telling me how to do it. Our team has seven members—six chiefs and me!"

The projects team that Mallory is working on has a deadline to meet that

C A S E
INCIDENT

is only six weeks away. Currently the team is at least two weeks behind schedule. Everyone is aware that there's a problem but no one seems to be able to solve it. What is especially frustrating to Mallory is that neither Lin Chen nor Joyce Rothman is showing any leadership. Lin is preoccupied with a number of other projects, and Joyce can't seem to control Sean and Harlow's strong personalities.

Questions

1. Discuss cross-functional teams in terms of their propensity to create conflict.
2. What techniques or procedures might help reduce conflict on cross-functional teams?
3. If you were Mallory, is there anything you could do to lessen the conflict on the core project? Elaborate.

VIDEO
CASE

ABCNEWS

Conflict in Professional Sports

Professional sports aren't like they used to be. Twenty years ago, teams were loyal to their fans and their athletes. Today, teams move if their communities don't build superstadiums or provide attractive incentives to keep them, and athletes jump ship to go to the team that offers the most bucks.

This case focuses on the growing conflict between the owners of professional sports teams and the athletes they employ. This includes professional baseball, football, hockey, and basketball. It's a conflict over money and who is going to get it, and increasingly, negotiations are breaking down and seasons are being curtailed. In 1994, for instance, the baseball season had to be cut short and the playoffs and World Series canceled because the millionaire players and the billionaire owners couldn't reach an agreement. The owners say they can't make enough money and blame the greedy players. Meanwhile, the players blame owners who are trying to limit the players' share of a growing revenue base.

Al Michaels, an ABC sports commentator, says, "There is so much money available right now, and the question has become: 'How do we split it?' I think if there's one word that sums up labor negotiations in sports these days it's mistrust or perhaps even distrust. The players think the owners are making a lot more money than the owners are contending they are making, and the players do not want to have anything to do with any sort of salary restriction. Of course, I'm talking about a salary cap. The owners, of course, would like to fix their costs, as would owners in any business, but the players are simply not buying into it and the players, for the most part, have won almost every labor negotiation to this point, and so they feel, at least until the baseball strike reached the point that it has reached, that they have had the upper hand."

One issue is revenue sharing. Another is the salary cap. Still another is free agency, and then there is the changing structure of ownership. Increasingly teams are being owned by large conglomerates (like Disney) or superrich individuals who have little motivation to settle negotiations on anything less than their terms. The same guy, for instance, owns Florida football, baseball, and hockey franchises. This is changing the leverage balance. For example, vertically integrated sports conglomerates own teams, ballparks, and television stations. The ballclub sells TV rights to its TV station at bargain rates, which transfers the profit from the ballpark where it has to be shared with the ballplayers. The team says that it isn't making enough money and that the profits are actually going to the TV station, which is owned by the same people.

Questions

1. What has changed in the past decade that has increased the number of impasses in professional sports' negotiations?

2. Analyze the 1994 baseball strike in terms of the conflict process.

3. If you were representing players in professional baseball, what, if anything, could you do to improve negotiation effectiveness?

4. What structural changes might make negotiations go more smoothly between professional sports' owners and the athletes?

Source: Based on "The Sports Industry's Money Disease," *ABC News Nightline;* aired October 3, 1994.

ROB PANCO: MANAGING GROUPS AND TEAMS

"I'm a big fan of teams," says Rob Panco. "When I came to Aslett, things were not as organized as well as they could have been. Of course, we were pretty small at the time. I decided to use teams as an organizing device for three reasons. First, functional specialization made teaming easy. I could take the separators or desk-top-publishing people and group them into common teams very easily. Second, teams allowed me greater control, and third, teams were good for the kind of work we did. We worked around projects. I thought cross-functional teams would be an effective way for us to meet our project goals." When asked if he had any people who weren't team players and, if so, how he handled it, Rob said, "I inherited one guy, Nick, who couldn't work well with others. No one wanted to work with him. I told him that he didn't have to be a team member but he had a responsibility to respect other projects. I isolated him as a team of one! Nick was a high maintenance person for me. He had a talent that I couldn't duplicate. He hurt morale when he copped his attitude. But I needed him and he was respected for his job competence."

On the subject of communication, Rob noted that he and his people at Aslett made increased use of electronics during his last few years there. Employees used an internal network to e-mail messages between each other. Rob worked with a consultant in the United Kingdom and communicated regularly with him via fax and e-mail as well as the telephone. But Rob is not an uncritical supporter of e-mail. "At AT&T I got so much e-mail, I couldn't read it all. It can become a party line with a lot of noise. From my standpoint, I think e-mail works well as a motivation tool. I could use it on Monday, for instance, to summarize the previous week's performance and to set the current week's goals." The UK example also reminded Rob of internal communication problems created by employees who came from different cultures. One of his British employees at Aslett, for example, had difficulty with the looseness and informality of his American peers. He viewed them as behaving "less than proper."

On leadership, Rob had some insightful comparisons between his managerial roles at AT&T versus Aslett. "At AT&T, I had responsibility but no authority because I managed peers. To be effective, I had to rely a lot on horse trading. At Aslett I had real authority." But he had some problems adjusting to this authority. "I'm friendly by nature. I had trouble creating distance between myself and my staff. This apparently confused people. They'd say, 'One minute Rob is my pal and then the next minute he's asking me where the pages are or why I missed a deadline.' I never figured out how to walk this tightrope very well." Rob also used the topic of leadership to explain his philosophy on empowering employees. "Realistically, there were some people I just couldn't delegate to. So I practiced *selective* empowerment. But overall, I wanted my people to take the ball and run with it because I saw empowerment as necessary if we were to grow. I looked at empowerment as an alternative to adding another level of management."

Although Rob doesn't consider himself a political animal, he clearly understands the importance of building a power base. For example, he noted that selection to the Leadership Continuity Program at AT&T gave him the clout to get the transfers he wanted when he wanted them. It also gave him influence with managers above him. But at a cost: Peers were jealous and it created conflicts with them. When asked if he did anything to increase his power at

AT&T, he quickly admitted to volunteering for committees and visible assignments. "Early in my career at AT&T, a boss told me to volunteer to work with upper managers. I asked 'why?' He said, 'It'll help at performance-appraisal time. The people who will be evaluating you and ranking you against others will know who you are.'"

Rob made a point to contrast politicking at Aslett and AT&T. "Look, politics occur everywhere. A certain amount is appropriate. At AT&T, however, it was individually-oriented. People kissed up to their boss to improve their personal status—to get a promotion or a salary increase. At Aslett, politics is more team-directed. It's used to get attention for a team or to protect the team's self-interest." When asked how the decline in business at Aslett in 1995 affected internal politics Rob replied, "I expected a lot of kissing-up to protect jobs. I expected to see overt examples of self-serving behavior. Growth provides excess resources. In decline, when those reserves are gone, I thought people would fight to get more of a shrinking resource pool. I was wrong. We experienced *increased* solidarity. For six to ten weeks, we had to put all our operating people on four-day work weeks and cut their pay by 20 percent. They didn't complain. Instead of backbiting, people came together as a team. They helped each other out and looked for ways to help management. They created an informal, cross-functional support network. People seemed to be wanting to make concessions to help the company survive."

On the topic of how Rob handles conflict, there was an obvious linkage back to his decision-making style. "When I see conflicts bubbling up, I sit back and analyze them. I don't do anything hastily. I want to think before I act. You can be too confrontational and make a situation worse. I want to get all the facts. So I'd talk privately with each individual involved in the conflict and ask him or her, 'What's going on?' Then I'd validate the information. Only then would I bring the parties together and try to find a resolution."

Questions

1. Evaluate Rob's solution to the problem of an employee who doesn't work well on teams.

2. Is there a conflict between being "boss" and being friendly with your staff? Discuss.

3. What do you think Rob means when he says that empowerment can be an alternative to adding another level of management?

4. What motivated Aslett employees to be cooperative when sales declined? What are the implications from your answer to when growth and profits return?

5. What do you think of Rob's conflict-handling orientation?

13

Part Four   The Organization System

FOUNDATIONS OF ORGANIZATION STRUCTURE

CHAPTER OUTLINE
What Is Organizational Structure?
Common Organizational Designs
New Design Options
Why Do Structures Differ?
Organizational Designs and Employee Behavior

> The dinosaur's eloquent lesson is that if some bigness is good, an overabundance of bigness is not necessarily better.
> —E.A. Johnston

LEARNING OBJECTIVES

After studying this chapter, you should be able to

1 Identify the six key elements that define an organization's structure

2 Explain the characteristics of a bureaucracy

3 Describe a matrix organization

4 Explain the characteristics of a "virtual" organization

5 Summarize why managers want to create boundaryless organizations

6 Contrast mechanistic and organic structural models

7 List the factors that favor different organizational structures

8 Explain the behavioral implications of different organizational designs

WHAT will tomorrow's large organization look like and what kind of people will it employ? If you want a prototype, consider the structure used by the organizing committee for the 1996 Summer Olympic Games in Atlanta.[1]

The Atlanta Committee for the Olympic Games (ACOG) was created in 1990, shortly after Atlanta won the bid for the Games. Headed by William Porter Payne (see photo), it began with literally half a dozen people. Yet it would grow to a peak of more than 88,000 (including volunteers), and then, in a matter of months, it would be closed down and essentially "go out of business." Full-time employees peaked at 4,500 during the Games in July. By August 30th, only 700 remained. And by January 1997, the ACOG employed fewer than 100 people. As one early employee described the task, it was equivalent to creating and dismantling a *Fortune* 500 company in a couple of years.

The task of putting an Olympics together is monumental. In Atlanta's case, this included raising money, signing up sponsors, building stadiums, installing security systems, creating marketing plans, printing tickets, hiring and training translators, and supervising tens of thousands of volunteers. To complete these tasks, the ACOG created a top-management team heading 13 units ranging from construction to security.

What kind of individuals are required to make an organization like this work? People who are flexible! They have to have the ability to make decisions on the fly, adjust to constantly changing situations, and feel comfortable in an environment where they know their workdays are numbered. But flexibility isn't something that's easy to teach. "You can't train people to be flexible," said Doris Issacs-Stallworth, ACOG's managing director of administration. "You have to hire people who are both specialists in their areas of expertise, such as marketing or finance, and yet who are able to pick up the slack wherever else they're needed." Issacs-Stallworth jokingly counted her three years with the Olympic committee in "dog years"—one year with ACOG being like seven in another organization.

Tomorrow's large organizations are very likely to be much more adaptable than ones with which we've become familiar. They'll look more like the structure of the ACOG than the traditional rigid bureaucracy, and the type of people they'll need will have to be, like those employed by the ACOG, highly flexible. Unfortunately, a lot of people are likely to have trouble adjusting to this need for flexibility. ◆

◆ An organization structure defines how job tasks are formally divided, grouped, and coordinated.

The theme of this chapter is that organizations have different structures and that these structures have a bearing on employee attitudes and behavior. More specifically, in the following pages, we define the key components that make up an organization's structure, present half a dozen or so structural design options from which managers can choose, identify the contingency factors that make certain structural designs preferable in varying situations, and conclude by considering the different effects that various organizational designs have on employee behavior.

What Is Organizational Structure?

organizational structure
How job tasks are formally divided, grouped, and coordinated.

An **organizational structure** defines how job tasks are formally divided, grouped, and coordinated. There are six key elements that managers need to address when they design their organization's structure. These are: work specialization, departmentalization, chain of command, span of control, centralization and decentralization, and formalization.[2] Exhibit 13-1 presents each of these elements as answers to an important structural question. The following sections describe these six elements of structure.

Work Specialization

Early in this century, Henry Ford became rich and famous by building automobiles on an assembly line. Every Ford worker was assigned a specific, repetitive task. For instance, one person would just put on the right-front wheel and someone else would install the right-front door. By breaking jobs up into small standardized tasks, which could be performed over and over again, Ford was able to produce cars at the rate of one every ten seconds, while using employees who had relatively limited skills.

Ford demonstrated that work can be performed more efficiently if employees are allowed to specialize. Today we use the term **work specialization** or *division of labor* to describe the degree to which tasks in the organization are subdivided into separate jobs.

work specialization
The degree to which tasks in the organization are subdivided into separate jobs.

The essence of work specialization is that, rather than an entire job being done by one individual, it is broken down into a number of steps, each step being completed by a separate individual. In essence, individuals specialize in doing part of an activity rather than the entire activity.

By the late 1940s, most manufacturing jobs in industrialized countries were being done with high work specialization. Management saw this as a means to make the most efficient use of its employees' skills. In most organizations, some tasks require highly developed skills; others can be performed by the untrained. If all workers were engaged in each step of, say, an organization's manufacturing process, all would have to have the skills necessary to

Exhibit 13-1 Six Key Questions That Managers Need to Answer in Designing the Proper Organizational Structure	The Key Question	The Answer Is Provided By
	1. To what degree are tasks subdivided into separate jobs?	Work specialization
	2. On what basis will jobs be grouped together?	Departmentalization
	3. To whom do individuals and groups report?	Chain of command
	4. How many individuals can a manager efficiently and effectively direct?	Span of control
	5. Where does decision-making authority lie?	Centralization and decentralization
	6. To what degree will there be rules and regulations to direct employees and managers?	Formalization

perform both the most demanding and the least demanding jobs. The result would be that, except when performing the most skilled or highly complex tasks, employees would be working below their skill levels. And since skilled workers are paid more than unskilled workers and their wages tend to reflect their highest level of skill, it represents an inefficient usage of organizational resources to pay highly skilled workers to do easy tasks.

Managers also looked for other efficiencies that could be achieved through work specialization. Employee skills at performing a task successfully increase through repetition. Less time is spent in changing tasks, in putting away one's tools and equipment from a prior step in the work process, and in getting ready for another. Equally important, training for specialization is more efficient from the organization's perspective. It is easier and less costly to find and train workers to do specific and repetitive tasks. This is especially true of highly sophisticated and complex operations. For example, could Cessna produce one Citation jet a year if one person had to build the entire plane alone? Not likely! Finally, work specialization increases efficiency and productivity by encouraging the creation of special inventions and machinery.

For much of the first half of this century, managers viewed work specialization as an unending source of increased productivity. And they were probably right. Because specialization was not widely practiced, its introduction almost always generated higher productivity. But by the 1960s, there became increasing evidence that a good thing can be carried too far. The point had been reached in some jobs where the human diseconomies from specialization—which surfaced as boredom, fatigue, stress, low productivity, poor quality, increased absenteeism, and high turnover—more than offset the economic advantages (see Exhibit 13-2 on page 480). In such cases, productivity could be increased by enlarging, rather than narrowing, the scope of job activities. Additionally, a number of companies found that by giving employees a variety of activities to do, allowing them to do a whole and complete job, and by putting them into teams with interchangeable skills, they often achieved significantly higher output with increased employee satisfaction.

Most managers today see work specialization as neither obsolete nor as an unending source of increased productivity. Rather, managers recognize the economies it provides in certain types of jobs and the problems it creates when it's carried too far. You'll find, for example, high work specialization

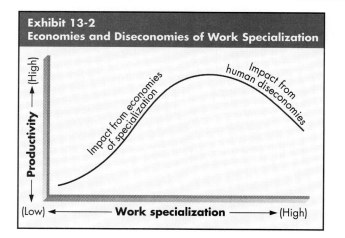

Exhibit 13-2
Economies and Diseconomies of Work Specialization

being used by McDonald's to efficiently make and sell hamburgers and fries, and by medical specialists in most health maintenance organizations. On the other hand, companies like Saturn Corporation have had success by broadening the scope of jobs and reducing specialization.

Departmentalization

Once you've divided jobs up through work specialization, you need to group these jobs together so common tasks can be coordinated. The basis by which jobs are grouped together is called **departmentalization**.

    One of the most popular ways to group activities is by *functions* performed. A manufacturing manager might organize his or her plant by separating engineering, accounting, manufacturing, personnel, and purchasing specialists into common departments. Of course, departmentalization by function can be used in all types of organizations. Only the functions change to reflect the organization's objectives and activities. A hospital might have departments devoted to research, patient care, accounting, and so forth. A professional football franchise might have departments entitled Player Personnel, Ticket Sales, and Travel and Accommodations. The major advantage to this type of grouping is obtaining efficiencies from putting like specialists together. Functional departmentalization seeks to achieve economies of scale by placing people with common skills and orientations into common units.

    Tasks can also be departmentalized by the type of *product* the organization produces. At Sun Petroleum Products, for instance, each of the three major product areas in the corporation (fuels, lubricants and waxes, and chemicals) is placed under the authority of a vice president who is a specialist in, and responsible for, everything having to do with his or her product line. Each, for example, would have his or her own manufacturing and marketing group. The major advantage to this type of grouping is increased accountability for product performance, since all activities related to a specific product are under the direction of a single manager. If an organization's activities are service rather than product related, each service would be autonomously grouped. For instance, an accounting firm could have departments for tax, management consulting, auditing, and the like. Each would offer a common array of services under the direction of a product or service manager.

departmentalization
The basis by which jobs are grouped together.

Health care facilities often use functional departmentalization in grouping work activities. Departments may include patient records, food service, admissions, accounting, radiology, pharmaceutical, and patient care. At River Hills West Healthcare Center in Pewaukee, Wisconsin, information technology helps coordinate activities among departments. The nurse shown here uses an electronic notepad to write in the name, dose, and time medication was given to a patient. This information is stored and instantly updated for the recordkeeping department.

Another way to departmentalize is on the basis of *geography* or territory. The sales function, for instance, may have western, southern, midwestern, and eastern regions. Each of these regions is, in effect, a department organized around geography. If an organization's customers are scattered over a large geographic area and have similar needs based on their location, then this form of departmentalization can be valuable.

At a Reynolds Metals aluminum tubing plant in upstate New York, production is organized into five departments: casting; press; tubing; finishing; and inspecting, packing, and shipping. This is an example of *process* departmentalization because each department specializes in one specific phase in the production of aluminum tubing. The metal is cast in huge furnaces; sent to the press department, where it is extruded into aluminum pipe; transferred to the tube mill, where it is stretched into various sizes and shapes of tubing; moved to finishing, where it is cut and cleaned; and finally arrives in the inspecting, packing, and shipping department. Since each process requires different skills, this method offers a basis for the homogeneous categorizing of activities.

Process departmentalization can be used for processing customers as well as products. If you've ever been to a state motor vehicles office to get a driver's license, you probably went through several departments before receiving your license. In one state, applicants must go through three steps, each handled by a separate department: (1) validation by motor vehicles division; (2) processing by the licensing department; and (3) payment collection by the treasury department.

A final category of departmentalization is to use the particular type of *customer* the organization seeks to reach. The sales activities in an office supply firm, for instance, can be broken down into three departments to service retail, wholesale, and government customers. A large law office can segment its staff on the basis of whether they service corporate or individual clients. The assumption underlying customer departmentalization is that customers in each department have a common set of problems and needs that can best be met by having specialists for each.

Large organizations may use all of the forms of departmentalization that we've described. A major Japanese electronics firm, for instance, organizes each of its divisions along functional lines and its manufacturing units around processes; it departmentalizes sales around seven geographic regions, and divides each sales region into four customer groupings. Two general trends, however, seem to be gaining momentum in the 1990s. First, customer departmentalization is growing in popularity. In order to better monitor the needs of customers and to be better able to respond to changes in those needs, many organizations have given greater emphasis to customer departmentalization. Xerox, for example, has eliminated its corporate marketing staff and placed marketing specialists out in the field.[3] This allows the company to better understand who their customers are and to respond faster to their requirements. The second trend is that rigid, functional departmentalization is being complemented by teams that cross over traditional departmental lines. As we described in chapter 8, as tasks have become more complex and more diverse skills are needed to accomplish those tasks, management has turned to cross-functional teams.

Chain of Command

Twenty years ago, the chain-of-command concept was a basic cornerstone in the design of organizations. As you'll see, it has far less importance today. But contemporary managers should still consider its implications when they decide how best to structure their organizations.

chain of command
The unbroken line of authority that extends from the top of the organization to the lowest echelon and clarifies who reports to whom.

authority
The rights inherent in a managerial position to give orders and to expect the orders to be obeyed.

unity of command
A subordinate should have only one superior to whom he or she is directly responsible.

The **chain of command** is an unbroken line of authority that extends from the top of the organization to the lowest echelon and clarifies who reports to whom. It answers questions for employees such as "To whom do I go if I have a problem?" and "To whom am I responsible?"

You can't discuss the chain of command without discussing two complementary concepts: *authority* and *unity of command*. **Authority** refers to the rights inherent in a managerial position to give orders and expect the orders to be obeyed. To facilitate coordination, each managerial position is given a place in the chain of command, and each manager is given a degree of authority in order to meet his or her responsibilities. The **unity-of-command** principle helps preserve the concept of an unbroken line of authority. It states that a person should have one and only one superior to whom he or she is directly responsible. If the unity of command is broken, a subordinate might have to cope with conflicting demands or priorities from several superiors.

Times change and so do the basic tenets of organizational design. The concepts of chain of command, authority, and unity of command have substantially less relevance today because of advancements in computer technology and the trend toward empowering employees. Just how different things are today is illustrated in the following excerpt from an article in *Business Week*.

◆ The concepts of chain of command, authority, and unity of command have substantially less relevance today because of advancements in computer technology and the trend toward empowering employees.

Puzzled, Charles Chaser scanned the inventory reports from his company's distribution centers one Wednesday morning in mid-March. According to the computer printouts, stocks of Rose Awakening Cutex nail polish were down to three days' supply, well below the three-and-a-half week stock Chesebrough-Pond's Inc. tries to keep on hand. But Chaser knew his Jefferson City (Missouri) plant had shipped 346 dozen bottles of the polish just two days before. Rose Awakening must be flying off store shelves, he thought. So Chaser turned to his terminal next to the production line and typed in instructions to produce 400 dozen more bottles on Thursday morning.

All in a day's work for a scheduling manager, right? Except for one detail: Chaser isn't management. He's a line worker—officially a "line co-ordinator"—one of hundreds who routinely tap the plant's computer network to track shipments, schedule their own workloads, and generally perform functions that used to be the province of management.[4]

A low-level employee today can access information in seconds that 20 years ago was available only to top managers. Similarly, computer technology increasingly allows employees anywhere in an organization to communicate with anyone else without going through formal channels. Moreover, the concepts of authority and maintaining the chain of command are increasingly less relevant as operating employees are being empowered to make decisions that previously were reserved for management. Add to this the popularity of self-managed and cross-functional teams and the creation of new structural designs that include multiple bosses, and the unity-of-command concept takes on less relevance. There are, of course, still many organizations that find they can be most productive by enforcing the chain of command. There just seem to be fewer of them nowadays.

Span of Control

How many subordinates can a manager efficiently and effectively direct? This question of **span of control** is important because, to a large degree, it determines the number of levels and managers an organization has. All things being equal, the wider or larger the span, the more efficient the organization. An example can illustrate the validity of this statement.

span of control
The number of subordinates a manager can efficiently and effectively direct.

Assume that we have two organizations, both of which have approximately 4,100 operative-level employees. As Exhibit 13-3 on page 484 illustrates, if one has a uniform span of four and the other a span of eight, the wider span would have two fewer levels and approximately 800 fewer managers. If the average manager made $40,000 a year, the wider span would save $32 million a year in management salaries! Obviously, wider spans are more efficient in terms of cost. However, at some point wider spans reduce effectiveness. That is, when the span becomes too large, employee performance suffers because supervisors no longer have the time to provide the necessary leadership and support.

Small spans have their advocates. By keeping the span of control to five or six employees, a manager can maintain close control.[5] But small spans have

Computer technology is increasing sales managers' span of control at Owens-Corning, a building supply manufacturer and retailer. The company has equipped its salespeople with computers loaded with software that provides up-to-date information about products, customers, and marketplace trends. The information empowers salespeople to manage their territory by making on-the-spot decisions on their own. Regional sales manager Charles Causey (left) expects the computer system to increase his span of control from 9 salespeople to 15.

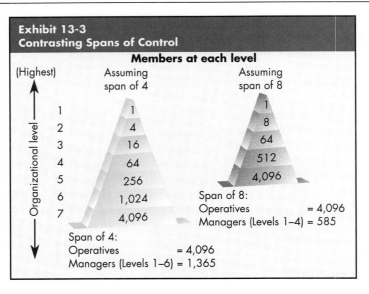

Exhibit 13-3
Contrasting Spans of Control

Members at each level

Organizational level	Assuming span of 4	Assuming span of 8
1 (Highest)	1	1
2	4	8
3	16	64
4	64	512
5	256	4,096
6	1,024	
7	4,096	

Span of 8:
Operatives = 4,096
Managers (Levels 1–4) = 585

Span of 4:
Operatives = 4,096
Managers (Levels 1–6) = 1,365

three major drawbacks. First, as already described, they're expensive because they add levels of management. Second, they make vertical communication in the organization more complex. The added levels of hierarchy slow down decision making and tend to isolate upper management. Third, small spans of control encourage overly tight supervision and discourage employee autonomy.

The trend in recent years has been toward larger spans of control. For example, the span for managers at companies such as General Electric and Reynolds Metals has expanded to ten or twelve subordinates—twice the number of 20 years ago.[6] Tom Smith, a regional manager with Carboline Co., oversees 27 people. His counterpart of 20 years ago would have typically managed 12 employees.[7]

Wide spans of control are consistent with recent efforts by companies to reduce costs, cut overhead, speed up decision making, increase flexibility, get closer to customers, and empower employees. However, to ensure that performance doesn't suffer because of these wider spans, organizations have been investing heavily in employee training. Managers recognize that they can handle a wider span when employees know their jobs inside and out or can turn to their co-workers when they have questions.

Centralization and Decentralization

In some organizations, top managers make all the decisions. Lower-level managers merely carry out top management's directives. At the other extreme, there are organizations where decision making is pushed down to those managers who are closest to the action. The former organizations are highly centralized; the latter are decentralized.

centralization
The degree to which decision making is concentrated at a single point in the organization.

The term **centralization** refers to the degree to which decision making is concentrated at a single point in the organization. The concept includes only formal authority, that is, the rights inherent in one's position. Typically, it's said that if top management makes the organization's key decisions with little or no input from lower-level personnel, then the organization is centralized. In contrast, the more that lower-level personnel provide input or are ac-

Exhibit 13-4

Source: S. Adams, *Dogbert's Big Book of Business*, DILBERT reprinted by permission of United Feature Syndicate, Inc.

tually given the discretion to make decisions, the more **decentralization** there is.

An organization characterized by centralization is an inherently different structural animal from one that is decentralized. In a decentralized organization, action can be taken more quickly to solve problems, more people provide input into decisions, and employees are less likely to feel alienated from those who make the decisions that affect their work lives.

Consistent with recent management efforts to make organizations more flexible and responsive, there has been a marked trend toward decentralizing decision making. In large companies, lower-level managers are closer to "the action" and typically have more detailed knowledge about problems than do top managers. Big retailers like Sears and JC Penney have given their store managers considerably more discretion in choosing what merchandise to stock. This allows those stores to compete more effectively against local merchants. Similarly, the Bank of Montreal grouped its 1,164 Canadian branches into 236 "communities," that is, a group of branches within a limited geographical area.[8] Each community is led by a community area manager, who

decentralization
Decision discretion is pushed down to lower-level employees.

typically works within a 20-minute drive of the other branches. These area managers can respond more quickly and more intelligently to problems in their communities than could some senior executive in Montreal. IBM Europe's chairperson Renato Riverso has similarly sliced the continent into some 200 autonomous business units, each with its own profit plan, employee incentives, and customer focus. "We used to manage from the top, like an army," said Riverso. "Now we're trying to create entities that drive themselves."[9]

From Concepts to *Skills*

Delegating Authority

If you're a manager and want to delegate some of your authority to someone else, how do you go about it? The following summarizes the primary steps you need to take.

1. *Clarify the assignment.* The place to begin is to determine what is to be delegated and to whom. You need to identify the person most capable of doing the task, then determine if he or she has the time and motivation to do the job.

   Assuming you have a willing and able subordinate, it is your responsibility to provide clear information on what is being delegated, the results you expect, and any time or performance expectations you hold.

   Unless there is an overriding need to adhere to specific methods, you should delegate only the end results. That is, get agreement on what is to be done and the end results expected, but let the subordinate decide on the means.

2. *Specify the subordinate's range of discretion.* Every act of delegation comes with constraints. You're delegating authority to act, but not *unlimited* authority. What you're delegating is authority to act on certain issues and, on those issues, within certain parameters. You need to specify what those parameters are so subordinates know, in no uncertain terms, the range of their discretion.

3. *Allow the subordinate to participate.* One of the best sources for determining how much authority will be necessary to accomplish a task is the subordinate who will be held accountable for that task. If you allow employees to participate in determining what is delegated, how much authority is needed to get the job done, and the standards by which they'll be judged, you increase employee motivation, satisfaction, and accountability for performance.

4. *Inform others that delegation has occurred.* Delegation should not take place in a vacuum. Not only do you and the subordinate need to know specifically what has been delegated and how much authority has been granted, but anyone else who may be affected by the delegation act also needs to be informed.

5. *Establish feedback controls.* The establishment of controls to monitor the subordinate's progress increases the likelihood that important problems will be identified early and that the task will be completed on time and to the desired specifications. For instance, agree on a specific time for completion of the task, and then set progress dates when the subordinate will report back on how well he or she is doing and any major problems that have surfaced. This can be supplemented with periodic spot checks to ensure that authority guidelines are not being abused, organization policies are being followed, and proper procedures are being met.

Employees' jobs at McDonald's restaurants are highly formalized. To provide customers with consistent product quality and fast service, workers are expected to follow defined food-preparation procedures. Learning these procedures is an important part of employee training at McDonald's Hamburger University training center, shown here.

Formalization

Formalization refers to the degree to which jobs within the organization are standardized. If a job is highly formalized, then the job incumbent has a minimum amount of discretion over what is to be done, when it is to be done, and how he or she should do it. Employees can be expected always to handle the same input in exactly the same way, resulting in a consistent and uniform output. There are explicit job descriptions, lots of organizational rules, and clearly defined procedures covering work processes in organizations where there is high formalization. Where formalization is low, job behaviors are relatively nonprogrammed and employees have a great deal of freedom to exercise discretion in their work. Since an individual's discretion on the job is inversely related to the amount of behavior in that job that is preprogrammed by the organization, the greater the standardization, the less input the employee has into how his or her work is to be done. Standardization not only eliminates the possibility of employees engaging in alternative behaviors, but it even removes the need for employees to consider alternatives.

The degree of formalization can vary widely between organizations and within organizations. Certain jobs, for instance, are well known to have little formalization. College book travelers—the representatives of publishers who call on professors to inform them of their company's new publications—have a great deal of freedom in their jobs. They have no standard sales "spiel," and the extent of rules and procedures governing their behavior may be little more than the requirement that they submit a weekly sales report and some suggestions on what to emphasize for the various new titles. At the other extreme, there are clerical and editorial positions in the same publishing houses where employees are required to "clock in" at their workstations by 8:00 A.M. or be docked a half-hour's pay and, once at that workstation, to follow a set of precise procedures dictated by management.

formalization
The degree to which jobs within the organization are standardized.

Common Organizational Designs

We now turn to describing three of the more common organizational designs found in use: the *simple structure*, the *bureaucracy*, and the *matrix structure*.

The Simple Structure

What do a small retail store, an electronics firm run by a hard-driving entrepreneur, a new Planned Parenthood office, and an airline in the midst of a companywide pilot's strike have in common? They probably all utilize the **simple structure**.

The simple structure is said to be characterized most by what it is not rather than what it is. The simple structure is not elaborated.[10] It has a low degree of departmentalization, wide spans of control, authority centralized in a single person, and little formalization. The simple structure is a "flat" organization; it usually has only two or three vertical levels, a loose body of employees, and one individual in whom the decision-making authority is centralized.

The simple structure is most widely practiced in small businesses in which the manager and the owner are one and the same. This, for example, is illustrated in Exhibit 13-5, an organization chart for a retail men's store. Jack Gold owns and manages this store. Although Jack Gold employs five full-time salespeople, a cashier, and extra personnel for weekends and holidays, he "runs the show."

The strength of the simple structure lies in its simplicity. It's fast, flexible, inexpensive to maintain, and accountability is clear. One major weakness is that it's difficult to maintain in anything other than small organizations. It becomes increasingly inadequate as an organization grows because its low formalization and high centralization tend to create information overload at the top. As size increases, decision making typically becomes slower and can eventually come to a standstill as the single executive tries to continue making all the decisions. This often proves to be the undoing of many small businesses. When an organization begins to employ 50 or 100 people, it's very difficult for the owner-manager to make all the choices. If the structure isn't changed and made more elaborate, the firm often loses momentum and can eventually fail. The simple structure's other weakness is that it's risky—everything depends on one person. One heart attack can literally destroy the organization's information and decision-making center.

simple structure
A structure characterized by a low degree of departmentalization, wide spans of control, authority centralized in a single person, and little formalization.

Exhibit 13-5
A Simple Structure (Jack Gold's Men's Store)

The simple structure isn't strictly limited to small organizations, it's just harder to make it work effectively in larger firms. One large company that seems to have succeeded with the simple structure is Nucor Corp., a $2.3 billion steel company that operates minimills in Indiana and Arkansas.[11] Its headquarters in Charlotte, North Carolina employs just 24 people. And there are only three levels between the company's president and mill workers. This lean structure has helped Nucor to become one of the most profitable steelmakers in the United States.

The Bureaucracy

Standardization! That's the key concept that underlies all bureaucracies. Take a look at the bank where you keep your checking account, the department store where you buy your clothes, or the government offices that collect your taxes, enforce health regulations, or provide local fire protection. They all rely on standardized work processes for coordination and control.

The **bureaucracy** is characterized by highly routine operating tasks achieved through specialization, very formalized rules and regulations, tasks that are grouped into functional departments, centralized authority, narrow spans of control, and decision making that follows the chain of command.

The primary strength of the bureaucracy lies in its ability to perform standardized activities in a highly efficient manner. Putting like specialties together in functional departments results in economies of scale, minimum duplication of personnel and equipment, and employees who have the opportunity to talk "the same language" among their peers. Furthermore, bureaucracies can get by nicely with less talented—and, hence, less costly—middle- and lower-level managers. The pervasiveness of rules and regulations substitutes for managerial discretion. Standardized operations, coupled with high formalization, allow decision making to be centralized. There is little need, therefore, for innovative and experienced decision makers below the level of senior executives.

One of the major weaknesses of a bureaucracy is illustrated in the following dialogue between four executives in one company: "Ya know, nothing happens in this place until we *produce* something," said the production executive. "Wrong," commented the research and development manager, "nothing happens until we *design* something!" "What are you talking about?" asked the marketing executive. "Nothing happens here until we *sell* something!" Finally, the exasperated accounting manager responded, "It doesn't matter what you produce, design, or sell. No one knows what happens until we *tally up the results*!" This conversation points up the fact that specialization creates subunit conflicts. Functional unit goals can override the overall goals of the organization.

The other major weakness of a bureaucracy is something we've all experienced at one time or another when having to deal with people who work in these organizations: obsessive concern with following the rules. When cases arise that don't precisely fit the rules, there is no room for modification. The bureaucracy is efficient only as long as employees confront problems that they have previously encountered and for which programmed decision rules have already been established.

The peak of bureaucracy's popularity was probably in the 1950s and 1960s. At that time, for instance, just about every major corporation in the

bureaucracy
A structure with highly routine operating tasks achieved through specialization, very formalized rules and regulations, tasks that are grouped into functional departments, centralized authority, narrow spans of control, and decision making that follows the chain of command.

world—firms such as IBM, General Electric, Volkswagen, Matsushita, and Royal Dutch Shell—was organized as a bureaucracy. Although the bureaucracy is currently out of fashion—critics argue that it can't respond rapidly to change and hinders employee initiative[12]—the majority of large organizations still take on basic bureaucratic characteristics, particularly specialization and high formalization. However, spans of control have generally been widened, authority has become more decentralized, and functional departments have been supplemented with an increased use of teams. Another trend is toward breaking bureaucracies up into smaller, though fully functioning, minibureaucracies.[13] These smaller versions, with 150 to 250 people, each have their own mission and profit goals. It's been estimated that about 15 percent of large corporations have taken this direction.[14] For instance, Eastman Kodak has transformed over 100 production units into separate businesses. ABB Asea Brown Boveri, a $32 billion corporation with 210,000 employees, has broken itself into 1,300 companies divided into almost 5,000 profit centers that are located in 140 different countries.

The Matrix Structure

matrix structure
A structure that creates dual lines of authority; combines functional and product departmentalization.

Another popular organizational design option is the **matrix structure**. You'll find it being used in advertising agencies, aerospace firms, research and development laboratories, construction companies, hospitals, government agencies, universities, management consulting firms, and entertainment companies.[15] Essentially, the matrix combines two forms of departmentalization: functional and product.

The strength of functional departmentalization lies in putting like specialists together, which minimizes the number necessary, while it allows the pooling and sharing of specialized resources across products. Its major disadvantage is the difficulty of coordinating the tasks of diverse functional specialists so that their activities are completed on time and within budget. Product departmentalization, on the other hand, has exactly the opposite benefits and disadvantages. It facilitates coordination among specialties to achieve on-time completion and meet budget targets. Furthermore, it provides clear responsibility for all activities related to a product, but with duplication of activities and costs. The matrix attempts to gain the strengths of each, while avoiding their weaknesses.

The most obvious structural characteristic of the matrix is that it breaks the unity-of-command concept. Employees in the matrix have two bosses—their functional department managers and their product managers. Therefore, the matrix has a dual chain of command.

◆ The matrix has a dual chain of command.

Exhibit 13-6 on page 492 shows the matrix form as used in a college of business administration. The academic departments of accounting, economics, marketing, and so forth are functional units. Additionally, specific programs (that is, products) are overlaid on the functions. In this way, members in a matrix structure have a dual assignment—to their functional department, and to their product groups. For instance, a professor of accounting who is teaching an undergraduate course reports to the director of undergraduate programs as well as to the chairperson of the accounting department.

The strength of the matrix lies in its ability to facilitate coordination when the organization has a multiplicity of complex and interdependent ac-

Exhibit 13-6
Matrix Structure for a College of Business Administration

Academic departments \ Programs	Undergraduate	Master's	Ph. D.	Research	Executive development	Community service
Accounting						
Administrative studies						
Finance						
Information and decision sciences						
Marketing						
Organizational behavior						
Quantitative methods						

tivities. As an organization gets larger, its information processing capacity can become overloaded. In a bureaucracy, complexity results in increased formalization. The direct and frequent contact between different specialties in the matrix can make for better communication and more flexibility. Information permeates the organization and more quickly reaches those people who need to take account of it. Furthermore, the matrix reduces bureaupathologies. The dual lines of authority reduce tendencies of departmental members to become so busy protecting their little worlds that the organization's overall goals become secondary.

There is also another advantage to the matrix. It facilitates the efficient allocation of specialists. When individuals with highly specialized skills are lodged in one functional department or product group, their talents are monopolized and underutilized. The matrix achieves the advantages of economies of scale by providing the organization with both the best resources and an effective way of ensuring their efficient deployment.

The major disadvantages of the matrix lie in the confusion it creates, its propensity to foster power struggles, and the stress it places on individuals.[16] When you dispense with the unity-of-command concept, ambiguity is significantly increased and ambiguity often leads to conflict. For example, it's frequently unclear who reports to whom, and it is not unusual for product managers to fight over getting the best specialists assigned to their products. Confusion and ambiguity also create the seeds of power struggles. Bureaucracy reduces the potential for power grabs by defining the rules of the game. When those rules are "up for grabs," power struggles between functional and product managers result. For individuals who desire security and absence from ambiguity, this work climate can produce stress. Reporting to more than one boss introduces role conflict, and unclear expectations introduce role ambiguity. The comfort of bureaucracy's predictability is absent, replaced by insecurity and stress.

OB in the News

Johnson & Johnson: It's Really 160 Companies!

Johnson & Johnson (J&J) has developed a remarkable record for developing new products. In spite of its size—its annual revenues are approaching $21 billion—36 percent of its current sales come from products introduced within the previous five years. How does this huge company generate such innovation and growth? By structuring itself more like a small entrepreneurial firm.

"We don't view ourselves as a big company," says its chairman, Ralph Larsen. "We view ourselves as 160 small companies."

A couple of decades ago, J&J was a consumer products firm. It made Band-Aids, baby powder, shampoos, and Tylenol. Today it still makes those consumer products but it gets two-thirds of its sales and most of its growth from pharmaceuticals and professional services. Two success

stories illustrate how J&J works.

J&J's management decided that interventional cardiology would become a huge business. To become involved in it, J&J created Interventional Systems. Starting with a general manager, a small staff, and no sales, they were told to create a business. Looking for opportunities, the new unit's managers discovered some medical specialists who had invented a tiny stainless steel scaffold that could be inserted inside a blocked artery using a balloon. This scaffold would allow blood to flow unimpeded. After investing heavily in clinical trials and in design and manufacturing processes, the scaffold was approved by the Federal Drug Administration in 1994. The next year this device brought J&J some $520 million in revenues and an estimated net earnings of some $200 million.

In the early 1980s, the market for contact lenses was dominated by Bausch & Lomb. J&J was on the verge of closing Vistakon, its contact lens division, when managers decided that they could develop a technology for making disposable contact lenses. The idea seemed preposterous at the time, since regular lenses were selling for $150 a pair. "It was a crazy idea," Larsen noted, "but there were people in our company who believed it could happen." Vistakon's managers spent five years and more than $200 million testing and developing the idea. Introduced in 1988, disposables were an immediate hit. The company now sells around $560 million worth every year, making J&J the world's leading contact lens maker.

Based on H. Rudnitsky, "One Hundred Sixty Companies for the Price of One," *Forbes*, February 26, 1996, pp. 56–62.

Take It to the Net

We invite you to visit the **Robbins** page on the Prentice Hall Web site at:

http://www.prenhall.com/robbinsorgbeh

for this chapter's World Wide Web exercise.

New Design Options

Since the early 1980s, senior managers in a number of organizations have been working to develop new structural options that can better help their firms compete effectively. In this section, we'll describe three such structural designs: the *team structure*, the *virtual organization*, and the *boundaryless organization*.

The Team Structure

As described in Chapter 8, teams have become an extremely popular means around which to organize work activities. When management uses teams as its central coordination device, you have a **team structure**. The primary characteristics of the team structure are that it breaks down departmental barriers and decentralizes decision making to the level of the work team. Team structures also require employees to be generalists as well as specialists.[17]

In smaller companies, the team structure can define the entire organization. For instance, Imedia, a 30-person marketing firm in New Jersey, is organized completely around teams which have full responsibility for most operational issues and client services.[18]

More often, particularly among larger organizations, the team structure complements what is typically a bureaucracy. This allows the organization to achieve the efficiency of bureaucracy's standardization, while gaining the flexibility that teams provide. To improve productivity at the operating level, for instance, companies like Chrysler, Saturn, Motorola, and Xerox have made extensive use of self-managed teams. On the other hand, when companies like Boeing or Hewlett-Packard need to design new products or coordinate major projects, they'll structure activities around cross-functional teams.

team structure
The use of teams as the central device to coordinate work activities.

The Virtual Organization

Why own when you can rent? That question captures the essence of the **virtual organization** (also sometimes called the *network* or *modular* organization), typically a small, core organization that outsources major business functions.[19] In structural terms, the virtual organization is highly centralized, with little or no departmentalization.

The prototype of the virtual structure is today's movie-making organization. In Hollywood's golden era, movies were made by huge, vertically integrated corporations.[20] Studios such as MGM, Warner Brothers, and 20th-Century Fox owned large movie lots and employed thousands of full-time specialists—set designers, camera people, film editors, directors, and even actors. Nowadays, most movies are made by a collection of individuals and small companies who come together and make films project by project. This structural form allows each project to be staffed with the talent most suited to its demands, rather than having to choose just from those people the studio employs. It minimizes bureaucratic overhead since there is no lasting organization to maintain. And it lessens long-term risks and their costs because there is no long term—a team is assembled for a finite period and then disbanded.

Companies like Nike, Reebok, Liz Claiborne, Emerson Radio, and Dell Computer are just a few of the thousands of companies that have found that they can do hundreds of millions of dollars in business without owning manufacturing facilities. Dell Computer, for instance, owns no plants and merely

virtual organization
A small, core organization that outsources major business functions.

Tour promoter RZO Productions used the virtual organization structure in organizing The Rolling Stones' Voodoo Lounge world tour. RZO employed 250 employees, such as stagehands, lighting and sound technicians, and truck drivers, on a contract basis for this specific tour. The organization was disbanded when the tour ended.

assembles computers from outsourced parts. National Steel Corp. contracts out its mail-room operations; AT&T farms out its credit card processing; and Mobil Oil Corporation has turned over maintenance of its refineries to another firm.

What's going on here? A quest for maximum flexibility. These virtual organizations have created networks of relationships that allow them to contract out manufacturing, distribution, marketing, or any other business function where management feels that others can do it better or more cheaply.

The virtual organization stands in sharp contrast to the typical bureaucracy that has many vertical levels of management and where control is sought through ownership. In such organizations, research and development are done in-house, production occurs in company-owned plants, and sales and marketing are performed by the company's own employees. To support all this, management has to employ extra personnel including accountants, human resource specialists, and lawyers. The virtual organization, however, outsources many of these functions and concentrates on what it does best. For most U.S. firms, that means focusing on design or marketing. Emerson Radio Corporation, for example, designs and engineers its televisions, stereos, and other consumer electronic products, but it contracts out its manufacture to Asian suppliers.

Exhibit 13-7 shows a virtual organization in which management outsources all of the primary functions of the business. The core of the organization is a small group of executives, whose job is to oversee directly any activities that are done in-house and to coordinate relationships with the other organizations that manufacture, distribute, and perform other crucial functions for the virtual organization. The arrows in Exhibit 13-7 represent those relationships typically maintained under contracts. In essence, managers in virtual structures spend most of their time coordinating and controlling external relations, typically by way of computer-network links.

The major advantage to the virtual organization is its flexibility. For instance, it allowed someone with an innovative idea and little money, such as

Exhibit 13-7
A Virtual Organization

Michael Dell and his Dell Computer firm, to successfully compete against large companies like IBM. The primary drawback to this structure is that it reduces management's control over key parts of its business.

The Boundaryless Organization

General Electric chairman, Jack Welch, coined the term **boundaryless organization** to describe his idea of what he wanted GE to become. Welch wanted to turn his company into a "$60 billion family grocery store."[21] That is, in spite of its monsterous size, he wanted to eliminate *vertical* and *horizontal* boundaries within GE and breakdown *external* barriers between the company and its customers and suppliers. The boundaryless organization seeks to eliminate the chain of command, have limitless spans of control, and replace departments with empowered teams.

Although GE hasn't yet achieved this boundaryless state—and probably never will—it has made significant progress toward this end. So have other companies like Hewlett-Packard, AT&T, and Motorola. Let's take a look at what a boundaryless organization would look like and what some firms are doing to make it a reality.[22]

By removing *vertical* boundaries, management flattens the hierarchy. Status and rank are minimized. And the organization looks more like a silo than a pyramid, where the grain at the top is no different than the grain at the bottom. Cross-hierarchical teams (which include top executives, middle managers, supervisors, and operative employees), participative decision-making practices, and the use of 360-degree performance appraisals (where peers and others above and below the employee evaluate his or her performance) are examples of what GE is doing to break down vertical boundaries.

Functional departments create *horizontal* boundaries. The way to reduce these barriers is to replace functional departments with cross-functional teams and to organize activities around processes. For instance, Xerox now develops new products through multidisciplinary teams that work in a single process

boundaryless organization
An organization that seeks to eliminate the chain of command, have limitless spans of control, and replace departments with empowered teams.

A global computer network allows Texas Instruments to communicate across intraorganizational boundaries in speeding new products to market. A company unit named Tiris, which produces tiny communications devices for security and identification purposes, is managed out of Bedford, England. Product designs are developed in the Netherlands and Germany, and the products are manufactured and assembled in Japan and Malaysia. Employees at all these locations send text, diagrams, and designs to each other using TI's networked computers. Shown here are assembly employees in Malaysia.

instead of around narrow functional tasks. Similarly, some AT&T units are now doing annual budgets based not on functions or departments but on processes such as the maintenance of a worldwide telecommunications network. Another way management can cut through horizontal barriers is to use lateral transfers and rotate people into and out of different functional areas. This turns specialists into generalists.

When fully operational, the boundaryless organization also breaks down barriers to *external* constituencies and barriers created by geography. Globalization, strategic alliances, supplier–organization and customer–organization linkages, and telecommuting are all examples of practices that reduce external boundaries. Coca-Cola, for instance, sees itself as a global corporation, not a U.S. or Atlanta company. Firms like NEC Corp., Boeing, and Apple Computer each have strategic alliances or joint partnerships with dozens of companies. These alliances blur the distinction between one organization and another as employees work on joint projects. Many organizations are also blurring the line between themselves and their suppliers. For instance, the CEO of Merix Corp., a 750-employee electronics firm, said, "We have people who work here that I thought were Merix employees. They have our badges, and I see them every day, but it turns out that they really work for our suppliers." Companies like AT&T and Northwest Airlines are allowing customers to perform functions that previously were done by management. For instance, some AT&T units are receiving bonuses based on customer evaluations of the teams that serve them. Northwest gives its frequent fliers ten $50 award certificates each year and tells these customers to distribute these awards to Northwest employees when they see them do something good. This practice, in essence, allows Northwest's customers to participate in employee appraisals. Finally, we suggest that telecommuting is blurring organizational boundaries. The security analyst with Merrill Lynch who does his job from his ranch in Montana or the software designer who works for a San Francisco company but does her job in Boulder, Colorado are just two examples of the millions of workers who are now doing their jobs outside the physical boundaries of their employers' premises.

The one common technological thread that makes the boundaryless organization possible is networked computers. They allow people to communicate across intraorganizational and interorganizational boundaries.[23] Electronic mail, for instance, enables hundreds of employees to share information simultaneously and allows rank-and-file workers to communicate directly with senior executives. And interorganizational networks now make it possible for Wal-Mart suppliers like Procter & Gamble and Levi Strauss to monitor inventory levels of laundry soap and jeans, respectively, because P&G's and Levi's computer systems are networked to Wal-Mart's system.

Why Do Structures Differ?

In the previous sections, we described a variety of organizational designs ranging from the highly structured and standardized bureaucracy to the loose and amorphous boundaryless organization. The other designs we discussed tend to exist somewhere between these two extremes.

Exhibit 13-8 reconceptualizes our previous discussions by presenting two extreme models of organizational design. One extreme we'll call the **mechanistic model**. It is generally synonymous with the bureaucracy in that it has extensive departmentalization, high formalization, a limited information network (mostly downward communication), and little participation by low-level members in decision making. At the other extreme is the **organic model**.

mechanistic model
A structure characterized by extensive departmentalization, high formalization, a limited information network, and centralization.

organic model
A structure that is flat, uses cross-hierarchical and cross-functional teams, has low formalization, possesses a comprehensive information network, and relies on participative decision making.

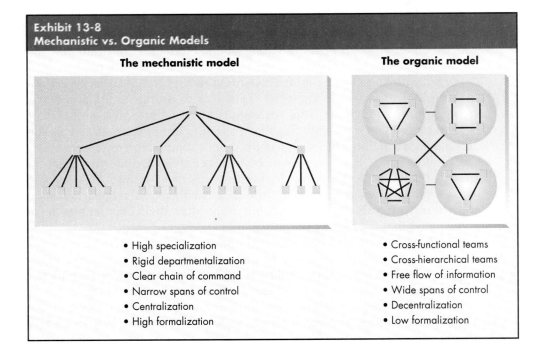

Exhibit 13-8
Mechanistic vs. Organic Models

The mechanistic model

The organic model

- High specialization
- Rigid departmentalization
- Clear chain of command
- Narrow spans of control
- Centralization
- High formalization

- Cross-functional teams
- Cross-hierarchical teams
- Free flow of information
- Wide spans of control
- Decentralization
- Low formalization

This model looks a lot like the boundaryless organization. It's flat, uses cross-hierarchical and cross-functional teams, has low formalization, possesses a comprehensive information network (utilizing lateral and upward communication as well as downward), and it involves high participation in decision making.[24]

With these two models in mind, we're now prepared to address the question: Why are some organizations structured along more mechanistic lines while others follow organic characteristics? What are the forces that influence the design that is chosen? In the following pages, we present the major forces that have been identified as causes or determinants of an organization's structure.[25]

Strategy

An organization's structure is a means to help management achieve its objectives. Since objectives are derived from the organization's overall strategy, it is only logical that strategy and structure should be closely linked. More specifically, structure should follow strategy. If management makes a significant change in its organization's strategy, the structure will need to be modified to accommodate and support this change.[26]

Most current strategy frameworks focus on three strategy dimensions—innovation, cost minimization, and imitation—and the structural design that works best with each.[27]

To what degree does an organization introduce major new products or services? An **innovation strategy** does not mean a strategy merely for simple or cosmetic changes from previous offerings but rather one for meaningful and unique innovations. Obviously, not all firms pursue innovation. This strategy may appropriately characterize 3M Co., but it certainly is not a strategy pursued by Reader's Digest.

An organization that is pursuing a **cost-minimization strategy** tightly controls costs, refrains from incurring unnecessary innovation or marketing expenses, and cuts prices in selling a basic product. This would describe the strategy pursued by Wal-Mart or the sellers of generic grocery products.

Organizations following an **imitation strategy** try to capitalize on the best of both of the previous strategies. They seek to minimize risk and maximize opportunity for profit. Their strategy is to move into new products or new markets only after viability has been proven by innovators. They take the successful ideas of innovators and copy them. Manufacturers of mass-marketed fashion goods that are rip-offs of designer styles follow the imitation strategy. This label also probably characterizes such well-known firms as IBM and Caterpillar. They essentially follow their smaller and more innovative competitors with superior products, but only after their competitors have demonstrated that the market is there.

Exhibit 13-9 describes the structural option that best matches each strategy. Innovators need the flexibility of the organic structure, while cost minimizers seek the efficiency and stability of the mechanistic structure. Imitators combine the two structures. They use a mechanistic structure in order to maintain tight controls and low costs in their current activities, while at the same time they create organic subunits in which to pursue new undertakings.

innovation strategy
A strategy that emphasizes the introduction of major new products and services.

cost-minimization strategy
A strategy that emphasizes tight cost controls, avoidance of unnecessary innovation or marketing expenses, and price cutting.

imitation strategy
A strategy that seeks to move into new products or new markets only after their viability has already been proven.

Exhibit 13-9 The Strategy–Structure Thesis

Strategy	Structural Option
Innovation	**Organic:** A loose structure; low specialization, low formalization, decentralized
Cost minimization	**Mechanistic:** Tight control; extensive work specialization, high formalization, high centralization
Imitation	**Mechanistic and organic:** Mix of loose with tight properties; tight controls over current activities and looser controls for new undertakings

Organization Size

A quick glance at the organizations we deal with regularly in our lives would lead most of us to conclude that size would have some bearing on an organization's structure. The more than 800,000 employees of the United States Postal Service, for example, do not neatly fit into one building, or into several departments supervised by a couple of managers. It's pretty hard to envision 800,000 people being organized in any manner other than one that contains a great deal of specialization, departmentalization, uses a large number of procedures and regulations to ensure uniform practices, and follows a high degree of decentralized decision making. On the other hand, a local messenger service that employs ten people and generates less than $300,000, a year in service fees is not likely to need decentralized decision making or formalized procedures and regulations.

There is considerable evidence to support that an organization's size significantly affects its structure.[28] For instance, large organizations—those typically employing 2,000 or more people—tend to have more specialization, more departmentalization, more vertical levels, and more rules and regulations than do small organizations. However, the relationship isn't linear. Rather, size affects structure at a decreasing rate. The impact of size becomes less important as an organization expands. Why is this? Essentially, once an organization has around 2,000 employees, it's already fairly mechanistic. An additional 500 employees will not have much impact. On the other hand, adding 500 employees to an organization that has only 300 members is likely to result in a shift toward a more mechanistic structure.

Technology

The term **technology** refers to how an organization transfers its inputs into outputs. Every organization has at least one technology for converting financial, human, and physical resources into products or services. The Ford Motor Co., for instance, predominantly uses an assembly-line process to make its products. On the other hand, colleges may use a number of instruction technologies—the ever-popular formal lecture method, the case analysis method, the experiential exercise method, the programmed learning method, and so forth. In this section we want to show that organizational structures adapt to their technology.

technology
How an organization transfers its inputs into outputs.

Numerous studies have been carried out on the technology–structure relationship.[29] The details of those studies are quite complex, so we'll go straight to "the bottom line" and attempt to summarize what we know.

The common theme that differentiates technologies is their *degree of routineness*. By this we mean that technologies tend toward either routine or nonroutine activities. The former are characterized by automated and standardized operations. Nonroutine activities are customized. They include such varied operations as furniture restoring, custom shoemaking, and genetic research.

> ◆ The common theme that differentiates technologies is their degree of routineness.

What relationships have been found between technology and structure? Although the relationship is not overwhelmingly strong, we find that routine tasks are associated with taller and more departmentalized structures. The relationship between technology and formalization, however, is stronger. Studies consistently show routineness to be associated with the presence of rule manuals, job descriptions, and other formalized documentation. Finally, there has been found to be an interesting relationship between technology and centralization. It seems logical that routine technologies would be associated with a centralized structure, whereas nonroutine technologies, which rely more heavily on the knowledge of specialists, would be characterized by delegated decision authority. This position has met with some support. However, a more generalizable conclusion is that the technology–centralization relationship is moderated by the degree of formalization. Formal regulations and centralized decision making are both control mechanisms and management can substitute one for the other. Routine technologies should be associated with centralized control if there is a minimum of rules and regulations. However, if formalization is high, routine technology can be accompanied by decentralization. So, we would predict that routine technology would lead to centralization, but only if formalization is low.

Environment

environment
Those institutions or forces outside the organization that potentially affect the organization's performance.

An organization's **environment** is composed of those institutions or forces that are outside the organization and potentially affect the organization's performance. These typically include suppliers, customers, competitors, government regulatory agencies, public pressure groups, and the like.

Why should an organization's structure be affected by its environment? Because of environmental uncertainty. Some organizations face relatively static environments—few forces in their environment are changing. There are, for example, no new competitors, no new technological breakthroughs by current competitors, or little activity by public pressure groups to influence the organization. Other organizations face very dynamic environments— rapidly changing government regulations affecting their business, new competitors, difficulties in acquiring raw materials, continually changing product preferences by customers, and so on. Static environments create significantly less uncertainty for managers than do dynamic ones. And since uncertainty is a threat to an organization's effectiveness, management will try to minimize it. One way to reduce environmental uncertainty is through adjustments in the organization's structure.[30]

Recent research has helped clarify what is meant by environmental uncertainty. It's been found that there are three key dimensions to any organization's environment. They are labeled capacity, volatility, and complexity.[31]

The *capacity* of an environment refers to the degree to which it can support growth. Rich and growing environments generate excess resources, which can buffer the organization in times of relative scarcity. Abundant capacity, for example, leaves room for an organization to make mistakes, while scarce capacity does not. In 1997, firms operating in the multimedia software business had relatively abundant environments, whereas those in the full-service brokerage business faced relative scarcity.

The degree of instability in an environment is captured in the *volatility* dimension. Where there is a high degree of unpredictable change, the environment is dynamic. This makes it difficult for management to predict accurately the probabilities associated with various decision alternatives. At the other extreme is a stable environment. The accelerated changes in Eastern Europe and the demise of the Cold War had dramatic effects on the U.S. defense industry in the early 1990s. This moved the environment of major defense contractors like McDonnell Douglas, Lockheed Martin, General Dynamics, and Northrop from relatively stable to dynamic.

Finally, the environment needs to be assessed in terms of *complexity*, that is, the degree of heterogeneity and concentration among environmental elements. Simple environments are homogeneous and concentrated. This might describe the tobacco industry, since there are relatively few players. It's easy for firms in this industry to keep a close eye on the competition. In contrast, environments characterized by heterogeneity and dispersion are called complex. This is essentially the current environment for firms competing in the internet-connection business. Every day there seems to be another "new kid on the block" with whom current internet access providers have to deal.

Exhibit 13-10 summarizes our definition of the environment along its three dimensions. The arrows in this figure are meant to indicate movement toward higher uncertainty. So organizations that operate in environments characterized as scarce, dynamic, and complex face the greatest degree of uncertainty. Why? Because they have little room for error, high unpredictability, and a diverse set of elements in the environment to monitor constantly.

Given this three-dimensional definition of environment, we can offer some general conclusions. There is evidence that relates the degrees of environmental uncertainty to different structural arrangements. Specifically, the more scarce, dynamic, and complex the environment, the more organic a

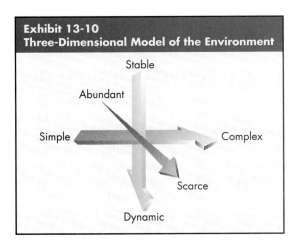

Exhibit 13-10
Three-Dimensional Model of the Environment

structure should be. The more abundant, stable, and simple the environment, the more the mechanistic structure will be preferred.

Summary

We've shown that four variables—strategy, size, technology, and environment—are the primary forces that determine whether an organization is mechanistic or organic. Now let's use our previous analysis to explain the evolution of structural designs throughout this century.

The industrial revolution encouraged economies of scale and the rise of the modern, large corporation. As companies grew from their original simple structures, they took on mechanistic characteristics and became bureaucracies. The rise of bureaucracy to become the dominant structure in industrialized nations from the 1920s through the 1970s can be largely explained by three facts. First, the environment was relatively stable and certain over this period. The monopoly power of the large corporations, coupled with little international competition, kept environmental uncertainty to a minimum. Second, economies of scale and minimal competition allowed these corporations to introduce highly routine technologies. And third, most of these large corporations chose to pursue cost minimization or imitation strategies—leaving innovation to the little guys. Combine these strategies with large size, routine technologies, and relatively abundant, stable, and simple environments, and you have a reasonably clear explanation for the rise and domination of the bureaucracy.

Things began to change in the 1970s, when the environment became significantly more uncertain. Oil prices quadrupled literally overnight in 1973. Inflation exploded into double digits in 1978 and 1979. Advances in computer technology—especially the availability of increasingly powerful systems at dramatically falling prices—began to lessen the advantage that accrued to large size. And, of course, competition moved to the global arena. To compete effectively, top management responded by restructuring their organizations. Some went to the matrix to give their companies increased flexibility. Some added team structures so they could respond more rapidly to change. Today, senior managers in most large corporations are debureaucratizing their organizations—making them more organic by reducing staff, cutting vertical levels, decentralizing authority, and the like—primarily because the environment continues to be uncertain. Managers realize that in a dynamic and changing environment, inflexible organizations end up as bankruptcy statistics.

Organizational Designs and Employee Behavior

We opened this chapter by implying that an organization's structure can have significant effects on its members. In this section, we want to directly assess just what those effects might be.

A review of the evidence linking organizational structures to employee performance and satisfaction leads to a pretty clear conclusion—you can't generalize! Not everyone prefers the freedom and flexibility of organic structures. Some people are most productive and satisfied when work tasks are standardized and ambiguity is minimized—that is, in mechanistic structures.

So any discussion of the effect of organizational design on employee behavior has to address individual differences. To illustrate this point, let's consider employee preferences for work specialization, span of control, and centralization.[32]

The evidence generally indicates that *work specialization* contributes to higher employee productivity but at the price of reduced job satisfaction. However, this statement ignores individual differences and the type of job tasks people do.

As we noted previously, work specialization is not an unending source of higher productivity. Problems start to surface, and productivity begins to suffer, when the human diseconomies of doing repetitive and narrow tasks overtake the economies of specialization. As the workforce has become more highly educated and desirous of jobs that are intrinsically rewarding, the point where productivity begins to decline seems to be reached more quickly than in decades past.

While more people today are undoubtedly turned off by overly specialized jobs than were their parents or grandparents, it would be naive to ignore the reality that there is still a segment of the workforce that prefers the routine and repetitiveness of highly specialized jobs. Some individuals want work that makes minimal intellectual demands and provides the security of routine. For these people, high work specialization is a source of job satisfaction. The empirical question, of course, is whether this represents 2 percent of the work force or 52 percent. Given that there is some self-selection operating in the choice of careers, we might conclude that negative behavioral outcomes from high specialization are most likely to surface in professional jobs occupied by individuals with high needs for personal growth and diversity.

A review of the research indicates that it is probably safe to say there is no evidence to support a relationship between *span of control* and employee performance. While it is intuitively attractive to argue that large spans might lead to higher employee performance because they provide more distant supervision and more opportunity for personal initiative, the research fails to support this notion. At this point it is impossible to state that any particular span of control is best for producing high performance or high satisfaction among subordinates. The reason is, again, probably individual differences. That is, some people like to be left alone, while others prefer the security of a boss who is quickly available at all times. Consistent with several of the contingency theories of leadership discussed in chapter 10, we would expect factors such as employees' experiences and abilities and the degree of structure in their tasks to explain when wide or narrow spans of control are likely to contribute to their performance and job satisfaction. However, there is some evidence indicating that a *manager's* job satisfaction increases as the number of subordinates he or she supervises increases.

We find fairly strong evidence linking *centralization* and job satisfaction. In general, organizations that are less centralized have a greater amount of participative decision making. And the evidence suggests that participative decision making is positively related to job satisfaction. But, again, individual differences surface. The decentralization–satisfaction relationship is strongest with employees who have low self-esteem. Because individuals with low self-esteem have less confidence in their abilities, they place a higher value on shared decision making, which means that they're not held solely responsible for decision outcomes.

Our conclusion: To maximize employee performance and satisfaction, individual differences, such as experience, personality, and the work task, should be taken into account. For simplicity's sake, it might help to keep in mind that individuals with a high degree of bureaucratic orientation (see Learning about Yourself Exercise at the end of this chapter) tend to place a heavy reliance on higher authority, prefer formalized and specific rules, and prefer formal relationships with others on the job. These people seem better suited to mechanistic structures. Those individuals with a low degree of bureaucratic orientation would probably fit better in organic structures. Additionally, cultural background influences preference for structure. Organizations operating with people from high power distance cultures, such as found in Greece, France, and most of Latin America, will find employees much more accepting of mechanistic structures than where employees come from low power distance countries. So you need to consider cultural differences along with individual differences when making predictions on how structure will effect employee performance and satisfaction.

Summary and Implications for Managers

The theme of this chapter has been that an organization's internal structure contributes to explaining and predicting behavior. That is, in addition to individual and group factors, the structural relationships in which people work have an important bearing on employee attitudes and behavior.

What's the basis for the argument that structure has an impact on both attitudes and behavior? To the degree that an organization's structure reduces ambiguity for employees and clarifies such concerns as "What am I supposed to do?" "How am I supposed to do it?" "To whom do I report?" and "To whom do I go if I have a problem?" it shapes their attitudes and facilitates and motivates them to higher levels of performance.

Of course, structure also constrains employees to the extent that it limits and controls what they do. For example, organizations structured around high levels of formalization and specialization, strict adherence to the chain of command, limited delegation of authority, and narrow spans of control give employees little autonomy. Controls in such organizations are tight and behavior will tend to vary within a narrow range. In contrast, organizations that are structured around limited specialization, low formalization, wide spans of control, and the like provide employees greater freedom and, thus, will be characterized by greater behavioral diversity.

Exhibit 13-11 visually summarizes what we've discussed in this chapter. Strategy, size, technology, and environment determine the type of structure an organization will have. For simplicity's sake, we can classify structural designs around one of two models: mechanistic or organic. The specific effect of structural designs on performance and satisfaction is moderated by employees' individual preferences and cultural norms.

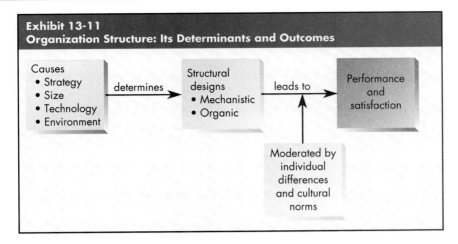

Exhibit 13-11
Organization Structure: Its Determinants and Outcomes

One last point: Managers need to be reminded that structural variables like work specialization, span of control, formalization, and centralization are objective characteristics that can be measured by organizational researchers. The findings and conclusions we've offered in this chapter, in fact, are directly a result of the work of these researchers. But employees don't objectively measure these structural characteristics! They observe things around them in an unscientific fashion and then form their own implicit models of what the organization's structure is like. How many people did they have to interview with before they were offered their jobs? How many people work in their departments and buildings? Is there an organization policy manual? If so, is it readily available and do people follow it closely? How is the organization and its top management described in newspapers and periodicals? Answers to questions such as these, when combined with an employee's past experiences and comments made by peers, lead members to form an overall subjective image of what their organization's structure is like. This image, though, may in no way resemble the organization's actual objective structural characteristics.

The importance of these **implicit models of organizational structure** should not be overlooked. As we noted in Chapter 3, people respond to their perceptions rather than objective reality. The research, for instance, on the relationship between many structural variables and subsequent levels of performance or job satisfaction is far from consistent. We explained some of this as being attributable to individual differences. However, an additional contributing cause to these inconsistent findings might be diverse perceptions of the objective characteristics. Researchers typically focus on actual levels of the various structural components, but these may be irrelevant if people interpret similar components differently. The bottom line, therefore, is to understand how employees interpret their organization's structure. That should prove a more meaningful predictor of their behavior than the objective characteristics themselves.

implicit models of organizational structure
Perceptions that people hold regarding structural variables formed by observing things around them in an unscientific fashion.

For Review

1. Why isn't work specialization an unending source of increased productivity?

2. All things being equal, which is more efficient, a wide or narrow span of control? Why?

3. In what ways can management departmentalize?

4. What is a matrix structure? When would management use it?

5. Contrast the network organization with the boundaryless organization.

6. What type of structure works best with an innovation strategy? A cost-minimization strategy? An imitation strategy?

7. Summarize the size–structure relationship.

8. Define and give an example of what is meant by the term *technology*.

9. Summarize the environment–structure relationship.

10. Explain the importance of the statement: "Employees form implicit models of organizational structure."

For Discussion

1. How is the typical large corporation of today organized in contrast to how that same organization was probably organized in the 1960s?

2. Do you think most employees prefer high formalization? Support your position.

3. If you were an employee in a matrix structure, what pluses do you think the structure would provide? What about minuses?

4. What could management do to make a bureaucracy more like a boundaryless organization?

5. What behavioral predictions would you make about people who worked in a "pure" boundaryless organization (if such a structure were ever to exist)?

Point

Small Is Beautiful

The Davids are beating up on the Goliaths. Big corporations are going the way of the dinosaurs because they're overly rigid, technologically obsolete, and too bureaucratic. They're being replaced by small, agile companies. These small organizations are the technology innovators, able to respond quickly to changing market opportunities, and have become the primary job generators in almost all developed countries.

In almost every major industry, the smaller and more agile firms are outperforming their larger competitors. In the airline industry, upstart Southwest Air continually outperforms the likes of American and United. The Fox Network has taken on ABC, CBS, and NBC with impressive results. In steel, small mini-mill operators like Nucor have proven to be far more efficient and responsive to change than big producers like U.S. Steel. And in the computer industry, giants like Digital and Apple are fighting for their lives against hundreds of small, entrepreneurial firms.

What's going on? The law of economies of scale is being repealed! The law of economies of scale argued that larger operations drove out smaller ones because, with large size, came greater efficiency. Fixed costs, for instance, could be spread over more units. Large companies could use standardization and mass production to produce the lowest-cost products. But that no longer applies because of market fragmentation, strategic alliances, and technology.

Niche markets have taken away the advantages of large size. Southwest can compete successfully against American and United because it doesn't try to match the big guys' full-service strategy. It doesn't use hubs, it doesn't transfer baggage, it doesn't compete in every market, it doesn't offer meals, and it provides no reserved seats.

Strategic alliances offer small firms the opportunity to share others' expertise and development costs, allowing little companies to compete with big ones. For example, many small North American book publishers don't have the money to develop marketing operations and sales staffs in Australia or Asia. By joining forces with publishers in those countries to market their books, they can behave like the big guys.

Technology is also taking away a lot of the advantage that used to go to size. Computer and satellite linkage and flexible manufacturing systems are examples of such technology. Quick & Reilly can execute orders as efficiently as Merrill Lynch through computer links to exchanges, even though it's a fraction of Merrill's size.

In today's increasingly dynamic environment, large size has become a serious handicap. It restricts the creativity to develop new products and services. It also limits job growth. More specifically, it's the small organizations that innovate and create jobs. For instance, the U.S. Bureau of the Census claims that the smallest firms—those with four or fewer employees—created virtually all the net new jobs in the United States between 1989 and 1991. These very small firms created 2.6 million net new jobs. In contrast, companies with 500 or more employees created only 122,000. All other business-size classes lost jobs.

Big companies are getting the message. They're laying off tens of thousands of employees. They're selling businesses that don't fit with their core competencies. And they're restructuring themselves to be more agile and responsive.

This argument is based on J. Case, "The Disciples of David Birch," *INC.*, January 1989, pp. 39–45; T. Peters, "Rethinking Scale," *California Management Review*, Fall 1992, pp. 7–28; and G. Gendron, "Small Is Beautiful! Big Is Best!" *INC.*, May 1995, pp. 39–49.

▄▶ *counterPoint* ◀▄

"Small Is Beautiful" Is a Myth!

It's now become the "conventional wisdom" to acknowledge that large organizations are at a disadvantage in today's dynamic environment. Their large size limits their agility. Additionally, competitive and technological forces have ganged up to take away the economies that derived from scale. Well, the conventional wisdom is wrong! The hard evidence shows that the importance of small businesses as job generators and as engines of technological dynamism has been greatly exaggerated. Moreover, large organizations have discovered how to become less rigid, more entrepreneurial, and less hierarchical while still maintaining the advantages that accrue to large size.

First, the research showing that small companies have been the prime job generators in recent years is flawed. The early data that were used exaggerated the incidence of startups and covered too short a period. It failed to recategorize companies once they grew or shrunk, which systematically inflated the relative importance of small firms. Additionally, the Bureau of the Census study classified all firms formed after 1989 in the 0-to-4-employee class, regardless of how many employees a firm had in 1991. Using the more common definition of small companies as those with fewer than 100 employees, the evidence indicates that the share of jobs held by small companies has remained virtually unchanged since the 1960s. The vast majority of job creation over time is contributed by a tiny fraction of new firms. Among the 245,000 U.S. businesses begun in 1985, 75 percent of the employment gains three years later were made by 735 companies (or .003 percent) of the group, and all of those 735 companies had more than 100 employees to begin with. This same pattern—new firms that are successful start out big—holds in the United Kingdom.

People like to cite computers as a high-tech industry dominated by innovative small firms. It isn't true. Only 5 percent of U.S. computer-related com-panies employ 500 workers or more (which includes companies like Intel and Microsoft), yet this 5 percent account for more than 90 percent of both jobs and sales in the industry. Incidentally, in Japan, computers have always been dominated by giants such as NEC, Toshiba, and Fujitsu.

It's true that the typical organization is getting smaller. The average American business establishment has shrunk dramatically during the last quarter-century—from 1,100 employees in 1967 to 630 in 1992. But what these number don't reveal is that these smaller establishments are increasingly part of a large, multilocation firm with the financial and technological resources to compete in a global marketplace. In other words, these smaller organizations are de facto part of the large enterprise, and this practice is going on throughout the world. For example, a study found that the 32 largest German manufacturing companies had in excess of a thousand legally independent subsidiaries and the number grew by almost 50 percent between 1971 and 1983.

Second, technology favors the big guys. Studies demonstrate that small firms turn out to be systematically backward when it comes to technology. For example, on every continent, the big companies are far more likely than the small ones to invest in computer-controlled factory automation.

Third, everyone agrees with the fact that large organizations are improving their flexibility by increasing their use of strategic alliances, interorganizational networks, and similar devices. For instance, Siemens, the huge German multinational, has strategic alliances with Fujitsu to make robotics, GTE in telecommunications, Philips to produce semiconductors, and with Microsoft to develop software. This worldwide trend, coupled with efforts to widen spans of control, decentralize decision making, cut vertical levels, and sell off or close operations that don't fit with the organization's primary purpose have made large firms increasingly agile and responsive.

This argument is based on B. Harrison, *Lean and Mean: The Changing Landscape of Corporate Power in the Age of Flexibility* (New York: Basic-Books, 1994). See also M.J. Mandel, "Land of the Giants," *Business Week*, September 11, 1995, pp. 34–35.

Learning about Yourself Exercise

Bureaucratic Orientation Test

Instructions: For each statement, check the response (either mostly agree or mostly disagree) that best represents your feelings.

	Mostly Agree	Mostly Disagree
1. I value stability in my job.	_____	_____
2. I like a predictable organization.	_____	_____
3. The best job for me would be one in which the future is uncertain.	_____	_____
4. The federal government would be a nice place to work.	_____	_____
5. Rules, policies, and procedures tend to frustrate me.	_____	_____
6. I would enjoy working for a company that employed 85,000 people worldwide.	_____	_____
7. Being self-employed would involve more risk than I'm willing to take.	_____	_____
8. Before accepting a job, I would like to see an exact job description.	_____	_____
9. I would prefer a job as a freelance house painter to one as a clerk for the Department of Motor Vehicles.	_____	_____
10. Seniority should be as important as performance in determining pay increases and promotion.	_____	_____
11. It would give me a feeling of pride to work for the largest and most successful company in its field.	_____	_____
12. Given a choice, I would prefer to make $50,000 per year as a vice president in a small company to $60,000 as a staff specialist in a large company.	_____	_____
13. I would regard wearing an employee badge with a number on it as a degrading experience.	_____	_____
14. Parking spaces in a company lot should be assigned on the basis of job level.	_____	_____
15. If an accountant works for a large organization, he or she cannot be a true professional.	_____	_____
16. Before accepting a job (given a choice), I would want to make sure that the company had a very fine program of employee benefits.	_____	_____
17. A company will probably not be successful unless it establishes a clear set of rules and procedures.	_____	_____
18. Regular working hours and vacations are more important to me than finding thrills on the job.	_____	_____
19. You should respect people according to their rank.	_____	_____
20. Rules are meant to be broken.	_____	_____

Turn to page A-29 for scoring directions and key.

Source: Adapted from A.J. DuBrin, *Human Relations: A Job Oriented Approach* 5th edition, © 1992. Reprinted with permission of Prentice Hall, Inc., Upper Saddle River, NJ.

Working with Others Exercise

Authority Figures

Purpose: To learn about one's experiences with and feelings about authority.
Time: Approximately 75 minutes.
Procedure:

1. Your instructor will separate class members into groups based on their birth order. Groups are formed consisting of "only children," "eldest," "middle," and "youngest," according to placement in families. Larger groups will be broken into smaller ones, with four or five members, to allow for freer conversation.

2. Each group member should talk about how he or she "typically reacts to the authority of others." Focus should be on specific situations that offer general information about how individuals deal with authority figures (for example, bosses, teachers, parents, or coaches). The group has 25 minutes to develop a written list of how the group generally deals with others' authority. Be sure to separate tendencies that group members share and those they do not.

3. Repeat Step 2 except this time discuss how group members "typically are as authority figures." Again make a list of shared characteristics.

4. Each group will share its general conclusions with the entire class.

5. Class discussion will focus on questions such as:
   a. What patterned differences have surfaced between the groups?
   b. What may account for these differences?
   c. What hypotheses might explain the connection between how individuals react to the authority of others and how they are as authority figures?

Source: This exercise is adapted from W.A. Kahn, "An Exercise of Authority," *Organizational Behavior Teaching Review*, vol. XIV, Issue 2, 1989–90, pp. 28–42. Reprinted with permission.

Ethical Dilemma Exercise

Employee Monitoring: How Far Is Too Far?

When does management's effort to control the actions of others become an invasion of privacy? Consider three cases.[33]

Employees at General Electric's answering center handle telephone inquiries from customers all day long. Those conversations are taped by GE and occasionally reviewed by its management.

The Internal Revenue Service's internal audit group monitors a computer log that shows employee access to taxpayers' accounts. This monitoring activity allows management to check and see what employees are doing on their computers.

The mayor of Colorado Springs, Colorado, reads the electronic mail messages that city council members send to each other from their homes.

Are any of these cases—monitoring calls, computer activities, or e-mail—an invasion of privacy? When does management overstep the bounds of decency and privacy by silently (even covertly) scrutinizing the behavior of its employees or associates?

Managers at GE and the IRS defend their practice in terms of ensuring quality, productivity, and proper employee behavior. GE can point to U.S. government statistics estimating that 10 million workers are being electronically monitored on their jobs. And silent surveillance of telephone calls can be used to help employees do their jobs better. One IRS audit of its Southeastern regional offices found that 166 employees took unauthorized looks at the tax returns of friends, neighbors, or celebrities. The mayor of Colorado Springs defended his actions by saying he was making sure that e-mail was not being used to circumvent his state's "open meeting" law that requires most council business to be conducted publicly.

When does management's need for information about employee performance cross over the line and interfere with a worker's right to privacy? For example, must employees be notified ahead of time that they will be monitored? Does management's right to protect its interests extend to electronic monitoring of every place a worker might be—bathrooms, locker rooms, and dressing rooms?

The ABB Way

C A S E

INCIDENT

If you ask Benny Karl-Erik Olsson where he is from today, he'll tell you Mexico. But nine months ago he was Venezuelan. Before that he was from Madrid, and before that, the 44-year-old executive was from Barcelona. In actuality, Olsson is of Swedish descent but born in South Africa.

Olsson's multiple ancestry is merely the result of having spent 20 years with Zurich-based ABB Asea Brown Boveri AG. Currently he's ABB's country manager in Mexico, one of 500 corporate missionaries that the worldwide builder of power plants, industrial factories, and infrastructure projects believes are essential to its survival against the likes of Siemens, General Electric, and Alcatel-Alsthom. These people—always multilingual—relocate from operation to operation, moving among the company's 5,000 profit centers in 140 countries. Their job? To cut costs, improve efficiency, and get local businesses in line with the ABB world view.

Few organizations have been as successful as ABB in creating a class of managers that gets global strategies to work with local operations. "Our strength comes from pulling together," says Percy Barnevik, the company's chairman and the person who masterminded the 1988 merger of a Swedish and Swiss firm that created ABB. He says, "if you can make this work real well, then you get a competitive edge out of the organization which is very, very difficult to copy."

Barnevik is trying to create a company with no geographic base—one that has many "home" markets and that can draw on expertise from around the globe. To glue the company together, he has created a set of managers like Olsson who can adapt to local cultures while executing ABB's global strategies.

Olsson's experience in Mexico illustrates some of the difficulties in trying to execute this unusual structural arrangement. ABB requires local business units, such as Mexico's motor factory, to report to Olsson and to a business area manager who sets motor strategy for ABB worldwide. The goals of the local factory can clash with worldwide priorities. It is up to managers like Olsson to sort out constant conflicts.

Olsson says his predecessor in Mexico too often made decisions that favored Mexican operations at the expense of ABB's worldwide businesses. For example, he had solicited bids from more than one ABB factory making equipment for power generators. That violated ABB's "allocation" rules, which dictate which ABB factories can supply other operations with components. Olsson's goal is to better balance the needs of the Mexican operations with needs of the overall corporation.

Questions

1. How would you classify the ABB structure? Defend your choice.
2. What are the advantages to this structure?
3. What are its disadvantages?
4. What kind of skills, abilities, and characteristics do you think are required to successfully do the type of job Olsson has?

This case is based on J. Guyon, "ABB Fuses Units with One Set of Values," The *Wall Street Journal*, October 2, 1996, p. A12.

ABCNEWS

The Palm Beach School District

Is Monica Yulhorn, superintendent of the Palm Beach School District, just the scapegoat for problems in her organization? Or is she the incompetent manager of a bloated bureaucracy, as her critics claim? Most of the evidence suggests Ms. Yulhorn is inept.

Palm Beach is the sixteenth largest school district in the United States. The district is projecting a $6 million shortfall this year and student test scores are down. Yet the district spends more per student than the national average. Here's a list of some of the criticism being directed at Ms. Yulhorn.

The district is wasting $100 million a year.

Yulhorn says she had to lay off 1,100 people because the district is short of funds. That's true but then she added back that many plus 2,600 more, calling some of them teachers, even though their jobs weren't in the classroom.

The district is paying more for supplies bought in bulk than could be obtained in retail stores.

Yulhorn is into dynasty building. Rather than using outside contractors to do work, she wants to hire more expensive and less qualified full-time people.

She wastes money on expensive consultants and travel for herself. For instance, in one five-month period, she hired 215 consultants and paid them $3.8 million, and a recent four-day convention in New Orleans cost the district $1,300.

Yulhorn isn't on top of what's happening in her district. Problems in communication occur between Yulhorn's office, area superintendents, principals, and teachers.

Yulhorn dismisses the comments made by outsiders and people she has fired. She says they're just angry and trying to further their self-interests. But the criticism is increasingly coming from within the school district. In a recent survey, 100 percent of the principals voted no confidence in Yulhorn; 98 percent of the assistant principals, 94 percent of the teachers, and even 84 percent of those on her own administrative staff voted no confidence.

Questions

1. What are the benefits of bureaucracy?
2. Would the employees in the Palm Beach School District be better off with less structure? Explain.
3. How does structure, in this case, shape the behavior of Ms. Yulhorn?

Source: Based on "School Budget Freeze," *ABC News Primetime*; aired on May 3, 1995.

WORK DESIGN

CHAPTER OUTLINE
Conceptual Frameworks for Analyzing Work Tasks
Technology and New Work Designs
Physical Working Conditions and Work Space Design
Work Redesign Options
Work Schedule Options

An optimist says,
"The glass is half
full." A pessimist
says, "It's half
empty." A
reengineering
consultant says,
"Looks like you've
got twice as much
glass as you need."
—Anonymous

LEARNING OBJECTIVES

After studying this chapter, you should be able to

1 Explain the job characteristics model

2 Contrast the social information processing model to the job characteristics model

3 Describe the role of the PDCA cycle in continuous improvement

4 Explain the current popularity of reengineering

5 Contrast reengineering and TQM

6 Describe the implications of flexible manufacturing systems on people who work within them

7 Identify who is affected by worker obsolescence

8 Explain the influence of work space design on employee behavior

9 Describe how a job can be enriched

10 Contrast the benefits and drawbacks to telecommuting from the employee's point of view

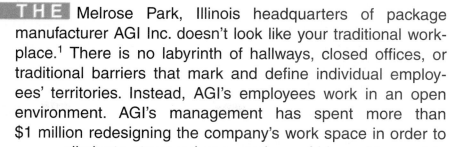

THE Melrose Park, Illinois headquarters of package manufacturer AGI Inc. doesn't look like your traditional workplace.[1] There is no labyrinth of hallways, closed offices, or traditional barriers that mark and define individual employees' territories. Instead, AGI's employees work in an open environment. AGI's management has spent more than $1 million redesigning the company's work space in order to eliminate structural connotations of hierarchies and to foster collaboration. Out went most of the walls, doors, and private offices, to be replaced with a relatively barrier-free environment.

The new offices are in a square with an oval track in the middle. Outside the oval is open space filled with modular office furniture. There are no walls, and the area is flooded with sunlight from skylights. Inside the oval's perimeter are executive offices with glass walls and no doors. And in the very center is a set of conference rooms where groups can meet and where tasks requiring privacy can be held. To further facilitate collaboration, no matter where employees are—at a co-worker's desk or on the plant floor—they have access to their computer files from the 32 computer terminals on the premises. Those employees who use laptops can plug into the company's network at any of 250 data ports.

AGI's CEO, Richard Block, planned the redesigned work space to encourage more participative problem solving and teamwork. He says it's working. Employees interact more often because there are fewer physical barriers. And the open workplace has encouraged the creation of ad hoc teams. For instance, when AGI's Atlanta account executive learned during a visit to headquarters that a client was disappointed with the color quality of a package, he brought his PowerBook down to film production and quickly assembled the production planner, printing supervisor, and a finishing supervisor. Then he called up his client file, including all correspondence, so he could compare the client's requests with AGI's production specifications. Once the group members solved the problem, they called the client for final approval.

Employees seem to like the open work space. By tearing down the physical barriers between workers and providing them with the information technology to work wherever necessary, employees find they can be more productive. And while some executives complained at first about the lack of privacy, they all now embrace the open environment. They have come to see how it makes their jobs easier. ◆

AGI is among a growing number of companies that are redesigning their work spaces in order to improve collaboration and communication. In this chapter, we discuss work space design in detail and explain how an employee's physical environment and work space layout can affect his or her work behavior. We also present several frameworks for analyzing jobs, demonstrate how technology is changing organizations and the jobs that people do, and conclude by showing how management can redesign jobs and work schedules in ways that can increase employee productivity and satisfaction.

Conceptual Frameworks for Analyzing Work Tasks

"Every day was the same thing," Frank Greer began. "Put the right passenger seat into Jeeps as they came down the assembly line, pop in four bolts locking the seat frame to the car body, then tighten the bolts with my electric wrench. Thirty cars and 120 bolts an hour, eight hours a day. I didn't care that they were paying me $18 an hour, I was going crazy. I did it for almost a year and a half. Finally, I just said to my wife that this isn't going to be the way I'm going to spend the rest of my life. My brain was turning to Jell-O on that job. So I quit. Now I work in a print shop and I make less than $12 an hour. But let me tell you, the work I do is really interesting. It challenges me! I look forward every morning to going to work again."

Frank Greer is acknowledging two facts we all know: (1) jobs are different and (2) some are more interesting and challenging than others. These facts have not gone unnoticed by OB researchers. They have responded by developing a number of **task characteristics theories** that seek to identify task characteristics of jobs, how these characteristics are combined to form different jobs, and the relationship of these task characteristics to employee motivation, satisfaction, and performance.

There are at least seven different task characteristics theories.[2] Fortunately, there is a significant amount of overlap between them.[3] For instance, Herzberg's motivation-hygiene theory and the research on the achievement need (both discussed in chapter 5) are essentially task characteristics theories. You'll remember that Herzberg argued that jobs that provided opportunities for achievement, recognition, responsibility, and the like would increase employee satisfaction. Similarly, McClelland demonstrated that high achievers performed best in jobs that offered personal responsibility, feedback, and moderate risks.

In this section, we review the three most important task characteristics theories—requisite task attributes theory, the job characteristics model, and the social information processing model.

Requisite Task Attributes Theory

The task characteristics approach began with the pioneering work of Turner and Lawrence in the mid-1960s.[4] They developed a research study to assess the effect of different kinds of jobs on employee satisfaction and absenteeism. They predicted that employees would prefer jobs that were complex and chal-

task characteristic theories
Seek to identify task characteristics of jobs, how these characteristics are combined to form different jobs, and their relationship to employee motivation, satisfaction, and performance.

lenging; that is, such jobs would increase satisfaction and result in lower absence rates. They defined job complexity in terms of six task characteristics: (1) variety; (2) autonomy; (3) responsibility; (4) knowledge and skill; (5) required social interaction; and (6) optional social interaction. The higher a job scored on these characteristics, according to Turner and Lawrence, the more complex it was.

Their findings confirmed their absenteeism prediction. Employees in high-complexity tasks had better attendance records. But they found no general correlation between task complexity and satisfaction—until they broke their data down by the background of employees. When individual differences in the form of urban-versus-rural background were taken into account, employees from urban settings were shown to be more satisfied with low-complexity jobs. Employees with rural backgrounds reported higher satisfaction in high-complexity jobs. Turner and Lawrence concluded that workers in larger communities had a variety of nonwork interests and thus were less involved and motivated by their work. In contrast, workers from smaller towns had fewer nonwork interests and were more receptive to the complex tasks of their jobs.

Turner and Lawrence's requisite task attributes theory was important for at least three reasons. First, they demonstrated that employees did respond differently to different types of jobs. Second, they provided a preliminary set of task attributes by which jobs could be assessed. And third, they focused attention on the need to consider the influence of individual differences on employees' reaction to jobs.

The Job Characteristics Model

Turner and Lawrence's requisite task attributes theory laid the foundation for what is today the dominant framework for defining task characteristics and understanding their relationship to employee motivation, performance, and satisfaction. That is Hackman and Oldham's **job characteristics model** (JCM).[5]

According to the JCM, any job can be described in terms of five core job dimensions, defined as follows:

1. **Skill variety**: The degree to which the job requires a variety of different activities so the worker can use a number of different skills and talent
2. **Task identity**: The degree to which the job requires completion of a whole and identifiable piece of work
3. **Task significance**: The degree to which the job has a substantial impact on the lives or work of other people
4. **Autonomy**: The degree to which the job provides substantial freedom, independence, and discretion to the individual in scheduling the work and in determining the procedures to be used in carrying it out
5. **Feedback**: The degree to which carrying out the work activities required by the job results in the individual obtaining direct and clear information about the effectiveness of his or her performance

Exhibit 14-1 offers examples of job activities that rate high and low for each characteristic.

Exhibit 14-2 on page 519 presents the model. Notice how the first three dimensions—skill variety, task identity, and task significance—combine to

---

job characteristics model
Identifies five job characteristics and their relationship to personal and work outcomes.

skill variety
The degree to which the job requires a variety of different activities.

task identity
The degree to which the job requires completion of a whole and identifiable piece of work.

task significance
The degree to which the job has a substantial impact on the lives or work of other people.

autonomy
The degree to which the job provides substantial freedom and discretion to the individual in scheduling the work and in determining the procedures to be used in carrying it out.

feedback
The degree to which carrying out the work activities required by a job results in the individual obtaining direct and clear information about the effectiveness of his or her performance.

Exhibit 14-1 Examples of High and Low Job Characteristics

Skill Variety

High variety	The owner-operator of a garage who does electrical repair, rebuilds engines, does body work, and interacts with customers
Low variety	A body shop worker who sprays paint eight hours a day

Task Identity

High identity	A cabinet maker who designs a piece of furniture, selects the wood, builds the object, and finishes it to perfection
Low identity	A worker in a furniture factory who operates a lathe solely to make table legs

Task Significance

High significance	Nursing the sick in a hospital intensive care unit
Low significance	Sweeping hospital floors

Autonomy

High autonomy	A telephone installer who schedules his or her own work for the day, makes visits without supervision, and decides on the most effective techniques for a particular installation
Low autonomy	A telephone operator who must handle calls as they come according to a routine, highly specified procedure

Feedback

High feedback	An electronics factory worker who assembles a radio and then tests it to determine if it operates properly
Low feedback	An electronics factory worker who assembles a radio and then routes it to a quality control inspector who tests it for proper operation and makes needed adjustments

Source: Adapted from G. Johns, *Organizational Behavior: Understanding and Managing Life at Work*, 4th ed. Copyright © 1981 by HarperCollins College Publishers. Reprinted by permission of Addison-Wesley Educational Publishers, Inc.

create meaningful work. That is, if these three characteristics exist in a job, we can predict that the incumbent will view the job as being important, valuable, and worthwhile. Notice, too, that jobs that possess autonomy give job incumbents a feeling of personal responsibility for the results and that, if a job provides feedback, employees will know how effectively they are performing. From a motivational standpoint, the model says that internal rewards are obtained by individuals when they *learn* (knowledge of results) that they *personally* (experienced responsibility) have performed well on a task that they *care* about (experienced meaningfulness).[6] The more that these three psychological states are present, the greater will be employees' motivation, performance, and satisfaction, and the lower their absenteeism and likelihood of leaving the organization. As Exhibit 14-2 shows, the links between the job dimensions and the outcomes are moderated or adjusted by the strength of the individual's growth need, that is, by the employee's desire for self-esteem and self-actualization. This means that individuals with a high growth need are more likely to experience the psychological states when their jobs are enriched than are their counterparts with a low growth need. Moreover, they will respond more positively to the psychological states when they are present than will individuals with a low growth need.

motivating potential score
A predictive index suggesting the motivation potential in a job.

The core dimensions can be combined into a single predictive index, called the **motivating potential score** (MPS). Its computation is shown in Exhibit 14-3.

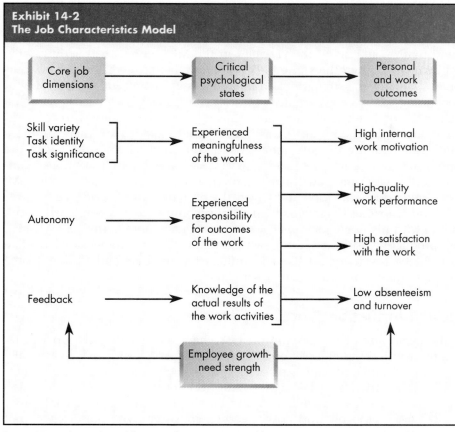

Exhibit 14-2
The Job Characteristics Model

Source: J.R. Hackman, G.R. Oldham, *Work Design,* (excerpted from pages 78–80.) © 1980 by Addison-Wesley Publishing Co., Inc. Reprinted by permission of Addison-Wesley Longman Inc.

Jobs that are high on motivating potential must be high on at least one of the three factors that lead to experienced meaningfulness, and they must be high on both autonomy and feedback. If jobs score high on motivating potential, the model predicts that motivation, performance, and satisfaction will be positively affected, while the likelihood of absence and turnover will be lessened.

The job characteristics model has been well researched. Most of the evidence supports the general framework of the theory—that is, there is a multiple set of job characteristics and these characteristics impact behavioral outcomes.[7] But there is still considerable debate around the five specific core dimensions in the JCM, the multiplicative properties of the MPS, and the validity of growth-need strength as a moderating variable.

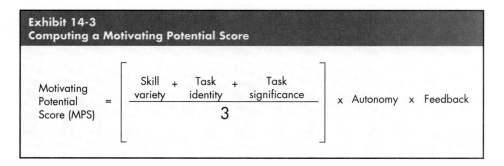

Exhibit 14-3
Computing a Motivating Potential Score

$$\text{Motivating Potential Score (MPS)} = \left[\frac{\text{Skill variety} + \text{Task identity} + \text{Task significance}}{3} \right] \times \text{Autonomy} \times \text{Feedback}$$

There is some question as to whether or not task identity adds to the model's predictive ability,[8] and there is evidence suggesting that skill variety may be redundant with autonomy.[9] Furthermore, a number of studies have found that by adding all the variables in the MPS, rather than adding some and multiplying by others, the MPS becomes a better predictor of work outcomes.[10] Finally, the strength of an individual's growth needs as a meaningful moderating variable has recently been called into question.[11] Other variables, such as the presence or absence of social cues, perceived equity with comparison groups, and propensity to assimilate work experience,[12] may be more valid in moderating the job characteristics–outcome relationship. Given the current state of research on moderating variables, one should be cautious in unequivocally accepting growth-need strength as originally included in the JCM.

Where does this leave us? Given the current state of evidence, we can make the following statements with relative confidence: (1) People who work on jobs with high-core job dimensions are generally more motivated, satisfied, and productive than are those who do not. (2) Job dimensions operate through the psychological states in influencing personal and work outcome variables rather than influencing them directly.[13]

Social Information Processing Model

At the beginning of this section on task characteristics theories, do you remember Frank Greer complaining about his former job on the Jeep assembly line? Would it surprise you to know that one of Frank's best friends, Russ Wright, is still working at Jeep, doing the same job that Frank did, and that Russ thinks his job is perfectly fine? Probably not! Why? Because, consistent with our discussion of perception in chapter 3, we recognize that people can look at the same job and evaluate it differently. The fact that people respond to their jobs as *they perceive them* rather than to the *objective* jobs themselves is the central thesis in our third task characteristics theory. It's called the **social information processing (SIP) model**.[14]

◆ People can look at the same job and evaluate it differently.

social information processing (SIP) model
Employees adopt attitudes and behaviors in response to the social cues provided by others with whom they have contact.

The SIP model argues that employees adopt attitudes and behaviors in response to the social cues provided by others with whom they have contact. These others can be co-workers, supervisors, friends, family members, or customers. For instance, Gary Ling got a summer job working in a British Columbia sawmill. Since jobs were scarce and this one paid particularly well, Gary arrived on his first day of work highly motivated. Two weeks later, however, his motivation was quite low. What happened was that his co-workers consistently bad-mouthed their jobs. They said the work was boring, that having to clock in and out proved management didn't trust them, and that supervisors never listened to their opinions. The objective characteristics of Gary's job had not changed in the two-week period; rather, Gary had reconstructed reality based on messages he had received from others.

A number of studies generally confirm the validity of the SIP model.[15] For instance, it has been shown that employee motivation and satisfaction can be manipulated by such subtle actions as a co-worker or boss commenting on the existence or absence of job features like difficulty, challenge, and autonomy. So managers should give as much (or more) attention to employees' perceptions of their jobs as to the actual characteristics of those jobs. They might spend more time telling employees how interesting and important their jobs are. And managers should also not be surprised that newly hired employees and people transferred or promoted to a new position are more likely to be receptive to social information than are those with greater seniority.

Technology and New Work Designs

We introduced the term *technology* in the previous chapter's discussion of why structures differ. We said it was how an organization transfers its inputs into outputs. In recent years, the term has become widely used by economists, managers, consultants, and business analysts to describe machinery and equipment that utilizes sophisticated electronics and computers to produce those outputs.

The common theme among new technologies in the workplace is that they substitute machinery for human labor in transforming inputs into outputs. This substitution of capital for labor has been going on essentially nonstop since the industrial revolution began in the mid-1800s. For instance, the introduction of electricity allowed textile factories to introduce mechanical looms that could produce cloth far faster and more cheaply than was previously possible when the looms were powered by individuals. But it's been the computerization of equipment and machinery in the last quarter-century that has been the prime mover in reshaping the twentieth-century workplace. Automated teller machines, for example, have replaced tens of thousands of human tellers in banks. Ninety-eight percent of the spot welds on new Ford Tauruses are performed by robots, not people. Many cars now come equipped with on-board computers that diagnose problems in seconds that used to take hours for mechanics to diagnose. IBM has built a plant in Austin, Texas, that can produce laptop computers without the help of a single worker. Everything from the time parts arrive at the IBM plant to the final packing of finished products is completely automated. And an increasing number of companies, small and large alike, are turning to multimedia and interactive technology for employee training.

This book is concerned with the behavior of people at work. No coverage of this topic today would be complete without discussing how recent

THE WALL STREET JOURNAL

COCHRAN!

"Cool! A keyboard that writes without a printer."

Exhibit 14-4

Source: *Wall Street Journal*, October 11, 1995. With permission from Cartoon Features Syndicate.

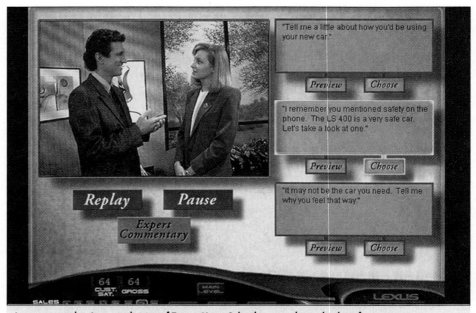

"Tell me a little about how you'd be using your new car."

Preview   Choose

"I remember you mentioned safety on the phone. The LS 400 is a very safe car. Let's take a look at one."

Preview   Choose

"It may not be the car you need. Tell me why you feel that way."

Preview   Choose

Replay   Pause

Expert Commentary

Luxury car maker Lexus, a division of Toyota Motor Sales, has turned to technology for training its salespeople. Computerized simulation exercises help salespeople develop their interpersonal skills through buyer/seller role-playing simulations. Trainees learn how to conduct honest negotiations with buyers, how to treat customers with respect and courtesy, and how to tailor a presentation to a customer's specific interest, as shown in this photo. The company's Fact Lab provides product information about Lexus and competing models, equipping salespeople with the knowledge necessary to achieve the Lexus goal of "complete customer satisfaction."

advances in technology are changing the workplace and affecting the work lives of employees. In this section, we'll look at four specific issues related to technology and work. These are TQM and continuous improvement processes, reengineering, flexible manufacturing systems, and worker obsolescence.

Continuous Improvement Processes

In chapter 1, we described total quality management (TQM) as a philosophy of management that's driven by the constant attainment of customer satisfaction through the continuous improvement of all organizational processes. Managers in many organizations, especially in North America, have been criticized for accepting a level of performance that is below perfection. TQM, however, argues that *good* isn't *good enough*! To dramatize this point, it's easy to assume that 99.9 percent error-free performance represents the highest standards of excellence. Yet it doesn't look so impressive when you recognize that this standard would result in the U.S. Post Office losing 2,000 pieces of mail per hour, or U.S. doctors performing 500 incorrect surgical operations per week, or two plane crashes per day at O'Hare Airport in Chicago![16]

TQM programs seek to achieve continuous process improvements so that variability is constantly reduced. When you eliminate variations, you increase the uniformity of the product or service. This, in turn, results in lower costs and higher quality. For instance, Advanced Filtration Systems Inc., of Champaign, Illinois, recently cut the number of product defects—as determined by a customer quality audit—from 26.5 per 1,000 units to zero over four years.

And that occurred during a period when monthly unit production tripled and the number of workers declined by 20 percent.

Continuous improvement runs counter to the more historical American management approach of seeing work projects as being linear—with a beginning and an end. For example, American managers traditionally looked at cost cutting as a short-term project. They set a goal of cutting costs by 20 percent, achieved it, and then said: "Whew! Our cost cutting is over." The Japanese, on the other hand, have regarded cost control as something that never ends. The search for continual improvement creates a race without a finish line.

The search for never-ending improvement requires a circular approach rather than a linear one. This is illustrated in the Plan-Do-Check-Act (PDCA) cycle shown in Exhibit 14-5.[17] Management plans a change, does it, checks the results and, depending on the outcome, acts to standardize the change or begin the cycle of improvement again with new information. This cycle treats all organizational processes as being in a constant state of improvement.

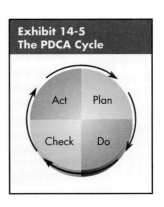

**Exhibit 14-5
The PDCA Cycle**

Eaton Corporation, a major manufacturer of automobile components, has adopted the PDCA cycle throughout the company.[18] Management encourages its workers to take thousands of small steps to incrementally improve the products they make and the processes used to make them. This extends to office workers who haggle over utility rates, challenge local tax assessments, scrutinize inventories, and eliminate paperwork. Continuous improvement helped Eaton increase its annual productivity between 1983 and 1992 by 3 percent a year compared to the U.S. average of 1.9 percent.

As literally tens of thousands of organizations introduce TQM and continuous process improvement, what does it mean for employees and their jobs? It means they're no longer able to rest on their previous accomplishments and successes. So, for some people, they may experience increased stress from a work climate that no longer accepts complacency with the status quo. A race with no finish line means a race that's never over, which creates constant tension. While this tension may be positive for the organization (remember *functional conflict* from chapter 12), the pressures from an unrelenting search for process improvements can create anxiety and stress in some employees. Probably the most significant implication for employees is that management will look to them as the prime source for improvement ideas. Employee involvement programs, therefore, are part and parcel of TQM. Empowered work teams who have hands-on involvement in process improvement, for instance, are widely used in those organizations that have introduced TQM.

Reengineering Work Processes

We also introduced reengineering in chapter 1. We described it as considering how things would be done if you could start all over from scratch.

The term *reengineering* comes from the historical process of taking apart an electronics product and designing a better version. Michael Hammer coined the term for organizations. When he found companies using computers simply to automate outdated processes, rather than finding fundamentally better ways of doing things, he realized the same principles could be applied to business. So, as applied to organizations, reengineering means management should start with a clean sheet of paper—rethinking and redesigning those processes by which the organization creates value and does work, ridding itself of operations that have become antiquated in the computer age.[19]

KEY ELEMENTS Three key elements of reengineering are identifying an organization's distinctive competencies, assessing core processes, and reorganizing horizontally by process.

distinctive competencies
Defines what it is that the organization is more superior at delivering than its competition.

An organization's **distinctive competencies** define what it is that the organization is more superior at delivering than its competition. Examples might include superior store locations, a more efficient distribution system, higher-quality products, more knowledgeable sales personnel, or superior technical support. Dell Computer, for instance, differentiates itself from its competitors by emphasizing high-quality hardware, comprehensive service and technical support, and low prices. Why is identifying distinctive competencies so important? Because it guides decisions regarding what activities are crucial to the organization's success.

Management also needs to assess the core processes that clearly add value to the organization's distinctive competencies. These are the processes that transform materials, capital, information, and labor into products and services that the customer values. When the organization is viewed as a series of processes, ranging from strategic planning to after-sales customer support, management can determine to what degree each adds value. Not surprisingly, this **process value analysis** typically uncovers a whole lot of activities that add little or nothing of value and whose only justification is "we've always done it this way."

process value analysis
Determination to what degree each organizational process adds value to the organization's distinctive competencies.

Reengineering requires management to reorganize around horizontal processes. This means cross-functional and self-managed teams. It means focusing on processes rather than functions. So, for instance, the vice president/marketing might become the "process owner of finding and keeping customers."[20] And it also means cutting out levels of middle management. As Hammer pointed out, "Managers are not value-added. A customer never buys a product because of the caliber of management. Management is, by definition, indirect. So if possible, less is better. One of the goals of reengineering is to minimize the necessary amount of management."[21]

WHY REENGINEERING NOW? Isn't reengineering something management should have been doing all along? Why has it become such a hot topic in the 1990s? The answers, according to Michael Hammer, are a changing global environment and organizational structures that had gotten top heavy.[22]

Traditional mechanistic organizations worked fine in times of stable growth. Activities could be fragmented and specialized to gain economic efficiencies. This described the environment faced by most North American organizations in the 1950s, 1960s, and much of the 1970s. But most organizations today operate in global conditions of overcapacity. Customers are much more informed and sophisticated than they were 30 years ago. Moreover, markets, production, and capital are all globally mobile. Investors in Australia, for example, can put their money into opportunities in Japan, Canada, or anywhere else in the world if they see better returns than they can get at home. Global customers now demand quality, service, and low cost. If *you* can't provide it, they'll get it from someone else.

Work specialization, functional departments, narrow spans of control, and the like drove down direct labor costs but the bureaucracies they created had massive overhead costs. That is, to coordinate all the fragmentation and specialization, the organization had to create numerous levels of middle management to glue together the fragmented pieces. So while bureaucracies drove down costs at the operating level, they required increasingly expensive coordinating systems. Those organizations that introduced teams, decentralized decisions, widened spans of control, and flattened structures became more efficient and challenged the traditional ways of doing things.

REENGINEERING VS. TQM   Is reengineering just a another term for TQM? No! They do have some common characteristics.[23] They both, for instance, emphasize processes and satisfying the customer. After that, they diverge radically. This is evident in their goals and the means they use for achieving their goals.

TQM seeks incremental improvements, while reengineering looks for quantum leaps in performance. That is, the former is essentially about improving something that is basically okay; the latter is about taking something that is irrelevant, throwing it out, and starting over. And the means the two approaches use are totally different. TQM relies on bottom-up, participative decision making in both the planning of a TQM program and its execution. Reengineering, on the other hand, is initially driven by top management. When reengineering is complete, the workplace is largely self-managed. But getting there is a very autocratic, nondemocratic process. Reengineering's supporters argue that it has to be this way because the level of change that the process demands is highly threatening to people and they aren't likely to accept it voluntarily. When top management commits to reengineering, employees have no choice. As Hammer is fond of saying, "you either get on the train, or we'll run over you with the train."[24] Of course, autocratically imposed change is likely to face employee resistance. While there is no easy solution to the resistance that top-down change creates, some of the techniques presented in chapter 17 in our discussion of overcoming resistance to change can be helpful.

IMPLICATIONS FOR EMPLOYEES   Reengineering is rapidly gaining momentum in business and industry.[25] A recent survey found that, among manufacturing firms, 44 percent of respondents indicated they are now reengineering or considering doing so. Among utilities and insurance companies, the responses were 48 and 52 percent, respectively.

Some of the companies that have implemented reengineering in at least some of their divisions include Motorola, Xerox, Ford, Banc One, Banca di

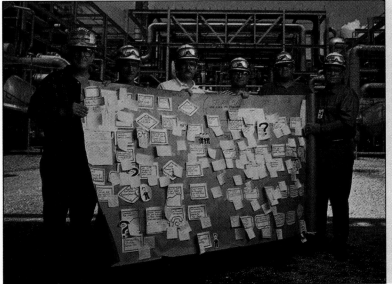

Top management at Union Carbide's industrial chemicals division led the drive to reengineer work processes in plant and equipment maintenance, which accounted for 30 percent of costs. Directed to work in teams and to set ambitious cost-cutting goals, employees (shown here) worked out the details of their new work process by developing new repair and maintenance procedures. The reengineering effort saved Union Carbide $20 million, 50 percent more than management's target. Companywide, Union Carbide has used reengineering to cut $400 million out of fixed costs over a recent three-year period.

America e di Italia, AT&T, Siemens, KPMG Peat Marwick, Hallmark, and the Commonwealth life insurance group. Hallmark, for instance, cut the time it takes to get a new product to market down from two years to a few months.[26] And Commonwealth now has 1,100 people doing the work that 1,900 used to do, even though its business has risen 25 percent.[27]

Reengineering's popularity isn't surprising. In today's highly competitive global marketplace, companies are finding that they're forced to reengineer their work processes if they're going to survive. And employees will "have to get on the train."

Lots of people are going to lose their jobs as a direct result of reengineering efforts. Just how many depends on the pace at which organizations adopt the new techniques. Some experts say that reengineering will eliminate from 1 million to 2.5 million jobs each year for the foreseeable future.[28] Undoubtedly much of the downsizing movement can be directly traced to reengineering efforts. But regardless of the number, the impact won't be uniform across the organization. Staff support jobs, especially middle managers, will be most vulnerable. So, too, will clerical jobs in service industries. For instance, one knowledgeable observer predicts that reengineering will reduce employment in commercial banks and thrift institutions by 30 to 40 percent during the 1990s.[29]

◆ Those employees that keep their jobs after reengineering will find that they aren't the same jobs any longer.

Those employees that keep their jobs after reengineering will find that they aren't the same jobs any longer. These new jobs will typically require a wider range of skills, include more interaction with customers and suppliers, offer greater challenge, contain increased responsibilities, and provide higher pay. However, the three to five-year period it takes to implement reengineering is usually tough on employees. They suffer from uncertainty and anxiety associated with taking on new tasks and having to discard long-established work practices and formal social networks.

Flexible Manufacturing Systems

They look like something out of a science-fiction movie in which remote-controlled carts deliver a basic casting to a computerized machining center. With robots positioning and repositioning the casting, the machining center calls upon its hundreds of tools to perform varying operations that turn the casting into a finished part. Completed parts, each a bit different from the others, are finished at a rate of one every 90 seconds. Neither skilled machinists nor conventional machine tools are used. Nor are there any costly delays for changing dies or tools in this factory. A single machine can make dozens or even hundreds of different parts in any order management wants. Welcome to the world of **flexible manufacturing systems**.[30]

flexible manufacturing system Integration of computer-aided design, engineering, and manufacturing to produce low-volume products at mass-production costs.

In a global economy, those manufacturing organizations that can respond rapidly to change have a competitive advantage. They can, for instance, better meet the diverse needs of customers and deliver products faster than their competitors. When customers were willing to accept standardized products, fixed assembly lines made sense. But nowadays, flexible technologies are increasingly necessary to compete effectively.

The unique characteristic of flexible manufacturing systems is that by integrating computer-aided design, engineering, and manufacturing, they can produce low-volume products for customers at a cost comparable to what had been previously possible only through mass production. Flexible manufactur-

A flexible manufacturing system at IBM's plant in Charlotte, North Carolina, can produce 27 different computer products at the same time. The automated assembly lines are controlled by computer instructions that vary based on diverse customer needs. The computers also give employees assembly instructions. This flexible system brings efficiency to IBM's manufacturing process and helps the company deliver products to customers more quickly than competitors.

ing systems are, in effect, repealing the laws of economies of scale. Management no longer has to mass-produce thousands of identical products to achieve low per-unit production costs. With flexible manufacturing, when management wants to produce a new part, it doesn't change machines—it just changes the computer program.

Some automated plants can build a wide variety of flawless products and switch from one product to another on cue from a central computer. John Deere, for instance, has a $1.5 billion automated factory that can turn out ten basic tractor models with as many as 3,000 options without plant shutdowns for retooling. National Bicycle Industrial Co., which sells its bikes under the Panasonic brand, uses flexible manufacturing to produce any of 11,231,862 variations on 18 models of racing, road, and mountain bikes in 199 color patterns and an almost unlimited number of sizes. This allows Panasonic to provide almost customized bikes at mass-produced prices.[31]

What do flexible manufacturing systems mean for people who have to work within them? They require a different breed of industrial employee.[32] Workers in flexible manufacturing plants need more training and higher skills. This is because there are fewer employees, so each has to be able to do a greater variety of tasks. For instance, at a flexible Carrier plant in Arkansas, which makes compressors for air conditioners, all employees undergo six weeks of training before they start their jobs. This training includes learning to read blueprints, math such as fractions and metric calculations, statistical process-control methods, some computer skills, and solving the problems involved in dealing with fellow workers. In addition to higher skills, employees in flexible plants are typically organized into teams and given considerable decision-making discretion. Consistent with the objective of high flexibility, these plants tend to have organic structures. They decentralize authority into the hands of the operating teams.

Worker Obsolescence

Changes in technology have cut the shelf life of most employees' skills. A factory worker or clerical employee in the 1950s could learn one job and be reasonably sure that his or her skills would be adequate to do that job for most of his or her work life. That certainly is no longer true. New technologies driven by computers, reengineering, TQM, and flexible manufacturing systems are changing the demands of jobs and the skills employees need to do them.

Repetitive tasks like those traditionally performed on assembly lines and by low-skilled office clerks will continue to be automated. And a good number of jobs will be upgraded. For instance, as most managers and professionals take on the task of writing their own memos and reports using word processing software, the traditional secretary's job will be upgraded to become more of an administrative assistant. Those secretaries that aren't equipped to take on these expanded roles will be displaced.

Reengineering, as we previously noted, is producing significant increases in employee productivity. The redesign of work processes is achieving higher output with fewer workers. And these reengineered jobs require different skills. Employees who are computer illiterate, have poor interpersonal skills, or can't work autonomously will increasingly find themselves ill prepared for the demands of new technologies.

Keep in mind that the obsolescence phenomenon doesn't exclude managers. Those middle managers who merely acted as conduits in the chain of command between top management and the operating floor are being eliminated. And new skills—for example, coaching, negotiating, and building teams—are becoming absolute necessities for every manager.

Finally, software is changing the jobs of many professionals, including lawyers, doctors, accountants, financial planners, and librarians.[33] Software programs will allow laypeople to use specialized knowledge to solve routine problems themselves or opt for a software-armed paraprofessional. Particularly vulnerable are those professionals who do standardized jobs. A lot of legal work, for instance, consists of writing standard contracts and other routine activities. These tasks will be done inside law firms by computers and paralegals; they might even be done by clients themselves, using software designed to prepare wills, trusts, incorporations, and partnerships. Software packages, such as TurboTax, will continue to take a lot of work away from professional accountants. And hospitals are using software to help doctors make their diagnoses. Punch in a patient's age, sex, lab results, and symptoms; answer a set of structured questions; and a $995 program called Illiad will draw on its knowledge of nine subspecialties of internal medicine to diagnose the patient's problem. These examples demonstrate that even the knowledge of highly trained professionals can become obsolete. As the world changes, professionals will also need to change if they're to survive.

> ◆ Software is changing the jobs of many professionals, including lawyers, doctors, accountants, financial planners, and librarians.

Physical Working Conditions and Work Space Design

Did you ever try to study for an exam in a library when the temperature was uncomfortably high? Or have you tried studying at home while family or friends talked loudly in an adjacent room? Did you find it hard to concentrate? If so, then you understand how employees might similarly be affected by their physical work setting.

Architects, industrial engineers, and office designers have known for decades that factors like temperature, noise level, and the physical layout of the work space influence an employee's performance. But it's only been in the past couple of decades that OB researchers have come to the same conclusion. The following briefly summarizes the research evidence linking the physical environment and work space design to employee performance and satisfaction.[34]

Physical Environment

At the turn of the century, "sweat shops" were common. Employees regularly toiled under adverse conditions such as extreme temperatures, poor lighting, polluted air, or cramped work spaces. Few employees in developed countries face such conditions today. We tend to take for granted that organizations will provide their employees with safe, healthy, and comfortable physical workplaces. Yet environmental conditions vary considerably from office to office and from factory to factory. Moreover, the evidence indicates that even relatively modest variations in temperature, noise, lighting, or air quality can exert appreciable effects on employee performance and attitudes.[35] As you review the evidence, keep in mind that these issues are probably more important today than they were just ten or twenty years ago. Why? Because so many people now work at home, and few home offices have had the benefit of professional layout and design that typically goes into most formal workplaces.

◆ Even relatively modest variations in temperature, noise, lighting, or air quality can exert appreciable effects on employee performance and attitudes.

TEMPERATURE   The effects of heat on performance of people performing heavy *physical* activities have been well documented.[36] But there are negative effects on employees doing *mental* tasks as well.[37] In contrasting individuals working in 95-degree (F) temperatures versus 70 degrees, the former condition produced more errors, with the difference becoming especially great as the number of hours of exposure extended beyond three.

The effects of cold are not as severe. The performance of manual tasks is not affected until skin temperatures fall below 55 degrees. On mental tasks, the available evidence suggests that cold is relatively unimportant.[38]

Temperature is one variable where large individual differences exist. One person's "heavenly" temperature is someone else's "hell." So, to maximize productivity, it's important that employees work in an environment in which temperature is regulated so as to fall within an individual's acceptable range. This implies some justification for creating individualized, temperature-controlled work spaces. It also suggest that organizations have dress codes that are flexible enough to allow employees to dress according to their own physical needs.

NOISE   Noise intensity or loudness is measured by decibels, which is a logarithmic scale. A 10-decibel difference in intensity is actually a tenfold difference in sound level. The evidence from noise studies indicates that constant or predictable noises do not *generally* cause deterioration in work performance.[39] If there is, it is at levels of about 90 decibels, which is equivalent to the noise generated by a subway train at 20 feet. To put this in perspective, the typical decibel level in an accounting office is less than 60 decibels, and the noise levels in printing press plants are rarely in excess of 85 decibels.[40]

In contrast, the effects of unpredictable noise appear to be uniformly negative. Such noises tend to interfere with an employee's ability to concentrate and pay attention.[41] Loud and unpredictable noises also tend to increase excitation and lead to reduced job satisfaction.[42]

Most offices and factories have noise levels in the low to moderate range. However, where levels are high or unpredictable, organizations should consider installing sound-absorbent surfaces (such as acoustical ceilings, carpets, and drapes) and equipment reflecting recent developments in white-sound technology that mask noise.

LIGHTING You know how reading in the dark puts a strain on your eyes. You undoubtedly study better with good light rather than dim illumination. But what is the optimum lighting level? And does performance improve in a linear fashion as light intensity goes from low to moderate to high?

The right light intensity depends upon task difficulty and required accuracy.[43] For difficult tasks that require attention to detail, illumination levels as high as 100 to 150 footcandles are typically appropriate. This would include activities like keyboarding, number verification, and proofreading. Difficult inspection tasks, such as checking for flaws in automobile paint, might require 500 footcandles. Loading and unloading materials, on the other hand, can be done effectively with 20 footcandles of light.

The right level of light intensity also is dependent on employee age.[44] Gains in performance at higher levels of illumination are greater for older than younger employees.

Finally, the benefits from increased lighting are not linear.[45] The benefits are greatest at relatively low levels of illumination, and decrease in magnitude as lighting increases to moderate and then high levels. You should expect only modest effects from increased lighting once some minimal level of illumination has been attained.

AIR QUALITY It's a well-established fact that breathing polluted air has adverse effects on personal health.[46] Polluted air in cities such as Los Angeles, Phoenix, Denver, Mexico City, and Athens bring on headaches, burning eyes, fatigue, irritability, depression, and impaired judgment. To the extent that various pollutants are found in higher concentrations in work settings than in the community at large, employees can be at serious personal health risk.

In regard to job performance, the evidence indicates that several pollutants can reduce output or accuracy on many tasks. For example, exposure to carbon monoxide at concentrations commonly found along major roads has been found to significantly slow human reaction time and to reduce manual dexterity. This argues for organizations that have polluted workplaces to install air filtration equipment. Such filters can remove up to 99.75 percent of airborne particulate matter.

The trend toward smoke-free workplaces is a response to the negative effects of passive smoke. For instance, nonsmokers exposed to high concentrations of cigarette smoking (i.e., passive smoke) report increased feelings of irritation, fatigue, and anxiety.

A final note: People seem to adjust to polluted air. People become less concerned about, and feel less threatened by, high levels of pollution following prolonged exposure to such conditions.

Work Space Design

Now we turn to the actual design of the employee's work space. Specifically, we'll look at how the amount of that work space, its arrangement or layout, and the degree of privacy it provides affect an employee's performance and satisfaction.

SIZE Size is defined by the square feet per employee. While you might think that the task to be accomplished would be the major factor in determining how much space is provided for an employee, this is not the case. Status is the most important determinant of space.[47] At least in North America, the higher an individual is in the organization's hierarchy, the more space he or she typically gets.

The fact that status and space are highly correlated demonstrates the symbolic value that the amount of space one controls plays. By merely walking into a manager's office and visually calculating his or her office size, you can immediately gauge this manager's authority level.

In the management ranks, office space may be the most cherished and fought over reward that the organization offers, after money and titles. Because it connotes achievement and rank, it is not unusual for organizations, especially large ones, to define square footage for each level in the hierarchy. Senior executives, for instance, may be assigned 800 square feet plus 300 square feet for a private secretary's office. A section manager may get 400 square feet, a unit manager 120, and supervisors only 80 square feet. Clerical personnel may be relegated to sharing an eight-person office. Again, there is no necessary relationship between square footage required to do one's job and the job assigned. And because status is the key determinant of workspace size, deviations from this pattern are likely to decrease job satisfaction for those individuals who perceive themselves on the short end of the discrepancy.

ARRANGEMENT While size measures the amount of space per employee, arrangement refers to the distance between people and facilities. As we'll show, the arrangement of one's workplace is important primarily because it significantly influences social interaction.

Furniture on wheels gives employees of Minneapolis-based ad agency Fallon McElligott flexibility in arranging their work space according to their task needs. For privacy, employees work in their office cubicles from desks that are specially equipped with a computer, files, and phone. But when art directors, space buyers, account managers, and copywriters need to team up for brainstorming sessions, they wheel their desks into an open area the agency calls "virtual" space.

There is a sizeable amount of research that supports that you're more likely to interact with those individuals who are physically close.[48] An employee's work location, therefore, is likely to influence the information to which one is privy and one's inclusion or exclusion from organization events. Whether you are on a certain grapevine network or not, for instance, will be largely determined by where you are physically located in the organization.

One topic that has received a considerable amount of attention is office arrangements, specifically the placement of the desk and where the office-holder chooses to sit.[49] Unlike factory floors, individuals typically have some leeway in laying out their office furniture. And the arrangement of an office conveys nonverbal messages to visitors. A desk between two parties conveys formality and the authority of the officeholder, while setting chairs so individuals can sit at right angles to each other conveys a more natural and informal relationship.

PRIVACY As described at the opening of this chapter, AGI Inc. redesigned its employee work space to reduce privacy and increase communication. AGI is one among many organizations that have replaced traditional hierarchical work spaces with open offices.[50]

Privacy is in part a function of the amount of space per person and the arrangement of that space. But it also is influenced by walls, partitions, and other physical barriers. Most employees desire a large degree of privacy in their jobs (especially in managerial positions, where privacy is associated with status). Yet most employees also desire opportunities to interact with colleagues, which are restricted as privacy increases.

◆ Open offices, with minimal opportunity for privacy, are now being widely implemented.

Open offices, with minimal opportunities for privacy, are now being widely implemented. "From Manhattan towers to Silicon Valley tilt-ups, from behemoths, such as Mobil, IBM, and Procter & Gamble, to tiny startups, business is embracing new office designs for the twenty-first century."[51] These new office designs are consistent with the trend toward creating "work anywhere, anytime" offices, all made possible by advanced technology.[52] The merging of voice mail, e-mail, fax, the World Wide Web, and private intranets makes it possible for organizations to tear down traditional walls and allow people to work in open offices, in their car, at home, or even in a client's office.

There is growing evidence that the desire for privacy is a strong one on the part of many people.[53] Privacy limits distractions, which can be particularly bothersome for people doing complex tasks. Yet the trend is clearly toward less privacy at the workplace. Further research is needed to determine whether or not organizational efforts to open work spaces and individual preferences for privacy are incompatible and result in lower employee performance and satisfaction.

Summary and an Integrative Model

"In and of itself, [physical working conditions and workspace design] does not appear to have a substantial motivational impact on people. In other words, it does not induce people to engage in specific behaviors, but it can make certain behaviors easier or harder to perform. In this way, the effectiveness of people may be enhanced or reduced."[54] So it's probably most accurate to think

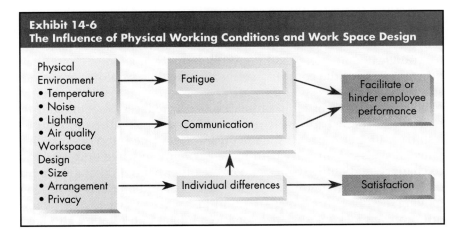

Exhibit 14-6
The Influence of Physical Working Conditions and Work Space Design

of the variables we've discussed in this section as ones that facilitate or hinder the opportunity for employees to optimize their performance.

Exhibit 14-6 summarizes the points made in this section. Work settings and conditions can directly influence an employee's satisfaction, taking into consideration individual differences. Work settings and conditions may also indirectly facilitate or hinder an employee's performance. When the work setting is poorly designed or uncomfortable for the employee, it can contribute to fatigue and hinder communication. Tired employees have difficulty in achieving both quantity and quality of output. Similarly, noise levels or physical partitions make it difficult for employees to interact or form informal group ties. But reactions are moderated by individual differences such as temperature preferences, length of time one has been exposed to polluted air, need for status, and need for social interaction.

Work Redesign Options

What are some of the options managers have at their disposal if they want to redesign or change the makeup of employee jobs? The following discusses four options: job rotation, job enlargement, job enrichment, and team-based designs.

Job Rotation

If employees suffer from overroutinization of their work, one alternative is to use **job rotation** (or what many now call *cross-training*). When an activity is no longer challenging, the employee is rotated to another job, at the same level, that has similar skill requirements.[55]

job rotation
The periodic shifting of a worker from one task to another.

G.S.I. Transcomm Data Systems Inc. in Pittsburgh uses job rotation to keep its staff of 110 people from getting bored.[56] Over one two-year period, nearly 20 percent of Transcomm's employees made lateral job switches. Management believes the job rotation program has been a major contributor to cutting employee turnover from 25 percent to less than 7 percent a year. Brazil's Semco SA makes extensive use of job rotation. "Practically no one," says Semco's president, "stays in the same position for more than two or three years. We try to motivate people to move their areas completely from time to time so they don't get stuck to the technical solutions, to ways of doing things in which they have become entrenched."[57] Mike Conway, CEO of

America West Airlines, describes how his company fully cross-trains their customer service representatives. He says America West does it "to give the employees a better job, to give them more job variety. It's more challenging, and for those who are interested in upward mobility, it exposes them to about 16 different areas of the company versus the one they would be exposed to if we specialized."[58]

The strengths of job rotation are that it reduces boredom and increases motivation through diversifying the employee's activities. Of course, it can also have indirect benefits for the organization since employees with a wider range of skills give management more flexibility in scheduling work, adapting to changes, and filling vacancies. On the other hand, job rotation is not without its drawbacks. Training costs are increased, and productivity is reduced by moving a worker into a new position just when his or her efficiency at the prior job was creating organizational economies. Job rotation also creates disruptions. Members of the work group have to adjust to the new employee. The supervisor may also have to spend more time answering questions and monitoring the work of the recently rotated employee. Finally, job rotation can demotivate intelligent and ambitious trainees who seek specific responsibilities in their chosen specialty.

Job Enlargement

job enlargement
The horizontal expansion of jobs.

More than 35 years ago, the idea of expanding jobs horizontally, or what we call **job enlargement**, grew in popularity. Increasing the number and variety of tasks that an individual performed resulted in jobs with more diversity. Instead of only sorting the incoming mail by department, for instance, a mail sorter's job could be enlarged to include physically delivering the mail to the various departments or running outgoing letters through the postage meter.

Efforts at job enlargement met with less than enthusiastic results.[59] As one employee who experienced such a redesign on his job remarked, "Before I had one lousy job. Now, through enlargement, I have three!" However, there have been some successful applications of job enlargement. For example, U.S. Shoe Co. created modular work areas to replace production lines in over half of its factories. In these work areas, workers perform two or three shoe-making steps instead of only one, as in traditional production lines. The result has been footwear produced more efficiently and with greater attention to quality.[60]

A red jacket worn by an employee at a Marriott hotel used to identify the employee as a doorman. But red jacket wearers at the Marriott Hotel in Schaumburg, Illinois, are now known as "guest service associates." To increase employee job satisfaction, the hotel has enlarged the doorman's job to include the tasks of bellman, front-desk clerk, and concierge. Job enlargement is also part of Marriott's strategy to improve service quality through programs such as First 10, which focuses on giving customers excellent service during their first 10 minutes at the hotel.

So, while job enlargement attacked the lack of diversity in overspecialized jobs, it did little to instill challenge or meaningfulness to a worker's activities. Job enrichment was introduced to deal with the shortcomings of enlargement.

Job Enrichment

Job enrichment refers to the vertical expansion of jobs. It increases the degree to which the worker controls the planning, execution, and evaluation of his or her work. An enriched job organizes tasks so as to allow the worker to do a complete activity, increases the employee's freedom and independence, increases responsibility, and provides feedback, so an individual will be able to assess and correct his or her own performance.[61]

job enrichment
The vertical expansion of jobs.

Lawrence Buettner enriched the jobs of employees in his international trade banking department at First Chicago Corporation.[62] His department's chief product is commercial letters of credit—essentially a bank guarantee to stand behind huge import and export transactions. When he took over the department of 300 employees, he found paperwork crawling along a document "assembly line," with errors creeping in at each handoff. And employees did little to hide the boredom they were experiencing in their jobs. Buettner replaced the narrow, specialized tasks that employees were doing with enriched jobs. Each clerk is now a trade expert who can handle a customer from start to finish. After 200 hours of training in finance and law, the clerks became full-service advisers who could turn around documents in a day while advising clients on such arcane matters as bank procedures in Turkey and U.S. munitions' export controls. And the results? Productivity has more than tripled, employee satisfaction has soared, and transaction volume has risen more than 10 percent a year. Additionally, increased skills have translated into higher pay for the employees who are performing the enriched jobs. These trade service representatives, some of whom had come to the bank directly out of high school, now earn from $25,000 to $50,000 a year.

The First Chicago example shouldn't be taken as a blanket endorsement of job enrichment. The overall evidence generally shows that job enrichment reduces absenteeism and turnover costs and increases satisfaction, but on the critical issue of productivity, the evidence is inconclusive.[63] In some situations, such as at First Chicago, job enrichment increases productivity; in others, it decreases it. However, even when productivity goes down, there does seem to be consistently more conscientious use of resources and a higher quality of product or service.

Team-Based Work Designs Revisited

Increasingly, people are doing work in groups and teams. What, if anything, can we say about the design of group-based work to try to improve employee performance in those groups? We know a lot more about individual-based work design than we do about design at the group level,[65] mostly because the wide popularity of teams—specifically assigning tasks to a group of individuals instead of to a single person—is a relatively recent phenomenon. That said, the best work in this area offers two sets of suggestions.[66]

First, the JCM recommendations seem to be as valid at the group level as they are at the individual level. Managers should expect a group to perform at a high level when (1) the group task requires members to use a variety of rela-

From Concepts to Skills

Designing Enriched Jobs

How does management enrich an employee's job? The following suggestions, based on the job characteristics model, specify the types of changes in jobs that are most likely to lead to improving their motivating potential.[64]

1. *Combine tasks.* Managers should seek to take existing and fractionalized tasks and put them back together to form a new and larger module of work. This increases skill variety and task identity.

2. *Create natural work units.* The creation of natural work units means that the tasks an employee does form an identifiable and meaningful whole. This increases employee "own-ership" of the work and improves the likelihood that employees will view their work as meaningful and important rather than as irrelevant and boring.

3. *Establish client relationships.* The client is the user of the product or service that the employee works on (and may be an "internal customer" as well as someone outside the organization). Wherever possible, managers should try to establish direct relationships between workers and their clients. This increases skill variety, autonomy, and feedback for the employee.

4. *Expand jobs vertically.* Vertical expansion gives employees responsibilities and control that were formerly reserved to management. It seeks to partially close the gap between the "doing" and the "controlling" aspects of the job, and it increases employee autonomy.

5. *Open feedback channels.* By increasing feedback, employees not only learn how well they are performing their jobs, but also whether their performance is improving, deteriorating, or remaining at a constant level. Ideally, this feedback about performance should be received directly as the employee does the job, rather than from management on an occasional basis.

tively high-level skills; (2) the group task is a whole and meaningful piece of work, with a visible outcome; (3) the outcomes of the group's work on the task have significant consequences for other people; (4) the task provides group members with substantial autonomy for deciding how they do the work; and (5) work on the task generates regular, trustworthy feedback about how well the group is performing.

Second, group composition is critical to the success of the work group. Consistent with findings described in chapter 8, managers should try to ensure that the following four conditions are met: (1) Individual members have the necessary task-relevant expertise to do their work; (2) the group is large enough to perform the work; (3) members possess interpersonal as well as task skills; and (4) membership is moderately diverse in terms of talents and perspectives.

Work Schedule Options

Susan Ross is your classic "morning person." She rises each day at 5 A.M. sharp, full of energy. On the other hand, as she puts it, "I'm usually ready for bed right after the 7 P.M. news."

Susan's work schedule as a claims processor at Hartford Insurance is flexible. It allows her some degree of freedom as to when she comes to work and when she leaves. Her office opens at 6 A.M. and closes at 7 P.M. It's up to her how she schedules her eight-hour day within this 13-hour period. Because Susan is a morning person and also has a seven-year-old son who gets out of school at 3 P.M. every day, she opts to work from 6 A.M. to 3 P.M. "My work hours are perfect. I'm at the job when I'm mentally most alert, and I can be home to take care of Sean after he gets out of school."

Most people work an eight-hour day, five days a week. They start at a fixed time and leave at a fixed time. But a number of organizations have introduced alternative work schedule options as a way to improve employee motivation, productivity, and satisfaction.

Compressed Workweek

The most popular form of **compressed workweek** is four ten-hour days.[67] The 4–40 program was conceived to allow workers more leisure time and shopping time, and to permit them to travel to and from work at non–rush-hour times. Supporters suggest that such a program can increase employee enthusiasm, morale, and commitment to the organization; increase productivity and reduce costs; reduce machine downtime in manufacturing; reduce overtime, turnover, and absenteeism; and make it easier for the organization to recruit employees.

compressed workweek
A four-day week, with employees working ten hours a day.

Currently about 25 percent of major U.S. companies offer a four-day schedule for at least some of their workers.[68] This is double what it was in the late 1980s. And a recent national survey found that two-thirds of working adults would prefer a four-day workweek to the standard five-day schedule.[69]

Proponents argue that the compressed workweek may positively affect productivity in situations in which the work process requires significant start-up and shutdown periods.[70] When start-up and shutdown times are a major factor, productivity standards take these periods into consideration in determining the time required to generate a given output. Consequently, in such cases, the compressed workweek will increase productivity even though worker performance is not affected, simply because the improved work scheduling reduces nonproductive time.

The evidence on 4–40 program performance is generally positive.[71] While some employees complain of fatigue near the end of the day, and about the difficulty of coordinating their jobs with their personal lives—the latter a problem especially for working mothers—most like the 4–40 program. In one study, for instance, when employees were asked whether they wanted to continue their 4–40 program, which had been in place for six months, or go back to a traditional five-day week, 78 percent wanted to keep the compressed workweek.[72]

Shorter Workweek

How does a reduced four-day, 32-hour workweek sound? What if it included a 20 percent cut in pay? A number of Western European countries are considering the former as a solution to high unemployment. But if unions have their way, it won't be with any pay cut.[73]

Western Europe has 20 million unemployed workers. In an effort to deal with this problem, countries such as Germany, France, Spain, and Belgium are seriously considering spreading the available work among more people by cutting the workweek 20 percent.

With the jobless rate nearly 12 percent and rising in France and Germany, political pressures are building for this proposal. Volkswagen, for instance, has given an ultimatum to the union that represents its 103,000 workers: Accept a four-day workweek with a 20 percent drop in pay, or nearly every third job will be cut.

It's not clear at this point whether or not the 32-hour workweek will become the new standard in Western Europe. Moreover, even if it does, it isn't certain that employees will have to take a commensurate cut in pay. Proposals currently being considered at the federal level include having employers absorb the full cost—paying workers for 40 hours, even if they work only 32; having the government pick up the tab; or some combination of cost sharing among workers, employers, and government.

The impact on employees of a shorter workweek can only be speculative at this time. While the program would create more jobs, employees are likely to focus on how it affects them individually rather than the positive effect on their country's employment. A 20 percent cut in hours, with no cut in pay, should have generally positive effects on employee satisfaction and negative effects on productivity. If the cut in hours is matched with a 20 percent reduction in pay, satisfaction is likely to drop.

Flextime

Flextime is a scheduling option that allows employees, within specific parameters, to decide when to go to work. Susan Ross's work schedule at Hartford Insurance is an example of flextime. But what specifically is flextime?

flextime
Employees work during a common core time period each day but have discretion in forming their total workday from a flexible set of hours outside the core.

Flextime is short for flexible work hours. It allows employees some discretion over when they arrive at and leave work. Employees have to work a specific number of hours a week, but they are free to vary the hours of work within certain limits. As shown in Exhibit 14-7, each day consists of a common core, usually six hours, with a flexibility band surrounding the core. For example, exclusive of a one-hour lunch break, the core may be 9 A.M. to 3 P.M., with the office actually opening at 6 A.M. and closing at 6 P.M. All employees are required to be at their jobs during the common core period, but they are allowed to accumulate their other two hours before and/or after the core time. Some flextime programs allow extra hours to be accumulated and turned into a free day off each month.

Flextime has become an extremely popular scheduling option. For instance, a recent study of firms with more than 1,000 employees found that 53 percent offered employees the option of flextime.[74]

The benefits claimed for flextime are numerous. They include reduced absenteeism, increased productivity, reduced overtime expenses, a lessening in

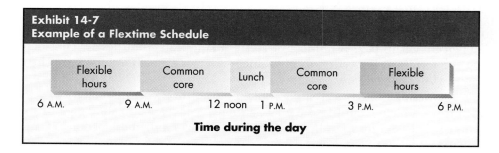

Exhibit 14-7
Example of a Flextime Schedule

Flexible hours	Common core	Lunch	Common core	Flexible hours

6 A.M.   9 A.M.   12 noon   1 P.M.   3 P.M.   6 P.M.

Time during the day

hostility toward management, reduced traffic congestion around work sites, elimination of tardiness, and increased autonomy and responsibility for employees that may increase employee job satisfaction.[75] But beyond the claims, what's flextime's record?

Most of the performance evidence stacks up favorably. Flextime tends to reduce absenteeism and frequently improves worker productivity,[76] probably for several reasons. Employees can schedule their work hours to align with personal demands, thus reducing tardiness and absences, and employees can adjust their work activities to those hours in which they are individually more productive.

Flextime's major drawback is that it's not applicable to every job. It works well with clerical tasks where an employee's interaction with people outside his or her department is limited. It is not a viable option for recep-

Netscape

Back | Forward | Home | Reload | Images | Open | Print | Find | Stop

Go to: http//www.prenhall.com/phbusiness

OB in the News

The Growing Popularity of Alternative Work Schedules

Alternative work schedules, which not too long ago were viewed as disruptions to the office workplace and as a "mothers only" perk, have become an important strategic tool as organizations try to offer the flexibility their employees need in a changing society.

Bank of America, San Francisco, for example, has 12,000 workers who use flextime, 4,800 on compressed workweeks, 2,000 who job share, 1,300 who work at home at least one day a week, and 500 part-time employees.

A business unit of Continental Corp. in upstate New York has 200 of its 207 employees on alternative schedules. Bechtel Corp., the worldwide construction firm, makes extensive use of compressed workweeks.

Three societal changes are driving this alternative work schedule movement. First, fewer women are at home to provide care for children or elderly parents. Second, there is less willingness of people to be married to a job. And third, changing technology like networked computers, phones, and faxes make the location where work is performed less relevant.

Based on M.A. Verespej, "The Anytime, Anywhere Workplace," *Industry Week*, July 4, 1994, pp. 37–40.

Take It to the Net

We invite you to visit the Robbins page on the Prentice Hall Web site at:

http://www.prenhall.com/robbinsorgbeh

for this chapter's World Wide Web exercise.

tionists, sales personnel in retail stores, or similar jobs where comprehensive service demands that people be at their work stations at predetermined times.

Job Sharing

job sharing
The practice of having two or more people split a 40-hour-a-week job.

A recent work scheduling innovation is **job sharing**. It allows two or more individuals to split a traditional 40-hour-a-week job. So, for example, one person might perform the job from 8 A.M. to noon, while another performs the same job from 1 P.M. to 5 P.M.; or the two could work full, but alternate, days.

Although job sharing is growing in popularity, it is less widespread than flextime. Only about 30 percent of large organizations offer this option.[77] And in contrast to flextime, only a very small percentage of employees actually use the option.[78] Xerox is one organization that does. Laura Meier and Lori Meagher, for instance, share a sales management position at Xerox.[79] Both are mothers of preschoolers and wanted greater flexibility, but they didn't want to give up their managerial careers at Xerox. So now Laura oversees their eight sales reps on Thursdays and Fridays, Lori has the job on Mondays and Tuesdays, and the two women work alternate Wednesdays.

From management's standpoint, job sharing allows the organization to draw upon the talents of more than one individual in a given job. A bank manager who oversees two job sharers describes it as an opportunity to get two heads, but "pay for one."[80] It also opens up the opportunity to acquire skilled workers—for instance, women with young children and retirees—who might not be available on a full-time basis. From the employee's viewpoint, job sharing increases flexibility. As such, it can increase motivation and satisfaction for those to whom a 40-hour-a-week job is just not practical.

Telecommuting

telecommuting
Employees do their work at home on a computer that is linked to their office.

It might be close to the ideal job for many people. No commuting, flexible hours, freedom to dress as you please, and little or no interruptions from colleagues. It's called **telecommuting** and refers to employees who do their work at home on a computer that is linked to their office.[81] Currently, about 10 million people work at home in the United States doing things like taking orders over the phone, filling out reports and other forms, and processing or analyzing information.[82] Telecommuting is presently the fastest-growing trend in work scheduling. One projection, for instance, predicts that by the year 2000, more than 60 million American workers—about half the workforce—will do some kind of work at home.[83] Employers have been enthusiastic about the concept, claiming it enhances worker productivity, improves the organization's ability to retain valuable employees, and increases employee loyalty.

◆ Telecommuting is presently the fastest-growing trend in work scheduling.

American Express Travel Services is one organization whose experience with telecommuting has been very positive.[84] In 1993, 100 AmEx travel agents in 15 locations were telecommuters. The company can connect these people's homes to American Express's phone and data lines for a modest one-time expense of $1,300 each, including hardware. Once in place, calls to AmEx's reservation service are seamlessly routed to workers at home, where they can look up fares and book reservations on PCs. The typical telecommuting agent at AmEx handles 26 percent more calls at home than at the office. Why? One agent thinks it's due to an absence of distractions: "I don't feel like I'm working any harder. It's just that I don't have Suzy next to me telling me her husband is a jerk. I'm not worried about who's going into the boss's office, or noticing who's heading to the bathroom for the tenth time today." Additionally, as more agents become telecommuters and free up office space, the company will generate substantial savings in rent. For instance, in New York City, it costs AmEx nearly $4,400 a year to rent the 125 square feet of space each travel agent occupies.

Not all employees embrace the idea of telecommuting. After the massive Los Angeles earthquake in January 1994, many L.A. firms began offering telecommuting for their workers.[85] It was popular for a week or two, but that soon faded. Many workers complained they were missing out on important meetings and informal interactions that led to new policies and ideas. The vast majority were willing to put up with two- and three-hour commutes, while bridges and freeways were being rebuilt, in order to maintain their social contacts at work.

The long-term future of telecommuting depends on some questions for which we don't yet have definitive answers. For instance, will employees who do their work at home be at a disadvantage in office politics? Might they be less likely to be considered for salary increases and promotions? Is being out of sight equivalent to being out of mind? Will non–work-related distractions like children, neighbors, and the close proximity of the refrigerator significantly reduce productivity for those without superior will power and discipline?

Summary and Implications for Managers

An understanding of work design can help managers design jobs that positively affect employee motivation. For instance, jobs that score high in motivating potential increase an employee's control over key elements in his or her work. Therefore, jobs that offer autonomy, feedback, and similar complex task characteristics help to satisfy the individual goals of those employees who desire greater control over their work. Of course, consistent with the social information processing model, the perception that task characteristics are complex is probably more important in influencing an employee's motivation than the objective task characteristics themselves. The key, then, is to provide employees with cues that suggest that their jobs score high on factors such as skill variety, task identity, autonomy, and feedback.

Technology is changing people's jobs and their work behavior. TQM and its emphasis on continuous process improvement can increase employee stress as individuals find that performance expectations are constantly being increased. Reengineering is eliminating millions of jobs and completely reshaping the jobs of those who remain. Flexible manufacturing systems require employees to learn new skills and accept increased responsibilities. And technology is making many job skills obsolete and shortening the life span of almost all skills—technical, administrative, and managerial. Work conditions and design variables such as temperature, noise, lighting, air quality, work space size, interior layout and arrangement, and degree of privacy can directly influence employee satisfaction. In addition, they indirectly affect employee productivity by influencing communication and employee fatigue.

Alternative work schedule options such as the compressed workweek, shorter workweeks, flextime, job sharing, and telecommuting have grown in popularity in recent years. They have become an important strategic tool as organizations try to increase the flexibility their employees need in a changing workplace.

For Review

1. Describe three jobs that score high on the JCM. Describe three jobs that score low.

2. What are the implications of the social information processing model for predicting employee behavior?

3. What are the implications for employees of a continuous improvement program?

4. What are the implications for employees of a reengineering program?

5. What are flexible manufacturing systems?

6. How could you design an office so as to increase the opportunity for employees to be productive?

7. What can you do to improve employee performance on teams through work design?

8. What are the advantages of flextime from an employee's perspective? From management's perspective?

9. What are the advantages of job sharing from an employee's perspective? From management's perspective?

10. From an employee's perspective, what are the pros and cons to telecommuting?

For Discussion

1. Reengineering needs to be autocratically imposed in order to overcome employee resistance. This runs directly counter to the model of a contemporary manager who is a good listener, a coach, motivates through employee involvement, and who possesses strong team support skills. Can these two positions be reconciled?

2. How has technology changed the manager's job over the past 20 years?

3. Would you want a full-time job telecommuting? How do you think most of your friends would feel about such a job? Do you think telecommuting has a future?

4. What can management do to improve employees' perceptions that their jobs are interesting and challenging?

5. What are the implications of worker obsolescence on (a) society; (b) management practice; and (c) you, as an individual, planning a career?

The Notion of Jobs Is Becoming Obsolete

Prior to 1800, very few people had a job. People worked hard raising food or making things at home. They had no regular hours, no job descriptions, no bosses, and no employee benefits. Instead, they put in long hours on shifting clusters of tasks, in a variety of locations, on a schedule set by the sun and the weather and the needs of the day. It was the industrial revolution and the creation of large manufacturing companies that brought about the concept of what we have come to think of as *jobs*. But the conditions that created "the job" are disappearing. Customized production is pushing out mass production; most workers now handle information, not physical products; and competitive conditions are demanding rapid response to changing markets. Although economists and social analysts continue to talk about the disappearance of jobs in certain countries or industries, they're missing a more relevant point: What's actually disappearing is *the job itself.*

In a fast-moving economy, jobs are rigid solutions to an elastic problem. We can rewrite a person's job description occasionally, but not every week. When the work that needs doing changes constantly—which increasingly describes today's world—organizations can't afford the inflexibility that traditional jobs bring with it.

In the near future, very few people will have jobs as we have come to know them. In place of jobs, there will be part-time and temporary work situations. Organizations will be transformed from a structure built out of jobs into a field of work needing to be done. These organizations will be essentially made up of "hired guns"—contingent employees (temporaries, part-timers, consultants, and contract workers) who join project teams created to complete a specific task. When that task is finished, the team disbands. People will work on more than one team at a time, keeping irregular hours, and maybe never meeting their co-workers face-to-face. Computers, pagers, cellular phones, modems, and the like will allow people to work for multiple employers, at the same time, in locations throughout the world. Few of these employees will be working nine to five at specific work spots, and they'll have little of the security that their grandfathers had, who worked for U.S. Steel, General Motors, Sears, Bank of America, or similar large bureaucracies. In place of security and predictability, they'll have flexibility and autonomy. They'll be able to put together their own place-time combinations to support their diverse work, family, lifestyle, and financial needs.

This argument is based on W. Bridges, *JobShift* (Reading, MA: Addison-Wesley, 1994).

counterPoint

Jobs Are the Essence of Organizational Life

The central core to any discussion of work or organizational behavior is the concept of a job. It is the aggregation of tasks that defines an individual's duties and responsibilities.

When an organization is created, managers have to determine what tasks need to be accomplished for the organization to achieve its goals and who will perform those tasks. These decisions precede the hiring of a workforce. Remember, it's the tasks that determine the need for people, not the other way around. Job analysis is the formal process managers use to define the jobs within the organization and the behaviors that are necessary to perform those jobs. For instance, what are the duties of a purchasing specialist, grade 3, who works for International Paper? What minimal knowledge, skills, and abilities are necessary for adequate performance of a grade 3 purchasing specialist's job? How do the requirements for a purchasing specialist, grade 3, compare with those for a purchasing specialist, grade 2, or a purchasing analyst? These are questions that job analysis can answer.

Can you conceive of an organization without jobs? No more than you can conceive of a car without an engine. There are no doubt changes taking place in organizations that are requiring managers to redefine what a job is. For instance, today's jobs often include extensive customer interaction as well as team responsibilities. In many cases, organizations are having to make job descriptions more flexible to reflect the more dynamic nature of work today. Because it's inefficient to rewrite job descriptions on a weekly basis, managers are rethinking what makes up a job and defining jobs in more fluid terms. But the concept of jobs continues to be at the core of any work design effort and a fundamental cornerstone to understanding formal work behavior in organizations.

For those who believe that the concept of jobs is on the wane, all they need to do is look to the trade union movement and its determination to maintain clear job delineations. Labor unions have a vested interest in the status quo and will fight hard to protect the security and predictability that traditional jobs provide. Moreover, if it looked like the jobless society was to become a widespread reality, politicians would be under strong pressure to create legislation to outlaw it. A world of part-time and temporary employment is a threat to the stability of our society. Working people want stability and predictability, and they will look to their elected representatives to protect that. Those politicians who ignore this desire face the wrath of the electorate.

Learning about Yourself Exercise

Is an Enriched Job for You?

INSTRUCTIONS People differ in what they like and dislike in their jobs. Listed below are twelve pairs of jobs. For each pair, indicate which job you would prefer. Assume that everything else about the jobs is the same—pay attention only to the characteristics actually listed for each pair of jobs. If you would prefer the job in Column A, indicate how much you prefer it by putting a check mark in a blank to the left of the Neutral point. If you prefer the job in Column B, check one of the blanks to the right of Neutral. Check the Neutral blank only if you find the two jobs equally attractive or unattractive. Try to use the Neutral blank rarely.

Column A		Column B
1. A job that offers little or no challenge.	Strongly prefer A Neutral Strongly prefer B	A job that requires you to be completely isolated from co-workers.
2. A job that pays well.	Strongly prefer A Neutral Strongly prefer B	A job that allows considerable opportunity to be creative and innovative.
3. A job that often requires you to make important decisions.	Strongly prefer A Neutral Strongly prefer B	A job in which there are many pleasant people to work with.
4. A job with little security in a somewhat unstable organization.	Strongly prefer A Neutral Strongly prefer B	A job in which you have little or no opportunity to participate in decisions that affect your work.
5. A job in which greater responsibility is given to those who do the best work.	Strongly prefer A Neutral Strongly prefer B	A job in which greater responsibility is given to loyal employees who have the most *seniority*.
6. A job with a supervisor who sometimes is highly critical.	Strongly prefer A Neutral Strongly prefer B	A job that does not require you to use much of your talent.
7. A very routine job.	Strongly prefer A Neutral Strongly prefer B	A job in which your co-workers are not very friendly.
8. A job with a supervisor who respects you and treats you fairly.	Strongly prefer A Neutral Strongly prefer B	A job that provides constant opportunities for you to learn new and interesting things.
9. A job that gives you a real chance to develop yourself personally.	Strongly prefer A Neutral Strongly prefer B	A job with excellent vacation and fringe benefits.
10. A job in which there is a real chance you could be laid off.	Strongly prefer A Neutral Strongly prefer B	A job with very little chance to do challenging work.
11. A job with little freedom and independence to do your work in the way you think best.	Strongly prefer A Neutral Strongly prefer B	A job with poor working conditions.

12. A job with very satisfying teamwork.

Strongly   Neutral   Strongly
prefer A   prefer B

A job that allows you to use your skills and abilities to the fullest extent.

Turn to page A-29 for scoring directions and key.

Source: J.R. Hackman and G.R. Oldham, *The Job Diagnostic Survey: An Instrument for the Diagnosis of Jobs and the Evaluation of Job Redesign Projects.* Technical Report No. 4 (New Haven, Conn.: Yale University, Department of Administrative Sciences, 1974). Reprinted with permission.

Working with Others Exercise

Analyzing and Redesigning Jobs

Break into groups of five to seven members each. Each student should describe the worst job he or she has ever had. Use any criteria you want to select one of these jobs for analysis by the group.

Members of the group will analyze the job selected by determining how well it scores on the job characteristics model. Use the following scale for your analysis of each job dimension:

7 = Very high
6 = High
5 = Somewhat high
4 = Moderate
3 = Somewhat low
2 = Low
1 = Very low

Following are sample questions that can guide the group in its analysis of the job in question:

◆ *Skill variety*: Describe the different identifiable skills required to do this job. What is the nature of the oral, written, and/or quantitative skills needed? Physical skills? Does the jobholder get the opportunity to use all of his or her skills?

◆ *Task identity*: What is the product that the jobholder creates? Is he or she involved in its production from beginning to end? If not, is he or she involved in a particular phase of its production from beginning to end?

◆ *Task significance*: How important is the product? How important is the jobholder's role in producing it? How important is the jobholder's contribution to the people he or she works with? If the jobholder's job were eliminated, how inferior would the product be?

◆ *Autonomy*: How much independence does the jobholder have? Does he or she have to follow a strict schedule? How closely is he or she supervised?

◆ *Feedback*: Does the jobholder get regular feedback from his or her supervisor? From peers? From subordinates? From customers? How about intrinsic performance feedback when doing the job?

Using the formula in Exhibit 14-3, calculate the job's motivating potential. Then using the suggestions offered in the chapter for redesigning jobs, describe specific actions management could take to increase this job's motivating potential.

Calculate the costs to management of redesigning the job in question. Do the benefits exceed the costs?

Conclude the exercise by having a representative of each group share his or her group's analysis and redesign suggestions with the entire class. Possible topics for class discussion might include: similarities in the jobs chosen, problems in rating job dimensions, and the cost-benefit assessment of design changes.

Source: This exercise is based on W.P. Ferris, "Enlivening the Job Characteristics Model," in C. Harris and C.C. Lundberg, *Proceedings of the 29th Annual Eastern Academy of Management Meeting*; Baltimore, MD; May 1992, pp. 125–28.

Reengineering the College Experience

C A S E
INCIDENT

At the turn of the century, less than 2 percent of high school graduates went on to college. For the most part, college in those days was an elitist experience reserved for children of the upper class. Today, in places like the United States, approximately 60 percent of high school graduates continue on to college. In the 1990s, in much of the world, higher education has become a product for the masses.

Although higher educational institutions now serve a much broader and diverse audience, the structure of colleges and their basic curricula have not changed much since the turn of the century. Critics claim that the typical undergraduate experience—four years of course work, broken down into eight or twelve terms, with students taking three to six courses per term, taught mostly by full-time instructors who lecture to their classes—makes little sense today. For example, we realize knowledge isn't compartmentalized by narrow departmental specialties nor into three-unit segments, but that's how it tends to be taught. Additionally, while lecturing made sense a century ago, it is a rather outdated means for transferring information when students have ready access to libraries and on-line databases. Critics also challenge a number of other well-established practices of colleges and universities: expansive campuses with dormitories and other facilities for resident students when, in fact, most students commute; accreditation processes that legitimize the faculty's academic credentials, the importance of research, the use of full-time over part-time faculty, and the granting of tenure; the heavy subsidizing of public education by taxpayers; and the unresponsiveness of faculty and administrators to the need for change.

What would a college look like if it were reengineered? Vassar College, for instance, recently announced that it was eliminating tenure for new faculty. National University in San Diego breaks its curriculum into monthly courses that are offered all year around, and taught almost entirely by working practitioners rather than full-time faculty. Some colleges are experimenting with team-teaching classes with faculty from diverse disciplines. But these represent only incremental changes. True reengineering would require creating an entire new structure and curriculum from scratch.

Questions

1. List as many characteristics of your college as you can that you think hinder its effectiveness in the 1990s.

2. What do you think a reengineered college structure and curriculum would look like?

3. In times of dramatic societal change, colleges and universities remain relatively stable. College campuses haven't changed much from those that your parents or grandparents might have encountered. What changes have occurred that have either been incremental or introduced by newly developed colleges? In times when almost every business firm is having to completely overhaul its traditional practices, why do most established colleges and universities continue to operate as they always have?

VIDEO CASE

ABCNEWS

Spying on Employees

Big Brother is watching you! Some corporations have been spying on employees at work, and even in instances when they're not at work. Sheraton Hotels is doing it. So is Kmart.

Francklin Etienne and Brad Fair were among dozens of Sheraton employees secretly videotaped at work—and not just while they were doing their jobs. Brad, for instance, was taped undressing in the employees' locker room. Francklin was "caught" reading a book during his scheduled break. Sheraton officials defend their actions by saying secret videotaping did result in nabbing one drug-dealing employee. However, Etienne, a Haitian immigrant, can't reconcile this action by his employer and the U.S. preoccupation with freedom. He says, "When I found out I was on the tape, I said to myself, 'Where is the privacy they're always talking about? Where is the freedom they're talking about?'"

Lew Hubble's experience at a Kmart warehouse was more personal. He learned that two co-workers whom he had befriended were actually private investigators hired by Kmart to compile reports on employees by going to local bars with them, visiting them at their homes, and the like. These reports contained information that had little or nothing to do with employees' jobs. For instance, one such report said that an employee had fathered another employee's child, and the report identified the employees by name. Kmart management wouldn't speak about these actions on the record, but managers defended their use of private investigators by saying they were hired to help break up an "inside" theft ring. Said one warehouse employee, "What takes place in that warehouse, they have a right to know. They do not have a right to know what goes on in my bedroom, in my living room."

These aren't isolated examples. It has been estimated that at least 6 million American workers are spied on at work each year. This spying takes various forms—listening in on phone calls, videotaping work areas, reviewing computer entries, and monitoring e-mail, and there's little that employees can do to stop management from spying on them, on or off company property. There is a federal law to keep employers from listening to workers' personal phone calls, but other than that, there is almost no protection from prying eyes on the job.

Questions

1. When does spying cross the line from effective management controls to invasion of employee privacy?

2. Would your perception of Sheraton's or Kmart's management be any

better if it had told employees ahead of time that they might be videotaped anywhere or that undercover private investigators had been hired to monitor illegal activities by employees? Discuss.

3. Do you think the decrease in employee morale and trust as a result of these spying practices is offset by reductions in property loss and gains in productivity (for example, by identifying and terminating employees who steal or use illegal drugs)?

4. Personal digital assistants, networked computers, and similar new technologies are only likely to make it easier for employers to monitor employees. How do you feel about this? What controls, if any, do you expect your employer to implement to protect your privacy and freedoms?

Source: Based on "Employers Spying on Employees," *ABC News World News Tonight*, aired on March 28, 1994.

HUMAN RESOURCE POLICIES AND PRACTICES

CHAPTER OUTLINE

Selection Practices
Training and Development Programs
Performance Evaluation
The Union—Management Interface
International Human Resource Practices: Selected Issues
Managing Diversity in Organizations

After listening to my employees, I have to conclude that I have only three types of people working for me: Stars, All-Stars, and Superstars! How is it possible for all my people to be above average?
—An Anonymous Boss

LEARNING OBJECTIVES

After studying this chapter, you should be able to

1 Contrast job descriptions with job specifications

2 Identify the key skills for effective interviewing

3 List the advantages of performance simulation tests over written tests

4 Define three skill categories

5 Describe how career planning has changed in the last decade

6 Explain the purposes of performance evaluation

7 Describe the potential problems in performance evaluation and actions that can correct these problems

8 Clarify how the existence of a union affects employee behavior

9 Describe characteristics of a family-friendly workplace

IMAGINE that you're in your final term in college. After considerable effort, you've secured an interview with the company you've long wanted to work for. Just to get to this interview stage is an accomplishment because the company receives 12,000 résumés a month and hires less than 3 percent of all prospects. The first few minutes of the interview goes as you expected. You're asked about your college experience, your favorite classes, your interests. Then, suddenly, the interviewer asks you several questions you've never even thought about: Why are manhole covers round? How many gas stations are there in the United States? How much water flows through the Mississippi daily? Suppose you have a balloon filled with air that's underwater and at equilibrium. What happens when you lower the balloon by 10 feet?

Welcome to an interview with Microsoft Corp.[1] The world's leader in software has grown more than threefold since 1990. In recent years, it has been hiring at the rate of 3,000 new employees annually, most right out of college. The preceding questions are typical of what Microsoft job applicants encounter. As the director of Microsoft's recruiting, David Pritchard, explained in describing why his people ask such strange questions, "We're not looking for the 'right' answer. We're looking for the method." He wants people who can demonstrate a logical reasoning process.

Microsoft's management is determined to hire the best and brightest. The company wants applicants who are smart, creative, and who demonstrate the flexibility to continually learn. "In this industry," said Pritchard, "things are changing on a daily basis, and if you're not capable of learning new things, you won't be successful."

Pritchard makes it clear that he and his staff believe that careful hiring is critical to the future success of Microsoft. "The best thing we can do for our competitors is hire poorly. If I hire a bunch of bozos, it will hurt us, because it takes time to get rid of them. They start infiltrating the organization and then they themselves start hiring people of lower quality. At Microsoft, we are always looking to hire people who are better than we are." ◆

icrosoft's rigorous interviews illustrate how human resource policies and practices can affect important organizational behavior outcomes. In this chapter, we discuss a number of human resource concerns that add key pieces to our puzzle as we attempt to explain and predict employee behavior.[2] Specifically, we look at selection practices, training and development programs, performance evaluation, and union–management relations.

Selection Practices

The objective of effective selection is to match individual characteristics (ability, experience, and so on) with the requirements of the job.[3] When management fails to get a proper match, both employee performance and satisfaction suffer. In this search to achieve the right individual–job fit, where does management begin? The answer is to assess the demands and requirements of the job. The process of assessing the activities within a job is called *job analysis*.

Job Analysis

job analysis
Developing a detailed description of the tasks involved in a job, determining the relationship of a given job to other jobs, and ascertaining the knowledge, skills, and abilities necessary for an employee to perform the job successfully.

job description
A written statement of what a jobholder does, how it is done, and why it is done.

job specification
States the minimum acceptable qualifications that an employee must possess to perform a given job successfully.

Job analysis involves developing a detailed description of the tasks involved in a job, determining the relationship of a given job to other jobs, and ascertaining the knowledge, skills, and abilities necessary for an employee to successfully perform the job.[4]

How is this information attained? Exhibit 15-1 describes the more popular job analysis methods.

Information gathered by using one or more of the job analysis methods results in the organization being able to create a **job description** and **job specification**. The former is a written statement of what a jobholder does, how it is done, and why it is done. It should accurately portray job content, environment, and conditions of employment. The job specification states the minimum acceptable qualifications that an employee must possess to perform a given job successfully. It identifies the knowledge, skills, and abilities needed to do the job effectively. So job descriptions identify characteristics of the job, while job specifications identify characteristics of the successful job incumbent.

Exhibit 15-1 Popular Job Analysis Methods

1. **Observation Method.** An analyst watches employees directly or reviews films of workers on the job.
2. **Individual Interview Method.** Selected job incumbents are extensively interviewed, and the results of a number of these interviews are combined into a single job analysis.
3. **Group Interview Method.** Same as individual except that a number of job incumbents are interviewed simultaneously.
4. **Structured Questionnaire Method.** Workers check or rate the items they perform in their jobs from a long list of possible task items.
5. **Technical Conference Method.** Specific characteristics of a job are obtained from "experts," who typically are supervisors with extensive knowledge of the job.
6. **Diary Method.** Job incumbents record their daily activities in a diary.

The job description and specification are important documents for guiding the selection process. The job description can be used to describe the job to potential candidates. The job specification keeps the attention of those doing the selection on the list of qualifications necessary for an incumbent to perform a job and assists in determining whether or not candidates are qualified.

Selection Devices

What do application forms, interviews, employment tests, background checks, and personal letters of recommendation have in common? Each is a device for obtaining information about a job applicant that can help the organization determine whether or not the applicant's skills, knowledge, and abilities are appropriate for the job in question. In this section, we review the more important of these selection devices—interviews, written tests, and performance simulation tests.

INTERVIEWS Do you know anyone who has gotten a job without at least one interview? You may have an acquaintance who got a part-time or summer job through a close friend or relative without having to go through an interview, but such instances are rare. Of all the selection devices that organizations use to differentiate candidates, the interview continues to be the one most frequently used.[5]

The interview also seems to carry a great deal of weight. That is, not only is it widely used, but its results tend to have a disproportionate amount of influence on the selection decision. The candidate who performs poorly in the employment interview is likely to be cut from the applicant pool, regardless of his or her experience, test scores, or letters of recommendation. Conversely, "all too often, the person most polished in job-seeking techniques, particularly those used in the interview process, is the one hired, even though he or she may not be the best candidate for the position."[6]

> ◆ The candidate who performs poorly in the employment interview is likely to be cut from the applicant pool, regardless of her experience, test scores, or letters of recommendation.

These findings are important because of the unstructured manner in which the selection interview is frequently conducted. The unstructured interview—short in duration, causal, and made up of random questions—has been proven to be an ineffective selection device.[7] The data gathered from such interviews are typically biased and often unrelated to future job performance. Without structure, a number of biases can distort results. These biases include interviewers tending to favor applicants who share their attitudes, giving unduly high weight to negative information, and allowing the order in which applicants are interviewed to influence evaluations.[8] By having interviewers use a standardized set of questions, providing interviewers with a uniform method of recording information, and standardizing the rating of the applicant's qualifications, the variability in results across applicants is reduced and the validity of the interview as a selection device is greatly enhanced.

The evidence indicates that interviews are most valuable for assessing an applicant's intelligence, level of motivation, and interpersonal skills.[9] When these qualities are related to job performance, the validity of the interview as a selection device is increased. For example, these qualities have demonstrated relevance for performance in upper managerial positions. This may explain

Qualified applicants seeking employment at The Bulldog Group are interviewed by the company's founding partner Ellie Rubin (at left). Because the Toronto marketing firm specializes in interactive communications such as kiosks and CD-ROM publishing, candidates must have experience in graphic design or video production and demonstrate technical proficiency in at least four, but preferably nine, specialized software programs. During interviews, applicants must also convince Rubin they possess a host of generalist skills. Her ideal employee is a "professional eclectic," a person who is creative, flexible, analytical, communicative, willing to learn, and thinks independently but can work with team members.

why applicants for senior management positions typically undergo dozens of interviews with executive recruiters, board members, and other company executives before a final decision is made. It can also explain why organizations that design work around teams may similarly put applicants through an unusually large number of interviews.

WRITTEN TESTS Typical written tests are tests of intelligence, aptitude, ability, interest, and integrity. Long popular as selection devices, they have generally declined in use since the late 1960s. The reason is that such tests have frequently been characterized as discriminating, and many organizations have not validated, or cannot validate, such tests as being job related.

Tests in intellectual ability, spatial and mechanical ability, perceptual accuracy, and motor ability have shown to be moderately valid predictors for many semiskilled and unskilled operative jobs in industrial organizations.[10] Intelligence tests have proven to be particularly good predictors for jobs that require cognitive complexity.[11] Japanese auto makers, when staffing plants in the United States, have relied heavily on written tests to predict candidates that will be high performers.[12] Getting a job with Toyota, for instance, can take up to three days of testing and interviewing. Written tests typically focus on skills such as reading, mathematics, mechanical dexterity, and ability to work with others.

As ethical problems have increased in organizations, integrity tests have gained popularity. These are paper-and-pencil tests that measure factors such as dependability, carefulness, responsibility, and honesty. The evidence is im-

From Concepts to Skills

Selection Interviewing

The interview is made up of four stages. It begins with *preparation*, followed by the *opening*, a period of *questioning and discussion*, and a *conclusion*.[13]

1. *Preparation.* Prior to meeting the applicant, you should review his or her application form and résumé. You also should review the job description and job specification of the position for which the applicant is interviewing.

Next, structure the agenda for the interview. Specifically, use the standardized questions provided to you or prepare a set of questions you want to ask the applicant. Standardized questions make comparisons between candidates easier. Choose questions that can't be merely answered with only a yes or no. Inquiries that begin with *how* or *why* tend to stimulate extended answers. Avoid leading questions that telegraph the desired response (such as "Would you say you have good interpersonal skills?") and bipolar questions that require the applicant to select an answer from only two choices (such as "Do you prefer working with people or working alone?"). In most cases, questions relating to marital and family status, age, race, religion, sex, ethnic background, credit rating, and arrest record are prohibited by law unless you can demonstrate that they are in some way related to job performance. So avoid them. In place of asking "Are you married?" or "Do you have children?" you might ask "Are there any reasons why you might not be able to work overtime several times a month?" Of course, to avoid discrimination, you have to ask this question of both male and female candidates. Since the best predictor of future behavior is past behavior, the best questions tend to be those that focus on previous experiences that are relevant to the current job. Examples might include: "What have you done in previous jobs that demonstrates your creativity?" "Think about a time when you had to motivate an employee to perform a job task that he or she disliked but that you needed the individual to do. How did you handle that situation?" By asking questions about how candidates have handled situations in the past similar to those they will face on the job, a more valid prediction can be made.

2. *Opening.* Assume the applicant is tense and nervous. If you're going to get valid insights into what the applicant is really like, you'll need to put him or her at ease. Introduce yourself. Be friendly. Begin with a few simple questions or statements that can break the ice; for example, "Did you run into much traffic coming over?"

Once the applicant is fairly relaxed, you should provide a brief orientation. Preview what topics will be discussed, how long the interview will take, and explain if you'll be taking notes. Encourage the applicant to ask questions.

3. *Questioning and Discussion.* The questions you developed during the preparation stage will provide a general road map to guide you. Make sure you cover them all. Additional questions should arise from the answers to the standardized questions. Select follow-up questions that naturally flow from the answers given.

Follow-up questions should seek to probe deeper into what the applicant says. If you feel that the applicant's response is superficial or inadequate, seek elaboration. Encourage greater response by saying, "Tell me more about that issue." If you need to clarify information, say something like, "You said working overtime was OK *sometimes*. Can you tell me specifically when you'd be willing to work overtime?" If the applicant doesn't directly answer your question, follow up by repeating the question or paraphrasing it. Finally, never underestimate the power of silence in an interview. One of the biggest errors that inexperienced interviewers make is that they talk too much. You're not learning anything about the candidate when you're doing the talk-

(continued)

ing. Pause for at least a few seconds after the applicant appears to have finished an answer. Your silence encourages the applicant to continue talking.

4. *Concluding.* Once you're through with the questions and discussions, you're ready to wrap up the interview. Let the applicant know this fact with a statement like, "Well, that covers all the questions I have. Is there anything about the job or our organization that I haven't answered for you?" Then let the applicant know what's going to happen next. When can he or she expect to hear from you? Will you write or phone? Are there likely to be more follow-up interviews?

Before you consider the interview complete, write your evaluation while it is fresh in your mind. Ideally, you kept notes or recorded the applicant's answers to your questions and made comments of your impressions. Now that the applicant is gone, take the time to assess the applicant's responses.

---

pressive that these tests are powerful in predicting supervisory ratings of job performance and counterproductive employee behavior on the job such as theft, discipline problems, and excessive absenteeism.[14]

PERFORMANCE SIMULATION TESTS What better way is there to find out if an applicant can do a job successfully than by having him or her do it? That's precisely the logic of performance simulation tests.

Performance simulation tests have increased in popularity during the past two decades. Undoubtedly the enthusiasm for these tests comes from the fact that they are based on job analysis data and, therefore, they more easily meet the requirement of job relatedness than do most written tests. Performance simulation tests are made up of actual job behaviors rather than surrogates, as are written tests.

◆ **What better way is there to find out if an applicant can do a job successfully than by having him or her do it?**

The two best-known performance simulation tests are work sampling and assessment centers. The former is suited to routine jobs, whereas the latter is relevant for the selection of managerial personnel.

work sampling
Creating a miniature replica of a job to evaluate the performance abilities of job candidates.

Work sampling is an effort to create a miniature replica of a job. Applicants demonstrate that they possess the necessary talents by actually doing the tasks. By carefully devising work samples based on job analysis data, the knowledge, skills, and abilities needed for each job are determined. Then each work sample element is matched with a corresponding job performance element. For instance, a work sample for a job where the employee has to use computer spreadsheet software would require the applicant to actually solve a problem using a spreadsheet.

The results from work sample experiments are impressive. Studies almost consistently demonstrate that work samples yield validities superior to written aptitude and personality tests.[15]

assessment centers
A set of performance simulation tests designed to evaluate a candidate's managerial potential.

A more elaborate set of performance simulation tests, specifically designed to evaluate a candidate's managerial potential, is administered in **assessment centers**. In assessment centers, line executives, supervisors, and/or trained psychologists evaluate candidates as they go through two to four days of exercises that simulate real problems that they would confront on the job. Based on a list of descriptive dimensions that the actual job incumbent has to meet, activities might include interviews, in-basket problem-solving exercises, group discussions, and business decision games. For instance, a candidate

Exhibit 15-2
Source: *Chronicle of Higher Education*, February 10, 1995.
© 1995 Mark Litzler.

might be required to play the role of a manager who must decide how to respond to ten memos in his or her in-basket within a two-hour period.

How valid is the assessment center as a selection device? The evidence on the effectiveness of assessment centers is extremely impressive. They have consistently demonstrated results that predict later job performance in managerial positions.[16]

Training and Development Programs

Competent employees don't remain competent forever. Skills deteriorate and can become obsolete. That's why organizations spend billions of dollars each year on formal training. For instance, it was reported that U.S. corporations with 100 or more employees spent $52.2 billion in one recent year on formal training for 47.3 million workers.[17] Xerox alone spends over $300 million a year on training and retraining its employees.[18] Motorola, Federal Express, Andersen Consulting, Corning, and Singapore Airlines all spend a minimum of 3 percent of their payroll costs on training.[19] And thousands of small companies are investing heavily in employee training.[20]

Intensified competition, technological changes, and the search for improved productivity are motivating management to increase expenditures for training. Engineers need to update their knowledge of mechanical and electrical systems. Hourly workers attend seminars on problem solving, quality improvement, and team-building skills. Clerical personnel take courses to learn how to fully utilize the latest software programs on their computers. And executives themselves participate in workshops to learn how to become more effective leaders or develop strategic plans for their divisions. Today, people at all levels in organizations are involved in formal training.

In this section, we look at the type of skills that training can improve; then we review various skill training methods, as well as the career development programs that can prepare individuals for a future that's different from today.

Skill Categories

We can dissect skills into four general categories: basic literacy, technical, interpersonal, and problem solving. Most training activities seek to modify one or more of these skills.

BASIC LITERACY   A recent report by the U.S. Department of Education found that 90 million American adults have limited literacy skills, and about 40 million can read little or not at all![21] The American Management Association reports that one out of three applicants tested for jobs by its members in 1995 lacked sufficient reading or math skills to perform the jobs they were seeking.[22] Most workplace demands require a tenth- or eleventh-grade reading level, but about 20 percent of Americans between the ages of 21 and 25 can't read at even an eighth-grade level.[23] And in many Third World countries, few workers can read or have gone beyond the equivalent of the third grade.

Organizations are increasingly having to provide basic reading and math skills for their employees. For instance, William Dudek runs a small manufacturing firm on Chicago's north side.[24] His 35 employees make metal clips, hooks, and clasps used in household appliances and automotive components. When Dudek tried to introduce some basic quality management principles in his plant, he noticed that many of his employees seemed to disregard the written instructions, and only a few could calculate percentages or plot a simple graph. After confirming his employees' lack of basic skills, he hired an instructor, and had classes in English and mathematics taught to his employees in the firm's cafeteria. Dudek said that this training, which cost him $15,000 in its first year, made his employees more efficient and that they now work better as a team.

TECHNICAL   Most training is directed at upgrading and improving an employee's technical skills. This applies as much to white-collar as to blue-collar jobs. Jobs change as a result of new technologies and improved methods. Today's employee working in an automated manufacturing plant needs a broad range of technical skills from math, science and computers to advanced assembly techniques and quality management tools such as statistical process control.[25] Few jobs go unaffected. Postal sorters have had to undergo technical training in order to learn to operate automatic sorting machines. Many auto repair personnel have had to undergo extensive training to fix and maintain recent models with front-wheel-drive trains, electronic ignitions, fuel injection, and other innovations. And millions of clerical personnel in the past decade have had to be trained to operate and interface with a computer terminal.

INTERPERSONAL Almost all employees belong to a work unit. To some degree, their work performance depends on their ability to effectively interact with their co-workers and their boss. Some employees have excellent interpersonal skills, but others require training to improve theirs. This includes learning how to be a better listener, how to communicate ideas more clearly, and how to be a more effective team player.

One of the fastest growing areas of interpersonal skill development is diversity training.[26] The two most popular types of this training focus on increasing awareness and building skills. *Awareness training* tries to create an understanding of the need for, and meaning of, managing and valuing diversity. *Skill-building training* educates employees about specific cultural differences in the workplace. Companies leading the way in diversity training include American Express, Avon, Corning, Hewlett-Packard, Monsanto, Motorola, Pacific Gas & Electric, US West, and Xerox.

PROBLEM SOLVING Managers as well as many employees who perform nonroutine tasks have to solve problems on the job. When people require these skills but are deficient in them, they can participate in problem-solving training. This would include activities to sharpen their logic, reasoning, and problem-defining skills, as well as their abilities to assess causation, develop alternatives, analyze alternatives, and select solutions. Problem-solving training has become a basic part of almost every organizational effort to introduce self-managed teams or implement TQM.

Training Methods

Most training takes place on the job. This preference can be attributed to the simplicity and, usually, lower cost of on-the-job training methods. However, on-the-job training can disrupt the workplace and result in an increase in errors as learning proceeds. Also, some skill training is too complex to learn on the job. In such cases, it should take place outside the work setting.[27]

◆ Most training takes place on the job.

ON-THE-JOB TRAINING Popular on-the-job training methods include job rotation and understudy assignments. *Job rotation* involves lateral transfers that enable employees to work at different jobs. Employees get to learn a wide variety of jobs and gain increased insight into the interdependency between jobs and a wider perspective on organizational activities. New employees frequently learn their jobs by understudying a seasoned veteran. In the trades, this is usually called an *apprenticeship*. In white-collar jobs, it is called a *coaching*, or *mentor*, relationship. In each, the understudy works under the observation of an experienced worker, who acts as a model whom the understudy attempts to emulate.

Both job rotation and understudy assignments apply to the learning of technical skills. Interpersonal and problem-solving skills are acquired more effectively by training that takes place off the job.

OFF-THE-JOB TRAINING   There are a number of off-the-job training methods that managers may want to make available to employees. The more popular are classroom lectures, videos, and simulation exercises. *Classroom lectures* are well suited for conveying specific information. They can be used effectively for developing technical and problem-solving skills. *Videos* can also be used to explicitly demonstrate technical skills that are not easily presented by other methods. Interpersonal and problem-solving skills may be best learned through *simulation exercises* such as case analyses, experiential exercises, role playing, and group interaction sessions. Complex computer models, such as those used by airlines in the training of pilots, are another kind of simulation exercise, which in this case is used to teach technical skills. So, too, is *vestibule training*, in which employees learn their jobs on the same equipment they will be using, only the training is conducted away from the actual work floor. Exhibit 15-3 describes the results from a survey of off-the-job instructional methods used for employee training.

Off-the-job training can rely on outside consultants, local college or trade school faculty, or in-house personnel. Most of you are probably familiar with the fact that McDonald's has been training thousands of its managers and future managers since 1961 at its Hamburger University.[28] The heart of Hamburger U's curriculum is a two-week program that combines operations enhancement, equipment management, and interpersonal skills training for restaurant managers and franchisees. But you don't have to be a multibillion-dollar corporation to make a major commitment to in-house training. Granite Rock, Inc., a producer of construction and paving materials, spends nearly 1 percent of gross sales and a whopping 4.2 percent of payroll on training, and has even created its own internal university.[29] Granite Rock University offers more than 50 courses and seminars for company employees on everything from enhancing self-esteem to the mechanics of mobile hydraulic equipment.

Exhibit 15-3   Popularity among Instructional Methods

Method	Percentage
Percentage of organizations using these methods for employee training	
Videotapes	95
Lectures	93
One-on-one instruction	76
Role plays	63
Games	58
Computer-based training	58
Audiotapes	54
Self-assessment/self-testing instruments	53
Case studies	52

Based on a national survey of U.S. companies with at least 100 employees.

Source: Reprinted with permission from the October 1993 issue of *TRAINING* Magazine. © 1993, Lakewood Publications, Minneapolis, MN. All rights reserved.

Individualize Training to Fit the Employee's Learning Style

The way that you process, internalize, and remember new and difficult material isn't necessarily the same way that I do. This fact means that effective training should be individualized to reflect the learning style of the employee.[30]

Some examples of different learning styles include reading, watching, listening, and participating. Some people absorb information better when they read about it. They're the kind of people who can learn to use computers by sitting in their study and reading manuals. Some people learn best by observation. They watch others and then emulate the behaviors they've seen. Such people can watch someone use a computer for a while, then copy what they've seen. Listeners rely heavily on their auditory senses to absorb information. They would prefer to learn how to use a computer by listening to an audiotape. People who prefer a participating style learn by doing. They want to sit down, turn on the computer, and gain hands-on experience by practicing.

You can translate these styles into different learning methods. To maximize learning, readers should be given books or other reading material to review; watchers should get the opportunity to observe individuals modeling the new skills either in person or on video; listeners will benefit from hearing lectures or audiotapes; and participants will benefit most from experiential opportunities where they can simulate and practice the new skills.

These different learning styles are obviously not mutually exclusive. In fact, good teachers recognize that their students learn differently and, therefore, provide multiple learning methods. They assign readings before class; give lectures; use visual aids to illustrate concepts; and have students participate in group projects, case analyses, role plays, and experiential learning exercises. If you know the preferred style of an employee, you can design his or her training program to optimize this preference. If you don't have that information, it's probably best to design the program to use a variety of learning styles. Overreliance on a single style places individuals who don't learn well from that style at a disadvantage.

Hilton Hotels offers employees a variety of training methods to accommodate individual learning styles and involves employees in developing training programs. Employee feedback helped Hilton design its video-based training series shown here. Hilton's huge investment in training and recognition that employees learn differently pay big dividends. Its workforce is the benchmark for service excellence in the hospitality industry.

Career Development

Few human resource issues have changed as much in the past couple of decades as the role of the organization in its employees' careers.[31] Twenty years ago, when a person was more likely to spend his or her entire work years with the same employer, most medium-sized and large organizations engaged in extensive employee career planning. It focused exclusively on developing employees for opportunities within the specific organization. For instance, they would develop sophisticated replacement charts that would identify potential promotion candidates for key internal positions. They'd also offer a wide range of in-house career development programs to prepare employees for promotions. Companies like Aetna Life, General Electric, Merrill Lynch, and Toshiba still invest heavily in this form of career planning. But as more and more organizations downsize their operations, reengineer processes, and restructure themselves to increase flexibility, they're shifting career development responsibility to their employees. Consistent with the employee empowerment movement, an increasing number of organizations are empowering employees to manage their own careers. Apple Computer, for instance, supports employees with workshops, career counseling, and tuition-reimbursement programs. But employees are told they have to take responsibility for planning their personal career track. It's not their manager's or the company's job to define their future. In those cases where it becomes evident that an employee's personal goals can't be fulfilled at Apple, company counselors even help the individual prepare for a future outside Apple.

In spite of this shifting of responsibility trend, there are definite benefits that accrue to organizations that offer career development programs.[32] These include ensuring the right people will be available for meeting changing staffing requirements, increasing workforce diversity, and providing employees with more realistic job expectations. In this section, we provide a brief historical review of the changing role that organizations are playing in employee career development. Then we describe both the organization's and employee's responsibilities for career development today.

First, however, let's define what we mean by the term *career*. A **career** is "the evolving sequence of a person's work experiences over time."[33] This definition does not imply advancement or success or failure. Any work, paid or unpaid, pursued over an extended period of time can constitute a career. In addition to formal job work, it may include schoolwork, homemaking, or volunteer work.[34]

A BRIEF LOOK BACKWARDS Management's role in career development has undergone significant changes in recent years. It has gone from paternalism—in which the organization took responsibility for managing its employees' careers—to supporting individuals as they take personal responsibility for their future.

For much of the twentieth century, companies recruited young workers with the intent that they would spend their entire career inside that single organization. For those with the right credentials and motivation, they created promotion paths dotted with ever increasing responsibility. Employers would provide the training and opportunities, and employees would respond by demonstrating loyalty and hard work. For most organizations today, this for-

---

◆ An increasing number of organizations are empowering employees to manage their own careers.

---

career
A sequence of positions occupied by a person during the course of a lifetime.

malized, employer-directed program of career planning has been discarded. It's been replaced by self-directed careers. The new compact between employers and employees transfers responsibility for career development from the organization to the employee. So today's employees are becoming more concerned than ever with keeping their skills, abilities, and knowledge current and preparing for tomorrow's new tasks. They are beginning to see learning as a lifelong process. Increasingly, today's employees are balancing current work responsibilities with taking courses during their off hours. In the same way that TQM emphasizes continuous improvement, self-directed careers require continuous training and learning.

What happened? Why have so many organizations moved out of the business of providing career guidance for their employees? Several forces seem to be at work.[35] For instance, organizational efforts toward creating lifetime employment have, for the most part, been discarded. Employers don't want to invest in expensive career planning programs for short-term employees. And employees aren't motivated to learn organization-specific skills that may not be compatible with the skills needed by other organizations. Additionally, bureaucracies were designed to carve out well-defined career paths for their members. They created narrow, functional specialists located in a multilayered hierarchy. As bureaucracies have been dismantled—often replaced by cross-functional teams, flat structures, and outsourced activities—so too have career-planning programs.

THE ORGANIZATION'S RESPONSIBILITIES What, if any, responsibility does the organization have for career development under these new rules? Amoco Corp.'s career development program is a model for modern companies.[36] It's designed around employee self-reliance and to help employees reflect on their marketability both inside and outside the Chicago-based oil company. All workers are encouraged to participate in a half-day introduction to the program and full-day self-assessment and self-development sessions. The company supports its employees by providing information—a worldwide electronic job-posting system, a network of career advisers, and a worldwide directory of Amoco employees and their skills from which company managers can search for candidates for job openings. But the whole program is voluntary and assumes that it's the employees' responsibility to maintain his or her employability.

The essence of a progressive career development program is built on providing support for employees to continually add to their skills, abilities, and knowledge. This support includes:

1. *Clearly communicating the organization's goals and future strategies.* When people know where the organization is headed, they're better able to develop a personal plan to share in that future.
2. *Creating growth opportunities.* Employees should have the opportunity to get new, interesting, and professionally challenging work experiences.
3. *Offering financial assistance.* The organization should offer tuition reimbursement to help employees keep current.
4. *Providing the time for employees to learn.* Organizations should be generous in providing paid time off from work for off-the-job training. Additionally, workloads should not be so demanding that they pre-

clude employees from having the time to develop new skills, abilities, and knowledge.

THE EMPLOYEE'S RESPONSIBILITIES Today's employees should manage their own careers like entrepreneurs managing a small business. They should think of themselves as self-employed, even if employed in a large organization.[37] In a world of "free agency," the successful career will be built on maintaining flexibility and keeping skills and knowledge up-to-date. The following suggestions are consistent with the view that you, and only you, hold primary responsibility for your career.[38]

1. *Know yourself.* Know your strengths and weaknesses. What talents can you bring to an employer? Personal career planning begins by being honest with yourself.

2. *Manage your reputation.* Without appearing as a braggart, let others both inside and outside your current organization know about your achievements. Make you and your accomplishments visible.

3. *Build and maintain network contacts.* In a world of high mobility, you need to develop contacts. Join national and local professional associations, attend conferences, and network at social gatherings.

4. *Keep current.* Develop those specific skills and abilities that are in high demand. Avoid learning organization-specific skills that can't be transferred quickly to other employers.

5. *Balance your specialist and generalist competencies.* You need to stay current within your technical specialty. But you also need to develop general competencies that give you the versatility to react to an ever-changing work environment. Overemphasis in a single functional area or even in a narrow industry can limit your mobility.

6. *Document your achievements.* Employers are increasingly looking to what you've accomplished rather than the titles you've held. Seek jobs and assignments that will provide increasing challenges and that will also offer objective evidence of your competencies.

7. *Keep your options open.* Always have contingency plans prepared that you can call on when needed. You never know when your group will be eliminated, your department downsized, your project canceled, or your company acquired in a takeover. "Hope for the best but be prepared for the worst" may be cliché, but it's still not bad advice.

Performance Evaluation

Would you study differently or exert a different level of effort for a college course graded on a pass-fail basis than for one where letter grades from A to F are used? When I ask that question of students, I usually get an affirmative answer. Students typically tell me that they study harder when letter grades are at stake. Additionally, they tell me that when they take a course on a pass-fail basis, they tend to do just enough to ensure a passing grade.

This finding illustrates how performance evaluation systems influence behavior. Major determinants of your in-class behavior and out-of-class studying effort in college are the criteria and techniques your instructor uses to evaluate your performance. Of course, what applies in the college context also applies to employees at work. In this section, we show how the choice of a performance evaluation system and the way it's administered can be an important force influencing employee behavior.

Purposes of Performance Evaluation

Performance evaluation serves a number of purposes in organizations (see Exhibit 15-4 for survey results on primary uses of evaluations).[39] Management uses evaluations for general *human resource decisions*. Evaluations provide input into such important decisions as promotions, transfers, and terminations. Evaluations *identify training and development needs*. They pinpoint employee skills and competencies that are currently inadequate but for which programs can be developed to remedy. Performance evaluations can be used as a *criterion against which selection and development programs are validated*. Newly hired employees who perform poorly can be identified through performance evaluation. Similarly, the effectiveness of training and development programs can be determined by assessing how well those employees who have participated do on their performance evaluation. Evaluations also fulfill the purpose of *providing feedback to employees* on how the organization views their performance. Furthermore, performance evaluations are used as the *basis for reward allocations*. Decisions as to who gets merit pay increases and other rewards are frequently determined by performance evaluations.

Each of these functions of performance evaluation is important. Yet their importance to us depends on the perspective we're taking. Several are clearly relevant to human resource management decisions. But our interest is in organizational behavior. As a result, we shall be emphasizing performance evaluation in its role as a mechanism for providing feedback and as a determinant of reward allocations.

Performance Evaluation and Motivation

In chapter 5, considerable attention was given to the expectancy model of motivation. We argued that this model currently offers one of the best explanations of what conditions the amount of effort an individual will exert on his or her job. A vital component of this model is performance, specifically the effort–performance and performance–reward linkages.

Exhibit 15-4 Primary Uses of Performance Evaluations

Use	Percent*
Compensation	85.6
Performance feedback	65.1
Training	64.3
Promotion	45.3
Human resource planning	43.1
Retention/discharge	30.3
Research	17.2

*Based on responses from 600 organizations.

Source: Based on "Performance Appraisal: Current Practices and Techniques," *Personnel*, May–June 1984, p.57.

But what defines *performance*? In the expectancy model, it's the individual's performance evaluation. To maximize motivation, people need to perceive that the effort they exert leads to a favorable performance evaluation and that the favorable evaluation will lead to the rewards that they value.

Following the expectancy model of motivation, if the objectives that employees are expected to achieve are unclear, if the criteria for measuring those objectives are vague, and if the employees lack confidence that their efforts will lead to a satisfactory appraisal of their performance or believe that there will be an unsatisfactory payoff by the organization when their performance objectives are achieved, we can expect individuals to work considerably below their potential.

What Do We Evaluate?

The criteria or criterion that management chooses to evaluate, when appraising employee performance, will have a major influence on what employees do. Two examples illustrate this.

In a public employment agency, which served workers seeking employment and employers seeking workers, employment interviewers were appraised by the number of interviews they conducted. Consistent with the thesis that the evaluating criteria influence behavior, interviewers emphasized the *number* of interviews conducted rather than the *placements* of clients in jobs.[40]

A management consultant specializing in police research noticed that, in one community, officers would come on duty for their shift, proceed to get into their police cars, drive to the highway that cut through the town, and speed back and forth along this highway for their entire shift. Clearly this fast cruising had little to do with good police work, but this behavior made considerably more sense once the consultant learned that the community's city council used mileage on police vehicles as an evaluative measure of police effectiveness.[41]

The performance of game testers in the quality assurance department of Interplay Productions, a producer of computer games, is evaluated on individual task outcomes. The goal of game testers is to find "bugs" in the programming of the games. When they find a flaw, testers must be able to tell the programmers how they spotted the flaw. They score extra points when they can also suggest how to fix the problem. Criteria for advancement in the company include the ability of game testers to explain a complex computer problem in simple terms and to generate ideas for new games.

These examples demonstrate the importance of criteria in performance evaluation. This, of course, begs the question: What should management evaluate? The three most popular sets of criteria are individual task outcomes, behaviors, and traits.

INDIVIDUAL TASK OUTCOMES If ends count, rather than means, then management should evaluate an employee's task outcomes. Using task outcomes, a plant manager could be judged on criteria such as quantity produced, scrap generated, and cost per unit of production. Similarly, a salesperson could be assessed on overall sales volume in his or her territory, dollar increase in sales, and number of new accounts established.

BEHAVIORS In many cases, it's difficult to identify specific outcomes that can be directly attributable to an employee's actions. This is particularly true of personnel in staff positions and individuals whose work assignments are intrinsically part of a group effort. In the latter case, the group's performance may be readily evaluated, but the contribution of each group member may be difficult or impossible to identify clearly. In such instances, it is not unusual for management to evaluate the employee's behavior. Using the previous examples, behaviors of a plant manager that could be used for performance evaluation purposes might include promptness in submitting his or her monthly reports or the leadership style that the manager exhibits. Pertinent salesperson behaviors could be average number of contact calls made per day or sick days used per year.

TRAITS The weakest set of criteria, yet one that is still widely used by organizations, is individual traits.[42] We say they are weaker than either task outcomes or behaviors because they are farthest removed from the actual performance of the job itself. Traits such as having "a good attitude," showing "confidence," being "dependable" or "cooperative," "looking busy," or possessing "a wealth of experience" may or may not be highly correlated with positive task outcomes, but only the naive would ignore the reality that such traits are frequently used in organizations as criteria for assessing an employee's level of performance.

Who Should Do the Evaluating?

Who should evaluate an employee's performance? The obvious answer would seem to be his or her immediate boss! By tradition, a manager's authority typically has included appraising subordinates' performance. The logic behind this tradition seems to be that since managers are held responsible for their subordinates' performance, it only makes sense that these managers do the evaluating of that performance. But that logic may be flawed. Others may actually be able to do the job better.

IMMEDIATE SUPERIOR As we implied, about 95 percent of all performance evaluations at the lower and middle levels of the organization are conducted by the employee's immediate boss.[43] Yet a number of organizations are recognizing the drawbacks to using this source of evaluation. For instance, many bosses feel unqualified to evaluate the unique contributions of each of their subordinates. Others resent being asked to "play God" with their employees' careers. Additionally, with many of today's organizations using self-managed teams, telecommuting, and other organizing devices that distance bosses from their employees, an employee's immediate superior may not be a reliable judge of that employee's performance.

PEERS   Peer evaluations are one of the most reliable sources of appraisal data. Why? First, peers are close to the action. Daily interactions provide them with a comprehensive view of an employee's job performance. Second, using peers as raters results in a number of independent judgments. A boss can offer only a single evaluation, but peers can provide multiple appraisals. And the average of several ratings is often more reliable than a single evaluation. On the downside, peer evaluations can suffer from co-workers' unwillingness to evaluate one another and from biases based on friendship or animosity.

SELF-EVALUATION   Having employees evaluate their own performance is consistent with values such as self-management and empowerment. Self-evaluations get high marks from employees themselves; they tend to lessen employees' defensiveness about the appraisal process; and they make excellent vehicles for stimulating job performance discussions between employees and their superiors. However, as you might guess, they suffer from overinflated assessment and self-serving bias. Moreover, self-evaluations are often low in agreement with superiors' ratings.[44] Because of these serious drawbacks, self-evaluations are probably better suited to developmental uses than evaluative purposes.

IMMEDIATE SUBORDINATES   A fourth judgment source is an employee's immediate subordinates. For instance, Datatec Industries, a maker of in-store computer systems, uses this form of appraisal.[45] The company's president says it's consistent with the firm's core values of honesty, openness, and employee empowerment.

Immediate subordinates' evaluations can provide accurate and detailed information about a manager's behavior because the evaluators typically have frequent contact with the evaluatee. The obvious problem with this form of rating is fear of reprisal from bosses given unfavorable evaluations. Therefore, respondent anonymity is crucial if these evaluations are to be accurate.

THE COMPREHENSIVE APPROACH: 360-DEGREE EVALUATIONS   The latest approach to performance evaluation is the use of 360-degree evaluations.[46] It provides for performance feedback from the full circle of daily contacts that an employee might have, ranging from mailroom personnel to customers to bosses to peers (see Exhibit 15-5). The number of appraisals can be as few as three or four evaluations or as many as 25; with most organizations collecting five to ten per employee.

A recent survey found 26 percent of U.S. companies using some form of 360-degree feedback as part of the review process.[47] This includes companies like Alcoa, Du Pont, Levi Strauss, Honeywell, UPS, Sprint, Amoco, AT&T, and W.L. Gore & Associates.

What's the appeal of 360-degree evaluations? They fit well into organizations that have introduced teams, employee involvement, and TQM programs. By relying on feedback from co-workers, customers, and subordinates,

Exhibit 15-5
360-Degree Evaluations

The primary objective of the 360-degree performance evaluation is to pool feedback from all of the employee's customers

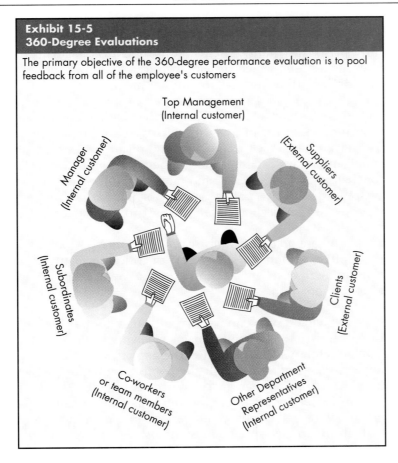

Source: Adapted from *Personnel Journal*, November 1994, p. 100.

these organizations are hoping to give everyone more of a sense of participation in the review process and gain more accurate readings on employee performance.

Methods of Performance Evaluation

The previous sections explained *what* we evaluate and *who* should do the evaluating. Now we ask: *How* do we evaluate an employee's performance? That is, what are the specific techniques for evaluation? This section reviews the major performance evaluation methods.

WRITTEN ESSAYS Probably the simplest method of evaluation is to write a narrative describing an employee's strengths, weaknesses, past performance, potential, and suggestions for improvement. The written essay requires no complex forms or extensive training to complete. But the results often reflect the ability of the writer. A good or bad appraisal may be determined as much by the evaluator's writing skill as by the employee's actual level of performance.

CRITICAL INCIDENTS **Critical incidents** focus the evaluator's attention on those behaviors that are key in making the difference between executing a job effectively and executing it ineffectively. That is, the appraiser writes

critical incidents
Evaluating those behaviors that are key in making the difference between executing a job effectively and executing it ineffectively.

down anecdotes that describe what the employee did that was especially effective or ineffective. The key here is that only specific behaviors, not vaguely defined personality traits, are cited. A list of critical incidents provides a rich set of examples from which the employee can be shown those behaviors that are desirable and those that call for improvement.

graphic rating scales
An evaluation method where the evaluator rates performance factors on an incremental scale.

GRAPHIC RATING SCALES One of the oldest and most popular methods of evaluation is the use of **graphic rating scales**. In this method, a set of performance factors, such as quantity and quality of work, depth of knowledge, cooperation, loyalty, attendance, honesty, and initiative, is listed. The evaluator then goes down the list and rates each on incremental scales. The scales typically specify five points, so a factor like *job knowledge* might be rated 1 ("poorly informed about work duties") to 5 ("has complete mastery of all phases of the job").

Why are graphic ratings scales so popular? Though they don't provide the depth of information that essays or critical incidents do, they are less time consuming to develop and administer. They also allow for quantitative analysis and comparison.

behaviorally anchored rating scales
An evaluation method where actual job-related behaviors are rated along a continuum.

BEHAVIORALLY ANCHORED RATING SCALES **Behaviorally anchored rating scales** (BARS) combine major elements from the critical incident and graphic rating scale approaches: The appraiser rates the employees based on items along a continuum, but the points are examples of actual behavior on the given job rather than general descriptions or traits.

BARS specify definite, observable, and measurable job behavior. Examples of job-related behavior and performance dimensions are found by asking participants to give specific illustrations of effective and ineffective behavior regarding each performance dimension. These behavioral examples are then translated into a set of performance dimensions, each dimension having varying levels of performance. The results of this process are behavioral descriptions, such as *anticipates, plans, executes, solves immediate problems, carries out orders*, and *handles emergency situations*.

MULTIPERSON COMPARISONS Multiperson comparisons evaluate one individual's performance against the performance of one or more others. It is a relative rather than an absolute measuring device. The three most popular comparisons are group order ranking, individual ranking, and paired comparisons.

group order ranking
An evaluation method that places employees into a particular classification such as quartiles.

The **group order ranking** requires the evaluator to place employees into a particular classification, such as top one-fifth or second one-fifth. This method is often used in recommending students to graduate schools. Evaluators are asked whether the student ranks in the top 5 percent of the class, the next 5 percent, the next 15 percent, and so forth. But when used by managers to appraise employees, managers deal with all their subordinates. Therefore, if a rater has 20 subordinates, only four can be in the top fifth and, of course, four must also be relegated to the bottom fifth.

individual ranking
An evaluation method that rank-orders employees from best to worst.

The **individual ranking** approach rank-orders employees from best to worst. If the manager is required to appraise 30 subordinates, this approach assumes that the difference between the first and second employee is the same as that between the twenty-first and twenty-second. Even though some of the employees may be closely grouped, this approach allows for no ties. The result is a clear ordering of employees, from the highest performer down to the lowest.

The **paired comparison** approach compares each employee with every other employee and rates each as either the superior or the weaker member of the pair. After all paired comparisons are made, each employee is assigned a summary ranking based on the number of superior scores he or she achieved. This approach ensures that each employee is compared against every other, but it can obviously become unwieldy when many employees are being compared.

paired comparison
An evaluation method that compares each employee with every other employee and assigns a summary ranking based on the number of superior scores that the employee achieves.

Multiperson comparisons can be combined with one of the other methods to blend the best from both absolute and relative standards. For example, in an effort to deal with grade inflation, Dartmouth College recently changed its transcripts to include not only a letter grade but also class size and class average.[48] So a prospective employer or graduate school can now look at two students who each got a B in their physical geology courses and draw considerably different conclusions about each because next to one grade it says the average grade was a C, while next to the other it says the average grade was a B+. Obviously, the former student performed relatively better than did the latter.

Potential Problems

While organizations may seek to make the performance evaluation process free from personal biases, prejudices, and idiosyncrasies, a number of potential problems can creep into the process. To the degree that the following factors are prevalent, an employee's evaluation is likely to be distorted.

SINGLE CRITERION The typical employee's job is made up of a number of tasks. An airline flight attendant's job, for example, includes welcoming passengers, seeing to their comfort, serving meals, and offering safety advice. If performance on this job were assessed by a single criterion measure—say, the time it took to provide food and beverages to a hundred passengers—the result would be a limited evaluation of that job. More important, flight attendants whose performance evaluation included assessment on only this single criterion would be motivated to ignore those other tasks in their job. Similarly, if a football quarterback were appraised only on his percentage of completed passes, he would be likely to throw short passes and only in situations where he felt assured that they would be caught. Our point is that where employees are evaluated on a single job criterion, and where successful performance on that job requires good performance on a number of criteria, employees will emphasize the single criterion to the exclusion of other job-relevant factors.

LENIENCY ERROR Every evaluator has his or her own value system that acts as a standard against which appraisals are made. Relative to the true or actual performance an individual exhibits, some evaluators mark high and others low. The former is referred to as positive **leniency error**, and the latter as negative leniency error. When evaluators are positively lenient in their appraisal, an individual's performance becomes overstated, that is, rated higher

leniency error
The tendency to evaluate a set of employees too high (positive) or too low (negative).

than it actually should be. This results in inflated evaluations—a problem widely acknowledged to exist in U.S. organizations.[49] A negative leniency error understates performance, giving the individual a lower appraisal than deserved.

If all individuals in an organization were appraised by the same person, there would be no problem. Although there would be an error factor, it would be applied equally to everyone. The difficulty arises when we have different raters with different leniency errors making judgments. For example, assume that Jones and Smith are performing the same job for different supervisors, but they have absolutely identical job performance. If Jones's supervisor tends to err toward positive leniency, while Smith's supervisor errs toward negative leniency, we might be confronted with two dramatically different evaluations.

HALO ERROR   The halo effect or error, as we noted in chapter 3, is the tendency for an evaluator to let the assessment of an individual on one trait influence his or her evaluation of that person on other traits. For example, if an employee tends to be dependable, we might become biased toward that individual to the extent that we will rate him or her high on many desirable attributes.[50]

People who design teaching appraisal forms for college students to fill out to evaluate the effectiveness of their instructors each semester must confront the halo error. Students tend to rate a faculty member as outstanding on all criteria when they are particularly appreciative of a few things he or she does in the classroom. Similarly, a few bad habits—like showing up late for lectures, for example, or being slow in returning papers, or assigning an extremely demanding reading requirement—might result in students' evaluating the instructor as "lousy" across the board.

similarity error
Giving special consideration when rating others to those qualities that the evaluator perceives in himself or herself.

SIMILARITY ERROR   When evaluators rate other people giving special consideration to those qualities that they perceive in themselves, they are making a **similarity error**. For example, evaluators who perceive themselves as aggressive may evaluate others by looking for aggressiveness. Those who demonstrate this characteristic tend to benefit, while others are penalized.[51]

Again, this error would tend to wash out if the same evaluator appraised all the people in the organization. However, interrater reliability obviously suffers when various evaluators are utilizing their own similarity criteria.

LOW DIFFERENTIATION   It's possible that, regardless of whom the appraiser evaluates and what traits are used, the pattern of evaluation remains the same. It's possible that the evaluator's ability to appraise objectively and accurately has been impeded by social differentiation, that is, the evaluator's style of rating behavior.

It has been suggested that evaluators may be classified as (1) high differentiators, who use all or most of the scale; or (2) low differentiators, who use a limited range of the scale.[52]

Low differentiators tend to ignore or suppress differences, perceiving the universe as being more uniform than it really is. High differentiators, on the other hand, tend to utilize all available information to the utmost extent and thus are better able to perceptually define anomalies and contradictions than are low differentiators.[53]

This finding tells us that evaluations made by low differentiators need to be carefully inspected and that the people working for a low differentiator have a high probability of being appraised as being significantly more homogeneous than they really are.

FORCING INFORMATION TO MATCH NONPERFORMANCE CRITERIA While rarely advocated, it is not an infrequent practice to find the formal evaluation taking place *following* the decision as to how the individual has been performing. This may sound illogical, but it merely recognizes that subjective, yet formal, decisions are often arrived at prior to the gathering of objective information to support those decisions.[54] For example, if the evaluator believes that the evaluation should not be based on performance, but rather on seniority, he or she may be unknowingly adjusting each "performance" evaluation so as to bring it into line with the employee's seniority rank. In this and other similar cases, the evaluator is increasing or decreasing performance appraisals to align with the nonperformance criteria actually being utilized.

Overcoming the Problems

Just because organizations can encounter problems with performance evaluations should not lead managers to give up on the process. Some things can be done to overcome most of the problems we have identified.[55]

USE MULTIPLE CRITERIA Since successful performance on most jobs requires doing a number of things well, all those "things" should be identified and evaluated. The more complex the job, the more criteria that will need to be identified and evaluated. But everything need not be assessed. The critical activities that lead to high or low performance are the ones that need to be evaluated.

EMPHASIZE BEHAVIORS RATHER THAN TRAITS Many traits often considered to be related to good performance may, in fact, have little or no performance relationship. For example, traits like loyalty, initiative, courage, reliability, and self-expression are intuitively appealing as desirable characteristics in employees. But the relevant question is: Are individuals who are evaluated as high on those traits higher performers than those who rate low? We can't answer this question easily. We know that there are employees who rate high on these characteristics and are poor performers. We can find others who are excellent performers but do not score well on traits such as these. Our conclusion is that traits like loyalty and initiative may be prized by managers, but there is no evidence to support that certain traits will be adequate synonyms for performance in a large cross section of jobs.

Another weakness of trait evaluation is the judgment itself. What is "loyalty"? When is an employee "reliable"? What you consider "loyalty," I may not. So traits suffer from weak interrater agreement.

DOCUMENT PERFORMANCE BEHAVIORS IN A DIARY By keeping a diary of specific critical incidents for each employee, evaluations tend to be more accurate.[56] Diaries, for instance, tend to reduce leniency and halo errors because they encourage the evaluator to focus on performance-related behaviors rather than traits.

USE MULTIPLE EVALUATORS   As the number of evaluators increases, the probability of attaining more accurate information increases. If rater error tends to follow a normal curve, an increase in the number of appraisers will tend to find the majority congregating about the middle. You see this approach being used in athletic competitions in such sports as diving and gymnastics. A set of evaluators judges a performance, the highest and lowest scores are dropped, and the final performance evaluation is made up from the cumulative scores of those remaining. The logic of multiple evaluators applies to organizations as well.

If an employee has had ten supervisors, nine having rated her excellent and one poor, we can discount the value of the one poor evaluation. Therefore, by moving employees about within the organization so as to gain a number of evaluations or by using multiple assessors (as provided in 360-degree appraisals), we increase the probability of achieving more valid and reliable evaluations.

EVALUATE SELECTIVELY   It has been suggested that appraisers should evaluate in only those areas in which they have some expertise.[57] If raters make evaluations on only those dimensions on which they are in a good position to rate, we increase the interrater agreement and make the evaluation a more valid process. This approach also recognizes that different organizational levels often have different orientations toward ratees and observe them in different settings. In general, therefore, we would recommend that appraisers should be as close as possible, in terms of organizational level, to the individual being evaluated. Conversely, the more levels that separate the evaluator and evaluatee, the less opportunity the evaluator has to observe the individual's behavior and, not surprisingly, the greater the possibility for inaccuracies.

The specific application of these concepts would result in having immediate supervisors, co-workers, subordinates, or some combination of these

Raychem, a producer of electronics and electrical equipment, uses multirater assessments in evaluating on-the-job performance. Former Raychem CEO Robert Saldich was evaluated by his team of top managers. They agreed in their evaluations that Saldich needed to improve in the area of contingency planning. Saldich was surprised by what he learned. He knew he was weak in contingency planning, but he was not aware that his weakness was so obvious to his top managers.

people provide the major input into the appraisal and having them evaluate those factors they are best qualified to judge. For example, it has been suggested that when professors are evaluating secretaries within a university, they use such criteria as judgment, technical competence, and conscientiousness, whereas peers (other secretaries) use such criteria as job knowledge, organization, cooperation with co-workers, and responsibility.[58] Using both professors and peers as appraisers is a logical and reliable approach, since it results in having people appraise only those dimensions on which they are in a good position to make judgments.

TRAIN EVALUATORS If you can't *find* good evaluators, the alternative is to *make* good evaluators. There is substantial evidence that training evaluators can make them more accurate raters.[59]

Common errors such as halo and leniency have been minimized or eliminated in workshops where managers practice observing and rating behaviors. These workshops typically run from one to three days, but allocating many hours to training may not always be necessary. One case has been cited where both halo and leniency errors were decreased immediately after exposing evaluators to explanatory training sessions lasting only five minutes.[60] But the effects of training do appear to diminish over time.[61] This suggests the need for regular refresher sessions.

PROVIDE EMPLOYEES WITH DUE PROCESS The concept of *due process* can be applied to appraisals to increase the perception that employees are treated fairly.[62] Three features characterize due process systems: (1) Individuals are provided with adequate notice of what is expected of them; (2) all relevant evidence to a proposed violation is aired in a fair hearing so individuals affected can respond; and (3) the final decision is based on the evidence and free from bias.

There is considerable evidence that evaluation systems often violate employees' due process by providing them with infrequent and relatively general performance feedback, allowing them little input into the appraisal process, and knowingly introducing bias into performance ratings. However, where due process has been part of the evaluation system, employees report positive reactions to the appraisal process, perceive the evaluation results as more accurate, and express increased intent to remain with the organization.

Providing Performance Feedback

For many managers, few activities are more unpleasant than providing performance feedback to employees.[63] In fact, unless pressured by organizational policies and controls, managers are likely to ignore this responsibility.[64]

Why the reluctance to give performance feedback? There seem to be at least three reasons. First, managers are often uncomfortable discussing performance weaknesses directly with employees. Given that almost every employee could stand to improve in some areas, managers fear a confrontation when presenting negative feedback. This apparently even applies when people give negative feedback to a computer! Bill Gates reports that Microsoft recently conducted a project that required users to rate their experience with a computer. "When we had the computer the users had worked with ask for an evaluation of its performance, the responses tended to be positive. But when we had a second computer ask the same people to evaluate their encounters with the first machine, the people were significantly more critical. Their reluctance to criticize the first computer 'to its face' suggested that they didn't want to hurt its feelings, even though they knew it was only a machine."[65] Second, many employees tend to become defensive when their weaknesses are pointed out. Instead of accepting the feedback as constructive and a basis for improving performance, some employees challenge the evaluation by criticizing the manager or redirecting blame to someone else. Finally, employees tend to have an inflated assessment of their own performance. Statistically speaking, half of all employees must be below-average performers. But the evidence indicates that the average employee's estimate of his or her own performance level generally falls around the 75th percentile.[66] So even when managers are providing good news, employees are likely to perceive it as not good enough!

> ◆ The average employee's estimate of his or her own performance level generally falls around the 75th percentile.

The solution to the performance feedback problem is not to ignore it, but to train managers in how to conduct constructive feedback sessions. An effective review—one in which the employee perceives the appraisal as fair, the manager as sincere, and the climate as constructive—can result in the employee leaving the interview in an upbeat mood, informed about the performance areas in which he or she needs to improve, and determined to correct the deficiencies.[67] In addition, the performance review should be designed more as a counseling activity than a judgment process. This can best be accomplished by allowing the review to evolve out of the employee's own self-evaluation.

What About Team Performance Evaluations?

Performance evaluation concepts have been almost exclusively developed with only individual employees in mind. This reflects the historic belief that individuals are the core building block around which organizations are built. But as we've described throughout this book, more and more organizations are restructuring themselves around teams. In those organizations using teams, how should they evaluate performance? Four suggestions have been offered for designing a system that supports and improves the performance of teams.[68]

1. *Tie the team's results to the organization's goals.* It's important to find measurements that apply to important goals that the team is supposed to accomplish.

2. *Begin with the team's customers and the work process the team follows to satisfy customers' needs.* The final product the customer receives can be evaluated in terms of the customer's requirements. The transactions between teams can be evaluated based on delivery and quality. And the process steps can be evaluated based on waste and cycle time.

3. *Measure both team and individual performance.* Define the roles of each team member in terms of accomplishments that support the team's work process. Then assess each member's contribution and the team's overall performance.

4. *Train the team to create its own measures.* Having the team define its objectives and those of each member ensures everyone understands their role on the team and helps the team develop into a more cohesive unit.

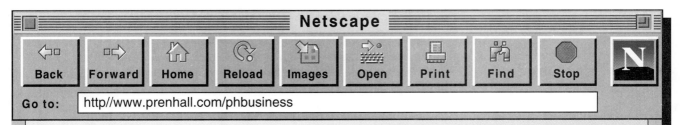

OB in the News

Employees Dislike Reviews, Even When They're Favorable

Employees don't like performance reviews. Managers don't either. Almost every major survey finds that the employees who get performance evaluations and most supervisors who give them rate the process as a resounding failure.

There has always been criticism of the performance evaluation process. But that criticism seems to be louder nowadays than ever.

In spite of all the potential benefits that can accrue from performance evaluations, critics claim they're not working. "Most of the time, it's just a ritual that managers go through," says a retired human resources executive. "They pull out last year's review, update it and do it quickly."

Experts say evaluation systems often don't work because most were designed primarily by personnel specialists with limited input from managers who use the system and even less input from the employees.

One problem: Not only don't employees like to hear bad news, but even when a review is generally positive, many seem to hear only the negatives. Another problem: Many supervisors hate giving negative feedback. They're uncomfortable saying anything negative and fear retribution from their employees. For instance, researchers in Philadelphia found that 98 percent of 151 area managers encountered some type of aggression after giving employees negative appraisals. For many supervisors, the easy way out is just to rate employees as "excellent" in all categories, which, of course, undermines much of the value of evaluations.

Despite all the inadequacies of performance evaluation systems, only a few organizations have actually eliminated their written appraisal forms. The primary reason seems to be that they provide documentation to help the organization defend itself in wrongful discharge lawsuits. But organizations are experimenting with modifications to the traditional annual performance review conducted by a supervisor. A growing number of companies, especially those with employees working in teams, have changed to the 360-degree appraisal. More and more companies require managers to formally review employees at least twice a year and informally provide feedback on a year-round basis.

Based on T.D. Schellhardt, "It's Time to Evaluate Your Work, and All Involved Are Groaning," *Wall Street Journal*, November 19, 1996, p. A1.

Take It to the Net

We invite you to visit the Robbins page on the Prentice Hall Web site at:

http://www.prenhall.com/robbinsorgbeh

for this chapter's World Wide Web exercise.

The Union–Management Interface

labor union
An organization, made up of employees, that acts collectively to protect and promote employee interests.

Labor unions are a vehicle by which employees act collectively to protect and promote their interests. Currently, in the United States, approximately 15 percent of the workforce belongs to and is represented by a union. This number is considerably higher in other countries. For instance, the comparable figures for Canada and Australia are 37 percent and 41 percent, respectively.

For employees who are members of a labor union, wage levels and conditions of employment are explicitly articulated in a contract that is negotiated, through collective bargaining, between representatives of the union and the organization's management. Where a labor union exists, it influences a number of organizational activities.[69] Recruitment sources, hiring criteria, work schedules, job design, redress procedures, safety rules, and eligibility for training programs are examples of activities that are influenced by unions. American labor unions, having to contend with declining job markets in industries where they were historically strong—such as steel, autos, rubber—have focused their attention in recent years on improving stagnant wages, discouraging corporate downsizings, minimizing the outsourcing of jobs, and coping with job obsolescence.[70]

The most obvious and pervasive area of labor's influence is wage rates and working conditions. Where unions exist, performance evaluation systems tend to be less complex because they play a relatively small part in reward decisions. Wage rates, when determined through collective bargaining, emphasize seniority and downplay performance differences.

Exhibit 15-6 shows what impact a union has on an employee's performance and job satisfaction. The union contract affects motivation through

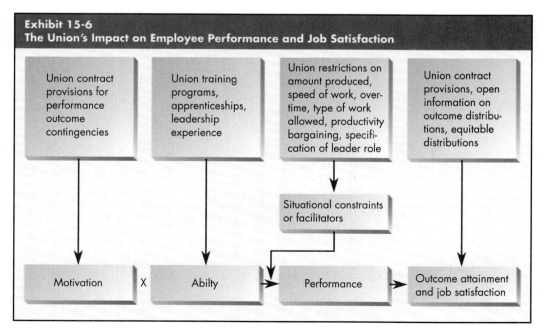

Exhibit 15-6
The Union's Impact on Employee Performance and Job Satisfaction

Source: T.H. Hammer, "Relationships Between Local Union Characteristics and Worker Behavior and Attitudes," *Academy of Management Journal*, December 1978, p. 573.

determination of wage rates, seniority rules, layoff procedures, promotion criteria, and security provisions. Unions can influence the competence with which employees perform their jobs by offering special training programs to their members, by requiring apprenticeships, and by allowing members to gain leadership experience through union organizational activities. The actual level of employee performance will be further influenced by collective bargaining restrictions placed on the amount of work produced, the speed with which work can be done, overtime allowances per worker, and the kind of tasks a given employee is allowed to perform.

The research evaluating the specific effect of unions on productivity is mixed.[71] Some studies found that unions had a positive effect on productivity as a result of improvements in labor–management relations as well as improvements in the quality of the labor force. In contrast, other studies have shown that unions negatively impact on productivity by reducing the effectiveness of some productivity enhancing managerial practices and by contributing to a poorer labor–management climate. The evidence, then, is too inconsistent to draw any meaningful conclusions.

Are union members more satisfied with their jobs than their nonunion counterparts? The answer to this question is more complicated than a simple "Yes" or "No." The evidence consistently demonstrates that unions have only indirect effects on job satisfaction.[72] They increase pay satisfaction but negatively affect satisfaction with the work itself (by decreasing job scope perceptions), satisfaction with co-workers and supervision (through less favorable perceptions of supervisory behavior), and satisfaction with promotions (through the lower importance placed on promotions).

International Human Resource Practices: Selected Issues

Many of the human resource policies and practices discussed in this chapter have to be modified to reflect societal differences.[73] To illustrate this point, let's briefly look at the problem of selecting managers for foreign assignments and the importance of performance evaluation in different cultures.

Selection

The global corporation increasingly needs managers who have experience in diverse cultures and who are sensitive to the challenges of international operations. At Ford Motor Co., for instance, an international assignment is a requirement for a rising executive's career. But many domestic managers don't have the attitudes or characteristics associated with successful international executives. One selection technique that an increasing number of companies are using is the Overseas Assignment Inventory (OAI). This 85-item questionnaire assesses 15 predictors: motivations, expectations, open-mindedness, respect for others' beliefs, trust in people, flexibility, tolerance, personal control, patience, adaptability, self-confidence/initiative, sense of humor, interpersonal interest, interpersonal harmony, and spouse/family communication. Results are compared against a database of more than 10,000 previous test takers. Research indicates that using the OAI as a prescreening device eliminates about 40 percent of traditional overseas assignment problems.[74]

Performance Evaluation

We previously examined the role that performance evaluation plays in motivation and in affecting behavior. Caution must be used, however, in generalizing across cultures. Why? Because many cultures are not particularly concerned with performance appraisal or, if they are, they don't look at it the same way as do managers in the United States or Canada.

Let's look at three cultural dimensions: a person's relationship to the environment, time orientation, and focus of responsibility.

U.S. and Canadian organizations hold people responsible for their actions because people in these countries believe that they can dominate their environment. In Middle Eastern countries, on the other hand, performance evaluations aren't likely to be widely used since managers in these countries tend to see people as subjugated to their environment.

Some countries, such as the United States, have a short-term time orientation. Performance evaluations are likely to be frequent in such a culture—at least once a year. In Japan, however, where people hold a long-term time frame, performance appraisals may occur only every five or ten years.

Israel's culture values group activities much more than does the United States or Canada. So, while North American managers emphasize the individual in performance evaluations, their counterparts in Israel are much more likely to emphasize group contributions and performance.

Managing Diversity in Organizations

United Parcel Service (UPS) has taken a rather unique approach to managing diversity. It's giving its managers a crash course in hard times.[75] The company believes that its managers aren't truly able to understand someone's problems unless they're in their shoes. So each year, UPS assigns 40 middle- and upper-level managers to month-long community internships that require them to live and work in poor communities. In McAllen, Texas, they assist poor Mexican-Americans and Latin American refugees. In Chicago, they live in a church and work with young people and their families. In Chattanooga, Tennessee, they provide aid to poor families, the disabled, and the severely retarded. In New York, they help unwed teenage mothers find jobs; they visit mental patients, and teach poor children. All of this is intended to help UPS managers better understand employees and customers from diverse backgrounds. One group of nine UPS managers, for instance, recently put in 60-hour weeks in McAllen, Texas, setting up a mobile library for migrant children, setting the plans for a sewing shop to provide jobs, and developing a video at a local clinic to educate indigent patients about health and nutrition.

The UPS program is unconventional. When we look at what companies like Aetna, American Express, Avon Products, Corning, Du Pont, Johnson & Johnson, Motorola, Quaker Oats, Xerox, and other prominent proponents of diversity are doing, we find a number of common characteristics. For the most part, their programs tend to emphasize creating family-friendly workplaces, providing diversity training, and developing mentoring programs.

Family-Friendly Workplaces

In today's diverse workforce, more and more employees are females, single parents, stepparents, individuals responsible for aging relatives, or members of two-career households. And these employees have different needs than the traditional stereotype of a working dad, with a stay-at-home wife and two kids. An increasing number of organizations are responding to their diverse workforce by creating family-friendly workplaces.

The U.S. workforce is now 46 percent female. More and more fathers want to actively participate in the care and raising of their children. As the baby-boom generation ages, many are finding themselves having to care for elderly parents. These three facts translate into an increasing number of employees who are attempting to juggle family obligations along with their job responsibilities. In the United States, the federal government acknowledged this fact when, in 1993, Congress passed the Family and Medical Leave Act. Its key provision is allowing up to 12 weeks of unpaid leave for employees following childbirth or adoption, or to care for a seriously ill child, spouse, or parent. The act also requires employers to continue health benefits during this leave and guarantees employees the same or a comparable job upon return. In much of Western Europe, such family-leave laws have been in place for decades.

So what's a **family-friendly workplace**? The term refers to an umbrella of work/family programs such as on-site day-care, child-care and elder-care referrals, flexible hours, compressed workweeks, job sharing, telecommuting, temporary part-time employment, and relocation assistance for employees' family members.[76]

Creating a family-friendly work climate was initially motivated by management's concern to improve employee morale and productivity and to reduce absenteeism. At Quaker Oats, for instance, 60 percent of employees admitted being absent at least three days a year because of children's illnesses and 56 percent said they were unable to attend company-related functions or work overtime because of child-care problems.[77] However, the overall evidence indicates that the major benefit to creating a family-friendly workplace is that it makes it easier for employers to recruit and retain first-class workers.[78]

For many parents, the ultimate determinant of whether they are able to work or not is the availability of child care. Fel-Pro, one of the world's largest makers of gaskets for automobiles and industrial uses, is a model of what a company can do for the children of its employees.[79] When children of Fel-Pro employees turn two, they are eligible to attend the professionally staffed Fel-Pro day-care center located adjacent to the company's plant. After the children start school, Fel-Pro day-care sends professionally trained caregivers to the home to take care of them if they get sick. If a child is having difficulty in school, the company provides testing and individual tutoring for a modest cost. And the company runs a summer day camp for children of employees. Buses pick up kids at the factory every weekday morning during the summer and return them every evening.

As the population ages, an increasing number of employees find themselves with responsibility for caring for parents or grandparents.[80] Employees who spend time worrying about elder care have less time for, and are less focused on, work-related issues. Therefore many organizations are widening child-care concerns to cover all dependents including elderly family members.

One of the more interesting findings related to family-friendly workplaces is its appeal to both sexes. The common assumption is that family-friendly programs are used mostly by women. The evidence suggests not. Workers of both sexes make trade-offs for family; and men are as likely as

family-friendly workplace
Companies that offer an umbrella of work/family programs such as on-site day-care, child-care and elder-care referrals, flexible hours, compressed workweeks, job sharing, telecommuting, temporary part-time employment, and relocation assistance for employees' family members.

Lancaster Labs, an analytical-testing laboratory, has expanded its day care facility for children to include care for the elderly. Its on-site intergenerational family center provides adult day care for up to 25 elderly or handicapped relatives of employees as well as day care for 151 children. Lancaster credits the child care center with the company's 94 percent retention rate of working moms, up from about 50 percent before the center was introduced. Lancaster surveys employees each year to learn what they want to add to the company's flexible benefits programs.

women to seek these programs.[81] Similarly, men are increasingly rejecting relocation, overnight travel, and overtime to spend more time with their families. For instance, at Du Pont, 41 percent of men in management or professional jobs told their supervisors they weren't available for relocation; and 19 percent told their bosses they would not take a job that required extensive travel. Among those in manufacturing jobs at Du Pont, 39 percent of men refused to work overtime in order to spend more time with family.[82]

Diversity Training

The centerpiece of most diversity programs is training. For instance, a 1994 survey found that 56 percent of U.S. organizations with more than 100 employees conducted some kind of diversity training in the prior year.[83] Diversity training programs are generally intended to provide a vehicle for increasing awareness and examining stereotypes. Participants learn to value individual differences, increase their cross-cultural understanding, and confront stereotypes.[84]

The typical program lasts from half a day to three days in length and includes role playing exercises, lectures, discussions, and group experiences. For example, Xerox has worked with Cornell University's theatre department to create a set of short plays that increases awareness of work-related racial and gender conflicts. The show has been presented to more than 1,300 Xerox managers.[85] A training exercise at Hartford Insurance that sought to increase sensitivity to aging asked participants to respond to the following four questions: (1) If you didn't know how old you are, how old would you guess you are? In other words, how old do you feel inside? (2) When I was 18, I thought middle age began at age _____. (3) Today, I think middle age begins at age _____. (4) What would be your first reaction if someone called you an older worker?[86] Answers to these questions were then used to analyze age-related stereotypes. In another program designed to raise awareness of the power of stereotypes, each participant was asked to write an anonymous paper detailing all groups—women, born-again Christians, blacks, gays, Hispanics, men—to which they had attached stereotypes.[87] They were also asked to explain why they'd had trouble working with certain groups in the past. Based on responses, guest speakers were brought into the class to shatter the stereotypes directed at each group. This was followed by extensive discussion.

Mentoring Programs

We previously discussed mentors briefly in chapter 2. A **mentor** is a senior employee who sponsors and supports a less experienced employee (a protégé). The mentoring role includes coaching, counseling, and sponsorship.[88] As a coach, mentors help to develop their protégés' skills. As counselors, mentors provide support and help bolster the protégés' self-confidence. As sponsors, mentors actively intervene on behalf of their protégés, lobby to get them visible assignments, and politick to get them rewards such as promotions and salary increases.

mentor
A senior employee who sponsors and supports a less experienced employee (a protégé).

Is mentoring important? For those who want to get ahead, it seems to be. Business school graduates who have had mentors early in their career are promoted faster, make higher salaries, and are more satisfied with their career progress later in life.[89] And more than half the men who make it to executive positions report they had a mentor along the way.[90]

Formal mentoring programs are particularly important for minorities and women. Why? Because the evidence indicates that individuals from these groups are less likely to be informally chosen as protégés than are white males and thus are less likely to accrue the benefits of mentorship.[91] Mentors tend to select protégés who are similar to themselves on criteria such as background, education, gender, race, ethnicity, and religion. "People naturally move to mentor and can more easily communicate with those with whom they most closely identify."[92] In the United States, for instance, upper-management positions in most organizations have been traditionally staffed by white males, so it's hard for minorities and women to be selected as protégés. In addition, in terms of cross-gender mentoring, senior male managers may select male protégés to minimize problems such as sexual attraction or gossip. So organizations have responded by replacing informal mentoring relationships with formal programs and providing training and coaching for potential mentors of special groups such as minorities and women.

Summary and Implications for Managers

An organization's human resource policies and practices represent important forces for shaping employee behavior and attitudes. In this chapter, we specifically discussed the influence of selection practices, training and development programs, performance evaluation systems, and the existence of a union.

Selection Practices

An organization's selection practices will determine who gets hired. If properly designed, they will identify competent candidates and accurately match them to the job. The use of the proper selection devices will increase the probability that the right person will be chosen to fill a slot.

While employee selection is far from a science, some organizations fail to design their selection systems so as to maximize the likelihood that the right person–job fit will be achieved. When errors are made, the chosen candidate's performance may be less than satisfactory. Training may be necessary to improve the candidate's skills. At the worst, the candidate will prove unacceptable and a replacement will need to be found. Similarly, where the selection process results in the hiring of less qualified candidates or individuals who don't fit into the organization, those chosen are likely to feel anxious, tense, and uncomfortable. This, in turn, is likely to increase dissatisfaction with the job.

Training and Development Programs

Training programs can affect work behavior in two ways. The most obvious is by directly improving the skills necessary for the employee to successfully complete his or her job. An increase in ability improves the employee's potential to perform at a higher level. Of course, whether that potential becomes realized is largely an issue of motivation.

A second benefit from training is that it increases an employee's self-efficacy. As you'll remember from chapter 5, self-efficacy is a person's expectation that he or she can successfully execute the behaviors required to produce an outcome.[93] For employees, those behaviors are work tasks and the outcome is effective job performance. Employees with high self-efficacy have strong expectations about their abilities to perform successfully in new situations. They're confident and expect to be successful. Training, then, is a means to positively affect self-efficacy because employees may be more willing to undertake job tasks and exert a high level of effort. Or in expectancy terms (see chapter 5), individuals are more likely to perceive their effort as leading to performance.

We also discussed career development in this chapter. We noted the significant decline in formal programs intended to guide an employee's career within a single organization. But employees still value career planning and development. So organizations can increase employee commitment, loyalty, and satisfaction by encouraging and guiding employees in developing a self-managed career plan, and by clearly communicating the organization's goals and future strategies, giving employees growth experiences, offering financial assistance to help employees keep their knowledge and skills current, and providing paid time off from work for off-the-job training.

Performance Evaluation

A major goal of performance evaluation is to assess accurately an individual's performance contribution as a basis for making reward allocation decisions. If the performance evaluation process emphasizes the wrong criteria or inaccurately appraises actual job performance, employees will be over- or underrewarded. As demonstrated in chapter 5, in our discussion of equity theory, this can lead to negative consequences such as reduced effort, increases in absenteeism, or search for alternative job opportunities. In addition, the content of the performance evaluation has been found to influence employee performance and satisfaction.[94] Specifically, performance and satisfaction are increased when the evaluation is based on behavioral, results-oriented criteria, when career issues as well as performance issues are discussed, and when the subordinate has an opportunity to participate in the evaluation.

Union–Management Interface

The existence of a union in an organization adds another variable in our search to explain and predict employee behavior. The union has been found to be an important contributor to employees' perceptions, attitudes, and behavior.

The power of the union surfaces in the collective bargaining agreement that it negotiates with management. Much of what an employee can and cannot do on the job is formally stipulated in this agreement. In addition, the informal norms that union cohesiveness fosters can encourage or discourage high productivity, organizational commitment, and morale.

For Review

1. What is job analysis? How is it related to those the organization hires?

2. What are assessment centers? Why do you think they might be more effective for selecting managers than traditional written tests?

3. Describe several on-the-job training methods and several off-the-job methods.

4. What can organizations do to help employees develop their careers?

5. What can individuals do to foster their own career development?

6. Why do organizations evaluate employees?

7. What are the advantages and disadvantages of the following performance evaluation methods: (1) written essays, (b) graphic rating scales, and (c) behaviorally anchored rating scales?

8. How can management effectively evaluate individuals when they work as part of a team?

9. How can an organization's performance evaluation system affect employee behavior?

10. What impact do unions have on an organization's reward system?

For Discussion

1. If you were the dean of a college of business, how would you determine which job candidates would be effective teachers?

2. If you were the dean of a college of business, how would you evaluate the performance of your faculty members?

3. What relationship, if any, is there between job analysis and performance evaluation?

4. What problems, if any, can you see developing as a result of using 360-degree evaluations?

5. Your company's president has asked you to identify things your firm might do to improve its track record for hiring and keeping female managers. What suggestions would you make?

Cross-Cultural Training Doesn't Work

Academics seem to take it as a truism that the expanding global marketplace has serious implications for management practice. As a result, they have become strong advocates for the necessity of cross-cultural training. But most corporations don't provide cross-cultural training for employees. Studies indicate, for instance, that only 30 percent of American managers who are sent on foreign assignments scheduled to last from one to five years receive any cross-cultural training before their departure.

Why don't most organizations provide their managers with cross-cultural training? We propose two possible explanations. One is that top managers believe that "managing is managing," so *where* it is done is irrelevant. The other explanation is that top management doesn't believe that cross-cultural training is effective.

Contrary to the evidence, many senior managers continue to believe that managerial skills are perfectly transferable across cultures. A good manager in New York or Los Angeles, for instance, should be equally effective in Paris or Hong Kong. In organizations where this belief dominates, you won't find any concern with cross-cultural training. Moreover, there is likely to be little effort made to select candidates for foreign assignments based on their ability to fit into, or adapt to, a specific culture. Selection decisions for overseas postings in these organizations are primarily made using a single criterion: the person's domestic track record.

It's probably fair to say that most senior managers today recognize that cultural differences do affect managerial performance. But their organizations still don't provide cross-cultural training because these managers doubt the effectiveness of this training. They argue that people can't learn to manage in a foreign culture after only a few weeks or months of training. An understanding of a country's culture is something one assimilates over many years based on input from many sources. It is not something that lends itself to short-term learning, no matter how intensive a training program might be.

Given the previous arguments, it would be surprising to find organizations offering cross-cultural training. We submit that top executives of organizations typically take one of three approaches in dealing with the selection of managerial personnel for staff foreign assignments. One approach is to ignore cultural differences. They don't worry about them, and make their selection decisions based solely on individuals' previous managerial records. Another approach is to hire nationals to manage foreign operations. Since cross-cultural training isn't effective, when a firm such as Xerox needs an executive to fill a key post in Italy, it might be best served by hiring an Italian. This solution has become even easier for North American firms in recent years as the number of foreigners in American and Canadian business schools has increased. For instance, there are now literally thousands of Italians, Arabs, Germans, Japanese, and other foreign nationals who have graduate business degrees from American universities, understand American business practices, and have returned to their homelands. The third solution to the problem is to either hire nationals or intensively train people to be expert advisors to management. AT&T, as a case in point, sent one executive and his family to Singapore for a lengthy stay to soak up the atmosphere and learn about the Singaporian way of doing business. He then returned to New York as the resident expert on Singapore. When problems involving that country arise, he is called upon to provide insight.

The evidence in this argument is drawn from J.S. Black and M. Mendenhall, "Cross-Cultural Training Effectiveness: A Review and a Theoretical Framework for Future Research," *Academy of Management Review*, January 1990, pp. 113–36; and A. Kupfer, "How to Be a Global Manager," *Fortune*, March 14, 1988, p. 52.

counterPoint

Cross-Cultural Training Is Effective

Yes, it's true that most corporations don't provide cross-cultural training. And that's a mistake! Clearly, the ability to adapt to the cultural differences in a foreign assignment is important to managerial success. Moreover, contrary to what many managers believe, cross-cultural training is very effective. Let's elaborate on this second point.

A comprehensive review of studies that specifically looked at the effectiveness of cross-cultural training shows overwhelming evidence that this training fosters the development of cross-cultural skills and leads to higher performance. Training has been shown to improve an individual's relationships with host nationals, to allow that person to adjust more rapidly to a new culture, and to improve his or her work performance. In addition, training significantly reduces expatriate failure rates. For instance, without training, 68 out of every 100 Americans transferred to Saudi Arabia will come home early because of their inability to cross the cultural chasm. Shell Oil, however, put 800 American employees through training before sending them to a petrochemical operation in Saudi Arabia and only three didn't survive the cultural adjustment.

Although these results are impressive, they don't say anything about the type of training the employee received. Does that make a difference?

There is a variety of training techniques available to prepare people for foreign work assignments. They range from documentary programs that merely expose people to a new culture through written materials on the country's sociopolitical history, geography, economics, and cultural institutions, to intense interpersonal experience training, where individuals participate in role-playing exercises, simulated social settings, and similar experiences to "feel" the differences in a new culture.

One research study looked at the effectiveness of these two approaches on a group of American managers. These managers, who worked for an electronic products firm, were sent on assignment to Seoul, South Korea. Twenty of them received no training, 20 got only the documentary program, and 20 received only interpersonal experience training. The training activities were all completed in a three-day period. All participants, no matter which group they were in, received some language training, briefings covering company operations in South Korea, and a cursory three-page background description of the country. The results of this study confirmed the earlier evidence that cross-cultural training works. Specifically, the study found that managers who received either form of training were better performers and perceived less need to adjust to the new culture than those who received no such training. Additionally, neither method proved superior to the other.

In another study with civilian employees in a U.S. military agency, participants were grouped so they received either a documentary orientation, experiential training, some combination of the two, or no training at all. Findings from this study again confirmed the value of cross-cultural training. Either type of training proved to be more effective than no training in improving cross-cultural knowledge and behavioral performance, and the combination approach was found to be the most effective.

The evidence in this argument is drawn from J.S. Black and M. Mendenhall, "Cross-Cultural Training Effectiveness: A Review and a Theoretical Framework for Future Research," *Academy of Management Review*, January 1990, pp. 113–36; P.C. Earley, "Intercultural Training for Managers: A Comparison of Documentary and Interpersonal Methods," *Academy of Management Journal*, December 1987, pp. 685–98; S. Caudron, "Surviving Cross-Cultural Shock," *Industry Week*, July 6, 1992, pp. 35–38; J.S. Lublin, "Companies Use Cross-Cultural Training to Help Their Employees Adjust Abroad," *Wall Street Journal*, August 4, 1992, p. B1; and J.K. Harrison, "Individual and Combined Effects of Behavior Modeling and the Cultural Assimilator in Cross-Cultural Management Training," *Journal of Applied Psychology*, December 1992, pp. 952–62.

Learning about Yourself Exercise

How Good Are Your Interviewing Skills?

Each of us is likely to undergo dozens of job interviews during our lifetime. Do you know how to make the best of those interview situations?

To assess your interview skills, answer the following statements using a scale of 1 (never) to 5 (always):

1. I think about the clothes I will wear at least a day before the interview and carefully select attire that will be consistent with the impression I want to make.

2. I prepare for the interview by researching the organization and gaining as much information as I can about the interviewer, the unit in which I would be working, and my potential boss.

3. I am precisely on time for the interview or a few minutes early.

4. I size-up my interviewer and his or her work area very early in the interview and tailor my body language and verbal responses to fit the situation.

5. I have carefully thought through answers to questions regarding my career goals, education, experience, and other questions I might be asked.

6. I have identified issues that are important in my decision and have questions about these issues that I'm prepared to ask the interviewer.

7. After the interview's conclusion, I send a formal thank-you letter to the interviewer.

Turn to page A-29 for scoring direction and key.

Source: Based on D.A. De Cenzo and S.P. Robbins, *Human Resource Management*, 5th edition (New York: Wiley, 1996), pp. 517–19.

Working with Others Exercise

Evaluating Performance and Providing Feedback

Objective   To experience the assessment of performance and observe the providing of performance feedback.

Time   Approximately 30 minutes.

Procedure   A class leader is to be selected. He or she may be either a volunteer or someone chosen by your instructor. The class leader will preside over the class discussion and perform the role of manager in the evaluation review.

Your instructor will leave the room. The class leader is then to spend up to 15 minutes helping the class to evaluate your instructor. Your instructor understands that this is only a class exercise and is prepared to accept criticism (and, of course, any praise you may want to convey). Your instructor also recognizes that the leader's evaluation is actually a composite of many students' input. So be open and honest in your evaluation and have confidence that your instructor will not be vindictive.

Research has identified seven performance dimensions to the college instructor's job: (1) instructor knowledge, (2) testing procedures, (3) student–teacher relations, (4) organizational skills, (5) communication skills, (6) subject relevance, and (7) utility of assignments. The discussion of your instructor's performance should focus on these seven dimensions. The leader may want to take notes for personal use but will not be required to give your instructor any written documentation.

When the 15-minute class discussion is complete, the leader will invite the instructor back into the room. The performance review will begin as soon as the instructor walks through the door, with the class leader becoming the manager and the instructor playing himself or herself.

When completed, class discussion will focus on performance evaluation criteria and how well your class leader did in providing performance feedback.

Ethical Dilemma Exercise

Ethics Training: Smoke or Substance?

Approximately 80 percent of the largest U.S. corporations have formal ethics programs, and 44 percent of these firms provide ethics training.* Most college and university programs in business now require courses in ethics or have added an ethics component to their courses in marketing, finance, and management.

What do proponents of ethics training expect to achieve with these programs? Ethics educators include among their goals stimulating moral thought, recognizing ethical dilemmas, creating a sense of moral obligation, developing problem-solving skills, and tolerating or reducing ambiguity. But can you teach ethics in college? The evidence is mixed. Let's briefly review the evidence presented by both sides.

Critics argue that ethics are based on values, and value systems are fixed at an early age. By the time people reach college, their ethical values are already established. The critics also claim that ethics cannot be formally taught, but must be learned by example. Leaders set ethical examples by what they say and do. If this is true, then ethics training is relevant only as part of leadership training.

Supporters of ethics training argue that values can be learned and changed after early childhood. And even if they couldn't, ethics training would be effective because it gets employees to think about ethical dilemmas and become more aware of the ethical issues underlying their actions. Supporters of ethics training point to the research evidence on the last point: A comprehensive analysis of the effectiveness of ethics training programs found that they improved students' ethical awareness and reasoning skills.

A recent survey of employees in companies that provide ethics training showed generally positive results. Overall, 73 percent of the respondents found the training useful either *frequently* or *occasionally* in guiding their decisions or conduct at work. Only 3 percent stated it was *never* useful.

Can colleges and universities teach ethics? Should business firms be spending money on ethics training programs? What do *you* think?

*The information in this exercise is from G.L. Pamental, "The Course in Business Ethics: Can It Work?" *Journal of Business Ethics*, July 1989, pp. 547–51; P.F. Miller and W.T. Coady, "Teaching Work Ethics," *Education Digest*, February 1990, pp. 54–55; D. Rice and C. Dreilinger, "Rights and Wrongs of Ethics Training," *Training and Development Journal*, May 1990, pp. 103–08; J. Weber, "Measuring the Impact of Teaching Ethics to Future Managers: A Review, Assessment, and Recommendations," *Journal of Business Ethics*, March 1990, pp. 183–90; and R. Goodell, *Ethics in American Business: Policies, Programs and Perceptions*. Report of a Landmark Survey of U.S. Employees (Washington, DC: Ethics Resource Center, 1994).

"I Can't Work on Sundays"

Most Americans understand that the law protects employees against discrimination based on gender or race bias. But Title VII of the federal civil rights laws also prohibits discrimination on the basis of religion. A manager at a Wal-Mart store in Springfield, Missouri didn't understand this fact and his company settled a religious discrimination lawsuit out of court brought by a former employee.

The former employee, Scott Hamby, said he was forced to quit Wal-Mart in 1993 after refusing to work on Sunday, his Sabbath. While denying any wrongdoing, Wal-Mart settled Mr. Hamby's claim with a cash settlement. It also agreed to immediately train Wal-Mart managers in charge of hiring and scheduling in its 2,173 stores on employees' rights to have their religious beliefs "reasonably accommodated," prepare a computer-based manual describing employees' rights and religious harassment, and hire 30 to 40 regional trainers on the subject.

The Wal-Mart incident may be a harbinger of future problems for many employers, especially in industries such as transportation, public safety, and retailing where weekend work is often an expected part of the job. The problem may also be exacerbated in the Midwest and South, where voters in recent years have repealed laws requiring businesses to close on Sundays.

The courts have said that employers must "reasonably accommodate" requests to observe the Sabbath or other religious days unless the request would cause "undue hardship" to the business. The employees' religious beliefs are assumed to be sincerely held unless proved otherwise.

Questions

1. Is there anything an employer could do at the time of hiring that could legally deter this problem from occuring?
2. Why do you think gender and race bias in the United States has received more attention than religious bias?
3. How could training to reduce religious discrimination fit in as part of diversity training?
4. What might a training program look like that seeks to eliminate discrimination on the basis of religion? Be specific.

This case is based on M.A. Jacobs, "Workers' Religious Beliefs May Get New Attention," *Wall Street Journal*, August 22, 1995, p. B1.

Reverse Discrimination?

VIDEO CASE

ABCNEWS

It's an increasing problem—white males who feel victimized because of their race and gender. The results of one recent poll showed that one out of every ten white males today feels that he's been a victim of reverse discrimination.

For years, women and minorities have been the victims of discrimination, often placing the blame on white males for keeping them out of jobs and power positions. Now the tables seem to have turned. White men are bitterly complaining that affirmative action programs are giving their jobs and promotions to women and minorities, even when these individuals are less qualified.

Although corporate America and academic institutions across the United States have their share of disgruntled white males, it's in government agencies where growing numbers of white men say they feel most vulnerable and most threatened. During one recent year, for example, over 4,000 men filed discrimination complaints with the Equal Employment Opportunity Commission. More than half of these complaints came from white males. Two U.S. Forest Service workers in California are representative of the types of complaints being made. One said, "How would you feel, working, and they'd say, you know, you're really good, but we have to hire someone else because of their birthright or their gender. It felt really bad. It was unfair." A California court ordered that region of the U.S. Forest Service to open up its all-male workforce to women, angering many longtime male employees. In the consent decree signed by the Forest Service, it promised that it would give 43 percent of its jobs to women. Although the Forest Service insists that its hiring practices have always been in full compliance with the Equal Opportunity Employment laws, many female forestry workers argue that had the California court not opened up the workplace to women, they'd still be on the outside looking in at an all-male Forest Service. Without the protection and action offered by affirmative action laws and regulations, these women say they wouldn't have had a chance for jobs or promotions.

In contrast, white males are complaining that these types of actions are really a form of reverse discrimination. For instance, at the Department of Defense, a number of white males aren't sure how to react to a memo that reportedly advised them that in the future "special permission would be required for the promotion of all white men without disabilities." At the National Park Service, a top official commented about a job applicant who was a *cum laude* Harvard graduate with Peace Corps experience, but "unfortunately, he is white, which is too bad."

Questions

1. How valid do you think these complaints are by white males?
2. Analyze this case in the context of employers trying to improve the diversity within their workforce.
3. What do you think are the behavioral implications for reverse discrimination on white males? On women and minorities?

Source: Based on "They Need Not Apply—Discrimination Against White Men," *ABC News 20/20*; aired on November 18, 1994.

16

ORGANIZATIONAL CULTURE

CHAPTER OUTLINE
Institutionalization: A Forerunner of Culture
What Is Organizational Culture?
What Does Culture Do?
Creating and Sustaining Culture
How Employees Learn Culture

In any organization, there are the ropes to skip and the ropes to know.
—R. Ritti and
G. Funkhouser

LEARNING OBJECTIVES

After studying this chapter, you should be able to

1 Describe institutionalization and its relationship to organizational culture

2 Define the common characteristics making up organizational culture

3 Contrast strong and weak cultures

4 Identify the functional and dysfunctional effects of organizational culture on people and the organization

5 Explain the factors determining an organization's culture

6 List the factors that maintain an organization's culture

7 Clarify how culture is transmitted to employees

8 Outline the various socialization alternatives available to management

FROM Mazda Motor Corp's Hiroshima headquarters, its president is trying to change his company's corporate culture.[1] The president, Henry Wallace (see photo), has his work cut out for him. Mazda's internal culture closely mirrors Japan's national culture. The company values indirect communication, loyalty, obedience, and relationships. Mr. Wallace believes these cultural values, which worked in the company's favor in the postwar years, are outdated in the current, highly competitive, global economy. He was brought in by Ford Motor Co., which owns controlling interest in Mazda, in the spring of 1996 to turn around declining sales and return Mazda to profitability. In 1995, Mazda made only 771,000 cars, half the number it made in 1990.

Mr. Wallace, a gangly Scot, stands out like a sore thumb in Japan. As the only foreigner running a Japanese company of any size, he is a celebrity and a curiosity. His outsider status provides him both advantages and disadvantages. Since foreigners are always expected to act differently, he is given more leeway in introducing non-Japanese practices at Mazda. But he lacks fluency in Japanese and his efforts to inject more English into the workplace and change established organizational norms is raising anxiety levels. Many Mazda employees feel Wallace just doesn't understand the way Japanese do things and the unique culture of Mazda.

Mr. Wallace faces an organizational culture where people are afraid to speak up in meetings and where employees and parts suppliers are set for life. Wallace wants to change this. He has turned carefully staged meetings into freewheeling brainstorming sessions. He expects people to ask questions and to challenge ideas. This doesn't come easy to Mazda employees. He has forced Mazda staff members to use more marketing data to back up new-product proposals. He's injecting more English, the international business language, into the company. Although he hasn't laid anyone off yet, he talks about it as a possibility, and that's raising concerns throughout the company. But one of his biggest challenges is breaking up Japan's traditional system of longtime, family-like relationships with suppliers. Hundreds of suppliers get blueprints from Mazda and build parts to company specifications. Although suppliers give Mazda loyalty and obedience, Wallace

593

believes Mazda suffers in terms of price, quality, and delivery schedules. He wants to reduce the number of suppliers that Mazda works with and increase competition among those that are left. "If the president [of Mazda] were a Japanese, he would have some sympathy toward us," complains the head of a small supplier. "He would think: 'You have been working so hard for Mazda.' Even in times of difficulties, he would take care so that as many companies as possible would survive." ◆

A strong organizational culture like that found at Mazda provides employees with a clear understanding of "the way things are done around here." It provides stability to an organization. But, as evidenced at Mazda, it can also be a major barrier to change. In this chapter, we show that every organization has a culture and, depending on its strength, it can have a significant influence on the attitudes and behaviors of organization members.

Institutionalization: A Forerunner of Culture

The idea of viewing organizations as cultures—where there is a system of shared meaning among members—is a relatively recent phenomenon. Until the mid-1980s, organizations were, for the most part, simply thought of as rational means by which to coordinate and control a group of people. They had vertical levels, departments, authority relationships, and so forth. But organizations are more. They have personalities too, just like individuals. They can be rigid or flexible, unfriendly or supportive, innovative or conservative. General Electric offices and people *are* different from the offices and people at General Mills. Harvard and MIT are in the same business—education—and separated only by the width of the Charles River, but each has a unique feeling and character beyond its structural characteristics. Organizational theorists now acknowledge this by recognizing the important role that culture plays in the lives of organization members. Interestingly, though, the origin of culture as an independent variable affecting an employee's attitudes and behavior can be traced back 50 years ago to the notion of **institutionalization**.[2]

institutionalization
When an organization takes on a life of its own, apart from any of its members, and acquires immortality.

When an organization becomes institutionalized, it takes on a life of its own, apart from its founders or any of its members. Ross Perot created Electronic Data Systems (EDS) in the early 1960s, but he left in 1987 to found a new company, Perot Systems. EDS, now part of General Motors, has continued to thrive despite the departure of its founder. Sony, Eastman Kodak, and Timex Corporation are examples of organizations that have existed beyond the life of any one member.

◆ When an organization becomes institutionalized, it takes on a life of its own, apart from its founders or any of its members.

Additionally, when an organization becomes institutionalized, it becomes valued for itself, not merely for the goods or services it produces. It acquires immortality. If its original goals are no longer relevant, it doesn't go out of business. Rather, it redefines itself. When the demand for Timex's watches declined, the company merely redirected itself into the consumer electronics business—making, in addition to watches, clocks, computers, and health-care products such as digital thermometers and blood pressure testing devices. Timex took on an existence that went beyond its original mission to manufacture low-cost mechanical watches.

Institutionalization operates to produce common understandings among members about what is appropriate and, fundamentally, meaningful behavior.[3] So when an organization takes on institutional permanence, acceptable modes of behavior become largely self-evident to its members. As we'll see, this is essentially the same thing that organizational culture does. So an understanding of what makes up an organization's culture, and how it is created, sustained, and learned will enhance our ability to explain and predict the behavior of people at work.

What Is Organizational Culture?

A number of years back, I asked an executive to tell me what he thought *organizational culture* meant and he gave me essentially the same answer that a Supreme Court Justice once gave in attempting to define pornography: "I can't define it, but I know it when I see it." This executive's approach to defining organizational culture isn't acceptable for our purposes. We need a basic definition to provide a point of departure for our quest to better understand the phenomenon. In this section, we propose a specific definition and review several peripheral issues that revolve around this definition.

A Definition

There seems to be wide agreement that **organizational culture** refers to a system of shared meaning held by members that distinguishes the organization from other organizations.[4] This system of shared meaning is, on closer examination, a set of key characteristics that the organization values. The most recent research suggests that there are seven primary characteristics that, in aggregate, capture the essence of an organization's culture.[5]

organizational culture
A common perception held by the organization's members; a system of shared meaning.

1. *Innovation and risk taking.* The degree to which employees are encouraged to be innovative and take risks.

A people orientation is a key characteristic that captures the essence of Birkenstock Footwear's organizational culture. Birkenstock's management supports employees' desires to participate in causes they believe in. When employees wanted to heighten the company's environmental consciousness, management responded by allowing them to spend an hour each week working on environmental projects and gave them the resources to develop an in-house environmental library, compile a guide to nontoxic resources, and organize monthly meetings with other businesses to share ideas on conservation products and issues.

2. *Attention to detail.* The degree to which employees are expected to exhibit precision, analysis, and attention to detail.

3. *Outcome orientation.* The degree to which management focuses on results or outcomes rather than on the techniques and processes used to achieve these outcomes.

4. *People orientation.* The degree to which management decisions take into consideration the effect of outcomes on people within the organization.

5. *Team orientation.* The degree to which work activities are organized around teams rather than individuals.

6. *Aggressiveness.* The degree to which people are aggressive and competitive rather than easygoing.

7. *Stability.* The degree to which organizational activities emphasize maintaining the status quo in contrast to growth.

Each of these characteristics exists on a continuum from low to high. Appraising the organization on these seven characteristics, then, gives a composite picture of the organization's culture. This picture becomes the basis for feelings of shared understanding that members have about the organization, how things are done in it, and the way members are supposed to behave. Exhibit 16-1 demonstrates how these characteristics can be mixed to create highly diverse organizations.

Culture Is a Descriptive Term

Organizational culture is concerned with how employees perceive the characteristics of an organization's culture, not with whether or not they like them. That is, it is a descriptive term. This is important because it differentiates this concept from that of job satisfaction.

Research on organizational culture has sought to measure how employees see their organization: Does it encourage teamwork? Does it reward innovation? Does it stifle initiative?

In contrast, job satisfaction seeks to measure affective responses to the work environment. It is concerned with how employees feel about the organization's expectations, reward practices, and the like. Although the two terms undoubtedly have overlapping characteristics, keep in mind that the term *organizational culture* is descriptive, while *job satisfaction* is evaluative.

Do Organizations Have Uniform Cultures?

Organizational culture represents a common perception held by the organization's members. This was made explicit when we defined culture as a system of *shared* meaning. We should expect, therefore, that individuals with different backgrounds or at different levels in the organization will tend to describe the organization's culture in similar terms.[6]

Acknowledgment that organizational culture has common properties does not mean, however, that there cannot be subcultures within any given culture. Most large organizations have a dominant culture and numerous sets of subcultures.[7]

A **dominant culture** expresses the core values that are shared by a majority of the organization's members. When we talk about an *organization's* culture, we are referring to its dominant culture. It is this macro view of culture that gives an organization its distinct personality.[8] **Subcultures** tend to

dominant culture
Expresses the core values that are shared by a majority of the organization's members.

subcultures
Minicultures within an organization, typically defined by department designations and geographical separation.

Exhibit 16-1 Contrasting Organizational Cultures

Organization A

This organization is a manufacturing firm. Managers are expected to fully document all decisions; and "good managers" are those who can provide detailed data to support their recommendations. Creative decisions that incur significant change or risk are not encouraged. Because managers of failed projects are openly criticized and penalized, they try not to implement ideas that deviate much from the status quo. One lower-level manager quoted an often used phrase in the company: "If it ain't broke, don't fix it."

There are extensive rules and regulations in this firm that employees are required to follow. Managers supervise employees closely to ensure there are no deviations. Management is concerned with high productivity, regardless of the impact on employee morale or turnover.

Work activities are designed around individuals. There are distinct departments and lines of authority, and employees are expected to minimize formal contact with other employees outside their functional area or line of command. Performance evaluations and rewards emphasize individual effort; although seniority tends to be the primary factor in the determination of pay raises and promotions.

Organization B

This organization is also a manufacturing firm. Here, however, management encourages and rewards risk taking and change. Decisions based on intuition are valued as much as those that are well rationalized. Management prides itself on its history of experimenting with new technologies and its success in regularly introducing innovative products. Managers or employees who have a good idea are encouraged to "run with it." And failures are treated as "learning experiences." The company prides itself on being market driven and rapidly responsive to the changing needs of its customers.

There are few rules and regulations for employees to follow, and supervision is loose because management believes that its employees are hardworking and trustworthy. Management is concerned with high productivity, but believes that this comes through treating its people right. The company is proud of its reputation as being a good place to work.

Job activities are designed around work teams and team members are encouraged to interact with people across functions and authority levels. Employees talk positively about the competition between teams. Individuals and teams have goals, and bonuses are based on achievement of these outcomes. Employees are given considerable autonomy in choosing the means by which the goals are attained.

develop in large organizations to reflect common problems, situations, or experiences that members face. These subcultures are likely to be defined by department designations and geographical separation. The purchasing department, for example, can have a subculture that is uniquely shared by members of that department. It will include the **core values** of the dominant culture plus additional values unique to members of the purchasing department. Similarly, an office or unit of the organization that is physically separated from the organization's main operations may take on a different personality. Again, the core values are essentially retained but modified to reflect the separated unit's distinct situation.

core values
The primary or dominant values that are accepted throughout the organization.

If organizations had no dominant culture and were composed only of numerous subcultures, the value of organizational culture as an independent variable would be significantly lessened because there would be no uniform interpretation of what represented appropriate and inappropriate behavior. It is the "shared meaning" aspect of culture that makes it such a potent device for guiding and shaping behavior. But we cannot ignore the reality that many organizations also have subcultures that can influence the behavior of members.

Strong vs. Weak Cultures

It has become increasingly popular to differentiate between strong and weak cultures.[9] The argument here is that strong cultures have a greater impact on employee behavior and are more directly related to reduced turnover.

strong cultures
Cultures where the core values are intensely held and widely shared.

In a **strong culture**, the organization's core values are both intensely held and widely shared.[10] The more members who accept the core values and the greater their commitment to those values is, the stronger the culture is. Consistent with this definition, a strong culture will have a great influence on the behavior of its members because the high degree of sharedness and intensity creates an internal climate of high behavioral control. For example, Seattle-based Nordstrom has developed one of the strongest service cultures in the retailing industry. Nordstrom employees know in no uncertain terms what is expected of them and these expectations go a long way in shaping their behavior.

One specific result of a strong culture should be lower employee turnover. A strong culture demonstrates high agreement among members about what the organization stands for. Such unanimity of purpose builds cohesiveness, loyalty, and organizational commitment. These qualities, in turn, lessen employees' propensity to leave the organization.[11]

Culture vs. Formalization

A strong organizational culture increases behavioral consistency. In this sense, we should recognize that a strong culture can act as a substitute for formalization.

The core value of enhancing people's lives through sports and fitness is intensely held and widely shared by Nike employees. Nike founder Philip Knight has created a strong sports-oriented culture and promotes it through company practices such as paying employees extra for biking to work instead of driving. Nike is recognized worldwide as an athlete's company that hires former college, professional, and Olympic athletes to design and market its shoes and clothing for sports enthusiasts. Nike headquarters in Beaverton, Oregon, is a 74-acre campus with walking and jogging trails and buildings named for sports heroes such as the Joan Benoit Samuelson Center, the Bo Jackson Fitness Center, and the Joe Paterno Day Care Center.

From Concepts to Skills

How to "Read" an Organization's Culture

The ability to read and assess an organization's culture can be a valuable skill.[12] If you're looking for a job, you'll want to choose an employer whose culture is compatible with your values and in which you'll feel comfortable. If you can accurately assess a prospective employer's culture before you make your decision, you may be able to save yourself a lot of grief and reduce the likelihood of making a poor choice. Similarly, you'll undoubtedly have business transactions with numerous organizations during your professional career. You'll be trying to sell a product or service, negotiate a contract, arrange a joint venture, or merely be seeking out who in an organization controls certain decisions. The ability to assess another organization's culture can be a definite plus in successfully completing these pursuits.

For the sake of simplicity, we'll approach the problem of reading an organization's culture from that of a job applicant. We'll assume you're interviewing for a job. Here's a list of things you can do to help learn about a potential employer's culture:

◆ Observe the physical surroundings. Pay attention to signs, pictures, style of dress, length of hair, degree of openness between offices, and office furnishings and arrangements.

◆ Who did you meet with? Just the person who would be your immediate supervisor? Or potential colleagues, managers from other departments, or senior executives? And based on what they revealed, to what degree do people other than the immediate supervisor have input to the hiring decision?

◆ How would you characterize the style of the people you met? Formal? Casual? Serious? Jovial?

◆ Does the organization have formal rules and regulations printed in a personnel policy manual? If so, how detailed are these policies?

◆ Ask questions of the people with whom you meet. The most valid and reliable information tends to come from asking the same questions of many people (to see how closely their responses align) and by talking with boundary spanners. Boundary spanners are employees whose work links them to the external environment and includes jobs such as human resource interviewer, salesperson, purchasing agent, labor negotiator, public relations specialist, and company lawyer. Questions that will give you insights into organizational processes and practices might include:

◆ What is the background of the founders?

◆ What is the background of current senior managers? What are their functional specializations? Were they promoted from within or hired from outside?

◆ How does the organization integrate new employees? Is there an orientation program? Training? If so, could you describe these features?

◆ How does your boss define his or her job success? (Amount of profit? Serving customers? Meeting deadlines? Acquiring budget increases?)

◆ How would you define fairness in terms of reward allocations?

◆ Can you identify some people here who are on the "fast track"? What do you think has put them on the fast track?

◆ Can you identify someone who seems to be considered a deviant in the organization? How has the organization responded to this person?

◆ Can you describe a decision that someone made here that was well received?

◆ Can you describe a decision that didn't work out well? What were the consequences for the decision maker?

◆ Could you describe a crisis or critical event that has occurred recently in the organization? How did top management respond? What was learned from this experience?

In chapter 13, we discussed how formalization's rules and regulations act to regulate employee behavior. High formalization in an organization creates predictability, orderliness, and consistency. Our point is that a strong culture achieves the same end without the need for written documentation. Therefore, we should view formalization and culture as two different roads to a common destination. The stronger an organization's culture, the less management need be concerned with developing formal rules and regulations to guide employee behavior. Those guides will be internalized in employees when they accept the organization's culture.

Organizational Culture vs. National Culture

We opened this chapter by describing the challenges facing Mazda's new president as he tries to change Mazda's organizational culture. But we also saw how Japan's national culture was closely intertwined with Mazda's corporate culture. Throughout this book we've argued that national differences—that is, national cultures—must be taken into account if accurate predictions are to be made about organizational behavior in different countries. It seems appropriate at this point, then, to ask the question: Does national culture override an organization's culture? Is an IBM facility in Germany, for example, more likely to reflect German ethnic culture or IBM's corporate culture?

The research indicates that national culture has a greater impact on employees than does their organization's culture.[13] German employees at an IBM facility in Munich, therefore, will be influenced more by German culture than by IBM's culture. These findings, incidentally, are consistent with what the new president at Mazda found—that Japan's national culture has strongly shaped this company's organizational culture, and that Japanese employees resist Ford-type cultural values. Our conclusion: As influential as organizational culture is to understanding the behavior of people at work, national culture is even more so.

The preceding conclusion has to be qualified to reflect the self-selection that goes on at the hiring stage. IBM, for example, may be less concerned with hiring the "typical Italian" for its Italian operations than in hiring an Italian who fits within the IBM way of doing things.[14] Historically, Italians who have a high need for autonomy are more likely to go to Olivetti than IBM. Why?

Japan's electronic giant Matsushita Electric Company recognizes that national culture has a greater impact on employees than does organization culture. Matsushita tries to accommodate national cultural values in managing its 150 plants in 38 countries throughout Southeast Asia, North America, Europe, the Middle East, Latin America, and Africa. At its plants in Malaysia, the company offers special ethnic food in its cafeterias for Muslim Malays, Chinese, and Indian employees and accommodates Muslim religious customs by providing special prayer rooms at each plant and allowing two prayer sessions per shift.

Because Olivetti's organizational culture is informal and nonstructured. It has tended to allow employees considerably more freedom than IBM does.[15] In fact, Olivetti seeks to hire individuals who are impatient, risk taking, and innovative—qualities in job candidates that IBM's Italian operations historically sought to exclude in new hires.

What Does Culture Do?

We've alluded to organizational culture's impact on behavior. We've also explicitly argued that a strong culture should be associated with reduced turnover. In this section, we will more carefully review the functions that culture performs and assess whether culture can be a liability for an organization.

Culture's Functions

Culture performs a number of functions within an organization. First, it has a boundary-defining role; that is, it creates distinctions between one organization and others. Second, it conveys a sense of identity for organization members. Third, culture facilitates the generation of commitment to something larger than one's individual self-interest. Fourth, it enhances social system stability. Culture is the social glue that helps hold the organization together by providing appropriate standards for what employees should say and do. Finally, culture serves as a sense-making and control mechanism that guides and shapes the attitudes and behavior of employees. It is this last function that is of particular interest to us.[16] As the following quote makes clear, culture defines the rules of the game:

> Culture by definition is elusive, intangible, implicit, and taken for granted. But every organization develops a core set of assumptions, understandings, and implicit rules that govern day-to-day behavior in the workplace. . . . Until newcomers learn the rules, they are not accepted as full-fledged members of the organization. Transgressions of the rules on the part of high-level executives or front-line employees result in universal disapproval and powerful penalties. Conformity to the rules becomes the primary basis for reward and upward mobility.[17]

The role of culture in influencing employee behavior appears to be increasingly important in the 1990s.[18] As organizations have widened spans of control, flattened structures, introduced teams, reduced formalization, and empowered employees, the *shared meaning* provided by a strong culture ensures that everyone is pointed in the same direction.

As we show later in this chapter, who receives a job offer to join the organization, who is appraised as a high performer, and who gets the promotion are strongly influenced by the individual–organization "fit"—that is, whether the applicant or employee's attitudes and behavior are compatible with the culture. It's not a coincidence that employees at Disney theme parks appear to be almost universally attractive, clean, and wholesome looking, with bright smiles. That's the image Disney seeks. The company selects employees who will maintain that image. And once on the job, a strong culture, supported by formal rules and regulations, ensures that Disney theme-park employees will act in a relatively uniform and predictable way.

Culture as a Liability

We are treating culture in a nonjudgmental manner. We haven't said that it's good or bad, only that it exists. Many of its functions, as outlined, are valuable for both the organization and the employee. Culture enhances organizational commitment and increases the consistency of employee behavior. These are clearly benefits to an organization. From an employee's standpoint, culture is valuable because it reduces ambiguity. It tells employees how things are done and what's important. But we shouldn't ignore the potentially dysfunctional aspects of culture, especially a strong one, on an organization's effectiveness.

BARRIER TO CHANGE Culture is a liability when the shared values are not in agreement with those that will further the organization's effectiveness. This is most likely to occur when the organization's environment is dynamic. When the environment is undergoing rapid change, the organization's entrenched culture may no longer be appropriate. So consistency of behavior is an asset to an organization when it faces a stable environment. It may, however, burden the organization and make it difficult to respond to changes in the environment. This helps to explain the challenges that executives at companies like IBM, Eastman Kodak, and General Dynamics have had in recent years in adapting to upheavals in their environment. These companies have strong cultures that worked well for them in the past. But these strong cultures become barriers to change when "business as usual" is no longer effective. As a case in point, when Louis Gerstner left RJR Nabisco in 1993 to become head of IBM, he made turning around IBM's conservative, risk-aversive culture his highest priority. After three years of focused attention, he seems to be finally succeeding.[19] For many organizations with strong cultures, practices that led to previous successes can lead to failure when those practices no longer match up well with environmental needs.[20]

BARRIER TO DIVERSITY Hiring new employees who, because of race, gender, ethnic, or other differences, are not like the majority of the organization's members creates a paradox.[21] Management wants new employees to accept the organization's core cultural values. Otherwise, these employees are unlikely to fit in or be accepted. But at the same time, management wants to openly acknowledge and demonstrate support for the differences that these employees bring to the workplace.

Strong cultures put considerable pressure on employees to conform. They limit the range of values and styles that are acceptable. In some instances, such as the recent Texaco case (which was settled on behalf of 1,400 employees for $176 million) where senior managers made disparaging remarks about minorities, a strong culture that condones prejudice can even undermine formal corporate diversity policies.[22]

Organizations seek out and hire diverse individuals because of the alternative strengths these people bring to the workplace. Yet these diverse behaviors and strengths are likely to diminish in strong cultures as people attempt to fit in. Strong cultures, therefore, can be liabilities when they effectively eliminate those unique strengths that people of different backgrounds bring to the organization. Moreover, strong cultures can also be liabilities when they support institutional bias or become insensitive to people who are different.

BARRIER TO MERGERS AND ACQUISITIONS Historically, the key factors that management looked at in making merger or acquisition decisions were related to financial advantages or product synergy. In recent years, cultural compatibility has become the primary concern.[23] While a favorable financial statement or product line may be the initial attraction of an acquisition candidate, whether the acquisition actually works seems to have more to do with how well the two organizations' cultures match up.

A number of mergers consummated in the 1990s already have failed or show signs of failing. And the primary cause is conflicting organizational cultures.[24] Time Inc.'s merger with Warner Communications in 1990 has had trouble from the start. Time's culture was conservative and paternalistic, while Warner's was a "high-risk, high-reward" culture of deal making.[25] Employees from the two companies don't trust each other and the combined Time Warner has never seen the synergies that the premerger pundits predicted. AT&T's 1991 acquisition of NCR and Matsushita's 1991 acquisition of MCA are other visible examples of culture-based merger failures. And few deals made more sense in financial terms than the October 1993 merger of Price Club and Costco Wholesale. The combined Price/Costco would have had the clout to compete directly with Wal-Mart's Sam's Club. But the marriage failed. The Price and Costco people couldn't work together. Said one analyst, "The Price guys had much more of a real estate strip-mall mentality. The Costco guys were the type who started working at grocery stores bagging groceries when they were 10 years old and worked their way up the ladder."[26] It was a very short marriage. Price and Costco broke up in August 1994.

Creating and Sustaining Culture

An organization's culture doesn't pop out of thin air. Once established, it rarely fades away. What forces influence the creation of a culture? What reinforces and sustains these forces once they are in place? We answer both of these questions in this section.

How a Culture Begins

An organization's current customs, traditions, and general way of doing things are largely due to what it has done before and the degree of success it has had with those endeavors. This leads us to the ultimate source of an organization's culture: its founders.[27]

The founders of an organization traditionally have a major impact on that organization's early culture. They have a vision of what the organization should be. They are unconstrained by previous customs or ideologies. The small size that typically characterizes new organizations further facilitates the founders' imposition of their vision on all organizational members.

Microsoft's culture is largely a reflection of co-founder and current CEO, Bill Gates. Gates is personally aggressive, competitive, and highly disciplined. Those are the same characteristics often used to describe the software giant he heads. Other contemporary examples of founders who have had an immeasurable impact on their organization's culture are Akio Morita at Sony, Ted Turner at Turner Broadcasting Systems, Fred Smith at Federal Express, Mary Kay at Mary Kay Cosmetics, and Richard Branson at the Virgin Group.

OB in the News

Chung Ju Yung and the Company He Created: Hyundai

Hyundai is a $45 billion-a-year business empire made up of more than 40 companies in fields ranging from ships to semiconductors, motor vehicles to computers, engineering to robots, petrochemicals to department stores. The Hyundai group is a disciplined, militaristic organization. The man who made it this way is Chung Ju Yung.

Chung was born in 1915, one of seven children from an impoverished peasant farm family. Following World War II, Chung set up an auto repair business. He called it "Hyundai," which means *modern* in Korean. From this small beginning, the giant empire began. Throughout the company's growth, Chung's style shaped its culture. Family loyalty and authoritarianism reign. "The boss is still the boss," says Kim Yung Duc, president of Hyundai Corp. U.S.A.

At the height of his powers, Chung was a fearsome figure. There are rumors that a stretcher used to be a fixture in Hyundai's executive boardroom because Chung would sometimes punch out underlings who wouldn't listen to him or do what he wanted.

Hyundai may represent an extreme in feudal obedience but it evolved into what Chung's executives call the "Hyundai Spirit." A manual given to new recruits states: "The hard work of the creator [Chung] and the courage of the pioneer have helped us open the way for the expansion, sophistication and internationalization of the industrial society of our country." In Hyundai lore and literature, Chung is quoted nearly as much as the Chinese, two decades ago, invoked Mao Zedong.

"Everything at Hyundai is run on a fairly military basis," says a U.S. consultant. "They have an armory in the yard. The guys who are educated all know what they have to do if war breaks out."

If you want to understand Hyundai's fierce, competitive style, its feudal obedience, or its disciplined, militaristic nature, you don't need to go any further than looking at its founder, Chung Ju Yung.

Based on D. Kirk, "The Humbling of Chairman Chung," *Asia, Inc.*, April 1994, pp. 24–29.

Take It to the Net

We invite you to visit the Robbins page on the Prentice Hall Web site at:

http://www.prenhall.com/robbinsorgbeh

for this chapter's World Wide Web exercise.

Keeping a Culture Alive

Once a culture is in place, there are practices within the organization that act to maintain it by giving employees a set of similar experiences.[28] For example, many of the human resource practices discussed in the previous chapter reinforce the organization's culture. The selection process, performance evaluation criteria, training and career development activities, and promotion procedures ensure that those hired fit in with the culture, reward those who support it, and penalize (and even expel) those who challenge it. Three forces play a particularly important part in sustaining a culture: selection practices, the actions of top management, and socialization methods. Let's take a closer look at each.

SELECTION The explicit goal of the selection process is to identify and hire individuals who have the knowledge, skills, and abilities to perform the jobs within the organization successfully. Typically, more than one candidate will be identified who meets any given job's requirements. When that point is reached, it would be naive to ignore that the final decision as to who is hired will be significantly influenced by the decision maker's judgment of how well the candidates will fit into the organization. This attempt to ensure a proper match, whether purposely or inadvertently, results in the hiring of people who have values essentially consistent with those of the organization, or at least a good portion of those values.[29] Additionally, the selection process provides information to applicants about the organization. Candidates learn about the organization and, if they perceive a conflict between their values and those of the organization, they can self-select themselves out of the applicant pool. Selection, therefore, becomes a two-way street, allowing employer or applicant to abrogate a marriage if there appears to be a mismatch. In this way, the selection process sustains an organization's culture by selecting out those individuals who might attack or undermine its core values.

◆ The final decision as to who is hired will be significantly influenced by the decision maker's judgment of how well the candidates will fit into the organization.

Applicants for entry-level positions in brand management at Procter & Gamble (P&G) experience an exhaustive application and screening process. Their interviewers are part of an elite cadre who have been selected and trained extensively via lectures, videotapes, films, practice interviews, and role plays to identify applicants who will successfully fit in at P&G. Applicants are interviewed in depth for such qualities as their ability to "turn out high volumes of excellent work," "identify and understand problems," and "reach thoroughly substantiated and well-reasoned conclusions that lead to action." P&G values rationality and seeks applicants who think that way. College applicants receive two interviews and a general knowledge test on campus before being flown back to Cincinnati for three more one-on-one interviews and a group interview at lunch. Each encounter seeks corroborating evidence of the traits that the firm believes correlate highly with "what counts" for success at P&G.[30] Applicants for positions at Compaq Computer are carefully chosen for their ability to fit into the company's teamwork-oriented culture. As one executive put it, "We can find lots of people who are competent. . . . The No. 1 issue is whether they fit into the way we do business."[31] At Compaq, that means job candidates who are easy to get along with and who feel comfortable with the company's consensus management style. To increase the likelihood that loners and those with big egos get screened out, it's not unusual for an applicant to be interviewed by 15 people, who represent all departments of the company and a variety of seniority levels.[32]

TOP MANAGEMENT   The actions of top management also have a major impact on the organization's culture.[33] Through what they say and how they behave, senior executives establish norms that filter down through the organization as to whether risk taking is desirable; how much freedom managers should give their subordinates; what is appropriate dress; what actions will pay off in terms of pay raises, promotions, and other rewards; and the like.

For example, look at Xerox Corp.[34] Its chief executive from 1961 to 1968 was Joseph C. Wilson. An aggressive, entrepreneurial type, he oversaw Xerox's staggering growth on the basis of its 914 copier, one of the most successful products in American history. Under Wilson, Xerox had an entrepreneurial environment, with an informal, high-camaraderie, innovative, bold, risk-taking culture. Wilson's replacement as CEO was C. Peter McColough, a Harvard MBA with a formal management style. He instituted bureaucratic controls and a major change in Xerox's culture. When McColough stepped down in 1982, Xerox had become stodgy and formal, with lots of politics and turf battles and layers of watchdog managers. His replacement was David T. Kearns. He believed the culture he inherited hindered Xerox's ability to compete. To increase the company's competitiveness, Kearns trimmed Xerox down by cutting 15,000 jobs, delegated decision making downward, and refocused the organization's culture around a simple theme: boosting the quality of Xerox products and services. By his actions and those of his senior managerial cadre, Kearns conveyed to everyone at Xerox that the company valued and rewarded quality and efficiency. When Kearns retired in 1990, Xerox still had its problems. The copier business was mature and Xerox had fared badly in developing computerized office systems. The current CEO, Paul Allaire, has again sought to reshape Xerox's culture. Specifically, he has reorganized the corpora-

Through her words and actions, Laura Henderson (left) has created a culture that values employees as the company's greatest asset. Henderson, founder of Prospect Associates, a health research and communications firm, gives her employees an enormous amount of flexibility in scheduling their work. She offers employees flextime, telecommuting, and part-time options; allows them to bring their children to work when necessary; and realigns employees' jobs to help them cope during difficult times in their lives. Henderson believes such flexibility helps her attract and keep the best employees, giving her small firm a competitive advantage.

tion around a worldwide marketing department, has unified product development and manufacturing divisions, and has replaced half of the company's top-management team with outsiders. Allaire seeks to reshape Xerox's culture to focus on innovative thinking and out-hustling the competition.

SOCIALIZATION No matter how good a job the organization does in recruiting and selection, new employees are not fully indoctrinated in the organization's culture. Maybe most important, because they are unfamiliar with the organization's culture, new employees are potentially likely to disturb the beliefs and customs that are in place. The organization will, therefore, want to help new employees adapt to its culture. This adaptation process is called **socialization**.[35]

All Marines must go through boot camp, where they "prove" their commitment. Of course, at the same time, the Marine trainers are indoctrinating new recruits in the "Marine way." New Sanyo employees go through an intensive five-month training program (trainees eat and sleep together in company-subsidized dorms and are required to vacation together at company-owned resorts) where they learn the Sanyo way of doing everything—from how to speak to superiors to proper grooming and dress.[36] The company considers this program essential for transforming young employees, fresh out of school, into dedicated *kaisha senshi*, or corporate warriors. Starbucks, the rapidly growing gourmet-coffee chain, doesn't go to the extreme that Sanyo does, but it seeks the same outcome.[37] All new employees go through 24 hours of training. Just for an entry-level job in a retail store making coffee? Yes! Classes cover everything necessary to make new employees brewing consultants. They learn the Starbucks philosophy, the company jargon (including phrases such as "half-decaf double tall almond skim mocha"), and even how to help customers make decisions about beans, grind, and espresso machines. The result is employees who understand Starbucks' culture and who project an enthusiastic and knowledgeable interface with customers.

As we discuss socialization, keep in mind that the most critical socialization stage is at the time of entry into the organization. This is when the organization seeks to mold the outsider into an employee "in good standing." Those employees who fail to learn the essential or pivotal role behaviors risk being labeled "nonconformists" or "rebels," which often leads to expulsion. But the organization will be socializing every employee, though maybe not as explicitly, throughout his or her entire career in the organization. This further contributes to sustaining the culture.

Socialization can be conceptualized as a process made up of three stages: prearrival, encounter, and metamorphosis.[38] The first stage encompasses all the learning that occurs before a new member joins the organization. In the second stage, the new employee sees what the organization is really like and confronts the possibility that expectations and reality may diverge. In the third stage, the relatively long-lasting changes take place. The new employee masters the skills required for his or her job, successfully performs his or her new roles, and makes the adjustments to his or her work group's values and norms.[39] This three-stage process impacts on the new employee's work productivity, commitment to the organization's objectives, and eventual decision to stay with the organization. Exhibit 16-2 on page 608 depicts this process.

The **prearrival stage** explicitly recognizes that each individual arrives with a set of values, attitudes, and expectations. These cover both the work to be done and the organization. For instance, in many jobs, particularly profes-

socialization
The process that adapts employees to the organization's culture.

prearrival stage
The period of learning in the socialization process that occurs before a new employee joins the organization.

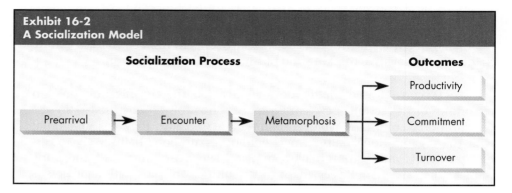

Exhibit 16-2
A Socialization Model

Socialization Process

Prearrival → Encounter → Metamorphosis

Outcomes

Productivity

Commitment

Turnover

sional work, new members will have undergone a considerable degree of prior socialization in training and in school. One major purpose of a business school, for example, is to socialize business students to the attitudes and behaviors that business firms want. If business executives believe that successful employees value the profit ethic, are loyal, will work hard, and desire to achieve, they can hire individuals out of business schools who have been premolded in this pattern. But prearrival socialization goes beyond the specific job. The selection process is used in most organizations to inform prospective employees about the organization as a whole. In addition, as noted previously, the selection process also acts to ensure the inclusion of the "right type"—those who will fit in. "Indeed, the ability of the individual to present the appropriate face during the selection process determines his ability to move into the organization in the first place. Thus, success depends on the degree to which the aspiring member has correctly anticipated the expectations and desires of those in the organization in charge of selection."[40]

Upon entry into the organization, the new member enters the **encounter stage**. Here the individual confronts the possible dichotomy between her expectations—about her job, her co-workers, her boss, and the organization in general—and reality. If expectations prove to have been more or less accurate, the encounter stage merely provides a reaffirmation of the perceptions gained earlier. However, this is often not the case. Where expectations and reality differ, the new employee must undergo socialization that will detach her from her previous assumptions and replace them with another set that the organization deems desirable. At the extreme, a new member may become totally disillusioned with the actualities of her job and resign. Proper selection should significantly reduce the probability of the latter occurrence.

Finally, the new member must work out any problems discovered during the encounter stage. This may mean going through changes—hence, we call this the **metamorphosis stage**. The options presented in Exhibit 16-3 are alternatives designed to bring about the desired metamorphosis. Note, for example, that the more management relies on socialization programs that are formal, collective, fixed, serial, and emphasize divestiture, the greater the likelihood that newcomers' differences and perspectives will be stripped away and replaced by standardized and predictable behaviors. Careful selection by management of newcomers' socialization experiences can—at the extreme—create conformists who maintain traditions and customs, or inventive and creative individualists who consider no organizational practice sacred.

We can say that metamorphosis and the entry socialization process is complete when the new member has become comfortable with the organization and his job. He has internalized the norms of the organization and his

encounter stage
The stage in the socialization process in which a new employee sees what the organization is really like and confronts the possibility that expectations and reality may diverge.

metamorphosis stage
The stage in the socialization process in which a new employee adjusts to his or her work group's values and norms.

Exhibit 16-3 Entry Socialization Options

Formal vs. Informal   The more a new employee is segregated from the ongoing work setting and differentiated in some way to make explicit his or her newcomer's role, the more formal socialization is. Specific orientation and training programs are examples. Informal socialization puts the new employee directly into his or her job, with little or no special attention.

Individual vs. Collective   New members can be socialized individually. This describes how it's done in many professional offices. They can also be grouped together and processed through an identical set of experiences, as in military boot camp.

Fixed vs. Variable   This refers to the time schedule in which newcomers make the transition from outsider to insider. A fixed schedule establishes standardized stages of transition. This characterizes rotational training programs. It also includes probationary periods, such as the eight- to ten-year "associate" status used by accounting and law firms before deciding on whether or not a candidate is made a partner. Variable schedules give no advanced notice of their transition timetable. Variable schedules describe the typical promotion system, where one is not advanced to the next stage until he or she is "ready."

Serial vs. Random   Serial socialization is characterized by the use of role models who train and encourage the newcomer. Apprenticeship and mentoring programs are examples. In random socialization, role models are deliberately withheld. The new employee is left on his or her own to figure things out.

Investiture vs. Divestiture   Investiture socialization assumes that the newcomer's qualities and qualifications are the necessary ingredients for job success, so these qualities and qualifications are confirmed and supported. Divestiture socialization tries to strip away certain characteristics of the recruit. Fraternity and sorority "pledges" go through divestiture socialization to shape them into the proper role.

Source: Based on J. Van Maanen, "People Processing: Strategies of Organizational Socialization," *Organizational Dynamics*, Summer 1978, pp. 19–36; and E.H. Schein, Organizational Culture," *American Psychologist*, February 1990, p. 116.

work group, and understands and accepts these norms. The new member feels accepted by his peers as a trusted and valued individual, is self-confident that he has the competence to complete the job successfully, and understands the system—not only his own tasks, but the rules, procedures, and informally accepted practices as well. Finally, he knows how he will be evaluated, that is, what criteria will be used to measure and appraise his work. He knows what is expected, and what constitutes a job "well done." As Exhibit 16-2 shows, successful metamorphosis should have a positive impact on the new employee's productivity and his commitment to the organization, and reduce his propensity to leave the organization.

Summary: How Cultures Form

Exhibit 16-4, on page 610, summarizes how an organization's culture is established and sustained. The original culture is derived from the founder's philosophy. This, in turn, strongly influences the criteria used in hiring. The actions of the current top management set the general climate of what is acceptable behavior and what is not. How employees are to be socialized will depend

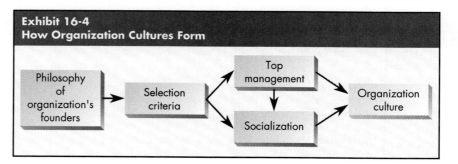

Exhibit 16-4
How Organization Cultures Form

both on the degree of success achieved in matching new employees' values to those of the organization's in the selection process and on top management's preference for socialization methods.

How Employees Learn Culture

Culture is transmitted to employees in a number of forms, the most potent being stories, rituals, material symbols, and language.

Stories

During the days when Henry Ford II was chairman of the Ford Motor Co., one would have been hard pressed to find a manager who hadn't heard the story about Mr. Ford reminding his executives, when they got too arrogant, that "it's my name that's on the building." The message was clear: Henry Ford II ran the company!

Nordstrom employees are fond of the following story. It strongly conveys the company's policy toward customer returns: When this specialty retail chain was in its infancy, a customer came in and wanted to return a set of automobile tires. The sales clerk was a bit uncertain how to handle the problem. As the customer and sales clerk spoke, Mr. Nordstrom walked by and overheard the conversation. He immediately interceded, asking the customer how much he had paid for the tires. Mr. Nordstrom then instructed the clerk to take the tires back and provide a full cash refund. After the customer had received his refund and left, the perplexed clerk looked at the boss. "But, Mr. Nordstrom, we don't sell tires!" "I know," replied the boss, "but we do whatever we need to do to make the customer happy. I mean it when I say we have a no-questions-asked return policy." Nordstrom then picked up the telephone and called a friend in the auto parts business to see how much he could get for the tires.

Stories such as these circulate through many organizations. They typically contain a narrative of events about the organization's founders, rule breaking, rags-to-riches successes, reductions in the workforce, relocation of employees, reactions to past mistakes, and organizational coping.[41] These stories anchor the present in the past and provide explanations and legitimacy for current practices.[42]

Rituals

rituals
Repetitive sequences of activities that express and reinforce the key values of the organization, what goals are most important, which people are important and which are expendable.

Rituals are repetitive sequences of activities that express and reinforce the key values of the organization, what goals are most important, which people are important and which are expendable.[43]

College faculty members undergo a lengthy ritual in their quest for permanent employment—tenure. Typically, the faculty member is on probation for six years. At the end of that period, the member's colleagues must make one of two choices: extend a tenured appointment or issue a one-year terminal contract. What does it take to obtain tenure? It usually requires satisfactory teaching performance, service to the department and university, and scholarly activity. But, of course, what satisfies the requirements for tenure in one department at one university may be appraised as inadequate in another. The key is that the tenure decision, in essence, asks those who are tenured to assess whether the candidate has demonstrated, based on six years of performance, whether he or she fits in. Colleagues who have been socialized properly will have proved themselves worthy of being granted tenure. Every year, hundreds of faculty members at colleges and universities are denied tenure. In some cases, this action is a result of poor performance across the board. More often, however, the decision can be traced to the faculty member's not doing well in those areas that the tenured faculty believe are important. The instructor who spends dozens of hours each week preparing for class and achieves outstanding evaluations by students but neglects his or her research and publication activities may be passed over for tenure. What has happened, simply, is that the instructor has failed to adapt to the norms set by the department. The astute faculty member will assess early on in the probationary period what attitudes and behaviors his or her colleagues want and will then proceed to give them what they want. And, of course, by demanding certain attitudes and behaviors, the tenured faculty have made significant strides toward standardizing tenure candidates.

One of the best-known corporate rituals is Mary Kay Cosmetics' annual award meeting.[44] Looking like a cross between a circus and a Miss America pageant, the meeting takes place over a couple of days in a large auditorium, on a stage in front of a large, cheering audience, with all the participants dressed in glamorous evening clothes. Saleswomen are rewarded with an array of flashy gifts—gold and diamond pins, fur stoles, pink Cadillacs—based on success in achieving sales quota. This "show" acts as a motivator by publicly

A ritual at Mary Kay Cosmetics is the annual sales meeting. Recognizing high achievement is an important part of the company's culture, which values hard work and determination. The ritual of praise and recognition honors the beauty consultants' accomplishments in meeting their sales quotas, which contribute to the success of the company.

Exhibit 16-5

Drawing by Mick Stevens in *The New Yorker*, October 3, 1994. Copyright © 1994 by The New Yorker Magazine, Inc. Reprinted by permission.

"I don't know how it started, either. All I know is that it's part of our corporate culture."

recognizing outstanding sales performance. In addition, the ritual aspect reinforces Mary Kay's personal determination and optimism, which enabled her to overcome personal hardships, found her own company, and achieve material success. It conveys to her salespeople that reaching their sales quota is important and that through hard work and encouragement they too can achieve success.

Material Symbols

The headquarters of package manufacturer AGI doesn't look like your typical head office operation. As we noted in chapter 14, there are few individual work areas. It is essentially made up of open, common areas and meeting rooms. This informal corporate headquarters conveys to employees that AGI values openness, equality, creativity, and flexibility.

Some corporations provide their top executives with chauffeur-driven limousines and, when they travel by air, unlimited use of the corporate jet. Others may not get to ride in limousines or private jets but they might still get a car and air transportation paid for by the company. Only the car is a Chevrolet (with no driver) and the jet seat is in the economy section of a commercial airliner.

The layout of corporate headquarters, the types of automobiles top executives are given, and the presence or absence of corporate aircraft are a few examples of material symbols. Others include the size of offices, the elegance of furnishings, executive perks, and dress attire.[45] These material symbols convey to employees who is important, the degree of egalitarianism desired by top management, and the kinds of behavior (for example, risk taking, conservative, authoritarian, participative, individualistic, social) that are appropriate.

Language

Many organizations and units within organizations use language as a way to identify members of a culture or subculture. By learning this language, members attest to their acceptance of the culture and, in so doing, help to preserve it.

The following are examples of terminology used by employees at Dialog, a California-based data redistributor: *accession number* (a number assigned to each individual record in a database); KWIC (a set of key-words-in-context); and *relational operator* (searching a database for names or key terms in some order). Librarians are a rich source of terminology foreign to people outside their profession. They sprinkle their conversations liberally with acronyms like ARL (Association for Research Libraries), OCLC (a center in Ohio that does cooperative cataloging), and OPAC (for on-line patron accessing catalog). When Louis Gerstner left RJR Nabisco to head up IBM, he had to learn a whole new vocabulary which included: *the Orchard* (IBM's Armonk, New York corporate headquarters, which was once an apple orchard); *big iron* (mainframe computers); *hypo* (a high-potential employee); *a one performer* (an employee with IBM's top performance rating); and *PROFS* (Professional Office Systems, IBM's internal electronic mail system).[46]

Organizations, over time, often develop unique terms to describe equipment, offices, key personnel, suppliers, customers, or products that relate to its business. New employees are frequently overwhelmed with acronyms and jargon that, after six months on the job, have become fully part of their language. Once assimilated, this terminology acts as a common denominator that unites members of a given culture or subculture.

Summary and Implications for Managers

Exhibit 16-6 depicts organizational culture as an intervening variable. Employees form an overall subjective perception of the organization based on such factors as degree of risk tolerance, team emphasis, and support of people. This overall perception becomes, in effect, the organization's culture or personality. These favorable or unfavorable perceptions then affect employee performance and satisfaction, with the impact being greater for stronger cultures.

Just as people's personalities tend to be stable over time, so too do strong cultures. This makes strong cultures difficult for managers to change. When a culture becomes mismatched to its environment, management will want to change it. But as the Point-Counterpoint debate for this chapter demonstrates, changing an organization's culture is a long and difficult process. The result, at least in the short term, is that managers should treat their organization's culture as relatively fixed.

One of the more important managerial implications of organizational culture relates to selection decisions. Hiring individuals whose values don't align with those of the organization are likely to lead to employees who lack motivation and commitment and who are dissatisfied with their jobs and the

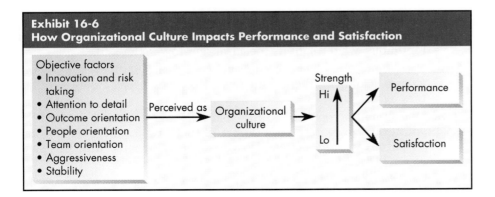

Exhibit 16-6
How Organizational Culture Impacts Performance and Satisfaction

Objective factors
- Innovation and risk taking
- Attention to detail
- Outcome orientation
- People orientation
- Team orientation
- Aggressiveness
- Stability

Perceived as → Organizational culture → Strength (Hi / Lo) → Performance / Satisfaction

organization.[47] Not surprisingly, employee "misfits" have considerably higher turnover rates than individuals who perceive a good fit.[48]

We should also not overlook the influence socialization has on employee performance. An employee's performance depends to a considerable degree on knowing what he should or should not do. Understanding the right way to do a job indicates proper socialization. Furthermore, the appraisal of an individual's performance includes how well the person fits into the organization. Can he or she get along with co-workers? Does he or she have acceptable work habits and demonstrate the right attitude? These qualities differ between jobs and organizations. For instance, on some jobs, employees will be evaluated more favorably if they are aggressive and outwardly indicate that they are ambitious. On another job, or on the same job in another organization, such an approach may be evaluated negatively. As a result, proper socialization becomes a significant factor in influencing both actual job performance and how it's perceived by others.

For Review

1. What is the relationship between institutionalization, formalization, and organizational culture?
2. What's the difference between job satisfaction and organizational culture?
3. Can an employee survive in an organization if he or she rejects its core values? Explain.
4. How can an outsider assess an organization's culture?
5. What defines an organization's subcultures?
6. Contrast organizational culture with national culture.
7. How can culture be a liability to an organization?
8. How does a strong culture affect an organization's efforts to improve diversity?
9. What benefits can socialization provide for the organization? For the new employee?
10. How is language related to organizational culture?

For Discussion

1. Contrast individual personality and organizational culture. How are they similar? How are they different?
2. Is socialization brainwashing? Explain.
3. If management sought a culture characterized as innovative and autonomous, what might its socialization program look like?
4. Can you identify a set of characteristics that describes your college's culture? Compare them with several of your peers. How closely do they agree?
5. "We should be opposed to the manipulation of individuals for organizational purposes, but a degree of social uniformity enables organizations to work better." Do you agree or disagree with this statement? Discuss.

The Case against Cultural Change

That an organization's culture is made up of relatively stable characteristics would imply that culture is very difficult for management to change. Such a conclusion would be correct.

An organization's culture develops over many years and is rooted in deeply held values to which employees are strongly committed. In addition, there are a number of forces continually operating to maintain a given culture. These would include written statements about the organization's mission and philosophy, the design of physical spaces and buildings, the dominant leadership style, hiring criteria, past promotion practices, entrenched rituals, popular stories about key people and events, the organization's historic performance evaluation criteria, and the organization's formal structure.

Selection and promotion policies are particularly important devices that work against cultural change. Employees chose the organization because they perceived their values to be a "good fit" with the organization. They become comfortable with that fit and will strongly resist efforts to disturb the equilibrium. The terrific difficulties that organizations like General Motors, AT&T, and the U.S. Postal Service have had in trying to reshape their cultures attest to this dilemma. These organizations historically tended to attract individuals who desired and flourished in situations that were stable and highly structured. Those in control in organizations will also select senior managers who will continue the current culture. Even attempts to change a culture by going outside the organization to hire a new chief executive are unlikely to be effective. The evidence indicates that the culture is more likely to change the executive than the other way around. Why? It's too entrenched, and change becomes a potential threat to member self-interest. In fact, a more pragmatic view of the relationship between an organization's culture and its chief executive would be to note that the practice of filling senior-level management positions from current managerial employees ensures that those who run the organization have been fully indoctrinated in the organization's culture. Promoting from within provides stability and lessens uncertainty. When Exxon's board of directors selects as a new chief executive officer an individual who has spent 30 years in the company, it virtually guarantees that the culture will continue unchanged.

Our argument, however, should not be viewed as saying that culture can never be changed. In the unusual case when an organization confronts a survival-threatening crisis—a crisis that is universally acknowledged as a true life-or-death situation—members of the organization will be responsive to efforts at cultural change. For instance, it was only when General Motors' and AT&T's executives were able to successfully convey to employees the crises faced from competitors that these organizations' cultures began to show signs of adaptation. However, anything less than a crisis is unlikely to be effective in bringing about cultural change.

How to Change an Organization's Culture

Changing an organization's culture is extremely difficult, but cultures *can* be changed. For example, Lee Iacocca came to Chrysler Corp. in 1978, when the company appeared to be only weeks away from bankruptcy. It took him about five years but, in what is now a well-worn story, he took Chrysler's conservative, inward-looking, and engineering-oriented culture and changed it into an action-oriented, market-responsive culture.

The evidence suggests that cultural change is most likely to take place when most or all of the following conditions exist:

A dramatic crisis. This is the shock that undermines the status quo and calls into question the relevance of the current culture. Examples of these crises might be a surprising financial setback, the loss of a major customer, or a dramatic technological breakthrough by a competitor. Executives at Pepsi-Cola and Ameritech even admit to creating crises in order to stimulate cultural change in their organizations.*

Turnover in leadership. New top leadership, which can provide an alternative set of key values, may be perceived as more capable of responding to the crisis. This would definitely be the organization's chief executive but also might need to include all senior management positions. The hiring of outside CEOs at IBM (Louis Gerstner) and General Motors (Jack Smith) illustrate attempts to introduce new leadership.

Young and small organization. The younger the organization is, the less entrenched its culture will be. Similarly, it's easier for management to communicate its new values when the organization is small. This again helps explain the difficulty that multibillion-dollar corporations have in changing their cultures.

Weak culture. The more widely held a culture is and the higher the agreement among members on its values, the more difficult it will be to change. Conversely, weak cultures are more amenable to change than strong ones.

If conditions support cultural change, you should consider the following suggestions:

1. Have top-management people become positive role models, setting the tone through their behavior.
2. Create new stories, symbols, and rituals to replace those currently in vogue.
3. Select, promote, and support employees who espouse the new values that are sought.
4. Redesign socialization processes to align with the new values.
5. Change the reward system to encourage acceptance of a new set of values.
6. Replace unwritten norms with formal rules and regulations that are tightly enforced.
7. Shake up current subcultures through transfers, job rotation, and/or terminations.
8. Work to get peer group consensus through utilization of employee participation and creation of a climate with a high level of trust.

Implementing most or all of these suggestions will not result in an immediate or dramatic shift in the organization's culture. For, in the final analysis, cultural change is a lengthy process—measured in years rather than months. But if the question is, "Can culture be changed?" the answer is "Yes!"

*B. Dumaine, "Times Are Good? Create a Crisis," *Fortune*, June 28, 1993, pp. 123–30.

What Kind of Organizational Culture Fits You Best?

For each of the following statements, circle the level of agreement or disagreement that you personally feel:

SA = Strongly Agree
A = Agree
U = Uncertain
D = Disagree
SD = Strongly disagree

1. I like being part of a team and having my performance assessed in terms of my contribution to the team. SA A U D SD
2. No person's needs should be compromised in order for a department to achieve its goals. SA A U D SD
3. I like the thrill and excitement from taking risks. SA A U D SD
4. If a person's job performance is inadequate, it's irrelevant how much effort he or she made. SA A U D SD
5. I like things to be stable and predictable. SA A U D SD
6. I prefer managers who provide detailed and rational explanations for their decisions. SA A U D SD
7. I like to work where there isn't a great deal of pressure and where people are essentially easygoing. SA A U D SD

Turn to page A-30 for scoring direction and key.

Rate Your Classroom Culture

Listed here are ten statements. Score each statement by indicating the degree to which you agree with it. If you strongly agree, give it a five. If you strongly disagree, give it a 1.

1. My classmates are friendly and supportive. _____
2. My instructor is friendly and supportive. _____
3. My instructor encourages me to question and challenge him or her as well as other students. _____
4. My instructor clearly expresses his or her expectations to the class. _____
5. I think the grading system used by my instructor is based on clear standards of performance. _____
6. My instructor's behavior during examinations demonstrates his or her belief that students are honest and trustworthy. _____

7. My instructor provides regular and rapid feedback on my performance. _____

8. My instructor uses a strict bell curve to allocate grades. _____

9. My instructor is open to suggestions on how the course might be improved. _____

10. My instructor makes me want to learn. _____

Add up your score for all the statements except number eight. For number eight, reverse the score (strongly agree = 1; strongly disagree = 5) and add it to your total. Your score will fall between ten and fifty.

A high score (thirty-seven or above) describes an open, warm, human, trusting, and supportive culture. A low score (twenty-five or below) describes a closed, cold, task-oriented, autocratic, and tense culture.

Form groups of 5 to 7 members each. Compare your scores. How close do they align? Discuss and resolve discrepancies.

Ethical Dilemma Exercise

Cultural Factors and Unethical Behavior

An organization's culture socializes people. It subtly conveys to members that certain actions are acceptable, even though they are illegal. For instance, when executives at General Electric, Westinghouse, and other manufacturers of heavy electrical equipment illegally conspired to set prices in the early 1960s, the defendants invariably testified that they came new to their jobs, found price fixing to be an established way of life, and simply entered into it as they did into other aspects of their job. One GE manager noted that every one of his bosses had directed him to meet with the competition: "It had become so common and gone on for so many years that I think we lost sight of the fact that it was illegal."*

The strength of an organization's culture has an influence on the ethical behavior of its managers. A strong culture will exert more influence on managers than a weak one. If the culture is strong and supports high ethical standards, it should have a very powerful positive influence on a manager's ethical behavior. However, in a weak culture, managers are more likely to rely on subculture norms to guide their behavior. So work groups and departmental standards will more strongly influence ethical behavior in organizations that have weak overall cultures.

It is also generally acknowledged that the content of a culture affects ethical behavior. Assuming this is true, what would a culture look like that would shape high ethical standards? What could top management do to strengthen that culture? Do you think it's possible for a manager with high ethical standards to uphold those standards in an organizational culture that tolerates, or even encourages, unethical practices?

*As described in P.C. Yeager, "Analyzing Corporate Offenses: Progress and Prospects," in W.C. Frederick and L.E. Preston (eds.), *Business Ethics: Research Issues and Empirical Studies* (Greenwich, CT: JAI Press, 1990), p. 174.

Cultural Change Efforts at the U.S. Postal Service

When Marvin Runyon was appointed Postmaster General in 1992, he promised to transform the U.S. Postal Service's culture. He said all the right things: streamlining management, moving away from authority-based leadership, empowering employees, holding postal managers and workers more accountable for their performance, and introducing cross-functional work teams to encourage formerly disparate operations to work more closely together. Runyon noted the need for change to overcome the public's perception that the Postal Service was inefficient. And he drove home the threat of competition from United Parcel Service, Federal Express, and electronic mail.

Good intentions aside, Runyon has essentially had no impact on changing the Postal Service culture. "Absolutely nothing has changed," says the national president of one labor union that represents about 240,000 active letter carriers. "Employee empowerment seemed like a good idea for about 60 days, until management figured out that it meant actually giving up some of their power and letting workers have a say."

The Postal Service has long had labor problems with its workforce of more than 700,000 career employees. Workers routinely file grievances over such things as denied requests for time off or unrequested overtime assignments. While union–management relations have been strained for decades, they seem to have reached new lows in recent years. Grievances are at all time highs. For instance, in 1995, 73,300 grievances could not be resolved at the workplace level. By contrast, the United Auto Workers, which represents about 800,000 employees, had only a thousand grievances that failed to get resolved at the plant level.

An example of the severe actions management is taking against workers, according to labor union officials, was a letter carrier with a spotless ten-year record who was fired for refusing to work overtime on a day when he had to pick up his child at school. Management at the Postal Service claims it is just getting tough with employees who abuse the system. It admits that efforts to revamp the service's authoritarian culture have not been as successful as it had hoped but that the number of grievances filed by workers should not be used as evidence that efforts to change the Postal Service have failed. Union leaders see things differently. They believe management is entrenched in its command-and-control style, wants to remind employees who's boss, and seeks to lessen the power of the unions.

Three notable sets of events seem to be at the heart of current labor–management tensions at the Postal Service. First is automation. The average salary for bargaining-unit employees was $45,000 in 1995. Over time, the service wants to cut labor costs through the use of letter-sorting equipment and bar code readers. Disruption of current jobs and anxiety about future jobs worry the unions. For instance, automation at the San Francisco Mail Processing and Distribution Center forced 600 of 2,400 unionized workers to change shifts or jobs. In some cases, workers had to move to jobs at lower pay levels. The second set of events revolve around contract negotiations. The 1994 round of negotiations with the Postal Service's four unions may have set an all-time record for intransigence. Only one of the four unions reached an agreement with the service without going to arbitration. In one set of negotiations, the letter carriers' union had requested a moderate pay and benefits increase, arguing that its members performed jobs comparable to UPS and

Federal Express delivery personnel and therefore deserved comparable pay hikes. Management countered with a demand for a pay cutback, arguing that the job performed by letter carriers was comparable to that of "uniformed delivery personnel such as pizza deliverers," a phrase that infuriated the union and its membership. An arbitrator eventually awarded carriers a 1.2 percent salary increase with a $950 lump-sum increase the first year. Finally, there are problems related to downsizing. Soon after becoming Postmaster General, Runyon offered managers an attractive early retirement package. He hoped to cut some 30,000 managers from what critics had long characterized as a bloated organization structure. But craft workers, the people who actually move the 180 billion pieces of mail each year, fought to be included in the retirement package. The end result was that 48,000 workers retired, many of them experienced craft workers and front-line supervisors, and overtime hours nearly doubled as remaining workers were forced to take up the slack.

Questions

1. Describe the Postal Service's current culture.
2. How might cultural change efforts be different in public-sector organizations than in for-profit business firms?
3. What suggestions would you have for top management that could help it enlist the unions in their cultural change efforts?
4. Discuss the specific suggestions you would make to top management that could help it succeed in changing the Postal Service's culture into the one originally described by Runyon.

Source: Based on D. Stamps, "Going Nowhere: Cultural Change at the Postal Service Fizzles," *Training*, July 1996, pp. 26–34.

When Good Cops Go Bad

Michael Dowd is a corrupt cop. This case is about Dowd and the culture within the New York Police Department that allowed him to abuse his authority position for six years.

Michael Dowd tells his story: "When you're a cop, you're the boss in the street. Who in their right mind, if they're doing something wrong, is going to say to a cop, 'You can't do this, you can't do that?' Nobody. You feel indestructible. I figured, 'If they haven't caught me by now, forget it.' I could do anything. I could do anything."

Dowd worked a tough neighborhood where drug deals were regularly going down. "You see money in wads in their pockets, you know, hundreds, thousands of dollars at a time, you know, and I'm taking home $340 a week at a time, so, you know, you notice those things."

But Dowd did more than notice. He joined the other side. He became a drug dealer himself. Starting slow—drinking on the job as a rookie, fixing traffic tickets—it escalated to the point where he was making as much as $8,000 to $10,000 a week through illegal activities. He stole money from corpses at crime scenes, robbed drug dealers, and dealt cocaine.

Didn't anyone pick up on Dowd's underworld activities? Yes, Joe Trimboli did. He was an investigator in the NYPD Internal Affairs (IA) Department. Trimboli suspected that as many as 15 to 20 cops were involved with Dowd and requested help in his investigation. He was turned down by his bosses. After continually pressing IA to pursue what Trimboli felt sure was a group of corrupt cops, IA shut down all of Trimboli's investigations and removed him from the Dowd case. Why? The best answer seems to lie in the history of the NYPD. It had suffered a major corruption scandal in 1986. It didn't want another scandal. The word from the mayor's office was "keep corruption out of the headlines."

Dowd and others like him were able to engage in corrupt practices for years largely because of the underwritten code of silence. When asked why other police officers in his command, who knew what he was doing, didn't turn him in, Dowd said, "Because I'm still a cop. Cops don't turn on other cops. Cops don't want to be labeled as rats. Cops depend on one another to survive out there."

Questions

1. How can an organization's culture condone or discourage illegal activities?
2. What, in the NYPD's culture, do you think supported bad cops?
3. If you were the new police chief in New York, what could you do to change the culture to make it less tolerant of unlawful activities?

Source: Based on "The Tarnished Shield," *ABC News Turning Point*; aired on September 14, 1994.

ROB PANCO: WORKING WITHIN THE ORGANIZATION SYSTEM

"The structures of AT&T and Aslett were as different as night and day," Rob Panco said. "AT&T was pure hierarchy. Everyone was very cognizant of your rank in the organization. It wasn't unusual for someone to say to me, for instance, 'Your're only second level. Be careful about challenging fourth levels in a meeting.' Rank was everything. In fact, I remember traveling with a higher level manager one time. When we picked up our rent-a-car at the airport, he said, 'You're the grunt. You drive.' At AT&T, they never let you forget where you are in the pecking order. In contrast, Aslett was very informal. We were a flat organization. People could come to me and not get their heads cut off. I didn't pay much attention to rank. Then again, I was in charge. If I had been Bob Allen [CEO of AT&T], I might have thought that AT&T was a lot less hierarchical. My perspective was from down below."

Most people are familiar with how large companies like AT&T go about the selection process. These companies historically hired young people for entry-level positions and let them grow up through the ranks. College grades and aptitude test scores were given a great deal of weight in the selection decision. During the past decade, AT&T has undergone major changes as a result of deregulation. Tens of thousands of people have been laid off. In contrast to past practices, new hires have often come from the outside to fill middle- and upper-level managerial slots because the necessary skills and perspectives weren't available inside AT&T. For instance, in 1990, the company hired Richard Bodman, president of Washington National Insurance, to become AT&T's senior vice president in charge of corporate strategy and development. In 1991, Alex Mandl, former chairman of Sea-Land Service, joined AT&T as its chief financial officer; and Jerre Stead, chairman of Square D Co., was brought in as president of AT&T's Business Communications Systems unit. More recently, AT&T chose John R. Walter, a printing executive at R.R. Donnelley & Sons with no expertise in telecommunications, to become corporate president and chief operating officer in 1996.

Aslett's small size and project form of structure allowed Rob Panco to hire in a much more informal and direct way. About half of Aslett's new hires came from current employee referrals. Once hired, the referral typically becomes the new employee's sponsor. That is, the sponsor helps the new employee adjust to his or her job. Most other new hires came from the pool of freelancers that the company used. When an opening came up, the best freelancers were usually looked at first as possible full-time employees. By hiring from this pool, Rob says he already had first-hand evidence of their performance capability so he didn't have to do much screening. Their prior work became the test. But among referrals, Rob relied on work samples. For instance, candidates for jobs as designers and electronic page makers had to take a half-hour test where they could demonstrate their skills. Rob noted that all new hires from the freelancers pool also had sponsors. They were usually the team leader from the freelancer's previous project. All new employees were told explicitly what was expected of them. They were then on probation for six months. At the end of six months, they were reviewed. Performance reviews after that were on their service anniversary.

When business slowed in 1995, hiring was curtailed. When natural attrition wasn't enough to get the payroll down, Rob's challenge became deciding whom to let go. "Actually the hiring and layoff decisions were very similar. For instance,

622

should I let the newest employees go first? Would I keep a high performing part-timer over a poorer performing full-timer? I chose to use two factors in guiding my decision—what skills were most critical and who were the most competent.

When asked if Aslett's culture changed when the growth stopped, Rob replied, "Yeah, I think so. The operating people took more ownership. They were more focused. They pulled together and took more initiative. During growth, we surpressed ownership. There was psuedo-empowerment, but I wasn't really letting go. Maybe if we had let employees participate sooner, business might have been better."

The way that AT&T and Aslett conducted performance evaluations also provides a good illustration of the differences between the two organizations. According to Rob, "evaluations are a game at AT&T. They have great tools but they don't teach managers how to use them." The evaluation procedure is fairly standardized: Individuals are rated by their boss and ranked from 1 to n in their group. A modified bell curve is used. Ten percent are allocated to the highest category (outstanding performers), with five percent having to be labeled as low performers and placed on probation. Of course, there is considerable politicking and negotiating over rankings. Time in rank, for instance, carries a lot of weight."

"I'm a wimp. I don't like rating people," confides Rob. "I used a metric system of ratings because it's better than subjective appraisals, but I don't like ranking people." Rob then described the standardized form he used, which broke employee performance down into four categories: personal (individual) performance; teammanship; contribution to quality; and personal development. "The first three were about equal—they were worth about 30 percent each. Personal development was a tiebreaker." Within each category, Rob made a list and rated people on (1) accomplishments made during the period and (2) areas for improvement. "I'll admit that I might have handled the process wrong. I didn't ask employees for their input until the end of the review session. I should have begun by asking people for a self-appraisal."

Aslett's small size created very different problems for Rob than for managers at AT&T. "At a company the size of AT&T, no one person makes that much of a difference," Rob stated. "But in a small company like Aslett, each person is critical. If someone doesn't come to work, it can really effect the whole organization. This makes each person at Aslett close to the heart. My people needed to buy into the organization more than is necessary at an AT&T."

Questions

1. Is it a law of structural design that large size (like AT&T) must result in a hierarchical-driven organization? Discuss.
2. Assess the pros and cons of filling job vacancies with referrals made by current employees.
3. Contrast the ways that structure constrains low-level employees at AT&T with operating personnel at Aslett.
4. Evaluate the effectiveness of the performance appraisal system Rob put in place at Aslett. Did it help or hinder employee motivation? Discuss.
5. How can "sponsors" influence the attitudes and behavior of new hires?
6. Some researchers note a "layoff-survivor syndrome" following downsizing: Those people who remain complain of fatigue and exhibit increased levels of anxiety and stress. Why didn't this happen at Aslett?

17

ORGANIZATIONAL CHANGE AND STRESS MANAGEMENT

CHAPTER OUTLINE

Forces for Change

Managing Planned Change

What Can Change Agents Change?

Resistance to Change

Approaches to Managing Organizational Change

Contemporary Change Issues for Today's Managers

Work Stress and Its Management

> Most people hate any change that doesn't jingle in their pockets.
> —Anonymous

LEARNING OBJECTIVES

After studying this chapter, you should be able to

1 Describe forces that act as stimulants to change

2 Contrast first-order and second-order change

3 Summarize sources of individual and organizational resistance to change

4 Identify properties of innovative organizations

5 List characteristics of a learning organization

6 Describe potential sources of stress

7 Explain individual difference variables that moderate the stress–outcome relationship

TODAY'S changing and competitive workplace is increasing the stress levels among workers and managers alike. For instance, a recent survey of U.S. workers found that 46 percent felt their jobs were extremely stressful and 34 percent had seriously thought about quitting their jobs in the previous 12 months because of workplace stress.[1] In Asia, more and more managers are showing signs of chronic fatigue and burnout, and there is growing concern among senior executives in Asia that burned-out managers can mean a burned-out company.[2]

Many executives thrive under pressure and enjoy the adrenalin rush that comes from competition and achievement. But human beings can burn out and that's apparently happening among a growing number of Asian managers. They're showing signs of chronic fatigue—moodiness, lethargy, erratic behavior, physical ailments, and increased family problems. The chief executive of Hongkong Telecom believes that stressed-out managers aren't good for their companies or shareholders. He says it leads "in most cases to greatly reduced efficiency in even the best of individuals and almost inevitably to decreased productivity."

Stress seems to be a problem regardless of whether the economy is strong or weak. In Thailand, for example, the economy is robust. But Thais working in highly competitive sectors such as advertising, securities, and consumer products are showing signs of stress and burnout. In contrast, the Japanese economy is stagnant. Yet managers there continue to put in 80-plus hours per week and push themselves toward burnout.

Japanese managers have long considered workaholism and evidence of work-related stress as a badge of honor. The Japanese even have a name for the "disease"—*karoshi* or death from overwork. Japanese managers prided themselves on having no social life and an inability to talk about any subject except business. Recent downsizing efforts by Japanese companies are only making matters worse. Lifetime employment with continuous advancement is being replaced by performance-related expectations. Merit pay plans are being installed. Noncontributors are getting coarse hints—such as hefty pay cuts—to shape up or ship out.

Companies bulging at the seams with excess middle managers, now faced with more efficient foreign competitors, can no longer afford to keep unproductive people. And lower-level managers are finding their workloads increased. This downsizing climate is only heightening workplace stress.

The Japanese government has begun to speak out against this culture of overwork, as the negative impact that stress is having on productivity can no longer be ignored. The government now wants Japan's workers and managers to get a life, enjoy their families, take vacations, produce less and consume more. Not surprisingly, in a climate of cutbacks, few Japanese are listening. And apparently their peers in Thailand, Hong Kong, Malaysia, and other booming Asian economies aren't getting the message either. ◆

This chapter is about change and stress. We describe environmental forces that are requiring managers to implement comprehensive change programs. We also consider why people and organizations often resist change and how this resistance can be overcome. We review various processes for managing organizational change. We also discuss contemporary change issues for today's managers. Then we move to the topic of stress. We elaborate on the sources and consequences of stress. Finally, we conclude this chapter with a discussion of what individuals and organizations can do to better manage stress levels.

Forces for Change

More and more organizations today face a dynamic and changing environment. This, in turn, is requiring these organizations to adapt. "Change or die!" is the rallying cry among today's managers worldwide. Exhibit 17-1 summarizes six specific forces that are acting as stimulants for change.

In a number of places in this book, we've discussed the changing *nature of the workforce*. For instance, almost every organization is having to adjust to a multicultural environment. Human resource policies and practices have to change in order to attract and keep this more diverse workforce. And many companies are having to spend large amounts of money on training to upgrade reading, math, computer, and other skills of employees.

As noted in chapter 14, *technology* is changing jobs and organizations. The substitution of computer control for direct supervision, for instance, is resulting in wider spans of control for managers and flatter organizations. Sophisticated information technology is also making organizations more responsive. Companies like AT&T, Motorola, General Electric, and Chrysler can now develop, make, and distribute their products in a fraction of the time it took them a decade ago. And, as organizations have had to become more adaptable, so too have their employees. As we noted in our discussion of groups and organization design, many jobs are being reshaped. Individuals doing narrow, specialized, and routine jobs are being replaced by work teams whose members can perform multiple tasks and actively participate in team decisions.

We live in an "age of discontinuity." In the 1950s and 1960s, the past was a pretty good prologue to the future. Tomorrow was essentially an ex-

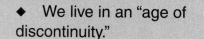

◆ We live in an "age of discontinuity."

Exhibit 17-1 Forces for Change

Force	Examples
Nature of the workforce	• More cultural diversity • Increase in professionals • Many new entrants with inadequate skills
Technology	• More computers and automation • TQM programs • Reengineering programs
Economic shocks	• Security market crashes • Interest rate fluctuations • Foreign currency fluctuations
Competition	• Global competitors • Mergers and consolidations • Growth of specialty retailers
Social trends	• Increase in college attendance • Delayed marriages by young people • Increase in divorce rate
World politics	• Collapse of Soviet Union • U.S. embargo of Libya • Black rule of South Africa

tended trend line from yesterday. That's no longer true. Beginning in the early 1970s, with the overnight quadrupling of world oil prices, *economic shocks* have continued to impose changes on organizations. In recent years, for instance, interest rates have become more volatile and the economies of individual countries have become more interdependent. When interest rates rise, for example, the market for new home loans and refinancings declines. For many mortgage brokerage firms, revenues decline and layoffs ensue. Similarly, the profitability of U.S. security firms such as Merrill Lynch and Dean Witter is increasingly linked to the health of foreign economies and markets.

Competition is changing. The global economy means that competitors are as likely to come from across the ocean as from across town. Heightened competition also means that established organizations need to defend themselves against both traditional competitors who develop new products and services and small, entrepreneurial firms with innovative offerings. Successful organizations will be the ones that can change in response to the competition. They'll be fast on their feet, capable of developing new products rapidly and getting them to market quickly. They'll rely on short production runs, short product cycles, and an ongoing stream of new products. In other words, they'll be flexible. They will require an equally flexible and responsive workforce that can adapt to rapidly and even radically changing conditions.

Take a look at *social trends* during the past generation. They suggest changes that organizations have to adjust for. For instance, there has been a clear trend in marriage and divorce during the past two decades. Young people are delaying marriage, and half of all marriages are ending in divorce. One obvious result of this social trend is an increasing number of single households and demand for housing by singles. If you're in the house-building business, this is an important factor in determining the size and design of homes. Similarly, the expansion of single households has increased demand for single-portion quantities of frozen meals, which is highly relevant to organizations like ConAgra's Healthy Choice division or Pillsbury's Green Giant.

We've called for seeing OB in a global context throughout this book. While business schools have been preaching a global perspective since the early 1980s, no one—not even the strongest proponents of globalization— could have imagined how *world politics* would change in recent years. A few examples make the point: the fall of the Berlin Wall, the reunification of Germany, Iraq's invasion of Kuwait, and the breakup of the Soviet Union. Almost every major U.S. defense contractor, for instance, has had to rethink its business and make serious changes in response to the demise of the Soviet Union and a shrinking Pentagon budget. Companies like Hughes Electronics, Lockheed Martin, Raytheon, and Northrop Grumman have each cut tens of thousands of jobs since the early 1990s.

Managing Planned Change

A group of employees that works in a small retail women's clothing store confronted the owner: "The air pollution in this store from cigarette smoking has gotten awful," said their spokeswoman. "We won't continue to work here if you allow smoking in the store. We want you to post no-smoking signs on the entrance doors and not allow any employee to smoke on the floor. If people have to smoke, they can go into the mall." The owner listened thoughtfully to the group's ultimatum and agreed to its request. The next day the owner posted the no-smoking signs and advised all of the employees of the new rule.

A major automobile manufacturer spent several billion dollars to install state-of-the-art robotics. One area that would receive the new equipment was quality control. Sophisticated computer-controlled equipment would be put in place to significantly improve the company's ability to find and correct de-

AT&T has adapted to changes in the global economic and political arenas by reorganizing into three separate global companies, laying off 40,000 employees, and seizing opportunities for growth in new markets. Following the passage of the North American Free Trade Agreement, AT&T began exporting fiber optic cable produced at its Atlanta, Georgia, plant to Mexico. NAFTA is helping AT&T's entry into the Mexican market, which has been dominated by global competitors such as Alcatel of France and Ericsson of Sweden.

fects. Since the new equipment would dramatically change the jobs of the people working in the quality control area, and since management anticipated considerable employee resistance to the new equipment, executives were developing a program to help people become familiar with the equipment and to deal with any anxieties they might be feeling.

Both of the previous scenarios are examples of **change**. That is, both are concerned with making things different. However, only the second scenario describes a planned change. In this section, we want to clarify what we mean by planned change, describe its goals, contrast first-order and second-order change, and consider who is responsible for bringing about **planned change** in an organization.

Many changes in organizations are like the one that occurred in the retail clothing store—they just happen. Some organizations treat all change as an accidental occurrence. However, we're concerned with change activities that are proactive and purposeful. In this chapter, we address change as an intentional, goal-oriented activity.

What are the goals of planned change? Essentially there are two. First, it seeks to improve the ability of the organization to adapt to changes in its environment. Second, it seeks to change employee behavior.

If an organization is to survive, it must respond to changes in its environment. When competitors introduce new products or services, government agencies enact new laws, important sources of supply go out of business, or similar environmental changes take place, the organization needs to adapt. Efforts to stimulate innovation, empower employees, and introduce work teams are examples of planned-change activities directed at responding to changes in the environment.

Since an organization's success or failure is essentially due to the things that its employees do or fail to do, planned change also is concerned with changing the behavior of individuals and groups within the organization. In this chapter, we review a number of techniques that organizations can use to get people to behave differently in the tasks they perform and in their interactions with others.

It also helps to think of planned change in terms of order of magnitude.[3] **First-order change** is linear and continuous. It implies no fundamental shifts in the assumptions that organizational members hold about the world or how the organization can improve its functioning. In contrast, **second-order change** is a multidimensional, multilevel, discontinuous, radical change involving reframing of assumptions about the organization and the world in which it operates. Mikio Kitano, director of all production engineering at Toyota, is introducing first-order change in his company.[4] He's pursuing slow, subtle, incremental changes in production processes to improve the efficiency of Toyota's plants. On the other hand, Boeing's top executives have recently committed themselves to radically reinventing their company.[5] Responding to a massive airline slump, aggressive competition from Airbus, and the threat of Japanese competitors, this second-order change process at Boeing includes slashing costs by up to 30 percent, reducing the time it takes to make a 737 from 13 months to 6 months, dramatically cutting inventories, putting the company's entire workforce through a four-day course in "competitiveness," and bringing customers and suppliers into the once secret process of designing new planes.

Who in organizations are responsible for managing change activities? The answer is **change agents**. Change agents can be managers or nonmanagers, employees of the organization or outside consultants.

change
Making things different.

planned change
Change activities that are intentional and goal oriented.

first-order change
Linear and continuous.

second-order change
Change that is multidimensional, multilevel, discontinuous, and radical.

change agents
Persons who act as catalysts and assume the responsibility for managing change activities.

Typically we look to senior executives as agents of change. CEO Bob Allen has been a primary change agent at AT&T. Mikio Kitano is one at Toyota. The primary change agent at Boeing is its CEO, Philip Condit.

For major change efforts, top managers are increasingly turning to temporary outside consultants with specialized knowledge in the theory and methods of change. Consultant change agents can offer a more objective perspective than insiders can. However, they are disadvantaged in that they often have an inadequate understanding of the organization's history, culture, operating procedures, and personnel. Outside consultants are also more willing to initiate second-order changes—which can be a benefit or a disadvantage—because they don't have to live with the repercussions. In contrast, internal staff specialists or managers, especially those who've spent many years with the organization, are often more cautious because they fear offending long-term friends and associates.

What Can Change Agents Change?

What can a change agent change? The options essentially fall into four categories: structure, technology, physical setting, and people.[6] (See Exhibit 17-2.) Changing *structure* involves making an alteration in authority relations, coordination mechanisms, job redesign, or similar structural variables. Changing *technology* encompasses modifications in the way work is processed and in the methods and equipment used. Changing the *physical setting* covers altering the space and layout arrangements in the workplace. Changing *people* refers to changes in employee attitudes, skills, expectations, perceptions, and/or behavior.

Changing Structure

In chapter 13, we discussed structural issues such as work specialization, span of control, and various organizational designs. But organizational structures

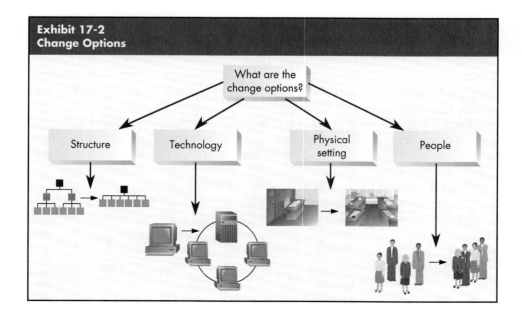

Exhibit 17-2
Change Options

What are the change options?

Structure · Technology · Physical setting · People

are not set in concrete. Changing conditions demand structural changes. As a result, the change agent might need to modify the organization's structure.

An organization's structure is defined by how tasks are formally divided, grouped, and coordinated. Change agents can alter one or more of the key elements in an organization's design. For instance, departmental responsibilities can be combined, vertical layers removed, and spans of control widened to make the organization flatter and less bureaucratic. More rules and procedures can be implemented to increase standardization. An increase in decentralization can be made to speed up the decision-making process.

Change agents can also introduce major modifications in the actual structural design. This might include a shift from a simple structure to a team-based structure or the creation of a matrix design. Change agents might consider redesigning jobs or work schedules. Job descriptions can be redefined, jobs enriched, or flexible work hours introduced. Still another option is to modify the organization's compensation system. Motivation could be increased by, for example, introducing performance bonuses or profit sharing.

Changing Technology

Most of the early studies in management and organizational behavior dealt with efforts aimed at technological change. At the turn of the century, for example, scientific management sought to implement changes based on time-and-motion studies that would increase production efficiency. Today, major technological changes usually involve the introduction of new equipment, tools, or methods; automation; or computerization.

Competitive factors or innovations within an industry often require change agents to introduce new equipment, tools, or operating methods. For example, many aluminum companies have significantly modernized their plants in recent years to compete more effectively. More efficient handling equipment, furnaces, and presses have been installed to reduce the cost of manufacturing a ton of aluminum.

Automation is a technological change that replaces people with machines. It began in the industrial revolution and continues as a change option today. Examples of automation are the introduction of automatic mail sorters by the U.S. Postal Service and robots on automobile assembly lines.

As noted in previous chapters, the most visible technological change in recent years has been expanding computerization. Many organizations now have sophisticated management information systems. Large supermarkets have converted their cash registers into input terminals and linked them to computers to provide instant inventory data. The office of 1998 is dramatically different from its counterpart of 1978, predominantly because of computerization. This is typified by desktop microcomputers that can run hundreds of business software packages and network systems that allow these computers to communicate with one another.

Changing the Physical Setting

The layout of work space should not be a random activity. Typically, management thoughtfully considers work demands, formal interaction requirements, and social needs when making decisions about space configurations, interior design, equipment placement, and the like.

For example, by eliminating walls and partitions, and opening up an office design, it becomes easier for employees to communicate with each other. Similarly, management can change the quantity and types of lights, the level of heat or cold, the levels and types of noise, and the cleanliness of the work area, as well as interior design dimensions like furniture, decorations, and color schemes.

Changing People

The final area in which change agents operate is in helping individuals and groups within the organization to work more effectively together. This category typically involves changing the attitudes and behaviors of organizational members through processes of communication, decision making, and problem solving. As you'll see later in this chapter, the concept of *organizational development* has come to encompass an array of interventions designed to change people and the nature and quality of their work relationships. We review these people-changing interventions in our discussion of organizational development.

Resistance to Change

One of the most well-documented findings from studies of individual and organizational behavior is that organizations and their members resist change. In a sense, this is positive. It provides a degree of stability and predictability to behavior. If there weren't some resistance, organizational behavior would take on characteristics of chaotic randomness. Resistance to change can also be a source of functional conflict. For example, resistance to a reorganization plan or a change in a product line can stimulate a healthy debate over the merits of the idea and result in a better decision. But there is a definite downside to resistance to change. It hinders adaptation and progress.

◆ One of the most well-documented findings from studies of individual and organizational behavior is that organizations and their members resist change.

Resistance to change doesn't necessarily surface in standardized ways. Resistance can be overt, implicit, immediate, or deferred. It is easiest for management to deal with resistance when it is overt and immediate. For instance, a change is proposed and employees quickly respond by voicing complaints, engaging in a work slowdown, threatening to go on strike, or the like. The greater challenge is managing resistance that is implicit or deferred. Implicit resistance efforts are more subtle—loss of loyalty to the organization, loss of motivation to work, increased errors or mistakes, increased absenteeism due to "sickness"—and hence more difficult to recognize. Similarly, deferred actions cloud the link between the source of the resistance and the reaction to it. A change may produce what appears to be only a minimal reaction at the time it is initiated, but then resistance surfaces weeks, months, or even years later. Or a single change that in and of itself might have little impact becomes the straw that breaks the camel's back. Reactions to change can build up and then explode in some response that seems totally out of proportion to the change action it follows. The resistance, of course, has merely been deferred and stockpiled. What surfaces is a response to an accumulation of previous changes.

**Exhibit 17-3
Sources of Individual Resistance to Change**

Let's look at the sources of resistance. For analytical purposes, we've categorized them by individual and organizational sources. In the real world, the sources often overlap.

Individual Resistance

Individual sources of resistance to change reside in basic human characteristics such as perceptions, personalities, and needs. The following summarizes five reasons why individuals may resist change. (See Exhibit 17-3.)

HABIT   Every time you go out to eat, do you try a different restaurant? Probably not. If you're like most people, you find a couple of places you like and return to them on a somewhat regular basis.

As human beings, we're creatures of habit. Life is complex enough; we don't need to consider the full range of options for the hundreds of decisions we have to make every day. To cope with this complexity, we all rely on habits or programmed responses. But when confronted with change, this tendency to respond in our accustomed ways becomes a source of resistance. So when your department is moved to a new office building across town, it means you're likely to have to change many habits: waking up ten minutes earlier, taking a new set of streets to work, finding a new parking place, adjusting to the new office layout, developing a new lunchtime routine, and so on.

SECURITY   People with a high need for security are likely to resist change because it threatens their feelings of safety. When Sears announces it's laying off 50,000 people or Ford introduces new robotic equipment, many employees at these firms may fear that their jobs are in jeopardy.

ECONOMIC FACTORS   Another source of individual resistance is concern that changes will lower one's income. Changes in job tasks or established work routines also can arouse economic fears if people are concerned that they won't be able to perform the new tasks or routines to their previous standards, especially when pay is closely tied to productivity.

FEAR OF THE UNKNOWN   Changes substitute ambiguity and uncertainty for the known. The transition from high school to college is typically such an

Exhibit 17-4

Source: Dilbert by Scott Adams. August 3, 1996. DILBERT reprinted by permission of United Feature Syndicate, Inc.

experience. By the time we're seniors in high school, we understand how things work. You might not have liked high school, but at least you understood the system. Then you move on to college and face a whole new and uncertain system. You have traded the known for the unknown and the fear or insecurity that goes with it.

Employees in organizations hold the same dislike for uncertainty. If, for example, the introduction of TQM means production workers will have to learn statistical process control techniques, some may fear they'll be unable to do so. They may, therefore, develop a negative attitude toward TQM or behave dysfunctionally if required to use statistical techniques.

SELECTIVE INFORMATION PROCESSING As we learned in chapter 3, individuals shape their world through their perceptions. Once they have created this world, it resists change. So individuals are guilty of selectively processing information in order to keep their perceptions intact. They hear what they want to hear. They ignore information that challenges the world they've created. To return to the production workers who are faced with the introduction of TQM, they may ignore the arguments their bosses make in explaining why a knowledge of statistics is necessary or the potential benefits the change will provide them.

Organizational Resistance

Organizations, by their very nature, are conservative.[7] They actively resist change. You don't have to look far to see evidence of this phenomenon. Government agencies want to continue doing what they have been doing for years, whether the need for their service changes or remains the same. Organized religions are deeply entrenched in their history. Attempts to change church doctrine require great persistence and patience. Educational institutions, which exist to open minds and challenge established doctrine, are themselves extremely resistant to change. Most school systems are using essentially the same teaching technologies today as they were 50 years ago. The majority of business firms, too, appear highly resistant to change.

Six major sources of organizational resistance have been identified.[8] They are shown in Exhibit 17-5.

STRUCTURAL INERTIA Organizations have built-in mechanisms to produce stability. For example, the selection process systematically selects certain

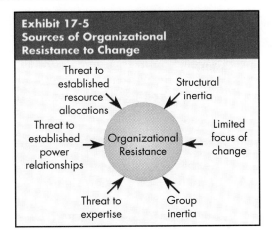

Exhibit 17-5
Sources of Organizational
Resistance to Change

people in and certain people out. Training and other socialization techniques reinforce specific role requirements and skills. Formalization provides job descriptions, rules, and procedures for employees to follow.

The people who are hired into an organization are chosen for fit; they are then shaped and directed to behave in certain ways. When an organization is confronted with change, this structural inertia acts as a counterbalance to sustain stability.

LIMITED FOCUS OF CHANGE Organizations are made up of a number of interdependent subsystems. You can't change one without affecting the others. For example, if management changes the technological processes without simultaneously modifying the organization's structure to match, the change in technology is not likely to be accepted. So limited changes in subsystems tend to get nullified by the larger system.

GROUP INERTIA Even if individuals want to change their behavior, group norms may act as a constraint. An individual union member, for instance, may be willing to accept changes in his job suggested by management. But if union norms dictate resisting any unilateral change made by management, he's likely to resist.

THREAT TO EXPERTISE Changes in organizational patterns may threaten the expertise of specialized groups. The introduction of decentralized personal computers, which allow managers to gain access to information directly from a company's mainframe, is an example of a change that was strongly resisted by many information systems departments in the early 1980s. Why? Because decentralized end-user computing was a threat to the specialized skills held by those in the centralized information systems departments.

THREAT TO ESTABLISHED POWER RELATIONSHIPS Any redistribution of decision-making authority can threaten long-established power relationships within the organization. The introduction of participative decision making or self-managed work teams is the kind of change that is often seen as threatening by supervisors and middle managers.

THREAT TO ESTABLISHED RESOURCE ALLOCATIONS Those groups in the organization that control sizable resources often see change as a threat. They tend to be content with the way things are. Will the change, for instance, mean a reduction in their budgets or a cut in their staff size? Those that most benefit from the current allocation of resources often feel threatened by changes that may affect future allocations.

Overcoming Resistance to Change

Six tactics have been suggested for use by change agents in dealing with resistance to change.[9] Let's review them briefly.

EDUCATION AND COMMUNICATION Resistance can be reduced through communicating with employees to help them see the logic of a change. This tactic basically assumes that the source of resistance lies in misinformation or poor communication: If employees receive the full facts and get any misunderstandings cleared up, resistance will subside. Communication can be achieved through one-on-one discussions, memos, group presentations, or reports. Does it work? It does, provided that the source of resistance is inadequate communication and that management–employee relations are characterized by mutual trust and credibility. If these conditions don't exist, the change is unlikely to succeed.

PARTICIPATION It's difficult for individuals to resist a change decision in which they participated. Prior to making a change, those opposed can be brought into the decision process. Assuming that the participants have the expertise to make a meaningful contribution, their involvement can reduce resistance, obtain commitment, and increase the quality of the change decision. However, against these advantages are the negatives: potential for a poor solution and great time consumption.

◆ It's difficult for individuals to resist a change decision in which they participated.

FACILITATION AND SUPPORT Change agents can offer a range of supportive efforts to reduce resistance. When employee fear and anxiety are high, employee counseling and therapy, new-skills training, or a short paid leave of absence may facilitate adjustment. The drawback of this tactic is that, as with the others, it is time consuming. Additionally, it's expensive, and its implementation offers no assurance of success.

NEGOTIATION Another way for the change agent to deal with potential resistance to change is to exchange something of value for a lessening of the resistance. For instance, if the resistance is centered in a few powerful individuals, a specific reward package can be negotiated that will meet their individual needs. Negotiation as a tactic may be necessary when resistance comes from a powerful source. Yet one cannot ignore its potentially high costs. Additionally, there is the risk that, once a change agent negotiates with one party to avoid resistance, he or she is open to the possibility of being blackmailed by other individuals in positions of power.

MANIPULATION AND COOPTATION Manipulation refers to covert influence attempts. Twisting and distorting facts to make them appear more attractive,

Michael Ying, chairman of Esprit Asia Holdings, learned that communication can help overcome resistance to change. Ying, in trying to integrate Esprit's Asian and European operations, recognized major differences in the way they managed people and the business. The European operation was nationalistic, autocratic, and had rigid structures, whereas the Asian operation was more open-minded and willing to learn. During visits with the European managers, Ying communicated his common-sense approach to problem solving and listened to the Europeans' concerns. This communication helped the Europeans to become receptive to Ying's plan of merging the two operations.

withholding undesirable information, and creating false rumors to get employees to accept a change are all examples of manipulation. If corporate management threatens to close down a particular manufacturing plant if that plant's employees fail to accept an across-the-board pay cut, and if the threat is actually untrue, management is using manipulation. Cooptation, on the other hand, is a form of both manipulation and participation. It seeks to "buy off" the leaders of a resistance group by giving them a key role in the change decision. The leaders' advice is sought, not to seek a better decision, but to get their endorsement. Both manipulation and cooptation are relatively inexpensive and easy ways to gain the support of adversaries, but the tactics can backfire if the targets become aware that they are being tricked or used. Once discovered, the change agent's credibility may drop to zero.

COERCION Last on the list of tactics is coercion, that is, the application of direct threats or force upon the resisters. If the corporate management mentioned in the previous discussion really is determined to close a manufacturing plant if employees don't acquiesce to a pay cut, then coercion would be the label attached to its change tactic. Other examples of coercion are threats of transfer, loss of promotions, negative performance evaluations, and a poor letter of recommendation. The advantages and drawbacks of coercion are approximately the same as those mentioned for manipulation and cooptation.

The Politics of Change

No discussion of resistance to change would be complete without a brief mention of the politics of change. Because change invariably threatens the status quo, it inherently implies political activity.[10]

Internal change agents typically are individuals high in the organization who have a lot to lose from change. They have, in fact, risen to their positions of authority by developing skills and behavioral patterns that are favored by the organization. Change is a threat to those skills and patterns. What if they are no longer the ones the organization values? This creates the potential for others in the organization to gain power at their expense.

Politics suggests that the impetus for change is more likely to come from outside change agents, employees who are new to the organization (and have less invested in the status quo), or from managers slightly removed from the main power structure. Those managers who have spent their entire careers with a single organization and eventually achieve a senior position in the hierarchy are often major impediments to change. Change, itself, is a very real threat to their status and position. Yet they may be expected to implement changes to demonstrate that they're not merely caretakers. By acting as change agents, they can symbolically convey to various constituencies—stockholders, suppliers, employees, customers—that they are on top of problems and adapting to a dynamic environment. Of course, as you might guess, when forced to introduce change, these long-time power holders tend to implement first-order changes. Radical change is too threatening.

Power struggles within the organization will determine, to a large degree, the speed and quantity of change. You should expect that long-time career executives will be sources of resistance. This, incidentally, explains why boards of directors that recognize the imperative for the rapid introduction of second-order change in their organizations frequently turn to outside candidates for new leadership.[11]

Approaches to Managing Organizational Change

Now we turn to several popular approaches to managing change. Specifically, we discuss Lewin's classic three-step model of the change process and present the action research model.

Lewin's Three-Step Model

Kurt Lewin argued that successful change in organizations should follow three steps: **unfreezing** the status quo, *movement* to a new state, and **refreezing** the new change to make it permanent.[12] (See Exhibit 17-6.) The value of this model can be seen in the following example when the management of a large oil company decided to reorganize its marketing function in the western United States.

The oil company had three divisional offices in the West, located in Seattle, San Francisco, and Los Angeles. The decision was made to consolidate the divisions into a single regional office to be located in San Francisco. The reorganization meant transferring over 150 employees, eliminating some duplicate managerial positions, and instituting a new hierarchy of command. As you might guess, a move of this magnitude was difficult to keep secret. The

unfreezing
Change efforts to overcome the pressures of both individual resistance and group conformity.

refreezing
Stabilizing a change intervention by balancing driving and restraining forces.

From Concepts to Skills

Assessing the Climate for Change

Why do some change programs succeed and others fail? One major factor is change readiness.[13] Research by Symmetrix, a Massachusetts consulting firm, identified 17 key elements to successful change. The more affirmative answers you get to the following questions, the greater the likelihood that change efforts will succeed.

1. Is the sponsor of change high up enough to have power to effectively deal with resistance?

2. Is day-to-day leadership supportive of the change and committed to it?

3. Is there a strong sense of urgency from senior management about the need for change and is it shared by the rest of the organization?

4. Does management have a clear vision of how the future will look different from the present?

5. Are there objective measures in place to evaluate the change effort and are reward systems explicitly designed to reinforce them?

6. Is the specific change effort consistent with other changes going on within the organization?

7. Are functional managers willing to sacrifice their personal self-interest for the good of the organization as a whole?

8. Does management pride itself on closely monitoring changes and actions taken by competitors?

9. Is the importance of the customer and a knowledge of customer needs well accepted by everyone in the workforce?

10. Are managers and employees rewarded for taking risks, being innovative, and looking for new solutions?

11. Is the organizational structure flexible?

12. Are communication channels open both downward and upward?

13. Is the organization's hierarchy relatively flat?

14. Has the organization successfully implemented major changes in the recent past?

15. Is employee satisfaction and trust in management high?

16. Is there a high degree of cross-boundary interactions and cooperation between units in the organization?

17. Are decisions made quickly, taking into account a wide variety of suggestions?

rumor of its occurrence preceded the announcement by several months. The decision itself was made unilaterally. It came from the executive offices in New York. Those people affected had no say whatsoever in the choice. For those in Seattle or Los Angeles, who may have disliked the decision and its consequences—the problems inherent in transferring to another city, pulling youngsters out of school, making new friends, having new co-workers, undergoing the reassignment of responsibilities—their only recourse was to quit. In actuality, less than 10 percent did.

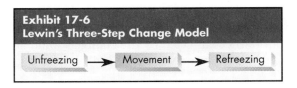

Exhibit 17-6
Lewin's Three-Step Change Model

Unfreezing → Movement → Refreezing

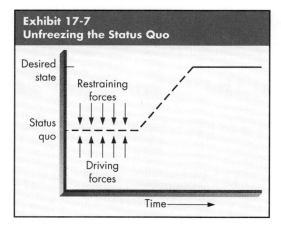

Exhibit 17-7
Unfreezing the Status Quo

driving forces
Forces that direct behavior away from the status quo.

restraining forces
Forces that hinder movement away from the status quo.

The status quo can be considered to be an equilibrium state. To move from this equilibrium—to overcome the pressures of both individual resistance and group conformity—unfreezing is necessary. It can be achieved in one of three ways. (See Exhibit 17-7.) The **driving forces**, which direct behavior away from the status quo, can be increased. The **restraining forces**, which hinder movement from the existing equilibrium, can be decreased. A third alternative is to *combine the first two approaches.*

The oil company's management could expect employee resistance to the consolidation. To deal with that resistance, management could use positive incentives to encourage employees to accept the change. For instance, increases in pay can be offered to those who accept the transfer. Very liberal moving expenses can be paid by the company. Management might offer low-cost mortgage funds to allow employees to buy new homes in San Francisco. Of course, management might also consider unfreezing acceptance of the status quo by removing restraining forces. Employees could be counseled individually. Each employee's concerns and apprehensions could be heard and specifically clarified. Assuming that most of the fears are unjustified, the counselor could assure the employees that there was nothing to fear and then demonstrate, through tangible evidence, that restraining forces are unwarranted. If resistance is extremely high, management may have to resort to both reducing resistance and increasing the attractiveness of the alternative if the unfreezing is to be successful.

Once the consolidation change has been implemented, if it is to be successful, the new situation needs to be refrozen so that it can be sustained over time. Unless this last step is taken, there is a very high chance that the change will be short-lived and that employees will attempt to revert to the previous equilibrium state. The objective of refreezing, then, is to stabilize the new situation by balancing the driving and restraining forces.

How could the oil company's management refreeze its consolidation change? By systematically replacing temporary forces with permanent ones. For instance, management might impose a permanent upward adjustment of salaries or permanently remove time clocks to reinforce a climate of trust and confidence in employees. The formal rules and regulations governing behavior of those affected by the change should also be revised to reinforce the new situation. Over time, of course, the work group's own norms will evolve to sustain the new equilibrium. But until that point is reached, management will have to rely on more formal mechanisms.

Action Research

Action research refers to a change process based on the systematic collection of data and then selection of a change action based on what the analyzed data indicate.[14] Their importance lies in providing a scientific methodology for managing planned change.

The process of action research consists of five steps: diagnosis, analysis, feedback, action, and evaluation. You'll note that these steps closely parallel the scientific method.

DIAGNOSIS The change agent, often an outside consultant in action research, begins by gathering information about problems, concerns, and needed changes from members of the organization. This diagnosis is analogous to the physician's search to find what specifically ails a patient. In action research, the change agent asks questions, interviews employees, reviews records, and listens to the concerns of employees.

ANALYSIS The information gathered during the diagnostic stage is then analyzed. What problems do people key in on? What patterns do these problems seem to take? The change agent synthesizes this information into primary concerns, problem areas, and possible actions.

FEEDBACK Action research includes extensive involvement of the change targets. That is, the people who will be involved in any change program must be actively involved in determining what the problem is and participating in creating the solution. So the third step is sharing with employees what has been found from steps one and two. The employees, with the help of the change agent, develop action plans for bringing about any needed change.

ACTION Now the "action" part of action research is set in motion. The employees and the change agent carry out the specific actions to correct the problems that have been identified.

EVALUATION Finally, consistent with the scientific underpinnings of action research, the change agent evaluates the effectiveness of the action plans. Using the initial data gathered as a benchmark, any subsequent changes can be compared and evaluated.

Action research provides at least two specific benefits for an organization. First, it's problem focused. The change agent objectively looks for problems and the type of problem determines the type of change action. While this may seem intuitively obvious, a lot of change activities aren't done this way. Rather, they're solution centered. The change agent has a favorite solution—for example, implementing flextime, teams, or a management by objectives program—and then seeks out problems that his or her solution fits. Second, because action research so heavily involves employees in the process, resistance to change is reduced. In fact, once employees have actively partici-

action research
A change process based on systematic collection of data and then selection of a change action based on what the analyzed data indicate.

pated in the feedback stage, the change process typically takes on a momentum of its own. The employees and groups that have been involved become an internal source of sustained pressure to bring about the change.

Organizational Development

organizational development (OD)
A collection of planned-change interventions, built on humanistic-democratic values, that seeks to improve organizational effectiveness and employee well-being.

No discussion of managing change would be complete without including organizational development. **Organizational development (OD)** is not an easily defined single concept. Rather, it's a term used to encompass a collection of planned-change interventions built on humanistic-democratic values that seek to improve organizational effectiveness and employee well-being.[15]

The OD paradigm values human and organizational growth, collaborative and participative processes, and a spirit of inquiry.[16] The change agent may be directive in OD; however, there is a strong emphasis on collaboration. Concepts such as power, authority, control, conflict, and coercion are held in relatively low esteem among OD change agents. The following briefly identifies the underlying values in most OD efforts.

1. *Respect for people.* Individuals are perceived as being responsible, conscientious, and caring. They should be treated with dignity and respect.
2. *Trust and support.* The effective and healthy organization is characterized by trust, authenticity, openness, and a supportive climate.
3. *Power equalization.* Effective organizations deemphasize hierarchical authority and control.
4. *Confrontation.* Problems shouldn't be swept under the rug. They should be openly confronted.
5. *Participation.* The more that people who will be affected by a change are involved in the decisions surrounding that change, the more they will be committed to implementing those decisions.

What are some of the OD techniques or interventions for bringing about change? In the following pages, we present five interventions that change agents might consider using.

Change agent George Fisher, CEO of Eastman Kodak, is applying the underlying values of organizational development in boosting employee morale and reigniting the company's growth. When Fisher took the top job at Kodak, the company was suffering from a series of restructurings, a dispirited workforce, a rigid hierarchy, and huge debts. While past Kodak CEOs tended to be autocratic and inaccessible, Fisher (right in photo) is rebuilding the company through respect for people, trust and support, openness, the sharing of power, and participation.

SENSITIVITY TRAINING It can go by a variety of names—laboratory training, **sensitivity training**, encounter groups, or T-groups (training groups)—but all refer to a method of changing behavior through unstructured group interaction. Members are brought together in a free and open environment in which participants discuss themselves and their interactive processes, loosely directed by a professional behavioral scientist. The group is process oriented, which means that individuals learn through observing and participating rather than being told. The professional creates the opportunity for participants to express their ideas, beliefs, and attitudes. He or she does not accept—in fact, overtly rejects—any leadership role.

The objectives of the T-groups are to provide the subjects with increased awareness of their own behavior and how others perceive them, greater sensitivity to the behavior of others, and increased understanding of group processes. Specific results sought include increased ability to empathize with others, improved listening skills, greater openness, increased tolerance of individual differences, and improved conflict resolution skills.

If individuals lack awareness of how others perceive them, then the successful T-group can affect more realistic self-perceptions, greater group cohesiveness, and a reduction in dysfunctional interpersonal conflicts. Furthermore, it will ideally result in a better integration between the individual and the organization.

sensitivity training
Training groups that seek to change behavior through unstructured group interaction.

SURVEY FEEDBACK One tool for assessing attitudes held by organizational members, identifying discrepancies among member perceptions, and solving these differences is the **survey feedback** approach.

Everyone in an organization can participate in survey feedback, but of key importance is the organizational family—the manager of any given unit and those employees who report directly to him or her. A questionnaire is usually completed by all members in the organization or unit. Organization members may be asked to suggest questions or may be interviewed to determine what issues are relevant. The questionnaire typically asks members for their perceptions and attitudes on a broad range of topics, including decision-making practices; communication effectiveness; coordination between units; and satisfaction with the organization, job, peers, and their immediate supervisor.

survey feedback
The use of questionnaires to identify discrepancies among member perceptions; discussion follows and remedies are suggested.

The data from this questionnaire are tabulated with data pertaining to an individual's specific "family" and to the entire organization and distributed to employees. These data then become the springboard for identifying problems and clarifying issues that may be creating difficulties for people. In some cases, the manager may be counseled by an external change agent about the meaning of the responses to the questionnaire and may even be given suggested guidelines for leading the organizational family in group discussion of the results. Particular attention is given to the importance of encouraging discussion and ensuring that discussions focus on issues and ideas and not on attacking individuals.

Finally, group discussion in the survey feedback approach should result in members identifying possible implications of the questionnaire's findings. Are people listening? Are new ideas being generated? Can decision making, interpersonal relations, or job assignments be improved? Answers to questions like these, it is hoped, will result in the group agreeing upon commitments to various actions that will remedy the problems that are identified.

process consultation
Consultant gives a client insights into what is going on around the client, within the client, and between the client and other people; identifies processes that need improvement.

PROCESS CONSULTATION   No organization operates perfectly. Managers often sense that their unit's performance can be improved, but they are unable to identify what can be improved and how it can be improved. The purpose of **process consultation** is for an outside consultant to assist a client, usually a manager, "to perceive, understand, and act upon process events" with which he or she must deal.[17] These might include work flow, informal relationships among unit members, and formal communication channels.

Process consultation (PC) is similar to sensitivity training in its assumption that organizational effectiveness can be improved by dealing with interpersonal problems and in its emphasis on involvement. But PC is more task directed than sensitivity training.

Consultants in PC are there to "give the client 'insight' into what is going on around him, within him, and between him and other people."[18] They do not solve the organization's problems. Rather, the consultant is a guide or coach who advises on the process to help the client solve his or her own problems.

The consultant works with the client in *jointly* diagnosing what processes need improvement. The emphasis is on "jointly" because the client develops a skill at analyzing processes within his or her unit that can be continually called on long after the consultant is gone. Additionally, by having the client actively participate in both the diagnosis and the development of alternatives, there will be greater understanding of the process and the remedy and less resistance to the action plan chosen.

Importantly, the process consultant need not be an expert in solving the particular problem that is identified. The consultant's expertise lies in diagnosis and developing a helping relationship. If the specific problem uncovered requires technical knowledge outside the client's and consultant's expertise, the consultant helps the client to locate such an expert and then instructs the client in how to get the most out of this expert resource.

team building
High interaction among team members to increase trust and openness.

TEAM BUILDING   As we've noted in numerous places throughout this book, organizations are increasingly relying on teams to accomplish work tasks. **Team building** utilizes high-interaction group activities to increase trust and openness among team members.[19]

Team building can be applied within groups or at the intergroup level where activities are interdependent. For our discussion, we emphasize the intragroup level and leave intergroup development to the next section. As a result, our interest concerns applications to organizational families (command groups), as well as to committees, project teams, self-managed teams, and task groups.

Not all group activity has interdependence of functions. To illustrate, consider a football team and a track team:

> Although members on both teams are concerned with the team's total output they function differently. The football team's output depends synergistically on how well each player does his particular job in concert with his teammates. The quarterback's performance depends on the performance of his linemen and receivers, and ends on how well the quarterback throws the ball, and so on. On the other hand, a track team's performance is determined largely by the mere addition of the performances of the individual members.[20]

Team building is applicable to the case of interdependence, such as in football. The objective is to improve coordinative efforts of members, which will result in increasing the team's performance.

The activities considered in team building typically include goal setting, development of interpersonal relations among team members, role analysis to clarify each member's role and responsibilities, and team process analysis. Of course, team building may emphasize or exclude certain activities depending on the purpose of the development effort and the specific problems with which the team is confronted. Basically, however, team building attempts to use high interaction among members to increase trust and openness.

It may be beneficial to begin by having members attempt to define the goals and priorities of the team. This will bring to the surface different perceptions of what the team's purpose may be. Following this, members can evaluate the team's performance—how effective is the team in structuring priorities and achieving its goals? This should identify potential problem areas. This self-critique discussion of means and ends can be done with members of the total team present or, where large size impinges on a free interchange of views, may initially take place in smaller groups followed up by the sharing of their findings with the total team.

Team building can also address itself to clarifying each member's role on the team. Each role can be identified and clarified. Previous ambiguities can be brought to the surface. For some individuals, it may offer one of the few opportunities they have had to think through thoroughly what their job is all about and what specific tasks they are expected to carry out if the team is to optimize its effectiveness.

Still another team-building activity can be similar to that performed by the process consultant, that is, to analyze key processes that go on within the team to identify the way work is performed and how these processes might be improved to make the team more effective.

INTERGROUP DEVELOPMENT A major area of concern in OD is the dysfunctional conflict that exists between groups. As a result, this has been a subject to which change efforts have been directed.

Intergroup development seeks to change the attitudes, stereotypes, and perceptions that groups have of each other. For example, in one company, the engineers saw the accounting department as composed of shy and conservative types, and the human resources department as having a bunch of "ultra-liberals who are more concerned that some protected group of employees might get their feelings hurt than with the company making a profit." Such stereotypes can have an obvious negative impact on the coordinative efforts between the departments.

intergroup development
OD efforts to change the attitudes, stereotypes, and perceptions that groups have of each other.

Although there are several approaches for improving intergroup relations,[21] a popular method emphasizes problem solving.[22] In this method, each group meets independently to develop lists of its perception of itself, the other group, and how it believes the other group perceives it. The groups then share their lists, after which similarities and differences are discussed. Differences are clearly articulated, and the groups look for the causes of the disparities.

Are the groups' goals at odds? Were perceptions distorted? On what basis were stereotypes formulated? Have some differences been caused by misunderstandings of intentions? Have words and concepts been defined differently by each group? Answers to questions like these clarify the exact nature of the conflict. Once the causes of the difficulty have been identified, the groups can move to the integration phase—working to develop solutions that will improve relations between the groups.

Subgroups, with members from each of the conflicting groups, can now be created for further diagnosis and to begin to formulate possible alternative actions that will improve relations.

Contemporary Change Issues for Today's Managers

Talk to managers. Read the popular business periodicals. What you'll find is that two issues have risen above the rest as current change topics. They are stimulating organizational *innovation* and creating a *learning organization*. In the following pages, we take a look at these topics. Then we address the question: Is managing change culture bound?

Innovation

The relevant question is: How can an organization become more innovative? The standard toward which many organizations strive is that achieved by the 3M Co.[23] It has developed a reputation for being able to stimulate innovation over a long period of time. 3M has a stated objective that 30 percent of its sales are to come from products less than four years old. In 1995, the figure was 32 percent. In one recent year alone, 3M launched more than 200 new products.

What's the secret of 3M's success? What can other organizations do to clone 3M's track record for innovation? While there is no guaranteed formula, certain characteristics surface again and again when researchers study innovative organizations. We've grouped them into structural, cultural, and human resource categories. Our message to change agents is that they should consider introducing these characteristics into their organization if they want to create an innovative climate. Before we look at these characteristics, however, let's clarify what we mean by innovation.

innovation
A new idea applied to initiating or improving a product, process, or service.

DEFINITION We said change refers to making things different. **Innovation** is a more specialized kind of change. Innovation is a new idea applied to initiating or improving a product, process, or service.[24] So all innovations involve change, but not all changes necessarily involve new ideas or lead to significant improvements. Innovations in organizations can range from small incremental improvements, such as RJR Nabisco's extension of the Oreo product line to include double stuffs and chocolate-covered Oreos, up to radical breakthroughs, such as the Amazon.Com bookstore on the Internet. Keep in mind that while our examples are mostly of product innovations, the concept of innovation also encompasses new production process technologies, new structures or administrative systems, and new plans or programs pertaining to organizational members.

SOURCES OF INNOVATION *Structural variables* have been the most studied potential source of innovation.[25] A comprehensive review of the structure–innovation relationship leads to the following conclusions.[26] First, organic structures positively influence innovation. Because they're lower in vertical differentiation, formalization, and centralization, organic organizations facilitate the flexibility, adaptation, and cross-fertilization that make the adoption of innovations easier. Second, long tenure in management is associated with innovation. Managerial tenure apparently provides legitimacy and knowledge of how to accomplish tasks and obtain desired outcomes. Third, innovation is nurtured where there are slack resources. Having an abundance of resources allows an organization to afford to purchase innovations, bear the cost of instituting innovations, and absorb failures. Finally, interunit communication is high in innovative organizations.[27] These organizations are high users of committees, task forces, cross-functional teams, and other mechanisms that facilitate interaction across departmental lines.

Innovative organizations tend to have similar *cultures*. They encourage experimentation. They reward both successes and failures. They celebrate mistakes. At Hewlett-Packard, for instance, CEO Lewis Platt has successfully built a corporate culture that supports people who try something that doesn't work out.[28] Platt, himself, protects people who stick their neck out, fearful that to do otherwise would stifle the risk-taking culture he encourages among his managers. Unfortunately, in too many organizations, people are rewarded for the absence of failures rather than for the presence of successes. Such cultures extinguish risk taking and innovation. People will suggest and try new ideas only where they feel such behaviors exact no penalties. Managers in innovative organizations recognize that failures are a natural by-product of venturing into the unknown. When Babe Ruth set his record for home runs in one season, he also led the league in strikeouts. And he is remembered for the former, not the latter!

Within the *human resources* category, we find that innovative organizations actively promote the training and development of their members so that they keep current, offer high job security so employees don't fear getting fired for making mistakes, and encourage individuals to become champions of change. Once a new idea is developed, **idea champions** actively and enthusiastically promote the idea, build support, overcome resistance, and ensure that the innovation is implemented.[29] The evidence indicates that champions

idea champions
Individuals who take an innovation and actively and enthusiastically promote the idea, build support, overcome resistance, and ensure it is implemented.

Aluminum Company of America is an innovative organization that encourages experimentation. Alcoa has installed touch-screen computer terminals at its plants to help educate employees about their 401(k) retirement planning and funding options. The terminals make it easy for employees to play "what if?" games by modeling different retirement investment choices and their potential returns.

have common personality characteristics: extremely high self-confidence, persistence, energy, and a tendency to take risks. Idea champions also display characteristics associated with transformational leadership. They inspire and energize others with their vision of the potential of an innovation and through their strong personal conviction in their mission. They are also good at gaining the commitment of others to support their mission. In addition, idea champions have jobs that provide considerable decision-making discretion. This autonomy helps them introduce and implement innovations in organizations.[30]

Given the status of 3M as a premier product innovator, we would expect it to have most of the properties we've identified. And it does. The company is so highly decentralized that it has many of the characteristics of small, organic organizations. The structure relies on extensive redundancy. For instance, every division, department, and product group has its own labs—many of which are deliberately duplicating the work of others. And consistent with the need for cross-fertilization of ideas, the company holds internal trade shows where divisions will show their technologies to employees of other divisions. All of 3M's scientists and managers are challenged to "keep current." Idea champions are created and encouraged by allowing scientists and engineers to spend up to 15 percent of their time on projects of their own choosing. And if a 3M scientist comes up with a new idea but finds resistance within the researcher's own division, he or she can apply for a $50,000 grant from an internal venture-capital fund to further develop the idea. The company encourages its employees to take risks—and rewards the failures as well as the successes. And 3M's management has the patience to see ideas through to successful products. It invests nearly 7 percent of company sales revenue (more than $1 billion a year) in research and development, yet management tells its R&D people that *not everything is going to work*. It also fosters a culture that allows people to defy their supervisors. For instance, each new employee and his or her supervisor take a one-day orientation class where, among other things, stories are told of victories won by employees despite the opposition of their boss. Finally, while 3M incurred its first layoffs in decades during 1995, the company still continues to be a model of corporate stability. The average tenure for company officers is 31 years and the overall annual turnover rate within the company is a miniscule 3 percent.

◆ What TQM was to the 1980s and reengineering was to the early 1990s, the learning organization has become to the late 1990s.

Creating a Learning Organization

What TQM was to the 1980s and reengineering was to the early 1990s, the learning organization has become to the late 1990s. It has developed a groundswell of interest from managers and organization theorists looking for new ways to successfully respond to a world of interdependence and change.[31] In this section, we describe what a learning organization looks like and methods for managing learning.

learning organization
An organization that has developed the continuous capacity to adapt and change.

WHAT'S A LEARNING ORGANIZATION? A **learning organization** is an organization that has developed the continuous capacity to adapt and change. Just as individuals learn, so too do organizations. "All organizations learn, whether they consciously choose to or not—it is a fundamental requirement for their sustained existence."[32] However, some organizations, such as Xerox,

Corning, Federal Express, Ford, General Electric, Motorola, and Wal-Mart, just do it better than others.

Most organizations engage in what has been called **single-loop learning**.[33] When errors are detected, the correction process relies on past routines and present policies. In contrast, learning organizations use **double-loop learning**. When an error is detected, it's corrected in ways that involve the modification of the organization's objectives, policies, and standard routines. Like second-order change described at the beginning of this chapter, double-loop learning challenges deep-rooted assumptions and norms within an organization. In this way, it provides opportunities for radically different solutions to problems and dramatic jumps in improvement.

Exhibit 17-8 summarizes the five basic characteristics of a learning organization. It's an organization where people put aside their old ways of thinking, learn to be open with each other, understand how their organization really works, form a plan or vision that everyone can agree upon, and then work together to achieve that vision.[34]

Proponents of the learning organization envision it as a remedy for the three fundamental problems inherent in traditional organizations: fragmentation, competition, and reactiveness.[35] First, *fragmentation* based on specialization creates "walls" and "chimneys" that separate different functions into independent and often warring fiefdoms. Second, an overemphasis on *competition* often undermines collaboration. Members of the management team compete with one another to show who is right, who knows more, or who is more persuasive. Divisions compete with one another when they ought to cooperate to share knowledge. Team project leaders compete to show who is the best manager. And third, *reactiveness* misdirects management's attention to problem solving rather than creation. The problem solver tries to make something go away, while a creator tries to bring something new into being. An emphasis on reactiveness pushes out innovation and continuous improvement and, in its place, encourages people to run around "putting out fires."

It may help to better understand what a learning organization is if you think of it as an *ideal* model that builds on a number of *previous OB concepts*. No company has successfully achieved all the characteristics described in Exhibit 17-8. As such, you should think of a learning organization as an ideal to strive toward rather than a realistic description of structured activity. Notice, too, how learning organizations draw on previous OB concepts such as TQM,

single-loop learning
Errors are corrected using past routines and present policies.

double-loop learning
Errors are corrected by modifying the organization's objectives, policies, and standard routines.

Exhibit 17-8 Characteristics of a Learning Organization

1. There exists a shared vision which everyone agrees on.
2. People discard their old ways of thinking and the standard routines they use for solving problems or doing their jobs.
3. Members think of all organizational processes, activities, functions, and interactions with the environment as part of a system of interrelationships.
4. People openly communicate with each other (across vertical and horizontal boundaries) without fear of criticism or punishment.
5. People sublimate their personal self-interest and fragmented departmental interests to work together to achieve the organization's shared vision.

Source: Based on P.M. Senge, *The Fifth Discipline* (New York: Doubleday, 1990).

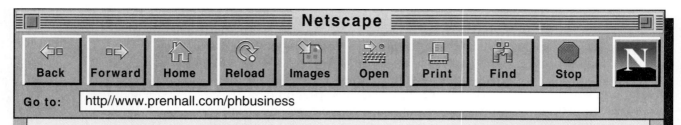
OB in the News

The U.S. Army Is Becoming a Learning Organization

The U.S. Army isn't the typical example that comes to mind when you think of what a learning organization might look like. But think again.

The army's environment has changed dramatically since the days of the Vietnam conflict. For one thing, the Soviet threat, which was a major justification for the army's military buildup, is largely gone. Army soldiers are more likely to be involved in feeding children in Somalia, peacekeeping in Haiti, or helping put out forest fires in the Pacific Northwest than fighting a war. And its new mission is reflected in its budget. The army's annual appropriation dropped from $90 billion in 1989 to $60 billion in 1994. Meanwhile, the number of troops in uniform have been downsized from 780,000 to less than 500,000. Clearly, it's no longer "business as usual" in the U.S. Army.

The army's high command has redesigned its structure to reflect its new mission. The old army was said to be an organization "designed by geniuses to be run by idiots." That rigid, hierarchical, command-and-control structure was fine when the army's single purpose was combat related. Authority was centralized at the Pentagon, and orders were passed down to the field. Officers weren't expected to innovate or make adjustments. But that type of structure doesn't fit with the changing role of the military. The new army is putting into place an adaptive and flexible structure to match its more varied objectives.

Along with the new structure is a major program to make the army's culture more egalitarian. Everyone from PFCs to brigadier generals has gone through team training to learn how to make decisions in the field and even to question authority (a previously unheard of idea). Senior officers are required to go through something called the After Action Review (AAR)—a public performance appraisal—where decisions are openly critiqued by subordinates. The potential for public embarrassment in an AAR would never have been allowed in the old army.

The bottom line is that the U.S. Army is becoming a learning organization. It's developing soldiers, especially officers, who can adapt rapidly to different tasks and missions. The new army seeks to be able to quickly improvise in complex and ambiguous situations. Its soldiers will be prepared to play a multiple set of changing roles—fighting, peacekeeping, peacemaking, humanitarian rescue, nation building, or whatever—and be able to change those roles quickly as need.

Source: Based on L. Smith, "New Ideas from the Army (Really)," *Fortune*, September 19, 1994, pp. 203–12.

Take It to the Net

We invite you to visit the Robbins page on the Prentice Hall Web site at:

http://www.prenhall.com/robbinsorgbeh

for this chapter's World Wide Web exercise.

organizational culture, the boundaryless organization, functional conflict, and transformational leadership. For instance, the learning organization adopts TQM's commitment to continuous improvement. Learning organizations are also characterized by a specific culture that values risk taking, openness, and growth. It seeks "boundarylessness" through breaking down barriers created by hierarchical levels and fragmented departmentation. A learning organization supports the importance of disagreements, constructive criticism, and other forms of functional conflict. And transformational leadership is needed in a learning organization to implement the shared vision.

MANAGING LEARNING How do you change an organization to make it into a continual learner? What can managers do to make their firms learning organizations?

Establish a strategy. Management needs to make explicit its commitment to change, innovation, and continuous improvement.

Redesign the organization's structure. The formal structure can be a serious impediment to learning. By flattening the structure, eliminating or combining departments, and increasing the use of cross-functional teams, interdependence is reinforced and boundaries between people are reduced.

Reshape the organization's culture. As noted earlier, learning organizations are characterized by risk taking, openness, and growth. Management sets the tone for the organization's culture both by what it says (strategy) and what it does (behavior). Managers need to demonstrate by their actions that taking risks and admitting failures are desirable traits. That means rewarding people who take chances and make mistakes. And management needs to encourage functional conflict. "The key to unlocking real openness at work," says one expert on learning organizations, "is to teach people to give up having to be in agreement. We think agreement is so important. Who cares? You have to bring paradoxes, conflicts, and dilemmas out in the open, so collectively we can be more intelligent than we can be individually."[36]

Managing Change: It's Culture Bound!

A number of change issues we've discussed are culture bound. To illustrate, let's briefly look at five questions: (1) Do people believe change is possible? (2) If it is possible, how long will it take to bring it about? (3) Is resistance to change greater in some cultures than in others? (4) Does culture influence how change efforts will be implemented? (5) Do successful idea champions do things differently in different cultures?

Do people believe change is possible? Remember that cultures vary in terms of beliefs about their ability to control their environment. In cultures where people believe that they can dominate their environment, individuals will take a proactive view of change. This would describe the United States and Canada. In many other countries, such as Iran and Saudi Arabia, people see themselves as subjugated to their environment and thus will tend to take a passive approach toward change.

If change is possible, how long will it take to bring it about? A culture's time orientation can help us answer this question. Societies that focus on the long term, such as Japan, will demonstrate considerable patience while waiting for positive outcomes from change efforts. In societies with a short-term focus, such as the United States and Canada, people expect quick improvements and will seek change programs that promise fast results.

These Chinese couples prefer Western-style dancing over *t'ai chi,* the traditional meditative morning exercise. But in the workplace, Chinese workers are more resistant to change, holding fast to their past traditions. Significant cultural differences challenge foreign companies operating in China. They face China's rigid hierarchical structure, where the idea of younger managers telling older workers what to do is unheard of and employees work in state-controlled companies that provide no incentives for advancement.

Is resistance to change greater in some cultures than in others? Resistance to change will be influenced by a society's reliance on tradition. Italians, as an example, focus on the past, while Americans emphasize the present. Italians, therefore, should generally be more resistant to change efforts than their American counterparts.

Does culture influence how change efforts will be implemented? Power distance can help with this issue. In high-power-distance cultures, such as the Philippines or Venezuela, change efforts will tend to be autocratically implemented by top management. In contrast, low-power-distance cultures value democratic methods. We'd predict, therefore, a greater use of participation in countries such as Denmark and Israel.

Finally, do successful idea champions do things differently in different cultures? The evidence indicates that the answer is "Yes."[37] People in collectivist cultures, in contrast to individualistic cultures, prefer appeals for cross-functional support for innovation efforts; people in high-power-distance cultures prefer champions to work closely with those in authority to approve innovative activities before work is conducted on them; and the higher the uncertainty avoidance of a society, the more champions should work within the organization's rules and procedures to develop the innovation. These findings suggest that effective managers will alter their organization's championing strategies to reflect cultural values. So, for instance, while idea champions in the United States might succeed by ignoring budgetary limitations and working around confining procedures, champions in Venezuela, Greece, Italy, or other cultures high in uncertainty avoidance will be more effective by closely following budgets and procedures.

Work Stress and Its Management

Most of us are aware that employee stress is an increasing problem in organizations. We hear about postal workers killing co-workers and supervisors and then we learn job-related tensions were a major cause. Friends tells us they're stressed out from greater workloads and having to work longer hours because of downsizing at their company. We read surveys where employees complain about the stress created in trying to balance work and family responsibilities. In this section we'll look at the causes and consequences of stress, and then consider what individuals and organizations can do to reduce it. (See Exhibit 17-9 for a ranking of jobs based on stress scores.)

What Is Stress?

Stress *is a dynamic condition in which an individual is confronted with an opportunity, constraint, or demand related to what he or she desires and for which the outcome is perceived to be both uncertain and important.*[38] This is a complicated definition. Let's look at its components more closely.

Stress is not necessarily bad in and of itself. While stress is typically discussed in a negative context, it also has a positive value. It is an opportunity when it offers potential gain. Consider, for example, the superior performance that an athlete or stage performer gives in "clutch" situations. Such individuals often use stress positively to rise to the occasion and perform at or near their maximum.

More typically, stress is associated with **constraints** and **demands**. The former prevent you from doing what you desire. The latter refers to the loss of

stress
A dynamic condition in which an individual is confronted with an opportunity, constraint, or demand related to what he or she desires and for which the outcome is perceived to be both uncertain and important.

constraints
Forces that prevent individuals from doing what they desire.

demands
The loss of something desired.

Exhibit 17-9   The Most Stressful Jobs

How do jobs rate in terms of stress? The following shows how selected occupations ranked in an evaluation of 250 jobs. Among the criteria used in the rankings were: overtime, quotas, deadlines, competitiveness, physical demands, environmental conditions, hazards encountered, initiative required, stamina required, win-lose situations, and working in the public eye.

Rank Score	Stress Score	Rank Score	Stress Score
1. U.S. president	176.6	47. Auto salesperson	56.3
2. Firefighter	110.9	50. College professor	54.2
3. Senior executive	108.6	60. School principal	51.7
6. Surgeon	99.5	103. Market research	
10. Air traffic controller	83.1	analyst	42.1
12. Public relations		104. Personnel recruiter	41.8
executive	78.5	113. Hospital	
16. Advertising account		administrator	39.6
executive	74.6	119. Economist	38.7
17. Real estate agent	73.1	122. Mechanical engineer	38.3
20. Stockbroker	71.7	124. Chiropractor	37.9
22. Pilot	68.7	132. Technical writer	36.5
25. Architect	66.9	149. Retail salesperson	34.9
31. Lawyer	64.3	173. Accountant	31.1
33. General physician	64.0	193. Purchasing agent	28.9
35. Insurance agent	63.3	229. Broadcast technician	24.2
42. Advertising		245. Actuary	20.2
salesperson	59.9		

Source: Reprinted by permission of *The Wall Street Journal*, © 1996 Dow Jones & Company, Inc. All rights reserved worldwide.

something desired. So when you take a test at school or you undergo your annual performance review at work, you feel stress because you confront opportunities, constraints, and demands. A good performance review may lead to a promotion, greater responsibilities, and a higher salary. But a poor review may prevent you from getting the promotion. An extremely poor review might even result in your being fired.

Two conditions are necessary for potential stress to become actual stress.[39] There must be uncertainty over the outcome and the outcome must be important. Regardless of the conditions, it is only when there is doubt or uncertainty regarding whether the opportunity will be seized, the constraint removed, or the loss avoided that there is stress. That is, stress is highest for those individuals who perceive that they are uncertain as to whether they will win or lose and lowest for those individuals who think that winning or losing is a certainty. But importance is also critical. If winning or losing is an unimportant outcome, there is no stress. If keeping your job or earning a promotion doesn't hold any importance to you, you have no reason to feel stress over having to undergo a performance review.

Understanding Stress and Its Consequences

What causes stress? What are its consequences for individual employees? Why is it that the same set of conditions that creates stress for one person seems to have little or no effect on another person? Exhibit 17-11 provides a model that can help to answer questions such as these.[40]

Exhibit 17-10

THE FAR SIDE copyright 1990 & 1991 FARWORKS, INC./Dist. by UNIVERSAL PRESS SYNDICATE. Reprinted with permission. All rights reserved.

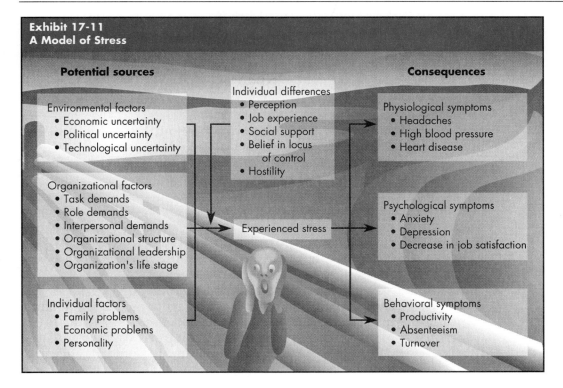

Exhibit 17-11
A Model of Stress

Potential sources

Environmental factors
• Economic uncertainty
• Political uncertainty
• Technological uncertainty

Organizational factors
• Task demands
• Role demands
• Interpersonal demands
• Organizational structure
• Organizational leadership
• Organization's life stage

Individual factors
• Family problems
• Economic problems
• Personality

Individual differences
• Perception
• Job experience
• Social support
• Belief in locus of control
• Hostility

Experienced stress

Consequences

Physiological symptoms
• Headaches
• High blood pressure
• Heart disease

Psychological symptoms
• Anxiety
• Depression
• Decrease in job satisfaction

Behavioral symptoms
• Productivity
• Absenteeism
• Turnover

The model identifies three sets of factors—environmental, organizational, and individual—that act as *potential* sources of stress. Whether they become *actual* stress depends on individual differences such as job experience and personality. When stress is experienced by an individual, its symptoms can surface as physiological, psychological, and behavioral outcomes.

Potential Sources of Stress

As the model in Exhibit 17-11 shows, there are three categories of potential stressors: environmental, organizational, and individual. Let's take a look at each.[41]

ENVIRONMENTAL FACTORS Just as environmental uncertainty influences the design of an organization's structure, it also influences stress levels among employees in that organization. Changes in the business cycle create *economic uncertainties*. When the economy is contracting, for example, people become increasingly anxious about their security. *Political uncertainties* don't tend to create stress among North Americans as they do for employees in countries like Haiti or Iraq. The obvious reason is that the United States and Canada have stable political systems where change is typically implemented in an orderly manner. Yet political threats and changes, even in countries like the United States and Canada, can be stress inducing. For instance, threats by Quebec to separate from Canada and become a distinct, French-speaking country increase stress among many Canadians, especially among Quebecers with little or no skills in the French language. *Technological uncertainty* is a third type of environmental factor that can cause stress. Because new innovations can make an employee's skills and experience obsolete in a very short

period of time, computers, robotics, automation, and similar forms of technological innovation are a threat to many people and cause them stress.

ORGANIZATIONAL FACTORS There is no shortages of factors within the organization that can cause stress. Pressures to avoid errors or complete tasks in
a limited time period, work overload, a demanding and insensitive boss, and
unpleasant co-workers are a few examples. (See Exhibit 17-12.) We've categorized these factors around task, role, and interpersonal demands; organizational structure; organizational leadership; and the organization's life stage.[42]

Task demands are factors related to a person's job. They include the design of the individual's job (autonomy, task variety, degree of automation),
working conditions, and the physical work layout. Assembly lines can put
pressure on people when their speed is perceived as excessive. The more interdependence between a person's tasks and the tasks of others, the more potential stress there is. Autonomy, on the other hand, tends to lessen stress. Jobs
where temperatures, noise, or other working conditions are dangerous or undesirable can increase anxiety. So, too, can working in an overcrowded room
or in a visible location where interruptions are constant.

Role demands relate to pressures placed on a person as a function of the
particular role he or she plays in the organization. Role conflicts create expectations that may be hard to reconcile or satisfy. Role overload is experienced
when the employee is expected to do more than time permits. Role ambiguity
is created when role expectations are not clearly understood and the employee is not sure what he or she is to do.

Interpersonal demands are pressures created by other employees. Lack of
social support from colleagues and poor interpersonal relationships can cause
considerable stress, especially among employees with a high social need.

Organizational structure defines the level of differentiation in the organization, the degree of rules and regulations, and where decisions are made. Excessive rules and lack of participation in decisions that affect an employee are
examples of structural variables that might be potential sources of stress.

Organizational leadership represents the managerial style of the organization's senior executives. Some chief executive officers create a culture characterized by tension, fear, and anxiety. They establish unrealistic pressures to
perform in the short run, impose excessively tight controls, and routinely fire
employees who don't "measure up."

Exhibit 17-12 Primary Causes of Stress at Work

What factors cause the most stress on the job? A *Wall Street Journal* survey reported:

Factor	Percentage Response*
Not doing the kind of work I want to	34
Coping with current job	30
Working too hard	28
Colleagues at work	21
A difficult boss	18

*Percentages exceed 100 as a result of some multiple responses.

Source: "Worries at Work," *The Wall Street Journal*, April 7, 1988, p. 27. Reprinted by permission of The *Wall Street Journal*, © 1988 Dow Jones & Company, Inc. All rights reserved worldwide.

Organizations go through a cycle. They're established, they grow, become mature, and eventually decline. An *organization's life stage*—that is, where it is in this four-stage cycle—creates different problems and pressures for employees. The establishment and decline stages are particularly stressful. The former is characterized by a great deal of excitement and uncertainty, while the latter typically requires cutbacks, layoffs, and a different set of uncertainties. Stress tends to be least in maturity where uncertainties are at their lowest ebb.

INDIVIDUAL FACTORS The typical individual only works about 40 to 50 hours a week. The experiences and problems that people encounter in those other 120-plus nonwork hours each week can spill over to the job. Our final category, then, encompasses factors in the employee's personal life. Primarily, these factors are family issues, personal economic problems, and inherent personality characteristics.

National surveys consistently show that people hold *family* and personal relationships dear. Marital difficulties, the breaking off of a relationship, and discipline troubles with children are examples of relationship problems that create stress for employees that aren't left at the front door when they arrive at work.

Economic problems created by individuals overextending their financial resources is another set of personal troubles that can create stress for employees and distract their attention from their work. Regardless of income level—people who make $80,000 a year seem to have as much trouble handling their finances as those who earn $18,000—some people are poor money managers or have wants that always seem to exceed their earning capacity.

Studies in three diverse organizations found that stress symptoms reported prior to beginning a job accounted for most of the variance in stress symptoms reported nine months later.[43] This led the researchers to conclude that some people may have an inherent tendency to accentuate negative aspects of the world in general. If true, then a significant individual factor influencing stress is a person's basic dispositional nature. That is, stress symptoms expressed on the job may actually originate in the person's *personality*.

STRESSORS ARE ADDITIVE A fact that tends to be overlooked when stressors are reviewed individually is that stress is an additive phenomenon.[44] Stress builds up. Each new and persistent stressor adds to an individual's stress level. A single stressor may seem relatively unimportant in and of itself, but if it is added to an already high level of stress, it can be "the straw that breaks the camel's back." If we want to appraise the total amount of stress an individual is under, we have to sum up his or her opportunity stresses, constraint stresses, and demand stresses.

Individual Differences

Some people thrive on stressful situations, while others are overwhelmed by them. What is it that differentiates people in terms of their ability to handle stress? What individual difference variables moderate the relationship between *potential* stressors and *experienced* stress? At least five variables—perception, job experience, social support, belief in locus of control, and hostility— have been found to be relevant moderators.

PERCEPTION   In chapter 3, we demonstrated that employees react in response to their perception of reality rather than to reality itself. Perception, therefore, will moderate the relationship between a potential stress condition and an employee's reaction to it. One person's fear that he'll lose his job because his company is laying off personnel may be perceived by another as an opportunity to get a large severance allowance and start his own business. Similarly, what one employee perceives as a challenging job may be viewed as threatening and demanding by others.[45] So the stress potential in environmental, organizational, and individual factors doesn't lie in their objective condition. Rather, it lies in an employee's interpretation of those factors.

JOB EXPERIENCE   Experience is said to be a great teacher. It can also be a great stress reducer. Think back to your first date or your first few days in college. For most of us, the uncertainty and newness of these situations created stress. But as we gained experience, that stress disappeared or at least significantly decreased. The same phenomenon seems to apply to work situations. That is, experience on the job tends to be negatively related to work stress. Two explanations have been offered.[46] First is the idea of selective withdrawal. Voluntary turnover is more probable among people who experience more stress. Therefore, people who remain with the organization longer are those with more stress-resistant traits, or those who are more resistant to the stress characteristics of their organization. Second, people eventually develop coping mechanisms to deal with stress. Because this takes time, senior members of the organization are more likely to be fully adapted and should experience less stress.

SOCIAL SUPPORT   There is increasing evidence that social support—that is, collegial relationships with co-workers or supervisors—can buffer the impact of stress.[47] The logic underlying this moderating variable is that social support acts as a palliative, mitigating the negative effects of even high-strain jobs.

For individuals whose work associates are unhelpful or even actively hostile, social support may be found outside the job. Involvement with family, friends, and community can provide the support—especially for those with a high social need—that is missing at work and this can make job stressors more tolerable.

BELIEF IN LOCUS OF CONTROL   Locus of control was introduced in chapter 2 as a personality attribute. Those with an internal locus of control believe they control their own destiny. Those with an external locus believe their lives are controlled by outside forces. Evidence indicates that internals perceive their jobs to be less stressful than do externals.[48]

When internals and externals confront a similar stressful situation, the internals are likely to believe that they can have a significant effect on the results. They, therefore, act to take control of events. Externals are more likely to be passive and defensive. Rather than do something to reduce the stress, they acquiesce. So externals, who are more likely to feel helpless in stressful situations, are also more likely to experience stress.

HOSTILITY For much of the 1970s and 1980s, a great deal of attention was directed at the Type A personality.[49] In fact, throughout the 1980s, it was undoubtedly the most frequently used moderating variable related to stress.

As noted in chapter 2, the Type A personality is characterized by feeling a chronic sense of time urgency and by an *excessive* competitive drive. The Type A individual is "*aggressively* involved in a *chronic, incessant* struggle to achieve more and more in less and less time, and if required to do so, against the opposing efforts of other things or other persons."[50]

Until recently, researchers believed that Type A's were more likely to experience stress on and off the job. More specifically, Type A's were widely believed to be at higher risk for heart disease. A closer analysis of the evidence, however, has produced new conclusions.[51] By looking at various components of Type A behavior, it's been found that only the hostility and anger associated with Type A behavior are actually related to heart disease. The chronically angry, suspicious, and mistrustful person is the one at risk.

So just because a person is a workaholic, rushes around a lot, and is impatient or competitive does not mean that he or she is unduly susceptible to heart disease or the other negative effects of stress. Rather, it's the quickness to anger, the persistently hostile outlook, and the cynical mistrust of others that are harmful.

Consequences of Stress

Stress shows itself in a number of ways. For instance, an individual who is experiencing a high level of stress may develop high blood pressure, ulcers, irritability, difficulty in making routine decisions, loss of appetite, accident proneness, and the like. These can be subsumed under three general categories: physiological, psychological, and behavioral symptoms.[52]

PHYSIOLOGICAL SYMPTOMS Most of the early concern with stress was directed at physiological symptoms. This was predominately due to the fact that the topic was researched by specialists in the health and medical sciences. This research led to the conclusion that stress could create changes in metabolism, increase heart and breathing rates, increase blood pressure, bring on headaches, and induce heart attacks.

The link between stress and particular physiological symptoms is not clear. There are few, if any, consistent relationships.[53] This is attributed to the complexity of the symptoms and the difficulty of objectively measuring them. But of greater relevance is the fact that physiological symptoms have the least direct relevance to students of OB. Our concern is with behaviors and attitudes. Therefore, the two other categories of symptoms are more important to us.

◆ Job dissatisfaction is "the simplest and most obvious psychological effect" of stress.

PSYCHOLOGICAL SYMPTOMS Stress can cause dissatisfaction. Job-related stress can cause job-related dissatisfaction. Job dissatisfaction, in fact, is "the simplest and most obvious psychological effect" of stress.[54] But stress shows itself in other psychological states—for instance, tension, anxiety, irritability, boredom, and procrastination.

The evidence indicates that when people are placed in jobs that make multiple and conflicting demands or in which there is a lack of clarity as to the incumbent's duties, authority, and responsibilities, both stress and dissatisfaction are increased.[55] Similarly, the less control people have over the pace of their work, the greater the stress and dissatisfaction. While more research is needed to clarify the relationship, the evidence suggests that jobs that provide a low level of variety, significance, autonomy, feedback, and identity to incumbents create stress and reduce satisfaction and involvement in the job.[56]

BEHAVIORAL SYMPTOMS Behaviorally related stress symptoms include changes in productivity, absence, and turnover, as well as changes in eating habits, increased smoking or consumption of alcohol, rapid speech, fidgeting, and sleep disorders.

There has been a significant amount of research investigating the stress–performance relationship. The most widely studied pattern in the stress–performance literature is the inverted-U relationship.[57] This is shown in Exhibit 17-13.

The logic underlying the inverted U is that low to moderate levels of stress stimulate the body and increase its ability to react. Individuals then often perform their tasks better, more intensely, or more rapidly. But too much stress places unattainable demands or constraints on a person, which result in lower performance. This inverted-U pattern may also describe the reaction to stress over time, as well as to changes in stress intensity. That is, even moderate levels of stress can have a negative influence on performance over the long term as the continued intensity of the stress wears down the individual and saps his or her energy resources. An athlete may be able to use the positive effects of stress to obtain a higher performance during every Saturday's game in the fall season, or a sales executive may be able to psych herself up for her presentation at the annual national meeting. But moderate levels of stress experienced continually over long periods of time, as typified by the emergency room staff in a large urban hospital, can result in lower performance. This may explain why emergency room staffs at such hospitals are frequently rotated and why it is unusual to find individuals who have spent the bulk of their career in such an environment. In effect, to do so would expose the individual to the risk of "career burnout."

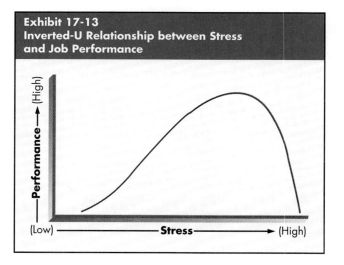

Exhibit 17-13
Inverted-U Relationship between Stress and Job Performance

In spite of the popularity and intuitive appeal of the inverted-U model, it doesn't get a lot of empirical support.[58] At this point in time, managers should be careful in assuming this model accurately depicts the stress–performance relationship.

Managing Stress

From the organization's standpoint, management may not be concerned when employees experience low to moderate levels of stress. The reason, as we showed earlier, is that such levels of stress may be functional and lead to higher employee performance. But high levels of stress, or even low levels sustained over long periods of time, can lead to reduced employee performance and, thus, require action by management.

While a limited amount of stress may benefit an employee's performance, don't expect employees to see it that way. From the individual's standpoint, even low levels of stress are likely to be perceived as undesirable. It's not unlikely, therefore, for employees and management to have different notions of what constitutes an acceptable level of stress on the job. What management may consider as "a positive stimulus that keeps the adrenalin running" is very likely to be seen as "excessive pressure" by the employee. Keep this in mind as we discuss individual and organizational approaches toward managing stress.[59]

INDIVIDUAL APPROACHES An employee can take personal responsibility for reducing his or her stress level. Individual strategies that have proven effective include implementing time management techniques, increasing physical exercise, relaxation training, and expanding the social support network.

Many people manage their time poorly. The things they have to accomplish in any given day or week are not necessarily beyond completion if they manage their time properly. The well-organized employee, like the well-organized student, can often accomplish twice as much as the person who is poorly organized. So an understanding and utilization of basic *time management* principles can help individuals better cope with tensions created by job demands.[60] A few of the more well-known time management principles are: (1) making daily lists of activities to be accomplished; (2) prioritizing activities by importance and urgency; (3) scheduling activities according to the priorities set; and (4) knowing your daily cycle and handling the most demanding parts of your job during the high part of your cycle when you are most alert and productive.[61]

Noncompetitive physical exercise such as aerobics, walking, jogging, swimming, and riding a bicycle have long been recommended by physicians as a way to deal with excessive stress levels. These forms of *physical exercise* increase heart capacity, lower at-rest heart rate, provide a mental diversion from work pressures, and offer a means to "let off steam."[62]

Individuals can teach themselves to reduce tension through *relaxation techniques* such as meditation, hypnosis, and biofeedback. The objective is to reach a state of deep relaxation, where one feels physically relaxed, somewhat detached from the immediate environment, and detached from body sensations.[63] Fifteen or twenty minutes a day of deep relaxation releases tension and provides a person with a pronounced sense of peacefulness. Importantly, significant changes in heart rate, blood pressure, and other physiological factors result from achieving the deep relaxation condition.

As we noted earlier in this chapter, having friends, family, or work colleagues to talk to provides an outlet when stress levels become excessive. Expanding your *social support network,* therefore, can be a means for tension reduction. It provides you with someone to hear your problems and to offer a more objective perspective on the situation. Research also demonstrates that social support moderates the stress–burnout relationship.[64] That is, high support reduces the likelihood that heavy work stress will result in job burnout.

ORGANIZATIONAL APPROACHES Several of the factors that cause stress—particularly task and role demands, and organizational structure—are controlled by management. As such, they can be modified or changed. Strategies that management might want to consider include improved personnel selection and job placement, use of realistic goal setting, redesigning of jobs, increased employee involvement, improved organizational communication, and establishment of corporate wellness programs.

While certain jobs are more stressful than others, we learned earlier in this chapter that individuals differ in their response to stress situations. We know, for example, that individuals with little experience or an external locus of control tend to be more prone to stress. *Selection and placement* decisions should take these facts into consideration. Obviously, while management shouldn't restrict hiring to only experienced individuals with an internal locus, such individuals may adapt better to high-stress jobs and perform those jobs more effectively.

◆ **The use of goals can reduce stress as well as provide motivation.**

We discussed *goal setting* in chapter 5. Based on an extensive amount of research, we concluded that individuals perform better when they have specific and challenging goals and receive feedback on how well they are progressing toward these goals. The use of goals can reduce stress as well as provide motivation. Specific goals that are perceived as attainable clarify performance expectations. Additionally, goal feedback reduces uncertainties as to actual job performance. The result is less employee frustration, role ambiguity, and stress.

Redesigning jobs to give employees more responsibility, more meaningful work, more autonomy, and increased feedback can reduce stress because these factors give the employee greater control over work activities and lessen dependence on others. But as we noted in our discussion of work design, not all employees want enriched jobs. The right redesign, then, for employees with a low need for growth might be less responsibility and increased specialization. If individuals prefer structure and routine, reducing skill variety should also reduce uncertainties and stress levels.

Role stress is detrimental to a large extent because employees feel uncertain about goals, expectations, how they'll be evaluated, and the like. By giving these employees a voice in those decisions that directly affect their job performances, management can increase employee control and reduce this role stress. So managers should consider *increasing employee involvement* in decision making.[65]

Increasing formal *organizational communication* with employees reduces uncertainty by lessening role ambiguity and role conflict. Given the importance that perceptions play in moderating the stress–response relationship, management can also use effective communications as a means to shape employee perceptions. Remember that what employees categorize as demands, threats, or opportunities are merely an interpretation, and that interpretation can be affected by the symbols and actions communicated by management.

Our final suggestion is to offer organizationally supported **wellness programs**. These programs focus on the employee's total physical and mental condition.[66] For example, they typically provide workshops to help people quit smoking, control alcohol use, lose weight, eat better, and develop a regular exercise program (see Exhibit 17-14). The assumption underlying most wellness programs is that employees need to take personal responsibility for their physical and mental health. The organization is merely a vehicle to facilitate this end.

Organizations, of course, aren't altruistic. They expect a payoff from their investment in wellness programs. And most of those firms that have introduced wellness programs have found significant benefits. For instance, Johnson & Johnson calculated the following annual savings in insurance premiums when an employee exchanges bad habits for healthy ones: quitting smoking ($1,110); starting to exercise ($260); lowering cholesterol from 240 to 190 milligrams ($1,200); and slimming down from obese to normal weight ($177).[67]

wellness programs
Organizationally supported programs that focus on the employee's total physical and mental condition.

Exhibit 17-14 Award-Winning Wellness Programs

Each year, the C. Everett Koop National Health Awards honor companies with outstanding wellness programs. The following highlights some recent winners, chosen because their plans offered a range of services and generated the biggest savings.

Aetna	Boasts five state-of-the art health clubs with 7,600 enrollees. Exercisers cost $282 less per year to insure than couch potatoes.
L.L. Bean	Pays up to $200 to employees whose families quit smoking or take prenatal classes. The company's annual insurance premiums are $2,000 per worker, half the national average.
Coors	Pays bonuses for healthy habits. Employees can use the award—a maximum of $500 per family—to buy extra holidays or pay for financial planning.
Dow	Backs in Action program encourages exercise, dieting, and ergonomics. The company has decreased on-the-job strains and sprains up to 90 percent.
Quaker Oats	Grants bonuses of as much as $500 for families who exercise, shun smoking, and wear seat belts. Employees can keep the money or invest in added benefits.
Steelcase	Tested 4,000 workers for everything from seat-belt use to cholesterol. By promoting healthy lifestyles, the furniture maker expects to save $20 million over ten years.
Union Pacific Corporation	Motivates stubborn, secretive workers to talk about their health risks and change their habits. Its $1.2-million-a-year investment in wellness programs generates a 3-to-1 return.

Source: S. Tully, "America's Healthiest Companies," *Fortune*, June 12, 1995, p. 99. © 1995 Time Inc. All rights reserved.

Summary and Implications for Managers

The need for change has been implied throughout this text. "A casual reflection on change should indicate that it encompasses almost all our concepts in the organizational behavior literature. Think about leadership, motivation, organizational environment, and roles. It is impossible to think about these and other concepts without inquiring about change."[68]

If environments were perfectly static, if employees' skills and abilities were always up-to-date and incapable of deteriorating, and if tomorrow was always exactly the same as today, organizational change would have little or no relevance to managers. But the real world is turbulent, requiring organizations and their members to undergo dynamic change if they are to perform at competitive levels.

Managers are the primary change agents in most organizations. By the decisions they make and their role-modeling behaviors, they shape the organization's change culture. For instance, management decisions related to structural design, cultural factors, and human resource policies largely determine the level of innovation within the organization. Similarly, management decisions, policies, and practices will determine the degree to which the organization learns and adapts to changing environmental factors.

We found that the existence of work stress, in and of itself, need not imply lower performance. The evidence indicates that stress can be either a positive or negative influence on employee performance. For many people, low to moderate amounts of stress enable them to perform their jobs better, by increasing their work intensity, alertness, and ability to react. However, a high level of stress, or even a moderate amount sustained over a long period of time, eventually takes its toll and performance declines. The impact of stress on satisfaction is far more straightforward. Job-related tension tends to decrease general job satisfaction.[73] Even though low to moderate levels of stress may improve job performance, employees find stress dissatisfying.

For Review

1. What is meant by the phrase "we live in an age of discontinuity"?

2. "Resistance to change is an irrational response." Do you agree or disagree? Explain.

3. Why is participation considered such an effective technique for lessening resistance to change?

4. Why does change so frequently become a political issue in organizations?

5. How does Lewin's three-step model of change deal with resistance to change?

6. What changes can an organization that has a history of "following the leader" make to foster innovation?

7. "Learning organizations attack fragmentation, competitiveness, and reactiveness." Explain this statement.

8. What characteristics distinguish organizational development?

9. How are opportunities, constraints, and demands related to stress? Give an example of each.

10. What can organizations do to reduce employee stress?

For Discussion

1. How have changes in the workforce during the past 20 years affected organizational policies?

2. "Managing today is easier than at the turn of the century because the years of real change took place between the Civil War and World War I." Do you agree or disagree? Discuss.

3. Are all managers change agents? Discuss.

4. Discuss the link between learning theories discussed in chapter 3 and the issue of organizational change.

5. Discuss the link between second-order change and double-loop learning.

Change Is an Episodic Activity

The study of planned organizational change has, with very few exceptions, viewed it as an episodic activity. That is, it starts at some point, proceeds through a series of steps, and culminates in some outcome that those involved hope is an improvement over the starting point. When change is seen as an episodic activity, it has a beginning, a middle, and an end.

Both Lewin's three-step model and action research follow this perspective. In the former, change is seen as a break in the organization's equilibrium. The status quo has been disturbed, and change is necessary to establish a new equilibrium state. The objective of refreezing is to stabilize the new situation by balancing the driving and restraining forces. Action research begins with a diagnostic assessment in which problems are identified. These problems are then analyzed, and shared with those who are affected, solutions are developed, and action plans are initiated. The process is brought to closure by an evaluation of the action plan's effectiveness. Even though supporters of action research recognize that the cycle may need to go through numerous iterations, the process is still seen as a cycle with a beginning and an end.

Some experts have argued that organizational change should be thought of as balancing a system made up of five interacting variables within the organization—people, tasks, technology, structure, and strategy. A change in any one variable has repercussions on one or more of the others. Again, this perspective is episodic in that it treats organizational change as essentially an effort to sustain an equilibrium. A change in one variable begins a chain of events that, if properly managed, requires adjustments in the other variables to achieve a new state of equilibrium.

Another way to conceptualize the episodic way of looking at change is to think of managing change as analogous to captaining a ship. The organization is like a large ship traveling across the calm Mediterranean Sea to a specific port. The ship's captain has made this exact trip hundreds of times before with the same crew. Every once in a while, however, a storm will appear, and the crew has to respond. The captain will make the appropriate adjustments—that is, implement changes—and, having maneuvered through the storm, will return to calm waters. Managing an organization should therefore be seen as a journey with a beginning and an end, and implementing change as a response to a break in the status quo and needed only in occasional situations.

Change Is an Ongoing Activity

The episodic approach may be the dominant paradigm for handling planned organizational change, but it has become obsolete. It applies to a world of certainty and predictability. The episodic approach was developed in the 1950s and 1960s, and it reflects the environment of those times. It treats change as the occasional disturbance in an otherwise peaceful world. However, this paradigm has little resemblance to the 1990s environment of constant and chaotic change.

If you want to understand what it's like to manage change in today's organizations, think of it as equivalent to permanent white-water rafting.* The organization is not a large ship, but more akin to a 40-foot raft. Rather than sailing a calm sea, this raft must traverse a raging river made up of an uninterrupted flow of permanent white-water rapids. To make things worse, the raft is manned by ten people who have never worked together or traveled the river before, much of the trip is in the dark, the river is dotted by unexpected turns and obstacles, the exact destination of the raft is not clear, and at irregular intervals the raft needs to pull to shore, where some new crew members are added and others leave. Change is a natural state and managing change is a continual process. That is, managers never get the luxury of escaping the white-water rapids.

To get a feeling for what managers are facing, think of what it would be like to attend a college that had the following structure: Courses vary in length. When you sign up for a course, however, you don't know how long it will last. It might go for two weeks or thirty weeks. Furthermore, the instructor can end a course any time he or she wants, with no prior warning. If that isn't frustrating enough, the length of the class changes each time it meets—sometimes it lasts twenty minutes, while other times it runs for three hours—and determination of when the next class meeting will take place is set by the instructor during the previous class. And one more thing: The exams are all unannounced, so you have to be ready for a test at any time.

A growing number of managers are coming to accept that their jobs are much like what a student would face in such a college. The stability and predictability of the episodic perspective don't exist. Nor are disruptions in the status quo only occasional, temporary, and followed by a return to an equilibrium state. Managers today face constant change, bordering on chaos. They are being forced to play a game they've never played before, governed by rules that are created as the game progresses. To manage in this dynamic arena, they are moving toward creating learning organizations.

*This perspective is based on P.B. Vaill, *Managing as a Performing Art: New Ideas for a World of Chaotic Change* (San Francisco: Jossey-Bass, 1989).

Learning about Yourself Exercise

Managing-in-a-Turbulent-World Tolerance Test

Instructions

Listed below are some statements a 37-year-old manager made about his job at a large, successful corporation. If your job had these characteristics, how would you react to them? After each statement are five letters, A to E. Circle the letter that best describes how you think you would react according to the following scale:

A   *I would enjoy this very much: it's completely acceptable.*

B   *This would be enjoyable and acceptable most of the time.*

C   *I'd have no reaction to this feature one way or another, or it would be about equally enjoyable and unpleasant.*

D   *This feature would be somewhat unpleasant for me.*

E   *This feature would be very unpleasant for me.*

1. I regularly spend 30 to 40 percent of my time in meetings.   A B C D E

2. A year and a half ago, my job did not exist, and I have been essentially inventing it as I go along.   A B C D E

3. The responsibilities I either assume or am assigned consistently exceed the authority I have for discharging them.   A B C D E

4. At any given moment in my job, I have on the average about a dozen phone calls to be returned.   A B C D E

5. There seems to be very little relation in my job between the quality of my performance and my actual pay and fringe benefits.   A B C D E

6. About two weeks a year of formal management training is needed in my job just to stay current.   A B C D E

7. Because we have very effective equal employment opportunity in my company and because it is thoroughly multinational, my job consistently brings me into close working contact at a professional level with people of many races, ethnic groups, and nationalities and of both sexes.   A B C D E

8. There is no objective way to measure my effectiveness.   A B C D E

9. I report to three different bosses for different aspects of my job, and each has an equal say in my performance appraisal.   A B C D E

10. On average, about a third of my time is spent dealing with unexpected emergencies that force all scheduled work to be postponed.   A B C D E

11. When I have to have a meeting of the people who report to me, it takes my secretary most of a day to find a time when we are all available, and even then, I have yet to have a meeting where everyone is present for the entire meeting. A B C D E

12. The college degree I earned in preparation for this type of work is now obsolete, and I probably should go back for another degree. A B C D E

13. My job requires that I absorb 100 to 200 pages per week of technical materials. A B C D E

14. I am out of town overnight at least one night per week. A B C D E

15. My department is so interdependent with several other departments in the company that all distinctions about which departments are responsible for which tasks are quite arbitrary. A B C D E

16. I will probably get a promotion in about a year to a job in another division that has most of these same characteristics. A B C D E

17. During the period of my employment here, either the entire company or the division I worked in has been reorganized every year or so. A B C D E

18. Although there are several possible promotions I can see ahead of me, I have no real career path in an objective sense. A B C D E

19. Although there are several possible promotions I can see ahead of me, I think I have no realistic chance of getting to the top levels of the company. A B C D E

20. Although I have many ideas about how to make things work better, I have no direct influence on either the business policies or the personnel policies that govern my division. A B C D E

21. My company has recently put in an "assessment center" where I and all other managers will be required to go through an extensive battery of psychological tests to assess our potential. A B C D E

22. My company is a defendant in an antitrust suit, and if the case comes to trial, I will probably have to testify about some decisions that were made a few years ago. A B C D E

23. Advanced computer and other electronic office technology is continually being introduced into my division, necessitating constant learning on my part. A B C D E

24. The computer terminal and screen I have in my office can be monitored in my bosses' offices without my knowledge. A B C D E

Turn to page A-30 for scoring directions and key.

Source: From P.B. Vaill, *Managing as a Performing Art: New Ideas for a World of Chaotic Change* (San Francisco: Jossey-Bass, 1989), pp. 8–9. Reproduced with permission of the publisher. All rights reserved.

Working with Others Exercise

The Beacon Aircraft Company

Objectives

1. To illustrate how forces for change and stability must be managed in organizational development programs.
2. To illustrate the effects of alternative change techniques on the relative strength of forces for change and forces for stability.

The Situation

The marketing division of the Beacon Aircraft Company has gone through two reorganizations in the past two years. Initially, its structure changed from a functional to a matrix form. But the matrix structure did not satisfy some functional managers. They complained that the structure confused the authority and responsibility relationships.

In reaction to these complaints, the marketing manager revised the structure back to the functional form. This new structure maintained market and project groups, which were managed by project managers with a few general staff personnel. But no functional specialists were assigned to these groups.

After the change, some problems began to surface. Project managers complained that they could not obtain adequate assistance from functional staff members. It not only took more time to obtain necessary assistance, but it also created problems in establishing stable relationships with functional staff members. Since these problems affected their services to customers, project managers demanded a change in the organizational structure—probably again toward a matrix structure. Faced with these complaints and demands from project managers, the vice president is pondering another reorganization. He has requested an outside consultant to help him in the reorganization plan.

The Procedure

1. Divide yourselves into groups of five to seven and take the role of consultants.
2. Each group identifies the driving and resisting forces found in the firm. List these forces in the spaces provided.

The Driving Forces	The Resisting Forces
_____	_____
_____	_____
_____	_____
_____	_____
_____	_____
_____	_____

3. Each group develops a set of strategies for increasing the driving forces and another set for reducing the resisting forces.

4. Each group prepares a list of changes it wants to introduce.

5. The class reassembles and hears each group's recommendations.

Source: Adapted from Kae H. Chung and Leon C. Megginson, *Organizational Behavior,* Copyright © 1981 by Kae H. Chung and Leon Megginson. Reprinted by permission of HarperCollins Publishers, Inc.

The Germans Come to Alabama

CASE INCIDENT

One day in the spring of 1994, two Mercedes managers participated in an Outward-Bound-type of team-building exercise in the Austrian Alps. This exercise was just one of their boss's, Andreas Renschler, ideas on how to shake up the culture at Mercedes-Benz.

Renschler is the fast-rising executive who is overseeing the development of Mercedes's first mass-market sport-utility vehicle (the All Activity Vehicle or AAV), which will be produced at the company's first big foreign plant in Vance, Alabama. As president of Mercedes-Benz U.S. International Inc., Renschler is trying to bring to the company's U.S. operations what his bosses are trying to do in Germany—to transform the once ponderous luxury car maker into an efficient worldwide competitor.

Renschler's relative youth—he's in his late 30s—was a major reason he was selected for this job. He's not steeped in the Mercedes culture, where costs have always been sublimated to engineering excellence. In his six years with the company, and assistant to the CEO, he helped plan the current corporate turnaround and became known as a creative problem solver and idea generator. He also planned strategies for light trucks in Europe and Latin America and ran the feasibility study for the AAV. But he has a tough job ahead of him. While Japanese transplants typically copy plants back home and assemble existing models at first, Renschler will have to simultaneously debug a product, a manufacturing process, and a workforce. "It's a prescription for disaster," says one manufacturing consultant. "There are too many variables."

As part of a plan to adapt the best operating techniques of other companies, Renschler has hired managers from Chrysler, Ford, Mitsubishi, Honda, Nissan, Toyota, Saturn, Subaru, and Isuzu. Unfortunately, their diverse backgrounds make it hard to mesh their styles. For instance, one Toyota alum spent Thanksgiving weekend of 1993 in an Alabama motel with a dozen German and American colleagues, debating a factory layout. German engineers wanted a sprawling E-shaped building with departments linked by complex conveyors. After endless wrangling, those with Japanese experience prevailed, and the group settled on a compact, rectangular design.

To shape his diverse group into a team, Renschler is going all out to erase Mercedes's stiff formality and encourage bonds. The team-building exercise in the Alps, for instance, was designed to help meet this objective. Renschler is also pushing changes in Mercedes's traditional product-development process. To save time and money, the AAV will have 100 primary suppliers versus 1,000 for the current E-class sedan. In addition, suppliers get a freer hand in designing parts, sometimes adapting off-the-shelf components rather than always starting from scratch as in the past. Also, rather than make suppliers bid for business annually as Mercedes usually does, Renschler has been offering multiyear contracts in return for annual 5 percent price cuts.

Renschler's aggressive change program has won him his share of enemies within the company. "Lots of people are envious" of his rise or are threatened by the changes he's pushing, says one insider, and some are quietly hoping for him to fail.

Questions

1. "If it ain't broke, don't fix it." Why doesn't Renschler accept this adage?

2. Is Renschler trying to implement too much change too fast? Support your position.

3. Do you think Renschler's innovations at Vance will succeed? Explain your position.

Based on D. Woodruff, "Mercedes' Maverick in Alabama," *Business Week*, September 11, 1995, pp. 64–65; and B.S. Moskal, "Not the Same Old Mercedes," *Industry Week*, October 7, 1996, pp. 12–21.

The Changing World of Corporate Loyalty

The list of blue chip companies handing out pink slips is growing. Sears Roebuck announces 50,000 jobs will be eliminated; IBM says it will cut 63,000 jobs; AT&T says 40,000 jobs have to go. And entire job categories are dissolving before our eyes. Between 1986 and 1994, banks eliminated 41,000 tellers. Most of those tellers were replaced by ATMs. Increasingly, there is no such thing as job security. The following comments by Albert Dunlap, former chairman and CEO of Scott Paper Co., while harsh, capture the essence of the new employee–employer arrangement. Dunlap, incidentally, has built a reputation for cutting jobs; hence, his nickname, Chain Saw Al. He begins by defending his nickname.

"It's not offensive because I've gone into companies that have had very poor results. The company before I joined Scott, they lost $277 million and were on credit watch, and I was forced to fire about 35 percent of the people, but 65 percent of the people have a more secure future than they've ever had before, and that's what people don't realize. I'm the doctor. I didn't create the problem.

"The reason to be in business is to make money for your shareholders. The shareholders own the company. They take all the risks. No company ever gives the shareholders their money back when they go bust, and you have an awesome responsibility to see that they get the proper return for their risk.

"The free enterprise system is very efficient when it's allowed to perform. America was becoming unproductive in global economies. American companies were failing. Because people have come in and made the tough decisions, American companies are now becoming successful. They're becoming global giants. And over time, they will create considerably more employment. And yes, some people have to lose their jobs, but as I said before, that's a lot better than everyone losing their jobs.

"The world has changed over the last 20 years. But business is not a social experiment. You exist in business to be competitive, to come out with the best products, the best facilities, and to create a future for your people, and the companies that do well must have good products, must have good employee relations, because it all figures into the future of the company. And you know, socialism has failed the world over, but yet we in America now want to reinstitute socialism into our economic situation and I think that's dead wrong.

"The business role is to provide as secure a future for its employees as it can, and within doing that, some people lose their job. That has happened since the beginning of time. And because people didn't take their responsibilities to run efficient corporations seriously, we're in the situation we are now. And the last person that should arbitrate it is the government, the largest business in America with the worst balance sheet, the poorest management, services people don't want, and a bloated cost structure."

Questions

1. Do you think Al Dunlap is accurately describing today's business climate?
2. Why do people who claim to support capitalism come down so hard in criticizing the things Dunlap says and does?
3. What are the implications of Dunlap's comments for today's employees?

Source: Based on "Corporate Layoffs and the Fate of American Workers," *ABC News Nightline*; aired February 14, 1996.

ROB PANCO: MANAGING CHANGE

"If it ain't broke and it ain't outdated, leave it alone. We change when we have to." That, according to Rob Panco, was his philosophy toward dealing with change. This philosophy, Rob admits, may have been a liability for him at Aslett. He contrasted Aslett with AT&T.

"AT&T and Bell Labs have been going through a great deal of change since the federal government deregulated the phone monopoly. Since Bob Allen took over, he's done some terrific things. I have a lot of respect for him. The first thing he did was create autonomous divisions with their own presidents and decentralize decision-making authority. My impression, however, is that the commitment for change at AT&T was high at both the very top of the company and among lower-level managers. The problem was middle management. The typical 55-year-old middle manager, with 30 years in the company, was threatened by the changes Allen proposed. There was considerable factional resistance to change. For instance, product managers and sales teams were very resistant. It's not a coincidence that the company used downsizing in the early 1990s to retire a lot of those rigid middle managers."

In his first 18 months at Aslett, Rob tried to create a climate that supported the growth and changes that were going on (including the use of desktop publishing, digital technology, and CD-ROM formats). Ironically, when downsizing came, the employees may have handled it better than he did. The workers showed little resistance to the change. "The crisis actually brought employees closer together. They helped each other out more. They looked for ways to cut costs. Their trust in management also seemed to significantly increase. They seemed to better understand that the changes we were making were for the best interests of the company." When asked if there was any one individual who couldn't handle the change very well, Rob said, "It might have been me. I'm a forward-looking person. That means growth to me. I don't deal well with constraints and limitations. I could orchestrate survival, but it's not my preference. Especially coming off such rapid growth. When the growth curve flattened, it took the fun out of the job."

According to Rob, Aslett's rapid growth created a great deal of stress among employees, especially at those critical times when projects were coming to completion. "People had to put in a lot of overtime. The hours were long. At the end of a project, it could get pretty crazy for members of a team. I didn't assume stress was normal. I wanted to help my people relieve it. As it got close to crunch time, I'd bring the team together and ask them to open up and tell me of any potential personal problems—like a child's christening they had to attend or a parent who had an upcoming operation. I wanted to know all the problems ahead of time so we could focus full attention on the project deadline. When the deadline neared, I often brought in snacks, lunch, and similar things to break the tension and show I was concerned. If someone became too stressed out, I'd send them home early with pay. Once a major project was over, I frequently told people to take a couple of days off, again with pay. I wanted them to spend the time necessary to get their personal lives back in order."

Was stress a problem at Aslett when business made a downturn? "No," says Rob. "Those people who couldn't handle it tended to self-select themselves out. They were the ones who voluntarily left. And fortunately, those who left voluntarily tended to be in areas where we were overstaffed. I also think we benefited by hiring right. We sought people who understood small companies. They had personalities that tended to adapt pretty well to the shifting fortunes of a small business. Looking back, I think growth was more of a threat and stress inducer for employees than downsizing. When we were growing, people seemed to have difficulty giving up responsibilities and having their work divied off to new hires. During cutbacks, there was a bit of the 'Am I next?' concern, but our people seemed to rally around our problems. They used the cutbacks as an opportunity to learn new skills and to build cooperative links with the others who remained."

Questions

1. What do you think about Rob's philosophy toward change?
2. Contrast the challenges of implementing change at Aslett with implementing change at AT&T.
3. What might explain Rob's observation that lower-level managers at AT&T were more accepting of change than middle managers?
4. What could Rob have done to make Aslett into a learning organization? Or is it already a learning organization?
5. Can you explain why employees at Aslett responded to the downsizing the way they did?

THE HISTORICAL EVOLUTION
OF ORGANIZATIONAL BEHAVIOR

Why study history? Oliver Wendell Holmes answered that question succinctly when he said, "When I want to understand what is happening today or try to decide what will happen tomorrow, I look back." By *looking back* at the history of organizational behavior, you gain a great deal of insight into how the field got to where it is today. It'll help you understand, for instance, how management came to impose rules and regulations on employees, why many workers in organizations do standardized and repetitive tasks on assembly lines, and why a number of organizations in recent years have replaced their assembly lines with team-based work units. In this appendix, you'll find a brief description of how the theory and practice of organizational behavior have evolved.

So where do we start? Human beings and organized activities have been around for thousands of years, but we needn't go back beyond the eighteenth or nineteenth century to find OB's roots.

Early Practices

There is no question that hundreds of people helped to plant the "seeds" from which the OB "garden" has grown.[1] Three individuals, however, were particularly important in promoting ideas that would eventually have a major influence in shaping the direction and boundaries of OB: Adam Smith, Charles Babbage, and Robert Owen.

Adam Smith

Adam Smith is more typically cited by economists for his contributions to classical economic doctrine, but his discussion in *The Wealth of Nations*,[2] published in 1776, included a brilliant argument on the economic advantages that organizations and society would reap from the division of labor (also called work specialization). Smith used the pin-manufacturing industry for his examples. He noted that ten individuals, each doing a specialized task, could produce about 48,000 pins a day among them. He proposed, however, that if each were working separately and independently, the ten workers together would be lucky to make ten pins in one day. If each had to draw the wire, straighten it, cut it, pound heads for each pin, sharpen the point, and solder the head and pin shaft, it would be quite a feat to produce ten pins a day!

Smith concluded that division of labor raised productivity by increasing each worker's skill and dexterity, by saving time that is commonly lost in changing tasks, and by encouraging the creation of labor-saving inventions and machinery. The extensive development of assembly-line production processes during this century has undoubtedly been stimulated by the economic advantages of work specialization cited over two centuries ago by Adam Smith.

Charles Babbage

Charles Babbage was a British mathematics professor who expanded on the virtues of division of labor first articulated by Adam Smith. In his book *On the Economy of Machinery and Manufactures*,[3] published in 1832, Babbage added the following to Smith's list of the advantages that accrue from division of labor:

1. It reduces the time needed for learning a job.
2. It reduces the waste of material during the learning stage.
3. It allows for the attainment of high skill levels.
4. It allows a more careful matching of people's skills and physical abilities with specific tasks.

Moreover, Babbage proposed that the economies from specialization should be as relevant to doing mental work as physical labor. Today, for example, we take specialization for granted among professionals. When we have a skin rash, we go to a dermatologist. When we buy a home, we consult a lawyer who specializes in real estate. The professors you encounter in your business school classes specialize in areas such as tax accounting, entrepreneurship, marketing research, and organizational behavior. These applications of division of labor were unheard of in eighteenth-century England. But contemporary organizations around the world—in both manufacturing and service industries—make wide use of division of labor.

Robert Owen

Robert Owen was a Welsh entrepreneur who bought his first factory in 1789, at the age of 18. He is important in the history of OB because he was one of the first industrialists to recognize how the growing factory system was demeaning to workers.

Repulsed by the harsh practices he saw in factories—such as the employment of young children (many under the age of ten), 13-hour workdays, and miserable working conditions—Owen became a reformer. He chided factory owners for treating their equipment better than their employees. He criticized them for buying the best machines but then employing the cheapest labor to run them. Owen argued that money spent on improving labor was one of the best investments that business executives could make. He claimed that showing concern for employees both was profitable for management and would relieve human misery.

For his time, Owen was an idealist. What he proposed was a utopian workplace that would reduce the suffering of the working class. He was more than a hundred years ahead of his time when he argued, in 1825, for regulated hours of work for all, child labor laws, public education, company-furnished meals at work, and business involvement in community projects.[4]

The Classical Era

The classical era covered the period from about 1900 to the mid-1930s. It was during this period that the first general theories of management began to evolve. The classical contributors—who include Frederick Taylor, Henri Fayol, Max Weber, Mary Parker Follett, and Chester Barnard—laid the foundation for contemporary management practices.

Scientific Management

The typical United Parcel Service (UPS) driver today makes 120 stops during his or her work shift. Every step on that driver's daily route has been carefully studied by UPS industrial engineers to maximize efficiency. Every second taken up by stoplights, traffic, detours, doorbells, walkways, stairways, and coffee breaks has been documented by UPS engineers so as to cut wasted time. It's no accident, for instance, that all UPS drivers tap their horns when they approach a stop in hopes that the customer will hurry to the door seconds sooner. It's also no accident that all UPS drivers walk to a customer's door at the brisk pace of three feet per second and knock first lest seconds be lost searching for the doorbell.

Today's UPS drivers are following principles that were laid down more than 85 years ago by Frederick W. Taylor in his *Principles of Scientific Management*.[5] In this book, Taylor described how the scientific method could be used to define the "one best way" for a job to be done. In this section, we review his work.

As a mechanical engineer at the Midvale and Bethlehem Steel companies in Pennsylvania, Taylor was consistently appalled at the inefficiency of workers. Employees used vastly different techniques to do the same job. They were prone to "taking it easy" on the job. Taylor believed that worker output was only about one-third of what was possible. Therefore, he set out to correct the situation by applying the scientific method to jobs on the shop floor. He spent more than two decades pursuing with a passion the "one best way" for each job to be done.

It's important to understand what Taylor saw at Midvale Steel that aroused his determination to improve the way things were done in the plant. At the time, there were no clear concepts of worker and management responsibilities. Virtually no effective work standards existed. Employees purposely worked at a slow pace. Management decisions were of the "seat-of-the-pants" nature, based on hunch and intuition. Workers were placed on jobs with little or no concern for matching their abilities and aptitudes with the tasks they were required to do. Most important, management and workers considered themselves to be in continual conflict. Rather than cooperating to their mutual benefit, they perceived their relationship as a zero-sum game—any gain by one would be at the expense of the other.

Taylor sought to create a mental revolution among both the workers and management by defining clear guidelines for improving production efficiency. He defined four principles of management, listed in Exhibit A-1; he argued that following these principles would result in the prosperity of both management and workers. Workers would earn more pay, and management more profits.

Probably the most widely cited example of scientific management has been Taylor's pig iron experiment. The average daily output of 92-pound pigs

Exhibit A-1 Taylor's Four Principles of Management

1. Develop a science for each element of an individual's work. (Previously, workers used the "rule-of-thumb" method.)
2. Scientifically select and then train, teach, and develop the worker. (Previously, workers chose their own work and trained themselves as best they could.)
3. Heartily cooperate with the workers so as to ensure that all work is done in accordance with the principles of the science that has been developed. (Previously, management and workers were in continual conflict.)
4. Divide work and responsibility almost equally between management and workers. Management takes over all work for which it is better suited than the workers. (Previously, almost all the work and the greater part of the responsibility were thrown upon the workers.)

loaded onto rail cars was 12.5 tons per worker. Taylor was convinced that by scientifically analyzing the job to determine the one best way to load pig iron, the output could be increased to between 47 and 48 tons per day.

Taylor began his experiment by looking for a physically strong subject who placed a high value on the dollar. The individual Taylor chose was a big, strong Dutch immigrant, whom he called Schmidt. Schmidt, like the other loaders, earned $1.15 a day, which even at the turn of the century, was barely enough for a person to survive on. As the following quotation from Taylor's book demonstrates, Taylor used money—the opportunity to make $1.85 a day—as the primary means to get workers like Schmidt to do exactly as they were told:

> "Schmidt, are you a high-priced man?" "Vell, I don't know vat you mean." "Oh, yes you do. What I want to know is whether you are a high-priced man or not." "Vell, I don't know vat you mean." "Oh, come now, you answer my questions. What I want to find out is whether you are a high-priced man or one of these cheap fellows here. What I want to know is whether you want to earn $1.85 a day or whether you are satisfied with $1.15, just the same as all those cheap fellows are getting." "Did I vant $1.85 a day? Vas dot a high-priced man? Vell, yes. I vas a high-priced man."[6]

Using money to motivate Schmidt, Taylor went about having him load the pig irons, alternating various job factors to see what impact the changes had on Schmidt's daily output. For instance, on some days Schmidt would lift the pig irons by bending his knees, whereas on other days he would keep his legs straight and use his back. He experimented with rest periods, walking speed, carrying positions, and other variables. After a long period of scientifically trying various combinations of procedures, techniques, and tools, Taylor succeeded in obtaining the level of productivity he thought possible. By putting the right person on the job with the correct tools and equipment, by having the worker follow his instructions exactly, and by motivating the worker through the economic incentive of a significantly higher daily wage, Taylor was able to reach his 48-ton objective.

Another Taylor experiment dealt with shovel sizes. Taylor noticed that every worker in the plant used the same-sized shovel, regardless of the material he was moving. This made no sense to Taylor. If there was an optimum weight that would maximize a worker's shoveling output over an entire day, then Taylor thought the size of the shovel should vary depending on the weight of the material being moved. After extensive experimentation, Taylor found that 21 pounds was the optimum shovel capacity. To achieve this optimum weight, heavy material like iron ore would be moved with a small-faced shovel and light material like coke with a large-faced shovel. Based on Taylor's findings, supervisors would no longer merely tell a worker to "shovel that pile over there." Depending on the material to be moved, the supervisor would now have to determine the appropriate shovel size and assign that size to the worker. The result, of course, was again significant increases in worker output.

Using similar approaches in other jobs, Taylor was able to define the one best way for doing each job. He could then, after selecting the right people for the job, train them to do it precisely in this one best way. To motivate workers, he favored incentive wage plans. Overall, Taylor achieved consistent improvements in productivity in the range of 200 percent or more. He reaffirmed the role of managers to plan and control and that of workers to perform as they were instructed. *The Principles of Scientific Management*, as well as papers that Taylor wrote and presented, spread his ideas not only in the United States, but also in France, Germany, Russia, and Japan. One of the biggest boosts in interest in scientific management in the United States came during a 1910 hearing on railroad rates before the Interstate Commerce Commission. Appearing before the commission, an efficiency expert claimed that railroads could save a million dollars a day (equivalent to about $16 million a day in 1998 dollars) through the application of scientific management! The early acceptance of scientific management techniques by U.S. manufacturing companies, in fact, gave them a comparative advantage over foreign firms that made U.S. manufacturing efficiency the envy of the world—at least for 50 years or so!

Administrative Theory

Administrative theory describes efforts to define the universal functions that managers perform and principles that constitute good management practice. The major contributor to administrative theory was a French industrialist named Henri Fayol.

Writing at about the same time as Taylor, Fayol proposed that all managers perform five management functions: They plan, organize, command, coordinate, and control.[7] The importance of this simple insight is underlined when we acknowledge that almost every introductory management textbook today uses these same five functions, or a very close variant of them, as a basic framework for describing what managers do.

In addition, Fayol described the practice of management as something distinct from accounting, finance, production, distribution, and other typical business functions. He argued that management was an activity common to all human undertakings in business, in government, and even in the home. He then proceeded to state 14 principles of management that could be taught in schools and universities. These principles are shown in Exhibit A-2.

Structural Theory

While Taylor was concerned with management at the shop level (or what we today would describe as the job of a supervisor) and Fayol focused on general management functions, the German sociologist Max Weber (pronounced *Vay-*

Exhibit A-2 Fayol's 14 Principles of Management

1. *Division of Work.* This principle is the same as Adam Smith's "division of labor." Specialization increases output by making employees more efficient.

2. *Authority.* Managers must be able to give orders. Authority gives them this right. Along with authority, however, goes responsibility. Whenever authority is exercised, responsibility arises.

3. *Discipline.* Employees must obey and respect the rules that govern the organization. Good discipline is the result of effective leadership, a clear understanding between management and workers regarding the organization's rules, and the judicious use of penalties for infractions of the rules.

4. *Unity of Command.* Every employee should receive orders from only one superior.

5. *Unity of Direction.* Each group of organizational activities that have the same objective should be directed by one manager using one plan.

6. *Subordination of Individual Interests to the General Interests.* The interests of any one employee or group of employees should not take precedence over the interests of the organization as a whole.

7. *Remuneration.* Workers must be paid a fair wage for their services.

8. *Centralization.* Centralization refers to the degree to which subordinates are involved in decision making. Whether decision making is centralized (to management) or decentralized (to subordinates) is a question of proper proportion. The problem is to find the optimum degree of centralization for each situation.

9. *Scalar Chain.* The line of authority from top management to the lowest ranks represents the scalar chain. Communications should follow this chain. However, if following the chain creates delays, cross-communications can be allowed if agreed to by all parties and superiors are kept informed.

10. *Order.* People and materials should be in the right place at the right time.

11. *Equity.* Managers should be kind and fair to their subordinates.

12. *Stability of Tenure of Personnel.* High employee turnover is inefficient. Management should provide orderly personnel planning and ensure that replacements are available to fill vacancies.

13. *Initiative.* Employees who are allowed to originate and carry out plans will exert high levels of effort.

14. *Esprit de Corps.* Promoting team spirit will build harmony and unity within the organization.

ber) was developing a theory of authority structures and describing organizational activity as based on authority relations.[8] He was one of the first to look at management and organizational behavior from a structural perspective.

Weber described an ideal type of organization that he called a bureaucracy. Bureaucracy was a system characterized by division of labor, a clearly defined hierarchy, detailed rules and regulations, and impersonal relationships. Weber recognized that this "ideal bureaucracy" didn't exist in reality but, rather, represented a selective reconstruction of the real world. He meant it to be taken as a basis for theorizing about work and how work could be done in large groups. His theory became the design prototype for large organizations. The detailed features of Weber's ideal bureaucratic structure are outlined in Exhibit A-3.

Exhibit A-3 Weber's Ideal Bureaucracy

1. *Job Specialization.* Jobs are broken down into simple, routine, and well-defined tasks.
2. *Authority Hierarchy.* Offices or positions are organized in a hierarchy, each lower one being controlled and supervised by a higher one.
3. *Formal Selection.* All organizational members are to be selected on the basis of technical qualifications demonstrated by training, education, or formal examination.
4. *Formal Rules and Regulations.* To ensure uniformity and to regulate the actions of employees, managers must depend heavily on formal organizational rules.
5. *Impersonality.* Rules and controls are applied uniformly, avoiding involvement with personalities and personal preferences of employees.
6. *Career Orientation.* Managers are professional officials rather than owners of the units they manage. They work for fixed salaries and pursue their careers within the organization.

"Social Man" Theory

People like Taylor, Fayol, and Weber could be faulted for forgetting that human beings are the central core of every organization and that human beings are social animals. Mary Parker Follett and Chester Barnard were two theorists who saw the importance of the social aspects of organizations. Their ideas were born late in the scientific management period but didn't achieve any large degree of recognition until the 1930s.[9]

MARY PARKER FOLLETT Mary Parker Follett was one of the earliest writers to recognize that organizations could be viewed from the perspective of individual and group behavior.[10] A transitionalist writing during the time when scientific management dominated, Follett was a social philosopher who proposed more people-oriented ideas. Her ideas had clear implications for organizational behavior. Follett thought that organizations should be based on a group ethic rather than individualism. Individual potential, she argued, remained only potential until released through group association. The manager's job was to harmonize and coordinate group efforts. Managers and workers should view themselves as partners—as part of a common group. Therefore, managers should rely more on their expertise and knowledge than on the formal authority of their position to lead subordinates.

Follett's humanistic ideas have influenced the way we look at motivation, leadership, power, and authority today. In fact, Japanese organization and management styles, which came into vogue in North America and Europe in the late 1970s, are indebted to Follett. They place a heavy emphasis on group togetherness and team effort.

CHESTER BARNARD Like Henri Fayol, Chester Barnard was a practitioner. He joined the American Telephone and Telegraph system in 1909 and became president of New Jersey Bell in 1927. Barnard had read Weber and was influenced by his writings. But unlike Weber, who had a mechanistic and impersonal view of organizations, Barnard saw organizations as social systems that require human cooperation. He expressed his views in *The Functions of the Executive*,[11] published in 1938.

Barnard viewed organizations as made up of people who have interacting social relationships. Managers' major roles were to communicate and to stimulate subordinates to high levels of effort. A major part of an organization's success, as Barnard saw it, depended on obtaining cooperation from its personnel. Barnard also argued that success depended on maintaining good relations with people and institutions outside the organization with whom the organization regularly interacted. By recognizing the organization's dependence on investors, suppliers, customers, and other external constituencies, Barnard introduced the idea that managers had to examine the environment and then adjust the organization to maintain a state of equilibrium. So, for instance, regardless of how efficient an organization's production might be, if management failed to ensure a continuous input of materials and supplies or to find markets for its outputs, then the organization's survival would be threatened. Much of the current interest in how the environment affects organizations and their employees can be traced to ideas initially suggested by Barnard.

The Behavioral Era

The "people side" of organizations came into its own during the period we'll call the behavioral era. As we show, this era was marked by the human relations movement and the widespread application in organizations of behavioral science research. While this behavioral era really didn't begin to roll until the 1930s, two earlier events deserve brief mention because they played an important part in the application and development of organizational behavior. These are the birth of the "personnel office" around the turn of the century and the creation of the field of industrial psychology with the publication of Hugo Münsterberg's textbook in 1913.

The Birth of the "Personnel Office"

In response to the growth of trade unionism at the turn of the century, a few firms—for example, H.J. Heinz, Colorado Fuel & Iron, and International Harvester—created the position of "welfare secretary." Welfare secretaries were supposed to assist workers by suggesting improvements in working conditions, housing, medical care, educational facilities, and recreation. These people, who were the forerunners of today's personnel or human resource management directors, acted as a buffer between the organization and its employees. The B. F. Goodrich Co. developed the first employment department in 1900, but its responsibilities consisted only of hiring. In 1902, the National Cash Register Company established the first comprehensive labor department responsible for wage administration, grievances, employment and working conditions, health conditions, recordkeeping, and worker improvement.

The Birth of Industrial Psychology

Hugo Münsterberg created the field of industrial psychology with the publication of his text *Psychology and Industrial Efficiency*[12] in 1913. In it, he argued for the scientific study of human behavior to identify general patterns and to explain individual differences. Interestingly, Münsterberg saw a link between scientific management and industrial psychology. Both sought increased efficiency through scientific work analyses and through better alignment of individual skills and abilities with the demands of various jobs.

Münsterberg suggested the use of psychological tests to improve employee selection, the value of learning theory in the development of training methods, and the study of human behavior in order to understand what techniques are most effective for motivating workers. Much of our current knowledge of selection techniques, employee training, work design, and motivation is built on Münsterberg's work.

The Magna Carta of Labor

Following the stock market crash of 1929, the United States and much of the world's economy entered the Great Depression. To help relieve the effects of the depression on the U.S. labor force, President Franklin Roosevelt supported the Wagner Act, which was passed in 1935. This act recognized unions as the authorized representatives of workers, able to bargain collectively with employers in the interests of their members. The Wagner Act would prove to be the Magna Carta of labor. It legitimized the role of trade unions and encouraged rapid growth in union membership. In response to this legislation, managers in industry became much more open to finding new ways to handle their employees. Having lost the battle to keep unions out of their factories, management began to try to improve working conditions and seek better relations with its workforce. A set of studies done at Western Electric's Hawthorne plant would be the prime stimulus for the human relations movement that swept American industry from the late 1930s through the 1950s.

Human Relations

The essence of the human relations movement was the belief that the key to higher productivity in organizations was increasing employee satisfaction. In addition to the Hawthorne studies, three people played important roles in conveying the message of human relations: Dale Carnegie, Abraham Maslow, and Douglas McGregor. In this section, we briefly review each man's contribution. But first, we'll briefly describe the very influential Hawthorne studies.

THE HAWTHORNE STUDIES Without question, the most important contribution to the human relations movement within organizational behavior came out of the Hawthorne studies undertaken at the Western Electric Company's Hawthorne Works in Cicero, Illinois. These studies, originally begun in 1924 but eventually expanded and carried on through the early 1930s, were initially devised by Western Electric industrial engineers to examine the effect of various illumination levels on worker productivity. Control and experimental groups were established. The experimental group was presented with varying illumination intensities, while the control group worked under a constant intensity. The engineers had expected individual output to be directly related to the intensity of light. However, they found that as the light level was increased in the experimental group, output for both groups rose. To the surprise of the engineers, as the light level was dropped in the experimental group, productivity continued to increase in both groups. In fact, a productivity decrease was observed in the experimental group only when the light intensity had been reduced to that of moonlight. The engineers concluded that illumination intensity was not directly related to group productivity, but they could not explain the behavior they had witnessed.

The Western Electric engineers asked Harvard professor Elton Mayo and his associates in 1927 to join the study as consultants. Thus began a relationship that would last through 1932 and encompass numerous experiments covering the redesign of jobs, changes in the length of the workday and workweek, introduction of rest periods, and individual versus group wage plans.[13] For example, one experiment was designed to evaluate the effect of a group piecework incentive pay system on group productivity. The results indicated that the incentive plan had less effect on a worker's output than did group pressure and acceptance and the concomitant security. Social norms or standards of the group, therefore, were concluded to be the key determinants of individual work behavior.

Scholars generally agree that the Hawthorne studies had a large and dramatic impact on the direction of organizational behavior and management practice. Mayo's conclusions were that behavior and sentiments were closely related, that group influences significantly affected individual behavior, that group standards established individual worker output, and that money was less a factor in determining output than were group standards, group sentiments, and security. These conclusions led to a new emphasis on the human factor in the functioning of organizations and the attainment of their goals. They also led to increased paternalism by management.

The Hawthorne studies have not been without critics. Attacks have been made on their procedures, analyses of findings, and the conclusions they drew.[14] However, from a historical standpoint, it's of little importance whether the studies were academically sound or their conclusions justified. What is important is that they stimulated an interest in human factors.

DALE CARNEGIE Dale Carnegie's book *How to Win Friends and Influence People*[15] was read by millions during the 1930s, 1940s, and 1950s. During this same period, tens of thousands of managers and aspiring managers attended his management speeches and seminars. So Carnegie's ideas deserve attention because of the wide audience they commanded.

Carnegie's essential theme was that the way to success was through winning the cooperation of others. He advised his audience to: (1) make others feel important through a sincere appreciation of their efforts; (2) strive to make a good first impression; (3) win people to their way of thinking by letting others do the talking, being sympathetic, and "never telling a man he is wrong"; and (4) change people by praising their good traits and giving the offender the opportunity to save face.[16]

ABRAHAM MASLOW Few students of college age have not been exposed to the ideas of Abraham Maslow. A humanistic psychologist, Maslow proposed a theoretical hierarchy of five needs: physiological, safety, social, esteem, and self-actualization.[17] From a motivation standpoint, Maslow argued that each step in the hierarchy must be satisfied before the next can be activated, and that once a need was substantially satisfied, it no longer motivated behavior. Moreover, he believed that self-actualization—that is, achieving one's full potential—was the summit of a human being's existence. Managers who accepted Maslow's hierarchy attempted to alter their organizations and management practices to reduce barriers to employees' self-actualization.

DOUGLAS MCGREGOR Douglas McGregor is best known for his formulation of two sets of assumptions—Theory X and Theory Y—about human nature.[18] Briefly, Theory X rests on an essentially negative view of people. It assumes that they have little ambition, dislike work, want to avoid responsibility, and need to be closely directed to work effectively. Theory Y, on the other hand, rests on a positive view of people. It assumes they can exercise self-direction, accept responsibility, and consider work to be as natural as rest or play. McGregor personally believed that Theory Y assumptions best captured the true nature of workers and should guide management practice. As a result, he argued that managers should free up their employees to unleash their full creative and productive potential.

Behavioral Science Theorists

The final category within the behavioral era encompasses a group of researchers who, as Taylor did in scientific management, relied on the scientific method for the study of organizational behavior. Unlike members of the human relations movement, the behavioral science theorists engaged in objective research of human behavior in organizations. They carefully attempted to keep their personal beliefs out of their work. They sought to develop rigorous research designs that could be replicated by other behavioral scientists in the hope that a science of organizational behavior could be built.

A full review of the contributions made by behavioral science theorists would cover hundreds of pages, since their work makes up a large part of today's foundations of organizational behavior. But to give you the flavor of their work, we'll briefly summarize the contributions of a few of the major theorists.

JACOB MORENO Jacob Moreno created an analytical technique called sociometry for studying group interactions.[19] Members of a group were asked whom they liked or disliked, and whom they wished to work with or not work with. From these data, collected in interviews, Moreno was able to construct sociograms that identified attraction, repulsion, and indifference patterns among group members. Moreno's sociometric analysis has been used in organizations to create cohesive and high-performing work teams.

B.F. SKINNER Few behavioral scientists' names are more familiar to the general public than that of B.F. Skinner. His research on operant conditioning and behavior modification had a significant effect on the design of organizational training programs and reward systems.[20]

Essentially, Skinner demonstrated that behavior is a function of its consequences. He found that people will most likely engage in desired behavior if they are rewarded for doing so; these rewards are most effective if they immediately follow the desired response; and behavior that is not rewarded, or is punished, is less likely to be repeated.

DAVID MCCLELLAND Psychologist David McClelland tested the strength of individual achievement motivation by asking subjects to look at a set of somewhat ambiguous pictures and to write their own story about each picture. Based on these projective tests, McClelland found he was able to differentiate people with a high need to achieve—individuals who had a strong desire to succeed or achieve in relation to a set of standards—from people with a low need to achieve.[21] His research has been instrumental in helping organizations better match people with jobs and in redesigning jobs for high achievers so as to maximize their motivation potential. In addition, McClelland and his associates have successfully trained individuals to increase their achievement drive. For instance, in India, people who underwent achievement training worked longer hours, initiated more new business ventures, made greater investments in productive assets, employed a larger number of employees, and saw a greater increase in their gross incomes than did a similar group who did not undergo achievement training.

FRED FIEDLER Leadership is one of the most important and extensively researched topics in organizational behavior. The work of Fred Fiedler on the subject is significant for its emphasis on the situational aspects of leadership as well as for its attempt to develop a comprehensive theory of leadership behavior.[22]

From the mid-1960s through the late 1970s, Fiedler's contingency model dominated leadership research. He developed a questionnaire to measure an individual's inherent leadership orientation and identified three contingency variables that, he argued, determined what type of leader behavior is most effective. In testing his model, Fiedler and his associates studied hundreds of groups. Dozens of researchers have attempted to replicate his results. Although some of the predictions from the model have not stood up well under closer analysis, Fiedler's model has been a major influence on current thinking and research about leadership.

FREDERICK HERZBERG With the possible exception of the Hawthorne studies, no single stream of research has had a greater impact on undermining the recommendations of scientific management than the work of Frederick Herzberg.[23]

Herzberg sought an answer to the question: What do individuals want from their jobs? He asked hundreds of people that question in the late 1950s, and then carefully analyzed their responses. He concluded that people preferred jobs that offered opportunities for recognition, achievement, responsibility, and growth. Managers who concerned themselves with things like company policies, employee pay, creating narrow and repetitive jobs, and developing favorable working conditions might placate their workers, but they wouldn't motivate them. According to Herzberg, if managers want to motivate their people, they should redesign jobs to allow workers to perform more and varied tasks. Much of the current interest in enriching jobs and improving the quality of work life can be traced to Herzberg's research.

J. RICHARD HACKMAN AND GREG OLDHAM While Herzberg's conclusions were greeted with enthusiasm, the methodology he used for arriving at those conclusions was far less enthusiastically embraced. It would be the work of J. Richard Hackman and Greg Oldham in the 1970s that would provide an explanation of how job factors influence employee motivation and satisfaction, and would offer a valid framework for analyzing jobs.[24] Hackman and Oldham's research also uncovered the core job dimensions—skill variety, task identity, task significance, autonomy, and feedback—that have stood up well as guides in the design of jobs. More specifically, Hackman and Oldham found that among individuals with strong growth needs, jobs that score high on these five core dimensions lead to high employee performance and satisfaction.

OB Today: A Contingency Perspective

We've attempted to demonstrate in this appendix that the present state of organizational behavior encompasses ideas introduced dozens, and sometimes hundreds, of years ago. So don't think of one era's concepts as *replacing* an earlier era's; rather, view them as *extensions* and *modifications* of earlier ideas. As United Parcel Service demonstrates, many of Taylor's scientific management principles can be applied today with impressive results. Of course, that doesn't mean that those principles will work as well in other organizations. If there is anything we've learned over the last quarter of a century, it's that few ideas—no matter how attractive—are applicable to *all* organizations or to *all* jobs or to *all* types of employees. Today, organizational behavior must be studied and applied in a contingency framework.

Baseball fans know that a batter doesn't *always* try for a home run. It depends on the score, the inning, whether runners are on base, and similar contingency variables. Similarly, you can't say that students always learn more in small classes than in large ones. An extensive body of educational research tells us that *contingency* factors such as course content and teaching style of the instructor influence the relationship between class size and learning effectiveness. Applied to organizational behavior, contingency theory recognizes that there is no "one best way" to manage people in organizations and no single set of simple principles that can be applied universally.[25]

A contingency approach to the study of OB is intuitively logical. Why? Because organizations obviously differ in size, objectives, and environmental uncertainty. Similarly, employees differ in values, attitudes, needs, and experiences. So it would be surprising to find that there are universally applicable principles that work in *all* situations. But, of course, it's one thing to say "it all depends" and another to say *what* it all depends upon.

The most popular OB topics for research investigation in recent years have been theories of motivation, leadership, work design, and job satisfaction.[26] But while the 1960s and 1970s saw the development of new theories, the emphasis since has been on refining existing theories, clarifying previous assumptions, and identifying relevant contingency variables.[27] That is, researchers have been trying to identify the "what" variables and which ones are relevant for understanding various behavioral phenomena. This essentially reflects the maturing of OB as a scientific discipline. The near-term future of OB research is likely to continue to focus on fine-tuning current theories so as to better help us understand those situations where they're most likely to be useful.

Summary

While the seeds of organizational behavior were planted more than 200 years ago, current OB theory and practice are essentially products of the twentieth century.

Frederick Taylor's principles of scientific management were instrumental in engineering precision and standardization into people's jobs. Henri Fayol defined the universal functions that all managers perform and the principles that constitute good management practice. Max Weber developed a theory of authority structures and described organizational activity based on authority relations.

The "people side" of organizations came into its own in the 1930s, predominately as a result of the Hawthorne studies. These studies led to a new emphasis on the human factor in organizations and increased paternalism by management. In the late 1950s, managers' attention was caught by the ideas of people like Abraham Maslow and Douglas McGregor, who proposed that organization structures and management practices had to be altered so as to bring out the full productive potential of employees. Motivation and leadership theories offered by David McClelland, Fred Fiedler, Frederick Herzberg, and other behavioral scientists during the 1960s and 1970s provided managers with still greater insights into employee behavior.

Almost all contemporary management and organizational behavior concepts are contingency based. That is, they provide various recommendations dependent upon situational factors. As a maturing discipline, current OB research is emphasizing the refinement of existing theories.

Appendix B

RESEARCH IN ORGANIZATIONAL BEHAVIOR

A few years back, a friend was all excited because he had read about the findings from a research study that finally, once and for all, resolved the question of what it takes to make it to the top in a large corporation. I doubted there was any simple answer to this question but, not wanting to dampen his enthusiasm, I asked him to tell me of what he had read. The answer, according to my friend, was *participation in college athletics*. To say I was skeptical of his claim is a gross understatement, so I asked him to tell me more.

The study encompassed 1,700 successful senior executives at the 500 largest U.S. corporations. The researchers found that half of these executives had played varsity-level college sports.[1] My friend, who happens to be good with statistics, informed me that since fewer than 2 percent of all college students participate in intercollegiate athletics, the probability of this finding occurring by mere chance is less than one in 10 million! He concluded his analysis by telling me that, based on this research, I should encourage my management students to get into shape and to make one of the varsity teams.

My friend was somewhat perturbed when I suggested that his conclusions were likely to be flawed. These executives were all males who attended college in the 1940s and 1950s. Would his advice be meaningful to females in the 1990s? These executives also weren't your typical college students. For the most part, they had attended elite private colleges like Princeton and Lehigh, where a large proportion of the student body participates in intercollegiate sports. And these "jocks" hadn't necessarily played football or basketball; many had participated in golf, tennis, baseball, cross-country running, crew, rugby, and similar minor sports. Moreover, maybe the researchers had confused the direction of causality. That is, maybe individuals with the motivation and ability to make it to the top of a large corporation are drawn to competitive activities like college athletics.

My friend was guilty of misusing research data. Of course, he is not alone. We are all continually bombarded with reports of experiments that link certain substances to cancer in mice and surveys that show changing attitudes toward sex among college students, for example. Many of these studies are carefully designed, with great caution taken to note the implications and limitations of the findings. But some studies are poorly designed, making their conclusions at best suspect, and at worst meaningless.

Rather than attempting to make you a researcher, the purpose of this appendix is to increase your awareness as a consumer of behavioral research. A knowledge of research methods will allow you to appreciate more fully the care in data collection that underlies the information and conclusions presented in this text. Moreover, an understanding of research methods will make you a more skilled evaluator of those OB studies you will encounter in business and professional journals. So an appreciation of behavioral research is important because (1) it's the foundation upon which the theories in this text are built, and (2) it will benefit you in future years when you read reports of research and attempt to assess their value.

Purpose of Research

Research is concerned with the systematic gathering of information. Its purpose is to help us in our search for the truth. While we will never find ultimate truth—in our case, that would be to know precisely how any person would behave in any organizational context—ongoing research adds to our body of OB knowledge by supporting some theories, contradicting others, and suggesting new theories to replace those that fail to gain support.

Research Terminology

Researchers have their own vocabulary for communicating among themselves and with outsiders. The following briefly defines some of the more popular terms you're likely to encounter in behavioral science studies.[2]

VARIABLE   A *variable* is any general characteristic that can be measured and that changes in either amplitude, intensity, or both. Some examples of OB variables found in this text are job satisfaction, employee productivity, work stress, ability, personality, and group norms.

HYPOTHESIS   A tentative explanation of the relationship between two or more variables is called a *hypothesis*. My friend's statement that participation in college athletics leads to a top executive position in a large corporation is an example of a hypothesis. Until confirmed by empirical research, a hypothesis remains only a *tentative* explanation.

DEPENDENT VARIABLE   A *dependent variable* is a response that is affected by an independent variable. In terms of the hypothesis, it is the variable that the researcher is interested in explaining. Referring back to our opening example, the dependent variable in my friend's hypothesis was executive succession. In organizational behavior research, the most popular dependent variables are productivity, absenteeism, turnover, job satisfaction, and organizational commitment.[3]

INDEPENDENT VARIABLE   An *independent variable* is the presumed cause of some change in the dependent variable. Participating in varsity athletics was the independent variable in my friend's hypothesis. Popular independent variables studied by OB researchers include intelligence, personality, job satisfaction, experience, motivation, reinforcement patterns, leadership style, reward allocations, selection methods, and organization design.

You may have noticed we said that job satisfaction is frequently used by OB researchers as both a dependent and an independent variable. This is not an error. It merely reflects that the label given to a variable depends on its place in the hypothesis. In the statement "Increases in job satisfaction lead to reduced turnover," job satisfaction is an independent variable. However, in the statement "Increases in money lead to higher job satisfaction," job satisfaction becomes a dependent variable.

MODERATING VARIABLE A *moderating variable* abates the effect of the independent variable on the dependent variable. It might also be thought of as the contingency variable: If X (independent variable), then Y (dependent variable) will occur, but only under conditions Z (moderating variable). To translate this into a real-life example, we might say that if we increase the amount of direct supervision in the work area (X), then there will be a change in worker productivity (Y), but this effect will be moderated by the complexity of the tasks being performed (Z).

CAUSALITY A hypothesis, by definition, implies a relationship. That is, it implies a presumed cause and effect. This direction of cause and effect is called *causality*. Changes in the independent variable are assumed to *cause* changes in the dependent variable. However, in behavioral research, it's possible to make an incorrect assumption of causality when relationships are found. For example, early behavioral scientists found a relationship between employee satisfaction and productivity. They concluded that a happy worker was a productive worker. Follow-up research has supported the relationship, but disconfirmed the direction of the arrow. The evidence more correctly suggests that high productivity leads to satisfaction rather than the other way around.

CORRELATION COEFFICIENT It's one thing to know that there is a relationship between two or more variables. It's another to know the *strength* of that relationship. The term *correlation coefficient* is used to indicate that strength, and is expressed as a number between -1.00 (a perfect negative relationship) to $+1.00$ (a perfect positive correlation).

When two variables vary directly with one another, the correlation will be expressed as a positive number. When they vary inversely—that is, one increases as the other decreases—the correlation will be expressed as a negative number. If the two variables vary independently of each other, we say that the correlation between them is zero.

For example, a researcher might survey a group of employees to determine the satisfaction of each with his or her job. Then, using company absenteeism reports, the researcher could correlate the job satisfaction scores against individual attendance records to determine whether employees who are more satisfied with their jobs have better attendance records than their counterparts who indicated lower job satisfaction. Let's suppose the researcher found a correlation coefficient between satisfaction and attendance of $+0.50$. Would that be a strong association? There is, unfortunately, no precise numerical cutoff separating strong and weak relationships. A standard statistical test would need to be applied to determine whether or not the relationship was a significant one.

A final point needs to be made before we move on: A correlation coefficient measures only the strength of association between two variables. A high value does *not* imply causality. The length of women's skirts and stock market prices, for instance, have long been noted to be highly correlated, but one should be careful not to infer that a causal relationship between the two exists. In this instance, the high correlation is more happenstance than predictive.

THEORY The final term we introduce in this section is *theory*. Theory describes a set of systematically interrelated concepts or hypotheses that purports to explain and predict phenomena. In OB, theories are also frequently referred to as *models*. We use the two terms interchangeably.

There are no shortages of theories in OB. For instance, we have theories to describe what motivates people, the most effective leadership styles, the best way to resolve conflicts, and how people acquire power. In some cases, we have half a dozen or more separate theories that purport to explain and predict a given phenomenon. In such cases, is one right and the others wrong? No! They tend to reflect science at work—researchers testing previous theories, modifying them, and, when appropriate, proposing new models that may prove to have higher explanatory and predictive powers. Multiple theories attempting to explain common phenomena merely attest that OB is an active discipline, still growing and evolving.

Evaluating Research

As a potential consumer of behavioral research, you should follow the dictum of *caveat emptor*—let the buyer beware! In evaluating any research study, you need to ask three questions.[4]

Is it valid? Is the study actually measuring what it claims to be measuring? Many psychological tests have been discarded by employers in recent years because they have not been found to be valid measures of the applicants' ability to successfully do a given job. But the validity issue is relevant to all research studies. So, if you find a study that links cohesive work teams with higher productivity, you want to know how each of these variables was measured and whether it is actually measuring what it is supposed to be measuring.

Is it reliable? Reliability refers to consistency of measurement. If you were to have your height measured every day with a wooden yardstick, you'd get highly reliable results. On the other hand, if you were measured each day by an elastic tape measure, there would probably be considerable disparity between your height measurements from one day to the next. Your height, of course, doesn't change from day to day. The variability is due to the unreliability of the measuring device. So if a company asked a group of its employees to complete a reliable job satisfaction questionnaire, and then repeat the questionnaire six months later, we'd expect the results to be very similar—provided nothing changed in the interim that might significantly affect employee satisfaction.

Is it generalizable? Are the results of the research study generalizable to groups of individuals other than those who participated in the original study? Be aware, for example, of the limitations that might exist in research that uses college students as subjects. Are the findings in such studies generalizable to full-time employees in real jobs? Similarly, how generalizable to the overall work population are the results from a study that assesses job stress among ten nuclear power plant engineers in the hamlet of Mahone Bay, Nova Scotia?

Research Design

Doing research is an exercise in trade-offs. Richness of information typically comes with reduced generalizability. The more a researcher seeks to control for confounding variables, the less realistic his or her results are likely to be. High precision, generalizability, and control almost always translate into higher costs. When researchers make choices about whom they'll study, where their research will be done, the methods they'll use to collect data, and so on, they must make some concessions. Good research designs are not perfect, but they do carefully reflect the questions being addressed. Keep these facts in mind as we review the strengths and weaknesses of five popular research designs: case studies, field surveys, laboratory experiments, field experiments, and aggregate quantitative reviews.

CASE STUDY You pick up a copy of Soichiro Honda's autobiography. In it he describes his impoverished childhood; his decisions to open a small garage, assemble motorcycles, and eventually build automobiles; and how this led to the creation of one of the largest and most successful corporations in the world. Or you're in a business class and the instructor distributes a 50-page handout covering two companies: Compaq Computer and Digital Equipment Corporation (DEC). The handout details the two firms' histories, describes their product lines, production facilities, management philosophies, and marketing strategies, and includes copies of their recent balance sheets and income statements. The instructor asks the class members to read the handout, analyze the data, and determine why Compaq has been more successful in recent years than DEC.

Soichiro Honda's autobiography and the Compaq and DEC handouts are case studies. Drawn from real-life situations, case studies present an in-depth analysis of one setting. They are thorough descriptions, rich in details about an individual, a group, or an organization. The primary source of information in case studies is obtained through observation, occasionally backed up by interviews and a review of records and documents.

Case studies have their drawbacks. They're open to the perceptual bias and subjective interpretations of the observer. The reader of a case is captive to what the observer/case writer chooses to include and exclude. Cases also trade off generalizability for depth of information and richness of detail. Since it's always dangerous to generalize from a sample of one, case studies make it difficult to prove or reject a hypothesis. On the other hand, you can't ignore the in-depth analysis that cases often provide. They are an excellent device for initial exploratory research and for evaluating real-life problems in organizations.

FIELD SURVEY A questionnaire made up of approximately a dozen items sought to examine the content of supervisory training programs in billion-dollar corporations. Copies of the questionnaire, with a cover letter explaining the nature of the study, were mailed to the corporate training officers at 250 corporations randomly selected from the *Fortune* 500 list; 155 officers responded to it. The results of this survey found, among other things, that the most common training topic was providing performance evaluation feedback to employees (92 percent of the surveyed companies selected this topic as the most common aspect of their program). This was closely followed by developing effective delegation skills (90 percent) and listening skills (83 percent).[5]

The preceding study illustrates a typical field survey. A sample of respondents (in this case, 250 corporate training officers) was selected to represent a larger group that was under examination (corporate training officers in *Fortune* 500 firms). The respondents were then surveyed using a questionnaire or interviewed to collect data on particular characteristics (the content of supervisory training programs) of interest to the researcher. The standardization of response items allows for data to be easily quantified, analyzed, and summarized, and for the researcher to make inferences from the representative sample about the larger population.

The field survey provides economies for doing research. It's less costly to sample a population than to obtain data from every member of that population. Moreover, as the supervisory training program example illustrates, field surveys provide an efficient way to find out how people feel about issues or how they say they behave. These data can then be easily quantified. But the field survey has a number of potential weaknesses. First, mailed questionnaires rarely obtain 100 percent returns. Low response rates call into question whether conclusions based on respondents' answers are generalizable to non-respondents. Second, the format is better at tapping respondents' attitudes and perceptions than behaviors. Third, responses can suffer from social desirability; that is, people saying what they think the researcher wants to hear. Fourth, since field surveys are designed to focus on specific issues, they're a relatively poor means of acquiring depth of information. Finally, the quality of the generalizations is largely a factor of the population chosen. Responses from executives at *Fortune* 500 firms, for instance, tell us nothing about small- or medium-sized firms or not-for-profit organizations. In summary, even a well-designed field survey trades off depth of information for breadth, generalizability, and economic efficiencies.

LABORATORY EXPERIMENT The following study is a classic example of the laboratory experiment. A researcher, Stanley Milgram, wondered how far individuals would go in following commands. If subjects were placed in the role of a teacher in a learning experiment and told by an experimenter to administer a shock to a learner each time that learner made a mistake, would the subjects follow the commands of the experimenter? Would their willingness to comply decrease as the intensity of the shock was increased?

To test these hypotheses, Milgram hired a set of subjects. Each was led to believe that the experiment was to investigate the effect of punishment on memory. Their job was to act as teachers and administer punishment whenever the learner made a mistake on the learning test.

Punishment was administered by an electric shock. The subject sat in front of a shock generator with 30 levels of shock—beginning at zero and progressing in 15-volt increments to a high of 450 volts. The demarcations of these positions ranged from "Slight Shock" at 15 volts to "Danger: Severe Shock" at 450 volts. To increase the realism of the experiment, the subjects received a sample shock of 45 volts and saw the learner—a pleasant, mild-mannered man about 50 years old—strapped into an "electric chair" in an adjacent room. Of course, the learner was an actor, and the electric shocks were phony, but the subjects didn't know this.

Taking his seat in front of the shock generator, the subject was directed to begin at the lowest shock level and to increase the shock intensity to the next level each time the learner made a mistake or failed to respond.

When the test began, the shock intensity rose rapidly because the learner made many errors. The subject got verbal feedback from the learner: At 75 volts, the learner began to grunt and moan; at 150 volts, he demanded to be released from the experiment; at 180 volts, he cried out that he could no longer stand the pain; and at 300 volts, he insisted that he be let out, yelled about his heart condition, screamed, and then failed to respond to further questions.

Most subjects protested and, fearful they might kill the learner if the increased shocks were to bring on a heart attack, insisted they could not go on with their job. Hesitations or protests by the subject were met by the experimenter's statement, "You have no choice, you must go on! Your job is to punish the learner's mistakes." Of course, the subjects did have a choice. All they had to do was stand up and walk out.

The majority of the subjects dissented. But dissension isn't synonymous with disobedience. Sixty-two percent of the subjects increased the shock level to the maximum of 450 volts. The average level of shock administered by the remaining 38 percent was nearly 370 volts.[6]

In a laboratory experiment such as that conducted by Milgram, an artificial environment is created by the researcher. Then the researcher manipulates an independent variable under controlled conditions. Finally, since all other things are held equal, the researcher is able to conclude that any change in the dependent variable is due to the manipulation or change imposed on the independent variable. Note that, because of the controlled conditions, the researcher is able to imply causation between the independent and dependent variables.

The laboratory experiment trades off realism and generalizability for precision and control. It provides a high degree of control over variables and precise measurement of those variables. But findings from laboratory studies are often difficult to generalize to the real world of work. This is because the artificial laboratory rarely duplicates the intricacies and nuances of real organizations. Additionally, many laboratory experiments deal with phenomena that cannot be reproduced or applied to real-life situations.

FIELD EXPERIMENT The following is an example of a field experiment. The management of a large company is interested in determining the impact that a four-day workweek would have on employee absenteeism. To be more specific, management wants to know if employees working four ten-hour days have lower absence rates than similar employees working the traditional five-day week of eight hours each day. Because the company is large, it has a number of manufacturing plants that employ essentially similar workforces. Two of these are chosen for the experiment, both located in the greater Cleveland area. Obviously, it would not be appropriate to compare two similar-sized plants if one is in rural Mississippi and the other is in urban Copenhagen because factors such as national culture, transportation, and weather might be more likely to explain any differences found than changes in the number of days worked per week.

In one plant, the experiment was put into place—workers began the four-day week. At the other plant, which became the control group, no changes were made in the employees' five-day week. Absence data were gathered from the company's records at both locations for a period of 18 months. This extended time period lessened the possibility that any results would be distorted by the mere novelty of changes being implemented in the experimental plant. After 18 months, management found that absenteeism had dropped by 40 percent at the experimental plant, and by only 6 percent in the control plant. Because of the design of this study, management believed that the larger drop in absences at the experimental plant was due to the introduction of the compressed workweek.

The field experiment is similar to the laboratory experiment, except it is conducted in a real organization. The natural setting is more realistic than the laboratory setting, and this enhances validity but hinders control. Additionally, unless control groups are maintained, there can be a loss of control if extraneous forces intervene—for example, an employee strike, a major layoff, or a corporate restructuring. Maybe the greatest concern with field studies has to do with organizational selection bias. Not all organizations are going to allow outside researchers to come in and study their employees and operations. This is especially true of organizations that have serious problems. Therefore, since most published studies in OB are done by outside researchers, the selection bias might work toward publication of studies conducted almost exclusively at successful and well-managed organizations.

Our general conclusion is that, of the four research designs we've discussed, the field experiment typically provides the most valid and generalizable findings and, except for its high cost, trades off the least to get the most.

AGGREGATE QUANTITATIVE REVIEWS What relationship, if any, is there between employee gender and occupational stress? There have been a number of individual field surveys and qualitative reviews of these surveys that have sought to throw light on this question. Unfortunately, these various studies produced conflicting results.

To try to reconcile these conflicts, researchers at Michigan State University identified all published correlations between gender and stress in work-related contexts.[7] After discarding reports that had inadequate information, nonquantitative data, and failed to include both men and women in their sample, the researchers narrowed their set to 15 studies that included data on 9,439 individuals. Using an aggregating technique called *meta-analysis*, the researchers were able to integrate the studies quantitatively and conclude that there are no differences in experienced stress between men and women in a work setting.

The gender–stress review done by the Michigan State researchers illustrates the use of meta-analysis, a quantitative form of literature review that enables researchers to look at validity findings from a comprehensive set of individual studies, and then apply a formula to them to determine if they consistently produced similar results.[8] If results prove to be consistent, it allows researchers to conclude more confidently that validity is generalizable. Meta-analysis is a means for overcoming the potentially imprecise interpretations of qualitative reviews. Additionally, the technique enables researchers to identify potential moderating variables between an independent and a dependent variable.

In the past dozen years, there's been a surge in the popularity of this research method. Why? It appears to offer a more objective means for doing traditional literature reviews. While the use of meta-analysis requires researchers to make a number of judgment calls, which can introduce a considerable amount of subjectivity into the process, there is no arguing that meta-analysis reviews have now become widespread in the OB literature.

Ethics in Research

Researchers are not always tactful or candid with subjects when they do their studies. For instance, questions in field surveys may be perceived as embarrassing by respondents or as an invasion of privacy. Also, researchers in laboratory studies have been known to deceive participants as to the true purpose of their experiment "because they felt deception was necessary to get honest responses."[9]

The "learning experiments" conducted by Stanley Milgram were widely criticized by psychologists on ethical grounds. He lied to subjects, telling them his study was investigating learning, when, in fact, he was concerned with obedience. The shock machine he used was a fake. Even the "learner" was an accomplice of Milgram's who had been trained to act as if he were hurt and in pain.

Professional associations like the American Psychological Association, the American Sociological Association, and the Academy of Management have published formal guidelines for the conduct of research. Yet the ethical debate continues. On one side are those who argue that strict ethical controls can damage the scientific validity of an experiment and cripple future research. Deception, for example, is often necessary to avoid contaminating results. Moreover, proponents of minimizing ethical controls note that few subjects have been appreciably harmed by deceptive experiments. Even in Milgram's highly manipulative experiment, only 1.3 percent of the subjects reported negative feelings about their experience. The other side of this debate focuses on the rights of participants. Those favoring strict ethical controls argue that no procedure should ever be emotionally or physically distressing to subjects, and that, as professionals, researchers are obliged to be completely honest with their subjects and to protect the subjects' privacy at all costs.

Now, let's take a look at a sampling of ethical questions relating to research. Do you think Milgram's experiment was unethical? Would you judge it unethical for a company to anonymously survey its employees with mail questionnaires on their intentions to quit their present job? Would your answer be any different if the company coded the survey responses to identify those who didn't reply so they could send them follow-up questionnaires? Would it be unethical for management to hide a video camera on the production floor to study group interaction patterns (with the goal of using the data to design more effective work teams) without first telling employees that they were subjects of research?

Summary

The subject of organizational behavior is composed of a large number of theories that are research based. Research studies, when cumulatively integrated, become theories, and theories are proposed and followed by research studies designed to validate them. The concepts that make up OB, therefore, are only as valid as the research that supports them.

The topics and issues in this text are for the most part largely research derived. They represent the result of systematic information gathering rather than merely hunch, intuition, or opinion. This doesn't mean, of course, that we have all the answers to OB issues. Many require far more corroborating evidence. The generalizability of others is limited by the research methods used. But new information is being created and published at an accelerated rate. To keep up with the lastest findings, we strongly encourage you to regularly review the latest research in organizational behavior. The more academic work can be found in journals such as the *Academy of Management Journal, Academy of Management Review, Administrative Science Quarterly, Human Relations, Journal of Applied Psychology, Journal of Management*, and *Leadership Quarterly*. For more practical interpretations of OB research findings, you may want to read the *Academy of Management Executive, California Management Review, Harvard Business Review, Organizational Dynamics*, and the *Sloan Management Review*.

SCORING KEYS FOR "LEARNING ABOUT YOURSELF" EXERCISES

Chapter 1: How Does Your Ethical Behavior Rate?

Give yourself 1 point for each N answer, 2 points for each S answer, 3 points for each O answer, and 4 points for each R answer. Now total your score. It will fall somewhere between 15 and 60 points. Since all of the items in this exercise are considered unethical, the lower your score the higher your ethical standards.

Chapter 2: What's Your Learning Style?

This instrument measures cognitive, affective and motivational elements that affect learning. While all 13 items did not prove statistically meaningful, it is possible to identify your dominant or preferred learning style from this questionnaire.

Pragmatic learners prefer to learn applications first and then learn the theory underlying applications. Real-world problem-solving is your forte. To calculate your pragmatic score, add up your circled answers to questions 1 and 5, and reverse the number for question 11 (5 becomes 1, 4 becomes 2, etc.).

Discovery learners prefer instructors to allow them to discover the underlying principles rather than tell them the principles in a lecture. Question 9 taps this style.

Critical inquirers prefer to know the why behind the subject and go beyond the factual material. They want analysis, synthesis, and evaluation. They see learning as an intellectual pursuit. To calculate your critical inquiry score, add up your circled answers to questions 6 and 10, and reverse the number for question 13.

Lack of commitment refers to people who are unwilling to spend the time it takes to master a subject. To calculate your lack of commitment score, add up your circled answers to questions 7, 8, and 11.

Now place your scores below and compute the average:

Calculated score

Pragmatic learner	_____	divided by 3	= _____
Discovery learner	_____	transfers to	= _____
Critical inquiry	_____	divided by 3	= _____
Lack of commitment	_____	divided by 3	= _____

On which learning style did you score *lowest*? That tells you your preferred learning style. Note, for instance, that a relatively high score on the pragmatic scale suggests you like abstract ideas and theory.

No one style is better than any other. The value of this exercise is to help you better understand yourself. You can then use this information to help guide you in selecting among learning techniques and methods.

Chapter 3: Decision-Making Style Questionnaire

Mark each of your responses on the following scales. Then use the point value column to arrive at your score. For example, if you answered a to the first question, you would check 1a in the feeling column. This response receives zero points when you add up the point value column. Instructions for classifying your scores are indicated following the scales.

Sensation	Point Value	Intuition	Point Value	Thinking	Point Value	Feeling	Point Value
2b _____	1	2a _____	2	1b _____	1	1a _____	0
4a _____	1	4b _____	1	3b _____	2	3a _____	1
5a _____	1	5b _____	1	7b _____	1	7a _____	1
6b _____	1	6a _____	0	8a _____	0	8b _____	1
9b _____	2	9a _____	2	10b _____	2	10a _____	1
12a _____	1	12b _____	0	11a _____	2	11b _____	1
15a _____	1	15b _____	1	13b _____	1	13a _____	1
16b _____	2	16a _____	0	14b _____	0	14a _____	1

Maximum Point Value	(10)		(7)		(9)		(7)

Write *intuition* if your intuition score is equal to or greater than your sensation score. Write *sensation* if your sensation score is greater than your intuition score. Write *feeling* if your feeling score is greater than your thinking score. Write *thinking* if your thinking score is greater than your feeling score.

A high score on *intuition* indicates you see the world in holistic terms. You tend to be creative. A high score on *sensation* indicates that you are realistic and see the world in terms of facts. A high score on *feeling* means you make decisions based on gut feeling. A high score on *thinking* indicates a highly logical and analytical approach to decision making.

Chapter 4: What Do You Value?

Transfer the numbers for each of the 16 items to the appropriate column; then add up the two numbers in each column.

	Professional	Financial	Family	Social
	1. _____	2. _____	3. _____	4. _____
	9. _____	10. _____	11. _____	12. _____
Totals	_____	_____	_____	_____
	Community	Spiritual	Physical	Intellectual
	5. _____	6. _____	7. _____	8. _____
	13. _____	14. _____	15. _____	16. _____
Totals	_____	_____	_____	_____

The higher the total in any value dimension, the higher the importance you place on that value set. The closer the numbers are in all eight dimensions, the more well rounded you are.

Chapter 5: What Motivates You?

To determine your dominant needs—and what motivates you—place the number 1 through 5 that represents your score for each statement next to the number for that statement.

Achievement	Power	Affiliation
1. _____	2. _____	3. _____
4. _____	5. _____	6. _____
7. _____	8. _____	9. _____
10. _____	11. _____	12. _____
13. _____	14. _____	15. _____
Totals: _____	_____	_____

Add up the total of each column. The sum of the numbers in each column will be between 5 and 25 points. The column with the highest score tells you your dominant need.

Chapter 6: How Equity Sensitive Are You?

Sum up the points you allocated to the following items: 1B; 2A; 3B; 4A; and 5B. Your total will be between zero and 50.

Researchers have identified three equity-sensitive groups. They are labeled and defined as follows:

◆ Benevolents—Individuals who prefer that their outcome/input ratios be less than the comparison others.

◆ Equity Sensitives—Individuals who prefer outcome/input ratios to be equal.

◆ Entitleds—Individuals who prefer that their outcome/input ratios exceed those of the comparison others.

Based on data from more than 3,500 respondents, the researchers have found that scores less than 29 are classified as Entitleds; those between 29 and 32 are Equity Sensitives; and those with scores above 32 are Benevolents.

What does all this mean? First, not all individuals are equity sensitive. Second, equity theory predictions are most accurate with individuals in the Equity Sensitives group. And third, Benevolents actually prefer lower outcome/input ratios and tend to provide higher levels of inputs than either Equity Sensitives or Entitleds.

Chapter 7: Are You Attracted to the Group?

Add up your scores for items 4, 6, 7, 8, 9, 10, 14, 17, 19, and 20. Obtain a corrected score by subtracting the score for each of the remaining questions from 10. For example, if you marked 3 for item 1, you would obtain a corrected score of 7 (10 − 3). Add the corrected scores together with the total obtained on the 10 items scored directly. The higher your score, the more positive are your feelings about the group.

Chapter 8: Do Others See Me as Trustworthy?

Add up your total score for the seven statements. The following provides general guidelines for interpreting your score.

$$57-70 \text{ points} = \text{You're seen as highly trustworthy.}$$
$$21-56 \text{ points} = \text{You're seen as moderately trustworthy.}$$
$$7-20 \text{ points} = \text{You're rated low on this characteristic.}$$

Chapter 9: Listening Self-Inventory

The correct answers to the 15 questions, based on listening theory, are as follows: (1) No; (2) No; (3) No; (4) Yes; (5) No; (6) No; (7) No; (8) No; (9) No; (10) No; (11) No; (12) Yes; (13) Yes; (14) No; (15) Yes. To determine your score, add up the number of incorrect answers, multiply by 7, and subtract that total from 105. If you scored between 91 and 105, you have good listening habits. Scores of 77 to 90 suggest significant room for improvement. Scores below 76 indicate that you're a poor listener and need to work hard on improving this skill.

Chapter 10: What's Your Basic Leadership Style?

Count the number of situations to which you responded by marking A. This is your *delegating* score. Similarly, count the number of situations to which you responded B, C, and D. These are your *participating, selling,* and *telling* scores, respectively.

These responses align with Hersey and Blanchard's situational leadership model. Your basic or preferred leadership style is the response that you selected most often.

Chapter 11: How Political Are You?

According to the author of this instrument, a complete organizational politician will answer "true" to all ten questions. Organizational politicians with fundamental ethical standards will answer "false" to questions 5 and 6, which deal with deliberate lies and uncharitable behavior. Individuals who regard manipulation, incomplete disclosure, and self-serving behavior as unacceptable will answer "false" to all or almost all of the questions.

Chapter 12: What Is Your Primary Conflict-Handling Intention?

To determine your primary conflict-handling intention, place the number 1 through 5 that represents your score for each statement next to the number for that statement. Then total up the columns.

Competing	Collaborating	Avoiding	Accommodating	Compromising
1. __	4. __	6. __	3. __	2. __
5. __	9. __	10. __	11. __	8. __
7. __	12. __	15. __	14. __	13. __
Totals __	__	__	__	__

Your primary conflict-handling intention is the category with the highest total. Your fall-back intention is the category with the second-highest total.

Chapter 13: Bureaucratic Orientation Test

Give yourself one point for each statement for which you responded in the bureaucratic direction:

1. Mostly agree	11. Mostly agree
2. Mostly agree	12. Mostly disagree
3. Mostly disagree	13. Mostly disagree
4. Mostly agree	14. Mostly agree
5. Mostly disagree	15. Mostly disagree
6. Mostly disagree	16. Mostly agree
7. Mostly agree	17. Mostly disagree
8. Mostly agree	18. Mostly agree
9. Mostly disagree	19. Mostly agree
10. Mostly agree	20. Mostly disagree

A very high score (15 or over) suggests that you would enjoy working in a bureaucracy. A very low score (5 or lower) suggests that you would be frustrated by working in a bureaucracy, especially a large one.

Chapter 14: Is an Enriched Job for You?

This questionnaire taps the degree to which you have a strong versus weak desire to obtain growth satisfaction from your work. Each item on the questionnaire yields a score from 1 to 7 (that is, "Strongly prefer A" is scored 1; "Neutral" is scored 4; and "Strongly prefer B" is scored 7). To obtain your individual growth need strength score, average the 12 items as follows:

Numbers 1, 2, 7, 8, 11, 12 (direct scoring)

Numbers 3, 4, 5, 6, 9, 10 (reverse scoring)

Average scores for typical respondents are close to the midpoint of 4.0. Research indicates that if you score high on this measure, you will respond positively to an enriched job. Conversely, if you score low, you will tend *not* to find enriched jobs satisfying or motivating.

Chapter 15: How Good Are Your Interviewing Skills?

Add up your score for the seven statements. Your score will range between 7 and 35. The higher your score, the better your interviewing skills. For instance, scores of 30 or higher indicate you should do pretty well in job interviews.

You can use this questionnaire to identify areas where you can improve your interview skills. If you scored 3 or less on any statement, you should consider what you can do to improve that score.

Chapter 16: What Kind of Organizational Culture Fits You Best?

For items 5 and 6, score as follows:

$$
\begin{aligned}
\text{Strongly agree} &= +2 \\
\text{Agree} &= +1 \\
\text{Uncertain} &= 0 \\
\text{Disagree} &= -1 \\
\text{Strongly disagree} &= -2
\end{aligned}
$$

For items 1, 2, 3, 4, and 7, reverse the score (Strongly agree $= -2$, and so on). Add up your total. Your score will fall somewhere between $+14$ and -14.

What does your score mean? The higher your score (positive), the more comfortable you'll be in a formal, mechanistic, rule-oriented, and structured culture. This is often associated with large corporations and government agencies. Negative scores indicate a preference for informal, humanistic, flexible, and innovative cultures, which are more likely to be found in research units, advertising firms, high-tech companies, and small businesses.

Chapter 17: Managing-in-a-Turbulent-World Tolerance Test

Score 4 points for each A, 3 for each B, 2 for each C, 1 for each D, and 0 for each E. Compute the total, divide by 24, and round to one decimal place.

While the results are not intended to be more than suggestive, the higher your score, the more comfortable you seem to be with change. The test's author suggests analyzing scores as if they were grade-point averages. In this way, a 4.0 average is an A, a 2.0 is a C, and scores below 1.0 flunk.

Using replies from nearly 500 MBA students and young managers, the range of scores was found to be narrow—between 1.0 and 2.2. The average score was between 1.5 and 1.6—equivalent to a D+/C− grade! If these scores are generalizable to the work population, clearly people are not very tolerant of the kind of changes that come with a turbulent environment. However, this sample is now nearly a decade old. We should expect average scores today to be higher as people have become more accustomed to living in a dynamic environment.

Appendix D

Part-Ending Video Cases: The Knitting Factory

Welcome to KnitMedia, LLC*

KnitMedia, LLC, is an alternative music and entertainment company head-quartered in the TriBeCa section of New York City. It is perhaps best known for its live-performance club, the Knitting Factory; its syndicated college radio show; and its critically acclaimed independent record label. The company produces live performances, concert tours, music festivals, its record label, a music publishing business, and multimedia (radio, television, Internet, and video conference) interactive performances.

Founded in 1987 by Milwaukee native Michael Dorf, the Knitting Factory was initially an art gallery/performance space that sold teas, coffee, and a small selection of foods. From its beginnings, it had a tremendous influence on the New York music scene. *Billboard* magazine called it the "world capital of new music: experimental jazz and rock, contemporary classical and ethnic sounds, as well as—and most important—various hybrid forms."

Michael Dorf started the Knitting Factory shortly after he left Wisconsin Law School and moved to New York City in 1986. He was looking to earn enough money to survive while promoting Swamp Thing, the band he managed, and his record company, Flaming Pie. He and friend Louis Spitzer had often talked about opening a performance space and art gallery. Together they rented and renovated a space in New York City and opened their club in February of 1987.

The club knit together various media and various types of music. Michael and Louis ran the art gallery during the day, spoken-word performances on Wednesdays, jazz on Thursdays, and anything-that-would-go on the weekends. Unlike most avant-garde clubs, which were nonprofit and sponsored by grants, the Knitting Factory was a for-profit venture. Seeking help, Michael contacted singer-songwriter Paul McMahon, who started booking artists on the weekends. Michael quickly learned the music scene and booked Wayne Horvitz to play at the club. Horvitz contibuted by programming the Thursday night jazz performances. Musician John Zorn visited the club and asked to debut a new project there. Because the club was fully booked, Michael suggested a midnight concert. That concert resulted in the club's first standing-room-only audience.

In June 1987, the Knit enjoyed its first major corporate sponsorship when the Bigelow Tea Company sponsored the Tea and Comprovisations festival. Louis Spitzer left the club, and Bob Appel, part owner of Flaming Pie Records, became Michael's partner. Flaming Pie put out eight records and albums and a guide to the music scene. Michael and Bob then started the *Live at the Knitting Factory* radio series, which they sold to 30 record stations. By 1990,

*Source: The following sources were referenced for this introductory section. B. Bambarger, *Billboard,* February 1, 1997, p. 1. P. Watrous, *The Village Voice,* June 30, 1987. J. Wolf, *Wall Street Journal,* April 9, 1991.

TDK Tapes was sponsoring the show, which was carried by more than 200 stations.

In mid-1989, Michael and Bob made a deal with A&M Records to do a series of recordings called *Live at the Knitting Factory.* They used a new technology in which they split the signal between the recording studio and the club's sound system. This allowed them to take the live recordings and mix the sound for the records while simultaneously mixing it for the customers in the club. The relationship with A&M eventually ended because the volume of records sold was relatively low for a major record company (but not for an independent) and because A&M was sold to Polygram.

During the summer of 1988, the Knit produced a jazz festival as an alternative to New York City's JVC Jazz Festival. The JVC festival had started to move from its jazz roots to more pop-jazz and popular music. The Knitting Factory's jazz festival, sponsored by Vinylmania, a West Village record store, earned a lot of press attention (the *New York Times,* the *New Yorker,* the *Nation,* and the *Village Voice*). When an article about the festival appeared in the Dutch newspaper *de Volksgraant* (similar to the *New York Times* "Arts and Leisure" section), Michael was invited to stage a jazz festival in Holland. Michael and Bob picked the European artists and took 30 musicians from New York to play in the Holland show.

Inspired by the idea of playing in Holland, Dorf put together a series of uptown concerts at Lincoln Center for the Knit's second summer jazz festival. Although press coverage was good, crowds were disappointing because big names such as Ella Fitzgerald and Dizzy Gillespie were playing at the same time at Avery Fischer Hall.

Their success in Holland encouraged Michael and Bob to produce a 24-city European tour. Although the tour lost quite a bit of money, it still generated over 100 favorable reviews in the European press, increased Knitting Factory record sales in Europe, and brought European tourists to the the Knitting Factory club in New York City. Michael and Bob were asked to put on more tours, beginning an annual tradition of European tours that had greater financial success. In 1991, they embarked on their first American tour, during which they promoted their Knitting Factory Works record label. In 1993, they opened an office in Amsterdam to promote and service the Knitting Factory Works brand and book Knitting Factory Festival Tours in Europe.

The success of jazz festivals in New York led to the Macintosh New York Music Festival in 1995 and 1996, and 1996's Heineken What Is Jazz? Festival. The Macintosh festival was sponsored by Apple Computer Company and featured live broadcasts of performances over the Internet to more than two million people around the world. The Knitting Factory was the first company to cybercast live, multi-camera music over the Internet; it has cybercast artists such as Yoko Ono, Throwing Muses, the Corrs, Ken Nordine, Groove Collective, Riverdance, and Medeski Martin & Wood. KnitMedia's popular Web site **http://www.knittingfactory.com** is highly trafficked. It has won several high technology awards, including *Newsweek's* "Virtual City" Cyberspace award and *Microsoft Network's* "Site of the Week."

The Knit has promoted many artists who have become very successful, including John Zorn, Wayne Horvitz, They Might Be Giants, Indigo Girls, Sonic Youth, the Lounge Lizards, Vernon Reid, Bill Frisell, Marc Ribot, Melvin Gibbs, Galaxie 500, Cassandra Wilson, and the Pixies. It has created a unique niche market for fringe music with these and other artists. "KnitMedia is at the center of an international music movement," the *Wall Street Journal* reported, and it intends to remain on the forefront of interactive entertainment and new media. Funds from investors will enable the company to continue its growth.

Questions

1. What actions did Michael Dorf take to make KnitMedia a success? Why did these actions make a difference?

2. List three critical management skills that Michael demonstrated as he built the Knitting Factory and the KnitMedia organization? Why were these skills important?

3. Why do you think the Knitting Factory has become so popular around the world?

Part One: Introduction

The Knitting Factory started as a two-man company. Michael Dorf and his partner did all the work and made all the decisions, dividing the work by interest and talent. But as the company grew, more people were needed, and as more people came on staff, Michael was able to relinquish many of his routine tasks. He still works hard at a variety of tasks, changing hats often and shifting gears quickly as he goes about his day. He is constantly on the run, meeting with his employees, with the artists that play at the Knitting Factory, and with his sponsors. He must also deal with problems that arise, take phone calls, and deal with voluminous correspondence. In addition, he has to plan for the growth of the company and its various businesses. Much of his communication tends to be face-to-face and verbal, and his position as CEO requires that he play the various roles of the top manager: interpersonal, informational, and decisional.

Michael's interpersonal role flows directly from his position as the CEO of KnitMedia. This role as a figurehead in ceremonial tasks such as meeting with visitors or employees is an important aspect of his position. As a leader, he must help his employees meet the organizations goals. This role requires that he find, hire, and promote staff, as well as coach and direct people. He must also meet with suppliers, artists, city government officials, and others to get the variety of information he needs.

In his informational role, Michael seeks and receives information and shares it with others within the organization and outside it. As controller he must monitor the organization's performance.

In his role as decision maker, Michael commits the Knitting Factory to courses of action: He initiates new projects, resolves conflicts, allocates resources, and negotiates. He must also be something of a behavioral scientist to understand his employees and know how best to develop and motivate them.

The Knitting Factory's employees reflect the company's multicultural appeal and its talent for attracting people motivated by their love of music, not money. Sascha von Oretzen is from Germany. Sascha learned that the Knitting Factory was looking for a recording engineer, a position for which she trained in Germany; she walked into the office and was hired immediately. Operations Manager Ed Greer is from Northern Ireland. The Knitting Factory has been able to hire high-quality people they couldn't otherwise afford, because of their love of music. For instance, an out-of-work lawyer works for them for a few hundred dollars a week because he loves the music business in general and the Knitting Factory in particular.

Musicians from around the world come to the Knitting Factory to perform. The avant-garde music for which the Knitting Factory has an international reputation, is enjoyed around the world. As a consequence, Michael began a series of concert tours in Europe and is in the process of opening Knitting Factory branches in cities around the world. Rather than take the franchise approach of a Hard Rock Café, Michael intends to develop clubs that combine experimental, avant-garde jazz with local music. In this way, the clubs will retain the unique Knitting Factory image, which has always reflected the local cutting-edge music scene by providing a home for local artists to create, explore, and develop their work.

Of course, international expansion presents challenges to any organization. Often, for example, there are problems due to cultural differences. Working to avoid these types of problems, the Knitting Factory opened an office in Amsterdam to organize European tours and to develop relations with local European bands, music agents, promoters, and retailers. The office books artists and promotes both them and Knitting Factory Works recordings to the European and Asian markets. Because of the increasing popularity of Knitting Factory music in Japan, it became evident to Michael that he needed to expand to Japan. In preparation, he took Japanese lessons to better understand the Japanese culture. In addition, the Knitting Factory draws on its multicultural staff's knowledge of local customs.

Finally, Michael has gained an extensive understanding of the music business in Europe, where he manages all of KnitMedia's business opportunities. His personal goal is to give all nationalities with their various styles of music an opportunity to play together and to create world music. Instead of allowing American musicians to dominate, he plans on booking local bands, other unusual combinations, and American talent in equal proportions.

A problem that faces all expanding organizations is the need to institute broader controls. Michael Dorf envisions a transnational organization in which central control over those aspects of the organization that should be standardized will combine with local control of those areas that should be based on distinct market considerations. For the Knitting Factory, this plan means that international clubs will respond to local musical tastes while retaining the essence of what makes them Knitting Factory clubs. In addition, it means that the financial function will be centralized in New York. Daily tracking of its financial position will be made possible by Internet technology. Financial information can be e-mailed overnight to New York on a daily basis. In this way, Michael Dorf can monitor financial information and make informed decisions for the management of his various enterprises.

Questions

1. What can you say about Michael's management style?
2. Based on what you've learned from the text, what is your assessment of Mike's efforts to expand to other countries and become global?
3. What challenges face KnitMedia as it moves into the future?

Part Two: The Individual

The Knitting Factory's success can be attributed to its founder Michael Dorf and the fact that he has been able to bring together a group of smart, highly qualified people. They share a love of music for which the Knitting Factory is known—cutting-edge rock, jazz, and alternative music—and share a similar value system of which artistic integrity is an important component. Most of them also wear multiple hats. For example, Ed Greer, who is now club manager of the Knitting Factory and director of KnitWork Operations, continues to perform as a musician at the club. Ed's prior work at the club included sound engineer, and then a production manager. Ed also supervised construction when the club moved from Houston Street to Leonard Street, its present location. He eventually took the role of club manager, managing the club, bars, shows, and physical premises. In his new role as general manager, he will also establish the new clubs the company is planning to open.

Michael Dorf promotes individual decision making by his staff. In his role as club manager and operations director, Ed Greer makes the operating decisions for the Knitting Factory club and the Knitting Factory Works recording studio. Ed hires the staff for the club and, in conjunction with the bar manager, hires the bar staff. He and Ken Ashworth, executive vice president and chief operation officer, and Rachel McBeth, business manager, hire the other managers.

Rachel got her job with the Knitting Factory by responding to an ad in the *New York Times*. She has an extensive background in the music business that started when she was a psychology student at Berkeley, where she worked on concert production for the student union association. Her production experience led to a job with a recording industry trade magazine publisher. When her employer bought an electronic music magazine, Rachel came to New York City to run the record producer's office. She was the business administrator for the Big Apple Circus before she joined the Knitting Factory, and now is responsible for the company's financial management.

Although individuals typically are given assignments by Michael Dorf, they have the freedom to decide how to get these jobs done. This latitude allows employees to be innovative and creative and fosters a positive work climate and attitude toward work. Moreover, as more people are added, job responsibilities change, so that people have the opportunity to grow and develop their talents and abilities. As a result, they have a very positive attitude toward work and are highly motivated. In general, the people who work at the Knitting Factory are supportive of each other. Rather than being competitive, they help each other put on good shows and keep the club running smoothly. They are focused on producing quality work, and tend to work together as co-workers, rather than as bosses and employees.

The Knitting Factory has a value-based work ethic, and key to that value system is maintaining a core of artistic integrity. Michael Dorf wants to promote music with integrity and to run his business with integrity. His sense of values, for example, led him to decline a sponsor because advertising was required that violated his sense of artistic integrity. He generously pays the bands who perform at the club, and although he often loses money, he retains and is noted for his integrity.

Naturally, people are motivated by a variety of factors. The opportunity to excel in one's work is highly motivating to many people. The Knitting Factory provides this opportunity to its employees. It is made up of people who love music and who value being able to share that music with others. It also offers them the opportunity to hear and meet great musicians. Working with people who share the same values and goals contributes to the motivation of those who work at the Knitting Factory.

Unlike many companies, however, the Knitting Factory is not able to motivate people with financial incentives. Its cash flow constricts its ability to pay high salaries or benefits. There are no profit-sharing nor major health care benefits, and often payroll is somewhat irregular. However, Michael Dorf is generous, especially with Christmas bonuses.

Michael Dorf also spends a lot of time thinking about how to deal with his employees. "The textbook doesn't always teach you how to deal with other human beings and motivate them," says Michael. "I spend hours thinking about that. Managing people is difficult. I've developed a lot of patience." Michael motivates his staff mainly with his vision of what the Knitting Factory is and what it will be in the future. It is a powerful vision. That vision includes being a major force in the music business; having Knitting Factory clubs all over the world; producing cyber-concerts; building a record label with a global franchise; being part of a digital Knitting Factory community; and expanding into television, film, and new media.

Questions

1. Based on your reading, how would you characterize Mike's management style? How is it effective or ineffective? Explain.
2. Is the Knitting Factory an organization for which you would like to work? Would you be motivated to excel? Why or why not? Explain.
3. What personality types do you think would be particularly suited to work for Mike Dorf? Explain.
4. What role do Mike's ethics play in the development of the Knitting Factory? In what ways is this manifested?

Part Three: The Group

The Knitting Factory provides a home for eclectic jazz-rock street music groups. In these groups, everyone has a role to play, much as in the Knitting Factory organization. In general, the Knitting Factory is made up of two groups, the day staff and the night staff. The day staff handles the running of the KnitMedia office, the finances, the record label, the tours, and the festivals. The night staff runs the Knitting Factory club. Due to their different hours, the day and night people form different task groups that don't often interact. As a result, they also form different friendship groups and are not close with each other. As Rachel McBeth described it, "Because our hours are different we don't all work together and, of course, our environments are different; there's not that same camaraderie. The office staff tends to group with the office staff, and the club staff tends to group with the club staff."

Among the day staff, individuals come together as small groups, especially as teams form to work on various projects. These teams are typically made up of people from different functional areas, depending on what skills are needed. For instance, in-house art director Liz Leggett is on any team that has to do with graphics work, whether it be the Knitting Factory Club, the Knitting Factory Works record label, or the festivals put on by the Knitting Factory.

Communication is an important aspect of Michael Dorf's management style, therefore, he holds regular meetings every Wednesday afternoon. These meetings grew out of an off-site rock-climbing retreat that Michael held for his managers. As part of a goal-setting exercise, each person was asked to identify the mission and strategy of the club. Everyone was surprisingly in sync, recalls Rachel McBeth. "We all, as a group, had almost identical impressions of what we were doing and what the point was and our mission per se. And I thought that was inspiring."

Wednesday meetings are held so that each area can communicate information and so that everyone knows what everyone else is doing. Michael Dorf also holds regular weekly meetings with his club operations people—Rachel, Ed, the box office manager, and the two night managers—to go through the next week or so of shows, staffing, operational issues, and the like. Michael also meets daily with Rachel to go over the day-to-day finances, cash flow problems, and any pertinent operational problems. In this way, he has better control over the operation and is able to find solutions before problems get out of hand. Rachel, who has been invaluable in helping Michael gain control of the finances, complements Michael: He focuses on the artistic side of the business and she watches the dollars.

Although the Knitting Factory is known as a sophisticated user of high technology, with live video conferences and cyberspace concerts, surprisingly enough, Michael Dorf cannot rely on e-mail as a mode of communication because not all his people are e-mail friendly. Says Dorf, "Some people I know read their e-mail all the time. Others don't, so people who I know are working on e-mail a lot, I e-mail. Mark is e-mail friendly. Ken is e-mail friendly. JW is less e-mail friendly, so with JW sometimes I'll put a little yellow sticky right on his computer."

Michael is a charismatic leader whose creative ideas energize people. He inspires them to implement both his ideas and their own and provides an environment in which they can exercise their own independence, creativity, and innovative talents. He also has a passion for excellence that motivates his staff to excel. But perhaps his most important trait is his visionary skill. He has created a vision of what KnitMedia can be and has drawn others to that vision. He has communicated that vision not only to his employees, but to his investors, as well. He is developing the skill of sharing power in a growing organization, and he also seems to recognize his strengths and weaknesses and has the wisdom to hire those who can compensate for the latter. "Before I hired Rachel," Dorf said, "I was always having cash problems, not being able to pay the bills, not having enough money to do things. Rachel smoothes out our cash flow problems and pays the bills on time."

Conflict, of course, exists in every organization. In the Knitting Factory, it stems from Michael Dorf's workaholic pace. Everyone works hard even though resources are stretched thin, and because of the frenetic pace of activity, a lot of disagreements fall by the wayside because there is no time to deal with them. But when conflicts cannot be resolved by the people experiencing them, Dorf steps in.

Questions

1. Discuss the value of teamwork as it relates to the Knitting Factory.

2. How would you describe the norms of the KnitMedia organization? How do these norms affect the organization's performance?

3. What are the advantages and disadvantages of the communications process at KnitMedia? Does the process promote groupthink or effective communications? Explain.

4. Referring to the video, the cases you've read thus far, and the text, discuss the effectiveness of Mike's handling the conflict over the waste basket. What other ways could this problem have been solved?

Part Four: The Organization System

KnitMedia has a formal organizational chart designed for the company of the future and a more informal chart that reflects the reality of today's organizational structure. Currently, there is not a lot of middle management in the company. In the club, there are more levels, whereas other areas have only a few. Although the formal chart has only a few people reporting directly to Michael Dorf, in reality he interacts with everyone on a day-to-day basis. He gets involved in everything that goes out from the organization because from an art direction standpoint, Michael believes that everything needs to reflect the Knitting Factory persona.

Dorf has described the organization as a campfire, with himself in the middle spitting out the sparks. He realizes, however, that the organization is really structured somewhat differently. "In the end, I'm at the top of this pyramid and, you know, I'd love to say I'm in the middle of this circle and there's all this happening to me but I'm sure, in reality, at this point, I'm more at the top." As with most entrepreneurs, Michael has problems letting go. He realizes this, however, and is now delegating more decision-making authority to associates, as well as giving a great deal of autonomy to the staff in how they get the work done.

The Knitting Factory is a pioneer in the use of technology for entertainment purposes and that technology can also be used to monitor and control the organization. Soon, Michael will be able to interact with staff in any part of the world. An accounting software program will enhance the financial system, and a monitoring system will enable Michael to have a closer control of the clubs. It can also be used to facilitate the flow of work in a chaotic atmosphere in which tasks fly at people from all directions.

The pace at the Knitting Factory is fast and people are under constant time pressure. There are continual cash flow problems, which means that money is tight and resources are stretched thin. This creates a lot of pressure in a company that offers daily live shows and puts out two new CDs each month. People manage the stress in various ways. Rachel McBeth manages her stress by going upstairs to see the shows. Michael Dorf handles his stress by exercising, running, rock climbing, and taking a yearly trip with his college buddies. Ken Ashworth seems to thrive on the stress. Says Ken, "When you're sort of caught up in the chaos of working and the thrill of doing more and more and more and the excitement of it, plus everybody else around you is working at the same pitch, almost like a group thing, that everybody wants to keep working and doing better sort of to support the artists, to support the company."

The Knitting Factory continues to develop organically. As the work changes and the need for particular skills arises, Michael finds the types of people the organization needs. The growth of the company has caused job descriptions to change. Job tasks are now divided among more people and tasks are more focused. Realizing the dynamics of these changes, Michael does not judge a new employee's work performance on the performance of the previous employee; although the titles are often the same, the work is usually very different. Because of the nature of the work—the fast pace and the stretched resources—and the existing culture of hard work and excellence, Michael cannot afford to keep people who are not working out. He will not tolerate poor work, and, if after one-on-one counseling the work problems cannot be resolved, Michael makes changes. As he says, "If ultimately the job doesn't work out, they're not accomplishing what my expectations are, then we'll have to make a change. Usually, it becomes pretty obvious."

The Knitting Factory's culture is defined by the alternative music that it promotes. Artistic integrity means that the Knit does not book popular rock or pop groups, even though these groups would bring in more money. The Knit stays true to its values. It has created a niche that now brings in music lovers from all over the world. That niche drives its club, its brand, its music festivals, its record label, and its Siberia music business. It has created a valuable image with its vision of a knitting together a mosaic of various kinds of music. Michael and his people share the same values about the music and a vision about the Knitting Factory's future. They see the Knitting Factory's organizational culture spreading around the world. Michael will soon be able to tap into the huge music market in London and other cities around the world. He plans to open clubs in London and Los Angeles as the first step in this vision of a global music organization built around the Knitting Factory brand.

Questions

1. What differences do you see between the formal and informal KnitMedia organization?

2. How does the Knit's organizational structure facilitate and impede its work and productivity?

3. What role has technology played in the development and performance of KnitMedia?

Part Five: Organizational Dynamics

KnitMedia is facing a world of unprecedented change. It recently raised funds to bring its vision of a global music business to fruition. In the next year, KnitMedia plans to double in size. First, the company intends to expand its record label on a global level. With new financing, KnitMedia can invest in artists, marketing, and promotions. It recently entered into a joint venture with Sony Music and Columbia Records to better market and distribute its recorded products worldwide.

The company also intends to launch a network of Knitting Factory clubs in strategic global markets. This will be called the Knitwork. They will begin the Knitwork by opening clubs in two critical markets, Los Angeles and London. The London club will be a strategic alliance with the South Bank Centre, which comprises Royal Festival Hall and Queen Elizabeth Hall. Additional clubs will be opened the following year in Dublin, Paris, Tokyo, and Toronto, with new clubs opening each year thereafter. The clubs will not only highlight local talent and cater to local tastes, they will also act as an outlet for KnitMedia's other artists and products. This gives it a distinct competitive advantage over other music companies and record labels.

The Knitwork will knit the network of Knitting Factory communities together with an interactive virtual connection between each club. This digital musical community will allow KnitMedia to create global meeting places and interactive live broadcasts of concerts, thus creating a venue where music consumers can interact with KnitMedia's products. KnitMedia is positioned to exploit the rapid technological change in the music industry as it competes for a larger share of existing markets and continues to gain shares in new and emerging markets.

This rapid growth means lots of changes in the KnitMedia organization. As CEO of this growing company, Michael Dorf is also aware that this means changes that will have profound implications on how the company operates now and how it will be structured in the future. It also means that his employees will be affected by these organizational changes. He wonders how to keep everyone motivated and how to retain the unique Knitting Factory culture that he established. "How can I ensure that all of these people will continue to feel the same sort of shared vision and then make sure that they're inspiring everyone underneath?"

As the organization grows, personnel will take on new areas of responsibility and new people will join the organization. Ed Greer will become general manager and will manage the new Knitting Factory clubs as they come on board. Michael and his business manager, Rachel McBeth, have named John Lewis to replace Ed as club manager.

Growth also impacts space, and the company's physical space is becoming crowded. The club moved from Houston Street to a much larger space on Leonard Street. Currently the office is in the basement of the building and is pretty crowded. Michael has to share his office and conference room with others because of the lack of office space. New positions will be needed as a result of the company's plans to expand existing businesses and develop new ones. Michael and his people are cognizant of the fact that the physical layout of a company can affect the company's culture. Steve Smith, publicity director, reflected on the company's growth, "I'm curious about how it will affect us and I think obviously that's going to be some reflection of the physical space itself. I mean, are we going to have offices? Are we going to have doors? Is it going to become more of a professional working environment?"

Michael Dorf doesn't want the company to be like a large corporation. He recognizes, however, that growth means that there have to be control systems in place to manage that growth. "As much as I don't want to turn this into a gross corporate feeling and vibe, there has to be some sort of rigidity to the communication process and the reporting process that's going to allow us to grow and have controls. At the same time, it's very exciting that we're thinking about it now a little bit more analytically."

By planning ahead, Michael can manage the process better than if he just let it happen. He can begin to determine what the company should look and feel like and still retain the Knitting Factory culture. For example, if he wants an open company feel, he may decide not to have doors. When Al Gamper took over CIT Financial Services Corporation, one of the first things he did was to take the doors off the hinges. Gamper wanted to change the company from a closed-door culture to one with an open-door culture. Managing the physical space has an impact on the employees and the culture that develops.

KnitMedia is all about music, about new music around the world, cutting-edge alternative pop and jazz. The Knitting Factory clubs are a conduit between artists who create, explore, and develop this avant-garde music and consumers of music and musical entertainment. As Michael puts it, "The clubs are still going to be where live music is most likely to be experienced, so that's an important base of our business. But how the other media develop over time, I don't know; and that's exciting because I'm glad I don't know where we're going to be in 10 years."

Questions

1. What forces are acting as a stimulant for the change that KnitMedia is facing or is going to face? Explain.

2. What do you anticipate as sources of individual resistance to change and as sources of organizational resistance to change in KnitMedia? Why? What can be done to mitigate these factors?

3. What advice would you give to Michael Dorf to help him in his efforts toward planned change? Explain.

Chapter 1

[1] D. Milbank, "Managers Are Sent to 'Charm Schools' to Discover How to Polish Up Their Acts," *Wall Street Journal,* December 14, 1990, p. B1.

[2] S. Sherman, "Are You As Good As the Best in the World?" *Fortune,* December 13, 1993, p. 96. This point is elaborated in J. Pfeffer, "Producing Sustainable Competitive Advantage through the Effective Management of People," *Academy of Management Executive,* February 1995, pp. 55–69.

[3] M. Rothman, "Into the Black," *INC.,* January 1993, p. 59.

[4] C. Hymowitz, "Five Main Reasons Why Managers Fail," *Wall Street Journal,* May 2, 1988, p. 25.

[5] Milbank, "Managers Are Sent to 'Charm Schools' to Discover How to Polish Up Their Acts."

[6] S.A. Waddock, "Educating Tomorrow's Managers," *Journal of Management Education,* February 1991, pp. 69–96; and K.F. Kane, "MBAs: A Recruiter's-Eye View," *Business Horizons,* January–February 1993, pp. 65–71.

[7] H. Fayol, *Industrial and General Administration* (Paris: Dunod, 1916).

[8] H. Mintzberg, *The Nature of Managerial Work* (New York: Harper & Row, 1973).

[9] R.L. Katz, "Skills of an Effective Administrator," *Harvard Business Review,* September–October 1974, pp. 90–102.

[10] F. Luthans, "Successful vs. Effective Real Managers," *Academy of Management Executive,* May 1988, pp. 127–32; and F. Luthans, R.M. Hodgetts, and S.A. Rosenkrantz, *Real Managers* (Cambridge, MA: Ballinger, 1988).

[11] See, for instance, J.E. Garcia and K.S. Keleman, "What Is Organizational Behavior Anyhow?" paper presented at the 16th Annual Organizational Behavior Teaching Conference, Columbia, MO, June 1989.

[12] See, for instance, A. Kohn, "You Know What They Say . . ." *Psychology Today,* April 1988, pp. 36–41.

[13] E.E. Lawler III and J.G. Rhode, *Information and Control in Organizations* (Pacific Palisades, CA: Goodyear, 1976), p. 22.

[14] R. Weinberg and W. Nord, "Coping with 'It's All Common Sense'," *Exchange,* 7, no. 2 (1982), 29–33; R.P. Vecchio, "Some Popular (But Misguided) Criticisms of the Organizational Sciences," *Organizational Behavior Teaching Review,* 10, no. 1 (1986–87), 28–34; and M.L. Lynn, "Organizational Behavior and Common Sense: Philosophical Implications for Teaching and Thinking," paper presented at the 14th Annual Organizational Behavior Teaching Conference, Waltham, MA, May 1987.

[15] See, for instance, R.R. Thomas Jr., "From Affirmative Action to Affirming Diversity," *Harvard Business Review,* March–April 1990, pp. 107–17; B. Mandrell and S. Kohler-Gray, "Management Development That Values Diversity," *Personnel,* March 1990, pp. 41–47; J. Dreyfuss, "Get Ready for the New Work Force," *Fortune,* April 23, 1990, pp. 165–81; and I. Wielawski, "Diversity Makes Both Dollars and Sense," *Los Angeles Times,* May 16, 1994, p. II-3.

[16] See S. Pedigo, "Diversity in the Workforce: Riding the Tide of Change," *The Wyatt Communicator,* Winter 1991, pp. 4–11.

[17] Dreyfuss, "Get Ready for the New Work Force," p. 168.

[18] See, for instance, P.L. McLeod and S.A. Lobel, "The Effects of Ethnic Diversity on Idea Generation in Small Groups," paper presented at the Annual Academy of Management Conference, Las Vegas, August 1992.

[19] J.S. McClenahen, "The Edge of Light," *Industry Week,* January 3, 1994, p. 11.

[20] See, for instance, M. Sashkin and K.J. Kiser, *Putting Total Quality Management to Work* (San Francisco: Berrett-Koehler, 1993); and J.R. Hackman and R. Wageman, "Total Quality Management: Empirical, Conceptual, and Practical Issues," *Administrative Science Quarterly,* June 1995, pp. 309–42.

[21] M. Hammer and J. Champy, *Reengineering the Corporation: A Manifesto for Business Revolution* (New York: HarperBusiness, 1993); and J. Champy, *Reengineering Management* (New York: HarperBusiness, 1995).

[22] B. Dumaine, "The New Non-Manager Managers," *Fortune,* February 22, 1993, pp. 80–84.

[23] "Wanted: Teammates, Crew Members, and Cast Members—But No Employees," *Wall Street Journal,* April 30, 1996, p. A1.

[24] M. Sashkin, "Participative Management Is an Ethical Imperative," *Organizational Dynamics,* Spring 1984, pp. 5–22.

[25] See, "What Self-Managing Teams Manage," *Training,* October 1995, p. 72.

[26] M. Kaeter, "The Age of the Specialized Generalist," *Training,* December 1993, pp. 48–53; and N. Templin, "Auto Plants, Hiring Again, Are Demanding Higher-Skilled Labor," *Wall Street Journal,* March 11, 1994, p. A1.

[27] See, for example, W.J. Byron, "Coming to Terms with the New Corporate Contract," *Business Horizons,* January–February 1995, pp. 8–15; "U.S. Labor Gets Flexible. . . ," *Business Week,* January 15, 1996, p. 22; J. Templeman, "A Continent Swarming with Temps," *Business Week,* April 8, 1996, p. 54; D. Hulme, "Temps Catch on in Japan," *Asian Business,* April 1996, pp. 57–58; T. Price, "Pioneering a New Age of Flexibility," *Asian Business,* April 1996, pp. 59–60; J.W. Verity, "Let's Order Out for Technology," *Business Week,* May 13, 1996, p. 47; and T. Egan, "A Temporary Force to Be Reckoned With," *New York Times,* May 20, 1996, p. C1.

[28] E.J. Ottensmeyer and G. McCarthy, *Ethics in the Workplace* (New York: McGraw Hill, 1996).

[29] R.R. Sims, "The Challenge of Ethical Behavior," *Journal of Business Ethics,* July 1992, pp. 505–13.

[30] See, for example, M.J. Driver, "Cognitive Psychology: An Interactionist View," R.H. Hall, "Organizational Behavior: A Sociological Perspective," and C. Hardy, "The Contribution of Political Science to Organizational Behavior," all in J.W. Lorsch (ed.), *Handbook of Organizational Behavior* (Englewood Cliffs, NJ: Prentice Hall, 1987), pp. 62–108.

[31] D. Tjosvold, "Controversy for Learning Organizational Behavior," *Organizational Behavior Teaching Review,* 11, no. 3 (1986–87), 51–59; and L.F. Moore, D.C. Limerick, and P.J. Frost, "Debating the Issue: Increasing Understanding of the 'Close Calls' in Organizational Decision Making," *Organizational Behavior Teaching Review,* 14, no. 1 (1989–90), 37–43.

[32] S.R. Rhodes and R.M. Steers, *Managing Employee Absenteeism* (Reading, MA: Addison-Wesley, 1990).

[33] Cited in "Expensive Absenteeism," *Wall Street Journal,* July 29, 1986, p. 1.

[34] M. Mercer, "Turnover: Reducing the Costs," *Personnel,* December 1988, pp. 36–42; and R. Darmon, "Identifying Sources of Turnover Cost," *Journal of Marketing,* April 1990, pp. 46–56.

[35] See, for example, D.R. Dalton and W.D. Todor, "Functional Turnover: An Empirical Assessment," *Journal of Applied Psychology,* December 1981, pp. 716–21; and G.M. McEvoy and W.F. Cascio, "Do Good or Poor Performers Leave? A Meta-Analysis of the Relationship between Performance and Turnover," *Academy of Management Journal,* December 1987, pp. 744–62.

[36] Cited in "You Often Lose the Ones You Love," *Industry Week,* November 21, 1988, p. 5.

[37] H.J. Leavitt, *Managerial Psychology,* rev. ed. (Chicago: University of Chicago Press, 1964), p. 3.

[38] Cited in "You Often Lose the Ones You Love."

[39] H.J. Leavitt, *Managerial Psychology,* rev. ed., p. 3.

Chapter 2

[1] Based on B. Vlasic and D. Woodruff, "Chrysler's Most Valuable Player?" *Business Week,* January 22, 1996, pp. 64–65.

[2] Reported in M. Galen, "Myths about Older Workers Cost Business Plenty," *Business Week,* December 20, 1993, p. 83.

[3] "American Business and Older Workers: A Road Map to the 21st Century," a report prepared for the American Association of Retired Persons by DYG, Inc., 1995; and "Valuing Older Workers: A Study of Costs and Productivity," a report prepared for the American Association of Retired Persons by ICF Inc., 1995.

[4] S.R. Rhodes, "Age-Related Differences in Work Attitudes and Behavior: A Review and Conceptual Analysis," *Psychological Bulletin,* March 1983, pp. 328–67; J.L. Cotton and J.M. Tuttle, "Employee Turnover: A Meta-Analysis and Review with Implications for Research," *Academy of Management Review,* January 1986, pp. 55–70; and D.R. Davies, G. Matthews, and C.S.K. Wong, "Ageing and Work," in C.L. Cooper and I.T. Robertson (eds.), *International Review of Industrial and Organizational Psychology,* vol. 6 (Chichester, England: Wiley, 1991), pp. 183–87.

[5] Rhodes, "Age-Related Differences in Work Attitudes and Behavior," pp. 347–49; R.D. Hackett, "Age, Tenure, and Employee Absenteeism," *Human Relations,* July 1990, pp. 601–19; and Davies, Matthews, and Wong, "Ageing and Work," pp. 183–87.

[6] Cited in K. Labich, "The New Unemployed," *Fortune,* March 8, 1993, p. 43.

[7] G.M. McEvoy and W.F. Cascio, "Cumulative Evidence of the Relationship between Employee Age and Job Performance," *Journal of Applied Psychology,* February 1989, pp. 11–17.

[8] A.L. Kalleberg and K.A. Loscocco, "Aging, Values, and Rewards: Explaining Age Differences in Job Satisfaction," *American Sociological Review,* February 1983, pp. 78–90; R. Lee and E.R. Wilbur, "Age, Education, Job Tenure, Salary, Job Characteristics, and Job Satisfaction: A Multivariate Analysis," *Human Relations,* August 1985, pp. 781–91; and Davies, Matthews, and Wong, "Ageing and Work," pp. 176–83.

[9] K.M. Kacmar and G.R. Ferris, "Theoretical and Methodological Considerations in the Age-Job Satisfaction Relationship," *Journal of Applied Psychology,* April 1989, pp. 201–07; and G. Zeitz, "Age and Work Satisfaction in a Government Agency: A Situational Perspective," *Human Relations,* May 1990, pp. 419–38.

[10] See, for example, E. Maccoby and C. Nagy Jacklin, *The Psychology of Sex Differences* (Stanford, CA: Stanford University Press, 1974); A.H. Eagly and L.L. Carli, "Sex Researchers and Sex-Typed Communications as Determinants of Sex Differences in Influenceability: A Meta-Analysis of Social Influence Studies," *Psychological Bulletin,* August 1981, pp. 1–20; J.S. Hyde, "How Large Are Cognitive Gender Differences?" *American Psychologist,* October 1981, pp. 892–901; and P. Chance, "Biology, Destiny, and All That," *Across the Board,* July–August 1988, pp. 19–23.

[11] R.P. Quinn, G.L. Staines, and M.R. McCullough, *Job Satisfaction: Is There a Trend?* Document 2900-00195, (Washington, D.C.: U.S. Government Printing Office, 1974).

[12] See, for example, B. Kantrowitz, P. Wingert, and K. Robins, "Advocating a 'Mommy Track'," *Newsweek,* March 13, 1989, p. 45; and S. Shellenbarger, "More Job Seekers Put Family Needs First," *Wall Street Journal,* November 15, 1991, p. B1.

[13] T.W. Mangione, "Turnover—Some Psychological and Demographic Correlates," in R.P. Quinn and T.W. Mangione (eds.), *The 1969–70 Survey of Working Conditions* (Ann Arbor: University of Michigan, Survey Research Center, 1973); and R. Marsh and H. Mannari, "Organizational Commitment and Turnover: A Predictive Study," *Administrative Science Quarterly,* March 1977, pp. 57–75.

[14] See, for instance, K.R. Garrison and P.M. Muchinsky, "Attitudinal and Biographical Predictors of Incidental Absenteeism," *Journal of Vocational Behavior,* April 1977, pp. 221–30; G. Johns, "Attitudinal and Nonattitudinal Predictors of Two Forms of Absence from Work," *Organizational Behavior and Human Performance,* December 1978, pp. 431–44; J.P. Leigh, "Sex Differences in Absenteeism," *Industrial Relations,* Fall 1983, pp. 349–61; K.D. Scott and E.L. McClellan, "Gender Differences in Absenteeism," *Public Personnel Management,* Summer 1990, pp. 229–53; and A. VandenHeuvel and M. Wooden, "Do Explanations of

Absenteeism Differ for Men and Women?" *Human Relations,* November 1995, pp. 1309–29.

15 See, for instance, M. Tait, M.Y. Padgett, and T.T. Baldwin, "Job and Life Satisfaction: A Reevaluation of the Strength of the Relationship and Gender Effects as a Function of the Date of the Study," *Journal of Applied Psychology,* June 1989, pp. 502–07; and R.A. Douthitt, "The Division of Labor within the Home: Have Gender Roles Changed?" *Sex Roles,* June 1989, pp. 693–704.

16 Garrison and Muchinsky, "Attitudinal and Biographical Predictors of Incidental Absenteeism"; C.J. Watson, "An Evaluation and Some Aspects of the Steers and Rhodes Model of Employee Attendance," *Journal of Applied Psychology,* June 1981, pp. 385–89; R.T. Keller, "Predicting Absenteeism from Prior Absenteeism, Attitudinal Factors, and Nonattitudinal Factors, *Journal of Applied Psychology,* August 1983, pp. 536–40; J.M. Federico, P. Federico, and G.W. Lundquist, "Predicting Women's Turnover as a Function of Extent of Met Salary Expectations and Biodemographic Data," *Personnel Psychology,* Winter 1976, pp. 559–66; Marsh and Mannari, "Organizational Commitment and Turnover"; and D.R. Austrom, T. Baldwin, and G.J. Macy, "The Single Worker: An Empirical Exploration of Attitudes, Behavior, and Well-Being," *Canadian Journal of Administrative Sciences,* December 1988, pp. 22–29.

17 M.E. Gordon and W.J. Fitzgibbons, "Empirical Test of the Validity of Seniority as a Factor in Staffing Decisions," *Journal of Applied Psychology,* June 1982, pp. 311–19; M.E. Gordon and W.A. Johnson, "Seniority: A Review of Its Legal and Scientific Standing," *Personnel Psychology,* Summer 1982, pp. 255–80; M.A. McDaniel, F.L. Schmidt, and J.E. Hunter, "Job Experience Correlates of Job Performance," *Journal of Applied Psychology,* May 1988, pp. 327–30; and M.A. Quinones, J.K. Ford, and M.S. Teachout, "The Relationship between Work Experience and Job Performance: A Conceptual and Meta-Analytic Review," *Personnel Psychology,* Winter 1995, pp. 887–910.

18 Garrison and Muchinsky, "Attitudinal and Biographical Predictors of Incidental Absenteeism"; N. Nicholson, C.A. Brown, and J.K. Chadwick-Jones, "Absence from Work and Personal Characteristics," *Journal of Applied Psychology,* June 1977, pp. 319–27; and R.T. Keller, "Predicting Absenteeism from Prior Absenteeism, Attitudinal Factors, and Nonattitudinal Factors, *Journal of Applied Psychology,* August 1983, pp. 536–40.

19 P.O. Popp and J.A. Belohlav, "Absenteeism in a Low Status Work Environment," *Academy of Management Journal,* September 1982, p. 681.

20 H.J. Arnold and D.C. Feldman, "A Multivariate Analysis of the Determinants of Job Turnover," *Journal of Applied Psychology,* June 1982, p. 352.

21 R.D. Gatewood and H.S. Field, *Human Resource Selection* (Chicago: Dryden Press, 1987).

22 J.A. Breaugh and D.L. Dossett, "The Effectiveness of Biodata for Predicting Turnover," paper presented at the National Academy of Management Conference, New Orleans, August 1987.

23 A.G. Bedeian, G.R. Ferris, and K.M. Kacmar, "Age, Tenure, and Job Satisfaction: A Tale of Two Perspectives," *Journal of Vocational Behavior,* February 1992, pp. 33–48.

24 L.E. Tyler, *Individual Differences: Abilities and Motivational Directions* (Englewood Cliffs, NJ: Prentice Hall, 1974).

25 M.D. Dunnette, "Aptitudes, Abilities, and Skills," in M.D. Dunnette (ed.), *Handbook of Industrial and Organizational Psychology* (Chicago, IL: Rand McNally, 1976), pp. 478–83.

26 D. Lubinski and R.V. Dawis, "Aptitudes, Skills, and Proficiencies," in M.D. Dunnette and L.M. Hough (eds.), *Handbook of Industrial & Organizational Psychology,* vol. 3, 2nd ed. (Palo Alto, CA: Consulting Psychologists Press, 1992), pp. 30–33.

27 J.E. Hunter and R.F. Hunter, "Validity and Utility of Alternative Predictors of Job Performance," *Psychological Bulletin,* January 1984, pp. 72–98; J.E. Hunter, "Cognitive Ability, Cognitive Aptitudes, Job Knowledge, and Job Performance," *Journal of Vocational Behavior,* December 1986, pp. 340–62; W.M. Coward and P.R. Sackett, "Linearity of Ability–Performance Relationships: A Reconfirmation," *Journal of Applied Psychology,* June 1990, pp. 297–300; and M.J. Ree, J.A. Earles, and M.S. Teachout, "Predicting Job Performance: Not Much More Than *g*," *Journal of Applied Psychology,* August 1994, pp. 518–24.

28 Hunter and Hunter, "Validity and Utility of Alternative Predictors of Job Performance," pp. 73–74.

29 E.A. Fleishman, "Evaluating Physical Abilities Required by Jobs," *Personnel Administrator,* June 1979, pp. 82–92.

30 G.W. Allport, *Personality: A Psychological Interpretation* (New York: Holt, Rinehart & Winston, 1937), p. 48.

31 Cited in R. Bolton, *People Skills* (Englewood Cliffs, NJ: Prentice Hall, 1979), p. 260.

32 Reported in R.L. Hotz, "Genetics, Not Parenting, Key to Temperament, Studies Say," *Los Angeles Times,* February 20, 1994, p. A1.

33 See T.J. Bouchard Jr., D.T. Lykken, M. McGue, N.L. Segal, and A. Tellegen, "Sources of Human Psychological Differences—The Minnesota Study of Twins Reared Apart," *Science,* October 12, 1990, pp. 223–38; T.J. Bouchard Jr. and M. McGue, "Genetic and Rearing Environmental Influences on Adult Personality: An Analysis of Adopted Twins Raised Apart," *Journal of Personality* 58 (1990), pp. 263–92; D.T. Lykken, T.J. Bouchard Jr., M. McGue, and A. Tellegen, "Heritability of Interests: A Twin Study," *Journal of Applied Psychology,* August 1993, pp. 649–61; and R.D. Arvey and T.J. Bouchard Jr., "Genetics, Twins, and Organizational Behavior," in B.M. Staw and L.L. Cummings, *Research in Organizational Behavior,* vol. 16 (Greenwich, CT: JAI Press, 1994), pp. 65–66.

34 See B.M. Staw and J. Ross, "Stability in the Midst of Change: A Dispositional Approach to Job Attitudes," *Journal of Applied Psychology,* August 1985, pp. 469–80; and B.M. Staw, N.E. Bell, and J.A. Clausen, "The Dispositional Approach to Job Attitudes: A Lifetime Longitudinal Test," *Administrative Science Quarterly,* March 1986, pp. 56–77.

35 R.C. Carson, "Personality," in M.R. Rosenzweig and L.W. Porter (eds.), *Annual Review of Psychology,* vol. 40 (Palo Alto, CA: Annual Reviews, 1989), pp. 228–29.

36 L. Sechrest, "Personality," in M.R. Rosenzweig and L.W. Porter (eds.), *Annual Review of Psychology,* vol. 27 (Palo Alto, CA: Annual Reviews, 1976), p. 10.

[37] Ibid.

[38] See A.H. Buss, "Personality as Traits," *American Psychologist,* November 1989, pp. 1378–88.

[39] G.W. Allport and H.S. Odbert, "Trait Names, A Psycholexical Study," *Psychological Monographs,* no. 47 (1936).

[40] R.B. Cattell, "Personality Pinned Down," *Psychology Today,* July 1973, pp. 40–46.

[41] See A.J. Vaccaro, "Personality Clash," *Personnel Administrator,* September 1988, pp. 88–92; and R.R. McCrae and P.T. Costa Jr., "Reinterpreting the Myers-Briggs Type Indicator from the Perspective of the Five Factor Model of Personality," *Journal of Personality,* March 1989, pp. 17–40.

[42] G.N. Landrum, *Profiles of Genius* (New York: Prometheus, 1993).

[43] See, for example, J.M. Digman, "Personality Structure: Emergence of the Five-Factor Model," in M.R. Rosenzweig and L.W. Porter (eds.), *Annual Review of Psychology,* vol. 41 (Palo Alto, CA: Annual Reviews, 1990), pp. 417–40; O.P. John, "The 'Big Five' Factor Taxonomy: Dimensions of Personality in the Natural Language and in Questionnaires," in L.A. Pervin (ed.), *Handbook of Personality Theory and Research* (New York: Guilford Press, 1990), pp. 66–100; M.K. Mount, M.R. Barrick, and J.P. Strauss, "Validity of Observer Ratings of the Big Five Personality Factors," *Journal of Applied Psychology,* April 1994, pp. 272–80; and P.J. Howard and J.M. Howard, "Buddy, Can You Paradigm?" *Training & Development Journal,* September 1995, pp. 28–34.

[44] M.R. Barrick and M.K. Mount, "The Big Five Personality Dimensions and Job Performance: A Meta-Analysis," *Personnel Psychology* 44 (1991), pp. 1–26; and M.R. Barrick and M.K. Mount, "Autonomy as a Moderator of the Relationships between the Big Five Personality Dimensions and Job Performance," *Journal of Applied Psychology,* February 1993, pp. 111–18.

[45] Mount, Barrick, and Strauss, "Validity of Observer Ratings of the Big Five Personality Factors," p. 272.

[46] J.B. Rotter, "Generalized Expectancies for Internal versus External Control of Reinforcement," *Psychological Monographs* 80, no. 609 (1966).

[47] See P.E. Spector, "Behavior in Organizations as a Function of Employee's Locus of Control," *Psychological Bulletin,* May 1982, pp. 482–97; and G.J. Blau, "Locus of Control as a Potential Moderator of the Turnover Process," *Journal of Occupational Psychology,* Fall 1987, pp. 21–29.

[48] R.T. Keller, "Predicting Absenteeism from Prior Absenteeism, Attitudinal Factors, and Nonattitudinal Factors," *Journal of Applied Psychology,* August 1983, pp. 536–40.

[49] Spector, "Behavior in Organizations as a Function of Employee's Locus of Control," p. 493.

[50] R.G. Vleeming, "Machiavellianism: A Preliminary Review," *Psychological Reports,* February 1979, pp. 295–310.

[51] R. Christie and F.L. Geis, *Studies in Machiavellianism* (New York: Academic Press, 1970), p. 312; and N.V. Ramanaiah, A. Byravan, and F.R.J. Detwiler, "Revised Neo Personality Inventory Profiles of Machiavellian and Non-Machiavellian People," *Psychological Reports,* October 1994, pp. 937–38.

[52] Christie and Geis, *Studies in Machiavellianism.*

[53] Based on J. Brockner, *Self-Esteem at Work* (Lexington, MA: Lexington Books, 1988), chapters 1–4.

[54] See M. Snyder, *Public Appearances/Private Realities: The Psychology of Self-Monitoring* (New York: W.H. Freeman, 1987).

[55] Ibid.

[56] M. Kilduff and D.V. Day, "Do Chameleons Get Ahead? The Effects of Self-Monitoring on Managerial Careers," *Academy of Management Journal,* August 1994, pp. 1047–60.

[57] R.N. Taylor and M.D. Dunnette, "Influence of Dogmatism, Risk-Taking Propensity, and Intelligence on Decision-Making Strategies for a Sample of Industrial Managers," *Journal of Applied Psychology,* August 1974, pp. 420–23.

[58] I.L. Janis and L. Mann, *Decision Making: A Psychological Analysis of Conflict, Choice, and Commitment* (New York: Free Press, 1977).

[59] N. Kogan and M.A. Wallach, "Group Risk Taking as a Function of Members' Anxiety and Defensiveness," *Journal of Personality,* March 1967, pp. 50–63.

[60] M. Friedman and R.H. Rosenman, *Type A Behavior and Your Heart* (New York: Alfred A. Knopf, 1974), p. 84 (emphasis in original).

[61] Ibid., pp. 84–85.

[62] Ibid, p. 86.

[63] F. Kluckhohn and F.L. Strodtbeck, *Variations in Value Orientations* (Evanston, IL: Row Peterson, 1961).

[64] Friedman and Rosenman, *Type A Behavior and Your Heart,* p. 86.

[65] J.L. Holland, *Making Vocational Choices: A Theory of Vocational Personalities and Work Environments,* 2nd ed. (Englewood Cliffs, NJ: Prentice Hall, 1985).

[66] See, for example, A.R. Spokane, "A Review of Research on Person-Environment Congruence in Holland's Theory of Careers," *Journal of Vocational Behavior,* June 1985, pp. 306–43; D. Brown, "The Status of Holland's Theory of Career Choice," *Career Development Journal,* September 1987, pp. 13–23; J.L. Holland and G.D. Gottfredson, "Studies of the Hexagonal Model: An Evaluation (or, The Perils of Stalking the Perfect Hexagon)," *Journal of Vocational Behavior,* April 1992, pp. 158–70; and T.J. Tracey and J. Rounds, "Evaluating Holland's and Gati's Vocational-Interest Models: A Structural Meta-Analysis," *Psychological Bulletin,* March 1993, pp. 229–46.

[67] W. McGehee, "Are We Using What We Know about Training?—Learning Theory and Training," *Personnel Psychology,* Spring 1958, p.2.

[68] I.P. Pavlov, *The Work of the Digestive Glands,* trans. W.H. Thompson (London: Charles Griffin, 1902).

[69] B.F. Skinner, *Contingencies of Reinforcement* (East Norwalk, CT: Appleton-Century-Crofts, 1971).

[70] A. Bandura, *Social Learning Theory* (Englewood Cliffs, NJ: Prentice Hall, 1977).

[71] T.W. Costello and S.S. Zalkind, *Psychology in Administration* (Englewood Cliffs, NJ: Prentice Hall, 1963), p. 193.

[72] F. Luthans and R. Kreitner, *Organizational Behavior Modification and Beyond,* 2nd ed. (Glenview, IL: Scott, Foresman, 1985).

[73] A. Halcrow, "Incentive! How Three Companies Cut Costs," *Personnel Journal,* February 1986, p. 12.

[74] D. Willings, "The Absentee Worker," *Personnel and Training Management,* December 1968, pp. 10–12.

[75] B.H. Harvey, J.F. Rogers, and J.A. Schultz, "Sick Pay vs. Well Pay: An Analysis of the Impact of Rewarding Employees for Being on the Job," *Public Personnel Management Journal,* Summer 1983, pp. 218–24.

[76] M.S. Forbes Jr., "There's a Better Way," *Forbes,* April 26, 1993, p. 23.

[77] Cited in *Training,* October 1995, p. 38.

[78] From A. Belohlav, *The Art of Disciplining Your Employees* (Englewood Cliffs, NJ: Prentice Hall, 1985); and R.H. Lussier, "A Discipline Model for Increasing Performance," *Supervisory Management,* August 1990, pp. 6–7.

[79] See, for instance, C.C. Manz and H.P. Sims, "Self-Management as a Substitute for Leadership: A Social Learning Theory Perspective," *Academy of Management Review,* July 1980, pp. 361–67; and S.E. Markham and I.S. Markham, "Self-Management and Self-Leadership Reexamined: A Levels-of-Analysis Perspective," *Leadership Quarterly,* Fall 1995, pp. 343–60.

[80] G.P. Latham and C.A. Frayne, "Self-Management Training for Increasing Job Attendance: A Follow-Up and a Replication," *Journal of Applied Psychology,* June 1989, pp. 411–16.

Chapter 3

[1] Based on R. Lane, "Don't Mess with Marilyn," *Forbes,* December 4, 1995, pp. 106–12.

[2] D.C. McClelland and J.W. Atkinson, "The Projective Expression of Needs: The Effect of Different Intensities of the Hunger Drive on Perception," *Journal of Psychology,* vol. 25 (1948), pp. 205–22.

[3] H.H. Kelley, "Attribution in Social Interaction," in E. Jones, et al. (eds.), *Attribution: Perceiving the Causes of Behavior* (Morristown, NJ: General Learning Press, 1972).

[4] See L. Ross, "The Intuitive Psychologist and His Shortcomings," in L. Berkowitz (ed.), *Advances in Experimental Social Psychology,* vol. 10 (Orlando, FL: Academic Press, 1977), pp. 174–220; and A.G. Miller and T. Lawson, "The Effect of an Informational Option on the Fundamental Attribution Error," *Personality and Social Psychology Bulletin,* June 1989, pp. 194–204.

[5] S. Nam, *Cultural and Managerial Attributions for Group Performance,* unpublished doctoral dissertation; University of Oregon. Cited in R.M. Steers, S.J. Bischoff, and L.H. Higgins, "Cross-Cultural Management Research," *Journal of Management Inquiry,* December 1992, pp. 325–26.

[6] D.C. Dearborn and H.A. Simon, "Selective Perception: A Note on the Departmental Identification of Executives," *Sociometry,* June 1958, pp. 140–44. Some of the conclusions in this classic study have recently been challenged in J.P. Walsh, "Selectivity and Selective Perception: An Inves-
tigation of Managers' Belief Structures and Information Processing," *Academy of Management Journal,* December 1988, pp. 873–96; M.J. Waller, G.P. Huber, and W.H. Glick, "Functional Background as a Determinant of Executives' Selective Perception," *Academy of Management Journal,* August 1995, pp. 943–74; and J.S. Bunderson, "Work History and Selective Perception: Fine-Tuning What We Know," in D.P. Moore (ed.), *Academy of Management Best Papers Proceedings* (Vancouver, BC, Academy of Management Conference, 1995), pp. 459–63.

[7] S.E. Asch, "Forming Impressions of Personality," *Journal of Abnormal and Social Psychology,* July 1946, pp. 258–90.

[8] J.S. Bruner and R. Tagiuri, "The Perception of People," in E. Lindzey (ed.), *Handbook of Social Psychology* (Reading, MA: Addison–Wesley, 1954), p. 641.

[9] See, for example, C.M. Judd and B. Park, "Definition and Assessment of Accuracy in Social Stereotypes," *Psychological Review,* January 1993, pp. 109–28.

[10] See, for example, S.T. Fiske, D.N. Beroff, E. Borgida, K. Deaux, and M.E. Heilman, "Use of Sex Stereotyping Research in Price Waterhouse vs. Hopkins," *American Psychologist,* 1991, pp. 1049–60; G.N. Powell, "The Good Manager: Business Students' Stereotypes of Japanese Managers versus Stereotypes of American Managers," *Group & Organizational Management,* 1992, pp. 44–56; and K.J. Gibson, W.J. Zerbe, and R.E. Franken, "Job Search Strategies for Older Job Hunters: Addressing Employers' Perceptions," *Canadian Journal of Counseling,* 1992, pp. 166–76.

[11] See, for example, E.C. Webster, *Decision Making in the Employment Interview* (Montreal: McGill University, Industrial Relations Center, 1964).

[12] See, for example, L. Jussim, "Self-Fulfilling Prophecies: A Theoretical and Integrative Review," *Psychological Review,* October 1986, pp. 429–45; D. Eden, *Pygmalion in Management* (Lexington, MA: Lexington, 1990); and D. Eden, "Leadership and Expectations: Pygmalion Effects and Other Self-Fulfilling Prophecies," *Leadership Quarterly,* Winter 1992, pp. 271–305.

[13] D. Eden and A.B. Shani, "Pygmalion Goes to Boot Camp: Expectancy, Leadership, and Trainee Performance," *Journal of Applied Psychology,* April 1982, pp. 194–99.

[14] See, for example, R.D. Bretz Jr., G.T. Milkovich, and W. Read, "The Current State of Performance Appraisal Research and Practice: Concerns, Directions, and Implications," *Journal of Management,* June 1992, pp. 323–24; and P.M. Swiercz, M.L. Icenogle, N.B. Bryan, and R.W. Renn, "Do Perceptions of Performance Appraisal Fairness Predict Employee Attitudes and Performance?" in D.P. Moore (ed.), *Proceedings of the Academy of Management* (Atlanta: Academy of Management, 1993), pp. 304–08.

[15] D. Kipnis, *The Powerholders* (Chicago: University of Chicago Press, 1976).

[16] See J.P. Near and M.P. Miceli, "Whistle-Blowers in Organizations: Dissidents or Reformers?" in L.L. Cummings and B.M. Staw (eds.), *Research in Organizational Behavior,* vol. 9 (Greenwich, CT: JAI Press, 1987), pp. 321–68.

[17] See H.A. Simon, "Rationality in Psychology and Economics," *The Journal of Business,* October 1986, pp. 209–24;

and A. Langley, "In Search of Rationality: The Purposes Behind the Use of Formal Analysis in Organizations," *Administrative Science Quarterly,* December 1989, pp. 598–631.

[18] For a review of the rational model, see E.F. Harrison, *The Managerial Decision-Making Process,* 4th ed. (Boston: Houghton Mifflin, 1995), pp. 75–85.

[19] W. Pounds, "The Process of Problem Finding," *Industrial Management Review,* Fall 1969, pp. 1–19.

[20] J.G. March, *A Primer on Decision Making* (New York: Free Press, 1994), pp. 2–7.

[21] T.M. Amabile, "A Model of Creativity and Innovation in Organizations," in B.M. Staw and L.L. Cummings (eds.), *Research in Organizational Behavior,* Vol. 10 (Greenwich, CT: JAI Press, 1988), p. 126.

[22] Cited in C.G. Morris, *Psychology: An Introduction,* 9th ed. (Upper Saddle River, NJ: Prentice Hall, 1996), p. 344.

[23] M.A. Colgrove, "Stimulating Creative Problem Solving: Innovative Set," *Psychological Reports,* vol. 22 (1968), pp. 1205–11.

[24] See M. Stein, *Stimulating Creativity,* vol. 1 (New York: Academic Press, 1974).

[25] E. deBono, *Lateral Thinking: Creativity Step by Step* (New York: Harper & Row, 1971).

[26] W.J.J. Gordon, *Synectics* (New York: Harper & Row, 1961).

[27] D.L. Rados, "Selection and Evaluation of Alternatives in Repetitive Decision Making," *Administrative Science Quarterly,* June 1972, pp. 196–206.

[28] M. Bazerman, *Judgment in Managerial Decision Making,* 3rd ed. (New York: Wiley, 1994), p. 5.

[29] See H.A. Simon, *Administrative Behavior,* 3rd ed. (New York: Free Press, 1976); and J. Forester, "Bounded Rationality and the Politics of Muddling Through," *Public Administration Review,* January–February 1984, pp. 23–31.

[30] W.H. Agor, "The Logic of Intuition: How Top Executives Make Important Decisions," *Organizational Dynamics,* Winter 1986, p. 5; W.H. Agor (ed.), *Intuition in Organizations* (Newbury Park, CA: Sage Publications, 1989); O. Behling and N.L. Eckel, "Making Sense Out of Intuition," *Academy of Management Executive,* February 1991, pp. 46–47; and V. Johnson, "Intuition in Decision-Making," *Successful Meetings,* February 1993, pp. 148–51.

[31] Behling and Eckel, "Making Sense Out of Intuition," pp. 46–54.

[32] As described in H.A. Simon, "Making Management Decisions: The Role of Intuition and Emotion," *Academy of Management Executive,* February 1987, pp. 59–60.

[33] Agor, "The Logic of Intuition," p. 9.

[34] Ibid., p. 15.

[35] See, for example, M.D. Cohen, J.G. March, and J.P. Olsen, "A Garbage Can Model of Organizational Choice," *Administrative Science Quarterly,* March 1972, pp 1–25.

[36] See J.G. Thompson, *Organizations in Action* (New York: McGraw-Hill, 1967), p. 123.

[37] C.E. Lindholm, "The Science of 'Muddling Through,'" *Public Administration Review,* Spring 1959, pp. 79–88.

[38] A. Tversky and K. Kahneman, "Judgment Under Uncertainty: Heuristics and Biases," *Science,* September 1974, pp. 1124–31.

[39] See B.M. Staw, "The Escalation of Commitment to a Course of Action," *Academy of Management Review,* October 1981, pp. 577–87; and D.R. Bobocei and J.P. Meyer, "Escalating Commitment to a Failing Course of Action: Separating the Roles of Choice and Justification," *Journal of Applied Psychology,* June 1994, pp. 360–63.

[40] A.J. Rowe, J.D. Boulgarides, and M.R. McGrath, *Managerial Decision Making,* Modules in Management Series (Chicago: SRA, 1984), pp. 18–22.

[41] S.N. Chakravarty and A. Feldman, "The Road Not Taken," *Forbes,* August 30, 1993, pp. 40–41.

[42] A. Wildavsky, *The Politics of the Budgetary Process* (Boston: Little Brown & Co., 1964).

[43] N.J. Adler, *International Dimensions of Organizational Behavior,* 2nd ed. (Boston: Kent Publishing, 1991), pp. 160–68.

[44] G.F. Cavanagh, D.J. Moberg, and M. Valasquez, "The Ethics of Organizational Politics," *Academy of Management Journal,* June 1981, pp. 363–74.

[45] See, for example, T. Machan, ed., *Commerce and Morality* (Totowa, NJ: Rowman and Littlefield, 1988).

[46] L.K. Trevino, "Ethical Decision Making in Organizations: A Person-Situation Interactionist Model," *Academy of Management Review,* July 1986, pp. 601–17; and L.K. Trevino and S.A. Youngblood, "Bad Apples in Bad Barrels: A Causal Analysis of Ethical Decision-Making Behavior," *Journal of Applied Psychology,* August 1990, pp. 378–85.

[47] See L. Kohlberg, *Essays in Moral Development: The Philosophy of Moral Development,* vol. 1 (New York: Harper & Row, 1981); L. Kohlberg, *Essays in Moral Development: The Psychology of Moral Development,* vol. 2 (New York: Harper & Row, 1984); and R.S. Snell, "Complementing Kohlberg: Mapping the Ethical Reasoning Used by Managers for Their Own Dilemma Cases," *Human Relations,* January 1996, pp. 23–50.

[48] W. Chow Hou, "To Bribe or Not to Bribe?" *Asia, Inc.,* October 1996, p. 104.

Chapter 4

[1] Based on J.L. Seglin, "The Happiest Workers in the World," *INC.: The State of Small Business 1996,* May 1996, pp. 62–76.

[2] Ibid.

[3] See, for instance, studies cited in A.F. Chelte, J. Wright, and C. Tausky, "Did Job Satisfaction Really Drop During the 1970s?" *Monthly Labor Review,* November 1982, pp. 33–36; "Job Satisfaction High in America, Says Conference Board Study," *Monthly Labor Review,* February 1985, p. 52; and C. Hartman and S. Pearlstein, "The Joy of Working," *INC.,* November 1987, pp. 61–66. See also "Wyatt WorkAmerica," published by The Wyatt Company, 1990.

[4] See "Job Satisfaction High in America," p. 52; and "America's Workers and Job Satisfaction," *Manpower Argus,* March 1996, p. 7.

[5] G.L. Staines and R.P. Quinn, "American Workers Evaluate the Quality of Their Jobs," *Monthly Labor Review,* January 1979, pp. 3–12.

[6] Chelte, Wright, Tausky, "Did Job Satisfaction Really Drop?"; and B.M. Staw, N.E. Bell, and J.A. Clausen, "The Dispositional Approach to Job Attitudes: A Lifetime Longitudinal Test," *Administrative Science Quarterly,* March 1986, pp. 56–77.

[7] J.L. Seglin, "The Happiest Workers in the World," p. 64; and "Satisfaction at Work," *Business Week,* June 24, 1996, p. 28.

[8] S.L. Wilk, L.B. Desmarais, and P.R. Sackett, "Gravitation to Jobs Commensurate With Ability: Longitudinal and Cross-Sectional Tests," *Journal of Applied Psychology,* February 1995, pp. 79–85.

[9] M. Rokeach, *The Nature of Human Values* (New York: Free Press, 1973), p. 5.

[10] See, for instance, P.E. Connor and B.W. Becker, "Personal Values and Management: What Do We Know and Why Don't We Know More?" *Journal of Management Inquiry,* March 1994, p. 68.

[11] L.M. Keller, T.J. Bouchard, Jr., R.D. Arvey, N.L. Segal, and R.V. Dawis, "Work Values: Genetic and Environmental Influences," *Journal of Applied Psychology,* February 1992, pp. 79–88.

[12] M. Rokeach and S.J. Ball-Rokeach, "Stability and Change in American Value Priorities, 1968–1981," *American Psychologist,* May 1989, pp. 775–84.

[13] M. Rokeach, *The Nature of Human Values,* p.6.

[14] Ibid.

[15] J.M. Munson and B.Z. Posner, "The Factorial Validity of a Modified Rokeach Value Survey for Four Diverse Samples," *Educational and Psychological Measurement,* Winter 1980, pp. 1073–79; and W.C. Frederick and J. Weber, "The Values of Corporate Managers and Their Critics: An Empirical Description and Normative Implications," in W.C. Frederick and L.E. Preston (eds.), *Business Ethics: Research Issues and Empirical Studies* (Greenwich, CT: JAI Press, 1990), pp. 123–44.

[16] Frederick and Weber, "The Values of Corporate Managers and Their Critics."

[17] Ibid., p. 132.

[18] See, for example, D.J. Cherrington, S.J. Condie, and J.L. England, "Age and Work Values," *Academy of Management Journal,* September 1979, pp. 617–23; J.A. Raelin, "The '60s Kids in the Corporation: More Than Just 'Daydream Believers,'" *Academy of Management Executive,* February 1987, pp. 21–30; L. Zinn, "Move Over, Boomers," *Business Week,* December 14, 1992, pp. 74–82; A. Harmon, "For GenX, the *Angst* Is On-Line," *Los Angeles Times,* April 28, 1993, p. A1; S. Ratan, "Generational Tension in the Office: Why Busters Hate Boomers," *Fortune,* October 4, 1993, pp. 56–70; P. O'Toole, "Redefining Success," *Working Woman,* November 1993, pp. 49–55, 100; B. Filipczak, "It's Just a Job: Generation X at Work," *Training,* April 1994, pp. 21–27; R. Rowe and W.E. Snizek, "Gender Differences in Work Values: Perpetuating the Myth," *Work and Occupations,* May 1995, pp. 215–29; and R. Maynard, "A Less-

Stressed Work Force," *Nation's Business,* November 1996, pp. 50–52.

[19] As noted to your author by R. Volkema and R.L. Neal Jr., of American University, this model may also be limited in its application to minority populations and recent immigrants to North America.

[20] R.E. Hattwick, Y. Kathawala, M. Monipullil, and L. Wall, "On the Alleged Decline in Business Ethics," *Journal of Behavioral Economics,* Summer 1989, pp. 129–43.

[21] B.Z. Posner and W.H. Schmidt, "Values and the American Manager: An Update Updated," *California Management Review,* Spring 1992, p. 86.

[22] See, for instance, D.A. Ralston, D.H. Holt, R.H. Terpstra, and Y. Kai-cheng, "The Impact of Culture and Ideology on Managerial Work Values: A Study of the United States, Russia, Japan, and China," in D.P. Moore (ed.), *Academy of Management Best Paper Proceedings* (Vancouver, BC; August 1995), pp. 187–91.

[23] G. Hofstede, *Culture's Consequences: International Differences in Work Related Values* (Beverly Hills, CA: Sage, 1980); G. Hofstede, *Cultures and Organizations: Software of the Mind* (London: McGraw-Hill, 1991); and G. Hofstede, "Cultural Constraints in Management Theories," *Academy of Management Executive,* February 1993, pp. 81–94.

[24] Hofstede called this dimension masculinity versus femininity, but we've changed his terms because of their strong sexist connotation.

[25] N.J. Adler, "Cross-Cultural Management Research: The Ostrich and the Trend," *Academy of Management Review,* April 1983, pp. 226–32.

[26] L. Godkin, C.E. Braye, and C.L. Caunch, "U.S.-Based Cross Cultural Management Research in the Eighties," *Journal of Business and Economic Perspectives,* vol. 15 (1989), pp. 37–45; and T.K. Peng, M.F. Peterson, and Y.P. Shyi, "Quantitative Methods in Cross-National Management Research: Trends and Equivalence Issues," *Journal of Organizational Behavior,* vol. 12 (1991), pp. 87–107.

[27] S.J. Breckler, "Empirical Validation of Affect, Behavior, and Cognition as Distinct Components of Attitude," *Journal of Personality and Social Psychology,* May 1984, pp. 1191–1205.

[28] See R.D. Arvey and T.J. Bouchard, Jr., "Genetics, Twins, and Organizational Behavior," in B.M. Staw and L.L. Cummings (eds.), *Research in Organizational Behavior,* vol. 16 (Greenwich, CT: JAI Press, 1994), pp. 66–68 for evidence demonstrating a genetic basis for attitude development and expression.

[29] P.P. Brooke Jr., D.W. Russell, and J.L. Price, "Discriminant Validation of Measures of Job Satisfaction, Job Involvement, and Organizational Commitment," *Journal of Applied Psychology,* May 1988, pp. 139–45.

[30] See, for example, S. Rabinowitz and D.T. Hall, "Organizational Research in Job Involvement," *Psychological Bulletin,* March 1977, pp. 265–88; G.J. Blau, "A Multiple Study Investigation of the Dimensionality of Job Involvement," *Journal of Vocational Behavior,* August 1985, pp. 19–36; and N.A. Jans, "Organizational Factors and Work Involvement," *Organizational Behavior and Human Decision Processes,* June 1985, pp. 382–96.

31 Based on G.J. Blau and K.R. Boal, "Conceptualizing How Job Involvement and Organizational Commitment Affect Turnover and Absenteeism," *Academy of Management Review,* April 1987, p. 290.

32 G.J. Blau, "Job Involvement and Organizational Commitment as Interactive Predictors of Tardiness and Absenteeism," *Journal of Management,* Winter 1986, pp. 577–84; and K. Boal and R. Cidambi, "Attitudinal Correlates of Turnover and Absenteeism: A Meta Analysis," paper presented at the meeting of the American Psychological Association, Toronto, Canada, 1984.

33 G. Farris, "A Predictive Study of Turnover," *Personnel Psychology,* Summer 1971, pp. 311–28.

34 Blau and Boal, "Conceptualizing," p. 290.

35 See, for instance, P.W. Hom, R. Katerberg, and C.L. Hulin, "Comparative Examination of Three Approaches to the Prediction of Turnover," *Journal of Applied Psychology,* June 1979, pp. 280–90; H. Angle and J. Perry, "Organizational Commitment: Individual and Organizational Influence," *Work and Occupations,* May 1983, pp. 123–46; and J.L. Pierce and R.B. Dunham, "Organizational Commitment: Pre-Employment Propensity and Initial Work Experiences," *Journal of Management,* Spring 1987, pp. 163–78.

36 Hom, Katerberg, and Hulin, "Comparative Examination"; and R.T. Mowday, L.W. Porter, and R.M. Steers, *Employee Organization Linkages: The Psychology of Commitment, Absenteeism, and Turnover* (New York: Academic Press, 1982).

37 L.W. Porter, R.M. Steers, R.T. Mowday, and P.V. Boulian, "Organizational Commitment, Job Satisfaction, and Turnover Among Psychiatric Technicians," *Journal of Applied Psychology,* October 1974, pp. 603–09.

38 L. Festinger, *A Theory of Cognitive Dissonance* (Stanford, CA: Stanford University Press, 1957).

39 A.W. Wicker, "Attitude versus Action: The Relationship of Verbal and Overt Behavioral Responses to Attitude Objects," *Journal of Social Issues,* Autumn 1969, pp. 41–78.

40 Ibid., p. 65.

41 T.A. Heberlein and J.S. Black, "Attitudinal Specificity and the Prediction of Behavior in a Field Setting," *Journal of Personality and Social Psychology,* April 1976, pp. 474–79.

42 H. Schuman and M.P. Johnson, "Attitudes and Behavior," in A. Inkeles (ed.), *Annual Review of Sociology* (Palo Alto, CA: Annual Reviews, 1976), pp. 161–207.

43 R.H. Fazio and M.P. Zanna, "Direct Experience and Attitude-Behavior Consistency," in L. Berkowitz (ed.), *Advances in Experimental Social Psychology* (New York: Academic Press, 1981), pp. 161–202.

44 L.R. Kahle and H.J. Berman, "Attitudes Cause Behaviors: A Cross-Lagged Panel Analysis," *Journal of Personality and Social Psychology,* March 1979, pp. 315–21; and C.L. Kleinke, "Two Models for Conceptualizing the Attitude-Behavior Relationship," *Human Relations,* April 1984, pp. 333–50.

45 D.J. Bem, "Self-Perception Theory," in L. Berkowitz (ed.), *Advances in Experimental Social Psychology,* vol. 6 (New York: Academic Press, 1972), pp. 1–62.

46 See, for example, C.A. Kiesler, R.E. Nisbett, and M.P. Zanna, "On Inferring One's Belief from One's Behavior," *Journal of Personality and Social Psychology,* April 1969, pp. 321–27.

47 R. Abelson, "Are Attitudes Necessary?" in B.T. King and E. McGinnies (eds.), *Attitudes, Conflicts, and Social Change* (New York: Academic Press, 1972), p. 25.

48 See, for example, G.E. Lyne, "How to Measure Employee Attitudes," *Training and Development Journal,* December 1989, pp. 40–43; and P. Hise, "The Motivational Employee-Satisfaction Questionnaire," *INC.,* February 1994, pp. 73–75.

49 P. Hise, "The Motivational Employee-Satisfaction Questionnaire."

50 I. Barmash, "More Substance Than Show," *Across the Board,* May 1993, pp. 43–45.

51 See G. Gallup, "Employee Research: From Nice to Know to Need to Know," *Personnel Journal,* August 1988, pp. 42–43; and T. Lammers, "The Essential Employee Survey," *INC.,* December 1992, pp. 159–61.

52 This box is based on P.G. Zimbardo, E.B. Ebbesen, and C. Maslach, *Influencing Attitudes and Changing Behavior* (Reading, MA: Addison-Wesley, 1977); R.E. Petty and J.T. Cacioppo, *Attitudes and Persuasion: Central and Peripheral Routes to Persuasion* (New York: Springer-Verlag, 1984); and A. Bednar and W. H. Levie, "Attitude-Change Principles," in C. Fleming and W.H. Levie, *Instructional Message Design: Principles from the Behavioral and Cognitive Sciences,* 2nd ed. (Englewood Cliffs, NJ: Educational Technology Publications, 1993).

53 M. Crawford, "The New Office Etiquette," *Canadian Business,* May 1993, pp. 22–31.

54 Cited in A. Rossett and T. Bickham, "Diversity Training: Hope, Faith and Cynicism," *Training,* January 1994, p. 40.

55 This section is based on A. Rossett and T. Bickham, "Diversity Training," pp. 40–46.

56 For problems with the concept of job satisfaction, see R. Hodson, "Workplace Behaviors," *Work and Occupations,* August 1991, pp. 271–90; and H.M. Weiss and R. Cropanzano, "Affective Events Theory: A Theoretical Discussion of the Structure, Causes and Consequences of Affective Experiences at Work," in B.M. Staw and L.L. Cummings (eds), *Research in Organizational Behavior,* vol. 18 (Greenwich, CT: JAI Press, 1996), pp. 1–3.

57 The Wyatt Company's 1989 national WorkAmerica study identified 12 dimensions of satisfaction: work organization, working conditions, communications, job performance and performance review, co-workers, supervision, company management, pay, benefits, career development and training, job content and satisfaction, and company image and change.

58 See J.L. Price and C.W. Mueller, *Handbook of Organizational Measurement* (Marshfield, MA: Pitman Publishing, 1986), pp. 223–27.

59 V. Scarpello and J.P. Campbell, "Job Satisfaction: Are All the Parts There?" *Personnel Psychology,* Autumn 1983, pp. 577–600.

60 E.A. Locke, "The Nature and Causes of Job Satisfaction," in M.D. Dunnette (ed.), *Handbook of Industrial and Organiza-*

tional Psychology (Chicago: Rand McNally, 1976), pp. 1319–28.

[61] R.A. Katzell, D.E. Thompson, and R.A. Guzzo, "How Job Satisfaction and Job Performance Are and Are Not Linked," in C.J. Cranny, P.C. Smith, and E.F. Stone (eds.), *Job Satisfaction* (New York: Lexington Books, 1992), pp. 195–217.

[62] L.A. Witt and L.G. Nye, "Gender and the Relationship Between Perceived Fairness of Pay or Promotion and Job Satisfaction," *Journal of Applied Psychology,* December 1992, pp. 910–17.

[63] See, for example, D.C. Feldman and H.J. Arnold, "Personality Types and Career Patterns: Some Empirical Evidence on Holland's Model," *Canadian Journal of Administrative Science,* June 1985, pp. 192–210.

[64] For the data on this issue, see Staw, Bell, and Clausen, "The Dispositional Approach to Job Attitudes"; R.D. Arvey, T.J. Bouchard, Jr., N.L. Segal, and L.M. Abraham, "Job Satisfaction: Environmental and Genetic Components," *Journal of Applied Psychology,* April 1989, pp. 187–92; B. Gerhart, "How Important Are Dispositional Factors as Determinants of Job Satisfaction? Implications for Job Design and Other Personnel Programs," *Journal of Applied Psychology,* August 1987, pp. 366–73; R.D. Arvey, G.W. Carter, and D.K. Buerkley, "Job Satisfaction: Dispositional and Situational Influences," in C.L. Cooper and I.T. Robertson (eds.), *International Review of Industrial and Organizational Psychology,* vol. 6 (Chichester, England: John Wiley, 1991), pp. 359–83; T.J. Bouchard, Jr., R.D. Arvey, L.M. Keller, and N.L. Segal, "Genetic Influences on Job Satisfaction: A Reply to Cropanzano and James," *Journal of Applied Psychology,* February 1992, pp. 89–93; T.A. Judge, "Dispositional Perspective in Human Resources Research," in G.R. Ferris and K.M. Rowland (eds.), *Research in Personality and Human Resources Management,* vol. 10 (Greenwich, CT: JAI Press, 1992); R.D. Arvey and T.J. Bouchard, Jr., "Genetics, Twins, and Organizational Behavior," in B.M. Staw and L.L. Cummings (eds.), *Research in Organizational Behavior;* T.A. Judge and S. Watanabe, "Another Look at the Job Satisfaction-Life Satisfaction Relationship," *Journal of Applied Psychology,* December 1993, pp. 939–48; and R.D. Arvey, B.P. McCall, T.J. Bouchard, Jr., and P. Taubman, "Genetic Influences on Job Satisfaction and Work Values," *Personality and Individual Differences,* July 1994, pp. 21–33.

[65] G. Bassett, "The Case Against Job Satisfaction," *Business Horizons,* May–June 1994, p. 65.

[66] A.H. Brayfield and W.H. Crockett, "Employee Attitudes and Employee Performance," *Psychological Bulletin,* September 1955, pp. 396–428; F. Herzberg, B. Mausner, R.O. Peterson, and D.F. Capwell, *Job Attitudes: Review of Research and Opinion* (Pittsburgh: Psychological Service of Pittsburgh, 1957); V.H. Vroom, *Work and Motivation* (New York: John Wiley, 1964); G.P. Fournet, M.K. Distefano, Jr., and M.W. Pryer, "Job Satisfaction: Issues and Problems," *Personnel Psychology,* Summer 1966, pp. 165–83.

[67] Vroom, *Work and Motivation;* and M.T. Iaffaldano and P.M. Muchinsky, "Job Satisfaction and Job Performance: A Meta-Analysis," *Psychological Bulletin,* March 1985, pp. 251–73.

[68] See, for example, J.B. Herman, "Are Situational Contingencies Limiting Job Attitude–Job Performance Relationship?", *Organizational Behavior and Human Performance,* October 1973, pp. 208–24; and M.M. Petty, G.W. McGee, and J.W. Cavender, "A Meta-Analysis of the Relationship Between Individual Job Satisfaction and Individual Performance," *Academy of Management Review,* October 1984, pp. 712–21.

[69] C.N. Greene, "The Satisfaction–Performance Controversy," *Business Horizons,* February 1972, pp. 31–41; E.E. Lawler III, *Motivation in Organizations* (Monterey, CA: Brooks/Cole, 1973); and Petty, McGee, and Cavender, "A Meta-Analysis of the Relationship Between Individual Job Satisfaction and Individual Performance."

[70] C. Ostroff, "The Relationship Between Satisfaction, Attitudes, and Performance: An Organizational Level Analysis," *Journal of Applied Psychology,* December 1992, pp. 963–74.

[71] Locke, "The Nature and Causes of Job Satisfaction," p. 1331; S.L. McShane, "Job Satisfaction and Absenteeism: A Meta-Analytic Re-Examination," *Canadian Journal of Administrative Science,* June 1984, pp. 61–77; R.D. Hackett and R.M. Guion, "A Reevaluation of the Absenteeism–Job Satisfaction Relationship," *Organizational Behavior and Human Decision Processes,* June 1985, p. 340–81; K.D. Scott and G.S. Taylor, "An Examination of Conflicting Findings on the Relationship Between Job Satisfaction and Absenteeism: A Meta-Analysis," *Academy of Management Journal,* September 1985, pp. 599–612; R.D. Hackett, "Work Attitudes and Employee Absenteeism: A Synthesis of the Literature," paper presented at 1988 National Academy of Management Conference, Anaheim, CA, August 1988; and R.P. Steel and J.R. Rentsch, "Influence of Cumulation Strategies on the Long-Range Prediction of Absenteeism," *Academy of Management Journal,* December 1995, pp. 1616–34.

[72] F.J. Smith, "Work Attitudes as Predictors of Attendance on a Specific Day," *Journal of Applied Psychology,* February 1977, pp. 16–19.

[73] Brayfield and Crockett, "Employee Attitudes"; Vroom, *Work and Motivation;* J. Price, *The Study of Turnover* (Ames: Iowa State University Press, 1977); and W.H. Mobley, R.W. Griffeth, H.H. Hand, and B. M. Meglino, "Review and Conceptual Analysis of the Employee Turnover Process," *Psychological Bulletin,* May 1979, pp. 493–522.

[74] See, for example, C.L. Hulin, M. Roznowski, and D. Hachiya, "Alternative Opportunities and Withdrawal Decisions: Empirical and Theoretical Discrepancies and an Integration," *Psychological Bulletin,* July 1985, pp. 233–50; and J.M. Carsten and P.E. Spector, "Unemployment, Job Satisfaction, and Employee Turnover: A Meta-Analytic Test of the Muchinsky Model," *Journal of Applied Psychology,* August 1987, pp. 374–81.

[75] D.G. Spencer and R.M. Steers, "Performance as a Moderator of the Job Satisfaction–Turnover Relationship," *Journal of Applied Psychology,* August 1981, pp. 511–14.

[76] T.A. Judge, "Does Affective Disposition Moderate the Relationship Between Job Satisfaction and Voluntary Turnover?" *Journal of Applied Psychology,* June 1993, pp. 395–401.

[77] S.M. Puffer, "Prosocial Behavior, Noncompliant Behavior, and Work Performance Among Commission Salespeople," *Journal of Applied Psychology,* November 1987, pp. 615–21; J. Hogan and R. Hogan, "How to Measure Employee Reliability," *Journal of Applied Psychology,* May 1989, pp. 273–79; and C.D. Fisher and E.A. Locke, "The New Look in Job Satisfaction Research and Theory," in C.J. Cranny, P.C. Smith, and E.F. Stone (eds.), *Job Satisfaction,* 165–94.

[78] See D. Farrell, "Exit, Voice, Loyalty, and Neglect as Responses to Job Dissatisfaction: A Multidimensional Scaling Study," *Academy of Management Journal,* December 1983, pp. 596–606; C.E. Rusbult, D. Farrell, G. Rogers, and A.G. Mainous III, "Impact of Exchange Variables on Exit, Voice, Loyalty, and Neglect: An Integrative Model of Responses to Declining Job Satisfaction," *Academy of Management Journal,* September 1988, pp. 599–627; M.J. Withey and W.H. Cooper, "Predicting Exit, Voice, Loyalty, and Neglect," *Administrative Science Quarterly,* December 1989, pp. 521–39; and D. Farrell, C. Rusbult, Y-H Lin, and P. Bernthall, "Impact of Job Satisfaction, Investment Size, and Quality of Alternatives on Exit, Voice, Loyalty, and Neglect Responses to Job Dissatisfaction: A Cross-Legged Panel Study," in L.R. Jauch and J.L. Wall (eds.), *Proceedings of the 50th Annual Academy of Management Conference,* San Francisco, 1990, pp. 211–15.

[79] R.B. Freeman, "Job Satisfaction as an Economic Variable," *American Economic Review,* January 1978, pp. 135–41.

Chapter 5

[1] S. Desker-Shaw, "Revving Up Asia's Workers," *Asian Business,* February 1996, pp. 41–44.

[2] R. Katerberg and G.J. Blau, "An Examination of Level and Direction of Effort and Job Performance," *Academy of Management Journal,* June 1983, pp. 249–57.

[3] A. Maslow, *Motivation and Personality* (New York: Harper & Row, 1954).

[4] See, for example, E.E. Lawler III and J.L. Suttle, "A Causal Correlation Test of the Need Hierarchy Concept," *Organizational Behavior and Human Performance,* April 1972, pp. 265–87; D.T. Hall and K.E. Nougaim, "An Examination of Maslow's Need Hierarchy in an Organizational Setting," *Organizational Behavior and Human Performance,* February 1968, pp. 12–35; and J. Rauschenberger, N. Schmitt, and J.E. Hunter, "A Test of the Need Hierarchy Concept by a Markov Model of Change in Need Strength," *Administrative Science Quarterly,* December 1980, pp. 654–70.

[5] A.K. Korman, J.H. Greenhaus, and I.J. Badin, "Personnel Attitudes and Motivation," in M.R. Rosenzweig and L.W. Porter (eds.), *Annual Review of Psychology* (Palo Alto, CA: Annual Reviews, 1977), p. 178.

[6] Ibid., p. 179.

[7] M.A. Wahba and L.G. Bridwell, "Maslow Reconsidered: A Review of Research on the Need Hierarchy Theory," *Organizational Behavior and Human Performance,* April 1976, pp. 212–40.

[8] D. McGregor, *The Human Side of Enterprise* (New York: McGraw-Hill, 1960). For an updated analysis of Theory X and Theory Y constructs, see R.J. Summers and S.F. Cronshaw, "A Study of McGregor's Theory X, Theory Y and the Influence of Theory X, Theory Y Assumptions on Causal Attributions for Instances of Worker Poor Performance," in S.L. McShane (ed.), *Organizational Behavior,* ASAC 1988 Conference Proceedings, vol. 9, Part 5. Halifax, Nova Scotia, 1988, pp. 115–23.

[9] F. Herzberg, B. Mausner, and B. Snyderman, *The Motivation to Work* (New York: John Wiley, 1959).

[10] R.J. House and L.A. Wigdor, "Herzberg's Dual-Factor Theory of Job Satisfaction and Motivations: A Review of the Evidence and Criticism," *Personnel Psychology,* Winter 1967, pp. 369–89; D.P. Schwab and L.L. Cummings, "Theories of Performance and Satisfaction: A Review," *Industrial Relations,* October 1970, pp. 403–30; and R.J. Caston and R. Braito, "A Specification Issue in Job Satisfaction Research," *Sociological Perspectives,* April 1985, pp. 175–97.

[11] D. Guest, "What's New in Motivation," *Personnel Management,* May 1984, pp. 20–23.

[12] C.P. Alderfer, "An Empirical Test of a New Theory of Human Needs," *Organizational Behavior and Human Performance,* May 1969, pp. 142–75.

[13] M. Haire, E.E. Ghiselli, and L.W. Porter, "Cultural Patterns in the Role of the Manager," *Industrial Relations,* February 1963, pp. 95–117.

[14] C.P. Schneider and C.P. Alderfer, "Three Studies of Measures of Need Satisfaction in Organizations," *Administrative Science Quarterly,* December 1973, pp. 489–505.

[15] J.P. Wanous and A. Zwany, "A Cross-Sectional Test of Need Hierarchy Theory," *Organizational Behavior and Human Performance,* May 1977, pp. 78–97.

[16] D.C. McClelland, *The Achieving Society* (New York: Van Nostrand Reinhold, 1961); J.W. Atkinson and J.O. Raynor, *Motivation and Achievement* (Washington, D.C.: Winston, 1974); D.C. McClelland, *Power: The Inner Experience* (New York: Irvington, 1975); and M.J. Stahl, *Managerial and Technical Motivation: Assessing Needs for Achievement, Power, and Affiliation* (New York: Praeger, 1986).

[17] McClelland, *The Achieving Society.*

[18] See, for example, A. Mehrabian, "Measures of Achieving Tendency," *Educational and Psychological Measurement,* Summer 1969, pp. 445–51; H.J.M. Hermans, "A Questionnaire Measure of Achievement Motivation," *Journal of Applied Psychology,* August 1970, pp. 353–63; and J.M. Smith, "A Quick Measure of Achievement Motivation," *British Journal of Social and Clinical Psychology,* June 1973, pp. 137–43.

[19] See W.D. Spangler, "Validity of Questionnaire and TAT Measures of Need for Achievement: Two Meta-Analyses," *Psychological Bulletin,* July 1992, pp. 140–54.

[20] D.C. McClelland and D.G. Winter, *Motivating Economic Achievement* (New York: Free Press, 1969).

[21] McClelland, *Power;* McClelland and D.H. Burnham, "Power Is the Great Motivator," *Harvard Business Review,* March–April 1976, pp. 100–10; and R.E. Boyatzis, "The Need for Close Relationships and the Manager's Job," in D.A. Kolb, I.M. Rubin, and J.M. McIntyre, *Organizational Psychology: Readings on Human Behavior in Organizations,* 4th ed. (Englewood Cliffs, NJ: Prentice Hall, 1984), pp. 81–86.

[22] Ibid.

23 J.B. Miner, *Studies in Management Education* (New York: Springer, 1965).

24 D. Kipnis, "The Powerholder," in J.T. Tedeschi (ed.), *Perspectives in Social Power* (Chicago: Aldine, 1974), pp. 82–123.

25 D. McClelland, "Toward a Theory of Motive Acquisition," *American Psychologist*, May 1965, pp. 321–33; and D. Miron and D.C. McClelland, "The Impact of Achievement Motivation Training on Small Businesses," *California Management Review*, Summer 1979, pp. 13–28.

26 R. de Charms, *Personal Causation: The Internal Affective Determinants of Behavior* (New York: Academic Press, 1968).

27 E.L. Deci, *Intrinsic Motivation* (New York: Plenum, 1975); R.D. Pritchard, K.M. Campbell, and D.J. Campbell, "Effects of Extrinsic Financial Rewards on Intrinsic Motivation," *Journal of Applied Psychology*, February 1977, pp. 9–15; E.L. Deci, G. Betly, J. Kahle, L. Abrams, and J. Porac, "When Trying to Win: Competition and Intrinsic Motivation," *Personality and Social Psychology Bulletin*, March 1981, pp. 79–83; and P.C. Jordan, "Effects of an Extrinsic Reward on Intrinsic Motivation: A Field Experiment," *Academy of Management Journal*, June 1986, pp. 405–12. See also J.M. Schrof, "Tarnished Trophies," *U.S. News & World Report*, October 25, 1993, pp. 52–59.

28 W.E. Scott, "The Effects of Extrinsic Rewards on 'Intrinsic Motivation': A Critique," *Organizational Behavior and Human Performance*, February 1976, pp. 117–19; B.J. Calder and B.M. Staw, "Interaction of Intrinsic and Extrinsic Motivation: Some Methodological Notes," *Journal of Personality and Social Psychology*, January 1975, pp. 76–80; and K.B. Boal and L.L. Cummings, "Cognitive Evaluation Theory: An Experimental Test of Processes and Outcomes," *Organizational Behavior and Human Performance*, December 1981, pp. 289–310.

29 G.R. Salancik, "Interaction Effects of Performance and Money on Self-Perception of Intrinsic Motivation," *Organizational Behavior and Human Performance*, June 1975, pp. 339–51; and F. Luthans, M. Martinko, and T. Kess, "An Analysis of the Impact of Contingency Monetary Rewards on Intrinsic Motivation," *Proceedings of the Nineteenth Annual Midwest Academy of Management*, St. Louis, 1976, pp. 209–21.

30 J.B. Miner, *Theories of Organizational Behavior* (Hinsdale, IL: Dryden Press, 1980), p. 157.

31 H.J. Arnold, "Effects of Performance Feedback and Extrinsic Reward upon High Intrinsic Motivation," *Organizational Behavior and Human Performance*, December 1976, pp. 275–88.

32 B.M. Staw, "Motivation in Organizations: Toward Synthesis and Redirection," in B.M. Staw and G.R. Salancik (eds.), *New Directions in Organizational Behavior* (Chicago: St. Clair, 1977), p. 76.

33 B.J. Calder and B.M. Staw, "Self-Perception of Intrinsic and Extrinsic Motivation," *Journal of Personality and Social Psychology*, April 1975, pp. 599–605.

34 E.A. Locke, "Toward a Theory of Task Motivation and Incentives," *Organizational Behavior and Human Performance*, May 1968, pp. 157–89.

35 P.C. Earley, P. Wojnaroski, and W. Prest, "Task Planning and Energy Expended: Exploration of How Goals Influence Performance," *Journal of Applied Psychology*, February 1987, pp. 107–14.

36 G.P. Latham and G.A. Yukl, "A Review of Research on the Application of Goal Setting in Organizations," *Academy of Management Journal*, December 1975, pp. 824–45; E.A. Locke, K.N. Shaw, L.M. Saari, and G.P. Latham, "Goal Setting and Task Performance," *Psychological Bulletin*, January 1981, pp. 125–52; A.J. Mento, R.P. Steel, and R.J. Karren, "A Meta-Analytic Study of the Effects of Goal Setting on Task Performance: 1966–1984," *Organizational Behavior and Human Decision Processes*, February 1987, pp. 52–83; M.E. Tubbs "Goal Setting: A Meta-Analytic Examination of the Empirical Evidence," *Journal of Applied Psychology*, August 1986, pp. 474–83; P.C. Earley, G.B. Northcraft, C. Lee, and T.R. Lituchy, "Impact of Process and Outcome Feedback on the Relation of Goal Setting to Task Performance," *Academy of Management Journal*, March 1990, pp. 87–105; and E.A. Locke and G.P. Latham, *A Theory of Goal Setting and Task Performance* (Englewood Cliffs, NJ: Prentice Hall, 1990).

37 J.M. Ivancevich and J.T. McMahon, "The Effects of Goal Setting, External Feedback, and Self-Generated Feedback on Outcome Variables: A Field Experiment," *Academy of Management Journal*, June 1982, pp. 359–72.

38 See, for example, G.P. Latham, M. Erez, and E.A. Locke, "Resolving Scientific Disputes by the Joint Design of Crucial Experiments by the Antagonists: Application to the Erez-Latham Dispute Regarding Participation in Goal Setting," *Journal of Applied Psychology*, November 1988, pp. 753–72.

39 M. Erez, P.C. Earley, and C.L. Hulin, "The Impact of Participation on Goal Acceptance and Performance: A Two-Step Model," *Academy of Management Journal*, March 1985, pp. 50–66.

40 J.R. Hollenbeck, C.R. Williams, and H.J. Klein, "An Empirical Examination of the Antecedents of Commitment to Difficult Goals," *Journal of Applied Psychology*, February 1989, pp. 18–23. See also J.C. Wofford, V.L. Goodwin, and S. Premack, "Meta-Analysis of the Antecedents of Personal Goal Level and of the Antecedents and Consequences of Goal Commitment," *Journal of Management*, September 1992, pp. 595–615; and M.E. Tubbs, "Commitment as a Moderator of the Goal-Performance Relation: A Case for Clearer Construct Definition," *Journal of Applied Psychology*, February 1993, pp. 86–97.

41 A. Bandura, "Self-Efficacy: Toward a Unifying Theory of Behavioral Change," *Psychological Review*, May 1977, pp. 191–215; and M.E. Gist, "Self-Efficacy: Implications for Organizational Behavior and Human Resource Management," *Academy of Management Review*, July 1987, pp. 472–85.

42 E.A. Locke, E. Frederick, C. Lee, and P. Bobko, "Effect of Self-Efficacy, Goals, and Task Strategies on Task Performance," *Journal of Applied Psychology*, May 1984, pp. 241–51; and M.E. Gist and T.R. Mitchell, "Self-Efficacy: A Theoretical Analysis of Its Determinants and Malleability," *Academy of Management Review*, April 1992, pp. 183–211.

43 A. Bandura and D. Cervone, "Differential Engagement in Self-Reactive Influences in Cognitively-Based Motivation,"

Organizational Behavior and Human Decision Processes, August 1986, pp. 92–113.

44 See J.C. Anderson and C.A. O'Reilly, "Effects of an Organizational Control System on Managerial Satisfaction and Performance," *Human Relations,* June 1981, pp. 491–501; and J.P. Meyer, B. Schacht-Cole, and I.R. Gellatly, "An Examination of the Cognitive Mechanisms by Which Assigned Goals Affect Task Performance and Reactions to Performance," *Journal of Applied Social Psychology,* vol. 18, No. 5, 1988, pp. 390–408.

45 R.M. Steers and L.W. Porter, *Motivation and Work Behavior,* 2nd ed. (New York: McGraw-Hill, 1979), p. 13.

46 E.A. Locke, "Latham vs. Komaki: A Tale of Two Paradigms," *Journal of Applied Psychology,* February 1980, pp. 16–23.

47 J.S. Adams, "Inequity in Social Exchanges," in L. Berkowitz (ed.), *Advances in Experimental Social Psychology* (New York: Academic Press, 1965), pp. 267–300.

48 P.S. Goodman, "An Examination of Referents Used in the Evaluation of Pay," *Organizational Behavior and Human Performance,* October 1974, pp. 170–95; S. Ronen, "Equity Perception in Multiple Comparisons: A Field Study," *Human Relations,* April 1986, pp. 333–46; R.W. Scholl, E.A. Cooper, and J.F. McKenna, "Referent Selection in Determining Equity Perception: Differential Effects on Behavioral and Attitudinal Outcomes," *Personnel Psychology,* Spring 1987, pp. 113–27; and T.P. Summers and A.S. DeNisi, "In Search of Adams' Other: Reexamination of Referents Used in the Evaluation of Pay," *Human Relations,* June 1990, pp. 497–511.

49 C.T. Kulik and M.L. Ambrose, "Personal and Situational Determinants of Referent Choice," *Academy of Management Review,* April 1992, pp. 212–37.

50 See, for example, E. Walster, G.W. Walster, and W.G. Scott, *Equity: Theory and Research* (Boston: Allyn & Bacon, 1978); and J. Greenberg, "Cognitive Reevaluation of Outcomes in Response to Underpayment Inequity," *Academy of Management Journal,* March 1989, pp. 174–84.

51 P.S. Goodman and A. Friedman, "An Examination of Adams' Theory of Inequity," *Administrative Science Quarterly,* September 1971, pp. 271–88; R.P. Vecchio, "An Individual-Differences Interpretation of the Conflicting Predictions Generated by Equity Theory and Expectancy Theory," *Journal of Applied Psychology,* August 1981, pp. 470–81; J. Greenberg, "Approaching Equity and Avoiding Inequity in Groups and Organizations," in J. Greenberg and R.L. Cohen (eds.), *Equity and Justice in Social Behavior* (New York: Academic Press, 1982), pp. 389–435; R.T. Mowday, "Equity Theory Predictions of Behavior in Organizations," in R.M. Steers and L.W. Porter (eds.), *Motivation and Work Behavior,* 4th ed. (New York: McGraw-Hill, 1987), pp. 89–110; E.W. Miles, J.D. Hatfield, and R.C. Huseman, "The Equity Sensitive Construct: Potential Implications for Worker Performance," *Journal of Management,* December 1989, pp. 581–88; and R.T. Mowday, "Equity Theory Predictions of Behavior in Organizations," in R. Steers and L.W. Porter (eds.), *Motivation and Work Behavior,* 5th ed. (New York: McGraw-Hill, 1991), pp. 111–31.

52 J. Greenberg and S. Ornstein, "High Status Job Title as Compensation for Underpayment: A Test of Equity Theory," *Journal of Applied Psychology,* May 1983, pp. 285–97; and J. Greenberg, "Equity and Workplace Status: A Field Experiment," *Journal of Applied Psychology,* November 1988, pp. 606–13.

53 See, for instance, B.H. Sheppard, R.J. Lewicki, and J.W. Minton, *Organizational Justice: The Search for Fairness in the Workplace* (New York: Lexington Books, 1992); and J. Greenberg, *The Quest for Justice on the Job* (Thousand Oaks, CA: Sage, 1996).

54 See, for example, R.C. Dailey and D.J. Kirk, "Distributive and Procedural Justice as Antecedents of Job Dissatisfaction and Intent to Turnover," *Human Relations,* March 1992, pp. 305–16; D.B. McFarlin and P.D. Sweeney, "Distributive and Procedural Justice as Predictors of Satisfaction With Personal and Organizational Outcomes," *Academy of Management Journal,* August 1992, pp. 626–37; and M.A. Korsgaard, D.M. Schweiger, and H.J. Sapienza, "Building Commitment, Attachment, and Trust in Strategic Decision-Making Teams: The Role of Procedural Justice," *Academy of Management Journal,* February 1995, pp. 60–84.

55 P.S. Goodman, "Social Comparison Process in Organizations," in B.M. Staw and G.R. Salancik (eds.), *New Directions in Organizational Behavior* (Chicago: St. Clair, 1977), pp. 97–132; and J. Greenberg, "A Taxonomy of Organizational Justice Theories," *Academy of Management Review,* January 1987, pp. 9–22.

56 V.H. Vroom, *Work and Motivation* (New York: John Wiley, 1964).

57 See, for example, H.G. Heneman III and D.P. Schwab, "Evaluation of Research on Expectancy Theory Prediction of Employee Performance," *Psychological Bulletin,* July 1972, pp. 1–9; T.R. Mitchell, "Expectancy Models of Job Satisfaction, Occupational Preference and Effort: A Theoretical, Methodological and Empirical Appraisal," *Psychological Bulletin,* November 1974, pp. 1053–77; and L. Reinharth and M.A. Wahba, "Expectancy Theory as a Predictor of Work Motivation, Effort Expenditure, and Job Performance," *Academy of Management Journal,* September 1975, pp. 502–37.

58 See, for example, L.W. Porter and E.E. Lawler III, *Managerial Attitudes and Performance* (Homewood, IL: Richard D. Irwin, 1968); D.F. Parker and L. Dyer, "Expectancy Theory as a Within-Person Behavioral Choice Model: An Empirical Test of Some Conceptual and Methodological Refinements," *Organizational Behavior and Human Performance,* October 1976, pp. 97–117; H.J. Arnold, "A Test of the Multiplicative Hypothesis of Expectancy-Valence Theories of Work Motivation," *Academy of Management Journal,* April 1981, pp. 128–41; and W. Van Eerde and H. Thierry, "Vroom's Expectancy Models and Work-Related Criteria: A Meta-Analysis," *Journal of Applied Psychology,* October 1996, pp. 575–86.

59 Vroom refers to these three variables as expectancy, instrumentality, and valence, respectively.

60 P.M. Muchinsky, "A Comparison of Within- and Across-Subjects Analyses of the Expectancy-Valence Model for

Predicting Effort," *Academy of Management Journal,* March 1977, pp. 154–58.

61 R.J. House, H.J. Shapiro, and M.A. Wahba, "Expectancy Theory as a Predictor of Work Behavior and Attitudes: A Re-evaluation of Empirical Evidence," *Decision Sciences,* January 1974, pp. 481–506.

62 L.H. Peters, E.J. O'Connor, and C.J. Rudolf, "The Behavioral and Affective Consequences of Performance-Relevant Situational Variables," *Organizational Behavior and Human Performance,* February 1980, pp. 79–96; M. Blumberg and C.D. Pringle, "The Missing Opportunity in Organizational Research: Some Implications for a Theory of Work Performance," *Academy of Management Review,* October 1982, pp. 560–69; D.A. Waldman and W.D. Spangler, "Putting Together the Pieces: A Closer Look at the Determinants of Job Performance," *Human Performance,* vol. 2, 1989, pp. 29–59; and J. Hall, "Americans Know How to Be Productive If Managers Will Let Them," *Organizational Dynamics,* Winter 1994, pp. 33–46.

63 For other examples of models that seek to integrate motivation theories, see H.J. Klein, "An Integrated Control Theory Model of Work Motivation," *Academy of Management Review,* April 1989, pp. 150–72; and E.A. Locke, "The Motivation Sequence, the Motivation Hub, and the Motivation Core," *Organizational Behavior and Human Decision Processes,* December 1991, pp. 288–99.

64 N.J. Adler, *International Dimensions of Organizational Behavior,* 2nd ed. (Boston: PWS-Kent Publishing, 1991), p. 152.

65 G. Hofstede, "Motivation, Leadership, and Organization: Do American Theories Apply Abroad?," *Organizational Dynamics,* Summer 1980, p. 55.

66 Ibid.

67 I. Harpaz, "The Importance of Work Goals: An International Perspective," *Journal of International Business Studies,* First Quarter 1990, pp. 75–93.

68 G.E. Popp, H.J. Davis, and T.T. Herbert, "An International Study of Intrinsic Motivation Composition," *Management International Review,* January 1986, pp. 28–35.

69 This section is based on F.J. Landy and W.S. Becker, "Motivation Theory Reconsidered," in L.L. Cummings and B.M. Staw (eds.), *Research in Organizational Behavior,* Vol. 9 (Greenwich, CT: JAI Press, 1987), pp. 24–35.

Chapter 6

1 P. Simao, "Eureka!" *Canadian Business,* June 1996, pp. 66–69.

2 P.F. Drucker, *The Practice of Management* (New York: Harper & Row, 1954).

3 See, for instance, S.J. Carroll and H.L. Tosi, *Management by Objectives: Applications and Research* (New York, Macmillan, 1973); and R. Rodgers and J.E. Hunter, "Impact of Management by Objectives on Organizational Productivity," *Journal of Applied Psychology,* April 1991, pp. 322–36.

4 See, for instance, R.C. Ford, F.S. MacLaughlin, and J. Nixdorf, "Ten Questions About MBO," *California Management Review,* Winter 1980, p. 89; T.J. Collamore, "Making MBO Work in the Public Sector," *Bureaucrat,* Fall 1989, pp. 37–40; G. Dabbs, "Nonprofit Businesses in the 1990s:

Models for Success," *Business Horizons,* September–October 1991, pp. 68–71; R. Rodgers and J.E. Hunter, "A Foundation of Good Management Practice in Government: Management by Objectives," *Public Administration Review,* January–February 1992, pp. 27–39; and T.H. Poister and G. Streib, "MBO in Municipal Government: Variations on a Traditional Management Tool," *Public Administration Review,* January/February 1995, pp. 48–56.

5 See, for instance, C.H. Ford, "MBO: An Idea Whose Time Has Gone?" *Business Horizons,* December 1979, p. 49; R. Rodgers and J.E. Hunter, "Impact of Management by Objectives on Organizational Productivity," *Journal of Applied Psychology,* April 1991, pp. 322–36; and R. Rodgers, J.E. Hunter , and D.L. Rogers, "Influence of Top Management Commitment on Management Program Success," *Journal of Applied Psychology,* February 1993, pp. 151–55.

6 S. Navarette, "Multiple Forms of Employee Recognition," *At Work,* July/August 1993, pp. 9–10.

7 Cited in S. Caudron, "The Top 20 Ways to Motivate Employees," *Industry Week,* April 3, 1995, pp. 15–16. See also B. Nelson, "Try Praise," *INC.,* September 1996, p. 115.

8 "Look, Movie Tickets: With Budgets Tight, Alternatives to Pay Increases Emerge," *Wall Street Journal,* September 27, 1994, p. A1.

9 Cited in *Asian Business,* December 1994, p. 3.

10 R. Levering and M. Moskowitz, "The Ten Best Companies to Work for in America," *Business and Society Review,* Spring 1993, p. 29.

11 B. Saporito, "The Revolt Against 'Working Smarter,'" *Fortune,* July 21, 1986, pp. 58–65; "Quality Circles: Rounding Up Quality at USAA," *AIDE Magazine,* Fall 1983, p. 24; and J. Kerr, "The Informers," *INC.,* March 1995, pp. 50–61.

12 J.L. Cotton, *Employee Involvement* (Newbury Park, CA: Sage, 1993), pp. 3 and 14.

13 Ibid., p. 3.

14 See, for example, the increasing body of literature on empowerment such as R.C. Ford and M.D. Fottler, "Empowerment: A Matter of Degree," *The Academy of Management Executive,* August 1995, pp. 21–31; and G.M. Spreitzer, "Psychological Empowerment in the Workplace: Dimensions, Measurement, and Validation," *Academy of Management Journal,* October 1995, pp. 1442–65.

15 M. Sashkin, "Participative Management Is an Ethical Imperative," *Organizational Dynamics,* Spring 1984, pp. 5–22.

16 R. Tannenbaum, I.R. Weschler, and F. Massarik, *Leadership and Organization: A Behavioral Science Approach* (New York: McGraw-Hill, 1961), pp. 88–100.

17 E. Locke and D. Schweiger, "Participation in Decision Making: One More Look," in B.M. Staw (ed.), *Research in Organizational Behavior,* Vol. 1, Greenwich, CT: JAI Press, 1979; E.A. Locke, D.B. Feren, V.M. McCaleb, K.N. Shaw, and A.T. Denny, "The Relative Effectiveness of Four Methods of Motivating Employee Performance," in K.D. Duncan, M.M. Gruneberg, and D. Wallis (eds.), *Changes in Working Life* (London: Wiley, 1980), pp. 363–88; K.L. Miller and P.R. Monge, "Participation, Satisfaction, and Productivity: A Meta-Analytic Review," *Academy of Management Journal,*

December 1986, pp. 727–53; J.A. Wagner III and R.Z. Gooding, "Effects of Societal Trends on Participation Research," *Administrative Science Quarterly,* June 1987, pp. 241–62; J.A. Wagner III and R.Z. Gooding, "Shared Influence and Organizational Behavior: A Meta-Analysis of Situational Variables Expected to Moderate Participation-Outcome Relationships," *Academy of Management Journal,* September 1987, pp. 524–41; J.L. Cotton, D.A. Vollrath, K.L. Froggatt, M.L. Lengnick-Hall, and K.R. Jennings, "Employee Participation: Diverse Forms and Different Outcomes," *Academy of Management Review,* January 1988, pp. 8–22; C.R. Leana, E.A. Locke, and D.M. Schweiger, "Fact and Fiction in Analyzing Research on Participative Decision Making: A Critique of Cotton, Vollrath, Froggatt, Lengnick-Hall, and Jennings," *Academy of Management Review,* January 1990, pp. 137–46; J.W. Graham and A. Verma, "Predictors and Moderators of Employee Responses to Employee Participation Programs," *Human Relations,* June 1991, pp. 551–68; J.A. Wagner III, "Participation's Effects on Performance and Satisfaction: A Reconsideration of Research Evidence," *Academy of Management Review,* April 1994, pp. 312–30; G.P. Latham, D.C. Winters, and E.A. Locke, "Cognitive and Motivational Effects of Participation: A Mediator Study," *Journal of Organizational Behavior,* January 1994, pp. 49–63; C. Doucouliagos, "Worker Participation and Productivity in Labor-Managed and Participatory Capitalist Firms: A Meta-Analysis," *Industrial and Labor Relations Review,* October 1995, pp. 58–77; and C. Pavett and T. Morris, "Management Styles Within a Multinational Corporation: A Five Country Comparative Study," *Human Relations,* October 1995, pp. 1171–91.

[18] J.L. Cotton, *Employee Involvement,* p. 114.

[19] See, for example, M. Poole, "Industrial Democracy: A Comparative Analysis," *Industrial Relations,* Fall 1979, pp. 262–72; IDE International Research Group, *European Industrial Relations* (Oxford, UK: Clarendon, 1981); E.M. Kassalow, "Employee Representation on U.S., German Boards," *Monthly Labor Review,* September 1989, pp. 39–42; T.H. Hammer, S.C. Currall, and R.N. Stern, "Worker Representation on Boards of Directors: A Study of Competing Roles," *Industrial and Labor Relations Review,* Winter 1991, pp. 661–80; and P. Kunst and J. Soeters, "Works Council Membership and Career Opportunities," *Organization Studies,* vol. 12, no. 1, 1991, pp. 75–93.

[20] J.D. Kleyn and S. Perrick, "Netherlands," *International Financial Law Review,* February 1990, pp. 51–56.

[21] J.L. Cotton, *Employee Involvement,* pp. 129–30 and 139–40.

[22] Ibid., p. 140.

[23] Ibid., p. 59.

[24] See, for example, G.W. Meyer and R.G. Stott, "Quality Circles: Panacea or Pandora's Box?" *Organizational Dynamics,* Spring 1985, pp. 34–50; M.L. Marks, P.H. Mirvis, E.J. Hackett, and J.F. Grady, Jr., "Employee Participation in a Quality Circle Program: Impact on Quality of Work Life, Productivity, and Absenteeism," *Journal of Applied Psychology,* February 1986, pp. 61–69; E.E. Lawler III and S.A. Mohrman, "Quality Circles: After the Honeymoon," *Organizational Dynamics,* Spring 1987, pp. 42–54; R.P. Steel and R.F. Lloyd, "Cognitive, Affective, and Behavioral Outcomes

of Participation in Quality Circles: Conceptual and Empirical Findings," *Journal of Applied Behavioral Science,* vol. 24, no. 1, 1988, pp. 1–17; T.R. Miller, "The Quality Circle Phenomenon: A Review and Appraisal," *SAM Advanced Management Journal,* Winter 1989, pp. 4–7; K. Buch and R. Spangler, "The Effects of Quality Circles on Performance and Promotions," *Human Relations,* June 1990, pp. 573–82; P.R. Liverpool, "Employee Participation in Decision-Making: An Analysis of the Perceptions of Members and Nonmembers of Quality Circles," *Journal of Business and Psychology,* Summer 1990, pp. 411–22, and E.E. Adams, Jr., "Quality Circle Performance," *Journal of Management,* March 1991, pp. 25–39.

[25] J.L. Cotton, *Employee Involvement,* p. 76.

[26] Ibid., p. 78.

[27] Ibid., p. 87.

[28] See K.M. Young (ed.), *The Expanding Role of ESOPs in Public Companies* (New York: Quorum, 1990); J.L. Pierce and C.A. Furo, "Employee Ownership: Implications for Management," *Organizational Dynamics,* Winter 1990, pp. 32–43; J. Blasi and D.L. Druse, *The New Owners: The Mass Emergence of Employee Ownership in Public Companies and What It Means to American Business* (Champaign, IL: Harper Business, 1991); F.T. Adams and G.B. Hansen, *Putting Democracy to Work: A Practical Guide for Starting and Managing Worker-Owned Businesses* (San Francisco: Berrett-Koehler, 1993); and A.A. Buchko, "The Effects of Employee Ownership on Employee Attitudes: An Integrated Causal Model and Path Analysis," *Journal of Management Studies,* July 1993, pp. 633–56.

[29] J.L. Pierce and C.A. Furo, "Employee Ownership"; C.H. Farnsworth, "One Employee Buyout That Actually Worked," *New York Times,* February 5, 1995, p. F4; A. Bernstein, "Should Avis Try Harder—For Its Employees?" *Business Week,* August 12, 1996, pp. 68–69.

[30] A.A. Buchko, "The Effects of Employee Ownership on Employee Attitudes.

[31] C.M. Rosen and M. Quarrey, "How Well Is Employee Ownership Working?" *Harvard Business Review,* September–October 1987, pp. 126–32.

[32] J.L. Pierce and C.A. Furo, "Employee Ownership."

[33] See data in D. Stamps, "A Piece of the Action," *Training,* March 1996, p. 66.

[34] T.R. Miller, "The Quality Circle Phenomenon," p. 5.

[35] J.L. Pierce and C.A. Furo, "Employee Ownership," p. 32; and A. Bernstein, "Why ESOP Deals Have Slowed to a Crawl," *Business Week,* March 18, 1996, pp. 101–02.

[36] Cited in T. Ehrenfeld, "Cashing In," *INC.,* July 1993, pp. 69–70.

[37] J. Fierman, "The Perilous New World of Fair Pay," *Fortune,* June 13, 1994, p. 63.

[38] G. Steinmetz, "German Banks Note the Value of Bonuses," *Wall Street Journal,* May 9, 1995, p. A17.

[39] J.A. Byrne, "Deliver—Or Else," *Business Week,* March 27, 1995, pp. 36–38.

[40] Based on S.E. Gross and J.P. Bacher, "The New Variable Pay Programs: How Some Succeed, Why Some Don't," *Compen-*

sation & Benefits Review, January–February 1993, p. 51; and J.R. Schuster and P.K. Zingheim, "The New Variable Pay: Key Design Issues," *Compensation & Benefits Review,* March–April 1993, p. 28.

41 J.A. Byrne, "That Eye-Popping Executive Pay," *Business Week,* April 25, 1994, p. 58.

42 J. O'C. Hamilton, "Levi's Pot O' Gold," *Business Week,* June 24, 1996, p. 44.

43 See, for instance, S.C. Hanlon, D.G. Meyer, and R.R. Taylor, "Consequences of Gainsharing," *Group & Organization Management,* March 1994, pp. 87–111; J.G. Belcher, Jr., "Gainsharing and Variable Pay: The State of the Art," *Compensation & Benefits Review,* May–June 1994, pp. 50–60; and T.M. Welbourne and L.R. Gomez Mejia, "Gainsharing: A Critical Review and a Future Research Agenda," *Journal of Management,* vol. 21; no. 3, 1995, pp. 559–609.

44 See J.L. Cotton, *Employee Involvement,* pp. 89–113; and W. Imberman, "Boosting Plant Performance with Gainsharing," *Business Horizons,* November–December 1992, p. 79.

45 M. Fein, "Work Measurement and Wage Incentives," *Industrial Engineering,* September 1973, pp. 49–51.

46 B. Wysocki, Jr., "Unstable Pay Becomes Ever More Common," *Wall Street Journal,* December 4, 1995, p. A1.

47 W. Zellner, "Trickle-Down Is Trickling Down at Work," *Business Week,* March 18, 1996, p. 34.

48 Ibid.

49 "Bonus Pay in Canada," *Manpower Argus,* September 1996, p. 5.

50 D. Beck, "Implementing a Gainsharing Plan: What Companies Need to Know," *Compensation & Benefits Review,* January–February 1992, p. 23.

51 W. Imberman, "Boosting Plant Performance with Gainsharing."

52 Cited in "Pay for Performance," *Wall Street Journal,* February 20, 1990, p. 1.

53 These examples are cited in A. Gabor, "After the Pay Revolution, Job Titles Won't Matter," *New York Times,* May 17, 1992, p. F5; "Skilled-Based Pay Boosts Worker Productivity and Morale," *Wall Street Journal,* June 23, 1992, p. A1; L. Wiener, "No New Skills? No Raise," *U.S. News & World Report,* October 26, 1992, p. 78; and M.A. Verespej, "New Responsibilities? New Pay!" *Industry Week,* August 15, 1994, p. 14.

54 G.E. Ledford, Jr., "Paying for the Skills, Knowledge, and Competencies of Knowledge Workers," *Compensation & Benefits Review,* July–August 1995, pp. 55–62.

55 M. Rowland, "For Each New Skill, More Money," *New York Times,* June 13, 1993, p. F16.

56 E.E. Lawler III, G.E. Ledford, Jr., and L. Chang, "Who Uses Skill-Based Pay, and Why," *Compensation & Benefits Review,* March–April 1993, p. 22.

57 "Tensions of a New Pay Plan," *New York Times,* May 17, 1992, p. F5.

58 Cited in E.E. Lawler III, S.A. Mohrman, and G.E. Ledford, Jr., *Creating High Performance Organizations: Practices and Results in the Fortune 1000* (San Francisco: Jossey-Bass, 1995).

59 "Skill-Based Pay Boosts Worker Productivity and Morale, *Wall Street Journal,* June 23, 1992, p. A1.

60 E.E. Lawler III, G.E. Ledford, Jr., and L. Chang, "Who Uses Skill-Based Pay, and Why."

61 M. Rowland, "It's What You Can Do That Counts," *New York Times,* June 6, 1993, p. F17.

62 Ibid.

63 See, for instance, "When You Want to Contain Costs and Let Employees Pick Their Benefits: Cafeteria Plans," *INC.,* December 1989, p. 142; "More Benefits Bend with Workers' Needs," *Wall Street Journal,* January 9, 1990, p. B1; R. Thompson, "Switching to Flexible Benefits," *Nation's Business,* July 1991, pp. 16–23; and A.E. Barber, R.B. Dunham, and R.A. Formisano, "The Impact of Flexible Benefits on Employee Satisfaction: A Field Study," *Personnel Psychology,* Spring 1992, pp. 55–75.

64 E.E. Lawler III, "Reward Systems," in Hackman and Suttle (eds.), *Improving Life at Work,* p. 182.

65 R. Thompson, "Switching to Flexible Benefits," p. 17.

66 "When You Want to Contain Costs and Let Employees Pick Their Benefits."

67 H. Bernstein, "New Benefit Schemes Can Be Deceiving," *Los Angeles Times,* May 14, 1991, p. D3.

68 See, for instance, M. Alpert, "The Care and Feeding of Engineers," *Fortune,* September 21, 1992, pp. 86–95; and G. Poole, "How to Manage Your Nerds," *Forbes ASAP,* December 1994, pp. 132–36.

69 See, for example, B. Geber, "The Flexible Work Force," *Training,* December 1993, pp. 23–30; M. Barrier, "Now You Hire Them, Now You Don't," *Nation's Business,* January 1994, pp. 30–31; J. Fierman, "The Contingency Work Force," *Fortune,* January 24, 1994, pp. 30–36; and D.C. Feldman, H.I. Doerpinghaus, and W.H. Turnley, "Managing Temporary Workers: A Permanent HRM Challenge," *Organizational Dynamics,* Autumn 1994, pp. 49–63.

70 "Six Million Americans Say Jobs Are Temporary," *Manpower Argus,* November 1995, p. 2.

71 G. Fuchsberg, "Parallel Lines," *Wall Street Journal,* April 21, 1993, p. R4; and A. Penzias, "New Paths to Success," *Fortune,* June 12, 1995, pp. 90–94.

72 D. Hage and J. Impoco, "Jawboning the Jobs," *U.S. News & World Report,* August 9, 1993, p. 53.

73 M.P. Cronin, "One Life to Live," *INC.,* July 1993, pp. 56–60.

Chapter 7

1 Based on M. Stevenson, "Be Nice for a Change," *Canadian Business,* November 1993, pp. 81–85.

2 L.R. Sayles, "Work Group Behavior and the Larger Organization," in C. Arensburg, et al. (eds.), *Research in Industrial Relations* (New York: Harper & Row, 1957), pp. 131–45.

3 B.W. Tuckman, "Developmental Sequences in Small Groups," *Psychological Bulletin,* June 1965, pp. 384–99; B.W. Tuckman and M.C. Jensen, "Stages of Small-Group Development Revisited," *Group and Organizational Studies,* December 1977, pp. 419–27; and M.F. Maples, "Group Development: Extending Tuckman's Theory," *Journal for Specialists in Group Work,* Fall 1988, pp. 17–23.

[4] R.C. Ginnett, "The Airline Cockpit Crew," in J.R. Hackman (ed.), *Groups That Work (and Those That Don't)* (San Francisco: Jossey-Bass, 1990).

[5] C.J.G. Gersick, "Time and Transition in Work Teams: Toward a New Model of Group Development," *Academy of Management Journal,* March 1988, pp. 9–41; C.J.G. Gersick, "Marking Time: Predictable Transitions in Task Groups," *Academy of Management Journal,* June 1989, pp. 274–309; E. Romanelli and M.L. Tushman, "Organizational Transformation as Punctuated Equilibrium: An Empirical Test," *Academy of Management Journal,* October 1994, pp. 1141–66; and B.M. Lichtenstein, "Evolution or Transformation: A Critique and Alternative to Punctuated Equilibrium," in D.P. Moore (ed.), *Academy of Management Best Paper Proceedings;* National Academy of Management Conference; Vancouver, BC, 1995, pp. 291–95.

[6] See J.L. Moreno, "Contributions of Sociometry to Research Methodology in Sociology," *American Sociological Review,* June 1947, pp. 287–92. Also J.W. Hart and R. Nath, "Sociometry in Business and Industry: New Developments in Historical Perspective," *Group Psychotherapy, Psychodrama and Sociometry,* Vol. 32 (1979), pp. 128–49.

[7] N.M. Tichy, M.L. Tushman, and C. Fombrun, "Social Network Analysis for Organizations," *Academy of Management Review,* October 1979, pp. 507–19; and N. Tichy and C. Fombrun, "Network Analysis in Organizational Settings," *Human Relations,* November 1979, pp. 923–65.

[8] D. Krackhardt and L.W. Porter, "The Snowball Effect: Turnover Embedded in Communication Networks," *Journal of Applied Psychology,* February 1986, pp. 50–55.

[9] R.E. Nelson, "The Strength of Strong Ties: Social Networks and Intergroup Conflict in Organizations," *Academy of Management Journal,* June 1989, pp. 377–401.

[10] H. Ibarra, "Personal Networks of Women and Minorities in Management: A Conceptual Framework," *Academy of Management Review,* January 1993, pp. 56–87.

[11] This model is based on the work of P.S. Goodman, E. Ravlin, and M. Schminke, "Understanding Groups in Organizations," in L.L. Cummings and B.M. Staw (eds.), *Research in Organizational Behavior,* Vol. 9 (Greenwich, CT: JAI Press, 1987), pp. 124–28; J.R. Hackman, "The Design of Work Teams," in J.W. Lorsch (ed.), *Handbook of Organizational Behavior* (Englewood Cliffs, NJ: Prentice Hall, 1987), pp. 315–42; G.R. Bushe and A.L. Johnson, "Contextual and Internal Variables Affecting Task Group Outcomes in Organizations," *Group and Organization Studies,* December 1989, pp. 462–82; and M.A. Campion, G.J. Medsker, and A.C. Higgs, "Relations Between Work Group Characteristics and Effectiveness: Implications for Designing Effective Work Groups," *Personnel Psychology,* Winter 1993, pp. 823–50.

[12] F. Friedlander, "The Ecology of Work Groups," in J.W. Lorsch (ed.) *Handbook of Organizational Behavior,* pp. 301–14; P.B. Paulus and D. Nagar, "Environmental Influences on Groups," in P. Paulus (ed.), *Psychology of Group Influence,* 2nd ed. (Hillsdale, NJ: Erlbaum, 1989); and E. Sundstrom and I. Altman, "Physical Environments and Work-Group Effectiveness," in L.L. Cummings and B.M.

Staw (eds.), *Research in Organizational Behavior,* Vol. 11 (Greenwich, CT: JAI Press, 1989), pp. 175–209.

[13] See, for example, J. Krantz, "Group Processes Under Conditions of Organizational Decline," *The Journal of Applied Behavioral Science,* Vol. 21, No. 1, 1985, pp. 1–17.

[14] Hackman, "The Design of Work Teams," pp. 325–26.

[15] See, for instance, G.R. Oldham and Y. Fried, "Employee Reactions to Workspace Characteristics," *Journal of Applied Psychology,* February 1987, pp. 75–80; and R.A. Baron, "The Physical Environment of Work Settings: Effects on Task Performance, Interpersonal Relations, and Job Satisfaction," in B.M. Staw and L.L. Cummings (eds.), *Research in Organizational Behavior,* Vol. 16 (Greenwich, CT: JAI Press, 1994), pp. 1–46.

[16] Cited in A.D. Szilagyi, Jr., and M.J. Wallace, Jr., *Organizational Behavior and Performance,* 4th ed. (Glenview, IL: Scott, Foresman, 1987), p. 223.

[17] See M. Hill, "Group Versus Individual Performance. Are N+1 Heads Better Than One?" *Psychological Reports,* April 1982, pp. 517–39; and A. Tziner and D. Eden, "Effects of Crew Composition on Crew Performance: Does the Whole Equal the Sum of Its Parts?" *Journal of Applied Psychology,* February 1985, pp. 85–93.

[18] M.E. Shaw, *Contemporary Topics in Social Psychology* (Morristown, NJ: General Learning Press, 1976), pp. 350–51.

[19] S. Lieberman, "The Effects of Changes in Roles on the Attitudes of Role Occupants," *Human Relations,* November 1956, pp. 385–402.

[20] See S.L. Robinson, M.S. Kraatz, and D.M. Rousseau, "Changing Obligations and the Psychological Contract: A Longitudinal Study," *Academy of Management Journal,* February 1994, pp. 137–52.

[21] E.H. Schein, *Organizational Psychology,* 3rd ed. (Englewood Cliffs, NJ: Prentice Hall, 1980), p. 24.

[22] See M.F. Peterson, et al., "Role Conflict, Ambiguity, and Overload: A 21-Nation Study," *Academy of Management Journal,* April 1995, pp. 429–52.

[23] P.G. Zimbardo, C. Haney, W.C. Banks, and D. Jaffe, "The Mind Is a Formidable Jailer: A Pirandellian Prison," *New York Times,* April 8, 1973, pp. 38–60.

[24] For a recent review of the research on group norms, see J.R. Hackman, "Group Influences on Individuals in Organizations," in M.D. Dunnette and L.M. Hough (eds.), *Handbook of Industrial & Organizational Psychology,* 2nd edition, Vol. 3 (Palo Alto, CA: Consulting Psychologists Press, 1992), pp. 235–50.

[25] A. Harlan, J. Kerr, and S. Kerr, "Preference for Motivator and Hygiene Factors in a Hypothetical Interview Situation: Further Findings and Some Implications for the Employment Interview," *Personnel Psychology,* Winter 1977, pp. 557–66.

[26] Adapted from Goodman, Ravlin, and Schminke, "Understanding Groups in Organizations," p. 159.

[27] See, for instance, G. Blau, "Influence of Group Lateness on Individual Lateness: A Cross-Level Examination," *Academy of Management Journal,* October 1995, pp. 1483–96.

[28] D.C. Feldman, "The Development and Enforcement of Group Norms," *Academy of Management Journal,* January

1984, pp. 47–53; and K.L. Bettenhausen and J.K. Murnighan, "The Development of an Intragroup Norm and the Effects of Interpersonal and Structural Challenges," *Administrative Science Quarterly*, March 1991, pp. 20–35.

29 C.A. Kiesler and S.B. Kiesler, *Conformity* (Reading, MA: Addison-Wesley, 1969).

30 Ibid, p. 27.

31 S.E. Asch, "Effects of Group Pressure upon the Modification and Distortion of Judgments," in H. Guetzkow (ed.), *Groups, Leadership and Men* (Pittsburgh: Carnegie Press, 1951), pp. 177–90.

32 R. Keyes, *Is There Life After High School?* (New York: Warner Books, 1976).

33 W.F. Whyte, "The Social Structure of the Restaurant," *American Journal of Sociology*, January 1954, pp. 302–08.

34 Cited in J.R. Hackman, "Group Influences on Individuals in Organizations," p. 236.

35 O.J. Harvey and C. Consalvi, "Status and Conformity to Pressures in Informal Groups," *Journal of Abnormal and Social Psychology*, Spring 1960, pp. 182–87.

36 J.A. Wiggins, F. Dill, and R.D. Schwartz, "On 'Status-Liability,'" *Sociometry*, April–May 1965, pp. 197–209.

37 J. Greenberg, "Equity and Workplace Status: A Field Experiment," *Journal of Applied Psychology*, November 1988, pp. 606–13.

38 E.J. Thomas and C.F. Fink, "Effects of Group Size," *Psychological Bulletin*, July 1963, pp. 371–84; A.P. Hare, *Handbook of Small Group Research* (New York: Free Press, 1976); and M.E. Shaw, *Group Dynamics: The Psychology of Small Group Behavior*, 3rd ed. (New York: McGraw-Hill, 1981).

39 See D.R. Comer, "A Model of Social Loafing in Real Work Groups," *Human Relations*, June 1995, pp. 647–67.

40 W. Moede, "Die Richtlinien der Leistungs-Psychologie," *Industrielle Psychotechnik*, Vol. 4 (1927), pp. 193–207. See also D.A. Kravitz and B. Martin, "Ringelmann Rediscovered: The Original Article," *Journal of Personality and Social Psychology*, May 1986, pp. 936–41.

41 See, for example, J.A. Shepperd, "Productivity Loss in Performance Groups: A Motivation Analysis," *Psychological Bulletin*, January 1993, pp. 67–81; and S.J. Karau and K.D. Williams, "Social Loafing: A Meta-Analytic Review and Theoretical Integration," *Journal of Personality and Social Psychology*, October 1993, pp. 681–706.

42 S.G. Harkins and K. Szymanski, "Social Loafing and Group Evaluation," *Journal of Personality and Social Psychology*, December 1989, pp. 934–41.

43 See P.C. Earley, "Social Loafing and Collectivism: A Comparison of the United States and the People's Republic of China," *Administrative Science Quarterly*, December 1989, pp. 565–81; and P.C. Earley, "East Meets West Meets Mideast: Further Explorations of Collectivistic and Individualistic Work Groups," *Academy of Management Journal*, April 1993, pp. 319–48.

44 Thomas and Fink, "Effects of Group Size"; Hare, *Handbook;* Shaw, *Group Dynamics;* and P. Yetton and P. Bottger, "The

Relationships Among Group Size, Member Ability, Social Decision Schemes, and Performance," *Organizational Behavior and Human Performance*, October 1983, pp. 145–59.

45 See, for example, P.S. Goodman, E.C. Ravlin, and L. Argote, "Current Thinking About Groups: Setting the Stage for New Ideas," in P.S. Goodman and Associates, *Designing Effective Work Groups* (San Francisco: Jossey-Bass, 1986), pp. 15–16; and R.A. Guzzo and G.P. Shea, "Group Performance and Intergroup Relations in Organizations," in M.D. Dunnette and L.M. Hough, eds., *Handbook of Industrial & Organizational Psychology*, 2nd edition, Vol. 3 (Palo Alto, CA: Consulting Psychologists Press, 1992), pp. 288–90.

46 Shaw, *Contemporary Topics*, p. 356.

47 W.E. Watson, K. Kumar, and L.K. Michaelsen, "Cultural Diversity's Impact on Interaction Process and Performance: Comparing Homogeneous and Diverse Task Groups," *Academy of Management Journal*, June 1993, pp. 590–602.

48 B.E. McCain, C.A. O'Reilly III, and J. Pfeffer, "The Effects of Departmental Demography on Turnover: The Case of a University," *Academy of Management Journal*, December 1983, pp. 626–41; W.G. Wagner, J. Pfeffer, and C.A. O'Reilly III, "Organizational Demography and Turnover in Top-Management Groups," *Administrative Science Quarterly*, March 1984, pp. 74–92; J. Pfeffer and C.A. O'Reilly III, "Hospital Demography and Turnover Among Nurses," *Industrial Relations*, Spring 1987, pp. 158–73; C.A. O'Reilly III, D.F. Caldwell, and W.P. Barnett, "Work Group Demography, Social Integration, and Turnover," *Administrative Science Quarterly*, March 1989, pp. 21–37; S.E. Jackson, J.F. Brett, V.I. Sessa, D.M. Cooper, J.A. Julin, and K. Peyronnin, "Some Differences Make a Difference: Individual Dissimilarity and Group Heterogeneity as Correlates of Recruitment, Promotions, and Turnover," *Journal of Applied Psychology*, August 1991, pp. 675–89; M.F. Wiersema and A. Bird, "Organizational Demography in Japanese Firms: Group Heterogeneity, Individual Dissimilarity, and Top Management Team Turnover," *Academy of Management Journal*, October 1993, pp. 996–1025; F.J. Milliken and L.L. Martins, "Searching for Common Threads: Understanding the Multiple Effects of Diversity in Organizational Groups," *Academy of Management Review*, April 1996, pp. 402–33.

49 For some of the controversy surrounding the definition of cohesion, see J. Keyton and J. Springston, "Redefining Cohesiveness in Groups," *Small Group Research*, May 1990, pp. 234–54.

50 I. Summers, T. Coffelt, and R.E. Horton, "Work-Group Cohesion," *Psychological Reports*, October 1988, pp. 627–36; and B. Mullen and C. Cooper, "The Relation Between Group Cohesiveness and Performance: An Integration," *Psychological Bulletin*, March 1994, pp. 210–27.

51 Based on J.L. Gibson, J.M. Ivancevich, and J.H. Donnelly Jr., *Organizations*, 8th ed. (Burr Ridge, IL: Irwin, 1994), p. 323.

52 I.D. Steiner, *Group Process and Productivity* (New York: Academic Press, 1972).

53 R.B. Zajonc, "Social Facilitation," *Science*, March 1965, pp. 269–74.

54 C.F. Bond, Jr. and L.J. Titus, "Social Facilitation: A Meta-Analysis of 241 Studies," *Psychological Bulletin,* September 1983, pp. 265–92.

55 V.F. Nieva, E.A. Fleishman, and A. Rieck, "Team Dimensions: Their Identity, Their Measurement, and Their Relationships." Final Technical Report for Contract No. DAHC 19-C-0001. Washington, DC: Advanced Research Resources Organizations, 1978.

56 See, for example, J.R. Hackman and C.G. Morris, "Group Tasks, Group Interaction Process and Group Performance Effectiveness: A Review and Proposed Integration," in L. Berkowitz (ed.), *Advances in Experimental Social Psychology* (New York: Academic Press, 1975), pp. 45–99; and R. Saavedra, P.C. Earley, and L. Van Dyne, "Complex Interdependence in Task-Performing Groups," *Journal of Applied Psychology,* February 1993, pp. 61–72.

57 J. Galbraith, *Organizational Design* (Reading, MA: Addison-Wesley, 1977).

58 See N.R.F. Maier, "Assets and Liabilities in Group Problem Solving: The Need for an Integrative Function," *Psychological Review,* April 1967, pp. 239–49; G.W. Hill, "Group versus Individual Performance: Are N+1 Heads Better Than One?" *Psychological Bulletin,* May 1982, pp. 517–39; and A.E. Schwartz and J. Levin, "Better Group Decision Making," *Supervisory Management,* June 1990, p. 4.

59 See, for example, R.A. Cooke and J.A. Kernaghan, "Estimating the Difference Between Group versus Individual Performance on Problem-Solving Tasks," *Group & Organization Studies,* September 1987, pp. 319–42; and L.K. Michaelsen, W.E. Watson, and R.H. Black, "A Realistic Test of Individual versus Group Consensus Decision Making," *Journal of Applied Psychology,* October 1989, pp. 834–39.

60 See, for example, W.C. Swap and Associates, *Group Decision Making* (Newbury Park, CA: Sage, 1984).

61 I.L. Janis, *Groupthink* (Boston: Houghton Mifflin, 1982); and C.P. Neck and G. Moorhead, "Groupthink Remodeled: The Importance of Leadership, Time Pressure, and Methodical Decision-Making Procedures," *Human Relations,* May 1995, pp. 537–58.

62 Janis, *Groupthink.*

63 Ibid.

64 C.R. Leana, "A Partial Test of Janis' Groupthink Model: Effects of Group Cohesiveness and Leader Behavior on Defective Decision Making," *Journal of Management,* Spring 1985, pp. 5–17; and G. Moorhead and J.R. Montanari, "An Empirical Investigation of the Groupthink Phenomenon," *Human Relations,* May 1986, pp. 399–410.

65 See D.J. Isenberg, "Group Polarization: A Critical Review and Meta-Analysis," *Journal of Personality and Social Psychology,* December 1986, pp. 1141–51; J.L. Hale and F.J. Boster, "Comparing Effect Coded Models of Choice Shifts," *Communication Research Reports,* April 1988, pp. 180–86; and P.W. Paese, M. Bieser, and M.E. Tubbs, "Framing Effects and Choice Shifts in Group Decision Making," *Organizational Behavior and Human Decision Processes,* October 1993, pp. 149–65.

66 See, for example, N. Kogan and M.A. Wallach, "Risk Taking as a Function of the Situation, the Person, and the Group," in *New Directions in Psychology,* Vol. 3 (New York: Holt, Rinehart and Winston, 1967); and M.A. Wallach, N. Kogan, and D.J. Bem, "Group Influence on Individual Risk Taking," *Journal of Abnormal and Social Psychology,* Vol. 65 (1962), pp. 75–86.

67 R.D. Clark III, "Group-Induced Shift Toward Risk: A Critical Appraisal," *Psychological Bulletin,* October 1971, pp. 251–70.

68 A.F. Osborn, *Applied Imagination: Principles and Procedures of Creative Thinking* (New York: Scribner's, 1941). See also P.B. Paulus, M.T. Dzindolet, G. Poletes, and L.M. Camacho, "Perception of Performance in Group Brainstorming: The Illusion of Group Productivity," *Personality and Social Psychology Bulletin,* February 1993, pp. 78–89.

69 See A.L. Delbecq, A.H. Van deVen, and D.H. Gustafson, *Group Techniques for Program Planning: A Guide to Nominal and Delphi Processes* (Glenview, IL: Scott, Foresman, 1975); and W.M. Fox, "Anonymity and Other Keys to Successful Problem-Solving Meetings," *National Productivity Review,* Spring 1989, pp. 145–56.

70 See, for instance, A.R. Dennis and J.S. Valacich, "Computer Brainstorms: More Heads Are Better Than One," *Journal of Applied Psychology,* August 1993, pp. 531–37; R.B. Gallupe and W.H. Cooper, "Brainstorming Electronically," *Sloan Management Review,* Fall 1993, pp. 27–36; and R.B. Gallupe, W.H. Cooper, M-L. Grise, and L.M. Bastianutti, "Blocking Electronic Brainstorms," *Journal of Applied Psychology,* February 1994, pp. 77–86.

71 S.P. Robbins and P.L. Hunsaker, *Training in Interpersonal Skills,* 2nd ed. (Upper Saddle River, NJ: Prentice Hall, 1996), pp. 168–84.

72 T.P. Verney, "Role Perception Congruence, Performance, and Satisfaction," in D.J. Vredenburgh and R.S. Schuler (eds.), *Effective Management: Research and Application,* Proceedings of the 20th Annual Eastern Academy of Management, Pittsburgh, PA, May 1983, pp. 24–27.

73 Ibid.

74 M. Van Sell, A.P. Brief, and R.S. Schuler, "Role Conflict and Role Ambiguity: Integration of the Literature and Directions for Future Research," *Human Relations,* January 1981, pp. 43–71; and A.G. Bedeian and A.A. Armenakis, "A Path-Analytic Study of the Consequences of Role Conflict and Ambiguity," *Academy of Management Journal,* June 1981, pp. 417–24.

75 Shaw, *Group Dynamics.*

76 B. Mullen, C. Symons, L. Hu, and E. Salas, "Group Size, Leadership Behavior, and Subordinate Satisfaction," *Journal of General Psychology,* April 1989, pp. 155–70.

Chapter 8

1 J.M. Schrof, "Team Chemistry Sets," *U.S. News & World Report,* August 5, 1996, pp. 53–56.

2 See, for example, D. Tjosvold, *Team Organization: An Enduring Competitive Advantage* (Chichester, England: Wiley, 1991); J. Lipnack and J. Stamps, *The TeamNet Factor* (Essex Junction, VT: Oliver Wight, 1993); J.R. Katzenbach and D.K. Smith, *The Wisdom of Teams* (Boston: Harvard Business School Press, 1993); and S.A. Mohrman, S.G. Cohen,

and A.M. Mohrman, Jr., *Designing Team-Based Organizations* (San Francisco: Jossey-Bass, 1995).

3 K. Kelly, "The New Soul of John Deere," *Business Week,* January 31, 1994, pp. 64–66.

4 This section is based on J.R. Katzenbach and D.K. Smith, *The Wisdom of Teams,* pp. 21, 45, and 85; and D.C. Kinlaw, *Developing Superior Work Teams* (Lexington, MA: Lexington Books, 1991), pp. 3–21.

5 J.H. Shonk, *Team-Based Organizations* (Homewood, IL: Business One Irwin, 1992); and M.A. Verespej, "When Workers Get New Roles," *Industry Week,* February 3, 1992, p. 11.

6 M.L. Marks, P.H. Mirvis, E.J. Hackett, and J.F. Grady, Jr., "Employee Participation in a Quality Circle Program: Impact on Quality of Work Life, Productivity, and Absenteeism," *Journal of Applied Psychology,* February 1986, pp. 61–69; T.R. Miller, "The Quality Circle Phenomenon: A Review and Appraisal," *SAM Advanced Management Journal,* Winter 1989, pp. 4–7; and E.E. Adams, Jr., "Quality Circle Performance," *Journal of Management,* March 1991, pp. 25–39.

7 See, for example, C.C. Manz and H.P. Sims, Jr., *Business Without Bosses: How Self-Managing Teams Are Building High Performance Companies* (New York: Wiley, 1993); J.R. Barker, "Tightening the Iron Cage: Concertive Control in Self-Managing Teams," *Administrative Science Quarterly,* September 1993, pp. 408–37; and S.G. Cohen, G.E. Ledford, Jr., and G.M. Spreitzer, "A Predictive Model of Self-Managing Work Team Effectiveness," *Human Relations,* May 1996, pp. 643–76.

8 J. Hillkirk, "Self-Directed Work Teams Give TI Lift," *USA Today,* December 20, 1993, p. 8B; and M.A. Verespej, "Worker-Managers," *Industry Week,* May 16, 1994, p. 30.

9 J.S. Lublin, "Trying to Increase Worker Productivity, More Employers Alter Management Style," *Wall Street Journal,* February 13, 1992, p. B1.

10 J. Hillkirk, "Self-Directed Work Teams."

11 "A Conversation with Charles Dull," *Organizational Dynamics,* Summer 1993, pp. 57–70.

12 T.B. Kirker, "Edy's Grand Ice Cream," *Industry Week,* October 18, 1993, pp. 29–32.

13 R. Zemke, "Rethinking the Rush to Team Up," *Training,* November 1993, pp. 55–61.

14 See, for instance, T.D. Wall, N.J. Kemp, P.R. Jackson, and C.W. Clegg, "Outcomes of Autonomous Workgroups: A Long-Term Field Experiment," *Academy of Management Journal,* June 1986, pp. 280–304; and J.L. Cordery, W.S. Mueller, and L.M. Smith, "Attitudinal and Behavioral Effects of Autonomous Group Working: A Longitudinal Field Study," *Academy of Management Journal,* June 1991, pp. 464–76.

15 See J. Lipnack and J. Stamps, *The TeamNet Factor,* pp. 14–17; G. Taninecz, "Team Players," *Industry Week,* July 15, 1996, pp. 28–32; and D.R. Denison, S.L. Hart, and J.A. Kahn, "From Chimneys to Cross-Functional Teams: Developing and Validating a Diagnostic Model," *Academy of Management Journal,* August 1996, pp. 1005–23.

16 D. Woodruff, "Chrysler's Neon: Is This the Small Car Detroit Couldn't Build?" *Business Week,* May 3, 1993, pp. 116–26.

17 T.B. Kinni, "Boundary-Busting Teamwork," *Industry Week,* March 21, 1994, pp. 72–78.

18 "Cross-Functional Obstacles," *Training,* May 1994, pp. 125–26.

19 This section is largely based on K. Hess, *Creating the High-Performance Team* (New York: Wiley, 1987); J.R. Katzenbach and D.K. Smith, *The Wisdom of Teams,* pp. 43–64; and K.D. Scott and A. Townsend, "Teams: Why Some Succeed and Others Fail," *HRMagazine,* August 1994, pp. 62–67.

20 For a more detailed breakdown on team skills, see M.J. Stevens and M.A. Campion, "The Knowledge, Skill, and Ability Requirements for Teamwork: Implications for Human Resource Management," *Journal of Management,* Summer 1994, pp. 503–30.

21 C. Margerison and D. McCann, *Team Management: Practical New Approaches* (London: Mercury Books, 1990).

22 B. Dumaine, "Payoff from the New Management," *Fortune,* December 13, 1993, pp. 103–10.

23 See S.T. Johnson, "Work Teams: What's Ahead in Work Design and Rewards Management," *Compensation & Benefits Review,* March–April 1993, pp. 35–41; and A.M. Saunier and E.J. Hawk, "Realizing the Potential of Teams Through Team-Based Rewards," *Compensation & Benefits Review,* July–August 1994, pp. 24–33.

24 F.K. Sonnenberg, "Trust Me . . . Trust Me Not," *Industry Week,* August 16, 1993, pp. 22–28. For a more elaborated definition, see L.T. Hosmer, "Trust: The Connecting Link Between Organizational Theory and Philosophical Ethics," *Academy of Management Review,* April 1995, pp. 379–403.

25 P.L. Schindler and C.C. Thomas, "The Structure of Interpersonal Trust in the Workplace," *Psychological Reports,* October 1993, pp. 563–73. A similar, four-dimensional definition is offered in A.K. Mishra, "Organizational Responses to Crisis: The Centrality of Trust," in R.M. Kramer and T.R. Tyler, *Trust in Organizations* (Thousand Oaks, CA: Sage, 1996), pp. 264–70.

26 Schindler and Thomas, "The Structure of Interpersonal Trust in the Workplace."

27 J.K. Butler and R.S. Cantrell, "A Behavioral Decision Theory Approach to Modeling Dyadic Trust in Superiors and Subordinates," *Psychological Reports,* August 1984, pp. 19–28.

28 Based on F. Bartolome, "Nobody Trusts the Boss Completely—Now What?" *Harvard Business Review,* March–April 1989, pp. 135–42; and P. Pascarella, "15 Ways to Win People's Trust," *Industry Week,* February 1, 1993, pp. 47–51.

29 D. Harrington-Mackin, *The Team Building Tool Kit* (New York: AMACOM, 1994), p. 53.

30 T.D. Schellhardt, "To Be a Star Among Equals, Be a Team Player," *Wall Street Journal,* April 20, 1994, p. B1.

31 Ibid.

32 Ibid.

33 "Teaming Up for Success," *Training,* January 1994, p. S41.

34 B. Geber, "The Bugaboo of Team Pay," *Training,* August 1995, pp. 27 and 34.

35 D.C. Kinlaw, *Developing Superior Work Teams,* p. 43.

36 B. Krone, "Total Quality Management: An American Odyssey," *The Bureaucrat,* Fall 1990, p. 37.

37 *Profiles in Quality: Blueprints for Action from 50 Leading Companies* (Boston: Allyn & Bacon, 1991), pp. 71–72 and 76–77.

38 See the review of the literature in S.E. Jackson, V.K. Stone, and E.B. Alvarez, "Socialization Amidst Diversity: The Impact of Demographics on Work Team Oldtimers and Newcomers," in L.L. Cummings and B.M. Staw (eds.), *Research in Organizational Behavior,* Vol. 15 (Greenwich, CT: JAI Press, 1993), p. 64.

39 R.M. Stogdill, "Group Productivity, Drive, and Cohesiveness," *Organizational Behavior and Human Performance,* February 1972, pp. 36–43. See also M. Mayo, J.C. Pastor, and J.R. Meindl, "The Effects of Group Heterogeneity on the Self-Perceived Efficacy of Group Leaders," *Leadership Quarterly,* Summer 1996, pp. 265–84.

40 J.E. McGrath, *Groups: Interaction and Performance* (Englewood Cliffs, NJ: Prentice Hall, 1984).

41 This idea is proposed in S.E. Jackson, V.K. Stone, and E.B. Alvarez, "Socialization Amidst Diversity," p. 68.

42 This section is based on M. Kaeter, "Repotting Mature Work Teams," *Training,* April 1994 (Supplement), pp. 4–6.

Chapter 9

1 This opening section is based on J. Ritter, "Poor Fluency in English Means Mixed Signals," *USA Today,* January 18, 1996, p. 1A. For an analysis of how communication problems cause aviation disasters, see also C. Linde, "The Quantitative Study of Communicative Success . . . ," *Language in Society,* Summer, 1988, pp. 375–99.

2 See, for example, K.W. Thomas and W.H. Schmidt, "A Survey of Managerial Interests with Respect to Conflict," *Academy of Management Journal,* June 1976, p. 317.

3 W.G. Scott and T.R. Mitchell, *Organization Theory: A Structural and Behavioral Analysis* (Homewood, IL: Richard D. Irwin, 1976).

4 D.K. Berlo, *The Process of Communication* (New York: Holt, Rinehart & Winston, 1960), pp. 30–32.

5 Ibid., p. 54.

6 Ibid., p. 103.

7 J.C. McCroskey, J.A. Daly, and G. Sorenson, "Personality Correlates of Communication Apprehension," *Human Communication Research,* Spring 1976, pp. 376–80.

8 B.H. Spitzberg and M.L. Hecht, "A Competent Model of Relational Competence," *Human Communication Research,* Summer 1984, pp. 575–99.

9 See, for example, L. Stafford and J.A. Daly, "Conversational Memory: The Effects of Instructional Set and Recall Mode on Memory for Natural Conversations," *Human Communication Research,* Spring 1984, pp. 379–402.

10 J.A. Daly and J.C. McCrosky, "Occupational Choice and Desirability as a Function of Communication Apprehension," paper presented at the annual meeting of the International Communication Association, Chicago, 1975.

11 J.A. Daly and M.D. Miller, "The Empirical Development of an Instrument of Writing Apprehension," *Research in the Teaching of English,* Winter 1975, pp. 242–49.

12 R.L. Simpson, "Vertical and Horizontal Communication in Formal Organizations," *Administrative Science Quarterly,* September 1959, pp. 188–96; and B. Harriman, "Up and Down the Communications Ladder," *Harvard Business Review,* Steptember–October 1974, pp. 143–51.

13 B. Smith, "FedEx's Key to Success," *Management Review,* July 1993, pp. 23–24.

14 See, for instance, J.W. Newstrom, R.E. Monczka, and W.E. Reif, "Perceptions of the Grapevine: Its Value and Influence," *Journal of Business Communication,* Spring 1974, pp. 12–20; and S.J. Modic, "Grapevine Rated Most Believable," *Industry Week,* May 15, 1989, p. 14.

15 K. Davis, "Management Communication and the Grapevine," *Harvard Business Review,* September–October 1953, pp. 43–49.

16 H. Sutton and L.W. Porter, "A Study of the Grapevine in a Governmental Organization," *Personnel Psychology,* Summer 1968, pp. 223–30.

17 K. Davis, cited in R. Rowan, "Where Did That Rumor Come From?" *Fortune,* August 13, 1979, p. 134.

18 L. Hirschhorn, "Managing Rumors," in L. Hirschhorn (ed.), *Cutting Back* (San Francisco: Jossey-Bass, 1983), pp. 49–52.

19 R.L. Rosnow and G.A. Fine, *Rumor and Gossip: The Social Psychology of Hearsay* (New York: Elsevier, 1976).

20 See, for instance, J.G. March and G. Sevon, "Gossip, Information and Decision Making" in J.G. March (ed.), *Decisions and Organizations* (Oxford: Blackwell, 1988), pp. 429–42; M. Noon and R. Delbridge, "News from Behind My Hand: Gossip in Organizations," *Organization Studies,* Vol. 14, No. 1, 1993, pp. 23–36; and N. DiFonzo, P. Bordia, and R.L. Rosnow, "Reining in Rumors," *Organizational Dynamics,* Summer 1994, pp. 47–62.

21 R.L. Birdwhistell, *Introduction to Kinesics* (Louisville, KY: University of Louisville Press, 1952).

22 J. Fast, *Body Language* (Philadelphia: M. Evan, 1970), p. 7.

23 Reported in "On Line," *The Chronicle of Higher Education,* October 27, 1995, p. A23.

24 See R.L. Daft and R.H. Lengel, "Information Richness: A New Approach to Managerial Behavior and Organization Design," in B.M. Staw and L.L. Cummings (eds.), *Research in Organizational Behavior,* vol. 6 (Greenwich, CT: JAI Press, 1984), pp. 191–233; R.E. Rice and D.E. Shook, "Relationships of Job Categories and Organizational Levels to Use of Communication Channels, Including Electronic Mail: A Meta-Analysis and Extension," *Journal of Management Studies,* March 1990, pp. 195–229; R.E. Rice, "Task Analyzability, Use of New Media, and Effectiveness," *Organization Science,* November 1992, pp. 475–500; S.G. Straus and J.E. McGrath, "Does the Medium Matter? The Interaction of

Task Type and Technology on Group Performance and Member Reaction," *Journal of Applied Psychology,* February 1994, pp. 87–97; J. Webster and L.K. Trevino, "Rational and Social Theories as Complementary Explanations of Communication Media Choices: Two Policy-Capturing Studies," *Academy of Management Journal,* December 1995, pp. 1544–72.

25 R.L. Daft, R.H. Lengel, and L.K. Trevino, "Message Equivocality, Media Selection, and Manager Performance: Implications for Information Systems," *MIS Quarterly,* September 1987, pp. 355–68.

26 J. DeLorean, quoted in S.P. Robbins, *The Administrative Process* (Englewood Cliffs, NJ: Prentice Hall, 1976), p. 404.

27 S.I. Hayakawa, *Language in Thought and Action* (New York: Harcourt Brace Jovanovich, 1949), p. 292.

28 This box is based on S.P. Robbins and P.L. Hunsaker, *Training in InterPersonal Skills: TIPS for Managing People at Work,* 2nd ed. (Upper Saddle River, NJ: Prentice Hall, 1996), Chapter 3; and data in R.C. Huseman, J.M. Lahiff, and J.M. Penrose, *Business Communication: Strategies and Skills* (Chicago: Dryden Press, 1988), pp. 380 and 425.

29 M. Young and J.E. Post, "Managing to Communicate, Communicating to Manage: How Leading Companies Communicate With Employees," *Organizational Dynamics,* Summer 1993, pp. 31–43.

30 L. Tabak, "Quality Controls," *Hemispheres,* September 1996, pp. 33–34.

31 Ibid.

32 Ibid.

33 Ibid.

34 See D. Tannen, *You Just Don't Understand: Women and Men in Conversation* (New York: Ballentine Books, 1991); and D. Tannen, *Talking from 9 to 5* (New York: William Morrow, 1995).

35 M.L. LaGanga, "Are There Words That Neither Offend Nor Bore?" *Los Angeles Times,* May 18, 1994, p. II-27.

36 Cited in J. Leo, "Falling for Sensitivity," *U.S. News & World Report,* December 13, 1993, p. 27.

37 R.E. Axtell, *Gestures: The Do's and Taboos of Body Language Around the World* (New York: Wiley, 1991).

38 See M. Munter, "Cross-Cultural Communication for Managers," *Business Horizons,* May–June 1993, pp. 75–76.

39 N. Adler, *International Dimensions of Organizational Behavior,* 2nd ed. (Boston: PWS-Kent, 1991), pp. 83–84.

40 See, for instance, R. Hotch, "Communication Revolution," *Nation's Business,* May 1993, pp. 20–28; G. Brockhouse, "I Have Seen the Future . . . ," *Canadian Business,* August 1993, pp. 43–45; R. Hotch, "In Touch Through Technology," *Nation's Business,* January 1994, pp. 33–35; and P. LaBarre, "The Other Network," *Industry Week,* September 19, 1994, pp. 33–36.

41 A. LaPlante, "TeleConfrontationing," *Forbes ASAP,* September 13, 1993, p. 117.

42 See, for example. R.S. Schuler, "A Role Perception Transactional Process Model for Organizational Communication-Outcome Relationships," *Organizational Behavior and Human Performance,* April 1979, pp. 268–91.

43 J.P. Walsh, S.J. Ashford, and T.E. Hill, "Feedback Obstruction: The Influence of the Information Environment on Employee Turnover Intentions," *Human Relations,* January 1985, pp. 23–46.

44 S.A. Hellweg and S.L. Phillips, "Communication and Productivity in Organizations: A State-of-the-Art Review," in *Proceedings of the 40th Annual Academy of Management Conference,* Detroit, 1980, pp. 188–92.

45 R.R. Reilly, B. Brown, M.R. Blood, and C.Z. Malatesta, "The Effects of Realistic Previews: A Study and Discussion of the Literature," *Personnel Psychology,* Winter 1981, pp. 823–34.

Chapter 10

1 D. Darlin, "To Whom Do Our Schools Belong?" *Forbes,* September 23, 1996, pp. 66–76.

2 R.M. Stogdill, *Handbook of Leadership: A Survey of the Literature* (New York: Free Press, 1974), p. 259.

3 For a review of the controversies, see G. Yukl, "Managerial Leadership: A Review of Theory and Research," *Journal of Management,* June 1989, pp. 252–53.

4 A. Zaleznik, "Excerpts from 'Managers and Leaders: Are They Different'?" *Harvard Business Review,* May–June 1986, p. 54.

5 J.P. Kotter, "What Leaders Really Do," *Harvard Business Review,* May–June 1990, pp. 103–11; and J.P. Kotter, *A Force for Change: How Leadership Differs from Management* (New York: Free Press, 1990).

6 V.H. Vroom, "The Search for a Theory of Leadership," in J.W. McGuire (ed.), *Contemporary Management: Issues and Viewpoints* (Englewood Cliffs, NJ: Prentice Hall, 1974), p. 396.

7 J.G. Geier, "A Trait Approach to the Study of Leadership in Small Groups," *Journal of Communication,* December 1967, pp. 316–23.

8 S.A. Kirkpatrick and E.A. Locke, "Leadership: Do Traits Matter?" *Academy of Management Executive,* May 1991, pp. 48–60.

9 G.H. Dobbins. W.S. Long, E.J. Dedrick, and T.C. Clemons, "The Role of Self-Monitoring and Gender on Leader Emergence: A Laboratory and Field Study," *Journal of Management,* September 1990, pp. 609–18; and S.J. Zaccaro, R.J. Foti, and D.A. Kenny, "Self-Monitoring and Trait-Based Variance in Leadership: An Investigation of Leader Flexibility Across Multiple Group Situations," *Journal of Applied Psychology,* April 1991, pp. 308–15.

10 G. Yukl and D.D. Van Fleet, "Theory and Research on Leadership in Organizations," in M.D. Dunnette and L.M. Hough (eds.), *Handbook of Industrial & Organizational Psychology,* 2nd ed., vol. 3 (Palo Alto, CA: Consulting Psychologists Press, 1992), p. 150.

11 R.G. Lord, C.L. DeVader, and G.M. Alliger, "A Meta-Analysis of the Relation Between Personality Traits and Leadership Perceptions: An Application of Validity Generalization Procedures," *Journal of Applied Psychology,* August

1986, pp. 402–10; Dobbins, Long, Dedrick, and Clemons, "The Role of Self-Monitoring and Gender on Leader Emergence"; and Kirkpatrick and Locke, "Leadership."

12 See T. Mulligan, "It's All a Matter of How to Crack Whip," *Los Angeles Times,* April 3, 1993, p. D1.

13 R.M. Stogdill and A.E. Coons (eds.), *Leader Behavior: Its Description and Measurement,* Research Monograph No. 88 (Columbus: Ohio State University, Bureau of Business Research, 1951). This research is updated in S. Kerr, C.A. Schriesheim, C.J. Murphy, and R.M. Stogdill, "Toward a Contingency Theory of Leadership Based upon the Consideration and Initiating Structure Literature," *Organizational Behavior and Human Performance,* August 1974, pp. 62–82; and C.A. Schriesheim, C.C. Cogliser, and L.L. Neider, "Is It 'Trustworthy'? A Multiple-Levels-of-Analysis Reexamination of an Ohio State Leadership Study, with Implications for Future Research," *Leadership Quarterly,* Summer 1995, pp. 111–45.

14 R. Kahn and D. Katz, "Leadership Practices in Relation to Productivity and Morale," D. Cartwright and A. Zander (eds.), *Group Dynamics: Research and Theory,* 2nd ed. (Elmsford, NY: Row, Paterson, 1960).

15 R.R. Blake and J.S. Mouton, *The Managerial Grid* (Houston: Gulf, 1964).

16 See, for example, R.R. Blake and J.S. Mouton, "A Comparative Analysis of Situationalism and 9,9 Management by Principle," *Organizational Dynamics,* Spring 1982, pp. 20–43.

17 See, for example, L.L. Larson, J.G. Hunt, and R.N. Osborn, "The Great Hi-Hi Leader Behavior Myth: A Lesson from Occam's Razor," *Academy of Management Journal,* December 1976, pp. 628–41; and P.C. Nystrom, "Managers and the Hi-Hi Leader Myth," *Academy of Management Journal,* June 1978, pp. 325–31.

18 See G. Ekvall and J. Arvonen, "Change-Centered Leadership: An Extension of the Two-Dimensional Model," *Scandinavian Journal of Management,* vol. 7, no. 1, 1991, pp. 17–26; M. Lindell and G. Rosenqvist, "Is There a Third Management Style?" *The Finnish Journal of Business Economics,* vol. 3, 1992, pp. 171–98; and M. Lindell and G. Rosenqvist, "Management Behavior Dimensions and Development Orientation," *Leadership Quarterly,* Winter 1992, pp. 355–77.

19 See, for instance, P.M. Podsakoff, S.B. MacKenzie, M. Ahearne, and W.H. Bommer, "Searching for a Needle in a Haystack: Trying to Identify the Illusive Moderators of Leadership Behavior," *Journal of Management,* vol. 1, no. 3, 1995, pp. 422–70.

20 F.E. Fiedler, *A Theory of Leadership Effectiveness* (New York: McGraw-Hill, 1967).

21 S. Shiflett, "Is There a Problem with the LPC Score in LEADER MATCH?" *Personnel Psychology,* Winter 1981, pp. 765–69.

22 F.E. Fiedler, M.M. Chemers, and L. Mahar, *Improving Leadership Effectiveness: The Leader Match Concept* (New York: John Wiley, 1977).

23 L.H. Peters, D.D. Hartke, and J.T. Pohlmann, "Fiedler's Contingency Theory of Leadership: An Application of the Meta-Analysis Procedures of Schmidt and Hunter," *Psychological Bulletin,* March 1985, pp. 274–85; C.A. Schriesheim, B.J. Tepper, and L.A. Tetrault, "Least Preferred Co-Worker Score, Situational Control, and Leadership Effectiveness: A Meta-Analysis of Contingency Model Performance Predictions," *Journal of Applied Psychology,* August 1994, pp. 561–73; and R. Ayman, M.M. Chemers, and F. Fiedler, "The Contingency Model of Leadership Effectiveness: Its Levels of Analysis," *Leadership Quarterly,* Summer 1995, pp. 147–67.

24 See, for instance, R.W. Rice, "Psychometric Properties of the Esteem for the Least Preferred Coworker (LPC) Scale," *Academy of Management Review,* January 1978, pp. 106–18; C.A. Schriesheim, B.D. Bannister, and W.H. Money, "Psychometric Properties of the LPC Scale: An Extension of Rice's Review," *Academy of Management Review,* April 1979, pp. 287–90; and J.K. Kennedy, J.M. Houston, M.A. Korgaard, and D.D. Gallo, "Construct Space of the Least Preferred Co-Worker (LPC) Scale," *Educational & Psychological Measurement,* Fall 1987, pp. 807–14.

25 See E.H. Schein, *Organizational Psychology,* 3rd ed. (Englewood Cliffs, NJ: Prentice Hall, 1980), pp. 116–17; and B. Kabanoff, "A Critique of Leader Match and Its Implications for Leadership Research," *Personnel Psychology,* Winter 1981, pp. 749–64.

26 F.E. Fiedler and J.E. Garcia, *New Approaches to Effective Leadership: Cognitive Resources and Organizational Performance* (New York: John Wiley & Sons, 1987).

27 Ibid, p. 6.

28 See R.P. Vecchio, "Theoretical and Empirical Examination of Cognitive Resource Theory," *Journal of Applied Psychology,* April 1990, pp. 141–47; and F.W. Gibson, F.E. Fiedler, and K.M. Barrett, "Stress, Babble, and the Utilization of the Leader's Intellectual Abilities," *Leadership Quarterly,* Summer 1993, pp. 189–208.

29 P. Hersey and K.H. Blanchard, "So You Want to Know Your Leadership Style?" *Training and Development Journal,* February 1974, pp. 1–15; and P. Hersey and K.H. Blanchard, *Management of Organizational Behavior: Utilizing Human Resources,* 6th ed. (Englewood Cliffs, NJ: Prentice Hall, 1993).

30 Hersey and Blanchard, *Management of Organizational Behavior,* p. 171.

31 P. Hersey and K. H. Blanchard, "Grid Principles and Situationalism: Both! A Response to Blake and Mouton," *Group and Organization Studies,* June 1982, pp. 207–10.

32 R.K. Hambleton and R. Gumpert, "The Validity of Hersey and Blanchard's Theory of Leader Effectiveness," *Group & Organizational Studies,* June 1982, pp. 225–42; C.L. Graeff, "The Situational Leadership Theory: A Critical View," *Academy of Management Review,* April 1983, pp. 285–91; R.P. Vecchio, "Situational Leadership Theory: An Examination of a Prescriptive Theory," *Journal of Applied Psychology,* August 1987, pp. 444–51; J.R. Goodson, G.W. McGee, and J.F. Cashman, "Situational Leadership Theory: A Test of Leadership Prescriptions," *Group & Organization Studies,* December 1989, pp. 446–61; W. Blank, J.R. Weitzel, and S.G. Green, "A Test of the Situational Leadership Theory," *Personnel Psychology,* Autumn 1990, pp. 579–97; and W.R.

Norris and R.P. Vecchio, "Situational Leadership Theory: A Replication," *Group & Organization Management,* September 1992, pp. 331–42.

33 Vecchio, "Situational Leadership Theory"; and Norris and Vecchio, "Situational Leadership Theory."

34 W. Blank, J.R. Weitzel, and S.G. Green, "A Test of the Situational Leadership Theory."

35 F. Dansereau, J. Cashman, and G. Graen, "Instrumentality Theory and Equity Theory as Complementary Approaches in Predicting the Relationship of Leadership and Turnover Among Managers," *Organizational Behavior and Human Performance,* October 1973, pp. 184–200; and G. Graen, M. Novak, and P. Sommerkamp, "The Effects of Leader–Member Exchange and Job Design on Productivity and Satisfaction: Testing a Dual Attachment Model," *Organizational Behavior and Human Performance,* August 1982, pp. 109–31.

36 G. Graen and J. Cashman, "A Role-Making Model of Leadership in Formal Organizations: A Development Approach," in J.G. Hunt and L.L. Larson (eds.), *Leadership Frontiers* (Kent, OH: Kent State University Press, 1975), pp. 143–65; R. Liden and G. Graen, "Generalizability of the Vertical Dyad Linkage Model of Leadership," *Academy of Management Journal,* September 1980, pp. 451–65; and R.C. Liden, S.J. Wayne, and D. Stilwell, "A Longitudinal Study of the Early Development of Leader–Member Exchanges," *Journal of Applied Psychology,* August 1993, pp. 662–74.

37 D. Duchon, S.G. Green, and T.D. Taber, "Vertical Dyad Linkage: A Longitudinal Assessment of Antecedents, Measures, and Consequences," *Journal of Applied Psychology,* February 1986, pp. 56–60; R.C. Liden, S.J. Wayne, and D. Stilwell, "A Longitudinal Study on the Early Development of Leader–Member Exchanges"; R.J. Deluga and J.T. Perry, "The Role of Subordinate Performance and Ingratiation in Leader–Member Exchanges," *Group & Organization Management,* March 1994, pp. 67–86; and A.S. Phillips and A.G. Bedeian, "Leader-Follower Exchange Quality: The Role of Personal and Interpersonal Attributes," *Academy of Management Journal,* August 1994, pp. 990–1001.

38 See, for example, G. Graen, M. Novak, and P. Sommerkamp, "The Effects of Leader–Member Exchange"; T. Scandura and G. Graen, "Moderating Effects of Initial Leader–Member Exchange Status on the Effects of a Leadership Intervention," *Journal of Applied Psychology,* August 1984, pp. 428–36; R.P. Vecchio and B.C. Gobdel, "The Vertical Dyad Linkage Model of Leadership: Problems and Prospects," *Organizational Behavior and Human Performance,* August 1984, pp. 5–20; T.M. Dockery and D.D. Steiner, "The Role of the Initial Interaction in Leader–Member Exchange," *Group and Organization Studies,* December 1990, pp. 395–413; G.B. Graen and M. Uhl-Bien, "Relationship-Based Approach to Leadership: Development of Leader–Member Exchange (LMX) Theory of Leadership Over 25 Years: Applying a Multi-Level Multi-Domain Perspective," *Leadership Quarterly,* Summer 1995, pp. 219–47; and R.P. Settoon, N. Bennett, and R.C. Liden, "Social Exchange in Organizations: Perceived Organizational Support, Leader–Member Exchange, and Employee Reciprocity," *Journal of Applied Psychology,* June 1996, pp. 219–27.

39 A. Jago, "Leadership: Perspectives in Theory and Research," *Management Science,* March 1982, p. 331.

40 R.J. House, "A Path-Goal Theory of Leader Effectiveness," *Administrative Science Quarterly,* September 1971, pp. 321–38; R.J. House and T.R. Mitchell, "Path-Goal Theory of Leadership," *Journal of Contemporary Business,* Autumn 1974, p. 86; and R.J. House, "Retrospective Comment," in L.E. Boone and D.D. Bowen (eds.), *The Great Writings in Management and Organizational Behavior,* 2nd ed. (New York: Random House, 1987), pp. 354–64.

41 See J. Indik, "Path-Goal Theory of Leadership: A Meta-Analysis," paper presented at the National Academy of Management Conference, Chicago, August 1986; R.T. Keller, "A Test of the Path-Goal Theory of Leadership with Need for Clarity as a Moderator in Research and Development Organizations," *Journal of Applied Psychology,* April 1989, pp. 208–12; and J.C. Wofford and L.Z. Liska, "Path-Goal Theories of Leadership: A Meta-Analysis," *Journal of Management,* Winter 1993, pp. 857–76.

42 See M.G. Evans, "R.J. House's 'A Path-Goal Theory of Leader Effectiveness,'" *Leadership Quarterly,* Fall 1996, pp. 305–09; and C.A. Schriesheim and L.L. Neider, "Path-Goal Leadership Theory: The Long and Winding Road," *Leadership Quarterly,* Fall 1996, pp. 317–21.

43 V.H. Vroom and P.W. Yetton, *Leadership and Decision-Making* (Pittsburgh: University of Pittsburgh Press, 1973).

44 V.H. Vroom and A.G. Jago, *The New Leadership: Managing Participation in Organizations* (Englewood Cliffs, NJ: Prentice Hall, 1988). See also V.H. Vroom and A.G. Jago, "Situation Effects and Levels of Analysis in the Study of Leader Participation," *Leadership Quarterly,* Summer 1995, pp. 169–81.

45 See, for example, R.H.G. Field, "A Test of the Vroom-Yetton Normative Model of Leadership," *Journal of Applied Psychology,* October 1982, pp. 523–32; C.R. Leana, "Power Relinquishment versus Power Sharing: Theoretical Clarification and Empirical Comparison of Delegation and Participation," *Journal of Applied Psychology,* May 1987, pp. 228–33; J.T. Ettling and A.G. Jago, "Participation Under Conditions of Conflict: More on the Validity of the Vroom-Yetton Model," *Journal of Management Studies,* January 1988, pp. 73–83; and R.H.G. Field and R.J. House, "A Test of the Vroom-Yetton Model Using Manager and Subordinate Reports," *Journal of Applied Psychology,* June 1990, pp. 362–66.

46 Dobbins, Long, Dedrick, and Clemons, "The Role of Self-Monitoring and Gender on Leader Emergence"; and S.J. Zaccaro, R.J. Foti, and D.A. Kenny, "Self-Monitoring and Trait-Based Variance in Leadership: An Investigation of Leader Flexibility Across Multiple Group Situations," *Journal of Applied Psychology,* April 1991, pp. 308–15.

47 S. Kerr and J.M. Jermier, "Substitutes for Leadership: Their Meaning and Measurement," *Organizational Behavior and Human Performance,* December 1978, pp. 375–403; J.P. Howell and P.W. Dorfman, "Substitutes for Leadership: Test of a Construct," *Academy of Management Journal,* December 1981, pp. 714–28; J.P. Howell, P.W. Dorfman, and S. Kerr, "Leadership and Substitutes for Leadership," *Journal of Applied Behavioral Science,* vol. 22, no. 1, 1986, pp. 29–46; J.P. Howell, D.E. Bowen, P.W. Dorfman, S. Kerr, and

P.M. Podsakoff, "Substitutes for Leadership: Effective Alternatives to Ineffective Leadership," *Organizational Dynamics,* Summer 1990, pp. 21–38; P.M. Podsakoff, B.P. Niehoff, S.B. MacKenzie, and M.L. Williams, "Do Substitutes for Leadership Really Substitute for Leadership? An Empirical Examination of Kerr and Jermier's Situational Leadership Model," *Organizational Behavior and Human Decision Processes,* February 1993, pp. 1–44; P.M. Podsakoff and S.B. MacKenzie, "An Examination of Substitutes for Leadership Within a Levels-of Analysis Framework," *Leadership Quarterly,* Fall 1995, pp. 289–328; P.M. Podsakoff, S.B. MacKenzie, and W.H. Bommer, "Transformational Leader Behaviors and Substitutes for Leadership as Determinants of Employee Satisfaction, Commitment, Trust, and Organizational Citizenship Behaviors," *Journal of Management,* vol. 22, no. 2, 1996, pp. 259–98; and P.M. Podsakoff, S.B. MacKenzie, and W.H. Bommer, "Meta-Analysis of the Relationships Between Kerr and Jermier's Substitutes for Leadership and Employee Attitudes, Role Perceptions, and Performance," *Journal of Applied Psychology,* August 1996, pp. 380–99.

48 B. Karmel, "Leadership: A Challenge to Traditional Research Methods and Assumptions," *Academy of Management Review,* July 1978, pp. 477–79.

49 Schein, *Organizational Psychology,* p. 132.

50 See L.R. Anderson, "Toward a Two-Track Model of Leadership Training: Suggestions from Self-Monitoring Theory," *Small Group Research,* May 1990, pp. 147–67.

51 C. Margerison and R. Glube, "Leadership Decision-Making: An Empirical Test of the Vroom and Yetton Model," *Journal of Management Studies,* February 1979, pp. 45–55.

52 See, for instance, J.C. McElroy, "A Typology of Attribution Leadership Research," *Academy of Management Review,* July 1982, pp. 413–17; J.R. Meindl and S.B. Ehrlich, "The Romance of Leadership and the Evaluation of Organizational Performance," *Academy of Management Journal,* March 1987, pp. 91–109; J.C. McElroy and J.D. Hunger, "Leadership Theory as Causal Attribution of Performance," in J.G. Hunt, B.R. Baliga, H.P. Dachler, and C.A. Schriesheim (eds.), *Emerging Leadership Vistas* (Lexington, MA: Lexington Books, 1988); B. Shamir, "Attribution of Influence and Charisma to the Leader: The Romance of Leadership Revisited," *Journal of Applied Social Psychology,* March 1992, pp. 386–407; and J.R. Meindl, "The Romance of Leadership as a Follower-Centric Theory: A Social Constructionist Approach," *Leadership Quarterly,* Fall 1995, pp. 329–41.

53 R.G. Lord, C.L. DeVader, and G.M. Alliger, "A Meta-Analysis of the Relation Between Personality Traits and Leadership Perceptions."

54 G.N. Powell and D.A. Butterfield, "The "High-High" Leader Rides Again!" *Group and Organization Studies,* December 1984, pp. 437–50.

55 J.R. Meindl, S.B. Ehrlich, and J.M. Dukerich, "The Romance of Leadership," *Administrative Science Quarterly,* March 1985, pp. 78–102.

56 J. Pfeffer, *Managing With Power* (Boston: Harvard Business School Press, 1992), p. 194; and M. Loeb, "An Interview with Warren Bennis: Where Leaders Come From," *Fortune,* September 19, 1994, p. 241.

57 J.A. Conger and R.N. Kanungo, "Behavioral Dimensions of Charismatic Leadership," in J.A. Conger, R.N. Kanungo and Associates, *Charismatic Leadership* (San Francisco: Jossey-Bass, 1988), p. 79.

58 R.J. House, "A 1976 Theory of Charismatic Leadership," in J.G. Hunt and L.L. Larson (eds.), *Leadership: The Cutting Edge* (Carbondale: Southern Illinois University Press, 1977), pp. 189–207.

59 W. Bennis, "The 4 Competencies of Leadership," *Training and Development Journal,* August 1984, pp. 15–19.

60 Conger and Kanungo, "Behavioral Dimensions of Charismatic Leadership," pp. 78–97.

61 B. Shamir, R.J. House, and M.B. Arthur, "The Motivational Effects of Charismatic Leadership: A Self-Concept Theory," *Organization Science,* November 1993, pp. 577–94.

62 R.J. House, J. Woycke, and E.M. Fodor, "Charismatic and Noncharismatic Leaders: Differences in Behavior and Effectiveness," in Conger and Kanungo, *Charismatic Leadership,* pp. 103–04; D.A. Waldman, B.M. Bass, and F.J. Yammarino, "Adding to Contingent-Reward Behavior: The Augmenting Effect of Charismatic Leadership," *Group & Organization Studies,* December 1990, pp. 381–94; and S.A. Kirkpatrick and E.A. Locke, "Direct and Indirect Effects of Three Core Charismatic Leadership Components on Performance and Attitudes," *Journal of Applied Psychology,* February 1996, pp. 36–51.

63 J.A. Conger and R.N. Kanungo, "Training Charismatic Leadership: A Risky and Critical Task," in Conger and Kanungo, *Charismatic Leadership,* pp. 309–23.

64 R.J. Richardson and S.K. Thayer, *The Charisma Factor: How to Develop Your Natural Leadership Ability* (Englewood Cliffs, NJ: Prentice Hall, 1993).

65 J.M. Howell and P.J. Frost, "A Laboratory Study of Charismatic Leadership," *Organizational Behavior and Human Decision Processes,* April 1989, pp. 243–69.

66 House, "A 1976 Theory of Charismatic Leadership."

67 J.A. Conger, *The Charismatic Leader: Behind the Mystique of Exceptional Leadership* (San Francisco: Jossey-Bass, 1989); R. Hogan, R. Raskin, and D. Fazzini, "The Dark Side of Charisma"; in K.E. Clark and M.B. Clark (eds.), *Measures of Leadership* (West Orange, NJ: Leadership Library of America, 1990); D. Sankowsky, The Charismatic Leader as Narcissist: Understanding the Abuse of Power," *Organizational Dynamics,* Spring 1995, pp. 57–71; and J. O'Connor, M.D. Mumford, T.C. Clifton, T.L. Gessner, and M.S. Connelly, "Charismatic Leaders and Destructiveness: An Historiometric Study," *Leadership Quarterly,* Winter 1995, pp. 529–55.

68 G.P. Zachary, "How 'Barbarian' Style of Philippe Kahn Led Borland Into Jeopardy," *Wall Street Journal,* June 2, 1994, p. A1.

69 See, for instance, J.M. Burns, *Leadership* (New York: Harper & Row, 1978); B.M. Bass, *Leadership and Performance Beyond Expectations* (New York: Free Press, 1985); B.M. Bass, "From Transactional to Transformational Leadership: Learning to Share the Vision," *Organizational Dynamics,* Winter 1990, pp. 19–31; F.J. Yammarino, W.D. Spangler, and B.M. Bass, "Transformational Leadership and Performance: A Longi-

tudinal Investigation," *Leadership Quarterly,* Spring 1993, pp. 81–102; and J.M. Howell and B.J. Avolio, "Transformational Leadership, Transactional Leadership, Locus of Control, and Support for Innovation: Key Predictors of Consolidated-Business-Unit Performance," *Journal of Applied Psychology,* December 1993, pp. 891–902.

70 B.M. Bass, "Leadership: Good, Better, Best," *Organizational Dynamics,* Winter 1985, pp. 26–40; and J. Seltzer and B.M. Bass, "Transformational Leadership: Beyond Initiation and Consideration," *Journal of Management,* December 1990, pp. 693–703.

71 B.J. Avolio and B.M. Bass, "Transformational Leadership, Charisma and Beyond," working paper, School of Management, State University of New York, Binghamton, 1985, p. 14.

72 Cited in B.M. Bass and B.J. Avolio, "Developing Transformational Leadership: 1992 and Beyond," *Journal of European Industrial Training,* January 1990, p. 23.

73 J.J. Hater and B.M. Bass, "Supervisors' Evaluation and Subordinates' Perceptions of Transformational and Transactional Leadership," *Journal of Applied Psychology,* November 1988, pp. 695–702.

74 Bass and Avolio, "Developing Transformational Leadership."

75 This definition is based on M. Sashkin, "The Visionary Leader," in J.A. Conger and R.N. Kanungo (eds.), *Charismatic Leadership,* pp. 124–25; B. Nanus, *Visionary Leadership* (New York: Free Press, 1992), p. 8; and N.H. Snyder and M. Graves, "Leadership and Vision," *Business Horizons,* January–February 1994, p. 1.

76 B. Nanus, *Visionary Leadership,* p. 8.

77 P.C. Nutt and R.W. Backoff, "Crafting Vision." A working paper. College of Business; Ohio State University; July 1995, p. 4.

78 B. Nanus, *Visionary Leadership,* pp. 178–79.

79 N.H. Snyder and M. Graves, "Leadership and Vision," p. 2.

80 Cited in L.B. Korn, "How the Next CEO Will Be Different," *Fortune,* May 22, 1989, p. 157.

81 J.C. Collins and J.I. Porras, *Built to Last: Successful Habits of Visionary Companies* (New York: HarperBusiness, 1994).

82 P.C. Nutt and R.W. Backoff, "Crafting Vision," pp. 5–7.

83 Cited in L. Larwood, C.M. Falbe, M.P. Kriger, and P. Miesing, "Structure and Meaning of Organizational Vision," *Academy of Management Journal,* June 1995, pp. 740–69.

84 Cited in B. Nanus, *Visionary Leadership,* pp. 141, 173, 178; and P.C. Nutt and R.W. Backoff, "Crafting Vision," pp. 1 and 3.

85 Based on M. Sashkin, "The Visionary Leader," pp. 128–30.

86 The material in this section is based on J. Grant, "Women as Managers: What They Can Offer to Organizations," *Organizational Dynamics,* Winter 1988, pp. 56–63; S. Helgesen, *The Female Advantage: Women's Ways of Leadership* (New York: Doubleday, 1990); A.H. Eagly and B.T. Johnson, "Gender and Leadership Style: A Meta-Analysis," *Psy-chological Bulletin,* September 1990, pp. 233–56; A.H. Eagly and S.J. Karau, "Gender and the Emergence of Leaders: A Meta-Analysis," *Journal of Personality and Social Psychology,* May 1991, pp. 685–710; J.B. Rosener, "Ways Women Lead," *Harvard Business Review,* November–December 1990, pp. 119–25; "Debate: Ways Men and Women Lead," *Harvard Business Review,* January–February 1991, pp. 150–60; A.H. Eagly, M.G. Makhijani, and B.G. Klonsky, "Gender and the Evaluation of Leaders: A Meta-Analysis," *Psychological Bulletin,* January 1992, pp. 3–22; A.H. Eagly, S.J. Karau, and B.T. Johnson, "Gender and Leadership Style Among School Principals: A Meta-Analysis," *Educational Administration Quarterly,* February 1992, pp. 76–102; L.R. Offermann and C. Beil, "Achievement Styles of Women Leaders and Their Peers," *Psychology of Women Quarterly,* March 1992, pp. 37–56; T. Melamed and N. Bozionelos, "Gender Differences in the Personality Features of British Managers," *Psychological Reports,* December 1992, pp. 979–986; G.N. Powell, *Women & Men in Management,* 2nd ed. (Thousand Oaks, CA: Sage, 1993); R.L. Kent and S.E. Moss, "Effects of Size and Gender Role on Leader Emergence," *Academy of Management Journal,* October 1994, pp. 1335–46; C. Lee, "The Feminization of Management," *Training,* November 1994, pp. 25–31; H. Collingwood, "Women as Managers: Not Just Different—Better," *Working Woman,* November 1995, p. 14; and J.B. Rosener, *America's Competitive Secret: Women Managers* (New York: Oxford University Press, 1995).

87 See, for instance, M. Frohman, "Nothing Kills Teams Like Ill-Prepared Leaders," *Industry Week,* October 2, 1995, pp. 72–76.

88 S. Caminiti, "What Team Leaders Need to Know," *Fortune,* February 20, 1995, pp. 93–100.

89 Ibid., p. 93.

90 Ibid., p. 100.

91 N. Steckler and N. Fondas, "Building Team Leader Effectiveness: A Diagnostic Tool," *Organizational Dynamics,* Winter 1995, p. 20.

92 R.S. Wellins, W.C. Byham, and G.R. Dixon, *Inside Teams* (San Francisco: Jossey-Bass, 1994), p. 318.

93 N. Steckler and N. Fondas, "Building Team Leader Effectiveness," p. 21.

94 C.D. Orth, H.E. Wilkinson, and R.C. Benfari, "The Manager's Role as Coach and Mentor," *Organizational Dynamics,* Spring 1987, p. 67.

95 See W.W. Burke, "Leadership as Empowering Others," in S. Srivastva and Associates, *Executive Power* (San Francisco: Jossey-Bass, 1986); J.A. Conger and R.N. Kanungo, "The Empowerment Process: Integrating Theory and Practice," *Academy of Management Review,* July 1988, pp. 471–82; J. Greenwald, "Is Mr. Nice Guy Back?" *Time,* January 27, 1992, pp. 42–44; J. Weber, "Letting Go Is Hard to Do," *Business Week,* November 1, 1993, pp. 218–19; and L. Holpp, "Applied Empowerment," *Training,* February 1994, pp. 39–44.

96 See, for instance, D.A. Waldman, "A Theoretical Consideration of Leadership and Total Quality Management," *Leadership Quarterly,* Spring 1993, pp. 65–79.

97 For problems with empowerment, see J.A. Belasco and R.C. Stayer, "Why Empowerment Doesn't Empower: The Bankruptcy of Current Paradigms," *Business Horizons,* March–April 1994, pp. 29–40; L. Holpp, "If Empowerment Is So Good, Why Does It Hurt?" *Training,* March 1995, pp. 52–57; and M.M. Broadwell, "Why Command and Control Won't Go Away," *Training,* September 1995, pp. 63–68.

98 R.E. Kelley, "In Praise of Followers," *Harvard Business Review,* November–December 1988, pp. 142–48; E.P. Hollander, "Leadership, Followership, Self, and Others," *Leadership Quarterly,* Spring 1992, pp. 43–54; and I. Challeff, *The Courageous Follower: Standing Up To and For Our Leaders* (San Francisco: Berrett-Koehler, 1995).

99 Kelley, "In Praise of Followers."

100 For a review of the cross-cultural applicability of the leadership literature, see R.S. Bhagat, B.L. Kedia, S.E. Crawford, and M.R. Kaplan, "Cross-Cultural Issues in Organizational Psychology: Emergent Trends and Directions for Research in the 1990s," in C.L. Cooper and I.T. Robertson (eds.), *International Review of Industrial and Organizational Psychology,* vol. 5 (Chichester, England: John Wiley & Sons, 1990), pp. 79–89.

101 "Military-Style Management in China," *Asia Inc.,* March 1995, p. 70.

102 This section is based on R.M. Sapolsky and J.C. Ray, "Styles of Dominance and Their Endocrine Correlates Among Wild Olive Baboons," *American Journal of Primatology,* vol. 18, no. 1, 1989, pp. 1–13; A. Booth, G. Shelley, A. Mazur, G. Tharp, and R. Kittok, "Testosterone, and Winning and Losing in Human Competition," *Hormones and Behavior,* December 1989, pp. 556–71; W.F. Allman, "Political Chemistry," *U.S. News & World Report,* November 2, 1992, pp. 62–65; E.L. Andrews, "A Skin Patch to Increase Testosterone," The *New York Times,* November 2, 1992, p. C2; P.D. Kramer, *Listening to Prozac* (New York: Penguin, 1993); M. Konner, "Out of the Darkness," *New York Times Magazine,* October 2, 1994, pp. 70–73; M. Chase, "More Are Listening to Prozac to Keep Their Business Edge," *Wall Street Journal,* March 27, 1995, p. B1; R. Langreth, "High Anxiety: Rivals Threaten Prozac's Reign," The *Wall Street Journal,* May 9, 1996, p. B1; and W.F. Allman, "The Serotonin Candidate," *Forbes ASAP,* September 23, 1996, pp. 133–40.

103 This section is based on R.B. Morgan, "Self- and Co-Worker Perceptions of Ethics and Their Relationships to Leadership and Salary," *Academy of Management Journal,* February 1993, pp. 200–14; J.B. Ciulla, "Leadership Ethics: Mapping the Territory," *Business Ethics Quarterly,* January 1995, pp. 5–28; E.P. Hollander, "Ethical Challenges in the Leader–Follower Relationship," *Business Ethics Quarterly,* January 1995, pp. 55–65; J.C. Rost, "Leadership: A Discussion About Ethics," *Business Ethics Quarterly,* January 1995, pp. 129–42; and R.N. Kanungo and M. Mendonca, *Ethical Dimensions of Leadership* (Thousand Oaks, CA: Sage Publications, 1996).

104 J.M. Burns, *Leadership* (New York: Harper & Row, 1978).

105 J.M. Howell and B.J. Avolio, "The Ethics of Charismatic Leadership: Submission or Liberation?" *Academy of Management Executive,* May 1992, pp. 43–55.

Chapter 11

1 Based on L. Jaroff, "Assembly-Line Sexism?" *Time,* May 6, 1996, pp. 56–58.

2 R.M. Kanter, "Power Failure in Management Circuits," *Harvard Business Review,* July–August 1979, p. 65.

3 J. Pfeffer, "Understanding Power in Organizations," *California Management Review,* Winter 1992, p. 35.

4 Based on B.M. Bass, *Bass & Stogdill's Handbook of Leadership,* 3rd ed. (New York: Free Press, 1990).

5 J.R.P. French, Jr., and B. Raven, "The Bases of Social Power," in D. Cartwright (ed.), *Studies in Social Power* (Ann Arbor: University of Michigan, Institute for Social Research, 1959), pp. 150–67. For an update on French and Raven's work, see D.E. Frost and A.J. Stahelski, "The Systematic Measurement of French and Raven's Bases of Social Power in Workgroups," *Journal of Applied Social Psychology,* April 1988, pp. 375–89; T.R. Hinkin and C.A. Schriesheim, "Development and Application of New Scales to Measure the French and Raven (1959) Bases of Social Power," *Journal of Applied Psychology,* August 1989, pp. 561–67; and G.E. Littlepage, J.L. Van Hein, K.M. Cohen, and L.L. Janiec, "Evaluation and Comparison of Three Instruments Designed to Measure Organizational Power and Influence Tactics," *Journal of Applied Social Psychology,* January 16–31, 1993, pp. 107–25.

6 D. Kipnis, *The Powerholders* (Chicago: University of Chicago Press, 1976), pp. 77–78.

7 R.E. Emerson, "Power–Dependence Relations," *American Sociological Review,* vol. 27 (1962), pp. 31–41.

8 P. Burrows, "Micron's Comeback Kid," *Business Week,* May 13, 1996, pp. 70–74.

9 H. Mintzberg, *Power In and Around Organizations* (Englewood Cliffs, NJ: Prentice Hall, 1983), p. 24.

10 R.M. Cyert and J.G. March, *A Behavioral Theory of the Firm* (Englewood Cliffs, NJ: Prentice Hall, 1963).

11 C. Perrow, "Departmental Power and Perspective in Industrial Firms," in M.N. Zald (ed.), *Power in Organizations* (Nashville, TN: Vanderbilt University Press, 1970).

12 Adapted from J. Pfeffer, *Managing With Power* (Boston: Harvard Business School Press, 1992), pp. 63–64.

13 Adapted from R.M. Kanter, "Power Failure in Management Circuits," *Harvard Business Review,* July–August 1979, p. 67.

14 See, for example, D. Kipnis, S.M. Schmidt, C. Swaffin-Smith, and I. Wilkinson, "Patterns of Managerial Influence: Shotgun Managers, Tacticians, and Bystanders," *Organizational Dynamics,* Winter 1984, pp. 58–67; T. Case, L. Dosier, G. Murkison, and B. Keys, "How Managers Influence Superiors: A Study of Upward Influence Tactics," *Leadership and Organization Development Journal,* vol. 9, no. 4, 1988, pp. 25–31; D. Kipnis and S.M. Schmidt, "Upward-Influence Styles: Relationship with Performance Evaluations, Salary, and Stress," *Administrative Science Quarterly,* December 1988, pp. 528–42; G. Yukl and C.M. Falbe, "Influence Tactics and Objectives in Upward, Downward, and Lateral Influence Attempts," *Journal of Applied Psychology,* April 1990, pp. 132–40; B. Keys and T. Case, "How to Become an Influential Manager," *Academy*

of Management Executive, November 1990, pp. 38–51; D.A. Ralston, D.J. Gustafson, L. Mainiero, and D. Umstot, "Strategies of Upward Influence: A Cross-National Comparison of Hong Kong and American Managers," *Asia Pacific Journal of Management,* October 1993, pp. 157–75; G. Yukl, H. Kim, and C.M. Falbe, "Antecedents of Influence Outcomes," *Journal of Applied Psychology,* June 1996, pp. 309–17; K.E. Lauterbach and B.J. Weiner, "Dynamics of Upward Influence: How Male and Female Managers Get Their Way," *Leadership Quarterly,* Spring 1996, pp. 87–107; and K.R. Xin and A.S. Tsui, "Different Strokes for Different Folks? Influence Tactics by Asian-American and Caucasian-American Managers," *Leadership Quarterly,* Spring 1996, pp. 109–32.

[15] This section is adapted from Kipnis, Schmidt, Swaffin-Smith, and Wilkinson, "Patterns of Managerial Influence."

[16] P.P. Poole, "Coalitions: The Web of Power," in *Research and Application, Proceedings of the 20th Annual Eastern Academy Conference.* D.J. Vredenburgh and R.S. Schuler (eds.), Effective Management: *Academy of Management,* Pittsburgh, May 1983, pp. 79–82.

[17] See Pfeffer, *Power in Organizations,* pp. 155–57.

[18] For recent reviews of the literature, see L.F. Fitzgerald and S.L. Shullman, "Sexual Harassment: A Research Analysis and Agenda for the 1990s," *Journal of Vocational Behavior,* February 1993, pp. 5–27; and M.L. Lengnick-Hall, "Sexual Harassment Research: A Methodological Critique," *Personnel Psychology,* Winter 1995, pp. 841–64.

[19] S. Silverstein and S. Christian, "Harassment Ruling Raises Free-Speech Issues," *Los Angeles Times,* November 11, 1993, p. D2.

[20] The following section is based on J.N. Cleveland and M.E. Kerst, "Sexual Harassment and Perceptions of Power: An Under-Articulated Relationship," *Journal of Vocational Behavior,* February 1993, pp. 49–67.

[21] S.A. Culbert and J.J. McDonough, *The Invisible War: Pursuing Self-Interest at Work* (New York: John Wiley, 1980), p. 6.

[22] Mintzberg, *Power In and Around Organizations,* p. 26.

[23] D.J. Vredenburgh and J.G. Maurer, "A Process Framework of Organizational Politics," *Human Relations,* January 1984, pp. 47–66.

[24] D. Farrell and J.C. Petersen, "Patterns of Political Behavior in Organizations," *Academy of Management Review,* July 1982, p. 405. For a thoughtful analysis of the academic controversies underlying any definition of organizational politics, see A. Drory and T. Romm, "The Definition of Organizational Politics: A Review," *Human Relations,* November 1990, pp. 1133–54.

[25] Farrell and Peterson, "Patterns of Political Behavior," pp. 406–07; and A. Drory, "Politics in Organization and Its Perception Within the Organization," *Organization Studies,* vol. 9, no. 2, 1988, pp. 165–79.

[26] Pfeffer, *Power in Organizations.*

[27] K.K. Eastman, "In the Eyes of the Beholder: An Attributional Approach to Ingratiation and Organizational Citizenship Behavior," *Academy of Management Journal,* October 1994, pp. 1379–91.

[28] See, for example, G. Biberman, "Personality and Characteristic Work Attitudes of Persons with High, Moderate, and Low Political Tendencies," *Psychological Reports,* October 1985, pp. 1303–10; and G.R. Ferris, G.S. Russ, and P.M. Fandt, "Politics in Organizations," in R.A. Giacalone and P. Rosenfeld (eds.), *Impression Management in the Organization* (Hillsdale, NJ: Lawrence Erlbaum Associates, 1989), pp. 155–56.

[29] Farrell and Petersen, "Patterns of Political Behavior," p. 408.

[30] S.C. Goh and A.R. Doucet, "Antecedent Situational Conditions of Organizational Politics: An Empirical Investigation," paper presented at the Annual Administrative Sciences Association of Canada Conference, Whistler, B.C., May 1986; C. Hardy, "The Contribution of Political Science to Organizational Behavior," in J.W. Lorsch (ed.), *Handbook of Organizational Behavior* (Englewood Cliffs, NJ: Prentice Hall, 1987), p. 103; and G.R. Ferris and K.M. Kacmar, "Perceptions of Organizational Politics," *Journal of Management,* March 1992, pp. 93–116.

[31] See, for example, Farrell and Petersen, "Patterns of Political Behavior," p. 409; P.M. Fandt and G.R. Ferris, "The Management of Information and Impressions: When Employees Behave Opportunistically," *Organizational Behavior and Human Decision Processes,* February 1990, pp. 140–58; and Ferris, Russ, and Fandt, "Politics in Organizations," p. 147.

[32] M.R. Leary and R.M. Kowalski, "Impression Management: A Literature Review and Two-Component Model," *Psychological Bulletin,* January 1990, pp. 34–47.

[33] S.P. Robbins and P.L. Hunsaker, *Training in InterPersonal Skills: TIPS for Managing People at Work,* 2nd ed. (Upper Saddle River, NJ: Prentice Hall, 1996), pp. 131–34.

[34] Ibid., p. 34.

[35] See, for instance, B.R. Schlenker, *Impression Management: The Self-Concept, Social Identity, and Interpersonal Relations* (Monterey, CA: Brooks/Cole, 1980); W.L. Gardner and M.J. Martinko, "Impression Management in Organizations," *Journal of Management,* June 1988, pp. 321–38; D.C. Gilmore and G.R. Ferris, "The Effects of Applicant Impression Management Tactics on Interviewer Judgments," *Journal of Management,* December 1989, pp. 557–64; Leary and Kowalski, "Impression Management: A Literature Review and Two-Component Model," pp. 34–47; S.J. Wayne and K.M. Kacmar, "The Effects of Impression Management on the Performance Appraisal Process," *Organizational Behavior and Human Decision Processes,* February 1991, pp. 70–88; E.W. Morrison and R.J. Bies, "Impression Management in the Feedback-Seeking Process: A Literature Review and Research Agenda," *Academy of Management Review,* July 1991, pp. 522–41; S.J. Wayne and R.C. Liden, "Effects of Impression Management on Performance Ratings: A Longitudinal Study," *Academy of Management Journal,* February 1995, pp. 232–60; and C.K. Stevens and A.L. Kristof, "Making the Right Impression: A Field Study of Applicant Impression Management During Job Interviews," *Journal of Applied Psychology,* October 1995, pp. 587–606.

[36] M. Snyder and J. Copeland, "Self-Monitoring Processes in Organizational Settings," in Giacalone and Rosenfeld, *Impression Management in the Organization,* p. 11; and E.D. Long and G.H. Dobbins, "Self-Monitoring, Impression

Management, and Interview Ratings: A Field and Laboratory Study," in J.L. Wall and L.R. Jauch, eds., *Proceedings of the 52nd Annual Academy of Management Conference;* Las Vegas, August 1992, pp. 274–78.

37 Leary and Kowalski, "Impression Management," p. 40.

38 Gardner and Martinko, "Impression Management in Organizations," p. 333.

39 R.A. Baron, "Impression Management by Applicants During Employment Interviews: The 'Too Much of a Good Thing' Effect," in R.W. Eder and G.R. Ferris (eds.), *The Employment Interview: Theory, Research, and Practice* (Newbury Park, CA: Sage Publishers, 1989), pp. 204–15.

40 Ferris, Russ, and Fandt, "Politics in Organizations."

41 Baron, "Impression Management by Applicants During Employment Interviews"; Gilmore and Ferris, "The Effects of Applicant Impression Management Tactics on Interviewer Judgments"; and Stevens and Kristof, "Making the Right Impression: A Field Study of Applicant Impression Management During Job Interviews."

42 Gilmore and Ferris, "The Effects of Applicant Impression Management Tactics on Interviewer Judgments."

43 K.M. Kacmar, J.E. Kelery, and G.R. Ferris, "Differential Effectiveness of Applicant IM Tactics on Employment Interview Decisions," *Journal of Applied Social Psychology,* August 16–31, 1992, pp. 1250–72.

44 Stevens and Kristof, "Making the Right Impression: A Field Study of Applicant Impression Management During Job Interviews."

45 This section is based on B.E. Ashforth and R.T. Lee, "Defensive Behavior in Organizations: A Preliminary Model," *Human Relations,* July 1990, pp. 621–48.

46 This figure is based on G.F. Cavanagh, D.J. Moberg, and M. Valasquez, "The Ethics of Organizational Politics," *Academy of Management Journal,* June 1981, pp. 363–74.

47 R.M. Kanter, *Men and Women of the Corporation* (New York: Basic Books, 1977).

48 See, for instance, C.M. Falbe and G. Yukl, "Consequences for Managers of Using Single Influence Tactics and Combinations of Tactics," *Academy of Management Journal,* August 1992, pp. 638–52.

49 P.A. Wilson, "The Effects of Politics and Power on the Organizational Commitment of Federal Executives," *Journal of Management,* Spring 1995, pp. 101–18.

50 See, for example, M.A. Rahim, "Relationships of Leader Power to Compliance and Satisfaction with Supervision: Evidence from a National Sample of Managers," *Journal of Management,* December 1989, pp. 545–56.

51 J.G. Bachman, D.G. Bowers, and P.M. Marcus, "Bases of Supervisory Power: A Comparative Study in Five Organizational Settings," in A.S. Tannenbaum (ed.), *Control in Organizations* (New York: McGraw-Hill, 1968), p. 236.

52 J. Pfeffer, *Managing With Power,* p. 137.

53 G.R. Ferris and K.M. Kacmar, "Perceptions of Organizational Politics."

54 A. Drory, "Perceived Political Climate and Job Attitudes," *Organization Studies,* vol. 14, no. 1, 1993, pp. 59–71.

Chapter 12

1 J. Barron, "Shea & Gould Partners Vote to Break Up the Law Firm," *New York Times,* January 29, 1994, p. 17; and M. Geyelin and E. Felsenthal, "Irreconcilable Differences Force Shea & Gould Closure," *Wall Street Journal,* January 31, 1994, p. B1.

2 See, for instance, C.F. Fink, "Some Conceptual Difficulties in the Theory of Social Conflict," *Journal of Conflict Resolution,* December 1968, pp. 412–60. For an updated review of the conflict literature, see J.A. Wall, Jr. and R.R. Callister, "Conflict and Its Management," *Journal of Management,* vol. 21, no. 3, 1995, pp. 515–58.

3 L.L. Putnam and M.S. Poole, "Conflict and Negotiation," in F.M. Jablin, L.L. Putnam, K.H. Roberts, and L.W. Porter (eds.), *Handbook of Organizational Communication: An Interdisciplinary Perspective* (Newbury Park, CA: Sage, 1987), pp. 549–99.

4 K.W. Thomas, "Conflict and Negotiation Processes in Organizations," in M.D. Dunnette and L.M. Hough (eds.), *Handbook of Industrial and Organizational Psychology,* 2nd ed., vol. 3 (Palo Alto, CA: Consulting Psychologists Press, 1992), pp. 651–717.

5 G. Smith, "How to Lose Friends and Influence No One," *Business Week,* January 25, 1993, pp. 42–43.

6 See A.C. Amason, "Distinguishing the Effects of Functional and Dysfunctional Conflict on Strategic Decision Making: Resolving a Paradox for Top Management Teams," *Academy of Management Journal,* February 1996, pp. 123–48.

7 This section is based on S.P. Robbins, *Managing Organizational Conflict: A Nontraditional Approach* (Englewood Cliffs, NJ: Prentice Hall, 1974), pp. 31–55.

8 L.R. Pondy, "Organizational Conflict: Concepts and Models," *Administrative Science Quarterly,* September 1967, p. 302.

9 See, for instance, R.L. Pinkley, "Dimensions of Conflict Frame: Disputant Interpretations of Conflict," *Journal of Applied Psychology,* April 1990, pp. 117–26; and R.L. Pinkley and G.B. Northcraft, "Conflict Frames of Reference: Implications for Dispute Processes and Outcomes," *Academy of Management Journal,* February 1994, pp. 193–205.

10 R. Kumar, "Affect, Cognition and Decision Making in Negotiations: A Conceptual Integration," in M.A. Rahim (ed.), *Managing Conflict: An Integrative Approach* (New York: Praeger, 1989), pp. 185–94.

11 Ibid.

12 P.J.D. Carnevale and A.M. Isen, "The Influence of Positive Affect and Visual Access on the Discovery of Integrative Solutions in Bilateral Negotiations," *Organizational Behavior and Human Decision Processes,* February 1986, pp. 1–13.

13 Thomas, "Conflict and Negotiation Processes in Organizations."

14 Ibid.

15 See R.J. Sternberg and L.J. Soriano, "Styles of Conflict Resolution," *Journal of Personality and Social Psychology,* July 1984, pp. 115–26; R.A. Baron, "Personality and Organizational Conflict: Effects of the Type A Behavior Pattern and Self-Monitoring," *Organizational Behavior and Human Deci-*

sion Processes, October 1989, pp. 281–96; and R.J. Volkema and T.J. Bergmann, "Conflict Styles as Indicators of Behavioral Patterns in Interpersonal Conflicts," *Journal of Social Psychology,* February 1995, pp. 5–15.

16. Thomas, "Conflict and Negotiation Processes in Organizations."

17. See, for instance, R.A. Cosier and C.R. Schwenk, "Agreement and Thinking Alike: Ingredients for Poor Decisions," *Academy of Management Executive,* February 1990, pp. 69–74; K.A. Jehn, "Enhancing Effectiveness: An Investigation of Advantages and Disadvantages of Value-Based Intragroup Conflict," *International Journal of Conflict Management,* July 1994, pp. 223–38; and R.L. Priem, D.A. Harrison, and N.K. Muir, "Structured Conflict and Consensus Outcomes in Group Decision Making," *Journal of Management,* vol. 21, no. 4, 1995, pp. 691–710.

18. See, for instance, C.J. Loomis, "Dinosaurs?" *Fortune,* May 3, 1993, pp. 36–42.

19. I.L. Janis, *Victims of Groupthink* (Boston: Houghton Mifflin, 1972).

20. J. Hall and M.S. Williams, "A Comparison of Decision-Making Performances in Established and Ad-Hoc Groups," *Journal of Personality and Social Psychology,* February 1966, p. 217.

21. R.L. Hoffman, "Homogeneity of Member Personality and Its Effect on Group Problem-Solving," *Journal of Abnormal and Social Psychology,* January 1959, pp. 27–32; and R.L. Hoffman and N.R.F. Maier, "Quality and Acceptance of Problem Solutions by Members of Homogeneous and Heterogeneous Groups," *Journal of Abnormal and Social Psychology,* March 1961, pp. 401–07.

22. See T.H. Cox and S. Blake, "Managing Cultural Diversity: Implications for Organizational Competitiveness," *Academy of Management Executive,* August 1991, pp. 45–56; T.H. Cox, S.A. Lobel, and P.L. McLeod, "Effects of Ethnic Group Cultural Differences on Cooperative Behavior on a Group Task," *Academy of Management Journal,* December 1991, pp. 827–47; P.L. McLeod and S.A. Lobel, "The Effects of Ethnic Diversity on Idea Generation in Small Groups," paper presented at the Annual Academy of Management Conference, Las Vegas, August 1992; and C. Kirchmeyer and A. Cohen, "Multicultural Groups: Their Performance and Reactions with Constructive Conflict," *Group & Organization Management,* June 1992, pp. 153–70.

23. R.E. Hill, "Interpersonal Compatibility and Work Group Performance Among Systems Analysts: An Empirical Study," *Proceedings of the Seventeenth Annual Midwest Academy of Management Conference,* Kent, OH, April 1974, pp. 97–110.

24. D.C. Pelz and F. Andrews, *Scientists in Organizations* (New York: John Wiley, 1966).

25. H. Lenk, "Konflikt und Leistung in Spitzensportmannschafter: Isozometrische Strukturen von WettKampfachtern in Ruden," *Soziale Welt,* vol. 15 (1964), pp. 307–43.

26. A. Tannenbaum, "Control Structure and Union Functions," *American Journal of Sociology,* May 1956, pp. 127–40.

27. For studies that focus on the dysfunctional consequences of conflict, see the *Journal of Conflict Resolution* and the *International Journal of Conflict Management.*

28. K. Jehn, "A Multimethod Examination of the Benefits and Detriments of Intragroup Conflict," *Administrative Science Quarterly,* June 1995, pp. 256–82.

29. This section is based on F. Sommerfield, "Paying the Troops to Buck the System," *Business Month,* May 1990, pp. 77–79; W. Kiechel III, "How to Escape the Echo Chamber," *Fortune,* June 18, 1990, pp. 129–30; and B. Angelo, "Musical Chairs in Maryland," *Time,* August 26, 1991, p. 21. See also E. van de Vliert and C.K.W. de Dreu, "Optimizing Performance by Conflict Stimulation," *International Journal of Conflict Management,* July 1994, pp. 211–22.

30. J.A. Wall, Jr., *Negotiation: Theory and Practice* (Glenview, IL: Scott, Foresman, 1985).

31. R.E. Walton and R.B. McKersie, *A Behavioral Theory of Labor Negotiations: An Analysis of a Social Interaction System* (New York: McGraw-Hill, 1965).

32. Thomas, "Conflict and Negotiation Processes in Organizations."

33. This model is based on R.J. Lewicki, "Bargaining and Negotiation," *Exchange: The Organizational Behavior Teaching Journal,* vol. 6, no. 2, 1981, pp. 39–40; and B.S. Moskal, "The Art of the Deal," *Industry Week,* January 18, 1993, p. 23.

34. M.H. Bazerman and M.A. Neale, *Negotiating Rationally* (New York: Free Press, 1992), pp. 67–68.

35. These suggestions are based on J.A. Wall, Jr. and M.W. Blum, "Negotiations," *Journal of Management,* June 1991, pp. 278–82.

36. Ibid.

37. C. Watson and L.R. Hoffman, "Managers as Negotiators: A Test of Power versus Gender as Predictors of Feelings, Behavior, and Outcomes," *Leadership Quarterly,* Spring 1996, pp. 63–85.

38. See N.J. Adler, *International Dimensions of Organizational Behavior,* 2nd ed. (Boston: PWS-Kent, 1991), pp. 179–217.

39. K.D. Schmidt, *Doing Business in France* (Menlo Park, CA: SRI International, 1987).

40. S. Lubman, "Round and Round," *The Wall Street Journal,* December 10, 1993, p. R3.

41. E.S. Glenn, D. Witmeyer, and K.A. Stevenson, "Cultural Styles of Persuasion," *Journal of Intercultural Relations,* Fall 1977, pp. 52–66.

42. J. Graham, "The Influence of Culture on Business Negotiations," *Journal of International Business Studies,* Spring 1985, pp. 81–96.

43. J.A. Wall, Jr. and M.W. Blum, "Negotiations," pp. 283–87.

44. For a review of the literature on intergroup relations, see M.B. Brewer and R.M. Kramer, "The Psychology of Intergroup Attitudes and Behavior," in M.R. Rosenzweig and L.W. Porter, *Annual Review of Psychology,* vol. 36 (Palo Alto, CA: Annual Reviews, 1985), pp. 219–43; and R.M. Kramer, "Intergroup Relations and Organizational Dilemmas: The Role of Categorization Processes," in L.L. Cummings and

B.M. Staw, *Research in Organizational Behavior,* vol. 13 (Greenwich, CT: JAI Press, 1991), pp. 191–228.

[45] J.M. Brett and J.K. Rognes, "Intergroup Relations in Organizations," in P.S. Goodman and Associates (eds.), *Designing Effective Work Groups* (San Francisco: Jossey-Bass, 1986), p. 205.

[46] J.D. Thompson, *Organizations in Action* (New York: McGraw-Hill, 1967), pp. 54–55.

[47] C. Perrow, "A Framework for the Comparative Analysis of Organizations," *American Sociological Review,* April 1967, pp. 194–208.

[48] P.R. Lawrence and J.W. Lorsch, *Organization and Environment* (Homewood, IL: R.D. Irwin, 1969), pp. 34–39.

[49] J. Galbraith, *Designing Complex Organizations* (Reading, MA: Addison-Wesley, 1973).

[50] Brett and Rognes, "Intergroup Relations in Organizations," p. 212.

[51] K.W. Thomas, "Toward Multidimensional Values in Teaching: The Example of Conflict Behaviors," *Academy of Management Review,* July 1977, p. 487.

Chapter 13

[1] D. Greising, "The Virtual Olympics," *Business Week,* April 29, 1996, pp. 64–66; and B. Filipczak, "The Other Olympic Training Challenge," *Training,* July 1996, pp. 42–46.

[2] See, for instance, R.L. Daft, *Organization Theory and Design,* 5th ed. (St. Paul, MN: West Publishing, 1995).

[3] J.H. Sheridan, "Sizing Up Corporate Staffs," *Industry Week,* November 21, 1988, p. 47.

[4] J.B. Treece, "Breaking the Chains of Command," *Business Week/The Information Revolution 1994,* p. 112.

[5] See, for instance, L. Urwick, *The Elements of Administration* (New York: Harper & Row, 1944), pp. 52–53.

[6] J.S. McClenahen, "Managing More People in the '90s," *Industry Week,* March 20, 1989, p. 30.

[7] J.R. Brandt, "Middle Management: Where the Action Will Be," *Industry Week,* May 2, 1994, p. 31.

[8] A. Ross, "BMO's Big Bang," *Canadian Business,* January 1994, pp. 58–63.

[9] J.B. Levine, "For IBM Europe, 'This Is the Year of Truth,'" *Business Week,* April 19, 1993, p. 45.

[10] H. Mintzberg, *Structure in Fives: Designing Effective Organizations* (Englewood Cliffs, NJ: Prentice Hall, 1983), p. 157.

[11] S. Baker, "Can Nucor Forge Ahead—And Keep Its Edge?" *Business Week,* April 4, 1994, p. 108.

[12] See, for instance, the interview with Edward Lawler in "Bureaucracy Busting," *Across the Board,* March 1993, pp. 23–27.

[13] W.E. Halal, "From Hierarchy to Enterprise: Internal Markets Are the New Foundation of Management," *The Executive,* November 1994, pp. 69–83.

[14] Cited in *At Work,* May–June 1993, p. 3.

[15] K. Knight, "Matrix Organization: A Review," *Journal of Management Studies,* May 1976, pp. 111–30; and L.R. Burns and D.R. Wholey, "Adoption and Abandonment of Matrix

Management Programs: Effects of Organizational Characteristics and Interorganizational Networks," *Academy of Management Journal,* February 1993, pp. 106–38.

[16] See, for instance, S.M. Davis and P.R. Lawrence, "Problems of Matrix Organization," *Harvard Business Review,* May–June 1978, pp. 131–42.

[17] M. Kaeter, "The Age of the Specialized Generalist," *Training,* December 1993, pp. 48–53.

[18] L. Brokaw, "Thinking Flat," *INC.,* October 1993, p. 88.

[19] See, for instance, E.A. Gargan, "'Virtual' Companies Leave the Manufacturing to Others," *New York Times,* July 17, 1994, p. F5; D.W. Cravens, S.H. Shipp, and K.S. Cravens, "Reforming the Traditional Organization: The Mandate for Developing Networks," *Business Horizons,* July–August 1994, pp. 19–27; R.T. King, Jr., "The Virtual Company," *Wall Street Journal,* November 14, 1994, p. 85; R.E. Miles and C.C. Snow, "The New Network Firm: A Spherical Structure Built on Human Investment Philosophy," *Organizational Dynamics,* Spring 1995, pp. 5–18; and G.G. Dess, A.M.A. Rasheed, K.J. McLaughlin, and R.L. Priem, "The New Corporate Architecture," *Academy of Management Executive,* August 1995, pp. 7–20.

[20] "Why Every Business Will Be Like Show Business," *INC.,* March 1995, pp. 64–78.

[21] "GE: Just Your Average Everyday $60 Billion Family Grocery Store," *Industry Week,* May 2, 1994, pp. 13–18.

[22] This section is based on P. LaBarre, "The Seamless Enterprise," *Industry Week,* June 19, 1995, pp. 22–34; and R. Ashkenas, D. Ulrich, T. Jick, and S. Kerr, *The Boundaryless Organization: Breaking the Chains of Organizational Structure* (San Francisco: Jossey-Bass, 1995).

[23] See J. Lipnack and J. Stamps, *The TeamNet Factor* (Essex Junction, VT: Oliver Wight Publications, 1993); J.R. Wilke, "Computer Links Erode Hierarchical Nature of Workplace Culture," *The Wall Street Journal,* December 9, 1993, p. A1; and T.A. Stewart, "Managing in a Wired Company," *Fortune,* July 11, 1994, pp. 44–56.

[24] T. Burns and G.M. Stalker, *The Management of Innovation* (London: Tavistock, 1961); and J.A. Courtright, G.T. Fairhurst, and L.E. Rogers, "Interaction Patterns in Organic and Mechanistic Systems," *Academy of Management Journal,* December 1989, pp. 773–802.

[25] This analysis is referred to as a contingency approach to organization design. See, for instance, J.M. Pennings, "Structural Contingency Theory: A Reappraisal," in B.M. Staw and L.L. Cummings (eds.), *Research in Organizational Behavior,* vol. 14 (Greenwich, CT: JAI Press, 1992), pp. 267–309.

[26] The strategy–structure thesis was originally proposed in A.D. Chandler, Jr., *Strategy and Structure: Chapters in the History of the Industrial Enterprise* (Cambridge, MA: MIT Press, 1962). For an updated analysis, see T.L. Amburgey and T. Dacin, "As the Left Foot Follows the Right? The Dynamics of Strategic and Structural Change," *Academy of Management Journal,* December 1994, pp. 1427–52.

[27] See R.E. Miles and C.C. Snow, *Organizational Strategy, Structure, and Process* (New York: McGraw-Hill, 1978); D. Miller, "The Structural and Environmental Correlates of Business

Strategy," *Strategic Management Journal,* January–February 1987, pp. 55–76; and D.C. Galunic and K.M. Eisenhardt, "Renewing the Strategy-Structure-Performance Paradigm," in B.M. Staw and L.L. Cummings (eds.), *Research in Organizational Behavior,* vol. 16 (Greenwich, CT: JAI Press, 1994), pp. 215–55.

28 See, for instance, P.M. Blau and R.A. Schoenherr, *The Structure of Organizations* (New York: Basic Books, 1971); D.S. Pugh, "The Aston Program of Research: Retrospect and Prospect," in A.H. Van de Ven and W.F. Joyce (eds.), *Perspectives on Organization Design and Behavior* (New York: John Wiley, 1981), pp. 135–66; R.Z. Gooding and J.A. Wagner III, "A Meta-Analytic Review of the Relationship Between Size and Performance: The Productivity and Efficiency of Organizations and Their Subunits," *Administrative Science Quarterly,* December 1985, pp. 462–81; and A.C. Bluedorn, "Pilgrim's Progress: Trends and Convergence in Research on Organizational Size and Environments," *Journal of Management,* Summer 1993, pp. 163–92.

29 See J. Woodward, *Industrial Organization: Theory and Practice* (London: Oxford University Press, 1965); C. Perrow, "A Framework for the Comparative Analysis of Organizations," *American Sociological Review,* April 1967, pp. 194–208; J.D. Thompson, *Organizations in Action* (New York: McGraw-Hill, 1967); J. Hage and M. Aiken, "Routine Technology, Social Structure, and Organizational Goals," *Administrative Science Quarterly,* September 1969, pp. 366–77; and C.C. Miller, W.H. Glick, Y. Wang, and G.P. Huber, "Understanding Technology–Structure Relationships: Theory Development and Meta-Analytic Theory Testing," *Academy of Management Journal,* June 1991, pp. 370–99.

30 See F.E. Emery and E. Trist, "The Causal Texture of Organizational Environments," *Human Relations,* February 1965, pp. 21–32; P. Lawrence and J.W. Lorsch, *Organization and Environment: Managing Differentiation and Integration* (Boston: Harvard Business School, Division of Research, 1967); M. Yasai-Ardekani, "Structural Adaptations to Environments," *Academy of Management Review,* January 1986, pp. 9–21; and A.C. Bluedorn, "Pilgrim's Progress."

31 G.G. Dess and D.W. Beard, "Dimensions of Organizational Task Environments," *Administrative Science Quarterly,* March 1984, pp. 52–73; E.A. Gerloff, N.K. Muir, and W.D. Bodensteiner, "Three Components of Perceived Environmental Uncertainty: An Exploratory Analysis of the Effects of Aggregation," *Journal of Management,* December 1991, pp. 749–68; and O. Shenkar, N. Aranya, and T. Almor, "Construct Dimensions in the Contingency Model: An Analysis Comparing Metric and Non-Metric Multivariate Instruments," *Human Relations,* May 1995, pp. 559–80.

32 See, for instance, L.W. Porter and E.E. Lawler III, "Properties of Organization Structure in Relation to Job Attitudes and Job Behavior," *Psychological Bulletin,* July 1965, pp. 23–51; L.R. James and A.P. Jones, "Organization Structure: A Review of Structural Dimensions and Their Conceptual Relationships with Individual Attitudes and Behavior," *Organizational Behavior and Human Performance,* June 1976, pp. 74–113; D.R. Dalton, W.D. Todor, M.J. Spendolini, G.J. Fielding, and L.W. Porter, "Organization Structure and Per-

formance: A Critical Review," *Academy of Management Review,* January 1980, pp. 49–64; W. Snizek and J.H. Bullard, "Perception of Bureaucracy and Changing Job Satisfaction: A Longitudinal Analysis," *Organizational Behavior and Human Performance,* October 1983, pp. 275–87; and D.B. Turban and T.L. Keon, "Organizational Attractiveness: An Interactionist Perspective," *Journal of Applied Psychology,* April 1994, pp. 184–93.

33 J. Markoff, "The Snooping Mayor," *New York Times,* May 4, 1990, p. B1; G. Bylinsky, "How Companies Spy on Employees," *Fortune,* November 4, 1991, pp. 131–40; D. Warner, "The Move to Curb Worker Monitoring," *Nation's Business,* December 1993, pp. 37–38; and M. Picard, "Working Under an Electronic Thumb," *Training,* February 1994, pp. 47–51.

Chapter 14
1 Based on J. Macht, "When the Walls Come Tumbling Down," *Inc. Technology,* No. 2, 1995, pp. 70–72.

2 R.M. Steers and R.T. Mowday, "The Motivational Properties of Tasks," *Academy of Management Review,* October 1977, pp. 645–58.

3 D.G. Gardner and L.L. Cummings, "Activation Theory and Job Design: Review and Reconceptualization," in B.M. Staw and L.L. Cummings (eds.), *Research in Organizational Behavior,* Vol. 10 (Greenwich, CT: JAI Press, 1988), p. 100.

4 A.N. Turner and P.R. Lawrence, *Industrial Jobs and the Worker* (Boston: Harvard University Press, 1965).

5 J.R. Hackman and G.R. Oldham, "Motivation Through the Design of Work: Test of a Theory," *Organizational Behavior and Human Performance,* August 1976, pp. 250–79.

6 J.R. Hackman, "Work Design," in J.R. Hackman and J.L. Suttle (eds.), *Improving Life at Work* (Santa Monica, CA: Goodyear, 1977), p. 129.

7 See "Job Characteristics Theory of Work Redesign," in J.B. Miner, *Theories of Organizational Behavior* (Hinsdale, IL: Dryden Press, 1980), pp. 231–66; B.T. Loher, R.A. Noe, N.L. Moeller, and M.P. Fitzgerald, "A Meta-Analysis of the Relation of Job Characteristics to Job Satisfaction," *Journal of Applied Psychology,* May 1985, pp. 280–89; W.H. Glick, G.D. Jenkins, Jr., and N. Gupta, "Method versus Substance: How Strong Are Underlying Relationships Between Job Characteristics and Attitudinal Outcomes?" *Academy of Management Journal,* September 1986, pp. 441–64; Y. Fried and G.R. Ferris, "The Validity of the Job Characteristics Model: A Review and Meta-Analysis," *Personnel Psychology,* Summer 1987, pp. 287–322; S.J. Zaccaro and E.F. Stone, "Incremental Validity of an Empirically Based Measure of Job Characteristics," *Journal of Applied Psychology,* May 1988, pp. 245–52; and R.W. Renn and R.J. Vandenberg, "The Critical Psychological States: An Underrepresented Component in Job Characteristics Model Research," *Journal of Management,* vol. 21, no. 2, 1995, pp. 279–303.

8 See R.B. Dunham, "Measurement and Dimensionality of Job Characteristics," *Journal of Applied Psychology,* August 1976, pp. 404–09; J.L. Pierce and R.B. Dunham, "Task Design: A Literature Review," *Academy of Management Review,* January 1976, pp. 83–97; D.M. Rousseau, "Technological Differences in Job Characteristics, Employee Satisfaction,

and Motivation: A Synthesis of Job Design Research and Sociotechnical Systems Theory," *Organizational Behavior and Human Performance,* October 1977, pp. 18–42; and Y. Fried and G.R. Ferris, "The Dimensionality of Job Characteristics: Some Neglected Issues," *Journal of Applied Psychology,* August 1986, pp. 419–26.

[9] Fried and Ferris, "The Dimensionality of Job Characteristics."

[10] See, for instance, Fried and Ferris, "The Dimensionality of Job Characteristics;" and M.G. Evans and D.A. Ondrack, "The Motivational Potential of Jobs: Is a Multiplicative Model Really Necessary?" in S.L. McShane (ed.), *Organizational Behavior,* ASAC Conference Proceedings, vol. 9, Part 5, Halifax, Nova Scotia, 1988, pp. 31–39.

[11] R.B. Tiegs, L.E. Tetrick, and Y. Fried, "Growth Need Strength and Context Satisfactions as Moderators of the Relations of the Job Characteristics Model," *Journal of Management,* September 1992, pp. 575–93.

[12] C.A. O'Reilly and D.F. Caldwell, "Informational Influence as a Determinant of Perceived Task Characteristics and Job Satisfaction," *Journal of Applied Psychology,* April 1979, pp. 157–65; R. V. Montagno, "The Effects of Comparison Others and Prior Experience on Responses to Task Design," *Academy of Management Journal,* June 1985, pp. 491–98; and P.C. Bottger and I. K-H. Chew, "The Job Characteristics Model and Growth Satisfaction: Main Effects of Assimilation of Work Experience and Context Satisfaction," *Human Relations,* June 1986, pp. 575–94.

[13] Hackman, "Work Design," pp. 132–33.

[14] G.R. Salancik and J. Pfeffer, "A Social Information Processing Approach to Job Attitudes and Task Design," *Administrative Science Quarterly,* June 1978, pp. 224–53; J.G. Thomas and R.W. Griffin, "The Power of Social Information in the Workplace," *Organizational Dynamics,* Autumn 1989, pp. 63–75; and M.D. Zalesny and J.K. Ford, "Extending the Social Information Processing Perspective: New Links to Attitudes, Behaviors, and Perceptions," *Organizational Behavior and Human Decision Processes,* December 1990, pp. 205–46.

[15] See, for instance, J. Thomas and R.W. Griffin, "The Social Information Processing Model of Task Design: A Review of the Literature," *Academy of Management Journal,* October 1983, pp. 672–82; and M.D. Zalesny and J.K. Ford, "Extending the Social Information Processing Perspective: New Links to Attitudes, Behaviors, and Perceptions," *Organizational Behavior and Human Decision Processes,* December 1990, pp. 205–46; and G.W. Meyer, "Social Information Processing and Social Networks: A Test of Social Influence Mechanisms," *Human Relations,* September 1994, pp. 1013–45.

[16] See, for example, T.H. Berry, *Managing the Total Quality Transition* (New York: McGraw Hill, 1991); D. Ciampa, *Total Quality* (Reading, MA: Addison-Wesley, 1992); W.H. Schmidt and J.P. Finnegan, *The Race Without a Finish Line* (San Francisco: Jossey-Bass, 1992); and T.B. Kinni, "Process Improvement," *Industry Week,* January 23, 1995, pp. 52–58.

[17] M. Sashkin and K.J. Kiser, *Putting Total Quality Management to Work* (San Francisco: Berrett-Koehler, 1993), p. 44.

[18] T.F. O'Boyle, "A Manufacturer Grows Efficient By Soliciting Ideas from Employees," *Wall Street Journal,* June 5, 1992, p. A1.

[19] M. Hammer and J. Champy, *Reengineering the Corporation: A Manifesto for Business Revolution* (New York: Harper-Business, 1993). See also J. Champy, *Reengineering Management: The Mandate for New Leadership* (New York: HarperBusiness, 1995); and M. Hammer and S.A. Stanton, *The Reengineering Revolution* (New York: HarperBusiness, 1995).

[20] R. Karlgaard, "ASAP Interview: Mike Hammer," *Forbes ASAP,* September 13, 1993, p. 70.

[21] Ibid.

[22] "The Age of Reengineering," *Across the Board,* June 1993, pp. 26–33.

[23] Ibid., p. 29.

[24] Ibid., p. 33.

[25] Cited in "The Bigger Picture: Reorganizing Work," *Industry Week,* August 2, 1993, p. 24.

[26] "The Age of Reengineering," p. 31.

[27] A. Ehrbar, "'Reengineering' Gives Firms New Efficiency, Workers the Pink Slip," *Wall Street Journal,* March 16, 1993, p. A1.

[28] Ibid.

[29] Ibid.

[30] See, for instance, O. Port, "Moving Past the Assembly Line," *Business Week/Reinventing America Special Issue,* November 1992, pp. 177–80; D.M. Upton, "The Management of Manufacturing Flexibility," *California Management Review,* Winter 1994, pp. 72–89; G. Bylinsky, "The Digital Factory," *Fortune,* November 14, 1994, pp. 96–100; and P. Coy, "The Technology Paradox," *Business Week,* March 6, 1995, pp. 76–84.

[31] S. Moffat, "Japan's New Personalized Production," *Fortune,* October 22, 1990, p. 44.

[32] See E. Norton, "Small, Flexible Plants May Play Crucial Role in U.S. Manufacturing," *Wall Street Journal,* January 13, 1993, p. A1.

[33] P.E. Ross, "Software as Career Threat," *Forbes,* May 22, 1995, pp. 240–46.

[34] For an excellent review of this literature, see R.A. Baron, "The Physical Environment of Work Settings: Effects on Task Performance, Interpersonal Relations, and Job Satisfaction," in B.M. Staw and L.L. Cummings, *Research in Organizational Behavior,* vol. 16 (Greenwich, CT: JAI Press, 1994), pp. 1–46.

[35] P.A. Bell, J.D. Fisher, A. Baum, and T.E. Green, *Environmental Psychology,* 3rd ed. (New York: Holt, Rinehart & Winston, 1990).

[36] See, for instance, E.J. McCormick and D. Ilgen, *Industrial Psychology,* 7th ed. (Englewood Cliffs, NJ: Prentice Hall, 1980), p. 388; and P.A. Bell, R.J. Loomis, and J.C. Cervone, "Effects of Heat, Social Facilitation, Sex Differences, and Task Difficulty on Reaction Time," *Human Factors,* January 1982, pp. 19–24.

[37] B.J. Fine and J.L. Kobrick, "Effects of Altitude and Heat on Complex Cognitive Tasks," *Human Factors*, February 1978, pp. 115–22.

[38] McCormick and Ilgen, *Industrial Psychology*, p. 390.

[39] Ibid., p. 391.

[40] Ibid.

[41] R.A. Baron, "The Physical Environment of Work Settings," p. 16.

[42] P.A. Bell, J.D. Fisher, A. Baum, and T.E. Green, *Environmental Psychology*.

[43] J.D. Wineman, "Office Design and Evaluation: An Overview," *Environment and Behavior*, May 1982, p. 276; and P.R. Boyce, S.M. Berman, B.L. Collins, A.L. Lewis, and M.S. Rea, *Lighting and Human Performance: A Review*. Lighting Equipment Division National Electrical Manufacturers Association and Lighting Research Institute, London, England (cited in R.A. Baron, "The Physical Environment of Work Settings").

[44] P.C. Hughes, "Lighting the Office," *The Office*, vol. 84, no. 3, 1976, p. 127.

[45] R.A. Baron, "The Physical Environment of Work Settings," p. 20.

[46] This section is based on R.A. Baron, "The Physical Environment of Work Settings," pp. 23–25.

[47] J. Pfeffer, *Organizations and Organization Theory* (Boston: Pitman, 1982), p. 261.

[48] See, for example, L.S. Festinger, S. Schachter, and K. Back, *Social Pressures in Informal Groups* (Stanford, CA: Stanford University Press, 1950).

[49] See, for example, R.L. Zweigenhaft, "Personal Space in the Faculty Office Desk Placement and the Student-Faculty Interaction," *Journal of Applied Psychology*, August 1976, pp. 529–32; D.E. Campbell, "Interior Office Design and Visitor Response," *Journal of Applied Psychology*, December 1979, pp. 648–53; P.C. Morrow and J.C. McElroy, "Interior Office Design and Visitor Response: A Constructive Replication," *Journal of Applied Psychology*, October 1981, pp. 646–50; and G.R. Oldham, "Effects of Changes in Workspace Partitions and Spatial Density on Employee Reactions: A Quasi-Experiment," *Journal of Applied Psychology*, May 1988, pp. 253–58.

[50] M.A. Verespej, "Welcome to the New Work Place," *Industry Week*, April 15, 1996, pp. 24–30.

[51] J. O'C. Hamilton, "The New Workplace," *Business Week*, April 29, 1996, p. 108.

[52] Ibid., p. 109.

[53] R.A. Baron, "The Physical Environment of Work Settings," p. 33.

[54] J.I. Porras and P.J. Robertson, "Organizational Development: Theory, Practice, and Research," in M.D. Dunnette and L.M. Hough, *Handbook of Industrial & Organizational Psychology*, 2nd ed., vol. 3 (Palo Alto, CA: Consulting Psychologists Press, 1992), p. 734.

[55] J.E. Rigdon, "Using Lateral Moves to Spur Employees," *Wall Street Journal*, May 26, 1992, p. B1.

[56] B.G. Posner, "Role Changes," *INC.*, February 1990, pp. 95–98.

[57] C. Garfield, "Creating Successful Partnerships with Employees," *At Work*, May/June 1992, p. 8.

[58] Ibid.

[59] See, for instance, data on job enlargement described in M.A. Campion and C.L. McClelland, "Follow-Up and Extension of the Interdisciplinary Costs and Benefits of Enlarged Jobs," *Journal of Applied Psychology*, June 1993, pp. 339–51.

[60] Related in personal communication with the author.

[61] J.R. Hackman and G.R. Oldham, *Work Redesign* (Reading, MA: Addison Wesley, 1980).

[62] Cited in *U.S. News & World Report*, May 31, 1993, p. 63.

[63] See, for example, J.R. Hackman and G.R. Oldham, *Work Redesign*; J.B. Miner, *Theories of Organizational Behavior* (Hinsdale, IL: Dryden Press, 1980), pp. 231–66; R.W. Griffin, "Effects of Work Redesign on Employee Perceptions, Attitudes, and Behaviors: A Long-Term Investigation," *Academy of Management Journal*, June 1991, pp. 425–35; and J.L. Cotton, *Employee Involvement* (Newbury Park, CA: Sage, 1993), pp. 141–72.

[64] J.R. Hackman, "Work Design," in J.R. Hackman and J.L. Suttle (eds.), *Improving Life at Work* (Santa Monica, CA: Goodyear, 1977), pp. 132–33.

[65] R.W. Griffin and G.C. McMahan, "Motivation Through Job Design," in J. Greenberg, ed. *Organizational Behavior: The State of the Science* (Hillsdale, NJ: Lawrence Erlbaum Associates, 1994), pp. 36–38.

[66] J.R. Hackman, "The Design of Work Teams," in J.W. Lorsch, ed., *Handbook of Organizational Behavior* (Englewood Cliffs, NJ: Prentice Hall, 1987), pp. 324–27.

[67] See, for example, P.T. Kilborn, "In Their Quest for Efficiency, Factories Scrap 5-Day Week," *The New York Times*, June 4, 1996, p. A1.

[68] G. Fuchsberg, "Four-Day Workweek Has Become a Stretch for Some Employees," *Wall Street Journal*, August 3, 1994, p. A1.

[69] Reported in Ibid.

[70] E.J. Calvasina and W.R. Boxx, "Efficiency of Workers on the Four-Day Workweek," *Academy of Management Journal*, September 1975, pp. 604–10.

[71] See, for example, J.C. Latack and L.W. Foster, "Implementation of Compressed Work Schedules: Participation and Job Redesign as Critical Factors for Employee Acceptance," *Personnel Psychology*, Spring 1985, pp. 75–92; and J.W. Seybolt and J.W. Waddoups, "The Impact of Alternative Work Schedules on Employee Attitudes: A Field Experiment," paper presented at the Western Academy of Management Meeting, Hollywood, CA, April 1987.

[72] J.C. Goodale and A.K. Aagaard, "Factors Relating to Varying Reactions to the 4-Day Work Week," *Journal of Applied Psychology*, February 1975, pp. 33–38.

[73] This section is based on T. Roth, "Europe Ponders the Shorter Workweek," *Wall Street Journal*, November 12, 1993, p. A11.

[74] Cited in C.M. Solomon, "Job Sharing: One Job, Double Headache?" *Personnel Journal,* September 1994, p. 90.

[75] D.R. Dalton and D.J. Mesch, "The Impact of Flexible Scheduling on Employee Attendance and Turnover," *Administrative Science Quarterly,* June 1990, pp. 370–87; and K.S. Kush and L.K. Stroh, "Flextime: Myth or Reality," *Business Horizons,* September–October 1994, p. 53.

[76] See, for example, D.A. Ralston and M.F. Flanagan, "The Effect of Flextime on Absenteeism and Turnover for Male and Female Employees," *Journal of Vocational Behavior,* April 1985, pp. 206–17; D.A. Ralston, W.P. Anthony, and D.J. Gustafson, "Employees May Love Flextime, But What Does It Do to the Organization's Productivity?" *Journal of Applied Psychology,* May 1985, pp. 272–79; J.B. McGuire and J.R. Liro, "Flexible Work Schedules, Work Attitudes, and Perceptions of Productivity," *Public Personnel Management,* Spring 1986, pp. 65–73; P. Bernstein, "The Ultimate in Flextime: From Sweden, by Way of Volvo," *Personnel,* June 1988, pp. 70–74; and D.R. Dalton and D.J. Mesch, "The Impact of Flexible Scheduling on Employee Attendance and Turnover," *Administrative Science Quarterly,* June 1990, pp. 370–87.

[77] Cited in Solomon, "Job Sharing," p. 90.

[78] "Job-Sharing: Widely Offered, Little Used," *Training,* November 1994, p. 12.

[79] "Teaming Up to Manage," *Working Woman,* September 1993, pp. 31–32.

[80] S. Shellenbarger, "Two People, One Job: It Can Really Work," *Wall Street Journal,* December 7, 1994, p. B1.

[81] See, for example, R. Maynard, "The Growing Appeal of Telecommuting," *Nation's Business,* August 1994, pp. 61–62; F.A.E. McQuarrie, "Telecommuting: Who Really Benefits?" *Business Horizons,* November–December 1994, pp. 79–83; and M. Hequet, "Virtually Working," *Training,* August 1996, pp. 29–35.

[82] A. LaPlante, "Telecommuting: Round Two. Voluntary No More," *Forbes ASAP,* October 9, 1995, p. 133.

[83] M. Hequet, "Virtually Working," p. 30.

[84] "American Express: Telecommuting," *Fortune,* Autumn 1993, pp. 24–28.

[85] S. Silverstein, "Telecommuting Boomlet Has Few Follow-Up Calls," *Los Angeles Times,* May 16, 1994, p. A1.

Chapter 15

[1] This opening vignette is based on R. Carpenter, "Geek Logic," *Canadian Business,* August 1995, pp. 57–58; and D. Pritchard, "Wired for Hiring: Microsoft's Slick Recruiting Machine," *Fortune,* February 5, 1996, pp. 123–24.

[2] For a review of the evidence linking HRM practices to organizational performance, see B. Becker and B. Gerhart, "The Impact of Human Resource Management on Organizational Performance: Progress and Prospects," *Academy of Management Journal,* August 1996, pp. 779–801; and J.T. Delaney and M.A. Huselid, "The Impact of Human Resource Management Practices on the Perceptions of Organizational Performance," *Academy of Management Journal,* August 1996, pp. 949–69.

[3] See, for instance, C.T. Dortch, "Job-Person Match," *Personnel Journal,* June 1989, pp. 49–57; and S. Rynes and B. Gerhart, "Interviewer Assessments of Applicant 'Fit': An Exploratory Investigation," *Personnel Psychology,* Spring 1990, pp. 13–34.

[4] See, for example, J.V. Ghorpade, *Job Analysis: A Handbook for the Human Resource Director* (Englewood Cliffs, NJ: Prentice Hall, 1988).

[5] R.L. Dipboye, *Selection Interviews: Process Perspectives* (Cincinnati: South-Western Publishing, 1992), p. 6; and J.E. Rigdon, "Talk Isn't Cheap," *Wall Street Journal,* February 27, 1995, p. R13.

[6] T.J. Hanson and J.C. Balestreri-Spero, "An Alternative to Interviews," *Personnel Journal,* June 1985, p. 114.

[7] See A.I. Huffcutt and W. Arthur, Jr., "Hunter and Hunter (1984) Revisited: Interview Validity for Entry-Level Jobs," *Journal of Applied Psychology,* April 1994, pp. 184–90; M.A. McDaniel, D.L. Whetzel, F.L. Schmidt, and S.D. Maurer, "The Validity of Employment Interviews: A Comprehensive Review and Meta-Analysis," *Journal of Applied Psychology,* August 1994, pp. 599–616; and J.M. Conway, R.A. Jako, and D.F. Goodman, "A Meta-Analysis of Interrater and Internal Consistency Reliability of Selection Interviews," *Journal of Applied Psychology,* October 1995, pp. 565–79.

[8] R.L. Dipboye, *Selection Interviews,* pp. 42–44.

[9] W.F. Cascio, *Applied Psychology in Personnel Management,* 4th ed. (Englewood Cliffs, NJ: Prentice Hall, 1991), p. 271.

[10] E.E. Ghiselli, "The Validity of Aptitude Tests in Personnel Selection," *Personnel Psychology,* Winter 1973, p. 475.

[11] R.J. Herrnstein and C. Murray, *The Bell Curve: Intelligence and Class Structure in American Life* (New York: Free Press, 1994); and M.J. Ree, J.A. Earles, and M.S. Teachout, "Predicting Job Performance: Not Much More Than *g*," *Journal of Applied Psychology,* August 1994, pp. 518–24.

[12] J. Flint, "Can You Tell Applesauce From Pickles?" *Forbes,* October 9, 1995, pp. 106–08.

[13] This box is based on W.C. Donaghy, *The Interview: Skills and Applications* (Glenview, IL: Scott, Foresman, 1984), pp. 245–80; J.M. Jenks and B.L.P. Zevnik, "ABCs of Job Interviewing," *Harvard Business Review,* July–August 1989, pp. 38–42; E.D. Pulakos and N. Schmitt, "Experience-Based and Situational Interview Questions: Studies of Validity," *Personnel Psychology,* Summer 1995, pp. 289–308; and M. Barrier, "Interviews: The War of Wits," *Nation's Business,* June 1996, p. 20

[14] D.S. Ones, C. Viswesvaran, and F.L. Schmidt, "Comprehensive Meta-Analysis of Integrity Test Validities: Findings and Implications for Personnel Selection and Theories of Job Performance," *Journal of Applied Psychology,* August 1993, pp. 679–703.

[15] J.J. Asher and J.A. Sciarrino, "Realistic Work Sample Tests: A Review," *Personnel Psychology,* Winter 1974, pp. 519–33; and I.T. Robertson and R.S. Kandola, "Work Sample Tests: Validity, Adverse Impact and Applicant Reaction," *Journal of Occupational Psychology,* Spring 1982, pp. 171–82.

[16] G.C. Thornton, *Assessment Centers in Human Resource Management* (Reading, MA: Addison-Wesley, 1992).

[17] Cited in *Training,* October 1995, p. 38.

18 Cited in J.C. Szabo, "Training Workers for Tomorrow," *Nation's Business,* March 1993, pp. 22–32.

19 R. Henkoff, "Companies That Train Best," *Fortune,* March 22, 1993, p. 64; and "How SIA Nurtures High Fliers," *Asian Business,* December 1993, p. 44.

20 M.E. Mangelsdorf, "Ground-Zero Training," *INC.,* February 1993, pp. 82–93.

21 Cited in M. Hequet, "The Union Push for Lifelong Learning," *Training,* March 1994, p. 31.

22 G. Koretz, "A Crash Course in the Three Rs?" *Business Week,* May 20, 1996, p. 26.

23 Reported in *From School to Work* (Princeton, NJ: Educational Testing Service, 1990).

24 J.C. Szabo, "Honing Workers' Basic Skills," *Nation's Business,* May 1994, p. 69.

25 M. Salter, "The New Blue Collar Elite," *Canadian Business: Special Technology Issue,* June 1995, pp. 55–57.

26 See, For instance, S.E. Jackson (ed.), *Diversity in the Workplace* (New York: Guilford Press, 1992); M. Lee, "Diversity Training Grows at Small Firms," *Wall Street Journal,* September 2, 1993, p. B2; H.B. Karp, "Choices in Diversity Training," *Training,* August 1994, pp. 73–74; S. Rynes and B. Rosen, "What Makes Diversity Programs Work," *HRMagazine,* October 1994, pp. 67–73; and S. Nelton, "Nurturing Diversity," *Nation's Business,* June 1995, pp. 25–27.

27 For an extended discussion of on-the-job and off-the-job training methods, see D. DeCenzo and S.P. Robbins, *Human Resource Management,* 5th ed. (New York: Wiley, 1996), pp. 243–45.

28 D. Schaaf, "Inside Hamburger University," *Training,* December 1994, pp. 18–24.

29 Cited in N.K. Austin, "Where Employee Training Works," *Working Woman,* May 1993, p. 23.

30 D.A. Kolb, "Management and the Learning Process," *California Management Review,* Spring 1976, pp. 21–31; and B. Filipczak, "Different Strokes: Learning Styles in the Classroom," *Training,* March 1995, pp. 43–48.

31 See H. Lancaster, "You, and Only You, Must Stay in Charge of Your Employability," *Wall Street Journal,* November 15, 1994, p. B1; B. Filipczak, "You're On Your Own: Training, Employability, and the New Employment Contract," *Training,* January 1995, pp. 29–36; and M.B. Arthur, P.H. Claman, and R.J. DeFillippi, "Intelligent Enterprise, Intelligent Careers," *The Executive,* November 1995, pp. 7–20.

32 See, for example, P.O. Benham, Jr., "Developing Organizational Talent: The Key to Performance and Productivity," *SAM Advanced Management Journal,* January 1993, pp. 34–39.

33 M.B. Arthur, D.T. Hall, and B.S. Lawrence (eds.), *Handbook of Career Theory* (Cambridge: Cambridge University Press, 1989), p. 8.

34 D.T. Hall, *Careers in Organizations* (Santa Monica, CA: Goodyear, 1976), pp. 3–4.

35 See R.A. McGowan, "Career Deinstitutionalization." Working Paper 14–95. Faculty of Administrative Studies; York University; North York, Ontario, 1995.

36 M. Hequet, "Flat and Happy?" *Training,* April 1995, pp. 29–34.

37 G. Johns, *Organizational Behavior: Understanding and Managing Life at Work,* 4th ed. (New York: HarperCollins, 1996), p. 622.

38 Based on P. Hirsch, *Pack Your Own Parachute: How to Survive Mergers, Takeovers, and Other Corporate Disasters,* (Reading, MA: Addison-Wesley, 1987); R. Henkoff, "Winning the New Career Game," *Fortune,* July 12, 1993, pp. 46–49; and H. Lancaster, "As Company Programs Fade, Workers Turn to Guild-Like Groups," *Wall Street Journal,* January 16, 1996, p. B1.

39 See J.N. Cleveland, K.R. Murphy, and R.E. Williams, "Multiple Uses of Performance Appraisal: Prevalence and Correlates," *Journal of Applied Psychology,* February 1989, pp. 130–35; J.F. Milliman, B. Nathan, and A.M. Mohrman, "Conflicting Appraisal Purposes of Managers and Subordinates and Their Effect on Performance and Satisfaction;" paper presented at the National Academy of Management meeting; Miami, Florida, 1991; and J.F. Milliman, S. Nason, K. Lowe, N-H. Kim, and P. Huo, "An Empirical Study of Performance Appraisal Practices in Japan, Korea, Taiwan, and the U.S.," in D.P. Moore (ed.), *Academy of Management Best Paper Proceedings* (Vancouver, BC, 1995).

40 P.M. Blau, *The Dynamics of Bureaucracy,* rev. ed. (Chicago: University of Chicago Press, 1963).

41 "The Cop-Out Cops," *National Observer,* August 3, 1974.

42 A.H. Locher and K.S. Teel, "Appraisal Trends," *Personnel Journal,* September 1988, pp. 139–45.

43 G.P. Latham and K.N. Wexley, *Increasing Productivity Through Performance Appraisal* (Reading, MA: Addison-Wesley, 1981), p. 80.

44 See Review in R.D. Bretz, Jr., G.T. Milkovich, and W. Read, "The Current State of Performance Appraisal Research and Practice: Concerns, Directions, and Implications," *Journal of Management,* June 1992, p. 326.

45 "Appraisals: Reverse Reviews," *INC.,* October 1992, p. 33.

46 See, for instance, J.F. Milliman, R.A. Zawacki, C. Norman, L. Powell, and J. Kirksey, "Companies Evaluate Employees From All Perspectives," *Personnel Journal,* November 1994, pp. 99–103; G. Yukl and R. Lepsinger, "How to Get the Most Out of 360-Degree Feedback," *Training,* December 1995, pp. 45–50; H. Lancaster, "Performance Reviews Are More Valuable When More Join In," *Wall Street Journal,* July 9, 1996, p. B1; and D. Antonioni, "Designing an Effective 360-Degree Appraisal Feedback Process," *Organizational Dynamics,* Autumn 1996, pp. 24–38.

47 Cited in R.J. Newman, "Job Reviews Go Circle," *U.S. News & World Report,* November 1, 1993, pp. 42–43.

48 D. Goldin, "In a Change of Policy, and Heart, Colleges Join Fight Against Inflated Grades," *The New York Times,* July 4, 1995, p. Y-10.

49 R.D. Bretz, Jr., G.T. Milkovich, and W. Read, "The Current State of Performance Appraisal Research and Practice," p. 333. See also J.S. Kanne, H.J. Bernardin, P. Villanova, and J. Peyrefitte, "Stability of Rater Leniency: Three Studies," *Academy of Management Journal,* August 1995, pp. 1036–51.

50 For a review of the role of halo error in performance evaluations, see W.K. Balzer and L.M. Sulsky, "Halo and Performance Appraisal Research: A Critical Evaluation," *Journal of Applied Psychology,* December 1992, pp. 975–85.

51 See T.A. Judge and G.R. Ferris, "Social Context of Performance Evaluation Decisions," *Academy of Management Journal,* February 1993, pp. 80–105.

52 A. Pizam, "Social Differentiation—A New Psychological Barrier to Performance Appraisal," *Public Personnel Management,* July–August 1975, pp. 244–47.

53 Ibid., pp. 245–46.

54 See D.J. Woehr and J. Feldman, "Processing Objective and Question Order Effects on the Causal Relation Between Memory and Judgment in Performance Appraisal: The Tip of the Iceberg," *Journal of Applied Psychology,* April 1993, pp. 232–41.

55 See, for example, W.M. Fox, "Improving Performance Appraisal Systems," *National Productivity Review,* Winter 1987–88, pp. 20–27.

56 See J. Greenberg, "Determinants of Perceived Fairness of Performance Evaluations," *Journal of Applied Psychology,* May 1986, pp. 340–42; and B.P. Maroney and M.R. Buckely, "Does Research in Performance Appraisal Influence the Practice of Performance Appraisal? Regretfully Not!" *Public Personnel Management,* Summer 1992, pp. 185–96.

57 W.C. Borman, "The Rating of Individuals in Organizations: An Alternate Approach," *Organizational Behavior and Human Performance,* August 1974, pp. 105–24.

58 Ibid.

59 See, for instance, D.E. Smith, "Training Programs for Performance Appraisal: A Review," *Academy of Management Review,* January 1986, pp. 22–40; D.C. Martin and K. Bartol, "Training the Raters: A Key to Effective Performance Appraisal," *Public Personnel Management,* Summer 1986, pp. 101–09; and T.R. Athey and R.M. McIntyre, "Effect of Rater Training on Rater Accuracy: Levels-of-Processing Theory and Social Facilitation Theory Perspectives," *Journal of Applied Psychology,* November 1987, pp. 567–72.

60 H.J. Bernardin, "The Effects of Rater Training on Leniency and Halo Errors in Student Rating of Instructors," *Journal of Applied Psychology,* June 1978, pp. 301–08.

61 Ibid.; and J.M. Ivancevich, "Longitudinal Study of the Effects of Rater Training on Psychometric Error in Ratings," *Journal of Applied Psychology,* October 1979, pp. 502–08.

62 M.S. Taylor, K.B. Tracy, M.K. Renard, J.K. Harrison, and S.J. Carroll, "Due Process in Performance Appraisal: A Quasi-Experiment in Procedural Justice," *Administrative Science Quarterly,* September 1995, pp. 495–523.

63 J.S. Lublin, "It's Shape-Up Time for Performance Reviews," *Wall Street Journal,* October 3, 1994, p. B1.

64 Much of this section is based on H.H. Meyer, "A Solution to the Performance Appraisal Feedback Enigma," *Academy of Management Executive,* February 1991, pp. 68–76.

65 B. Gates, *The Road Ahead* (New York: Viking, 1995), p. 86.

66 R.J. Burke, "Why Performance Appraisal Systems Fail," *Personnel Administration,* June 1972, pp. 32–40.

67 B.R. Nathan, A.M. Mohrman, Jr., and J. Milliman, "Interpersonal Relations as a Context for the Effects of Appraisal Interviews on Performance and Satisfaction: A Longitudinal Study," *Academy of Management Journal,* June 1991, pp. 352–69.

68 J. Zigon, "Making Performance Appraisal Work for Teams," *Training,* June 1994, pp. 58–63.

69 Much of the material in this section was adapted from T.H. Hammer, "Relationship Between Local Union Characteristics and Worker Behavior and Attitudes," *Academy of Management Journal,* December 1978, pp. 560–77.

70 See B.B. Auster and W. Cohen, "Rallying the Rank and File," *U.S. News & World Report,* April 1, 1996, pp. 26–28; and M.A. Verespej, "Wounded and Weaponless," *Industry Week,* September 16, 1996, pp. 46–58.

71 See J.B. Arthur and J.B. Dworkin, "Current Topics in Industrial and Labor Relations Research and Practice," *Journal of Management,* September 1991, pp. 530–32.

72 See, for example, C.J. Berger, C.A. Olson, and J.W. Boudreau, "Effects of Unions on Job Satisfaction: The Role of Work-Related Values and Perceived Rewards," *Organizational Behavior and Human Performance,* December 1983, pp. 289–324; and M.G. Evans and D.A. Ondrack, "The Role of Job Outcomes and Values in Understanding the Union's Impact on Job Satisfaction: A Replication," *Human Relations,* May 1990, pp. 401–18.

73 See, for instance, M. Mendonca and R.N. Kanungo, "Managing Human Resources: The Issue of Cultural Fit," *Journal of Management Inquiry,* June 1994, pp. 189–205.

74 W. Lobdell, "Who's Right for an Overseas Position?" *World Trade,* April–May 1990, pp. 20–26.

75 K. Murray, "Listening to the Other America, *New York Times,* April 25, 1993, p. F25.

76 See, for instance, A. Saltzman, "Family Friendliness, *U.S. News & World Report,* February 22, 1993, pp. 59–66; M. Galen, "Work & Family," *Business Week,* June 28, 1993, pp. 80–88; S. Hand and R.A. Zawacki, "Family-Friendly Benefits: More Than a Frill," *HRMagazine,* October 1994, pp. 79–84; S. Nelton, "Adjusting Benefits for Family Needs," *Nation's Business,* August 1995, pp. 27–28; L.T. Thomas and D.C. Ganster, "Impact of Family-Supportive Work Variables on Work-Family Conflict and Strain: A Control Perspective," *Journal of Applied Psychology,* February 1995, pp. 6–15; and K.H. Hammonds, "Balancing Work and Family," *Business Week,* September 16, 1996, pp. 74–80.

77 Cited in M.A. Verespej, "People-First Policies," *Industry Week,* June 21, 1993, p. 20.

78 S. Shellenbarger, "Data Gap," *Wall Street Journal,* June 21, 1993, p. R6.

79 R. Levering and M. Moskowitz, "The Ten Best Companies to Work for in America," *Business and Society Review,* Spring 1993, pp. 31–32.

80 S. Shellenbarger, "The Aging of America Is Making 'Elder Care' a Big Workplace Issue," *The Wall Street Journal,* February 16, 1994, p. A1.

81 See S.J. Lambert, "An Investigation of Workers' Use and Appreciation of Supportive Workplace Policies," in D.P.

Moore (ed.), *Academy of Management Best Paper Proceedings* (Vancouver, BC, 1995), pp. 136–40; and T. Lewin, "Workers of Both Sexes Make Trade-Offs for Family, Study Shows," *The New York Times*, October 29, 1995, p. Y14.

82 Cited in T. Lewin, "Workers of Both Sexes Make Trade-Offs for Family, Study Shows."

83 Cited in J. Gordon, "Different From What? Diversity as a Performance Issue," *Training*, May 1995, p. 27.

84 See, for example, M. Galen, "Diversity: Beyond the Numbers Game," *Business Week*, August 14, 1995, pp. 60–61.

85 L.E. Wynter, "Theatre Program Tackles Issues of Diversity," The *Wall Street Journal*, April 18, 1991, p. B1.

86 B. Hynes-Grace, "To Thrive, Not Merely Survive," in *Textbook Authors Conference Presentations* (Washington, DC: October 21, 1992), sponsored by the American Association of Retired Persons, p. 12.

87 "Teaching Diversity: Business Schools Search for Model Approaches," *Newsline*, Fall 1992, p. 21.

88 See, for example, K.E. Kram, *Mentoring at Work: Developmental Relationships in Organizational Life* (Glenview, IL: Scott, Foresman, 1985).

89 G. Dreher and R. Ash, "A Comparative Study of Mentoring Among Men and Women in Managerial, Professional, and Technical Positions," *Journal of Applied Psychology*, October 1990, pp. 539–46; and W. Whitely, T. Dougherty, and G. Dreher, "Relationship of Career Mentoring and Socioeconomic Origin to Managers' and Professionals' Early Career Progress," *Academy of Management Journal*, June 1991, pp. 331–51.

90 Reported in G. Johns, *Organizational Behavior: Understanding and Managing Life at Work*, p. 620.

91 See, for example, B.R. Ragins, "Barriers to Mentoring: The Female Manager's Dilemma," *Human Relations*, January 1989, pp. 1–22; B.R. Ragins and D. McFarlin, "Perceptions of Mentor Roles in Cross-Gender Mentoring Relationships," *Journal of Vocational Behavior*, December 1990, pp. 321–39; and D.A. Thomas, "The Impact of Race on Managers' Experiences of Developmental Relationships: An Intra-Organizational Study," *Journal of Organizational Behavior*, November 1990, pp. 539–46.

92 J.A. Wilson and N.S. Elman, "Organizational Benefits of Mentoring," *The Executive*, November 1990, p. 90.

93 A. Bandura, "Self-Efficacy: Towards a Unifying Theory of Behavioral Change," *Psychological Review*, March 1977, pp. 191–215; and P.C. Earley, "Self or Group? Cultural Effects of Training on Self-Efficacy and Performance," *Administrative Science Quarterly*, March 1994, pp. 89–117.

94 B.R. Nathan, A.M. Mohrman, Jr., and J. Milliman, "Interpersonal Relations as a Context for the Effects of Appraisal Interviews on Performance and Satisfaction: A Longitudinal Study."

Chapter 16

1 S. Sugawara, "A Stranger in a Strange Land? Making Changes at Mazda," *International Herald Tribune*, October 11, 1996, p. 1.

2 P. Selznick, "Foundations of the Theory of Organizations," *American Sociological Review*, February 1948, pp. 25–35.

3 See L.G. Zucker, "Organizations as Institutions," in S.B. Bacharach (ed.), *Research in the Sociology of Organizations* (Greenwich, CT: JAI Press, 1983), pp. 1–47; A.J. Richardson, "The Production of Institutional Behaviour: A Constructive Comment on the Use of Institutionalization Theory in Organizational Analysis," *Canadian Journal of Administrative Sciences*, December 1986, pp. 304–16; L.G. Zucker, *Institutional Patterns and Organizations: Culture and Environment* (Cambridge, MA: Ballinger, 1988); and R.L. Jepperson, "Institutions, Institutional Effects, and Institutionalism," in W.W. Powell and P.J. DiMaggio (eds.), *The New Institutionalism in Organizational Analysis* (Chicago: University of Chicago Press, 1991), pp. 143–63.

4 See, for example, H.S. Becker, "Culture: A Sociological View," *Yale Review*, Summer 1982, pp. 513–27; and E.H. Schein, *Organizational Culture and Leadership* (San Francisco: Jossey-Bass, 1985), p. 168.

5 This seven-item description is based on C.A. O'Reilly III, J. Chatman, and D.F. Caldwell, "People and Organizational Culture: A Profile Comparison Approach to Assessing Person–Organization Fit," *Academy of Management Journal*, September 1991, pp. 487–516; and J.A. Chatman and K.A. Jehn, "Assessing the Relationship Between Industry Characteristics and Organizational Culture: How Different Can You Be?" *Academy of Management Journal*, June 1994, pp. 522–53. For a description of other popular measures, see A. Xenikou and A. Furnham, "A Correlational and Factor Analytic Study of Four Questionnaire Measures of Organizational Culture," *Human Relations*, March 1996, pp. 349–71.

6 The view that there will be consistency among perceptions of organizational culture has been called the "integration" perspective. For a review of this perspective and conflicting approaches, see D. Meyerson and J. Martin, "Cultural Change: An Integration of Three Different Views," *Journal of Management Studies*, November 1987, pp. 623–47; and P.J. Frost, L.F. Moore, M.R. Louis, C.C. Lundberg, and J. Martin (eds.), *Reframing Organizational Culture* (Newbury Park, CA: Sage Publications, 1991).

7 See J.M. Jermier, J.W. Slocum, Jr., L.W. Fry, and J. Gaines, "Organizational Subcultures in a Soft Bureaucracy: Resistance Behind the Myth and Facade of an Official Culture," *Organization Science*, May 1991, pp. 170–94; S.A. Sackmann, "Culture and Subcultures: An Analysis of Organizational Knowledge," *Administrative Science Quarterly*, March 1992, pp. 140–61; and R.F. Zammuto, "Mapping Organizational Cultures and Subcultures: Looking Inside and Across Hospitals," paper presented at the 1995 National Academy of Management Conference, Vancouver, BC, August 1995.

8 T.A. Timmerman, "Do Organizations Have Personalities?" paper presented at the 1996 National Academy of Management Conference; Cincinnati, OH, August 1996.

9 See, for example, G.G. Gordon and N. DiTomaso, "Predicting Corporate Performance From Organizational Culture," *Journal of Management Studies*, November 1992, pp. 793–98.

10 Y. Wiener, "Forms of Value Systems: A Focus on Organizational Effectiveness and Cultural Change and Maintenance," *Academy of Management Review*, October 1988, p. 536.

[11] R.T. Mowday, L.W. Porter, and R.M. Steers, *Employee-Organization Linkages: The Psychology of Commitment, Absenteeism, and Turnover* (New York: Academic Press, 1982).

[12] See N.J. Adler, *International Dimensions of Organizational Behavior,* 2nd ed. (Boston: PWS-Kent Publishing, 1991), pp. 58–60.

[13] Ideas in this box were influenced by A.L. Wilkins, "The Culture Audit: A Tool for Understanding Organizations," *Organizational Dynamics,* Autumn 1983, pp. 24–38; and H.M. Trice and J.M. Beyer, *The Cultures of Work Organizations* (Englewood Cliffs, NJ: Prentice Hall, 1993), pp. 358–62.

[14] S.C. Schneider, "National vs. Corporate Culture: Implications for Human Resource Management," *Human Resource Management,* Summer 1988, p. 239.

[15] Ibid.

[16] See C.A. O'Reilly and J.A. Chatman, "Culture as Social Control: Corporations, Cults, and Commitment," in B.M. Staw and L.L. Cummings (eds.), *Research in Organizational Behavior,* vol. 18 (Greenwich, CT: JAI Press, 1996), pp. 157–200.

[17] T.E. Deal and A.A. Kennedy, "Culture: A New Look Through Old Lenses," *Journal of Applied Behavioral Science,* November 1983, p. 501.

[18] J. Case, "Corporate Culture," *INC.,* November 1996, pp. 42–53.

[19] W.J. Cook, "The Turnaround Artist," *U.S. News & World Report,* June 17, 1996, pp. 55–58.

[20] See, for instance, D. Miller, "What Happens After Success: The Perils of Excellence," *Journal of Management Studies,* May 1994, pp. 11–38.

[21] See C. Lindsay, "Paradoxes of Organizational Diversity: Living Within the Paradoxes," in L.R. Jauch and J.L. Wall (eds.), *Proceedings of the 50th Academy of Management Conference* (San Francisco, 1990), pp. 374–78; and T. Cox, Jr., *Cultural Diversity in Organizations: Theory, Research & Practice* (San Francisco: Berrett-Koehler, 1993), pp. 162–70.

[22] "Texaco: Lessons From a Crisis-In-Progress," *Business Week,* December 2, 1996, p. 44.

[23] A.F. Buono and J.L. Bowditch, *The Human Side of Mergers and Acquisitions: Managing Collisions Between People, Cultures, and Organizations* (San Francisco: Jossey-Bass, 1989); Y. Weber and D.M. Schweiger, "Top Management Culture Conflict in Mergers and Acquisitions: A Lesson From Anthropology," *The International Journal of Conflict Management,* January 1992, pp. 1–17; and S. Cartwright and C.L. Cooper, "The Role of Culture Compatibility in Successful Organizational Marriages," *Academy of Management Executive,* May 1993, pp. 57–70.

[24] P.L. Zweig, "The Case Against Mergers," *Business Week,* October 30, 1995, pp. 122–30.

[25] J. Marchese, "Time Warp," *Business Month,* September 1990, pp. 32–40; and L. Landro, "It May Be Hollywood, But Happy Endings Are Unusual in Mergers," *Wall Street Journal,* August 2, 1995, p. A1.

[26] P.L. Zweig, "The Case Against Mergers," p. 130.

[27] E.H. Schein, "The Role of the Founder in Creating Organizational Culture," *Organizational Dynamics,* Summer 1983, pp. 13–28.

[28] See, for example, J.R. Harrison and G.R. Carroll, "Keeping the Faith: A Model of Cultural Transmission in Formal Organizations," *Administrative Science Quarterly,* December 1991, pp. 552–82.

[29] See B. Schneider, "The People Make the Place," *Personnel Psychology,* Autumn 1987, pp. 437–53; J.A. Chatman, "Matching People and Organizations: Selection and Socialization in Public Accounting Firms," *Administrative Science Quarterly,* September 1991, pp. 459–84; D.E. Bowen, G.E. Ledford, Jr., and B.R. Nathan, "Hiring for the Organization, Not the Job," *Academy of Management Executive,* November 1991, pp. 35–51; B. Schneider, H.W. Goldstein, and D.B. Smith, "The ASA Framework: An Update," *Personnel Psychology,* Winter 1995, pp. 747–73; and A.L. Kristof, "Person-Organization Fit: An Integrative Review of Its Conceptualizations, Measurement, and Implications," *Personnel Psychology,* Spring 1996, pp. 1–49.

[30] R. Pascale, "The Paradox of 'Corporate Culture': Reconciling Ourselves to Socialization," *California Management Review,* Winter 1985, pp. 26–27.

[31] "Who's Afraid of IBM?" *Business Week,* June 29, 1987, p. 72.

[32] Ibid.

[33] D.C. Hambrick and P.A. Mason, "Upper Echelons: The Organization as a Reflection of Its Top Managers," *Academy of Management Review,* April 1984, pp. 193–206; B.P. Niehoff, C.A. Enz, and R.A. Grover, "The Impact of Top-Management Actions on Employee Attitudes and Perceptions," *Group and Organization Studies,* September 1990, pp. 337–52; and H.M. Trice and J.M. Beyer, "Cultural Leadership in Organizations," *Organization Science,* May 1991, pp. 149–69.

[34] "Culture Shock at Xerox," *Business Week,* June 22, 1987, pp. 1, 6–10; and T. Vogel, "At Xerox, They're Shouting 'Once More into the Breach,'" *Business Week,* July 23, 1990, pp. 62–63.

[35] See, for instance, N.J. Allen and J.P. Meyer, "Organizational Socialization Tactics: A Longitudinal Analysis of Links to Newcomers' Commitment and Role Orientation," *Academy of Management Journal,* December 1990, pp. 847–58; J.P. Wanous, *Organizational Entry,* 2nd ed. (New York: Addison-Wesley, 1992); G.T. Chao, A.M. O'Leary-Kelly, S. Wolf, H.J. Klein, and P.D. Gardner, "Organizational Socialization: Its Content and Consequences," *Journal of Applied Psychology,* October 1994, pp. 730–43; and J.S. Black and S.J. Ashford, "Fitting In or Making Jobs Fit: Factors Affecting Mode of Adjustment for New Hires," *Human Relations,* April 1995, pp. 421–37.

[36] J. Impoco, "Basic Training, Sanyo Style," *U.S. News & World Report,* July 13, 1992, pp. 46–48.

[37] B. Filipczak, "Trained by Starbucks," *Training,* June 1995, pp. 73–79.

[38] J. Van Maanen and E.H. Schein, "Career Development," in J.R. Hackman and J.L. Suttle (eds.), *Improving Life at Work* (Santa Monica, CA: Goodyear, 1977) pp. 58–62.

[39] D.C. Feldman, "The Multiple Socialization of Organization Members," *Academy of Management Review,* April 1981, p. 310.

[40] Van Maanen and Schein, "Career Development," p. 59.

[41] D.M. Boje, "The Storytelling Organization: A Study of Story Performance in an Office-Supply Firm," *Administrative Science Quarterly,* March 1991, pp. 106–26; and C.H. Deutsch, "The Parables of Corporate Culture," *The New York Times,* October 13, 1991, p. F25.

[42] A.M. Pettigrew, "On Studying Organizational Cultures," *Administrative Science Quarterly,* December 1979, p. 576.

[43] Ibid. See also K. Kamoche, "Rhetoric, Ritualism, and Totemism in Human Resource Management," *Human Relations,* April 1995, pp. 367–85.

[44] Cited in J.M. Beyer and H.M. Trice, "How an Organization's Rites Reveal Its Culture," *Organizational Dynamics,* Spring 1987, p. 15.

[45] A. Rafaeli and M.G. Pratt, "Tailored Meanings: On the Meaning and Impact of Organizational Dress," *Academy of Management Review,* January 1993, pp. 32–55.

[46] "LOB, Anyone?" *Business Week,* October 4, 1993, p. 94.

[47] J.A. Chatman, "Matching People and Organizations: Selection and Socialization in Public Accounting Firms," pp. 459–84; and B.Z. Posner, "Person–Organization Values Congruence: No Support for Individual Differences as a Moderating Influence," *Human Relations,* April 1992, pp. 351–61.

[48] J.E. Sheridan, "Organizational Culture and Employee Retention," *Academy of Management Journal,* December 1992, pp. 1036–56.

Chapter 17

[1] Reported in T.D. Schellhardt, "The Pressure's On," *Wall Street Journal,* February 26, 1996, p. R4.

[2] Z. Abdoolcarim, "Executive Stress a Company Killer," *Asian Business,* August 1995, pp. 22–26.

[3] A. Levy, "Second-Order Planned Change: Definition and Conceptualization," *Organizational Dynamics,* Summer 1986, pp. 4–20.

[4] K.L. Miller, "The Factory Guru Tinkering With Toyota," *Business Week,* May 17, 1993, pp. 95–97.

[5] J.S. McClenahen, "Condit Takes a Hike," *Industry Week,* December 2, 1996, pp. 12–16.

[6] Based on H.J. Leavitt, "Applied Organization Change in Industry," in W. Cooper, H. Leavitt, and M. Shelly (eds.), *New Perspectives on Organization Research* (New York: John Wiley, 1964); and P.J. Robertson, D.R. Roberts, and J.I. Porras, "Dynamics of Planned Organizational Change: Assessing Empirical Support for a Theoretical Model," *Academy of Management Journal,* June 1993, pp. 619–34.

[7] R.H. Hall, *Organizations: Structures, Processes, and Outcomes,* 4th ed. (Englewood Cliffs, NJ: Prentice Hall, 1987), p. 29.

[8] D. Katz and R.L. Kahn, *The Social Psychology of Organizations,* 2nd ed. (New York: John Wiley & Sons, 1978), pp. 714–15.

[9] J.P. Kotter and L.A. Schlesinger, "Choosing Strategies for Change," *Harvard Business Review,* March-April 1979, pp. 106–14.

[10] See J. Pfeffer, *Managing With Power: Politics and Influence in Organizations* (Boston: Harvard Business School Press, 1992), pp. 7, and 318–20.

[11] See, for instance, W. Ocasio, "Political Dynamics and the Circulation of Power: CEO Succession in U.S. Industrial Corporations, 1960–1990," *Administrative Science Quarterly,* June 1994, pp. 285–312.

[12] K. Lewin, *Field Theory in Social Science* (New York: Harper & Row, 1951).

[13] This box is based on T.A. Stewart, "Rate Your Readiness to Change," *Fortune,* February 7, 1994, pp. 106–10.

[14] See, for example, A.B. Shani and W.A. Pasmore, "Organization Inquiry: Towards a New Model of the Action Research Process," in D.D. Warrick (ed.), *Contemporary Organization Development: Current Thinking and Applications* (Glenview, IL: Scott, Foresman, 1985), pp. 438–48.

[15] For a sampling of various OD definitions, see J.I. Porras and P.J. Robertson, "Organizational Development: Theory, Practice, and Research," in M.D. Dunnette and L.M. Hough (eds.), *Handbook of Industrial & Organizational Psychology,* 2nd ed., vol. 3 (Palo Alto: Consulting Psychologists Press, 1992), pp. 721–23.

[16] L.D. Brown and J.G. Covey, "Development Organizations and Organization Development: Toward an Expanded Paradigm for Organization Development," in R.W. Woodman and W.A. Pasmore (eds.), *Research in Organizational Change and Development,* vol. 1 (Greenwich, CT: JAI Press, 1987), p. 63; and W.A. Pasmore and M.R. Fagans, "Participation, Individual Development, and Organizational Change: A Review and Synthesis," *Journal of Management,* June 1992, pp. 375–97.

[17] E.H. Schein, *Process Consultation: Its Role in Organizational Development* (Reading, MA: Addison-Wesley, 1969), p. 9.

[18] Ibid.

[19] See, for instance, P.F. Buller, "The Team Building-Task Performance Relation: Some Conceptual and Methodological Refinements," *Group and Organization Studies,* September 1986, pp. 147–68; and D. Eden, "Team Development: Quasi-Experimental Confirmation Among Combat Companies," *Group and Organization Studies,* September 1986, pp. 133–46.

[20] N. Margulies and J. Wallace, *Organizational Change: Techniques and Applications* (Glenview, IL: Scott, Foresman, 1973), 99–100.

[21] See, for example, E.H. Neilsen, "Understanding and Managing Intergroup Conflict," in J.W. Lorsch and P.R. Lawrence (eds.), *Managing Group and Intergroup Relations* (Homewood, IL: Irwin-Dorsey, 1972), pp. 329–43.

[22] R.R. Blake, J.S. Mouton, and R.L. Sloma, "The Union–Management Intergroup Laboratory: Strategy for Resolving Intergroup Conflict," *Journal of Applied Behavioral Science,* no. 1 (1965), pp. 25–57.

[23] Discussions of the 3M Co. in this chapter are based on K. Labich, "The Innovators," *Fortune,* June 6, 1988, p. 49;

R. Mitchell, "Masters of Innovation," *Business Week,* April 10, 1989, p. 58; K. Kelly, "The Drought Is Over at 3M," *Business Week,* November 7, 1994, pp. 140–41; T.A. Stewart, "3M Fights Back," *Fortune,* February 5, 1996, pp. 94–99; and T.D. Schellhardt, "David in Goliath," *Wall Street Journal,* May 23, 1996, p. R14.

24 See, for instance, A. Van de Ven, "Central Problems in the Managment of Innovation," *Management Science,* Vol. 32, 1986, pp. 590–607; and R.M. Kanter, "When a Thousand Flowers Bloom: Structural, Collective and Social Conditions for Innovation in Organizations," in B.M. Staw and L.L. Cummings (eds.), *Research in Organizational Behavior,* vol. 10 (Greenwich, CT: JAI Press, 1988), pp. 169–211.

25 F. Damanpour, "Organizational Innovation: A Meta-Analysis of Effects of Determinants and Moderators," *Academy of Management Journal,* September 1991, p. 557.

26 Ibid., pp. 555–90.

27 See also P.R. Monge, M.D. Cozzens, and N.S. Contractor, "Communication and Motivational Predictors of the Dynamics of Organizational Innovation," *Organization Science,* May 1992, pp. 250–74.

28 J.H. Sheridan, "Lew Platt: Creating a Culture for Innovation," *Industry Week,* December 19, 1994, pp. 26–30.

29 J.M. Howell and C.A. Higgins, "Champions of Change," *Business Quarterly,* Spring 1990, pp. 31–32; and D.L. Day, "Raising Radicals: Different Processes for Championing Innovative Corporate Ventures," *Organization Science,* May 1994, pp. 148–72.

30 J.M. Howell and C.A. Higgins, "Champions of Change."

31 See, for example, P.M. Senge, *The Fifth Discipline* (New York: Doubleday, 1990); D.Q. Mills and B. Friesen, "The Learning Organization," *European Management Journal,* June 1992, pp. 146–56; M. Dodgson, "Organizational Learning: A Review of Some Literatures," *Organization Studies,* vol. 14, no. 3, 1993; D.A. Garvin, "Building a Learning Organization," *Harvard Business Review,* July–August 1993, pp. 78–91; J.W. Slocum, Jr., M. McGill, and D.T. Lei, "The New Learning Strategy: Anytime, Anything, Anywhere," *Organizational Dynamics,* Autumn 1994, pp. 33–47; and F.J. Barrett, "Creating Appreciative Learning Cultures," *Organizational Dynamics,* Autumn 1995, pp. 36–49.

32 D.H. Kim, "The Link Between Individual and Organizational Learning," *Sloan Management Review,* Fall 1993, p. 37.

33 C. Argyris and D.A. Schon, *Organizational Learning* (Reading, MA: Addison-Wesley, 1978).

34 B. Dumaine, "Mr. Learning Organization," *Fortune,* October 17, 1994, p. 148.

35 F. Kofman and P.M. Senge, "Communities of Commitment: The Heart of Learning Organizations," *Organizational Dynamics,* Autumn 1993, pp. 5–23.

36 B. Dumaine, "Mr. Learning Organization," p. 154.

37 See S. Shane, S. Venkataraman, and I. MacMillan, "Cultural Differences in Innovation Championing Strategies," *Journal of Management,* vol. 21, no. 5, 1995, pp. 931–52.

38 Adapted from R.S. Schuler, "Definition and Conceptualization of Stress in Organizations," *Organizational Behavior and Human Performance,* April 1980, p. 189. For an updated review of definitions, see R.L. Kahn and P. Byosiere, "Stress in Organizations," in M.D. Dunnette and L.M. Hough, *Handbook of Industrial and Organizational Psychology,* 2nd ed., vol. 3 (Palo Alto, CA: Consulting Psychologists Press, 1992), pp. 573–80.

39 Ibid., p. 191.

40 This model is based on D.F. Parker and T.A. DeCotiis, "Organizational Determinants of Job Stress," *Organizational Behavior and Human Performance,* October 1983, p. 166, S. Parasuraman and J.A. Alutto, "Sources and Outcomes of Stress in Organizational Settings: Toward the Development of a Structural Model," *Academy of Management Journal,* June 1984, p. 333; and R.L. Kahn and P. Byosiere, "Stress in Organizations," p. 592.

41 This section is adapted from C.L. Cooper and R. Payne, *Stress at Work* (London: John Wiley, 1978); and Parasuraman and Alutto, "Sources and Outcomes of Stress in Organizational Settings," pp 330–50.

42 See, for example, D.R. Frew and N.S. Bruning, "Perceived Organizational Characteristics and Personality Measures as Predictors of Stress/Strain in the Work Place," *Journal of Management,* Winter 1987, pp. 633–46; and M.L. Fox, D.J. Dwyer, and D.C. Ganster, "Effects of Stressful Job Demands and Control of Physiological and Attitudinal Outcomes in a Hospital Setting," *Academy of Management Journal,* April 1993, pp. 289–318.

43 D.L. Nelson and C. Sutton, "Chronic Work Stress and Coping: A Longitudinal Study and Suggested New Directions," *Academy of Management Journal,* December 1990, pp. 859–69.

44 H. Selye, *The Stress of Life,* rev. ed. (New York: McGraw-Hill, 1956).

45 J.L. Xie and G. Johns, "Job Scope and Stress: Can Job Scope Be Too High?" *Academy of Management Journal,* October 1995, pp. 1288–1309.

46 S.J. Motowidlo, J.S. Packard, and M.R. Manning, "Occupational Stress: Its Causes and Consequences for Job Performance," *Journal of Applied Psychology,* November 1987, pp. 619–20.

47 See, for instance, J.J. House, *Work Stress and Social Support* (Reading, MA: Addison Wesley, 1981); S. Jayaratne, D. Himle, and W.A. Chess, "Dealing with Work Stress and Strain: Is the Perception of Support More Important Than Its Use?" *The Journal of Applied Behavioral Science,* vol. 24, no. 2, 1988, pp. 191–202; R.C. Cummings, "Job Stress and the Buffering Effect of Supervisory Support," *Group & Organization Studies,* March 1990, pp. 92–104; C.L. Scheck, A.J. Kinicki, and J.A. Davy, "A Longitudinal Study of a Multivariate Model of the Stress Process Using Structural Equations Modeling," *Human Relations,* December 1995, pp. 1481–1510; and M.R. Manning, C.N. Jackson, and M.R. Fusilier, "Occupational Stress, Social Support, and the Cost of Health Care," *Academy of Management Journal,* June 1996, pp. 738–50.

48 See L.R. Murphy, "A Review of Organizational Stress Management Research," *Journal of Organizational Behavior Management,* Fall-Winter 1986, pp. 215–27.

49 M. Friedman and R.H. Rosenman, *Type A Behavior and Your Heart* (New York: Alfred A. Knopf, 1974).

50 Ibid., pp. 84.

51 R. Williams, *The Trusting Heart: Great News About Type A Behavior* (New York: Times Books, 1989).

52 Schuler, "Definition and Conceptualization of Stress," pp. 200–205; and R.L. Kahn and P. Byosiere, "Stress in Organizations," pp. 604–10.

53 See T.A. Beehr and J.E. Newman, "Job Stress, Employee Health, and Organizational Effectiveness: A Facet Analysis, Model, and Literature Review," *Personnel Psychology*, Winter 1978, pp. 665–99; and B.D. Steffy and J.W. Jones, "Workplace Stress and Indicators of Coronary-Disease Risk," *Academy of Management Journal*, September 1988. pp. 686–98.

54 B.D. Steffy and J.W. Jones, "Workplace Stress and Indicators of Coronary-Disease Risk," p. 687.

55 C.L. Cooper and J. Marshall, "Occupational Sources of Stress: A Review of the Literature Relating to Coronary Heart Disease and Mental Ill Health," *Journal of Occupational Psychology*, vol. 49, no. 1 (1976), pp. 11–28.

56 J.R. Hackman and G.R. Oldham, "Development of the Job Diagnostic Survey," *Journal of Applied Psychology*, April 1975, pp. 159–70.

57 See, for instance, J.M. Ivancevich and M.T. Matteson, *Stress and Work* (Glenview, IL: Scott, Foresman, 1981); and R.D. Allen, M.A. Hitt, and C.R. Greer, "Occupational Stress and Perceived Organizational Effectiveness in Formal Groups: An Examination of Stress Level and Stress Type," *Personnel Psychology*, Summer 1982, pp. 359–70.

58 S.E. Sullivan and R.S. Bhagat, "Organizational Stress, Job Satisfaction and Job Performance: Where Do We Go From Here?" *Journal of Management*, June 1992, pp. 361–64.

59 The following discussion has been influenced by J.E. Newman and T.A. Beehr, "Personal and Organizational Strategies for Handling Job Stress," *Personnel Psychology*, Spring 1979, pp. 1–38; A.P. Brief, R.S. Schuler, and M. Van Sell, *Managing Job Stress*; R.L. Rose and J.F. Veiga, "Assessing the Sustained Effects of a Stress Management Intervention on Anxiety and Locus of Control," *Academy of Management Journal*, March 1984, pp. 190–98; J.M. Ivancevich and M.T. Matteson, "Organizational Level Stress Management Interventions: A Review and Recommendations," *Journal of Organizational Behavior Management*, Fall–Winter 1986, pp. 229–48; M.T. Matteson and J.M. Ivancevich, "Individual Stress Management Interventions: Evaluation of Techniques," *Journal of Management Psychology*, January 1987, pp. 24–30; J.M. Ivancevich, M.T. Matteson, S.M. Freedman, and J.S. Phillips, "Worksite Stress Management Interventions," *American Psychologist*, February 1990, pp. 252–61; R. Maturi, "Stress *Can* Be Beaten," *Industry Week*, July 20, 1992, pp. 23–26; and P. Froiland, "What Cures Job Stress?" *Training*, December 1993, pp. 32–36.

60 T.H. Macan, "Time Management: Test of a Process Model," *Journal of Applied Psychology*, June 1994, pp. 381–91.

61 See, for example, M.E. Haynes, *Practical Time Management: How to Make the Most of Your Most Perishable Resource* (Tulsa, OK: PennWell Books, 1985).

62 J. Kiely and G. Hodgson, "Stress in the Prison Service: The Benefits of Exercise Programs," *Human Relations*, June 1990, pp. 551–72.

63 E.J. Forbes and R.J. Pekala, "Psychophysiological Effects of Several Stress Management Techniques," *Psychological Reports*, February 1993, pp. 19–27; and G. Smith, "Meditation, the New Balm for Corporate Stress," *Business Week*, May 10, 1993, pp. 86–87.

64 D. Etzion, "Moderating Effects of Social Support on the Stress–Burnout Relationship," *Journal of Applied Psychology*, November 1984, pp. 615–22; and Jackson, Schwab, and Schuler, "Toward an Understanding of the Burnout Phenomenon."

65 S.E. Jackson, "Participation in Decision Making as a Strategy for Reducing Job-Related Strain," *Journal of Applied Psychology*, February 1983, pp. 3–19; and P. Froiland, "What Cures Job Stress?"

66 See, for instance, R.A. Wolfe, D.O. Ulrich, and D.F. Parker, "Employee Health Management Programs: Review, Critique, and Research Agenda," *Journal of Management*, Winter 1987, pp. 603–15; D.L. Gebhardt and C.E. Crump, "Employee Fitness and Wellness Programs in the Workplace," *American Psychologist*, February 1990, pp. 262–72; and C.E. Beadle, "And Let's Save 'Wellness.' It Works," *New York Times*, July 24, 1994, p. F9.

67 S. Tully, "America's Healthiest Companies," *Fortune*, June 12, 1995, p. 104.

68 P.S. Goodman and L.B. Kurke, "Studies of Change in Organizations: A Status Report," in P.S. Goodman (ed.), *Change in Organizations* (San Francisco: Jossey-Bass, 1982), pp. 1–2.

69 R.L. Kahn and P. Byosiere, "Stress in Organizations," pp. 605–08.

Appendix A

1 See, for instance, D.A. Wren, *The Evolution of Management Thought*, 4th ed. (New York: John Wiley & Sons, 1994), especially Chapters 13–18.

2 A. Smith, *An Inquiry into the Nature and Causes of the Wealth of Nations* (New York: Modern Library, 1937; orig. pub. 1776).

3 C. Babbage, *On the Economy of Machinery and Manufactures* (London: Charles Knight, 1832).

4 R.A. Owen, *A New View of Society* (New York: E. Bliss & White, 1825).

5 F.W. Taylor, *Principles of Scientific Management* (New York: Harper & Brothers, 1911).

6 Ibid., p. 44.

7 H. Fayol, *Industrial and General Administration* (Paris: Dunod, 1916).

8 M. Weber, *The Theory of Social and Economic Organizations*, ed. T. Parsons, trans. A.M. Henderson and T. Parsons (New York: Free Press, 1947).

9 Wren, *The Evolution of Management Thought*, chapter 14.

10 See, for example, M.P. Follett, *The New State: Group Organization the Solution of Popular Government* (London: Longmans, Green & Co., 1918). See also the review forum on

Mary Parker Follett in *Organization,* February 1996, pp. 147–80.

11 C.I. Barnard, *The Functions of the Executive* (Cambridge, MA: Harvard University Press, 1938).

12 H. Münsterberg, *Psychology and Industrial Efficiency* (Boston: Houghton Mifflin, 1913).

13 E. Mayo, *The Human Problems of an Industrial Civilization* (New York: Macmillan, 1933); and F.J. Roethlisberger and W.J. Dickson, *Management and the Worker* (Cambridge, MA: Harvard University Press, 1939).

14 See, for example, A. Carey, "The Hawthorne Studies: A Radical Criticism," *American Sociological Review,* June 1967, pp. 403–16; R.H. Franke and J. Kaul, "The Hawthorne Experiments: First Statistical Interpretations," *American Sociological Review,* October 1978, pp. 623–43; B. Rice, "The Hawthorne Defect: Persistence of a Flawed Theory," *Psychology Today,* February 1982, pp. 70–74; J.A. Sonnenfeld, "Shedding Light on the Hawthorne Studies," *Journal of Occupational Behavior,* April 1985, pp. 111–30; and S.R.G. Jones, "Was There a Hawthorne Effect?" *American Journal of Sociology,* November 1992, pp. 451–68.

15 D. Carnegie, *How to Win Friends and Influence People* (New York: Simon & Schuster, 1936).

16 Wren, *The Evolution of Management Thought,* p. 336.

17 A. Maslow, *Motivation and Personality* (New York: Harper & Row, 1954).

18 D. McGregor, *The Human Side of Enterprise* (New York: McGraw-Hill, 1960).

19 J.L. Moreno, "Contributions of Sociometry to Research Methodology in Sociology," *American Sociological Review,* June 1947, pp. 287–92.

20 See, for instance, B.F. Skinner, *Science and Human Behavior* (New York: Free Press, 1953); and B.F. Skinner, *Beyond Freedom and Dignity* (New York: Knopf, 1972).

21 D.C. McClelland, *The Achieving Society* (New York: Van Nostrand Reinhold, 1961); and D.C. McClelland and D.G. Winter, *Motivating Economic Achievement* (New York: Free Press, 1969).

22 F.E. Fiedler, *A Theory of Leadership Effectiveness* (New York: McGraw-Hill, 1967).

23 F. Herzberg, B. Mausner, and B. Snyderman, *The Motivation to Work* (New York, John Wiley, 1959); and F. Herzberg, *The Managerial Choice: To Be Efficient or to Be Human,* rev. ed (Salt Lake City: Olympus, 1982).

24 J.R. Hackman and G.R. Oldham, "Development of the Job Diagnostic Survey," *Journal of Applied Psychology,* April 1975, pp. 159–70.

25 See, for instance, J.M. Shepard and J.G. Hougland, Jr., "Contingency Theory: 'Complex Man' or 'Complex Organization'?" *Academy of Management Review,* July 1978, pp. 413–27; and H.L. Tosi, Jr., and J.W. Slocum, Jr., "Contingency Theory: Some Suggested Directions," *Journal of Management,* Spring 1984, pp. 9–26.

26 C.A. O'Reilly III, "Organizational Behavior: Where We've Been, Where We're Going," in M.R. Rosenzweig and L.W. Porter (eds.), *Annual Review of Psychology,* vol. 42 (Palo Alto, CA: Annual Reviews, Inc., 1991), pp. 429–30.

27 Ibid., pp. 427–58.

Appendix B

1 J.A. Byrne, "Executive Sweat," *Forbes,* May 20, 1985, pp. 198–200.

2 This discussion is based on material presented in E. Stone, *Research Methods in Organizational Behavior* (Santa Monica, CA: Goodyear, 1978).

3 B.M. Staw and G.R. Oldham, "Reconsidering Our Dependent Variables: A Critique and Empirical Study," *Academy of Management Journal,* December 1978, pp. 539–59; and B.M. Staw, "Organizational Behavior: A Review and Reformulation of the Field's Outcome Variables," in M.R. Rosenzweig and L.W. Porter (eds.), *Annual Review of Psychology,* vol. 35 (Palo Alto, CA: Annual Reviews, 1984), pp. 627–66.

4 R.S. Blackburn, "Experimental Design in Organizational Settings," in J.W. Lorsch (ed.), *Handbook of Organizational Behavior* (Englewood Cliffs, NJ: Prentice Hall, 1987), pp. 127–28.

5 G.G. Alpander, "Supervisory Training Programmes in Major U.S. Corporations," *Journal of Management Development,* vol. 5, no. 5, 1986, pp. 3–22.

6 S. Milgram, *Obedience to Authority* (New York: Harper & Row, 1974). For a critique of this research, see T. Blass, "Understanding Behavior in the Milgram Obedience Experiment: The Role of Personality, Situations, and Their Interactions," *Journal of Personality and Social Psychology,* March 1991, pp. 398–413.

7 J.J. Martocchio and A.M. O'Leary, "Sex Differences in Occupational Stress: A Meta-Analytic Review," *Journal of Applied Psychology,* June 1989, pp. 495–501.

8 See, for example, R.A. Guzzo, S.E. Jackson, and R.A. Katzell, "Meta-Analysis Analysis," in L.L. Cummings and B.M. Staw (eds.), *Research in Organizational Behavior,* vol. 9 (Greenwich, CT: JAI Press, 1987), pp. 407–42; A.L. Beaman, "An Empirical Comparison of Meta-Analytic and Traditional Reviews," *Personality and Social Psychology Bulletin,* June 1991, pp. 252–57; and G.E. Ledford, Jr. and E.E. Lawler, III, "Research on Employee Participation: Beating a Dead Horse?" *Academy of Management Review,* October 1994, pp. 633–36.

9 For more on ethical issues in research, see T.L. Beauchamp, R.R. Faden, R.J. Wallace, Jr., and L. Walters (eds.), *Ethical Issues in Social Science Research* (Baltimore, MD: Johns Hopkins University Press, 1982); and D. Baumrind, "Research Using Intentional Deception," *American Psychologist,* February 1985, pp. 165–74.

Illustration Credits

Indexes

Name Index

Note: Page numbers preceded with "E:" refer to the *Endnotes* section; numbers preceded with "A:" refer to the *Appendixes*.

Zaleznik, A., 346, E:21
Zalkind, S.S., E:4
Zammuto, R.F., E:37
Zander, A., E:22
Zanna, M.P., E:8
Zawacki, R.A., E:35
Zeitz, G., E:2

Zellner, W., E:15
Zemke, R., 303, E:19
Zerbe, W.J., E:5
Zevnik, B.L.P., E:34
Zhou, J., 411, 426
Zigon, J., E:35
Zimbardo, P.G., 254, E:8, 16

Zingheim, P.K., E:15
Zinn, L., E:7
Zucker, L.G., E:37
Zwany, A., E:10
Zweig, P.L., E:38
Zweigenhaft, R.L., E:33

Organization Index

ABB Asea Brown Boveri, 490, 511-12
ABC Company, 143-44, 507
Academy of Management, A:23
ACTUP, 408
Advanced Filtration Systems, Inc., 522
Aetna Life & Casualty, 288, 391, 562, 580, 663
AGI Inc., 515-16, 532, 612
Aid Association for Lutherans, 289
Airbus, 629
Alcatel, 628
Allied-Signal, 214, 328
Allstate, 317
Aluminum Company of America (Alcoa), 568, 647
Amana Refrigeration, Inc., 298, 299
American Airlines, 213, 214, 309, 341-42, 349, 353, 373
American Express, 8, 127, 559, 580
American Express Travel Services, 540-41
American Management Association, 558
American Psychological Association, A:23
American Safety Razor, 218
American Sociological Association, A:23
American Steel & Wire, 218
American Telephone and Telegraph (see AT&T)
America West Airlines, 534
Ameritech, 616
Amoco Corp., 563, 568
Amy's Ice Creams, 249
Andersen Consulting, 557
Anheuser-Busch, 214, 449
Apple Computer, 54, 229, 284, 292, 370, 372, 376, 391, 433, 457, 458, 496, 507, 562
Arco Chemical Company, 329
Arthur Andersen & Co., 1
Asia Department Store, 383
Aslett Corporation, M.E., 39, 234, 235, 236, 474, 475, 622-23, 674-75
Atlanta Committee for the Olympic Games (ACOG), 477-78
AT&T, 8, 38-39, 54, 106, 223, 284, 296, 306, 474-75, 494, 495, 496, 526, 568, 586, 603, 615, 622, 623, 626, 628, 630, 672, 674, A:7

Universal Card, 218
Australian Airlines, 284
Autodesk, 25
Avianca, 309
Avis Corporation, 212
Avon Products, 559, 580

B.F. Goodrich Co., A:8
Banca di America e di Italia, 525-26
Banc One, 525
BankAmerica, 358
Bankers Trust, 215
Bank of America, 246, 539, 543
Bank of Montreal, 485
Barrick Gold Corporation, 203, 204
Bausch & Lomb, 491
Bayerische Vereinsbank, 215
Beacon Aircraft Co., 670
Bechtel Corp., 539
Bell Atlantic, 297
Bell & Howell, 218
Bell Labs, 674
Ben & Jerry's Homemade, Inc., 118, 127-28
Bethlehem Steel, A:3
Binney & Smith (Canada), 163-64
Birkenstock Footwear, 595
Black Diamond Equipment, 50
Blockbuster Video, 376
BMW, 41, 289
Boeing Company, 249, 289, 493, 496, 629, 630
Bookman's Used Books, 214-15
Borland International, 372
BP Exploration, 148
Bristol-Myers Squibb, 438
British Airways, 23
Bucknell University, 321
Bulldog Group, The, 554
Burger King, 12
Business Week, 482

Canada Trust, 326
CAP Gemini Sogeti, 223
Carboline Co., 484
Carrier, 527
Caterpillar, 17, 358, 498
CBS, 507
Center for Creative Leadership, 2, 11
Chadick & Kimball, 458
Champion Spark Plug, 218

Chesebrough-Pond's Inc., 482
Chicago Bulls, 184
Childress Buick, 208
Chrysler Corporation, 2, 17, 35, 41-42, 50, 284, 289, 370, 391, 493, 616, 626, 671
Cincinnati Milacron, 218
CitiBank, 8
Citicorp, 54-55
Coca-Cola Company, 8, 13, 231, 496
Colgate-Palmolive, 231
Colorado Fuel & Iron, A:8
Commonwealth, 526
Compaq Computer, 605, A:19
ConAgra, 628
Conrail, 381
Conseco, 231
Continental Corp., 539
Control Data, 214, 392
Convex Computer Corporation, 206-7
Coors Brewing, 288, 663
Cornell University, 582
Corning, 557, 559, 580, 649
Costco Wholesale, 603

Daewoo Group, 3
Dallas Cowboys, 186
Dan Air, 309
Datatec Industries, 568
Dayton Hudson, 284
Dean Witter, 627
Dell Computer, 452, 493, 494, 495, 524
Delta Air Lines, 213, 373
DHL Ltd., 167
Dialog, 612
Dickinson, Stilwell, and Gardner, 280
Digital Computer, 392, 467, 507
Digital Equipment Corporation (DEC), 14, 214, A:19
Disney, 216, 601
Disneyland, 376
Donnelly Corporation, 208
Dorsey Trailers Inc., 89-90, 103
Douglas Aircraft Co., 289
Dow, 106, 247, 663
Du Pont, 106, 568, 580, 582

E.F. Hutton, 467
Eastern Airlines, 467

Glindex A Combined Glossary/Subject Index

D

Decentralization *Decision discretion is pushed down to lower-level employees,* 484-86

Decisional roles *Roles that include those of entrepreneur, disturbance handler, resource allocator, and negotiator,* 4

Decision making
    alternatives, 110-13
    behavioral, 107-16
    behavior and, 121-22
    biases, 111-13
    choices, 111-13
    ethics and, 117-20
    group, 267-73
    heuristics, 111-12
    individual, 103, 267-68
    intuitive, 109-10
    national culture and, 116-17
    optimizing model, 104-05
    perception and, 103
    problem identification, 110
    programmed, 115
    rational, 104-05
    satisficing, 108-09
    styles, 113-14, 125

Decisions *Choices made from among two or more alternatives,* 103

Decoding *Retranslating a sender's communication message,* 313

Defensive behaviors *Reactive and protective behaviors to avoid action, blame, or change,* 323, 420-21

Delegation of authority, 486

Demands *The loss of something desired,* 653-54

Demography, group, 262

Departmentalization *The basis by which jobs are grouped together,* 480-82

Dependency *B's relationship to A when A possesses something that B requires,* 396-97, 400-02

Dependent variable *A response that is affected by an independent variable,* 23

Design, organizational (*see* Organizational structure *and* Work design)

Development, group, 241-45

Development-oriented leader *One who values experimentation, seeking new ideas, and generating and implementing change,* 351-53

Devil's advocate, 444

Directive leader, 361-62

Discipline, 76, 77 (*see also* Punishment)

Discrimination, gender, 591 (*see also* Diversity *and* Sexual harassment)

Dissatisfaction, job, 156-57 (*see also* Job satisfaction)

Disseminator role, 4-5

Dissonance, cognitive, 144-46

Distinctive competencies *Defines what it is that the organization is more superior at delivering than its competition,* 524

Distinctiveness, 95

Distortions, sources of, 313-14

Distributive
    bargaining *Negotiation that seeks to divide up a fixed amount of resources; a win-lose situation,* 450-51
    justice *Perceived fairness of the amount and allocation of rewards among individuals,* 186-87

Disturbance handlers, 4-5

Diversity, gender (*see also* Sexual harassment)
    communication style, 330, 342-43
    leadership style, 377-78
    negotiation style, 454

Diversity, workforce,
    attitudes and, 149-50
    biographical characteristics and, 42-45
    challenge in, 13-14
    cliques and, 264
    change, force for, 627
    communication, 330-32
    conflict and, 446
    culture as barrier to, 602
    exercises, 32-34
    flexible benefits and, 633-34
    gender (*see* Diversity, gender)
    global village, and, 11-12
    group demography and, 262-63
    international, 12-13
    intranational, 13-14
    managing, 580-83
    melting pot approach to, 13-14
    motivation and, 224
    organizational culture as barrier to, 602
    sexual harassment and, 395-96, 408-10, 428-31
    stereotypes and, 99-100
    training, 582-83
    value of, 13-14
    work teams and, 299-300

Divestiture socialization, 609

Division of labor, 478-80

Dominant culture *Expresses the core values that are shared by a majority of the organization's members,* 596

Double-loop learning *Errors are corrected by modifying the organization's objectives, policies, and standard routines,* 649

Downward communication, 315

Driving forces *Forces that direct behavior away from the status quo,* 640

Due process, in performance evaluation, 575

Dysfunctional conflict *Conflict that hinders group performance,* 436-37, 447, 468

E

Economic uncertainties, 627

Economy, influence of, 633

Education to reduce resistance to change, 636 (*see also* Training)

Effective
    listening, 324
    managers, 6-7

Effectiveness *Achievement of goals,* 23

Efficiency *The ratio of effective output to the input required to achieve it,* 23

Effort, 102, 168 (*see also* Motivation)

Electronic
    communications, 334-35
    mail (e-mail), 321-23, 334-35
    meetings *Meetings where members interact on computers; allowing for anonymity of comments and aggregating of votes,* 272

Emergent clusters *Informal, unofficial groups,* 245

Emotional intelligence, 87

Emotional stability *A personality dimension that characterizes someone as calm, enthusiastic, secure (positive) versus tense, nervous, depressed, and insecure (negative),* 55

Employee
    involvement *A participative process that uses the entire capacity of employees and is designed to encourage increased commitment to the organization's success,* 208-14
    monitoring, ethics of, 510-11
    -oriented leader *One who emphasizes interpersonal relations,* 351
    stock ownership plans *Company-established benefit plans in which employees acquire stock as part of their benefits,* 212, 213

Empowerment *Putting employees in charge of what they do,* 16-17, 379-81

Encoding *Converting a communication message to symbolic form,* 312

factors are adequate, people will not be dissatisfied, 173
Hypothesis, A:16

I

Idea champions *Individuals who take an innovation and actively and enthusiastically promote the idea, build support, overcome resistance, and ensure it is implemented,* 647-48
Identity
    role, 252
    task, 517, 518
Illegitimate political behavior *Extreme political behavior that violates the implied rules of the game,* 410
Imitation strategy *A strategy that seeks to move into new products or new markets only after their viability has already been proven,* 498
Implicit models of organization structure *Perceptions that people hold regarding structural variables formed by observing things around them in an unscientific fashion,* 505
Impression management *The process by which individuals attempt to control the impression others form of them,* 416-20
Incentives (*see* Compensation plans *and* Motivation)
Independent variable *The presumed cause of some change in the dependent variable,* 26
Individual
    behavior, 26
    decision making, 103-20, 121-22
    differences, 10-12, 31, 657-59
    factors in stress, 657, 661-62
    ranking *An evaluation method that rank-orders employees from best to worst,* 570-71
    resistance to change, 633-34
    socialization, 609
Individualism *A national culture attribute describing a loosely knit social framework in which people emphasize only the care of themselves and their immediate family,* 138
Individual-level variables, 26
Industrial psychology, A:8-9
Inertia, group, 635
Influence (*see* Power)
Informal
    group *A group that is neither formally structured nor organizationally determined; appears in response to the need for social contact,* 240

network *The communication grapevine,* 316, 318-20
    social arrangement norms, 256
    socialization, 609
    status, 259
Informational roles *Roles that include monitoring, disseminating, and spokesperson activities,* 4
Initiating structure *The extent to which a leader is likely to define and structure his or her role and those of subordinates in the search for goal attainment,* 350
Innovation *A new idea applied to initiating or improving a product, process, or service* (*see also* Change), 646-48
Innovation strategy *A strategy that emphasizes the introduction of major new products and services,* 498
Institutionalization *When an organization takes on a life of its own, apart from any of its members, and acquires immortality,* 594-95
Instrumental values *Preferable modes of behavior or means of achieving one's terminal values,* 135
Integrative
    case, 37-39, 234-37, 474-75, 622-23, 674-75
    departments, 463
    bargaining *Negotiation that seeks one or more settlements that can create a win-win solution,* 450-51
Integrity *Honesty and truthfulness,* 294
Intellectual ability *That required to do mental activities,* 46-48, 87
Intentions *Decisions to act in a given way in a conflict episode,* 441-43
Interacting groups *Typical groups, where members interact with each other face-to-face,* 271
Interactionist view of conflict *The belief that conflict is not only a positive force in a group but that it is absolutely necessary for a group to perform effectively,* 435-36
Interdependence, 457-58
Interest group *Those working together to attain a specific objective with which each is concerned,* 240
Interests, influence on perception, 91
Intergroup
    development *OD efforts to improve interactions between groups,* 645-46
    relations, 456-63
Intermittent reinforcement *A desired behavior is reinforced often enough to make the behavior worth repeating,*

but not every time it is demonstrated, 73
Internals *Individuals who believe that they control what happens to them,* 56
International diversity (*see* National culture)
Interpersonal
    demands, stress and, 653-54
    roles *Roles that include figurehead, leadership, and liaison activities,* 4
    skills, 1-2
Interviews, 100-01, 553-54, 555-56, 588
Intrinsic motivation, 178-79
Intuition *A feeling not necessarily supported by research,* 11-12, 109-10
Intuitive decision making *An unconscious process created out of distilled experience,* 109-10
Involvement, employee, 208-14
Investiture socialization, 609
IQ, 46-48
Isolates *Individuals who are not connected to a social network,* 245

J

Jargon, 325
Job analysis *Developing a detailed description of the tasks involved in a job, determining the relationship of a given job to other jobs, and ascertaining the knowledge, skills, and abilities necessary for an employee to perform the job successfully,* 552-53
Job characteristics model (JCM) *Identifies five job characteristics and their relationship to personal and work outcomes,* 517-20, A:12-13
Job description *A written statement of what a jobholder does, how it is done, and why it is done,* 552
Job enlargement *The horizontal expansion of jobs,* 534-35
Job enrichment *The vertical expansion of jobs,* 535, 536, 545
Job involvement *The degree to which a person identifies with his or her job, actively participates in it, and considers his or her performance important to self-worth,* 142
Job obsolescence, 543, 544
Job-personality fit, 66-68
Job redesign (*see* Work design)
Job rotation *The periodic shifting of a worker from one task to another,* 533-34, 559
Job satisfaction *A general attitude*

ROBBINS
Organizational Behavior 8/E
Prentice-Hall, Inc.

**YOU SHOULD CAREFULLY READ THE TERMS AND CONDITIONS BEFORE USING THE DISKETTE PACKAGE.
USING THIS DISKETTE PACKAGE INDICATES YOUR ACCEPTANCE
OF THESE TERMS AND CONDITIONS.**

Prentice-Hall, Inc. provides this program and licenses its use. You assume responsibility for the selection of the program to achieve your intended results, and for the installation, use, and results obtained from the program. This license extends only to use of the program in the United States or countries in which the program is marketed by authorized distributors.

LICENSE GRANT

You hereby accept a nonexclusive, nontransferable, permanent license to install and use the program ON A SINGLE COMPUTER at any given time. You may copy the program solely for backup or archival purposes in support of your use of the program on the single computer. You may not modify, translate, disassemble, decompile, or reverse engineer the program, in whole or in part.

TERM

The License is effective until terminated. Prentice-Hall, Inc. reserves the right to terminate this License automatically if any provision of the License is violated. You may terminate the License at any time. To terminate this License, you must return the program, including documentation, along with a written warranty stating that all copies in your possession have been returned or destroyed.

LIMITED WARRANTY

THE PROGRAM IS PROVIDED "AS IS" WITHOUT WARRANTY OF ANY KIND, EITHER EXPRESSED OR IMPLIED, INCLUDING, BUT NOT LIMITED TO, THE IMPLIED WARRANTIES OR MERCHANTABILITY AND FITNESS FOR A PARTICULAR PURPOSE. THE ENTIRE RISK AS TO THE QUALITY AND PERFORMANCE OF THE PROGRAM IS WITH YOU. SHOULD THE PROGRAM PROVE DEFECTIVE, YOU (AND NOT PRENTICE-HALL, INC. OR ANY AUTHORIZED DEALER) ASSUME THE ENTIRE COST OF ALL NECESSARY SERVICING, REPAIR, OR CORRECTION. NO ORAL OR WRITTEN INFORMATION OR ADVICE GIVEN BY PRENTICE-HALL, INC., ITS DEALERS, DISTRIBUTORS, OR AGENTS SHALL CREATE A WARRANTY OR INCREASE THE SCOPE OF THIS WARRANTY.

SOME STATES DO NOT ALLOW THE EXCLUSION OF IMPLIED WARRANTIES, SO THE ABOVE EXCLUSION MAY NOT APPLY TO YOU. THIS WARRANTY GIVES YOU SPECIFIC LEGAL RIGHTS AND YOU MAY ALSO HAVE OTHER LEGAL RIGHTS THAT VARY FROM STATE TO STATE.

Prentice-Hall, Inc. does not warrant that the functions contained in the program will meet your requirements or that the operation of the program will be uninterrupted or error-free.

However, Prentice-Hall, Inc. warrants the diskette(s) on which the program is furnished to be free from defects in material and workmanship under normal use for a period of ninety (90) days from the date of delivery to you as evidenced by a copy of your receipt.

The program should not be relied on as the sole basis to solve a problem whose incorrect solution could result in injury to person or property. If the program is employed in such a manner, it is at the user's own risk and Prentice-Hall, Inc. explicitly disclaims all liability for such misuse.

LIMITATION OF REMEDIES

Prentice-Hall, Inc.'s entire liability and your exclusive remedy shall be:
1. the replacement of any diskette not meeting Prentice-Hall, Inc.'s "LIMITED WARRANTY" and that is returned to Prentice-Hall, or
2. if Prentice-Hall is unable to deliver a replacement diskette that is free of defects in materials or workmanship, you may terminate this agreement by returning the program.

IN NO EVENT WILL PRENTICE-HALL, INC. BE LIABLE TO YOU FOR ANY DAMAGES, INCLUDING ANY LOST PROFITS, LOST SAVINGS, OR OTHER INCIDENTAL OR CONSEQUENTIAL DAMAGES ARISING OUT OF THE USE OR INABILITY TO USE SUCH PROGRAM EVEN IF PRENTICE-HALL, INC. OR AN AUTHORIZED DISTRIBUTOR HAS BEEN ADVISED OF THE POSSIBILITY OF SUCH DAMAGES, OR FOR ANY CLAIM BY ANY OTHER PARTY.

SOME STATES DO NOT ALLOW FOR THE LIMITATION OR EXCLUSION OF LIABILITY FOR INCIDENTAL OR CONSEQUENTIAL DAMAGES, SO THE ABOVE LIMITATION OR EXCLUSION MAY NOT APPLY TO YOU.

GENERAL

You may not sublicense, assign, or transfer the license of the program. Any attempt to sublicense, assign or transfer any of the rights, duties, or obligations hereunder is void.

This Agreement will be governed by the laws of the State of New York.

Should you have any questions concerning this Agreement, you may contact Prentice-Hall, Inc. by writing to:
Director of New Media
Higher Education Division
Prentice-Hall, Inc.
1 Lake Street
Upper Saddle River, NJ 07458

Should you have any questions concerning technical support, you may write to:
New Media Production
Higher Education Division
Prentice-Hall, Inc.
1 Lake Street
Upper Saddle River, NJ 07458

YOU ACKNOWLEDGE THAT YOU HAVE READ THIS AGREEMENT, UNDERSTAND IT, AND AGREE TO BE BOUND BY ITS TERMS AND CONDITIONS. YOU FURTHER AGREE THAT IT IS THE COMPLETE AND EXCLUSIVE STATEMENT OF THE AGREEMENT BETWEEN US THAT SUPERSEDES ANY PROPOSAL OR PRIOR AGREEMENT, ORAL OR WRITTEN, AND ANY OTHER COMMUNICATIONS BETWEEN US RELATING TO THE SUBJECT MATTER OF THIS AGREEMENT.